CONWAY'S

ALL THE WORLD'S FIGHTING SHIPS 1906-1921

The dreadnought in peace and war: the ceremonial of a visit to Malta by the Austro-Hungarian *Viribus Unitis* and *Tegetthoff*, 26 May 1914, contrasts with the grim scene of North Sea patrol duty for the British 5th Battle Squadron (*Queen Elizabeth* class) in 1918.

G Pawlak (top); CPL

CONWAY'S

ALL THE WORLD'S FIGHTING SHIPS 1906-1921

NAVAL INSTITUTE PRESS

Editorial Director
ROBERT GARDINER
Editor
RANDAL GRAY
Contributors
PRZEMYSŁAW BUDZBON (Russia)
N J M CAMPBELL (German capital ships)
ALDO FRACCAROLI (Italy)
NORMAN FRIEDMAN (United States of America, Japan)
ANDRZEJ V MACH (China, Greece, Turkey, Minor Navies – Cambodia, Egypt, Liberia, Morocco, Persia, Siam)
ANTONY PRESTON (Great Britain)
ROBERT L SCHEINA (Argentina, Brazil, Chile, Peru, Minor Navies – Colombia, Cuba, Dominican Republic, Ecuador, Mexico, Paraguay, Uruguay, Venezuela)
ERWIN SIECHE (Austria-Hungary, Germany – except capital ships)
ADAM ŚMIGIELSKI (with the assistance of Andrzej M Jaskuła – France, Minor Navies – Belgium, Costa Rica, Haiti, Honduras, Nicaragua, San Salvador, Sarawak, Zanzibar)
IAN STURTON (Netherlands, Portugal, Spain)
MAREK TWARDOWSKI (Minor Navies – Bulgaria, Estonia, Latvia, Poland, Rumania, Yugoslavia)
KARL-ERIK WESTERLUND (Denmark, Norway, Sweden, Minor Navies – Finland)
Line drawings
By Przemysław Budzbon, Adam Śmigielski, Marek Twardowski
Book design
By Dave Mills
Index
By Patricia Moore

First published in 1985 by Conway Maritime Press Ltd,
24 Bride Lane, Fleet Street, London EC4Y 8DR

Published and distributed in the United States of America and Canada by the Naval Institute Press, Annapolis, Maryland 21402

Library of Congress Catalog Card No. 84-42782

ISBN 0-87021-907-3

Manufactured in the United Kingdom

Contents

Foreword

This volume completes the *Conway's All the World's Fighting Ships* series, and with it the monumental task of describing all the major warships from the advent of the ironclad down to the present day. As with the rest of the series, the aim is three-fold: to provide a single manageable source of information on the warships of the period; to make that information as detailed, reliable and up-to-date as possible by the critical use of both new research and published material; to fill out the bare technical data, wherever possible, with notes on the rationale of the design, and to give an overview of the political and economic factors affecting the navies themselves.

SCOPE

The period runs from the introduction of the *Dreadnought* to the Washington Naval Treaty, which effectively called a halt to the post-war naval construction race, although the coverage is designed to dovetail exactly into the 1860–1905 and 1922–1946 volumes, so the commencement and finishing dates may vary slightly from section to section. Submarines as a type were omitted from the 1860–1905 volume, so even those vessels built before 1906 are given a full class entry. As ever, the emphasis is on *fighting ships,* but compared with previous volumes there are fewer exclusions, and more space is devoted to riverine vessels and other small and often obscure craft. The vast number of auxiliary warships taken up during the Great War posed a significant problem, and in most cases no more than a nominal list has been possible, but preference was given to the lesser known vessels, and navies otherwise poorly represented in English-language publications. This volume also contains more information on the careers of the ships and the naval actions of the period.

ORGANISATION

The basic pattern of the 1860–1905 volume has been followed, with the Great Powers – those with a battlefleet – preceding the Coast Defence Navies, which are grouped geographically. The Minor Navies consist of those countries which operated only small craft and are listed alphabetically. British Colonial and Dominion Forces will be found under 'Great Britain', usually in the British classes to which they belonged.

The order within each country is standard: a general introduction, followed by a statement of fleet strength in 1906, then the post-1906 classes in type and chronological order. The type divisions have been standardised and reduced to Capital Ships, Monitors, Cruisers, Destroyers and Torpedo-Boats, Submarines, Small Surface Ships, Auxiliary Warships, and Miscellaneous. For the Coast Defence Navies this is further simplified to Major Surface Ships, Submarines, Small Surface Ships, and Miscellaneous, while the Minor Navies are simply listed as Post-1906 Additions to differentiate the new vessels from the 1906 Fleet Strength table. Within all these categories a more precise designation is given in the heading to each class table, and sections are subdivided accordingly.

THE CLASS TABLES

The presentation of information follows previous volumes, and in most cases is self-explanatory. However, readers should note the following points:

1. Where two tonnages, speeds and ranges are quoted for submarines, the first applies to the surfaced condition and the second as submerged.

2. Gun armament is given in the traditional form, namely: number of barrels – size of guns/calibre (number of mountings × number of barrels per mount). For example, '8–15in/42 (4×2)' means eight 42-calibre 15-inch guns in four twin mountings. However, in this volume mountings are only described if they are not singles, in order to save space. An attempt has also been made to follow the practice of the navy concerned as to whether guns are given metric or imperial designations, but *nominal* equivalents are given for all calibres above about 3in or 100mm (since smaller weapons rarely have exact equivalents). This leads to certain anomolies and apparent inconsistencies, but will facilitate rapid reference for any reader, whatever his preferred unit of measurement.

3. Metric–Imperial equivalents have also been given for armour thicknesses, but it is the first which is usually the officially listed figure followed by an approximate equivalent in brackets.

ILLUSTRATIONS

Classes of ship of cruiser-size and upward are usually represented by both a photograph and a line drawing. Wherever possible these are complementary, depicting either different sister-ships, or the same ship at different times, and the captions are dated as accurately as possible.

All the line drawings were specially commissioned for this book and are mostly reproduced to the international standard 1/1250 scale. The exceptions are clearly marked – those at 1/1500 would otherwise have been too large to print horizontally, and those at 1/750 would have been too small to be worth reproducing. There are also a few very small Russian vessels reproduced at 1/200 scale.

THE SERIES

Although chronologically this is the second volume it is the last to be published, and since the series has been continuously developed and improved, it is important to bear this in mind when referring to any part of the work. The 1860–1905 volume was not only the series prototype, but necessarily broke more new ground than any subsequent volume, so its shortcomings are all the more apparent. We are very grateful to the many readers who submitted additional information, corrections and suggested improvements to '1860–1905', and our original intention was to include an appendix at the end of this volume to utilise this material. However, in attempting to chronicle the 1906–1921 period in the maximum amount of detail, this volume expanded to the point where an appendix became impossible, so a fully revised edition of '1860–1905' at some future date seems the best solution. Nevertheless we have been able to incorporate much additional and amended information, where appropriate, into the 1906 Fleet Strength tables, so where there is a discrepancy readers are advised to follow the later work. Similarly information that supplements or amplifies the 1922–1946 volume has also been included wherever possible.

Ships transferred from one navy to another have usually been listed in full detail under country of origin, but in general readers will have to use their common sense when cross-referencing, either between countries in this volume, or between other parts of the series. For example, there are many accepted variations in orthography for countries which do not use the Roman Alphabet (particularly Russia, China, Turkey and Greece), so different authors have employed different systems, and it has not always been possible to standardise. Similarly, in some odd cases, especially relating to opinion and interpretation, information from different authors cannot be reconciled and the variations have been allowed to stand. Even after sixty years certain historical details continue to cause disagreement and it is as well for the reader to accept that even warship data is not a simple matter of objective truth or falsehood.

As originally conceived, this series is now completed, but the process of improvement will continue, so additional information for later revised editions is always welcome. Looking to the future, a similar, but somewhat modified, volume covering 1816 to 1859 is in the initial stages of preparation, and even earlier periods seem possible subjects for the *Fighting Ships* approach. All correspondence relating to any volume in the series should be addressed to Conway Maritime Press Ltd, 24 Bride Lane, Fleet Street, London EC4Y 8DR, Great Britain.

ACKNOWLEDGEMENTS

For help with photographs we are indebted to the following individuals and organisations: Herr Baumgartner, F F Bilzer, P Budzbon, R A Burt, Aldo Fraccaroli, Norman Friedman, Pierre Hervieux, F J IJsseling, Vic Jeffrey of the Royal Australian Navy, B Lemachko, John M Maber, Jerzy Micinksi, J Navarret, G Pawlik, Antony Preston, Dr Jurgen Röhwer of the BfZ, R L Scheina, Erwin Sieche, Marek Twardowski, the US Navy, the US Naval Institute, and K-E Westerlund.

Robert Gardiner

Abbreviations

AA, anti-aircraft
A-H, Austria-Hungary
AMC, armed merchant cruiser
ANZAC, Australian New Zealand Army Corps (created 25 April 1915)
approx, approximately
AS(W), anti-submarine (warfare or weapon)
aw, above-water

BEF, British Expeditionary Force
BCF, Battle Cruiser Force
BCS, Battle Cruiser Squadron
bhp, brake horsepower
BL, breech-loader; breech-loading
BLR, breech-loading rifle
BS, Battle Squadron
BU, broken up
BuShips, Bureau of Ships (US)

c, circa
C, compound
cal, calibre (usually expressed as an oblique stroke after the bore diameter, eg '12in/45 (cal)'
CE, compound expansion
Ch, Chantiers
CL, centreline
cm, centimetre(s)
CM, care and maintenance
CMB, coastal motor boat
CNS, Chief of Naval Staff
comm, commissioned
comp, completed
conv, converted
CP, centre pivot
crh, calibre radius head
CR, compound reciprocating
C&R, Construction and Repair
CS, Cruiser Squadron
CT, conning tower
cwt, hundredweight
cyl, cylindrical (of boilers); cylinder(s) (of engines)

DA, direct action
DC, depth charge
DCT, depth charge thrower, or director control tower
DE, double expansion
DF, Destroyer Flotilla
disp, displacement
DNC, Director of Naval Construction
DP, dual purpose
DYd, Dockyard

E-in-C, Engineer-in-Chief, (RN)
EOC, Elswick Ordnance Company

fps, fs, feet per second
ft, feet; foot
fwd, forward

gal, gallon(s)
GB, Great Britain
grt, gross registered tons

HA, high-angle
HC, heavy calibre
HDML, habour defence motor launch
HM, His Majesty's
HMS, His Majesty's Ship
HN, Harvey nickel (armour)
hp, horsepower
HP, high pressure
HQ, headquarters
HS, harbour service
HT, high tensile (steel)

ihp, indicated horsepower
IJN, Imperial Japanese Navy
in, inch(es)
inc, including

KC Krupp cemented,
KNC, Krupp non-cemented
kt(s), knot(s)
kW, kilowatts

LA, low-angle
lb, pound(s)
LCS, Light Cruiser Squadron
loco, locomotive
LP, low pressure
lwl, load waterline

m, metre(s)
M, Model (for French guns)
MAS, *motobarca armata silurante* (Italian torpedo-armed motor launch)
MC, medium calibre
MG, machine gun(s)
min, minute(s)
Mk, Mark
ML, muzzle-loader; muzzle-loading, or motor launch
MLR, muzzle-loading rifle
mm, millimetre(s)
MTB, motor torpedo-boat

NC, non-cemented
nhp, nominal horsepower
nm, nautical miles
No, number
NS, nickel steel
N Yd, Navy Yard

oa, overall

P&S, port and starboard
pdr, pounder(s)
pp, between perpendiculars
psi, pounds per square inch

QF, quick-firing

RAF, Royal Air Force (formed 1 April 1918)
RAN, Royal Australian Navy
RCN, Royal Canadian Navy
rds, rounds
RF, rapid-fire (or -firing)
RGF, Royal Gun Factory
RIN, Royal Indian Navy

RL, rocket launcher
RML, rifled muzzle-loading; rifled muzzle-loader
RN, Royal Navy
RNAS, Royal Naval Air Service (1914–18)
RNVR, Royal Naval Volunteer Reserve
RNZN, Royal New Zealand Navy
RPC, Remote Power Control
rpg, rounds per gun

SB, smoothbore (gun) or shipbuilders, shipbuilding
shp, shaft horsepower
S/m, submarine
SNO, Senior Naval Officer
STT, Stabilimento Tecnico Triestino
sub, submerged

t, ton(s)
TB, torpedo-boat
TBD, torpedo-boat destroyer
TE, triple expansion
TGB, torpedo gunboat
TL, torpedo launcher(s)
TRV, torpedo recovery vessel
TS, training ship
TT, torpedo tube(s)

US, United States
USA, United States of America
USN, United States Navy
USS, United States Ship

VC, vertical compound
VQE, vertical quadruple expansion
VTE, vertical triple expansion

W, West
Wks, Works
wl, waterline
W/T, wireless telegraphy

yd(s), yard(s)

Great Britain

AND EMPIRE FORCES

In 1906 the Royal Navy was just beginning to feel the effects of its dynamic new First Sea Lord, Sir John Fisher. But there were underlying causes for the technological ferment, which owed nothing to the driving force of Fisher. The great partnership between the Admiralty and the naval armaments industry had come to full flower, to a point where even the Royal Dockyards were at such a peak of efficiency that they could compete on an equal footing with private yards. Sir William White, the Director of Naval Construction (1885–1901), had taken the reputation of British designs to the forefront of world opinion, so that exports helped to keep building costs competitive. Even more important, the emergence of the German Imperial Navy as a new threat provided a political spur to maintain the rate of expansion started by the Naval Defence Act in 1889. The pace of technical advance had paradoxically slowed sufficiently to permit a period of consolidation. Armour was no longer changing almost yearly, and so there was no race between gun calibre and protection to bedevil the designers. The Parsons steam turbine was now proven, and needed only the endorsement of the Admiralty to displace reciprocating engines. And last of all, after four decades of largely theoretical discussion of warship design, there was now the practical experience of the Russo-Japanese War of 1904–5 to shape ideas about how warships should fight.

The Fisher dictum 'Build First and Build Fast, Each One Better than the Last' made a rousing slogan, and industry responded magnificently by turning out large numbers of ships at astonishingly short intervals. But, as one commentator had said, the flame of genius burned uncertainly in Fisher, and in his enthusiasm for the new technology he showed surprisingly little understanding of its implications. Thus the basic design of the *Dreadnought* was repeated in two classes, before any valid lessons could be learned from the prototype. Similarly the new armoured cruisers (later spuriously promoted to 'battlecruisers') were repeated with no attempt to eradicate any weaknesses. Speed was Fisher's god, and in his zeal to increase speed in every category he created severe problems. The time given to prepare designs for the new destroyers, for example, was ludicrously short, and as a result the Navy was saddled with ships of considerably less utility than the previous class – and at higher cost. The mania for speed soon infected the whole Navy, and it became the habit to credit ships with absurdly high speeds on trials. The policy of deception spread to other areas, and the battlecruisers in particular were credited with spurious fighting qualities. As is so often the case, the deceivers ultimately came to believe their own deception, thereby defeating whatever object Fisher may have had in mind.

The other dangerous flaw in Fisher's doctrines was his conviction that there was no longer any need for cruising ships, whether cruisers or escort craft. His drastic pruning of the gunboats and old cruisers proved premature, and quite a number condemned to the scrapheap in 1904 were later reprieved, but there was soon a crucial shortage of fast modern cruisers for the two vital tasks of commerce protection and scouting for the battlefleet. The hope that big destroyers could perform these functions proved false, and it was soon necessary to resume cruiser construction. Commerce protection in any case had little or no part in Fisher's view of the future. Despite his far-sighted prediction in 1904 that submarines would be used against shipping, he showed no inclination to find a counter to this threat.

CAPITAL SHIPS

Although soon overshadowed by the subsequent battlecruisers HMS *Dreadnought* was a remarkable technical achievement, and reflected great credit on the Engineer-in-Chief's Department. The Navy accepted his case for adopting the Parsons steam turbine even though the first large turbine-driven liner had not yet run her trials. Despite her novelty the ship did not suffer any mishaps, and she had exactly the revolutionary effect that Fisher had hoped, raising the speed of the battlefleet by three knots and increasing gunpower by 250 per cent. The *Invincible* class armoured cruisers or battlecruisers were just as successful *in terms of design*, and achieved exactly what the DNC had been asked to do. What was faulty was the tactical assumptions made by Fisher – that they could take part in capital ship actions while having no more protection than the previous classes of armoured cruiser. The accelerated pace of construction prevented a sober evaluation of both battleship and battlecruiser designs, so that a number of less than adequate ships joined the Fleet before detailed improvements could be incorporated. Thus battleship design did not begin to 'shake down' until the *King George V* class of 1911–12; but from there it was a comparatively short step to the *Queen Elizabeth*, an enormous improvement in all-round fighting power and equal in most respects to the best foreign ships.

The outbreak of war in August 1914 effectively froze battleship design as the Cabinet rightly assumed that the Grand Fleet had an ample margin of superiority, particularly with the acquisition of three more ships from Turkey and Chile (with another on the stocks). Nevertheless work started on forward planning for the postwar period, to take advantage of practical experience. Thus by 1917–18 there was a large body of experience based on battle damage and reports from the Fleet, and it needed only a further period of trials against surrendered German ships to test these concepts. The result was that by 1920–21 the DNC was in a position to proceed with a new series of capital ships, had the Washington Treaty not intervened. Had they been built they would have been as big an advance over existing designs as the *Dreadnought* had been over the *Lord Nelson*, only 16 years earlier.

In battle British capital ships earned a poor reputation, not all of it deserved. The poor quality of ammunition (see below) and the lack of flash-protection to magazines stemmed from mistakes made by other departments in the Admiralty organisation, and the faulty tactical use of the battlecruisers is the worst of many such examples. Fisher's reluctance to form a Naval Staff was eventually overcome by Winston Churchill in 1912 but too late to avoid many of these problems. The Fleet's big guns generally proved satisfactory, and its machinery gave comparatively little trouble, despite four years of very hard use, much more than pre-war designers had ever imagined. The designer's nightmare, restrictions on dimensions, caused the early dreadnoughts to have less side protection than was considered ideal, but the thin deck armour stemmed from a failure at high level to perceive the full effect of long-range gunnery. The increase in battle range dictated by

The Spithead Review of 1911 *CPL*

improvements to torpedoes was noted, but the risk of long-range shells diving through thin deck armour was apparently not taken so seriously.

Postwar examination of surrendered German capital ships was to show that the alleged superiority of German design was largely imaginary. The examination of the *Baden* in 1920–21 showed a remarkable similarity to the *Revenge*, and a detailed comparision showed only minor differences, and by no means all favourable to the German ship. Even the inferior designs which followed the *Dreadnought* had better seakeeping and were more reliable than their German counterparts.

CRUISERS

The big armoured cruiser was already doomed, but a misreading of the results of the Battle of Tsushima in May 1905 caused Fisher and others to think of them swooping down on crippled battleships. The battlecruisers was so much more powerful, however, that it quickly made the big cruiser obsolete. This left a gap for what the Victorian Navy called the 2nd Class cruiser, but Fisher mistakenly believed that this category was also obsolete; protection of trade could be left to the battlecruiser, and scouting for the Fleet could be left to destroyers. This was soon proved to be absurdly wrong, for the battlecruiser was far too expensive to be built in sufficient numbers to guard merchant shipping, and destroyers were too small for scouting duties. The much despised small cruiser had therefore to be reinstated, but the *Bristol* design (launched in 1910) was soundly conceived, and the resulting 'Town' classes were fine ships, robust enough to scout for the Fleet in all weathers and having sufficient fuel and gunpower to operate on the trade routes. War service amply proved their qualities, and it was no coincidence that the only new wartime design was called an 'Improved *Birmingham*'.

The very lightly built scout cruisers were outclassed by the new classes of faster destroyers, which could easily outstrip them in anything but the worst weather. To provide more powerful leaders for the flotillas and at the same time increase numbers for fleet scouting, the 'Town' design gave way to a new type of 'light armoured cruiser', a misnomer for a light cruiser with splinter-proof protection to her vitals. The *Arethusa* class (launched in 1913) proved successful, and by a progressive increase in dimensions the design was developed throughtout the war. To sum up, British cruisers turned out to be considerably superior to their German opponents, better armed and more seaworthy. Even the cramped *Arethusa* design performed outstanding service in the North Sea, and proved a sound basis for expansion.

DESTROYERS

From the 'River' class onwards the Royal Navy set a world-beating standard in destroyer design, preferring robust construction and seakeeping to unrealistic speeds. The only exception to this was, inevitably, at Fisher's behest, with a series of ambitious but unsuccessful designs. The big flotilla leader *Swift* of 1907 was to be the replacement for light cruisers but proved too fragile. Her speed proved a disappointment and the cost was exorbitant. The same could be said of the 'Tribal' group, elegant but frail and woefully short of endurance, even by contemporary destroyer standards. Although Fisher publicised the alleged virtues of the 'Tribals' and the *Swift* the Admiralty was so disappointed that it reverted to the previous policy as fast as it could, concentrating on a realistic sea speed and heavy gunpower to defeat German torpedo-boat attacks on the battlefleet. By 1914 the British standard destroyer was a powerful unit, and at Jutland the British flotillas repeatedly drove off German attacks by superior gunpower. They also proved excellent seaboats, capable of keeping at sea in the most vile conditions, whereas the German torpedo-craft were always limited by bad weather. The proof of excellence is that the standard destroyer in wartime was very little different from the pre-war 'L' and 'M' designs. Like the light cruisers there was a progressive improvement, and the basic design was only abandoned in 1916 on the basis of false intelligence reports.

SUBMARINES

The advent of the submarine was a result of pressure from abroad, and the decision was made in 1900 to buy Holland's design from the Electric Boat Co. British improvements quickly led to the 'A', 'B' and 'C' classes. Although Fisher embraced the new craft with characteristic enthusiasm, he was inclined to view them as mainly useful in harbour defence, providing him with an excuse to get rid of observation mines. The result was a curb on dimensions, and the 'C' class were put into quantity production when a progressive increase in size would have yielded better results. After a delay the error was put right; the 'D' class were a great improvement, and led to the 'E' class, a sturdy design which bore the brunt of the underwater war until 1917. The Admiralty chafed at the monopoly which had been given to Vickers, and partly to break what was regarded as a stranglehold and partly to satisfy criticism of Vickers/DNC designs from within the service, a series of competitive designs was ordered, including one from France and one from Italy. Unfortunately the war prevented this ambitious experiment from being properly evaluated, and the foreign designs were handed over to Italy to solve the logistic problems.

Wartime developments were much more random than in the surface fleet. Attempts to build 'fleet' submarines capable of operating with the Grand Fleet produced the 'J' and 'K' classes. The latter class attracted notoriety through a series of spectacular accidents, but this should not obscure the great technological achievement in producing a 24-knot, heavily armed submarine. Like the battlecruisers, the 'K boats' paid the penalty for a faulty tactical concept, but their design was not defective. The 'E' class proved easily adaptable as minelayers, and their success with deck guns in the Turkish Sea of Marmora in 1915–16 led to the grotesque 'M' class, with a 12in gun. After so many freaks the Admiralty finally returned to an improved 'E' design, the 'L' class, as the standard production design in the second half of the war. When Fisher returned to the Admiralty in 1914 he placed large orders for 'H' class boats in the United States and Canada, and this Electric Boat design became the basis for a British-designed 'H'.

Fisher's enthusiasm actually generated more submarines than the Royal Navy could man, and incidentally caused confusion in the shipyards until a few cancellations and re-allocations of contracts restored order.

MONITORS AND MINOR WAR VESSELS

Fisher galvanised the shipbuilding industry with massive orders late in 1914, and in the process created several new types of warship. Monitors had disappeared in the previous century, but the name was revived for a new type of bombardment vessel, using battleship guns. British forces were fighting in so many theatres that monitors proliferated, some using old cruiser guns, others using American 14in. Another category revived from a previous era was the sloop: initially designed for humdrum support duties with the Fleet, such as towing liberty boats and minesweeping, but when the onslaught on shipping started in 1915 these 'Flower' class proved ideal as tough and weatherly anti-submarine escorts. A totally new type of craft was the P-boat, intended to be an escort destroyer but designed with low freeboard to resemble a submarine. They were intended for the East Coast, and turned out to be good anti-submarine escorts. Like the 'Flowers' many were completed as decoys in the war against the U-boats. A vast number of merchant ships were taken up as naval auxiliaries. The best-known were the Armed Merchant Cruisers (AMCs) but much more important were the multitude of minelayers, depot ships, stores ships, balloon ships etc, which were vital to the support of naval operations in almost every part of the world.

LIGHT TORPEDO CRAFT

The original steam-powered torpedo-boat had already been eclipsed by the destroyer, and an attempt by Fisher to revive the concept showed the limitations of very flimsy high-speed hulls. Thereafter interest lapsed, but after the outbreak of war the potential of the fast motor (petrol-engined) boat was tapped. The Coastal Motor Boat (CMB) promised a new dimensions to naval warfare, but the results were meagre for the large amount of money and effort expended; they proved useful only when used on special assignments.

INDUSTRY AND SHIPBUILDING

It has become the fashion to talk of Britain's economic decline in this period, as if industry had become incapable of supplying the Navy's requirements. Nothing could be further from the truth, for although the British economy was no longer expanding, the defence industry was competitive, efficient and innovative. The Fisher building programmes posed a challenge to shipbuilding and engineering which it met handsomely, producing radically new ships and more powerful machinery at remarkably short notice. The story of the 15in gun is well-known; the Navy could ask the Elswick Ordnance Company to go from 13.5in to 15in calibre without a protracted period of trials and evaluation, knowing that the risk of failure was minimal. In wartime the exertions of industry were even more remarkable. Once the weaknesses of the armour-piercing shell and the instability of nitrocellulose propellant were identified, industry was able to put the problem right very quickly. The sheer volume of wartime shipbuilding was overwhelming, and if any criticism can be levelled, it must be at the Government for its prodigality. There was a failure to treat mercantile shipping as a war asset, manifesting itself in a total shutdown not only of new-building, but also salvage and repair of damaged ships. The excuse was that the war would be short, and therefore that resources should be concentrated on naval construction. Not until 1916 did the Admiralty decide to build up a force of ocean salvage tugs, and the need for mass-produced merchant ships took equally long to be acknowledged. The replacement programme did not begin to produce results until 1918, when the worst of the crisis was over, but the new salvage organisation played a vital role during the grim months of mid-1918.

WEAPONS

The legacy of the Victorian Navy was an excellent arms industry, which continued to provide reliable guns and torpedoes. The Royal Navy was probably the first to recognise that ballistics are improved by increasing the weight of the shell, rather than increasing the velocity of the gun. Attempts to improve shooting merely by lengthening the barrel and raising muzzle velocity produced unsatisfactory 12in and 6in guns, but subsequent guns had greatly improved accuracy at extreme range. The 13.5in gun combined greater accuracy with good barrel-life, qualities which were continued in the 15in and 18in. The wire-wound gun was liable to 'droop' and was undoubtedly inferior in quality to the Krupp all-steel method of construction, but what should be borne in mind is the relative cost. The Krupp gun (like German warships in general) was a high-quality product and therefore expensive. It also took longer to manufacture than its equivalent in Britain. The Royal Navy, on the other hand, with a very large inventory of ships, needed cost-effective guns which could be produced in the quantities required. Proof of which argument was correct did not emerge until after 1914: the German Navy never received its pre-war quota of heavy guns, whereas the RN could meet all its wartime needs and still supply spare guns to the Army for use in France.

The cruiser and destroyer guns proved effective, and required comparatively minor improvements in the light of war experience. A large number of gun-types existed, thanks to the thriving pre-war export market. Another way of obtaining more light guns was to strip the armament of the older warships. As the war went on various Victorian veterans were paid off to release their crews, and the older ships kept in commission were stripped of light guns to arm minor warships, particularly trawlers and drifters, and merchant ships.

Torpedoes were by and large reliable, even the older models dating from the 1880s. The introduction of the 21in torpedo, with its Hardcastle heater, made torpedo warfare much more effective. Range increased dramatically, forcing battle ranges up to 10,000 yards, and the larger warhead was much more destructive. However various marks of 18in torpedo continued to be specified for new construction right through the war.

The least satisfactory weapons in the British inventory were mines. The reason is mainly the lack of interest shown by Fisher in the subject. Despite having made his reputation as an expert in mine warfare he came to believe that they were purely defensive, and therefore unimportant. As a result little was done to develop new types; the British Elia, the standard moored mine, was of Italian design and built under licence. Instead of the electro-chemical 'horn' firing device used in German and other foreign mines, the 'BE' had a cumbersome crossbar mechanical lever, which frequently failed to be actuated. The poor performance of mines led the Admiralty to acquire a number of mines from the Russians, and a copy of the German Herz horn mine was put in hand. The latter, known as the H2, became available in sufficient numbers towards the end of 1916, at which point it became worthwhile to start large-scale offensive mining in enemy waters.

The mining offensive proved highly successful. In 1918 the world's first magnetic influence mine, the 'M Sinker', was introduced. Although early examples were faulty, the concrete-cased 'M Sinker' added to the effectiveness of the mine offensive against the Flanders U-boats. Closely related to mines were depth-charges, which were introduced in 1916. Production was stepped up in 1917, to permit their use by every type of anti-submarine vessel. In addition to the standard depth-charge, a number of weapons were developed to fire hydrostatically controlled projectiles.

OPERATIONS 1914–1918

The history of the Royal Navy in the First World War is largely one of disappointments and frustrations, but equally there were some outstanding successes. The expectations of a decisive fleet action in the North Sea proved illusory, and even the full engagement at Jutland on 31 May 1916 left the Grand Fleet feeling that it had been cheated of victory. And yet the Royal Navy never yielded control of the sea at any time. The lack of a pre-war Staff has been mentioned, but its lack was not felt until 1916, when it became painfully clear that the Royal Navy had not developed *administrative* techniques to deal with the U-boat crisis. In fact the Navy had done remarkably little to devise any sort of strategy. There had been clear recognition that Germany would be the enemy, and the capital ship building programmes were designed to counter the High Seas Fleet. What was not done, however, was to frame any sort of strategic aims; certainly in August 1914 the Navy was far less certain than the Army about what it was to do.

A vague approach to strategy was accompanied by a haphazard

approach to tactics. Long-range gunnery was preached constantly but the implications for fire control and ship-to-ship communications were not examined. There was a total failure to devise countermeasures to the submarine, despite Fisher's frequent predictions on the subject, and no attempt was made to develop shore bombardment, a vital corollary of a maritime strategy. On the credit side, the mine threat was recognised in 1909, when the Admiralty bought its first trawlers for conversion to minesweepers. By 1911 the RNR Trawler Section was established as a cadre for expansion in wartime, with 80 vessels earmarked by August 1914.

The Naval Staff resolutely set its face against convoy, for pre-war thinking had been against it. Instead 'offensive' patrols by larger and larger numbers of escorts were organised, a colossal and largely ineffectual effort. The Q-ships, or disguised mercantile conversions, achieved little for all their bravery and energy. Sanity only prevailed in the spring of 1917, when officers of the Trade Division succeeded in persuading the Cabinet Secretary, Maurice Hankey, that convoy of merchant ships was the only countermeasure likely to succeed.

Despite bombastic claims that the British Army was the 'largest shell to be fired by the Navy' there had been no detailed planning for amphibious warfare. When the big landings in the Dardanelles got underway the results of this neglect became all too obvious. Naval officers had no knowledge of storing merchant ships, and no techniques had been developed for shore bombardment. This was in sharp contrast to the Victorian Navy, which constantly carried out landings and bombardments, with considerable success.

Despite its failure to produce a clear-cut victory Jutland was a considerable achievement, and with a little more luck and better staff-work would have been a great one. The High Seas Fleet was fully aware that it had narrowly escaped destruction, and the efficiency of the surface fleet decayed rapidly in 1917. In fairness to all navies, there had been no action between *major* fleets between Lissa in 1866 and Tsushima in 1905. The latter provided a great number of lessons for those clever enough to extract them, but the difference in fighting power between the new dreadnoughts and the old-fashioned ships of the Russian and Japanese Navies persuaded people that the lessons were irrelevant. In fact virtually all the lessons of 1914–18 were foreshadowed by Tsushima. Jutland in particular gave the British the warning that they needed about poor quality armour-piercing shells and propellant, but it also drew attention to faulty tactics and command procedures. Thereafter there was much less centralised control, better night-fighting techniques and better damage control, to name only a few points. On paper the losses appeared severe, but apart from the tragic loss of so many lives, the only surprise sinking was that of the battlecruiser *Queen Mary*; her consorts *Invincible* and *Indefatigable* were fighting at ranges at which their side armour could easily be penetrated, and the same can be said of the three armoured cruisers, which should not have been there. On the credit side the battleships *Marlborough* and *Warspite* got home despite severe damage, and the Grand Fleet was largely intact, ready to fight in the same waters the next day. The same could not be said of the High Sea Fleet, which had no intention of offering battle next day. The Grand Fleet's losses were soon replaced by new ships, making the margin over the High Seas Fleet even bigger.

During 1917 the Grand Fleet replaced its faulty projectiles and cordite, and at the same time perfected new techniques of concentrating fire. The biggest step forward, again dictated by Jutland experience, was the provision of an integral air element, at first by flying spotters and fighters off turret platforms and then by getting aircraft carriers to sea. Seaplane carriers had been at sea since 1914 but their clumsy seaplanes were of little use in Fleet scouting. Fighters were needed to shoot down Zeppelin airships before they could give away the Fleet's position, and spotters were needed to locate the enemy and to spot fall of shot at long ranges. This meant wheeled aircraft, capable of landing back on deck if possible. By the Armistice the Grand Fleet had over 500 aircraft embarked in capital ships, cruisers and carriers, and the Royal Navy had the most advanced naval air arm in the world.

Although the Grand Fleet saw little action in four years, and had to keep morale up by frequent sweeps through the North Sea, the light forces were almost continuously engaged from 1914 to 1918. The Harwich Force and the Dover Patrol fought numerous fierce and sometimes bloody actions against German light cruisers and torpedo-boats. The Auxiliary Patrol and the escort forces were under ceaseless strain, not only from U-boats but also from hit-and-run attacks by surface ships. In spite of the hazards only one German action against light forces could be described as a total success, when in October 1917 the fast minelayers *Brummer* and *Bremse* sank the destroyers *Mary Rose* and *Strongbow* and then destroyed their Scandinavian convoy. Contemporary memoirs, and in particular 'Taffrail's' (alias Captain Taprell Dorling of the Harwich Force) and E Keble Chatterton's quasi-official histories give vivid accounts of the Navy and Merchant Navy efforts.

Once the remedy of convoy had been accepted, and with it the corollary of tight control over shipping, the Royal Navy began to win the U-boat war, and by the spring of 1918 victory was clearly within sight. The Navy's primary task, to keep the Atlantic supply-line open, had been achieved. British forces sank 133 U-boats out of the 178 lost from all causes. It was only to be regretted that so much blood and treasure had been expended before wisdom prevailed. Like the British war effort as a whole, the naval war had been characterised by profligacy. Too many aims had been pursued, and the British Government never reconciled the diverging needs of a maritime strategy versus a land strategy – the attempt to try and do both came close to losing the war, and certainly accomplished the downfall of the British Empire.

INNOVATIONS

For a service that is frequently described as reactionary and obscurantist, the Royal Navy pioneered an enormous number of ideas during the War. The anti-torpedo 'bulge' dated from before 1914, but proved a vital antidote to the torpedo. The hydrophone was the first underwater sensor, and by the end of 1918 the first Asdic (later to be called Sonar) was ready to be tested. The magnetic mine has already been mentioned, and the depth-charge, but there are many lesser examples, including the paravane. The Royal Navy produced the world's

The Grand Fleet at Scapa Flow 1917 *CPL*

One of the Royal Navy's most significant innovations was the pioneering of naval air power, including the operation of aircraft from relatively small ships, such as the cruiser *Sydney* seen here.
By courtesy of Antony Preston

largest gun, the 18in, and pioneered ultra-long-range gunnery off the Belgian coast. Its destroyers were universally recognised as the best in the world, as witness the fact that the *Shakespeare* and 'V & W' designs were the basis of post-war developments in every navy. Naval aviation, in embryo before 1914, was taken to unimagined efficiency in only four years; the Royal Navy was the first to build a ship from the keel up as an aircraft carrier. By September 1914 the Admiralty's famous code-breaking Room 40 and the first radio intercept stations were in existence.

POST-WAR DEVELOPMENTS

The only operations of any importance were the limited conflicts of 1918–20 in the Baltic and the Black Sea against the Bolshevik Revolution. The Baltic intervention started almost immediately after the Armistice, although naval forces had previously been stored at Archangel to safeguard the large quantities of war material landed there for the Russian armed forces. The Baltic operations were at times fierce, involving 238 vessels in all, and losses included a light cruiser, two destroyers and a submarine, whereas the Black Sea operations were mainly limited to providing gunfire support to the 'White' armies and eventually covering their withdrawal. Operations in the White Sea led to the loss of two monitors during the withdrawal in 1919.

Clearly the enormously bloated Navy had to be reduced in size quickly, for the dockyards were overcrowded with a motley collection of Victorian hulks. As foreign battleships now boasted guns up to 16in calibre there could be no place in the battle line for 12in-gunned ships. This meant the scrapping of all the earlier dreadnoughts as well as the pre-dreadnoughts. The same went for the armoured cruisers and the older light cruisers, but the bulk of the newer light cruisers were fit for further service. The problem with destroyers was that many of the modern craft particularly the 'M' class, were worn-out by extremely hard service. The same applied to submarines. In November 1918 the submarine strength included: 1 'B' class, 29 'C' class, 3 'D' class, 29 'E' class, 4 'V' class, 3 'F' class, 10 'G' class, 10 *H 1* class, 11 *H 21* class (plus 13 fitting-out), 6 'J' class (including 1 with RAN), 14 'K' class (plus *K 26* completing), 1 'M' class (plus *M 2*, *M 3* completing), 15 'L' class (plus 14 completing, and 7 *L 50* class), 6 'R' class (plus 4 completing). By the end of 1919 only four 'C's were left, no 'D's, 'V's or 'F's, and some of the 'E' and 'K' classes had gone; by the end of 1920 the 'G's had gone and only 16 'E' remained.

The rundown of sloops, minesweepers, P-boats etc was even more rapid, and large numbers had gone by 1920. The need to re-establish the fishing fleet was particularly urgent. Preliminary orders for demobilisation were drafted as early as July 1918 and by February 1919 the return of requisitioned vessels was well under way. After August 1919 the only civilian ships still under Admiralty control were those retained to help in mine clearance. Many minesweepers and sloops were converted to small merchant ships, but comparatively few went to foreign navies.

The category in most urgent need of replacement was capital ships. Even the 15in-gunned ships were now outclassed by the latest American and Japanese designs. It was also imperative to learn the lessons of the war, and an urgent programme of trials was put in hand in 1920, using German ships salvaged from Scapa Flow, particularly the *Baden*, which had been recovered almost intact. She was stripped and minutely examined, a turret was removed for separate examination, and finally she was subjected to careful firing tests, using the latest armour-piercing shells and propellants. The experience was then used in the preparation of new designs of battlecruisers and battleships, to follow the *Hood*. The so-called 1921–22 capital ships were the only ships in the world to incorporate the lessons of Jutland as well as other lessons learned from German ships. The delegates sent to the Washington Conference in 1921 had strict orders not to return without securing permission to build new ships equal or superior to the latest foreign designs.

The Washington Treaty and its after-effects fall outside the scope of this volume, but with hindsight we can see that the decline of the Royal Navy was inevitable. The immense exertions of 1914–18, on land and sea, left Britain financially exhausted. The overwhelming financial burdens were never lifted, and continued to inhibit the rebuilding of the Fleet. It is significant that when the delegates argued at Washington for the retention of the four 'G 3' battlecruisers, the Cabinet had already informed the Admiralty that they would not be built.

ROYAL NAVY 1914–1918

	August 1914	War construction	Losses
Dreadnoughts	22	13	2
Pre-dreadnoughts	41	–	10
Battlecruisers	10	5	3
Cruisers	49	–	14
Light cruisers	65	54	8
Aircraft carriers	1	16	3
Cruiser minelayers	7	2	3
Destroyers	221	329	66
Torpedo boats	109	–	10
Submarines	73	98	56
Sloops etc	15	257	21
Monitors	–	39	4

FLEET STRENGTH 1906

BATTLESHIPS

Name	Launched	Disp (load)	Fate
Rupert turret ram			
RUPERT	12.3.72	5440t	Sold 7.07
Devastation class turret ships			
DEVASTATION	12.7.71	9330t	Sold for BU 12.5.08
THUNDERER	25.3.72	9330t	Sold for BU 13.7.09
Dreadnought turret ship			
DREADNOUGHT	8.3.75	10,886t	Sold for BU 14.7.08
Belleisle class central battery ship			
ORION	23.1.79	4870t	HS 1910, sold 7.13
Colossus class turret ships			
COLOSSUS	21.3.82	9420t	Sold for BU 6.10.08
EDINBURGH	18.3.82	9420t	Sold for BU 11.10.08
Conqueror class turret ships			
CONQUEROR	8.9.81	6200t	Sold for BU 9.4.07
HERO	27.10.85	6200t	Sunk as target 18.2.08
'Admiral' class barbette ships			
COLLINGWOOD	22.11.82	9500t	Sold for BU 11.5.09
ANSON	17.2.86	10,600t	Sold for BU 13.7.09
CAMPERDOWN	24.11.85	10,600t	Sold for BU 11.7.11
HOWE	28.4.85	10,300t	Sold for BU 10.11.10
RODNEY	8.10.84	10,300t	Sold for BU 16.6.09
BENBOW	15.6.85	10,600t	Sold for BU 13.7.09
Victoria class turret ship			
SANS PAREIL	9.5.87	10,470t	Sold for BU 9.4.07
Trafalgar class turret ships			
TRAFALGAR	20.9.87	12,590t	Sold for BU 9.3.11
NILE	27.3.85	12,590t	Sold for BU 9.7.12
Royal Sovereign class			
EMPRESS OF INDIA	7.5.91	14,150t	Sunk as target 4.11.13
RAMILLIES	1.3.92	14,150t	Sold for BU 7.10.13
REPULSE	27.2.92	14,150t	Sold for BU 27.7.11
RESOLUTION	28.5.92	14,150t	Sold for BU 2.4.14
REVENGE	3.11.92	14,150t	Renamed *Redoubtable* 1913, sold for BU 6.11.19
ROYAL OAK	5.11.92	14,150t	Sold for BU 14.1.14
ROYAL SOVEREIGN	26.2.91	14,150t	Sold for BU 7.10.13
Hood turret ship			
HOOD	30.7.91	14,150t	Sunk as blockship 4.11.14
Centurion class			
CENTURION	3.8.92	10,500t	Sold for BU 12.7.10
BARFLEUR	10.8.92	10,500t	Sold for BU 12.7.10
Renown			
RENOWN	8.5.95	12,350t	Sold for BU 2.4.14
Majestic class			
CAESAR	2.9.96	14,820t	Sold for BU 8.11.21
HANNIBAL	28.4.96	14,820t	Sold for BU 28.1.20
ILLUSTRIOUS	17.9.96	14,820t	Sold for BU 18.6.20
JUPITER	18.11.95	14,820t	Sold for BU 15.1.20
MAJESTIC	31.1.95	14,820t	Torpedoed 27.5.15
MAGNIFICENT	19.12.94	14,820t	Sold for BU 9.5.21
MARS	30.3.96	14,820t	Sold for BU 9.5.21
PRINCE GEORGE	22.8.95	14,820t	Sold for BU 21.9.21
VICTORIOUS	19.10.95	14,820t	Sold for BU 19.12.22
Canopus class			
ALBION	21.6.98	13,150t	Sold for BU 11.12.19
CANOPUS	12.10.97	13,150t	Sold for BU 18.2.20
GLORY	11.3.99	13,150t	Sold for BU 19.12.22
GOLIATH	25.3.98	13,150t	Torpedoed 13.5.15
OCEAN	5.7.98	13,150t	Mined 18.3.15
VENGEANCE	25.7.99	13,150t	Sold for BU 1.12.21
Formidable class			
FORMIDABLE	17.11.98	14,500t	Torpedoed 1.1.15
IRRESISTIBLE	15.12.98	14,500t	Mined 18.3.15
IMPLACABLE	11.3.99	14,500t	Sold for BU 8.11.21
London class			
BULWARK	18.10.99	14,500t	Blown up 26.11.14
LONDON	21.9.99	14,500t	Sold for BU 4.6.20
VENERABLE	8.3.02	14,150t	Sold for BU 4.6.20
QUEEN	8.3.02	14,150t	Sold for BU 4.9.20
PRINCE OF WALES	25.3.02	14,150t	Sold for BU 12.4.20
Duncan class			
ALBEMARLE	5.3.01	13,440t	Sold for BU 19.11.19
CORNWALLIS	13.7.01	13,745t	Torpedoed 9.1.17
DUNCAN	21.3.01	13,640t	Sold for BU 18.2.20
EXMOUTH	31.8.01	13,500t	Sold for BU 15.2.20
MONTAGU	5.3.01	13,420t	Wrecked 30.5.06
RUSSELL	19.2.01	13,270t	Mined 27.3.16
King Edward VII class			
AFRICA	20.5.05	15,740t	Sold for BU 30.6.20
BRITANNIA	10.12.04	15,810t	Torpedoed 9.11.18
COMMONWEALTH	13.5.03	15,610t	Sold for BU 18.11.21
DOMINION	25.8.03	15,645t	Sold for BU 9.5.21
HIBERNIA	17.6.05	15,795t	Sold for BU 8.11.21
HINDUSTAN	19.12.03	15,885t	Sold for BU 9.5.21
KING EDWARD VII	23.7.03	15,630t	Mined 6.1.16
NEW ZEALAND	4.2.04	15,585t	Renamed *Zealandia* 1911, sold for BU 8.11.21
Swiftsure class			
SWIFTSURE	12.1.03	11,800t	Sold for BU 18.6.20
TRIUMPH	15.1.03	11,985t	Torpedoed 25.5.15
Lord Nelson class			
LORD NELSON	4.9.06	16,090t	Sold for BU 4.6.20
AGAMEMNON	23.6.06	15,925t	Sold for BU 24.1.27

Rupert
Port guardship at Bermuda 1904–07; sold there in 1907.

Devastation class
Devastation had been in Reserve since 1902; she was stricken from the Effective List in 1907 and sold May 1908. *Thunderer* had been in Reserve since 1900 and was removed from the Effective List in 1907; sold 1909.

Dreadnought
Had been in Reserve since 1905, and was lying at the Kyles of Bute; sold 1908.

Orion
Served a brief commission in December 1906 but went back into Reserve; converted to storeship 1910 and renamed *Orontes*. Sold at Malta 1913.

Colossus class
Colossus put up for sale in September 1906 but not towed away until October 1908. *Edinburgh* was in Special Reserve at Chatham in 1906; used as target to test armour and shells in 1908; sold 1910.

Conqueror class
Conqueror was laid up at Rothesay until sold in 1907. *Hero* was used as a target from November 1907, and was finally sunk off the Kentish Knock on 18 February 1908.

'Admiral' *class*
Collingwood was laid up at East Kyle, and *Anson* was in 'B' Reserve at Chatham; both sold 1909. *Camperdown* was removed from Effective List in 1908 and stationed at Harwich as submarine depot ship; sold 1911. *Howe* lay in Fleet Reserve in the Hamoaze until sold. *Rodney* was in Chatham Special Reserve from July 1906 until sold. *Benbow* in 'B' Reserve at Devonport until sold.

Victoria class
Sans Pareil in Fleet Reserve until sold in 1907.

Trafalgar class
Trafalgar in Reserve at Devonport; from March 1907 to April 1909 served as turret and torpedo drillship; then joined 4th Division, Home Fleet at the Nore until sold. *Nile* was in Reserve with nucleus crew; joined 4th Division, Home Fleet, then 'E' Division in 1911.

Royal Sovereign class
All seven spent their last years in Home waters, and six were finally paid off in 1911–13. In September 1906 *Revenge* replaced *Colossus* as gunnery TS at Portsmouth. Following serious collision damage in 1912 she was refitted with modern fire control. Her guns were temporarily relined to fire 10in shells, and then relined once again to fire 12in shells. In April 1913 reduced to Material Reserve and towed to the Motherbank, but in October 1914 she was brought back into service to bombard German positions on the Belgian coast. Renamed *Redoubtable* on 2 August 1915 to free her name for a new ship. She was fitted with 'bulges' to protect her against torpedo attack and had an early form of minesweeping gear fitted to her bows. Paid off in October 1915 when sufficient monitors were available. Subsequently recommissioned as tender to HMS *Victory* 1918–19. Armament in 1915: 4–12in, 6–6in, about 12–12pdr AA.

Hood
Passed into Fleet Reserve from September 1904 at Devonport; became part of Home Fleet Commmissioned Reserve, February 1907 until July 1910, when

she became a receiving ship at Queenstown (with all 6in guns removed). Removed from Effective List 1911 but put into Material Reserve for use as a target. In 1913 she was fitted with the first experimental 'bulges' for protection against torpedoes, and was put on the Sale List in August 1914. On 4 November 1914 she was scuttled to fill a gap in the defences of Portland harbour.

Centurion class
Centurion was in full commission until August 1905, and then went into Commissioned Reserve at Portsmouth. In May 1907 she became a special service ship with reduced crew; in April 1909 formed part of the 4th Division, Home Fleet but towed to Motherbank in June 1909.

Barfleur joined Commissioned Reserve in January 1905, and a month later took a relief crew for *Vengeance* out to China. Flagship of Portsmouth Reserve from May 1905 but refitted 1905–6. Recommissioned March 1907 with nucleus crew; joined 4th Division of Home Fleet in April 1909 until towed to Motherbank two months later.

Renown
Joined Commissioned Reserve in February 1905; in April–October 1905 converted as Royal Yacht to carry the Prince and Princess of Wales to India (all 6in guns removed). Reverted to Commissioned Reserve in May 1906 and joined 4th Division of Home Fleet in 1907. Tender to HMS *Victory* in October 1909 and acted as stokers' TS (slightly damaged in collision with water carrier *Aid*, 26 September 1911); put into Care & Maintenance in January 1913; towed to Motherbank December 1913.

Majestic class
Load displacements varied, and the tonnage in the table above is the legend figure. *Caesar* was the flagship, Rear-Admiral, Channel Fleet from December 1905; in February 1907 she became temporary flagship of the Atlantic Fleet but joined the Home Fleet at Devonport in May 1907. Refitted at Devonport 1907–8 and in May 1909 went to the Home Fleet at the Nore (temporary flagship of Vice-Admiral 3rd anu 4th Divisions). In April 1911 transferred to Devonport, with 3rd Division, Home Fleet; in March 1912 she was part of the 4th Division, Home Fleet with a nucleus crew, and remained with the Home Fleet until the outbreak of war. Brought to full commission in 7th Battle Squadron in the Channel. From 1915 to 1918 she was on the North America and West Indies Station, carrying out Atlantic patrols. In 1918 she went to the Mediterranean, passing through the Dardenelles after the Armistice to support operations in the Black Sea against the Bolsheviks.

Hannibal paid off at Devonport in August 1905. Refitted and converted to burn oil fuel, and fire control fitted, 1906; recommissioned October 1906 in Reserve as part of Channel Fleet. Transferred to Devonport as part of Home Fleet in July 1907, where she remained until 1914 (strucked submerged reef off Devon coast in August 1909 and suffered severe damage; collided with *TB 105* in October 1909). Refitted 1911–12. She was intended to recommission into the 9th Battle Squadron but went to the Humber as guardship in August 1914, and later moved to Scapa Flow. She was then disarmed at Dalmur to provide 12in turrets for the new monitors *Prince Eugene* and *Sir John Moore*, and was converted to a troopship (4–6in guns); went to the Mediterranean in September 1915. In 1916–19 she served in the East Indies and in Egypt. Sold January 1920.

Illustrious was in full commission in the Channel Fleet until September 1908 (flagship of Rear-Admiral from November 1906). Went into Reserve at Portsmouth, but was transferred to 3rd Fleet at Devonport in 1912 (commissioned for 1912 Manoeuvres as flagship Vice-Admiral, 2nd Battle Squadron). Commissioned in August 1914 as guardship and served at Loch Ewe, Lough Swilly, the Tyne and the Humber in succession, but by May 1915 she had joined the Southern Fleet in the Channel. In 1916 she was disarmed and reduced to harbour service as an ammunition ship on the Tyne; in 1917 she was moved to Portsmouth, where she remained until paid off in March 1920.

Jupiter joined the Commissioned Reserve at Portsmouth in August 1905; in October 1908 she was part of the Home Fleet with a nucleus crew (flagship February–June 1909 and then second flagship of 3rd Division, Home Fleet). Refitted 1909–10 with fire control for main armament and became sea-going gunnery TS at the Nore. In January 1913 became part of 3rd Fleet at Pembroke and Devonport. On the outbreak of war she joined the 7th Battle Squadron as guardship for the Humber (later the Tyne). Sent to Archangel as an icebreaker, and established a record by being the first ship to arrive so early in the year (February 1915). She returned to the Channel Fleet in May 1915, and subsequently served in the East Indies and Egypt. She remained in commission for special service but by 1918 she was an accommodation ship at Devonport. Paid off in 1919.

Majestic was in commission with the Atlantic Fleet from August 1906, but she went into Commissioned Reserve at the Nore in October 1906. Refitted at Chatham with fire control and radio, before joining the Home Fleet at Devonport. In 3rd Fleet at Devonport from May 1912 (in collision with her sister *Victorious* in July 1912) and remained there until outbreak of war. Commissioned at Devonport for 7th Battle Squadron, and in October 1914 was part of ocean escort for Canadian troop convoy. Served with Channel Fleet and Dover Patrol (bombarded Belgian coast early in 1915). Went to Mediterranean to act as 'mine-bumper' in Dardanelles operations. Took part in the big bombardment of 18 March 1915, and became flagship of Admiral Nicholson on 26 May. Next day she was torpedoed twice by *U 21* while providing gunfire support off Gaba Tepe. She rolled over and sank within 7 minutes, but with only 40 casualties.

Magnificent joined the Commissioned Reserve at Chatham in November 1906, and temporarily wore flag of Commander-in-Chief in November 1907. Converted to burn oil fuel and fitted with fire control in 1907–8 and then became second flagship of the Home Fleet from August 1908 to January 1909. Reduced to nucleus crew as flagship of the Home Fleet at the Nore in February 1909 and then wore flag of Vice-Admiral, 3rd and 4th Divisions (sternwalk damaged in collision in December 1910). Became tender to *Vivid* (turret drill ship) in February 1911, and sea-going gunnery TS at Devonport in May 1912. She became an independent command in September 1912 (slightly damaged by grounding in June 1913) and joined the 3rd Fleet at Devonport in July 1913. Commissioned for the 9th Battle Squadron in August 1914 and stationed in Humber. Later moved to Scapa Flow as guardship, but in February 1915 arrived at Belfast to be disarmed, as her 12in turrets were required for the new monitors *General Craufurd* and *Prince Eugene*. She was used as a troop transport and took part in the Suvla Bay landings in September 1915, and on her return was reduced to various subsidiary duties. By 1918 she was an ammunition store at Rosyth. She was paid off in 1919.

Mars was in Commissioned Reserve at Portsmouth in 1906 but recommissioned in the Channel Fleet late that year for a short spell, and again in March–May 1907. Refitted 1908–9 and 1911–12, and until outbreak of war was in the 4th Division, Home Fleet. Earmarked for 9th Battle Squadron but was sent to the Humber as guardship in August 1914. In February 1915 arrived with *Magnificent* at Harland & Wolff's yard in Belfast, where her 12in turrets were removed for installation in the monitors *Earl of Peterborough* and *Sir Thomas Picton*. As a troop transport she went to the Mediterranean in September 1915 and covered the Anzac and Cape Helles evacuations in January 1916. Paid off in 1916 and became a depot ship at Invergordon.

Prince George was serving with the Channel Fleet in 1906, but from March 1907 to February 1909 was flagship of the Portsmouth Division of the Home Fleet. She was refitted with radio in 1909, and in December 1909 suffered severe damage in a collision with HMS *Shannon*. Reduced to nucleus crew in December 1910 and refitted, but moved to Devonport in 1911. In June 1912 formed part of 7th Battle Squadron and remained part of 3rd Fleet until 1914. Commissioned as flagship of the 7th Battle Squadron in 8 August 1914 and was stationed in the Channel. Sent to Dardanelles to act as 'mine-bumper', and during the 1915 bombardments suffered severe damage from Turkish gunfire and had to be repaired at Malta. During Cape Helles evacuation she was hit by a torpedo which failed to explode. Paid off at Chatham early in 1916 and disarmed; she was used as an auxiliary sickbay, destroyer depot ship and other subsidiary duties, being renamed *Victorious II* in July 1918. Reverted to her original name in February 1919 and was sold in 1921 but foundered off Kamperduin (Camperdown) on 30 December 1921 while on passage to Germany for BU. Armament in 1915 included some 6pdr AA guns added.

Victorious was serving in the Atlantic Fleet in 1906 but in January 1907 she became part of the Home Fleet at Chatham. She reduced to a nucleus crew in March 1909 and was refitted to burn oil fuel, and had fire control and radio added. From April 1909 with Nore Division, Home Fleet, and temporary flagship. In collision with *Majestic* in fog on June 1910, sustaining damage to sternwalk and starboard engine. Transferred to Devonport Division January 1911–May 1912, then became part of 3rd Fleet. Started short refit December 1913 and earmarked for 9th BS in August 1914, but sent to the Humber as guardship. Sent to Elswick on Tyne in February 1915 to be disarmed, providing 12in turrets for monitors *Prince Rupert* and *General Wolfe*. Converted to repair ship in March 1916 and stationed at Scapa Flow until 1919. Renamed *Indus II* in 1920.

Canopus Class
Albion was serving with Channel Fleet, but in April 1906 she was in Commissioned Reserve at Chatham, undergoing an engine and boiler refit, lasting until December. She joined the Home Fleet temporarily at Portsmouth in February 1907 and then a month later joined the Atlantic Fleet. Refitted 1908–9 and in August 1909 became Parent Ship of 4th Division, Home Fleet at the Nore; 3rd Fleet, Nore from May 1912, and refitted at Chatham; stationed at Pembroke in 1913. Joined 8th BS, Channel Fleet in August 1914, then sent to Cape of Good Hope and East Africa until February 1915, when she was sent to Dardanelles. Damaged by Turkish shellfire during bombardments on 28 April and 2 May 1915, including grounding off Gaba Tepe. Transported troops to Salonika in October 1915, and then returned Home to be stationed on East Coast as guardship, and in 1918 was sent to Devonport, where she was laid up as an accommodation ship.

Canopus was serving in the Channel Fleet in 1906, and during that year was refitted with fire control, but in May 1907 was reduced to nucleus crew at Portsmouth as part of the Home Fleet. Refitted in 1907–8 and recommissioned for the Mediterranean Fleet from April 1908 to December 1909, before returning to 4th Division, Home Fleet. From May 1912 in reserve at the Nore but in 1913–14 was at Pembroke as part of the 3rd Fleet. On 7 August 1914 she commissioned in the 8th Battle Squadron for service in the Channel, but on 23 August went to Cape St Vincent as guardship. In October 1914 she went to the South American Station for service as guardship at Port Stanley and the Abrolhos Rocks. During this period she was part of Rear-Admiral Cradock's force, but because of an erroneous report that she could only make 13kts Cradock left her behind when he offered battle to Von Spee's squadron. She then returned to Port Stanley and beached herself on the mudflats, sent some of her 12pdr guns ashore, and established spotting stations ashore. On the morning of 8 December her 12in guns fired some ranging salvoes at the German cruisers, but no hits were reported. Went to Dardanelles in January 1915 and took part in the bombardments of 2 and 18 March, as well as the blockade of Smyrna and the main landings. Returned to Home Waters early in 1916 and was paid off at Chatham. Served as accommodation ship until sold. In 1917 8 main deck 6in guns replaced by 4 on battery deck; light AA also added in place of 12pdrs and 3pdrs.

Glory was in the Channel Fleet until October 1906 but then went into Commissioned Reserve at Portsmouth (Home Fleet). Refitted March–July 1907 with fire control, magazine cooling and machinery and boilers overhauled. Joined the Mediterranean Fleet until April 1909 and then reduced to nucleus crew in 4th Division of Home Fleet. In 3rd Fleet at Nore from May 1912 and transferred to Portsmouth in April 1913. Joined 8th Battle Squadron in Channel in August 1914, and escorted Canadian convoy in October 1914 before going to North America and West Indies Station as flagship. To Mediterranean Fleet in June 1915, covering Suez Canal, Egyptian waters and the East Indies. Sent to Archangel in 1916 and remained there as guardship until 1919, when she returned to Rosyth. There she was renamed *Crescent* in April 1920 while acting as a depot ship. In 1917 8 main deck 6mm guns replaced by 4 on battery deck, as in *Canopus*.

Goliath had just joined the Channel Fleet in 1906, but reduced to nucleus crew in March 1907 after being fitted with fire control. Machinery overhauled August 1907–February 1908 and then went to Malta (*en route* one of her propeller shafts fractured, necessitating a 4-month repair). Joined 4th Fleet at Nore in April 1909, and then 3rd Fleet in 1913–14. Commissioned in the 8th Battle Squadron for service in the Channel in August 1914 and then went to Loch Ewe as guardship. Covered landing of marines at Ostend and in September 1914 went to East Indies. In November 1914 took part in Rufiji River operations against the *Königsberg*, and then went to the Dardanelles in April 1915. Provided gunfire support at Cape Helles and was damaged on 25 April and 2 May. On the night of 13 May she was torpedoed by the Turkish torpedo-boat *Muavenet* and sank quickly with the loss of 570 men.

Ocean joined the Channel Fleet from January 1906 to June 1908, and then went to the Mediterranean. Refitted with fire control in 1908–9. Joined 4th Division of Home Fleet in February 1910 at Nore, but in 1913–14 was stationed at Pembroke. Joined 8th Battle Squadron in 14 August and went to Queenstown, then in September 1914 went to East Indies. In October 1914 took part in Persian Gulf operations, and was then sent to the Mediterranean. Took part in various bombardments in the Dardanelles in February–March 1915. On 18 March 1915 was damaged by gunfire and then hit a floating mine. She was abandoned about 1930 and sank 3 hours later.

Vengeance joined the Channel Fleet in May 1906 after machinery repairs. Went to Home Fleet in May 1908 (damaged in collision with merchantman, June 1908), and joined Home Fleet at the Nore in February 1909 (grounded in Thames in that month, and collided with destroyer *Biter* in November 1910). Became parent ship to Special Service ships, and in April 1909 became gunnery drill ship. In 1912–13 served with the 8th Battle Squadron and in 1913–14 became gunnery TS. At the outbreak of war joined the 8th BS in the Channel and on Atlantic patrols. In Novemebr 1914 went to West Africa for operations against the Cameroons, and then to Egypt, and Cape Verde. At Gibraltar in January 1915 she became the flagship of Admiral de Robeck and went to the Dardanelles. Took part in the bombardments and the Cape Helles landing on 25 April, and later in November 1915 returned to Egypt. Served in East Indies, Egypt, East Africa and the Cape of Good Hope, returning home in 1917. She was rearmed, losing 4 main deck 6in casemate guns and having 4–6in in open shields sited on the battery deck. She then became an ordnance depot at Devonport until paid off in 1919.

Formidable class

Formidable was serving in the Mediterranean Fleet in 1906 but in April 1908 she was transferred to the Channel Fleet. After a refit at Chatham from August 1908 to April 1909 joined 1st Division, Home Fleet and then the Atlantic Fleet until May 1912. Reduced to nucleus crew and joined 5th Squadron of the 2nd Fleet at the Nore (developed serious machinery defects after hard steaming nucleus crew). Served in the 5th Battle Squadron from 1912 to 1914. Remained in 5th BS on outbreak of war, and while on Channel patrol off Portland Bill on 1 January 1915 she was torpedoed by *U 24*. She sank quickly in bad weather, with the loss of 547 men out of 780.

Irresistible was in the Mediterranean in 1906 and remained there until January 1908 when she joined the Channel Fleet (collided with a schooner in May 1908). In 1909 she joined the Nore Division and then reduced to nucleus crew in May 1910. From 1912 to 1914 served in the 5th Battle Squadron. Served on Channel patrols from outbreak of war, as part of 5th BS. Sent to Dardanelles in 1915, she gave gunfire support from 26 February onwards. On 18 March she struck a mine in Erenkui Bay (at about 1615); after being abandoned under the Turkish guns she was sunk by gunfire at about 1930.

Implacable served in the Mediterranean until May 1908 and then returned to Chatham for refit before joining the Channel Fleet. From 1912 she was in the 5th Battle Squadron. Served with remainder of 5th BS on Channel patrols until ordered to Dardanelles in March 1915. Distinguished herself by giving very close support during the Cape Helles landings on 25 April and later. Ordered to Adriatic in May 1915 to reinforce the Italian Navy, but later went to the East Indies. On her return to Home waters in 1917, 4 main deck casemates on either side were replaced by 2–6in guns on the battery deck. She then served with the Northern Patrol until the Armistice and was paid off in 1919.

London class

Bulwark commissioned at Devonport on 18 March 1907 as flagship of the Mediterranean Fleet, having had a long refit immediately after completion for the adding of fire control. In February 1907 became flagship of the Home Fleet (grounded with slight damage, October 1907). After refit went to Channel Fleet in August 1908 and then Home Fleet, being reduced to nucleus crew at the Nore in March 1910. From 1912 to 1914 with 5th Battle Squadron, and from the outbreak of war carried out Channel patrols. On 26 November 1914 while loading ammunition at Sheerness she was destroyed by an internal explosion, probably caused by careless handling of black powder charges on the upper deck. Only 12 men survived.

London was in the Mediterranean in 1906 but returned to the Nore in 1907. In June 1908 became flagship of Rear-Admiral, Channel Fleet and then Rear-Admiral Atlantic Fleet in 1910. Reduced to nucleus crew in 3rd Battle Squadron in May 1912 but was transferred to 5th BS at the Nore for experiments with seaplanes. During these trials a 'hydro-aeroplane' took off from a ramp over the forecastle. She remained with the 5th BS until the outbreak of war. Served on Channel patrols from August 1914 and then went to the Dardanelles to replace losses. Transferred to Adriatic in May 1915 to stiffen Italian resistance and remained at Taranto until 1917, when she returned home for conversion to a minelayer. When she joined the 1st Minelaying Squadron in January 1918 the 12in guns had been removed from the forward turret, the after turret had been replaced by a 6in gun, and the entire main deck aft had been converted to a mine deck carrying rails for 240 mines. In 1919 she was a reserve depot.

Venerable was serving as flagship of the Mediterranean Fleet in 1906 but was relieved by the *Prince of Wales* in August 1907. After a long refit at Chatham she joined the Atlantic Fleet in October 1909. In May 1912 reduced to nucleus crew in 5th Battle Squadron. Served on Channel patrols from outbreak of war, and bombarded Belgian coast up to October 1914, and again in March 1915. Ordered to the Dardanelles in May 1915 to relieve the *Queen Elizabeth*. Took part in Suvla operations 14–21 August 1915 but was then transferred to Adriatic to help the Italian Navy contain the Austrians. Returned to Home waters early in 1918 and reduced to harbour service until paid off in 1919.

Prince of Wales was in the Mediterranean at the beginning of 1906 but returned in May to join Commissioned Reserve at Portsmouth for refit. Returned to Mediterranean in September 1906 as flagship of Rear-Admiral, and from November 1908 transferred to Atlantic Fleet as C-in-C's flagship. Flagship of Vice-Admiral, 3rd Battle Squadron, 1st Fleet from May 1912, and then flagship, Rear-Admiral, 2nd Fleet at Portsmouth. From 1912 to 1914 serving with 5th BS. Served on Channel patrols from August 1914 and then to Dardanelles in May 1915, including Anzac landings on 25 April. Ordered to Adriatic on 12 May 1915 with three sisters, and remained there until the beginning of 1918. Reduced to harbour service on her return.

Queen was in the Mediterranean in 1906 and became flagship in February 1907. Transferred to Atlantic Fleet in December 1908, and in May 1912 joined 3rd Battle Squadron, 1st Fleet. Up to the outbreak of war was serving with the 5th BS. From August 1914 took part in Channel patrols, but was ordered to the Dardanelles in March 1915. She covered the Anzac landing on 25 April and was then ordered to the Adriatic. She remained at Taranto as a base ship until 1918, but before she returned home her 4–12in guns were removed and transferred to the Italian Navy.

Duncan class

Albemarle was in the Channel Fleet in 1906, but became flagship, Rear-Admiral of the Atlantic Fleet in February 1907, and then flagship, Rear-Admiral at Gibraltar in January 1909. Reduced to nucleus crew in February 1910 at the Nore, but in October 1910 became flagship, Rear-Admiral at Portsmouth. After long refit she joined the 4th Battle Squadron, Home Fleet at the end of 1912. In May 1913 she became gunnery tender at Portsmouth while serving with 6th BS. Joined the Grand Fleet in August 1914 and served on the Northern Patrol. In February 1915 joined 6th BS of Channel Fleet and later the 3rd BS. On 11 November 1915 while heavily loaded with spare ammunition she was badly damaged by bad weather in the Pentland Firth, losing her bridge. After repairs she returned to Scapa Flow in December 1915 and was sent to North Russia to act as an icebreaker to get supplies through to Archangel. Between September 1916 and May 1917 her main deck casemate guns were replaced by 4–6in on the battery deck, but from May 1917 to November 1918 she served as an overflow ship to the naval barracks at Devonport, in reserve.

Cornwallis was with the Channel Fleet in 1906 but transferred to the Atlantic

London as a minelayer 1918 — *By courtesy of John M Maber*

Fleet in February 1907. Joined the Mediterranean Fleet in August 1910, and in June 1912 returned home to the 4th Battle Squadron, Home Fleet, where she remained until 1914. On the outbreak of war she joined the 6th BS, Channel Fleet but went to the Dardanelles in January 1915, becoming the first Allied warship to open fire on 18 February. She took part in all the operations, and during the final evacuation fired 500 rounds of 12in and 6000 rounds of 6in shell. On 9 January 1917 east of Malta she was hit three times by torpedoes from *U 32* but remained afloat long enough for all but 15 men to be taken off.

Duncan was with the Channel Fleet in 1906, and ran aground on Lundy while trying to help her sister *Montague*. Joined the Atlantic Fleet in February 1907 and then to Mediterranean Fleet in November 1908. Flagship of Rear-Admiral, Mediterranean Fleet from August 1912 for June 1912 and then joined 4th Battle Squadron, 1st Fleet in Home Waters. Gunnery tender at Portsmouth from May 1913. Joined 6th BS, 2nd Fleet on the outbreak of war and worked with the Northern Patrol. In November 1915 joined 3rd BS and moved later to Portland and Dover. To Mediterranean in 1915 but played no major part in the Dardanelles opeations. Returned home in 1917 and went into reserve to provide manpower for other ships.

Exmouth was flagship of the Home (later Channel) Fleet in 1906, but reduced to nucleus crew in April 1907 before recommissioning as flagship of the Atlantic Fleet. Flagship, Mediterranean Fleet from November 1908, and in July 1912 became flagship of Vice-Admiral, 4th Battle Squadron, Home Fleet. Became gunnery TS at Devonport in July 1913. Joined 6th BS, Grand Fleet on outbreak of war, and then worked on Northern Patrol as part of the 3rd BS. In November 1914 went to Portland, where with the *Lord Nelson*s and seven *Formidable*s reformed the Channel Fleet. She bombarded Zeebrugge on 21 November and in May 1915, after being fitted with extra-heavy nets, was sent to the Dardanelles. As flagships of Admiral Nicholson at Kephalo she was the only battleship allowed to remain off the beaches after the torpedoing of the *Goliath*, *Majestic* and *Triumph*. Returned home in 1917 and paid off into reserve.

Montagu was serving with the Channel Fleet in 1906. On 30 May 1906 while in thick fog she ran hard aground on Lundy Island. She proved beyond salvage, but her guns and other equipment were recovered, leaving the wreck to be broken up where it lay.

Russell was in the Home Fleet (Channel Fleet from April 1906) but transferred to the Atlantic Fleet in February 1907 and then to the Mediterranean Fleet in July 1909. Returned to the 1st Fleet in Home Waters in August 1912 and joined the 2nd Fleet at the Nore in September 1913. Joined the Grand Fleet in August 1914 as flagship, 6th Battle Squadron. With 3rd BS later took part in the Northern Patrol, and in November 1914 joined Channel Fleet at Portland. After bombarding the Belgian coast was ordered to the Dardanelles. In November 1915 with the *Hibernia* she was kept at Mudros in support, and only took part in the evacuation on 7 January 1916. Mined off Malta on 27 April 1916 with the loss of 126 lives.

King Edward VII class

Africa commissioned for the Atlantic Fleet on completion in November 1906, but transferred to the Channel Fleet in February 1907. In April 1909 joined 2nd Division, Home Fleet and became temporary flagship of Rear-Admiral. Reduced to nucleus crew at Nore in November 1911 and became flagship of 3rd and 4th Divisions of Home Fleet (relieved by *King Edward VII* in August 1911). Back in full commission with 3rd Battle Squadron in May 1912, having been fitted the previous month with temporary seaplane runway over her forecastle. Temporarily attached to 4th BS, Mediterranean Fleet in February 1913 and rejoined 3rd BS in July. With rest of 3rd BS joined the Grand Fleet in August 1914 (where they were known as the 'Wobbly Eight'). Moved from Scapa Flow to the Nore in May 1916. Refitted in 1917 with all 6in guns in main deck battery replaced by 4–6in a deck higher. Attached to 9th Cruiser Squadron from April 1917 to November 1918, and reduced to accommodation ship in April 1919.

Britannia commissioned for the Atlantic Fleet in December 1906, and transferred in February 1907 to Channel Fleet. In April 1909 became flagship of Vice-Admiral, 2nd Division of Home Fleet; joined 3rd Battle Squadron in Mediterranean temporarily before returning to 2nd Division, 1st Fleet. On outbreak of war went with 3rd BS to the Grand Fleet; ran aground on Inchkeith in January 1915 and suffered severe damage. Torpedoed off Cape Trafalgar by *UB 50* on 9 November 1918; she stayed afloat for 3½ hours but suffered a number of casualties from toxic smoke. In 1917 all 6in guns in battery replaced by 4–6in on shelter deck.

Commonwealth was serving in the Atlantic Fleet in 1906, but transferred to the Channel Fleet in May 1907 (suffered two accidents, a collision with *Albemarle* in February 1907 and a grounding in August 1907). Home Fleet, 2nd Division from April 1909, and went to Mediterranean temporarily in 1913. Joined the Grand Fleet with rest of 3rd Battle Squadron in August 1914, but was refitted December 1914–February 1915. Major reconstruction early in 1918, with 6in batteries replaced by 4–6in a deck higher, tripod foremast with director control, and anti-torpedo bulges. From 1919 to 1921 served as sea-going gunnery TS at Invergordon.

Dominion was serving in the Atlantic Fleet in 1906; ran aground in the Gulf of St Lawrence in August 1906 and was repaired at Bermuda. Joined Home Fleet in April 1909; 2nd Battle Squadron in May 1912. In October 1913 went with 3rd Battle Squadron to Mediterranean. With 3rd BS joined Grand Fleet in August 1914 and became temporary flagship of Vice-Admiral, August–September 1915. Attacked unsuccessfully by a U-boat in May 1916, and spent remainder of war based on the Thames. Accommodation ship at Chatham from April 1918.

Commonwealth 1920 following reconstruction — *By courtesy of John M Maber*

Agamemnon as a target ship — *By courtesy of John M Maber*

Hibernia commissioned in the Atlantic Fleet in January 1907 but transferred the following month to the Channel Fleet as flagship, Rear-Admiral. In January 1909 became flagship, Vice-Admiral. In March 1909 became flagship of Rear-Admiral, Home Fleet, 2nd Division. Reduced to nucleus crew at Nore in January 1912. In May 1912 she was fitted with temporary runway over forecastle, and from this Cdr Sampson made the first seaplane flight from a British warship on 4 May. At the time she was flagship, Rear-Admiral, 3rd Battle Squadron. Joined Grand Fleet in August 1914, but in November 1915 went to Dardanelles as flagship of Admiral Fremantle and acted as stand-by battleship at Kephalo. Became accommodation ship at Nore in 1919. In 1917 all 6in guns were removed from the battery and 4–6in replaced them on the shelter deck.

Hindustan was serving in the Atlantic Fleet in 1906; Channel Fleet from January 1907, and 2nd Division, Home Fleet from April 1909. In May 1912 joined 3rd Battle Squadron (temporarily joined 4th BS). Served with Grand Fleet August 1914–May 1916 and then stationed at Nore. From late 1914 to May 1918 stationed in Swin as depot ship for ships taking part in the Zeebrugge and Ostend raids.

King Edward VII was undergoing repairs in 1906 and in March 1907 recommissioned as flagship of the Channel Fleet. In March 1909 she became flagship of Vice-Admiral, 2nd Division of Home Fleet; relieved by *Hercules* in June 1911 and reduced to nucleus crew at Nore in August 1911 as flagship, Vice-Admiral 3rd and 4th Divisions. Joined 3rd Battle Squadron in May 1912 and spent short while in Mediterranean. Joined Grand Fleet as flagship of 3rd BS under Vice-Admiral Bradford; relieved by *Dominion* but rejoined on 2 August. On 6 January 1916, mined off Cape Wrath; both engine rooms flooded and she capsized some 12 hours later.

New Zealand was in the Atlantic Fleet in 1906 but joined the Channel Fleet in June 1907. In March 1909 she joined 2nd Division, Home Fleet and temporarily wore flag of Rear-Admiral. On December 1911 she was renamed *Zealandia* and joined 3rd Battle Squadron in May 1912. Joined Grand Fleet in August 1914 and then to Mediterranean in November 1915. Refitted in 1918 similar to *Commonwealth* but without bulges. Accommodation ship at Portsmouth in 1919.

Swiftsure class

Swiftsure was serving with the Home Fleet in 1906 but transferred to the Channel Fleet from July 1906 to October 1908. To Mediterranean March 1909–May 1912 and then returned to join 3rd Fleet at Portsmouth. Refitted September 1912–March 1913 before going out as flagship, East Indies. In August 1914 began Red Sea patrols and escorted Indian troopships to Aden. In November 1914 became flagship of forces defending Suez Canal (fired on Turkish troops at Kantara). Sent to Dardanelles in March 1915, and carried out several successful bombardments. Attacked by U-boat unsuccessfully in September 1915, and after evacuation returned home. Placed in reserve at Chatham, and in 1917 all armament was removed in preparation for her conversion to a blockship for use in the projected Belgian Coast attack. Conversion was cancelled and she was used later as an overflow ship. Used as a target in 1919.

Triumph was with the Channel Fleet in 1906, but transferred to the Mediterranean from March 1909 to May 1912. Joined 3rd Fleet at the Nore before going out to China in April 1913 to relieve the *Tamar* at Hong Kong. When war broke out she was in reserve but was recommissioned with the crews of various gunboats. Took part in operations against Tsingtao with Japanese warships, but was ordered to the Mediterranean in January 1915. Took part in the attacks on the Dardanelles forts from 18 February, and one of her picket boats destroyed HM Submarine *E 15* off Kephez. On 25 May 1915 while firing off Gaba Tepe she was torpedoed by *U 21*; she capsized within half an hour and sank with the loss of 73 men.

Lord Nelson class
Lord Nelson joined the Nore Division of the Home Fleet on completion in December 1908, but with a nucleus crew. In May 1912 joined the 2nd Battle Squadron and (temporarily in September 1913, 4th BS). Became flagship of the Channel Fleet after the outbreak of war, covering the passage of the BEF to France. To Dardanelles in February 1915, and became flagship of Vice-Admiral Wester Wemyss until 22 December 1915 (and then Sir John de Robeck until June 1916). Became flagship in Eastern Mediterranean and Aegean. After the Armistice passed through the Dardanelles into the Black Sea, where she remained flagship until April 1919. Returned home in May 1919 and paid off at Sheerness.

Agamemnon joined Nore Division of Home Fleet on completion in June 1908 (damaged by grounding in February 1911) and joined 4th Battle Squadron temporarily in September 1913. Served with 5th BS in Channel after outbreak of war, but in February 1915 went to Dardanelles with *Lord Nelson*. Took part in all the bombardments and was struck by over 50 projectiles. On 5 May 1916 shot down Zeppelin *LZ 85* at Salonika (with a 6pdr), her station after the evacuation. With her sister remained on stand-by at Mudros or Salonika in case of a break-out by the German battlecruiser *Goeben*, but when the break-out did occur in January 1918 both ships were absent. The Turkish Armistice was signed on board, and she returned to Chatham in February 1919. Converted to a radio-controlled target and recommissioned in April 1923. Paid off at Portsmouth in December 1926 and relieved by *Centurion*. The only major alteration to either ship was the raising of their funnels to reduce smoke interference in 1917.

LARGE CRUISERS

Name	Launched	Disp (load)	Fate
Blake class			
BLAKE	23.11.89	9150t	Depot ship 8.07, sold for BU 9.6.22
BLENHEIM	26.5.94	9150t	Depot ship 5.08, sold for BU 13.7.26
Edgar class			
CRESCENT	30.3.92	7700t	Depot ship 1917, sold for BU 22.9.21
EDGAR	24.11.90	7350t	Sold for BU 9.5.21
ENDYMION	22.7.91	7350t	Sold for BU 16.3.21
GIBRALTAR	27.4.92	7700t	Depot ship 6.15, sold for BU 9.23
GRAFTON	30.1.92	7350t	Sold for BU 1.7.20
HAWKE	11.3.91	7350t	Torpedoed 15.10.14
ROYAL ARTHUR	26.2.91	7700t	Depot ship 1915, sold for BU 22.9.21
ST GEORGE	23.6.92	7700t	Depot ship 3.10, sold for BU 1.7.20
THESEUS	8.9.92	7350t	Sold for BU 1921, resold 8.11.21
Powerful class			
POWERFUL	24.7.95	14,200t	HS 1912, sold for BU 31.8.29
TERRIBLE	27.5.95	14,200t	Disarmed 1915, HS 1.18, sold for BU 7.32
Diadem class			
AMPHITRITE	5.1.98	11,000t	Sold for BU 12.4.20
ANDROMEDA	30.4.97	11,000t	HS 9.13, sold for BU 8.56
ARGONAUT	24.1.98	11,000t	HS 1916, sold for BU 5.20
ARIADNE	22.4.98	11,000t	Torpedoed 26.7.17
DIADEM	21.10.96	11,000t	HS 1918, sold for BU 9.5.21
EUROPA	20.3.97	11,000t	Sold 15.9.20
NIOBE	20.2.97	11,000t	RCN 1910, HS 10.15, BU 1922
SPARTIATE	27.10.98	11,000t	HS 1913, sold for BU 7.32
Cressy class			
ABOUKIR	16.5.00	12,000t	Torpedoed 22.9.14
BACCHANTE	21.2.01	12,000t	Sold for BU 1.7.20
CRESSY	4.12.99	12,000t	Torpedoed 22.9.14
EURYALUS	20.5.01	12,000t	Sold for BU 1.7.20
HOGUE	13.8.00	12,000t	Torpedoed 22.9.14
SUTLEJ	18.11.99	12,000t	Sold for BU 9.5.21

Name	Launched	Disp (load)	Fate
Drake class			
DRAKE	5.3.01	14,150t	Torpedoed 2.10.17
GOOD HOPE	21.2.01	14,150t	Sunk by gunfire 1.11.14
KING ALFRED	28.10.01	14,150t	Sold for BU 30.1.20
LEVIATHAN	3.7.01	14,150t	Sold for BU 3.3.20
Monmouth class			
BEDFORD	31.8.01	9800t	Wrecked 21.8.10
BERWICK	20.9.02	9800t	Sold for BU 1.7.20
CORNWALL	29.10.02	9800t	Sold for BU 7.6.20
CUMBERLAND	16.12.02	9800t	Sold for BU 9.5.21
DONEGAL	4.9.02	9800t	Sold for BU 1.7.20
ESSEX	29.8.01	9800t	Sold for BU 8.11.21
KENT	6.3.01	9800t	Sold for BU 6.20
LANCASTER	22.3.02	9800t	Sold for BU 3.3.20
MONMOUTH	13.11.01	9800t	Sunk by gunfire 1.11.14
SUFFOLK	15.1.03	9800t	Sold for BU 1.7.20
Devonshire class			
ANTRIM	8.10.03	10,850t	Sold for BU 19.12.22
ARGULL	3.4.04	10,850t	Wrecked 28.10.15
CARNARVON	7.10.03	10,850t	Sold for BU 8.11.21
DEVONSHIRE	30.4.04	10,850t	Sold for BU 9.5.21
HAMPSHIRE	4.9.03	10,850t	Mined 5.6.16
ROXBURGH	19.1.04	10,850t	Sold 8.11.21
Duke of Edinburgh class			
BLACK PRINCE	14.6.04	13,550t	Sunk by gunfire 31.5.16
DUKE OF EDINBURGH	8.11.04	13,550t	Sold for BU 12.4.20
Warrior class			
ACHILLES	17.6.05	13,550t	Sold for BU 9.5.21
COCHRANE	20.5.05	13,550t	Wrecked 14.11.18
NATAL	30.9.05	13,550t	Blew up 30.12.15
WARRIOR	25.11.05	13,550t	Foundered in tow after gunfire damage, 1.6.16
Minotaur class			
DEFENCE	24.4.07	14,600t	Sunk by gunfire 31.5.16
MINOTAUR	6.6.06	14,600t	Sold for BU 12.4.20
SHANNON	20.9.06	14,600t	Sold for BU 12.12.22

Blake class
Both ships were struck off the Effective List in 1906 and converted to depot ships for destroyers, with armament reduced to 4–6in, 4–4in and 4–12pdrs. During the war *Blake* served with the Grand Fleet destroyers (2nd Destroyer Flotilla and then 11th DF), while *Blenheim* served Mediterranean flotillas and was sent to Mudros in March 1915 for the Dardanelles operations.

Edgar class
Crescent returned from Cape and West Africa Station in 1907 and recommissioned in June 1907 in Portsmouth Division of Home Fleet 4th Cruiser Squadron 1909–13, recommissioning 1 February 1913 in Queenstown Training Squadron. In August 1914 joined 10th CS (Northern Patrol) until February 1915, when she was sent to Hoy as guardship. Paid off in November 1915 and disarmed as depot ship; attached to Grand Fleet 1917–18 and paid off at Rosyth 1920.

Edgar was serving as Boys' TS in 4th Cruiser Squadron but on her return from the North America and West Indies Station in May 1909 was paid off into reserve at the Nore. Recommissioned in March 1913 for the Queenstown Training Squadron until August 1914, when she joined the 10th CS. She and her sisters were proving too frail for work in Northern waters, and they were paid off at the end of 1914 to provide 9.2in Mk VI and their CP III mountings for a new class of monitors. The need for bombarding ships in the Dardanelles then led to them being fitted with anti-torpedo bulges. Single 6in guns were mounted in place of the 9.2in forward and aft, changing the armament to 12–6in. Other guns were added during 1915–18, probably light AA, but details are lacking. *Edgar* and her three sisters arrived at the Dardanelles in mid-1915, and remained in the Mediterranean until the Armistice. She was at Gibraltar in November 1918 and returned to Queenstown in 1919, where she paid off.

Endymion was serving as a tender to HMS *Wildfire* at Sheerness for gunnery training in 1906, where she remained until 1912, when she joined the 3rd Fleet at Portsmouth. Commissioned in March 1913 as flagship, Vice-Admiral commanding the Queenstown Training Squadron; 10th Cruiser Squadron, August 1914–February 1915 and then rearmed and bulged for service in the Dardanelles. Served in the Aegean in 1918 but returned to the Nore, where she paid off early in 1920.

Gibraltar remained in reserve at Portsmouth from 1905 to 1908 and then joined the Home Fleet at Devonport until 1912. In 1908 she carried drafts of troops to Australia and in 1910–11 escorted the new Australian destroyers *Parramatta* and *Yarra* out to Australia. Commissioned for Queenstown Training Squadron in February 1913 and in August 1914 joined 10th Cruiser Squadron. Early in 1915 disarmed and converted to depot ship for the Northern Patrol at Swarback Minns in the Shetlands (arrived June 1915). Later formed part of the anti-submarine school at Portland, and served as a destroyer depot ship in 1919–22.

Endymion about 1916 showing Dardanelles equipment and bulges *CPL*

Grafton served as tender to HMS *Excellent* 1905–13; joined Queenstown Training Squadron April 1913; 10th Cruiser Squadron August 1914–February 1915 and then rearmed and bulged. Sent to Dardanelles mid-1915. Damaged by a torpedo hit on 11 June 1917 but returned to Malta for repairs. Served in Aegean 1918 and went to Black Sea 1919, acting as depot ship for British ships supporting the White Russians. Paid off at the end of 1919.

Hawke was Boys' TS in 4th Cruiser Squadron on North America and West Indies Station but returned and paid off in August 1906, going to the Nore torpedo school until 1907, when she joined the Home Fleet at the Nore. Stationed with Home Fleet at Portsmouth 1908–13, and on 20 September 1911 lost her ram bow in collision with the liner *Olympic* in the Solent. She was repaired but without a stiffened ram. Commissioned in the Queenstown Training Squadron in February 1913, then 10th CS in August 1914. Torpedoed and sunk with the loss of 524 men (only 70 survivors) by *U 9* on 15 October 1914.

Royal Arthur paid off as a flagship 4th Cruiser Squadron in May 1906 and went into reserve at Portsmouth; 4th CS, Home Fleet 1909–12 and then commissioned in August 1913 in Queenstown Training Squadron. In August 1914 to 10th CS but reduced to guardship at Scapa Flow in February 1915 and then became a depot ship for submarines. Operating with 12th Submarine Flotilla in 1918 and 1st Flotilla in 1919; paid off in December 1920.

St George was serving as Boys' TS in 4th Cruiser Squadron, but after May 1906 she went into reserve at Devonport. Converted to a destroyer depot ship at Chatham in 1909–10, and recommissioned as depot ship for 3rd Destroyer Flotilla at the Nore in March 1910. Suffered minor damage from grounding off Sheerness in June 1910. Served with 6th DF 1912–13 and then 9th DF 1913–14. Formed part of the Humber Patrol from November 1914, but in 1917 was converted to support submarines, and went to the Aegean in 1918–19 with 2nd Submarine Flotilla. Paid off early 1920.

Theseus was a tender to HMS *Cambridge* at Devonport from 1905–13, and joined Queenstown Training Squadron in February 1913. In 10th Cruiser Squadron August 1914–February 1915, and then rearmed and bulged for service in the Dardanelles. Returned from the Mediterranean 1916 and sent to White Sea. In 1918 she went to the Aegean as depot ship for trawlers and then to the Black Sea in 1919, returning home to pay off in February 1920.

Powerful class

Both these expensive ships spent most of their time in reserve, *Powerful* being laid up as a harbour TS at Devonport in 1912; she was renamed *Impregnable* in November 1919. *Terrible* was disarmed and used to carry troops to the Dardanelles in 1915–16 and then became an accommodation ship at Portsmouth, where she remained for many years after the war.

Blake as a depot ship *By courtesy of John M Maber*

Diadem class

Amphitrite was in reserve at Chatham in 1906 but recommissioned for the Home Fleet in February 1907. In March 1910 attached to HMS *Vivid* at Devonport as Stokers' TS. Recommissioned for 9th Cruiser Squadron in August 1914 and stationed at Cape Verde February–June 1915; laid up at Portsmouth from June 1915 but then converted to minelayer. On completion in August 1917 she was armed with only 4–6in and 1–4in AA gun, and carried 354 mines. She replaced her sister *Ariadne* on the Dover Barrage in November 1917, laying a total of 5053 mines. In April 1918 operated with US Navy, laying mines in Northern Barrage. Collision with destroyer HMS *Nessus* September 1918. Paid off June 1919.

Andromeda returned from China and paid off in July 1906 into reserve at Chatham. With Home Fleet at Devonport 1907–10, taking relief crew for *Bedford* out to China. 4th Fleet, Devonport 1910–12 and then reserve 1913. Recommissioned as Boys' TS at Devonport in September 1913; renamed *Impregnable II* in November 1919 until paid off in March 1929; became part of Torpedo School in March 1931 and renamed *Defiance*, and survived until 1956.

Argonaut was in reserve at Chatham but was refitted for Special Service June–September 1906 and joined Home Fleet at Portsmouth in October. Paid off in February 1911 and recommissioned February 1912 for 3rd Fleet until paid off in April 1914. Joined 9th Cruiser Squadron and stationed off Cape Finisterre from August 1914 to July 1915. Captured the German merchant ship *Graecia* on 10 October 1914. Laid up at Portsmouth in October 1915 and used as a hospital ship until 1917. Accommodation ship for stokers in 1918 and sold 1920.

Ariadne recommissioned from Portsmouth reserve into 3rd Fleet 1912 but was reduced to Stokers' TS at Portsmouth 1913–14. Continued in this capacity but was transferred to Devonport October 1915. Converted to minelayer 1916–17, similar to *Amphitrite* but carrying 400 mines. Recommissioned March 1917 at Devonport and laid 708 mines in the Dover Barrage and Heligoland Bight, but on 26 July 1917 she was torpedoed and sunk by *UC 65* off Beachy Head (38 lives lost).

Diadem was flagship of Vice-Admiral, China Station until returning home to pay off in April 1907. Joined Home Fleet at Portsmouth 1907–12 and then 3rd Fleet (refitted 1909). From 1914 served as Stokers' TS at Portsmouth; closed from October 1915 to January 1918 but then re-opened; put up for sale January 1921.

Europa was in reserve at Devonport but recommissioned in November 1907 for the Home Fleet; paid off February 1910 but joined 3rd Fleet from November 1911 to outbreak of war, when she joined 9th Cruiser Squadron, and was stationed off Cape Finisterre as flagship until June 1915. Flagship at Mudros July 1915–1919 and paid off at Malta in March 1920. Bought by G F Bletto for conversion to an emigrant carrier, but sank in a gale off Corsica in January 1921; wreck later raised and BU.

Niobe was flagship of Rear-Admiral Reserve Squadron from 1905 to 1909

Amphitrite 1918 as a minelayer *By courtesy of John M Maber*

(refitted 1908). Recommissioned April 1909 in 4th Division, Home Fleet at Devonport, and paid off September 1910. Sold to Canadian Government 6 September 1910 and arrived at Halifax, Nova Scotia 22 October. Ran aground on Cape Sable 29 July 1911 and had to be towed off by HMS *Cornwall*. Sent to New York in October 1914 and then to Bermuda from February to August 1915; paid off at Halifax in October 1915 and disarmed as a depot ship. She was badly damaged by the ammunition explosion in Halifax Narrows on 6 December 1917, losing her funnels, ventilators and masts, but continued in service until sold in 1922.

Spartiate was in reserve at Portsmouth until November 1907 and then underwent a refit before joining the 4th Division, Home Fleet in April 1909. With 3rd Fleet at Portsmouth 1912–13 and then became Stokers' TS. Renamed *Fisgard* in June 1915 until put up for sale in January 1932.

Cressy class

Aboukir was refitting at Chatham until March 1907, when she recommissioned for the 3rd Cruiser Squadron, Mediterranean Fleet. Paid off at Devonport in March 1909 and recommissioned in July for 6th CS, Mediterranean Fleet. Joined 4th CS, Home Fleet in December 1912 but transferred to 6th CS 1913 and then 7th CS 1913–14. Was in reserve at outbreak of war, but was recommissioned with reservists for Cruiser Force 'C' in Southern North Sea (the 'Broad Fourteens' Patrol). Torpedoed and sunk by *U 9* on 22 September 1914 with heavy loss of life.

Bacchante was refitting at Portsmouth in 1906, and recommissioned as flagship 3rd Cruiser Squadron, Mediterranean Fleet in November 1916. Flagship 6th CS 1909–12 and then 3rd Fleet, Nore 1912–14. Sent to Humber in August 1914 as guardship, but shortly afterwards became flagship of Cruiser Force 'C'. Saw action in Heligoland Bight on 28 August 1914 and escorted convoy to Gibraltar in October. To Suez Canal in February 1915 and Dardanelles April 1915. Returned to home waters late in 1916 and was damaged in collision with HMS *Achilles* in the Irish Sea in February 1917. Flagship 9th CS at Gibraltar April 1917–November 1918, and paid off into reserve at Chatham in April 1919. Placed on sale list April 1920.

Cressy was in reserve in 1906 but was refitted and joined 4th Cruiser Squadron, North America and West Indies Station as Boys' TS in 1907. Joined 3rd Fleet at Nore August 1909–April 1910; in reserve at Chatham 1910–11 and then joined 4th Division, Home Fleet. Joined Cruiser Force 'C' in August 1914 and was torpedoed and sunk by *U 9* on 22 September 1914 while trying to rescue survivors from HMS *Aboukir*, 560 lives were lost.

Euryalus returned to Portsmouth as flagship of Vice-Admiral Australia Station and paid off in March 1906. From May 1906 to 1909 she was Boys' TS in 4th Cruiser Squadron, North America and West Indies Station, and then joined 3rd Division, Home Fleet at Portsmouth until 1910. Transferred to 4th Division, Home Fleet at Devonport 1911–13, then 3rd Division in reserve at the Nore until the outbreak of war. Joined Cruiser Force 'C' in August 1914. Escorted troop convoy to Gibraltar in October 1914; to Suez Canal February 1915; Smyrna March 1915; Dardanelles April 1915. Returned to Suez Canal in December 1915 and from 1916 to 1919 was flagship, East Indies, supporting the Arab Revolt in 1917. Went to Hong Kong at end of 1917, where it was proposed to convert her to a minelayer but this was cancelled, and she paid off at Hong Kong in 1918. Returned to be laid up in reserve at the Nore in April 1919 and was put on the sale list in January 1920.

Hogue returned from China in 1906 and recommissioned as Boys' TS, 4th Cruiser Squadron, North America and West Indies Station from 1906 to May 1908. In reserve at Devonport 1908–9 (coal bunker explosion October 1909); 3rd Division, Home Fleet at the Nore 1909–12. Refitted at Chatham 1912–13 and then joined Home Fleet at Nore from September 1913. With Cruiser Force 'C' from outbreak of war and torpedoed and sunk by *U 9* while trying to rescue survivors of HMS *Aboukir* on 22 September 1914. She had been in action at Heligoland Bight on 28 August 1914, and towed damaged cruiser HMS *Arethusa* home.

Sutlej returned from China in May 1906 and then served (with a short spell in reserve) as Boys' TS in 4th Cruiser Squadron, North America and West Indies Station until 1909. Flagship 3rd Fleet at Devonport 1909–10; suffered boiler explosion on manoeuvres in July 1910. In reserve at Devonport 1911–12, then 6th CS 1912–13, 7th CS 1913 and 6th CS 1913–14, going into reserve in June 1914. Joined 9th CS in August 1914, but transferred to 11th CS in Ireland in February 1915. Sent to Santa Cruz in February 1916 and joined 9th CS in September 1916. Renamed *Crescent II* as depot ship at Rosyth in January 1918 (she had been laid up there as an accommodation ship in 1917); reverted to *Sutlej* in 1919 before being put on sale list.

Drake class

Drake was flagship, 2nd Cruiser Squadron, Atlantic Fleet in 1906, but in 1908 became flagship of 1st CS. Transferred to 5th CS 1910, Home Fleet. Reduced to reserve at Portsmouth in 1913 but recommissioned for July 1914 Test Mobilisation. In January 1915 joined 6th CS, Grand Fleet, and was refitted in October. From 1916 used for ocean escort, and was refitted, with all lower deck casemate 6in guns replaced by four in shields on the shelter deck p&s. On 2 October 1917 she was torpedoed by *U 79* off Rathlin Island, Northern Ireland. She drifted into Rathlin Sound and sank, but without heavy loss of life. Demolition of the wreck was started *c*1970.

Good Hope was flagship, 1st Cruiser Squadron, Atlantic Fleet in 1906, and in 1908 visited South Africa as flagship 2nd CS. Went into reserve 1913 but recommissioned in July 1914 Test Mobilisation. Joined 6th CS in August 1914 with her three siters. Sent to South Atlantic as flagship of Rear-Admiral Sir Christopher Cradock. At the Battle of Coronel on 1 November 1914 she and her squadron were annihilated by Vice-Admiral von Spee's cruisers *Scharnhorst* and *Gneisenau*. *Good Hope* appears to have suffered an internal explosion towards the end of the action, and sank with all hands.

Leviathan returned from the Mediterranean at the end of 1906, and after a refit joined the 5th Cruiser Squadron in 1907. Paid off into reserve 1908 but recommissioned for 4th CS 1909. In reserve at Chatham 1913 but recommissioned for Test Mobilisation in July 1914 and joined 6th CS immediately on outbreak of war. Joined 5th CS in December 1914 until relieved by *Defence* in January 1915, when she reverted to 6th CS. Flagship, North America and West Indies Squadron from October 1915, and recommissioned for same command in January 1918. Paid off into reserve 1919.

King Alfred recommissioned as flagship, China Station in January 1906, where she remained until relieved by the *Minotaur* in 1913. On her return she joined the reserve at Portsmouth. After the Test Mobilisation she went to war with the 6th Cruiser Squadron but joined 9th CS, Grand Fleet in October 1915. Covered Atlantic convoys in 1917 and in January 1918 she and *Leviathan* escorted US troop convoys across Atlantic. Both ships were probably refitted like the *Drake*, with lower deck 6in casemate guns replaced by 6in guns in shields on the shelter deck, and light AA armament in place of the numerous light guns.

Monmouth class

Bedford was serving in the Atlantic Fleet, and on her return in 1906 paid off into reserve at Chatham. She commissioned for the China Station in February 1907 and was recommissioned at Hong Kong by a relief crew in March 1909. Wrecked at Quelpart Island in the China Sea on 21 August 1910 (18 lives lost); wreck sold for BU 10 October 1910.

Berwick paid off from 2nd Cruiser Squadron, Atlantic Fleet in March 1906, and then joined Home Fleet. On 2 April 1908 rammed and sank HMS *Tiger* during night exercises off the Isle of Wight. Refitted 1908–9 at Portsmouth and recommissioned for 4th CS, West Indies Station in April 1909. Served with Training Squadron in West Indies in 1912 and was still on the North America and West Indies Station in August 1914. Captured German merchantman *Spreewald* in South Atlantic on 10 September 1914 and carried out patrols and escort duty from 1915 and 1918. Joined 8th Light Cruiser Squadron in 1919 before paying off. In common with most of her sisters she probably had her lower 6in casemate guns replaced by two single shielded guns p&s on the shelter deck by 1917.

Cornwall paid off from 2nd Cruiser Squadron, Atlantic Fleet in December 1906 and was then refitted during 1907 for service as Cadets' TS from January 1908. Suffered damage by running aground on Cape Sable, Nova Scotia while trying to tow HMCS *Niobe* on 31 July 1911, and was repaired at Halifax. Returned for the July 1914 Naval Review and Test Mobilisation, and immediately joined 5th CS. She captured the German merchantman *Syra* on 6 August 1914 and was sent to South Atlantic in September to patrol between Madeira and Pernambuco. Part of squadron assembled to catch von Spee's squadron after Coronel and with HMS *Glasgow* sank the light cruiser *Leipzig* during the Battle of the Falklands on 8 December 1914. Took part in operations off South West Africa in January 1915 and then went to East Africa in April, and then the Dardanelles. Transferred to China Station January–April 1916 but returned to convoy duty in the Atlantic in 1917, joining North America and West Indies Squadron in September 1917 until the Armistice. Cadets' TS in 1919 until paid off for disposal. Probably rearmed with 12–6in (six lower deck casemates suppressed and 4–6in added on shelter deck) in 1917.

Cumberland paid off from 2nd Cruiser Squadron, Atlantic Fleet in December 1906 and joined Home Fleet in 1907 as Cadets' TS (refitted 1907–8). Was present at Spithead in July 1914 and was sent to West Africa immediately after the outbreak of war. At Duala in the Cameroons on 27 September 1914 captured 10 German merchantmen. On her return home in January 1915 joined 6th CS and spent remainder of war on ocean escort duties. Paid off at Queenstown in April 1920.

Donegal commissioned from Devonport reserve for China Station in February 1906 but ran aground near Suez on 2 March and had to return home for repairs at Chatham. Home Fleet at Devonport June 1906–1909 and then 4th Cruiser Squadron until 1911. Collided with merchant ship off Gibraltar in December 1909. Joined Training Squadron 1912 and then 3rd CS in 1913. Destroyed derelict merchantman *Volturno* by gunfire in October 1913. After outbreak of war served with 3rd CS at Sierra Leone, but in January 1915 joined 6th CS, Grand Fleet, and then, in November 1915, 7th CS escorting convoys to the White Sea (Archangel). With 2nd CS from May 1916, then 9th CS in September. Went to North America and West Indies Station in September 1917 but returned to Devonport in June 1918, where she paid off.

Essex paid off from 2nd Cruiser Squadron, Atlantic Fleet in March 1906. Went into commissioned reserve, and had an explosion in a 6in gun accident in July. Recommissioned for 4th CS in September 1909 and transferred to Training Squadron in 1912. Refitted 1913 and recommissioned in 4th CS, West Indies in January 1914. Served in Noth Atlantic from August 1914, capturing German merchantman on 10 August, and another on 7 September 1916. In West Indies from November 1916 to January 1915. Stationed in Canary Islands from January 1916, capturing a German merchantman in May 1916. Believed to have been rearmed in 1917, with lower casemate 6in guns moved up two decks. Put on sale list in April 1921.

Kent was on China Station from 1906 to 1913, and returned to Portsmouth for refit in August 1913. Sent to Falklands in September 1914 and took part in the Battle of the Falklands on 8 December 1914, sinking the light cruiser *Nurnberg*. On 14 March 1915 with HMS *Glasgow* discovered the *Dresden* at Mas a Fuera in Chile, and sank her. Sent to China Station in March 1915 but returned home in May 1915. Escorted Channel convoys in June 1918 and in July 1918 went to China. Sent to Vladivostok in January 1919 during American and Japanese operations against Bolshevik Russia. Put on sale list at Hong Kong in March 1920. She had been rearmed in 1917, with lower 6in casemate guns moved up two decks.

Lancaster paid off from 3rd Cruiser Squadron, Mediterranean Fleet in March 1906 but recommissioned a day later with a relief crew. Joined 6th CS in March 1909 and returned home in 1912 to join 5th CS. In 1913 she went to the West Indies as part of 4th CS, and after the outbreak of war returned to join the 7th CS, Grand Fleet in 1915. To Pacific in April 1916 and in 1918 became flagship of the Eastern Squadron. Partially dismantled at Birkenhead in 1919 before being put up for sale. Partially rearmed in 1916, with lower 6in casemate guns moved up two decks.

Monmouth was serving in 1st Cruiser Squadron, Channel Fleet but paid off into reserve at Devonport at the end of January 1906. Recommissioned for China Station in April 1906, and transferred to 3rd Fleet in 1913. Commissioned for 5th CS in August 1914 and sent to Pernambuco. With the flagship HMS *Good Hope* she was sunk by von Spee's squadron off Coronel on 1 November 1914 (lost with all hands).

Suffolk was serving with 3rd Cruiser Squadron, Mediterranean Fleet; refitted 1907–8. Recommissioned for 6th CS, Mediterranean Fleet 1909, paying off at Devonport for refit in October 1912. Recommissioned February 1913 at Devonport as flagship of 4th CS (Rear-Admiral Cradock; transferred flag to *Good Hope* in August 1914). Chased German light cruiser *Karlsruhe* in August

1914, but without success; captured a German merchantman on 8 August 1914. Served on North America and West Indies Station from 1915 to 1916, then to China Station as flagship from August 1917 to November 1918. Went to Vladivostok in 1918–19 to cover operations against Bolshevik Russia. On her return home in 1919 she became Cadets' TS until placed on sale list in April 1920.

Devonshire class
Antrim was serving with 1st Cruiser Squadron, Channel Fleet, but joined 2nd CS in March 1907, then Atlantic Fleet in September 1908. Became part of 3rd Division, Home Fleet at the Nore in April 1909. Was flagship of Rear-Admiral, 3rd CS from December 1912 and joined Grand Fleet in August 1914. Captured a German merchantman on 6 August 1914 and was unsuccessfully attacked by a U-boat on 9 October. Sent to Archangel in June 1916 and was then sent to North America and West Indies Station; paid off in December 1917 but returned during August–November 1918. In reserve at the Nore 1919 but refitted as W/T and Asdic trials ship, recommissioning in March 1920 (she carried out the first sea trials of Asdic). Cadets' TS 1922 until paid off for sale.

Argyll commissioned in January 1906 for the 1st Cruiser Squadron, Channel Fleet, then joined 5th CS, Atlantic Fleet in March 1909, but was detached in 1911 for duty as escort to the Royal Yacht SS *Medina*. Joined 3rd CS in March 1912; damaged by grounding in Plymouth Sound in December 1912. Joined Grand Fleet in August 1914 and captured a German merchantman on the 6th. Wrecked on the Bell Rock off Dundee on 28 October 1915 (no lives lost).

Carnarvon was serving in 3rd Cruiser Squadron, Mediterranean Fleet until paid off in March 1907. Recommissioned in 2nd CS, Atlantic Fleet in June 1907; reduced to 3rd Division, Home Fleet in April 1909. Transferred to 2nd Fleet at Devonport in March 1912 and was flagship 5th CS to outbreak of war. Went to Cape Verde in August 1914, capturing a German merchantman on the 24th. To Montevideo in October 1914. Led cruisers during Battle of Falklands on 12 December. Tore her bottom plating on a shoal near the Abrolhos Rocks in February 1916 and had to be repaired at Rio de Janeiro. Served on North America and West Indies Station from March 1915 to November 1918. Cadets' TS from 1919 until put on sale list in March 1921.

Devonshire was serving in 1st Cruiser Squadron, Channel Fleet but in March 1907 transferred to Atlantic Fleet. In 3rd Division, Home Fleet at Devonport from August 1909 to 1912; 5th CS 1912–13; 3rd CS 1913–16. Sent to Scapa Flow August 1914, capturing a German merchantman on the 6th. Refitted at Cromarty in September 1914. Operated off Norway in April 1916. Stationed at Nore in 1916, joining 7th CS in July 1916; to North America and West Indies Station from December 1916 to the end of 1918. Put on sale list May 1920.

Hampshire was serving in 1st Cruiser Squadron, Channel Fleet and paid off for refit at Portsmouth in December 1908. Recommissioned in 3rd Division, Home Fleet in August 1909, and then in December 1911 for 6th CS, Mediterranean Fleet. Sent to China in 1912 until outbreak of war. Captured German merchantman on 11 August 1914 and took part in hunt for the *Emden*. Joined Grand Fleet in December 1914, becoming part of 7th CS in January 1915. Sent to White Sea to protect shipping in November 1915. Serving with 2nd CS in 1916 and took part in Battle of Jutland, 31 May 1916. Embarked Lord Kitchener and his staff for mission to North Russia but struck a mine off the Shetlands on 5 June 1916, foundering with the lost of all but 12 men.

Roxburgh was serving in 1st Cruiser Squadron, Channel Fleet until December 1908 and was then refitted at Devonport. Recommissioned for 3rd Division, Home Fleet in August 1909; 5th CS from June 1912. Stood by the stranded merchantman SS *Ludgate* off the coast of Morocco in December 1912. Joined 3rd CS from February 1913 and joined Grand Fleet in August 1914. Captured a German merchantman on 6 August 1914. Refitted January 1915; hit by torpedo from *U 39* on 20 June 1915 but escaped with serious damage to bow. After repairs completed in April 1916 served in Norwegian waters. To North America and West Indies Station from September 1916 until Armistice, and while escorting a convoy off Northern Ireland on 12 February 1918 rammed and sank *U 89*. Into reserve at Portsmouth in June 1919 but recommissioned as W/T trials ship until paid off in February 1920.

Duke of Edinburgh class
Black Prince served with 2nd CS until 1907, then 1st CS 1907–08; 5th CS (Atlantic Fleet) 1908–12; 3rd CS 1912–13. She captured a German merchantman in the Red Sea in August 1914. Stationed at Gibraltar in November 1914 but joined the Grand Fleet (1st CS) the following month. Sunk by gunfire from German battleships during the night action at Jutland, 31 May 1916 (all hands lost).

Duke of Edinburgh served in 2nd Cruiser Squadron, Atlantic Fleet after completion but transferred to 1st CS in 1907; 5th CS 1908–12, during which time she rescued survivors of SS *Delhi* at Cape Spartel in December 1911. Joined 3rd CS 1912–13 and then 1st CS, Mediterranean Fleet 1913–14. Captured a German merchantman in Red Sea in August 1914 and went to the Persian Gulf in November 1914. Joined 1st CS, Grand Fleet in December 1914 and saw action at Jutland. Joined 2nd CS in June 1916 and escorted Atlantic convoys in 1917. Sent to North America and West Indies Station August–November 1918, and on her return was stationed in the Humber at Immingham, E Coast of England (June 1919); put up for sale in March 1920.

In March 1916 both ships had their armament altered, with all 6in removed from the lower deck battery and replaced by three p&s in shields between the main deck 9.2in turrets (total now 6–9.2in, 6–6in). In May 1917 *Duke of Edinburgh* was given two more 6in in embrasures on the forecastle deck, as in the *Iron Duke* class. The foremast was replaced by a tripod mast at the time, and some of the light guns may have been replaced by AA guns.

Warrior class
Achilles joined the 5th Cruiser Squadron, Home Fleet on completion and went to Baltic on official visit to Russia in 1908. Joined 3rd Fleet at Portsmouth in 1909, and remained with that Squadron until 1919. Gun explosion aboard in November 1914. Missed Jutland as she was refitting at the time, but with the armed boarding steamer *Dundee* sank the German disguised raider *Leopard* in the North Sea on 16 March 1917. On ocean escort duties 1917–18 but reduced to Stokers' TS by the Armistice. On sale list July 1920.

Cochrane joined 5th Cruiser Squadron on completion but transferred to 2nd CS in 1909. Escorted Royal Yacht *Medina* 1911–12. Went to Scapa Flow with Grand Fleet in August 1914 and saw action at Jutland. On North America and West Indies Station 1917 and then to Archangel May–September 1918. Ran aground in the Mersey on 14 November 1918 and became a total loss. Wreck demolished by June 1919.

Natal joined 5th Cruiser Squadron at the Nore in 1907; 2nd CS 1909 thereafter, escorting Royal Yacht *Medina* in 1911–12 and carrying body of Whitelaw Reid to New York (US Ambassador to Great Britain). Joined Grand Fleet in August 1914 and was refitted at Cromarty in January 1915. While lying there on 31 December 1915 she was destroyed by an internal explosion (faulty cordite) and 404 lives were lost.

Warrior joined 5th Cruiser Squadron at Nore and then 2nd CS from 1909 to 1913; 1st CS, Mediterranean Fleet 1913–14, and was sent to Adriatic in August 1914 to try to prevent the breakout of the German battlecruiser *Goeben*. Returned to Egype to defend the Suez Canal. To Gibraltar and then Sierra Leone in November and joined Grand Fleet in December 1914. Heavily damaged by German gunfire during the opening action at Jutland, 31 May 1916; taken in tow by seaplane carrier HMS *Engadine* but foundered next day. To reduce smoke interference *Warrior* had the fore funnel raised by 6ft to clear the charthouse, but by 1910 all four funnels were raised, the sisters followed suit. In 1916–17 the two survivors were given tripod foremasts and may have had smaller guns replaced by AA weapons.

Minotaur class
Defence joined 5th Cruiser Squadron in February 1909 but transferred to 1st CS in July (Home Fleet); escorted Royal Yacht *Medina* November–December 1912, and then went to China Station as flagship. Joined 1st CS as flagship in 1913, and took part in hunt for *Goeben* and *Breslau* in August 1914. Stationed off Dardanelles in September but sent to South Atlantic to reinforce Rear-Admiral Cradock's squadron; diverted to Cape of Good Hope in November 1914. Became flagship 1st CS, Grand Fleet, in January 1915 and was sunk by gunfire of German battleship *Friedrich der Grosse* at Jutland, 31 May 1916. All hands (893 officers and men) lost as a result of cordite charges catching fire in the ammunition passages.

Minotaur joined 5th Cruiser Squadron on completion in May 1908 but transferred to 1st CS the following April. Flagship, China Station 1910–14 and after outbreak of war escorted Australian troop convoys in November 1914. Became flagship at Cape of Good Hope but returned home in December 1914 for refit before joining 2nd CS early in 1916. Present at Jutland. Paid off into reserve in June 1919 until sold.

Shannon commissioned as flagship Rear-Admiral, 5th Cruiser Squadron in March 1908 but transferred to 2nd CS in April 1909. Damaged in collision with HMS *Prince George* in Portsmouth in December 1909. Recommissioned March 1912 as flagship 3rd CS, reverting to 2nd CS in 1913. Joined Grand Fleet in August 1914 and was refitted at Cromarty in November 1914. Present at Jutland, but went to Murmansk in November 1916. Escorted Atlantic convoys 1917–18, and paid off into reserve 1920. Accommodation ship attached to HMS *Actaeon* until paid off in 1922.

Funnels were raised 15ft in 1909, and in 1917 *Minotaur* and *Shannon* received tripod foremasts. Light armament was probably reduced at this time, and at least one AA gun was added.

LIGHT CRUISERS

Name	Launched	Disp (load)	Fate
Medea class			
MEDEA	9.6.88	2800t	Sold for BU 2.4.14
MEDUSA	11.6.88	2800t	HS 1910, sold for BU 1920, and resold 21.10.21
Barham class			
BARHAM	11.9.89	1830t	Sold for BU 19.2.14.
Pearl class			
PHILOMEL	28.8.90	2575t	To RNZN 1914, HS 1921, sold 17.1.47
WALLAROO	5.2.90	2575t	HS 1906, guardship 19.11.14; depot ship 3.19, sold for BU 27.2.20
Apollo class			
AEOLUS	13.11.91	3600t	Sold for BU 26.5.14
ANDROMACHE	14.8.90	3400t	Minelayer 1907, BU 1920
APOLLO	10.2.91	3400t	Minelayer 1907, BU 1920

Name	Launched	Disp (load)	Fate
BRILLIANT	24.6.91	3600t	Scuttled as blockship 23.4.18
INDEFATIGABLE	12.3.91	3600t	Sold for BU 26.5.14
INTREPID	20.6.91	3600t	Minelayer 1907, scuttled as blockship 23.4.18
IPHIGENIA	19.11.91	3600t	Minelayer 1907, scuttled as blockship 23.4.18
LATONA	22.5.90	3400t	Minelayer 1907, sold 1920
MELAMPUS	2.8.90	3400t	Sold for BU 9.5.11
NAIAD	29.9.90	3400t	Minelayer 1907, sold 1922
PIQUE	13.12.90	3600t	Sold for BU 9.5.11
RAINBOW	25.3.91	3600t	To RCN 4.8.10; sold for BU 1920
RETRIBUTION	6.8.91	3600t	Sold for BU 4.4.11
SAPPHO	9.5.91	3400t	Sold for BU 3.21
SCYLLA	17.10.91	3400t	Sold for BU 2.4.14
SIRIUS	27.10.90	3600t	Scuttled as blockship 23.4.18
SPARTAN	25.2.91	3600t	HS 1906, sold 7.31
TERPSICHORE	30.10.90	3400t	Sold for BU 28.5.14
THETIS	13.12.90	3400t	Minelayer 1907, sunk as blockship 23.4.18
TRIBUNE	24.2.91	3400t	Sold for BU 9.5.11
Astraea class			
ASTRAEA	17.3.93	4360t	Sold for BU 1.7.20
BONAVENTURE	2.12.92	4360t	Depot ship 4.08, sold for BU 12.4.20
CAMBRIAN	31.1.93	4360t	HS 3.16, renamed *Vivid* 9.21, sold for BU 21.2.23
CHARYBDIS	15.6.93	4360t	Converted to cargo carrier 3.18, sold for BU 27.1.22
FLORA	21.11.93	4360t	HS 4.15, renamed *Indus II*, sold 12.12.22
FORTE	9.12.93	4360t	Sold for BU 2.4.14
FOX	15.6.93	4360t	Sold for BU 14.7.20
HERMIONE	7.11.93	4360t	Sold 25.10.21
Eclipse class			
DIANA	5.12.95	5600t	Sold for BU 1.7.20
DIDO	20.3.96	5600t	HS 1.14, sold 16.12.26
DORIS	3.3.96	5600t	Sold for BU 20.2.19
ECLIPSE	19.7.94	5600t	HS 1916, sold for BU 8.21
ISIS	27.6.96	5600t	Sold for BU 26.2.20
JUNO	16.11.95	5600t	Sold for BU 24.9.20
MINERVA	23.9.95	5600t	Sold for BU 5.10.20
TALBOT	25.4.95	5600t	Sold for BU 6.12.91
VENUS	5.9.95	5600t	Sold for BU 22.9.21
Arrogant class			
ARROGANT	26.5.96	5750t	Depot ship 6.11, sold for BU 13.11.23
FURIOUS	3.12.96	5750t	HS 6.15, sold for BU 5.23
GLADIATOR	18.12.96	5750t	Sunk in collision 25.4.08
VINDICTIVE	9.12.97	5750t	Scuttled as blockship 10.5.18, salved 16.8.20 and BU
Hermes and Challenger classes			
HERMES	7.4.98	5600t	Seaplane carrier 1912
HIGHFLYER	4.6.98	5600t	Sold for BU 6.21
HYACINTH	27.10.98	5600t	Sold for BU 11.23
CHALLENGER	27.5.02	5600t	Sold for BU 31.5.20
ENCOUNTER	18.6.02	5600t	Lent to RNZN 7.12, transferred permanently 12.19, HS 5.23, scuttled 9.32
Pelorus class			
PANDORA	17.1.00	2200t	Sold for BU 7.13
PELORUS	15.12.96	2135t	Depot ship 1916, sold for BU 6.5.20
PEGASUS	4.3.97	2135t	Sunk by gunfire 20.9.14
PERSEUS	15.7.97	2135t	Sold for BU 26.5.14

Name	Launched	Disp (load)	Fate
PACTOLUS	21.12.96	2135t	Depot ship 9.12, sold for BU 25.10.21
PIONEER	28.6.99	2200t	To RAN 28.12.12, sold 1924, scuttled 19.2.31
POMONE	25.11.97	2135t	HS 1.10, sold for BU 25.10.22
PROMETHEUS	20.10.98	2135t	Sold for BU 28.5.14
PROSERPINE	5.12.96	2135t	Sold for BU 30.11.19
PSYCHE	19.7.98	2135t	To RAN 1.7.15, sold for BU 6.22
PYRAMUS	15.5.97	2135t	Sold for BU 21.4.20
'Gem' class			
AMETHYST	5.11.03	3000t	Sold for BU 1.10.20
DIAMOND	6.1.04	3000t	Sold for BU 9.5.21
SAPPHIRE	17.3.04	3000t	Sold for BU 9.5.21
TOPAZE	23.7.03	3000t	Sold for BU 22.9.21
Adventure class			
ADVENTURE	9.9.04	2670t	Sold for BU 3.3.20
ATTENTIVE	24.11.04	2670t	Sold for BU 12.4.20
Forward class			
FORWARD	27.8.04	2850t	Sold for BU 27.7.21
FORESIGHT	8.10.04	2850t	Sold for BU 3.3.20
Pathfinder class			
PATHFINDER	16.7.04	2940t	Torpedoed 5.9.14
PATROL	13.10.04	2940t	Sold for BU 21.4.20
Sentinel class			
SENTINEL	19.4.04	2895t	Sold for BU 18.1.23
SKIRMISHER	7.2.05	2895t	Sold for BU 3.3.20

Medea class

Medea was laid up awaiting disposal in 1906, but she recommissioned at Devonport in April 1909 for service with the Mediterranean Fleet. Recommissioned May 1911 and paid off in 1913.

Medusa was laid up out of commission in 1906 but was brought back into service as a harbour hulk in 1910; used as a calibrating vessel at Bantry 1914–18.

Barham class

Barham had been with the Mediterranean Fleet since January 1905; recommissioned at Malta in January 1909 and again at Devonport in April 1911; paid off in 1913.

Pearl class

Philomel was laid up in Firth of Forth until February 1908, when she recommissioned for the Mediterranean Fleet. Commissioned again at Portsmouth July 1909 for the East Indies, returning in 1913 when her transfer to the Royal New Zealand Navy had been agreed. Handed over at Wellington 15 July 1914 and commissioned as seagoing TS. Served as convoy escort from August 1914 to April 1917, when she paid off. Disarmed and reduced to depot ship, and made her last sea voyage in 1921, when she steamed to Auckland to become a training hulk. Sold in January 1947 to Strongman Shipping Co and scuttled off Coromandel (India) 6 August 1949.

Wallaroo was attached to *Indus* in 1906 as TS for mechanicians, but was rearmed in August 1914 for service as guardship at Chatham. Renamed *Wallington* in March 1919, reverting to *Wallaroo* in March 1920, before being sold for BU.

Apollo class

Seven were converted to minelayers from 1906–1910, with armament reduced to 4–4.7in (12cm) and double sets of mine-tracks running from the break of the forecastle to the poop (for 100–140 mines). The first conversions, *Thetis* and *Iphigenia* are reported to have carried their mines slung from overhead travellers, but this method was found unsuitable and was replaced in them and the later conversions by a more conventional double trackway on the deck, allowing the sinkers to be winched aft and rolled off chutes projecting over the stern. Although too slow for operations in enemy waters they were successful, laying nearly 8000 mines in 22 operations in 1914–15. They were then replaced by larger cruiser-conversions, merchant ships and fast light cruisers and destroyers, and were reduced to subsidiary service.

Aeolus had been in Devonport Reserve since September 1905; recommissioned for Training Squadron in May 1911, then West Coast of America Station 1912–13; paid off 1913.

Andromache laid up out of commission in 1906, but taken in hand 1907 for conversion to a minelayer; completed conversion September 1909 at Chatham DYd. Operated out of Dover and Sheerness 1914–15, then became a depot ship in Mediterranean.

Apollo laid up out of commission in 1906, but converted to minelayer; completed conversion at Chatham DYd August 1909; war service as *Andromache* (depot ship to 4th DF January 1918).

Brilliant had been attached to the Coast Guard since December 1904 and was at Southampton in 1906; she then joined 4th CS on North America and West Indies Station, remaining there until she came home to pay off in 1913. Laid up for disposal in August 1914 but recommissioned as depot ship, and stationed on the Tyne until 1915, then moved to Lerwick until early 1918. Converted to blockship at Chatham and scuttled at Ostend.

Indefatigable had been in Portsmouth Reserve since May 1905; commissioned for 4th CS, North America and West Indies Station January 1906, and recommissioned 11 January 1910 when her name was changed to *Melpomene* (releasing her former name for the new battlecruiser); Training Squadron January 1912 to 1913, then paid off for disposal.

Intrepid laid up out of commission in 1906; converted to minelayer 1907–September 1910 at Chatham; depot ship 1916–17 (White Sea 1917) and then converted to blockship and scuttled at Zeebrugge.

Iphigenia returned from China in January 1906, reducing to Special Service at Portsmouth; converted to minelayer at Portsmouth November 1906 – December 1908; depot ship 1916–17 (White Sea 1917); fitted out as blockship and scuttled at Zeebrugge.

Latona was with Newfoundland Fishery Squadron from February 1905, returning to Portsmouth in May 1906 to begin conversion to minelayer. Completed conversion at Portsmouth June 1908; service as *Andromache* (depot ship in Mediterranean 1917) and sold at Malta for BU December 1920.

Naiad laid up out of commission in 1906; converted to minelayer 1907–October 1910 at Chatham DYd; service as *Andromache* (depot ship on Tyne 1917).

Rainbow laid up out of commission 1906–10; recommissioned August 1910 for newly established Royal Canadian Navy and stationed at Esquimalt, BC; remained there as depot ship 1914–18.

Sappho had been with Newfoundland Fishery Squadron from January 1905; joined Sheerness Reserve Squadron 1906, then commissioned for 4th CS, North America and West Indies Station May 1907; joined 1st Fleet as tender to flagship April 1912, a duty which lasted until 1915. Laid up 1915–1921.

Scylla had been with Newfoundland Fishery Squadron since January 1905, and then joined 4th CS, North America and West Indies Station in September 1906; returned home to pay off in 1913.

Sirius was in Devonport Reserve October 1905–February 1912, when she recommissioned for the Training Squadron; served briefly with 4th CS in 1912–13, then paid off into reserve; at Nore August 1914–1915, then to West Africa until early 1918; returned home and converted to blockship at Chatham; scuttled at Ostend.

Spartan was laid up out of commission, and in 1906 reduced to harbour service as an accommodation hulk at Devonport; renamed *Defiance II* in August 1921.

Terpsichore was on Cape of Good Hope Station April 1904–November 1906, then in reserve at Portsmouth until put on disposal list 1913.

Thetis was in reserve at Chatham from July 1905, then joined 3rd Division at Portsmouth. *Thetis* completed conversion to a minelayer at Portsmouth DYd in August 1907; depot ship 1916–17 then converted to blockship early 1918 and scuttled at Zeebrugge.

Melampus, Retribution and Tribune were laid up out of commission from 1906 until sold.

Astrea class

Astrea was serving on China Station in 1906, recommissioning at Hong Kong in September 1906, again at Colombo in September 1908 and September 1910. Returned to Home waters at the end of 1911, recommissioning in the 3rd Fleet at the Nore in June 1912. Recommissioned April 1913 for Cape of Good Hope and West Africa Station, where she remained throughout the war. Bombarded Dar-es-Salaam on 8 August 1914 and blockaded the *Königsberg* in the Rufiji Delta. Paid off on 1 July 1919 and sold for BU, but resold and BU in Germany.

Bonaventure returned from Pacific Squadron to pay off at Devonport in May 1906. Went to Haulbowline Dockyard, Cork for conversion to submarine depot ship, which was completed in April 1907.

Cambrian was serving on Australian Station in 1906, and recommissioned at Colombo in October 1907, September 1909 and 19 September 1911. Became flagship in 1913 and returned home to pay off early in 1914 and put on sale list, but reinstated in August 1914. Fitted out as Stokers' TS at Devonport and renamed *Harlech* on completion in March 1916.

Charybdis was in Commissioned Reserve at Chatham in 1906 following refit at Sheerness. Carried relief crew for *Astraea* out to Colombo in August 1908 but returned to Chatham to pay off two months later; rejoined Commissioned Reserve on her return. Transferred to 4th Division, Home Fleet at Nore in November 1910 and recommissioned in April 1913 in 3rd Fleet at Devonport. Joined 12th Cruiser Squadron in August 1914, but damaged in collision on 9 January 1915 and laid up at Bermuda. Commissioned for harbour service in 1917 and converted to cargo carrier in March 1918 for loan to mercantile operator. Returned to RN in January 1920, and sold at Bermuda in January 1922; resold 1923 and towed to Holland for BU in October 1923.

Flora was serving on China Station in 1906, recommissioning at Singapore in August 1907 and at Colombo in September 1909 and 1911. Returned home in 1913 and put on sale list 1914. Reduced to harbour service and renamed *Indus II* in April 1915.

Forte was serving on Cape of Good Hope and West Africa Station in 1906, returning home to pay off at Portsmouth in June 1907. Recommissioned immediately for Portsmouth Division of Home Fleet. Made up full complement at Portsmouth in April 1909 and relieved *Hermione* at the Cape. Recommissioned at Simonstown in April 1911 and returned home in 1913 to pay off at Chatham. Laid up in Kethole Reach and put on sale list. BU in Holland.

Fox was serving on East Indies Station in 1906 but paid off at Portsmouth in January 1907, recommissioning a day later for the Portsmouth Division of the Reserve Fleet. Repaired at Haulbowline and recommissioned there in May 1908 for the Devonport Division, Home Fleet. Relieved *Highflyer* in East Indies and left Devonport June 1908. Recommissioned at Muscat July 1910 and again at Aden in July 1912. Captured German merchant ships *Australia* (10 August 1914) and *Holtenfels* (11 August 1914), both off Colombo. Served in East Indies and Egyptian waters 1915–17, then Red Sea 1917–18, paying off in March 1919.

Hermione was in Commissioned Reserve at Portsmouth in 1906 but was refitted in 1907 and made up to full complement in April 1907 for the Cape Station. Ran aground at Zanzibar on 14 February 1909 but was refloated with only slight damage. Returned to Portsmouth in June and joined 3rd Division, Home Fleet in July 1909. Ran aground off Killingholme in the Humber on 6 August but was refloated after 8 hours. Recommissioned in June 1910 and made up full complement in September for naval airship duties at Barrow. On completion of this detached duty in January 1912 she reverted to 4th Division, Home Fleet. Recommissioned in July 1913 to relieve *Melpomene* in West Atlantic; relieved July 1914 by *Bristol* and then paid off. In August 1914 she became guardship at Southampton, but from December 1916 served as HQ ship for motor launches (MLs) and coastal motor boats (CMBs), a duty which ended in 1919. Sold in October 1921 but resold to Marine Society in 1922 and became TS *Warspite* in December 1922. Sold for BU in September 1940.

Eclipse class

Diana remained in the Mediterranean until 1913 and then transferred to 3rd Fleet at Devonport. Joined Cruiser Force 'G' in Channel in August 1914, capturing a German schooner on the 6th. 12th Cruiser Squadron, Channel from February 1915; China Station November 1915–August 1917, then to Red Sea and Indian Ocean until November 1918. Returned to Queenstown and paid off June 1919.

Dido was in Channel Fleet until 1907 and then Home Fleet at the Nore to 1909. Attached to 1st Battle Squadron 1909–10 and paid off in December for refit at Chatham. Joined Home Fleet, Nore September 1911 and then to 6th Submarine Flotilla from August 1912. In collision with HMS *Berwick* in 1913, and joined 3rd S/m Flotilla early in 1914. Remained at Harwich with her flotilla until 1916, when she became depot ship to the 10th Destroyer Flotilla until the Armistice. Joined Reserve Fleet at Portsmouth and paid off for disposal in February 1926.

Doris was in reserve at Devonport until 1909, but after a refit she joined the Atlantic Fleet until 1910. Served with Home Fleet 1910–14, and on 5 August 1914 captured a German merchantman. Then joined 11th Cruiser Squadron in Mediterranean, sinking a Turkish merchantman in December 1914. To Dardanelles 1915 and later operated in Aegean. In East Indies from March 1917 to November 1918, and was sold at Bombay.

Eclipse was in reserve at Portsmouth in 1906, and was attached to RN College, Osborne in 1907–12. Joined 3rd Fleet at Portsmouth 1912–13 and then at Devonport 1913–14. Escorted new Australian submarines *AE 1* and *AE 2* to Singapore early in 1914, and after outbreak of war joined Cruiser Force 'G' in Channel, capturing a German merchantman on 10 August 1914 and another on 10 September. Joined 12th Cruiser Squadron in February 1915 but reduced to accommodation ship for submarine flotillas by 1916. Laid up at Devonport 1918–19.

Isis served as Cadets' TS in 4th Cruiser Squadron, North America and West Indies Station until 1907 and then joined Home Fleet at Devonport until 1909. Attached to 1st Battle Squadron 1909–10 and joined Home Fleet at Devonport. Served in 4th CS 1911–14 (refitted 1913), and sank merchantman in collision in April 1914. Captured a German merchantman on 5 August 1914. Based in Ireland with 11th CS from February 1915; Bermuda 1916; North America and West Indies Station December 1916–November 1918. At Invergordon in 1919.

Juno served in the Channel Fleet until 1909, and was attached to 2nd Battle Squadron, Home Fleet until 1910. 3rd Fleet, Portsmouth 1910–11; Nore 1911–12; 4th Fleet, Nore 1912; attached to 7th BS 1912–13. With 11th Cruiser Squadron in Ireland from August 1914; Persian Gulf July 1915; East Indies January–November 1918, and returned home to pay off at the Nore in March 1920.

Minerva served in Mediterranean until 1912. Joined 3rd Fleet, Devonport 1912–13 and helped in salvage of submarine *B 2* in October 1912. Attached to 6th Destroyer Flotilla in 1913 and was at Portsmouth until outbreak of war. With 11th Cruiser Squadron in Ireland in August 1914, but joined 5th CS in September, capturing an Austrian merchantman off Finisterre the same month. To Suez Canal in November 1914, and then to Dardanelles November 1915; she sank the Turkish torpedo-boat *Demir-Hissar* off Chios on 17 April 1915. To China 1916; Red Sea and Indian Ocean January 1917; East Africa March 1917–1919. Returned to Queenstown and put on sale list in May 1920.

Talbot was in reserve at the Nore, but in 1906 was moved to Devonport. Served in the Channel Fleet 1907–9; attached to 2nd Battle Squadron 1909–10; stationed at Haulbowline, Cork 1911–12. Joined 3rd Fleet 1912–13, and ran aground in the Suez Canal in September 1912. Attached to 7th Destroyer Flotilla 1913 but reverted to 3rd Fleet at Devonport 1913–14. Joined Cruiser Force 'G' in August 1914 and captured a German merchantman off the Lizard in September. Joined 12th Cruiser Squadron in February 1915 and went to Dardanelles in April 1915; East Africa May 1916 to 1917; Cape of Good Hope 1918; Mediterranean 1919. Returned to Devonport in November 1919, and was put up for sale at Queenstown in 1920.

Venus served in the Mediterranean until 1908 and then joined the Atlantic Fleet until 1911. Attached to 7th Destroyer Flotilla until and then 1st DF in 1911; joined 3rd Fleet at Pembroke 1913 and went to Portsmouth in 1914. Joined 11th Cruiser Squadron in Ireland in August 1914; captured two German merchantmen in October and lost her foremast in a gale in November

1914. To Egypt 1916; Singapore March 1917; flagship East Indies 1919 until she returned home in May 1919 to pay off.

Arrogant class
Arrogant was serving with Atlantic Fleet in 1906, recommissioning at Devonport in September 1907. Recommissioned for 3rd Division, Home Fleet. Paid off May 1910 at Devonport for conversion to a submarine depot ship to relieve HMS *Mercury*.

Furious was in commission as a tender to HMS *Vernon* at Portsmouth in 1906, where she remained until paid off in March 1912. Laid up at the Motherbank from 1913 to June 1915, when she was renamed *Forte* and attached to *Vernon* as a hulk.

Gladiator was in reserve at Portsmouth in 1906 but recommissioned for Portsmouth Division, Home Fleet in May 1907. On 25 April 1908 collided with American liner *St Paul* in the Solent, sinking with the loss of 27 lives. Raised in October 1908 but was found to be beyond economical repair, and was sold for BU in August 1909.

Vindictive was in reserve but recommissioned in December 1906 for special service, and again in February 1907, April 1908 and May 1909. Refitted at Chatham December 1909–April 1910 for service in 3rd Division, Home Fleet at the Nore. Recommissioned for 4th Division September 1910 and remained at Nore until March 1912, when she recommissioned at Portsmouth to relieve *Furious* as tender to *Vernon*. In August 1914 joined 9th Cruiser Squadron, and captured two German merchantmen: *Schlesien* on 7 August and *Slawentzitz* on 8 September 1914. Left 9th CS in 1915 and was sent to SE Coast of America Station. From 1916 she served in the White Sea, returning late in 1917. Early in 1918 she was fitted out as an assault ship for the Zeebrugge Raid (most guns replaced by howitzers, flame-throwers and mortars, and gangways fitted on port side). Upperworks badly damaged by gunfire while she lay alongside Zeebrugge Mole on 23 April 1918. On her return she was refitted as a blockship and was scuttled in Ostend harbour on 10 May 1918. The wreck was raised on 16 August 1920 and sold for BU.

Hermes 1914 with aircraft equipment — *By courtesy of John M Maber*

Highflyer class
Hermes was flagship of the East Indies Station in 1906, but in 1907 she relieved *Hyacinth* as flagship on the Cape Station. Recommissioned at Simonstown in October 1908 and again at Ascension in December 1910. Relieved by *Hyacinth* in March 1913 and returned home to pay off in April 1913 and joining 3rd Fleet at the Nore. Converted at Chatham to depot ship for Naval Wing of Royal Flying Corps (subsequently Royal Naval Air Service), with launching platform forward and stowage platform aft for 3 seaplanes (only 2 carried). Recommissioned at Chatham in May 1913 but paid off in December after trials and manoeuvres. In August 1914 the stripped equipment was hurriedly reinstalled and she recommissioned on 31 August as part of the Nore Command. Torpedoed on 31 October 1914 off Ruylingen Bank by *U 27* and sank with the loss of 22 lives. She had been ferrying aircraft across to France.

Highflyer was in Devonport Reserve Division in 1906 but took part in the Annual Manoeuvres before commissioning at Devonport in November 1906 to relieve *Fox* on the East Indies Station. Paid off at Devonport in September 1908 but recommissioned a day later in Devonport Division, Home Fleet. Recommissioned July 1909 but paid off for refitting in November 1910. Commissioned for 3rd Division, Home Fleet at the Nore in December 1910. and then made up to full complement at Chatham in February 1911 to relieve *Hyacinth* as flagship on East Indies Station. Relieved by *Swiftsure* April 1913 and paid off at Chatham into 3rd Fleet, but recommissioned August 1913 as TS for Special Entry Cadets. Joined 9th Cruiser Squadron in August 1914, and later transferred to 5th CS. Sank the German armed merchant cruiser *Kaiser Wilhelm der Grosse* off the Rio d'Oro on 27 August 1914. Sent to Cape Verde 1914, then West Africa 1916, West Indies 1917 and East Indies 1918. Paid off at Bombay in march 1919 but recommissioned in July as flagship East Indies Station until paid off early in 1921. BU at Bombay.

Hyacinth was in Commissioned Reserve at Devonport in 1906 but made up to full complement in February 1907 for service as flagship, East Indies Station. Recommissioned at Bombay March 1909 and then paid off at Chatham for refitting in March 1911, and recommissioned February 1912 for 3rd Fleet at the Nore. Commissioned at Chatham February 1913 to relieve *Hermes* as flagship on Cape Station, where she remained after the outbreak of war. On 18 April 1915 she intercepted German merchantman *Rubens* which was trying to get supplies to the cruiser *Königsberg*. On 23 March 1916 she sank the SS *Tabora* at Dar-es-Salaam. On her return to Home waters she was paid off in August 1919 at Portsmouth.

Challenger class
Challenger had been on Australian Station and recommissioned at Singapore 21 July 1906, at Sydney 1 October 1908 and at Sydney 9 December 1910. Returned home and paid off at Devonport in October 1912, recommissioning immediately in 3rd Fleet (reserve). Recommissioned in 9th Cruiser Squadron in August 1914, based at Portland. Captured German steamer *Ulla Boog* at entrance to Bristol Channel before going out to West Africa for Cameroons operations in September 1914. Engaged in Rufiji River operations against *Königsberg* in 1915, and bombarded Dar es Salaam 13 June 1916 with *Pioneer*. Remained in East Africa until Armistice and returned to Portsmouth, paying off in April 1919. Sold May 1920 for BU.

Encounter had commissioned in December 1905 to relieve *Katoomba* and *Wallaroo* on Australian Station. Recommissioned at Colombo 1 January 1908, and on while being towed at Sydney on 5 January 1909 her pinnace was run down by SS *Dunmore* with the loss of 15 lives. Recommissioned at Colombo 15 April 1910 and was handed over to Royal Australian Navy in 1912, recommissioning at Sydney on 1 July 1912. Served on Pacific Station in 1914–15, capturing German sailing vessel *Elfriede* on 25 April 1915. China Station 1915–16, then returned to Pacific Station 1916–18. Permanently transferred to RAN 5 December 1919, becoming a receiving ship at Sydney. Renamed *Penguin* May 1923 as submarine depot ship, and relieved by *Platypus* in 1929. Paid off 15 August1929 and scuttled off Sydney Heads 14 September 1932.

Pelorus class
Most served on overseas stations before the outbreak of war. *Pandora* sold for BU in July 1913, followed by *Prometheus* in May 1914 *Pomone* had been reduced to harbour service as a TS at Dartmouth in January 1910; sold for BU in October 1922. *Pactolus* was converted to a submarine depot ship in September 1912, and served with 9th S/m Flotilla at Ardrossan 1914–18; sold for BU in May 1921.

Pegasus was on Cape of Good Hope Station in August 1914, and was sent to East Africa. While lying at Zanzibar with fires drawn on 20 September 1914 she was destroyed by the German light cruiser *Königsberg*.

Pelorus was on patrol in the Bristol Channel in August 1914, and was then sent to the Mediterranean. Converted to a depot ship in 1916 and sold for BU in May 1920.

Pioneer transferred to RAN in December 1912 and remained in Australian waters until early 1915. Served in East Africa until 1916, when she returned to Sydney to pay off and be laid up. Sold as a hulk in 1924 and scuttled in February 1931.

Proserpine served with 7th CS in the Channel Fleet from August 1914 and was sent to Egypt early in 1915. During 1915–18 she served in Mesopotamia and was sold for BU in Genoa in November 1919.

Psyche was in New Zealand in August 1914, and then went to China after being transferred to the RAN in July 1915. Sold for BU in Melbourne in June 1922.

Pyramus was in New Zealand in August 1914 and in early 1915 went to the Persian Gulf, and then the East Indies. Sold for BU in January 1920.

'Gem' *class*
Amethyst was leader of Harwich Force and Destroyer Command at outbreak of war but relieved by *Arethusa* just before Heligoland Bight action 28 August 1914; joined 1st Light Cruiser Squadron, Grand Fleet for remainder of year, and in 1915 transferred to Mediterranean, serving in the Dardanelles; South America Station 1916–18; sold for BU October 1920.

Diamond was Senior Officers' Ship, 3rd Flotilla 1911–12; attached to 5th Battle Squadron in Channel 1914–15, then worked with reformed 5th BS, Grand Fleet 1915–18; Mediterranean 1918, where she was used as a 'CMB carrier' with six 40ft CMBs carried in davits; sold for BU May 1921.

Sapphire was Senior Officer's Ship, 5th Flotilla 1911–12; attached to 4th Battle Squadron 1914–15 then Mediterranean 1915–16; East Indies 1916–18; sold for BU May 1921.

Topaze was Senior Officer's Ship, 4th Flotilla 1911–12; attached to 5th Battle Squadron, Channel, 1914–15; Mediterranean 1915–17; Red Sea 1917–18; sold for BU September 1921.

Adventure class
Adventure had been in Commissioned Reserve at the Nore since completion. In April 1907 she collided with and sank a sailing vessel off Sussex coast. Commissioned at Chatham in June 1907 as leader of 1st Torpedo Boat Destroyer Flotilla; recommissioned August 1909 and then refitted at Chatham in June 1910. On completion of refit joined 2nd Destroyer Flotilla, recommissioning at Devonport in April 1911. Refitted at Devonport in August 1912 and joined 3rd Light Cruiser Squadron for 1913 Manoeuvres. Commissioned at Devonport in July 1913 for 6th DF at Dover, where she remained until May 1915, when she temporarily joined 6th LCS in the Humber. Became flagship at Queenstown July 1915–November 1917, during which period she rescued crew of SS *Huronian* (26 December 1915). Escorted slow convoys to Gibraltar from April to November 1918 and then went to the Mediterranean, including a short spell in the Aegean in June 1919. Paid off at Immingham 12 August 1919, and while

laid up there in the Humber was rammed by a Hull trawler in January 1920. Sold March 1920 and towed to Morecambe by *Skirmisher* for BU.

Attentive went into reserve at the Nore on completion in June 1906. Commissioned at Chatham in March 1907 for Nore Division, Home Fleet. On 6 August 1907 collided with destroyer *Quail* off Portland. On 27 April 1908 was involved in double collision with destroyers, sinking the *Gala* (1 life lost) and holing the *Ribble*. On commissioning at Chatham in July 1909 she became leader of the 3rd Destroyer Flotilla but transferred to 2nd DF in 1910, and recommissioned at Devonport in October 1911. Refitted at Devonport in August 1912 and joined 3rd Light Cruiser Squadron for the 1913 Annual Manoeuvres. Commissioned at Devonport for 1st DF in July 1913, but transferred to 6th DF (Dover) early in 1914. Spent April 1914 in Ulster but spent most of the war with the Dover Patrol, including the Zeebrugge Raid on 25 April 1918. Sent to Gibraltar to escort convoys, and then sent to North Russia. Paid off in December 1918 and sold for BU.

Forward class

Foresight had been in reserve since completion, and joined Portsmouth Division, Home Fleet in March 1906; recommissioned for same service in February 1908. Made up to full complement at Portsmouth in October 1909 to lead 2nd Destroyer Flotilla, but joined 3rd DF at Nore in August 1910 and recommissioned in May 1911. Placed in reserve at Chatham early in 1912, and recommissioned at Chatham in May 1911 for service with 6th DF at Dover. Damaged destroyer *Falcon* in collision in November 1913. Served with Dover Patrol from August 1914, operating off Flanders coast in October 1914. Then served with 8th DF at Dover, including temporary duty with 6th Light Cruiser Squadron in Humber in May 1915. Sent to Mediterranean. Served in Aegean from July 1916 and rescued survivors of hospital ship *Britannic* in November 1916. Returned to Chatham to pay off in June 1919.

Forward joined Portsmouth Reserve on completion, but commissioned at Portsmouth in October 1907, relieving *Patrol* in Channel Fleet. Became leader of 2nd Destroyer Flotilla early in 1909, transferring to 4th DF in October, and then 3rd DF at the Nore in 1910 (recommissioning in June 1911). Refitted at Chatham in 1912 and then commissioned as leader of 3rd DF in June 1913, but detached to join 3rd Light Cruiser Squadron in 1913 Manoeuvres. Attached to 9th DF in 1914, and formed part of Shetland Patrol before outbreak of war. Present during German battlecruiser raid on Hartlepool in December 1914, then transferred to 7th DF in Humber. In 6th Light Cruiser Sqdn temporarily in Humber (May 1915) before leaving for Mediterranean. Served in Aegean from June 1916 to early 1919, returning to pay off at Sheerness in April 1919.

Pathfinder class

Pathfinder had been serving in Atlantic Fleet but in 1906 was attached to Channel Fleet for special service and in 1907 joined Home Fleet at the Nore. Commissioned at Chatham in January 1909 as leader of 1st Destroyer Flotilla and paid off in November 1910. Recommissioned at Chatham for 4th DF, Home Fleet (stationed at Portsmouth) but paid off into reserve 1912–13. Commissioned October 1913 as relief for *Amethyst* with 8th DF. Patrolling off Ulster in April 1914, and with 8th DF was stationed in the Firth of Forth from August 1914. Torpedoed off St Abbs Head on 5 September 1914 by *U 21* (259 lives lost).

Patrol was on particular service in 1906, and then joined Home Fleet after recommissioning in October 1907. Joined 3rd Fleet at Nore in 1908 but commissioned as temporary leader of 1st Destroyer Flotilla at Portsmouth in August 1909. With 3rd DF 1910, then refitted at Chatham in June 1910 before rejoining 1st DF. In reserve at Chatham 1912 and then stationed at Haulbowline in 1913–14. Commissioned 27 January 1914 at Portsmouth to relieve *Juno* in 9th DF, and served with her flotilla in the Forth and Tyne from August 1914. Present during Scarborough Raid in December 1914. Transferred to 7th DF, Humber, in 1915. To Irish Sea in 1918, but by the end of the year had rejoined the 9th DF at the Nore. Paid off there in April 1919.

Sentinel class

Sentinel was with the 3rd Cruiser Squadron in the Mediterranean in 1906, but was recalled for particular service with the Channel Fleet, being based at Devonport. In 1907 she was part of the Home Fleet (recommissioned in May 1909). She commissioned at Devonport in February 1910 as leader of the 5th Destroyer Flotilla, Home Fleet; refitted at Chatham in June 1910 and recommissioned at Devonport in April 1911. After refit at Portsmouth in 1912 joined 3rd Light Cruiser Squadron for the 1913 Manoeuvres before commissioning at Portsmouth as leader of the 9th DF. Transferred to 6th DF at Dover in 1913 but after outbreak of war joined 8th DF in the Forth. Temporarily joined 6th LCS in Humber before being sent to Mediterranean. Part of Aegean Squadron in 1918 and entered the Dardanelles on 12 November 1918 for service in Black Sea. Returned to Sheerness in April 1919 to pay off, but saw further service as Mechanics' TS at Chatham from July 1920 until the end of 1922.

Skirmisher was in reserve in 1906, having been moved from Portsmouth to Devonport. Commissioned in April 1907 as leader of 5th Destroyer Flotilla, Home Fleet, at Dover. With 2nd DF Home Fleet from 1909, recommissioning at Devonport in May 1909, and then joined 4th DF in August 1910. Refitted at Portsmouth in 1912 and was temporarily attached to 3rd Light Cruiser Squadron for 1913 Manoeuvres. Commissioned at Portsmouth in July 1913 as leader of 7th DF. Stationed at Immingham in December 1914, then temporary service with 6th LCS in the Humber in September 1915. Went to the Mediterranean in 1916 and served with Aegean Squadron in November 1918. On her return in June 1919 was stationed at Immingham (Humber).

DESTROYERS AND TORPEDO-BOATS

Name	Fate	Name	Fate
Yarrow 26-knotters: launched 1893, 275t			
HAVOCK	Sold 1912	HORNET	Sold 1909
Thornycroft 26-knotter: launched 1893–94, 280t			
DARING	Sold 1912		
Laird 26-knotters: launched 1893–94; 280t			
FERRET	Sunk as target 1911	LYNX	Sold 1912
Thornycroft 27-knotters: launched 1894–95, 265t			
ARDENT	Sold 1911	BOXER	Sunk in collision 8.2.18
BRUIZER	Sold 1914		
Yarrow 27-knotters: launched 1894, 255t			
CHARGER	Sold 1912	HASTY	Sold 1912
DASHER	Sold 1912		
Doxford 27-knotters: launched 1895, 260t			
HARDY	Sold 1911	HAUGHTY	Sold 1912
Palmer 27-knotter: launched 1895, 275t			
JANUS	Sold 1914	LIGHTNING	Mined 30.6.1915
PORCUPINE	Sold 1920		
Earle 27-knotters: launched 1895, 305t			
SALMON	Sold 1912	SNAPPER	Sold 1912
Laird 27-knotters: launched 1894, 290t			
BANSHEE	Sold 1912	DRAGON	sold 1912
CONTEST	Sold 1911		
White 27-knotters: launched 1894–95, 320t			
CONFLICT	Sold 1920	WIZARD	Sold 1920
TEAZER	Sold 1912		
Hanna Donald & Wilson 27-knotters: launched 1895, 275t			
FERVENT	Sold 1920	ZEPHYR	Sold 1920
Fairfield 27-knotters: launched 1895, 275t			
HANDY	Sold 1916	HUNTER	Sold 1912
HART	Sold 1912		
Hawthorn Leslie 27-knotters: launched 1895, 310t			
OPOSSUM	Sold 1920	SUNFISH	Sold 1920
RANGER	Sold 1920		
J & G Thompson 27-knotters: launched 1894, 280t			
ROCKET	Sold 1912	SURLY	Sold 1920
SHARK	Sold 1911		
Naval Construction & Armament Co 27-knotters: launched 1894–95, 300t			
SKATE	Sold 1907	STURGEON	Sold 1912
STARFISH	Sold 1912		
Armstrong 27-knotters: launched 1895, 320t			
SPITFIRE	Sold 1912	SWORDFISH	Sold 1910
Thames Iron Works 27-knotter: launched 1895, 310t			
ZEBRA	Sold 1914		
Thornycroft 30-knotters: launched 1896–99, 310t			
DESPERATE	Sold 1920	ARIEL	Wrecked 19.4.07
FAME	Sold 1921	COQUETTE	Mined 7.3.16
FOAM	Sold 1914	CYNTHIA	Sold 1920
MALLARD	Sold 1940	CYGNET	Sold 1920
ANGLER	Sold 1920	STAG	Sold 1921
Laird 30-knotters: launched 1895–1900, 355t			
QUAIL	Sold 1919	PANTHER	Sold 1920
THRASHER	Sold 1919	SEAL	Sold 1921
VIRAGO	Sold 1919	WOLF	Sold 1921
EARNEST	Sold 1920	ORWELL	Sold 1922
GRIFFON	Sold 1920	LIVELY	Sold 1922
LOCUST	Sold 1919	SPRIGHTLY	Sold 1921
Vickers 30-knotters: launched 1896–1900, 355t			
AVON	Sold 1920	LEOPARD	Sold 1919
BITTERN	Sunk in collision 4.4.18	VIXEN	Sold 1921
OTTER	Sold 1916		
Doxford 30-knotters: launched 1899–1901, 350t			
SYLVIA	Sold 1919	LEE	Wrecked 5.10.09
VIOLET	Sold 1920	SUCCESS	Wrecked 27.12.14
Fairfield 30-knotters: launched 1897–1900, 355t			
OSPREY	Sold 1919	LEVEN	Sold 1920
FAIRY	Lost 31.5.18	FALCON	Lost 1.4.18
GIPSY	Sold 1921	OSTRICH	Sold 1920
Palmer 30-knotters: launched 1896–1900, 370t–390t			
STAR	Sold 1919	FLIRT	Sunk 1916
WHITING	Sold 1919	SPITEFUL	Sold 1920
BAT	Sold 1919	PETEREL	Sold 1919
CRANE	Sold 1919	MYRMIDON	Lost 26.3.17
FLYING FISH	Sold 1919	SYREN	Sold 1920
FAWN	Sold 1919	KANGAROO	Sold 1920
Hawthorn Leslie 30-knotters: launched 1899–1901, 355t–385t			
CHEERFUL	mined 30.6.17	RACEHORSE	Sold 1920
MERMAID	Sold 1919	ROEBUCK	Sold 1919
GREYHOUND	Sold 1919		

Name	Fate	Name	Fate
Earle 30-knotters: launched 1898, 345t			
BULLFINCH	Sold 1919	DOVE	Sold 1920
John Brown/J & G Thompson 30-knotters: launched 1896–1900, 380t			
BRAZEN	Sold 1919	KESTREL	Sold 1921
ELECTRA	Sold 1920	THORN	Sold 1919
RECRUIT	Torpedoed 1.5.15	TIGER	Lost 2.4.08
VULTURE	Sold 1919	VIGILANT	Sold 1920
Thornycroft Special Design (33-knotter): launched 1898, 430t			
ALBATROSS	Sold 1921		
Cammell Laird Special Design (33-knotter): launched 1897, 465t			
EXPRESS	Sold 1921		
J & G Thompson Special Design (33-knotter): launched 1900, 470t			
ARAB	Sold 1919		
Hawthorn Leslie Turbine Prototype: launched 1902, 400t			
VELOX	Mined 25.10.15		
Ex-Chinese prize: launched 1898, 305t			
TAKU	Sold 1916		
'River' class (Palmer group): launched 1903–5, 550t			
ERNE	Wrecked 6.2.15	URE	Sold 1919
ETTRICK	Sold 1919	WEAR	Sold 1919
EXE	Sold 1920	SWALE	Sold 1919
CHERWELL	Sold 1919	ROTHER	Sold 1919
DEE	Sold 1919		
(Yarrow group): launched 1903–5, 590t			
USK	Sold 1920	WELLAND	Sold 1920
TEVIOT	Sold 1919	GALA	Lost in collision 27.4.08
RIBBLE	Sold 1920	GARRY	Sold 1919
(Hawthorn Leslie group): launched 1903–4, 550t			
DERWENT	Mined 2.5.17	BOYNE	Sold 1919
EDEN	Sunk in collision 18.6.16	DOON	Sold 1919
WAVENEY	Sold 1920	KALE	Mined 27.3.18
(Laird group): launched 1903–5, 550t			
FOYLE	Mined 15.3.17	LIFFEY	Sold 1919
ITCHEN	Torpedoed 6.7.17	MOY	Sold 1919
ARUN	Sold 1920	OUSE	Sold 1919
BLACKWATER	Sunk 6.4.09		
(Thornycroft group): launched 1903–4, 550t			
KENNET	Sold 1919	CHELMER	Sold 1920
JED	Sold 1920	COLNE	Sold 1919
(White group): launched 1905, 555t			
NESS	Sold 1919	NITH	Sold 1919
Thornycroft 125ft TBs: launched 1885–86, 60t			
TB 025	Sold 1919	TB 050	Sold 1920
TB 026	Sold 1919	TB 051	Sold *c*1913
TB 027	Sold 1919	TB 052	Sold 1919
TB 029	Sold 1919	TB 053	Sold 1913
TB 041	Sold 1919	TB 054	Sold 1919
TB 042	Sold 1919	TB 055	Sold 1920
TB 043	Sold 1919	TB 056	Lost 17.5.06
TB 044	Sold 1919	TB 057	Sold 1919
TB 046	Sold 1920	TB 058	Sold 1919
TB 047	Sold *c*1908	TB 059	Sold 1919
TB 048	Sold *c*1905	TB 060	Sold 1919
TB 049	Sold 1919		
Yarrow 125ft TBs: launched 1885–7, 60t			
TB 031	Sold 1913	TB 069	Sold *c*1910
TB 033	Sold 1919	TB 070	Sold 1919
TB 061	Sold 1909	TB 071	Sold 1923
TB 063	Sold 1919	TB 074	Sold 1920
TB 064	Sold 21.3.15	TB 076	Sold 1920
TB 065	Sold 1919	TB 077	Sold 1920
TB 066	Sold 1920	TB 078	Sold 1919
TB 067	Sold 1920	TB 079	Sold 1919
TB 068	Sold 1920		
White 125ft TBs: launched 1185–87, 60t–66t			
TB 035	Sold 1919	TB 037	Sold 1919
TB 036	Sold 1919	TB 038	Sold 1919
Yarrow 135ft TB: launched 1886, 105t			
TB 80	Sold 1921		
White 150ft TB: launched 1884, 137t			
TB 81	Sold 1921		
Yarrow 130ft TBs: launched 1884, 87t			
TB 82	Sold 1921	TB 85	Sold 1921
TB 83	Sold 1919	TB 86	Sold 1921
TB 84	Lost 17.4.06	TB 87	Sold 1920
Yarrow 140ft TBs: launched 1892–94, 105t			
TB 88	Sold 1919	TB 90	Lost 25.4.18
TB 89	Sold 1919		
Thornycroft 140ft TBs: launched 1892–94, 141t			
TB 91	Sold 1919	TB 93	Sold 1919
TB 92	Sold 1920		
White 140ft TBs: launched 1892–95, 130t			
TB 94	Sold 1919	TB 96	Sold 1919

Name	Fate	Name	Fate
TB 95	Sold 1919		
Laird 140ft TB: launched 1843, 130t			
TB 97	Sold 1920		
Ex-Royal Indian Marine TBs: launched 1887–89, 92t–96t			
TB 100	Sold 1909	TB 104	Sold 1920
TB 101	Sold 1920	TB 105	Sold 1920
TB 102	Sold 1909	TB 106	Sold 1910
TB 103	Sold 1909		
Thornycroft 160ft TBs: launched 1901–3, 200t			
TB 98	Sank 1907 but salved; sold 1920	TB 107–TB 112	Sold 1920
TB 99	Sold 1920	TB 113	Sold 1919
White 160ft TBs: launched 1902–5, 219t			
TB 114	Sold 1921	TB 116	Sold 1921
TB 115	Sold 1919	TB 117	Sunk 10.6.17
2nd Class TBs: launched 1884–89, 14t–16½t			
TB 5	Sold 1909	TB 38–TB 44	Sold 1907
TB 6	Deleted in 1907	TB 45–TB 48	Sold 1912
TB 9–TB 11	Hulked 1912	TB 49	Sold 1906
Old 2nd class TBs: launched 1878–86, 11t–14½t			
TB 51	Sold 1907	TB 80	Sold 1907
TB 65	Sold 1907	TB 82	Sold 1906
TB 69–TB 70	Sold 1906	TB 89	Sold 1907
TB 71	Sold 1909	TB 94	Sold 1906
TB 74	Sold 1906	TB 96	Sold 1906
TB 76–TB 78	Sold 1906	TB 99	Sold 1907
TB 80	Sold 1907	TB 100	Sold 1908
TB 82	Sold 1906		

By Admiralty Order of 30 August 1912 all the surviving 27-knotters became the 'A' class, while the 30-knotters were divided into 'B' class (four funnels), 'C' class (three) and 'D' class (two). The remaining classes were also fitted into the alphabetical system: the 'Rivers' became the 'E' class, 'Tribals' the 'F' class, *Beagles* the 'G' class, *Acorns* the 'H' class, *Acherons* the 'I' class, and the *Acastas* the 'K' class. The 'A' to 'E' class were organised into patrol flotillas and local defence flotillas, 6th (Dover), 7th (Humber), 8th (Forth) and 9th (Tyne), and local defence flotillas at the Nore, Portsmouth, Devonport, Pembroke and Queenstown.

In 1917–18 they were largely equipped with depth-charges for anti-submarine escort work. A 1909 survey credited most of them with only 20–23kts, and some as low as 17–18½kts.

Pre-1913 sales

Skate was put on the sale list in November 1905 but was used as a target for shore batteries at Shoeburyness; sold for BU in April 1907. *Hornet* was sold for BU in October 1909. *Swordfish* was sold for BU in October 1910. *Ferret* was surveyed and found to be worn out in 1907, so in December 1908 she was used in experiments, charging boom defences before being dismantled at Chatham DYd. She was sunk as a target in 1911. *Hardy, Contest* and *Shark* were sold for BU in July 1911. *Hart* was sold for BU at Hong Kong in 1912. *Daring, Lynx, Haughty, Banshee, Hunter, Rocket* and *Spitfire* were sold for BU in April 1912. *Havock, Charger, Dasher, Salmon, Snapper* and *Sturgeon* sold for BU in May 1912. *Hasty, Dragon* and *Teazer* were sold for BU in July 1912.

'A' class

Janus was sold for BU at Hong Kong in 1914. *Bruizer* was sold for BU in May 1914. *Zebra* was used in experiments in April 1913 to test effect of 4in lyddite shells on oil fuel; special tanks were fitted to simulate fuel tanks. Sold for BU in July 1914. *Boxer* was sunk in collision with SS *St Patrick* in the Channel, 8 February 1918. *Lightning* was mined in North Sea, 30 June 1915. *Handy* was put on the sale list at Hong Kong in 1914 and sold by 1916. *Porcupine, Conflict, Wizard, Fervent, Zephyr, Opossum, Ranger, Sunfish,* and *Surly* were all sold for BU March–May 1920.

'B' class

Thrasher sank *UC 39* with depth charges off East Coast, 8 February 1917; sold for BU in November 1919. *Locust* served with Scapa Flow Local Defence Flotilla from August 1914; sold for BU in June 1919. *Virago* was on China Station in August 1914; sold at Hong Kong October 1919. *Sprightly* was with Scapa Local Defence Flotilla from August 1914; sold for BU in July 1921. *Success* was wrecked off Fife Ness, 27 December 1914. *Myrmidon* was with the Dover Patrol (6th DF) from August 1914; sunk in collision with SS *Hamborn* in Channel, 26 March 1917. *Syren* had been wrecked off Berehaven in May 1905 but was salved and returned to service in 1906; with Dover Patrol from August 1914 and sold with *Spiteful* in September 1920. *Arab* and *Quail* sold for BU in July 1919; *Peterel* sold in August 1919; *Kangaroo* sold in March 1920; *Panther* sold in June 1920; *Orwell, Lively, Griffon* and *Earnest* sold in July 1920; *Seal* and *Express* sold March 1921; and *Wolf* sold July 1921.

'C' class

Bittern sunk in collision with SS *Kenilworth* in thick fog off Portland Bill, 4 April 1918 (lost with all hands). *Lee* ran ashore in Blacksod Bay, Ireland on 5 October 1909 and became a total loss; wreck sold in December. *Fairy* foundered in North Sea, 31 May 1918 after ramming *UC 75*. *Falcon* was hit on bridge by a German 8.2in shell off Ostend in August 1914 (24 killed out of total crew of 60); sunk in collision with naval trawler *John Fitzgerald*. *Cheerful* was mined off Shetlands, 30 June 1917. *Tiger* was sunk off Isle of Wight during night manoeuvres, 2 April 1908 (cut in two and 36 lives lost, while trying to cross the bows of the cruiser *Berwick*). *Velox* was mined off the Nab, 25 October 1915. *Flirt* was sunk on 27 October 1916 in night action with German destroyers in Dover Straits. *Recruit* was torpedoed by *UB 16* off Galloper light vessel, 1 June 1915. *Otter* was commissioned for a few months at Hong Kong but was paid off to provide seamen for other ships; sold locally for BU in October 1916. *Roebuck* and *Thorn* were BU at Portsmouth DYd in 1919. *Vulture* BU May 1919; *Bullfinch, Crane, Greyhound, Leopard, Star* sold June 1919; *Fawn, Mermaid, Sylvia* sold July 1919; *Bat, Flying Fish* sold August 1919; *Brazen, Osprey* and *Whiting* sold November 1919 (*Whiting* at Hong Kong); *Dove* sold January 1920; *Vigilant* sold February 1920; *Racehorse* sold March 1920; *Electra* and *Ostrich* sold April 1920; *Albatross* and *Violet* sold June 1920; *Avon* sold July 1920; *Leven* sold September 1920; *Kestrel* and *Vixen* sold March 1921. *Gipsy* and five drifters shelled *U 48*, which had run aground on the Goodwin Sands on 24 November 1917; sold March 1921 and her hulk was still extant as a pontoon at Dartmouth in 1937.

'D' class
Ariel was wrecked on Ricasoli Point while trying to enter Malta during a night exercise, 19 April 1907. *Coquette* was mined off East Coast, 7 March 1916. *Taku* was on China Station in August 1914; sold at Hong Kong for BU in October 1916 (there is no record of her being in commission after August 1914). *Mallard* was sold for BU in February 1920; *Cygnet, Cynthia* sold April 1920; *Angler, Desperate* sold May 1920; *Stag* sold March 1921 and *Fame* sold for BU at Hong Kong in August 1921.

'River' class
Served with 1st and 2nd Flotillas from 1909, but from 1910 replaced in the 2nd DF by the new *Acorn* class. In August 1914 most were allotted to the Patrol Flotillas, except *Chelmer, Colne, Jed, Kennet, Ribble, Usk* and *Welland*, which were on the China Station. After the fall of Tsingtao they were sent to the Mediterranean. In the 1913 reorganisation they became the 'E' class.

Gala was cut in two by the scout *Attentive* during night manoeuvres on 27 April 1908 near Outer Gabbard light vessel. *Blackwater* was sunk in collision with SS *Hero* off Dungeness, 6 April 1909. *Erne* was wrecked on Rattray Head, 6 February 1915. *Derwent* was mined off Le Havre, 2 May 1917. *Kale* was mined in the North Sea on 27 April 1918. *Foyle* was mined in the Dover Straits, 15 March 1917. *Itchen* was torpedoed by *U 99* in the North Sea, 6 July 1917. *Ettrick* had her bows blown off by a mine, July 1917; sold for BU May 1919. *Wear* was badly damaged in collision with a merchant ship in January 1907; served with Patrol Flotillas from August 1914; sold for BU November 1919.

Garry rammed and sank *U 18* (already damaged by a trawler) off Scapa Flow on 23 November 1914. Rammed and sank *UB 110* off Yorkshire coast on 19 July 1918; sold for BU October 1919. *Eden* ran aground off Dover in January 1910 and sank, but was salved and repaired; sunk in collision with SS *France* in the Channel, 18 June 1916. *Ouse* sank *UC 70* with depth charges off Whitby 28 August 1918 and with *Star* depth-charged *UB 115* off Sunderland on 29 September 1918; sold for BU October 1919. *Chelmer* went from China to Mediterranean late in 1914 and served with *Colne* at Anzac Cove, supporting the troops ashore. Returned to Home waters and sold for BU in June 1920. *Moy, Ness, Doon and Ure* sold for BU May 1919; *Liffey, Nith, Cherwell, Rother, Swale* and *Teviot* sold June 1919; *Dee* sold July 1919; *Boyne* sold August 1919; *Colne* sold November 1919; *Kennet* sold December 1919; *Waveney* and *Exe* sold February 1920; *Arun* and *Welland* sold June 1920; *Jed, Ribble* and *Usk* sold July 1920.

Torpedo-Boats
The 'oily wad' coastal destroyers were divided between the Local Defence Flotilla in the Firth of Forth (about 24 boats) and the LDFs at Newcastle, Sheerness and Portsmouth. *TB 98–TB 117* were also used for local defence, principally at Portsmouth. *TB 90–TB 97, TB 83, TB 88* and *TB 89* formed the local defence flotilla at Gibraltar. *TB 042, TB 044, TB 046, TB 063* and *TB 070* formed the local defence flotilla at Malta in August 1914 and were sent to defend the Suez Canal early in 1915, and saw action when the Turks attempted to cross the Canal. The remaining old TBs were used for various harbour duties in Home waters.

TB 046 ran out of coal while going from Port Said to Mudros and was wrecked on Lemnos, 27 December 1915; refloated and repaired; sold for BU 1920. *TB 056* foundered off Damietta on 17 May 1906 while in tow of *Arrogant; TB 059* used as target 1911 and sold 1912. *TB 064* wrecked in Aegean, 21 March 1915. *TB 84* sunk in collision with destroyer *Ardent*, 17 April 1906. *TB 90* capsized in heavy weather off Gibraltar 25 April 1918. *TB 96* sunk in collision with troopship *Tringa* off Gibraltar 1 November 1915. *TB 98* sank in 1907 but salved; sold for BU June 1920. *TB 117* sunk in collision with SS *Kamouraska* in the Channel, 10 June 1917.

The majority of the survivors were sold for BU between July and December 1919 or January and June 1920, except *TB 80–TB 82, TB 85, TB 86* and *TB 116* which were sold in October 1921.

GUNBOATS

Name	Fate	Name	Fate
Rattlesnake class torpedo gunboat: launched 1886, 550t			
RATTLESNAKE	Sold 1910		
Sharpshooter class torpedo gunboats: launched 1889–90, 735t			
GOSSAMER	Sold for BU 1920	SKIPJACK	Sold for BU 1920
SEAGULL	Sunk 30.9.18	SPANKER	Sold for BU 1920
SHELDRAKE	Sold 1907	SPEEDWELL	Sold for BU 1920
Alarm class torpedo gunboats: launched 1892–93, 810t			
ANTELOPE	Sold 1919	LEDA	Sold for BU 7.20
CIRCE	Sold for BU 7.20	NIGER	Torpedoed 11.11.14
HEBE	Sold for BU 22.10.19	ONYX	Sold 1924
JASON	Mined 7.4.17	SPEEDY	Mined 3.9.14
Halcyon class torpedo gunboats: launched 1893–94, 1070t			
DRYAD	BU 1920	HARRIER	BU 1920
HALCYON	BU 1920	HUSSAR	BU 1921
Plucky class iron gunboat: launched 1870, 212t			
PLUCKY	Sold 1928		
Ant class iron gunboats: launched 1870–74, 254t			
ANT	Sold 1926	COMET	Sold 1908
BADGER	Sold 1908	CUCKOO	Sold 1959
BLAZER	Sold 1919	KITE	Sold 1920
BLOODHOUND	Sold 1921	MASTIFF	Sold 1931
BONETTA	Sold 1909	PIKE	Sold 1920
BULLDOG	Sold 1906	SNAKE	HS 1907
BUSTARD	Sold 1923	SNAP	Sold 1909
Bouncer class steel gunboat: launched 1881, 265t			
INSOLENT	Foundered 1.7.22		
Medina class iron gunboats: launched 1876–77, 386t			
SABRINA	Sold 1922	TAY	Sold 1920
SLANEY	Sold 1919	TEES	Sold 1907
SPEY	Deleted *c*1915		
Bramble class composite gunboats: launched 1886, 715t			
RATTLER	Sold 1924		
Pigmy class composite gunboats: launched 1888, 755t			
PARTRIDGE	Sold 1912	PHEASANT	Sold 1906
PEACOCK	Sold 1906	PIGEON	Sold 1906
Redbreast class composite gunboats: launched 1889, 805t			
LAPWING	Sold 1910	RINGDOVE	Sold 1920
MAGPIE	Sold 1921	SPARROW	Sold 1922
REDBREAST	Sold 1910	THRUSH	Wrecked 11.4.19
REDPOLE	Sold 1906	WIDGEON	Sold 1906
Bramble class steel gunboats: launched 1898–99, 710t			
BRAMBLE	Sold 1920	DWARF	Sold 1926
BRITOMART	Sold 1920		
THISTLE	Sold 1926		
Nymphe class sloops: launched 1888–89, 1140t			
NYMPHE	Sold 1920	BUZZARD	Sold 1921
Alert class sloops: launched 1894, 960t			
ALERT	BU 1949	TORCH	Sold 1920
Phoenix class sloops: launched 1895, 1050t			
PHOENIX	Lost 18.9.06	ALGERINE	Sold 1919
Condor class sloops: launched 1898–1900, 980t			
MUTINE	Sold 1932	SHEARWATER	Sold 1922
RINALDO	Sold 1921	VESTAL	Sold 1921
ROSARIO	Sold 1921		
Cadmus class sloops: launched 1900–3, 1070t			
CADMUS	Sold 1921	FANTOME	Sold 1925
CLIO	Sold 1920	MERLIN	Sold 1923
ESPIEGLE	Sold 1923	ODIN	Sold 1920

Rattlesnake
She had been in Reserve since 1891 and was virtually a hulk at Portsmouth from 1905; removed from Effective List 1906, and according to most sources sold for BU 1910, but may have been still in use as a target in mine experiments in 1914.

Sharpshooter class
Apart from *Sheldrake* all were converted to minesweepers in 1909, retaining guns and fitted with kite winch and gallows on quarterdeck. *Gossamer* in commission as tender to *Pembroke* until 1907, then Home Fleet 1908. Converted to minesweeper 1909 and joined 1st Fleet from 1912. At the Armistice she was with 13th Minesweeping Flotilla at Oban. Sold with the other survivors of this class in February–March 1920. *Seagull* was a tender at Portsmouth until 1908, and was converted to minesweeper 1909; she was sunk in collision with SS *Corrib* in the Clyde. *Sheldrake* put on sale list 1906 and sold for BU in July 1907. *Skipjack* brought forward from Reserve in 1905 and refitted for Fishery Protection Squadron, serving from 1906 to 1908. Converted to minesweeper 1909. *Spanker* recommissioned from Reserve in 1906 and was with Home Fleet 1907–8 and was then converted to minesweeper. *Speedwell* in Reserve at Chatham 1906; Home Fleet 1907–9; converted to minesweeper 1909.

GREAT BRITAIN

Alarm class
Apart from the depot ship conversions all followed the *Sharpshooter* type minesweeper conversions in 1909. *Antelope* laid up at Motherbank 1905–8, but commissioned as submarine tender with Home Fleet in June 1910; reduced to harbour service at Devonport 1912 and sold for BU May 1919. *Circe* in Reserve at Devonport 1906, then commissioned for Home Fleet 1907–9; converted to minesweeper 1909. *Hebe* was RNR drillship at Southampton 1906; Home Fleet 1907–9 and then converted to submarine tender, recommissioning in May 1910. *Jason* in Chatham Reserve 1906; Home Fleet 1907–9 and then converted to minesweeper; she was mined off the West Coast of Scotland in 1917. *Leda* was RNR drillship in Clyde until 1906, then Coastguard 1907–8; collided with cruiser *Andromache* at Sheerness in February 1909 and had to be beached. Repaired and converted to minesweeper 1909. *Niger* was tender to *Vernon* at Portsmouth until 1909, when she underwent conversion to minesweeper. She was torpedoed by *U 12* off Deal in 1914. *Onyx* was laid up in 1906 and was converted in 1907 to submarine tender; renamed *Vulcan II* in June 1919. *Speedy* was serving with Coastguard at Harwich in 1906 and was damaged in collision with merchant ship off Falmouth in June 1906. Home Fleet 1907–9 and then converted to minesweeper. She was mined off the Humber in 1914.

Halcyon class
They were converted to minesweepers, like the *Sharpshooter* and *Alarm* classes in 1914–15. *Dryad* served as tender to Navigation School at Portsmouth 1906–14, and was converted to minesweeper after outbreak of war. Renamed *Hamadryad* in January 1918, having been attached to the 10th Cruiser Squadron in 1914–15, and then to Lowestoft. *Halcyon* was RNR drillship to 1908, then Fishery Protection service 1909–14. Converted to minesweeping 1914–15. *Harrier* was tender to Navigation School at Portsmouth 1906–14, then converted to minesweeper. *Hussar* was the Senior Officer's ship of the Mediterranean Minesweeping Force 1915–18. All sold for BU November 1919–December 1920.

Plucky class
Plucky was serving on miscellaneous duties by 1906; reduced to harbour service *c*1916 and renamed *Banterer*; sold for BU 1928.

Ant class
Ant was employed on miscellaneous duties by 1906; armed with 2–4.7in in August 1914 for bombarding Belgian coast; disarmed 1916 and converted to boom defence vessel; sold for BU June 1926. *Badger* sold for BU October 1908. *Blazer* employed on subsidiary duties by 1906; rearmed with 2–12pdr for Belgian coast bombardment in August 1914; disarmed 1916 and sold for BU August 1919. *Bloodhound* had been disarmed, but in August 1914 was rearmed with 2–6pdr; disarmed November 1915 and returned to harbour service; sold for BU June 1921. *Bonetta* converted to salvage vessel, renamed *Dispenser* and sold January 1909 for commercial service. *Bulldog* sold for BU July 1906. *Bustard* had been disarmed, but in August 1914 was rearmed with 1–6in and 1–4.7in for bombardment of Belgian coast. Disarmed October 1916 and returned to harbour service. Sold for BU March 1923. *Comet* reduced to subsidiary duties by 1906; sold for BU May 1908. *Cuckoo* was hulked as tender *Vivid* February 1912; became *Vivid II* January 1920, *YC 37* 1923 and sold for BU 1959. *Kite* had been disarmed but in August 1914 was rearmed with 1–6in and 1–4.7in for bombarding Belgian coast. Disarmed November 1915 and reverted to harbour services. Sold May 1920 for conversion to a dredger. *Mastiff* was renamed *Snapper* in 1914 to release name for the new destroyer and in August 1914 was rearmed with 2–4.7in and 1–12pdr for bombarding the Belgian coast. Disarmed and reverted to harbour service by 1916; sold for BU November 1931. *Pike* was stripped and used as a boom defence vessel at Southampton from 1908. Sold for BU March 1920. *Snake* converted to cable lighter *VC 15* in September 1907. *Snap* sold for BU May 1909.

Bouncer class
Insolent was disarmed and reduced to harbour service by 1906. Used as gate vessel from January 1918. Foundered 1 July 1922 in Portsmouth Harbour, and wreck sold for BU June 1925.

Medina class
Sabrina reduced to harbour service by 1906; renamed *Sabine* in 1916 to release name for new destroyer; became hulk *Vivid* late 1919 and sold for BU July 1922. *Slaney* sold for BU August 1919. *Spey* deleted *c*1915 and sold for BU 1923. *Tay* sold for BU October 1920. *Tees* sold for BU July 1907.

Bramble class
Rattler reduced to harbour service 1910; renamed *Dryad* 1919 and sold for BU 1924.

Pigmy class
Partridge at Simonstown in March 1912, where she was stripped for sale, and BU. *Peacock* and *Pheasant* sold for BU May 1906. *Pigeon* sold May 1906 for conversion to salvage vessel.

Redbreast class
Lapwing sold at Bombay for BU November 1910. *Magpie* had been reduced to harbour service in 1902 but was rearmed in 1915 and re-rated as a gunboat; reduced to depot ship in October 1915 and sold for BU 1921. *Readbreast* sold 1910. *Redpole* sold for BU May 1906. *Ringdove* converted to salvage vessel 1917 and renamed *Melita*. Sold for commercial service January 1920. *Sparrow* transferred to New Zealand Government in October 1906 as TS and renamed *Amokura*; sold as coal hulk 1922 and BU 1955. *Thrush* served with Coastguard from 1906; converted to cable ship 1915, then salvage vessel 1916. Wrecked off Northern Ireland in 1917. *Widgeon* sold for BU May 1906.

Bramble class
Bramble sold at Bombay for BU January 1920. *Britomart* sold at Bombay 1920 for conversion to passenger vessel. *Dwarf* sold for BU July 1926. *Thistle* sold with *Dwarf* 1926.

Nymphe class
Nymphe became base ship *Wildfire* at Sheerness 1906; in August 1914 bombarded Belgian coast; became diving tender *Gannet* March 1916; base ship *Pembroke* June 1917; sold for BU June 1920. *Buzzard* reduced to harbour service 1909 as *President;* lent to Marine Society 1918, sold for BU September 1921.

Alert class
Alert lent to Basra civil authorities in 1906; in 1915 formed part of the naval force in the Shatt-el-Arab. Sold to Basra Port Authority January 1926 for use as a pilot vessel; BU October 1949. *Torch* served in Pacific 1914–17; renamed *Firebrand* in August 1917 to release name for new destroyer and transferred to New Zealand government for harbour training duties. Sold locally for BU July 1920. *Phoenix* capsized in dock at Hong Kong on 18 September 1906 during typhoon. *Algerine* based at Esquimalt 1914–18, but from 1915 was reduced to harbour service. Sold for conversion to salvage vessel April 1919 and wrecked 1924.

Condor class
Mutine completed conversion to a survey ship in 1907. Paid off at Bermuda in August 1914 but recommissioned as a depot ship in December 1917; RNVR drillship September 1925, sold 1932. *Rinaldo* was on Cape of Good Hope Station until 1912. Guardship in Wash 1914–15, then sent to West and East Africa. Sold for BU October 1921. *Rosario* converted to submarine tender 1910–11 and stationed at Hong Kong from 1911. Sold locally 11 November 1921. *Shearwater* was at Esquimalt (Vancouver) in August 1914, and became tender to Canadian submarines *CC 1* and *CC 2* in 1915. Moved to Halifax, Nova Scotia 1917; sold May 1922 and renamed *Vedas*. *Vestal* was gunnery tender at Portsmouth in August 1914, and served briefly on Belgian coast before reverting to harbour service. Sold with *Rinaldo*.

Cadmus class
Cadmus was on China Station, remaining there until she paid off at Hong Kong August 1920. Sold for BU September 1921. *Clio* was on China Station in 1906; to Persian Gulf in August 1914, capturing German merchant ship *Paklat* the same month. Mesopotamia Campaign 1915, covering Army operations on the River Tigris. Paid off at Bombay August 1920 and sold for BU November 1920. *Espiegle* was Cadets' TS at Dartmouth until 1910, then East Indies from 1911. In August 1914 captured two German merchantmen, SS *Rappenfels* and SS *Furth*. Operated on Tigris from November 1914, co-operating with Indian troops in capture of Turkish positions and sinking Turkish motor boat. Sold for BU at Bombay September 1923. *Fantome* returned from West Indies early in 1906 and was converted to survey ship. Sold at Sydney NSW, 30 January 1925. *Merlin* recommissioned September 1906 after conversion to survey ship. Sold at Hong Kong 3 August 1923. *Odin* was drillship for Cape Naval Volunteer Corps at Simon's Bay 1905–10 and then went to East Indies. Persian Gulf August 1914, where she took part in the 1915–17 Mesopotamia Campaign. Red Sea patrols 1917–18, including the capture of German merchantman *Iltis* off Aden in March 1917. Sold at Bombay with *Clio* after both had blockaded the Somaliland coast 1919–20 and landed a naval brigade to demolish one of the 'Mad Mullah's' forts.

RIVER GUNBOATS

Name	Fate	Name	Fate
Heron class: launched 1897–8, 85t			
NIGHTINGALE	Sold 1919	SANDPIPER	Sold 1920
ROBIN	Sold 1928	SNIPE	Sold 1919
Woodcock class: launched 1897, 150t			
WOODCOCK	Sold 1928	WOODLARK	Sold 1928
Moorhen class: launched 1901, 180t			
MOORHEN	Sold 1933	TEAL	Sold 1931
Widgeon class: launched 1904, 195t			
WIDGEON	Sold 1931		
Kinsha class: purchased 1900, 616t			
KINSHA	Sold 1921		

Heron class
All served on the Yangtze and West Rivers until August 1914. Paid off December 1914 to provide crews for other ships. Only *Robin* recommissioned post-war, as *Nightingale* and *Snipe* sold locally in November 1919 and *Sandpiper* sold October 1920.

Woodcock class
Like the older gunboats they were paid off at Hong Kong in December 1914, but both served postwar, being sold for BU in 1928.

Moorhen class
Paid off at Hong Kong December 1914 and recommissioned post-war. *Moorhen* sold for BU August 1933 at Hong Kong and *Teal* sold at Shanghai October 1931.

Widgeon class
Paid off at Hong Kong December 1914 but recommissioned postwar and sold for BU at Shanghai October 1931.

Kinsha
Kinsha paid off at Hong Kong December 1914 and sold for BU at Shanghai April 1921. Temporary flagship of Rear-Admiral Yangtze Flotilla 1920–21 until relieved by *Bee*.

Kinsha 1909
By courtesy of Antony Preston

CAPITAL SHIPS

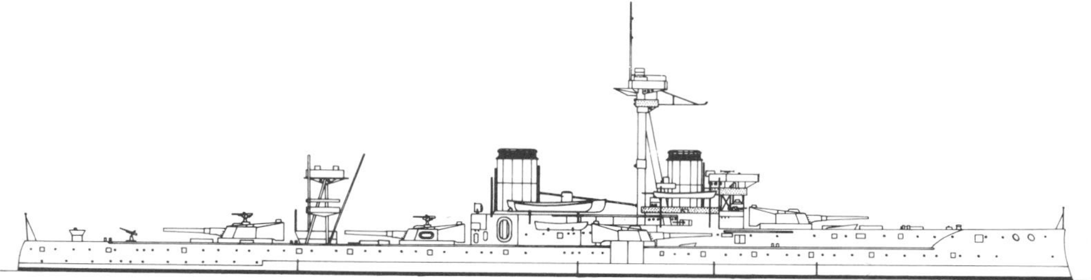

Dreadnought 1918

DREADNOUGHT *battleship*

Displacement:	18,110t load; 21,845t deep load
Dimensions:	527ft oa × 82ft × 31ft deep load *160.6m × 25.0m × 9.4m*
Machinery:	4-shaft Parsons turbines, 18 Babcock & Wilcox boilers, 23,000shp = 21kts. Coal 2900t, oil 1120t. Range 6620nm at 10kts
Armour:	11in–4in (280mm–100mm) belt, 11in (280mm) barbettes, turret faces and CT, 3in–1⅜in (76mm–35mm) decks
Armament:	10–12in (30.5cm)/45cal Mk X (5×2), 24/27 (from 1916 10)–12pdr (76mm) 18cwt, 5 (from 1916 4)–18in (45.7cm) TT sub (4 beam, 1 stern)
Complement:	695–773

Name	Builder	Laid down	Launched	Comp	Fate
DREADNOUGHT	Portsmouth DYd	2.10.05	10.2.06	12.06	Sold for BU 9.5.21

Although the broad outlines of the design history of HMS *Dreadnought* are too well known to require more than a brief summary, certain points about her are not common knowledge. She was a logical step in British battleship design rather than a sudden departure inspired by the fertile brain of Admiral Sir John Fisher. Deadman and Narbeth, the Constructors who worked on the *King Edward VII* design had pressed for a heavier armament then, and had proposed an all-12in gun armament for the *Lord Nelson* class. Although most historians claim that General Cuniberti's article in *Jane's Fighting Ships*' 1903 edition inspired the concept, it can have had little effect on the outcome as both the Gunnery Branch and the DNC's department had already reached the conclusion that a simplified one-calibre armament made sense; gunnery ranges were increasing to the point where 6in, 9.2in and 12in shell splashes could not be distinguished from one another. In 1904 the US Navy's designers started work on a ship with four twin 12in turrets and no secondary gun bigger than 3in, for exactly the same reasons, and experience in the Russo-Japanese War would very soon convince the Japanese to go the same way.

Fisher himself does not seem to have grasped the potential for long-range gunnery; what impressed him most about the sketch designs put before him was the economy of maintenance of a ship driven by steam turbines and carrying only one outfit of spares and ammunition. With a programme of increased expenditure planned Fisher was bound to be swayed by the argument that 30 *Dreadnoughts* would cost the same as 29 *Lord Nelsons* to run. What was in many ways a much more revolutionary and risky step was the proposal by the Engineer-in-Chief, Sir John Durston, to adopt 4-shaft Parsons turbines. With the backing of the DNC, Sir Philip Watts, the Parsons turbine won the day, despite the fact that the first RN destroyers with turbines had only gone to sea four years earlier, the first turbine-driven cruiser was not yet at sea, and the first large commercial turbine-driven ship had not even been laid down.

The high-ranking (and high-powered Committee on Designs first met on 3 January 1905 and reached the stage of making its final report only seven weeks later, a remarkably short time for such a complex series of decisions. In fact this haste, plus the lack of good professional engineering knowledge of weapons may have contributed to the mistakes which were made. Three distinguished captains agreed to site the tripod mast with its all-important fire control platform immediately abaft the forward funnel, where it would inevitably be smoked out at high speed. This was done merely to provide a convenient method of handling the boats, and taken with some recorded remarks by the Committee, confirms that neither Fisher nor his appointees had really grasped the implications of long-range gunnery. The same gunnery experts opted for an inconvenient layout of the five 12in turrets, with two wing turrets which had limited arcs of fire. A more serious weakness was the omission of the upper strake of 8in armour in previous designs. This was probably done to keep the displacement down, for political reasons, but it meant that at deep load (21,845t) with 2900t of coal on board the draught would rise to 31ft. At this draught the 11in belt was completely submerged, and the ship would be protected only by a 4ft strake of 8in armour. It was a failing of three designs which followed the *Dreadnought*, and was contrary to the wishes of the DNC.

When the ship appeared in 1906 her revolutionary appearance stifled such criticisms, however, and most commentators were at a loss to understand how a ship of such heavy armament and freeboard had been achieved on only a small increase in displacement over her predecessors. Herein lay the secret of the design, for the steam turbine machinery was about 300t lighter than reciprocating engines of the same power. Furthermore, the greater weight would have meant bigger engine rooms, and the true saving in weight was probably nearer 1000t. The constructors then contributed their part by designing an efficient hull-form to meet the unusually high speed of 21kts, using tank models at Haslar to achieve the best form.

The weight of hull structure and fittings was strictly controlled, and the steady reduction in weights which had been going on for a decade or more was maintained. For example, the hull weight was no greater than the *Majestic* (1894) despite an overall increase of 3000t. The newer model of 12in turret and turntable introduced in the *King Edward VII* also helped to keep weight down. The intention was to build the ship in a very short time, and so the hull structure was designed for simplicity, without losing the rigidity necessary to withstand the shock of eight-gun broadsides. Part of this 'streamlining' was the adoption of standard plates in varous sizes and thicknesses. These plates were ordered well in advance. The unpierced bulkheads and separate pumping and flooding arrangements used in the *Lord Nelsons* were repeated in order to speed construction, although their value in reducing vulnerability was also recognised.

The building of HMS *Dreadnought* in 14 months (for publicity purposes a basin trial after 12 months was treated as completion) set a record which has never been equalled, and although Fisher's drive helped to enthuse everyone connected with the project, most of the credit must go to the staff of Portsmouth Dockyard. The yard was already the most efficient in the country, having built the *Majestic* in 22 months and averaging only 31 months for battleships built between 1894 and 1904. Once authority was given to divert four

12in turrets from the *Lord Nelson* and *Agamemnon* the way was clear. The keel was laid on 2 October 1905, and the official start of trials was 3 October 1906, although the ship could not be called complete for another two months.

Sea trials were very satisfactory, as the high forecastle stayed dry and the full section amidships helped to damp the roll. Above all, the risk taken with the Parsons turbine more than justified itself as vibration was much reduced. Imitation is the most sincere form of flattery, and in all foreign navies work on 'dreadnoughts' started immediately. She gave her name to a new breed of battleship, and epitomised the naval arms race between Great Britain and Germany.

The ship's light secondary armament was subject to a number of changes during the trials period, but eventually settled in 1907: 10–12pdrs in pairs on the turret roofs and another 14 in the superstructure. She underwent very little modification during the war, apart from getting lower topmasts in 1915, and in late 1916 receiving the standard enlarged fire control position, searchlight control positions, and the removal of torpedo nets, etc.

She was flagship 4th Battle Squadron, Home Fleet in August 1914 and went to Scapa Flow. While engaged on a sweep in the North Sea on 18 March 1915 she rammed and sank *U 29* (K/Lt Otto Weddigen), making her the only battleship to have sunk a submarine. She received a major refit early in 1916, and in May 1916 became flagship, 3rd BS (*King Edward VII* class) stationed at Sheerness. Rejoined 4th BS, Grand Fleet as flagship in March 1918 until paid off in July. Went into reserve at Rosyth February 1919, and put on sale list March 1920.

Dreadnought about 1911
CPL

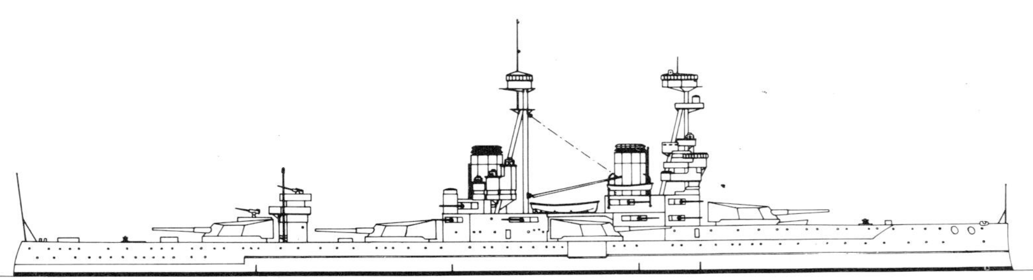

Superb 1918

The first class of battleships to follow the *Dreadnought* were virtually repeats of the design, with the same propulsion but some minor improvements. The tripod foremast was moved forward of the fore funnel, but a second tripod and spotting position was equally likely to be smoked out, as it was placed immediately forward of the second funnel. The puny armament of 12pdr (3in) guns was replaced by 4in QF, an altogether more credible defence against destroyer attack. Although the main armour belt was slightly thinner, overall protection was improved by the inclusion for the first time of a torpedo bulkhead, an inner longitudinal bulkhead designed to localise a torpedo hit.

The tall twin tripods gave the ships a more balanced profile than the *Dreadnought* but war service quickly showed the uselessness of the after fire control position and the exposed platforms for the 4in guns. Topmasts were reduced in height in 1915 with new, more powerful radio equipment, and in 1916 all 4in were removed from the turret roofs. New double-decked positions were provided in the superstructure, where they had good arcs of fire. In 1917 a 4in AA gun was added on the quarterdeck and a 3in on the after superstructure (in *Superb* the 4in AA gun was on the after 12in turret). Torpedo nets were removed, along with the stern TT, enclosed searchlight platforms were added, and a clinker screen (funnel cap) was added to the fore funnel. The torpedo nets had been removed in 1915, at the same

BELLEROPHON class *battleships*

Displacement:	18,800t load; 22,102t deep load
Dimensions:	526ft oa × 82ft 6in × 27ft 3in mean *160.3m × 25.2m × 8.3m*
Machinery:	4-shaft Parsons turbines, 18 Babcock & Wilcox or Yarrow boilers, 23,000shp = 20¾kts. Coal 2648t, oil 842t, patent fuel 170t. Range 5720nm at 10kts
Armour:	10in–15in (250mm–130mm) belt, 8in (200mm) bulkheads, 9in–5in 1(230mm–130mm) barbettes, 11in (280mm) turret faces, 11in–8in (280mm–200mm) CT, 4in–½in (100mm–15mm) decks
Armament:	10–12in (30.5cm)/45cal Mk X (5×2), 16–4in (10.2cm)/50 QF, 4–3pdr (47mm) saluting, 3–18in (45.7cm) TT sub (2 beam, 1 stern)
Complement:	733

Name	Builder	Laid down	Launched	Comp	Fate
BELLEROPHON	Portsmouth DYd	3.12.06	27.7.07	2.09	Sold for BU 8.11.21
SUPERB	Elswick	6.2.07	7.11.07	5.09	Sold for BU 12.12.23
TEMERAIRE	Devonport DYd	1.1.07	24.8.07	5.09	Sold for BU 7.12.21

Bellerophon about 1913

CPL

time that the after fire control position had been eliminated. By 1918 all three had been equipped to operate aircraft from platforms on 'A' and 'Y' turrets, a Sopwith Pup fighter and a 1½-Strutter reconnaissance machine. Although they suffered from the same weaknesses as the *Dreadnought* they were built rapidly to maintain the lead, and were successful ships which remained in front-line service until 1918.

Bellerophon was commissioned for the Home Fleet at the Nore in February 1909, and joined the 1st Division (collision with *Inflexible* at Portland in May 1911). In May 1912 joined 1st Battle Squadron, Home Fleet (collision with merchantman in August 1914). Joined 4th BS, Grand Fleet in August 1914 and saw action at Jutland, 31 May 1916. Went into reserve at Sheerness 1919, where she became a turret drillship. For disposal 1920. *Superb* commissioned at the end of May 1909 for 1st Division, 1st BS, Home Fleet. With the rest of 1st BS joined Grand Fleet in August 1914, and in 1915 became flagship, 4th BS; saw action at Jutland. Led Allied Fleet through Dardanelles in November 1918, but returned home to pay off into reserve in 1919, Thereafter became a turret drillship and after being stricken in 1920 was used as a target. *Temeraire* commissioned into 1st Division, Home Fleet in May 1909; joined 1st BS, Home Fleet in May 1912. After outbreak of war joined 4th BS, and saw action at Jutland; went to the Mediterranean in 1918 and then returned home in 1919 to become Cadets' sea-going TS until put up for sale late in 1921.

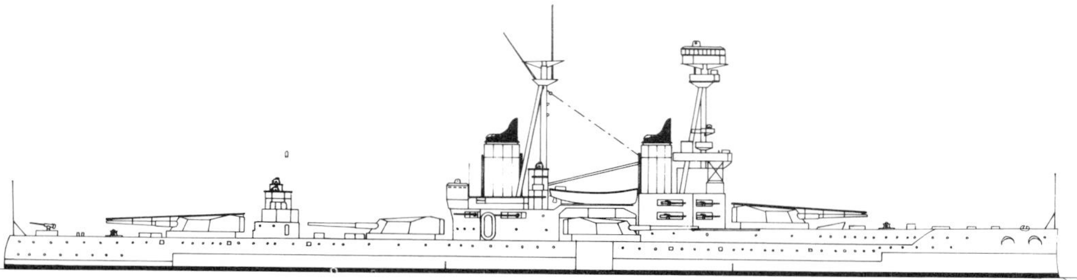

Collingwood 1918

ST VINCENT class *battleships*

Displacement: 19,560t load; 23,030t deep load
Dimensions: 536ft oa × 84ft × 27ft 11in
163.4m × 25.6m × 8.5m
Machinery: 4-shaft Parsons turbines, 18 Babcock & Wilcox or Yarrow boilers, 24,500shp = 21kts. Coal 2800t, oil 940t, patent fuel 190t. Range 6900nm at 10kts
Armour: 10in–7in (250mm–180mm) belt, 8in–4in (200mm–100mm) bulkheads, 9in–5in (230mm–130mm) barbettes, 11in (280mm) turret faces, 11in–8in (280mm–200mm) CT, 3in–¾in (75mm–20mm) decks
Armament: 10–12in (30.5cm)/50cal Mk XI (5×2), 20–4in (10.2cm)/50cal QF, 4–3pdr (47mm) saluting, 3–18in (45.7cm) TT sub (2 beam, 1 stern)
Complement: 718

Name	Builder	Laid down	Launched	Comp	Fate
COLLINGWOOD	Devonport DYd	3.2.07	7.11.08	4.10	Sold for BU 12.12.22
ST VINCENT	Portsmouth DYd	30.12.07	10.9.08	5.09	Sold for BU 1.12.21
VANGUARD	Vickers, Barrow	2.4.08	22.2.09	2.10	Sunk 9.7.17

The next class of battleships followed the lines of the *Bellerophon*s, largely to speed construction, but a new model of 12in gun was adopted. Horsepower was increased slightly to offset the rise in displacement, but a slight reduction in beam and draught, as well as more length helped as well. The 50cal Mk XII gun was not a success as its high muzzle velocity shortened barrel life and reduced accuracy at long range. As in the *Bellerophon*s the after fire control position was all but useless because of smoke interference.

Modifications before 1914 were restricted to lowering the topmasts and removing 2–4in guns from the roof of 'A' turret. By 1916 all three had lost their torpedo nets and in 1916–17 the fore funnel had been given a clinker screen (*Collingwood* had a clinker screen on the after funnel as well), the stern TT had been removed and a single 4in AA gun had replaced the 2–3in AA installed in 1915–16. *Collingwood* was also fitted with aircraft platforms and operated the standard Pup and 1½-Strutter aircraft in 1918. Both *St Vincent* and *Collingwood* had their bridgework and control tops enlarged, and the superstructure was built up, with 4in guns mounted on two levels. Searchlights were regrouped as well, being mounted in 'coffee pot' towers.

Collingwood was commissioned in April 1910 for 1st Division, Home Fleet. In February 1911 she grounded on an uncharted rock off Ferrol. In June 1912 she became flagship 1st Battle Squadron, and joined Grand Fleet in August 1914, saw action at Jutland, and shortly afterwards joined 4th BS. Joined Devonport Reserve after the Armistice and served as a gunnery TS until paid off. BU to comply with Washington Treaty. *St Vincent* was commissioned in 1st Division, Home Fleet in May 1910, becoming flagship a month later. Flagship 1st BS from May 1912 and joined the Grand Fleet in August 1914. Saw action at Jutland, and afterwards joined 4th BS. Joined Portsmouth Reserve 1919, acting as gunnery TS until finally paid off late 1919. BU to comply with Washington Treaty. *Vanguard* was commissioned in 1st Division, Home Fleet in March 1910; in 1st Battle Squadron from 5 May 1912, and then Grand Fleet from August 1914. Saw action at Jutland, with no casualties. Blew up at anchor in Scapa Flow on 9 July 1917, due to faulty ammunition (804 killed).

Vanguard as completed
CPL

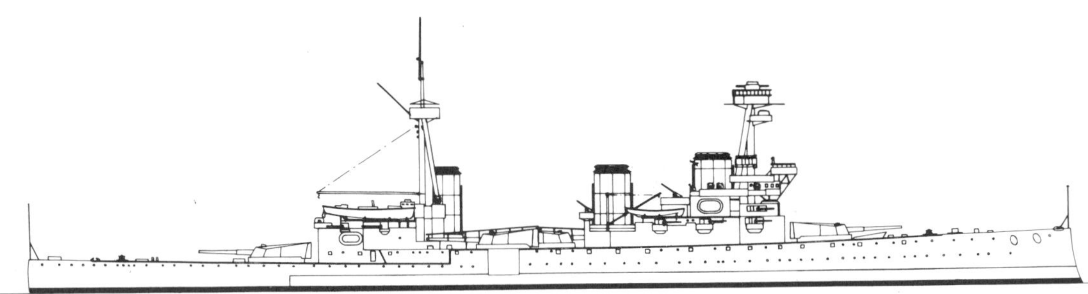

Inflexible 1918

Since the 1890s the armoured cruiser had risen in size and gunpower until it outstripped many 2nd and 3rd class battleships. The Royal Navy in particular built a series of enormously expensive cruisers, and in the last years before the advent of the *Dreadnought*, each class of battleship had its corresponding 'homologue': the *Minotaur* design, for example, had many of the *Lord Nelson* features. It was thus entirely logical that in 1902 Admiral Fisher should discuss with W H Gard the design of a new armoured cruiser to be built in parallel with the new battleship. As first conceived it would have 6in armour, 2 twin 9.2in turrets and 6 twin 7.5in turrets; speed would be 25kts with turbines developing 35,000shp. The Admiralty built the *Minotaur* class instead, but they were too slow by Fisher's standards.

The Russo-Japanese War gave fresh impetus to plans for a new armoured cruiser, especially as armoured cruisers had apparently proved capable of fighting battleships without suffering unduly. The appalling inefficiency and tactical ineptitude of the Russian Baltic Fleet was conveniently overlooked, and Fisher was not alone in thinking that speed offered sufficient protection against heavy shells. The Committee on Designs, as soon as it had finished with the *Dreadnought* design, turned to discussion of a specification for an armoured cruiser equivalent of the *Dreadnought*, having her 12in guns, the 6in armour of the *Minotaur* but the unheard-of speed of 25kts.

The design which emerged bore a strong resemblance to the most recent armoured cruisers, rather than to the *Dreadnought*, although clearly some of her features were repeated. With a much longer hull needed to accommodate the extra boilers and machinery it was possible to have the midships 12in turrets *en echelon*, which permitted broadside firing of the whole armament, but only four turrets could be included. The forecastle deck was carried aft for two-thirds of the lengths, giving high command to the midships turrets, and 4in QF Mk III guns replaced the 12pdr (3in) guns of the *Dreadnought*.

INVINCIBLE class *battlecruisers*

Displacement: 17,373t average load; 20,078t average deep load

Dimensions: 567ft oa × 78ft 6in × 26ft 2in mean
172.8m × 22.1m × 8.0m

Machinery: 4-shaft Parsons turbines, 31 Babcock & Wilcox or Yarrow boilers, 41,000shp = 25½kts. Coal 3085t, oil 710t–725t. Range 3090nm at 10kts

Armour: 6in–4in (150mm–100mm) belt, 7in–6in (180mm–150mm) bulkheads, 7in–2in (180mm–50mm) barbettes, 7in (180mm) turret faces, 10in–6in (250mm–150mm) CT, 2½in–¾in (65mm–20mm) decks

Armament: 8–12in (30.5cm)/45cal Mk X (4×2), 16–4in (10.2cm)/45cal Mk III QF, 7 Maxim MGs, 5–18in (45.7cm) TT sub (4 beam, 1 stern)

Complement: 784

Name	Builder	Laid down	Launched	Comp	Fate
INDOMITABLE	Fairfield	1.3.06	16.3.07	6.08	Sold 1922
INFLEXIBLE	Clydebank	5.2.06	26.6.07	10.08	Sold 1922
INVINCIBLE	Elswick	2.4.06	13.4.07	3.09	Sunk 31.5.16

The main drawings and detailed work were complete by 22 June 1905 and the first of class was laid down the following February. Although there was no question of emulating the building-time of the *Dreadnought* all three took little more than 26–32 months to build, a creditable time for large and novel ships. They were driven by no fewer than ten turbines, two HP and two LP ahead turbines, two HP and two LP astern sets and two HP cruising sets, with steam provided by 31 boilers. *Indomitable* reached a record speed of 25.3kts with 43,700shp over a period of three days, and all three were economical steamers. Like the *Dreadnought*, their twin balanced rudders made them handy ships with a small tactical diameter. They were capable of 25½kts at load draught and 24.6kts at deep load, while the average radius of action at 23kts was 2300 miles (rising to nearly 3100nm if oil fuel was used).

The *Invincible* class were later condemned as a badly conceived and poorly executed design. This, however, is a harsh judgement on the men who carried out Fisher's instructions. They produced a logical successor to the previous classes of armoured cruisers, with all-round improvements in speed, gunpower and range, and no sacrifice in protection. The trials were an outstanding success, showing that the ships met all specifications. If there is a valid criticisms of the design, it is the expense of the ships, for they cost nearly 50 per cent more than the *Minotaur* class.

The *Invincible* had been fitted with electrically driven 12in turrets, 'A' and 'Y' to Vickers' design and 'P' and 'Q' to Armstrongs' design. These installations did not prove a great success as the rate of 'creep' was too slow and uneven, and although conversion to hydraulic power was planned to take place in October 1912–May 1913 it did not happen until March 1914.

What was wrong with the *Invincible* class was their role. The validity of the armoured cruiser was already in doubt, and what the Royal Navy really needed was a cruiser capable of working with the Fleet. By giving the *Invincible* 12in guns instead of 9.2in or 10in the error was compounded, for she would inevitably be regarded as equivalent to a battleship. The introduction of the term 'battlecruiser' in 1912 was proof of this, and the term 'capital ship' was then used to cover both battleships and battlecruisers. It was asking a lot of any admiral to leave out of his battle line any ship armed with 12in guns, and it was only a matter of time before a battlecruiser's thin armour was exposed to a weight of shellfire it was never intended to face.

As completed all three ships had short funnels, following Fisher's insistence on reducing the silhouette to a minimum, but in 1910 *Indomitable* had her fore funnel raised, followed by *Inflexible* a year later, but *Invincible* did not follow suit until January 1915. From 1911 the 4in guns on turret roofs were fitted with canvas spray screens, and from August 1914 they underwent a variety of minor alterations. These included removal of torpedo nets, fitting of various rangefinder baffles on masts, addition of a 3in AA gun (at the after end of the shelter deck) and enlarging of the control platforms aloft. After Jutland the two survivors were given additional armour on the turret roofs and 1in armour was added over the crowns of the magazines. By 1918 both had a Sopwith Pup and a 1½-Strutter flying-off platforms on 'P' and 'Q' turrets.

Invincible commissioned in the 1st Cruiser Squadron, attached to 1st Division, Home Fleet. Refitted 1909–10 and in March 1911 reduced to nucleus crew at Portsmouth for further refit lasting until May 1911. Joined 1st Battle Cruiser Squadron in January 1913, and collided with submarine *C 34* in March. To Mediterranean between August and December 1913, and then paid off for refit from March to August 1914. On 3 August 1914 ordered to Queenstown to guard against German breakout, and then to Humber, to form 2nd BCS with *New Zealand*. At Battle of Heligoland Bight 28 August 1914, supporting light forces. Ordered to Falklands 4 November 1914, leaving Devonport on the 11th and arriving at Port Stanley on 7 December 1914 (flagship of Admiral Sturdee). The following day she and her sister destroyed Vice-Admiral

Invincible 1910

CPL

von Spee's armoured cruisers. *Scharnhorst* and *Gneisenau* (*Invincible* fired 513 12in shells). She was docked at Gibraltar on 1 January 1915 for two-month refit before joining Battlecruiser Force at Rosyth. Joined by *Indomitable* in March and by *Inflexible* in June, after which the class formed the 3rd BCS. Refitted in May 1916 and with her sisters was detached to Scapa Flow for gunnery exercises and to replace the 5th BS in the Grand Fleet. Flew the flag of Rear-Admiral The Hon Horace Hood, and engaged light cruisers of the German 2nd Scouting Group at 10,000yds. Although her fire disabled the *Wiesbaden* and *Pillau* and then inflicted two serious hits on the battlecruiser *Lützow*, her target, and the *Derfflinger* scored five hits on her. The last shell blew the roof off 'Q' turret and set fire to the cordite propellant. The flash quickly reached the magazine and the *Invincible* was blown in half by a massive explosion. All but 3 of her complement were lost, including the Admiral.

Indomitable commissioned in June 1908 and sailed a month later, carrying the Prince of Wales to Montreal. Following final completion she joined the Nore Division of the Home Fleet in October 1908. In 1st CS from March 1909, becoming flagship on 26 July 1909. Refitted 1910 and returned to 1st CS as flagship. Refitted November 1911–February 1912 and joined 2nd CS, Home Fleet (flagship February–December 1912) and then attached to 1st CS (became 1st BCS in January 1913), and transferred with *Invincible* to Mediterranean to form 2nd BCS. Started refit at Malta in July 1914 but ordered to get ready for sea during Sarajevo Crisis. With the rest of the Mediterranean Fleet hunted the *Goeben* and *Breslau* in August 1914 and then blockaded the Dardanelles. Bombarded the outer forts on 3 November 1914 with HMS *Indefatigable*. Returned to Grand Fleet at Rosyth in December 1914 and then underwent refit. On 24 January 1915 took part in the Battle of the Dogger Bank, when she opened fire at 16,250yds (she was the slowest of the class and still had 2crh shells). Fired 134 12in shells at *Blücher* at ranges down to 6000yds, as well as 2 12in at a Zeppelin airship, and in spite of machinery problems reached 25kts. She towed the crippled flagship *Lion* back to Rosyth. Damaged by an electrical fire, and repaired January–March 1915, and then joined 3rd BCS at Rosyth. With her sisters joined Grand Fleet in May 1916 and fought at Jutland. Hit *Derfflinger* three times and *Seydlitz* once during deployment phase, and later scored a hit on the pre-dreadnought *Pommern*. Altogether she fired 175 12in shells. Joined 2nd BS in June 1916 and remained in that squadron until paid off in March 1920; had been in Nore Reserve since February 1919.

Inflexible replaced *Jupiter* in Nore Division of Home Fleet on completion, but then underwent repairs to damage caused by gun trials (October 1908–January 1909). Joined 1st CS in March 1909 and suffered slight damage from a coal bunker explosion. In September 1909 became flagship of Sir Edward Seymour for visit to New York. Refitted October–December 1909; damaged May 1911 in collision with *Bellerophon* off Portland. After repairs became flagship 1st CS until May 1912. Commissioned as flagship of Admiral Berkely Milne, C-in-C Mediterranean Fleet in November 1912. Led hunt for *Goeben* and *Breslau* in August 1914 but ordered home on 18 August. A month later replaced *New Zealand* in 2nd BCS at Rosyth. Sailed with *Invincible* for refit at Devonport 5 November 1914 and sailed for Falklands six days later. During Battle of the Falklands fired 661 12in shells. On her return was sent to Mediterranean, and relieved *Indefatigable* as flagship of C-in-C. Bombarded outer Dardanelles forts, on 19 February and 15 March 1915, and during the attack on the 18th put two 14in guns out of action. Suffered superficial damage from Turkish gunfire, but was seriously damaged by a mine on 19 March, suffering flooding forward. Towed to Malta and repaired by May 1915 but then returned to Rosyth, where she joined her sisters in the 3rd BCS. Suffered no damage at Jutland, and spent remainder of the war in 3rd BCS. Collided with submarine *K 22* on 1 February 1918 during 'Battle of May Island', and was present at German surrender in November. Joined Nore Reserve in January 1919 and paid off at end of March 1920.

NEPTUNE *battleship*

Displacement: 19,680t load; 22,720t deep load

Dimensions: 546ft oa × 85ft × 28ft 6in max
166.4m × 25.9m × 8.7m

Machinery: 4-shaft Parsons steam turbines, 18 Yarrow boilers, 25,000shp = 21kts. Coal 2710t, oil 790t. Range 6330nm at 10kts

Armour: 10in–2½in (250mm–65mm) belt, 8in–4in (200mm–100mm) bulkheads, 9in–5in (230mm–130mm) barbettes, 11in (280mm) turret faces, 11in (280mm) CT, 3in–¾in (75mm–20mm) decks

Armament: 10–12in (30.5cm)/50cal Mk XI (5×2), 16–4in (10.2cm)/50cal Mk VIII, 4–3pdr (47mm), 3–18in (45.7cm) TT (2 beam, 1 stern)

Complement: 759

Name	Builder	Laid down	Launched	Comp	Fate
NEPTUNE	Portsmouth DYd	19.1.09	30.9.09	1.11	Sold for BU 9.22

British designers were aware that the disposition of guns in the *Dreadnought* and her successors was far from ideal, particularly in the light of developments abroad. The latest ships, the *St Vincents*, could only fire 8 guns on the broadside, whereas the American *Delaware* class and the Argentine *Moreno* class, for example, could fire 10 and 12 guns respectively. The solution chosen for the first ship of the 1908 Programme was far from satisfactory, but it was a step in the right direction. The wing turrets were staggered to give a limited degree of cross-deck firing, and to avoid too long a hull, 'X' turret was raised a deck level over 'Y', as in American ships. Cross-deck firing proved of limited value as it strained the hull, but the new layout did at least permit 10 guns to be fired on the broadside. Unfortunately all other theoretical advantages were not feasible; axial firing from the wing turrets caused unacceptable damage to the superstructure, and the superimposed turret could not fire directly aft because they concussed the gunlayers in 'Y' turret. The exposed positions for the 4in guns on turret roofs were abandoned, and the secondary guns were mounted in the superstructure. To keep the arcs for the 12in guns clear the boats were carried on a prominent 'flying bridge', but it was soon recognised that these were likely to be destroyed by gunfire, with the inevitable consequence that the wreckage would foul the guns below. For the first time cruising turbines were provided, to cut coal consumption at slow and medium speed. She was the fastest British battleship to date, making 22.7kts on trials and sustaining 21¾kts for 8 hours.

In 1912 her fore funnel was raised, and in 1913 twin searchlights were grouped on the forward superstructure. Shortly after the outbreak of war the forward flying bridge was removed, and in 1916 the twin searchlights were replaced by singles. At the same time a funnel cap or clinker screen was added to the fore funnel and the after fire control platform was removed. It has been found that the 4in guns were exposed, and the upper positions were enclosed by light steel structures. The stern TT was removed *c*1915.

She was commissioned in January 1911 for temporary Special Service, but in May became flagship of the C-in-C, Home Fleet. In May 1912 she joined the 1st Battle Squadron, in which she was still serving in August 1914. Collided with a merchant ship in April 1916, but was not seriously damaged and fought at Jutland, suffering no casualties. Transferred to 4th BS 1917, and paid off into Reserve 1919.

Neptune as completed *By courtesy of John M Maber*

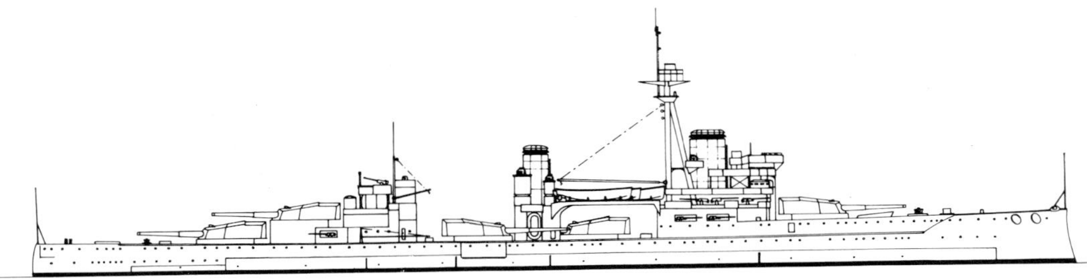

Hercules 1918

In 1908 a 'panic' started over allegations that Germany was laying down dreadnoughts in secret, to overtake the Royal Navy. Reports suggested that by the spring of 1912 there would be 21 German and 21 British dreadnoughts each, and the public debate become violently partisan. Ironically the Admiralty figures were contested most fiercely by Winston Churchill, then President of the Board of Trade. The Conservative opposition and the Navy League adopted as their slogan 'We Want Eight and we Won't Wait', demanding that the four capital ships proposed for 1909 should be increased to eight. The figures provided by naval intelligence and various informants who had visited Germany were incorrect, but they gave the Admiralty an excuse to ask for six ships. In fact this figure restored cuts imposed by the Liberal government. The Cabinet finally gave in to public agitation, and voted for all eight ships: two battleships similar to the *Neptune* and six much larger 13.5in-gunned ships.

COLOSSUS class *battleships*

Displacement:	20,225t load; 23,050t deep load
Dimensions:	546ft oa × 85ft × 28ft 9in max *166.4m × 25.9m × 8.8m*
Machinery:	4-shaft Parsons steam turbines, 18 Babcock & Wilcox (*Hercules* Yarrow) boilers, 25,000shp = 21kts. Coal 2900t, oil 800t. Range 6680nm at 10kts
Armour:	11in–7in (280mm–180mm) belt, 10in–4in (250mm–100mm) bulkheads, 11in–4in (280mm–100mm) barbettes, 11in (280mm) turret faces, 11in (280mm) CT, 4in–1¾in (100mm–45mm) decks
Armament:	10–12in (30.5cm)/50cal Mk XI (5×2), 16–4in (10.2cm)/50cal Mk VII, 4–3pdr (57mm), 3–21in (53.3cm) TT sub (beam and stern)
Complement:	755

Name	Builder	Laid down	Launched	Comp	Fate
COLOSSUS	Scotts	8.7.09	9.4.10	7.11	Sold for BU 7.28
HERCULES	Palmers	30.7.09	10.5.10	8.11	Sold for BU 11.21

The first two battleships were half-sisters to the *Neptune*, but with numerous minor changes. The layout of main armament was unchanged, but to save weight the arrangement of siting the tripod mast abaft the fore funnel was reintroduced. The midships 'P' and 'Q' turrets were closer together, permitting a longer forward superstructure and a better concentration of secondary guns. The 21in Hardcastle 'heater' torpedo also replaced the 18in, necessitating larger torpedo rooms below the waterline. It was vital to keep displacement down to avoid submerging the belt any further, and great efforts were made to improve protection on the gun positions and along the waterline. Unfortunately the designers were asked to do all this on the same length and beam as the *Neptune*, so the additional 1in armour on the belt and 2in on the barbettes could only result in thinner plating elsewhere. This was the last attempt to keep displacement down to an artificial limit, but the increase in size was accompanied by a big jump in gun calibre, which largely used up the additional margin created.

In 1912 the fore funnel was raised in both ships to keep smoke away from the bridge. The principal visual difference between the two ships was in the 4in gun battery: *Hercules* had shields to her light guns, while her sister had open ports with dropping lids. In 1915–16 both ships lost their torpedo nets and in 1917 the after flying deck was removed; other standard wartime changes were made during this period. Three 4in were replaced by one 4in AA and one 3in AA.

Colossus commissioned in August 1911 at Devonport for 2nd Division, Home Fleet; 2nd Battle Squadron May–December 1912, then 1st BS. From August 1914 she was flagship, 1st BS, and was the only Grand Fleet battleship hit at Jutland (two hits, five casualties); after repairs she joined the 4th BS. In 1919–20 she served as a Cadets' TS at Devonport, being painted in Victorian black, white and buff livery. She was stricken in 1920 but not sold for BU until July 1928.

Hercules commissioned in July 1911 at Portsmouth as flagship, 2nd Division, Home Fleet; flagship 2nd Battle Squadron July 1912–March 1913; damaged in collision with steamer, 22 March 1913. She joined the 1st BS in March 1913 but transferred to the 8th BS when she joined the Grand Fleet in August 1914; fought in the 6th Division at Jutland; flagship 4th BS 1916–18 and carried Allied Naval Commission to Kiel in November 1918.

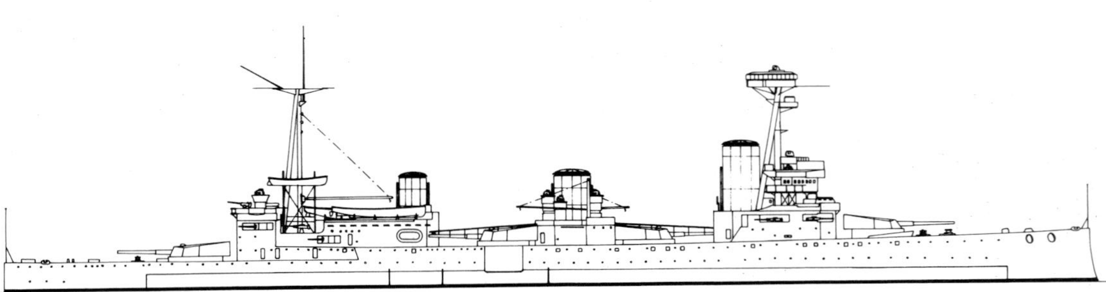

New Zealand 1918

The second ship of the 1908 Programme was to be a battlecruiser equivalent of the *Neptune*, but instead of taking the opportunity to remedy the weaknesses of the *Invincible*s they were virtually repeats of the design. The only excuse for building such a ship would be to speed up construction, but there was no justification for repeating the design when the Dominions of Australia and New Zealand voted money for their own capital ships. HMAS *Australia* was to become the flagship of the new Royal Australian Navy, but the *New Zealand* was presented to the RN on completion. For some reason the design was credited with much greater fighting power than the ship possessed – presumably the result of

INDEFATIGABLE class *battlecruisers*

Displacement:	18,500t (*Indefatigable* 18,470t) load; 22,110t (*Indefatigable* 22,080t) deep load
Dimensions:	590ft oa × 80ft × 26ft 6in mean *179.8m × 24.4m × 8.1m*
Machinery:	4-shaft Parsons turbines, 32 Babcock & Wilcox boilers, 44,000shp (*Indefatigable* 43,000shp) = 25kts. Coal 3170t, oil 840t (*Indefatigable* 3340t/870t). Range 6330nm at 10kts
Armour:	6in–4in (150mm–100mm) belt, 4in (100mm) bulkheads, 7in–3in (180mm–80mm) barbettes, 7in (180mm) turret faces, 10in (250mm) CT, 2½in–1in (65mm–25mm) decks
Armament:	8–12in (30.5mm)/45cal Mk X (4×2), 16–4in (10.2cm)/50cal Mk VII, 4–3pdr (47mm), 3–18in (45.7cm) TT (1 beam, 2 stern)
Complement:	800

Name	Builder	Laid down	Launched	Comp	Fate
INDEFATIGABLE	Devonport DYd	23.2.09	28.10.09	4.11	Sunk 31.5.16
AUSTRALIA	John Brown	23.6.10	25.10.11	6.13	Scuttled 12.4.24
NEW ZEALAND (RNZN)	Fairfield	20.6.10	1.7.11	11.12	Sold for BU 19.12.22

Australia as completed

CPL

official 'leaks' inspired by Admiral Fisher. To this day most reference books credit the ship with Mk XI 50cal 12in guns, whereas photos indicate the same Mk X turrets as the *Invincible* (a fact confirmed by official drawings and other primary sources). Even the normally well-informed Fred T Jane greatly exaggerated the scale of armour (8in belt, 3in decks and 10in on turrets) and a speed of 29–30kts. In fact she was simply a repeat *Invincible* lengthened to permit both 'P' and 'Q' turrets to fire on the broadside, but unlike the original, displaced 1000t less than her battleship equivalent, HMS *Neptune*. Some attempt was made to improve the armouring in the *Australia* and *New Zealand* by deleting the thin armour at bow and stern and thickening the belt abreast of 'A' and 'X' turrets to 5in. There was also an increase of 1000shp, with the result that they had less difficulty in exceeding the designed speed of 25kts. *Indefatigable* barely reached 25kts on trials, but by forcing the boilers she recorded 26.89kts with over 55,000shp. The other two exceeded 26kts on trials, and during the Dogger Bank HMS *New Zealand* is credited with developing 65,000shp.

The smoke nuisance was becoming evident by the time the *Indefatigable* was designed, and so she was given a tall fore funnel. In spite of the gap between the third funnel and the fire control position of the after tripod it still proved unuseable and during the war was dismantled. In October 1914 *New Zealand* had 1–3in/20cwt Mk I and 1–6pdr (57mm) Hotchkiss AA guns added on the after superstructure; *Indefatigable* and *Australia* each received 1–3in/20cwt Mk I AA gun in March 1915. After Jutland the two survivors were given 1in deck armour between 'P' and 'Q' barbettes and on the main deck in the wake of all four barbettes. They also received all the standard modifications to searchlights, range clocks and deflection scales, as well as enlarged fire control positions and bridgework (director platforms for the main armament had been added to the foremast in 1915–16 in all three ships). The stern 18in TT was removed from all three ships *c*1915. In June 1917 *Australia* was given an additional AA gun, a 4in Mk VII on a 60° mounting, and at about the same time *New Zealand* was modified in similar manner, losing her 6pdr AA gun. In 1918 both ships were fitted with aircraft platforms on 'P' and 'Q' turrets, to operate a Sopwith Camel fighter and a 1½-Strutter spotter, and on 4 April 1918 *Australia* successfully flew off the first 1½-Strutter from 'Q' turret. In February 1919 *New Zealand*'s 3in AA gun was replaced by 2–2pdr pompoms, and 4–4in secondary guns were removed (a fifth had been removed in 1917). *Australia* had both AA guns replaced by 2–4in QF Mk V on 80° mountings in January 1920.

Indefatigable was commissioned in February 1911 for the 1st Cruiser Squadron, which was renamed 1st Battle Cruiser Squadron in January 1913. In December 1913 transferred to Mediterranean, serving with 2nd BCS and in August 1914 took part in hunt for *Goeben* and *Breslau*. Bombarded Cape Helles, 3 November 1914 and became flagship of Admiral Carden until January 1915, when she was relieved by the *Inflexible*. After a short refit at Malta she returned to the Grand Fleet (2nd BCS) in February 1915. Was sunk by 11in shellfire from the *von der Tann* during the first phase of Jutland, 31 May 1916. Two shells apparently caused an explosion in 'X' magazine and she staggered out of line, sinking by the stern; then another salvo hit on the foredeck, causing a much more severe explosion which destroyed her.

Australia was completed on the Clyde in June 1913 and went out to Australia, where she became the flagship of the RAN. At the outbreak of war she became flagship of the North America and West Indies Station, and then became flagship of a combined Australian and New Zealand force assembled in the Pacific to prevent any incursion by von Spee's squadron. After the Falklands battle she joined in the search for Spee's supply ships and then joined the Grand Fleet as flagship of 2nd BCS. Missed Jutland as she had been damaged in collision with *New Zealand* in April 1916. She remained flagship of 2nd BCS until end of war, and then returned to Australia as flagship in 1919. Was declared surplus to tonnage under the Washington Disarmament Treaty in 1922 and was ceremonially scuttled off Sydney Heads on 12 April 1924.

New Zealand was completed in February 1912 and presented to the Royal Navy. In February 1913 she left on a world cruise of the Dominions, and on her return in December 1913 joined the 1st BCS for a cruise to the Baltic. Joined the Grand Fleet in August 1914 and served as flagship 2nd BCS in January–February 1915. At the Battle of the Dogger Bank she fired 147 12in shells, without any known result. She became Beatty's temporary flagship when the *Lion* was put out of action during the battle. In collision with the *Australia* on 22 April 1916 but repaired in time for Battle of Jutland. Hit by an 11in shell on 'X' turret but without serious damage or casualties; she fired more shells than any other dreadnought (420 12in) but scored only four hits. She joined the 1st BCS in June 1916 but was replaced by *Renown* in September 1916 and reverted to 2nd BCS for remainder of the war. In 1919 she carried Admiral Jellicoe on his tour of the Dominions, but was one of the ships listed for disposal under the Washington Treaty and was sold in December 1922.

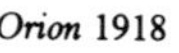

Orion 1918

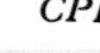

CPL

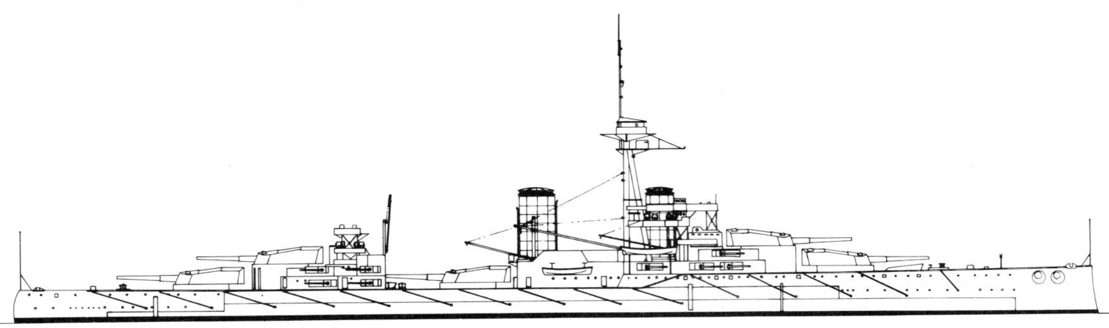

Monarch as completed

ORION class *battleships*

Displacement:	22,200t load; 25,870t deep load
Dimensions:	581ft oa × 88ft 6in × 24ft 11in mean *177.1m × 27.0m × 7.6m*
Machinery:	4-shaft Parsons turbines, 18 Babcock & Wilcox (*Monarch* Yarrow) boilers, 27,000shp = 21kts. Coal 3300t, oil 800t. Range 6730nm at 10kts
Armour:	12in–8in (300mm–200mm) belt, 10in–3in (250mm–75mm) bulkheads, 10in–3in (250mm–75mm) barbettes, 11in (280mm) turret faces, 11in (280mm) CT, 4in–1in (100mm–25mm) decks
Armament:	10–13.5in (34.3cm)/45cal Mk V (5×2), 16–4in (10.2cm)/50cal, BL Mk VII, 4–3pdr (47mm), 3–21in (53.3cm) TT sub (2 beam, 1 stern)
Complement:	752

Name	Builder	Laid down	Launched	Comp	Fate
CONQUEROR	Beardmore	5.4.10	1.5.11	11.12	Sold for BU 12.22
MONARCH	Armstrong	1.4.10	30.3.11	3.12	Sunk as target 1925
ORION	Portsmouth DYd	29.11.09	20.8.10	1.12	Sold for BU 12.22
THUNDERER	Thames IW	13.4.10	1.2.11	6.12	Sold for BU 12.26

Under the 1909 Programme four much larger battleships and one battlecruiser were approved. Dissatisfaction with the 50cal 12in gun led the Director of Naval Ordnance to press for a return to the 13.5in calibre last seen in the Naval Defence Act battleships. The increase in calibre not only gave greater range and much greater hitting power (at least 300lb greater shell weight) but improved shooting. By keeping the muzzle velocity down the designers were able to eliminate much of the tendency of the shell to 'wobble' in flight, improving accuracy at extreme range, and it had the additional benefit of reducing barrel wear. For comparatively small increase in weight and size the 13.5in/45cal gun offered a significant advantage over the German 12in and other foreign navies' guns. The provision of a heavier shell (1400lb instead of 1250lb) further improved the ballistics of the gun, and with 20° elevation (as against 15° previously) had no difficulty in ranging out to 24,000yds. There were other improvements in design, and clearly the new battleships benefited from a slight relaxation in the tempo of battleship building. The cumbersome layouts seen in the early dreadnoughts gave way to an all-centreline disposition, with superimposed turrets forward and aft (although the Admiralty's insistence on sighting hoods at the forward end of the turret caused unbearable blast effect on personnel in the lower turret, and so limited them to broadside arcs). Side armour was extended up to the main deck, thus curing a major weakness of all the early dreadnoughts, and splinter protection was given to the boats. There was one inexplicable weakness in the layout: the tripod mast was stepped between the funnels, as it had been in the *Dreadnought*, *Colossus* and *Hercules*. The problem of smoke interference with fire control was well known, and the only reason that can be found in the same one as before – it provided a convenient position to place the booms for handling the boats. However the majestic profile of the *Orion* class emphasized their impressive armament, and their design proved a good basis for a further five classes.

A weak point of the later British dreadnoughts was their lack of beam. As compared with German dreadnoughts there was insufficient beam to provide the scale of underwater protection found in German ships, and it is interesting to find that the DNC's staff did consider adding beam in order to improve subdivision against torpedo hits. If the original *Dreadnought* length: beam ratio had been preserved the *Orion*s would have had 91ft as against the 88½ft given to them. An increase was vetoed by the Naval Staff, who wished to restrict metacentric height and thereby improved the ship as a gunnery platform. Another factor was the need to keep speed at 21kts. Beam was only permitted to increase to the point where it provided initial stiffness and preserved the correct metacentric height.

Thunderer was the second ship to be fitted with the Scott Director system, which permitted the guns to be fired from the central fire control position, placed high on the tripod mast. When she fired in competition with the *Orion* in 1912 she scored six times as many hits as the *Orion* – both ships had started firing at the same time. All four ships received the usual wartime alterations: topmasts reduced and torpedo nets removed in 1915, fire control platforms extended and extra plating over magazines after Jutland and aeroplane platforms in 1917 (*Thunderer* had runways on 'B' and 'X' turrets, the rest had platforms on 'B' only). The original bridgework around the fore funnel proved totally inadequate, and by

Princess Royal preparing for trials 13 August 1912 *CPL*

1918 had been considerably extended. Fortunately the fore funnel served only a third of the boilers, so heat and smoke caused less trouble than in the earlier dreadnoughts.

Conqueror commissioned in November 1912 for service with the 2nd Battle Squadron. In August 1914 joined Home Fleet and sent to Scapa Flow. Bows seriously damaged in collision with *Monarch*, 27 December 1914. Fought at Jutland but sustained no damage or casualties. Retained in post-war Fleet but discarded to comply with Washington Treaty, and sold for BU in 1922.

Orion commissioned in January 1912 as flagship of Rear-Admiral, 2nd BS, Home Fleet. Damaged in collision when *Revenge* broke loose from her moorings and drifted across her bows. Joined Grand Fleet with 2nd BS in August 1914, and was present at Jutland as flagship of Rear-Admiral A C Leveson (no casualties). Served with Atlantic Fleet post-war but discarded under Washington Treaty and sold for BU in 1922.

Thunderer commissioned in June 1912 for Annual Manoeuvres, then joined 2nd BS, Home Fleet. Joined Grand Fleet in August 1914. Fought at Jutland and sustained no damage. Retained in post-war Fleet but under terms of the Washington Treaty became a cadets' TS 1922–26.

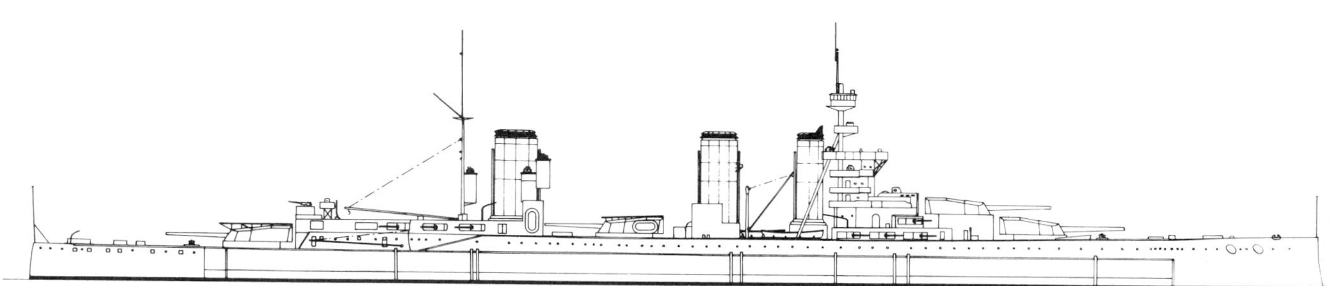

Lion 1918

The battlecruiser equivalents of the *Orion* class reflected their improvements in armament, with 13.5in guns on the centreline. They were 6kts faster, and to achieve that the shp was increased by over 150 per cent, but in spite of an increase of 7600t in displacement they had grave weaknesses. Instead of eliminating the midships 13.5in turret the after superimposed mounting was deleted, giving a cumbersome arrangement of magazine and shellroom between two groups of boilers, and restricted arcs of fire for 'Q' turret. The tripod mast was sited abaft the fore funnel, but whereas the *Orion* class had only 6 boilers served by that funnel, in the *Lion*s there were 14 boilers. The worst error, however, was to provide armour protection only against 11in shellfire, and only in limited areas. The vast hull was totally vulnerable to 12in shells, and in some areas the side armour could be pierced by 11in as well. The worst deficiencies were masked by a policy of official lying about the armour protection (leaks to the Press suggested a 'battleship scale' and the term 'capital ship' was coined, suggesting that they were fast battleships). But the problems with smoke could not be disguised; on her preliminary trials the *Lion*'s tripod became so hot that personnel could not leave the fire control platform. On the initiative of the new First Lord, Churchill, both the *Lion* and the incomplete Princess Royal were altered at a cost of £60,000. Official leaks also greatly exaggerated the speed of the class, *Princess Royal* being credited with 33½kts mean (34.7kts maximum) and *Lion* was credited with having exceeded 31kts. The truth is that neither ship was capable of 28kts except by forcing the machinery. Even when the *Princess Royal* was ordered to go for maximum power over the Polperro Mile in 1913 the staggering total of 96,240shp only yielded 28.06kts, and the strain on her machinery meant that she was ever after the 'lame duck' of the battlecruiser force.

The war service of the *Lion* and the 'Splendid Cats' kept them in the forefront of the action, and their reputation did not suffer until the near-loss of the *Lion* and the disaster to the *Queen Mary* at Jutland. Thanks to adroit manipulation of the Press they were regarded with affection by the public but they must surely be ton-for-ton the least satisfactory ships built for the RN in modern times. The faults of the original battlecruiser could be forgiven for lack of experience with new tactics and technology, but the *Lion*s were expensive second-rate ships.

LION class *battlecruisers*

Displacement:	26,270t load; 29,680t deep load
Dimensions:	700ft × 88ft 6in × 27ft 8in mean *213.4m × 27.0m × 8.4m*
Machinery:	4-shaft Parsons turbines, 42 Yarrow boilers, 70,000shp = 27kts. Coal 3500t, oil 1135t. Range 5610nm at 10kts
Armour:	9in–4in (230mm–100mm) belt, 4in (100mm) bulkheads, 9in–3in (230–75mm) barbettes, 9in (230mm) turret faces, 10in (250mm) CT, 2½in–1in (65mm–25mm) decks
Armament:	8–13.5in (34.3cm)/45cal Mk V (4×2), 16–4in (10.2cm)/50cal Mk VII, 4–3pdr (47mm), 2–21in (53.3cm) TT sub (beam)
Complement:	997

Name	Builder	Laid down	Launched	Comp	Fate
LION	Devonport DYd	29.9.09	6.8.10	5.12	Sold for BU 1.24
PRINCESS ROYAL	Vickers	2.5.10	24.4.11	11.12	Sold for BU 12.22

Only *Lion* had the fore funnel ahead of the tripod, until taken in hand in February 1912. Both ships commissioned with light pole masts, but these were soon stiffened by light struts. In 1915 these gave way to proper tripod legs (fabricated locally at Scapa Flow) as the masthead control platforms were enlarged. Nets were removed, searchlight platforms enclosed and other standard alterations were carried out as the War progressed. In 1918 both ships had aircraft platforms on 'Q' and 'X' turrets.

The secondary and anti-aircraft armament changed frequently:

Lion
Post-August 1914: 1–3pdr saluting gun lost overboard in gale.
October 1914: 6pdr Hotchkiss AA added.
January 1915: 3in/20cwt AA Mk I added.
April 1915: 2–3pdr removed.
July 1915: 6pdr AA replaced by second 3in/20cwt AA.
August 1915: last 3pdr removed
April 1917: 1–3in/20cwt AA received from *Princess Royal* (replacement), 1–4in/50 removed from port side aft, put on 60° mounting and given to *Princess Royal*.
May–June 1919: 4–3pdr saluting guns added.

Princess Royal
October 1914: 6pdr Hotchkiss AA added.
January 1915: 3in/20cwt AA Mk I added.
April 1915: 2–3pdr removed.
April 1917: 1–4in/50 removed from starboard aft, put on 60° AA mounting and remounted with gun from *Lion*, 2–3in/20cwt AA removed.
May–June 1919: 4–3pdrs added, 4in/50 AA replaced by 2–3in/20 AA Mk I and 2–2pdr AA Mk II (removed March 1922).

Lion commissioned in June 1912 for the 1st Cruiser Squadron (flagship from July 1912) and in January 1913 hoisted flag of 1st Battle Cruiser Squadron (Rear-Admiral Beatty). Joined Grand Fleet in August 1914 and took part in Heligoland Bight action against German light forces. At the Dogger Bank on 24 January 1915 she fired 243 shells, but scored only one hit on the *Blücher*, one on the *Derfflinger* and two on the *Seydlitz*, at a range of about 16,000yds. She was hit by 16 11in and 12in shells, and one 8.3in, suffering serious damage. The port engine room was flooded and eventually the starboard turbines stopped as well, and she had to be towed home by *Indomitable*. She was temporarily repaired at Rosyth, with more permanent repairs completed by Palmers before returning to service as flagship of the newly constituted Battle Cruiser Force (BCF). At Jutland she suffered much more serious damage, being hit by 13 12in shells from the *Lützow*. The most damaging hit started a fire in 'Q' turret which was only stopped from blowing up the magazine by the presence of mind of a fatally wounded Marine Officer, who gave the order to flood the magazine. On her return to Rosyth, 'Q' turret had to be removed for repairs, and she went to sea from 20 July to 23 September 1916 without it. In November 1916 she became flagship of Rear-Admiral Pakenham but remained with the battlecruisers until January 1918, during which time she led numerous sorties. Flagship 1st BCS 1919–23 but paid off under Washington Treaty and sold for BU in 1924.

Princess Royal commissioned in November 1912 for 1st CS, and joined 1st BCS in January 1913. Joined Grand Fleet in August 1914 and fought at Heligoland Bight, 28 August 1914. Sent to West Indies during hunt for von Spee's squadron, but returned to 1st BCS as flagship early in 1915. In action at Dogger Bank but without damage or casualties. At Jutland was hit by eight 12in and one 11in from *Derfflinger*, *Markgraf* and *Posen*, suffering 22 killed and 81 wounded. Numerous fires were started and two legs of the tripod foremast were badly hit, but the ship remained operational. Returned to Rosyth on 21 July 1916 after repairs. Remained with 1st BCS until 1922, and sold for BU in December 1922 to comply with Washington Treaty; resold and not BU until 1926.

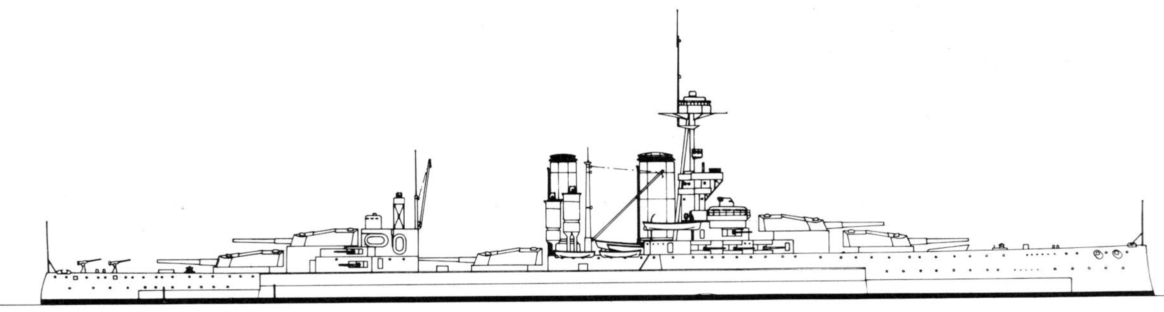

King George V 1918

The 'four battleships of the 1910 Programme were to have been repeat *Orion*s but fortunately the lessons from the *Lion*'s trials were available and the design was altered to a pole foremast stepped ahead of the fore funnel. It was widely felt that the 4in secondary guns should have been replaced by 6in, in the light of the growing threat from torpedo-boats and destroyers, but that would have meant an extra 2000t at a time when the Liberal Government was trying to reduce naval expenditure. However the increase in dimensions did permit a slight improvement in deck armour. With their tall, flat-sided funnels the *King George V* class were handsome ships. The lead ship and the *Centurion* were completed with a light pole foremast but the last pair were completed for director firing and had to have struts halfway up the mast. *Centurion* was then altered in similar fashion but *King George V* merely received stiffening flanges. She was finally given a full tripod in 1918. The three survivors received the full set of wartime modifications: removal of nets, searchlights enclosed in towers, enlarged bridgework etc, and were fitted to carry aircraft in 1918. Although the 13.5in Mk V gun was repeated in the new ships it was modified to fire a 1400lb shell, which further improved its long-range shooting. From 1915 2–4in AA guns were added on the quarterdeck, while 2–4in/50 BL on either side below the forecastle deck abreast of 'A' and 'B' turrets were removed when found to be unworkable in heavy weather.

KING GEORGE V class *battleships*

Displacement:	23,000t load; 25,700t deep load
Dimensions:	597ft 6in oa × 89ft × 28ft 8in mean *182.1m × 27.1m × 8.7m*
Machinery:	4-shaft Parsons turbines, 18 Babcock & Wilcox (*Audacious, Centurion* Yarrow) boilers, 31,000shp = 21kts. Coal 2870t–3150t, oil 800t. Range 6730nm at 10kts
Armour:	12in–8in (300mm–200mm) belt, 10in–4in (250mm–100mm) bulkheads, 10in–3in (250mm–75mm) barbettes, 11in (280mm) turret faces, 4in–1in (100mm–25mm) decks
Armament:	10–13.5in (34.3cm)/45cal Mk V (5×2), 16–4in (10.2cm)/50cal BL Mk VII, 4–3pdr (47mm), 3–21in (53.3cm) TT sub (2 beam, 1 stern)
Complement:	782

Name	Builder	Laid down	Launched	Comp	Fate
KING GEORGE V (ex-*Royal George*)	Portsmouth DYd	16.1.11	9.10.11	11.12	Sold for BU 12.26
CENTURION	Devonport DYd	16.1.11	18.11.11	5.13	Scuttled 1944
AUDACIOUS	Cammell Laird	2.11	14.9.12	10.13	Mined 27.10.14
AJAX	Scotts	27.2.11	21.3.12	3.13	Sold for BU 11.26

Ajax commissioned for the 2nd Battle Squadron, Home Fleet in October 1913. Joined the Grand Fleet in August 1914 and fought at Jutland. Went to Mediterranean late in 1918 and in 1919 supported White Russians in Black Sea. Remained with Mediterranean Fleet until 1924, when she returned to pay off into reserve at the Nore. Put on disposal list in 1926 and sold in 1926. *Audacious* commissioned in 1913 for 2nd BS, Home Fleet; Grand Fleet from August 1914 but sank after striking mines laid off Lough Swilly on 27 October 1914. In fact damage was comparatively light but progressive flooding outside the armoured citadel made her unmanageable as the weather worsened, and she foundered before she could be towed to safety.

Centurion collided with and sank an Italian merchantman on trials in December 1912; repairs delayed her commissioning until March 1913. After searchlight controls were fitted she commissioned formally into 2nd BS, Home Fleet in March 1913. Joined Grand Fleet in August 1914 and served throughout war with 2nd BS. Transferred to Mediterranean 1919 for operations in Black Sea. Returned from Mediterranean 1924 and went into reserve at Portsmouth until paid off in April 1926. Converted to radio-controlled target ship to replace *Agamemnon*, and used for guns up to 8in calibre until April 1941 at Plymouth. Converted to resemble the new *Anson* and sailed to India in 1942, then reduced to static AA battery in Suez Canal until 1944. Finally sunk as blockship in 'Mulberry' harbour off Normandy on 9 June 1944.

King George V joined 2nd BS, on completion in November 1912 as Flagship, Home Fleet. Joined Grand Fleet and became flagship of 2nd BS. From 1919 to 1923 was flagship of Devonport Reserve, and from 1923 to 1926 was gunnery TS. Sold for BU in December 1926 (with rest of class, to offset completion of *Nelson* and *Rodney*, under terms of Washington Treaty).

Centurion about 1917
CPL

Queen Mary as completed
CPL

QUEEN MARY *battlecruiser*

Displacement:	26,770t load; 31,650t deep load
Dimensions:	703ft 6in oa × 89ft × 28ft mean *214.4m × 27.1m × 8.5m*
Machinery:	4-shaft Parsons turbines, 42 Yarrow boilers, 75,000shp = 27½kts. Coal 3600t, oil 1170t. Range 5610nm at 10kts
Armour:	As *Lion* class (see notes)
Armament:	As *Lion* class
Complement:	997

Name	Builder	Laid down	Launched	Comp	Fate
QUEEN MARY	Palmers	6.3.11	20.3.12	8.13	Sunk 31.5.16

Although often listed as a third *Lion*, the battlecruiser ordered under the 1910 Programme was a half-sister with many internal improvements later extended in the *Tiger*. These included higher power, 1400lb shells for the main armament and a different arrangement of the 4in belt armour. However, apart from having round funnels and a single-decked 4in gun battery she appeared identical. Her battleship equivalents were the *King George V* class. On trials she made 28.1kts with 83,000shp. The heavier shells improved the accuracy of the guns but in spite of the great range of the 13.5in Mk V, sights only allowed for a maximum elevation of 15°. This was not rectified in the Grand Fleet and the battlecruisers until 1916, when super-elevation 6° prisms were fitted to the central sight in each turret (*Queen Mary* had been fitted before Jutland). Director control for the main armament was fitted in December 1915. Alterations to the ship included the addition of struts halfway up the pole foremast, lowering of topmasts, enlargement of masthead control positions and bridgework, but torpedo nets were still carried at Jutland. The 4–3pdr Hotchkiss saluting guns were removed early in 1915, and in October 1914 she had received 1–3in/20cal AA Mk I and a 6pdr Hotchkiss AA.

Her completion was delayed by industrial trouble and she did not finally commission until September 1913, when she joined 1st Cruiser Squadron (1st Battle Cruiser Squadron from January 1914). Joined Grand Fleet in August 1914 and was in action at Heligoland Bight on 28 August 1914. She was refitting during the Dogger Bank battle but rejoined 1st BCS shortly after. At Jutland she came under fire from *Derfflinger*. She had fired about 150 shells, and had scored 4 hits on the *Seydlitz*, when she was hit on 'Q' turret above the right-hand gun. That hit put the gun out of action but as the left-hand gun carried on firing the damage had not seriously harmed the ship. Then two more 12in shells hit, one in the vicinity of 'A' and 'B' turrets, and the other on 'Q'. Almost immediately 'A' and 'B' magazines exploded, destroying the forward part of the ship as far as the foremast. As the shattered hull listed to port a further explosition sent the remains to the bottom, only 38 minutes after the start of the battle. Hardly any survivors were found, and 1266 men lost their lives. The exact cause of loss cannot be identified for at 14,400yds her armour was vulnerable to shells plunging at 12°. However the near-disaster in the *Lion* showed that the poor quality of British cordite and the lack of flashtight doors made it all too easy for damage in the turret, barbette or working chamber to generate a flash which could detonate the magazine.

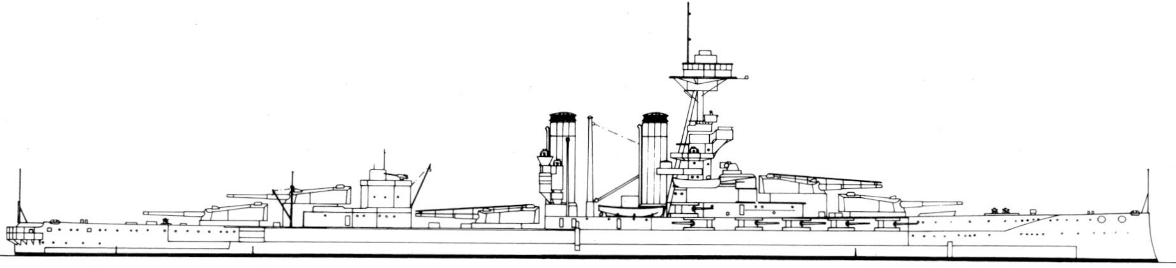

Iron Duke 1918

IRON DUKE class *battleships*

Displacement:	25,000t load; 29,560t deep load
Dimensions:	622ft 9in oa × 90ft × 29ft 6in mean *189.8m × 27.4m × 9.0m*
Machinery:	4-shaft Parsons turbines, 18 Babcock & Wilcox or Yarrow boilers, 29,000shp = 21¼kts. Coal 3250t, oil 1050t. Range 7780nm at 10kts
Armour:	12in–4in (300mm–100mm) belt, 8in–1½in (200mm–40mm) bulkheads, 10in–3in (250mm–75mm) barbettes, 11in (280mm) turret faces, 2½in–1in (65mm–25mm) decks
Armament:	10–13.5in (34.3cm)/45cal Mk V (5×2), 12–6in (15.2cm)/45cal BL Mk VII, 2–3in (76mm)/20 AA Mk I, 4–3pdr (47mm), 4–21in TT sub (beam)
Complement:	995–1022 (war)

Name	Builder	Laid down	Launched	Comp	Fate
IRON DUKE	Portsmouth DYd	12.1.12	12.10.12	3.14	Sold for BU 3.46
MARLBOROUGH	Devonport DYd	25.1.12	24.10.12	6.14	Sold for BU 6.32
BENBOW	Beardmore	30.5.12	12.11.13	10.14	Sold for BU 3.31
EMPEROR OF INDIA (ex-*Delhi*)	Vickers	31.5.12	27.11.13	11.14	Sunk as target 1.9.31

Growing pressure from the Fleet finally forced the Board of Admiralty to reintroduce the 6in secondary gun in the 1911 Programme battleships. The introduction of the 21in heater torpedo had given the torpedo more range, and it was clear to all but the most obstinate supporters of 'all-big-gun' theories that the 4in gun was no longer adequate. The fact that Fisher had retired from the post of First Sea Lord in 1910 also cleared the way for a less dogmatic approach to the problem. The 1911 battleships were generally similar to the King *George V* class, but 25ft longer and slightly beamier and deeper, the extra length being necessary to preserve buoyancy against the heavier weight of the 6in battery, both forward and aft. The extra length forward also moved the secondary guns further aft to reduce interference in bad weather. By the time the design was finalised the need for a big director and fire control top was recognised, and so the ships were given a heavy tripod foremast, but the funnels were much thinner than before, giving the *Iron Duke*s a distinctive look. They were the first ships to have AA guns, as 2–12pdr guns were mounted on the after superstructure, for use against airships.

Iron Duke ran her trials late in 1913 with torpedo nets but these were removed before she commissioned, and they were never installed in the rest of the class. The stern TT was finally dropped in this class but the sitting of the aftermost 6in gins – right aft under the quarterdeck – showed little appreciation of what could happen in rough weather. The purpose of the after pair of 6in guns was to fire at torpedo-boats silhouetted against the setting sun, but in practice the ports were washed out in anything short of flat calm. They and the forward guns were in revolving shields, which could be closed by hinged plates, but these proved too fragile and were constantly washed away. During the winter of 1914–15 it was found necessary to unship them completely and water then entered freely, finding its way below into messdecks and working spaces. Aboard the *Iron Duke* a cure was devised: dwarf walls at the rear of the gun battery and india-rubber joints between the revolving shield and the fixed plating of the embrasure. This worked well and was applied to the battery guns in the *Tiger* and the *Queen Elizabeth* class. The after 6in positions were totally useless and were removed early in the war. The embrasures were plated over and a new unarmoured embrasure was provided amidships above the original battery, port and starboard. After Jutland, in addition to the usual improvements to searchlights and fire control they received 820t of extra protection, 1in–2in on decks around the barbettes and some thickening of magazine bulkheads.

Emperor of India as completed CPL

As the only British dreadnought to be torpedoed the *Marlborough* provided interesting data. She was hit amidships and had a 70ft × 20ft hole blown in her side plating. At that point, abreast the boiler rooms, she was protected only by coal bunkers, as the 1in–1½in torpedo bulkhead only protected the magazines and engine rooms. In spite of that she kept station at 17kts, and was only forced to cease fire when her list to starboard prevented her guns from bearing. A day later, while making her way to the Humber, her draught had increased to 39ft and she could make only 10kts but she reached harbour.

Three of the class were scrapped to comply with the Washington Treaty, but *Iron Duke* was retained in 'demilitarised' state as a TS. This included removal of 'B' and 'Y' turrets as well as the belt armour, and sufficient boilers made inoperable to reduce speed to 18kts.

Iron Duke was completed in March 1914 and joined Home Fleet after trials. Briefly flagship of Sir George Callaghan but in August 1914 became flagship C-in-C Grand Fleet until November 1916. Fought at Jutland as part of 2nd BS, with which she remained until sent to Mediterranean in 1919. After supporting White Russians in Black Sea operations 1919–20 rejoined Mediterranean Fleet. Atlantic Fleet 1926–29 and then paid off for disarming and conversion to TS. Served with Home Fleet at Scapa Flow as depot ship 1939–45, but her remaining 13.5in and 6in guns were removed for use in shore defences. Badly damaged by near miss bombs on 17 October 1939 but repaired.

Marlborough completed June 1914 and joined Home Fleet as second flagship, but in August joined 1st BS, Grand Fleet as flagship. Torpedoed at Jutland but repaired on the Tyne in three months. With the rest of the class served in the Mediterranean until 1926, then Atlantic Fleet until 1929.

Benbow was completed in October 1914 and joined the Grand Fleet on 10 December 1914 for service with the 4th Battle Squadron. She was flagship of Sir Douglas Gamble until replaced by Sir Doveton Sturdee in February 1915. Fought at Jutland but suffered no damage. Went to Mediterranean 1919 and with her sisters provided gunfire support for White Russians in the Black Sea until 1920. Remained in Mediterranean until 1926 and then joined Atlantic Fleet until 1929, when she paid off for disposal.

Emperor of India was completed in November 1914 and joined Grand Fleet 4th BS a month later. Remained with 4th BS except for a short spell as flagship 1st BS, and went to Mediterranean 1919. Refitted 1922 and returned to Mediterranean Fleet until 1926, when she transferred to the Atlantic Fleet. Put on disposal list but sunk as gunnery target in 1931; raised and sold for BU 6.2.32.

Tiger 1918

It was becoming clear that British battlecruisers were an expensive and dubious investment, and under the 1911–12 Estimates there was provision for only one, an improved *Queen Mary*. Considerable attention was paid to correcting some of the obvious defects of the earlier ships, notably the layout of main armament and the provision of a good secondary armament. Unfortunately the quest for ever-higher speed led to an increase in power to 85,000shp with an overload limit of 108,000shp to boost speed from 28kts to 30kts. The folly of such a design criterion became evident on trials late in 1914; at 91,103shp the *Tiger* reached 28.38kts but 104,635shp pushed this up only to 29.07kts. As she burned about 1245t of fuel daily at 59,500shp, a huge increase in bunker capacity was necessary simply to give her an endurance comparable to the *Lion* class. If the Naval Staff had been content with the same machinery, or if the Engineer-in-Chief had been allowed to use small-tube boilers there might have been sufficient margin to give this fine ship the scale of protection she deserved. As things turned out she did not pay the worst penalty, but she was just as vulnerable to enemy shellfire as her half-sister *Queen Mary*.

The rearrangement of 'Q' turret transformed the appearance of the

TIGER *battlecruiser*

Displacement: 28,430t load; 35,710t deep load
Dimensions: 704ft oa × 90ft 6in × 28ft 6in mean
214.6m × 27.6m × 8.7m
Machinery: 4-shaft Brown-Curtis turbines, 39 Babcock & Wilcox boilers, 85,000shp = 28kts. Coal 2450t, oil 2450t. Range *c*4650nm at 10kts
Armour: Belt 9in–3in (230mm–75mm), bulkheads 4in–2in (100mm–50mm), barbettes 9in–1in (230mm–25mm), turret faces 9in, CT 10in, decks 3in–1in (75mm–25mm)
Armament: 8–13.5in (34.3cm)/45cal Mk V (4×2), 12–6in (15.2cm)/45cal BL Mk VII, 2–3in (76mm)/20 cwt AA Mk I, 4–3pdr (47mm) saluting 4–21in (53.3cm) TT sub (beam)
Complement: 1121

Name	Builder	Laid down	Launched	Comp	Fate
TIGER	John Brown	20.6.12	15.12.13	10.14	Sold for BU 2.32

Tiger January 1915 — CPL

ship, and the combination of a heavy tripod and three round, equally-spaced funnels made an extremely handsome profile. Although often claimed to be the result of the Japanese battlecruiser *Kongo*'s influence there is no evidence of this in Admiralty records. The details of *Tiger* had been settled before the *Kongo*'s design was complete, and what is more likely is that Vickers' chief designer was given details of the new ship's layout, so that he could incorporate them in the Japanese design. The secondary armament was very similar to the *Iron Duke* but instead of the useless pair of 6in guns right aft an additional embrasure was provided a deck above the main deck battery, at its forward end. Like other 13.5in–gunned ships HMS *Tiger* was fitted with 6° prisms in 1916 to permit her to use the full range of the guns. She was completed with 2–3in/20cwt AA guns and kept these until 1923, when they were replaced by 4–4in QF Mk V (reduced by 2 in November 1924). In January 1925 she was rearmed with 4–3in/20cwt AA Mk I. In March 1929 these were once again replaced by 3in AA, and in March–September 1928 a pair of 2pdr Mk II pompoms were carried. In March 1915 two of her 3pdr saluting guns were removed but they were replaced in May 1919. Apart from an aircraft platform on 'Q' turret she remained virtually unaltered, but in 1918 the fore topmast was moved to the derrick post between No 2 and No 3 funnel, destroying her elegant profile.

She was completed in October 1914 and joined the Grand Fleet on 6 November 1914, for service with 1st Battle Cruiser Squadron. At the Battle of the Dogger Bank on 24 January 1915 she was hit by six shells and suffered 10 killed and 11 wounded. One 11in hit 'Q' turret and splinters jammed the training gear and put the turret out of action. She was repaired by 8 February 1915. At Jutland she fired 303 heavy shells and scored 3 hits, but in return she was hit 15 times by heavy shell, killing 24 and wounding 46. Although 'Q' turret and 'X' barbette were holed there was no ammunition explosion. Repairs at Rosyth lasted from 3 June to 1 July 1916, and she rejoined the BCF. From 1919 to 1922 she served in the Atlantic Fleet BCS and from 1924 to 1929 served as sea-going gunnery TS. Replaced *Hood* in BCS 1929–31 and paid off on 30 March 1931 at Devonport.

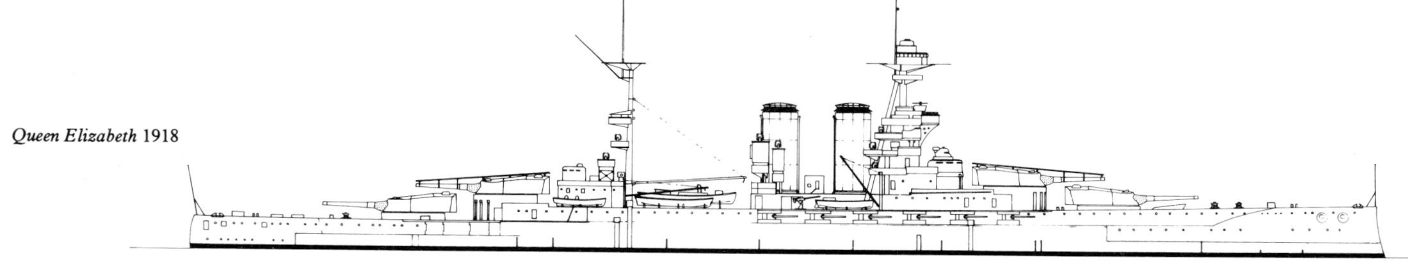

Queen Elizabeth 1918

QUEEN ELIZABETH class *battleships*

Displacement: 27,500t normal; 31,500t deep load

Dimensions: 645ft 9in oa × 90ft 6in × 28ft 9in mean
196.8m × 27.6m × 8.8m

Machinery: 4-shaft Parsons turbines (*Barham* and *Valiant* Brown Curtis), 24 Babcock & Wilcox (*Barham* and *Valiant* Yarrow) boilers, 56,000shp = 23kts. Oil 3400t. Range *c*4500nm at 10kts

Armour: Belt 13in–6in (330mm–150mm), bulkheads 6in–4in (150mm–100mm), barbettes 10in–4in (250mm–100mm), turret faces 13in (330mm), CT 11in (280mm), decks 13in (330mm)

Armament: 8–15in (38.1cm)/42cal Mk I (4×2), 14 (*Queen Elizabeth* 16)-6in (15.2cm)/45cal Mk XII, 2–3in (76mm)/20cwt AA Mk I, 4–3pdr (47mm) saluting, 4–21in (53.3cm) TT sub (beam)

Complement: 925–951

Name	Builder	Laid down	Launched	Comp	Fate
QUEEN ELIZABETH	Portsmouth DYd	21.10.12	16.10.13	1.15	Sold for BU 4.48
WARSPITE	Devonport DYd	31.10.12	26.11.13	3.15	Sold for BU 7.46
VALIANT	Fairfield	31.1.13	4.11.14	2.16	Sold for BU 3.48
BARHAM	John Brown	24.2.13	31.10.14	10.15	Sunk 25.11.41
MALAYA	Armstrong	20.10.13	18.3.15	2.16	Sold for BU 2.48
AGINCOURT	Portsmouth DYd	–	–	–	Cancelled 26.8.14

Under the 1912 Programme three battleships and a battlecruiser were planned. Originally intended to be improved *Iron Dukes*, growing unease about rumours that Germany was planning an increase in calibre plus the certainty that Japanese and American dreadnoughts were being armed with 14in guns, suggested that the new ships should be up-gunned. The gunmakers, the Elswick Ordnance Company, assured the Admiralty that a 15in gun, firing a 1920lb shell, was feasible. Because no 15in gun had yet been made it would be necessary to start the ships with no certainty that the new gun would be successful, but the Director of Naval Ordnance had no doubts at all. The only concession which Elswick could make was to hurry one gun 4 months ahead of the others, to allow proof-firing and the preparation of range tables in time for the lead ship. In the event DNO's confidence was more than justified as the 15in/42cal Mk I proved even more accurate than the 13.5in Mk V, with the same long barrel-life. What was more important was its greater hitting power and range, which promised to give the Royal Navy a comfortable margin for a few years.

New designs were hurriedly prepared, initially for a five-turret, 21kt ship similar to the *Iron Duke* in layout. It was soon realised, however, that a reduction of one turret would still give a broadside of more than 15,000lb, as against 14,000lb in the *Iron Duke*. The space thus saved could be used for additional boilers to give a speed of 24–25kts. War College studies had shown that a fast wing to the battlefleet would be far more effective than a force of battlecruisers. To achieve 25kts on 27,000t would be impossible if the ship were to be coal-fired, but the greater thermal efficiency of oil would solve the problem and at the same time reduce weight. The only practical objection was, of course, that oil fuel was imported from the Middle East whereas anthracite coal was available in Britain. After considerable thought the First Lord of the Admiralty, Churchill, made the momentous decision to buy shares in the Iranian oil companies, and thus secure access to the oilfields. Now that a fast wing to the battlefleet was possible there was little point in keeping the battlecruiser in the 1912 Programme, and in its place a fourth fast battleship was ordered to create a complete Fast Division. Then the Federated Malay States offered to pay for a fifth unit, and to commemorate the gift she was named *Malaya*. A sixth unit, *Agincourt*, was ordered under the 1914 Programme but as she had not been laid down the order was cancelled shortly after the outbreak of war.

Although a great step forward, the *Queen Elizabeth* design attempted too much on the displacement, and they were not as good as they might have been. All five were seriously overweight when built (33,500t–34,000t) and the refusal yet again to sanction small-tube boilers made 25kts impossible to achieve. It should be noted that the designed speed was 23kts, and 25kts was only intended to be reached at the overload rating of 72,000shp. In practice they were good for nearly 24kts at 71,000–76,000shp.

Queen Elizabeth was the only one to have the full outfit of 16–6in Mk XII guns, but the four guns under the quarterdeck suffered as badly as the same guns did in the *Iron Duke*. They were hurriedly removed and a single gun in a shield was resited port and starboard above the battery amidships, the remaining four ships being completed this way. As in the *Iron Duke*s the forward guns in the battery suffered severely in a seaway and the battery was modified in similar fashion, with dwarf walls inside the battery and india-rubber sealing joints to stop water finding its way between the revolving shield and the embrasure. In 1916 2–6in guns were replaced by 3in/20cwt AA Mk I guns. Like other dreadnoughts they were modified after Jutland, with range clocks and deflector scales, searchlights in towers and additional deck armour around the barbettes. *Queen Elizabeth* was the only one with a sternwalk but this was removed late in 1915 or early in 1916. *Barham* had a searchlight platform on the forebridge from completion until 1917, when it was replaced by a rangefinder. In 1915–16 *Warspite* and *Barham* had large rangefinder baffles fitted between the funnels and on the mainmast in an attempt to defeat German rangefinders but this futile addition was removed from both ships in 1917–18. In 1918 all five were fitted with aircraft platforms on 'B' and 'X' turrets. The *Queen Elizabeth* class were extremely handsome ships and a considerable improvement over previous British battleships in protection. At Jutland the presence of four of them saved Beatty's battlecruisers from a severe mauling. In view of some of the criticisms of British gunnery in that battle it is interesting to note that the Germans were astounded by the accuracy of *Valiant*'s shooting, and noted that it demonstrated how far ahead British fire control was over German equipment.

Barham was commissioned in August 1915 and joined the 5th Battle Squadron, Grand Fleet as flagship in October. Collided with *Warspite*, 1 December 1915 and repaired 8–23 December at Cromarty and Invergordon. Fought at Jutland when she fired 337 shells and was hit six times. She suffered severely from two hits but continued in action. Under repair 1 June–5 July 1916. Refitted Cromarty February–March 1917 and at Rosyth 7–23 February 1918. In 1920 became flagship 1st BS, Atlantic Fleet, and from 1924 in the Mediterranean Fleet. Partially modernised 1930–33; torpedoed off Sollum in the Mediterranean by *U 331*.

Malaya commissioned at Newcastle in February 1916 and joined 5th BS, Grand Fleet at Scapa Flow. Suffered slight damage in action at Jutland and completed repairs by 4 July. Damaged 22 November 1918 in collision with destroyer *Penn*. Visited Cherbourg for Peace Celebrations in April 1919 and the following year carried Allied Disarmament Commission to inspect German ports. In 1921 carried Prince Arthur of Connaught to India and paid courtesy visit to Malaya. From 1920 to 1924 served in Atlantic Fleet, thereafter Mediterranean Fleet. Partially modernised 1927–29 and again 1934–36. Served in Second World War until paid off early in 1945, and sold for BU in 1948.

Queen Elizabeth commissioned at Portsmouth in December 1914 and sent to Mediterranean in February 1915 for service in Dardanelles. She fired against the Narrows forts and in support of the landings from 25 February to 14 May 1915, a total of 86 15in and 71 6in shells. Lack of 15in shell limited her value in shore bombardment and the Admiralty had also issued firm orders that her guns were not to be worn out. Struck Admiral De Robeck's flag and left for Gibraltar on 14 May 1915, arriving at Scapa Flow on the 26th to join 5th BS. Refitted at Rosyth 22 May–4 June 1916 and so missed Jutland; June 1916 became temporary flagship of 5th BS. Refitted July 1916–February 1917 and recommissioned after conversion to Fleet Flagship. On 9–10 September 1917 wore temporarily flag of Admiral Mayo USN. Surrender of German High Seas Fleet signed on board 15 November 1918. Flagship Atlantic Fleet July 1919–July 1924, when she became flagship Mediterranean Fleet. Partially modernised 1926–27 and rebuilt 1937–41 for service in Second World War. Joined reserve in August 1945 and sold for BU in 1968.

Valiant commissioned at Govan in January 1916 and joined 5th BS at Scapa Flow on 3 March. Fought at Jutland without sustaining damage. Damaged in collision with *Warspite*, 24 August 1916 and repaired 26 August–18 September. From 1919 served with Atlantic Fleet and then Mediterranean Fleet. Partially modernised 1929–30, and rebuilt 1937–39 for service in Second World War. Paid off in July 1945 and sold for BU in 1948.

Warspite commissioned at Devonport in March 1915 and arrived at Scapa Flow in April to join 5th BS. Grounded, 16 September 1915 and repaired at Rosyth 17 September–20 November. In collision with *Barham*, 3 December 1915 and repaired at Devonport 11–21 December. Heavily damaged at Jutland suffering at least 15 11in and 12in hits and 5 5.9in hits. One pierced her 7½in upper belt, wrecking the port feed tank and causing the engine room to flood. Her helm jammed at a crucial moment in the action, causing her to turn circles under fire from the head of the German battle line but she managed to limp clear. She had to be detached because her speed was dropping, and made her own way back to Rosyth. Under repair 1 June–22 July 1916, but on 24 August was seriously damaged in a collision with the *Valiant*, requiring repairs from 26 August to 28 September. Flagship of 5th BS February 1918. Refitted at Rosyth 12 March–16 May 1918. Joined 1st BS Atlantic Fleet in 1919, then Mediterranean Fleet following partial modernisation 1924–26. Rebuilt 1934–37 for service in Second World War. Paid off into reserve finally in February 1945 and sold for BU in July 1946. She left Portsmouth in tow for Faslane but broke her tow and ran aground on 23 April 1947, so that salvage and scrapping took another nine years.

Malaya about 1920 *CPL*

Resolution 1924 CPL

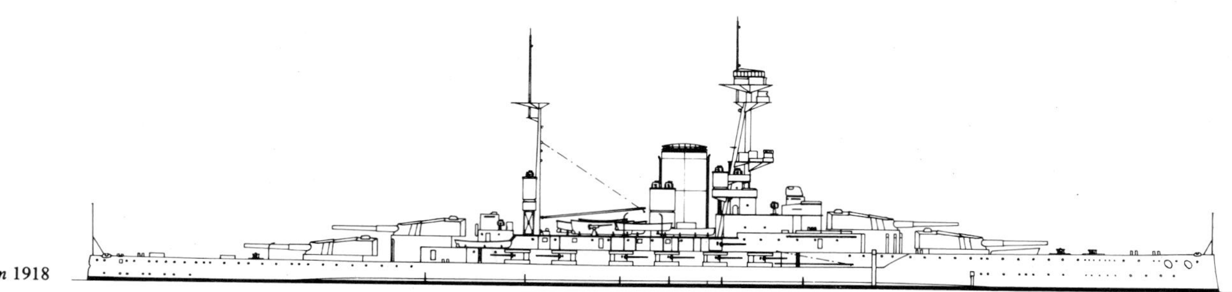

Resolution 1918

REVENGE class *battleships*

Displacement: 28,000t load; 31,000t deep load

Dimensions: 624ft 3in oa × 88ft 6in × 28ft 6in load
190.3m × 27.0m × 8.7m

Machinery: 4-shaft Parsons turbines, 18 Babcock & Wilcox or Yarrow boilers, 40,000shp = 23kts. Oil 3400t. Range 4200nm at 10kts

Armour: Belt 13in–1in (330mm–25mm), bulkheads 6in–4in (150mm–100mm), barbettes 10in–4in (250mm–100mm), turret faces 13in (330mm), CT 11in (280mm), decks 2in–1in (50mm–25mm)

Armament: 8–15in (38.1cm)/42cal Mk I (4×2), 14–6in (15.2cm)/45cal BL Mk XII, 2–3in (76mm)/20cwt AA Mk I, 4–3pdr (47mm), 4–21in (53.3cm) TT sub (beam)

Complement: 908–997

Name	Builder	Laid down	Launched	Comp	Fate
RAMILLIES	Beardmore	12.11.13	12.9.16	9.17	Sold for BU 2.48
RESOLUTION	Palmers	29.11.13	14.1.15	12.16	Sold for BU 5.48
REVENGE (ex-*Renown*)	Vickers	22.12.13	29.5.15	3.16	Sold for BU 9.48
ROYAL OAK	Devonport DYd	15.1.14	17.11.14	5.16	Torpedoed 14.10.39
ROYAL SOVEREIGN	Portsmouth DYd	15.1.14	29.4.15	5.16	Sold for BU 2.49
RENOWN	Palmers	–	–	–	Suspended 26.8.14
REPULSE	John Brown	–	–	–	Suspended 26.8.14
RESISTANCE	Devonport DYd	–	–	–	Cancelled 26.8.14

Although a later generation knew them as the *Royal Sovereign* class, Admiralty papers of the 1914–18 period always refer to the 1913 Programme battleships as the *Revenge* class. They were a cheaper design than the *Queen Elizabeth*s, with a speed of only 21½kts, and were to revert to coal and oil fuel, but in other respects resembled the previous design. During the design stage the aftermost 6in guns were suppressed and a weatherdeck 6in gun was substituted, as in the *Tiger*. In January 1915 the design was altered to oil fuel only and shp was increased from 31,000 to 40,000 to increase speed from 21½kts to 23kts. Fuel stowage changed from 3000t coal/1500t oil to 3400t oil but the change did little to increase endurance as load tonnage had gone up from 25,500t to 28,000t. Eight ships were planned but on 26 August 1914 work stopped on all new capital ships. The new First Sea Lord, Admiral Fisher, succeeded in getting contracts for two suspended, with a view to redesigning them as battlecruisers (see *Renown* class).

Although smaller than the *Queen Elizabeth*s the armour was better disposed, with the protective deck moved up to main deck level. Another improvement was to move the 6in guns further aft, and to ensure that the after pair of guns on either side bore aft. However they were still too close to the waterline, and this was the last class to have main deck batteries of this type. In March 1915 permission was given to fit anti-torpedo 'bulges' to the incomplete *Ramillies*. These were 7ft wide structures attached to the midships portion of the hull and faired into the lines to reduce drag. They were filled with compartments packed with steel tubes, oil fuel, water or air, and their purpose was to provide a bursting space for a torpedo warhead before it could inflict crippling damage on the main hull. The 'bulge' extended from the forward torpedo room to the after one and weighed some 2500t, including 773t of tubes (intended to offer resistance to the crushing effect of an explosion) and 194t of wood. The *Revenge* class were good gun platforms but tended to heel excessively when turning. The 'bulging' of *Ramillies* had the effect of reversing the original stability requirements, by increasing the beam and raising the metacentre. This gave the ship greater initial stability and improved the trim. However it did have the effect of making her roll too much, and after the war experiments were carried to find an improved form of bulge. *Revenge* was fitted with bulges October 1917–February 1918, followed by *Resolution* in late 1917–May 1918. The expected loss of speed did not occur, and the 'bulged' ships showed much less resistance at speed. On trials *Revenge*, without 'bulges' and displacing 30,750t, made 21.9kts with 42,650shp, whereas *Ramillies* at 33,000t made 21.5kts with 42,383shp.

Unlike the earlier dreadnoughts, which had twin balanced rudders, the new ships were given a single large rudder with a small auxiliary rudder ahead of it, on the centreline as well. This idea was intended to reduce vulnerability of the rudders to damage, to reduce resistance and to improve emergency hand-steering (hand-gear was connected only to the small rudder). In practice, however, the small rudder proved of very little use and it was later removed. The ships were completed with all the latest improvements, including director control for the 6in as well as the main armament, although secondary directors were not actually fitted until March–April 1917 (in *Ramillies* as late as June 1918). In common with all dreadnoughts their pumping, flooding and draining arrangements were extended and improved to cope with underwater damage. Extra 1in HT plating was fitted on the main deck over the magazines and on the transverse torpedo bulkheads, and flashtight scuttles were provided for both 15in and 6in ammunition handling systems. All ships received aircraft platforms on 'B' and 'X' turrets in 1918, and they received the usual searchlight towers, range clocks and deflection scales between 1916 and 1918.

Ramillies injured her rudder at her launch and was towed with great difficulty to Cammell Laird for repair. Commissioned May 1917 and joined 1st Battle Squadron, Grand Fleet in September. Sent to Mediterranean from 1920, and was stationed at Ismid with *Revenge* in June 1920 during the war between Greece and Turkey. Returned to join 2nd BS, Atlantic Fleet in 1924. Served in Second World War and sold for BU in 1948.

Resolution commissioned August 1916 and joined 1st BS, Grand Fleet in December 1916. Joined 2nd BS, Atlantic Fleet in April 1919, but in 1920 became flagship of 1st BS in Mediterranean. Saw service in Second World War, being sold for BU in 1948.

Revenge commissioned in February 1916 and the following month joined 1st BS, Grand Fleet. Fought at Jutland and became temporary flagship of Vice-Admiral Burney after torpedoing of *Marlborough*. Fired both 3in AA and 15in at Zeppelin during late stages of action. In November 1916 became flagship of Admiral Madden, second-in-command of Grand Fleet. Sent to Mediterranean in 1920, and was stationed at Ismid in June 1920 with

Ramillies during hostilities between Greece and Turkey. With 1st BS guarded British interests during seizure of Mudania the following month and then returned to join Atlantic Fleet. Served in Second World War and sold for BU in 1948.

Royal Oak commissioned for 4th BS, Grand Fleet in May 1916 and at the end of that month fought at Jutland. Reverted to 1st BS afterwards. Joined 2nd BS, Atlantic Fleet in 1919 but refitted in 1922. Served in Home Fleet from outbreak of Second World War but torpedoed by *U 47* in Scapa Flow on 14 October 1939.

Royal Sovereign commissioned in May 1916 for 1st BS, Grand Fleet but missed Jutland. With 1st BS transferred to Atlantic Fleet 1919. Served in Second World War but transferred to Soviet Navy on 30 May 1944 and renamed *Archangelsk*. Returned 9 February 1949 and sold for BU.

Erin 1915 CPL

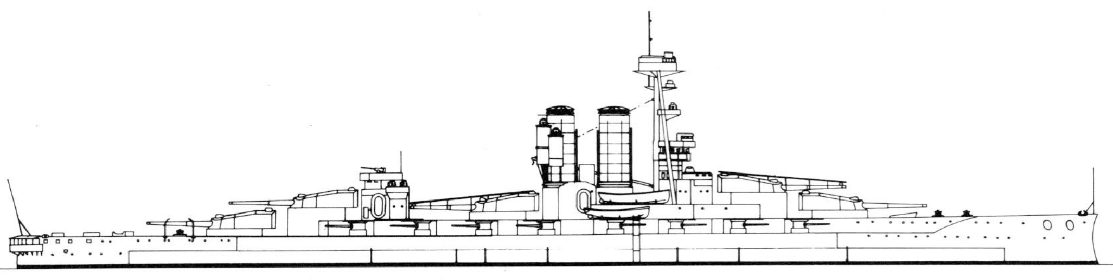

Erin 1918

When war broke out in August 1914 two battleships had nearly been completed for Turkey, and they were seized by order of the First Lord of the Admiralty, Winston Churchill. The first of these, the *Reshadieh* (ex-*Reshad V*) had been one of a pair ordered in 1911, but the *Reshad-i-Hammiss* was cancelled in 1912 and replaced by a purchase from Brazil (see below). The design was by Vickers' designer Thurston but was based on the *King George V*, with some features of the *Iron Duke*s. The hull was shorter and beamier, and the midships 'Q' 13.5in turret was a deck higher, which made for better shooting in a seaway, and the battery was marginally better arranged than in her British contemporaries. The short hull made for a tight turning circle. Although on paper nearly as good as the *Iron Duke*s on 2000t less, the *Erin* displayed the usual trade-off of qualities in private shipyard designs. The armour belt was 3in thinner and shallower than the *King George V*'s; with 1130t less coal she also had considerably less endurance, but this was adequate for North Sea operations, so did not reduce her effectiveness. Her appearance was unusual, with a pair of narrow funnels close together and a single tripod foremast with the legs trailing forward. She also had a 'plough' or 'cleaver' bow which was beginning to displace the more traditional ram type; this feature enhanced her looks and improved seakeeping. In 1917 she was given the standard modifications to fire control and searchlights, and in 1918 she was given aircraft platforms on 'B' and 'Q' turrets.

HMS *Erin* joined the 2nd Battle Squadron, Grand Fleet in September 1914; fought at Jutland and suffered no casualties. In 1919 became flagship, Nore Reserve until sold for BU in 1922 to comply with Washington Treaty.

ERIN *battleship*

Displacement:	22,780t load; 25,250t deep load
Dimensions:	559ft 6in oa × 91ft 7in × 28ft 5in mean *170.5m × 27.9m × 8.7m*
Machinery:	4-shaft Parsons turbines, 15 Babcock & Wilcox boilers, 26,500shp = 21kts. Coal 2120t, oil 710t. Range 5300nm at 10kts
Armour:	Belt 12–4in (300mm–100mm), bulkheads 8in–4in (200mm–100mm), barbettes 10in–3in (250mm–75mm), turret faces 11in (280mm), CT 12in (300mm), deck 3in–1½in (75mm–40mm)
Armament:	10–13.5in (34.5cm)/45cal Mk V (5×2), 16–6in (15.2cm)/50cal Mk XI, 6–6pdr (57mm), 2–3in (76mm)/20cwt AA Mk I, 4–21in (53.3cm) TT sub (beam)
Complement:	1070

Name	Builder	Laid down	Launched	Comp	Fate
ERIN (ex-*Reshadieh*)	Vickers	1.8.11	3.9.13	8.14	Sold for BU 12.22

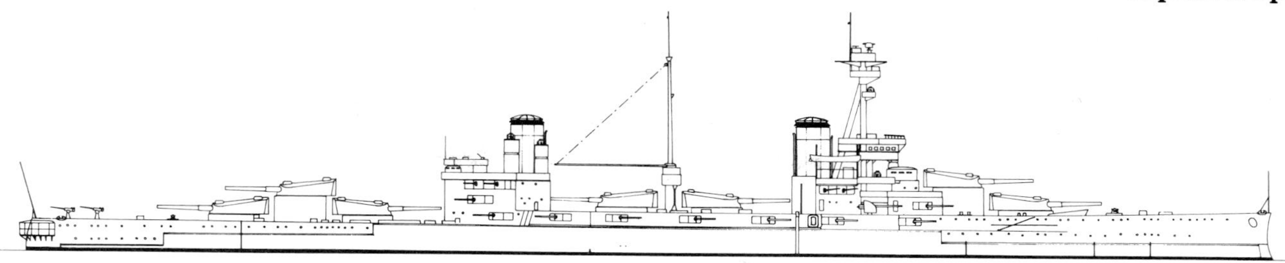
Agincourt 1918

This unusual battleship was the outcome of prolonged rivalry between the 'ABC' countries of South America, Argentina, Brazil and Chile. To answer the Argentine *Moreno* and *Rivadavia* (12–12in guns), ordered in 1910 in the United States, Brazil wished to have the most powerful ship in the world. Designs armed with 8–16in and 10–15in were looked at, but finally a 12–14in design had been accepted (to be built by Armstrong). At the last minute, however, a change of government led to the ship being cancelled, and in its place was to be built a ship with the maximum number of guns. Armstrongs' salesmen and designers were only too happy to oblige, and draw up plans for an immensely long ship with seven turrets, all on the centreline. The design was accepted, and she was laid down as the *Rio de Janeiro*, but in July 1912 the Brazilian Government began to look for a buyer for her. Turkey, smarting from her defeat in the Balkan War, bought her for £2,725,000 early in 1914 and renamed her *Sultan Osman I*. The ship was complete when war broke out and was being docked at Devonport, but Churchill ordered that she should be delayed until Turkey's position became clear. As soon as Turkey showed that she was friendly to Germany the ship was seized and incorporated into the RN as HMS *Agincourt*, giving her three owners in less than a year. She was also the longest battleship to serve in the RN to date and the last with 12in guns.

The ship required major alterations before she was fit to join the Grand Fleet. The massive flying deck between the funnels was removed, along with torpedo nets. The turrets were named after the days of the week instead of 'A', 'B', 'P' and 'Q' etc. As with the *Erin* the scale of protection and coal supply was not up to RN standards. In the Grand Fleet she was not highly regarded, partly because her non-standard equipment put her in dockyard hands frequently but principally because of her light protection and, as Oscar Parkes said, she was regarded as nothing more than a 'floating magazine with a tremendous volume of fire as her best protection'. The turrets were unusual in having all loading operations controlled by a single lever. The Elswick 'W' pattern 12in gun was not interchangeable with the similar Mk X in the early dreadnoughts.

In 1916 the tripod mainmast was removed and the topmast was restepped on the derrick post amidships, a considerable improvement to her profile. In 1918 her bridgework was enlarged and searchlights were regrouped in towers around the after funnel. To quell rumours that she would turn turtle if she fired all 14 guns together her gunnery officer ordered the 'Gin Palace' to fire full broadsides when she got her brief moment of action at the rear of the battle line at Jutland. In all 144 rounds of 12in were fired and onlookers recorded that the massive sheet of flame looked like a battlecruiser blowing up.

Taken over in August 1914 and after alterations joined the 4th Battle Squadron, Grand Fleet at sea on 7 September 1914. Transferred to 1st BS 1915 and fought at Jutland (no damage or casualties). Joined 2nd BS late 1918 but put on Disposal List 1919. Recommissioned at Rosyth 1921 for experimental work and then stripped for conversion to 'Mobile Naval Base' or large depot ship. This involved the removal of all but No 1 and No 2 turrets and the provision of extra oil fuel and ammunition stowage. Work was stopped late in 1921 (a rumoured resale to Brazil did not materialise) and she was sold for BU in 1922.

AGINCOURT *battleship*

Displacement: 27,500t load; 30,250t deep load

Dimensions: 671ft 6in oa × 89ft × 27ft mean
204.7m × 27.1m × 8.2m

Machinery: 4-shaft Parsons geared turbine, 22 Babcock & Wilcox boilers, 34,000shp = 22kts. Coal 3200t, oil 620t. Range *c*4500nm at 10kts

Armour: Belt 9in–4in (230mm–100mm), bulkheads 8in–4in (200mm–100mm), barbettes 9in–3in (230mm–75mm), turret faces 12in (300mm), decks 2½–1in (65mm–25mm), CT 12in (3000mm)

Armament: 14–12in (30.5cm)/45cal Mk XIII (7×2), 20–6in (15.2cm)/50cal Mk XI, 10–3in (76mm)/45cal QF, 2–3in (76mm)/20cwt AA Mk I, 3–21in (53.3cm) TT sub (2 beam, 1 stern)

Complement: 1115

Name	Builder	Laid down	Launched	Comp	Fate
AGINCOURT (ex-*Sultan Osman I*)	Armstrong	9.11	22.1.13	8.14	Sold for BU 12.22

Agincourt as completed
By courtesy of John M Maber

Canada about 1916 — *Aldo Fraccaroli Collection*

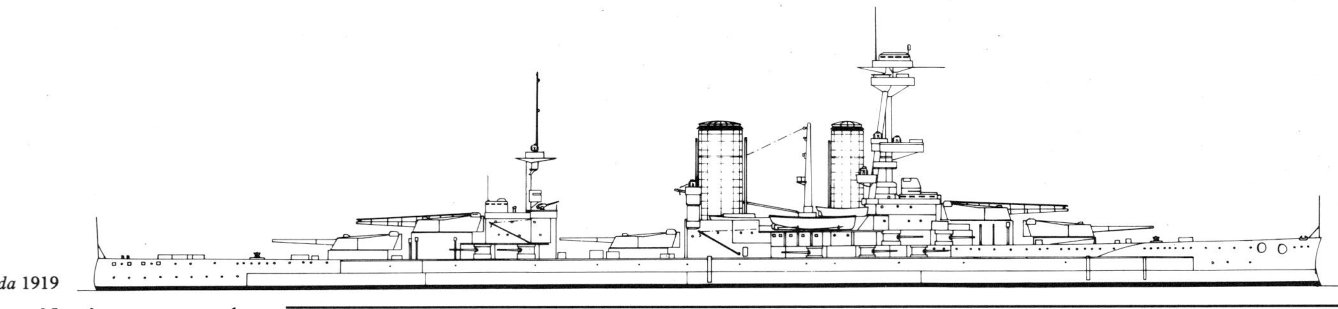

Canada 1919

The Chilean Navy's response to the Argentine and Brazilian battleships of 1910–11 was typically forthright: two much larger and altogether more powerful ships were ordered in Britain, armed with 14in guns. The *Almirante Latorre* was afloat and well advanced in August 1914, but her sister *Almirante Cochrane* was still on the stocks. As Chile was a friendly neutral and supplier of nitrates vital to the munitions industry there could be no question of seizure, and the *Latorre* was formerly purchased on 9 September 1914. Work was suspended on her sister, which was complete up to the forecastle deck, with boilers and engines installed and plated over but side armour not yet in place. Although suspended, her 14in guns were completed and put into reserve for her sister. She was formally taken over on 28 February 1918 for conversion to an aircraft carrier and renamed *Eagle*. The design was essentially similar to the *Iron Duke* but longer, with a shorter forecastle but a much longer quarterdeck. As they were intended to be fast the engine and boiler rooms occupied more space than in *Erin* or her British contemporaries. Although having the same freeboard as the *Iron Duke* class the *Canada*'s massive funnels and tall tripod seemed to make her lower in the water, particularly forward. During completion the funnels were reduced in height and a single pole mast was stepped on the after superstructure. In 1916 the after four 6in guns were removed because they were badly affected by blast from 'Q' turret. Like the other two purchased battleships she had a 'plough' bow. In 1918 she had aircraft platforms on 'B' and 'X' turrets.

Joined 4th Battle Squadron, Grand Fleet in October 1915. Fought at Jutland without damage or casualties, and then transferred to 1st BS. In 1919–20 refitted to Devonport and returned to Chile in April 1920 under her original name.

CANADA class *battleships*

Displacement: 28,600t load; 32,120t deep load
Dimensions: 661ft oa × 92ft × 29ft mean
201.5m × 28.0m × 8.8m
Machinery: 4-shaft Brown-Curtis (HP) and Parsons (LP) turbines, 21 Yarrow boilers, 37,000shp = 22¾kts. Coal 3300t, oil 520t. Range 4400nm at 10kts
Armour: Belt 9in–4in (230mm–100mm), bulkheads 4½in–3in (115mm–75mm), barbettes 10in–4in (250mm–100mm), turret faces 10in (250mm), CT 11in (280mm), decks 4in–1in (100mm–25mm)
Armament: 10–14in (35.6cm)/45cal Mk I (5×2), 16–6in (15.2cm)/50 Mk XI, 2–3in (76mm)/20cwt AA Mk I, 4–3pdr (47mm), 4–21in (53.3cm) TT sub (beam)
Complement: 1167

Name	Builder	Laid down	Launched	Comp	Fate
CANADA (ex-*Almirante Latorre*)	Armstrong	12.11	27.11.13	9.15	Returned to Chile 4.20
— (ex-*Almirante Cochrane*)	Armstrong	2.13	–	–	Completed as carrier *Eagle*

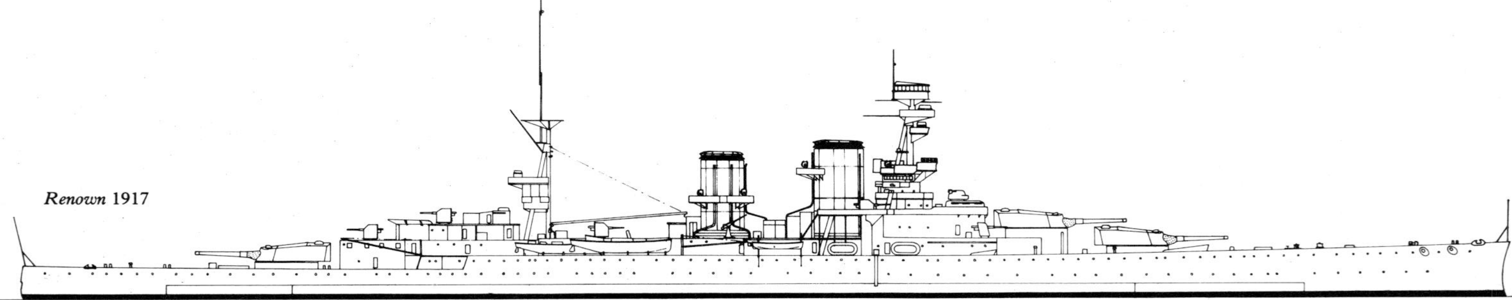

Renown 1917

The Admiralty had decided that there would be no more battlecruisers after HMS *Tiger* but they reckoned without the return of Lord Fisher to the post of First Sea Lord in October 1914. Capitalising on the apparent vindication of the *Invincible* class at the Battle of the Falklands he was able to persuade the Cabinet to overturn its decision to stop work on capital ships. In response to questions about the war being over before the ships were finished, Fisher promised to build them as fast as the *Dreadnought* ten years earlier. That boast proved impossible but the speed with which the two novel and complex ships were built was nonetheless a great tribute to the efficiency of British shipbuilding and the DNC's staff. As was to be expected Fisher's influence on the design was disastrous. He rightly sought to use as much material as possible from the two contracts already placed with Palmers and John Brown for *Revenge* class battleships, and built the design around existing gun mountings, six sets of turntables and twelve 15in guns, part of the outfit for the battleships. But the old admiral's belief that speed was the best protection led him to armour the two ships on the scale of the *Invincible*, despite the fact that they would be facing enemy capital ships armed with guns which could riddle 6in belt armour.

Speed was everything, and a speed of 32kts was to be achieved. The Engineer-in-Chief recommended the use of new lightweight machinery, with lighter turbines and small-tube boilers but as time was short the machinery of *Tiger* was duplicated, with three more boilers. Fisher's influence could also be detected in the choice of secondary armament. The ships were given five triple 4in mountings and two singles, arranged high up around the superstructure. The PXII mounting was very clumsy, with all three guns in separate sleeves, and they required exceptionally large crews, 32 men. In theory the arrangement of these mountings – one on either side of the forward superstructure, one on the centreline between the funnels and the mainmast, and two superfiring aft – gave a concentration of fire which was superior to a 6in battery, but this ignored realities as the triple mountings could not deliver a volume of fire and the 4in shell lacked range and stopping power.

When the *Repulse* joined the Grand Fleet in August 1916 (*Renown* joined a month later) the losses at Jutland had destroyed whatever reputation the battlecruisers had ever had,

RENOWN class *battlecruisers*

Displacement: 27,650t average load; 30,835t deep load
Dimensions: 794t oa × 90ft × 25ft 6in mean
242.0m × 27.4m × 7.8m
Machinery: 4-shaft Brown-Curtis turbines, 42 Babcock & Wilcox boilers, 112,000shp = 30kts. Oil 4243t. Range 3650nm at 10kts
Armour: Belt 6in–1½in (150mm–40mm), bulkheads 4in–3in (100mm–75mm), barbettes 7in–4in (180mm–100mm), turret faces 11in (280mm), CT 10in (250mm), decks 3in–½in (75mm–15mm)
Armament: 6–15in (38.1cm)/42cal Mk I (3×2), 17–4in (10.2cm)/44.3cal BL Mk IX (5×3, 2×1), 2–3in (76mm)/20cwt AA Mk I, 4–3pdr (47mm) saluting, 2–21in (53.3cm) TT sub (beam)
Complement: –

Name	Builder	Laid down	Launched	Comp	Fate
RENOWN	Fairfield	25.1.15	4.3.16	9.16	Sold for BU 3.48
REPULSE	John Brown	25.1.16	8.1.16	8.16	Sunk 10.12.41

and nobody could avoid the significance of the long double row of scuttles amidships, indicating a vast area of hull unprotected even by the thin strip of 6in armour. So poor an impression did they make that the C-in-C Sir John Jellicoe suggested in October 1916 that they should both receive additional protection, and a month later *Repulse* was taken in hand, followed by her sister in February 1917. This was only a palliative, taking the form of 500t of additional plating on decks, particularly over the crowns of magazines, over the engine rooms and over the steering gear.

Both ships had funnels of equal height when completed but after trials the forward one was raised by 6ft to cure interference from smoke. *Repulse* was the first capital ship to receive a flying-off platform, in the autumn of 1917, and Sqn Ldr Rutland flew a Sopwith Pup from the ship's 'B' turret on 1 October. On 8 October Rutland flew off again, this time off the back of 'Y' turret to demonstrate the platform's reversability. *Renown* was similarly fitted early in 1918. Both ships received the remainder of the standard modifications, but in addition extra stiffening had to be fitted internally as they proved to have been too lightly built. Even after the first round of modifications their protection was a constant source of worry, and in response to complaints from the C-in-C the DNC proposed various schemes for adding grating-type armour, a proper bulge etc. DNC then suggested that one ship could be given the 9in armour belt removed from the ex-Chilean battleship *Almirante Cochrane* (which was being converted to a carrier), while the second would have to wait longer for new 9in armour to be manufactured, or have one of the less orthodox types of protection. By July 1918 it had been decided to give *Repulse* the ex-Chilean armour and to re-armour *Renown*, the work to be done at Portsmouth. In fact *Renown* had to wait until 1923, but in December 1918 *Repulse* went into the dockyard for a three-year period of reconstruction. *Renown* received a short refit in 1919–20 to improve accommodation for the Prince of Wales' tour of the United States and Australasia. This included removal of one triple 4in and the installation of a squash court on the port side amidships. In 1923–26 she was given a new 9in belt, but instead of moving the 6in armour up above it, as had been done in *Repulse* it was omitted. In its place the ship was given more deck armour, but externally the ship could be distinguished from her sister by retaining the double row of scuttles.

Renown about 1919 CPL

Renown joined the Grand Fleet in September 1916, serving with 1st Battle Cruiser Squadron until 1919. Royal Tour 1920–21 and again to India 1921–22 before undergoing a lengthy refit 1923–26. Underwent massive reconstruction 1936–39 to serve as fast carrier escort and saw considerable service in Second World War. Sold for BU in 1948. *Repulse* was completed in August 1916 and joined 1st BCS, Grand Fleet. Briefly in action against German light forces in Heligoland Bight on 17 November 1917 (fired 54 shells, scoring one hit on light cruiser *Königsberg*). Refit December 1918–January 1921 at Portsmouth DYd and joined BCS, Atlantic Fleet from 1922. Like *Renown* she carried out several Royal Tours and made a world cruise. Refitted in 1936 and served with Home Fleet from the outbreak of the Second World War. Sunk with HMS *Prince of Wales* by Japanese torpedo-bombers (5 hits) off Malaya in December 1941.

Glorious 1918

COURAGEOUS class *light battlecruisers*

Displacement: 19,230t load; 22,690t deep load

Dimensions: 786ft 3in oa × 81ft × 23ft 4in mean
239.7m × 24.7m × 7.1m

Machinery: 4-shaft Parsons geared turbines, 18 Yarrow small-tube boilers, 90,000shp = 32kts. Oil 3160t. Range ?

Armour: Belt 3in–2in (75mm–50mm), bulkheads 3in–2in (75mm–25mm), barbettes 7in–3in (180mm–75mm), turret faces 13in–11in (330mm–280mm), CT 10in (250mm), decks 1½–¾in (40mm–20mm)

Armament: 4–15in (38.1cm)/42cal Mk I (2×2), 18–4in (10.2cm)/44.3cal BL Mk IX (6×3), 2–3in (76mm)/20cwt AA Mk I, 2–3pdr (47mm), 2–21in (53.3cm) TT sub (beam)

Complement: 828–842

Name	Builder	Laid down	Launched	Comp	Fate
COURAGEOUS	Armstrong, Elswick	28.3.15	5.2.16	1.17	Sunk 17.9.39
GLORIOUS	Harland & Wolff	1.5.15	20.4.16	1.17	Sunk 8.6.40

To get around the Cabinet ruling against new capital ships Fisher ordered early in 1915 three 'large light cruisers' which were in fact light battlecruisers intended to support his proposed Baltic landing. The precise role, like everything else connected with Fisher's Baltic plans, was never worked out, but it can be assumed that they were to provide gunfire support with their heavy guns and possibly to lure away German forces. To that end their high speed and shallow draught made sense, but as with the original battlecruisers, the result was a very expensive solution to the problem. The basis of the design was simply an enlargement of the current light cruisers, with 2in armour plating over 1in shell plating. Even the machinery was merely that of the light cruiser *Champion*, doubled to drive four shafts, and 18 boilers instead of 8. However the design showed that the RN was at last becoming aware of the benefits of more advanced machinery, for the combination of small-tube boilers and double helical geared turbines enabled the *Courageous* class to develop 90,000shp quite easily, when compared with the 42 large-tube boilers needed for 110,000shp in the *Renown* class. This feature in the design marked a victory for the DNC and E-in-C, who had been pressing the Naval Staff for some years to get away from heavy uneconomical machinery. The main improvement was to use small-diameter, fast-running turbines in place of large-diameter turbines.

The hull form was similar to the *Renown* class, with an integral 'bulge' taking the place of an internal anti-torpedo bulkhead. During construction an additional 1½in–1in torpedo bulkhead was worked in between the barbettes but as they ran inboard of the wing engine rooms they would have been only partially effective in limiting flooding. As Fisher had already initiated work on an 18in gun it was hoped to give the new ships an armament of two single 18in, but to get the first two ships into service quickly twin 15in were substituted.

The ships were designed to reach 32kts at a load tonnage of 17,400t, so that the trial speed of *Glorious*, 31¼kts at 21,270t with 88,550shp was highly creditable. Although not too lightly built the great length of the hull was a potential source of weakness. On 8 January 1917 while working up to full power during a trial the *Courageous* suffered buckling of the forecastle between the breakwater and the 15in barbette, as well as leaking fuel tanks, so she was given 130t of stiffening. Although no such damage was suffered in *Glorious*, she was also stiffened early in 1918. In addition to the torpedo bulkhead mentioned earlier, after Jutland both ships were given extra 1in plating on the main deck over the magazines. The single large funnel and long forecastle made them handsome ships but they were even bigger white elephants than the *Renown* and *Repulse*, for which no proper role could be imagined. In 1917 both ships were given 12 additional fixed TT (6×2), 3 twin abreast the mainmast and 2 twin around the after turret, port and starboard. Although *Glorious* managed to fire a torpedo from one of her submerged TT at full speed, in practice this was limited to 23kts as the guidebar was bent by the water pressure. When *Courageous* received four sets of mine rails on her quarterdeck in the spring of 1917 (known as 'Clapham Junction') she could lay 222 British Elia mines or 202 of the new HII type, but there is no record of her ever laying any.

Glorious about 1918 — CPL

Courageous could be distinguished from her sister by having her searchlights around the funnel on one level.

Courageous commissioned in January 1917 and joined the Grand Fleet, first with 3rd Light Cruiser Squadron and later 1st Cruiser Squadron. Converted to minelayer in April 1917, and order given for removal of rails 23 November 1917. On 17 November 1917 engaged (with *Glorious* and *Repulse*) German light forces in the Heligoland bight. Expended 92 15in shell, scoring a hit on the cruiser *Pillau* (shared with *Glorious*); out of 393 4in shells fired by both ships scored no hits. After the Armistice she was attached to the Gunnery School and later became flagship of the reserve. Converted to a carrier 1924–28 and was the first RN ship loss of the Second World War, being torpedoed by *U 29* on 17 September 1939 with the loss of 23 Swordfish planes and 514 of her 1200 crew.

Glorious commissioned in January 1917 as flagship 3rd LCS but then joined her sister in 1st LCS. In action on 17 November 1917, firing 57 15in shells. Attached to gunnery school at Devonport in 1919 and later became flagship of reserve. Converted to carrier 1924–30 and sunk by gunfire off Norway, 8 June 1940.

Furious as completed

FURIOUS *light battlecruiser*

Displacement:	19,513t load; 22,890t deep load
Dimensions:	786ft 6in oa × 88ft × 21ft mean *239.7m × 26.8m × 6.4m*
Machinery:	4-shaft Brown-Curtis geared turbines, 18 Yarrow boilers, 90,000shp = 31½kts. Oil 3393t.
Armour:	Belt 3in–2in (75mm–50mm), bulkheads 3in–2in (75mm–50mm), barbettes 7in–4in (180mm–100mm), turret faces 9in (230mm), CT 10in (250mm), decks 3in–¾in (75mm–20mm)
Armament:	2–18in (45.7cm)/40cal Mk I, 11–5.5in (14cm)/50 BL Mk I, 2–3in (75mm)/20cwt AA Mk I, 4–3pdr (47mm), 2–21in (53.3cm) TT sub (beam)
Complement:	880

Name	Builder	Laid down	Launched	Comp	Fate
FURIOUS	Armstrong	8.6.15	15.8.16	7.17	Converted to carrier 1917

The third light battlecruiser was given two single 18in guns, but care was taken to make the turret-ring the same size as the twin 15in mounting, so that if problems were encountered with the gun it would be possible to re-arm the ship with 15in guns. In fact the 18in gun was merely a much bigger version of the 15in, and apart from its massive muzzle blast, retained the good qualities of the smaller gun. Experience with the ex-Greek cruisers *Birkenhead* and *Chester* had demonstrated the qualities of the 5.5in gun, and the single mountings proved far more satisfactory than the triple 4in guns in the *Courageous* class. They were grouped two p&s of the foremast, p&s of the funnel, one on the centreline, p&s of the mainmast, and p&s abreast of the funnel at weatherdeck level.

The ship was nearly complete at Elswick when on 19 March 1917 it was decided by the Admiralty to convert her to a carrier to remedy the Grand Fleet's crucial shortage of aircraft. The after gun had been installed but the forward turret was still being assembled and the gun was still ashore. The turret was replaced by a hangar and sloping flying-off deck which extended to the forecastle, with two derricks for hoisting aircraft aboard. The ship was completed to the new design on 4 July 1917 and she joined the Fleet, but on 17 October further orders were issued to give her an after flight deck and hangar. This was a much more drastic conversion, and full details will be found under 'Aircraft Carriers'.

The hull was 7ft beamier than the *Courageous* class, but with a more pronounced 'bulge'. There was also a simpler form of main framing and structure. In appearance she would have resembled the *Courageous* class, apart from the massive 18in turrets. As with her half-sisters the torpedo armament was increased by the addition of four sets of triple 21in TT on the upper deck aft and two pairs on the upper deck forward. The triple tubes were subsequently removed, reducing the total to six TT, including the submerged tubes ahead of the forward barbette. On a full power trial she reached 31½kts with 94,000shp.

Joined Grand Fleet in July 1917 and carried out trials until November. On 2 August 1917 Sqn Cdr Dunning twice landed a Sopwith Pup on the flying-off deck but he was killed while attempting to repeat the success on 7 August. Went into dockyard hands for full conversion to carrier in December 1917.

Hood on sea trials 1920 — *By courtesy of John M Maber*

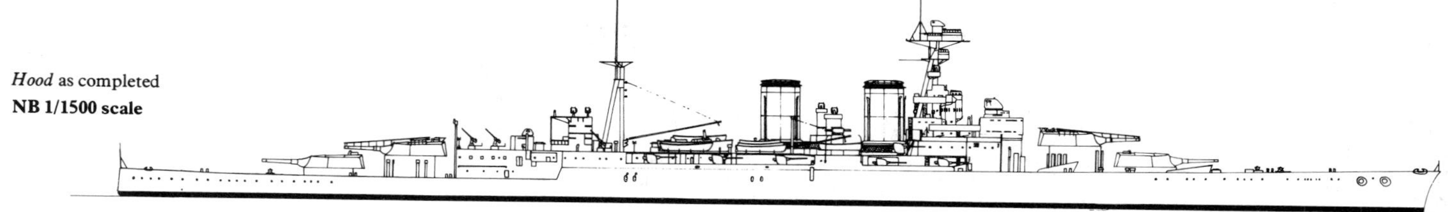

Hood as completed
NB 1/1500 scale

In November 1915 the Admiralty Board called for a design for an experimental battleship, with the lightest practicable draught and incorporating the latest ideas on underwater protection. The basis was to be the *Queen Elizabeth* class of fast battleships, but when the proposals were forwarded to the C-in-C, Admiral Jellicoe, he insisted that 30kt battlecruisers were more useful than battleships. The design was recast as a battlecruiser of 36,300t, with 8in belt armour and a speed of 32kts, but the loss of three battlecruisers at Jutland on the day the first ship was laid down (construction of three had been authorised in April 1916 and the fourth followed in July) caused all work to be stopped. The design was investigated and recast by early August 1916 as 37,500t, with a deeper belt. Later that month the DNC submitted his own modifications, which raised displacement to 40,600t and increased belt armour to 12in. Among other ideas looked at were triple 15in mountings, two triple and two twin, or three triples, with displacement increased to 40,900t–43,500t and speed cut to 30½kts–30¾kts. Finally, however, the 8-gun design was accepted, and so in effect the original idea of a bigger and faster *Queen Elizabeth* was finally achieved.

HOOD class *battlecruisers*

Displacement:	42,670t load; 45,200t deep load
Dimensions:	860ft oa × 104ft × 28ft 6in *262.1m × 31.7m × 8.7m*
Machinery:	4-shaft Brown-Curtis geared turbines, 24 Yarrow boilers, 144,000shp = 31kts. Oil 4000t. Range 4000nm at 10kts
Armour:	Belt 12in–5in (300mm–130mm), bulkheads 5in–4in (130mm–100mm), barbettes 12in–5in (300mm–130mm), turret faces 15in (380mm), CT 11in–9in (280mm–230mm), decks 3in–1½in (100mm–50mm)
Armament:	8–15in (38.1cm)/42cal Mk I (4×2), 12–5.5in (14cm)/50cal BL Mk I, 4–4in (10.2cm)/45cal QF Mk V AA, 4–3pdr (47mm), 6–21in (53.3cm) TT (2 sub beam; 4 aw beam)
Complement:	1477

Name	Builder	Laid down	Launched	Comp	Fate
HOOD	John Brown	31.5.16*	22.8.18	5.20	Sunk 24.5.41
RODNEY	Fairfield	9.10.16	–	–	Cancelled 1918
HOWE	Cammell Laird	16.10.16	–	–	Cancelled 1918
ANSON	Armstrong	9.11.17	–	–	Cancelled 1918

*Laid down for second time 1.9.16 (see notes)

The most obvious lesson learned since the outbreak of war was that secondary batteries needed to be a deck higher, and so the 5.5in guns were mainly at forecastle deck level, with two singles p&s abreast of the forward funnel giving even better command in bad weather. Seakeeping was improved by giving the hull pronounced sheer and flare. This flare was also intended to ensure that an incoming shell would not strike at 90°, and so in effect increased the armour's resistance to penetration. On 8 February 1917 the War Cabinet decided to proceed only with the *Hood* as intelligence showed that the Germans had stopped work on capital ships. *Rodney, Howe* and *Anson* were therefore suspended on 9 March. They lay on the stocks until October 1918, when the contractors were authorised to clear the slips, but the task of selling off armour and machinery continued until August 1919. So many changes had been made to their design that they would have differed considerably from the *Hood*. The belt would have been reduced to 11in, funnels would have been closer together and the mainmast would have been stepped close to the after funnel. A new type of 15in turret was also under consideration.

Before the *Hood* was completed four 5.5in guns at the after end of the battery were suppressed along with 4 of the 8 aw TT. The ship was by now considerably overweight with all the additions made in 1918–19, and it was having the effect of submerging the main belt and reducing freeboard. The 15in Mk II mounting differed from previous mountings in having 30° elevation. As in the 18in turret, sighting ports in the roof were replaced by rectangular ports cut in the face armour, and the crowns were much flatter than before. In the light of subsequent allegations about specific design faults 'known to a handful of senior officers' it is interesting to note that the DNC's advice in 1918 was that the ship reflected pre-Jutland ideas on the disposition of armour, and that the changes since August 1916 had done no more than remedy the worst defects. He went on to recommend that since it would be an unwarranted waste of money to break her up on the slip the best thing would be to get her out of the way, cancel her sisters and get on with building ships which benefited from wartime experience. The reputation of the 'Mighty *Hood*' was largely inflated by the press, which equated size with fighting power. Notwithstanding her weak protection against long-range gunfire, she embodied several novel features, and had the armour been concentrated where it did most good she would have been a much better ship.

HMS *Hood* commissioned on the Clyde in May 1920 as flagship of the Battle Cruiser Squadron. As the most prestigious unit of the RN she saw service all over the world but never received the modernisation which she needed. Served with Home Fleet and Force 'H' in the Second World War and blew up in action with *Bismarck* and *Prinz Eugen* on 24 May 1941.

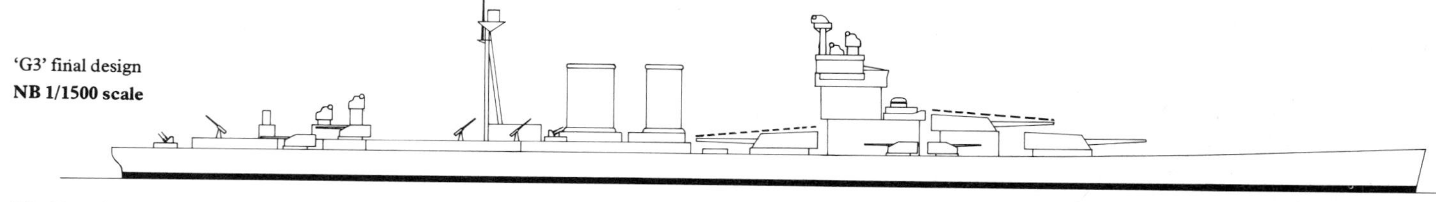

'G3' final design
NB 1/1500 scale

The Royal Navy was well aware that it had ended the War in an inferior position *vis á vis* the American and Japanese navies. Despite the enormous preponderance of numbers, the 12in-gunned dreadnoughts were quite outclassed, and even the 13.5in- and 15in-gunned ships were outclassed by the latest 14in- and 16in-gunned 'super-dreadnoughts' laid down during the War. Drastic reconstruction would remedy the worst deficiencies of the 15in-gunned ships, but what was needed was a new class of ships capable of facing 16in and even 18in gunfire. There was also an urgent need to incorporate war lessons: the *Hood* class,

'G 3' type *battlecruisers*

Displacement:	48,400t legend; 53,909t deep load
Dimensions:	856ft oa × 106ft × 35ft 8in deep *260.9m × 32.3m × 10.9m*
Machinery:	4-shaft single-reduction geared steam turbines, 20 small-tube boilers, 160,000shp = 31–32kts. Oil 5000t
Armour:	Belt 12in–14in (305mm–355mm), bulkheads 10in–12in (255mm–305mm), turret faces 17in (430mm), decks 4in–8in (100mm–200mm), CT 10in–14in (255mm–355mm)
Armament:	9–16in (40.6cm)/45cal Mk I (3×3), 16–6in (15.2cm)/50cal Mk XXIII (8×2), 6–4.7 (12cm)/43cal AA (6×1), 40–2pdr (40mm) pom-poms (10×4), 2–24.5in (62.2cm) TT sub (forward)
Complement:	1716

despite detailed improvements, was essentially a pre-Jutland design, and by 1921 there was a large body of fresh experience based on tests against German ships. The first design required was a class of four large battlcruisers, to be laid down in 1921. The concept which evolved was much closer to a fast battleship than anything previously considered and the US Navy's 'all-or-nothing' concept of protection was embraced.

The latest type of protection was to be used, namely an inclined internal armour belt and internal 'bulges' against torpedoes.

For the first time a triple turret was adopted to concentrate armament. The secondary armament was mounted in twin turrets. Various designs were drawn up, but all had in common a concentration of heavy armour over the vitals, with turrets grouped together to permit the maximum thickness of armour. They represented a big a step forward in fighting power as the *Dreadnought* had 17 years earlier, and they showed how much the size of capital ships had increased in little more than a decade.

After lengthy consideration, design 'G 3' (out of an alphabetical series) was accepted in February 1921), the final legend being approved in August 1921. Orders followed on 26 October – one each from Beardmore, John Brown, Fairfield and Swan Hunter (the last with machinery sub-contracted to Parsons) – but the orders were suspended on 18 November by Cabinet order. The threat of these ships being built was used as a bargaining counter during the Washington Conference, but it was quite clear by the end of 1921 that Britain was in a deepening financial crisis, and the Cabinet would not have permitted the programme to go ahead, even if the Americans and Japanese had refused to negotiate reductions in their fleets. Although the ships had not started construction the details of the design were sufficiently developed to provide a basis for the *Nelson* and *Rodney*, truncated versions carrying the same armament and scale of protection, but 8–9kts slower. Under the terms of the Treaty the four 'G 3's were cancelled on 13 February 1922. Names were never allocated, and the two sets of names often quoted are merely speculative: *St George, St Andrew, St David* and *St Patrick*; or *Invincible, Inflexible, Indomitable* and *Indefatigable*.

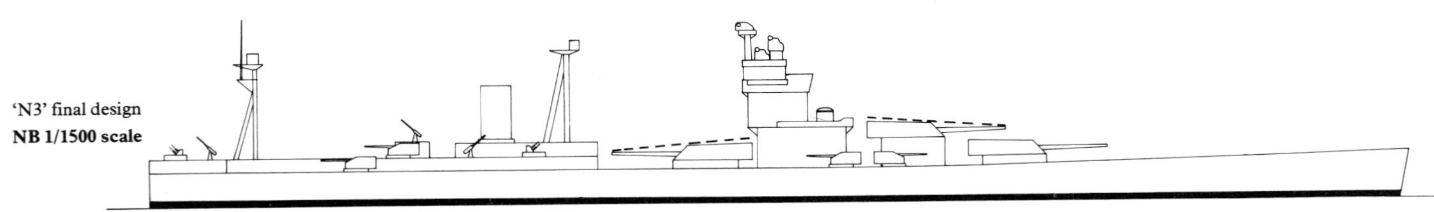

'N3' final design
NB 1/1500 scale

In addition to four battlecruisers for 1921 the Admiralty hoped to lay down four battleships in 1922. The design which evolved was broadly similar to the 'G 3' battlecruiser design, but with only half the horsepower, as speed was cut to 23–23½kts (the speed of the battlefleet). The main armament was to be three triple 18in, of a new 45cal type, firing a 2837lb shell at a muzzle velocity of 2837fps. Experience with the blast effects of the triple 16in was later to suggest that the theoretical power of the 18in would have been outranked by the appalling blast-effects on decks and superstructure.

'N 3' type *battleships*

Displacement:	48,500t normal
Dimensions:	820ft oa × 106ft × 32ft–33ft *250m × 32.3m × 9.9m–10.1m*
Machinery:	4-shaft single-reduction geared steam turbines, probably 80,000shp = 23–23½kts.
Armour:	Belt 13¾in–15in (340mm–380mm), bulkheads 14in (355mm), turret faces 18in (460mm), decks 8in (200mm), CT 15in (380mm)
Armament:	9–18in (45.7cm)/45cal Mk II (3×3), 16–6in (15.2cm)/50cal Mk XXII (8×2), 6–4.7 (12cm)/43cal AA (6×1), 40–2pdr (40mm) pom-poms (4×10)
Complement:	Not known

The four ships planned were still at an early design-stage when the Washington Treaty put an end to all plans for large capital ships. Like the 'G 3' design they would have been cancelled at the insistence of the Treasury, even without the Treaty, but they remain the most powerfully armed British battleships of all time.

MONITORS

Humber as completed

Three small river monitors had been ordered by Brazil from Vickers in January 1912, and the first, *Javary*, had started trials in October 1913. All three were ready by February 1914, but by this time the Brazilian Navy could not afford to pay for them and they were laid up in the Devonshire Dock at Barrow awaiting a buyer. Just before the outbreak of war the Admiralty made arrangements to buy them for £155,000 each to prevent them from falling into enemy hands, and they were formally taken over on 3 August 1914. Although nominally capable of 12kts none of them achieved double figures in RN service, although *Javary* had reached 11½kts in 1913. They were totally unsuited to operate in the open sea, as their shallow draught permitted them to be blown sideways.

The ships underwent a series of alterations, starting in September–October 1914 when they received additional 1in plating over the magazine. By the end of 1914 they had worn out their guns and serious thought was given to replacing the turrets with spares from the 'County' class armoured cruisers (the turret was a Vickers commercial variant of the RN twin 6in). The work would have been too complex and time-consuming and so *Severn* and *Mersey*'s turrets were removed entirely. In their place the ships were each given 2–6in BL Mk VII each, one forward and one aft. The 2–4.7in howitzers were moved from the quarterdeck to the boat deck. As *Humber*'s guns were not so badly worn she kept her turret, but in December 1914 she received an additional 6in Mk VII on the quarterdeck. *Severn* and *Mersey* were given a 3pdr AA gun in place of the after searchlight in September–October 1914. It was proposed early in 1919 to re-arm all three with triple 4in for service in North Russia but *Humber*

HUMBER class *monitors*

Displacement:	1260t Navy List; 1520t deep load
Dimensions:	266ft 9in oa × 49ft × 5ft 7½in deep *81.3m × 14.9m × 1.7m*
Machinery:	2-shaft TE, 2 boilers, 1450ihp = 9½kts. Coal 187t, oil 90t
Armour:	Belt 3in–1½in (75mm–40mm), bulkheads 1½in (40mm), barbette 3½in (90mm), turret face 4in (100mm)
Armament:	2–6in (15.2cm)/50cal BL Mk XIV (righthand) and Mk XV (lefthand) (1×2), 2–4.7in (12cm)/18cal howitzers, 4–3pdr (47mm), 6–7mm Hotchkiss MG
Complement:	140

Name	Builder	Laid down	Launched	Comp	Fate
SEVERN (ex-*Solimoes*)	Vickers	24.8.12	19.8.13	1.14	Sold for BU 5.21
HUMBER (ex-*Javary*)	Vickers	24.8.12	17.6.13	11.13	Sold 9.20
MERSEY (ex-*Madeira*)	Vickers	24.8.12	30.9.13	2.14	Sold for BU 5.21

was sent to Murmansk with her original armament, apart from a 3in/20cwt Mk II AA gun in place of the 3pdr AA. Her sisters were not altered as their orders were cancelled.

Humber was ready for RN service by 25 August 1914 and reached Dover four days later. Took part in Belgian coast operations October–November 1914 and then repaired at Chatham DYd. Remained in Medway until March 1915 and left for Mediterranean with her sisters, in company with the liner *Trent*. Arrived Malta 29 March but did not reach Gallipoli until June 1915. Refitted and given new guns at Alexandria in January 1916 and remained in Egyptian waters. Guardship at Akaba August 1917–February 1918 and sent to Mudros with her sisters in October 1918. Went through Dardanelles after Armistice and after three months at Istanbul returned home in March 1919. Refitted and left Devonport for Murmansk 20 May 1919. Left Archangel in September 1919 in tow, paying off at Chatham on 24 October. Sold in September 1920 to Dutch salvage company for conversion to a crane barge, and was still doing salvage work in 1938. Probably BU post 1945.

Severn commissioned in August 1914 and arrived at Dover on 29 August. Took part in Belgian coast operations in October–November 1914, then refitted at Chatham in November–December 1914. Ordered to Dardanelles in March 1915 but was diverted at Malta to go with *Mersey* to East Africa, to help destroy the cruiser *Königsberg* in the Rufiji River. Arrived at Mafia Island on 3 June and between 6 and 11 July destroyed the enemy with long-range gunfire. Remained off East African coast until April 1918 (refitted Durban April 1917), then sent to Egypt. Sent to Mudros in October 1918 and served on Danube for three months. Ordered home in March 1919 for service on Dvina River as part of White Sea Squadron, but remained at Devonport in C&M until moved to Queenstown (Cobh) in July 1919.

Mersey commissioned in August 1914 and served on Belgian coast operations until November 1914. Refitted at Chatham and then towed to Malta March–April 1915. Diverted with *Severn* to deal with *Königsberg* in East Africa. Refitted at Durham March 1916 and towed back to Mediterranean by liner *Trent*, March–May 1918. Sent to Mudros in October 1918 and then to Black Sea and Danube after Armistice. On her return to Devonport in May 1919 was paid off into C&M. Moved to Queenstown in July 1919 and sold in 1921.

Humber 1915

By courtesy of R A Burt

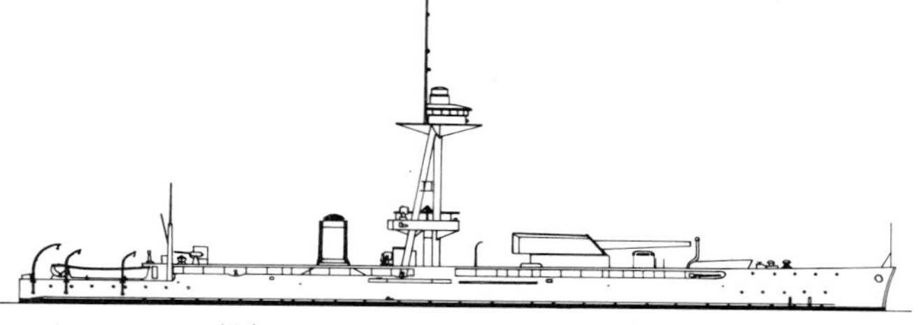

Roberts as completed

ABERCROMBIE class *monitors*

Displacement: 6150t legend/deep load
Dimensions: 334ft 6in oa × 90ft 2in × 10ft
102.0m × 27.4m × 3.1m
Machinery: 2-shaft QE, 2 Babcock & Wilcox boilers, 2000ihp = 10kts designed (*Raglan* 4-cyl VTE, 2310ihp = 6½kts, *Roberts* 3-cyl VTE, 1800ihp = 6kts actual)
Armour: Internal belt 4in (100mm), bulkheads 4in (100mm), barbette 8in (200mm), turret face 10in (250mm), decks 2in–1in (50mm–25mm)
Armament: 2–14in (35.6cm)/45cal Mk II (1×2), 2–12pdr (76mm)/18cwt QF Mk I, 1–3pdr (47mm) AA, 1–2pdr (40mm) AA, 4–.303in Maxim MGs
Complement: 198

Name	Builder	Laid down	Launched	Comp	Fate
ABERCROMBIE	Harland & Wolff, Belfast	12.12.14	15.4.15	5.15	Sold 1927
HAVELOCK	Harland & Wolff, Belfast	12.12.14	29.4.15	6.15	Sold 1927
RAGLAN	Harland & Wolff, Govan	1.12.14	29.4.15	6.15	Sunk 20.1.18
ROBERTS	Swan Hunter	17.12.14	15.4.16	6.15	Sold 1936

The makeshift fleet of old battleships and gunboats which bombarded the Belgian coast in October 1914 showed clearly that whatever opportunities might be presented for warships to influence events ashore, the Royal Navy lacked ships suited to the task. Thus when on 3 November 1914 the President of Bethlehem Steel, Charles M Schwab, called on Winston Churchill to offer four twin 14in turrets, the First Lord of the Admiralty saw the possibility of using them for shore bombardment. The guns were destined for the Greek ship *Salamis* but Schwab recognised that they would never get through the British blockade, and was quite happy to sell them to the British instead. Literally the following day the DNC was instructed to investigate the building of two 'armoured monitors' with a draught of 10ft, within four months.

The design, although pushed through very rapidly, incorporated the new anti-torpedo 'bulges' but in combination with the extremely bluff bow and stern, they made the monitors unwieldy and slow. Had Fisher been prepared to wait for the results of tank tests the proper power needed for 10kts speed (roughly double what had been specified) would have been available in time, but construction was rushed ahead.

Abercrombie April 1919
By courtesy of John M Maber

The builders were told to use whatever mercantile engines were available. To preserve secrecy the four monitors were referred to as the *Styx* class, but soon had numbers *M 1–M 4* until February 1915, when American names were allocated to commemorate the US origin of their guns. But the Schwab deal, with its flagrant breach of neutrality, had already drawn strong State Department protests, and the ships were hurriedly renamed: *M 1* was renamed *Admiral Farragut* in February 1915, then *Abercrombie* in May; *M 2* was renamed *General Grant* in February 1915, then *Havelock* in May; *M 3* was allocated the name *Robert E Lee* in February 1915 but commissioned as *M 3* on 3 June 1915 as the order cancelling her name had been issued on 31 May; the name *Lord Raglan* was approved for her on 19 June but shortened to *Raglan* four days later; *M 4* was named *Stonewall Jackson* in February 1915, then *Earl Roberts* in May, but shortened to *Roberts* on 22 June. Several variants such as *Lord Roberts* and *General Abercrombie* have been quoted but they were never official.

The 14in/45cal BL Mk II had a range of 19,900yds at 15° elevation and was electrically worked. The construction of the gun was considerably different from anything seen in the RN and it used nitro-cellulose tube (NCT) propellant. The first shells and charges were supplied from the USA, the nose-fused 4crh shells being made to British specifications. The US Navy subsequently supplied four similar 14in guns and in 1917 the Royal Gun Factory at Woolwich made two wire-wound versions, to replace worn-out guns in *Abercrombie*. Although called 'monitors' the new ships bore little resemblance to the low freeboard turret ships built in the 1860s, but the name had been applied to single-turreted ships built for coast defence and service in South American rivers, so the name was applied to the new ships. Their distinguishing features were a massive tripod mast and the large gun turret, and the diminutive funnel and bridge emphasized the bareness of the hull. All except *Raglan* had two derricks at the after end of the forecastle deck for handling seaplanes, making them the first British warships designed to carry aircraft. The secondary guns were carried below the forecastle, behind hinged bulwarks ahead of the 14in turret. In addition they carried a single 3pdr and a 2pdr pom-pom for air defence. They underwent few modifications, the first being to raise the funnel by 12ft at the first refit. To help the monitors provide routine harassing fire, a 6in Mk XII was added on the forecastle deck in *Abercrombie* and *Raglan* (in 1917 and 1916 respectively, *Raglan*'s gun being salvaged from *M 30*). In 1916 *Roberts* received a 6in QF Mk I on an improvised AA mounting, mounted at upper deck level on the starboard side aft, while the barrel and the trunnions projected through the forecastle deck. The 12pdrs were removed in 1915–16 and remounted on the forecastle deck on modified high-angle mountings. By 1918 they had the following armaments:

Abercrombie: 2–14in, 1–6in, 2–12pdr AA, 1–3in/20cwt AA, 1–3pdr AA, 1–2pdr AA.
Havelock: 2–14in, 2–12pdr AA, 2–3in/20cwt AA.
Raglan: 2–14in, 1–6in, 2–12pdr AA, 1–3pdr AA, 1–2pdr AA.
Roberts: 2–14in, 1–6in AA, 2–12pdr AA, 1–3in AA, 1–3pdr AA, 2–2pdr AA.

Although designed to operate seaplanes none of them did for any length of time as shore-based RNAS aircraft proved far better for spotting duties. Another problem was that each time the guns fired the seaplane had to be hoisted over the side to prevent blast damage. In September 1915 *Roberts* operated a Short 166, as did *Raglan* for several days in October 1916. *Abercrombie* carried out similar experiments with a Sopwith Schneider. In September 1917 *Raglan* carried a Short 184 seaplane on top of the 14in turret.

Abercrombie commissioned (as *Admiral Farragut*) in May 1915 and sailed for Dardanelles on 24 June in company with the cruiser *Theseus*, which gave her a tow to speed up the passage. On her arrival at Kephalo on 12 July 1915, she became flagship of supporting forces and immediately went into action against Turkish defences. She was hit frequently but suffered no serious damage. In September 1915 she and her sisters were formed into 1st Division, Special Squadron. After evacuation of Cape Helles in January 1916 went to Imbros, from where she fired sporadically against Turkish troops and positions. Refitted at Malta in May 1916 and returned to Imbros. In action on Salonika front October 1916 and then supported various Aegean operations before returning to Kephalo early in 1917. Refitted at Malta in May 1917 and again May 1918, when her guns were replaced, but saw very little action. Late in August 1918 she was near-missed by the same U-boat which torpedoed *Endymion*. Went through Dardanelles on Armistice Day 1918 and returned home in February 1919. In April she was sent to Immingham to await disposal (in C&M); paid off in May 1919 and disarmed at Portsmouth in June 1920. Sold for BU in May 1921 but retained by Admiralty and laid up at Portsmouth until June 1927 when she was resold and BU.

Havelock commissioned (as *General Grant*) in May 1915 and went to Dardanelles with cruiser *Juno*; joined 1st Division, Special Squadron in September. After evacuation from Cape Helles in January 1916 returned home, and was sent to Lowestoft in May to act as guardship against German raids. Refitted on Tyne in June 1917 but apart from AA firing and occasional false alarms saw no further action. Paid off into C&M at Immingham in May 1919 and disarmed at Portsmouth in June 1920. Sold in May 1921 but remained laid up at Portsmouth until sold for BU in June 1927.

Raglan commissioned (as *M 3*) in June 1915 and went to Dardanelles for bombardment duty, in company with cruiser *Diana*. Formed part of 1st Division, Special Squadron September 1915–January 1916. After evacuation served in Aegean. To Port Said in September 1917 for operations against Turks in Southern Palestine. In January 1917 returned to Imbros to guard against a breakout by the *Goeben* and *Breslau*, a duty which she shared with the *Abercrombie* and a number of small monitors as the 2nd Detached Squadron of the Aegean Squadron. Early on the morning of 20 January 1918 she came under accurate fire from first the *Breslau* and later the *Goeben*; she was set on fire and after being abandoned she sank on an even keel in shallow water (127 dead). Guns and other valuable equipment were salvaged.

Roberts commissioned (as *Stonewall Jackson*) in May 1915 and went to Dardanelles in company with cruiser *Endymion*. Formed part of 1st Division, Special Squadron September 1915–January 1916; returned home in February and sent to Yarmouth in May for service as guardship, but apart from air raids saw little action. Docked in June 1917 on the Tyne and then moved to Thames Estuary to take part in the projected Belgian landings (as a reserve monitor). Returned to Yarmouth in October, refitted at Portsmouth in July 1918 and paid off into C&M at Immingham in May 1919. Towed to Portsmouth in October 1920 but was not disarmed. Sold in May 1921 but retained by Admiralty for trials. In 1925 she was considered for conversion to an airship mooring mast and fuelling point, and in the early 1930s was used for trials of underwater protection for new construction. Sold for BU in September 1936.

General Wolfe with 18in gun 1918 CPL

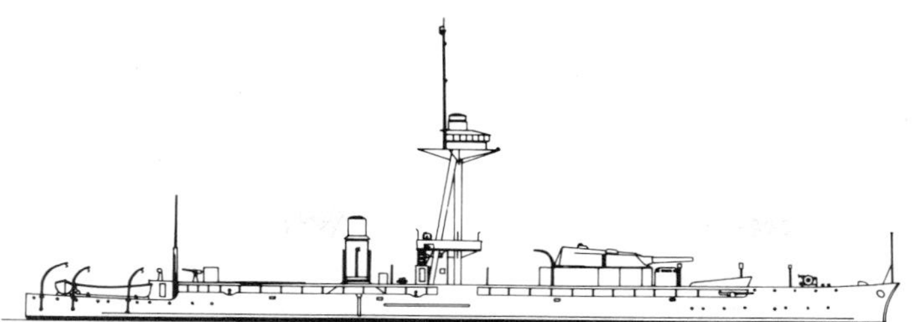

General Craufurd 1915

LORD CLIVE class *monitors*

Displacement: 6150t legend; 6150t deep load
Dimensions: 335ft 6in oa × 87ft 2in × 9ft 7in deep
102.3m × 26.6m × 2.9m
Machinery: 2-shaft 4-cyl (*Moore, Rupert* 3-cyl) VTE, 2 boilers, 2310ihp (*Wolfe, Moore* 2500ihp, *Rupert* 1600ihp) = 6½kts. Coal 356t
Armour: As *Abercrombie* class, except belt 6in (150mm), turret faces 10½in (270mm)
Armament: 2–12in (30.5cm)/35cal Mk VIII (1×2), 2–12pdr (76mm)/18cwt QF, 1–3pdr (47mm) AA, 1–2pdr (40mm) AA
Complement: 194

Name	Builder	Laid down	Launched	Comp	Fate
LORD CLIVE (*M 6*)	Harland & Wolff, Belfast	9.1.15	10.6.15	7.15	Sold for BU 10.27
GENERAL CRAUFURD (*M 7*)	Harland & Wolff, Belfast	9.1.15	8.7.15	8.15	Sold for BU 5.21
EARL OF PETERBOROUGH (*M 8*)	Harland & Wolff, Belfast	16.1.15	26.8.15	10.15	Sold for BU 11.21
SIR THOMAS PICTON (*M 12*)	Harland & Wolff, Belfast	16.1.15	30.9.15	15.11.15	Sold for BU 11.21
PRINCE EUGENE (*M 11*)	Harland & Wolff, Govan	1.2.15	14.7.15	9.15	Sold for BU 5.21
PRINCE RUPERT (*M 10*)	Hamilton	12.1.15	20.5.15	7.15	Sold for BU 5.23
SIR JOHN MOORE (*M 5*)	Scott	13.1.15	31.5.15	7.15	Sold for BU 11.21
GENERAL WOLFE (*M 9*)	Palmer	1.15	9.9.15	11.15	Sold for BU 5.21

The speed of building the 14in gun monitors encouraged Churchill to suggest on 11 December 1914 the construction of at least eight more. The First Lord hoped to make use of spare 13.5in and 15in guns but as all these spares lacked complete turrets they would take about a year before they were ready. There were, however, a number of pre-dreadnought battleships which were useless for anything but coast defence, and four of these would provide eight twin 12in turrets. The *Majestics*, being the oldest battleships on the Navy List, were chosen and, on the advice of Admiral Sir Percy Scott, the Elswick Ordnance Company was asked to increase elevation from 13½° to 30°, increasing range from 13,700yds to at least 21,300yds (24,500yds if 4crh shells were used). The guns were provided by *Victorious* (for *Prince Rupert* and *General Wolfe*), *Magnificent* (for *Lord Clive* and *General Craufurd*), *Hannibal* (*Prince Eugene* and *Sir John Moore*) and *Mars* (*Earl of Peterborough* and *Sir Thomas Picton*).

Although Churchill toyed with the idea of diesel engines and some other unorthodox ideas, haste was essential, and the design was virtually a repeat of the 14in type. As before the installed power was insufficient for the speed required and they made only 7kts–8kts on trials (6½kts was the maximum service speed). The designed AA armament was to have been 2–3in but as production was slow they were completed with a 3pdr and a 2pdr pom-pom on high-angle mountings. Like the 14in-gunned ships they were fitted to carry seaplanes aft but these were not embarked and the derricks were removed, but in August 1916 *General Craufurd* temporarily embarked a Short 184 seaplane for trials.

The 12in monitors' armament and equipment changed much more than the 14in-gunned ships, partly because dockyard facilities were closer but also because conditions off the Belgian coast changed constantly. The 12pdr armament was soon removed from the Dover Patrol ships, and replaced by four 6in QF abreast of the funnel (most removed from the battleship *Illustrious*). To provide more accommodation the open sides were plated in; these alterations were progressive, until by 1918 all except *Sir John Moore*, *Prince Rupert* and *General Wolfe* had their sides fully enclosed. In 1917 all the Dover ships were given smoke-making apparatus on the foretop, while the upperworks were painted in a chequer-board pattern. The Adriatic monitors were painted khaki to match the colour of the water in the lagoons, and *Sir Thomas Picton* received a 6in BL Mk XII abaft the funnel.

In 1918 three of the Dover Patrol monitors were converted to take an 18in gun each. A 384t fixed mounting was devised, enabling the gun to elevate to 45°, but trained to starboard, with only a limited 10° arc of train. The 12in twin turret was left in place to avoid having to ballast to restore trim, while the after part of the hull had to be specially stiffened to take the enormous weight. As there was no space below decks for additional magazines and shellrooms, sufficient shells for a day's firing (60 rounds) were stowed on the upper deck, with cordite in cases on the forecastle deck. The cordite was kept in water-jacketed tanks to solve the problem of cooling. The original plans called for the ships chosen, *Lord Clive*, and *Prince Eugene* to be taken in hand at Portsmouth in December 1917, complete stiffening in January 1918, ship the gun by March and finish trials in May 1918, at which point the third ship, *General Wolfe* would be taken in hand. In fact the guns and mountings were delayed, and when the first mounting arrived at Portsmouth in July 1918 it was installed in the *General Wolfe*, and she carried out firing trials off the Isle of Wight on 7 August. *Lord Clive* received her gun in August–September 1918 and ran trials in October, but *Prince Eugene* never received hers as the war ended before it could be fitted.

The following armaments were fitted to the class by November 1918:
Lord Clive: 1–18in, 2–12in, 4–4in, 2–3in AA, 3–2pdr AA.
General Wolfe: 1–18in, 2–12in, 2–6in, 2–3in AA, 2–2pdr AA.
Prince Eugene: 2–12in, 2–6in, 2–3in AA, 2–2pdr AA.
Sir John Moore: 2–12in, 4–4in, 2–12pdr AA, 2–3in AA, 2–2pdr.
General Craufurd: 2–12in, 4–6in, 2–12pdr AA, 2–3in AA, 2–2pdr.
Prince Rupert: 2–12in, 2–6in, 2–12pdr AA, 2–3in AA, 1–2pdr.
Sir Thomas Picton: 2–12in, 1–6in, 2–12pdr AA, 1–3in AA, 1–3pdr AA.
Earl of Peterborough: 2–12in, 2–12pdr AA, 2–3in AA, 1–2pdr.

Earl of Peterborough commissioned in September 1915 and left for the Mediterranean from Devonport in October, arriving at Mudros the following month. Transferred to Mytilene Squadron at Port Iero in February 1916, and took part in takeover of Greek Fleet in August 1916. Allocated to Adriatic Squadron in November 1916 and arrived at Venice, December. Started bombardments of Austrian positions in May 1917 and took part in 11th Battle of the Isonzo, August 1917. After prolonged action in support of Italian Army refitted at La Spezia in March–June 1918 and then went to Valona on Albanian front. After Armistice went to Venice as guardship, returning to Malta in February 1919 prior to her return home. Paid off in March 1919 and laid up at Immingham.

General Craufurd commissioned in August 1915 and joined Monitor Squadron at Dover. She carried out numerous bombardments on Belgian coast 1915–18, and was paid off in November 1918 at Sheerness. Remained at Nore with *Sir John Moore* and was recommissioned as a gunnery tender to 1st Fleet in January 1919. Offered for sale to Rumania later that year, but paid off again in spring of 1920 and put on sale list.

General Wolfe commissioned in October 1915 and joined Monitor Squadron at Dover in December. Rearmed with 18in gun at Portsmouth DYd 5 April–15 August 1918 and fired her first shells in September. Paid off at Sheerness in November 1918 and laid up in C&M at Immingham until sold in 1921.

Lord Clive was first of her class to commission, in July 1915. Although intended to be one of four 12in monitors for the Dardanelles she was allocated to the Monitor Squadron and arrived at Dover in August 1915. Modified for 18in gun at Portsmouth 5 December 1917–6 April 1918 but went back to Dover without the gun. Relieved *Roberts* at Yarmouth in July 1918 and then went to Portsmouth to receive her 18in gun, rejoining Dover Patrol on 13 August 1918. Paid off in November 1918 and laid up at Immingham until September 1920, when she was towed to Portsmouth for conversion. The 18in gun was removed in October–November 1920 and in its place was put a triple 15in open mounting, intended to test muzzle blast and interference in the proposed new triple 16in turret. Recommissioned in December and paid off in August 1921, to be laid up at Portsmouth until sold.

Prince Eugene commissioned in August 1915 and joined Monitor Squadron at Dover in September. Modified for rearming with 18in gun at Portsmouth 13 December 1917–7 April 1918 but returned to Dover without the gun. Went to Portsmouth on 17 October to receive the gun but three days later work stopped as armistice negotiations were already under way. Paid off in December 1918 and laid up in C&M at Immingham until sold.

Prince Rupert commissioned in June 1915 and was diverted from Dardanelles to Monitor Squadron of the Dover Patrol. Joined off Sheerness in August 1915 with *Lord Clive*. Docked in October 1917 at Portsmouth and then sent to Tees as guardship. Refitted at Jarrow in April 1918, and remained on the Tees as temporary tender to the submarine depot ship *Vulcan* until September 1919. Joined remaining monitors laid up at Immingham until May 1920, went to Chatham to become accommodation ship for dockyard police and boats' crews. In February 1922 took over from old *Achilles* as parent ship for the naval depot and renamed *Pembroke*.

Sir John Moore commissioned in July 1915 and was first of her class to join the Monitor Squadron at Dover later that month. Was also the last to leave, on 16 January 1919, going to the Nore. Recommissioned in January 1919 as gunnery tender with *General Craufurd* in 1st Fleet.

Sir Thomas Picton commissioned in October 1915 and went to Dardanelles, arriving at Mudros in November 1915. To Port Said in February 1916 and then to Aegean. Guns changed at Malta in February and in March 1917 was sent to Venice to support Italian Army. Refitted at Genoa March–June 1918. Sent to Fiume as guardship after Armistice and returned to Malta in February 1919. Paid off in May and laid up in C&M at Immingham, and then towed to Portsmouth for removal of guns and fittings before laid up in Spithead.

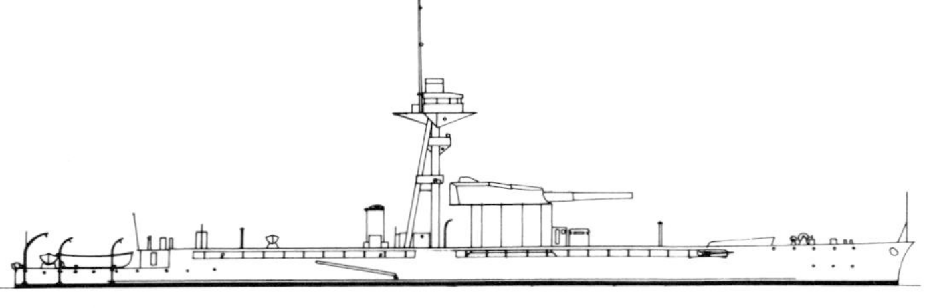

Marshal Soult as completed

MARSHAL SOULT class *monitors*

Displacement:	6670t legend; 6900t deep load
Dimensions:	355ft 8in oa × 90ft 3in × 10ft 5in deep *108.4m × 27.5m × 3.2m*
Machinery:	2-shaft 6-cyl MAN (*Soult* 8-cyl Vickers) diesels, 1500bhp = 9kts (6kts in service)
Armour:	Sloping internal belt 4in (100mm), bulkheads 4in (100mm), barbette 8in (200mm), turret face 13in (330mm), CT 6in (150mm), deck 4in–1in (100mm–25mm)
Armament:	2–15in (38.1cm)/42cal Mk I (1×2), 2–12pdr (76mm)/50cal 18cwt QF Mk I, 1–3pdr (47mm) AA
Complement:	187

Name	Builder	Laid down	Launched	Comp	Fate
MARSHAL NEY	Palmer	1.15	17.6.15	8.15	Sold for BU 1957
MARSHAL SOULT	Palmer	2.15	24.8.15	11.15	Sold for BU 7.46

In January 1915 the Admiralty decided to build two 15in-gunned monitors, in addition to the 12in already authorised. Although the hull had to be enlarged to accommodate the much heavier 15in mounting, draught was still to be no more than 10ft and beam was held at 90ft to enable them to be docked easily. The most severe technical problem encountered was the need to find room in a shallow hull for the ammunition trunk. As a result the barbette projected 17ft above the deck, giving the ships a much more impressive profile than the earlier monitors. Fisher wanted them to have diesel engines and so the engines of the fleet oilers *Trefoil* and *Turmoil* were commandeered. Unfortunately the mistakes in the previous classes were repeated; the installed power was too low for such a full-bodied hull form, and they were grossly underpowered for the displacement and almost impossible to steer. It had been hoped to use the turrets building for *Renown* and *Repulse* (the fourth turret for the original design) but they could not be ready before 1916. In their place turrets were diverted from *Ramillies*, allowing the ships to be completed by November 1915 at the latest. The provisional numbers *M 13* and *M 14* were allocated but names of Napoleonic marshals were chosen as a compliment to France.

The trials of *Marshal Ney* were disastrous as her MAN diesels were very difficult to start. Even when she was persuaded to start her speed was only 6kts instead of the 9kts expected. The results of machinery trials were so disheartening that the Admiralty seriously considered stopping work on both ships and transferring the turrets to other ships, but the trials of *Marshal Soult* were better and they were reprieved. Another scheme to arm them with the turrets from the battleship *Illustrious* or her sister *Caesar* was rejected. When completed both ships had diminutive funnels, which coupled with the tall tripod and massive turret gave them a bizarre look. *Ney* had her 15in turret removed in January–April 1916 (for *Terror*) at Elswick, and was then towed to Portsmouth, where she received a single 9.2in (23.4cm)/40cal BL Mk VIII and 4–6in/40cal QF Mk II. In March 1917 she was given a further pair, 2–6in/50cal BL Mk XI, and one of the 6in QF Mk Is was given to *Marshal Soult*. During *Soult*'s refit in 1917 she was also given 2–6in QF Mk I and a 3in/20cwt AA gun on the forecastle deck. More important was the raising of the axis of the 15in guns by 2ft to permit them to elevate to 30° and shoot to 30,000yds. In 1918 the 6in were replaced by 8–4in/44.4cal BL Mk IX in single shields amidships. The funnel was doubled in height, and searchlight positions and a control platform added aft. Two 2pdr AA guns were added aft. *Ney* was stripped of armament in 1920, but *Soult* remained very much in her 1918 state until disarmed in 1940.

Marshal Ney started trials in August 1915 and arrived at Sheerness early the following month. Served with Monitor Squadron at Dover until December 1916, when her engine trouble and appalling steering finally proved incurable. To stop German destroyers from raiding shipping in the Downs she was stripped of her 15in turret and given a lighter armament, for service as a permanent guardship. Took up station early in April 1917 and was missed by an air-launched torpedo on the 19th; drove off German destroyers during Ramsgate Raid on the 27th, and often engaged Zeppelins and bombers. Towed back to Sheerness in December 1918 and put on disposal list, but retained as base ship for MLs at Queensborough February–September 1919. Replaced *Arrogant* as depot ship for Submarine School at Fort Blockhouse from August 1920 (disarmed and tripod removed). From July 1922 at Devonport, replacing *Harlech* (ex-*Cambrian*) as Stoker Training Establishment; renamed *Vivid*. Remained there for another 35 years, being renamed *Drake* in January 1934. Renamed *Alaunia II* in 1947 and finally sold for BU 1957.

Marshal Soult was completed in October 1915 and left the Tyne in November, joining the Dover Patrol on the 6th. Alterations to 15in turret carried out at Elswick November 1916–March 1917 and refitted at Portsmouth January–April 1918. Returned to Chatham late in October and immediately sent to Portsmouth as tender to Gunnery School *Excellent*. Took up similar duties at Devonport from March 1919 to March 1921 and then paid off and removed from Effective List. Brought back into service to relieve *Glorious* as gunnery TS, and refitted May 1924–March 1925. Moved to Chatham in April 1926 to relieve *Erebus*, and remained there for 14 years. Although considered for return to active service her hull was in poor condition, so in March 1940 her turret was removed to be refurbished for the new monitor *Roberts*. From December 1940 she served as a trawler depot ship at Portsmouth until paid off in March 1946.

Marshal Ney about 1916 — *By courtesy of John M Maber*

See under Norway for original design

GORGON class *monitors*

Displacement: 5700t nominal; 5746t deep load
Dimensions: 310ft oa × 73ft 7in × 16ft 4in deep
94.5m × 22.4m × 5.0m
Machinery: 2-shaft VTE, 4 boilers, 4000ihp = 12kts. Coal 364t, oil 171t
Armour: Belt 7in–3in (180mm–100mm), bulkheads 4in–3in (100mm–75mm), barbettes 8in–6in (200mm–150mm), turret faces 8in (200mm), CT 8in (200mm), decks 2½in–1in (65mm–25mm)
Armament: 2–9.2in (23.4cm)/51.4cal Mk XII, 4–6in (15.2cm)/48.9cal Mk XVIII, 2–3in (76mm)/20cwt AA Mk I, 4–2pdr (40mm) AA (*Glatton* 4–3pdr (47mm) AA, 2–2pdr AA, instead 4–2pdr)
Complement: 305

Name	Builder	Laid down	Launched	Comp	Fate
GORGON (ex-*Nidaros*)	Elswick	11.6.13	9.6.14	6.18	Sold for BU 8.28
GLATTON (ex-*Bjorgvin*)	Elswick	26.5.13	8.8.14	9.18	Blew up 16.9.18

The Norwegian Government had ordered two coast defence battleships, the *Nidaros* and *Bjorgvin*, in January 1913, to be armed with 9.4in (24cm) and 5.9in (15cm) guns and capable of 15kts. The first named was launched on the Tyne in June 1914 and her sister just after the outbreak of war, and by November 1914 the Admiralty was negotiating with the Norwegians to take them over for conversion to monitors. The two-thirds of the contract price already paid was refunded and the ships were bought for a total of £370,000 each. In January 1915 the builders were given orders to begin the conversion, principally to modify the guns to take standard British shells, and to provide for additional fuel to increase endurance. In addition the boilers were converted to dual coal-oil-firing (see under Norway for details of original design). At first the work was given top priority but in May 1915, with 10–12 months' work still to do, work was suspended to expedite *Courageous* and *Furious*. In September 1917 Armstrongs were asked to complete the ships to a revised design, with wide anti-torpedo 'bulges'. The TT were removed, elevation of the main armament increased to 40° and a heavy tripod mast was fitted. Three of the guns had been completed as 9.4in and were relined to 9.2in, while No 4 gun was finished to the new calibre. With 40° elevation the new gun could range to 39,000yds with special 8crh shells (the 4crh shell fitted with a long ballistic cap), a range exceeded only by the 18in in the *General Wolfe* and *Lord Clive*. The ships were also give a new high-angle armament, an the result was a pair of highly effective monitors. Speed was now down by 2kts, thanks to the 'bulges' and *Gorgon* and *Glatton* made 13kts and 12½kts respectively on trials.

Glatton commissioned at Newcastle on 31 August 1918 and arrived at Dover 11 September. A week later, while she was lying in Dover harbour, her midships 6in magazine exploded and she caught fire. Attempts to scuttle her were impossible because the flames had taken hold, and Admiral Keyes ordered the destroyer *Cossack* to torpedo her. The first failed to detonate but the second blew a large hole in her starboard side. Two more 21in 'fish' from the *Myngs* were needed before she heeled over and sank (over half her crew were killed or injured). Although the Board of Enquiry reported in April 1919 that cork insulation might have been ignited by red-hot clinker and ash piled against the magazine bulkhead (the stokers being unaware that a magazine was on the other side) the Engineer-in-Chief and the DNC recorded their disagreement. Only when the *Gorgon*'s insulation was being stripped out did it become obvious that in some places the granulated cork had never been put in. Instead there were newspapers – far more likely to char and burst into flame than cork. Although the verdict of the enquiry was never formally reversed it seems clear that this was the cause of the magazine fire and explosion in *Glatton*. The wreck was raised May 1925–March 1926 and BU *in situ*.

Gorgon commissioned in May 1918 and arrived at Dover in June, taking part in several shoots against the Belgian coast batteries. She fired the last shell in four years of almost continuous bombardments on 15 October 1918. Sent to Portsmouth in November to await decision about her disposal; took part in trials to determine the cause of *Glatton*'s loss and her resale to Norway was discussed. To Devonport in April 1919 as temporary tender to *Vivid*, and paid off in August. In September 1919 joined Devonport Reserve. Sale to Argentina, Peru and Rumania was discussed in 1920 (Rumania offered *c*£60,000 for *Gorgon* and £140,000 for six 'M' class destroyers). Disarmed 1921 for use in further trials; towed back to Portsmouth in June 1922 and used as target for bombs and shells.

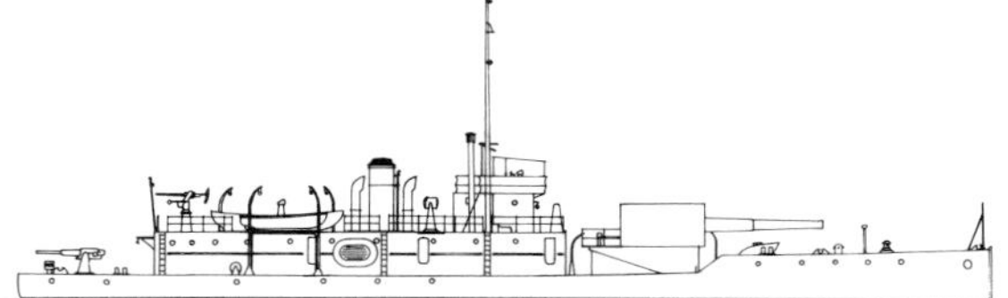

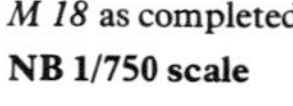

M 18 as completed
NB 1/750 scale

M 15 class *monitors*

Displacement: 540t legend; 650t deep load
Dimensions: 177ft 3in oa × 31ft × 6ft 7½in–7ft
54.0m × 9.4m × 2.0m–2.1m
Machinery: 2-shaft VTE, ? boilers, 800ihp (*M 21* 600ihp, *M 22* 650ihp) = 11kts
M 18–M 20, M 23, M 25, M 26–M 28 4 shafts, Bolinder 4-cyl semi-diesels, 640bhp (*M 26* 2-cyl, 480bhp, *M 27* 2-cyl, 560bhp)
M 24 4 shafts, Campbell 4-cyl paraffin engines, 640bhp
Armament: 1–9.2in (23.4cm)/46.7cal BL Mk X (*M 19–M 28* 31.5cal Mk VI), 1–12pdr (76mm)/18cwt QF Mk I, 1–6pdr (57mm) QF Mk I AA
Complement: 69

Name	Builder	Laid down	Launched	Comp	Fate
M 15	Wm Gray, Tees	3.15	28.4.15	6.15	Torpedoed 11.11.17
M 16	Wm Gray, Tees	3.15	3.5.15	6.15	Sold 1.20
M 17	Wm Gray, Tees	3.15	12.5.15	7.15	Sold 5.20
M 18	Wm Gray, Tees	3.15	15.5.15	7.15	Sold 1.20
M 19	Raylton Dixon, Tees	3.15	4.5.15	6.15	Sold 5.20
M 20	Raylton Dixon, Tees	3.15	11.5.15	7.15	Sold 1.20
M 21	Raylton Dixon, Tees	3.15	27.5.15	7.15	Mined 20.10.18
M 22	Raylton Dixon, Tees	3.15	10.6.15	8.15	Sold for BU 12.38
M 23	Raylton Dixon, Tees	3.15	17.6.15	7.15	Sold for BU 12.38
M 24	Raylton Dixon, Tees	3.15	9.8.15	10.15	Sold 1.20
M 25	Raylton Dixon, Tees	3.15	24.7.15	9.15	Scuttled 16.9.19
M 26	Raylton Dixon, Tees	3.15	24.8.15	10.15	Sold 1.20
M 27	Raylton Dixon, Tees	3.15	8.9.15	11.15	Scuttled 16.9.19
M 28	Raylton Dixon, Tees	3.15	28.6.15	8.15	Sunk 20.1.18

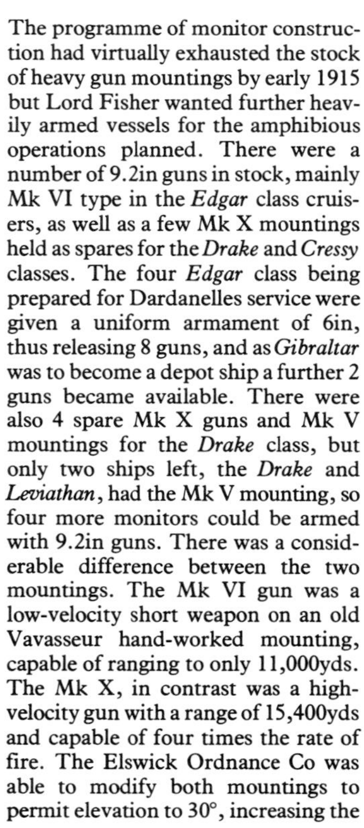

The programme of monitor construction had virtually exhausted the stock of heavy gun mountings by early 1915 but Lord Fisher wanted further heavily armed vessels for the amphibious operations planned. There were a number of 9.2in guns in stock, mainly Mk VI type in the *Edgar* class cruisers, as well as a few Mk X mountings held as spares for the *Drake* and *Cressy* classes. The four *Edgar* class being prepared for Dardanelles service were given a uniform armament of 6in, thus releasing 8 guns, and as *Gibraltar* was to become a depot ship a further 2 guns became available. There were also 4 spare Mk X guns and Mk V mountings for the *Drake* class, but only two ships left, the *Drake* and *Leviathan*, had the Mk V mounting, so four more monitors could be armed with 9.2in guns. There was a considerable difference between the two mountings. The Mk VI gun was a low-velocity short weapon on an old Vavasseur hand-worked mounting, capable of ranging to only 11,000yds. The Mk X, in contrast was a high-velocity gun with a range of 15,400yds and capable of four times the rate of fire. The Elswick Ordnance Co was able to modify both mountings to permit elevation to 30°, increasing the

Gorgon as completed CPL

range of the Mk VI to 16,300yds and 22,000yds for the Mk X (25,000yds with 4crh shells).

The requirements of the design were basic: draught about 6ft, speed 12kts and the simplest construction. Fisher was still anxious to get diesel engines into service, and he pressed for the use of the same Bolinder 'semi-diesel' as had been recommended for the large programme of 'X-lighter' landing barges. Only six of the 4-cylinder 'M' type were available and so two were given four of the 2-cylinder type. One ship received four paraffin engines by the Campbell Gas Co and the rest received conventional steam engines. The guns were allocated as follows: 2 from *Edgar* into *M 19* and *M 26*; 2 from *Theseus* into *M 21* and *M 27*; 2 from *Grafton* into *M 23* and *M 28*; 2 from *Endymion* into *M 24* and *M 25*; 2 from *Gibraltar* into *M 20* and *M 22*. One spare Mk X gun and its mounting was held at Malta, and a second had been sent out there before the Gallipoli landings, so *M 15* and *M 16* were sent out to be armed there; the other mountings were held at Portsmouth and were sent by road to Hartlepool.

In service their worst feature was their lively motion, which seriously impaired their ability to carry out accurate bombardments. As there was a serious shortage of heavy artillery on the Western Front, Admiral Bacon, commanding the Dover Patrol, ordered the 9.2in guns to be taken out from *M 25* (the only monitor then in service in September 1915) and the three (*M 24, M 26* and *M 27*) still fitting out at Middlesborough. Early in 1916 all four were sent to Portsmouth to receive lighter guns, 7.5in/50cal BL Mk III in *M 25* and *M 25* and 6in/40cal QF Mk I/II in *M 26* and *M 27*. the 7.5in guns were spares for *Triumph*, but when her sister *Swiftsure* began Atlantic patrols one of her spare guns was allocated to *M 26*. The two 6in guns had been removed from the *Redoubtable*, but *M 27*'s gun was soon replaced by a more modern Mk VII. When *M 21* and *M 23* came home in 1917 they also had their 9.2in replaced by 7.5in, but those left in the Mediterranean remained largely unaltered. The other alterations were mostly to close-range and AA anti-aircraft armament. By 1918 the following armaments were mounted:

M 16 1–9.2in, 1–3in AA
M 17 1–9.2in, 1–12pdr, 1–6pdr AA
M 18–M 20, M 22 1–9.2in, 1–3in AA, 1–6pdr AA
M 21, M 25 1–7.5in, 1–3in AA, 1–12pdr
M 23, M 24, M 26 1–7.5in, 1–3in AA, 1–12pdr, 2–2pdr
M 27 1–6in, 1–3in AA, 1–12pdr, 2–2pdr

For service in North Russia *M 27* had the 6in replaced by a triple 4in Mk IX similar to those in *Repulse* and *Renown*, while *M 24, M 26* and *M 27* had the 12pdr replaced by a 3in AA gun and *M 23–M 26* all received 2–3pdr AA in place of their 2pdrs.

M 15 was towed to Malta in July 1915 where she received her 9.2in Mk X gun before going on to Mudros. To Egypt after evacuation from Cape Helles in January 1916 and took part in defence of Suez Canal. Torpedoed off Gaza in 1917 by *UC 38* (26 dead).

M 16 towed to Malta with *M 15* to pick up her gun mounting and was based at Imbros August 1915–January 1916, then to Mytilene until November 1917 and then Stavros February–October 1918. Paid off at Mudros early 1919 and sold in 1920 to Anglo-Saxon Petroleum Co for conversion to small oil tanker, and renamed *Tiga*.

M 17 served in Mediterranean from August 1915 to October 1918 and in Black Sea March–September 1919 and then paid off at Mudros. Sold in 1920 for conversion to oil tanker *Toedjoe*.

M 18 served in Mediterranean October 1915–October 1918 and in Baltic April–June 1919 and then paid off at Malta. Sold in 1920 for conversion to tanker *Anam*.

M 19 served in Mediterranean July 1915–December 1915, then paid off at Mudros early 1919. Sold in 1920 for conversion to tanker *Delapan*. Badly damaged by gun explosion 4 December 1915.

M 20 served in Mediterranean August 1915–December 1918, then paid off at Malta 1919; sold for conversion to tanker *Lima* in 1920.

M 21 served in Mediterranean September 1915–September 1917, then sent home to join Dover Patrol in October. Struck two mines off Ostend on 20 October 1918 but towed back to Dover and sank about a mile from West Pier.

M 22 served in Mediterranean September 1915–December 1918 and then *Black Sea* June–September 1919 and then paid off at Malta. Towed home to Portsmouth and in October converted to minelayer 1920; renamed *Medea* in December 1925. Sold for BU in 1938 and wrecked near Trevose Head (Cornwall), 2 January 1939.

M 23 served in Mediterranean October 1915–May 1917; Dover Patrol June 1917–June 1918 and then ordered to North Russia for service with White Sea Squadron. Returned to Sheerness in November 1919 and converted to RNVR drillship *Claverhouse*, and stationed at Dundee from August 1922 until sold for BU in 1959.

M 24 served with Dover Patrol October 1915–June 1918, the White Sea until September 1919. Sold for conversion to tanker *Satoe* 1920.

M 25 served with Dover Patrol September 1915–June 1918, then White Sea Squadron. Abandoned and blown up in Dvina River on 16 September 1919 when level of river fell during evacuation of British forces.

M 26 served with Dover Patrol November 1915–December 1918. Paid off at Portsmouth and sold in 1920, for conversion to small tanker *Doewa*.

M 27 served with Dover Patrol December 1915–December 1918. Refitted at Chatham with triple 4in guns for service in White Sea. Left for Archangel in May 1919 but had to be abandoned and blown up on Dvina River with *M 25*.

M 28 served in Mediterranean from September 1915. Sunk with *Raglan* by gunfire of *Goeben* and *Breslau* at Imbros in 1918.

M 29 class *monitors*

Displacement: 355t legend; 580t deep load
Dimensions: 177ft 3in oa × 31ft × 5ft 11in deep
54.0m × 9.4m × 1.8m
Machinery: 2-shaft VTE, 400ihp = 9kts. Oil 45t
Armour: Nil, except 6in (150mm) on gunshield
Armament: 2–6in (15.2cm)/45cal BL Mk XII, 1–6pdr (57mm) AA
Complement: 72

Name	Builder	Laid down	Launched	Comp	Fate
M 29	Harland & Wolff, Belfast	3.15	22.5.15	6.15	Sold 19.46
M 30	Harland & Wolff, Belfast	3.15	23.6.15	7.15	Sunk 14.5.16
M 31	Harland & Wolff, Belfast	3.15	24.6.15	7.15	BU 1948
M 32	Workman Clark, Belfast	3.15	22.5.15	6.15	Sold 1.20
M 33	Workman Clark, Belfast	3.15	22.5.15	6.15	Extant 1984

Just after the 9.2in monitors had been ordered, the *Queen Elizabeth* class were instructed to land their main deck 6in guns. As only two could be resited in each ship there were 10 Mk XII guns available, so a slightly modified version of the *M 15* design was drawn up, armed with 2 single 6in guns. The 7t gun could range to 14,700yds at 17½° elevation, and the total weight of gun, mounting and ammunition came to only 62t as against 100t for the 9.2in guns. Using these approximate figures it was unwisely assumed that both displacement and draught could be scaled down by 18 per cent, as compared with the *M 15* hull. This was unfortunate as the designers had overlooked the need to provide sufficient deck area for two guns, and if the deck area could not be reduced the hull dimensions could not be reduced either. The result was a ship which bore no relation to her legend displacement of 355t and designed draught of 4ft. However, this alarming discrepancy did not affect them too badly, apart from a tendency to trim by the head which made steering difficult. Although the ex-*Queen Elizabeth* class guns were the basis for the design the guns actually allocated to the monitors turned out to be new construction mountings from Coventry Ordnance Works and most of the barrels came from Vickers. When *M 31* and *M 33* were sent to the White Sea they received a 3in/20cwt AA gun in place of the 6pdr.

M 29 served in Mediterranean from July 1915–December 1918 and in White Sea May–September 1919. Paid off and towed home. Laid up at

Devonport until converted to minelayer September 1923–January 1925, and named *Medusa* in December 1925. Commissioned in May 1925 as tender to *Egmont* at Malta. Converted to repair ship in May 1941; renamed *Talbot* September 1941 as depot ship for 10th Submarine Flotilla. Damaged by bombs in March 1942 and renamed *Medway II* in February 1944 when she became depot ship to 1st S/m Flotilla. Towed back home post-war and sold for BU in 1946.

M 30 served in Mediterranean from August 1915, and while blockading Gulf of Smyrna in 1916 was sunk by shore batteries.

M 31 served in Mediterranean August 1915–March 1919. Paid off at Mudros and towed home. White Sea May–September 1919. Completed conversion to minelayer at Portsmouth in January 1921 and assigned to HMS *Defiance*, the Torpedo School at Devonport. Named *Melpomene* in December 1925 an remained at Devonport, and althougn put on sales list in 1937 was unsold in September 1939 and returned to naval duties, serving as torpedo instruction vessel, with a single 21in TT on the forecastle. Renamed *Menelaus* in 1941 to avoid confusion with Free French ship of same name and BU in 1948.

M 32 served in Mediterranean July 1915–December 1918; paid off at Mudros early 1919. White Sea Squadron May–September 1919, and paid off for disposal. Sold 1920 for conversion to oil tanker *Ampat*.

M 33 served in Mediterranean July 1915–November 1918, then White Sea May–September 1919. Converted to minelayer at Pembroke May 1924–February 1925; named *Minerva* in December 1925; sales list from 1937 but reinstated in September 1939. Converted to boom defence workshop in November 1943 and towed to Clyde in December 1944. Returned to Portsmouth and served at Royal Clarence Yard, Gosport as hulk *C 23*, where she remains today.

M 29 as completed — *By courtesy of John M Maber*

Erebus 1916

EREBUS class *monitors*

Displacement: 8000t normal; 8450t deep load
Dimensions: 405ft oa × 88ft 2in × 11ft 8in deep
123.4m × 26.9m × 3.6m
Machinery: 2-shaft 4-cyl VTE, 4 Babcock & Wilcox boilers, 6000ihp = 12kts. Oil 784t
Armour: As *Abercrombie* class, except 4in (100mm) deck over magazine and 13in (330mm) on turret face
Armament: 2–15in (38.1cm)/42cal Mk I (1×2), 2–6in (15.2cm)/40cal QF Mk II, 2–12pdr (76mm), 1–3in (76mm)/20cwt AA Mk I, 4–.303in Maxim MGs
Complement: 204

Name	Builder	Laid down	Launched	Comp	Fate
EREBUS	Harland & Wolff, Govan	12.10.15	19.6.16	9.16	Sold for BU 1946
TERROR	Harland & Wolff, Belfast	26.10.15	18.5.16	8.16	Sunk 24.10.41

The urgent need for heavy bombardment ships to replace battleships in the Dardanelles led to an order being placed for four 15in-gunned monitors in May 1915 to supplement the *Marshal Ney* class. Designated *M 34–M 37*, they were to be built by Harland & Wolff (*M 34, M 35*), Swan Hunter (*M 36*) and Hamilton (*M 37*) and turrets were to be re-allocated from the battleship *Royal Oak*. The new Balfour-Jackson Admiralty Board reviewed priorities early in June 1915 and decided that the battleship programme could not be delayed, and so the four monitors were cancelled on 10 June. Then in August 1915 came the bad news of the *Marshal Ney*'s trials, and consideration was given to putting both the *Marshals*' turrets into new monitors. The outcome of this convoluted process was the first opportunity to incorporate lessons from the earlier monitors. At last sufficient power was stipulated to make a minimum of 10kts, and at 6000ihp this was more than twice the previous figure. The hull was made appreciably longer to accommodate the machinery but above all it secured a reasonably fine entrance and run (50° angle of entrance as compared with 120° in the 14in and 12in monitors). The hull aided propulsive efficiency and improved steering as well. The basic hull had the same beam as the *Marshals* but the 'bulge' was narrower and filled with crushing tubes to improve resistance to explosions. It proved impossible to restrict draught to 10ft but even 11ft was a small penalty to pay for all the other improvements in design. A proper bridge was provided and the funnel was tall enough and far enough back from the bridge to avoid smoke interference.

Terror as completed — *By courtesy of John M Maber*

Harland & Wolff's Govan yard had already started work on *M 34*, and material assembled for her and *M 35* was used wherever possible, particularly 4in armour. To speed construction *Marshal Ney*'s 15in turret was transferred to *Terror*, but as the Admiralty had now decided to retain *Marshal Soult* her turret was no longer available. Fortunately two spare turrets had been earmarked for *Furious* in case her 18in guns proved unsatisfactory, and one of these was brought forward for *Erebus*. After all the disappointments with previous monitors the machinery trials proved a great success: *Terror* made 13kts instead of the 12kts expected, and *Erebus* averaged 14kts. Both ships could make 12kts in service. Initially only *Erebus* had 2–6in QF Mk II but *Terror* was soon similarly armed, and by late 1917 both ships were given another pair on the forecastle deck. In the summer of 1918 both ships had the 6in replaced by eight single 4in/BL Mk IX and had 2–12pdr on high-angle mountings on a platform in place of the former CT. At the Armistice the armament for both ships was: 2–15in, 8–4in, 2–12pdr AA, 2–3in AA, 2–2pdr.

Erebus joined Monitor Squadron at Dover in September 1916. Docked in October 1917 and returned to duty and on the 28th was hit by German distance-controlled explosive boat (DCB) *FL 12*. Fortunately the 1540lb charge detonated on the 'bulge', blowing a 50ft hole in it but doing very little damage to the hull. She was back in service by 21 November and remained at Dover until after the Armistice. Tender to Chatham Gunnery School from January 1919 but sent to White Sea in July. While on her way home in October she was diverted to Copenhagen and supported operations in the Gulf of Finland, including the destruction of the German Iron Division at Libau in November 1919. Returned to Chatham on 31 December. Used in firing trials against surrendered German battleship *Baden* in August 1921 and then paid off into C&M at Chatham. After several years' service as drillship refitted in 1939 and saw widespread service in Second World War. Sold in 1946.

Terror joined Dover Patrol in August 1916 and took part in numerous bombardments of Belgian coast. She was lying at anchor off Dunkirk on the night of 18–19 October 1917 when she was hit by three torpedoes from the German torpedo-boats *A 59, A 60* and *A 61*. Two did considerable damage to her bow but the third hit on the bulge, and she managed to beach herself. Towed back to Dover and then to Portsmouth but was abandoned off Hastings on the night of the 27th. Reboarded and brought into Spithead next day, and took ten weeks to repair. After Armistice relieved *Marshall Soult* as Director and Fire Control TS, arriving at Portsmouth in January 1919. Used in firing trials against *Swiftsure* in July 1919 and then in 1920 against the submarines *UB 21* (September) and *U 141* (October), destroyers *V 82* (October) and *V 44* (December), cruiser *Nürnberg* (November), battleships *Baden* (February 1921 and later that year) and *Superb* (May 1922). Recommissioned as turret drillship at Portsmouth in May 1924 and saw service in Second World War. Sunk by Ju 87 dive-bombers off Derna in 1941.

CRUISERS

Bellona as completed

The need for small cruisers to work with the destroyer flotillas led to a new series of 'scouts' from 1906 onwards. They were built in three series, two under the 1907 Programme, two more under the 1909 Programme and three under the 1910 and 1911 Programmes. All were built at Pembroke DYd, and each class showed a slight improvement over the last. Although too small for ocean work they proved useful in the North Sea, but like the earlier 'scouts', too slow for the new generation of oil-fired destroyers capable of 27kts–29kts. The 'armour' was only partial plating over machinery. The first pair carried their guns p&s on a platform ahead of the bridge, two more at the break of the forecastle and two on the centreline aft. By 1916 four more 4in guns had been added in the waist and a 3in/20cwt AA gun. In 1918 the 3in gun was replaced by a 4in AA.

Bellona was SO's ship 2nd Flotilla 1909–1912. From August 1914 she was one of a number of light cruisers attached to the Grand Fleet without forming part of any particular Light Cruiser Squadron and in that capacity fought at Jutland. Converted to lay mines in June 1917 and laid 306 mines in four trips. Paid off 1919 and sold in 1921.

Boadicea was SO's ship 1st Flotilla 1909–12. She was later attached to Grand Fleet battle squadrons and fought at Jutland. Converted to minelayer in December 1917 and laid 184 mines in three trips. Paid off and reduced to harbour service at Dartmouth. Was to have been renamed *Pomone* in April 1920 but order cancelled and she remained there until sold in 1926.

BOADICEA class *scout cruisers*

Displacement: 3300t normal; 3800t deep load
Dimensions: 405ft oa × 41ft × 14ft normal
123.4m × 12.5m × 4.3m
Machinery: 4-shaft Parsons turbines, 12 Yarrow boilers, 18,000shp = 25kts. Coal 850t, oil 200t
Armour: Deck 1in (25mm), CT 4in (100mm)
Armament: 6–4in (10.2cm)/50cal BL Mk VIII, 4–3pdr (47mm), 2–18in (45.7cm) TT (deck, p&s)
Complement: 317

Name	Builder	Laid down	Launched	Comp	Fate
BOADICEA	Pembroke DYd	1.6.07	14.5.08	6.09	Sold for BU 7.26
BELLONA	Pembroke DYd	5.6.08	20.3.09	2.10	Sold for BU 5.21

Boadicea about 1914 — *Aldo Fraccaroli Collection*

The second pair of 'scouts' was built under the 1909 Programme, differed from the *Boadicea* class in having 21in TT and four more 4in guns, mounted in the waist. The armour on the deck was also slightly increased over the machinery.

Blanche was attached to the 1st Destroyer Flotilla 1911–12. She served with the Grand Fleet battle squadrons from August 1914 and was at Jutland. In March 1917 she was converted to lay 66 mines, and in 16 trips laid a total of 1238 mines. Paid off 1919 and sold for BU in 1921.

Blonde was SO's ship, 7th Flotilla in the Mediterranean 1911–12. She served with Grand Fleet battle squadrons from August 1914 to 1919 but was not present at Jutland. Converted to minelaying in September 1917 but laid no mines. Sold in 1920.

BLONDE class *scout cruisers*

Displacement: 3350t normal; 3850t deep load
Dimensions: 405ft oa × 41ft 6in × 15ft 6in max
123.4m × 12.6m × 4.7m
Machinery: 4-shaft Parsons turbines, 12 Yarrow boilers, 18,000shp = 24½kts. Coal 780t, oil 190t
Armour: Deck 1½in (40mm), CT 4in (100mm)
Armament: 10–4in (10.2cm)/50cal BL Mk VIII, 4–3pdr (47mm), 2–21in (53.3cm) TT (deck, p&s)
Complement: 314

Name	Builder	Laid down	Launched	Comp	Fate
BLONDE	Pembroke DYd	6.12.09	22.7.10	5.11	Sold for BU 5.20
BLANCHE	Pembroke DYd	12.4.09	25.11.09	11.10	Sold for BU 7.21

Bristol 1919

BRISTOL class *light cruisers*

Displacement:	4800t normal; 5300t deep load
Dimensions:	453ft oa × 47ft × 15ft 6in normal *138.1m × 14.3m × 4.7m*
Machinery:	4-shaft Parsons turbines (*Bristol* 2-shaft Brown-Curtis), 12 Yarrow boilers, 22,000shp = 25kts. Coal 1350t, oil 1250t. Range *c*5070nm at 16kts
Armour:	Deck 2in–¾in (50mm–20mm)
Armament:	2–6in (15.2cm)/50cal BL Mk XI, 10–4in (10.2cm)/50cal BL Mk VIII, 4–3pdr (47mm), 2–18in (45.7cm) TT sub (beam)
Complement:	480

Name	Builder	Laid down	Launched	Comp	Fate
BRISTOL	John Brown	23.3.09	23.2.10	12.10	Sold for BU 5.21
GLASGOW	Fairfield	25.3.09	30.9.09	9.10	Sold for BU 4.27
GLOUCESTER	Beardmore	15.4.09	28.10.09	10.10	Sold for BU 5.21
LIVERPOOL	Vickers	17.2.09	30.10.09	10.10	Sold for BU 5.21
NEWCASTLE	Elswick	14.4.09	25.11.09	9.10	Sold for BU 5.21

The *Bristol* class were the first true cruisers built for the RN since the turn of the century, for the big armoured cruisers had in reality been 2nd class battleships, with little thought given to the main roles of scouting and patrol work normally done by cruisers. To make matters worse Fisher had decreed that large destroyers like the *Swift* could perform the cruiser role, and only when it became painfully obvious that this was impossible did the Admiralty resume the design and construction of medium-sized cruisers. The original design was to have been armed with unshielded 4in guns but with the German 3rd class cruisers very much in mind the Board decreed that two 6in guns should be added. The guns were logically disposed, two shielded 6in forward and aft, and five shielded 4in p&s in the waist. For protection against shellfire they were given 2in plating over the magazines and machinery spaces, thinning to ¾in elsewhere. The machinery spaces had additional protection from coal bunkers.

The main drawbacks of the design proved to be the large metacentric height needed to preserve stability in the damaged state, and the cramped accommodation. The high metacentre made them very lively gun-platforms, while Fisher's insistence on placing officers' accommodation forward, however sound in the tactical sense, encroached on the ratings' already limited recreation space. After the ships were well advanced, firing trials against the old turret ship *Edinburgh* showed that such thin armoured decks by themselves offered no protection against modern high-explosive shells, as they could riddle the sides easily, and if they burst above the deck could send lethal splinters down through holes in the deck. These criticisms notwithstanding, the *Bristol* class gave a good account of themselves in service and provided the starting point for some of the most successful cruisers ever built for the RN. As the five ships spent so much time on foreign stations during the war and because they were comparatively cramped they never received the alterations given to later 'Town' classes. The main addition was a 3in/20cwt Mk II AA gun in 1915–16. As completed they had short funnels but smoke interference caused them to be raised, which improved draught as well.

Bristol was attached to 2nd Battle Squadron, Home Fleet on completion at the end of 1910. Ran aground in Plymouth Sound 22 December 1912. Joined 2nd Fleet January 1913, then 2nd Light Cruiser Squadron in July 1913, and 5th Cruiser Squadron in 1914. Joined 4th CS in August 1914 and sent to West Indies. Had brief skirmish with *Karlsruhe* on 6 August and sent to Falklands to join Admiral Stoddart's force at Port Stanley. Had fires drawn on morning of Falkland Islands battle but got underway later that day and with AMC *Macedonia* captured German colliers. Took part in hunt for *Dresden* during remainder of December 1914 and then went to Mediterranean. Adriatic 1916–17, then back to South American waters in 1918. Paid off into reserve at Portsmouth in June 1919; sales list May 1920 and sold in 1921.

Glasgow was attached to 2nd BS, Home Fleet 1910–11, then sent to South America 1911 (recommissioned there in September 1912). West Atlantic 1913; sent to South America in August 1914, where she captured German SS *Catherina* on 16 August. With AMC *Otranto* escaped destruction at Battle of Coronel 1 November 1914 and went to Port Stanley. Took part in Falkland Islands battle on 8 December and with *Cornwall* helped to sink *Leipzig*. Caught *Dresden* at Juan Fernandez Island and sank her 14 March 1915. Moved to Mediterranean; took part in hunt for raider *Möwe* in February and September 1916; with 8th LCS in Adriatic 1917–18. At Gibraltar June 1919 and returned to UK later that year. Paid off for disposal May 1920. Used as stokers' TS at Portsmouth 1921–26 (disarmed) January 1925); put on Disposal List March 1926 and sold in 1927.

Gloucester was attached to 1st BS, Home Fleet on completion; recommissioned for 2nd LCS in Mediterranean January 1913. On outbreak of war chased *Goeben* and *Breslau*; took part in hunt for *Emden* in November 1914 but returned to Mediterranean the same month. Was to join 2nd LCS, Grand Fleet, but detained to search off coast of Africa for German AMC *Kronprinz Wilhelm*. Joined 3rd LCS in February 1915 and captured German supply ship *Macedonia* the same month. Shelled Galway during Easter Uprising, April 1916; 2nd LCS before Jutland; from December 1916 to Armistice served in Adriatic with 8th LCS (apart from detached duty in East Indies in April 1917). Paid off into reserve at Devonport April 1919, then put on Disposal List in March 1920 and sold in 1921.

Liverpool attached to 1st BS, Home Fleet. Joined 2nd LCS 1913–14 but joined 5th CS on outbreak of war. In action at Heligoland Bight 26 August 1914, and had a man killed by fragments when the mined battleship *Audacious* finally blew up on 27 October 1914. Refitted November 1914 after condenser trouble, then joined 2nd LCS January–February 1915, when joined 3rd LCS at Rosyth. Search for *Kronprinz Wilhelm* off West Africa and then underwent boiler repairs at Liverpool in June 1915. Sent to Brindisi in November, remaining there till January 1918, then Aegean Squadron in November and passed through Dardanelles after the Armistice. Black Sea operations 1918–19 then into reserve at Devonport in June 1919. Paid off for disposal in March 1920 and sold in 1921.

Newcastle commissioned for China Station to replace *Bedford*; Shanghai Rebellion 23 June 1913. At Esquimalt in August 1914 and searched off South America for German AMC *Prinz Eitel Friedrich*. Pacific January 1915–November 1916, including capture of German prize *Mazatlan* in January 1916. At Mudros in 1917, East Indies March 1917, Adriatic in May 1917. Flagship of SE Coast of South America Station 1918–19; paid off at Nore in February 1920, placed on sale list December 1920 and sold in 1921.

Liverpool about 1911 — *Aldo Fraccaroli Collection*

Weymouth 1916 — *By courtesy of R A Burt*

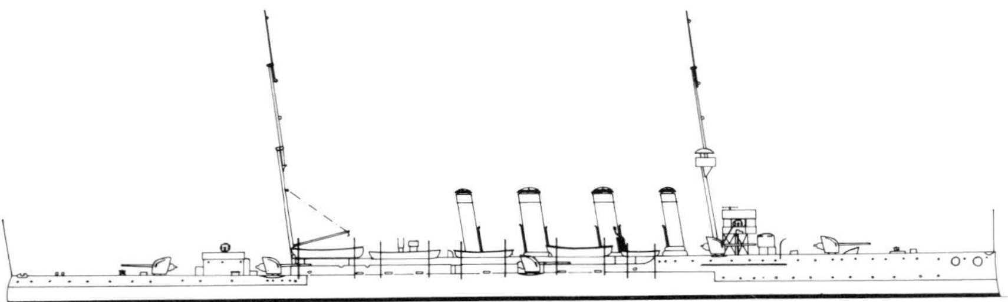

Weymouth as completed

WEYMOUTH class *light cruisers*

Displacement: 5250t normal; 5800t deep load
Dimensions: 453ft oa × 48ft 6in × 15ft 6in normal
138.1m × 14.6m × 4.7m
Machinery: 4-shaft Parsons compound–reaction (*Yarmouth* 2-shaft Brown-Curtis) turbines, 12 Yarrow boilers, 22,000shp = 25kts. Coal 1290t, oil 260t. Range *c*4500nm at 10kts
Armour: Deck 2in–¾in (50mm–20mm), CT 4in (100mm)
Armament: 8–6in (15.2cm)/50cal BL Mk XI, 4–3pdr (47mm), 2–21in (53.3cm) TT sub (beam)
Complement: 475

Name	Builder	Laid down	Launched	Comp	Fate
DARTMOUTH	Vickers	19.2.10	14.12.10	10.11	Sold for BU 12.30
FALMOUTH	Beardmore	21.2.10	20.9.10	9.11	Sunk 19.8.16
WEYMOUTH	Elswick	19.1.20	18.11.10	10.11	Sold for BU 10.28
YARMOUTH	London & Glasgow Co	27.1.10	12.4.11	4.12	Sold for BU 7.29

The mixed armament of the *Bristol* class was soon recognised as unsatisfactory, and to remedy this the 'Improved *Bristol* class' authorised under the 1909–1910 Estimates were given a uniform armament of 8–6in. There were also complaints about the waist guns being unworkable in a seaway, and in the new cruisers the forecastle was extended aft and a bulwark enclosed the waist guns. In addition to the forecastle gun two more were carried at the same level p&s of the bridge, giving them much better command. In 1915 a 3in AA gun was added on a platform between 2nd and 3rd funnel, and like other warships, topmasts were housed down or removed. All except *Falmouth* were fitted in 1917 with a tripod foremast and director control for the 6in guns, and searchlight control platforms were added aft. In 1918 aircraft platforms were fitted to *Weymouth* and *Yarmouth*, extending over the CT and forward 6in gun. Both *Weymouth* and *Dartmouth* carried an extra AA gun on the quarterdeck. Post-war the aircraft platforms were removed. When attached to the Signals School *Yarmouth* had a prominent lattice tower stepped between the 2nd and 3rd funnel, and the AA was resited on a platform at the end of the after superstructure. The tower was removed but a large cabin remained. The CT was removed from *Dartmouth* in 1917–18 to reduce topweight. The *Weymouth*s were a great improvement over the *Bristol*s and paved the way for even better ships. Being robust and well armed they saw widespread service and were retained in the post-war Fleet.

Dartmouth commissioned at Devonport for Atlantic Fleet and attached to 3rd Battle Squadron 1912–13. Mediterranean Cruise to Montenegro and Salonika 1913, then joined 2nd Light Cruiser Squadron for July 1913 Annual Manoeuvres. Recommissioned in September 1913 for East Indies, relieving *Perseus*. Docked Bombay in August 1914. Captured German tug *Adjutant* in October and operated in Indian Ocean in December. Appointed to 2nd LCS, Grand Fleet in January 1915 but remained in South Atlantic to search for *Karlsruhe* and returned to West Indies. To Dardanelles February 1915, then 8th LCS at Brindisi May 1915–1919 (torpedoed by *UC 25* on 15 May 1917 but reached harbour safely). Recommissioned in March 1919 for 7th LCS, South America. In Reserve at Devonport June 1921–September 1924 then paid off into dockyard control for refit. Recommissioned September 1926 for trooping duties. Flagship Vice-Admiral Reserve Fleet at Portsmouth April 1927–1928 (relieved by *Constance*), then trooping duties to Mediterranean and China. Reduced to reserve in June 1929 and acted as temporary accommodation hulk for *Defiance I* in January 1930. Paid off into dockyard control in May 1930 and sold in December.

Falmouth attached to 2nd BS, Home Fleet on commissioning and then in June 1913 appointed to 2nd LCS. Joined 5th CS in August 1914 and sank German merchantmen *Fasolt, Ochtum, Borkum* and *Hude* during that month. Joined 1st LCS as flagship in December, then 3rd LCS at Rosyth in February 1915. In action at Jutland, being hit by one shell; after battle became flagship until sunk. She was damaged by a torpedo from *U 66* on 19 August 1916 while screening Grand Fleet, and was towed to Flamborough Head, but was torpedoed again by *U 52* and sank next day.

Weymouth was attached to 3rd BS, Atlantic Fleet on commissioning, and from June 1913 2nd LCS, Mediterranean Fleet. Sent to Indian Ocean in August 1914 to hunt for *Emden* and then to East Africa for operations against the *Königsberg* in the Rufiji River from February to July 1915. To Adriatic in December 1915. Joined 6th LCS, Grand Fleet 1916–17, but was stationed at Bermuda in December 1916. 8th LCS at Brindisi 1917–19 (damaged by torpedo from Austrian *U 28* off Durazzo 2 October 1918). Paid off at Malta June 1919 and refitted to join 7th LCS in South America March 1920–January 1921. In reserve at Nore July 1921–December 1925 and then flagship Vice-Admiral Nore Reserve until paid off into dockyard control at Portsmouth in September 1927. On sales list and sold in 1928.

Yarmouth attached to 4th BS, Mediterranean Fleet on completion. China Station August 1913–August 1914 and then joined in hunt for *Emden*. Captured ex-Greek *Pontoporus*, one of *Emden*'s colliers in October 1914, and sank the collier *Markomannia*. 2nd LCS, Grand Fleet from December, then 3rd LCS, Rosyth in February 1915, being present at Jutland. Unsuccessfully attacked by U-boat in July 1916. Rejoined 2nd LCS 1918 and became temporary flagship at Cape in June 1919 before returning home for refit. With 7th LCS, South America 1919–20 then Nore Reserve from December 1920. Attached to Signals School at Portsmouth 1922–24, refitted December 1924–1925 and then undertook trooping runs in 1925–26. Signals School, Portsmouth once more in 1927; flagship of Rear-Admiral Submarines at Falmouth April–October 1928, then into C&M and put on sales list in November 1928.

In the third group of 'scouts' (the first two were ordered under the 1910 Programme and *Fearless* under 1911 Programme) there was little change from the previous class, except to thicken the shell plating amidships as partial protection against light gunfire, but even this modest improvement was insufficient to fit them for work with the Fleet. They could easily be distinguished from the earlier ships by their 'plough' bow. In 1916 *Active* received a 3in/20cwt Mk I AA gun. In 1918 *Active* and *Fearless* had 2–4in removed and *Fearless* received a 3in AA, like her sister.

Active was leader of 2nd Destroyer Flotilla in August 1914 and joined the Harwich Force. In 1915 transferred to Grand Fleet, then in 1916–17 led 4th DF at Portsmouth. Based at Queenstown (Cobh) 1917–18 and spent rest of war in Mediterranean. Paid off and sold in 1920.

Amphion was leader of 3rd DF at Harwich on the outbreak of war, and became the first casualty when early on the morning of 6 August she ran into a minefield laid by the *Konigin Luise,* which she and her flotilla had just sunk; 148 of her crew died.

Fearless was leader of 1st DF at Harwich from August 1914 to 1916 then became leader of 12th Submarine Flotilla, Grand Fleet ('K' class) until the end of war. She was involved in the 'Battle of May Island' on the night of 31 January 1918, ramming and sinking *K 17*.

ACTIVE class *scout cruisers*

Displacement: 3440t normal; 4000t deep load
Dimensions: 406ft oa × 41ft 6in × 15ft 7in max
123.8m × 12.6m × 4.7m
Machinery: 4-shaft Parsons turbines, 12 Yarrow boilers, 18,000shp = 25kts. Coal 780t, oil 190t
Armour: Deck 1in (25mm), CT 4in (100mm)
Armament: 10–4in (10.2cm)/50cal BL Mk VIII, 4–3pdr (47mm), 2–18in (45.7cm) TT (deck, p&s)
Complement: 321–325

Name	Builder	Laid down	Launched	Comp	Fate
ACTIVE	Pembroke DYd	27.7.10	14.3.11	12.11	Sold for BU 4.20
AMPHION	Pembroke DYd	15.3.11	4.12.11	3.13	Mined 6.8.14
FEARLESS	Pembroke DYd	15.11.11	12.6.12	10.13	Sold for BU 11.21

Active February 1915
CPL

Sydney about 1920
RAN, by courtesy of Vic Jeffery

In the three cruisers authorised for 1911 the weaknesses of the preceding classes were eliminated. On virtually the same dimensions seakeeping was improved by extending the forecastle aft for more than two-thirds of the length, and some side protection was worked in, all at the cost of only a slight increase in beam. A reduction in metacentric height also reduced rolling and improved shooting. The protective deck of the *Bristol* and *Weymouth* designs was retained, but only to maintain watertight integrity (3/8in over most of its length, ¾in over machinery and 1½in over the steering gear). A shell penetrating this deck would still have to penetrate three decks first, and would probably have detonated by the time it reached the so-called 'splinter deck'. The weight saved on deck plating was devoted to a 2in waterline belt of nickel steel on 1in shell plating. The protection thus became part of the main structure of the ship, enabling weight to be saved on framing. As this arrangement of double plating could not be given a double curvature the midships section in the new design was slab-sided. There had been dissatisfaction with the high-velocity Mk XI 6in gun, and so the new cruisers reverted to a RGF-designed 45cal lower-velocity gun, the Mk XII. It had the advantage of shooting more accurately and being nearly 2t lighter, with virtually the same range (14,000yds). In the *Sydney*'s report of the action against the *Emden* her CO commented most

CHATHAM class *light cruisers*

Displacement: 5400t normal; 6000t deep load
Dimensions: 458ft oa × 49ft × 16ft normal
139.6m × 14.9m × 4.9m
Machinery: 4-shaft Parsons (*Southampton* 2-shaft Brown-Curtis) turbines, 12 Yarrow boilers, 25,000shp = 25½kts. Coal 1240t, oil 260t. Range *c*4500nm at 16kts
Armour: Belt 2in (50mm) on 1in (25mm) plating, deck 1½in–3/8in (40mm–15mm), CT 4in (102mm)
Armament: 8–6in (15.2cm)/45cal BL Mk XII, 4–3pdr (47mm), 2–21in (53.3cm) TT sub (beam)
Complement: 475

Name	Builder	Laid down	Launched	Comp	Fate
CHATHAM	Chatham DYd	3.1.11	9.11.11	12.12	Sold for BU 7.26
DUBLIN	Beardmore	3.1.11	9.11.11	3.13	Sold for BU 7.26
SOUTHAMPTON	John Brown	6.4.11	16.5.12	11.12	Sold for BU 7.26
SYDNEY	London & Glasgow Co	11.2.11	29.8.12	6.13	BU 1929–30
MELBOURNE	Cammell Laird	14.4.11	30.5.12	1.13	Sold for BU 12.28
BRISBANE	Cockatoo DYd	25.1.13	30.9.15	11.16	Sold for BU 6.36

favourably on the advantage in range his ship enjoyed over the enemy, and on the ability of the armour to keep out German projectiles.

The *Chatham* class could easily be distinguished from the *Weymouths* by their long forecastle deck and the 'plough' bow. They were all given 3in AA guns in 1915 and in 1917–18 underwent numerous changes in appearance. The CT was removed to offset the additional weight of aircraft platforms in *Dublin, Melbourne, Sydney* and *Southampton*. All were fitted with a tripod and spotting platform for director firing, and had tall searchlight platforms added aft. The aircraft platforms were removed in 1919. Three more ships were ordered for the new Royal Australian Navy, two from British shipyards and a third, the *Brisbane*, to be built in Australia with British technical assistance. Apart from an initial period in the Pacific, the *Sydney* and *Melbourne* spent much of the war with the Grand Fleet, while *Brisbane* served with Allied forces in the Adriatic before returning home.

Chatham attached to 2nd Battle Squadron on commissioning; 1st Light Cruiser Squadron July 1913. With 2nd LCS in Mediterranean 1913–14, and detached to Red Sea on outbreak of war. Discovered whereabouts of *Königsberg* on 30 November 1914 and sank colliers to block her exit from the Rufiji Delta, and captured German merchantman *Prasident* in October 1914. To Dardanelles May 1915, the Grand Fleet from 1916 to 1918 as flagship, 3rd LCS. Damaged by mine off Norfolk coast, 26 May 1916 and towed stern-first to Chatham for repairs. Went into reserve at Nore 1918–20, and recommissioned in Royal New Zealand Navy, 11 September 1920. Returned to RN 1924 to become flagship 4th LCS, East Indies 1924–25. Paid off November 1925 at Devonport and sold in 1926.

Dublin attached to 1st BS on commissioning, then 1st LCS, Mediterranean from July 1913, and 2nd LCS September 1913 until end of 1914. Sent to Dardanelles in February 1915, and Brindisi in May. Damaged by torpedo hit from Austrian U-boat, 9 June 1915. Served with 2nd LCS, Grand Fleet 1916–18, including action at Jutland, where she was hit several times suffering 3 dead during night action. Commissioned for 6th LCS, African station in January 1920, then 3rd LCS, Mediterranean Fleet briefly in April, and returned to 6th LCS until 1924, when she returned home to pay off into Nore Reserve. Sold in 1926 and ran aground on her way to breakers, but was refloated in July 1927.

Southampton attached to 1st BS from February 1913. Flagship Commodore 1st LCS, Home Fleet July 1913–1915 (lost 1 man killed in boiler explosion at Govan in September 1913). Part of British squadron which visited Kiel in June 1914; fought at Heligoland Bight and Dogger Bank. Led 2nd LCS from February 1915 to 1917, including action at Jutland, where she sank the German torpedo boat *S 35* and torpedoed and sank the cruiser *Frauenlob*, and sustained severe damage in night action. 8th LCS 1917–19. Flagship 7th LCS, South America May 1919–1920, then refitted at Cape 1920–21. 4th LCS, East Indies September 1921–1924. Joined Material Reserve at Nore in August 1924 and put on sales list in August 1925, before being sold in 1926.

Brisbane served in Pacific 1916–17, then East Indies later in 1917, and covered convoys from Australia to UK in 1918. Joined Aegean Squadron in November 1918. Returned to Australia 1919. Became TS in June 1928 and put on Disposal List 1935. Paid off into dockyard control at Portsmouth, September 1935; on sales list in October and sold in 1936.

Melbourne served in Pacific 1913–14, then North America and West Indies Station August 1914–1916. Joined 2nd LCS, Grand Fleet, 1916 to Armistice. Left Spithead March 1919 in company with destroyers *Huon, Parramatta, Warrego* and *Yarra*. Relieved *Sydney* as Flagship RAN in October 1927 until February 1928, when she left for UK. Paid off at Portsmouth in April and sold later in 1928.

Sydney served in Pacific 1913–14, and took part in the New Guinea expedition in September 1914. Escorting ANZAC convoy in November 1914 when news of *Emden*'s attack on Cocos-Keeling Island caused her to be diverted. Engaged and sank the *Emden* on 9 November 1914 with only slight damage to herself. To North America and West Indies Station December 1914–1916, then 2nd LCS, Grand Fleet until the Armistice. Left for Australia in company with 'J' class submarines in March 1919. Refitted at Cockatoo Island DYd 1923; Flagship RAN September 1924–1927. Paid off in May 1928 and BU at Cockatoo Island 1929–30 (her foremast was preserved as a memorial in Sydney).

Birmingham in the early 1920s
CPL

BIRMINGHAM class *light cruisers*

Displacement:	5440t normal; 6040t deep (*Adelaide* 5550t; 6160t)
Dimensions:	457ft (*Adelaide* 462ft 9in) oa × 50ft × 16ft normal *139.3m (141.0m) × 15.2m × 4.9m*
Machinery:	4-shaft Parsons turbines, 12 Yarrow boilers, 25,000shp = 25½kts. Coal 1165t, oil 235t. Range 4140nm at 16kts
Armour:	As *Chatham* class
Armament:	9–6in (15.2cm)/45cal BL Mk XII, 4–3pdr (47mm), 2–21in (53.3cm) TT sub (beam)
Complement:	480

Name	Builder	Laid down	Launched	Comp	Fate
BIRMINGHAM	Elswick	10.6.12	7.5.13	2.14	Sold for BU 3.31
LOWESTOFT	Chatham DYd	29.7.12	28.4.13	4.14	Sold for BU 1.31
NOTTINGHAM	Pembroke DYd	13.6.12	18.4.13	4.14	Sunk 19.8.16
ADELAIDE	Cockatoo DYd	1.15	27.7.18	8.22	Sold for BU 1.49

For the 1912 Programme three near-repeats of the *Chatham* class were approved. The only alterations were to add a second 6in on the forecastle, side by side to improve ahead fire, and additional flare on the forecastle to reduce spray. Like the *Chatham* class they proved highly successful in service and they were retained in the post-war Fleet. *Lowestoft* was completed with a tripod foremast carrying a spotting platform, and in December 1914 a new light pattern of director was fitted. *Birmingham* was similarly fitted in 1916–17 but no photographs exist of *Nottingham* with a tripod so it must be assumed that she was lost unaltered. All three received 1–3in/20cwt Mk I AA gun in 1915, on a centreline platform abaft the funnels, but neither of the survivors received an aircraft platform. Searchlight positions were greatly altered, and by 1918 both ships had tall towers on the after superstructure. Details of *Adelaide*'s appearance changes will be found in the 1922–1946 Volume as she was not completed until 1922, but as completed she incorporated virtually all the wartime alterations made to her sisters.

Birmingham joined 1st Light Cruiser Squadron in 1914 and visited Kiel in June. Sank two German merchantmen in August 1914 and on 9 August rammed and sank *U 15* in the North Sea. Dogger Bank action in January, then joined 2nd LCS as flagship in February 1915. Attacked unsuccessfully by U-boat on 18 June 1915. Suffered splinter damage at Jutland in night action. Flagship 6th LCS 1919–20, then Nore Reserve 1920–22. Commissioned November 1923 as Flagship 6th LCS, Africa Station, relieving *Lowestoft*. After further service on foreign stations sold in 1931.

Lowestoft joined 1st LCS and sank German merchantman *Fernbellin* in August 1914. Dogger Bank action in January 1915, then joined 2nd LCS as flagship February 1915–1916. Flagship 8th LCS Mediterranean 1916–19, then 6th LCS, Africa Station until 1924 (flagship from August 1921). After further service on foreign stations sold in 1931.

Nottingham joined 1st LCS 1914 and visited Kiel in June. At Dogger Bank battle in January 1915. Joined 2nd LCS in February, and attacked unsuccessfully by U-boat, 20 June 1915. In action at Jutland but received only splinter hits. While sweeping at 20kts with Grand Fleet on 19 August 1916 was torpedoed three times by *U 52* and sank (38 dead).

Adelaide commissioned in August 1922, and saw service in Second World War. Sold in 1949.

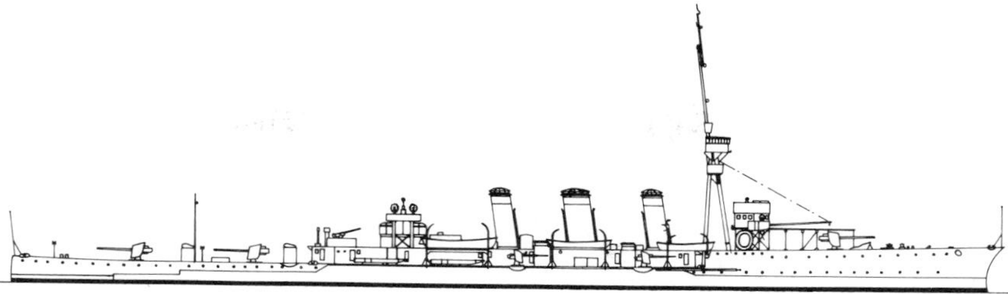

Royalist 1919

The grave shortage of cruisers capable of working with the Fleet was matched by a lack of ships for strengthening the flotillas. By 1911 the speed of destroyers had made it impossible for the 'Scouts' to lead a high-speed dash and that gap would widen with the introduction of what became the 'K' and 'L' classes. To examine the problem a Cruiser Committee was set up by the new First Lord, Churchill, late in 1911. Two basic lines of development were examined: a super-*Swift* or enlarged destroyer relying only on speed, or a super-*Active*, an enlarged scout with lower speed but some armour protection and a much heavier armament. As might be expected, Fisher wanted the super-*Swift* because of its alleged high speed (37kts), but Churchill backed the 'cruiser admirals' on the committee in their preference for an uprated 'Scout'. She would cost £285,000 as against £350,000 for a *Dartmouth*. By working in the armour as part of the longitudinal strength the DNC was able to increase the armour protection amidships. The E-in-C, Sir Henry Oram, proposed to use fast-running destroyer turbines and boilers to get speed up from 28 to 30 or even 31kts. The higher speed proved illusory as so much extra weight was worked into the design but even so a sea speed of 27½kts was a great improvement over previous cruisers. Many sources quote the installed power as 30,000shp. This was the designed hp, with an extra 10,000shp load but in practice the load shp came to be used as standard. Proposed armaments were 10–4in, as in the 'Scouts' or 5–6in, but ultimately a compromise of 2–6in and 6–4in was chosen. When presented to Parliament, Churchill described them as 'light armoured cruisers', to emphasise the protection for they were the smallest British warships to be protected by vertical armour. In practice the *Arethusa* class proved successful in the North Sea, although very cramped as a result of wartime additions. They would not have been able to replace the 'Towns' on overseas stations, as witness the fact that the *Arethusa*s disappeared very quickly after the war, whereas many of the older 'Towns' were kept on for some years.

The mixed armament was not a success, partly because the new pattern semi-automatic 4in QF Mk IV was prone to jam and partly because in a confused action their shell-splashes could not be distinguished from the 6in. In 1918 the *Galatea, Inconstant, Penelope, Phaeton* and *Royalist* had the after pair of 4in removed and an extra 6in installed on the centreline abaft the funnels. The 3pdr AA gun was replaced by a 3in/20cwt Mk I on the centreline aft in 1915, but in 1917 the *Aurora, Galatea, Inconstant, Phaeton* and

ARETHUSA class *light cruisers*

Displacement: 3750t load; 4400t deep load
Dimensions: 436ft oa × 39ft × 13ft 5in mean
132.9m × 11.9m × 4.1m
Machinery: 4-shaft Parsons (*Arethusa, Undaunted* Brown-Curtis) turbines, 8 boilers, 40,000shp = 28½kts. Oil 875t
Armour: Belt 3in–1in (75mm–25mm), deck 1in (25mm)
Armament: 2–6in (15.2cm)/45cal Mk XII, 6–4in (10.2cm)/45cal QF Mk IV, 1–3pdr (47mm) AA, 4–21in (53.3cm) TT aw (2×2)
Complement: 276–282

Name	Builder	Laid down	Launched	Comp	Fate
ARETHUSA	Chatham DYd	28.10.12	25.10.13	8.14	Mined 11.2.16
AURORA	Devonport DYd	24.10.12	30.9.13	9.14	Sold for BU 8.27
GALATEA	Beardmore	9.1.13	14.5.14	12.14	Sold for BU 10.21
INCONSTANT	Beardmore	3.4.14	6.7.14	1.15	Sold for BU 6.22
PENELOPE	Vickers	1.2.13	25.8.14	12.14	Sold for BU 10.24
PHAETON	Vickers	12.3.13	21.10.14	2.15	Sold for BU 1.23
ROYALIST	Beardmore	3.6.13	14.1.15	3.15	Sold for BU 8.22
UNDAUNTED	Fairfield	21.12.12	28.4.14	8.14	Sold for BU 4.23

Royalist were rearmed with two 3in AA p&s of the after control position. At about this time *Penelope* and *Undaunted* received a 4in AA gun, on the centreline ahead of the after 6in gun. As the ships fought mainly with light forces the torpedo armament was strengthened. In 1917 all were given an additional pair of 21in TT p&s at upper deck level, abreast of the after 6in. Later they were moved ahead of the original TT in all except *Aurora* and *Undaunted*. Although the appearance of the ships was much changed in detail the major difference came in 1917–18 when the pole foremast was replaced by a tripod carrying a spotting top and light director. All except *Undaunted* were fitted for minelaying at this time, with rails and chutes discharging over the stern. They carried 70–74 mines and laid over 2500 mines.

Four of the class were the first RN cruisers to take aircraft to sea, when in 1915 they were given a sloping runway over the forecastle to enable them to launch a French monoplane. They were intended to deal with the nuisance of Zeppelins, which kept sighting the Harwich Force, but the aircraft could not gain altitude fast enough to catch the airships and in August 1915 the platforms were removed. In 1917–18 the *Galatea, Phaeton, Royalist* and *Undaunted* were fitted with a winch on the quarterdeck for towing a kite balloon, and in 1918 all seven were given flying-off platforms over the forward 6in gun. *Undaunted* was completed at the end of August 1914 with her upper-works camouflaged, one of the first RN warships to be disguised in this way.

Arethusa commissioned in mid-August 1914 as flagship of the new Harwich Force and fought in the Heligoland Bight action on the 28th, during which she was badly damaged by gunfire. Escorted Cuxhaven

Phaeton as completed *CPL*

seaplane raid on 25 December 1914 and took part in Dogger Bank battle on 24 January 1915. Towed destroyer *Landrail* back from Bight after collision with *Undaunted*, April 1915. Fitted with aircraft platform until August 1915. Transferred to 5th Light Cruiser Squadron in June 1915 and covered the Borkum seaplane raid a month later. Took part in the chase and sinking of the German minelayer *Meteor*, 9 August 1915. Flagship, 5th LCS August 1915. Captured three German trawlers on 30 September 1915 and a further three on 7 October. Badly damaged by a mine off Felixstowe on 11 February 1916; taken in tow but broke loose and ran aground on the Cutler Shoal, where she broke her back.

Aurora was leader of 1st Flotilla in the Harwich Force from commissioning in September 1914 to February 1915, including action at Dogger Bank. Leader of 10th Destroyer Flotilla, February–June 1915, during which time she was fitted with aircraft platform (see above). Joined 5th LCS in June 1915 with which she remained until March 1918. Took part in sinking of *Meteor* in August and captured two trawlers in September and October 1915. Covered seaplane raid on Hoyer, 24 March 1916. Fitted for minelaying May 1917 and laid 212 mines in three trips including one in the Kattegat in March 1918. Transferred to 7th LCS in March 1918 and was present at surrender of High Seas Fleet in November 1918. In commissioned reserve at Devonport March 1919–August 1920 and then paid off in September for transfer to Royal Canadian Navy on 1 November 1920 at Devonport. Put into C&M at Halifax, 1 July 1922 and put on sales list 1 July 1927. Sold in 1927 and BU at Sorel, Quebec in 1928.

Galatea leader 2nd DF, Harwich Force December 1914–February 1915, then leader 1st Flotilla at Rosyth February 1915–September 1918. With *Phaeton* shot down Zeppelin *L 7* on 4 May 1916 and radioed first sighting of High Seas Fleet at Jutland (hit by one shell). Missed by torpedo from U-boat 12 July 1916. Fitted to lay 74 mines in November 1917 and laid 220 mines on three trips. Sent to Black Sea after Armistice, and *en route* collided with and sank SS *Moto* off Northumberland 10 December 1918. With 1st LCS served in Black Sea (joined November 1918) and returned April 1919 to join 2nd LCS. Paid off into reserve at Portsmouth in March 1920 and put on sales list the following year.

Inconstant joined 1st LCS at Rosyth in February 1915, remaining with the squadron until after the Armistice. Took part in search for *Meteor*, and fought at Jutland. Fitted to lay 74 mines in September 1917 and laid in all 370 mines (5 trips). Sent to Baltic early 1919 as SNO's ship, returning home in April 1919 to join 2nd LCS, Harwich Force. Paid off in October 1919 and then attached to 1st Submarine Flotilla until February 1922, including short spell as Atlantic Fleet Flagship. Paid off 16 February 1922 at Chatham and sold.

Penelope joined Harwich Force in December 1914 and took part in Hoyer Raid in March 1915. Fitted to launch seaplanes but platform removed in August 1915. Joined 5th LCS that month and captured or sank four German trawlers in September 1915. Rudder and steering gear wrecked by torpedo hit from *UB 29* off Norfolk coast 25 April 1916. Converted in November 1917 to lay 70 mines and laid 210 mines in three trips, including lay in Kattegat in February 1918. Joined 7th LCS, Grand Fleet in March 1918, and took part in surrender of High Seas Fleet in November. Paid off into reserve at Nore June 1919–19 February 1921 before being put on Disposal List April 1921–July 1923.

Phaeton served with 4th LCS, Grand Fleet, February–March 1915 and then sent to Dardanelles until September. Returned to join 1st LCS Grand Fleet. Shot down *L 7* with *Galatea* on 4 May and fought at Jutland later that month. Converted to lay 74 mines in August 1917, making five trips and laying 358 mines (including lay in Kattegat in March 1918). Transferred to 7th LCS, Grand Fleet, March 1918, then 2nd LCS, Harwich Force September 1919. Paid off for 12-month refit February 1920, and then went into Reserve at Devonport. Put on Disposal List May 1922.

Royalist joined 4th LCS, Grand Fleet in March 1915, then 1st LCS after February 1917 conversion to minelayer (74 mines). Made 16 trips and laid 1183 mines. Went to Baltic in January 1919 but returned in April to join 2nd LCS, Harwich Force. Paid off into Reserve at Portsmouth in January 1920, then put on Disposal List in May 1922.

Undaunted joined 3rd DF, Harwich Force as leader at the end of August 1914, and led her flotilla in successful action against German destroyers off Flanders coast on 17 October. Covered Cuxhaven Raid, 25 December 1914 and fought at Dogger Bank, 24 January 1915. Attacked unsuccessfully by U-boat off Dungeness in February and seriously damaged in collision with destroyer *Landrail* in April 1915. Joined 9th DF in August 1915 and captured German trawler in October. Covered Tondern Raid 24 March 1916 and later that day damaged severely in collision with *Cleopatra*. Repaired on the Tyne. Converted to lay 70 mines in April 1917 but laid no mines. Joined 7th LCS, Grand Fleet November 1918–March 1919. In Nore Reserve April 1919 but came out of reserve to carry drafts to Mediterranean February–May 1921 going back into Reserve until April 1922. Put on Disposal List then.

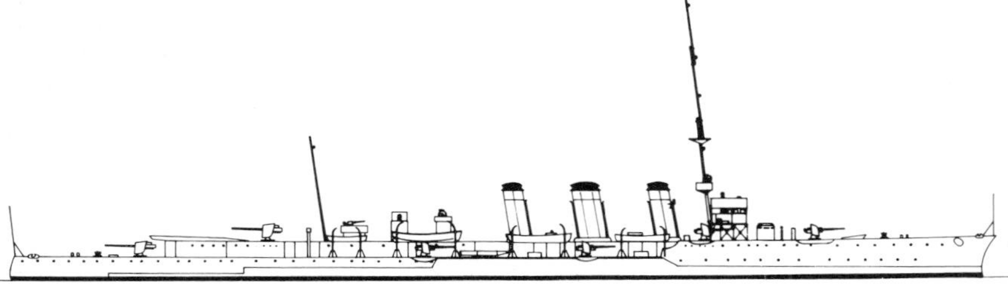

Caroline as completed

CAROLINE class *light cruisers*

Displacement: 4219t load; 4733t deep load
Dimensions: 446ft oa × 41ft 6in × 16ft mean
135.9m × 12.6m × 4.9m
Machinery: 4-shaft Parsons independent reduction (*Carysfort* Brown-Curtis) turbines, 8 Yarrow boilers, 40,000shp = 28½kts. Oil 916t
Armour: Belt 3in–1in (75mm–25mm), deck 1in (25mm), CT 6in (152mm)
Armament: 2–6in (15.2cm)/45cal Mk XII, 8–4in (10.2cm)/45 QF Mk IV, 1–13pdr (76.2mm) AA, 4–3pdr (47mm), 4–21in (53.3cm) TT aw (2×2)
Complement: 301

Name	Builder	Laid down	Launched	Comp	Fate
CAROLINE	Cammell Laird	28.1.14	29.9.14	12.14	HS 1924, extant 1984
CARYSFORT	Hawthorn Leslie	25.2.14	14.11.14	6.15	Sold for BU 8.31
CLEOPATRA	Cammell Laird	26.2.14	14.1.15	6.15	Sold for BU 6.31
COMUS	Swan Hunter	3.11.13	16.12.14	1.15	Sold for BU 7.34
CONQUEST	Scott	3.3.14	20.1.15	6.15	Sold for BU 8.30
CORDELIA	Pembroke DYd	21.7.13	23.2.14	1.15	Sold for BU 7.23

Another eight 'light armoured cruisers' were approved for the 1913 Programme, but the last two were completed to a different design. In essence the *Arethusa* design was repeated but 10ft longer and slightly beamier to improve stability. The logical arrangement of guns in the original design was changed to allow for an extra pair of 4in guns on the forecastle, while the 6in was moved aft to a superimposed position on the after deckhouse. Like the *Arethusa*s the designed power was 30,000shp, with 10,000shp extra for load. Being bigger than the *Arethusa* class they were generally more successful, apart from the useless pair of guns forward but with more beam they could be altered more easily. In 1916–17 these guns were replaced by a single 6in Mk XII, and a year later, when the foremast and CT were replaced by a tripod, spotting top and light director (like the *Arethusa* class) they were given a fourth 6in gun abaft the funnels, at forecastle deck level. At the same time the remaining 4in guns were removed and an extra pair of 21in TT was added p&s immediately behind the existing pair. The former Royal Horse Artillery 13pdr AA gun was replaced by the following guns:
Caroline, Caryfort, Comus: 2–3in/20cwt AA Mk I.
Cleopatra – 2–4in AA, 2–2pdr AA
Conquest – 1–4in AA, 2–2pdr AA
Cordelia – 1–4in AA only

In most ships the AA guns were abreast of the foremast, but *Conquest* and *Cordelia* had their AA guns abaft the central control platform.

Two of the class serving with the Harwich Force in 1915 (*Carysfort* and *Cleopatra*) were fitted with forecastle runways for launching French monoplanes against Zeppelins but these were removed by early 1916. An improved type was fitted in 1917–18 to *Caroline* and *Comus* but this was removed by late 1918; these two were also fitted with High Speed Sweeps (explosive paravanes) for use against U-boats. There were many minor alterations to the class. As the ships were grossly overweight they were lightened after the Armistice. In 1919 *Cordelia* received 2–3in/20cwt AA Mk I as in *Caroline* etc. In all

Cleopatra about 1918 *Aldo Fraccaroli Collection*

except *Cleopatra* and *Cordelia* the after control platform was removed and all searchlights were removed, but in 1920 she followed suit. *Conquest* was also rearmed with 2–3in AA in 1920, and *Carysfort, Comus* and *Cordelia* received 2–2pdr on the centreline on the after shelter deck. In 1924 *Conquest* had No 2 6in gun replaced by a deckhouse, and when *Caroline* was reduced to a training hulk she retained 1–6in, 3–4in and 2–12pdr.

Caroline joined 4th Destroyer Flotilla, Grand Fleet as leader in December 1914, then joined 1st LCS from February to November 1915. Joined 4th LCS early in 1916 and fought at Jutland 31 May 1916; served with 4th LCS until after the Armistice, and went with squadron to East Indies in June 1919. Paid off into Dockyard control February 1922 and in February 1924 became Harbour TS for Ulster Division RNVR at Belfast. Served as administrative centre for escorts based at Londonderry 1939–45 and returned to RNVR. Refitted by Harland & Wolff 1951 and still in existance (1984).

Carysfort joined 4th LCS, Grand Fleet on completion in August 1915. Relieved *Conquest* in 5th LCS, Harwich Force in April 1916. Flagship 7th LCS, Grand Fleet 1917. Collided with SS *Glentaise* off Orfordness in December 1917. Returned to 2nd LCS, Harwich Force April 1919 and sent to Baltic until 1920. Returned with 2nd LCS and joined Atlantic Fleet April 1921. Patrolling in Irish waters during Civil War 1922, and then sent to Turkey 1922–23 during war with Greece. Paid off into Reserve at Devonport in September but recommissioned for trooping duties a year later. Flagship, Devonport Reserve 1927. Trooping to China February–July 1929 and then SNO's ship, Devonport Reserve January 1930 until relieved by *Comus*. Paid off into dockyard control at Devonport in April 1931.

Cleopatra joined 5th LCS, Harwich Force on completion in June 1915, and replaced the lost *Arethusa* as Commodore Tyrwhitt's flagship in February 1916. Covered Tondern Raid 24 March 1916, during which she rammed and sank the German torpedo-boat *G 194* and suffered serious damage in a collision with *Undaunted*. In action with enemy destroyers 18 July and was mined off Thornton Ridge 4 August 1916. Underwent repairs and modernisation 1917 and recommissioned as Flagship, 7th LCS, Grand Fleet August 1918–March 1919. Rejoined 2nd LCS, Harwich Force April–October 1919, including operations in Baltic, then 1st LCS 1919–20. Recommissioned October 1920 for Atlantic Fleet until paid off into Nore Reserve 1921. Served temporarily in 3rd LCS in 1923 and then went into reserve at Devonport 1924–25. Recommissioned for 2nd LCS, Atlantic Fleet January 1925 until paid off into dockyard control, December 1926. Commissioned in Nore Reserve December 1927, becoming SNO's ship September 1928–March 1931. Trooping to Mediterranean October 1928 and to China in 1929. Paid off at Chatham into dockyard control in March 1931.

Comus joined 4th LCS, Grand Fleet in May 1915. Took part in sinking of raider *Greif*, 29 February 1916, and fought at Jutland. Joined 1st LCS March–April 1919 before being refitted at Rosyth. Recommissioned in October for 4th LCS and served in East Indies until June 1923 (temporary flagship 1921). Refitted at Portsmouth November 1922–July 1923 and then temporarily attached to 3rd LCS in Mediterranean until December 1924. Joined Nore Reserve until commissioned for 2nd LCS, Atlantic Fleet in September 1925 and after refit recommissioned for same service August 1927. Relieved by *Norfolk* in May 1930 and went into reserve at Devonport until December 1933 (SNO's ship from April 1931). Paid off into dockyard control at Devonport in December 1933.

Conquest joined 5th LCS, Harwich Force in June 1915, taking part in the sinking of *Meteor* in August 1915. Flagship 5th LCS March–April 1916 but then badly damaged by 12in shell hit during Lowestoft Raid, 25 April 1916. Sank enemy destroyer *S 20* off Belgian coast on 5 June 1917. Damaged by mine in July 1918 and paid off on the 13th for repairs lasting until April 1919. Went into reserve at Nore (including refit in 1921) until recommissioned in February 1922 as SNO's ship, 1st Submarine Flotilla, Atlantic Fleet and served until January 1927. Transferred to Mediterranean until April 1928, and went into commissioned reserve at Portsmouth until 1930, sold for BU in 1930 but broke adrift from tow in bad weather off Flamborough Head, 26 September 1930 and went missing with 6-man passage crew for two days before finishing the tow to Rosyth.

Cordelia joined 1st LCS, Grand Fleet in January 1915 and fought at Jutland. 4th LCS 1917–April 1919. Attached to Devonport Gunnery School in June and then into Nore Reserve until January 1920, when recommissioned for 2nd LCS, Atlantic Fleet. On patrol off Irish coast 1922 and paid off in December into Nore Reserve once again.

CALLIOPE class *light cruisers*

Displacement: 4228t normal; 4695t deep load
Dimensions: 446ft oa × 41ft 6in × 14ft 9in mean
135.9m × 12.6m × 4.5m
Machinery: 4-shaft (*Champion* 2-shaft) Parsons geared turbines, 6 Yarrow boilers, 37,500shp = 29½kts (*Champion* 40,000shp = 29kts). Oil 805t–895t
Armour: Belt 4in–1½in (100mm–40mm), deck 1in (25mm), CT 6in (150mm)
Armament: As *Caroline* class, except 2–21in (53.3cm) TT aw (beam)
Complement: 368

Name	Builder	Laid down	Launched	Comp	Fate
CALLIOPE	Chatham DYd	1.1.14	17.12.14	6.15	Sold for BU 8.31
CHAMPION	Hawthorn Leslie	9.3.14	29.5.15	12.15	Sold for BU 7.34

In the last two cruisers of the 1913 Programme the opportunity was taken to introduce gearing to improve the efficiency of the turbines. A 4-shaft arrangement was tried in the *Calliope* but the double helical type of gearing and the 2-shaft arrangement in *Champion* proved more successful. On trials she reached 28.2kts at 31,418shp and 29.5kts at 41,188shp, whereas the fastest direct-drive ships had only reached 29kts, at much higher revolutions. By rearranging the boilers it proved possible to reduce the funnels to two, marking the beginning of the classic 'C' class cruiser profile, with one fat fore funnel and a thinner after funnel. They were completed with the extra pair of 4in guns on the forecastle, but in 1916–17 these gave way to a third 6in gun. A year later a fourth 6in was mounted on a platform abaft the funnels, and the remaining 4in guns were removed. A light tripod was fitted and 4–21in TT (2×2) were added on either side amidships. The AA armament was also altered: *Calliope* received 2–3in/20cwt AA Mk I abreast of the tripod, while *Champion* had a 4in AA gun on the centreline abaft the after control position. In 1918 *Calliope* received a flying-off platform forward and had High Speed Sweeps fitted, while *Champion* received a winch for towing a kite balloon. In 1919 *Calliope* had her aircraft platform removed, and during the November 1919–March 1920

Champion about 1919 *CPL*

refit the above-water TT, searchlights and after control platform were removed to improve stability. At about this time *Calliope* was given 2-2pdr guns, and *Champion* followed suit in 1924. In 1926–27 *Champion* had her single 4in AA replaced by 2–3in AA and her above-water TT were removed, but she retained her after control platform.

Calliope commissioned as flagship 4th Light Cruiser Squadron, Grand Fleet. Suffered severe boiler room fire, 19 March 1916, but repaired in time for Jutland, where she suffered four shell hits. Helped to sink four trawler minesweepers off Jutland coast 1 September 1917. Commissioned March 1919 for 8th LCS, North America and West Indies Station and suffered another engine room fire while off the Azores, in October 1919. Repaired at Devonport November 1919–March 1920 and recommissioned for same service. Returned home December 1920 to refit and paid off at Nore in January 1921. In Nore Reserve October 1921 until recommissioned at Chatham for 2nd CS, Atlantic Fleet in May 1924. Trooping duties in 1925–26 and then paid off into dockyard control at the Nore for refit April 1926. In Nore Reserve but carried out trooping runs in 1927–28 and was SNO's ship from December 1927. Recommissioned at Chatham September 1928 for 3rd CS, Mediterranean Fleet. Paid off into reserve at Portsmouth January 1930, and a year later passed into dockyard control.

Champion was leader of 13th Destroyer Flotilla, Grand Fleet from December 1915 to early 1919, and served at Jutland (also Commodore 'D'). Joined 2nd LCS 1919 briefly but then attached to *Vernon* Torpedo School 1919–24. Refitted 1923 but paid off into dockyard control at Portsmouth October 1924. Recommissioned as Gunnery Firing Ship May 1925, and from 1928 attached to Signal School. Paid off into dockyard control in December 1933.

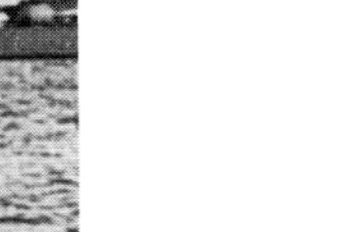

Chester 1917
CPL

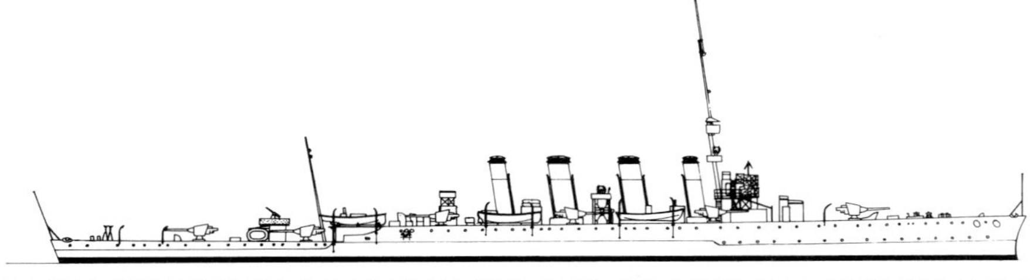

Chester 1916

BIRKENHEAD class *light cruisers*

Displacement: 5185t–5235t normal; 5795t–5845t deep load
Dimensions: 446ft oa × 50ft × 16ft normal
135.9m × 15.2m × 4.9m
Machinery: 4-shaft Parsons turbines, 12 Yarrow boilers, 25,000shp = 25½kts (*Chester* 31,000shp = 26½kts). Coal 1070t, oil 352t (*Chester* 1161t oil only)
Armour: As *Chatham* class
Armament: 10–5.5in (14cm)/50cal BL Mk I, 1–3in (76mm)/20cwt Mk I AA, 2–21in sub (beam)
Complement: *c*500 (*Chester c*450)

Name	Builder	Laid down	Launched	Comp	Fate
BIRKENHEAD (ex-*Antinavarhos Kontouriotis*)	Cammell Laird	27.3.14	18.1.15	5.15	Sold for BU 10.21
CHESTER (ex-*Lambros Katsonis*)	Cammell Laird	7.10.14	8.12.15	5.16	Sold for BU 11.21

After the Balkan War in 1912 the Greek Navy's British Chief of Staff, Rear-Admiral Sir Mark Kerr, proposed the construction of a modern squadron to protect the long coastline and large mercantile marine from any attempt by Turkey to avenge her recent defeat. Kerr wanted a fleet of destroyers and submarines to defend the Archipelago, backed up by seaplanes for reconnaissance and by light cruisers for additional gunpower to stiffen the surface forces. Out of this original and far-sighted scheme not much survived for the Greek Government insisted on buying a battlecruiser from Germany and a battleship from France, but at the beginning of 1914 an order was placed in Britain for two light cruisers and four destroyers. The order was placed with the newly formed Coventry Syndicate, a powerful consortium of John Brown, Fairfield, Cammell Laird and the Coventry Ordnance Works. The cruisers were to be copies of the *Chatham/Birmingham* design, but with a new 5.5in/50cal gun designed by Coventry Ordnance Works. It was about 13cwt lighter than the Royal Navy's latest 6in Mk XII, enabling ten to be carried instead of nine. At 85lb the shell was easier to handle, which made for a higher rate of fire, and as the range and penetration were only marginally less than the 6in it had a lot to recommend it. Another innovation was the provision in the design for 12pdr high-angle guns, among the first AA guns ever proposed. To meet a request for 26½kts the *Chester* was modified to burn only oil fuel. The Greek Government continued to pay the instalments on the two ships but by early 1915, when the *Antinavarhos Kontouriotis* had been launched, British hopes of an early victory had begun to fade, and the Admiralty Director of Contracts advised the Coventry Syndicate that HM Government would take over the two ships and a total of 38–5.5in guns and ammunition. The new names were allocated at this point and orders were given to Cammell Laird to supply builders' specifications and drawings.

As the ships conformed closely to Admiralty requirements, apart from the armament, very few changes were made to them. The two submerged TT were intended to fire a side-loading Elswick-pattern torpedo, but to save time standard Admiralty-pattern tubes and torpedoes were installed. The high-angle 12pdr guns were not available in 1915, and although there were plans to install 12½pdr guns on extemporised mountings, Vickers 3pdr AA guns were finally installed when the ships went to sea. The main visual distinction between the two ships was the mainmast, which was vertical in *Birkenhead* and raked in *Chester*. After Jutland both ships had the pole foremast replaced by a tripod, and in 1918 *Birkenhead* was fitted with an aircraft platform forward of the bridge, and a kite balloon winch aft. Her sister was fitted with a High Speed Sweep in 1918.

Birkenhead served with 3rd LCS

and fought at Jutland. In reserve at Portsmouth 1919 and paid off in May 1920 (resale to Greece considered but rejected).

Chester joined the Grand Fleet only three weeks before Jutland, and was scouting for Rear-Admiral Hood's battlecruisers when she came under withering fire from German light forces. The comparatively shallow gunshields permitted large numbers of splinters to cause havoc among her guncrews. One of the grislier aspects of this was that threequarters of the wounds were below the knee. Refitted and returned to 3rd LCS until Armistice. In Nore Reserve 1919 while her resale to Greece was discussed, but paid off in May 1920.

Castor in the mid 1920s — *CPL*

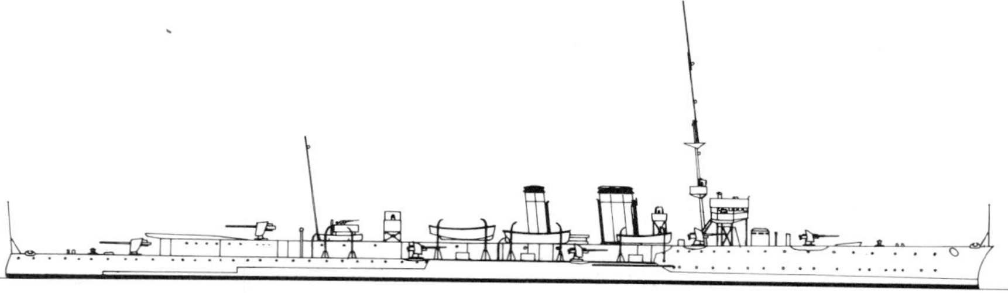
Cambrian class as completed with 4in guns on forecastle

The light cruisers ordered under the 1914–15 Programme were repeats of the *Calliope*, with the same layout. Only the *Cambrian*, last to be completed, incorporated the improved layout of the earlier class: 1–6in gun in place of the sided 2–4in on the forecastle. The other three were brought up to the same standard in 1916–17, and among other improvements a tripod with light director replaced the pole foremast. In 1917–18 all four lost the 6–4in guns in the waist, and received a fourth 6in gun abaft the funnels. The 13pdr on its extemporised AA mounting was replaced by 2–3in AA, p&s on the forecastle (*Cambrian* received a 4in AA aft on the centreline and 2–2pdr). *Canterbury* also received two pairs of 21in twin TT p&s, as the underwater TT had proved impossible to use at high speed. Post-war *Castor* received 2–2pdr and the 4in was replaced by 2–3in AA. Her deck TT were removed. In 1920–24 all four lost the after control tower and searchlight platform.

CAMBRIAN class *light cruisers*

Displacement: 4320t normal; 4799t deep load
Dimensions: 446ft oa × 41ft 6in × 14ft 10in mean
135.9m × 12.6m × 4.5m
Machinery: 4-shaft Parsons (*Canterbury* Brown-Curtis) geared turbines, 6 Yarrow boilers, 40,000shp = 28½kts. Oil 841t
Armour: Belt 3in–1½in (75mm–40mm), deck 1in (25mm), CT 6in (150mm)
Armament: 2–6in (15.2cm)/45cal BL Mk XIII, 8–4in (10.2cm)/45cal QF Mk IV, 4–3pdr (47mm), 1–13pdr (76.2mm) AA, 2–21in (53.3cm) TT sub (beam)
Complement: 368

Name	Builder	Laid down	Launched	Comp	Fate
CAMBRIAN	Pembroke DYd	8.12.14	3.3.16	5.16	Sold for BU 7.34
CANTERBURY	John Brown	14.10.14	21.12.15	5.16	Sold for BU 7.34
CASTOR	Cammell Laird	28.10.14	28.7.15	11.15	Sold for BU 7.36
CONSTANCE	Cammell Laird	25.1.15	12.9.15	1.16	Sold for BU 1.36

Cambrian joined 4th Light Cruiser Squadron from May 1916–1919, then North America and West Indies Station 1919–22. 2nd LCS, Atlantic Fleet August 1922–June 1924, including operations during Turkish Crisis 1922–23. Paid off into dockyard control in June 1924 for refit to 1926, then commissioned for 2nd LCS August 1926–1929. Trooping to China 1929 before paying off into Nore Reserve November 1929. Commissioned as SNO's ship March 1931; paid off into dockyard control at Sheerness in July 1933, and put on sales list.

Canterbury with 3rd BCS in 1916, including Battle of Jutland; 5th LCS, Harwich Force 1916–18, sinking torpedo-boat *S 20* by gunfire off Belgian coast, 5 June 1917. Aegean and Black Sea 1918–19, then commissioned at Portsmouth November 1919 for 1st LCS, Atlantic Fleet. Attached to Gunnery School, Portsmouth 1920–22, then Portsmouth Reserve 1922–24. Recommissioned at Portsmouth for 2nd CS, Atlantic Fleet May 1924, paying off into dockyard control for refit from June 1925. Recommissioned from Nore Reserve November 1926 for 2nd CS; trooping to China 1930–31, followed by Nore Reserve March 1931–December 1933, and trooping duty again from August 1932. Paid off in December 1933.

Castor commissioned November 1915 as Flagship, Commodore (D), 11th Destroyer Flotilla, Grand Fleet. Damaged at Jutland (10 casualties). To Black Sea 1919–20, then recommissioned April 1920 at Chatham for 2nd LCS, Atlantic Fleet, and served on Irish Patrol 1922. Gunnery School, Portsmouth 1923–24, Nore Reserve 1924–25. Refitted November 1925–September 1926 (into Nore Reserve), trooping to China from October 1927. Recommissioned at Devonport for China Station June 1928, Devonport Reserve from July 1930, paid off May 1935.

Constance with 4th LCS, Grand Fleet, January 1916–1919, including Jutland. 8th LCS, North America and West Indies Station 1919–26 and recommissioned at Devonport January 1923. Refitted Chatham September 1926–December 1927, then Flagship, Portsmouth Reserve. 5th CS, China Station 1928–November 1930, paying off into reserve at Portsmouth, March 1931–July 1935.

Concord 1928 partially disarmed
By courtesy of John M Maber

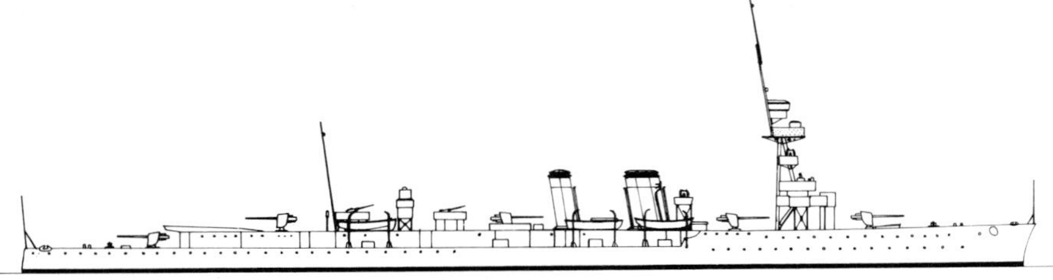
Centaur as completed

CENTAUR class *light cruisers*

Displacement:	4165t normal; 4870t deep load
Dimensions:	446ft oa × 42ft × 13ft 6in mean *135.9m × 12.8m × 4.1m*
Machinery:	4-shaft Parsons impulse-reaction geared turbines, 6 Yarrow boilers, 40,000shp = 29kts. Oil 824t
Armour:	Belt 3in–1¼in (75mm–30mm), deck 1in (25mm), CT 6in (150mm)
Armament:	5–6in (15.2cm)/45cal BL Mk XII, 1–13pdr (76.2mm), 2–3in (76mm)/20cwt Mk I AA, 2–21in (53.3cm) TT sub (team)
Complement:	437

Name	Builder	Laid down	Launched	Comp	Fate
CENTAUR	Vickers	24.1.15	6.1.16	8.16	Sold for BU 2.34
CONCORD	Vickers	1.2.15	1.4.16	12.16	Sold for BU 8.35

Although often described as ex-Turkish ships, the two *Centaur* class were additional units of the 1914–15 Programme to follow the *Cambrian* class. However to save time the builders were authorised to use two sets of machinery which had been ordered for a pair of Turkish scout cruisers, and out of this came the *Centaur* class. The opportunity was taken to incorporate all wartime lessons learned to date, principally the need for more 6in guns and director control. They were given 5–6in guns, one forward, one between foremast and fore funnel, one abaft the funnels and two superimposed aft, as in the *Caroline* class. They were also given a heavier tripod to take a large two-storey control top. Being the first light cruisers with an 'all-big gun armament' they were nicknamed 'Tyrwhitt's dreadnoughts' when they joined the Harwich Force. Distinguished from earlier two-funnelled cruisers by the gap between foremast and funnels. Being more modern they received fewer alterations, but in 1917–18 they were fitted with range clocks forward and aft. Searchlights removed from foremast and forward platform, and repositioned on after control platform. The 13pdr ex-Royal Horse Artillery AA gun was replaced by 2–2pdr pom-poms. Post-war the ships were partially disarmed, *Centaur* having her second 6in replaced by a deckhouse and *Concord* losing her second and fourth 6in guns. In 1931–32 *Concord* lost her 3in AA guns.

Centaur with 5th Light Cruiser Squadron, Harwich Force August 1916–March 1919, including the sinking of torpedo-boat *S 30* off Schouwen Bank January 1917, and being mined in June 1918. Repaired at Hull and sent to Baltic December 1918. 3rd LCS, Mediterranean March 1919–October 1923, recommissioning at Malta in June 1920 and at Gibraltar in March 1922. Paid off into Reserve at Devonport October 1923; refitted 1924–25 and recommissioned at Portsmouth 8 April 1925 as Commodore (D) Atlantic Fleet. Recommissioned February 1928 and September 1930; paid off into reserve at Portsmouth March 1932. On sales list 1933.

Concord joined 5th LCS, Harwich Force December 1916–March 1919. Recommissioned Devonport October 1919 for 3rd LCS, Mediterranean Fleet, and again in August 1921, until paid off in July 1923. Refitted at Devonport and commissioned May 1924 for 3rd CS, Mediterranean, attached to Australian Station 1925 and China Station 1925–26, returning to 3rd CS 1926–27. Reserve, Portsmouth from October 1927; trooping to China February 1928, then refitted October–November 1928 before joining Signals School at Portsmouth. Paid off into dockyard control January 1933 and put on sales list in November 1934.

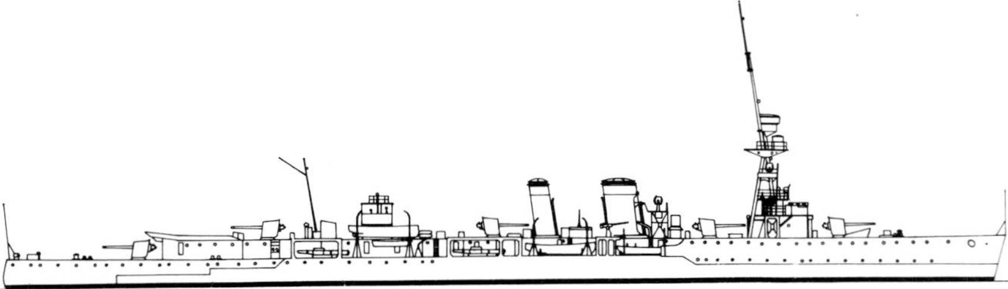
Caledon 1917

CALEDON class *light cruisers*

Displacement:	4120t normal; 4950t deep load
Dimensions:	450ft oa × 42ft 9in × 16ft 3in deep *137.2m × 13.0m × 5.0m*
Machinery:	2-shaft Parsons all-geared turbines, 6 Yarrow boilers, 40,000shp = 29kts. Oil 935t
Armour:	Belt 3in–1¼in (75mm–30mm) deck 1in (25mm) CT 6in (150mm)
Armament:	5–6in (15.2cm)/45cal BL Mk XII, 2–3in (76mm)/20cwt MK I AA, 4–3pdr (47mm), 8–21in (53.3cm) TT (4×2)
Complement:	400 (437 as flagship)

Name	Builder	Laid down	Launched	Comp	Fate
CALEDON	Cammell Laird	17.3.16	25.11.16	3.17	Sold for BU 1.48
CALYPSO	Hawthorn Leslie	7.2.16	24.1.17	6.17	Torpedoed 12.6.40
CARADOC	Scott	21.2.16	23.12.16	6.17	Sold for BU 4.46
CASSANDRA	Vickers	3.16	25.11.16	6.17	Mined 5.12.18

By late 1915, although 41 light cruisers were in service or nearly complete only 24 were available for the Grand Fleet (5 with the battle squadrons, 12 with destroyers). Accordingly, six 'Improved *Centaur*' class were ordered in December 1915, incorporating many wartime lessons, including a heavier armament of deck-mounted TT. They could easily be distinguished from the earlier ships by the raked bow. The improvements were mainly to improve seakeeping (a slightly longer forecastle (and to compensate for topweight 9in more beam). Like the *Centaurs* they proved remarkably tough ships. The fifth and sixth ships were held over to form part of the next class (see *Ceres*).

Caledon joined 6th Light Cruiser Squadron, Grand Fleet from March 1917, and then Flagship, 1st LCS under Commodore Cowan. In action 17 November 1917 against German outposts in the Heligoland Bight, when she was hit by a 12in shell. To Baltic January 1919; flagship 2nd LCS, Atlantic Fleet April 1919–August 1921, when she was relieved by *Curacoa*. Recommissioned at Chatham August 1921 for 2nd LCS; Irish Patrol 1922, but detached to Mediterranean September 1922. To Memel in January 1923 during rebellion in Lithuania, and collided with German pilot vessel at Cuxhaven February 1923. Served in Second World War and sold in 1948.

Calypso joined 6th LCS, Grand Fleet June 1917 and took part in Heligoland Bight action 17 November 1917, when the entire bridge personnel including CO were killed by a shell. To Baltic November 1918, and on 26 December with *Caradoc* and destroyers *Vendetta*, *Vortigern* and *Wakeful* captured Bolshevik destroyers *Avtroil* and *Spartak* off Reval. 3rd LCS, Mediterranean March 1919 recommissioning August 1922, January 1925 and August 1927. Served in Second World War and torpedoed south of Crete by the Italian submarine *Bagnolini* in 1940.

Caradoc with 6th LCS from June 1917–March 1919. Stranded on Fair Isle August 1917. To Baltic December 1918, and took part in capture of *Avtroil* and *Spartak* off Reval. With 3rd LCS February 1919–January 1921, recommissioning March 1923 and February 1926. Served in Second World War and sold in 1946.

Cassandra joined 6th LCS, Grand Fleet from June 1917. With *Caradoc* ran aground on Fair Isle 15 August 1917, and had to be towed to Lerwick for repairs. To Baltic November 1918 and sunk by mine in the Gulf of Finland 5 December 1918 (11 dead).

Calypso after the war
CPL

CERES class *light cruisers*

Displacement: 4190t normal; 5020t deep load
Dimensions: 450ft 3in oa × 43ft 5in × 14ft 8in mean
137.2m × 13.3m × 4.5m
Machinery: 2-shaft Brown-Curtis (*Curlew* Parsons) all-geared turbines, 6 Yarrow boilers, 40,000shp = 29kts. Oil 935t
Armour: Belt 3in–1½in (75mm–40mm), deck 1in (25mm), CT 3in (75mm)
Armament: As *Caledon* class, plus 2–2pdr (40mm) pom-pom AA
Complement: 460

Name	Builder	Laid down	Launched	Comp	Fate
CARDIFF (ex-*Caprice*)	Fairfield	22.7.16	12.4.17	6.17	Sold for BU 1.46
CERES	John Brown	11.7.16	24.3.17	6.17	Sold for BU 4.46
COVENTRY (ex-*Corsair*)	Swan Hunter	4.8.16	6.7.17	2.18	Sunk 14.9.42
CURACOA	Pembroke DYd	7.16	5.5.17	2.18	Sunk 2.10.42
CURLEW	Vickers	21.8.16	5.7.17	12.17	Sunk 26.5.40

When a new class of light cruisers was ordered in March–April 1916 the opportunity was taken to make a radical improvement to the *Centaur/Caledon* design. While no attempt was made to increase armament, by giving the hull 8in more beam and rearranging the guns it proved possible to increase fighting power. The tripod and bridgework were moved aft, allowing the second 6in to be moved from its restricted position to 'B' position, superimposed over 'A' gun. This, plus a longer forecastle gave the forward guns much better command in a seaway and enabled more firepower to be brought to bear across wider arcs.

Cardiff was Flagship 6th Light Cruiser Squadron from June 1917 and fought in Heligoland Bight action, 17 November 1917. She was chosen to lead the entire High Seas Fleet in to surrender, 21 November 1918. Flagship in the Baltic November 1918–early 1919, then 3rd LCS, Mediterranean 1919–29. Served in Second World War and sold in 1946.

Ceres with 6th LCS June 1917–1919, including service in Baltic November 1918–1919. 3rd LCS, Mediterranean 1919 (Black Sea 1920), recommissioning November 1920 and September 1922. Damaged in collision with destroyer USS *Fox* in entrance to Bosphorus April 1923. Served in Second World War and sold in 1946.

Coventry with 5th LCS, Harwich Force February 1918–May 1919, including service in Baltic December 1918. Commissioned for Atlantic Fleet May 1919, and in 1920 served as HQ ship for Naval Inter-Allied Disarmament Commission. Refitted 1920 for 2nd LCS and Rear-Admiral (D)'s flagship, Atlantic Fleet. Torpedo explosion in Malta March 1923 (2 dead). Served in Second World War as AA cruiser, and sunk by air attack off Tobruk in 1942.

Curacoa Flagship 5th LCS, Harwich Force February 1918–May 1919, then Flagship 1st LCS, Atlantic Fleet. Steering gear damaged by mine in Baltic May 1919, and relieved by *Delhi*; repaired at Chatham from June. 2nd LCS, Atlantic Fleet late 1919, recommissioning as flagship August 1921. Turkish Crisis 1922–23. Served in Second World War as AA cruiser, and rammed and sunk by RMS *Queen Mary* in 1942.

Curlew with 5th LCS, Harwich Force from December 1917. To Baltic January 1919, then temporary service with 1st LCS, Atlantic Fleet May–June 1919. In Devonport Reserve August 1919, but later moved to Rosyth for recommissioning April 1920 for 5th LCS, China Station. Recommissioned November 1922 for North America and West Indies Station; escorted *Repulse* on 1923 Royal Tour. Served in Second World War as AA cruiser, and sunk by air attack off Norway in 1943.

Cardiff about 1927
Aldo Fraccaroli Collection

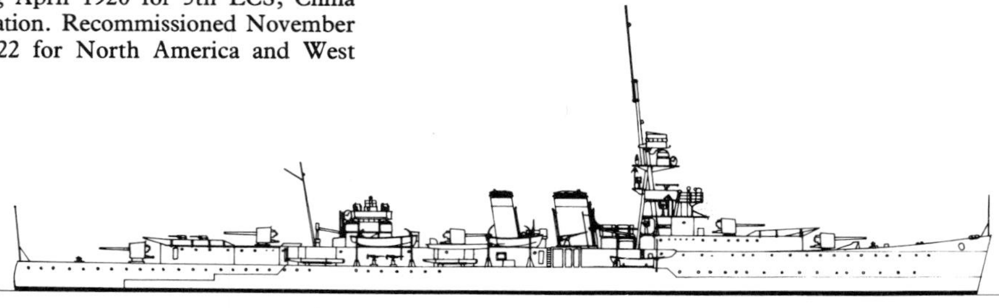

Calcutta as completed

CAPETOWN class *light cruisers*

Displacement: 4290t normal; 5250t deep load
Dimensions: 451ft 6in oa × 43ft 6in × 15ft 6in max
137.6m × 13.3m × 4.7m
Machinery: 2-shaft Parsons (*Carlisle, Colombo* Brown-Curtis) geared turbines, 6 Yarrow boilers, 40,000shp = 29kts. Oil 935t
Armour: As *Ceres* class
Armament: As *Ceres* class
Complement: 432

Name	Builder	Laid down	Launched	Comp	Fate
CAIRO	Cammell Laird	28.11.17	19.11.18	10.19	Torpedoed 12.8.42
CALCUTTA	Vickers	18.10.17	9.7.18	8.19	Sunk 1.6.41
CAPETOWN	Cammell Laird	23.2.18	18.6.19	4.22	Sold for BU 4.46
CARLISLE (ex-*Cawnpore*)	Fairfield	2.10.17	9.7.18	11.18	Sold for BU 1948
COLOMBO	Fairfield	8.12.17	18.12.18	7.10	Sold for BU 1.48

Five more light cruisers were ordered in June–July 1917, basically repeats of the *Ceres* class, but with a raised 'trawler' bow to prevent spray from blanketing 'A' and 'B' guns. All were completed post-war.

Cairo was Flagship, China Station October 1919–1921, then with 4th Light Cruiser Squadron, East Indies. Two men injured in gun explosion in May 1922. Served in Second World War as AA cruiser; torpedoed by Italian submarine *Axum* in Mediterranean in 1942.

Calcutta Flagship 8th LCS, North America and West Indies Station from August 1919, again in June 1921, September 1923 and May 1926. Served in Second World War as AA cruiser; sunk by air attack during evacuation of Crete in 1941.

Carlisle with aircraft hangar forward CPL

Capetown was towed to Pembroke DYd for completion and joined 8th LCS, North America and West Indies Station from April 1922. Served in Second World War and sold in 1946.

Carlisle completed on Armistice Day and joined Harwich Force. Commissioned March 1919 for 5th LCS, China Station, again January 1921 and February 1923. Served in Second World War as AA cruiser, and laid up as base ship late 1944, damaged beyond repair after an air attack. Sold for BU 1948.

Colombo with 5th LCS, China Station July 1919–March 1922, then 4th CS, East Indies. Served in Second World War as AA cruiser and sold in 1948.

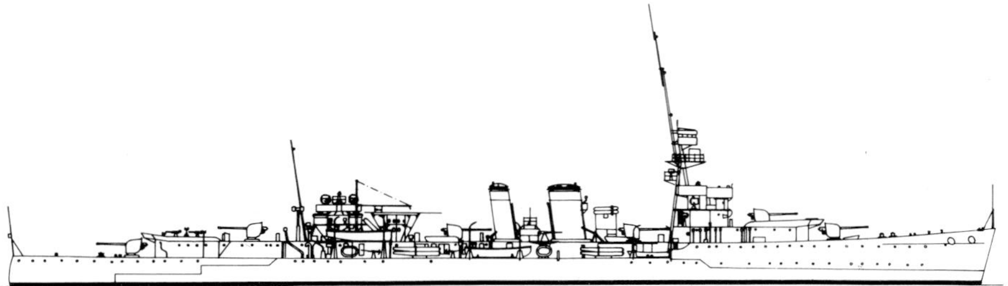

Delhi as completed

DANAE class *light cruisers*

Displacement: 4970t normal; 5870t deep load

Dimensions: 471ft oa × 45ft 6in × 16ft 6in deep
143.6m × 13.9m × 5.0m

Machinery: 2-shaft Brown-Curtis (*Dauntless, Diomede* Parsons) geared turbines, 6 Yarrow boilers, 40,000shp = 29kts. Oil 1050t

Armour: As *Ceres* class

Armament: 6–6in (15.2cm)/45cal BL Mk XII, 2–3in (76mm)/20cwt Mk I AA, 2–2pdr (40mm) pom-pom AA, (2×1), 12–21in (53.3cm) TT (4×3)

Complement: 450 (469 as flagship)

Name	Builder	Laid down	Launched	Comp	Fate
DANAE	Armstrong	11.12.16	26.1.18	6.18	Sold for BU 1.48
DAUNTLESS	Palmers	3.1.17	10.4.18	11.18	Sold for BU 2.46
DRAGON	Scott	1.17	29.12.17	8.18	Scuttled 8.7.44
2nd Group					
DELHI	Armstrong	29.10.17	23.8.18	5.19	Sold for BU 1.48
DESPATCH	Fairfield	8.7.18	24.9.19	6.22	Sold for BU 4.46
DIOMEDE	Vickers	3.6.18	29.4.19	10.22	Sold for BU 4.46
DUNEDIN	Armstrong	11.17	19.11.18	9.19	Torpedoed 24.11.41
DURBAN	Scott	1.18	29.5.19	11.21	Scuttled 9.6.44
DAEDALUS	Armstrong	1918	–	–	Cancelled 26.11.18
DARING	Beardsmore	1918	–	–	Cancelled 26.11.18
DESPERATE	Hawthorn Leslie	1918	–	–	Cancelled 26.11.18
DRYAD	Vickers	1918	–	–	Cancelled 26.11.18

In September 1916 three 'Improved *Ceres*' type were ordered, taking the original *Arethusa* concept to its limit. As before the hull was lengthened to enable an extra 6in gun to be fitted in between the foremast and the fore funnel. The reason was an erroneous intelligence report which suggested that new powerful German light cruisers were planned. The result was effective but the long asymmetrical profile had nothing of the balance of the 'C' classes. As beam was increased they were also able to accommodate triple TT, so gunpower was up by 20 per cent and torpedo armament by 50 per cent. In July 1917 a further three were ordered (2nd Group – *Delhi, Dunedin* and *Durban*), followed by six more in March 1918, but the last four were cancelled in November. All the second group were modified like the *Capetown* class, with 'trawler bows' for better seakeeping. In addition several had a conspicuous hangar abaft 'B' gun; This was later removed. *Diomede* had an experimental enclosed gunhouse for 'A' gun with 40° elevation. In 1920 it was proposed to complete *Despatch* as a royal yacht, with armament deleted and two boilers removed to reduce speed to 24kts. The forecastle deck would have been extended right aft, and the bow and stern would have been altered to resemble a yacht. Nothing came of this scheme.

Danae joined 5th Light Cruiser Squadron, Harwich Force in June 1918, the first one of the class to see war service. In Baltic 1919, then 1st LCS, Atlantic Fleet from September 1919. Served in Second World War; to Polish Navy as *Conrad* October 1944 and sold in 1948.

Despatch was to be launched 10 September 1919 but she stuck on the ways for two weeks. Towed to Chatham DYd for completion and then joined 5th LCS, China Station from June 1922. Served in Second World War and sold in 1946.

Dragon joined 5th LCS, Harwich Force in August 1918 and went to Baltic in 1919 before joining 1st LCS, Atlantic Fleet. Part of escort for Prince of Wales' visit to West Indies August 1919. Served in Second World War and lent to Polish Navy January 1943, and after torpedo damage scuttled as part of Mulberry Harbour in 1944.

Diomede was towed to Portsmouth DYd for completion and joined 5th LCS, China Station in October 1922. Served in Second World War and sold in 1946.

Dunedin commissioned for 1st LCS, Atlantic Fleet October 1920 and transferred to RNZN May 1924–March 1937 (relieving *Chatham*). Served in Second World War and torpedoed off coast of Brazil by *U 124* in 1941.

Durban was towed to Devonport for completion and joined 5th LCS, China Station November 1921. Served in the Second World War and scuttled as part of the Mulberry Harbour breakwater in 1944.

Dauntless with aircraft hangar
CPL

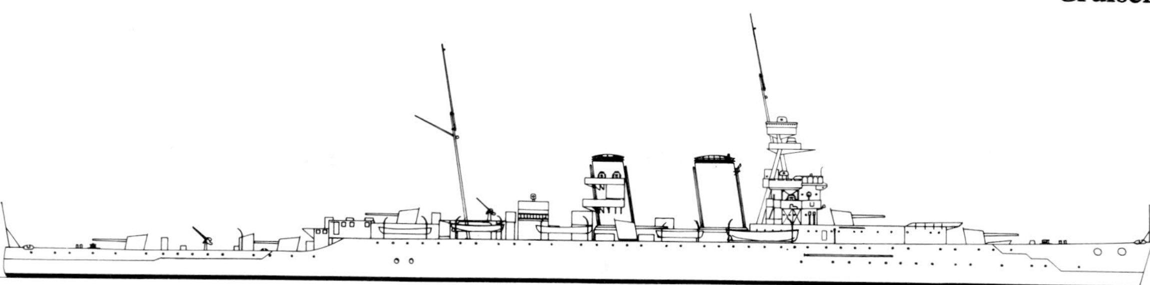

Frobisher as completed

A new class of cruisers was designed in 1915 to meet the threat of armed raiders in distant oceans, for the effort to hunt down the small number of German cruisers in August–December 1914 had seriously depleted the Grand Fleet's light cruiser squadrons and had disrupted movements of troopships. In June 1915 the Admiralty asked the DNC to prepare designs for an improved *Birmingham* with heavier armament, higher speed and more endurance. DNC's proposals were for a 9000t hull with a variety of armaments: 8–, 12– or 14–6in or a mixed armament of 2–9.2in and 8–6in. Two 9.2in were felt to offer poor chances of hitting at long distance, while the 6in would be outranged, so a uniform armament of 7.5in was chosen, firing a 200lb shell.

To assist operations in distant areas it was decided to make the four boilers in the after boiler room suitable for mixed coal-/oil-firing, while the old practice of using coal bunkers as protection was revived. The decision was made in 1917 to modify the boilers and turbines to boost power to 70,000shp, but not in *Cavendish* and *Hawkins* because they were too advanced. As things turned out *Raleigh* was the only one to have the higher performance as *Effingham* and *Frobisher* were altered to burn oil fuel only. Their mixed-firing boilers were replaced by two standard Yarrow small-tube boilers as in the forward boiler rooms, and power was increased to 65,000shp. In 1929 *Hawkins* was brought up to the same standard, with only 8 oil-fired boilers, but power boosted so that total power was only reduced to 55,000shp and more endurance was provided.

Although referred to as 'Improved *Birminghams*' the ships bore no resemblance to the 'Town' class, apart from having a long forecastle. The hull was based on the *Furious*, with sides sloped inboard at 10°, and 5ft 'bulges' covering the machinery spaces. The magazines were given 'box' protection, with 1in crowns and ½in sides, a light and economical form of internal armouring which was used in all later cruisers. With 25ft freeboard forward they were fine seaboats. The 7.5in BL VI was based on the old Mk I in the *Devonshire* class, but given 30° elevation, allowing shooting out to 22,000yds. In 1918 electrical training and elevation was provided but it remained a cumbersome mounting, with hand-loading for an extremely heavy shell. At the end of 1917 the *Cavendish* was earmarked for completion as an aircraft carrier, and she was renamed *Vindictive* in June 1918 to commemorate the old cruiser used as a blockship in the raids on Zeebrugge and Ostend. The *Hawkins* was completed with reasonable promptness but *Effingham* and *Frobisher* were given very low priority after the Armistice, being dockyard contracts.

CAVENDISH class *cruisers*

Displacement: 9750t normal; 12,190t deep load

Dimensions: 605ft oa × 65ft × 19ft 3in deep
184.4m × 19.8m × 5.9m

Machinery: 4-shaft geared turbines
Hawkins and *Cavendish* Parsons, 12 Yarrow boilers, 60,000shp = 30kts. Oil 1480t, coal 860t
Raleigh Brown-Curtis, 12 Yarrow boilers, 70,000shp = 31kts. Oil 1480t, coal 860t
Effingham and *Frobisher* Brown-Curtis, 10 Yarrow boilers, 65,000shp = 30½kts. Oil 2150t

Armour: Belt 3in–1½in (75mm–40mm), deck 1½in–1in (40mm–25mm), CT 3in (75mm)

Armament: 7–7.5in (19cm)/45cal BL Mk VI, 6–12pdr (76mm)/50cal QF Mk I, 4–3in (76mm)/20cwt Mk I AA, 4–3pdr (47mm), 6–21in (53.3cm) TT (2 sub beam; 4 aw fixed p&s)

Complement: 712

Name	Builder	Laid down	Launched	Comp	Fate
EFFINGHAM	Portsmouth DYd	2.4.17	8.6.21	7.25	Wrecked 18.5.40
FROBISHER	Devonport DYd	2.8.16	20.3.20	9.24	Sold for BU 3.49
HAWKINS	Chatham DYd	3.6.16	1.10.17	7.19	Sold for BU 8.47
RALEIGH	Beardmore	4.10.16	28.8.19	7.21	Wrecked 8.8.22
CAVENDISH	Harland & Wolff	29.6.18	17.1.18	10.18	Coverted to carrier *Vindictive* 6.18

Effingham completed in 1925. Reconstructed for service in Second World War but ran aground on uncharted rock near Harstad in Norway in 1940.

Frobisher's completion was delayed until 1924. Was reduced to training duties in 1939 but was rearmed for Second World War service and sold in 1949.

Hawkins served as Flagship 5th LCS, China Station from July 1919 and served in Second World War, being sold in 1947.

Raleigh commissioned in April 1921 as Flagship, 8th LCS on North America and West Indies Station, but in 1922 she became a private ship. Ran aground in thick fog on Point Armour, in the Belleisle Strait, Labrador in 1922. Although a large amount of equipment was salvaged she could not be refloated, and the wreck was abandoned (blown up in 1927 by a party from HMS *Calcutta*).

Hawkins about 1922 *CPL*

Enterprise in the late 1930s
CPL

EMERALD class *light cruisers*

Although described as enlarged 'D' class, the three light cruisers ordered in March 1918 had their origin in an exaggerated late-1917 staff requirement for ships capable of catching the fast minelayers *Brummer* and *Bremse*. For the first time in many years speed was the dominant criterion, not armament or range. The new ships, therefore, were to be capable of 33kts in light condition and 32kts deep, but would only have one more gun than the 'D' class. To get the maximum speed a high length: beam ratio was adopted, and to give the ships the ability to pursue at high speed in bad weather they were given 30ft freeboard forward. Instead of the 'trawler bow' in the latest 'C' and 'D' classes they were given a long, high forecastle with a prominent knuckle. Although no objections were raised to the somewhat sparse armament the Director of Naval Ordnance recommended that deck protection should be increased, and 1in plating was added on the lower deck over the engine rooms. Boilers were also broken up into groups to reduce the risk of being knocked out by a single shell or torpedo – a first step towards the unit system of the late 1930s. The machinery of the *Shakespeare* class flotilla leaders was duplicated, giving twice the power of the 'D' class. Only three ships could be ordered because of the shortage of labour and materials. *Euphrates* was cancelled in November 1918 and the construction of the other two slowed down after their launch.

Emerald was completed in 1926 and served in Second World War, being sold in 1948. *Enterprise* was completed in 1926 and served in Second World War; sold in 1946.

Displacement: 7300t light; 9450t deep load
Dimensions: 570ft oa × 54ft 6in × 18ft 6in mean
173.7m × 16.6m × 5.6m
Machinery: 4-shaft Brown-Curtis geared turbines, 8 Yarrow boilers, 80,000shp = 33kts. Oil 1600t
Armour: Belt 3in–1½in (75mm–40mm), deck 1in–½in (25mm–15mm)
Armament: 7–6in (15.2cm)/45cal BL Mk XII (*Emerald* 7×1; *Enterprise* 1×2, 5×1), 5–4in (10.2cm) AA, 4–3pdr (47mm), 3–2pdr (40mm) AA, 12–21in (53.3cm) TT (4×3)
Complement: 450

Name	Builder	Laid down	Launched	Comp	Fate
EMERALD	Armstrong	23.9.18	19.5.20	1.26	Sold for BU 6.48
ENTERPRISE	John Brown	28.6.18	23.12.19	4.26	Sold for BU 4.46
EUPHRATES	Fairfield	1918	–	–	Cancelled 26.11.18

1918 Cruiser Designs

After the 'E' class were approved erroneous intelligence reports suggested that a new class of German cruiser would carry 2–8.2in guns. The Board therefore asked the DNC to prepare new designs. The first, Design 'A' was simply a repeat 'E' hull with 7.5in guns.

Design 'A'
Displacement: 7700t
Dimensions: 570ft oa × 54ft 6in × 15ft 3in *(173.7m × 16.6m × 4.7m)*
Protection: As 'E' class
Machinery: 80,000shp = 33kts. Oil 1600t
Armament: 4–7.5in (19cm) Mk VI, 4–4in (10.2cm) AA, 12–21in (53.3cm) TT (4×3)

The alternative clearly owed some of its inspiration to the *Cavendish* class, with greater emphasis on range, but like the 'E' class, both designs emphasised high speed.

Design 'B'
Displacement: 8850t
Dimensions: 607ft oa × 58ft × 15ft 9in *(185.0m × 17.7m × 4.8m)*
Protection: As 'E' class
Machinery: 80,000shp = *c*30kts. Oil 2000t
Armament: 5–7.5in (19cm) Mk VI, 4–4in (10.2cm) AA, 12–21in (53.3cm) TT (4×3)

AIRCRAFT CARRIERS

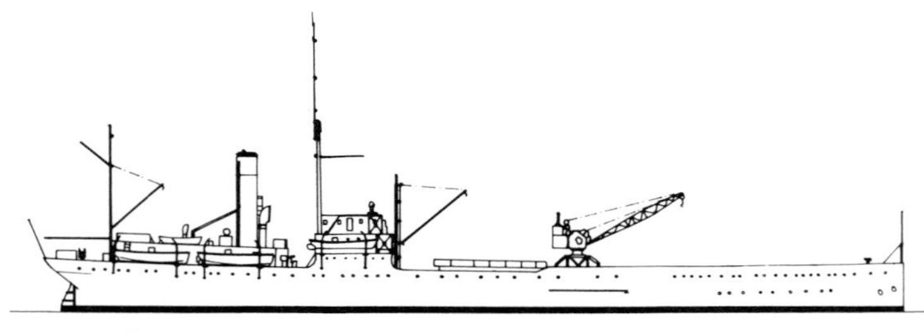

Ark Royal as completed

ARK ROYAL *aircraft carrier*

So many lessons were learned from the 1913 trials with the old cruiser *Hermes* that the First Lord of Admiralty allocated £81,000 in the 1914–15 Navy Estimates for the acquisition and conversion of a 'seaplane carrying ship'. A mercantile hull lying on the stocks at Blyth was chosen – a typical 'Black Sea tramp' or general bulk coal or grain carrier (not an oil tanker, as so often stated). The changes made by the Admiralty were so radical that the conversion amounted to construction from the keel up. Machinery was moved aft and a large 'aeroplane hold' or hangar 150ft × 45ft × 15ft took up most of the fore part of the hull. There were also workshops for working on engines and airframes, and to protect against an explosion of petrol vapour the hangar sides were isolated by cellular water spaces. A sliding hatch, 40ft × 30ft gave access to the upper deck, with aircraft hoisted in and out by two 3-ton steam-powered cranes.

Displacement: 7080t normal; 7450t load
Dimensions: 366ft oa × 50ft 10in × 18ft mean
111.6m × 15.5m × 5.5m
Machinery: 1-shaft TE, 2 cyl boilers, 3000ihp = 11kts. Oil 500t
Armament: 4–12pdr (76mm)/50cal QF Mk I, 2 MGs, 5 floatplanes, 2 landplanes
Complement: 180

Name	Builder	Laid down	Launched	Comp	Fate
ARK ROYAL	Blyth SB	7.11.13	5.9.14	12.14	Sold 1946

The ship was bought by the Admiralty in May 1914 and launched four months later. Her first aircraft were a pair of Type 807 Sopwith seaplanes, two Wright Pushers, a Short 135, and two Sopwith Tabloid landplanes. The seaplanes were to be launched from the deck on wheeled trolleys, as in *Hermes*, and to taxi alongside for recovery by crane. The landplanes were presumably intended to fly off in the same way but land ashore, which presumed that some method of carrying them back to the ship existed. Although slow the *Ark Royal* proved very useful, and the ideas incorporated into her design proved valid for later carriers.

Commissioned early in December 1914 and sailed for Dardanelles on 1 February 1915, arriving at Tenedos on the 17th. Although hampered by the poor performance of her seaplanes she provided much-needed reconnaissance for the bombardment of the Turkish forts. Involved in many operations March–April 1915 and covered the landings from 25 April onwards, but at the end of May was withdrawn to Imbros where she became in effect a depot ship for all aircraft based there (she was too vulnerable to U-boat attack to be risked at sea). To Mytilene and Salonika from November 1915 to March 1916, then back to Mudros as parent ship to No 2 Wing, RNAS. Two of her Sopwith Baby Seaplanes attempted to bomb *Goeben* in January 1918. To Syra as parent ship through Dardanelles after the Armistice and operated in the Black Sea, transporting aircraft to Batumi. Withdrawn at the end of 1919 to support Somaliland campaign against the 'Mad Mullah'. Sea of Marmora and Black Sea 1920, covering withdrawal of White Russian forces from Crimea, and carried aircraft to Basra, in the Persian Gulf. In reserve at Rosyth after refit November 1920–April 1921. Recommissioned September 1922 to take aircraft out to Mediterranean during the Chanak Crisis, refitting at Malta in April 1923 before returning to Dardanelles. Renamed *Pegasus* in December 1934 to release name for new carrier. Survived to fight in Second World in various capacities, and sold in December 1946 for conversion to Panamanian merchant ship. As *Anita I*, started conversion at Antwerp but the ship was sold for BU in June 1949.

EMPRESS *seaplane carrier*

Displacement: 2540t normal
Dimensions: 311ft pp × 40ft × 16ft
94.8m × 12.2m × c4.9m
Machinery: 3-shaft Parsons turbines, 2 return-tube boilers, *c*6000shp = 21kts
Armament: 2–4in (10.2cm), 1–6pdr (57mm) AA, 6 seaplanes
Complement: *c*250

Name	Builder	Laid down	Launched	Comp	Fate
EMPRESS	Denny	1906	13.4.07	6.07	Returned 1919

Requisitioned by Admiralty from South East and Chatham Railway Co 11 August 1914 and converted at Chatham DYd to operate three seaplanes. This involved stripping the after deck of all fittings and erecting a large canvas hangar, workshop and cranes aft. Later armed with 8–12pdr. Modified by Cunard at Liverpool to operate four seaplanes (1915).

Commissioned in RN 25 August 1914 and took part in Cuxhaven Raid on 25 December. Moved from North Sea to Queenstown in October 1915, then in 1916 to Egypt, where she operated from Port Said. Returned to her owners in November 1919.

Empress about 1918 with large hangar aft *CPL*

Riviera with canvas hangars as first converted *IWM*

RIVIERA *seaplane carrier*

Displacement: *c*2500t normal; 1783t gross
Dimensions: 316ft pp × 41ft × 16ft
96.3m × 12.5m × 4.9m
Machinery: 3-shaft Parsons turbines, 6 Babcock & Wilcox boilers, *c*6000shp = 20½kts. Coal 119t
Armament: 2–4in (10.2cm), 1–6pdr (57mm) AA, 4 seaplanes
Complement: *c*250

Name	Builder	Laid down	Launched	Comp	Fate
RIVIERA	Denny	1910	1.4.11	6.11	Returned 1919

The second of three fast Cross-Channel steamers taken over from the SE & CR on 11 August 1914, the *Riviera* was converted to a seaplane carrier at Chatham DYd for service with the RN. The aircraft which she carried at various times were: Sopwith Baby, Short 74 (on Cuxhaven Raid), Short 135 (No 136), Short 74s Nos 811 and 818, Short 184s Nos N 2929, N 2930, N 2943, N 2949. Commissioned at Chatham 13 August 1914 and took part in Cuxhaven Raid 25 December 1914. Dover Patrol 1915, and again 1917–18. Refitted and recommissioned June 1918 for Mediterranean. Paid off 21 May 1919 and returned to her owners. Served in Second World War as HMS *Laird's Isle* 1939–45.

ENGADINE *seaplane carrier*

Displacement: 1881t normal; 1676t gross
Dimensions: 316ft pp × 41ft × 16ft
96.3m × 12.5m × 4.9m
Machinery: 3-shaft Parsons turbines, 6 Babcock & Wilcox boilers, *c*6000shp = 21½kts. Coal 119t
Armament: 2–4in (10.2cm), 1–6pdr (57mm) AA, 4 seaplanes
Complement: *c*250

Name	Builder	Laid down	Launched	Comp	Fate
ENGADINE	Denny	1910	23.9.11	1912	Returned 1919

The last of three Cross-Channel steamers taken over on 11 August 1914 from the SE & CR Co, the *Engadine* was fitted out at Chatham DYd with a hangar for three seaplanes. Like the other conversions she was limited by the poor performance of the seaplanes, and several attempts to use the ships to attack shore targets were frustrated by the difficulties of handling the aircraft. Refitted by Cunard Co in 1915 to improve aircraft facilities, and then carried four seaplanes.

She commissioned at Chatham on 13 August 1914 and took part in Cuxhaven Raid on 25 December. With Grand Fleet 1915–17, and was used at Battle of Jutland, during which one of her seaplanes sighted the High Seas Fleet but failed to get the message through. She towed the damaged *Warrior* and saved 600 men when that ship sank. Attack on Tondern Zeppelin sheds 4 May 1916. To Mediterranean 1918; paid off November 1919 and returned to owners. She operated the following aircraft: Short 74 (1914); Short 184 (1916); Short 827, Short 830, Sopwith Schneider, Sopwith Baby (1916), Short 184s Nos 8050, 8065, 9073, N 2822, N 2944, N 9000, 8359 (at Jutland); Short Folders Nos 120, 121, 122 (October 1914).

Engadine about 1917
CPL

Campania as first converted 1915
By courtesy of John M Maber

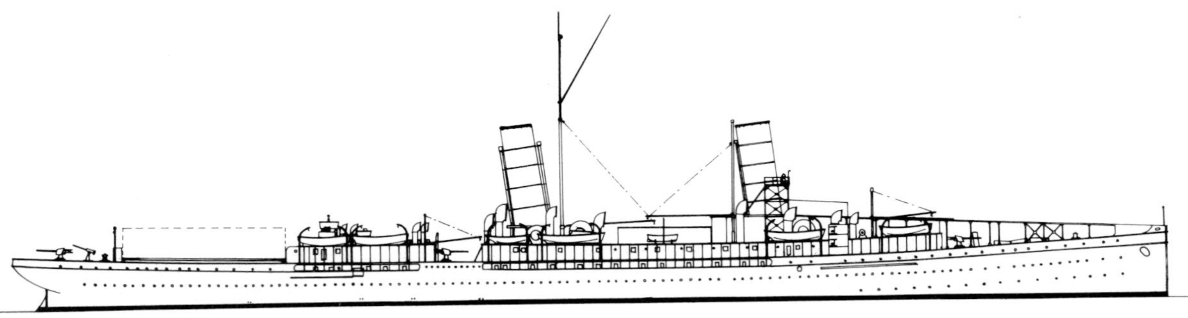

Campania 1916

In addition to the converted Cross-Channel steamers the Admiralty was anxious to acquire a larger hull for use as a seaplane carrier capable of working with the Grand Fleet. The only hull immediately available was the old Cunard record-breaker *Campania*, which was already in the hands of the breakers T W Ward, but only stripped of deck fittings. She was bought outright on 27 November 1914 and towed to Cammell Laird for a 5-month conversion to a seaplane carrier. The conversion was ambitious, with a 120ft flight deck forward, and a hangar and workshops. Unfortunately the old ship's machinery required constant attention, and keeping up with the Grand Fleet in all weathers was always a strain. The runway was found to be too short, and after unsuccessful trials the fore funnel was removed and replaced by twin flat-sided uptakes which permitted the runway to be extended to 200ft. In November 1915 she was fitted to launch a kite balloon aft. The first flight from her deck took place on 6 August 1915, with a Sopwith Schneider. She carried the following aircraft: Sopwith Schneider (1915); Short 184 (1916); Sopwith 1½-Strutter Nos 9722, A 6919–6922, N 5633, N 5635, N 5638 (1918); Fairey Campanias Nos N 1842, N 1850, N 2366, N 2372, N 2373 (1918).

She was commissioned on 17 April 1915 and joined the Grand Fleet. In hand for modifications November 1915–April 1916 at Birkenhead. She failed to receive the signal to raise steam and so missed the Battle of Jutland. She dragged her cables during a gale in the Firth of Forth, 5 November 1918 and drifted across the bows of the battleship *Revenge*, and foundered.

CAMPANIA *seaplane carrier*

Displacement: 18,000t normal; 12,884t gross
Dimensions: 622ft oa × 65ft × 26ft
189.6m × 19.8m × 7.9m
Machinery: 2-shaft 5-cyl TE, 28,000ihp = 21kts
Armament: 6–4.7in (12cm) QF, 1–3in (76mm) AA, 10 seaplanes
Complement: 600

Name	Builder	Laid down	Launched	Comp	Fate
CAMPANIA	Fairfield	18.92	8.9.93	18.93	Sunk 5.11.18

Pegasus about 1921
CPL

ANNE *seaplane carrier*

Displacement: 7000t normal; 4083t gross
Dimensions: 367ft pp × 47ft 6in × ?
111.9m × 14.5m × ?
Machinery: 1-shaft TE, ? = 11kts
Armament: 1–12pdr (76mm), 2 seaplanes
Complement: ?

Name	Builder	Laid down	Launched	Comp	Fate
ANNE (ex-*Aenne Rickmers*)	Rickmers	?	1911	?	Sold 1922

One of two German merchantmen seized at Port Said in August 1914. She was requisitioned for service under the Red Ensign in January 1915 and served under her original name, and operated with two seaplanes in the Eastern Mediterranean and the Aegean. Both pilots were French, while the observers were British, and for a while she served with the French seaplane squadron off the Syrian coast. She operated two Nieuport seaplanes at first, then a Short 184 and a Sopwith Schneider. While operating off Smyrna she had been torpedoed by a Turkish TB on 11 March 1915. Beached at Mudros and repaired by HMS *Reliance;* refloated and repaired at Alexandria May–June 1915. Commissioned in RN August 1915 and renamed next day. Served in vicinity of Port Said and in Red Sea. Paid off August 1917 and became a stores carrier, then as a fleet collier January 1918–January 1919. Returned to mercantile service 1922.

RAVEN II *seaplane carrier*

Displacement; 4678t gross
Dimensions: 390ft 6in pp × 51ft 6in × ?
119.0m × 15.7m × ?
Machinery: 1-shaft QE, ? = 10kts
Armament: 1–12pdr (76mm), 2 seaplanes
Complement: ?

Name	Builder	Laid down	Launched	Comp	Fate
RAVEN II (ex-*Rabenfels*)	Swan Hunter	?	1903	–	Sold 1923

German merchantman seized at Port Said in August 1914 and commissioned in RN 12 June 1915, but not renamed until August 1915. Carried two French seaplanes and operated with French Fleet in the Eastern Mediterranean for a while. The aircraft operated included the following: Short 184, Sopwith Schneider, Sopwith Baby, Short 827/830. Operated in Eastern Mediterranean 1915; damaged by German bombing attack on Port Said 1 September 1916. Served in Red Sea and Indian Ocean 1916–17. Renamed *Ravenrock* in January 1918 and used thereafter as a fleet collier, stores carrier and troopship until January 1921. Sold and returned to mercantile service 1922.

PEGASUS *seaplane carrier*

Displacement: 3300t normal; 2450t gross
Dimensions: 332ft oa × 43ft × 15ft
101.2m × 13.1m × 4.6m
Machinery: 2-shaft Brown-Curtis geared turbines, 6 cyl boilers, 9500shp = 20kts. Oil 300t
Armament: 2–3in (76mm)/20cwt Mk I AA, 2–12pdr (76mm) AA, 9 aircraft
Complement: 280

Name	Builder	Laid down	Launched	Comp	Fate
PEGASUS (ex-*Stockholm*)	John Brown	1914	9.6.17	8.17	Sold for BU 8.31

The last of the short-sea passenger ship conversions was in many ways the most sophisticated, because she completed last. As with the *Nairana* landplanes were stowed in the forward hangar, and seaplanes aft, to simplify handling. A variety of aircraft were carried: Beardmore WB IIIs Nos N 6104, N 6106, N 6107 (1917); Fairey Campania; Sopwith Camel 2F 1s (4 carried in October 1918); Fairey IIIC (White Sea 1919 and 'L' Flt of 267 Sqn – N 9253, N 9257); RAF in Dardanelles, 1922 – N 9230, N 9259 taken to Russia, N 9253, N 9257 to Mediterranean; Fairey IIIFDs (6 in 1922); Short 184s N 9290, N 9291, N 9292, N 9293 (Russia 1919).

The ship was bought on the stocks as SS *Stockholm* 27 February 1917 and renamed on 28 August 1917 after commissioning. Joined Grand Fleet until early 1919, when she was sent to Archangel to support operations against the Bolsheviks. Recommissioned at Rosyth 2 December 1919 and left for Mediterranean in March 1920. Ran aground off Kerch 9 March 1920 but she was on soft mud, was refloated with help of two tugs and an icebreaker. Remained with Mediterranean Fleet to 1923. From 1924 she was rated as an aircraft tender until sold.

ARGUS *aircraft carrier*

Displacement: 14,550t normal
Dimensions: 566ft oa × 68ft × 21ft
172.5m × 20.7m × 6.4m
Machinery: 4-shaft Parsons geared turbines, 12 cyl boilers, 20,000shp = 20kts. Oil 2000t
Armament: 6–4in (10.2cm) AA, 20 aircraft
Complement: 401

Name	Builder	Laid down	Launched	Comp	Fate
ARGUS (ex-*Conte Rosso*)	Beardmore	6.14	2.12.17	9.18	Sold for BU 12.46

The need for a large hull led to the purchase of the incomplete liner *Conte Rosso* ordered in 1914 for the Lloyd Sabaudo Line. She had been lying on the stocks since August 1914 and was bought in August 1916. With such a capacious hull it was possible for the first time to have a full length hangar and flight deck. The design and layout of flight deck were tried out in a wind-tunnel, and as a result a flush deck was adopted, with a small pilot house which could be lowered during flying operations. A dummy 'island' structure was tried out in the Firth of Forth in October 1918.

The first aircraft embarked were 18 Sopwith Cuckoo torpedo-dropping aircraft, and it was hoped to use the *Argus* in the projected 1919 attack on the High Seas Fleet in its harbours. The following aircraft were embarked: Sopwith Cuckoos (18 in October 1918); Sopwith Camel 2F 1s (1919), Sopwith 1½-Strutter (1919), Sopwith Pup (1919), Parnall Panthers (1919–20), Nieuport Nightjars (1922), Fairey IIIB seaplane (1922), Fairey Flycatcher No N 163 (for trials February 1923).

With a reasonable speed the wind-over-deck was adequate for aircraft launching under most conditions and she proved a great success, although too late to affect the war. Commissioned at Glasgow in September 1918 and embarked aircraft a month later before joining the Grand Fleet. From 1919 with Atlantic Fleet. Served in Second World War on subsidiary duties.

Argus after the war
CPL

Furious 1918
CPL

FURIOUS *aircraft carrier*

Armament: 10–5.5in (14cm)/55cal BL Mk I, 6–3in (76mm) AA , 8 aircraft
Other particulars: See under Capital Ships

As flying operations had proved almost impossible from the battle-cruiser *Furious* on 1 September 1917 it was decided to give her a full landing deck as well. In late November 1917 she was returned to her builders, who removed the remaining 18in gun and magazine, as well as the mainmast and the centreline 5.5in gun and TT. In their place was built a box hangar and flight deck 284ft × 70ft, level with the flying-off deck forward. To stop aircraft from flying into the funnel a large gantry was provided, with vertical cables acting as the first primitive crash barrier. The ship recommissioned at Rosyth on 15 March 1918 for the Flying Squadron of the Grand Fleet, and became Flagship of Rear-Admiral Phillimore, Admiral Commanding Aircraft. Landing trials began in April, using Sopwith Pups with skid undercarriages, but only 3 out of 13 landings were successful. The main problem was funnel gas, which caused draughts and eddies over the flight deck. Landings were therefore suspended once more, but the ship could still launch landplanes, and she embarked new aircraft: 1½-Strutters and 2F 1 Camels.

During a reconnaissance mission in June 1918 she was attacked by two seaplanes but drove them off with gunfire and managed to launch 2 Camels, which were recovered by destroyers. On 19 July 1918 flew off 7 Camels in successful attack on Zeppelin sheds at Tondern in Schleswig-Holstein. Baltic 1919 and then went into reserve at Rosyth from November 1919 until her massive reconstruction could begin. Served in Second World War and sold for BU January 1948.

BEN-MY-CHREE *seaplane carrier*

Displacement: 3888t normal; 2651t gross
Dimensions: 375ft pp × 46ft × *c*16ft
114.3m × 14.0m × c4.9m
Machinery: 3-shaft turbines, 14,000shp = 24½kts
Armament: 2–4in (10.2cm), 1–6pdr (57mm) AA, 4 seaplanes
Complement: *c*250

Name	Builder	Laid down	Launched	Comp	Fate
BEN-MY-CHREE	Vickers	1907	23.3.08	1908	Sunk 11.1.17

Requisitioned by the Admiralty 2 January 1915 and converted by Cammell Laird at Birkenhead, she was the fastest of the seaplane carrier conversions. Owned by the Isle of Man Steam Packet Co. When commissioned she was sent to Harwich for a short while, but soon went to the Dardanelles. She operated 4 Short 184s, and on 12 August 1915 one used a 14in torpedo to sink a Turkish merchantman, and again on the 17th. In September 1915 rescued 300 survivors from the torpedoed liner *Southland* and towed the ship to Mudros. In 1916 was based at Aden, before returning to Aegean. While anchored off Castellorizo she was set on fire by Turkish artillery, and blew up and sank.

VINDEX *seaplane carrier*

Like the *Ben-my-Chree* the *Viking* was one of the fastest short-sea steamers, being built for the Isle of Man Steam Packet Co's service between Fleetwood and Douglas. Taken over for the RN on 15 March 1915 and converted to seaplane carrier, but unlike the trio taken up in August 1914, the 1915 trio were given flying-off platforms to permit them to launch seaplanes with wheeled trolleys. On 3 November 1915 a Bristol Scout C, numbered 1255 and flown by Flt Lt Towler, made the first take-off from a British carrier. The 12pdr guns were later replaced by 2–4in AA. During her naval career she operated the following aircraft: Short 184s Nos 8033, 8346, N 1232; Sopwith Pups Nos 9921, N 6457, N 6458; Bristol Scout Cs No 1255 (1915), 3028 (1916); Bristol Scout D; Sopwith Babies (Tondern Raid). Commissioned September 1915 as HMS *Vindex* (renamed to avoid confusion with TBD); purchased outright from owners 11 October 1915. Served at the Nore and Harwich from 1915. Tondern Raid 4 May 1916. Mediterranean 1918–19 and paid off late 1919; sold back to owners February 1920. Served in the Second World War as a troopship.

Displacement: 2950t normal; 1957t gross
Dimensions: 361ft oa × 42ft × 13ft 3in
110.0m × 12.8m × 4.0m
Machinery: 3-shaft turbines, 11,000shp = 23kts
Armament: 4–12pdr (76mm)/50cal QF, 1–6pdr AA, 7 seaplanes
Complement: 218

Name	Builder	Laid down	Launched	Comp	Fate
VINDEX (ex-*Viking*)	Armstrong	1904	7.3.05	5.07	Returned 1920

MANXMAN *seaplane carrier*

The third of the steamers requisitioned in 1915 was the Midland Railway Co's *Manxman*, which ran between Heysham and Douglas. Bought by the Admiralty late in 1915 and converted at Chatham, with two hangars and a flying-off deck. She operated the following aircraft: Sopwith Baby floatplanes (January 1917); Sopwith Pups Nos 9913, 9943, 9945, N 6431, N 6444, N 6455 (1917); Sopwith Camels Nos N 6806, N 6807, N 6808 (1918); Short 184s Nos N 1788, N 1828, N 2803, N 2909 (1918). Commissioned 17 April 1916 and was at Rosyth with Grand Fleet to October 1917, then to Mediterranean. Paid off December 1919 and sold to Isle of Man Steam Packet Co in 1920. Served in Second World War as radar training ship.

Displacement: 2048t gross
Dimensions: 341ft oa × 43ft × *c*16ft
103.9m × 13.1m × c4.9m
Machinery: 3-shaft turbines, 6300shp = 21kts
Armament: 2–4in (10.2cm), 1–6pdr (57mm) AA, 8 seaplanes
Complement: 250

Name	Builder	Laid down	Launched	Comp	Fate
MANXMAN	Vickers	1903	15.6.04	1904	Sold 2.20

NAIRANA *seaplane carrier*

The *Nairana* had been ordered for Huddart Parker in January 1914 but had been suspended after being launched to clear the slipway in 1915. Requisitioned 27 February 1917 for completion as a carrier by the builders. She was similar to the 1915 conversions but incorporated many wartime improvements. Landplanes were accommodated forward, seaplanes aft. Three main workshops were installed, and a 95ft flying-off platform. She carried the following aircraft: Beardmore SB 3Ds Nos N 6105, N 6108, N 6110 (1917); Fairey Campanias (5, in White Sea); Sopwith Camels (2, in White Sea). Commissioned 25 August 1917 and served with Grand Fleet in 1918, then White Sea, Archangel in 1919. Sold 1920 to Tasmanian Steamship Co.

Displacement: 3070t normal; 3547t gross
Dimensions: 352ft oa × 45ft 6in × 14ft
107.3m × 13.9m × 4.3m
Machinery: 2-shaft Parsons geared turbines, 6 Babcock & Wilcox boilers, 6300shp = 20kts. Coal 293t
Armament: 2–12pdr (76mm), 2–12pdr (76mm) AA, 7 seaplanes and landplanes
Complement: 278

Name	Builder	Laid down	Launched	Comp	Fate
NAIRANA	Denny	1914	21.6.15	8.17	Sold 1920

VINDICTIVE *aircraft carrier*

In August 1917 it was decided to modify one of the new *Cavendish* class cruisers to carry 6 folding seaplanes, partly because opinion was divided as to the merits of the *Hermes* design. Being very similar in dimensions the cruiser would provide comparable results, and at the same time if unsuccessful could be reconverted to a cruiser. She was given a box hangar in place of 'B' gun, with a roof long enough (78ft long) to allow aircraft to fly off it. As in the *Furious'* second conversion an 'alighting' deck was built on abaft the funnels, 193ft × 57ft, extending as far back as No 7 gun (the wing 7.5in guns were left in place). A gangway about 8ft wide permitted aircraft to be moved along the port side between the flying-on deck and the hangar. Considerable modifications were needed between decks to handle fuel stowage, workshops and accommodation for flying personnel etc. To compensate for additional topweight she was given deeper 'bulges'. Surprisingly the presence of two funnels on the centreline did not make for a difficult landing when it was attempted, but the experiment was not repeated.

Commissioned in October 1918 for Flying Squadron, Grand Fleet. Sent to Baltic 1919 and on 6 July ran aground in Biorko Sound. She sustained serious damage to bottom plating and frames, and 2200t of gear had to be removed to refloat her. Repaired at Portsmouth August 1919–March 1920, then into reserve. Trooping duties 1920–23, then paid off and converted back to a cruiser 1923–25. Served in Second World War as repair ship. Sold for BU February 1946.

Armament: 4–7.5in (19cm)/45cal Mk VI, 4–3in (76mm), 4–12pdr (76mm) AA, 6–21in (53.3cm) TT (2 sub beam, 4 aw fixed p&s), 6 aircraft
Complement: 560
Other particulars: See *Cavendish* class cruisers

Vindictive about 1919 *CPL*

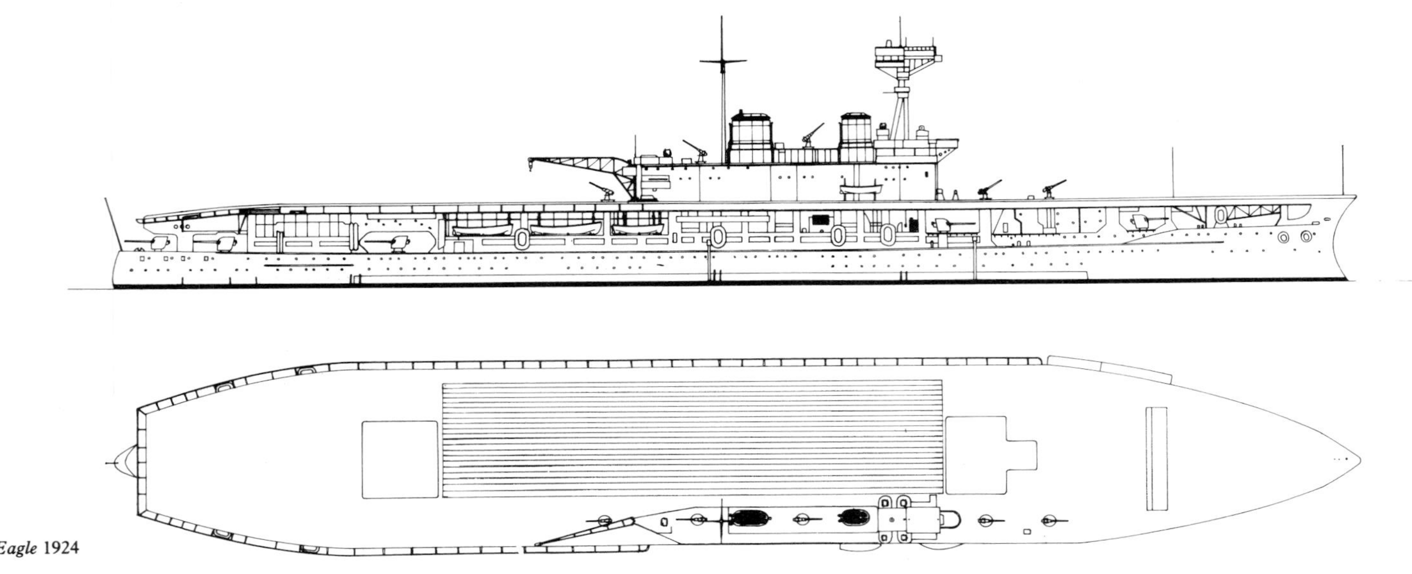

Eagle 1924

During the autumn of 1917 the problems encountered with *Furious* made it clear that a flush-decked carrier was essential. The *Argus* was in hand but was lightly armed and slow, and the C-in-C Grand Fleet demanded a larger and more battleworthy ship. The only hull which met this requirement was the incomplete Chilean battleship *Almirante Cochrane*. She was virtually complete to forecastle deck level, with boilers installed but no side armour. By the end of 1917 the DNC had completed plans for the re-design as a carrier, and on 28 February 1918 the ship was purchased and renamed *Eagle*. The builders promised delivery in March 1919 if given the highest priority but this was not given. The design allowed for *two* islands, p&s and each with a tripod mast. Hull stiffening was essential, and a new 4½in belt was installed before launch; in all 11,000t of armour, guns and barbettes, were exchanged for 4000t of new steel. Industrial disputes virtually stopped work from November 1918 to March 1919, but work was officially suspended by Admiralty order in October 1919 as the Board was seriously considering converting her back to a battleship for resale to Chile. However this was overruled as there was an urgent need to validate the concept of a starboard island (the double island arrangement having been discarded in March 1918) and the ship was to be used for flying trials. Approval having been given in November 1919 the builders finished the ship to the point where she could leave the yard in March 1920. However the open lift wells were plated over, only two after boilers were working and one funnel was in position and no guns were mounted. A wooden hut was erected on the 'island' as a navigation position and accommodation was provided for only 430 men.

Trials at Portsmouth were completed in April–October 1920, and she then paid off at Devonport DYd for completion (at Portsmouth March 1921–August 1922). Major changes included the conversion to oil fuel only 9–6in Mk XVII instead of 12 Mk XII, and a much longer island as a result of wind-tunnel testing. The hull was also to be bulged to a width of 105ft, making her the first RN ship which could not transit the Panama Canal. She did not go to sea until September 1923, but proved a great success in pioneering many new ideas. She served in the Second World War and was torpedoed in the Mediterranean by *U 73* in 1942 (160 killed).

EAGLE *aircraft carrier*

Displacement: 21,630t normal; 26,000t deep load

Dimensions: 667ft 6in oa × 94ft × 24ft 8in
203.5m × 28.7m × 7.5m

Machinery: 4-shaft Brown-Curtis geared turbines, 32 Yarrow boilers, 50,000shp = 22½kts. Coal 3200t, oil 1750t

Armour: Belt 4½in–1in (115mm–25mm), bulkheads 4in (100mm), decks 1½in–1in (40mm–24mm), gunshields 3in (75mm)

Armament: 12–6in (15.2cm)/45cal Mk XII, 4–4in (10.2cm)/45cal Mk V AA, 4–3pdr (47mm), 6–21in (53.3cm) TT (2×3), 21 aircraft

Complement: 950

Name	Builder	Laid down	Launched	Comp	Fate
EAGLE (ex-*Almirante Cochrane*)	Armstrong	20.2.13	8.6.18	4.20	Sunk 11.8.42

Eagle 1922

CPL

Hermes as completed

CPL

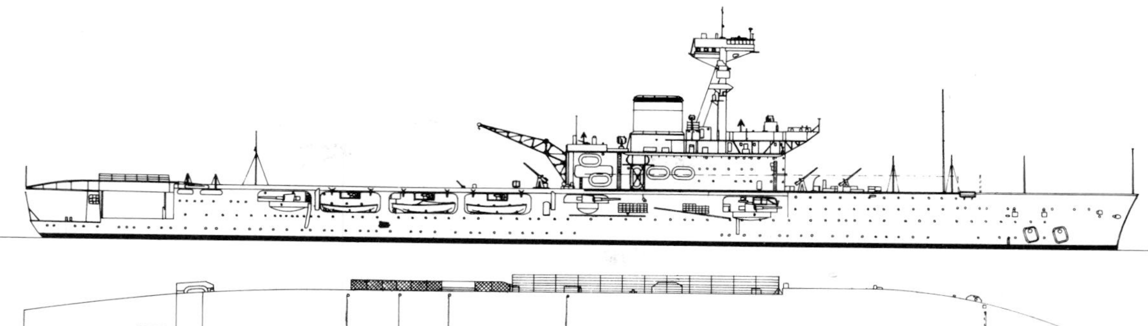

Hermes as completed

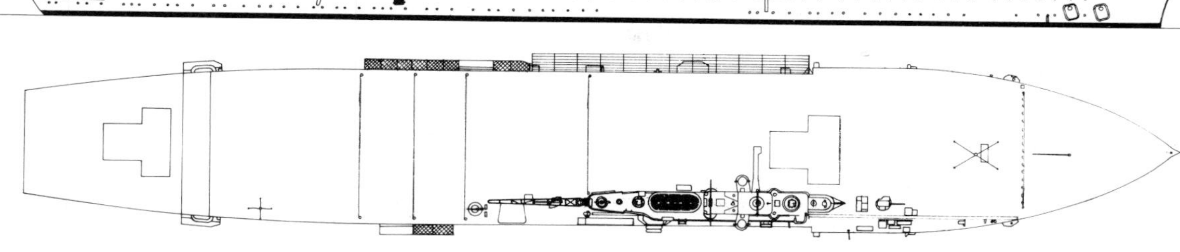

In 1917 the design of a 'proper' carrier, as against conversions, was put in hand. Although it has been claimed that the hull of a *Cavendish* class cruiser was adapted there is no resemblance between the two hulls, apart from a general similarity in the scale of protection, gunpower and machinery: standard light cruiser 2-shaft installation; 3in plating and light deck protection; 6in guns. These were, however, the logical outcome of the choice of such displacement and dimensions. To secure maximum area of flight deck the hull was given considerable flare. She proved an excellent seaboat, and her main drawback was her small aircraft complement – the result of being designed before the post-war generation of aircraft existed. The island superstructure was adopted, with a heavy tripod and director control position. In 1919 the 6in guns were exchanged for 5.5in, to ensure commonality with *Furious*. The order was placed in July 1917 but the ship was not laid down for another six months. She was launched to clear the slip and was towed to Devonport for completion in 1924. Served in Second World War and sunk by Japanese air attack off Ceylon in 1942.

HERMES *aircraft carrier*

Displacement: 10,850t normal; 13,000t deep load
Dimensions: 598ft oa × 70ft 3in × 18ft 6in
182.3m × 21.4m × 5.7m
Machinery: 2-shaft Parsons geared turbines, 6 Yarrow boilers, 40,000shp = 25kts. Oil 2000t
Armour: Belt 3in (75mm), deck 1in (25mm)
Armament: 10–6in (15.2cm)/45cal Mk XII, 4–4in (10.2cm) AA, 20 aircraft
Complement: 664

Name	Builder	Laid down	Launched	Comp	Fate
HERMES	Armstrong	15.1.18	11.9.19	2.24	Sunk 9.4.42

FURTHER CARRIER PROJECTS
Late in 1916 the Admiralty planned to build 12 '*Vindex* Type' carriers. This was replaced by 1917 plans to build two 'ocean' carriers and two North Sea/Mediterranean type. These four were confirmed by a War Cabinet order dated 8 February 1917 and orders for the large carriers were provisionally placed with Cammell Laird and Fairfield but cancelled soon after. The smaller pair were cancelled at the same time, and replaced by *Nairana* and *Pegasus*. The purchase of an unspecified hull for conversion and the building of another seaplane carrier were also cancelled in 1917, clearly as a result of conflicting priorities in the naval and mercantile building programmes.

CASPIAN SEA CONVERSIONS
During operations in support of 'White Russians' on the Caspian Sea in late 1918 and 1919 two Russian steamers were converted to small seaplane carriers:
Alader Yousannof, 1–12pdr, 2 aircraft. Commissioned January 1919 and handed over to White Russians in August 1919.
Orlionoch, 2–4in, 2 aircraft. Commissioned October 1918 and handed over to White Russians 24 August 1919.

DESTROYERS AND TORPEDO-BOATS

'TRIBAL' group *destroyers*

Displacement: *Afridi* 855t normal; *c*1000t deep load, *Cossack* 882t normal, *Ghurka* 872t normal, *Mohawk* 864t normal, *Tartar* 850t normal, *Amazon* 970t normal; *c*1200t deep load, *Saracen* 980t normal, *Crusader* 1045t normal, *Maori* 1026t normal, *Nubian* 998t normal, *Viking* 1090t normal, *Zulu* 1027t normal
Dimensions: *Afridi* 250ft pp × 24ft 6in × 10ft (average)
76.2m × 7.5m × 3.0m
Cossack, *Tartar* 207ft pp × 26ft × 10ft
82.3m × 7.9m × 3.0m
Ghurka 255ft pp × 25ft 6¾in × 10ft
77.7m × 7.8m × 3.0m
Mohawk 270ft pp × 25ft × 10ft
82.3m × 7.8m × 3.0m
Amazon 280ft 4in pp × 26ft 7½in × 10ft
85.4m × 8.1m × 3.0m
Saracen 272ft 1⁵/₈in pp × 26ft 1¹/₈in × 10ft
83.0m × 8.0m × 3.0m
Maori 279ft 11¾in pp × 27ft 1in × 10ft
85.3m × 8.3m × 3.0m
Nubian 280ft 2in pp × 26ft 8½in × 10ft
85.4m × 8.1m × 3.0m
Viking 280ft 2¾in pp × 27ft 5in × 10ft
85.4m × 8.4m × 3.0m
Zulu 280ft 1¼in pp × 27ft × 10ft
85.4m × 8.2m × 3.0m
Machinery: 3-shaft Parsons steam turbines, 5 Yarrow boilers in *Afridi*, *Ghurka*; 6 Yarrow in *Maori, Zulu, Viking;* 6 White-Foster in *Mohawk*, *Saracen;* 6 Thornycroft in *Tartar*, *Amazon* and *Nubian*; 5 Laird in *Cossack*, 14,000shp = 33kts. Oil 185t–216t
Armament: 2–4in (10.2cm)/45cal BL Mk IV (*Afridi, Cossack, Ghurka, Mohawk, Tartar* 3–12pdr/12cwt QF), 2–18in (45.7cm) TT (centreline)
Complement: 68

Name	Builder	Launched	Fate
AFRIDI	Armstrong	8.5.07	Sold 1919
COSSACK	Cammell Laird	16.2.07	Sold 1919
GHURKA	Hawthorn Leslie	29.4.07	Mined 8.2.17
MOHAWK	J S White	15.3.07	Sold 1919
TARTAR	Thornycroft	25.6.07	Sold 1921
AMAZON	Thornycroft	29.7.08	Sold 1919
SARACEN	J S White	31.3.08	Sold 1919
CRUSADER	J S White	20.3.09	Sold 1920
MAORI	Denny	24.5.09	Mined 7.5.15
NUBIAN	Thornycroft	21.4.09	Joined with *Zulu* to form *Zubian* 1916–17
VIKING	Palmer	14.9.09	Sold 1919
ZULU	Hawthorn Leslie	16.9.09	Joined with *Nubian* to form *Zubian* 1916–17

When Fisher became First Sea Lord in 1904 he quickly implemented his ideas; the future Fleet would comprise only fast capital ships and destroyers. In November 1904 he issued a directive for a new class of TBDs:
1. They must steam at 33kts for 8 hours
2. Oil fuel only
3. Armament of 2–12pdr and 5–3pdr
4. Stores for 7 days
The armament was modified to 3–12pdr/18cwt, and stores were cut to 4 days, but 33kts and oil fuel remained, and these conditions were the basis of the offer to various firms to tender. As had been the practice with earlier destroyers the builders were asked only to meet the main criteria, and were left a free hand in designing a destroyer to meet them. No two were alike, particularly as Fisher allowed only 11 days for a reply to the invitation to tender. It was not the right way to achieve success in stretching destroyer design to its limit – 7½kts more than the 'Rivers', and little experience with oil fuel. As might be expected the bids were high, and as an economy measure old 12pdr guns were substituted for the new 18cwt high-velocity gun. However the stores provision was raised to 28 days.

Five TBDs were ordered under the 1905–6 Estimates. For the following year five more were proposed (later cut to two, *Amazon* and *Saracen*). The firms were asked to include what the Board regarded as the best features from the boats already building. A similar procedure was followed with the five ordered under the 1907–8 Programme. White proposed a repeat *Saracen* with the same boilers but more powerful turbines for 15,500shp. Similarly Thornycroft proposed a repeat *Amazon*, either at a higher price or with more power. The trials were not the outstanding success for which Fisher was hoping. *Cossack* reached 33kts on a 6-hour trial but with high fuel consumption, and joined the Fleet a year late. *Afridi* needed over 21,000shp to reach her contract speed. They were not regarded as good seaboats, and compared with the 'Rivers' their endurance was miserable. *Afridi* and *Amazon* used 9½t of fuel each, raising steam for a trip from Harwich to Felixstowe and back, a distance of 6 miles in all. Each boat looked different: *Cossack* had three large funnels, *Afridi* and *Ghurka* three low; *Mohawk* had a turtleback forecastle, and with *Tartar, Saracen, Amazon, Nubian, Zulu, Crusader* and *Maori* had four funnels; while *Viking* had six (four of them paired together). *Mohawk*'s seakeeping was so poor that she was eventually rebuilt with a high forecastle. After numerous complaints the four-funnelled boats had the fore funnel raised to stop the bridges from being smoked out. In 1909 the early boats were given an extra pair of 12pdrs, and all received the new 18in Mk VII heater torpedo, with a maximum range of 3000yds at 41kts or 6000–7000yds at 31kts. The later boats were all armed with 2–4in guns from completion.

They formed the 6th Flotilla, and in February 1914 were sent to Dover having been reclassified as the 'F' class in October 1913. Their poor endurance prevented them from being used anywhere else, but with the Dover Patrol the 'Tribals' fought a hard war, losing four to enemy action, although the total loss was reduced to three by the creation of *Zubian* (see below). *Viking* mounted a 6in Mk VII BL temporarily to see if the 'Tribals' could be up-gunned, but it was removed late in 1916 after trials. Instead she and others received 2–4in QF Mk V and 2–2pdr pom-poms. *Afridi* was given 2–4.7in BL, 1–2pdr pom-pom, 1 Maxim MG and four depth-charge throwers. In September 1918 the survivors were fitted with two 14in TT at the break of the forecastle for close-range action. *Mohawk* left Dover Patrol in 1918 and was attached to 10th Submarine Flotilla to the Armistice.

Mohawk as completed — CPL

Viking was mined near the Colbart light vessel and lost her stern, but was towed into Chatham and rebuilt. *Nubian* during a night of action on 27 October 1916 tried to ram a German destroyer, but had her bow blown off and had to be run ashore on the South Foreland. After *Zulu* had her stern blown off by a mine on 8 November 1916 it was suggested that the two might be joined together. Chatham DYd achieved the task with some difficulty, not least because the hulls were not identical, but on 7 June 1917 a new destroyer called *Zubian* commissioned. She displaced 1050t and was armed with 2–4in QF Mk V, and could be distinguished by a clinker screen on the fore funnel. She is credited with sinking *UC 50* with depth-charges on 4 February 1918. *Afridi, Cossack, Mohawk, Amazon, Saracen, Viking* and *Zubian* were all sold for BU in May–December 1919, followed by *Crusader* in April 1920 and *Tartar* in May 1921.

TB 17, a Denny-built boat
NB 1/750 scale

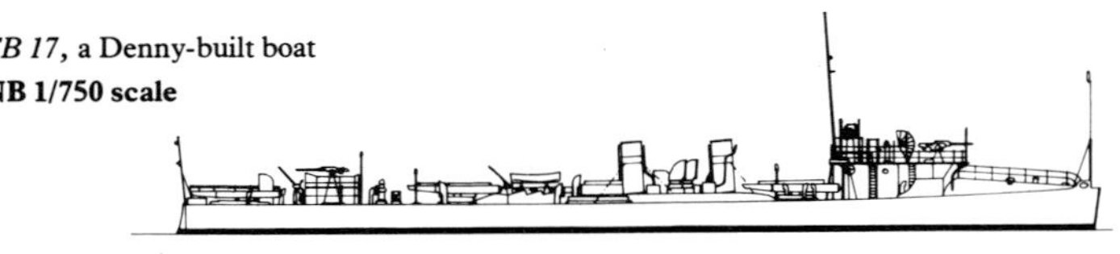

CRICKET class *coastal destroyers*

Displacement:	225t–255t normal; *c*400t deep load
Dimensions:	175–180ft oa × 17ft 6in–18ft × 6ft *53.3m–54.9m × 5.3m–5.5m × 1.8m*
Machinery:	3-shaft Parsons turbines, 2 Yarrow boilers, 3750shp = 26kts. Oil 20t–25t
Armament:	2–12pdr (76mm), 3–18in (45.7cm) TT (centreline)
Complement:	35

Name	Builder	Launched	Fate
CRICKET	J S White	23.1.06	*TB 1* (1906), sold 1920
DRAGONFLY	J S White	11.3.06	*TB 2* (1906), sold 1920
FIREFLY	J S White	1.9.06	*TB 3* (1906), sold 1920
SANDFLY	J S White	30.10.06	*TB 4* (1906), sold 1920
SPIDER	White	15.12.06	*TB 5* (1906), sold 1920
GADFLY	Thornycroft	24.6.06	*TB 6* (1906), sold 1920
GLOWWORM	Thornycroft	20.12.06	*TB 7* (1906), sold 1921
GNAT	Thornycroft	1.12.06	*TB 8* (1906), sold 1921
GRASSHOPPER	Thornycroft	18.3.07	*TB 9* (1906), sunk in collision
GREENFLY	Thornycroft	15.2.07	*TB 10* (1906), mined 10.6.15
MAYFLY	Yarrow	29.1.07	*TB 11* (1906), mined 7.3.16
MOTH	Yarrow	15.3.07	*TB 12* (1906), mined 10.6.15
TB 13	J S White	10.7.07	Sunk in collision 26.1.16
TB 14	J S White	26.9.07	Sold 1920
TB 15	J S White	19.11.07	Sold 1920
TB 16	J S White	23.12.07	Sold 1920
TB 17	Denny	21.12.07	Sold 1919
TB 18	Denny	15.2.08	Sold 1920
TB 19	Thornycroft	7.12.07	Sold 1921
TB 20	Thornycroft	21.1.08	Sold 1921
TB 21	Hawthorn Leslie	20.12.07	Sold 1920
TB 22	Hawthorn Leslie	1.2.08	Sold 1920
TB 23	Yarrow	5.12.07	Sold 1921
TB 24	Palmer	19.3.08	Sunk in collision 28.1.17
TB 25	J S White	28.8.08	Sold 1921
TB 26	J S White	28.8.08	Sold 1921
TB 27	J S White	29.9.08	Sold 1921
TB 28	J S White	29.10.08	Sold 1921
TB 29	Denny	29.9.08	Sold 1919
TB 30	Denny	29.9.08	Sold 1919
TB 31	Thornycroft	10.10.08	Sold 1921
TB 32	Thornycroft	23.11.08	Sold 1921
TB 33	Hawthorn Leslie	22.2.09	Sold 1922
TB 34	Hawthorn Leslie	22.2.09	Sold 1921
TB 35	Palmer	19.4.09	Sold 1922
TB 36	Palmer	6.5.09	Sold 1921

To supplement the 'Tribal' class destroyers the new First Sea Lord proposed to build 'coastal destroyers', driven by three-stage turbines and also using oil fuel. They were in fact very similar in size and armament to the latest series of

TB 26, a White-built boat — *By courtesy of John M Maber*

1st Class torpedo-boats *TB 98–TB 117*, and proved too frail to undertake ocean escort work. The first twelve, ordered late in 1905, were numbered *TB 1–TB 12* shortly after the trials of *Cricket* and *Dragonfly* in 1906, and re-rated as 1st Class TBs. A further twelve were ordered in November 1906 but never received names, and they were followed by another twelve in September 1907. Like all the early destroyers and TBs, there were numerous differences in appearance, but in general they had two short slim funnels and the third 18in TT was sited on the stern. The 'oily wads' were popular but lacked sufficient beam for the armament, and were too lightly built to undertake destroyers' duties. During the war they served with the North Sea Patrol Flotillas or with the Nore Local Defence Flotilla.

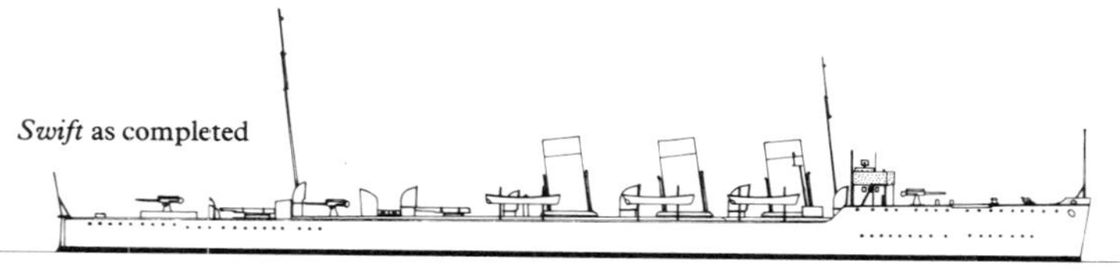

Swift as completed

SWIFT *flotilla leader*

Displacement: 2170t normal; 2390t deep load
Dimensions: 353ft 9in oa × 34ft 2in × 10ft 6in
107.8m × 10.4m × 3.2m
Machinery: 4-shaft Parsons turbines, 12 Laird boilers, 30,000shp = 35kts. Oil 282t
Armament: 4–4in (10.2cm)/45cal BL Mk VIII, 2–18in (45.7in) TT (centreline)
Complement: 126

Name	Builder	Launched	Fate
SWIFT (ex-*Flying Scud*)	Cammell Laird	7.12.07	Sold for BU BU 11.21

At Admiral Fisher's instigation the Controller asked DNC in October 1904 to produce a design for a destroyer based on the 'River' class but capable of 36kts, using turbines and oil or coal. The DNC's reply was predictable; the hull weight was inadequate, as it was no more than 20t heavier than the previous turbine-driven destroyer (HMS *Eden*) and would have less strength than the 30-knotters. In January 1905 a revised design was rushed through at two hours' notice: displacement was up to 1140t and 19,000shp would give 33½kts. To meet the First Sea Lord's request for 2½kts more a second legend was prepared shortly afterwards: 1350t and 29,000shp. The specialist firms were not happy with the invitation to tender, particularly as they were given only four weeks to produce a design. Only after considerable argument was the Cammell Laird design accepted in December 1905, but with the builders' proviso that many amendments would be needed. Guns were changed from 12pdr to 4in, sided on the forecastle and two on the centreline aft. The name *Flying Scud* was dropped in April 1906.

Trials proved that the design was over-ambitious, and despite endless changes of propellers, raising the funnels and other expedients she failed to reach her contract speed, and was good for just a fraction over 35kts. The cost was heavy oil consumption, over 27½t per hour. The absurd speeds of 38–39kts quoted in contemporary reference books can only be attributed to official lies put about at the First Sea Lord's instigation to cover up the failure of his favourite project. She was finally accepted in February 1920 after nearly two years of trials, and the Board graciously agreed to limit the penalties to £5000. In service she proved a good seaboat, but the full bow form and lack of flare made her wet. The flimsy bridge also made it hard for her to maintain full speed in a seaway, and the vast areas of steam pipes made her vulnerable to the smallest shells. Like Fisher's other favourites she was technically interesting but at £233,764 was a very expensive solution to the problem.

In 1912 she became leader or Captain (D)'s ship, 4th TBD Flotilla, and with the 'K' class became part of the Grand Fleet in August 1914. She proved too frail for service in Northern waters, and in July 1915 she had a brief refit (Egerton sweep gear added) and went south to the Dover Patrol (6th DF). In 1916 she was re-armed with a 6in BL on the forecastle in place of the 4in guns. Badly damaged in action with German destroyers in the Channel on 20 April 1917 in company with *Broke*. Repaired and rejoined Dover Patrol in July without the 6in gun (replaced by 2–4in QF Mk V). Her bridge had been enlarged and strengthened in 1916. Remained at Dover until Armistice and then paid off.

PALMER modified 30-knotter type *destroyers*

Displacement: 440t normal; *c*550t deep load
Dimensions: 215ft 6in pp × 21ft × 7ft
65.7m × 6.4m × 2.1m
Machinery: 2-shaft Parsons turbines, 4 Reed boilers, 7000shp = 26½kts. Oil ?
Armament: 3–12pdr (76mm)/12cwt, 2–18in (45.7cm) TT (centreline)
Complement: 64

Name	Builder	Launched	Fate
ALBACORE	Palmer	19.9.06	Sold for BU 8.19
BONETTA	Palmer	14.1.07	Sold for BU 6.20

Two destroyers were laid down by Palmer of Yarrow in September 1905 on speculation and completed in 1907. They were then bought in March 1909 as 'stock' boats to replace *Tiger* and *Lee*. They were in general similar to the standard 30-knotters, with turtleback forecastles, but had a more powerful armament of 3–12pdr, and had turbines and oil fuel. Listed as 'B' class from 1 October 1913. In August 1914 *Albacore* went to Scapa Flow as part of the Local Patrol Flotilla and at some time was severely damaged, losing her bow, but was rebuilt. *Bonetta* was a tender to the submarine flotillas in the Clyde and later the Tyne.

Repeat 'RIVER' class *destroyers*

Displacement: 550t light; 620t full load
Dimensions: 220ft pp × 23ft 6in × 9ft
67.1m × 7.2m × 2.7m
Machinery: 2-shaft Parsons turbines, 7000shp = 25½kts
Armament: 1–12pdr (76mm), 5–6pdr (57mm), 2–18in (45.7cm) TT (centreline)
Complement: 70

Name	Builder	Launched	Fate
STOUR	Cammell Laird	3.6.05	Sold for BU 8.19
TEST	Cammell Laird	6.5.05	Sold for BU 8.19

A number of firms had laid down 'River' class hulls in expectation of receiving orders, and when further orders were cancelled they were left on the builders' hands. Initially the Admiralty would have nothing to do with the problem, but after the loss of *Gala* and *Blackwater* it was decided to buy them at £50,000 each (as compared with a cost of £67,000–£87,000 for the original 'Rivers'). They ran trials satisfactorily in October 1909 and were bought two months later. As *Stour* and *Test* they formed part of the 'River' class (later the 'E' class). They served with the Patrol Flotillas from August 1914.

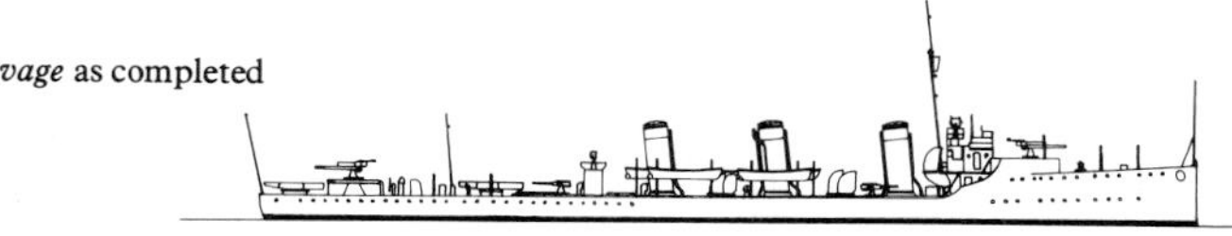

Savage as completed

BEAGLE class *destroyers*

Displacement: 945t (average) normal; *c*1100t deep load
Dimensions: 263ft 11¼in–275ft pp × 26ft 10in–28ft 1in × 8ft 6in (average)
80.4m–83.8m × 8.2m–8.6m × 2.6m
Machinery: 3-shaft Parsons turbines, 5 Yarrow (*Basilisk, Harpy* White-Forster) boilers, 14,300shp = 27kts. Coal 205t–236t
Armament: 1–4in (10.2cm)/45cal QF Mk VIII, 3–12pdr (76mm)/12cwt, 2–21in (53.3cm) TT (centreline, 4 torpedoes)
Complement: 96

Name	Builder	Launched	Fate
BEAGLE	John Brown	16.10.09	Sold for BU 11.21
BULLDOG	John Brown	13.11.09	Sold for BU 9.20
FOXHOUND	John Brown	11.12.09	Sold for BU 11.21
PINCHER	Denny	15.3.10	Wrecked 24.7.18
GRASSHOPPER	Fairfield	23.11.09	Sold for BU 11.21
MOSQUITO	Fairfield	27.1.10	Sold for BU 8.20
SCORPION	Fairfield	19.2.10	Sold for BU 10.21
SCOURGE	Hawthorn Leslie	11.2.10	Sold 5.21

Name	Builder	Launched	Fate
RACOON	Cammell Laird	15.2.10	Wrecked 9.1.18
RENARD	Cammell Laird	30.11.09	Sold for BU 8.20
WOLVERINE	Cammell Laird	15.1.10	Sunk in collision 12.12.17
RATTLESNAKE	London & Glasgow	14.3.10	Sold for BU 5.21
NAUTILUS	Thames Iron Works	30.3.10	Renamed *Grampus* 16.12.12, sold for BU 9.20
SAVAGE	Thornycroft	10.3.10	Sold for BU 5.21
BASILISK	J S White	9.2.10	Sold for BU 11.21
HARPY	J S White	27.11.09	Sold for BU 11.21

For the destroyers of the 1908–09 Programme the Admiralty decided against a repetition of the 'Tribals', partly because of their excessive cost but also because of their frailty. There was also a strong feeling against using oil fuel, which was then difficult to obtain. These arguments were reinforced by a report that a new German destroyer *G 137* had reached a mean speed of just over 33kts on a displacement of 372t for 4 hours. Understandably there was consternation at a coal-burner achieving the same speed as the oil-burning 'Tribals'. A sketch design was prepared in June 1908, but oil fuel was immediately deleted, and the final design was approved the following month. After orders had been placed a 4in Mk VIII was substituted for the 2–12pdr/12cwt mounted side-by-side on the forecastle. The new RGF Mk VIII 21in torpedo with the Hardcastle heater was adopted in this class. It ran at 50kts for 1000yds or 12,000yds at 30kts. A major improvement was the siting of the forecastle gun on a raised platform, but the after TT was frequently unusable right aft over the rudder (during the war it was replaced by a 3pdr AA gun in some boats). Like the 'Rivers' the *Beagle*s sacrificed nominal speed for a more realistic sea speed. In trials against the 'Tribals' they repeatedly showed superior endurance. Designated the 'G' class from October 1913.

They formed the 1st Destroyer Flotilla on completion in April-October 1910. In 1911 they became 5th DF and were sent to the Mediterranean, where they were at the outbreak of war. Six were recalled to Home waters late in 1914 but were then sent to the Dardanelles, where they were used temporarily as minesweepers. Recalled to Home waters late 1917.

Huon, Australian 'I' class *Vic Jeffery Collection*

ACORN class *destroyers*

Displacement: 772t normal; 970t deep load
Dimensions: 246ft oa × 25ft 3in–25ft 5½in × 8ft 6in deep
75.0m × 7.7m–7.8m × 2.6m
Machinery: 3-shaft Parsons (*Brisk* 2-shaft Brown-Curtis) turbines, 4 Yarrow (*Redpole, Rifleman, Ruby* White-Forster) boilers, 13,500shp = 27kts. Oil 170t
Armament: 2–4in (10.2cm) BL Mk VIII, 2–12pdr (76mm)/12cwt, 2–21in (53.3cm) (centreline)
Complement: 72

Name	Builder	Launched	Fate
ACORN	John Brown	1.7.10	Sold 11.21
ALARM	John Brown	29.8.10	Sold for BU 5.21
BRISK	John Brown	20.9.10	Sold 11.21
SHELDRAKE	Denny	18.1.11	Sold for BU 5.21
STAUNCH	Denny	29.10.10	Torpedoed 11.11.17
CAMELEON	Fairfield	1.6.10	Sold 12.21
COMET	Fairfield	23.6.10	Torpedoed 6.8.18
GOLDFINCH	Fairfield	12.7.10	Wrecked 19.2.15, wreck BU 4.19
NEMESIS	Hawthorn Leslie	9.8.10	To Japan 6.17–1919, sold for BU 11.21
NEREIDE	Hawthorn Leslie	6.9.10	Sold 12.21
NYMPHE	Hawthorn Leslie	31.1.11	Sold for BU 5.21
FURY	Inglis	25.4.11	Sold 11.21
HOPE	Swan Hunter	6.9.10	Sold for BU 2.20
LARNE	Thornycroft	23.8.10	Sold for BU 5.21
LYRA	Thornycroft	4.10.10	Sold for BU 5.21
MARTIN	Thornycroft	15.12.10	Sold for BU 8.20
MINSTREL	Thornycroft	2.2.11	To Japan 6.17–1919, sold for BU 12.21
REDPOLE	J S White	24.6.10	Sold for BU 5.21
RIFLEMAN	J S White	22.8.10	Sold for BU 5.21
RUBY	J S White	4.11.10	Sold for BU 5.21

For the 1909–10 Programme there was a reversion to oil fuel, but speed was to be the same as the *Beagle*s. For the first time a standard Admiralty design was the basis, enabling a larger number of firms to tender for contracts. The original design had three short funnels to reduce the silhouette but the fore funnel was raised during building; the armament was also increased from 3/4–12 pdr to 2–4in, one forward and one aft, with 12pdrs p–s at the break of the forecastle. The design was approved in July 1909 and the first of class, *Cameleon*, was laid down in December and completed in December 1910. The last, *Fury* was completed in February 1912 and they replaced the 'Rivers' in the 2nd Flotilla as they came into service. The 2nd DF became part of the Grand Fleet from August 1914 to the spring of 1916; the flotilla was sent to Devonport, but six were sent to the Mediterranean in 1915, followed by five more in 1916. By 1918 all the survivors were in the Mediterranean, and they had received a 3pdr AA gun and depth-charges. Reclassified as the 'H' class from October 1913.

Sheldrake during the war *CPL*

Admiralty 'I' class design

ACHERON class *destroyers*

Displacement: 778t legend; *c*990t deep load
Dimensions: 246ft oa × 25ft 8in × 9ft
75.0m × 7.8m × 2.7m
Machinery: 3-shaft Parsons turbines, 3 Yarrow boilers, 13,500shp = 27kts. Oil 178t (Yarrow 'specials' 16,000shp = 28kts; Thornycroft 'specials' 15,500shp = 29kts; *Firedrake* type 20,000shp = 32kts; White-Forster boilers in *Ferret, Forester*)
Armament: As *Acorn* class (3–18in TT in Australian 'specials')
Complement: 70

Name	Builder	Launched	Fate
Admiralty design			
GOSHAWK	Beardmore	18.10.11	Sold 11.21
HIND	John Brown	28.7.11	Sold 5.21
HORNET	John Brown	20.12.11	Sold 5.21
HYDRA	John Brown	19.2.12	Sold 5.21
DEFENDER	Denny	30.8.11	Sold 11.21
DRUID	Denny	4.12.11	Sold 5.21
SANDFLY	Swan Hunter	26.7.11	Sold for BU 5.21
JACKAL	Hawthorn Leslie	9.9.11	Sold for BU 9.20
TIGRESS	Hawthorn Leslie	20.12.11	Sold 5.21
LAPWING	Cammell Laird	29.7.11	Sold for BU 10.21
LIZARD	Cammell Laird	10.10.11	Sold 11.21
PHOENIX	Vickers	9.10.11	Torpedoed 14.5.18
FERRET	J S White	12.4.11	Sold 5.21
FORESTER	J S White	1.6.11	Sold 11.21
Yarrow 'specials'			
ARCHER	Yarrow	21.10.11	Sold 5.21
ATTACK	Yarrow	12.12.11	Mined 30.12.17
Thornycroft 'specials'			
ACHERON	Thornycroft	26.7.11	Sold 5.21
ARIEL	Thornycroft	26.9.11	Mined 2.8.18
Parsons 'specials'			
BADGER	Denny	11.7.11	Sold 5.21
BEAVER	Denny	6.10.11	Sold 5.21
Firedrake group of Yarrow 'specials'			
FIREDRAKE	Yarrow	9.4.12	Sold for BU 10.21
LURCHER	Yarrow	1.6.12	Sold for BU 6.22
OAK	Yarrow	5.9.12	Sold for BU 5.21
Australian type			
PARRAMATTA	Fairfield	9.2.10	BU 1929
WARREGO	Fairfield/ Cockatoo DYd	4.4.11	Hulked 1929, sank 22.7.31
YARRA	Denny	8.4.10	BU 1929
HUON (ex-*Derwent*)	Cockatoo DYd	19.12.14	Sunk as target 9.4.30
SWAN	Cockatoo DYd	11.12.15	BU 9.29
TORRENS	Cockatoo DYd	28.8.15	Sunk as target 24.11.30

The 20 destroyers in the 1910–11 Programme were to be repeats of the *Acorns*, but 6 'specials' were included to give the specialist firms a chance to improve performance. To try to match the latest German destroyers Yarrow's were given an order for 3 more, with a free hand to increase length and power. They were very similar to the standard boats but had more rake to the funnels and masts. The layout was identical to the *Acorns* but had two level-topped funnels. Although the fore funnel was set back from the bridge it was still too short to avoid smoking out the compass platform, and the standard boats had the fore funnel raised from September 1916. The *RAN* ordered 3 more Yarrow 'specials', but the design was modified by Sir John Biles. They were built by other yards to the modified design, and sections for a fourth was shipped out to Australia for assembly, and two more were built locally. They resembled the standard design but had two raked funnels. All the RN boats were redesignated the 'I' class in October 1913.

The design was submitted for approval in May 1910 and the lead boat, *Ferret*, was laid down in September. She commissioned in October 1911 and the last of the class, *Beaver* was completed in November 1912. They joined the 1st Flotilla in 1911–12 and became part of the Grand Fleet from August 1914 to the spring of 1916, when they were attached to the 3rd BS. To Portsmouth spring 1917 and then the majority were sent to the Mediterranean. *Ariel, Ferret* and *Sandfly* converted to minelayers 1917 and served with 20th Flotilla. *Ariel* rammed and sank *U 12* off Aberdeen on 10 March 1915, in company with *Attack* and *Acheron*. Converted to minelayer (40 mines replacing after TT and 4in gun temporarily) in 1917 and while operating with 20th Flotilla from Immingham was mined in Heligoland Bight. *Ferret* (40 'H' type or 'M' sinkers) and *Sandfly* were also converted to minelayers.

Garland as completed

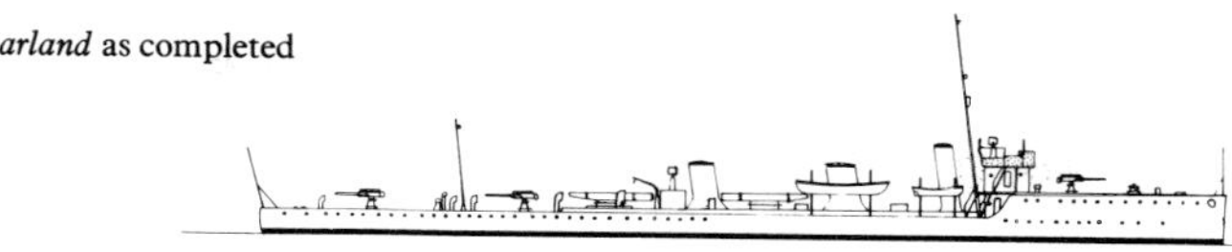

ACASTA class *destroyers*

Displacement: 1072t legend; *c*1300t deep load
Dimensions: 267ft 6in oa × 27ft × 9ft 6in
81.5m × 8.2m × 2.9m
Machinery: 2-shaft Parsons (*Garland* semi-geared; *Acasta, Achates, Ambuscade* Brown-Curtis) turbines, 4 Yarrow boilers, 24,500shp = 29kts. Oil 258t
Armament: 3–4in (10.2cm)/45cal BL Mk VIII, 2–21in (53.3cm) TT (4 torpedoes)
Complement: 73

Name	Builder	Launched	Fate
ACASTA (*King*)	John Brown	10.9.21	Sold for BU 5.21
ACHATES (*Knight*)	John Brown	14.11.12	Sold for BU 5.21
AMBUSCADE (*Keith*)	John Brown	25.1.13	Sold for BU 9.21
CHRISTOPHER (*Kite*)	Hawthorn Leslie	29.8.12	Sold for BU 5.21
COCKATRICE (*Kingfisher*)	Hawthorn Leslie	8.11.12	Sold for BU 5.21
CONTEST (*Kittiwake*)	Hawthorn Leslie	7.1.13	Torpedoed 18.9.17
SHARK (*Kestrel*)	Swan Hunter	30.7.12	Sunk 31.5.16
SPARROWHAWK (*Kingsmill*)	Swan Hunter	12.10.12	Sunk 1.6.16
SPITFIRE (*Keppel*)	Swan Hunter	23.12.12	Sold for BU 5.21
LYNX (*Koodoo*)	London & Glasgow	20.3.13	Mined 9.8.15
MIDGE (*Keitloa*)	London & Glasgow	22.5.13	Sold for BU 11.21
OWL (*Killer*)	London & Glasgow	7.7.13	Sold for BU 11.21
Thornycroft 'specials'			
HARDY (*Kelpie*)	Thornycroft	10.10.13	Sold for BU 5.21
PARAGON (*Katrine*)	Thornycroft	21.2.13	Torpedoed 18.3.17
PORPOISE (*Kennington*)	Thornycroft	7.7.13	Sold to Brazil 3.20
UNITY (*Kinsale*)	Thornycroft	18.9.13	Sold for BU 10.22
VICTOR (*Kingston*)	Thornycroft	28.11.13	Sold 1.23
Denny 'special'			
ARDENT (*Kenric*)	Denny	8.9.13	Sunk 1.6.16
Fairfield 'special'			
FORTUNE	Fairfield	17.3.13	Sunk 31.5.16
Parsons 'special'			
GARLAND (*Kenwulf*)	Cammell Laird	23.4.13	Sold for BU 9.21

The 1911–12 Programme destroyers were an expansion of the *Acherons*, but for the first time the 12pdr gun was dropped, being too light to inflict serious damage. A uniform armament of 4in was no more expensive in cost or weight. It had been hoped to raise speed to 32kts but E-in-C felt that this might be beyond some builders. It was also felt that many of the problems encountered in recent years had been through asking for too high a speed on a small displacement, so the requirement for 29kts was a reasonable compromise. The selection of names had been made before the first boat, *Shark*, was lauched in July 1912, but in 1913 it was decided to switch to alphabetical class-names, with each boat in the class having the same initial letter. It was proposed to rename all the older destroyers, and the 'K' names given in the table were allotted to the *Acastas*, but in accordance with a long-held superstition against changing a ship's name after her launch, they were never used, and the ships retained the original names.

Although the policy of building to a standard Admiralty design was continued several novel features were tried in the 'K' class. *Fortune* was given a clipper bow and had the second 4in gun on a platform between No 2 and No 3 funnels, a layout which would be continued in the 'L' class. In *Ardent* Denny Bros were allowed to try out their system of longitudinal framing, which gave much greater hull-strength while keeping weight down. She had only two funnels. With *Hardy* an attempt was made to install the first high-speed diesel engine in a destroyer. An 1800bhp Sulzer diesel was to be installed on a centre shaft, but when it became clear that it would not be ready the ship was accepted without diesels. *Garland* was given semi-geared turbines. Although speed and seakeeping were an improvement over the *Acorn* and *Acheron* classes their wide turning circle was a disappointment. This was cured by altering the rudder, cutting the diameter from nearly 1000yds to 700yds.

They joined the 4th Flotilla (led by *Swift*) on completion between November 1912 and June 1914 and joined the Grand Fleet on the outbreak of war. In the late summer of 1916 the flotilla moved to the Humber, then to Portsmouth at the end of the year, and to Devonport in spring 1917. At Portsmouth some boats joined the 6th DF and some were detached to the Dover Patrol. *Ardent* was sunk at Jutland; *Contest* was torpedoed by a U-boat in the Channel; *Lynx* was mined in the Moray Firth. *Paragon* was sunk by a German destroyer torpedo in a night action in the Straits of Dover. *Porpoise* was sold to Thornycroft in March 1920 to be refitted and resold to Brazil as *Alexandrino Dealenca*; renamed *Maranhao* 1927. *Shark* was sunk by gunfire and torpedo during daylight action at Jutland; *Sparrowhawk* collided with *Broke* at Jutland and had to be sunk by gunfire.

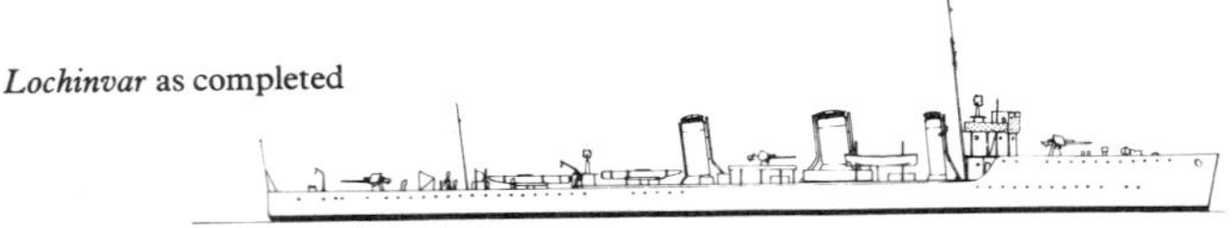

Lochinvar as completed

LAFOREY class *destroyers*

Displacement: 965t–1010t (normal); 1150t–1300t (deep load)

Dimensions: 268ft 10in oa × 27ft 8in × 10ft 6in
81.9m × 8.4m × 3.2m

Machinery: 2-shaft Parsons turbines (Brown-Curtis in Fairfield and Yarrow boats; all-geared turbines in *Leonidas* and *Lucifer*), 4 Yarrow (3 White-Forster in *Laurel* and *Liberty*; 3 Yarrow in Yarrow boats) boilers, 24,500shp = 29kts. Oil 268t

Armament: 3–4in (10.2cm)/45cal QF Mk IV, 1–.303in Maxim MG, 4–21in (53.3cm) TT (2×2; 4 torpedoes)

Complement: 73

Name	Builder	Launched	Fate
LLEWELLYN (ex-*Picton*)	Beardmore	30.10.13	Sold for BU 3.22
LENNOX (ex-*Portia*)	Beardmore	17.3.14	Sold for BU 10.21
LOYAL (ex-*Orlando*)	Denny	11.11.13	Sold for BU 11.21
LEGION (ex-*Viola*)	Denny	3.2.14	Sold for BU 5.21
LAFOREY (ex-*Florizel*)	Fairfield	28.3.13	Mined 25.3.17
LAWFORD (ex-*Ivanhoe*)	Fairfield	30.10.13	Sold for BU 8.22
LOUIS (ex-*Talisman*)	Fairfield	30.12.13	Wrecked 31.10.15
LYDIARD (ex-*Waverley*)	Fairfield	26.2.14	Sold for BU 11.21
LAERTES (ex-*Sarpedon*)	Swan Hunter	5.6.13	Sold 12.21
LYSANDER (ex-*Ulysses*)	Swan Hunter	18.8.13	Sold 6.22
LANCE (ex-*Daring*)	Thornycroft	25.2.14	Sold for BU 11.21
LOOKOUT (ex-*Dragon*)	Thornycroft	27.4.14	Sold 8.22
White 2-funnelled type			
LAUREL (ex-*Redgauntlet*)	J S White	6.5.13	Sold for BU 11.21
LIBERTY (ex-*Rosalind*)	J S White	15.9.13	Sold for BU 11.21
Yarrow 2-funnelled type			
LARK (ex-*Haughty*)	Yarrow	26.5.13	Sold 1.23
LANDRAIL (ex-*Hotspur*)	Yarrow	7.2.14	Sold for BU 12.21
LAVEROCK (ex-*Hereward*)	Yarrow	19.11.13	Sold for BU 5.21
LINNET (ex-*Havock*)	Yarrow	16.8.13	Sold 11.21
War emergency repeat 'L' class			
LOCHINVAR (ex-*Malice*)	Beardmore	9.10.15	Sold 11.21
LASSOO (ex-*Magic*)	Beardmore	24.8.15	Mined 13.8.16
Parsons 'specials'			
LEONIDAS (ex-*Rob Roy*)	Palmers	30.10.13	Sold for BU 5.21
LUCIFER (ex-*Rocket*)	Palmers	29.12.13	Sold 12.21

Laurel as completed — CPL

The step-by-step improvements in previous designs showed to good advantage in the destroyers of the 1912–13 Programme. Although originally given Shakespearian and Waverley Novel names they were all given 'L' names by Admiralty order of 30 September 1913, thus becoming the first alphabetical class under the new organisation. After some discussion about the possbility of finding a design cheaper than the *Acorns*, in January 1912 the Controller issued a fresh Staff Requirement for a twin-screw TBD with 24,500shp, 3–4in semi-automatic guns, two twin torpedo-tubes and three boilers. Following the success of the semi-geared turbines in *Badger* and *Beaver* (*Garland* had not been laid down) two, *Leonidas* and *Lucifer*, were to have 'all-geared' turbines. Frahm anti-rolling tanks were also approved.

As designed the 'Ls' had short level funnels like the *Acherons* but height was raised to 20ft during construction. The White and Yarrow boats were two-funnelled but the rest had three funnels. As built all were fitted to stow and lay 4 Vickers Elia Mk IV mines, but there is no record of them laying these mines, and when the Elia Mk IV was replaced by the 'H' type in 1917 there was no reason to retain the capability. *Lawford* and *Legion* were converted to lay 'H' mines in 1917. Two additional boats were ordered from Beardmore late in 1914. They were intended to be extra 'M' class vessels but to save time the builders were ordered to repeat the design of the two 'L's already in hand, and they were renamed *Lassoo* and *Lochinvar* in February 1915.

As they were completed they joined the 3rd DF at Harwich, and in 1917 the survivors were dispersed to Devonport and Portsmouth for convoy escort duties. Four were sent to the Mediterranean in 1915 and the survivors were recalled in 1916. *Lance* fired first shot of the war at sea, when *Amphion* and her flotilla intercepted the minelayer *Konigin Luise* off Harwich on 5 August 1914 (13hrs after the declaration of war). *Landrail* was very badly damaged in collision with the light cruiser *Undaunted*, August 1915, losing her bow; towed home stern first by *Mentor* and took five weeks to repair. *Legion, Undaunted, Loyal, Lennox* and *Lance* sank German torpedo-boats *S 115, S 117, S 118* and *S 119* off the Texel on 17 October 1914. *Legion* was converted to a minelayer during her 6-month repair following mine damage in November 1916. *Louis* was in the Mediterranean from early 1915, and was wrecked in Suvla Bay, being subsequently destroyed by Turkish shellfire.

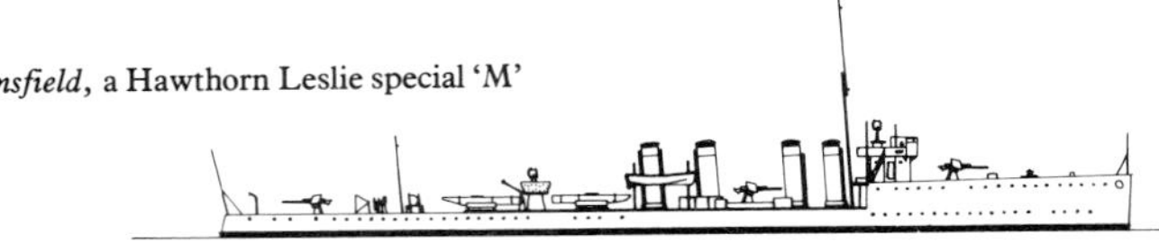

Mansfield, a Hawthorn Leslie special 'M'

'M' class *destroyers*

Displacement: Admiralty design 900t legend; *c*1100t deep load
Hawthorn Leslie boats 1055t legend
Thornycroft boats 980t legend
Yarrow boats 850t normal; 990t deep load

Dimensions: Admiralty design 273ft 4in oa × 26ft 8in × 8ft 6in
83.3m × 8.1m × 2.6m
Hawthorn Leslie boats 271ft 6in oa × 27ft × 10ft 6in
82.8m × 8.2m × 3.2m
Thornycroft boats 274ft 3in oa × 27ft 3in × 10ft
83.6m × 8.3m × 3.0m
Yarrow boats 269ft 6in oa × 25ft 7½in × 9ft 6in
82.1m × 7.8m × 2.9m

Machinery: Admiralty boats 3-shaft Parsons (*Milne, Moorsom, Morris* Brown-Curtis) turbines, 4 Yarrow boilers, 25,000shp = 34kts. Oil 278t
Hawthorn Leslie boats 2-shaft Parsons independent reduction turbines, 4 Yarrow boilers, 27,000shp = 35kts
Thornycroft boats 2-shaft Parsons independent reduction turbines, 4 Yarrow boilers, 26,500shp = 35kts
Yarrow boats 2-shaft Brown-Curtis turbines, 23,000shp = 35kts

Armament: 3–4in (10.2cm)/45cal QF Mk IV, 2–1pdr pom-pom, 4–21in (53.3cm) TT (2×2; 4 torpedoes)

Complement: Admiralty 80, Hawthorn Leslie 76, Thornycroft 82, Yarrow 79

Name	Builder	Launched	Fate
Admiralty design			
MATCHLESS	Swan Hunter	5.10.14	Sold for BU 10.21
MURRAY	Palmers	6.8.14	Sold 5.21
MYNGS	Palmer	24.9.14	Sold 5.21
MILNE	John Brown	5.10.14	Sold for BU 9.21
MOORSOM	John Brown	20.12.14	Sold for BU 11.21

Name	Builder	Launched	Fate
MORRIS	John Brown	19.11.14	Sold for BU 11.21
Hawthorn Leslie 'specials' (4-funnelled)			
MANSFIELD	Hawthorn Leslie	3.12.14	Sold 10.21
MENTOR	Hawthorn Leslie	21.8.14	Sold for BU 5.21
Thornycroft 'specials'			
MASTIFF	Thornycroft	5.9.14	Sold for BU 5.21
METEOR	Thornycroft	24.7.14	Sold for BU 5.21
Yarrow 'specials' (2-funnelled)			
MIRANDA	Yarrow	27.5.14	Sold for BU 10.21
MINOS	Yarrow	6.8.14	Sold for BU 8.20
MANLY	Yarrow	12.10.14	Sold 10.21
Unallocated orders			
MARKSMAN	–	–	Cancelled 1914
MENACE	–	–	Cancelled 1914
MONITOR	–	–	Cancelled 1914

The boats of the 1913–14 Programme were improved 'L's, with 6kts more speed, at the insistence of the new First Lord of the Admiralty, Winston Churchill. For the first time speed of delivery was all-important, as the Admiralty clearly recognised that war was imminent, and Thornycroft, White and Yarrow were asked to accept two orders each, with the first payment to be made in April 1913, before contracts were signed (delivery was to be in March 1914). Thus when in March 1913 the Controller issued invitations to tender, the three boats building at Thornycroft and the two each at Yarrow and Hawthorn Leslie were 'bought' as if they had been built on speculation. Two orders planned for J S White were not placed, however, and Thornycroft were given a third order. Geared turbines were favoured, but the E-in-C wished to wait until the trials results with *Leonidas* and *Lucifer* were available before making the switch to the 'all-geared' type. Similarly longitudinal framing would be examined after *Ardent* had finished her trials.

Excluding the seven 'stock' boats already building, the final order was for only six, three from John Brown, two from Palmer and one from Swan Hunter, making 13 instead of the normal 20 for a full flotilla. The reason was that money for the *Arethusa* class light cruisers had used up funds in the current Estimates – a decision which was justified on the dubious grounds that they would take over many of the duties of destroyers. The lead boat, *Miranda* was begun in October 1912 and completed in August 1914, followed by her sisters in October–November. She made 33kts in deep load condition, whereas *Minos* in light condition made 36kts on a 6-hour trial. The 'M' class were generally similar to the 'L' class in appearance, but with the midships gun on the deck, not on a 'bandstand' platform. The Yarrow boats had two funnels and the bridge carried well back from the forecastle. The Hawthorn Leslie boats had four funnels. The Admiralty boats had short funnels, and the Thornycroft boats could be distinguished by three taller flat-sided funnels. The design proved most successful and, with only slight modifications, was used for mass-production in the war which followed. They served with the Harwich Force 1914–17, four being lent to Dover Patrol 1916–17; most went to Mediterranean 1917–18, then returned to Grand Fleet or Dover Patrol. In spite of serving for less than four years they were worn out, and were soon laid up in Reserve. *Meteor* was converted to a minelayer 1917 for service with 20th Flotilla. *Marksman, Menace* and *Monitor* were projected for the 1914–15 Programme but were cancelled in favour of two *Lightfoot* class leaders.

Tipperary as completed — *CPL*

Marksman 1919

Abdiel 1916

LIGHTFOOT class *flotilla leaders*

Displacement:	1440t legend; *c*1700t deep load
Dimensions:	324ft 10in oa × 31ft 9in × 12ft *99.0m × 9.7m × 3.7m*
Machinery:	3-shaft Parsons (Brown-Curtis in *Marksman* and *Nimrod*) turbines, 4 Yarrow (White-Forster in *Lightfoot*) boilers, 36,000shp = 34½kts. Oil 515t
Armament:	4–4in (10.2cm)/45cal QF Mk IV, 2–1pdr or 1½pdr (20mm), 4–12in (53.3cm) TT (2×2; 4 torpedoes)
Complement:	104

Name	Builder	Launched	Fate
KEMPENFELT	Cammell Laird	1.5.15	Sold for BU 5.21
LIGHTFOOT	J S White	28.5.15	Sold for BU 5.21
MARKSMAN	Hawthorn Leslie	28.4.15	Sold for BU 11.21
NIMROD	Denny	12.4.15	Sold for BU 11.26
ABDIEL (ex-*Ithuriel*)	Cammell Laird	12.10.15	Sold for BU 1936
GABRIEL (ex-*Abdiel*)	Cammell Laird	23.12.15	Sold for BU 5.21
ITHURIEL (ex-*Gabriel*)	Cammell Laird	8.3.16	Sold for BU 11.21

Experience with the *Swift* and the comparatively low speed of the scout cruisers confirmed the need for a new type of flotilla leader, based on the destroyer. A conference of the War Staff in October 1913 proposed that a 'Tribal' class (*Crusader, Maori* or *Zulu*, or *Swift* herself) should be given Poulsen long-range wireless (150m range) and have the bridge enlarged to accommodate the additional Captain (D)'s staff. However the Controller instructed the DNC to prepare a legend for a leader not exceeding 1800t, a speed of 33–34kts, 4–4in guns and 4 'anti-airship pom-poms' etc. Accommodation would include Captain (D), an extra Lieutenat, a WO for signal duties and 8 extra staff. The design had machinery similar to the 'M' class. Although three were proposed, only two were approved: one each for the 1st and 3rd DF, a scout cruiser for the slower *Acorn* class in the 2nd DF, and *Swift* to lead 4th DF, all forming part of 1st Fleet. The design was approved in December 1913 and it was suggested that their names should conform to the new initial letter of the flotilla which they would lead, hence the names *Lightfoot* and *Marksman*. In April 1914 tenders were put out for two more, *Kempenfelt* and *Nimrod*, to be built under the 1914–15 Estimates. In August 1914 the 12–1pdr out of the total ordered for the 13 'M' class and the first two leaders were transferred to the Army for use in France, so the design was altered to 1½pdr guns instead, but in February 1915 Vickers 2pdr pom-poms were substituted.

The four leaders were successful, providing sufficient extra space for the administrative and signal staff essential to the running of a large flotilla. In November 1914 three more were ordered, but this time they were given the names of angels in Milton's *Paradise Lost*. One of them, *Gabriel* was selected in August 1915 for conversion to a minelayer but later the same month *Abdiel* took her place. She was given stowage for 80 mines, and when loaded sacrificed both sets of TT and Nos 3 and 4 guns. In mid-1918 the *Gabriel* was also converted to a minelayer, but only carried 60 mines. In 1917 *Lightfoot* was given two 14in TT for short-range 'cold' torpedoes for night action, p&s under the midships 'bandstand', and *Nimrod* was similarly converted.

FAULKNOR class *flotilla leaders*

Displacement:	1610t legend; 2000t deep load
Dimensions:	330ft 10in oa × 32ft 6in × 11ft 7in *100.8m × 9.9m × 3.5m*
Machinery:	3-shaft Parsons IR turbines, 6 White-Forster boilers, 30,000shp = 31kts. Coal 433t/Oil 83t
Armament:	6–4in (10.2cm)/45cal Mk VI, 1-1½pdr (20mm), 2–.303in Maxim MGs, 4–21in (53.3cm) TT (beam p&s; *Faulknor, Broke* 4×1, *Botha, Tipperary* 2×2)
Complement:	197

Name	Builder	Launched	Fate
BOTHA (ex-*Almirante Williams Rebolledo*)	J S White	2.12.14	To Chile 1920
BROKE (ex-*Almirante Goni*)	J S White	25.5.14	To Chile 1920
FAULKNOR (ex-*Almirante Simpson*)	J S White	26.2.14	To Chile 1920
TIPPERARY (ex-*Almirante Riveros*)	J S White	5.3.15	Sunk 1.6.16

Plans to use the new *Arethusa* class light cruisers as flotilla leaders were quickly dropped as the Grand Fleet was so short of scouting cruisers. There were, however, four big destroyers out of a batch of six ordered from J S White in Cowes by Chile in 1912. These were bought immediately on the outbreak of war; two were well advanced and the other two were on the stocks. The second pair, named *Botha* and *Tipperary* were bought in September 1914. The distribution of armament was altered; twin 21in TT instead of four singles, and single 4in guns on the forecastle and quarterdeck. In all four the 1½pdr guns were replaced by 2pdr Mk I pom-poms. In March 1918 *Broke* was rearmed with 2–4.7in (12cm)/45cal BL, one forward and one aft, retaining the 4in guns on either side of the bridge (a request for 6–4.7in BL had to be turned down because of the weight); the remaining two ships were similarly rearmed by the Armistice. *Tipperary* was sunk by gunfire at Jutland; the remaining three were refitted and sold back to Chile in May 1920, as *Almirante Uribe* (ex-*Broke*), *Almirante Williams* (ex-*Botha*) and *Almirante Riveros* (ex-*Faulknor*)

Melampus as completed

MEDEA class *destroyers*

Displacement: 1007t–1040t normal; *c*1200t deep load
Dimensions: As Admiralty 'M' class
Machinery: 3-shaft Brown-Curtis turbines, 3 Yarrow boilers, 25,000shp = 32kts. Oil as 'M' class
Armament: 3–4in (10.2cm)/45cal QF Mk VII, 4–21in (53.3cm) TT (2×2; 4 torpedoes)
Complement: 80

Name	Builder	Launched	Fate
MEDEA (ex-*Kriti*)	John Brown	30.1.15	Sold for BU 5.21
MEDUSA (ex-*Lesvos*)	John Brown	27.3.15	Lost 25.3.16
MELAMPUS (ex-*Chios*)	Fairfield	16.12.14	Sold for BU 9.21
MELPOMENE (ex-*Samos*)	Fairfield	1.2.15	Sold for BU 5.21

Late in 1913 four destroyers had been ordered for the Greek Navy (see light cruisers *Chester* and *Birkenhead*), and they were laid down early in 1914 as the *Kriti* and *Lesvos* (John Brown) and *Chios* and *Samos* (Fairfield). They were very similar to the Admiralty 'M' class, but had a raised fore funnel and carried the second 4in gun between No 1 and No 2 funnels. Internally they differed in having the double boiler room next to the engine room, and the accommodation was different. *Medea* was completed in June 1915 and joined 10th DF, Harwich Force. *Medusa* completed in July 1915 and joined Harwich Force; in March 1916 while screening seaplane carrier *Vindex* she was rammed by *Laverock*, and although an attempt was made to tow her home she had to be abandoned later. *Melampus* was completed in June 1915 and went to Harwich as tender to 8th S/m Flotilla. *Melpomene* completed in August 1915 and joined 10th DF, Harwich Force.

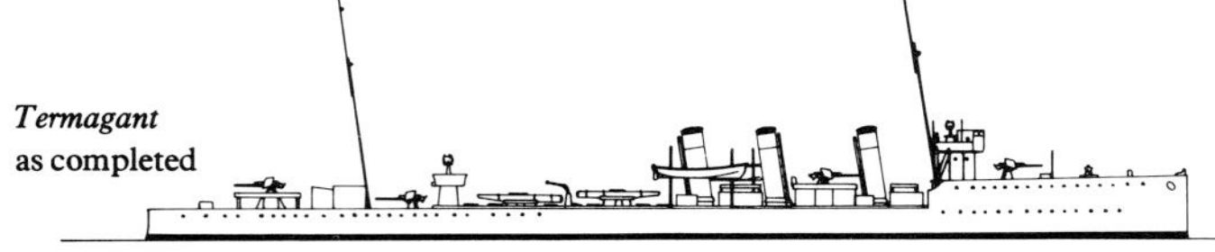
Termagant as completed

TALISMAN class *destroyers*

Displacement: 1098t normal; *c*1300t deep load
Dimensions: 309ft oa × 28ft 7in × 9ft 6in
94.2m × 8.7m × 2.9m
Machinery: 3-shaft Parsons turbines, 3 Yarrow boilers, 25,000shp = 32kts. Oil 237t
Armament: 5–4in (10.2cm)/45cal QF Mk IV, 4–21in (53.3cm) TT (2×2)
Complement: 102

Name	Builder	Launched	Fate
TALISMAN (ex-*Napier*)	Hawthorn Leslie	15.7.15	Sold for BU 4.21
TERMAGANT (ex-*Narbrough*)	Hawthorn Leslie	26.8.15	Sold for BU 5.21
TRIDENT (ex-*Offa*)	Hawthorn Leslie	20.11.15	Sold for BU 5.21
TURBULENT (ex-*Ogre*)	Hawthorn Leslie	5.1.16	Sunk 1.6.16

Although all sources, including Admiralty records, state that four destroyers were on order for Turkey in August 1914 modern historians claim that no trace of such an order exists in Turkish records (nor for the two 'E' class submarines listed later). This prompts the question of where these four destroyers originated. There are only two valid explanations: that Hawthorn Leslie had ordered material for four 'M' class hulls on speculation; or that some secret deal was still under negotiation between the British and the Turks, possibly under the aegis of the international arms dealer Sir Basil Zaharoff. However attractive this latter explanation might sound, it clashes with the known facts that the Young Turks were already heavily under German influence, and there is also the indisputable fact that no written evidence for these contracts has turned up, neither in Turkish nor British archives. The fact remains, however, that these were similar to the Greek 'M's, having the double boiler room transposed and the 4in gun between the first and second funnels, so did not conform to the Admiralty pattern. They also had two extra 4in QF Mk IV, two p&s on the forecastle, two aft and one on a centreline 'bandstand'. The original design had a pair of TT right aft, but as completed only the midships twin TT were retained, using Elswick light-pattern twin tubes. As they were intended to work with submarines they were given Poulsen long-range wireless, with tall mainmasts. Orders were placed in November 1914 and 'T' names were substituted in February 1915. *Turbulent* was completed on 12 May 1916 and was sunk in action at Jutland less than three weeks later, while serving with 10th DF, Harwich Force (cut in two by German battlecruiser, with 90 dead).

ARNO *destroyer*

Displacement: 600t normal; *c*750t deep load
Dimensions: 230ft pp × 22ft × 7ft
70.1m × 6.7m × 2.1m
Machinery: 2-shaft Parsons turbines, 4 boilers, 8000shp = 29kts. Coal ?
Armament: 4–12pdr (76mm)/50cal 18cwt, 3–18in (45.7cm) TT (2 beam, 1 centreline, 3×1; 3 torpedoes)
Complement:

Name	Builder	Launched	Fate
ARNO (ex-*Liz*)	Ansaldo, Genoa	22.12.14	Lost 23.3.18

The Italian Ansaldo shipyard was building a destroyer for the Portuguese Navy, to be called *Liz*, and for reasons which remain obscure she was bought by the Admiralty in March 1915 while fitting out at Genoa. As HMS *Arno* she was the only foreign-built warship to be purchased for the RN, and she served on escort duties in the Mediterranean after completion in June 1915. Sunk in collision with destroyer HMS *Hope* off the Dardanelles in 1918. She was generally similar to some of the 'River' class in appearance, with two tall funnels.

Arno as completed
CPL

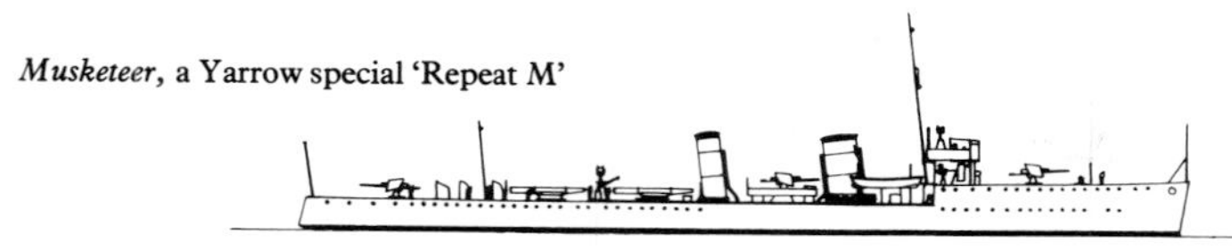
Musketeer, a Yarrow special 'Repeat M'

Repeat 'M' class *destroyers*

Displacement: Admiralty design 1025t legend; *c*1250t deep load
Thornycroft 'specials' 985t
Yarrow 'specials' 895t

Dimensions: Generally as original 'M' class but length increased 3in–4in (*7.5cm—10cm*) and beam up to 2in (5cm) in some boats, draught 8ft 6in load, 9ft 5in–9ft 7in deep
2.6m, 2.8m–2.9m

Machinery: Admiralty design 3-shaft Brown-Curtis or Parsons (geared in *Manners, Mandate, Magic, Moresby, Mary Rose, Menace*) turbines, 3 Yarrow boilers (White-Forster in J S White boats; Babcock & Wilcox in *Noble, Nizam, Nomad* and *Nonpareil*), 25,000shp = 34kts. Oil 266t
Thornycroft 'specials' 3-shaft turbines, 26,500shp = 35kts. Oil 254t
Yarrow 'specials' 2-shaft turbines, 23,000shp = 35kts. Oil 228t

Armament: As original 'M' class, but most completed with 1–2pdr (40mm) pom-pom

Complement: 80

Name	Builder	Launched	Fate
Admiralty design (1st order, 9.14)			
MONS	John Brown	1.5.15	Sold 11.21
MARNE	John Brown	29.5.15	Sold for BU 9.21
MYSTIC (ex-*Myrtle*)	Denny	26.6.15	Sold for BU 11.21
MAENAD	Denny	10.8.15	Sold for BU 9.21
MANNERS	Fairfield	15.6.15	Sold for BU 10.21
MANDATE	Fairfield	27.4.15	Sold for BU 9.21
MAGIC (ex-*Marigold*)	J S White	10.9.15	Sold for BU 9.21
MORESBY (ex-*Marlion*)	J S White	20.11.15	Sold for BU 5.21
MARMION	Swan Hunter	28.5.15	Sunk in collision 21.10.17
MARTIAL	Swan Hunter	1.7.15	Sold for BU 5.21
MARY ROSE	Swan Hunter	8.10.15	Sunk 17.10.17
MENACE	Swan Hunter	9.11.15	Sold for BU 1921
Thornycroft 'specials'			
MICHAEL	Thornycroft	19.5.15	Sold for BU 9.21
MILBROOK	Thornycroft	12.7.15	Sold for BU 9.21
MINION	Thornycroft	11.9.15	Sold for BU 11.21
MUNSTER (ex-*Monitor*)	Thornycroft	24.11.15	Sold for BU 11.21
Yarrow 'specials'			
MOON	Yarrow	23.4.15	Sold for BU 5.21
MORNING STAR	Yarrow	26.6.15	Sold 12.21
MOUNSEY	Yarrow	11.9.15	Sold for BU 11.21
MUSKETEER	Yarrow	12.11.15	Sold for BU 11.21
(2nd order, early 11.14) *Admiralty design*			
MAMELUKE	John Brown	14.8.15	Sold for BU 9.21
MARVEL	Denny	7.10.15	Sold for BU 5.21
MISCHIEF	Fairfield	12.10.15	Sold for BU 11.21
MINDFUL	Fairfield	24.8.15	Sold for BU 9.21
NONSUCH (ex-*Narcissus*)	Palmer	8.12.15	Sold for BU 5.21
NEGRO	Palmer	8.3.16	Sunk in collision 21.12.16
NESSUS	Swan Hunter	24.8.15	Sunk in collision 8.9.18

Name	Builder	Launched	Fate
Thornycroft 'specials'			
NEPEAN	Thornycroft	22.1.16	Sold for BU 11.21
NEREUS	Thornycroft	24.2.16	Sold for BU 11.21
Yarrow 'special'			
NERISSA	Yarrow	9.2.16	Sold for BU 11.21
(3rd order, late 11.14) *Admiralty design*			
NOBLE (ex-*Nisus*)	A Stephen	25.11.15	Sold for BU 11.21
NIZAM	A Stephen	6.4.16	Sold for BU 5.21
NOMAD	A Stephen	7.2.16	Sunk 31.5.16
NONPAREIL	A Stephen	16.5.16	Sold for BU 5.21
NORMAN	Palmer	20.3.16	Sold for BU 5.21
NORTHESK	Palmer	5.7.16	Sold for BU 5.21
NORTH STAR	Palmer	9.11.16	Sunk 23.4.18
NUGENT	Palmer	23.1.17	Sold for BU 5.21
OBEDIENT	Scott	6.11.15	Sold for BU 11.21
OBDURATE	Scott	21.1.16	Sold for BU 11.21
ONSLAUGHT	Fairfield	4.12.15	Sold for BU 10.21
ONSLOW	Fairfield	15.2.16	Sold for BU 10.21
OPAL	Doxford	11.9.15	Wrecked 21.1.18
OPHELIA	Doxford	13.10.15	Sold for BU 11.21
OPPORTUNE	Doxford	20.11.15	Sold for BU 12.23
ORACLE	Doxford	23.12.15	Sold for BU 10.21
ORESTES	Doxford	21.3.16	Sold for BU 10.21
ORFORD	Doxford	19.4.16	Sold for BU 10.21
ORPHEUS	Doxford	17.6.16	Sold for BU 11.21
OCTAVIA (ex-*Oryx*)	Doxford	21.6.16	Sold for BU 11.21
OSSORY	John Brown	9.10.15	Sold for BU 11.21
NESTOR	Swan Hunter	9.10.15	Sunk 31.5.16
(4th order, 2.15) *Admiralty design*			
NAPIER	John Brown	27.11.15	Sold for BU 11.21
NARBROUGH	John Brown	2.3.16	Wrecked 12.1.18
NARWHAL	Denny	30.12.15	Collision 1919, BU 1920
NICATOR	Denny	3.2.16	Sold for BU 5.21
NORSEMAN	Doxford	15.8.16	Sold for BU 5.21
OBERON	Doxford	29.9.16	Sold for BU 5.21
OBSERVER	Fairfield	1.5.16	Sold for BU 10.21
OFFA	Fairfield	7.6.16	Sold for BU 10.21
ORCADIA	Fairfield	26.7.16	Sold for BU 10.21
ORIANA	Fairfield	23.9.16	Sold for BU 10.21
ORIOLE	Palmer	31.7.16	Sold for BU 5.21
OSIRIS	Palmer	28.9.16	Sold for BU 5.21
PALADIN	Scott	27.3.16	Sold for BU 5.21
PARTHIAN	Scott	3.7.16	Sold for BU 11.21
PARTRIDGE	Swan Hunter	4.3.16	Sunk 12.12.17
PASLEY	Swan Hunter	15.4.16	Sold for BU 5.21

Offa, an Admiralty standard 'Repeat M'
CPL

Name	Builder	Launched	Fate
Thornycroft 'specials'			
PATRICIAN	Thornycroft	5.6.16	To RCN 1920, sold for BU 1929
PATRIOT	Thornycroft	20.4.16	To RCN 1920, sold for BU 1929
(5th order, 5.15) Admiralty design			
PLUCKY	Scott	21.4.16	Sold for BU 5.21
PORTIA	Scott	10.8.16	Sold for BU 5.21
PHEASANT	Fairfield	23.10.16	Mined 1.3.17
PHOEBE	Fairfield	20.11.16	Sold for BU 11.21
PIGEON	Hawthorn Leslie	3.3.16	Sold for BU 5.21
PLOVER	Hawthorn Leslie	3.3.16	Sold for BU 5.21
PENN	John Brown	8.4.16	Sold for BU 10.21
PEREGRINE	John Brown	29.5.16	Sold for BU 11.21
PELICAN	Beardmore	18.3.16	Sold for BU 11.21
PELLEW	Beardmore	8.5.16	Sold for BU 5.21
PETARD	Denny	24.3.16	Sold for BU 5.21
PEYTON	Denny	2.5.16	Sold for BU 5.21
PRINCE	A Stephen	26.7.16	Sold for BU 5.21
PYLADES	A Stephen	28.9.16	Sold for BU 5.21
MEDINA (ex-*Redmill*)	J S White	8.3.16	Sold for BU 5.21
MEDWAY (ex-*Medora*, ex-*Redwing*)	J S White	19.4.16	Sold for BU 5.21
Thornycroft 'specials'			
RAPID	Thornycroft	15.7.16	Sold for BU 4.27
READY	Thornycroft	26.8.16	Sold for BU 7.26
Yarrow 'specials'			
RELENTLESS	Yarrow	15.4.16	Sold for BU 11.26
RIVAL	Yarrow	14.6.16	Sold for BU 7.26

Twenty more 'M' class were ordered in September 1914, 16 of them to the Admiralty standard design but without the cruising turbines (to accelerate delivery – except in Fairfield, Swan Hunter and Fairfield boats). Another improvement was to put No 2 4in gun on a 'bandstand' as in the 'L' class. The doubling on the stempiece fitted as an emergency measure to the early 'M' class was now made standard to facilitate ramming of U-boats, but in the form of a single casting. The Yarrow 'specials' were similar to the *Miranda* but were 1ft longer on the waterline and had raked stems and sloping sterns. The only other variants built thereafter were Thornycroft 'specials', which resembled the Admiralty boats but had flat-sided funnels and higher freeboard. In the later Admiralty-designed boats the stem was raked and the bows were given more flare to improve seakeeping. Machinery was non-standard, with geared-turbines in a few, triple screws in most, and twin screws in some. In July 1916 the Admiralty restored order to a chaotic situation by ordering that all 3-shaft destroyers building were to be listed as Admiralty 'M' class, and future 2-shaft boats would be Admiralty 'R's; as a result *Redmill* and *Redwing* became *Medina* and *Medora* (renamed *Medway* two weeks later).

Although there were some complaints about poor finish they proved sturdy craft and gave good value in four hard years of war. Because of hard driving and particularly because their hulls had not been galvanized they were worn out by 1919 and very few survived the wholesale scrappings in 1921. In all 90 were built, 79 Admiralty boats, and 11 'specials'. All but four spent the war with the Grand Fleet flotillas. In January 1916 11th DF had 15, 12th had 5, but a year later the total had risen to 16, 18 and 25 respectively, and in addition there were 17 with 14th DF and 5 with 15th DF. Four served in Mediterranean 1917–18. *Marmion* was sunk in collision with destroyer *Tirade* off Lerwick. *Mary Rose* was sunk by the German light cruisers *Brummer* and *Bremse* in North Sea. *Negro* was sunk in the North Sea in collision with the flotilla leader *Hoste*. *Nessus* was sunk in the North Sea in collision with the cruiser *Amphitrite*. *Nomad* and *Nestor* were sunk by gunfire at Jutland. *North Star* was sunk by gunfire during the Zeebrugge Raid. *Partridge* was sunk by the gunfire of German destroyers in North Sea.

PARKER class *flotilla leaders*

Displacement:	1660t–1673t normal; *c* 1900t deep load
Dimensions:	As *Lightfoot* class
Machinery:	3-shaft Parsons IR turbines (Brown-Curtis in *Anzac*), 4 Yarrow boilers, 36,000shp = 34kts. Oil 515t
Armament:	4–4in (10.2cm)/45cal QF Mk IV, 2–2pdr (40mm) pom-poms, 4–21in TT (2×2)
Complement:	116

Name	Builder	Launched	Fate
GRENVILLE	Cammell Laird	17.6.16	Sold for BU 12.31
PARKER (ex-*Frobisher*)	Cammell Laird	19.4.16	Sold for BU 11.21
HOSTE	Cammell Laird	16.8.16	Lost 21.12.16
SAUMAREZ	Cammell Laird	14.10.16	Sold for BU 1.31
SEYMOUR	Cammell Laird	31.8.16	Sold for BU 1.30
ANZAC	Denny	11.1.17	To Australia 1919; sold for BU 8.35

Two repeat *Kempenfelt* class leaders were ordered in February 1915, *Grenville* and *Frobisher* (renamed *Parker* before launch), followed by orders for three more in July; in December 1915 a sixth was ordered from Denny Bros. Early in 1916 the C-in-C and Commodore (T) asked for modifications to future leaders, suggesting that they should have more freeboard, more guns bearing ahead and the bridge moved further aft. There was also a request for a slower roll, as the *Kempenfelts* had a very rapid period of roll. The DNC said that it would be extremely difficult to increase freeboard in most of the new leaders as frames were already being bent, but it might be feasible in *Saumarez* and *Anzac* (Nos 5 and 6), which could have 1ft higher forecastles. This was finally approved only for *Anzac*. The bridge could be moved 13ft aft by reducing the boiler rooms from three to two, allowing one 4in gun to be put on a superimposed platform in 'B' position. As the forward boiler room now had two boilers the forward uptakes were combined in one thicker funnel, which was raised to keep smoke clear of the compass platform. The new profile was a great improvement, and the *Parker* class were a great success.

Seymour was converted to a minelayer after completion. *Anzac*'s higher forecastle and squarer-section funnels made her easy to distinguish from her sisters. All were distinguishable by the thick tall fore funnel. *Hoste* was delivered on 13 November 1916 and her operational career lasted only 38 days. On 19 December, with the 13th DF she was screening the Grand Fleet during a sweep between Norway and the Shetlands when a stud on her steering engine fractured. While returning to Scapa Flow with the *Negro* as escort the two destroyers collided. Two depth-charges knocked off the *Hoste*'s stern detonated, blowing in the bottom plating of the *Negro* and demolishing the stern of the *Hoste*. The *Negro* foundered shortly afterwards with heavy loss of life but the *Marmion* and *Marvel* tried to tow the broken-backed *Hoste* home. She was finally abandoned after her crew had been taken off.

Saumarez during the war CPL

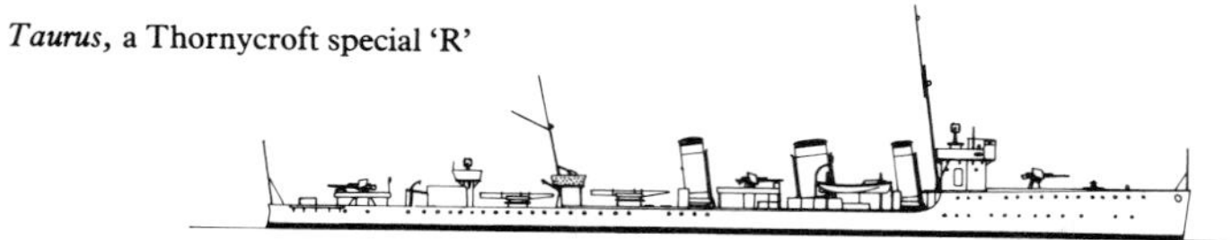
Taurus, a Thornycroft special 'R'

'R' class *destroyers*

Displacement: Admiralty design 975t normal; 1173t deep load
Thornycroft 'specials' 1035t normal
Yarrow 'specials' 930t normal

Dimensions: Admiralty design 276ft oa × 26ft 8in × 9ft
84.1m × 8.1m × 2.7m
Thornycroft 'specials' 274ft 3in oa × 27ft–27ft 3in × 9ft
83.6m × 8.2m–8.3m × 2.7m
Yarrow 'specials' 273ft 6in oa × 25ft 7½in × 9ft
83.4m × 7.8m × 2.7m

Machinery: Admiralty design 2-shaft Brown-Curtis (Parsons in Doxford, Hawthorn Leslie and Beardmore boats, except *Tancred*) turbines, 3 Yarrow (White-Forster in J S White boats) boilers, 27,000shp = 36kts. Oil 296t
Yarrow 'specials' 2-shaft Parsons direct-drive turbines, 27,000shp = 36kts

Armament: 3–4in (10.2cm)/45cal QF Mk IV, 1–2pdr (40mm) pom-pom, 4–21in (53.3cm) TT (2×2)

Complement: 82

Name	Builder	Launched	Fate
(6th order, 2 in 5.15, the rest in 7.15)			
RADSTOCK	Swan Hunter	3.6.16	Sold for BU 4.27
RAIDER	Swan Hunter	17.7.16	Sold for BU 4.27
ROMOLA	John Brown	14.5.16	Sold for BU 3.30
ROWENA	John Brown	1.7.16	BU 1937
RESTLESS	John Brown	12.8.16	BU 1936
RIGOROUS	John Brown	30.9.16	Sold for BU 11.26
ROCKET	Denny	2.7.16	Sold for BU 12.26
ROB ROY	Denny	28.8.16	Sold for BU 7.26
REDGAUNTLET	Denny	23.11.16	Sold for BU 7.27
REDOUBT	Doxford	28.10.16	Sold for BU 7.26
RECRUIT	Doxford	9.12.16	Mined 9.8.17
STURGEON	A Stephen	11.1.17	Sold for BU 12.26
SCEPTRE	A Stephen	18.4.17	Sold for BU 12.26
SALMON	Harland & Wolff	7.10.16	Renamed *Sable* 1933, BU 1937
SYLPH	Harland & Wolff	15.11.16	Sold for BU 12.26
SARPEDON	Hawthorn Leslie	1.6.16	Sold for BU 7.26
SABLE	J S White	28.6.16	Sold for BU 8.27
SETTER	J S White	18.8.16	Sunk in collision 17.5.17
SORCERESS	Swan Hunter	29.8.16	Sold for BU 4.27
Thornycroft 'specials'			
ROSALIND	Thornycroft	14.10.16	Sold for BU 7.26
RADIANT	Thornycroft	25.11.16	To Siam 1920
RETRIEVER	Thornycroft	15.1.17	Sold for BU 7.27
Yarrow 'specials'			
SABRINA	Yarrow	24.7.16	Sold for BU 11.26
STRONGBOW	Yarrow	30.9.16	Sunk 17.10.17
SURPRISE	Yarrow	25.11.16	Mined 23.12.17
SYBILLE	Yarrow	5.2.17	Sold for BU 11.26
(7th order, 12.15)			
Admiralty design			
SATYR	Beardmore	27.12.16	Sold for BU 12.26
SHARPSHOOTER	Beardmore	27.2.17	Sold for BU 4.27
SIMOOM	John Brown	30.10.16	Torpedoed 23.1.17
SKATE	John Brown	11.1.17	Sold for BU 7.47
STARFISH	Hawthorn Leslie	27.9.16	Sold for BU 4.28
STORK	Hawthorn Leslie	15.11.16	Sold for BU 10.27
SKILFUL	Harland & Wolff	3.2.17	Sold for BU 7.26
SPRINGBOK	Harland & Wolff	9.3.17	Sold for BU 12.26
Thornycroft 'specials'			
TAURUS	Thornycroft	10.3.17	Sold for BU 3.30
TEAZER	Thornycroft	21.4.17	Sold for BU 2.31
(8th order, 3.16)			
Admiralty design			
TANCRED	Beardmore	30.6.17	Sold for BU 5.28
TARPON	John Brown	10.3.17	Sold for BU 8.27
TELEMACHUS	John Brown	21.4.17	Sold for BU 7.27
TEMPEST	Fairfield	26.1.17	BU 1937
TETRARCH	Harland & Wolff	20.4.17	Sold for BU 7.34
TENACIOUS	Harland & Wolff	21.5.17	Sold for BU 6.28
THISBE	Hawthorn Leslie	8.3.17	BU 1936
THRUSTER	Hawthorn Leslie*	10.1.17	Sold for BU 3.37
TORMENTOR	A Stephen	22.5.17	Sold for BU 11.29
TORNADO	A Stephen	4.8.17	Mined 23.12.17
TORRENT	Swan Hunter	26.11.16	Mined 23.12.17
TORRID	Swan Hunter	10.2.17	Wrecked 16.3.37 on way to BU
Yarrow 'specials'			
TRUCULENT	Yarrow	24.3.17	Sold for BU 4.27
TYRANT	Yarrow	19.5.17	Sold 1938
ULLESWATER	Yarrow	4.8.17	Torpedoed 15.8.18

*Sub-contracted from Parsons

Raider, an Admiralty 'R' CPL

In July 1915 the Admiralty Board gave approval for all future destroyers to be engined with 2-shaft geared turbines, preferably Brown-Curtis. This far-sighted move was made only on the basis of the success of a year's service in *Leonidas* and *Lucifer*. The design for the next batch of destroyers was in other respects merely a duplication of the standard 'M' design, but with more flare and 1ft more freeboard on the forecastle. Other improvements were to put the after 4in gun on a 'bandstand', and a more robust bridge structure. The design which resulted was generally similar to the war-built 'M' class, with three round funnels. Because the bridge was 9ft wider than previously the 2pdr pom-poms formerly mounted at the end of the forecastle could not be mounted, and so a single pom-pom replaced the 20in searchlight on its platform between the TT. Some 'M' and 'R' class vessels had 2–14in (35.6cm) TT (one fixed on each beam) subsequently added at the break of the forecastle. The geared turbines were a great success, providing high speed with less cavitation and reduced fuel consumption. The lead-ship *Romola* maintained 36kts for 4 hours in light condition, and on her acceptance trials reached 32½kts in deep load condition. Comparative trials run between *Romola* and *Norman* showed that the 'R' class used 15 per cent less fuel at 18kts, and 28 per cent less at 25kts, resulting in an increase of 17.8 per cent and 40 per cent of range. The Yarrow 'specials' were the only units to retain direct-drive turbines. Oil fuel was also increased compared with the 'M' class.

The 51 boats of the class came into service from the autumn of 1916 through to the autumn of 1917, and suffered comparatively light losses. They were retained in the post-war fleet but being less seaworthy than the 'V&W' classes were progressively scrapped until only *Skate* survived to serve in the Second World War. *Tarpon* and *Telemachus* served as minelayers in 1917–18. *Radiant* was sold to Thornycroft June 1920 for resale to Thailand in September; renamed *Phra Ruang* and survived until mid-1960s. *Strongbow* was sunk by gunfire of *Bremse* and *Brummer* while escorting a Scandinavian convoy in 1917. *Simoom* was torpedoed by German destroyer *S 50* during action off Schouwen Bank in 1917. *Torrent* and her divison ran into a minefield near the Maass light buoy on 23 December 1917, and while assisting her *Surprise* struck a mine as well. *Tornado* tried to get clear but set off two more mines and sank with only one survivor, and only *Radiant* got home. *Ulleswater* was torpedoed by *UC 17* off the Dutch coast.

On January 1917 there were 2 'R' class with 11th DF, Grand Fleet, 1 with 14th DF, and 13 with 15th DF. A year later the total had risen to 8 with 11th DF, 1 with 14th DF, 10 with 15th DF (including Modified 'R's), 8 with Lerwick Force in the Shetlands, 8 with 13th DF, Battlecruiser Force and 21 with 10th DF, Harwich Force. Disposition at the Armistice was as follows: *Grand Fleet* 11th DF – 5 boats, 14th DF – 5 'R' and 'S' class, 15th DF – 18 boats; *Harwich Force* 10th DF – 24 boats.

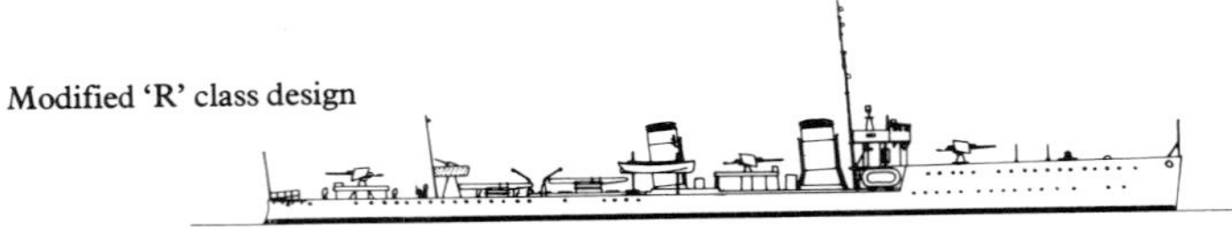
Modified 'R' class design

Modified 'R' class *destroyers*

Displacement: As 'R' class
Dimensions: As 'R' class
Machinery: 2-shaft Brown-Curtis (Parsons in *Urchin* and *Ursa*) single-reduction turbines, 3 Yarrow (White-Forster in *Trenchant* and *Tristram*) boilers, 27,000shp = 36kts. Oil 2976t
Armament: 3–4in (10.2cm)/45cal QF Mk V, 1–2pdr (40mm) pom-pom, 4–21in (53.3cm) TT (2×2)
Complement: 82

Name	Builder	Launched	Fate
ULSTER	Beardmore	10.10.17	Sold for BU 4.28
UNDINE	Fairfield	22.3.17	Sold for BU 4.28
TOWER	Swan Hunter	5.4.17	Sold for BU 5.28
TRENCHANT	J S White	23.12.16	Sold for BU 11.28
TRISTRAM	J S White	24.2.17	Sold for BU 5.21
TIRADE	Scott	21.4.17	Sold for BU 11.21
URSULA	Scott	2.8.17	Sold for BU 11.29
ULYSSES	Doxford	24.3.17	Lost 29.10.18
UMPIRE	Doxford	9.6.17	Sold for BU 1.30
URCHIN	Palmer	7.6.17	Sold for BU 1.30
URSA	Palmer	23.7.17	Sold for BU 7.26

Valentine after the war CPL

Broke (ex-*Rooke*) as completed CPL

Out of the last 26 'R' class ordered in March 1916 only 15 were completed to the original design. Despite all the minor improvements reports from the various commands and flotillas showed that bridges needed to be as far aft as possible, to protect personnel, and hulls needed to be stronger to cope with the exceptional stresses of constant hard driving in heavy weather. The 'Modifed R' class had No 1 and No 2 boiler rooms transposed, allowing the uptakes to be combined in one fatter funnel and making space for the forward gun and bridge to be moved aft. The new 4in Mk V QF gun had 30° elevation, increasing range from 10,000yds to 12,000yds, and rate of fire was 19–20 rounds/minute. *Trenchant*, the lead-ship, and her sister *Tristram* had their funnels made on thin plating, with distinctive ribs to strengthen them. *Undine* made 36½kts on trials, in light condition. They served with the Grand Fleet and the Harwich Force (7 in 13th DF at Armistice). *Ulysses* was sunk in collision with SS *Ellerie* in the Clyde on 29 October 1918.

'V' class *flotilla leaders*

Displacement: 1188t legend; 1400t deep load
Dimensions: 312ft × 29ft 6in × 10ft 6in
95.1m × 9.0m × 3.2m
Machinery: 2-shaft Brown-Curtis geared (Parsons IR in *Valentine* and *Valhalla*) turbines, 3 Yarrow (White-Forster in *Vampire*) boilers, 27,000shp = 34kts. Oil 367t
Armament: 4–4in (10.2cm)/45cal QF Mk V, 2–2pdr (40mm) pom-poms, 4–21in (53.3cm) TT (2×2)
Complement: 115

Name	Builder	Launched	Fate
VAMPIRE (ex-*Wallace*)	J S White	21.5.17	To Australia 1933; sunk 9.4.42
VALENTINE (ex-*Bruce*)	Cammell Laird	24.3.17	Sunk 15.5.40
VALHALLA (ex-*Douglas*)	Cammell Laird	22.5.17	Sold for BU 12.31
VALOROUS (ex-*Montrose*)	Denny	8.5.17	Sold for BU 3.47
VALKYRIE (ex-*Malcolm*)	Denny	13.3.17	BU 1936

The new 'R' class promised to be able to outstrip existing flotilla leaders and so the DNC was asked to design a new leader capable of a nominal speed of 34kts. The design which resulted was submitted in April 1916, and had the armament of the *Parker* class, but with superimposed guns aft as well as forward. Accommodation was better and the bridge was 15ft further aft, but the overall length was 15ft less. Even cost compared favourably, for at £200,000 the new leader would be £50,000 cheaper than the *Lightfoot* and only £6000 more than some of the Yarrow 'M' and 'R' class. The first two orders were placed with Denny Bros in April 1916, followed by three more from J S White and Cammell Laird in July, with delivery to be from June 1917. The new leaders were a great improvement over previous designs, with good seakeeping and a powerful armament, but ultimately served as divisional or half-leaders, as even more powerful leaders followed them into service quite quickly. They had a distinctive appearance, with a tall, thin fore funnel and a short fatter second funnel. They were distinguishable from the later 'V&W' boats by having a compass platform forward of the searchlight platform amidships. *Vampire* was completed with triple TT (2×3) in place of twins.

SHAKESPEARE class *flotilla leaders*

Displacement: 1554t legend; 2009t deep load
Dimensions: 329ft oa × 31ft 6in × 12ft 6in
100.3m × 9.6m × 3.8m
Machinery: 2-shaft Brown-Curtis geared turbines, 4 Yarrow boilers, 40,000shp = 36kts. Oil 500t
Armament: 5–4.7in (12cm)/45cal BL Mk I, 1–3in (76mm)/20cwt AA, 2–2pdr (40mm) pom-poms, 6–21in (53.3cm) TT (2×3)
Complement: 183

Name	Builder	Launched	Fate
SHAKESPEARE	Thornycroft	7.7.17	BU 1936
SPENSER	Thornycroft	22.9.17	BU 1936
WALLACE	Thornycroft	26.10.18	Sold for BU 3.45
KEPPEL	Thornycroft	23.4.20	Sold for BU 7.45
ROOKE	Thornycroft	16.9.20	Sunk 8.11.42
SAUNDERS	Thornycroft	–	Cancelled 4.19
SPRAGGE	Thornycroft	–	Cancelled 4.19

While the DNC was working on the design of the 'V' class leader Thornycroft submitted their own series of designs for a leader. As it happened the DNC had been instructed to work out designs for a larger type of leader to match rumoured new German destroyers armed with 5in guns, and he reported that the addition of 5in guns to the Thornycroft design would fit the new requirement very well. As there was no 5in gun in the Navy's inventory design of a new gun would take too long, and it was suggested that the Army's 4.7in field gun should be adopted instead. This was done, and as a result the new leaders carried five 4.7in, superimposed forward and aft, as in the 'V' leaders, and a fifth gun on a 'bandstand' between the funnels. With their two sets of triple 21in TT, this made the new leaders the most heavily armed destroyers in the world, and the addition of a 9ft rangefinder as well as torpedo sights on the bridge marked a vast improvement in fighting efficiency. With their massive flat-sided funnels and heavy armament the *Shakespeare* class made a great impression, particularly among other navies. The first two, *Shakespeare* and *Spenser*, were ordered in April 1916, followed by *Wallace* in April 1917 and the remainder in April 1918. Two were cancelled, and *Rooke* and *Keppel* were slowed down after the Armistice. Two more, *Barrington* and *Hughes*, were to be built by Cammell Laird because Thornycroft's Woolston yard was full to capacity in the spring of 1918, but the DNC decided that Cammell Laird would be unable to match the weight-saving techniques, and the orders were replaced by *Scott* class vessels with the same names.

Rooke was renamed *Broke* in April 1921; completed by Pembroke DYd in January 1925. *Shakespeare* was handed over (with *Spenser*, *Valkyrie*, *Vectis*, *Venturous* and some 'S' class) for BU in September 1936 in exchange for the old liner *Majestic* (later HMS *Caledonia*).

Campbell July 1935 *CPL*

SCOTT class *flotilla leaders*

Displacement: 1580t legend; 2050t deep load
Dimensions: 332ft 6in oa × 31ft 9in × 12ft 6in
101.3m × 9.7m × 3.8m
Machinery: 2-shaft Parsons (Brown-Curtis in *Stuart* and *Montrose*) IR geared turbines, 4 Yarrow boilers, 40,000shp = 36kts. Oil 500t
Armament: As *Shakespeare* class
Complement: 164

Name	Builder	Launched	Fate
SCOTT	Cammell Laird	18.10.17	Torpedoed 15.8.18
BRUCE	Cammell Laird	26.2.18	Sunk as target 22.11.39
DOUGLAS	Cammell Laird	8.5.18	Sold for BU 3.45
CAMPBELL	Cammell Laird	21.9.18	Cammell Laird 2.47
MALCOLM	Cammell Laird	29.5.19	Sold for BU 7.45
MACKAY (ex-*Claverhouse*)	Cammell Laird	21.12.18	Cammell Laird 2.47
STUART	Hawthorn Leslie	22.8.18	To Australia 1933, sold for BU 2.47
MONTROSE	Hawthorn Leslie	10.6.18	Sold for BU 1.46
BARRINGTON	Cammell Laird	–	Cancelled 12.18
HUGHES	Cammell Laird	–	Cancelled 12.18

A design of flotilla leader was prepared in the spring of 1916 to incorporate features of the *Shakespeare* class, but using standard Admiralty practice so that contracts could be given to other builders. It was suggested that Thornycroft's drawings should be given to Cammell Laird to enable them to achieve similar weight-reductions and *Barrington* and *Hughes* were in fact ordered to the *Shakespeare* design, but the DNC advised against this move as non-specialist builders were unlikely to be able to achieve similar standards, and the two were subsequently changed to standard Admiralty leaders. The design was very similar to the *Shakespeare*, but they were heavier and slower. On her acceptance trials *Scott* reached about 33kts at a displacement of 1716t, and in a comparative trial reached 36.63kts at 1770t. Machinery weighed about 70t more than in the Thornycroft boats. Externally the major difference was the funnels, which were round in the Admiralty design, instead of flat-sided. *Scott* was ordered in April 1916, followed by *Bruce* and *Douglas* in December, and the remainder in April 1917.

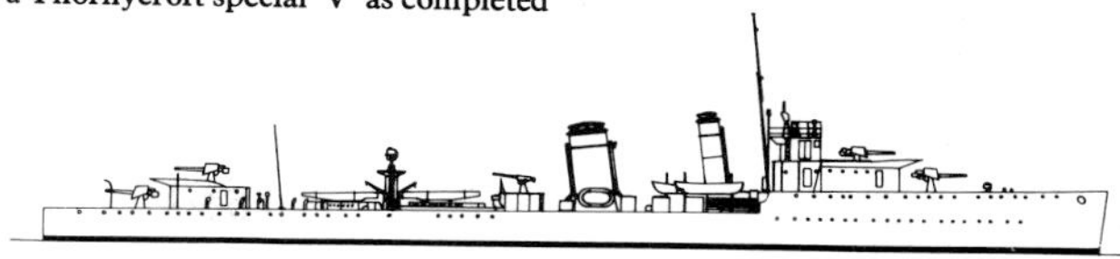

Viscount, a Thornycroft special 'V' as completed

'V' class *destroyers*

Displacement: Admiralty design 1100t light; 1490t deep load
Thornycroft 'specials' 1095t light; 1512t deep load
Dimensions: Admiralty design 312ft oa × 29ft 6in × 10ft 6in
95.1m × 9.0m × 3.2m
Thornycroft 'specials' 312ft oa × 30ft 8½in × 9ft 6in
95.1m × 9.4m × 2.9m
Machinery: 2-shaft Brown-Curtis single-reduction (Parsons IR in Doxford and Swan Hunter boats) geared turbines, 3 Yarrow (White-Forster in *Vectis* and *Vortigern*) boilers, 27,000shp = 34kts. Oil 367t (374t in *Viceroy* and *Viscount*)
Armament: 4–4in (10.2cm)/45cal, QF Mk V, 1–3in (76mm)/20cwt Mk I AA, 4–21in (53.3cm TT (2×2)
Complement: 134

Name	Builder	Launched	Fate
VANCOUVER	Beardmore	28.12.17	Renamed *Vimy* 4.28, sold for BU 3.47
VANESSA	Beardmore	16.3.18	Sold for BU 3.47
VANITY	Beardmore	3.5.18	Sold for BU 3.47
VANQUISHER	John Brown	18.8.17	Sold for BU 3.47
VANOC	John Brown	14.6.17	Sold for BU 7.45
VEGA	Doxford	1.9.17	Sold for BU 3.47
VELOX	Doxford	17.11.17	Sold for BU 2.47
VEHEMENT	Denny	6.7.17	Mined 1.8.18
VENTUROUS	Denny	21.9.17	BU 1936
VENDETTA	Fairfield	3.9.17	To Australia 10.33; scuttled 2.7.48
VENETIA	Fairfield	29.10.17	Mined 19.10.40
VERDUN	Hawthorn Leslie	21.8.17	Sold for BU 1946
VERSATILE	Hawthorn Leslie	31.10.17	Sold for BU 8.48
VERULAM	Hawthorn Leslie	3.10.17	Mined 4.9.19
VESPER	A Stephen	15.12.17	Sold for BU 3.3
VIDETTE	A Stephen	28.2.18	Sold for BU 3.47
VIOLENT	Swan Hunter	1.9.17	BU 1937
VIMIERA	Swan Hunter	22.6.17	Mined 9.1.42
VITTORIA	Swan Hunter	29.10.17	Torpedoed 1.9.19
VIVACIOUS	Yarrow	3.11.17	Sold for BU 3.47
VIVIEN	Yarrow	16.2.18	Sold for BU 2.47
VORTIGERN	J S White	15.10.17	Torpedoed 15.3.42
VECTIS	J S White	4.9.17	BU 1936
Thornycroft 'specials'			
VICEROY	Thornycroft	17.11.17	Sold for BU 6.48
VISCOUNT	Thornycroft	29.12.17	Sold 3.45, BU 1947

In response to claims by the C-in-C that the Germans were building large destroyers the Board decided in June 1916 that the next 26 destroyers should be repeats of the 'V' class 300ft leaders. Triple TT were suggested by the DNO but vetoed by Controller to avoid delays. However decks were to be made strong enough to take triple tubes. Bridges were strengthened in response to criticism from the Fleet, with canvas screens replaced by steel plating. All were ordered between June and August 1916. As completed they resembled the 'V' leaders closely, but without the compass platform ahead of the searchlight platform amidships. In January 1917 orders were given to complete *Vehement*, *Venturous*, *Vanoc* and *Vanquisher* as minelayers, with rails for 60 'H' or 'M Sinker' mines. Subsequently *Vimiera*, *Velox*, *Versatile*, *Vesper*, *Vittoria* and *Vortigern* were altered in similar fashion. From 1920 onwards all except the minelayers were rearmed with triple TT (the minelayers retained the after twin TT, making them 5-tube boats). *Vectis* and *Vortigern* had typical White ribbed funnels, while *Verdun*, *Versatile* and *Verulam* had prominent caging on their funnel-tops. *Viceroy* and *Viscount* had tall flat-sided second funnels.

The first boats came into service in August 1917 and the last in June 1918.

In January 1918 there was one with 11th DF (Grand Fleet), 14 with 13th DF (Battlecruiser Force) and some with 20th DF (minelaying). Many served in the Baltic 1919–20 and in 1921 there were 18 in 1st, 2nd, 5th and 6th DF (Atlantic Fleet) and five in 9th DF (Rosyth). *Vittoria* was torpedoed by Bolshevik submarine *Pantera* in the Baltic. *Vectis, Venturous* and *Violent* handed over to shipbreakers in part exchange for RMS *Majestic* 1936–37.

Windsor September 1933 — CPL

'W' class *destroyers*

Armament:	4–4in (10.2cm)/45cal QF Mk V, 1–3in (76mm) AA, 6–21in (53.3cm) TT (2×3)
Other details:	As 'V' class

Name	Builder	Launched	Fate
WAKEFUL	John Brown	6.10.17	Torpedoed 29.5.40
WATCHMAN	John Brown	2.11.17	Sold for BU 7.45
WALPOLE	Doxford	12.2.18	Sold for BU 2.45
WHITLEY (ex-*Whitby*)	Doxford	13.4.18	Bombed and beached 19.5.40
WALKER	Denny	29.11.17	Sold for BU 3.46
WESTCOTT	Denny	14.2.18	Sold for BU 1.46
WALRUS	Fairfield	27.12.17	Wrecked 12.2.38
WOLFHOUND	Fairfield	14.3.18	Sold for BU 2.48
WARWICK	Hawthorn Leslie	28.12.17	Torpedoed 20.2.44
WESSEX	Hawthorn Leslie	12.3.18	Bombed 24.5.40
VOYAGER	A Stephen	8.5.16	To Australia 1933, wrecked and scuttled 23.9.42
WHIRLWIND	Swan Hunter	15.12.17	Torpedoed 5.7.40
WRESTLER	Swan Hunter	25.2.18	Sold for BU 7.44
WINCHELSEA	J S White	15.12.17	Sold for BU 3.45
WINCHESTER	J S White	1.2.18	Sold for BU 3.46
WESTMINSTER	Scott	24.2.18	Sold for BU 3.47
WINDSOR	Scott	21.6.18	Sold for BU 3.47
WRYNECK	Palmer	13.5.18	Bombed 27.4.41
WATERHEN	Palmer	26.3.18	To Australia 1933, bombed 30.6.41
WAYFARER	Yarrow	–	Cancelled 1917
WOODPECKER	Yarrow	–	Cancelled 1917
Thornycroft 'specials'			
WOLSEY	Thornycroft	16.3.18	Sold for BU 3.47
WOOLSTON	Thornycroft	27.4.18	Sold for BU 2.47

In December 1916 orders were placed for 23 repeat 'V' class, but with the triple TT which had not been ready in time for the 'V's. They were virtually identical, the J S White boats having the same level topped and ribbed funnels as the *Vectis* and *Vortigern*, and the Thornycroft 'specials' having the same high freeboard and flat-sided after funnel as the *Viceroy* and *Viscount*. Two ordered from Yarrow, to be named *Wayfarer* and *Woodpecker*, were cancelled in April 1917 and replaced by 'S' class. In 1918 *Walker, Walrus, Warwick, Watchman* and *Whirlwind* were completed as minelayers.

They were completed between November 1917 and October 1918, and by the Armistice they were distributed between the 11th, 12th, 13th and 14th DFs (Grand Fleet) and 20th DF (Immingham). The *Warwick*, Vice-Admiral Keyes' flagship for the Zeebrugge Raid, was returning from the second attempt to block Ostend on 10 May 1918 when she was mined aft. Despite breaking her back the *Velox* was able to help her get back to Dover. Six went to the Baltic with 13th DF in November 1918 and several more went out in 1919. In 1921 there were four with 1st DF, two with 2nd DF, two with 4th DF, five with 5th DF and five with 6th DF (all with the Atlantic Fleet), and one with 9th DF (laid up at Rosyth).

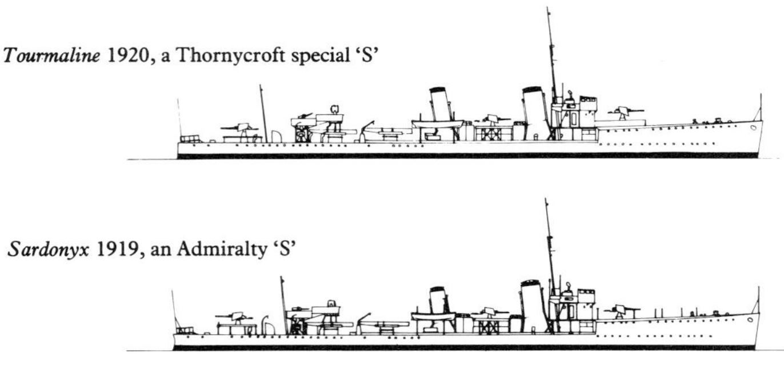

Tourmaline 1920, a Thornycroft special 'S'

Sardonyx 1919, an Admiralty 'S'

'S' class *destroyers*

Displacement:	Admiralty design 1075t legend Thornycroft 'specials' 1087t legend Yarrow 'specials' 930t legend
Dimensions:	Admiralty design 276ft oa × 26ft 8in × 9ft mean *84.1m × 8.1m × 2.7m* Thornycroft 'specials' 276ft oa × 27ft 4in × 10ft 6in *84.1m × 8.3m × 3.2m* Yarrow 'specials' 273ft 6in oa × 25ft 7½in × 10ft *83.4m × 7.8m × 3.0m*
Machinery:	Admiralty design: 2-shaft Brown-Curtis (Parsons in Palmer boats and *Tilbury, Tintagel* and *Strenuous*), single-reduction geared turbines, 3 Yarrow (White-Forster in J S White boats) boilers, 27,000shp = 36kts. Oil 301t
Armament:	3–4in (10.2cm)/45 cal QF Mk IV, 1–2pdr (40mm) pom-pom, 4–21in (53.3cm) TT (2×2). Thornycroft 'specials' had in addition 2–18in (45.7cm) TT at break of forecastle p&s
Complement:	90

Name	Builder	Launched	Fate
Admiralty design (1st order, 4.17)			
SIMOOM	John Brown	26.1.18	Sold 1.31
SCIMITAR	John Brown	27.2.18	Sold 6.47
SCOTSMAN	John Brown	30.3.18	BU 7.37
SCOUT	John Brown	27.4.18	Sold 3.46
SHARK	Swan Hunter	9.4.16	Sold 2.31
SPARROWHAWK	Swan Hunter	14.5.18	Sold 2.31
SPLENDID	Swan Hunter	10.7.18	Sold 1.31
SABRE	A Stephen	23.9.18	Sold 11.45
SALADIN	A Stephen	17.2.19	Sold 6.47
SIKH	Fairfield	7.5.18	Sold 7.27
SIRDAR	Fairfield	6.7.18	Sold 5.34
SOMME	Fairfield	10.9.18	Sold 8.32
SUCCESS	Doxford	29.6.18	To Australia 1919, sold for BU 6.37
SHAMROCK	Doxford	26.8.18	BU 1936
SHIKARI	Doxford	14.7.19	Sold 11.45
SENATOR	Denny	2.4.18	BU 1936
SEPOY	Denny	22.5.18	Sold 7.32
SERAPH	Denny	8.7.18	Sold 5.34
SWALLOW	Scott	1.8.18	BU 1936
SWORDSMAN	Scott	28.12.18	To Australia 1919, sold for BU 6.37
STEADFAST	Palmer	8.8.18	Sold 7.34
STERLING (ex-*Stirling*)	Palmer	8.10.18	Sold 8.32
TRIBUNE	J S White	28.3.18	Sold 12.31
TRINIDAD	J S White	8.4.18	Sold 3.32
Thornycroft 'specials'			
SPEEDY	Thornycroft	1.6.18	Sunk in collision 24.9.22
TOBAGO	Thornycroft	15.7.18	Mined 12.11.20, BU 1922
Yarrow 'specials'			
TORCH	Yarrow	16.3.18	Sold 11.29
TOMAHAWK	Yarrow	11.5.18	Sold for BU 6.28
TRYPHON	Yarrow	22.6.18	Ran aground 4.5.19, sold for BU 9.20
TUMULT	Yarrow	17.9.18	Sold 10.28
TURQUOISE	Yarrow	9.11.18	Sold 1.32
TUSCAN	Yarrow	1.3.19	Sold 8.32

Name	Builder	Launched	Fate
TYRIAN	Yarrow	2.7.19	Sold 2.30
Admiralty design (2nd order, 6.17)			
TACTICIAN	Beardmore	7.8.18	Sold 2.31
TARA	Beardmore	12.10.18	Sold 12.31
TASMANIA	Beardmore	22.11.18	To Australia 1919, sold for BU 6.37
TATTOO	Beardmore	28.12.18	To Australia 1919, sold for BU 1.37
SCYTHE	John Brown	25.4.18	Sold 11.31
SEABEAR	John Brown	6.7.18	Sold 2.31
SEAFIRE	John Brown	10.8.18	BU 1936
SEARCHER	John Brown	11.9.18	Sold 3.38
SEAWOLF	John Brown	2.11.18	Sold 2.31
SPORTIVE	Swan Hunter	19.9.18	BU 1936
STALWART	Swan Hunter	23.10.18	To Australia 1919, sold for BU 6.37
TILBURY	Swan Hunter	3.6.18	Sold 2.31
TINTAGEL	Swan Hunter	9.8.18	Sold 3.32
SARDONYX	A Stephen	27.5.19	BU 10.45
SATURN	A Stephen	–	Cancelled 1919
SYCAMORE	A Stephen	–	Cancelled 1919
STONEHENGE	Palmer	19.3.19	Wrecked 6.11.20
STORMCLOUD	Palmer	30.5.19	Sold 7.34
SPEAR	Fairfield	9.11.18	Sold 7.26
SPINDRIFT	Fairfield	30.12.18	Sold 7.36
SERAPIS	Denny	17.9.18	Sold 1.34
SERENE	Denny	30.11.18	BU 1936
SESAME	Denny	30.12.18	Sold 5.34
STRENUOUS	Scott	9.11.18	Sold 8.32
STRONGHOLD	Scott	6.5.19	Bombed 4.3.42
STURDY	Scott	26.6.19	Wrecked 30.10.40
TROJAN	J S White	20.7.18	BU 1936
TRUANT	J S White	18.9.18	Sold 11.31
TRUSTY	J S White	6.11.18	BU 1936
TURBULENT	Hawthorn Leslie	29.5.19	BU 1936
TENEDOS	Hawthorn Leslie	21.10.18	Bombed 5.4.42
THANET	Hawthorn Leslie	5.11.18	Bombed 27.1.42
THRACIAN	Hawthorn Leslie	5.3.20	BU 1947
Thornycroft 'specials'			
TORBAY	Thornycroft	6.3.18	To Canada 1928 as *Champlain*, BU 1937
TOREADOR	Thornycroft	7.12.18	To Canada 1928 as *Vancouver*, BU 1937
TOURMALINE	Thornycroft	12.4.19	Sold 11.31

When it was realised that reports of new German destroyer armaments had been exaggerated the Controller suggested in February 1917 that destroyer construction should revert to Modified 'R' class. They would be cheaper, faster to build, and 2kts faster. Several improvements were incorporated after consultation with Captains (D) and the various Commands. These included the provision of more TT, a 'trawler' bow or sharply sheered forecastle and a turtleback forecastle. The original proposal for the 18in TT was for single fixed tubes firing 'cold' torpedoes, but the Admiralty design was given training tubes, which meant that the forecastle plating had to be cut away to allow the tube to train. This made the boats very wet, for the open forecastle permitted spray to be thrown up over the bridge. In the Thornycroft design two tubes were fixed athwartships, firing through a narrow aperture, so the problem was avoided. The torpedoes were fired by the CO, who carried two trailing leads in his pockets, permitting him to fire at targets of opportunity. The Thornycroft boats also carried the forecastle gun on a raised platform, further improving seakeeping. As weight was critical in the Admiralty design it was soon realised that the weight of the single 18in TT was too much, and the later boats were completed without them, to permit the heavier Mk V 21in torpedoes to be carried in the midships TT. In June 1918 *Senator* was fitted with an aircraft platform aft, allowing an aircraft to take off when the destroyer went full speed astern.

Orders were placed for 24 boats in April 1917, followed by 33 more in June, but *Saturn* and *Sycamore* were cancelled in 1919. Only 19 were completed by the Armistice. The class were completed from April 1918 to October 1919 (apart from *Shikari*, completed at Chatham in March 1924 and *Thracian* completed at Sheerness in April 1922), and several served in the Baltic and Black Sea in 1919–20 and the Mediterranean in 1919–22. Being smaller and less heavily armed than the 'V&W' classes they were quickly consigned to the Reserve Fleet and comparatively few saw active service. Only a handful survived to serve in the Second World War. *Thracian* was beached at Hong Kong on 24 December 1941 but repaired by Japanese and recommissioned as *No 101* in September 1942. Returned to RN in September 1945 and BU. *Tobago* was mined in the Black Sea in 1920, sustaining serious damage to her engine room. She was patched up in the Arsenal at Istanbul and then towed 1000 miles to Malta DYd by the battleship *Centurion*, but when surveyed was found to be beyond economical repair, and was sold locally. *Turbulent*, *Senator*, *Swallow*, *Seafire*, *Serene*, *Sportive*, *Trojan*, *Trusty* and *Shamrock* handed over for BU in part exchange for RMS *Majestic* in August–November 1936.

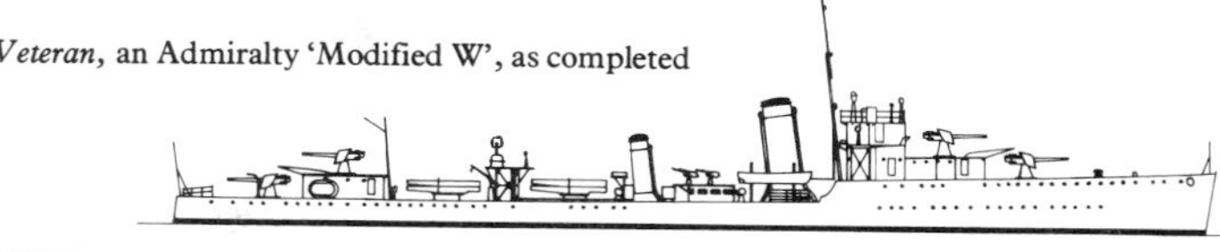

Veteran, an Admiralty 'Modified W', as completed

Modified 'W' class *destroyers*

Displacement: 1325t normal; 1508t deep load
Dimensions: As 'V' and 'W' classes
Machinery: 2-shaft Brown-Curtis geared (Parsons IR in Swan Hunter boats) turbines, 3 Yarrow (White-Forster in J S White boats) boilers, 27,000shp = 34kts. Oil 367t
Armament: 4–4.7in (12cm)/45cal BL Mk I, 1–3in (76mm)/20cwt Mk I AA or 2–2pdr (40mm) pom-poms, 6–21in (53.3cm) TT (2×3)
Complement: 127

Name	Builder	Launched	Fate
Admiralty design (1st order, 1.18)			
VANSITTART	Beardmore	17.4.19	Sold for BU 2.46
VIMY (ex-*Vantage*)	Beardmore	–	Cancelled 9.19
VOLUNTEER	Denny	17.4.19	Sold for BU 3.47
VOTARY	Denny	–	Cancelled 12.18
VENOMOUS (ex-*Venom*)	John Brown	21.12.18	Sold for BU 3.47
VERITY	John Brown	19.3.19	Sold for BU 3.47
WANDERER	Fairfield	7.8.18	Sold for BU 1.46
WARREN	Fairfield	–	Cancelled 9.19
WELCOME	Hawthorn Leslie	–	Cancelled 4.19
WELFARE	Hawthorn Leslie	–	Cancelled 4.19
WHITEHALL	Swan Hunter	11.9.19	Sold 10.45
WHITEHEAD	Swan Hunter	6.18	Cancelled 4.19
WREN	Yarrow	11.11.19	Bombed 27.7.40
WYE	Yarrow	1.18	Cancelled 9.19
Thornycroft 'specials'			
WISHART	Thornycroft	18.7.19	Sold for BU 3.45
WITCH	Thornycroft	11.11.19	Sold 7.46
Admiralty design (2nd order, 4.18)			
VASHON	Beardmore	–	Cancelled 11.18
VENGEFUL	Beardmore	–	Cancelled 11.18
VETERAN	John Brown	26.4.19	Torpedoed 26.9.42
VIGO	John Brown	–	Cancelled 11.18
VIRULENT	John Brown	–	Cancelled 11.18
VOLAGE	John Brown	–	Cancelled 11.18
VOLCANO	John Brown	–	Cancelled 11.18
WISTFUL (ex-*Vigorous*)	John Brown	–	Cancelled 11.18
WAGER	Denny	–	Cancelled 4.19
WAKE	Denny	–	Cancelled 11.18
WALDEGRAVE	Denny	–	Cancelled 11.18
WALTON	Denny	–	Cancelled 11.18
WHITAKER	Denny	–	Cancelled 11.18
WATSON	Fairfield	–	Cancelled 9.19
WAVE	Fairfield	–	Cancelled 11.18
WEAZEL	Fairfield	–	Cancelled 11.18
WHITE BEAR	Fairfield	–	Cancelled 11.18
WELLESLEY	Hawthorn Leslie	–	Cancelled 11.18
WHEELER	Scott	–	Cancelled 4.19
WHIP	Scott	–	Cancelled 11.18
WHIPPET	Scott	–	Cancelled 11.18
WHELP	Scott	–	Cancelled 9.19
WHITSHED	Swan Hunter	31.1.19	Sold for BU 2.47
WILD SWAN	Swan Hunter	17.5.19	Bombed 17.8.42
WILLOUGHBY	Swan Hunter	–	Cancelled 12.18
WINTER	Swan Hunter	–	Cancelled 12.18
WITHERINGTON	J S White	18.4.19	Sold 3.47
WOLVERINE	J S White	17.7.19	Sold 1.46
WORCESTER	J S White	20.4.19	Sold for BU 9.46
WEREWOLF	J S White (ex-Swan Hunter)	17.7.19	Cancelled 4.19

Name	Builder	Launched	Fate
WESTPHAL	J S White (ex-Swan Hunter)	–	Cancelled 4.19
WESTWARD HO	J S White (ex-Swan Hunter)	–	Cancelled 4.19
WRANGLER	J S White	–	Cancelled 9.19
YEOMAN	Yarrow	–	Cancelled 4.19
ZEALOUS	Yarrow	–	Cancelled 4.19
ZEBRA	Yarrow	–	Cancelled 4.19
ZODIAC	Yarrow	–	Cancelled 4.19

A Repeat 'W' class of 16 boats was ordered in January 1918, followed by 38 more in March–April, but only 9 of the first order and 7 of the second survived the wholesale cancellations which followed the Armistice. As before Thornycroft were permitted to build two to their own design, with added freeboard and more powerful machinery. The dimensions of the 'V&W' classes were followed but with a slightly different stern. In the second group the boiler rooms were transposed to improve watertight integrity, with the double room separated from the engine room to reduce the number of large compartments amidships. This resulted in a different silhouette, with a thick fore funnel and thin after funnel. The two sets of triple 21in TT were repeated but the 4.7in BL gun of the *Shakespeare* and *Scott* classes replaced the 4in QF Mk V, marking a major increase in gunpower. All were completed after the Armistice, most between April 1919 and July 1920, but *Whitehall* was towed to Chatham DYd and not completed until July 1924, *Wren* was completed at Pembroke DYd in January 1923 and *Worcester* was completed at Portsmouth in September 1922. The order for *Watson* was transferred to Devonport DYd and she is reported to have been launched in 1919 to clear the slip. Similarly *Werewolf*, *Westphal* and *Westward Ho* were transferred from J S White to Swan Hunter and *Wrangler* was transferred from J S White to Yarrow. As part of the November 1918 cancellation material for *Whelp* was transferred to Pembroke DYd, material for *Watson* to Devonport DYd, material for *Warren* to Chatham DYd and *Vigo*'s boilers were transferred to *Whelp*.

SUBMARINES

'HOLLAND' type *submarines*

Displacement: 113t surfaced; 122t submerged
Dimensions: 63ft 10in oa × 11ft 10in × 9ft 11in surfaced
19.5m × 3.6m × 3.0m
Machinery: 1 shaft, 4-cyl Wolseley petrol engine, 1 electric motor, 160hp/70hp = 7½kts/6kts. Range 500nm at 7kts surfaced
Armament: 1–18in (45.7cm) TT (bow, 3 torpedoes)
Complement: 8

Class (launched, fate):
No 1 (2.10.01, sold for BU 10.13, salvaged 9.82), *No 2* (21.2.02, sold for BU 10.13), *No 3* (9.5.02, sold for BU 10.13), *No 4* (23.5.02, foundered 3.9.21), *No 5* (10.6.02, foundered 8.8.12). All built by Vickers.

Although the First Sea Lord professed publicly that he saw no reason for the Royal Navy to have submarines the growing numbers of submarines in France and the United States caused unease. Thus when in the summer of 1900 the Electric Boat Co offered to build Holland-type submarines, negotiations quickly got under way. By November 1900 an outline agreement to build five boats under licence at Barrow had been concluded and the Treasury was asked to provide secret funding. A brief statement in the 1901–1902 Estimates announced the plans to build, and a firm order was given to Vickers in December 1900, followed by the keel-laying of *No 1* the following February. In fact *No 2* entered service first, as *No 1* was conducting exhaustive first-of-class trials. All five were in service by 1903, giving the Royal Navy vital experience for the design of its own boats. They were extremely primitive and could never be more than experimental craft, and yet they served for ten years without suffering any serious accidents.

No 1 was laid down in February 1901 and ran trials February–April 1902, although accepted she did not become operational for another year. Used for training and based at Fort Blockhouse until sold in 1913. She foundered in tow from Portsmouth and was rediscovered in April 1981. She has been raised and is now being restored at the Submarine Museum at Gosport. *No 4* was stricken in 1912 and foundered in tow, but was raised and later sunk as a gunnery target in 1914. *No 5* arrived at Portsmouth late in 1902 and served with the first flotilla at Fort Blockhouse until removed from the Effective List in August 1912. She foundered in tow to be BU.

A 11 before the war *CPL*

A 'Holland' boat alongside the depot ship *Hazard* *CPL*

'A' class *submarines*

Displacement: 190t surfaced; 205t–207t submerged
Dimensions: *A 1* 103ft 3in oa × 11ft 10in × 10ft 1in surfaced
31.5m × 3.6m × 3.1m
A 2–A 13 105ft 0½in oa × 12ft 8¾in × 10ft 8in surfaced
32.0m × 3.9m × 3.3m
Machinery: *A 1–A 12* 1 shaft, 16-cyl Wolseley petrol engine, 1 electric motor, 350hp/125hp = 9½kts/6kts (*A 2–A 4* 450hp/150hp = 10kts/7kts; *A 5–A 7* 550hp/150hp = 11½kts/7kts; *A 8–A 12* 600hp/150hp = 11kts/6kts)
A 13 1 shaft, 6-cyl heavy oil engine, 1 electric motor, 500hp/150hp = 11kts/6kts. Range 320nm at 10kts surfaced
Armament: *A 1–A 4* 1–18in (45.7cm) TT (bow, 3 torpedoes)
A 5–A 13 2–18in (45.7cm) TT (bow, 4 torpedoes)
Complement: 11

Class (launched, fate):
A 1 (ex-*No 6*, 9.7.02, sunk as target 8.11), *A 2* (16.4.03, wrecked 1.20), *A 3* (9.3.03, sunk as target 17.5.12), *A 4* (9.6.03, sold for BU 1.20), *A 5* (3.3.04, BU 1920), *A 6* (3.3.04, sold for BU 1.20), *A 7* (23.1.05, lost 16.1.14), *A 8* (23.1.05, sold for BU 10.20), *A 9* (8.2.05, BU 1920), *A 10* (8.2.05, sold for BU 4.19), *A 11* (8.3.05, BU 5.20), *A 12* (8.3.05, sold for BU 1.20), *A 13* (18.4.05, BU 1920). All built by Vickers.

A sixth improved unit of the 'Holland' class was so altered at the design stage that she became the prototype for the next class, the first all-British submarines. *A 1* was little more than a lengthened Holland, but from *A 2* onwards they were enlarged and from *A 5* carried a second TT in a side-by-side configuration. Another innovation was a proper conning tower, to avoid being swamped when running on the surface. Like the 'Hollands' their main defect was the small reserve of buoyancy. Although still largely experimental the 'A' boats were successful, and the survivors saw active service in 1914, even if only in the training role. Protracted trials with *A 13*'s Hornsby-Ackroyd vertical heavy oil engine led to the adoption of the diesel in due course, and the basic concepts remained unaltered for several years.

A 1 was laid down before Holland *No 1* had completed her trials, and came into service in July 1903. Unfortunately she was the first submarine casualty, being rammed and sunk on 18 March 1904 by the liner *Berwick Castle* off the Nab. Raised on 18 April 1904 she was never recommissioned, and was sunk as a target. *A 2* was wrecked while on the Sale List. *A 3* was rammed and sunk by *Hazard* on 2 February 1912 but raised and used as a target. *A 4* was sunk in collision on 16 October 1905, and although raised was not recommissioned. *A 7* was lost in Whitesand Bay when she dived into the mud. *A 8* foundered and sank in Plymouth Sound on 8 June 1905 but was raised and repaired; stricken July 1916 and sold in 1920.

'B' class *submarines*

Displacement:	287t surfaced; 316t submerged
Dimensions:	142ft 2¼in oa × 13ft 7in × 11ft 7in surfaced *43.3m × 4.1m × 3.4m*
Machinery:	1 shaft, 16-cyl Vickers petrol engine, electric motor, 600hp/290hp = 12kts/6kts. Range 1000nm at 8¾kts surfaced
Armament:	2–18in (45.7cm) TT (bow, 4 torpedoes)
Complement:	15

Class (launched, fate):
B 1 (25.10.04, sold for BU 5.21), *B 2* (30.10.05, sunk 4.10.12), *B 3* (31.10.05, sold for BU 12.19), *B 4* (14.11.05, sold for BU 4.19), *B 5* (14.11.05, sold for BU 8.21), *B 6* (30.11.05, sold for BU 1919 as *S 6*), *B 7* (30.11.05, sold for BU 1919 as *S 7*), *B 8* (23.1.06, sold for BU 1919 as *S 8*), *B 9* (24.1.06, sold for BU 1919 as *S 9*), *B 10* (23.3.06, sunk 9.8.16), *B 11* (21.2.06, sold for BU 1919 as *S 11*). All built by Vickers.

The successors to the 'A' class were very similar, the main improvements being the provision of a more substantial deck casing to improve surface performance and a bigger reserve of buoyancy. They were also fitted with a pair of hydroplanes at the forward end of the conning tower to improve underwater handling. This innovation was not repeated in subsequent classes, but 50 years later it was reintroduced in US nuclear submarines for the same reason. The six boats went to the Mediterranean (*B 6*–*B 11*) were not employed after the autumn of 1915 for lack of spares, and in order to make better use of them the Admiralty arranged with the Italian Navy to rebuild them as surface patrol boats at Venice in 1917. This involved removing the electric motors and batteries and building up the bow casing to form a forecastle. A small wheelhouse was provided, and a platform for a 12pdr gun. No note survives about their torpedo armament but presumably the tubes were not used. As *S 6*–*S 11* these patrol craft were employed in the Adriatic, and the survivors were sold at Malta in 1919.

B 2 was sunk in collision with SS *Amerika* in the Dover Strait. *B 10* was sunk in Venice DYd while undergoing conversion to surface patrol boat, by Austrian bombing attack. *B 11* was sent to the Mediterranean late in 1914, and on 1 December negotiated Turkish minefields and nets to sink the coast defence ship *Messudieh*.

'C' class design
NB 1/750 scale

'C' class *submarines*

Displacement:	287t–290t surfaced; 316t–320t submerged
Dimensions:	142ft 2¼in oa × 13ft 7in × 11ft 2in–11ft 6in *43.3m × 4.1m × 3.4m–3.5m*
Machinery:	1 shaft, 16-cyl Vickers petrol engine, 1 electric motor, 600hp/300hp = 13kts/7½kts. Range 1000nm at 8¾kts surfaced
Armament:	2–18in (45.7cm) TT (bow, 4 torpedoes)
Complement:	16

Class (launched, fate):
C 1 (10.7.06, sold for BU 10.20), *C 2* (10.7.06, sold for BU 10.20), *C 3* (3.10.06, expended 23.4.18), *C 4* (18.10.06, sold for BU 4.22), *C 5* (20.8.06, sold for BU 10.19), *C 6* (20.8.06, sold for BU 11.19), *C 7* (15.2.07, sold for BU 12.19), *C 8* (15.2.07, sold for BU 10.20), *C 9* (3.4.07, sold for BU 7.22), *C 10* (15.4.07, sold for BU 7.22), *C 11* (27.5.07, sunk 14.7.09), *C 12* (9.9.07, sold for BU 2.20), *C 13* (9.11.07, sold for BU 2.20), *C 14* (7.12.07, sold for BU 12.21), *C 15* (21.1.08, sold for BU 2.22), *C 16* (19.3.08, sold for BU 8.22), *C 17* (13.8.08, sold for BU 11.19), *C 18* (10.10.08, sold for BU 5.21), *C 19* (20.3.09, sold for BU 2.20), *C 20* (27.11.09, sold for BU 5.21), *C 21* (26.9.08, sold for BU 12.21), *C 22* (10.10.08, sold for BU 2.20), *C 23* (26.11.08, sold for BU 12.21), *C 24* (26.11.08, sold for BU 5.21), *C 25* (10.3.09, sold for BU 12.21), *C 26* (20.3.09, scuttled 4.4.18), *C 27* (22.4.09, scuttled 4.4.18), *C 28* (22.4.09, sold for BU 8.21), *C 29* (19.6.09, mined 29.8.15), *C 30* (19.7.09, sold for BU 8.21), *C 31* (2.9.09, lost by unknown cause 4.1.15), *C 32* (29.9.09, stranded 24.10.17), *C 33* (10.5.10, lost by unknown cause 4.8.15), *C 34* (8.6.10, torpedoed 21.7.17), *C 35* (2.11.09, scuttled 4.4.18), *C 36* (30.11.09, sold for BU 6.19), *C 37* (1.1.10, sold for BU 6.19), *C 38* (10.2.10, sold for BU 6.19). All built by Vickers, except *C 17*–*C 20*, *C 33*, *C 34* which were built by Chatham DYd.

Having built three classes of submarines the Admiralty felt confident in embarking on a large production-run from 1906. In retrospect the decision to build 38 submarines to what was essentially a small coastal design was a mistake, for it delayed the introduction of proper overseas patrol submarines. The blame rests largely with Fisher, who saw submarines as useful for harbour defence, as a substitute for minefields. However, in spite of their petrol engines and the lack of space and endurance they saw continuous war service. Six were built by Chatham DYd to ensure the Royal Dockyards' ability to keep up with progress in submarine design. Appearance was similar to the 'B' class, but without the diving planes amidships. Some were camouflaged late in the war.

C 1 was converted in 1918 to destroy the viaduct during the Zeebrugge Raid, but was kept in reserve. *C 3* was nominally attached to 6th Flotilla for Zeebrugge Raid, 23 April 1918, when she was loaded with explosives to blow up the viaduct connecting the Mole to the shore. *C 11* was sunk in collision with SS *Eddystone* off Cromer. *C 14* and *C 17* were also sunk in collisions (with Hopper *No 27* on 10 December 1913, and with HMS *Lurcher* in May 1917 respectively), but both were raised and repaired. *C 26*, *C 27* and *C 35* were sent on Detached Service to the Baltic from 1916, going out as deck cargo to Archangel, then by canal barge and rail to Lapvik on the Gulf of Finland. All were scuttled on 4 April 1918 off Helsingfors to avoid surrender to Germans. *C 32* was also sent to the Baltic in 1916; she was stranded and destroyed in Gulf of Riga.

B 2 before the war CPL

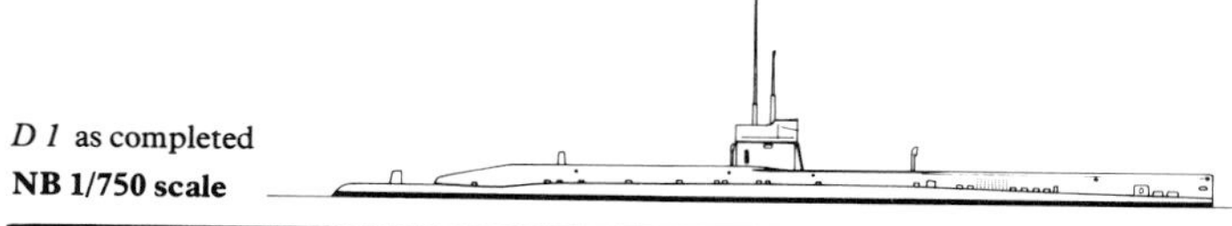
D 1 as completed
NB 1/750 scale

'D' class *submarines*

Displacement:	*D 1* 483t surfaced; 595t submerged *D 2* 489t surfaced; 603t submerged *D 3*–*D 8* 495t surfaced; 620t submerged
Dimensions:	*D 1* 163ft oa × 20ft 6in over tanks × 10ft 5in surfaced *49.7m × 6.2m × 3.2m* *D 2* 162ft 1in oa × 20ft 6in over tanks × 10ft 9½in surfaced *49.4m × 6.3m × 3.3m* *D 3*–*D 8* 164ft 7in oa × 20ft 5in over tanks × 11ft 5in surfaced *50.2m × 6.2m × 3.5m*
Machinery:	2 shafts, 6-cyl diesels, 2 electric motors, 1200hp/550hp = 14kts/9kts. Range 2500nm at 10kts surfaced
Armament:	3–18in (45.7cm) TT (2 bow, 1 stern, 6 torpedoes), 1–12pdr (76mm; *D 4* only)
Complement:	25

Class (launched, fate):
D 1 (16.5.08, sunk as target 23.10.18), *D 2* (25.5.10, sunk 25.11.14), *D 3* (17.10.10, sunk in error 15.3.18), *D 4* (27.5.11, sold for BU 12.21), *D 5* (28.8.11, mined 3.11.14), *D 6* (23.10.11, torpedoed 26.6.18), *D 7* (14.1.11, sold for BU 12.21), *D 8* (23.9.11, sold for BU 12.21). The last pair built by Chatham DYd and the rest by Vickers.

Approved 1906, and were the first British submarines with an overseas patrolling capability. Apart from the introduction of diesels most of the improvements stemmed from the big increase in displacement. More internal volume and a bigger crew lightened the work-load on a long patrol. The diesel engines also helped by eliminating the dangerous petrol vapour which had caused numerous explosions in the early boats. The adoption of saddle tanks increased internal space, while twin screws gave greater manoeuvrability. Earlier submarines had been fitted to receive radio messages but the 'D' class could transmit as well for the first time, an extendable mast being rigged by hand when needed. Although contemporary references suggest that the entire class were fitted with guns, and many with 2–12pdr, only *D 4* had one, on a platform which folded down into the casing. This arrangement was not a success, and later the gun was given a fixed position on deck. With their larger conning towers and full-length casings the 'D' class marked a clean break with the tiny 'A's, 'B's and 'C's. *D 1* was authorised under 1906–07 Estimates, *D 2* under 1908–09 Estimates and remainder under 1909–40 Estimates.

D 2 was sunk by German patrol boats off the Ems estuary. *D 3* was sunk in error by a French airship in the Channel. *D 6* was torpedoed by *UB 73* off Northern Ireland.

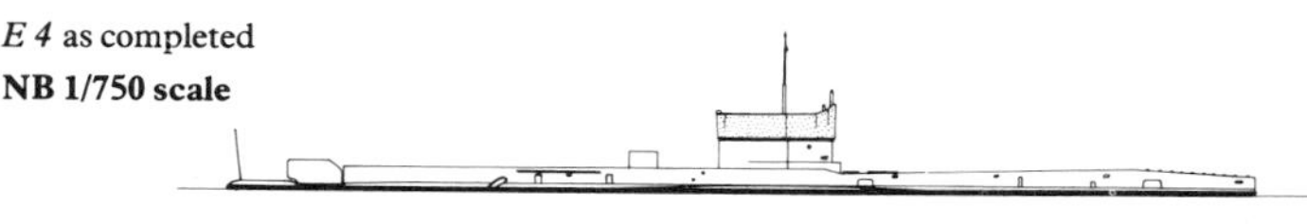
E 4 as completed
NB 1/750 scale

'E' class (E 1 group) *submarines*

Displacement:	655t surfaced; 796t submerged
Dimensions:	178ft 1in oa × 22ft 8⅝in × 12ft 6¼in mean *54.2cm × 6.9m × 3.8m*
Machinery:	2 shafts, 8-cyl Vickers diesels, 2 electric motors, 1600hp/840hp = 15kts/9kts. Range 3000nm at 10kts surfaced
Armament:	4–18in (45.7cm) TT (1 bow, 2 beam, 1 stern, 8 torpedoes), 1–12pdr (76mm)/18cwt
Complement:	30

Class (launched, fate):
E 1 (ex-*E 9*, 9.11.12, scuttled 8.4.18), *E 2* (ex-*D 10*, 23.11.12, sold for BU 1921), *E 3* (29.10.12, torpedoed 18.10.14), *E 4* (5.2.12, sold for BU 2.22), *E 5* (17.5.12, lost by unknown cause 7.3.16), *E 6* (12.11.12, mined 26.12.15), *E 7* (2.10.13, sunk 5.9.15), *E 8* (30.10.13, scuttled 4.8.18), *AE 1* (RAN, 18.6.13, lost 14.9.14), *AE 2* (RAN, 22.5.13, scuttled 30.4.15), *E 1*, *E 2*, *E 7* and *E 8* were built by Chatham DYd, the remainder by Vickers.

For the 1920–11 Programme the Admiralty ordered six enlarged and improved versions of the 'D's. There was little fundamental change for the 'D' class had proved most successful, but in response to requests from the Submarine Service the hull was enlarged to accommodate a pair of beam TT. It was felt that long-range attacks with bow tubes were not sufficiently accurate, whereas beam tubes permitted more accurate short-range shooting. For that reason the 'E' class were to be given single bow and stern tubes, and a pair of tubes amidships, firing p&s. The diesels were the standard Vickers 4-stroke type but *E 3* was given 2-stroke Carel diesels of Belgian manufacture. They were not successful, and after trials they were replaced by the standard type. An important innovation was the provision for the first time of two watertight bulkheads. When war broke out in August 1914 two boats of the 1911–12 Programme, *E 7* and *E 8*, were ordered to be built to the *E 1* design, rather than to the 'Improved E' design which was to follow. The design proved highly successful, and production continued right through to 1917. With their later successors they bore the brunt of the Allies' submarine offensive, losing nearly 50 per cent and scoring some of the outstanding successes of the war in the Sea of Marmora and the Baltic. *E 7* was fitted with 6pdr 1915, and *E 2* with 4in (supplied by Malta DYd for operations in Sea of Marmora).

E 1 was sent to Baltic in October 1914 and was scuttled off Helsingfors to avoid capture. *E 3* was torpedoed in the North Sea by *U 27*. *E 4* was sunk in collision with *E 41* on 15 August 1916, but although raised was apparently never recommissioned. *E 7* was trapped in anti-submarine nets in the Dardanelles and then destroyed by explosive charge from *UB 14*. *E 8* went to the Baltic and was scuttled off Helsingfors. *AE 1* was lost from unknown cause (probably struck underwater obstruction) off Bismarck Archipelago. *AE 2* was sent to the Mediterranean in March 1915 and had to be scuttled in Sea of Marmora after sustaining severe damage from Turkish torpedo-boat *Sultan Hissar*.

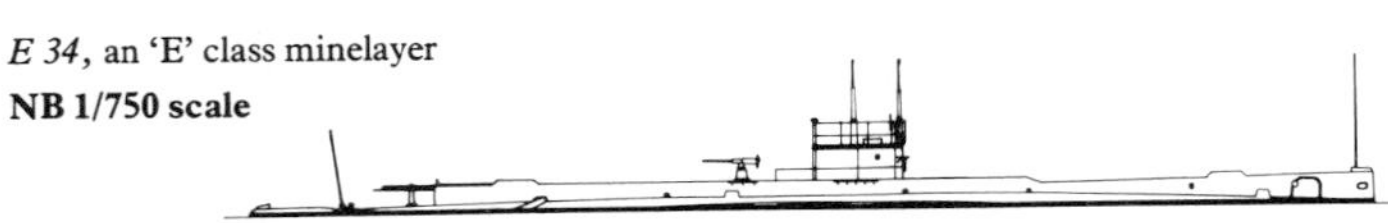

E 34, an 'E' class minelayer
NB 1/750 scale

'E' class (E 9 group) *submarines*

Displacement: 667t surfaced; 807t submerged
Dimensions: 181ft (182ft 6in from *E 19* onwards) × 15ft 1½in × 12ft 6in surfaced
55.2m (55.6m) × 4.6m × 3.8m
Machinery: As *E 1* group
Armament: 5–18in (45.7cm) TT (2 bow, 2 beam, 1 stern, 10 torpedoes), 1–12pdr (76mm)/18cwt
Minelayers 3–18in TT (2 bow, 1 stern), 20 mines
Complement: 30

Class (builders, launched, fate):
E 9 (Vickers, 29.11.13, scuttled 8.4.18), *E 10* (Vickers, 29.11.13, lost from unknown cause 18.1.15), *E 11* (Vickers, 23.4.14, sold for BU 3.21), *E 12* (Chatham DYd, 5.9.14, sold for BU 3.21), *E 13* (Chatham DYd, 22.9.14, sold for BU 12.21), *E 14* (Vickers, 7.7.14, mined 27.1.18), *E 15* (Vickers, 23.4.14, lost 15.4.15), *E 16* (Vickers, 23.9.14, mined 22.8.16), *E 17* (Vickers, 16.1.16, wrecked 6.1.16), *E 18* (Vickers, 4.3.15, sunk 24.5.16), *E 19* (Vickers, 13.5.15, scuttled 8.4.18), *E 20* (Vickers, 12.6.16, sunk 5.11.15), *E 21* (Vickers, 24.7.15, sold for BU 12.21), *E 22* (Vickers, 27.8.15, torpedoed 25.4.16), *E 23* (Vickers, 28.9.15, sold for BU 9.22), *E 25* (ex-Turkish, Beardmore, 23.8.15, sold for BU 12.21), *E 26* (ex-Turkish, Beardmore, 11.11.15, lost by unknown cause 6.7.16), *E 27* (Yarrow, 9.6.17, sold for BU 9.22), *E 28* (Yarrow,–, cancelled 4.15), *E 29* (Armstrong, 1.6.15, sold for BU 2.22), *E 30* (Armstrong, 29.6.15, lost by unknown cause 22.11.16), *E 31* (Scott, 23.8.15, sold for BU 9.22), *E 32* (White, 16.8.16, sold for BU 9.22), *E 33* (Thornycroft, 18.4.16, sold for BU 9.22), *E 35* (John Brown, 20.5.16, sold for BU 9.22), *E 36* (John Brown, 16.9.16, lost by unknown cause, 17.1.17), *E 37* (Fairfield, 2.9.15, lost by unknown cause 1.12.16), *E 38* (Fairfield, 13.6.16, sold for BU 9.22), *E 39* (Palmer, 18.5.16, sold for BU 10.21), *E 40* (Palmer, 9.11.16, sold for BU 12.21), *E 42* (Cammell Laird, 22.10.15, sold for BU 9.22), *E 43* (Swan Hunter, 11.11.15, sold for BU 1.21), *E 44* (Swan Hunter, 21.2.16, sold for BU 10.21), *E 47* (Fairfield, 29.5.16, lost by unknown cause 20.8.17), *E 48* (Fairfield, 2.8.16, sold for BU 7.28), *E 49* (Swan Hunter, 18.9.16, mined 12.3.17), *E 50* (John Brown, 13.11.16, mined 1.2.18), *E 52* (Denny, 25.1.17, sold for BU 1.21), *E 53* (Beardmore, 1916, sold for BU 9.22), *E 54* (Beardmore, 1916, sold for BU 12.21), *E 55* (Denny, 5.2.16, sold for BU 9.22), *E 56* (Denny, 19.6.16, sold for BU 6.23)
Minelayers – *E 24* (Vickers, 9.12.15, mined 24.3.16), *E 34* (Thornycroft, 27.1.17, mined 20.7.18), *E 41* (Cammell Laird, 22.10.15, sold for BU 9.22), *E 45* (Cammell Laird, 25.1.16, sold for BU 9.22), *E 46* (Cammell Laird, 4.4.16, sold for BU 9.22), *E 51* (Scott, 30.11.16, sold for BU 10.31).

Five more 'E' class were proposed for the 1911–12 Programme, but with numerous improvements suggested by experience with the 'D's and early 'E's. However in August 1914, to speed production the Admiralty proposed that *E 7* and *E 8* should be completed to the basic design, and that only the essential improvements should be incorporated into *E 9*. As mass-production was planned Chatham Dockyard's *E 12* was to be the pattern for all builders except Vickers. The *E 9* design was made 3ft longer to permit a second 18in TT in the bow. Although the 'D' class had their tubes 'over-and-under' to allow a finer bow-form, the 'Improved E' design reverted to a side-by-side configuration as this afforded more protection to the bow caps and shutters, and made for easier loading. The foremost watertight bulkhead was also moved 2ft aft to simplify loading. The engines were moved forward, the conning tower was enlarged to provide a steering position, and a third watertight bulkhead was povided. *E 9–E 11* and *E 14–E 16* were immediately approved to be built to this design but Chatham DYd produced a design which was a compromise between the original *E 1* class and the modified Vickers design. A single bow tube was the most important change, but as *E 12* became the pattern for wartime production at some stage the twin tubes must have been reinstated, for records show clearly that war-built 'E's had two TT forward.

When war broke out the contracts for *E 17* and *E 18* were authorised and had gone to Vickers, but Fisher was anxious to build many more submarines. On 11 November 1914 a conference between the Admiralty and representatives of the shipbuilders met to allocate future construction. Out of this came contracts for *E 19–E 56*: 6 from Vickers, 4 from Beardmore, 2 from Scott, 2 from Yarrow, 2 from Armstrong, 1 from White, 2 from Thornycroft, 3 from John Brown, 4 from Fairfield, 2 from Palmer, 4 from Cammell Laird, 1 from White, 2 from Scott and 3 from Denny. This total included two 'E' class already ordered for Turkey from Beardmore; they were re-allocated as *E 25* and *E 26*. *E 27* and *E 28* were cancelled in April 1915 to allow Yarrow to carry on with more important work, but *E 27* was reinstated in August. From *E 19* all were given a 'plough' bow to improve seakeeping, and a variety of guns were fitted, as supplies allowed. Experience in the Sea of Marmora showed the need for guns, and various weapons were hurriedly installed, such as *E 20*'s 6in howitzer (fitted by the builders), *E 11*'s 12pdr and *E 12*'s 4in (supplied by Malta DYd). Some of the North Sea boats received high-angle 3in or 12pdrs in 1916–17. Early in 1916 *E 22* was fitted with a launching ramp on her after superstructure to fly off two Sopwith Baby seaplanes; the idea was to launch them well inside the Heligoland Bight on a reconnaissance mission. In the Sea of Marmora several boats carried spare torpedoes lashed to the casing. The upper rudder was removed from all during the war.

E 9 went to the Baltic in October 1914 and was scuttled to avoid falling into German hands; *E 19* was scuttled at the same time. *E 13* was sent to the Baltic in August 1915. While trying to enter Baltic ran aground on Saltholm and after being disabled by German shellfire was interned on 18 August 1915; returned to RN in November 1918. *E 15*, while trying to get through to the Sea of Marmora ran aground off Kephez Point on 15 April 1915, and was disabled by gunfire. Numerous attempts were made to destroy her, including an attack by *B 6*, bombing and destroyer attack, and long-range bombardment, but on the night of 16 April she was destroyed by 14in torpedoes launched by battleships' picket boats. *E 18* was sunk off Bornholm by German decoy ship *K*. *E 41*, while exercising off Harwich on 15 August 1916 was rammed by the submerged *E 4*; both boats sank with heavy loss of life; subsequently raised by lifting craft.

E 11 1915 *CPL*

'S' class design
NB 1/750 scale

'S' class *submarines*

Displacement: 265t surfaced; 324t submerged
Dimensions: 148ft 1½in oa × 14ft 5in × 10ft 4½in mean
45.1m × 4.4m × 3.2m
Machinery: 2 shafts, Scott-FIAT 6-cyl diesels, 2 electric motors, 650hp/400hp = 13kts/8½kts. Range 1600nm at 8½kts surfaced
Armament: 2–18in (45.7cm) TT (bow, 4 torpedoes), 1–12pdr (76mm)
Complement: 18

Class (launched, fate):
S 1 (28.2.14, to Italy 25.10.15), *S 2* (14.4.15, to Italy 25.10.15), *S 3* (10.6.15, to Italy 25.10.15). All built by Scott.

In August 1911 a group of Admiralty officers visited FIAT-San Giorgio's works at La Spezia, and were shown the *Velilla* and *Medusa.* A month later, Scott's of Greenock, who had been FIAT-San Giorgio's UK licensees since 1909, offered to build a similar boat for £50,000. The tender was accepted that month and *S 1* was ordered. She was comparable to the 'C' class in size, and had the same armament, 2–18in TT and 4 torpedoes. Although slightly slower she had a high reserve of buoyancy and a ship-shape form. The main disadvantage was the length of time taken to dive, an inherent problem with the Laurenti type of double-hull construction. Although some sources suggest that the 'S' boats were not sufficiently seaworthy for North Sea operations there is no apparent reason why boats with such a high reserve of buoyancy should be poor seaboats; a more likely reason is the general lack of familiarity with Italian practice and equipment.

The design followed Laurenti's principles, with a partial double hull and a wide 'ducktail' stern. There were no fewer than ten watertight bulkheads, at a time when the 'E' class had only two. Two more boats were ordered in June 1913, but all three were transferred to the Italian Navy in 1915 as the RN had more submarines than it could find crews for. They served under the same numbers in Italian service.

'V' class *submarines*

Displacement:	*V 1* 386t surfaced; 453t submerged *V 2–V 4* 391t surfaced; 457t submerged
Dimensions:	*V 1* 144ft oa × 16ft 6in × 11ft 6in mean *43.9m × 5.0m × 3.5m* *V 2–V 4* 147ft 6in oa × 16ft 3in × 11ft 6in mean *45.0m × 5.0m × 3.5m*
Machinery:	2 shafts, Vickers 8-cyl diesels, 2 electric motors, 900hp/450hp (380hp in *V 2–V 4*), 14kts/8½kts. Range 3000nm at 9kts surfaced
Armament:	2–18in (45.7cm) TT (bow, 4 torpedoes), 1–12pdr (76mm)
Complement:	20

Class (launched, fate):
V 1 (23.7.14, sold for BU 11.21), *V 2* (17.2.15, sold for BU 11.21), *V 3* (1.4.15, sold for BU 10.20), *V 4* (25.11.15, sold for BU 10.20). All built by Vickers.

The February 1912 Submarine Committee recommended two new types for development, an overseas type displacing 1000t on the surface and a coastal type of 250t–300t. The large type emerged as the *Nautilus (qv)* and the coastal type emerged as the 'S' and 'F' types, but Vickers produced their own design to meet the requirement, and in the mood of experiment current in the RN Submarine Service it was accepted. There was a close resemblance to the 'S' design for the Vickers boats also adopted a partial double hull. It extended over about 75ft amidships, as against 45ft in the 'S' design. The battery capacity was low: 132 Exide cells as against 166 in the 'C' class. Even the 'A' class, on half the displacement, had 120 cells. The result was that the 'V' class were short of underwater endurance but in spite of that they had no difficulty in reaching their designed speed. Two types of electric motors were used: *V 1*'s were made by Laurence Scott with 300hp as designed, whereas *V 2–V 4*'s came from the Don Works, which had provided motors for previous classes.

V 2–V 4 differed from the prototype because two lots of two 21in frames had been added, in the battery tank compartment and the torpedo compartment respectively. As the foremost tank compartment was then shortened by two frames, the total increase in length was 3ft 6in. *V 1* was authorised under the 1912–13 Programme and ordered in March 1913 (Vickers had already started her on 11 December 1912). Three more were ordered in August 1913 under the 1913–14 Programme.

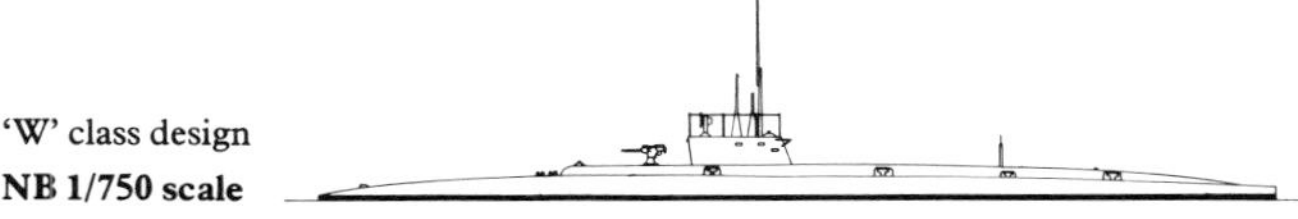
'W' class design
NB 1/750 scale

'W' class *submarines*

Displacement:	*W 1, W 2* 331t surfaced; 499t submerged *W 3, W 4* 321t surfaced; 479t submerged
Dimensions:	*W 1, W 2* 171ft 11in oa × 15ft 4¼in × 8ft 10½in mean *52.4m × 4.7m × 2.7m* *W 3, W 4* 149ft 11in oa × 17ft 10in × 9ft 4in mean *45.7m × 5.4m × 2.8m*
Machinery:	*W 1, W 4* 2 shafts, 8-cyl diesels, 2 electric motors, 710hp/480hp = 13kts/8½kts. Range 2500nm at 9kts surfaced *W 3, W 4* 2 shafts, 6-cyl diesels, 2 electric motors, 760hp/480hp = 13kts/8½kts
Armament:	*W 1, W 2* 2–18in (45.7cm) TT (bow, 2 torpedoes), 4–18in torpedoes in external drop-collars *W 3, W 4* 2–18in (45.7cm) TT (bow, 4 torpedoes), 1–3in (76mm) AA added in both
Complement:	18

V 3 as completed *By courtesy of John M Maber*

F 2 as completed *By courtesy of John M Maber*

Class (launched, fate):
W 1 (19.11.14, to Italy 23.8.16), *W 2* (15.2.15, to Italy 23.8.16), *W 3* (1.4.15, to Italy 23.8.16), *W 4* (25.11.15, to Italy 7.8.16). All built by Armstrong.

The same Admiralty team which visited FIAT-San Giorgio in 1911 also visited the Schneider yard at Toulon to inspect the French Navy's submarine *Pluviose* and various Schneider-Laubeuf designs. They concluded that the French boats were too long and too slow, and in particular they did not like the Drzwiecki drop-collars carried outside the casing. In spite of this adverse report two were ordered from Armstrong Whitworth, for no better reason than keeping a promise to the firm to order two submarines per year (however, there was great enthusiasm for foreign double-hulled designs in the Submarine Service). Two were therefore ordered under the 1912–13 Estimates, and keels of *W 1* and *W 2* were laid in October and December 1913 (order placed January 1913). Seven months later *W 3* and *W 4* were ordered from the same builders, but considerably modified by M Laubeuf to meet RN requirements.

In spite of delays in redrawing and redesign the first pair were built remarkably quickly, 15 and 17 months respectively. The principal difference between the two groups was the omission of the drop-collars in *W 3* and *W 4*. The engines were Schneider-Laubeuf diesels, but 8-cyl type in the first two and 6-cyl in the later pair. The chief complaint in service was poor habitability, caused mainly by the small diameter of the pressure hull (2ft 6in × 3ft 6in, less than the 'Hollands') but somewhat mitigated by the lack of internal framing. In their defence, however, the DNC commented that that they had unusually good control when diving, while the detailed design of flooding, venting and other subsidiary installations was practical and efficient. As the RN had a surplus of submarines and because these four boats, like the 'S' class, were non-standard, they were handed over to the Italian Navy in 1916, retaining their original numbers.

'F' class *submarines*

Displacement:	363t surfaced; 525t submerged
Dimensions:	151ft oa × 16ft 1¼in × 10ft 7in mean *46.0m × 4.9m × 3.2m*
Machinery:	2 shafts, 2 diesels, 2 electric motors, 900hp/400hp = 14kts/8¾kts. Range 3000nm at 9½kts surfaced
Armament:	3–18in (45.7cm) TT (2 bow, 1 stern, 6 torpedoes), 1–2pdr
Complement:	19

Class (builder, launched, fate):
F 1 (Chatham DYd, 31.3.15, BU 1920), *F 2* (White, 7.7.17, sold for BU 7.22), *F 3* (Thornycroft, 19.2.16, BU 1920).

Standard Admiralty coastal design built for comparison with the 'S', 'V' and 'W' types. Like them had double-hull features, and was based largely on the 'V' design, with improvements such as a stern TT. The Admiralty was most anxious to encourage the building of diesel engines, and so while *F 1* had the standard Vickers type, *F 2* had 6-cyl Nuremberg (MAN) type built under licence by J Samuel White, but *F 3* reverted to the Vickers type. The battery had 128 Exide cells. *F 1* was ordered under the 1913–14 Programme and laid down in January 1913. *F 2* and *F 3* came under the 1914–15 Programme but laying down dates are not known. Another three, *F 4–F 6* were projected in 1914 but cancelled after war broke out. Being very small these submarines saw relatively little service, apart from local defence.

NAUTILUS *submarine*

Displacement: 1441t surfaced; 2026t submerged
Displacement: 258ft 4½in oa × 26ft × 17ft 9in mean
78.8m × 7.9m × 5.4m
Machinery: 2 shafts, Vickers 12-cyl diesels, 2 electric motors, 3700hp/1000hp = 17kts/10kts. Range 5300nm at 11kts surfaced
Armament: 8–18in (45.7cm) TT (2 bow, 4 beam, 2 stern, 16 torpedoes), 1–3in (76mm) AA
Complement: 42

Class (builder, launched, fate):
Nautilus (Vickers, 31.12.14, sold for BU 6.22).

In reply to the 1912 Submarine Committee's recommendation that an overseas submarine be built, displacing 1000t and capable of 20kts on the surface, Vickers produced a design. Unfortunately their conclusion was that 17kts was the maximum to be hoped for, while displacement would be at least 1270t. The Admiralty was disappointed at this pessimistic view, but realised that Vickers had far more experience with diesels than any other builder, and even that experience was limited to four years' running with *A 13* and three years with *D 1*. The FIAT company, when approached through Scott's, agreed with Vickers and were most reluctant to guarantee even the 1850bhp proposed by Vickers for their new 12-cyl diesel. They suggested instead a steam turbine installation, which was rejected but used subsequently in *Swordfish*. Vickers were given a provisional order in October 1912 (covering design work) and laid the keel in March 1913, a month before the official order was received. As predicted development of the big diesel proved very slow, particularly under wartime conditions, and although she was launched at the end of 1914 she was not completed until October 1917 (having been numbered *N 1* in June). Although nominally in service with the 6th Flotilla at Portsmouth she never became operational and was used as a depot ship, supplying power to other submarines. This apparent failure conceals the fact that she was a giant step forward, not only in size but in power. The experience provided useful data for future developments.

Nautilus as completed — *By courtesy of John M Maber*

Swordfish during trials — *By courtesy of John M Maber*

SWORDFISH *submarine*

Displacement: 932t surfaced; 1105t submerged
Displacement: 231ft 3½in oa × 22ft 11in × 14ft 11in mean
70.5m × 7.0m × 4.5m
Machinery: 2-shaft Parsons geared impulse-reaction steam turbines, 2 electric motors, 1 Yarrow boiler, 4000hp/1400hp = 18kts/10kts. Range 3000nm at 8½kts surfaced
Armament: 2–21in (53.3cm) TT (bow, 2 torpedoes), 4–18in (45.7cm) TT (beam, 8 torpedoes), 2–3in (76mm)
Complement: *c*18

Class (builder, launched, fate):
Swordfish (Scott, 18.3.16, sold for BU 7.22).

Disappointed with the performance proposed for *Nautilus*, the Admiralty still hoped to build a 20kt submarine. The proposal put forward by Laurenti in mid-1912 was resurrected, for it promised 18kts on only 856t. What was known as the 'FIAT 140bis' design was developed by Scott's, with increased surface displacement, lower endurance and heavier armament. The order was placed in August 1913. In design it followed Laurenti principles closely, with a double hull for 75 per cent of the length. A small folding funnel was provided, with electrical control; once folded down the well was sealed hydraulically by a cover. Two 3in were provided forward and aft, also with disappearing mountings under watertight covers. Closing down the funnel took about 1½ minutes, and the rise in heat inside the boat proved to be no worse than in destroyers and light cruisers. Like the 'S' class, *Swordfish* had more watertight bulkheads than contemporary British designs. Other safety features which attracted favourable comment were the provision of safety buoys, a telephone buoy, a blowing arrangement with controls in the control room and forward and aft, and an emergency HP air line to all compartments.

She commissioned on 28 April 1916 as a tender to *Dolphin*, having been numbered *S 1* on 1 April. Although nominally operational with 4th Flotilla following acceptance in July 1916 her trials continued for five months. She tended to lose stability when surfacing, presumably because of the difficulty in clearing water from the free-flooding spaces in the upper part of the hull. She was eventually laid up at Portsmouth in January 1917 while her future was decided. Taken in hand on 27 June 1917 for conversion to a surface patrol boat, and reverted to the name *Swordfish* in July. A new raised forecastle and wheelhouse were built up, and a new taller, fixed funnel was stepped (armament 2–12pdr, depth-charges). The original steam plant was retained but the batteries were presumably replaced by ballast. Commissioned on 10 August 1917 and accepted two months later; served as tender to *Victory* but did not become operational until January 1918.

G 10 as completed
NB 1/750 scale

'G' class *submarines*

Displacement: 703t surfaced; 837t submerged
Dimensions: 187ft 1in oa × 22ft 8in × 13ft 4in mean
57.0m × 6.9m × 4.1m
Machinery: 2 shafts, Vickers 8-cyl diesels, 2 electric motors, 1600hp/840hp = 14¼kts/9kts. Range 2400nm at 12½kts surfaced.
Armament: 1–21in (53.3cm) TT (stern, 2 torpedoes), 4–18in (45.7cm) TT (2 bow, 2 beam, 8 torpedoes), 1–3in (76mm) AA
Complement: 30

Class (launched, fate):
Chatham DYd – *G 1* (14.8.15, sold for BU 2.20), *G 2* (23.12.15, sold for BU 2.20), *G 3* (22.1.16, sold for BU 11.21), *G 4* (23.10.15, sold for BU 6.28), *G 5* (23.11.15, sold for BU 10.22).
Armstrong – *G 6* (7.12.15, sold for BU 11.21), *G 7* (4.3.16, sunk 1.11.18)
Vickers – *G 8* (1.5.16, sunk by unknown cause 14.1.18), *G 9* (15.6.16, sunk in error 16.9.17), *G 10* (11.1.16, sold for BU 1.23), *G 11* (22.2.16, wrecked 22.11.18), *G 12* (24.3.16, sold for BU 2.20), *G 13* (18.7.16, sold for BU 1.23)
Scott – *G 14* (17.5.17, sold for BU 3.21)
White – *G 15* (–, cancelled 4.15).

The Admiralty, reacting to a rumour in 1913 that almost the whole German U-boat effort had been turned over to double-hulled overseas boats, was panicked into requesting a boat with displacement similar to the 'E' class, a partial double hull, a single 21in TT forward and two 18in beam tubes. Out of this emerged the 'G' class, 7 units being ordered under the 1914–15 Estimates: *G 1–G 7* were ordered pre-war and *G 8–G 13* ordered on 24 November 1914 as part of Fisher's expansion of the submarine force. The firms invited to tender for *G 6*, *G 7*, *G 14* and *G 15* were allowed to install their own diesels, so Armstrong Whitworth proposed to put MAN Nuremberg type in *G 6*, and Sulzers in *G 7*; Scott's proposed to put FIAT engines into *G 14* and White proposed to put their licence-built MAN type into *G 15* (cancelled in 1915). The impossibility of getting German diesels led to *G 6* and *G 7* being engined. with Vickers standard diesels. The standard 'G's had the same diesel as the 'E's, so to speed up production of existing 'E's Chatham DYd were allowed to divert the diesels ordered for *G 2–G 5* into *E 19–E 22*. The engines were presumably replaced by engines built at Chatham. During construction the armament was changed. The 21in tube was moved aft and two 18in bow tubes were substituted. The 'G's thus introduced the 21in torpedo to British submarines, although *Swordfish* had been ordered a year earlier.

'J' class *submarines*

Displacement: 1204t surfaced; 1820t submerged (*J 7* 1212t; 1820t)
Dimensions: 275ft 6in (*J 7* 274ft 9in) oa × 23ft × 14ft mean
84.0m (83.7m) × 7.0m × 4.3m
Machinery: 3 shafts, Vickers 12-cyl diesels, 3 electric motors, 3600hp/1350hp = 19½kts/9½kts. Range 5000nm at 12½kts surfaced
Armament: 6–18in (45.7cm) TT (4 bow, 2 beam, 12 torpedoes), 1–12pdr (76mm), 1–3in (76mm) AA (*J 5–J 7* 1–12pdr AA, 1–2pdr) (all except *J 3* rearmed with 1–4in)
Complement: 44

Class (launched, fate):
Portsmouth DYd – *J 1* (6.11.15, to Australia 25.3.19, sold for BU 2.24), *J 2* (6.11.15, to Australia 25.3.19, sold for BU 2.24), *J 3* (–, cancelled 4.15), *J 4* (–, cancelled 4.15)
Pembroke DYd – *J 3* (ex-*J 7*, 4.12.15, to Australia 25.3.19, sold for BU 2.24), *J 4* (ex-*J 8*, 2.2.16, to Australia 25.3.19, sold for BU 1.26)
Devonport DYd – *J 5* (9.9.15, to Australia 25.3.19, sold for BU 2.24), *J 6* (9.9.15, sunk in error 15.10.18), *J 7* (RAN, 21.2.17, sold for BU 11.29).

The continuing incorrect intelligence reports of 22kt U-boats so worried the C-in-C of the Grand Fleet that he lobbied successfully for yet another attempt at a fleet submarine, capable of keeping station with the battle fleet. Vickers, already wrestling with the engines for the *Nautilus*, did not propose to use the 1850hp diesel, and suggested instead that the standard 8-cyl engine could be enlarged to 12-cyl, but it would still take three, and although 20kts was the speed asked for, the records suggest that 19½kts was the accepted design-speed. Given the haste with which the design was to be prepared the Admiralty had no choice, and approved its one and only triple-shaft design in January 1915. The design was another partial double-hull type, with the double hull occupying 56 per cent of the length. As built the large free-flooding casing brought the bows down in a seaway, slowing the boat down, so it was sealed off. After some months in service all had their bows raised, and thereafter could make 17kts in the heaviest seas.

Originally eight boats were approved, all from the Royal Dockyards, but two from Portsmouth DYd, *J 3* and *J 4*, were cancelled and *J 7* and *J 8* were renumbered to fill the gap. A further boat was ordered for the RAN but she differed in important respects. The control room was moved from just forward of the beam TT to the motor room aft. The conning tower was therefore moved aft as well, but in other respects *J 7* was identical to her sisters. *J 1* was fitted to drop depth-charges from after casing.

K 3 as completed

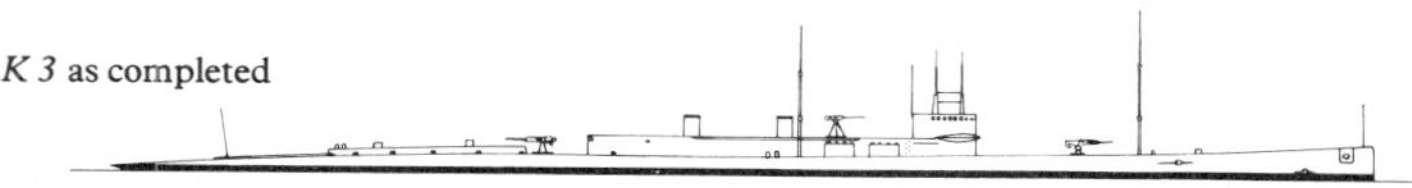

'K' class *submarines*

Displacement:	1980t surfaced; 2566t submerged
Dimensions:	330ft oa × 26ft 6⅝in × 17ft mean *100.6m × 8.1m × 5.2m*
Machinery:	2-shaft Brown-Curtis (*K3, K 4, K 8–K 10, K 17* Parsons) geared steam turbines, 2 Yarrow boilers, 4 electric motors, 10,500hp/1440hp = 24kts/9½kts. Range 3000nm at 13½kts surfaced
Armament:	10–18in (45.7cm) TT (4 bow, 4 beam, 1×2 revolving mount in superstructure, 18 torpedoes), 2–4in (10.2cm) QF 1–3in (76mm) AA
Complement:	59

Class (builder, launched, fate):
K 1 (Portsmouth DYd, 14.11.16, sunk following collision 17.11.17), *K 2* (Portsmouth DYd, 14.10.16, sold for BU 7.26), *K 3* (Vickers, 20.5.16, sold for BU 10.21), *K 4* (Vickers, 15.7.16, sunk in collision 31.1.18), *K 5* (Portsmouth DYd, 16.12.16, sunk by unknown cause 20.1.21), *K 6* (Devonport DYd, 31.5.16, sold for BU 7.26), *K 7* (Devonport DYd, 31.5.16, sold for BU 9.21), *K 8* (Vickers, 10.10,16, sold for BU 10.23), *K 9* (Vickers, 8.11.16, sold for BU 7.26), *K 10* (Vickers, 27.12.16, sold for BU 11.21), *K 11* (Armstrong, 16.8.16, sold for BU 11.21), *K 12* (Armstrong, 23.2.17, sold for BU 7.26), *K 13* (Fairfield, 11.11.16, renumbered *K 22* 3.17, sold for BU 12.26), *K 14* (Fairfield, 8.2.17, sold for BU 12.26), *K 15* (Scott, 31.10.17, sold for BU 8.24), *K 16* (Beardmore, 5.11.17, sold for BU 8.24), *K 17* (Vickers, 10.4.17, sunk in collision 31.1.18), *K 18* (Vickers, –, cancelled 1917), *K 19* (Vickers, –, cancelled 1917), *K 20* (Armstrong, –, cancelled 1917), *K 21* (Armstrong, –, cancelled 1917).

In the spring of 1915 the C-in-C Grand Fleet once again pressed for Fleet Submarines, this time capable of 24kts. To meet this demand two designs were examined, one from Vickers and the other from the DNC:

	Vickers Design	DNC Design
Displacement (surfaced)	2000t	1700t
Length (oa)	280ft	338ft
Beam	28ft	29ft
Draught (mean)	23ft	11ft
Armament	8–18in TT	8–21in TT
Power	14,000shp	10,000shp
Speed	23kts	24kts

The DNC design dated back two years, during discussions on *Swordfish* and *Nautilus*, and the difficulty of achieving 20kts on existing diesels. It had been extensively tested with models at AEW Haslar but had not been proceeded with. The Vickers proposal was produced in mid-April 1915, as an alternative to a diesel-electric design, which would need no fewer than eight of the new and untried 12-cyl 'J' class diesels. Being a knot slower and less heavily armed, as well as being 300t heavier than the Admiralty design, it was not accepted but Vickers were asked to develop the DNC's design into a new class of fleet submarine. Outline particulars and drawings were handed over early in May 1915, and *K 3* and *K 4* were ordered in June.

More boats were soon ordered: *K 1, K 2* and *K 5* in August 1915. After a lull another four (*K 15–K 18*) were ordered in February 1916; the last three were ordered in May 1916 but they and *K 18* were cancelled before they had been laid down, and the orders were replaced by 'M' class *M 1–M 4*. Had they been built with their designed armament they would have been the most powerful submarines in the world for some years, but during construction 18in TT were substituted to avoid the delay of having to design a new torpedo-tube. At this stage the revolving twin TT in the superstructure were added, for use at night, along with two 4in and a 3in high-angle gun. Displacement was now up to 1880t, and would increase by another 100t during building.

Although officially described as double-hulled they were more like the early Laubeuf boats, with an external hull abreast of the upper half of the pressure hull. A totally enclosed bridge deckhouse was provided for the first time, to protect personnel. Machinery occupied 35 per cent of the length. An 800hp 'E' class diesel drove a 700hp dynamo, providing auxiliary diesel-electric drive on the surface. This enabled the boat to get under way during the interval between surfacing and getting up steam. It had been hoped to provide a third shaft for this purpose, but it would have been very inefficient. For main electric drive two motors were geared to each shaft.

In service the early boats were found to be very wet, like the 'J' class, and so the bow was raised; a new steering position then had to be built over the wheelhouse to see over the big 'swan' bow. The superstructure TT were removed as they were too close to the waterline to be of any use. One 4in gun was dropped, and the remaining one and the 3in AA gun were moved to the superstructure. Although there was talk of fitting some with 5.5in guns and some references suggest that this happened to at least one boat, Admiralty records do not show a 5.5in gun issued to any submarines. As a class they acquired a lurid reputation for bad luck and poor design, but most of this can be attributed to the faulty conception which had led to them being built. Fleet submarines had to operate on the surface in close company with surface ships, making collisions highly likely. The funnels and watertight hatches could be closed down in 30 seconds but a comparatively small obstruction could jam a ventilator open, as happened on several occasions. The disastrous 'Battle of May Island' at the end of January 1918 was the result of navigational errors, not design. To mix squadrons of battlecruisers and light cruisers with submarines having 'the speed of a destroyer and the bridge facilities of a picket boat' was asking for trouble, especially when all were steaming fast at night, without lights. The 'K' class were a remarkable technical achievement, however, unmatched by the Germans or any of the Allies.

K 13 foundered on 29 January 1917 in the Gareloch while running trials, under contractors' control; salved in March and renumbered *K 22* before acceptance in May 1917. It was her jammed helm which set off the chain of collisions off May Island, 31 January 1918.

J 4 1919 — *RAN, by courtesy of Vic Jeffery*

K 12 with raised bow — *CPL*

Improved 'K' class *submarines*

Displacement:	2140t surfaced; 2530t submerged
Dimensions:	351ft oa × 28ft × 16ft mean *107.0m × 8.5m × 4.9m*
Machinery:	2-shaft Parsons geared steam turbines, 2 Yarrow boilers, 4 electric motors, 10,500hp/1440hp = 23½kts/9½kts
Armament:	6–21in (53.3cm) TT (bow, 12 torpedoes), 4–18in (45.7cm) TT (beam, 8 torpedoes), 3–4in (10.2cm) QF
Complement:	59

Class (launched, fate):
Armstrong – *K 23* (–, cancelled 26.11.18), *K 24* (–, cancelled 26.11.18), *K 25* (–, cancelled 26.11.18)

GREAT BRITAIN

K 26 as completed *CPL*

Vickers – *K 26* (26.8.19, sold for BU 3.31), *K 27* (–, cancelled 26.11.18), *K 28* (–, cancelled 26.11.18)

In this class the known defects of the 'K' class were eliminated as far as possible. Motors, batteries and beam TT remained the same but a much heavier bow salvo of 6–21in TT was provided. The bow was given more flare to improve seakeeping, and the superstructure was higher to protect funnels and uptakes. Other improvements were to extend the superstructure forward to form a gun platform and to move hydroplanes 16ft further aft, where they were less susceptible to damage. Faster diving was possible by moving some ballast tanks to the internal hull, below the waterline. Six were ordered early in 1918, but five were cancelled in November. The frames of *K 24*, *K 25* and *K 28* were then ordered on 31 December 1918 to be taken to Chatham for completion, but that was later rescinded as well. In 1920 *K 26* was towed to Chatham and completed in June 1923.

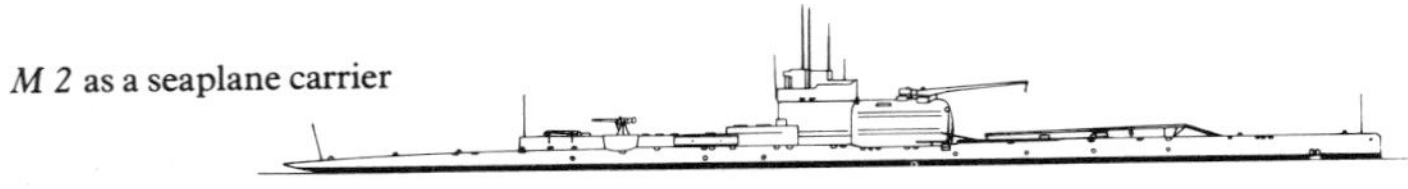
M 2 as a seaplane carrier

'M' class *submarines*

Displacement:	1594t surfaced; 1946t submerged
Dimensions:	295ft 9in (*M 3* 305ft 9in) oa × 24ft 8in × 15ft 11in (*M 3* 15ft 9in) mean *90.1m (93.2m) × 7.5m × 4.9m (4.8m)*
Machinery:	2-shafts, Vickers 12-cyl diesels, 2 electric motors, 2400hp/1600hp = 15kts/9kts. Range 3840nm at 10kts surfaced
Armament:	4–18in (*M 3* 21in) TT (bow, 8 torpedoes), 1–12in (30.5cm)/40cal Mk IX
Complement:	65

Class: (launched, fate):
M 1 (9.7.17, sunk in collision 12.11.25), *M 2* (19.10.18, foundered 26.1.32), *M 3* (19.10.18, sold for BU 2.32), *M 4* (20.7.19, cancelled 1918). The first pair were built by Vickers, and the other two by Armstrong.

Although often referred to as ex-'K' class, these four boats were a fresh design bearing no resemblance to the steam-driven 'K's, and were in fact replacement contracts for *K 18–K 21*, which had never been laid down. The exact date of ordering is not known, as the dates usually given, February 1916 *(M 1)*, May 1916 *(M 2)* and August 1916 *(M 3* and *M 4)* are the same as *K 18–M 21*. The true dates may be slightly later, as all four were laid down in July-December. The design was suggested by Commodore Hall, for a monitor submarine armed with a single 12in/23cal gun, to supplement torpedo attack. Fifty shells could be carried as against no more than eight torpedoes, and a round already loaded could be fired in 30 seconds from periscope depth, or 20 seconds breaking surface. The gun would also be available for shore bombardment. The idea was supported by a committee chaired by Admiral Tudor, but the boats were delayed as it was felt that such an idea in German hands might be dangerous. The committee talked of a 23cal 12in, and some sources talk of guns from the *Majestic* class, but the old Mk I, II and III 12in guns were 25cal, and the *Majestics*' Mk VIII guns were 35cal. In fact the 40cal Mk IX guns were part of a plentiful stock held for the *Formidable* group of pre-dreadnoughts.

After the initial delay *M 1* was accelerated, followed by *M 2–M 4*. The main engines and motors were identical to the 'L' class. *M 3* was lengthened by 10ft to permit 21in TT instead of 18in. The gun trials were highly successful, the 12in being able to elevate 20°, depress −5° and train 15°. The diving time was only 90 seconds. There was however, no role for them to play by 1918, and when *M 1* was completed in April 1919 it was suggested that *M 2–M 4* should be completed as oversea patrol submarines without 12in guns. This was vetoed by the First Sea Lord.

M 1 was the only one to see war service, being briefly with the 6th Flotilla to October 1918 and then 11th. Rammed and sunk 12 November 1925 off Start Point by SS *Vidar*. *M 2* became a seaplane carrier in April 1928 and foundered off Portland in 1933. *M 3* became a minelayer in 1927, and was sold in 1932. *M 4* was cancelled after the Armistice and was bought on after being launched to clear the slip in 1919 was bought by her builders in November 1921.

M 1 about 1919 *CPL*

'H' class *submarines*

Displacement:	364t surfaced; 434t submerged
Dimensions:	150ft 3in oa × 15ft 4in × 12ft 6in *45.8m × 4.7m × 3.8m*
Machinery:	2 shafts, diesels, 2 electric motors, 480hp/620hp = 13kt/11kts. Range 1600nm at 10kts surfaced
Armament:	4–18in (45.7cm) TT (bow, 6 torpedoes)
Complement:	22

Class (fate):
Canadian Vickers – *H 1* (sold 3.21), *H 2* (sold 1921), *H 3* (mined 15.7.16), *H 4* (sold 11.21), *H 5* (sunk in collision 3.6.18), *H 6* (interned 1916), *H 7* (sold 11.21), *H 8* (sold 11.21), *H 9* (sold 11.21), *H 10* (lost by unknown cause 19.1.18)
Fore River Co – *H 11* (sold for BU 1921), *H 12* (sold for BU 1922), *H 13* (to Chile 3.7.17), *H 14* (to Canada 6.19 as *CH 14*, BU 1925), *H 15* (to Canada 6.19 as *CH 15*, BU 1925), *H 16* (to Chile 3.7.17), *H 17* (to Chile 3.7.17), *H 18* (to Chile 3.7.17), *H 19* (to Chile 3.7.17), *H 20* (to Chile 3.7.17). Launch dates unknown.

In addition to the purchase of guns and armour for monitors, in November 1914 the Admiralty gave a contract to Bethlehem Steel to supply material for ten submarines similar to the US Navy's 'H' class. To get around the neutrality laws the boats were to be assembled by Canadian Vickers in Montreal, and a further ten were to be delivered 'after the war'. In fact the second batch were built at Bethlehem's Fore River yard, and were to be delivered unarmed to Canadian Vickers. The first ten boats were completed in May–June 1915, and their crossing of the Atlantic established a new record for submarines. The second batch was, however, subject to close scrutiny by the US Government, and it was made clear to the British that the boats could not be delivered, and they were held up until the United States entered the War in April 1917. In the meantime Bethlehem Steel had managed to send their engines, motors and other fittings to England for installation in the Vickers-built *H 21* class, so completion lagged far behind the first batch. As the entire batch were built in secrecy, launch dates were not logged in Admiralty records, and many details remain obscure. They were single-hulled, and had a small reserve of surface stability as a result, much like the 'B' and 'C' class. Nevertheless they gave good service. After America's entry into the war *H 11–H 20* were released but the Admiralty wished to compensate Chile for the ships requisitioned in 1914–15, and instructed the builders to deliver six of them to Chile.

H 6 ran aground on the Dutch coast on 8 January 1916 and was interned. Bought by the Royal Netherlands Navy in February 1916 she was numbered *O 8*.

Improved 'H' class *submarines*

Displacement:	423t surfaced; 510t submerged
Dimensions:	171ft 9in oa × 15ft 9in over fenders × 13ft 2½in mean *52.4m × 4.8m × 4.0m*
Machinery:	2 shafts, diesels, 2 electric motors, 480hp/620hp = 11½kts/10½kts
Armament:	4–21in (53.3cm) TT (bow, 6–8 torpedoes)
Complement:	22

Class (launched, fate):
Vickers – *H 21* (20.10.17, sold for BU 7.26), *H 22* (14.11.17, sold for BU 2.29), *H 23* (29.1.18, sold for BU 5.34), *H 24* (14.11.17, sold for BU 5.34), *H 25* (27.4.18, sold for BU 1929), *H 26* (15.11.17, sold for BU 4.28), *H 27* (25.9.18, sold for BU 8.35), *H 28* (12.3.18, sold for BU 9.44), *H 29* (8.6.18, foundered in dock 9.8.26, sold for BU 8.35), *H 30* (9.5.18, sold for BU 8.35), *H 31* (16.11.18, sunk 24.12.41), *H 32* (19.11.18, sold for BU 10.44)
Cammell Laird – *H 33* (24.8.18, sold for BU 1944), *H 34* (5.11.18, sold for BU 1945), *H 35* (–, cancelled 10.17), *H 36* (–, cancelled 10.17), *H 37* (–, cancelled 10.17), *H 38* (–, cancelled 10.17), *H 39* (–, cancelled 10.17)
Armstrong – *H 40* (–, cancelled 10.17), *H 41* (26.7.18, cancelled 1918), *H 42* (21.10.18, sunk in collision 23.2.22), *H 43* (3.2.19, sold for BU 1944), *H 44* (17.2.19, sold for BU 1944), *H 45* (–, cancelled 10.17), *H 46* (–, cancelled 10.17)
Beardmore – *H 47* (19.11.18, sunk in collision 9.7.29), *H 48* (31.3.19, sold for BU 8.35), *H 49* (15.7.19, sunk 27.10.40), *H 50* (25.10.19, sold for BU 1945)
Pembroke DYd – *H 51* (15.11.18, sold for BU 6.24), *H 52* (31.3.19, sold for BU 11.27)
Devonport DYd – *H 53* (–, cancelled 10.17), *H 54* (–, cancelled 10.17).

In January 1917 an order was placed with Vickers for 12 boats similar to the 'H' class but with 21in TT. Engines, main motors and major fittings were obtained from the United States. In June 1917 a second batch was ordered, 6 from Cammell Laird, 8 from Armstrong Whitworth, 4 from Beardmore, 2 from Pembroke DYd and 2 from Devonport DYd, using engines and motors made in England to US designs, but otherwise identical to those in *H 1–H 20* and *H 11–H 32*. The order was cut back when it was decided in October 1917 to build 12 'R' class (using many of the *H 21* class components). Another was cancelled shortly after the Armistice, so only 22 out of 34 were completed. The main differences between these and the earlier 'H' class resulted from fitting 21in TT; the hull was 21ft longer but the diameter of the pressure hull was the same. Displacement went up by 16 per cent. Despite their small reserve of surface stability, inherent in a single-hulled design, they were most successful and some survived to serve in the Second World War, although nominally restricted to training duties.

R 1 as completed
NB 1/750 scale

'R' class *submarines*

Displacement: 410t surfaced; 503t submerged
Dimensions: 163ft 9in oa × 15ft 3in × 11ft 6in mean
49.9m × 4.6m × 3.5m
Machinery: 1 shaft, diesel, electric motor, 240hp/1200hp (plus 25hp auxiliary electric motor) = 9½kts/15kts. Range 2000nm at 8kts surfaced
Armament: 6–18in (45.7cm) TT (bow, 12 torpedoes)
Complement: 22

Class (launched, fate):
Chatham DYd – *R 1* (25.4.18, sold for BU 1.23), *R 2* (25.4.18, sold for BU 2.23), *R 3* (8.6.18, sold for BU 2.23), *R 4* (8.6.18, sold for BU 5.34)
Pembroke DYd – *R 5* (–, cancelled 1919), *R 6* (–, cancelled 1919)
Vickers – *R 7* (14.5.18, sold for BU 2.23), *R 8* (28.6.18, sold for BU 2.23)
Armstrong – *R 9* (12.8.18, sold for BU 2.23), *R 10* (5.10.18, sold for BU 2.29)
Cammell Laird – *R 11* (16.3.18, sold for BU 2.23), *R 12* (9.4.18, sold 2.23).

This class, the first anti-submarine 'hunter-killers', were 30 years ahead of their time. In March 1917 the DNC's department submitted a design of submarine fast enough to overtake enemy submarines and sink them with torpedoes, rather than gunfire. The design was not approved, but later that year when Commodore (S) suggested the idea should be developed, it was resurrected and orders were placed in December (armament increased from four to six TT). The hull reverted to the 'spindle' shape of the 'Hollands' and 'A' to 'C' classes, and hull-sections were the same as the *H 21* class to save time (they were ordered in place of cancelled 'H' boats). The propulsion unit was a single 'H' engine, but a 'J' class 220-cell battery was used to boost underwater speed. An unusual step was the provision of a small 25hp auxiliary motor mounted on the shaft, for slow running. The bow compartment contained five powerful and sensitive hydrophones, with bearing measurement to allow torpedoes to be fired underwater. Although the single shaft made them hard to manoeuvre on the surface, the streamlined hull and large rudder gave them good underwater performance. Unfortunately the only engagement in which their unique capabilities could be used – *R 8*'s October 1918 attack on a U-boat – was marred by a faulty torpedo, and they were discarded early. Diving depth was 250ft (75m).

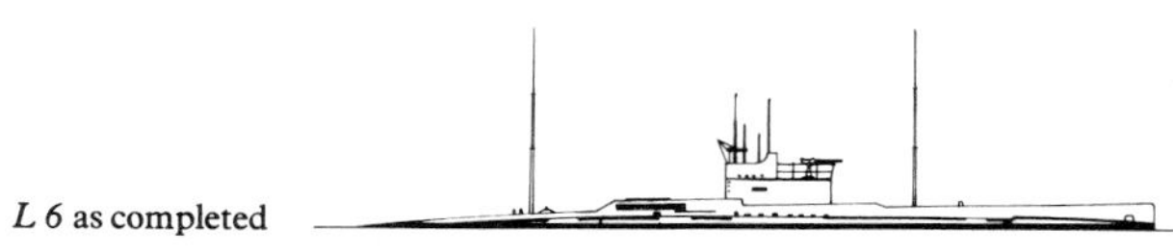
L 6 as completed

'L' class *submarines*

Displacement: 891t surfaced; 1074t submerged
Dimensions: 231ft 1in oa × 23ft 5½in × 13ft 3in mean
70.4m × 17.2m × 4.0m
Machinery: 2 shafts, diesels, 2 electric motors, 2400hp/1600hp = 17kts/10½kts. Range 3800nm at 10kts surfaced
Armament: 6–18in (45.7cm) TT (4 bow, 2 beam, 10 torpedoes), 1–4in (10.2cm)
Complement: 35

Class (launched, fate):
Vickers – *L 1* (ex-*E 57*, 10.5.17, sold for BU 1930), *L 2* (ex-*E 58*, 6.7.17, sold for BU 1930), *L 3* (1.9.17, sold for BU 1931), *L 4* (17.11.17, sold for BU 2.34)
Swan Hunter – *L 5* (26.1.18, sold for BU 1931)
Beardmore – *L 6* (14.1.18, sold for BU 1935)
Cammell Laird – *L 7* (24.4.17, sold for BU 1930), *L 8* (7.7.17, sold for BU 10.30).

By 1916 there was an urgent need for a design to replace the 'E' class, which despite its wartime improvements was six years old, and hard to 'stretch' to accommodate further improvements. After all the experiments with double- and partially double-hulled boats, the Admiralty reverted to the well-tried saddle-tank design, but with higher speeds. The first pair, *E 57* and *E 58* were only intended to be lengthened 'E's, but showed so many improvements that they were chosen as prototypes for a new class and numbered *L 1* and *L 2*. These had been ordered in February 1916 and laid down three months later.

L 3–L 8 were ordered in May 1916, and they were completed between November 1917 and March 1918. Armament varied: *L 1* had a 3in AA gun on a disappearing mounting, and initially some had no gun at all. Eventually all carried their 4in gun on a platform at the forward end of the conning tower, with its own access trunk.

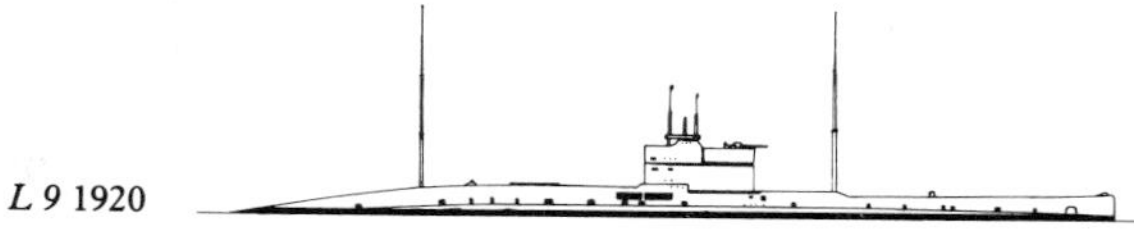
L 9 1920

L 9 class *submarines*

Displacement: 890t surfaced; 1080t submerged
Dimensions: 238ft 7in oa × 23ft 5½in × 13ft 3in without extra fuel
72.7m × 7.2m × 4.0m
Machinery: As 'L' class
Armament: 4–21in (53.3cm) TT (bow, 8 torpedoes), 2–18in (45.7cm) TT (beam, 2 torpedoes)
Minelayers 4–21in TT (bow), 14–16 mines (see notes)
Complement: 38

Class (launched, fate):
Denny – *L 9* (29.1.18, sold for BU 6.27), *L 10* (24.1.18, sunk by destroyer 30.10.18)
Fairfield – *L 15* (16.1.18, sold for BU 2.32), *L 16* (9.4.18, sold for BU 2.34)
Vickers – *L 18* (21.11.18, sold for BU 10.36), *L 19* (4.2.19, sold for BU 1937), *L 20* (23.9.18, sold for BU 1.35), *L 21* (11.10.19, sold for BU 2.39), *L 22* (25.10.19, sold for BU 8.35), *L 23* (1.7.19, sold for BU 1946), *L 24* (19.2.19, sunk in collision 14.1.24), *L 26* (29.5.19, sold for BU 1946), *L 27* (14.6.19, sold for BU 1946), *L 28* (–, cancelled 1919), *L 29* (–, cancelled 1919), *L 30* (–, cancelled 1919), *L 31* (–, cancelled 1919), *L 32* (23.8.19, cancelled 1919, sold for BU 3.20)
Swant Hunter – *L 33* (29.5.19, sold 1932)
Pembroke DYd – *L 34* (–, cancelled 1919), *L 35* (–, cancelled 1919)
Orders not placed – *L 36–L 49*
Minelayers (all Vickers-built) – *L 11* (26.2.18, sold for BU 2.32), *L 12* (16.3.18, sold for BU 2.32), *L 14* (10.6.18, sold for BU 5.34), *L 17* (13.5.18, sold for BU 2.34), *L 25* 13.2.19, sold for BU 1935).

War experience demanded a heavier bow salvo, and so the second batch of 'L' class was given 4–21in TT, although the beam 18in were retained to avoid having to enlarge the hull. The lead boat *L 9* was ordered in August 1916, followed by *L 10–L 35* in December (excluding the 'unlucky' *L 13*). Although it was planned to build *L 36–L 49* later, orders were not placed. Five boats were completed as minelayers, along the lines of the 'E' class, with vertical mine-chutes in the saddle tanks. *L 11*, *L 12*, *L 14* and *L 17* had 16 mine-tubes (16 mines) but *L 25* had only 14 tubes. From *L 12* onwards the 4in gun was raised to the bridge deck level, where it was served by an enclosed access trunk. This arrangement was intended to permit the 'L's to engage a U-boat out of torpedo-range, with the boat trimmed down. They were a great improvement over the 'E' class, particularly in accommodation. Three survived to the end of the Second World War on training duties. Seven were cancelled in 1918–19.

The main alterations were dictated by the change to 21in TT. The pressure hull was lengthened by 7ft 6in and a water-tight bulkhead was added abaft the bow TT to separate the tube compartment from the forward torpedo room. From *L 18* onwards 78t more fuel was carried, an improvement which was retro-fitted to the earlier 'L' class and *L 9–L 17*. No spare torpedoes were carried for the beam TT.

H 27 after the war — *CPL*

L 53 about 1930 CPL

L 50 class *submarines*

Displacement:	960t surfaced; 1150t submerged
Dimensions:	235ft oa × 23ft 5½in × 13ft 1½in mean *71.6m × 7.2m × 4.0m*
Machinery:	As 'L' class except range 4500nm at 8kts surfaced
Armament:	6–21in (53.3cm) TT (bow, 12 torpedoes), 2–4in (10.2cm) QF
Complement:	44

Class (builder, launched, fate):
L 50 (Cammell Laird, –, cancelled 1919), *L 51* (Cammell Laird, –, cancelled 1919), *L 52* (Armstrong, 18.12.18, sold for BU 1935), *L 53* (Armstrong, 12.8.19, sold for BU 1938), *L 54* (Denny, 20.8.19, sold for BU 1938), *L 55* (Fairfield, 21.9.18, sunk 9.6.19), *L 56* (Fairfield, 29.5.19, sold for BU 3.38), *L 57* (Fairfield, cancelled 1919), *L 58* (Fairfield, cancelled 1918), *L 59* (Beardmore, –, cancelled 1918), *L 60* (Cammell Laird, –, cancelled 1918), *L 61* (Cammell Laird, –, cancelled 1918), *L 62* (Fairfield, –, cancelled 1918), *L 63* (Scott, –, cancelled 1918), *L 64* (Scott, –, cancelled 1918), *L 65* (Swan Hunter, –, cancelled 1918), *L 66* (Swan Hunter, –, cancelled 1918), *L 67* (Armstrong, –, cancelled 1919), *L 68* (Armstrong, –, cancelled 1919), *L 69* (Beardmore, 6.12.18, sold for BU 2.39), *L 70* (Beardmore, –, cancelled 1919), *L 71* (Scott, 17.5.19, sold for BU 3.38), *L 72* (Scott, –, cancelled 1919), *L 73* (Denny, –, cancelled 1919), *L 74* (Denny, –, cancelled 1918).

An expansion of the 'L' design was authorised early in 1917, before any experience had been gained with *L 1—L 8*, but as that class was successful the *L 50* design simply provided heavier armament. *L 50–L 55* were ordered in January–February 1917, followed by *L 56–L 58* in April 1917 and *L 59–L 66* and *L 74* in April 1918, but most were in an early stage of building by the Armistice. *L 59–L 66 and L 74* were cancelled by Admiralty Order of 26 November 1918, followed by *L 50, L 51, L 57, L 58, L 67, L 68, L 70, L 72* and *L 73* in April 1919. The frames for *L 67* and *L 68* were used to build the Yugoslav *Hrabri* and *Nebojsa* in 1927. *L 53* was towed to Chatham DYd for completion in January 1925, *L 54* to Devonport DYd for completion in August 1924, and *L 69* to Devonport for completion in April 1923. They were easily distinguished from the earlier 'L' class by having a second 4in gun platform at the after end of the conning tower. The bow salvo was increased to 6–21in TT and the beam tubes were omitted.

L 55 completed in December 1918 and was sent to the Baltic early 1919. Sunk off Kronstadt in 1919 by Russian patrol craft, she was later raised, repaired and incorporated into Soviet Navy under the same number.

SMALL SURFACE WARSHIPS

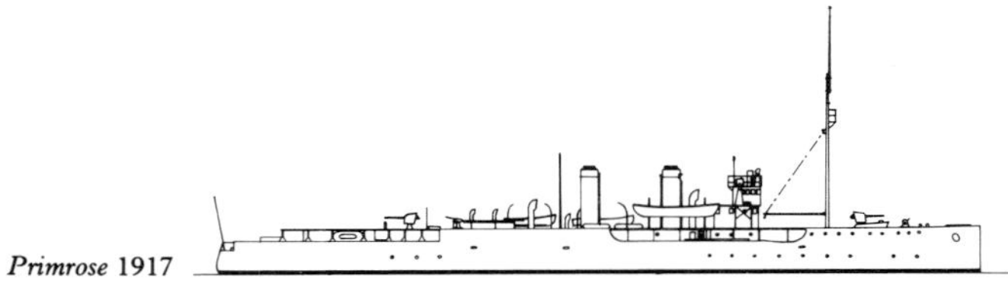

Primrose 1917

ACACIA class *fleet sweeping sloops*

Displacement:	1200t normal
Dimensions:	250ft pp × 33ft × 11ft *76.2m × 10.1m × 3.4m*
Machinery:	1-shaft TE, 2 boilers, 1800ihp = 16½kts. Coal 130t
Armament:	2–12pdr (76mm), 2–3pdr (47mm) AA
Complement:	90

Class (launched, fate):
Swan Hunter – *Acacia* (15.4.15, sold 9.22), *Anemone* (30.6.15, sold 9.22)
Earle – *Aster* (1.5.15, mined 4.7.17)
Scott – *Bluebell* (24.7.15, sold 5.30), *Daffodil* (17.8.15, sold 2.35), *Magnolia* (26.6.15, sold 7.32)
Barclay Curle – *Dahlia* (21.4.15, sold 7.32), *Daphne* (19.5.15, sold 1.23), *Foxglove* (30.3.15, sold for BU 9.46), *Hollyhock* (1.5.15, sold 10.30), *Lily* (6.6.15, sold 6.30), *Mallow* (13.7.15, RAN 7.19, sunk as target 1.8.35)
Lobnitz – *Honeysuckle* (29.4.15, sold 9.22), *Iris* (1.6.15, sold 1.20)
Connell – *Jonquil* (12.5.15, to Portugal 5.20), *Laburnum* (10.6.15, lost at Singapore 2.42)
Napier & Miller – *Larkspur* (11.5.15, sold 3.22)
McMillan – *Lavender* (12.6.15, torpedoed 4.5.17)
Greenock & Grangemouth – *Lilac* (29.4.15, sold 12.22)
Bow McLachlan – *Marigold* (27.5.15, sold 1.20), *Mimosa* (16.7.15, sold 11.22)
Simons – *Primrose* (29.6.15, sold 4.23)
Henderson – *Sunflower* (28.5.15, sold 27.1.21)
Dunlop Bremmer – *Veronica* 27.5.15, sold 22.2.35)

Soon after the outbreak of war in August 1914 the Admiralty realised the need for additional vessels capable of minesweeping, for general service, towing and the transport of libertymen and stores. The DNC produced a design based on mercantile scantlings, simple and robust, and capable of being built by non-specialist yards. By standardising on fittings building rates were accelerated and several were built in 19–21 weeks. Being single-screw ships they had large turning circles, and they carried steadying sail to assist in keeping their head to wind. To protect the ammunition it was carried in a lightly armoured 'box' magazine far aft; on several occasions the entire magazine was blown into the air by a mine-explosion without detonating the contents. Later vessels were fitted with treble-thickness plating around the bows and reinforced bulkheads forward. The first 12 ships were ordered on 1 January 1915, followed by another 12 on the 12th. They were delivered between May and September 1915. They were almost exclusively used on minesweeping until 1917, when they proved ideal for convoy escort.

AZALEA class *fleet sweeping sloops*

Displacement:	1210t normal
Armament:	2–4.7in (12cm), 2–3pdr (47mm) AA (some had 2–4in, 2–3pdr AA)
Other details:	As *Acacia* class

Class (launched, fate):
Barclay Curle – *Azalea* (10.9.15, sold 2.23), *Begonia* (26.8.15, lost 2.10.17)
Bow McLachlan – *Camellia* (25.9.15, sold 1.23)
Greenock & Grangemouth – *Carnation* (6.9.15, sold 1.22), *Clematis* (29.7.15, sold 2.31)
Lobnitz – *Heliotrope* (10.9.15, sold 1.35), *Myrtle* (11.10.15, mined 16.7.19)
Swan Hunter – *Jessamine* (9.9.15, sold 12.22), *Zinnia* (12.8.15, sold 4.20)
Napier & Miller – *Narcissus* (22.9.15, sold 9.22)
McMillan – *Peony* (27.10.15, sold 8.19), *Snowdrop* (7.10.15, sold 1.23)

A repeat order for minesweeping sloops was placed in May 1915, but with heavier armament, in view of the likelihood of German raids on the sweeping flotillas. It was hoped to provide 4.7in guns for them all, but the later ships had 4in. In other respects they were virtually identical, and came into service in September–December 1915. *Begonia* was converted to a Q-Ship or anti-submarine decoy, being rebuilt at Haulbowline near Queenstown 1916–17 to resemble a small coaster. She recommissioned on 9 August 1917 and used the names *Dolcis, Jessop* and *Q 10*. She was sunk in collision with the large U-boat *U 151* off Casablanca. *Myrtle* was mined in the Gulf of Finland during operations against the Bolsheviks. *Zinnia* was transferred to Belgium in April 1920 and retained her name.

ARABIS class *fleet sweeping sloops*

Displacement: 1250t normal
Dimensions: 268ft oa × 33ft 6in × 11ft
81.7m × 10.2m × 3.4m
Machinery: 1-shaft TE, 2 boilers, 2000ihp = 16kts. Coal 130t
Armament: 2–4.7in (12cm; six vessels had 2–4in, 10.2cm), 2–3pdr AA (47mm)
Complement: 90

Class (launched, fate):
Earle – *Alyssum* (5.11.15, mined 18.3.17), *Amaryllis* (9.12.15, sold 1.23)
Henderson – *Arabis* (6.11.15, sunk in action 10.2.16), *Asphodel* (21.12.15, to Denmark 16.6.20), *Berberis* (3.2.16, sold 1.23)
Barclay Curle – *Buttercup* (24.10.15, sold 2.20), *Campanula* (25.12.15, sold 9.22), *Celandine* (19.2.16, sold 1.23), *Cornflower* (30.3.16, bombed 19.12.41)
Lobnitz – *Crocus* (24.12.15, sold 7.30), *Cyclamen* (22.2.16, sold 7.32)
Napier & Miller – *Delphinium* (23.12.15, sold 10.33), *Genista* (22.2.16, torpedoed 23.10.16)
Greenock & Grangemouth – *Gentian* (23.12.15, mined 16.7.19), *Geranium* (8.11.15, RAN 1920, sunk as target 24.4.35)
Connell – *Gladiolus* (25.10.15, to Portugal 9.20), *Godetia* (8.1.16, sold 2.37), *Hydrangea* (2.3.16, sold 4.20)
Simons – *Lobelia* (7.3.16, sold 3.20), *Lupin* (31.5.16, sold 3.46)
Dunlop Bremner – *Marguerite* (23.11.15, RAN 1919, sunk as target 1.8.35), *Mignonette* (26.1.16, mined 17.3.17)
Bow McLachlan – *Myosotis* (4.4.16, sold 1.23)
McMillan – *Nasturtium* (21.12.15, mined 27.4.16)
Hamilton – *Nigella* (10.12.15, sold 11.22), *Pansy* (1.2.16, sold 1.20)
Workman Clark – *Pentstemon* (15.2.16, sold 4.20), *Petunia* (3.4.16, sold 12.22)
Swan Hunter – *Poppy* (9.11.15, sold 4.23), *Primula* (6.12.15, torpedoed 1.3.16)
Richardson Duck – *Rosemary* (22.11.15, sold 12.47)
Ropner – *Snapdragon* (21.12.15, sold 5.34)
C Rennoldson – *Valerian* (21.2.16, foundered 22.10.26)
Blyth Shipbuilding – *Verbena* (9.11.15, sold 10.33)
Irvine – *Wallflower (8.11.15, sold 8.31), Wisteria* (7.12.15, sold 1.31)

A slightly improved class was ordered in three batches in July 1915 to follow the *Azaleas*, with slightly more powerful machinery, which, it was hoped, would give ½kt more speed. All the improvements suggested from experience with the first batch were incorporated during construction, including the packing of some bow and wing compartments with 50t of cork to improve flotation in case of heavy damage. Eight more built for French Navy 1915–16.

Asphodel was transferred to Denmark and renamed *Fylla; Gladiolus* went to Portugal as *Republica*; *Geranium* was transferred to Australia in 1919. *Gentian* was mined in the Gulf of Finland during operations against the Bolsheviks. *Cornflower* was sold out commercially and taken back into naval service and lost during the fall of Singapore. *Rosemary* saw active service in the Second World War and was sold for BU in 1947.

AUBRIETIA class *convoy sloops*

Displacement: 1250t normal
Dimensions: As *Arabis* class
Machinery: 1-shaft TE, 2 boilers, 2500ihp = 17½kts. Coal 130t
Armament: As designed 3–12pdr (76mm), 2–3pdr (47mm) AA. As built 2–4in (10.2cm), 1–3pdr (47mm) AA
Complement: 92

Class (launched, fate):
Ordered 1.16:
Blyth – *Aubrietia* (17.6.16, sold 10.22)
Greenock & Grangemouth – *Heather* (16.6.16, sold 2.32)
Irvine – *Salvia* (16.6.16, torpedoed 20.6.17)
Lobnitz – *Tamarisk* (2.6.16, sold 10.22)
Richardson Duck – *Tulip* (15.7.16, torpedoed 30.4.17)
Ropner – *Viola* (14.7.16, sold 10.22)
Ordered 12.16:
Swan Hunter – *Andromeda* (6.17, to France 1917)
Blyth Shipbuilding – *Gaillardia* (19.5.17, mined 22.3.18)
Greenock & Grangemouth – *Hibiscus* (17.11.17, sold 1.23)
Hamilton – *Lychnis* (21.8.17, to RIM 9.21. BU 1946)
Irvine – *Montbretia* (3.9.17, sold 1.23)
Lobnitz – *Polyanthus* (24.9.17, sold 5.21)

A further order was placed for six sloops in January 1916, but it was hoped to improve their anti-submarine capabilities by disguising them as small merchant ships, with armament concealed. The earlier 'Flower' class ships had proved useful escorts but their unmistakable silhouette always betrayed them as warships, and it was hoped that a more mercantile silhouette would tempt U-boats to stay on the surface long enough for the sloops to get within gun-range. Six more were ordered in December. The builders were given a free hand to model the sloops on similar-sized ships which they had already built. This frequently resulted in unsuitable accommodation and internal arrangements, but was considered a necessary evil to make the disguise effective. Although not strictly Q-ships, in the sense that they were built as commissioned warships, they were incorporated into the decoy organisation, with 'Q' numbers and false identities. Their main problems were that when viewed from the bow or quarter their lines were much too fine for a mercantile hull, and if engaged by a U-boat their crews were too large to fake an 'abandon ship' routine.

Primula as completed — *By courtesy of John M Maber*

Andromeda was transferred to the French Navy before completion and renamed *Andromede*. *Lychnis* was transferred to the Royal Indian Marine and renamed *Cornwallis*.

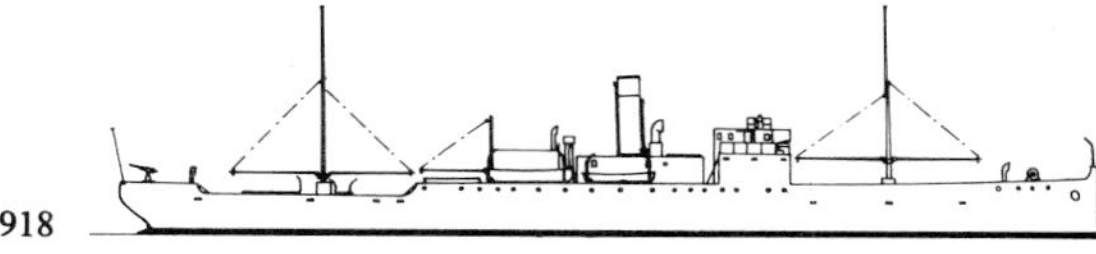

Coreopsis 1918

ANCHUSA class *convoy sloops*

Displacement: 1290t normal
Dimensions: 262ft 6in oa × 35ft × 11ft 6in
80.0m × 10.7m × 3.5m
Machinery: As *Aubrietia* class
Armament: 2–4in (10.2cm), 2–12pdr (76mm)
Complement: 92

Class (launched, fate):
Ordered 1.17:
Armstrong – *Anchusa* (21.4.17, torpedoed 16.7.18), *Bergamot* (5.5.17, torpedoed 13.8.17), *Candytuft* (19.5.17, torpedoed 18.11.17), *Ceanothus* (2.6.17, to RIM 5.22, wrecked 29.1.25)
Barclay Curle – *Convolvulus* (19.5.17, sold 1922), *Eglantine* (22.6.17, sold 12.21)
Simons – *Spiraea* (1.11.17, sold 9.22)
Workman Clark – *Syringa* (29.9.17, to Egypt 31.3.20)
Ordered 2.17:
Armstrong – *Arbutus* (8.9.17, torpedoed 8.9.17), *Auricula* (4.10.17, sold 2.23), *Bryony* (27.10.17, BU 1938), *Chrysanthemum* (10.11.17, RNVR drill ship, extant 1985)
Barclay Curle – *Coreopsis* (15.9.17, sold 9.22), *Cowslip* (19.10.17, torpedoed 25.4.18), *Dianthus* (1.12.17, sold 6.21), *Gardenia* (27.12.17, sold 1.23), *Gilia* (15.3.18, sold 1.23), *Harebell* (10.5.18, BU 1939)
Blyth Shipbuilding – *Ivy* (31.10.17, sold 2.20)
Greenock & Grangemouth – *Marjoram* (26.12.17, wrecked 1.21), *Mistletoe* (17.11.17, sold 1.21)
Hamilton – *Pelargonium* (18.3.18, sold 5.21)
Irvine – *Rhododendron* (15.10.17, torpedoed 5.5.18)
Lobnitz – *Saxifrage* — (29.1.18, RNVR drill ship *President* 1921, extant 1985)
Simons – *Silene* (13.3.18, sold 12.21)
Swan Hunter – *Sweetbriar* (5.10.17, sold 10.27), *Tuberose* (16.11.17, sold 1.23)
Workman Clark – *Windflower* (12.4.18, sold 10.27)

Similar to the *Aubrietia* type, and like them, varied according to the builders' ideas; Armstrongs had at least three designs, Barclay Curle at least two. When merchant ships were defensively armed many ships of these types received a dummy gun on the poop to maintain the disguise. In addition to concealed guns they had anti-submarine weapons, including depth-charges dropped through traps under the poop, and bomb-throwers of various types mounted on deck, usually behind breastworks where they could not be seen easily. The first six were ordered on 6 January 1917 (four from Armstrongs and two from Barclay Curle), followed by *Syringa* and *Spiraea* on the 13th and the remainder (*Arbutus* etc) on 21 February 1917, and they came into service between June 1917 and June 1918.

Ceanothus transferred to Indian Marine and renamed *Elphinstone*; wrecked off Nicobar Islands. *Syringa* sold to Egypt and renamed *Sollum*. *Chrysanthemum* converted to target towing tender May 1920; RNVR TS from 1938 and still moored off Embankment in London.

'24' class *fleet sweeping sloops*

Displacement: 1320t normal
Dimensions: 267ft 6in oa × 35ft × 10ft 6in
81.5m × 10.7m × 3.2m
Machinery: 1-shaft TE, 2 boilers, 2500ihp = 17kts. Coal 260t
Armament: 2–4in (10.2cm), 39 DCs
Complement: 82

Class (fate):
Swan Hunter – *Ard Patrick* (sold 1920), *Cicero* (sold for BU 12.20), *Flying Fox* (extant 1985), *Minoru* (sold 1920), *Orby* (sold 1922), *Rocksand* (sold 1922), *Spearmint* (sold 1922)
Barclay Curle – *Bend Or* (sold 1920), *Harvester* (sold 1922), *Iroquois* (sold 6.37), *Sefton* (sold 1922), *Silvio* (BU 1946), *Sir Bevis* (drill ship 1923)
Greenock & Grangemouth – *Donovan* (sold 1922), *Isinglass* (sold 1920), *Sanfoin* (sold 1922), *Sir Hugo* (sold for BU 12.21)
Osbourne Graham – *Ladas* (sold 1920), *Persimmon* (sold 1920), *Sir Visto* (sold 1920)
Blyth Shipbuilding – *Merry Hampton* (mined 14.11.44), *Ormonde* (sold for BU 8.37)

Launched June 1918–1919. A further class of 24 escort sloops was ordered between December 1916 and April 1917, modelled on the 'Flower' class but carrying the decoy principle to the ultimate, being double-ended, with identical deckhouses and gunshields forward and aft. Although named after famous racehorses they could easily be confused with the 'Racecourse' class minesweepers and so they became known officially as the '24' class, from the number planned. In fact only 22 were completed as *Galtee More* (ordered from Osbourne Graham but transferred to Swan Hunter) and *Sunstar* (Swan Hunter) were cancelled in December 1918. They proved indifferent seaboats, being inclined to roll, and were not rated as highly as the 'Flowers'. When dazzle-painted their course was extremely hard to determine, especially as *Ormonde, Iroquois, Silvio* and *Sir Bevis* had the mast abaft the funnel, whereas the others had it before. Ten were completed by the Armistice, and serving with sloop flotillas at Granton and Gibraltar.

Flying Fox became RNVR drill ship in March 1920 and is still extant at Bristol. *Sir Hugo* became depot ship in October 1919. *Iroquois* converted to survey ship 1922; handed over for BU in part exchange for RMS *Majestic*. *Merry Hampton* converted to a survey ship and renamed *Herald* in February 1923; scuttled at Seletar in February 1942 but repaired and recommissioned by the Japanese as *Heiyo* October 1942; mined in 1944. *Ormonde* converted to survey ship in March 1924. *Silvio* transferred to Australia in December 1924 for conversion to survey ship; recommissioned as HMAS *Moresby* in April 1925; rearmed 1940. *Sir Bevis* became RNVR drill ship *Irwell* in September 1923; renamed *Eaglet* 1926.

Ard Patrick as completed — *By courtesy of John M Maber*

P 52 about 1920 — *CPL*

P-BOAT type *patrol craft*

Displacement:	613t normal
Dimensions:	244ft 6in oa × 23ft 9in × 8ft *74.5m × 7.2m × 2.4m*
Machinery:	2-shaft steam turbines, 2 boilers, 3500shp = 20kts. Oil
Armament:	1–4in (10.2cm), 1–2pdr (40mm) AA, 2–14in (35.6cm) TT (deck p&s) (*P 52* 2–4in, 2–2pdr, no TT)
Complement:	50–54

Class (fate):
J S White – *P 11* (sold 12.21), *P 12* (sunk in collision 4.11.18), *P 40* (BU 1938), *P 52* (sold 5.23), *P 59* (sold 6.38)
Hamilton – *P 13* (sold 7.23), *P 38* (sold 5.38), *P 57* (to Egypt 21.5.20), *P 58* (sold 12.21)
Connell – *P 14* (sold 7.23)
Workman Clark – *P 15* (sold 11.21), *P 16* (sold 11.21), *P 17* (sold 11.21)
Inglis – *P 18* (sold 11.21), *P 39* (sold 9.22), *P 64* (sold 4.23)
Northumberland SB – *P 19* (sold 7.23), *P 20* (sold 5.23)
Russell – *P 21* (sold 11.21)
Caird – *P 22* (sold 12.23), *P 35* (sold 1.23)
Bartram – *P 23* (sold 7.23), *P 41* (sold 9.22)
Harland & Wolff, Govan – *P 24* (sold 12.21), *P 25* (sold 12.21)
Tyne Iron SB – *P 26* (mined 10.4.17), *P 50* (sold 12.21)
Eltringham – *P 27* (sold 7.23), *P 36* (sold 5.23)
R Thompson – *P 28* (sold 7.23), *P 49* (sold 1.23)
Gray – *P 29* (sold 7.23), *P 30* (sold 7.23), *P 37* (sold 2.24), *P 45* (sold 1.23)
Readhead – *P 31* (sold 12.26), *P 47* (sold 10.25), *P 48* (sold 5.23)
Harkess – *P 32* (sold 12.21), *P 46* (sold 10.25)
Napier & Miller – *P 33* (sold 12.21)
Barclay Curle – *P 34* (sold 12.21), *P 53* (sold 2.24), *P 54* (sold 2.24)

Launched October 1915–May 1918. Intended as utility destroyers, these were unorthodox craft with very low freeboard, sharply cutaway funnels and a small turning circle. A resemblance to large submarines was fostered, to give them a chance to close the range and sink by ramming or gunfire. Many were armed with single 14in TT facing aft, as it was hoped that they might be able to cripple German surface warships if attacked during one of the many East Coast raids (these TT were removed from old torpedo boats). The numbers *P 1–P 10* had already been used as pendant numbers for old battleships etc. *P 11–P 34* ordered May 1915, followed by *P 35–P 40* in February 1916, *P 41–P 54* in March 1916, *P 55–P 62* in April–May 1916 and *P 63–P 64* in June 1916. Ten of these were converted on the stocks and completed as PC-Boats.

All served with the Dover Patrol, Nore Local Defence Flotilla or Portsmouth Escort Force. *P 13* was renumbered *P 75* in August 1917. *P 57* was sold to Egypt and renamed *Raqib*. *P 38* was renamed *Spey* in February 1925 and used on fishery protection duties. Most were sold for BU in the early 1920s.

PC type, general appearance

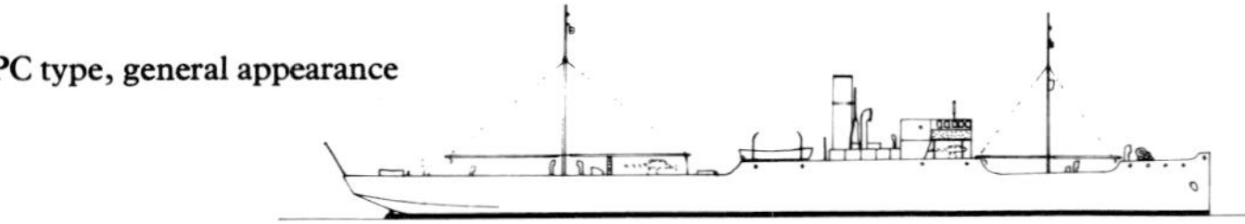

PC-BOAT type *decoy patrol boats*

Displacement:	682t–694t normal
Dimensions:	247ft oa × 25ft 6in × 8ft *75.3m × 7.8m × 2.4m*
Machinery:	As P-boats
Armament:	1–4in (10.2cm), 2–12pdr (76mm)
Complement:	50–55

Class (fate):
Caird – *PC 42* (sold 12.21), *PC 43* (sold 1.23)
Eltringham – *PC 44* (sold 4.23), *PC 65* (sold 1.23)
Tyne Iron SB – *PC 51* (sold 5.23)
Barclay Curle – *PC 55* (to RIM 2.22, sold 1935), *PC 56* (sold 7.23)
Workman Clark – *PC 60* (sold 2.24), *PC 61* (sold 4.23), *PC 69* (to RIM 5.8.21, lost 23.6.40), *PC 70* (sold 9.26)
Harland & Wolff, Govan – *PC 62* (sold 12.21)
Connell – *PC 63* (sold 5.23)
Harkess – *PC 66* (sold 7.23)
J S White – *PC 67* (sold 12.21), *PC 68* (sold 12.21), *PC 71* (sold 10.25), *PC 72* (sold 10.25), *PC 73* (sold 3.39), *PC 74* (sold 3.48)

Launched September 1916 – October 1918. The belief that Q-ships or decoys were the best counter to the U-boat threat led to an Admiralty order in December 1916 to complete 10 P-boats with a mercantile appearance, like the 'Flower-Q's. Although known for a while as PQ-boats the term PC-boat was finally chosen, and a further 10 were ordered, *PC 65–PC 70* in January 1917 and *PC 71–PC 74* in June. They were fully integrated in to the Q-ship system and used false names. There were severe topweight problems in fitting false upperworks and derricks etc to such a small hull, and many had wooden girdling added to improve stability. All were based at Pembroke from completion early in 1918. *PC 55* transferred to Royal Indian Marine and recommissioned in March 1922 (renamed *Baluchi* May 1922). *PC 69* transferred to Royal Indian Marine in August 1921 and renamed *Pathan* in May 1922; sunk off Bombay by internal explosion. *PC 73* renamed *Dart* in April 1925 and used for fishery protection duties. *PC 74* served in the Second World War as decoy ship *Chatsgrove* September–October 1939 then reverted to escort duties.

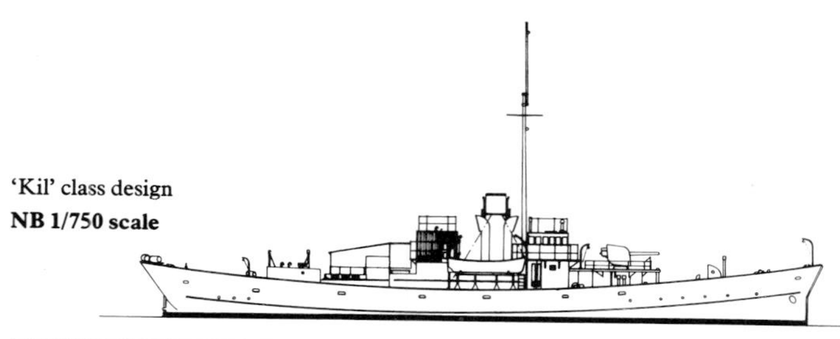
'Kil' class design
NB 1/750 scale

'KIL' class *patrol gunboats*

Displacement:	895t normal
Dimensions:	182ft oa × 30ft × 10ft 6in *55.5m × 9.1m × 3.2m*
Machinery:	1-shaft TE, 1 cylindrical boiler, 1400ihp = 13kts. Coal 330t
Armament:	1–4in (10.2cm)
Complement:	39

Class:
Smith's Dock – (3800–3815) *Kildary, Kildorough, Kilfenora, Kilgobnet, Kilclare, Kilchrenan, Kildavin, Kildorrey, Kilfullert, Kilkeel, Kilcock, Kildimo, Kildysart, Kilgarvan, Kilchreest, Kilham*
Smith's Dock – (4049–4069) *Killena, Killerig, Killiney, Killour, Killowen, Killybegs, Killygordon, Kilmacolm, Kilmacrennan, Kilmaine, Kilmallock, Kilmanahan, Kilmarnock, Kilmartin, Kilmead, Kilmelford, Kilmersdon, Kilmington, Kilmore, Kilmuckridge, Kilmun*
Hawthorn – (4001–4002) *Kilblane, Kilbarchan* (both cancelled 12.18)
George Brown – (4003–4006) *Kilberry, Kilbeggan, Kilbirnie, Kilbrachan* (cancelled 12.18)
Hall Russell – (4007–4012) *Kilbride, Kilbrittain* (cancelled 12.18), *Kilburn, Kilby, Kilcar, Kilcavan* (cancelled 12.18)
Cook, Welton & Gemmell – (4013–4026) *Kilchattan, Kilchvan, Kilclief, Kilclogher* (all completed), *Kilcolgan, Kilcommon, Kilconnell, Kilcoole, Kilcorney, Kilcot, Kilcreggan, Kilcullen, Kilcurrig, Kildale* (all cancelled 12.18)
Cochrane – (4027–4048) *Kildalkey, Kildangan, Kildare, Kildonan, Kildress, Kildwick, Kilfinny, Kilfree* (all completed), *Kilglass, Kilgowan, Kilkee, Kilkenny, Kilkenzie, Kilkerrin, Kilkhampton, Killadoon, Killagon, Killaloo, Killane, Killarney, Killary* and *Killegar* (all cancelled 12.18)

In mid-1917 it was decided to build a type of auxiliary escort vessel with greater speed, endurance and seakeeping than trawlers, and from July 1917 orders were placed with six trawler-builders for a series of 'fast trawlers' (reclassified as patrol gunboats in January 1918). Financial approval to build a total of 85 was given in November 1917, as well as a directive giving them priority over the Admiralty 'Strath', 'Castle' and 'Mersey' type trawlers (16 projected 'Castles' ordered from Smith's Dock were cancelled to allow them to take on gunboats 3800–3815, and the same builder was appointed 'parent firm' for the rest. In March 1918 a revision of priorities resulted in the cancellation of 30 gunboat contracts, but material was to be sent to Smith's Dock, who would henceforward be sole builder of the 'Kil' class. All vessels shown as cancelled, except *Kilbrachan* (George Brown) had been transferred to Smith's Dock by November 1918 (the *Kilbrachan* was cancelled in December 1918). To mislead U-boats they were given identical bow and stern, and they were given an angular stem and stern reminiscent of a 'paper boat'. Very few were completed by the Armistice, and all formed part of the Auxiliary Patrol, at least 11 being fitted for minesweeping.

The majority were completed without armament and went straight onto the Sale List, to be snapped up for mercantile conversion. *Kildress, Kilfree, Kildonan* and *Kildwick* were sold November 1919, followed by the remainder in February 1920. The only one retained by the RN was *Kilmun*, completed as a cable layer in February 1920. She was not sold until September 1946 and was wrecked in January 1950 as SS *Rask*. The first of class, *Kildary* was laid down in July 1917, launched 1 November 1917 and commissioned in December 1917. Cost varied from £18,000 to £20,000 for the hull and £19,700 for the machinery. Several were bought back into RN and Commonwealth naval service in an auxiliary role in the Second World War.

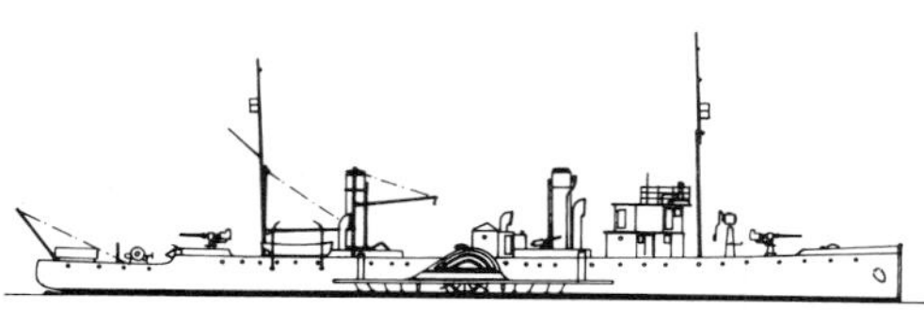
Kempton as completed

ASCOT class *paddle minesweepers*

Displacement:	810t normal
Dimensions:	245ft 9in oa × 29ft (58ft oa) × 7ft *74.9m × 8.8m (17.7m) × 2.1m*
Machinery:	Paddle-wheel diagonal compound steam, cyl boilers, 1500ihp = 14½kts. Coal 156t
Armament:	2–6pdr (57mm), 2–2pdr (40mm) pom-poms
Complement:	50

Class:
Ordered 9.15:
Ailsa SB – *Ascot, Atherstone, Chelmsford*
Ayrshire – *Chepstow, Croxton, Doncaster, Eglinton*
George Brown – *Epsom*
Clyde SB – *Eridge*
Dundee SB – *Gatwick*
Ferguson – *Kempton*
Fleming & Ferguson – *Lingfield*
Goole SB – *Ludlow*
Hamilton – *Melton*
Inglis – *Newbury*
McMillan – *Plumpton*
Murdoch & Murray – *Pontefract*
Ordered 10.15:
Ardrossan SB – *Cheltenham*
Dundee SB – *Goodwood*
Dunlop Bremner – *Haldon, Hurst*
Ordered 1.16:
Ayrshire – *Redcar*
Dunlop Bremner – *Sandown*
McMillan – *Totnes*

As a result of the success of hired paddlers as minesweepers the Admiralty ordered a design based on Ailsa SB's *Glen Usk*. They were named after race courses. The design included provision for two seaplanes, to help spot minefields from the air, but only *Eridge* and *Melton* had derricks and platforms fitted, and seaplanes were never used. They were completed between April and December 1916. *Ascot* was torpedoed by *UB 67* off the Faeroes 10 November 1918. *Kempton* was mined on 24 June 1917 while rescuing survivors of *Redcar* (also mined on the same day). *Ludlow* was mined off the Shipwash Shoal 29 December 1916. *Plumpton* was beached on the Belgian coast 19 October 1918 after being mined; she was subsequently BU where she lay. *Haldon* was sold for BU December 1921; *Croxton, Doncaster, Eglinton, Epsom, Eridge, Gatwick, Goodwood, Hurst, Newbury, Pontefract, Sandown* and *Totnes* were sold March–September 1922; *Lingfield* was sold in May 1923. *Atherstone, Chelmsford, Cheltenham, Chepstow* and *Melton* were sold August–November 1927 (*Atherstone* and *Melton* both returned to RN service in 1939–45, as AA ships *Queen of Kent* and *Queen of Thanet*). During the war the paddle 'sweepers' served with the Auxiliary Patrol, Fishery flag pendants superior to Admiralty Nos 881–904. Post-war they served in the Mine Clearance Service, bearing 'T' pendant numbers.

Leamington after the war *CPL*

BANBURY class *paddle minesweepers*

Displacement: 820t normal
Dimensions: 249ft oa × 29ft 6in × 7ft
76.1m × 9.0m × 2.1m
Machinery: As *Ascot* class
Armament: As *Ascot* class
Complement: 52

Class:
Ailsa SB – *Banbury, Harpenden*
Clyde SB – *Hexham*
Fleming & Ferguson – *Lanark, Lewes*
Dundee SB – *Shincliffe*
Dunlop Bremner – *Shirley*
Murdoch & Murray – *Wetherby*

In January 1917 eight slightly enlarged versions of the *Ascot* design known as the Improved Racecourse class, were ordered, and they were commissioned in January–June 1918. *Shirley* was sold in April 1919 for conversion to a ferry; *Lewes* and *Shincliffe* were sold for BU March 1922; *Banbury, Hexham* and *Lanark* were sold May–September 1923; *Wetherby* was sold in June 1924; *Harpenden* BU 1928.

FULMAR class *paddle minesweepers*

Particulars: Not known

Class:
Ailsa SB – *Fulmar, Gadwall, Pochard*
Murdoch & Murray – *Stormy Petrel, Tern*
No builder allocated – *Redshank, Shrike*

No details have survived for this design, but they would almost certainly have resembled the 'Racecourse' class. Ordered in 1918 and cancelled in December 1918; very little work had been done on them.

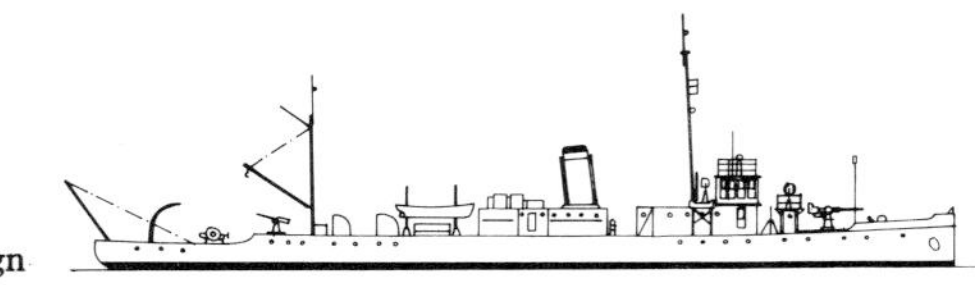
'Hunt' class design

'HUNT' class *minesweepers*

Displacement: 750t normal
Dimensions: 231ft oa × 28ft × 7ft
70.4m × 8.5m × 2.1m
Machinery: 2-shaft 3-cyl TE, 2 Yarrow boilers, 1800ihp = 16kts. Coal 140t
Armament: 2–12pdr (76mm), 2–6pdr (57mm) (many had only 1–12pdr, 1–6pdr)
Complement: 71

Class:
Ailsa SB – *Belvoir, Bicester*
Ardrossan SB – *Blackmorevale*
Bow McLachlan – *Cotswold, Cottesmore*
Clyde SB – *Cattistock, Croome*
Dunlop Bremner – *Dartmoor, Garth*
Fleming & Ferguson – *Hambledon, Heythrop*
Henderson – *Holderness, Meynell*
Lobnitz – *Muskerry, Oakley*
Napier & Miller – *Pytchley, Quorn*
Simons – *Southdown, Tedworth*
Murdoch & Murray – *Zetland*

The paddle 'sweepers ran the risk of catching moored mines in their paddle wheels, and to meet this objection the Admiralty decided early in 1916 that a class of twin-screw vessels was needed. Another complaint against the paddlers was their poor performance in bad weather. Ailsa SB was asked to submit a design, which became the basis for 20 ships ordered in mid-1916. Like the sloops, mercantile practice was followed to a great extent, greatly simplifying construction. They were most successful, being capable of undertaking escort duties as well as minesweeping. They were fitted with 'Quixo' patent davits for handling sweep gear, and were the world's first fleet minesweepers.

The lead-ship *Muskerry* came into service in January 1917, having been laid down in June 1916. The remainder were commissioned by August 1917. Most served in the 2nd and 3rd Minesweeping Flotillas at Granton. *Blackmorevale* was mined off Montrose 1 May 1918. *Belvoir, Croome, Hambledon, Heythrop, Meynell, Pytchley* and *Quorn* were sold for BU July–November 1922; *Bicester, Cattistock, Cotswold, Cottesmore, Dartmore, Garth, Muskerry, Oakley,* and *Zetland* were sold January–February 1923; *Holderness* was sold August 1924; *Southdown* was sold December 1926. *Tedworth* became a diving tender in August 1923; used for radar trials 1936 and sold for BU November 1946.

ABERDARE class *minesweepers*

Displacement: 800t normal
Dimensions: 231ft oa × 28ft 6in × 7ft 6in
70.4m × 8.7m × 2.3m
Machinery: 2-shaft TE, 2 Yarrow boilers, 2200ihp = 16kts. Coal 185t
Armament: 1–4in (10.2cm) QF, 1–12pdr (76mm) AA
Complement: 74

Class:
Ailsa SB – *Aberdare, Abingdon, Albury, Alresford, Ambleside, Amersham, Appledore, Leamingtan* (ex-*Aldeburgh*)
Ardrossan SB – *Badminton, Bagshot, Barnstaple, Swindon* (ex-*Bantry*)
Ayrshire – *Banchory, Bloxham* (ex-*Brixham*), *Bradfield, Burslem* (ex-*Blakeney*), *Goole* (ex-*Bridlington*)
Bow McLachlan – *Blackburn* (ex-*Burnham*), *Bootle* (ex-*Buckie*), *Caerleon, Camberley, Carstairs* (ex-*Cawsand*), *Caterham*
Dundee SB – *Battle, Fermoy, Forfar* (ex-*Fairburn*)
Eltringham – *Bury, Cheam, Gretna, Harrow, Havant, Huntley* (ex-*Helmsdale*), *Instow* (ex-*Infracombe*), *Gaddesdon, Gainsborough* (ex-*Gorleston*), *Northolt*
Simons – *Clonmel* (ex-*Stranraer*), *Elgin* (ex-*Troop*), *Sherborne* (ex-*Tarbert*), *Tiverton, Tonbridge, Tralee, Tring* (ex-*Teignmouth*), *Truro, Uppingham, Verwood* (ex-*Ventnor*), *Wem* (ex-*Walmer*), *Wexford*
Clyde SB – *Craigie, Derby* (ex-*Dawlish*), *Dorking, Dundalk, Dunoon, Fairfield, Forres* (ex-*Fowey*)
McMillan – *Cupar* (ex-*Rosslare*), *Sutton* (ex-*Salcombe*)
Dunlop Bremner – *Fareham, Faversham, Ford* (ex-*Fleetwood*), *Rugby* (ex-*Filey*)
Fairfield – *Irvine, Kendal, Kinross, Lydd* (ex-*Lydney*)
Harkess – *Longford* (ex-*Minehead*), *Marlow, Mistley* (ex-*Maryport*), *Monaghan* (ex-*Mullion*)
Fleming & Ferguson – *Mallaig, Malvern, Marazion, Munlochy* (ex-*Macduff*)
Inglis – *Nailsea* (ex-*Newquay*), *Newark* (ex-*Newlyn*), *Repton* (ex-*Wicklow*), *Weybourne*
Lobnitz – *Pangbourne* (ex-*Padstow*), *Penarth, Petersfield* (ex-*Portmadoc*), *Pinner* (ex-*Portreath*), *Pontypool* (ex-*Polperro*), *Prestatyn* (ex-*Porlock*), *Radley, Ross* (ex-*Ramsey*)
Murdoch & Murray – *Salford* (ex-*Shoreham*), *Saltash, Saltburn, Selkirk*
Napier & Miller – *Shrewsbury, Sligo, Widnes* (ex-*Withernsea*), *Yeovil*
C Rennoldson – *Stafford* (ex-*Staithes*), *Stoke* (ex-*Southwold*)
Cancelled 12.18 and later:
Ailsa SB – *Alton* (ex-*Arbroath*), *Ashburton*
Ardrossan SB – *Bideford, Bolton* (ex-*Beaumaris*)
Bow McLachlan – *Cashel* (ex-*Cley*), *Cavan* (ex-*Clovelly*), *Clifton, Crediton* (ex-*Colwyn*)
Clyde SB – *Athelney, Bala, Bathgate*
Dundee SB – *Beccles, Blickling*
Eltringham – *Curragh, Flint, Frome, Grays, Kew, Kingussie, Knowle, Naas*
Fleming & Ferguson – 2 unnamed vessels (projected)
Lobnitz – *Northrepps, Okehampton, Oundle, Radnor, Reading, Retford, Ringwood, Runcorn, Shifnal, Smethwick, Tain, Wembdon, Yealmpton*

The Admiralty incorporated certain improvements in a mass-produced version of the 'Hunts', which were to be built in large numbers from mid-1917. Sometimes called the 'later Hunts', these included a flush deck aft and heavier armament, but in other respects they were similar, and equally successful, although only 32 were in commission by the Armistice. Wholesale disposals followed, many for commercial conversion as coasters. Many were employed on post-war mine clearance duties, and several survived to serve in the Second World War. Six were completed as survey vessels, namely *Ambleside* (renamed *Beaufort*), *Amersham* (renamed *Collinson*), *Pinner* (renamed *Fitzroy*), *Radley* (renamed *Flinders*), *Uppingham* (renamed *Kellett*), *Verwood* (renamed *Crozier*), all of which were renamed in March 1919. Most of the original names were coastal towns, but it was decided that this could lead to confusion in signals, so on 25 June 1918 new names of inland towns were substituted where appropriate. *Fowey* was originally ordered from Dunlop Bremner but was transferred to Clyde SB and renamed *Forres*.

Cupar was mined off the Tyne 5 May 1919. *Kinross* was mined in the Aegean 16 June 1919. *Penarth* was mined in the North Sea 4 February 1919. *Petersfield* wrecked on Tung Yung Island, China 11 November 1931. *Crozier* transferred to South African Naval Forces 1921 and renamed *Protea* October 1922; sold October 1933. *Battle* and *Bloxham* were launched in 1919 to clear slips, and were sold incomplete subsequently. *Appledore, Bradfield, Fairfield, Instow, Monaghan, Repton* and *Salford* were sold March–November 1920; *Barnstaple, Swindon, Wem* and *Wexford* were sold April–December 1921; *Collinson, Banchory, Battle, Blackburn, Caerleon, Cheam, Clonmel, Craigie, Forfar, Gaddesdon, Munlochy, Pontypool* and *Sligo* were sold March–November 1922. *Havant* was sold to Siam (Thailand) in August 1922 and renamed *Chow Phraya*. *Badminton, Bloxham, Bootle, Bury, Camberley, Irvine, Longford* and *Prestatyn* were sold January–December 1923; *Faversham, Mallaig, Nailsea, Rugby, Shrewsbury* and *Tring* were sold October–November 1927; *Burslem, Dorking, Ford, Gainsborough, Gretna, Kendal, Leamington, Malvern, Marlow, Newark, Northolt, Sherborne, Stafford, Tonbridge, Truro, Weybourne* and *Yeovil* were sold Febuary–October 1928; *Tralee* was sold July 1929; *Marazion* was sold March 1933; *Carstairs* (renamed *Dryad* between January and August 1924) was sold April 1935, with *Caterham* and *Forres; Beaufort* and *Tiverton* were sold June–December 1938. *Goole* was completed September 1926 as RNVR drill ship *Irwell*; sold for BU 1962. *Abingdon* was bombed by Italian aircraft off

Malta 5 April 1942, and beached at Calcara; BU 1950. *Dundalk* was damaged by mine off Harwich 16 October 1940 and sank next day. *Dunoon* was mined in the North Sea 30 April 1940. *Fermoy* was sunk 4 May 1941 by bombs in Malta DYd later raised and BU. *Huntley* was sunk by air attack in the Eastern Mediterranean 31 January 1941. *Fitzroy* reverted to 'sweeper 1939; mined off Great Yarmouth 27 May 1942. *Stoke* was sunk off Tobruk by air attack 7 May 1941. *Widnes* was damaged by air attack 20 May 1941 and beached at Suda Bay, Crete; refloated by German Navy and renamed *UJ 2109*; sunk 17 October 1943 by RN destroyers. *Flinders* (accommodation ship from August 1940), *Kellett* (reverted to 'sweeper from 1939) and *Elgin* were sold March–August 1945; *Derby* and *Saltburn* were sold July–October 1946; *Aberdare, Albury, Alresford, Harrow, Lydd, Pangbourne, Ross* and *Sutton* were sold 1947; *Fareham* (depot ship *St Angelo II* 1944–45) was sold August 1948. *Bagshot* served as depot ship *Medway II* April 1945–February 1946; was sold *c*1949 and mined off Corfu 1 September 1951 while in tow.

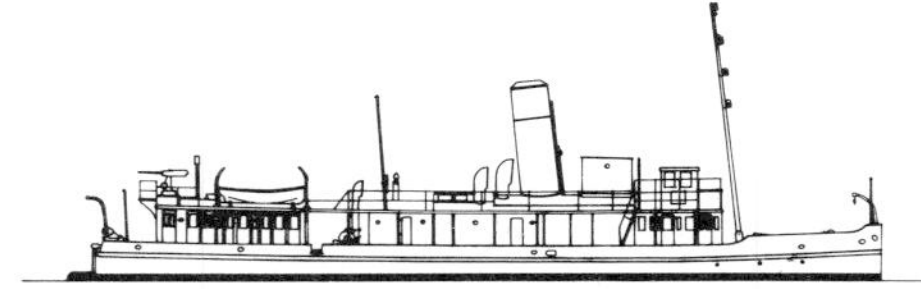

'Dance' class design
NB 1/750 scale

'DANCE' class *tunnel minesweepers*

Displacement:	*Cotillion* group 290t normal *Gavotte* group 265t
Dimensions:	130ft pp × 26ft 3in × 3ft 9in *39.6m × 8.0m × 1.1m*
Machinery:	2-shaft TE, 1 cyl boiler, 450ihp = 9½kts. Oil 37½t–41½t
Armament:	1–6pdr (*Gavotte, Tarantella* 1–12pdr, 1–6pdr; *Cotillion, Coverley, Pirouette, Quadrille, Sarabande* 1–3pdr)
Complement:	22–26

Class:
Cotillion group
Transferred 10.17:
Day Summers – *Cotillion* (ex-*T 92*), *Minuet* (ex-*T 93*)
Ferguson – *Coverley* (ex-*Roger de Coverley*) and *Quadrille*
Murdock & Murray – *Hornpipe, Mazurka*
Gavotte group transferred 12.17:
Goole SB – *Gavotte, Sarabande*
Rennie Forrest – *Pirouette*
Hamilton – *Tarantella* (ex-*T 95*)
Transferred 4.19:
Lytham SB – *Fandango* (ex-*T 98*), *Morris Dance* (ex-*T 99*), *Step Dance* (ex-*ET 11*), *Sword Dance* (ex-*ET 10*)

In July 1917 a requirement for shallow-draught minesweepers arose, to permit inshore sweeping at low tide. The Director of Auxiliary Vessels suggested that some of the 'tunnel tugs' building for the War Office for service in Mesopotamia could be adapted, as their draught was only 3ft 6in. Six currently under construction were then bought from the War Office in October 1917 at a cost of £169,350. In December 1917 four more were taken over at a cost of £4500 per ship, on the understanding that they would revert to the War Office after the end of the War. These 10 ships were converted during construction, being given a trawl winch and a light pattern of sweep gear. Despite being somewhat spartan in their accommodation they were successful, and all were based at Dunkirk in 1918, sweeping mines off the Flanders coast. In April 1919 another four were acquired for service in North Russia. They were specially modified for the extremes of weather at Archangel, with mosquito netting, as well as heaters to enable aircraft engines to be warmed up in cold weather. They were boarded up for the long voyage in tow.

Fandango was mined in the Dvina River on 3 July 1919, and *Sword Dance* on 24 June 1919. *Coverley* was known under her original name *Roger de Coverley* until 1918, and she was sold with *Cotillion, Hornpipe, Mazurka, Minuet, Quadrille, Morris Dance* and *Step Dance* in May 1920; *Gavotte, Pirouette, Sarabande* and *Tarantella* were returned to War Office in 1920 (*Tarantella* sold in 1921 for commercial use).

Cockchafer on the Yangtse in the mid 1920s *By courtesy of John M Maber*

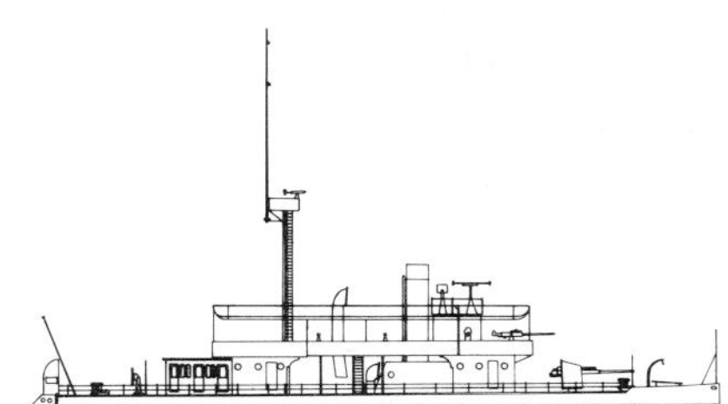

Butterfly as completed
NB 1/750 scale

'FLY' class *river gunboats*

Displacement:	98t normal
Dimensions:	126ft oa × 20ft × 2ft *38.4m × 6.1m × 0.6m*
Machinery:	1-shaft TE, 1 Yarrow boiler (mixed-firing), 175ihp = 9½kts. Coal 5t, oil 10t
Armament:	1–4in (10.2cm), 1–12pdr (76mm), 1–6pdr (57mm; in some), 1–3pdr (47mm) AA, 1–2pdr (40mm), 4 or 5 MGs
Complement:	22

Class:
Ordered 2.15:
Butterfly, Cranefly, Dragonfly, Firefly, Gadfly, Grayfly, Greenfly, Mayfly, Sawfly, Snakefly, Stonefly, Waterfly
Ordered 12.15:
Blackfly, Caddisfly, Hoverfly, Sedgefly. All built by Yarrow.

In February 1915 the Admiralty ordered 12 river gunboats from Messrs Yarrow for operations on the Tigris and Euphrates, but to camouflage their destination they were known as 'China gunboats'. The design was based on Yarrow's earlier river craft, with a single screw operating in a tunnel, using the Yarrow patent flap to prevent the tunnel from being emptied by the wash of another vessel. Another four vessels were ordered in December. The first dozen were laid down in February 1915, then dismantled and re-erected at Abadan on the Persian Gulf, being sent out in July–September 1915. The last four were laid down in December 1915 and sent out in April–September 1916. They were retained only briefly after the Armistice, but continued to serve on the Tigris and Euphrates under new ownership, some retaining a para-military role. *Firefly* entered service in November 1915 and was captured by the Turks during the advance on Baghdad on 1 December 1915. Recaptured on 26 February 1917, she was finally sunk on the Euphrates by insurgents 14 June 1924. *Gadfly* was transferred to the Air Ministry at Basra 1922, and *Grayfly* transferred to the War Department 1923. *Blackfly* was lost in collision with a bridge at Baghdad 26 May 1923 while on loan to Air Ministry. The remainder were sold locally in 1923.

'INSECT' class *river gunboats*

Displacement:	645t normal
Dimensions:	237ft 6in oa × 36ft × 4ft *72.4m × 11.0m × 1.2m*
Machinery:	2-shaft TE, 2 Yarrow boilers (mixed-firing), 2000ihp = 14kts. Coal 35t, oil 54t
Armament:	2–6in (15.2cm)/40cal QF Mk I/II, 2–12pdr (76mm) QF, 6–.303in Maxim MGs
Complement:	53

Class (fate):
Ailsa SB – *Aphis* (sold 1947), *Bee* (sold 3.39)
Barclay Curle – *Cicala* (bombed 21.12.41), *Cockchafer* (sold 1949), *Cricket* (bombed 29.6.41), *Glowworm* (sold for BU 9.28)
Lobnitz – *Gnat* (torpedoed 21.10.41), *Ladybird* (sunk 12.5.44)
Sunderland SB – *Mantis* (sold 1.40), *Moth* (scuttled 21.12.41)
Wood Skinner – *Scarab* (BU 1948), *Tarantula* (sunk as target 1.5.46). Launched 1915–16.

Twelve 'large China gunboats' were ordered in February 1915, for planned operations on the Danube against the Austro-Hungarian river flotilla. Designed and engined by Yarrow, with propellers in tunnels, they were in effect small monitors, being well armed for their displacement, and several survived to see distinguished service in the Second World War. In 1916–17 *Cicala, Cockchafer, Cricket* and *Glowworm* were rearmed temporarily with 6in QF Mk II on CP II anti-aircraft mountings (53½° elevation), for use against Zeppelins. None of the class fought on the Danube as Serbian resistance collapsed. The class was therefore used in other theatres, where their shallow draught and gunpower were needed to support land operations.

Aphis, Bee, Ladybird and *Scarab* sent to Port Said from November 1915 to April 1916, and *Gnat, Mantis, Moth* and *Tarantula* were towed out to the Persian Gulf early in 1916. *Cicala, Cockchafer, Cricket* and *Glowworm* were sent to the East Coast (*Cicala* and *Cricket* in the Humber, *Cockchafer* at Brightlingsea, and *Glowworm* at Lowestoft) to help defend against Zeppelin raids. In September 1918 the four on the East Coast were sent to North Russia for operations on the Dvina River. *Glowworm* was badly damaged by an exploding ammunition barge alongside at Bereznik, 24 August 1919. *Aphis* and *Ladybird* patrolled the Danube November 1918–March 1922 (*Glowworm* replaced *Aphis* in 1920). *Bee* and *Scarab* sent to Hong Kong in March 1918, followed by *Gnat* and *Tarantula*. *Cicala, Cockchafer, Cricket, Mantis* and *Moth* towed out from

The 55ft *CMB 98ED* with the 40ft *CMB 112* beyond *CPL*

England in 1920, leaving *Glowworm* on the Danube and *Aphis* and *Ladybird* laid up at Malta. *Cicala* was sunk by Japanese aircraft at Hong Kong. *Cricket* was crippled by bombing in the Mediterranean in 1941 and laid up at Port Said; hull stripped and sold for BU 1942. *Gnat* was torpedoed in the Mediterranean by *U 79*; laid up at Suez and sold for BU 1945 after being stripped for spares. *Ladybird* was sunk by air attack off Tobruk. *Moth* was scuttled at Hong Kong in 1941 but raised by the Japanese and recommissioned as *Suma*; mined in Yangtze 19 March 1945. *Tarantula* sunk as target off Trincomalee. *Aphis*, *Cockchafer* and *Scarab* were sold for BU 1947–49.

CMB 40ft type *coastal motor boats*

Displacement:	5t
Dimensions:	45ft oa × 8ft 6in × 2ft 6in–3ft *13.7m × 2.6m × 0.8m–0.9m*
Machinery:	*CMB 1–CMB 13* 1 shaft, 1–Thornycroft V-8 or V-12 petrol engine, 250bhp = 24.8kts *CMB 40–CMB 61* 1 shaft FIAT petrol engine, 275bhp = 35.13kts *CMB 112*, 1 shaft, Thornycroft V-12 petrol engine, = 37¾kts *CMB 121-CMB 123* 1 shaft, Green 12-cyl petrol engine, 275bhp = 37.79kts
Armament:	1–18in (45.7cm) TT (stern trough), 2 or 4–.303in Lewis MGs (1×2 or 2×2)
Complement:	2 or 3

Class (fate):
Thornycroft, Hampton – *CMB 1* (lost off Ostend 19.6.17), *CMB 2* (lost by fire 9.7.18), *CMB 3* (converted to *DCB 3* 7.18), *CMB 4–CMB 7, CMB 8* (scuttled 27.9.17), *CMB 9* (converted to DCB 1 7.18), *CMB 10* (lost by fire 7.5.18), *CMB 13* (converted to *DCB 2* 7.18), *CMB 40* (sunk by air attack 11.8.18), *CMB 41, CNB 42* (sunk by air attack 11.8.18), *CMB 47* (caught fire after air attack 11.8.18), *CMB 48, CMB 50* (scuttled 19.7.18), *CMB 55, CMB 56, CMB 112, CMB 121–CMB 123*
Tom Bunn, Rotherhithe – *CMB 11* (lost by fire after collision, 2.11.17), *CMB 12*
Taylor & Bates, Chertsey – *CMB 43, CMB 49*
J W Brooke, Lowestoft – *CMB 44, CMB 45, CMB 59*
Frank Maynard, Chiswick – *CMB 46, CMB 53, CMB 54*
Salter Bros, Oxford – *CMB 51, CMB 52, CMB 60, CMB 61*
Wills & Packham, Sittingbourne – *CMB 57, CMB 58*. Launched 1916.

Twelve were ordered in January 1916 and all were delivered by mid-August 1916, after Thornycroft had submitted designs based on pre-war hydroplanes. The hull was a stepped planing type and the torpedo was launched tail-first over the stern. The original specification called for CMBs (a camouflage designation) to be light enough for hoisting in light cruisers' davits, but only the 'scout' *Diamond* was used for this purpose. *CMB 40* became a nominal depot ship and was renamed *Osea* in June 1918. A further 16 boats of the *CMB 121* group were cancelled in November 1918. Five were converted to Distant Controlled Boats (DCBs), including two 40-footers not previously taken into naval service (*MB 1143* and *MB 1256*, which became *DCB 4* and *DCB 5*). The survivors were mostly sunk as targets or sold post-war, only *CMB 12* lasting until 1935. *CMB 4* was lent to the Imperial War Museum from 1921 to 1928 and then preserved at Hampton, and is now once again in IWM hands at Duxford.

CMB 55ft type *coastal motor boats*

Displacement:	11t
Dimensions:	60ft oa × 11ft × 3ft *18.3m × 3.4m × 0.9m*
Machinery:	2 shafts, petrol engines, 750bhp–900bhp = 34kts–42kts
Armament:	1 or 2–18in (45.7cm) TT (stern troughs), 4–.303in Lewis MGs, 4 DCs
Complement:	3–5

Class (fate):
Thornycroft, Hampton – *CMB 14A–CMB 17A, CMB 18A* (lost in collision 12.4.18), *CMB 21B, CMB 24A* (lost at Kronstadt 18.8.19), *CMB 25BD, CMB 26B, CMB 27A, CMB 28A, CMB 31BD, CMB 33A* (sunk in action off Ostend 12.4.18), *CMB 34A, CMB 36A, CMB 65A, CMB 76A, CMB 78E, CMB 80C, CMB 82C, CMB 83CE, CMB 87B, CMB 93E–CMB 97E, CMB 113CK, CMB 120F*
Taylor & Bates, Chertsey – *CMB 19A, CMB 68B, CMB 73B, CMB 74B, CMB 84C, CMB 86BD, CMB 114D* (caught fire and sank 4.23), CMB 115DE
Camper & Nicholson, Gosport – *CMB 19A, CMB 68B, CMB 73B, CMB 74B, CMB 84C, CMB 86BD, CMB 114D* (caught fire and sank 4.23), *CMB 115DE*
Camper & Nicholson, Gosport – *CMB 20A, CMB 37A, CMB 39B, CMB 69A, CMB 70A, CMB 72A, CMB 75B, CMB 77A, CMB 79A* (lost at Kronstadt 18.9.19), *CMB 81C, CMB 98ED, CMB 99ED* (lost by fire 1920), *CMB 39B* (lost by fire 28.4.18)
Wills & Packham, Sittingbourne – *CMB 22B, CMB 30B, CMB 63BD, CMB 64BD, CMB 116D, CMB 117D*
Salter Bros, Oxford – *CMB 23B, CMB 62BD, CMB 67A* (lost at Kronstadt 18.8.19)
Rowhedge Iron Works – *CMB 29A, CMB 35A, CMB 90BD–CMB 93BD*
Frank Maynard, Chiswick – *CMB 32A, CMB 38B, CMB 68BD, CMB 71A* (missing 15.10.18, believed foundered after collision off Belgian coast), *CMB 85C, CMB 88BD*
Builder unknown – *CMB 89BD*. Launched 1917 (*CMB 14A–CMB 18A*) – 1919 (except *CMB 1180–CMB 120F* 1922).

Enlarged versions of the 40-footers were ordered in mid-1916. They were generally similar, but to identify the wide variety of engine types used they were given the following suffixes:
A = Thornycroft V-12, 500bhp = 35¼kts
B = Green 12 engine, 550bhp = 37.06kts
C = Sunbeam engines, 900bhp = 41.19kts
D = Green 18 engines, 900bhp = *c*40kts
E = Thornycroft Y12 engines, 700bhp = 40.96kts
F = engines (unknown make)
BD = Green 12 engines, 500bhp = 35.10kts
CE = engines (unknown make)
CK = engines (unknown make)
DE = Green 18 engines, 900bhp = 40.67kts
ED = Thornycroft Y12 engines, 700bhp = approx. 40kts
The BD, CE, CK, DE and ED boats all carried two 18in torpedoes, the others one each. Disposal was much as the 40-footers, with six lasting until 1932.

CMB 70ft type *coastal motor boats*

Displacement:	24t
Dimensions:	72ft 6in oa × 14ft × 3ft 6in *22.1m × 4.3m × 1.1m*
Machinery:	2 shafts, petrol engines, = 26kts–36kts (see notes)
Armament:	6–.303in Lewis MGs, 4 DCs, 7 mines
Complement:	3–5

Class (fate):
Thornycroft, Hampton – *CMB 100M, CMB 102MT*
Thornycroft, Woolston (completed by Portsmouth DYd) – *CMB 101M*
Camper & Nicholson, Gosport – *CMB 103MT*((served in Second World War and preserved as relic), *CMB 104MT*. Launched 1919 (except *CMB 103MT* and *CMB 104MT* 1922)

Twelve minelaying CMBs were ordered in January 1918, capable of laying seven 'M Sinker' magnetic mines, or an alternative load of six torpedoes, but five were cancelled, *CMBs 105–CMB 111*. Post-war there were a number of experimental hulls, probably part of this programme, but completed by the builders for trials work. *MB 1265* was reported to have been towed from Woolston to Pembroke DYd for completion and *MB 1535*, building at Hampton, had triple 18in torpedo-troughs, 3 twin Lewis MGs and DCs, and was driven by a 24-cylinder Green engine. The variations in engines were:
M = Thornycroft Y12 engines, = 25.96bhp
MT = Thornycroft Y24 engines, = 36.6kts
CMB 102MT became depot ship *Hornet* in 1923 and survived the Second World War, with *CMB 103MT* and *CMB 104MT*, but the other two were deleted in 1920–21.

ML type, general appearance
NB 1/750 scale

ML type *motor launches*

Displacement:	34t (*ML 51–ML 580* 37t)
Dimensions:	75ft × 12ft × 4ft (*ML 51–ML 580* 80ft × 12ft 3in × 4ft) *22.9m × 3.7m × 1.2m (24.4m × 3.7m × 1.2m)*
Machinery:	2 shafts, petrol engines, 440bhp = 19kts
Armament:	1–13pdr (replaced by 1–3pdr in most)
Complement:	8

Class:
Ordered 4.15 from Elco, Bayonne, NY (placed through Canadian Vickers) – *ML 1–ML 50*
Ordered 6.15 from Elco – *ML 51–ML 550*
Ordered 7.17 from Elco – *ML 551–ML 580*. Launched in 1915 (except *ML 551* group 1918).

ML 19, ML 40, ML 52, ML 55, ML 64, ML 110, ML 424, ML 149, ML 197, ML 230, ML 247, ML 253, ML 254, ML 255, ML 278, ML 356, ML 403, ML 421, ML 431, ML 474, ML 534, ML 540, ML 541, ML 561 were war losses. *ML 114–ML 117, ML 38, ML 390, ML 392, ML 394, ML 396, ML 400, ML 402, ML 404, ML 442, ML 444, ML 446, ML 448–ML454, ML 456, ML 458–ML 460, ML 462, ML 464, ML 469–ML 472, ML 489, ML 491–ML 493, ML 543–ML 544, ML 547–ML 548* were transferred to the French Navy and renumbered in *V 1–V 73* series. *ML 18, ML 62, ML 121, ML 152, ML 191, ML 196, ML 434, ML 521, ML 566* were lost after the Armistice. *ML 97, ML 127, ML 229* were sold in damaged state. A total of 200 were sold in 1919, 127 were sold in 1920, and all but 8 were sold by 1924.

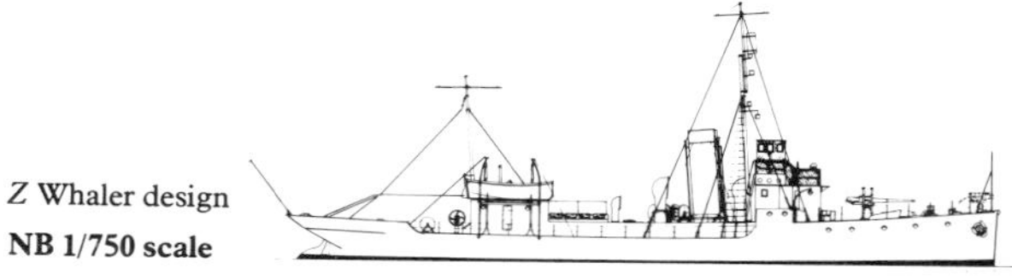

Z Whaler design
NB 1/750 scale

Z WHALER type *patrol craft*

Displacement:	336t normal; 346t full load
Dimensions:	132ft 9in oa × 25ft × 8ft 7in mean *40.5m × 7.6m × 2.6m*
Machinery:	1-shaft TE, 2 White-Forster boilers, 1200ihp = 13kts. Coal 60t
Armament:	1–12pdr (76mm) 18cwt (*Z 1* 1–12pdr, 1–6pdr AA)
Complement:	26

Class (fate):
Zedwhale (ex-*Meg*, ex-*Z 1*, sold 2.20), *Balena* (ex-*Z 2*, sold 4.20), *Beluga* (ex-*Z 3*, sold 4.20), *Bowhead* (ex-*Z 4*, sold 4.20), *Blackwhale* (ex-*Z 5*, mined 3.1.18), *Bullwhale* (ex-*Z 6*, sold 3.20), *Cachalot* (ex-*Z 7*, sold 1933), *Cowwhale* (ex-*Z 8*, sold 3.20), *Humpback* (ex-*Z 9*, sold 3.20), *Rorqual* (ex-*Z 10*, sold 3.20), *Rightwhale* (ex-*Z 11*, sold 3.20), *Icewhale* (ex-*Z 12*, sold 10.28), *Finwhale* (ex-*Z 13*, sold 3.20), *Pilotwhale* (ex-*Z 14*, sold 4.20), *Arctic Whale* (ex-*Z 15*, sold 4.20). All built by Smith's Dock in 1915.

Early in 1915 the threat from U-boats was driving the British Admiralty to ask for patrol craft to relieve destroyers from escort duties. This led to the officially designed 'P-boat', but there was also a need for a slower craft for escort and patrol work. Opinion favoured the whalecatcher, renowned for its manoeuvrability rather than its speed, and so on 15 March 1915 the Admiralty ordered Smith's Dock Company of Middlesbrough to stop all work in hand to leave themselves free to build 15 new escorts as fast as possible. The plans were to be provided by the departments of the Director of Naval Construction (DNC) and Engineer-in-Chief (E-in-C) but they were in fact adapted from a design ordered by the Imperial Russian Government. Delivery of the first vessel was planned to be three months after approval of the plans, followed by the remaining 14 at 10-day intervals, subject to the delivery of boilers and ancillary equipment. The principal features of the design were: rapid manoeuvring; minimum draught, to reduce risk from mines and torpedoes; maximum speed possible on the displacement; a stiffened stem to allow for ramming U-boats; a raised forecastle, stiffened to carry a 12pdr (3in) gun; subdivision into six watertight compartments and a watertight lower deck abaft the machinery, for maximum safety on the displacement. The Q-ships were already in being and it was felt that these armed whalecatchers should also try to look at innocuous as possible. The 12pdr was arranged to stow athwartships under a canvas cover and a dummy harpoon gun was provided to complete the disguise. For the same reason the searchlight on the navigating bridge was fitted with a canvas screen painted to resemble a wheelhouse. Admiralty records show no addition to the listed armament but they were undoubtedly given two depth-charges when these were issued in 1916 and the outfit presumably increased as more DCs became available in 1917–18.

They were formed into three squadrons, based at Stornoway, Shetland and Peterhead, although from time to time some were stationed in the Humber.

Although they lived up to their reputation for manoeuvrability their seaworthiness proved something of a disappointment, and was considered inferior to trawlers of the same tonnage. The decision was therefore made not to continue with the type.

X-LIGHTER type *landing craft*

Displacement:	160t (*X 1* series), 137t (*X 201* series) normal
Dimensions:	*X 1* series 105ft 6in pp × 21ft × 3ft 6in *32.2m × 6.4m × 1.1m* *X 201* series 98ft pp × 20ft × 3ft 6in *29.6m × 6.1m × 1.1m*
Machinery:	1-shaft Bolinder diesel engines, 60bhp (average) = ?kts (DX 1–25 unpowered)
Armament:	Nil

Class:
X 1–200 (ordered 2.15 from various builders; launched 4-7.15; most delivered by 8.15)
X 201–225 (ordered 2.16 from various builders; launched 6-9.16)
DX 1–DX 25 (launched late 1916)

Designed initially for Dardanelles by James Pollock & Sons of Faversham, who provided Bolinder diesels to a large number of sub-contractors. *DX 1–DX 25* were intended to be towed by X-lighters. One, *X 22* was used as a decoy vessel, and several were transferred to the Indian Government for operations in Mesopotamia. Most were sold or used for subsidiary duties by 1925, but 32 lasted until the Second World War.

There were also 90 Y-lighters built in February–June 1915, which were powered barges for ferrying troops and equipment, and 20 dumb barges built for Mesopotamia.

An X-lighter in action *CPL*

AUXILIARY WARSHIPS

The limitations of space severely restrict the amount of information that can be included on auxiliary warships. Therefore details are only given for vessels which were lost while serving under the White Ensign or which had particularly interesting careers.

ARMED MERCHANT CRUISERS

Name (tonnage, armament, fate):
Alcantara (15,831grt; 8–6in, 2–6pdr; sunk in action 29.2.16), *Almanzora, Alsatian, Ambrose* (depot ship from 10.15), *Andes, Aquitania, Arlanza, Armadale Castle, Avenger* (15,000grt; 8–6in, 2–3pdr; torpedoed 14.6.17), *Avoca, Bayano* (5948grt; 2–6in, torpedoed 11.3.15), *Berrima* (RAN, store carrier from 10.14), *Calgarian* (17,515grt; 8–6in; torpedoed 1.3.18), *Calyx* torpedoed 10.7.16 after release from naval service 6.15), *Caribbean* (accommodation ship from 6.15 and foundered 26.9.15), *Carmania, Caronia, Cedric, Celtic, Changuinola, City of London, Clan MacNaughton* (4985grt; 8–4.7in; mined 3.2.15), *Columbella, Digby* (to France as *Artois* 11.15–7.17), *Ebro, Edinburgh Castle, Empress of Asia, Empress of Britain, Empress of Japan, Empress of Russia, Eskimo* (released 7.15, and captured 26.7.16), *Gloucestershire, Hilary* (6239grt; 6–6in, 2–6pdr; torpedoed 25.5.17), *Hildebrand, Himalaya, India* (7940grt; armament

Laurentic as an AMC CPL

Bayano as a commissioned escort vessel CPL

A typical Q-ship, the '*Underwing*' (alias *Goodwin*) 1917 CPL

The converted paddle steamer *Clacton Belle* as a minesweeper CPL

unknown; torpedoed 8.8.15), *Kildonan Castle, Kinfauns Castle* (released 9.15 for trooping, then minelayer), *Laconia* (18,099grt; 8–6in; armed storeship from 8.16 and torpedoed 25.2.17), *Laurentic* (14,892grt; 8–6in, 2–6pdr; mined 25.1.17), *Lusitania* (30,396grt; returned to owners 8.14 without receiving armament and torpedoed 7.5.15), *Macedonia, Mantua, Marmora* (10,509grt; 8–4.7in; torpedoed 23.7.18), *Mauretania* (released 8/9.14 but taken up again as AMC 1.18), *Moldavia* (9500grt; 8–6in, 2–6;dr AA; torpedoed 23.5.18), *Morea, Motagua, Naldera, Narkunda* (work stopped 12.18), *Oceanic* (17,274grt; 8–4.7in; wrecked 8.9.14), *Olympic* (released 8/9.14 but taken up for conversion 31.3.17), *Ophir, Orama* (12,927grt; 8–6in (torpedoed 19.10.17), *Orbita, Orcoma, Oropesa* (to France as *Champagne* 12.15–7.17), *Orotava, Orvieto* (ex-minelayer, taken up 5.16), *Osiris* (released 10.14 but became depot ship 4.15), *Otranto* (12,128grt; 8–4.7in; wrecked 5.10.18 after collision), *Otway* (12,077grt; 8–6in, 2–6pdr; torpedoed 23.7.17), *Patia* (6103grt; 6–6in, 2–3pdr AA; torpedoed 13.6.18), *Patuca* (also served as balloon ship .17–12.18), *Princess* (ex-dummy battleship *Ajax*, taken up 1.16), *Teutonic, Victorian, Viknor, Virginian*.

COMMISSIONED ESCORT SHIPS

Name (tonnage, armament, fate):
Bayano, Bostonian (5626grt; 3–6in; taken up 6.17 and torpedoed 10.10.17), *Camito, Carrigan Head* (ex-squadron supply ship 8.14–4.16 and Q-ship 6.16–8.17), *Coronado, Discoverer, Knight Templar, Lepanto, Mechanician* (9044grt; 2–6in, 2–4in; taken up 6.17 and torpedoed 20.1.18), *Naneric, Quernmore* (7302grt; 3–6in; taken up 6.17 and torpedoed 31.7.17), *Sachem, Wyncote*.

ARMED BOARDING STEAMERS

Name (tonnage, armament, fate):
Alouette (ex-fleet messenger from 9.14 and taken up 7.15), *Amsterdam, Anglia* (taken up 8.14–4.15, then hospital ship and mined 17.11.15), *Caesarea, Cambria* (became hospital ship after 8.15), *Carron, City of Belfast, Duchess of Devonshire* (troopship from 1.19), *Duke of Albany* (1997grt; armament unknown; taken up 10.14 and torpedoed 25.8.16), *Duke of Clarence, Duke of Cornwall, Dundee* (2709grt; 2–4in; taken up 10.15 and torpedoed 3.9.17), *Fauvette* (2644grt; ex-store carrier taken up 3.15 and mined 9.3.16), *Fiona* (1611grt; 1–4in, 1–12pdr; taken up 10.14 and wrecked 6.9.17), *Grangemouth, Grive* (2037grt; 2–4.7in; flotilla supply ship 8.14–8.15, taken up again 2.16 and torpedoed 24.12.17), *Hazel, Heroic, King Orry, Lama, Louvain* (1830grt; 2–12pdr; taken up 10.14 and torpedoed 20.1.18), *Lunka, Partridge (Partridge II), Peel Castle, Perth, Prince Abbas* (served 6.15–5.16, subsequently sunk 9.7.17), *Richard Welford, Rowan, Royal Scot, Sarnia* (1498grt; 2–12pdr; taken up 11.14 and torpedoed 12.9.18), *Scotia, Snaefell* (1368grt; 2–12pdr; taken up 11.14 and torpedoed 5.6.18), *Stephen Furness* (1712grt; 2–4.7in; ex-squadron supply ship 12.14–3.16, torpedoed 13.12.17), *Suva, Tara* (1862grt; 3–6pdr; taken up 8.14 and torpedoed 5.11.15), *The Ramsey* (1443grt; 2–12pdr; taken up 10.14 and sunk in action 8.8.15), *Tithonus* (3463grt; 2–6in, 2–6pdr; taken up 2.16 and torpedoed 28.3.18), *Vienna* (ex-*accommodation ship 8—12.14, Q-ship 1—4.15*), *Woodnut, York*.

COASTGUARD AND FISHERY PROTECTION VESSELS

Name (fate):
Julia (ex-yacht purchased 4.01; examination service at Queenstown 1914–18; sold 11.20, *Argus* (launched 12.04; examination service at Berehaven 1914–18; sold 2.20), *Squirrel* (launched 12.04; cable ship 1914, and then based at Devonport and Falmouth; sold 11.21 as yacht), *Ringdove* (ex-*Thrush* class gunboat, transferred to Coastguard 1906; examination service at Queensferry, then in 11.15 completed conversion to salvage ship and renamed *Melita*), *Thrush* (ex-gunboat; converted to cable ship 1914 and based at Berehaven 1914–16; converted to salvage ship 1916), *Watchful* (launched 4.11; SO's ship for minesweepers at Sheerness to 1918; sold 5.20), *Safeguard* (launched 6.14 and based at Queenstown to 1918; sold 2.20).

Brenda, Freya, Goldseeker, Minna, Norna and *Vigilant* were former Scottish Fishery Board vessels, taken over in August 1914 for examination duties in Scottish waters.

SUBMARINE DECOY VESSELS (Q-SHIPS)

Commissioned name (false name(s), fate):
Acton (Gandy, Harelda, Q 34, Woffington), Albert H Whitman, Albert J Lutz, Amy B Silver, Arvonian (Alastair, Balfame, Bendish, Dorinda, Girdler, Santee (USN)), *Baron Rose (Sieux), Barranca (Echunga), Bayard (Ledger* No 898, *Q 20, Syren;* 220grt; taken up 1.17 and lost 29.3.17), *Blessing, Bracondale (Chagford,* 2095grt; armament unknown; taken up 5.17 and torpedoed 7.8.17), *Bradford City (Ballistan, Saros;* 3683grt; armament not known; taken up 10.15 and torpedoed 16.8.17), *Breadwinner (S 7, Seagull), Brig 1 (Emelia C), Brig 2 (Rosina Ferrara), Brig 3 (Santa Anna), Brig 4 (Margaret & Annie, Vera), Brig 5 (Salomea K), Brig 9 (Kostoula, Q 500, QS 9), Brig 10 (Helgoland, Horley, Q 17), Brig 11 (Gaelic, Gobo, Q 22), Brig 12 (Vassiliki), Chevington, Children's Friend, Cymric (Olive), Dargle (Bibby, Grabbitt, J J Bibby, Peggy, Q 29), Djerissa (Mallina, Solax, Woking), Dorando Pietri (S 5), Dorothy G Snow, Dreadnought II (Ledger No 897), Dunclutha (Champney, Stamford), Dunraven (Boverton;* 3117grt; 1–4in, 4–12pdr, 2–TT; taken up 6.17 and sank 10.8.17 after action damage), *Early Blossom (S 2), Eilian (Chromium), Eleuthera (Elizabeth), Energic (Cheerio, Mascot, S 1), Ethel & Millie (Boy Alfred, Ledger No 929, S 3;* 58grt; 1–6pdr; taken up 2.17 and sunk by gunfire 15.8.17), *Farnborough (Lodorer, Q 5, Sandyford), First Prize (Else, Prize, Q 21;* 227grt; sunk 14.8.17); *Fresh Hope (Edith E Cummins, Iroquois),* G & E *(Bird, Extirpator, Foam Crest, I'll Try, Ledger No 929, Nelson, S 3;* 61grt; 1–13pdr; taken up 8–9.15 and again 1.16; sunk 15.8.17), *George L Muir (Glm, George L Munro, Padre), Glen (Athos, Sidney), Glendevon, Glenfoyle (Donlevon, Stonecrop;* 1680grt; armament unknown; taken up 4.17 and sunk 18.9.17), *Glenisla, Glory, Goblin (Mana), Goodwin (Ballantral, Moderly, Underwing), Grantley, Harmonic (Cocksedge, Fairlight, Tricord), Hartside (Dunsany, Fairfax, Trioa), Helen M Coolen, Holkar, Hyanthes (Craven, Lorimer, Ooma), Ianthe (Manon), I'll Try, Imogene (Dorothy, Impey, Jeanette), Inverlyon, Kemes, Lady Olive (Q 18;* 701grt; 1–4in, 4–12pdr; taken up 11.16 and sunk 19.2.17 after

sinking *UC 18*), *Lady Patricia* (*Paxton, Q 25, Tosca, Sverige;* 1372grt; 1–4in, 2–12pdr; taken up 2.17 and sunk 20.5.17), *Laggan* (*Granmer, Pladda, Q 24*), *Lowtyne* (3231grt; armament not known; taken up 6.18 and sunk 10.6.18), *Maresfield* (*Chiswell, Sequax*), *Margaret Murray* (*Sarah Jones*), *Marshfort* (*Hillcollow, Huayna, Senley*), *Mary B Mitchell* (*Amaris, Arius, Brine, Cancalais, Eider, Jeanette, Marie Therese, Mary Y Jose, Mitchell, Neptun, Q 9*), *Mavis* (*Nyroca*), *Merops* (*Bellmore, Ilma, Maracaibo, Q 28, Steady, Toofa*), *Pargust* (*Friswell, Pangloss, Snail, Vittoria;* taken up 3.17 and lent to US Navy 10.17–4.18), *Penhallow* (*Century*), *Penshurst* (*Manford, Q 7;* 1191grt; 1–12pdr, 2–6pdr, 2–3pdr; taken up 11.15 and sunk 25.12.17), *Perim, Perugia* (*Moeraki, Q 1;* 4348grt; armament unknown; taken up 4.16 and sunk 3.12.16), *Pet, Peveril* (*Puma, Q 36, Stephenson;* 1459grt; armament unknown; taken up 2–4.15 and again 2.17, then sunk 6.11.17), *Pinta, Prevalent* (*Hurter*), *Prince Charles, Privet* (*Alcala, Island Queen, Q 19, Swisher*), *Probus* (*Elixir, Q 30, Ready, Thirza*), *Ravenstone* (*Donlevon*), *Record Reign, Remembrance* (*Lammeroo;* 3660grt; armament unknown; taken up 10.15 and sunk 14.8.16), *Resolute* (*Pamela, Rentoul*), *Result* (*Capulet, Dag, Ledger No 928*), *Revenge* (*Fame;* 39grt; armament unknown; taken up 1.16 and lost 19.11.16), *Rule* (*Baryta, Cassor, Ouse, Q 35*), *Sarah Colebrooke* (*Balham, Meryl*), *Starmount* (*Glenmay, Graveney, Tring*), *Stockforce* (*Charyce;* 732grt; 2–4in, 2–12pdr; taken up 2.17 and sank in tow 30.7.18 after damaging *UB 80* the same day), *Strumble* (*M 135;* 45grt; 1–12pdr; taken up 6.16 and sunk 4.5.17), *Suffolk Coast, Superior* (*Desmond, Superb*), *Tay & Tyne* (*Cheriton, Dundreary, Ledger No 928*), *Telesia* (*Commodore, Hobby Hawk, S 4*), *Thornhill* (*Margit, Wellholme, Werribee, Woganella*), *Vala* (*Q 8;* 1016grt; armament not known; taken up 8.15 and sunk by *UB 54* 21.8.17), *Vera Elizabeth* (*Alma*), *Victoria, Viola* (*Vereker, Violetta*), *Warner* (*Q 27;* 1273grt; armament not known; taken up 1.17 and sunk by *U 61* 13.3.17), *Wellholme* (*Danton;* 113grt; armament unknown; taken up 9.17 and sunk by U-boat 30.1.18), *Willow Branch* (*Bombala, Juggler, Vinetroe;* 3314grt; armament unknown; taken up 1.17 and sunk by U-boat 25.4.18), *Zylpha* (*Q 6;* 2917grt; armament unknown; taken up 9.15 and sunk 15.6.17 by U-boat), ? (Amber, Remo), ? (Defender), ? (Good Hope), ? (Lothian), ? (Margaretha), ? (Morning Star), ? (Sunshine, Strathallan), ? (Union, Union II), ? (Wadsworth), ? (Wild Rose, Strathearn).

All the above were ex-merchant vessels but in addition the following naval vessels served as decoys:

Sloops – *Begonia*, 6 *Aubrietia* class, 33 *Anchusa* class
PC-boats – 20 vessels
Commissioned escort ship – *Carrigan Head*
Armed boarding steamer – *Antwerp* (as *Vienna*)
Fleet Messengers – *Princess Ena, Redbreast*
Store carriers – *Baralong, Duncombe* (as *Derwent*), *Intaba, Lothbury* (as *Argo*), *M J Hedley, Westphalia, Wexford Coast, Wirral*
Yachts – *Brown Mouse, Lisette, Mona*
Trawlers – *Asama, Auk, Commissioner, Coot, Cormorant IV, Fort George, Gunner, Isaak Walton, King Lear, King Stephen, Oceanic II, Quickly, Rosskeen, Sea King, Speedwell II, Taranaki, Tenby Castle, Walter S Bailey*
Drifters – *Bellona II, Fizzer* (as *Violet*), *Imperator* (as *Impregnable*), *Kent County, Ocean Fisher, Principal*
Motor drifters – *Betsy Jamieson, Excel, Fisher Lassie II, Passaway, Thalia*
Tug – *Earl of Powis*
Salvage vessel – *Lyons*
Lighter – *X 22*
Submarine/trawler combinations – *Ratapiko* and *C 23*, *Taranaki* and *C 24*, *Wolsey* and *C 26*, *Princess Louise* and *C 27*, *Ariadne* and *C 29*, *Malta* and *C 33*; *C 14, C 16, C 21* and *C 34* were also used but their towing trawlers are unidentified.
Specially constructed decoy vessel – *Hyderabad* (also known as *Coral, Nicobar, SSS 966;* used as depot ship in North Russia 1919)

The number of U-boats actually sunk by Q-ships was relatively small. The best documented successes were: *Baralong* (sank *U 27* 19 August 1915), *Farnborough* (sank *U 68* 22 March 1916 and *U 38* 17 February 1917), *Inverlyon* (sank *UB 4* 15 August 1915), *Lady Olive* (sank *UC 18* 19 February 1917), *Pargust* (sank *UC 29* 7 June 1917), *Penshurst* (sank *UB 19* 30 November 1916 and *UB 37* 14 January 1917), *Prince Charles* (sank *U 36* 24 July 1915), *Privet* (sank *U 85* 12 March 1917 and *U 34* 9 November 1918, *Wyandra* (sank *U 41* 24 September 1915).

DUMMY CAPITAL SHIPS

Disguise (original name, period of service, fate):
'*St Vincent*' (ex-*City of Oxford*, 10.14–7.15, then converted to kite balloon ship), '*Collingwood*' (ex-*Michigan*, 10.14–, sunk as blockship at Mudros 1.1.16), '*Iron Duke*' (ex- *Montezuma*, 11.14–7.15, purchased as oiler *Abadol*), '*King George V*' (ex-*Ruthenia*, ex-*Lake Champlain*, 11.14–1.16, purchased as water carrier), '*Centurion*' (ex-*Tyrolia*, ex-*Lake Erie*, 10.14–6.16, purchased as oiler *Saxol*), '*Orion*' (ex-*Oruba*, 10.14 until expended as blockship at Mudros 1.1.16), '*Marlborough*' (ex-*Mount Royal*, 10.14–7.16, purchased as oiler *Rangol*), '*Audacious*' (ex-*Montcalm*, 10.14–1.16, purchased as oiler), '*Ajax*' (ex-*Princess*, ex-*Kronprinsessen Cecilie*, 11.14–1.16, converted to armed merchant cruiser), '*Vanguard*' (ex-*Perthshire*, 10.14–9.15, purchased as water carrier), '*Queen Mary*' (ex-*Cevic*, 10.14–9.15, became oiler *Bayol*), '*Indomitable*' (ex-*Manipur*, 11.14–1915, purchased as repair ship *Sandhurst*), '*Invincible*' (ex-*Patrician*, 11.14–1915, purchased as oiler *Teakol*), '*Tiger*' (ex-*Merion*, 12.14–5.15, torpedoed in Aegean 30.5.15).

MINELAYER CONVERSIONS

Name (particulars, fate):
Warships (see 1906 Fleet Strength table) – *Ariadne, Amphitrite* (see *Diadem* class cruisers), *London* (see *London* class battleships), *Euryalus* (see *Cressy* class cruisers), *Andromache, Apollo, Latona, Naiad, Thetis, Intrepid, Iphigenia* (see *Apollo* class cruisers)
Merchantmen – *Angora* (4298t; 3–4.7in, 2–6pdr AA, 320 mines; served 2.15–11.19), *Biarritz* (2495t; 2–12pdr, 180 mines; served 3.15–11.19), *Gazelle* (613t; 2–12pdr, 50 mines; ex-minesweeper, served 5–11.15), *Kinfauns Castle* (9664t; ex-AMC, ex-troopship, began conversion 7.18 at Millwall but cancelled 2.19), *Old Colony* (4779t; taken over 5.18 for conversion but cancelled 11.18 and sold for BU 3.20), *Orvieto* (12,130t; 4–4.7in, 1–3pdr AA, 600 mines; served 1.15–5.16, laying 3000 mines; AMC from 5.16), *Paris* (1774t; 1–4in, 1–12pdr, 1–6pdr AA, 140 mines; served 11.14–11.19), *Perdita* (543t; 1–12pdr, 1–6pdr AA, 100 mines; served 8.15–8.19), *Princess Irene* (5934t; 2–4.7in, 2–12pdr, 2–6pdr AA, 500 mines; commissioned 1.15 but destroyed by internal explosion at Sheerness 27.5.15), *Princess Margaret* (details as *Princess Irene*; served 12.14 onwards and purchased 6.19; sold for BU 5.29), *Wahine* (4436t; 2–14pdr, 2–6pdr AA, 180 mines; ex-fleet messenger, served 7.16–2.20), *Anglesey* (ex-*Anglia*; requisitioned 7.18 while under construction; incomplete at Armistice and conversion cancelled 12.18), *Sheppey* (ex-*Hibernia*; as *Anglesey*)
Converted trawlers – *Carmania II, King Emperor, Russell II, Scott, Shackleton, Welbeck, Osta, Ostrich, The Norman, Savitri, St Maurice, Pitfour, Erna, Hero, Kate Lewis, Strathcoe* (carried 24 mines each, and converted 5.15–6.18)
Converted paddle steamers (controlled minelayers) – *Albert Victor, Quince, America, Ireland, Medlar, The Lady Carmichael* (carried 8–10 mines, converted early 1918; *Flying Fish* and *Golden Eagle* conversions stopped in 11.18).

MINESWEEPER CONVERSIONS

Warships (see 1906 Fleet Strength table) – *Gossamer, Seagull, Skipjack, Spanker, Speedwell* (see *Sharpshooter* class torpedo gunboats), *Circe, Jason, Leda, Niger, Speedy* (see *Alarm* class torpedo gunboats), *Dryad, Halcyon, Harrier, Hussar* (see *Dryad* class torpedo gunboats)
Converted screw steamers – *Atlanta II, Clacton* (torpedoed 3.8.16), *Folkestone, Gazelle, Hythe, Lynn, Newmarket* (torpedoed 16.7.17), *Reindeer, Roedean* (lost 13.1.15), *St Seiriol* (mined 25.4.18), *Whitby Abbey*
Converted paddle steamers – *Aiglon, Albyn, Balmoral, Belle, Bickerstaffe, Bourne, Brighton Queen* (mined 6.10.15), *Britain, Caledonia, Cambridge, City of Rochester, Clacton Belle, Devonia, Duchess, Duchess of Buccleuch, Duchess of Fife, Duchess of Hamilton* (mined 29.11.15), *Duchess of Kent, Duchess of Montrose* (mined 18.3.17), *Duchess of Rothesay, Eagle III, Erin's Isle* (mined 7.2.19), *Fair Maid* (mined 9.11.16), *Glen Avon, Glen Cross, Glen Rosa, Glen Usk, Grenade, Greyhound II, Helper, Her Majesty, Isle of Arran, Junior, Jupiter II, Kenilworth, Kylemore, Lady Clare, Lady Evelyn, Lady Ismay* (mined 21.12.15), *Lady Moyra, Lady Rowena, London Belle, Lorna Doone, Marchioness of Breadalbane, Marchioness of Fife, Marmion II, Marsa* (lost 18.11.17), *Melcombe Regis, Mercury, Monarchy, Nepaulin* (mined 20.4.17), *Princess Beatrice, Queen Empress, Queen of the North* (mined 20.7.17), *Ravenswood, Redgauntlet II, Royal Pearl, Royal Ruby, Royal Sapphire, St Elvies, St Trillo, Slieve Bearnaigh, Snowdon, Southend Belle, Talla, Verdun/Verdun II, Walton Belle, Waverley, Way, Westward Ho/Western Queen, William Muir, Yarmouth Belle,* (*Cloghmore* and *Earl of Dunraven* started conversion in 1917 but were released; *Harlequin* and *Wanderer* taken up 1917–18)

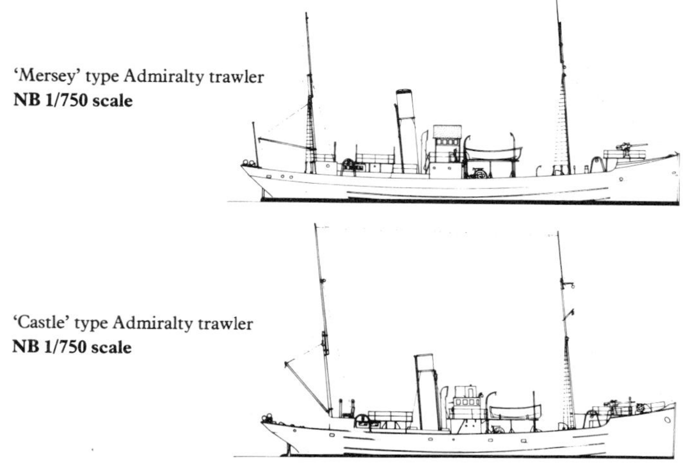

'Mersey' type Admiralty trawler
NB 1/750 scale

'Castle' type Admiralty trawler
NB 1/750 scale

ADMIRALTY TRAWLERS

A large programme of trawler-type vessels was undertaken during the war to provide cheap anti-submarine, minesweeping and utility patrol craft. Initially vessels were purchased for conversion: 10 *Military* class (*c*350t, 130ft × 24ft, *39.6m × 7.3m*) were purchased on the stocks December 1914–April 1915; 9 ex-Portuguese were bought in September 1915. The Admiralty also settled on three standard designs to be purpose-built, and these were known as the 'Mersey' (438t standard, 665t full load, 138ft 6in pp × 23ft 9in, *42.2m × 7.2m*,

11kts, 1–12pdr), 'Castle' (360t standard; 547t full load, 125ft pp × 23ft 6in, *38.1m × 7.2m*, 10½kts, 1–12pdr), and 'Strath' (311t standard; 429t full load, 115ft pp × 22ft, *35.1m × 6.7m*, 10kts, 1–12pdr) types. There were many detail variations within the three broad types, but all resembled commercial fishing vessels. Armament varied, but most had a 12pdr and many had 3.5in or 7.5in bomb-throwers; some had 12pdr AA guns and a few had 4in guns. They were ordered in three batches, each order comprising all three types: 250 in November 1916, 150 in 1917, and 140 in 1918. For the 'Mersey' type 69 were completed by the Armistice, 8 were completed without armament for post-war mine clearance, 35 were completed as fishing vessels, and 44 were cancelled, for a total of 156. The corresponding figures for 'Castle' and 'Strath' types were 127, 18, 52, 20, totalling 217, and 89, 14, 46, 18 totalling 167, respectively.

The Empire also contributed to the trawler programme with 12 Canadian vessels being ordered in January 1917 and 60 Canadian-built 'Castle' type being ordered January–July 1917. In India 6 vessels were purchased in March 1917, and 9 Indian-built 'Castle' type were ordered in the same year.

86ft wooden type Admiralty drifter
NB 1/750 scale

ADMIRALTY DRIFTERS

There were two basic patterns of naval drifter, the wooden-hulled type (*c*175t, 86ft × 19ft, *26.2m × 5.8m*, 9kts, 1–6pdr) and the steel-hulled version (*c*199t, 86ft × 18ft 6in, *26.2m × 5.6m*, 9kts, 1–6pdr). Of the wooden type 91 were launched 1918–20, and 100 similar Canadian-built craft were ordered in January 1917; 123 steel-hulled vessels were launched 1917–20 and 48 others were cancelled. All were named like the trawlers except the Canadian-built vessels which were numbered *CD 1–CD 100*.

AUXILIARY SMALL CRAFT

Auxiliary patrol yachts – 153 (requisitioned from 8.14)
Hired whalers – 1 (hired 1.15), 12 (purchased 1.15–8.17), 3 (ex-German prizes, seized 1914)
Hired trawlers – over 1400
Captured trawlers – 29 '5in' group (ex-German prizes), 17 'Axe' class (ex-Russian seized or handed over in the White Sea 8.18)
Hired drifters (including motor craft) – over 1000
Local patrol vessels – over 120
Requisitioned motor boats – over 200

MISCELLANEOUS

DEPOT SHIPS

Destroyer depot ships – *Hecla* (ex-*British Crown*), *Tyne* (ex-*Mariotis*), *Aquarius* (ex-*Hampstead*), *Leander, Blake, Blenheim, St George, Dido, Diligence* (ex-*Tabaristan*), *Greenwich, Woolwich*
Submarine depot ships – *Vulcan, Forth, Thames, Bonaventure, Hebe, Onyx, Arrogant, Pactolus, Rosario, Shearwater, Hazard, Pandora, Lucia* (ex-*Spreewald*), *Upolu* (RAN), *Titania, Ambrose, Adamant, Alecto, Maidstone, Platypus* (RAN)
Fleet repair ships – *Assistance, Cyclops* (ex-*Indrabarah*), *Sandhurst* (ex-dummy '*Indomitable*', ex-*Manipur*)
Torpedo sub-depot ships – *Abo, Sobo, Sokoto*

OILERS

Purpose-built – *Kharki, Mercedes, Petroleum, Isla, Burma, Attendant, Servitor, Carol, Ferol, Trefoil, Turmoil, Olympia, Delphinula* (ex-*Buyo Maru*), *Nucula* (ex-*Soyo Maru*), *Erivan, Mixol, Thermol*
Ex-dummy battleships (converted to oilers 1915–16) – *Abadol* (ex-'*Iron Duke*'), *Montcalm* (ex-'*Audacious*'), *Perthshire* (ex-'*Vanguard*'), *Rangol* (ex-'*Marlborough*'), *Ruthenia* (ex-'*King George V*'), *Saxol* (ex-'*Centurion*'), *Teakol* (ex-'*Invincible*')
Hired vessel – *Esturia*
Ex-Hoppers (converted 10.16) – *Barkol, Battersol, Blackol, Greenol, Purfol, Silverol*
Ex-dredger – *Dredgol*
War construction – *Appleleaf, Ashleaf, Beechleaf, Birchleaf, Brambleleaf, Briarleaf, Cherryleaf, Dockleaf, Elmleaf, Fernleaf, Hollyleaf, Laurelleaf, Orangeleaf, Palmleaf, Pearleaf, Plumleaf, Roseleaf, Boxleaf, Limeleaf, Birchol, Boxol, Creosol, Distol, Ebonol, Elderol, Elmol, Hickorol, Kimmerol, Larchol, Limol, Philol, Scotol, Viscol, Belgol, Celerol, Fortol, Francol, Montenol, Prestol, Rapidol, Serbol, Slavol, Vitol, Kurumba (RAN), Petrella, Petrobus, British Beacon, British Lantern, British Star, Red Dragon, Biloela (RAN), War Afridi, War Bahadur, War Bharata, War Brahmin, War Diwan, War Gaekwar, War Ghurka, War Hindoo, War Jemadar, War Krishna, War Mehtar, War Nawab, War Nizam, War Pathan, War Pindari, War Rajah, War Ranee, War Sepoy, War Shikari, War Sirdar, War Subadar, War Sudra*

SUPPORT SHIPS

Water tank vessels – *Chester, Elizabeth, Shamrock, Echo, Asp, Chub, Monkey, Tortoise, Aid, Blossom, Cherub, Clinker, Creole, Hesper, Minx, Faithful, Helpful, Provider, Ripple, Despatch, Pelter, Supply, Urgent, Zealous, Petronel, Innisfree, Innisinver, Innisjura, Innisshannon, Innistrahull, Innisulva, Gibraltar, Polshannon*
Store carriers – *Growler, Upnor, Industry, Bison, Reliance, Isleford, Bacchus*
Flotilla supply ships – *Albatross, Baron Herries, Intaba, Ortolan, Peregrine, Sorrento, Stork, Swift*
Squadron supply ships – *Alcinous, Baralong, Baron Ardrossan, Battenhall, Chantala, Chinkoa, Civilian, Clan MacGillivray, Clan MacQuarrie, Crown of Arragon, Crown of Castile, Crown of Galicia, Egret, Empire, Floridian, Glenturret, Hirondelle, Indrani, Intombi, Jabiru, Lakonia, Manco, Muritai, Netherby Hall, Palma, Peshawur, Statesman, Swanley, Torr Head, Tringa, Umgeni, Umtali, Vanellus, Whimbrel, Wildrake, Zaria*
Fleet messengers – *Alert, Alexandra, Aquilla, Arethusa II, Asteria, Barry, Borodino, Brighton, Brocklesby, C 64, C 65, Celtic Pride, Clifford, Curran, Devaney, Eblana, Elpiniki, Ermine, F A Tamplin, Floris, Gransha, Groningen, Hungerford, Invicta, Ibis, Killingholme, Nugget, Opulent, Osmanieh, Overton, Pebble, Petrolea, Polgowan, Polly Bridge, Portia, Princess Alberta, Princess Ena, Princess Maud, Princess of Wales, Princess Victoria, Race Fisher, Redbreast, River Fisher, Rosaleen, San Patricio, Saxon, Scandinavia, Silverfield, Skelwith Force, Spinel, Stamfordham, Sunik, Susetta, The Viceroy, Trent, Turquoise, Vitruvia, Wexford Coast, Wheatberry*
Store carriers – *Abercraig, Aire, Ardgarth, Ariadne Christine, Arleia, Armourer, Arrival, Asturian, Bangarth, Ben Nevis, Bernicia, Braeside, Brixham, Brook, Broomhill, Buccaneer, Burriana, Calder, Carlston, Carnalea, Cato, Chalkis, Charles Goodanew, Chesterfield, Cheviot, Clan Macrae, Clandeboye, Clermiston, Clifton Grove, Clydeburn, Clydesdale, Cornishman, Cortes, Cragside, Cunene, Derwent, Don, Dunvegan, Echo, Egba, Emerald, Endcliffe, Eros, Eskwood, Fairy, Farraline, Fernley, Ferryhill, Gertie, Gosforth, Hampshire, Harmodius, Harperley, Hebble, Helmsman, Hermiston, Hodder, Hova, Huntsclyde, Huntscraft, Huntsgulf, Immingham, Junin, Kassala, Larne, Leicester, Liberty, Lord Antrim, Lossie, Lucent, Lutterworth, M J Hedley, Macclesfield, Mersey, Moorgate, Nascopie, Nidd, Nigeria, Norfolk Coast, Notts, Ocean Transport, Palm Branch, Rayford, Rievaulx Abbey, Sea Serpent, Sibir, Skipper, Solfels, Sportsman, Staveley, Steersman, Stephen, Susquehanna, Tees, Teesider, Telamon, Theseus, Thespis, Trelawney, Trostan, Victor, Volana, Volhynia, Volturnus, War Castle, War Cypress, War Down, War Gascon, War Grange, War Lemur, War Magpie, War Mango, War Music, War Wolf, Waterland, Wearsider, Welshman, Wenning, Westborough, Westphalia, Wharfe, Whinhill, White Head, Wirral, Yarborough*
Miscellaneous vessels – *Abassieh, Acrrington, Alexis, Alhambra, Annandale, Argo (i), Argo (ii), Arno, Borderglen, Cordova, Cove, Daffodil, Edinburgh Castle, El Kahira, Eleanor, Etna, Forcados, Glengoil, Glenmore, Golden Eagle, Gothland, HC 9, HC 10, Harden, Haupiri, Hubbuck, Iris, Isle of Skye, John Pender, John Sanderson, King Edward, Lady Cory Wright, Lagos, Lord Morton, Magda, Mayumba, Medlar, Minia, Mona's Isle, Nautpur, Nigel, Peregrine II, Polish Monarch, Prince, Prince Abbas, Prince Edward, Princess Louise, Queen Victoria, Ramillies, Redstart, Spey, Sunhill, The Lady Carmichael, Victoria IV, White Swan, Winifred, Wrexham, Zephyr*

TUGS AND HARBOUR CRAFT

Pre-war tugs – fleet tugs (5 on Navy list in 8.14), dockyard tugs (12 built 1866–1890), paddle tugs (9 built 1899–1902, 3 built 1899–1900, 11 launched 1900–1908), small berthing tugs (16 purchased 1893–1904), *Rover* class (4 launched 1908–10), *Robust* class (10 launched 1908–15)
War construction tugs – *Pert* class (1 launched 1916), berthing tugs (10 purchased 2.15–1918), 'West' class (8 launched 1918–19), 'Poultry' class (8 launched 1919), 'Burn' class (2 launched 1919), 'Poet' class (2 launched 1919), boarding tugs (15 purchased 7.14–6.15), patrol tugs (13 hired 8–10.14), large screw tugs (over 150 requisitioned), small screw tugs (over 100 requisitioned), paddle tugs (over 50 requisitioned), rescue tugs (over ?? hired 1917–18), *Stoic* class (5 launched 1916–18), *Racia* type (3 launched 1918–19), *Resolve* class (*Sir David Hunter* type; 6 ordered 2.17), 'Saint' class (64 ordered 4–8.18, of which 18 were cancelled 12.18), ex-War Department tugs (over 50 transferred by 11.18), ferro-concrete tugs (24 ordered *c*1918, 12 cancelled)
Salvage vessels – 10 (acquired or converted 10.14–11.17)
Lifting craft – 6 (acquired 2.16–9.17)
Boom defence vessels – 11 pre-war craft; *BV 1–BV 60* (ordered 6.17–2.18, 10 cancelled).

United States of America

The period covered by this volume was a crucial one for the US Navy. By 1906 it had achieved great material strength, but it was still a rapidly developing organisation, with as yet little experience of fleet operations. Fifteen years later it was a modern Navy, much like the force which fought Japan in 1941.

The Fleet of 1906 was a very new one, and it did not possess the mass of supporting (or auxiliary) warships that would have marked a European fleet of comparable size. Nor did it have the same elaborate infrastructure. Although Congress was willing enough to approve new battleships, it baulked at the cruisers needed to support the battlefleet, and to scout for it. That was particularly apparent after 1903 as capital ships became more and more expensive. Repeated attempts to obtain scout cruisers, for example, were rebuffed, and the US Navy bought unusually large destroyers in hopes of using them partly as scouts. This cruiser shortage was apparent as late as the 1930s, and it accounts in part for the sheer size of the cruiser programme of 1940–42.

THE NAVY OF 1906

The bulk of the battlefleet, as it existed in 1906, had been laid down during the previous five years. Thus the US Navy had little practical experience of fleet operation. Instead, it had to rely on theoretical studies, primarily war games, carried out at the Naval War College at Newport, Rhode Island. The games tested both naval strategies and proposed new types of warships; in the period of this volume, examples included a battlecruiser or armoured cruiser with battleship armour, and a battleship armed primarily with torpedo tubes. Game experience (as well as fleet exercises) also exposed the main existing deficiency, a lack of scout cruisers.

One effect of the importance of the War College was that abstract strategic issues played a very large part in US naval development, much more so than, say, in the Royal Navy. From about 1904 onwards, a group of naval reformers, led by Captain (later Admiral) William S Sims, campaigned, in effect, for the triumph of the war planners and gamers, represented by the General Board, over the technicians, represented by the bureaus (such as the Bureau of Ordnance and the Bureau of Construction and Repair). At Newport in 1908 they charged that the existing battleship design, for the *Utah*, was grossly deficient because it had been completed under the bureau system. As a result, the General Board was given authority over warship characteristics (staff requirements), a power it held until 1945.

In a typical pre-1914 US naval scenario, a hostile power attempted to seize a base, either in Central America or in the Caribbean, before attacking the United States mainland or the territory of one of the South American states. The battlefleet was concentrated in the North Atlantic, and from 1903 onwards the General Board, the senior naval council, was increasingly interested in strategic scouting, ie in ships required to achieve contact with an approaching European fleet before it could seize its base. The approach of the Spanish fleet in 1898 was clearly the prototype for this scenario, but it is worth noting that there was no other major one.

The Navy of 1906, manned by 35,000 men, was still essentially a peacetime organisation. It had only just been concentrated into a single (North Atlantic) battlefleet, under a single Commander-in-Chief afloat. All operational orders were still issued by the civilian Secretary of the Navy, and there was no senior naval officer. Naval strategic policy was framed by a General Board of senior officers, headed by the Admiral of the Navy, George Dewey, the victor of Manila Bay, but it was only an advisory organisation. Ship design was coordinated by a Board on Construction consisting of the heads of the independent bureaus. It, too, reported to the Secretary.

This was a cumbersome arrangement, and there were several attempts at reform, all amounting to attempts to develop a true naval war staff. Finally in 1915 Secretary Josephus Daniels accepted the concept of a Chief of Naval Operations, choosing Admiral William S Benson, who he considered a relatively weak personality. A supporting office, which is still called OpNav, was formed in 1916. The catalytic event was America's entry into World War One: OpNav now had a naval war to fight, and it grew very powerful very rapidly. Secretary Daniels, who was himself a relatively strong personality, found himself depending on Admiral Benson, and the supremacy of the civilian Secretary was never really restored after 1918. This process went so far that the chief organisational issue after 1918 was the proper balance between OpNav and the General Board.

The single great strategic theme throughout this period, and indeed until 1941, was concentration of the battlefleet. Prior to 1906, the US Navy was distributed on 'stations' around the world to support American interests by 'showing the flag'. President Theodore Roosevelt and his advisers rejected this earlier policy: they wanted above all a fighting fleet. That implied concentration, and the problem of concentration was that the United States was a two-ocean power, with important interests in both oceans. Hence the extreme importance of the new Panama Canal (opened in 1914), which (at least in theory) allowed a single fleet to deal with threats in either ocean. It could not, however, solve the problem of *simultaneous* threats in both oceans. The problem of such threats was not really faced until just prior to World War Two, when another wave of naval expansion was designed to produce a 'two-ocean', ie a two-threat, Navy.

Such a policy might seem obvious, but the British example shows that it was not. Britain always had widely separated interests, but she could afford only one fleet. Under Lord Fisher, the Royal Navy essentially withdrew from the Far East under the cover of a treaty with Japan. The entente with France permitted her to withdraw most of the Mediterranean Fleet. More importantly, Britain was able to withdraw her large fleet of armoured cruisers, which had been required to counter Russian and French commerce raiders in the event of war. Thus, by 1906, although much of the British Empire was well East of Suez, the Royal Navy could be concentrated in home waters. When these guarantees lapsed after 1921, Britain could not continue to concentrate her fleet. For example, a large force was stationed in the Mediterranean, where it could join either the Atlantic Fleet or the China Station, depending upon the scenario.

Thus the United States was fortunate in that, although *in theory* she faced naval threats in both oceans, she could concentrate on only one at a time. Before 1918 the Fleet was concentrated in the Atlantic, primarily against Gemany. In theory, in the event of war with Japan, armoured cruisers in the Pacific would harass the Japanese until the main fleet could arrive, but this type of war plan was considered relatively unrealistic. After 1919 the Fleet was concentrated on the

Maryland class battleships of the inter-war US Pacific Fleet *CPL*

Pacific Coast, at San Pedro and ultimately at Pearl Harbor. The fact that, throughout the period from 1906 to 1939, there was a single battlefleet had a profound effect on US naval tactics. This fleet was so large that it could be divided into large squadrons for naval manoeuvres, in the course of which, carrier task force tactics were evolved. By contrast, between the World Wars the Royal Navy generally could not concentrate enough ships to test such concepts.

The US Navy of 1906 still reflected its origins in the 'New Navy' modernisation begun in 1882. By 1921 those traces had been swept away, and the Fleet that would face Japan two decades later existed in embryo form. Between these two dates several major (even traumatic) shifts in doctrine, and in the basic concept of naval operations, can be traced. In 1883 the rationale for naval organisation was fear of attack by the major European powers. The United States had proclaimed the Monroe Doctrine, barring further European expansion in the Western Hemisphere, in 1823, but without a strong navy she could not even hope to keep her own coastal cities inviolate. Moreover, until the early 1890s, the United States could not even consider herself supreme, in a naval sense, in her own hemisphere. The Navy was, then, primarily defensive in character. Americans still thought of Britain as a possible enemy, and the War of 1812 was a popular model for American naval strategy. For the first decade of her modern Navy, then, the United States built two major types of warship: the commerce-raiding cruiser and the coast defence monitor.

In 1889, however, a Policy Board proposed a new, Mahanian concept: the US Navy would engage potential invaders overseas. It would maintain a seagoing battlefleet, backed by a coast defence force. At the time, the proposed programme, which would have made the United States second only to Great Britain, was derided as absurd. However, it was largely realised over the next two decades: by 1906, at least in battleships, the United States was second only to Great Britain. From 1889 onwards, then, there was a subtle but important shift in the fundamental American naval strategy. A US battlefleet, suitably warned of the approach of a hostile invading fleet, would attempt to meet it on the high seas. As the Navy learned to its embarrassment in 1898, that in turn required long-range scout cruisers. A major exercise in 1903 showed how important (and difficult) scouting was, given the primary scenario of an enemy fleet attempting to seize a base in the New World. That is, the US fleet had to intercept the enemy force and bring it to battle before it could fortify its base, *eg* by defensive mining. In April–May 1914 the Atlantic Fleet concentrated 19 battleships off Mexico in The Vera Cruz Incident, covering 3000 marines (the Corps numbered 9991 then) landed at that port while 8 cruisers sailed down Mexico's Pacific coast. Vera Cruz was not relinquished until 25 November 1914.

THE PHILIPPINES AND THE PACIFIC

The other great consequence of the victory over Spain was US possession of the Philippine Islands. The defence of the Philippines was always the most difficult American naval task: there was no hope of stationing large naval forces in the area, and the sheer logistics of a fleet advance through the central Pacific were always daunting. At least from the end of the Russo-Japanese War, any friction with Japan almost automatically brought up the fear that Japan would seize the islands. It was probably typical of attitudes within the Navy that the General Board argued in 1915 that Japan wished to eject the United States because she considered the Philippines a rival foothold in the vast markets of Asia. At this time the General Board argued that, although the Philippines were the greatest single US naval liability, they could not be abandoned. Even were they to be made independent, the United States would still be responsible for their security. Much the same issue was raised in 1935, when isolationists in Congress passed a bill which would make the islands independent within a decade (*ie* by 1945), entirely in the hopes of keeping the United States out of any Pacific war.

From an operational point of view, the vast distances of a Pacific War presented enormous problems. They were emphasised by the 1904–5 misfortunes of the Russian Baltic Fleet, which had to steam almost halfway around the world before being destroyed by Japan at Tsushima. American concern with the logistics of Pacific operations was reflected in the construction of modern colliers designed specifically for replenishment at sea, and then of oilers for a similar role. Although the US Navy could not afford to maintain an adequate fleet train between wars, its planning for a war against Japan envisaged the wholesale conversion of civilian ships, a conversion programme which was implemented at the beginning of World War Two. To some extent, too, the round-the-world cruise of 16 US battleships (comprising the 'Great White Fleet') in 1907–9 was a demonstration that the United States could in fact project naval power into the Far East.

The rise of the Imperial German Navy almost paralleled that of the modern US Navy, and, as early as 1897, Theodore Roosevelt, who was then Assistant Secretary of the Navy, argued that, in her search for colonies abroad, Germany would almost inevitably come into collision with the United States. In 1898, a German squadron nearly came to blows with Admiral Dewey's fleet after the victory at Manila Bay, and the scenario of war against Germany was an important one for naval planners from then on. Perhaps more significantly, the size of the German Navy was used as a measure of the appropriate size of the US Navy.

That is, as the US Fleet grew, the issue of its ultimate size had to be addressed. Before World War One, there was no possibility of rivalling the greatest foreign navy, the Royal Navy, even though Britain was almost a hereditary enemy. The effort required was just too vast, and the goal too visionary. Germany was a very different matter. Not only was she a much more realistic goal in fiscal terms; her behaviour made Germany a much likelier enemy. The German archives show, remarkably, that Washington's concern with German intentions was matched by a series of official German studies of the requirements of a war in the Western Hemisphere, ie by just the ideas the US war planners attributed to the Kaiser and his advisers.

THE FIRST WORLD WAR

World War One transformed the political situation, first by making America much more defence-conscious, and then by radically changing the priorities of the US Navy when the latter actually entered the war in April 1917. The first development swept away the obstacles to naval expansion: in 1915 the General Board called for a new naval policy of parity with the greatest foreign power, ie with Britain. It argued that, whoever emerged victorious from the war would challenge the United States. The potential of war-weariness was dismissed. The Board also suggested that Japan, by making agreements with both Germany and the Allies, had ensured that she would continue to threaten the Philippines. In 1916 President Woodrow Wilson finally accepted the call for parity, and Congress passed a massive three-year programme, which included 10 battleships, 6 battlecruisers and 10 scout cruisers. Although this programme was never completed, the demand for parity became standard US naval policy.

During this period, the United States benefitted enormously from the rapid changes in warship, particularly battleship, design, which wiped out much of the advantage Britain had built up over the years since the advent of the *Dreadnought*. During 1905–1914 the British edge increased, partly because of the enormous strength of the British shipbuilding industry, and partly because, after Theodore Roosevelt left the Presidency, Congress was increasingly reluctant to buy new ships in sufficient numbers. However, once Britain entered World War One, she virtually ceased battleship construction, whereas the United States continued at prewar rates. Moreover, ships of wartime design were so much more than a match for earlier ships that the *effective* British postwar battlefleet was not too much larger than the US fleet built up from the *Nevada* onwards. Moreover, the American 16in gun was superior to the British 15in/42, so that the three *Maryland*s more than matched the wartime British 'R' class.

When war was declared on Germany on 6 April 1917, American naval policy shifted abruptly. Most of the US battlefleet remained in home waters, partly because the U-boat campaign had made oil fuel scarce in British waters. However, six coal-burning battleships did serve with the Grand Fleet as the 6th Battle Squadron. Other US battleships were based in Ireland to meet the threat of a German battlecruiser raid into the Atlantic. Submarines were based at Queenstown and in the Azores. American destroyers based at Queenstown and Brest served as convoy escorts, as did some of the pre-dreadnoughts and the big armoured cruisers.

In 1917 the ongoing US big-ship naval programme had to be suspended in favour of mass production of destroyers, sub-chasers, submarines, and merchant ships. The submarines were considered an ASW measure: they would patrol U-boat operational areas, submerged, in hopes of ambushing U-boats. American submarines operated in European waters in this role, and for a time it appeared that the United States would build an equivalent of the British R class ASW submarine. Destroyer production had a profound effect on the postwar US Navy, in that suddenly there were far more destroyers than the battlefleet required, and large numbers of new ones had to be laid up. At the same time, since cruisers were not part of the ASW programme, the war did not leave the Navy with any solution to its prewar cruiser shortage, and destroyers still had to carry out some cruiser scouting missions. Manpower grew to 450,000. Losses only amounted to the armoured cruiser *San Diego*, 2 destroyers, 2 submarines and 7 auxiliaries. Between 1906 and 1919 the US merchant marine more than doubled from about 5 million tons to almost 12 million tons. Wartime losses only came to 389,000 tons being dwarfed tenfold (4,030,949 tons) by new construction almost matching the British Empire's over the whole war.

The other great US contribution to the ASW war was the 1918 North Sea Mine Barrage, stretching from Scotland to Norway, and laid by a

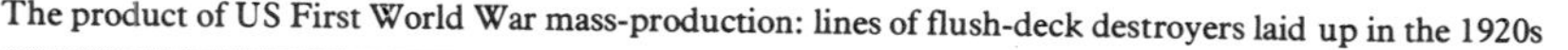

The product of US First World War mass-production: lines of flush-deck destroyers laid up in the 1920s *CPL*

scratch force led by the converted cruisers *Baltimore* and *San Francisco*. Between 5 and 7 U-boats sank in it. Like the sub-chaser programme, it was an example of what US mass-production technology could do. This immense field was cleared by the 'Bird' class sweepers immediately after the war. In 1919–20 a total of 14 US warships served under British command in the Baltic during the Allied intervention against the Bolsheviks. Destroyers assisted the French Navy's evacuation of 120,000 White Russian refugees from the Crimea in November 1920. The Asiatic Fleet played a less prominent role in the Allied operations at Vladivostok.

BRITISH INFLUENCE

Perhaps the most important effect of US participation in World War One was the shock effect of close contact with what was then the most advanced naval organisation in the world, the British Grand Fleet. For example, the US Navy, which before the war had been very proud of its gunnery, found its salvoes much less tightly bunched than those of the British. Admiral Sims' London Planning Group proposed a future construction programme that very nearly mirrored British practice. It called, for example, for a *Hood*-like fast battleship to be built in place of the planned lightly-armoured battlecruisers, and an 8in gun cruiser similar in theory to the British *Hawkins*. The former proposal was not adopted, but the 8in cruiser became the 'treaty' cruiser of the 1920s.

At this time, too, a British naval constructor, Stanley Goodall (later Director of Naval Construction), was seconded to the Bureau of Construction and Repair. He brought details of the *Hood*, of the British experience at Jutland, and of British aircraft carrier concepts. Consequences included the radical redesign of the US battlecruiser, and the earliest US aircraft carrier design.

POSTWAR PARITY

The 1916 programme was resumed in 1919, and the United States was soon engaged in a building race with Japan and Britain. The American objective appears to have been to achieve and then enforce parity, by means of a combination of new construction and agreements to reduce naval construction abroad. For example, new programmes were announced in 1919, but there is evidence that these announcements were intended largely to deter Britain from further construction of her own. The US efforts culminated in the Washington Naval Conference of 1921–22, at which the United States delegation proposed the 5:5:3 ratio of American, British, and Japanese capital ship tonnage.

In effect, British acceptance of the US proposals made parity a fact, and legitimised America's claim to be a first rank naval power. Because Congress had never been willing to buy large numbers of cruisers, parity (as of 1921) applied only to capital ships, and for the next decade the General Board annually proposed cruiser programme that would bring the United States to equality with Britain. The magnitude of the task daunted Congress; the Board attempted to reduce it by defining parity in terms of net cruiser *tonnage* rather than numbers. That is, the Royal Navy had large numbers of small cruisers. From a tonnage point of view, then, each new US 10,000 ton cruiser equated to two or more of the existing British ships, so that the *numbers* needed (which was what Congress noticed) were not so great.

For the US Navy, the main effects of the treaty were the cancellation of 7 battleships and 6 battlecruisers, and the disposal of all of the pre-dreadnoughts as well as of the earliest dreadnought battleships; one admiral is said to have remarked that the treaty destroyed more ships than those sunk by all the admirals of history. That is not altogether fair. The general disposal of obsolescent ships struck much harder at the Royal Navy, which lost much of its edge over the US fleet. Moreover, the ban on new construction prevented the Royal Navy from matching America's 'all or nothing' battleships. At the conference, there was much discussion of 'post Jutland battleships', with heavy deck armour, but (it appears) little comprehension that every US battleship from the *Nevada* onwards properly fell into this category. Nor is there any indication that the US delegation was aware of the great advantage the United States stood to gain by freezing the competition.

Similarly, the United States managed to abort a large Japanese building programme, and it is tempting to imagine that the conference was called as soon as the US Navy became aware of the nature of the Japanese programme. Again, it is by no means clear that this was the case. The US government did benefit greatly by its ability to read Japanese diplomatic code traffic during the conference, but it appears that the key issue was how far the Japanese could be pushed, not the technical details of their new ships.

FLEET STRENGTH 1906

BATTLESHIPS

No	Name	Launched	Disp (normal)	Fate
–	TEXAS	28.6.92	6135t	Renamed *San Marcos* 16.2.11, target 1911–12
Indiana class				
BB 1	INDIANA	28.2.93	10,288t	Sunk as target 1920
BB 2	MASSACHUSETTS	10.6.93	10,288t	Scuttled as target 1921
BB 3	OREGON	26.10.93	10,288t	Sold 1956
Iowa				
BB 4	IOWA	28.3.96	11,410t	Sunk as target 1923
Kearsarge class				
BB 5	KEARSARGE	24.3.98	11,540t	Sold 1955
BB 6	KENTUCKY	24.3.98	11,540t	Sold 1923
Illinois class				
BB 7	ILLINOIS	4.10.98	11,565t	Sold 1956
BB 8	ALABAMA	18.5.98	11,565t	Sunk as target 1921
BB 9	WISCONSIN	26.11.98	11,653t	Sold 1922
Maine class				
BB 10	MAINE	27.7.01	12,846t	Sold 1922
BB 11	MISSOURI	28.12.01	12,362t	Sold 1922
BB 12	OHIO	18.5.01	12,723t	Sold 1923
Virginia class				
BB 13	VIRGINIA	5.4.04	14,948t	Sunk as target 1923
BB 14	NEBRASKA	7.10.04	14,948t	Sold 1923
BB 15	GEORGIA	11.10.04	14,948t	Sold 1923
BB 16	NEW JERSEY	10.11.04	14,948t	Sunk as target 1923
BB 17	RHODE ISLAND	17.5.04	14,948t	Sold 1923
Connecticut class				
BB 18	CONNECTICUT	29.9.04	16,000t	Sold 1923
BB 19	LOUISIANA	27.8.04	16,000t	Sold 1923
Vermont class				
BB 20	VERMONT	31.8.05		Sold 1923
BB 21	KANSAS	12.8.05		Sold 1923
BB 22	MINNESOTA	8.4.05		Sold 1924
BB 25	NEW HAMPSHIRE	30.6.06		Sold 1923
Mississippi class				
BB 23	MISSISSIPPI	30.9.05		To Greece 30.7.14
BB 24	IDAHO	9.12.05		To Greece 30.7.14

Indiana class

Indiana and *Massachusetts* were renamed *Coast Battleship No 1* and *Coast Battleship No 2* on 29 March 1919. *Oregon* was used as a floating memorial from 1925 to 1942 and was sold for BU in December 1942. However work was stopped and she was employed as an ammunition hulk during the 1944 invasion of Guam, where she remained until sold.

Iowa
Renamed *Coast Battleship No 4* on 29 March 1919; used as a radio-controlled target ship until sunk.

Kearsarge class
Kearsarge was converted into a crane ship in 1920, and was renamed *Crane Ship No 1* in November 1941.

Illinois class
Illinois was used as an armoury and later an accommodation ship from 1921 to 1955. She was renamed *Prairie State* (IX 15) in January 1941.

Virginia class
New Jersey commissioned in May 1906, was off Cuba in 1907 during the insurrection, and landed marines at Vera Cruz on 22–23 April 1914.

Connecticut class
Both ships landed marines at Vera Cruz in April–May 1914. *Connecticut* landed 2nd Marine Regiment at Port-au-Prince, Haiti, on 4 August 1915.

Vermont class
Vermont, Minnesota and *New Hampshire* landed marines at Vera Cruz in April–May 1914.

Mississippi class
Mississippi took marines and 6 Curtiss 'hydroaeroplanes' from Pensacola to Vera Cruz 21–24 April 1914.

Modifications to pre-dreadnought classes
Pre-dreadnought battleships went through two series of modifications: immediately after the World Cruise of 1907–9, and during and just after World War One. The World Cruise coincided with two major developments: an increasing interest in very long-range gunfire, and a 'naval reform' movement bent on making the fleet more battleworthy. The major changes to existing ships were the installation of tall cage masts, to raise spotters aloft and thus make very long range fire possible; and the elimination of much existing top-hamper, particularly bridgework. The experience of the Russo-Japanese War was considered to have shown that extensive bridge structures served merely to burst shells, and thus to kill exposed personnel. Better to force vital personnel into the protection of the conning towers, which were enlarged, in the expectation that ships would be controlled from within, even in peacetime. To encourage officers to work from within their conning towers, the practice of building up windscreens around open bridges was banned.

In theory, the cage masts could sustain multiple hits, so that ships would be able to continue fire control (by spotting) through a battle. Most ships received two, again for survivability, although in some cases ships were initially fitted with only one. The first four battleships, which were considered obsolescent by 1909, received only cage mainmasts, the original pole foremasts being retained, although the enclosed pilot houses were eliminated. All of the slow-firing 6in/30 secondary guns were removed at this time and replaced by 12 rapid-fire 3in/50, including four on the turret tops. *Iowa*, which had no 6in secondaries, received 4–4in turret top guns, for a total of 10.

At this time, too, the ships were all painted dark grey, in place of their earlier white-and-buff colours. In theory, this change, too, resulted from cruise experience, but one cannot separate it from an increasing move towards greater war readiness within the Navy. The modifications did not affect the pre-dreadnoughts' gravest defect, the wetness of their secondary batteries.

As expected battle ranges increased after the World Cruise, it became standard practice to mount long-base rangefinders atop some of the turrets. These unprotected instruments would provide initial ranges, allowing the US fleet to make what were hoped to be early hits. In many cases shorter-base instruments were also mounted atop one or both of the cage masts.

The major World War One modification was the wholesale removal of hull-mounted guns in both battleships and armoured cruisers, not so much because of their wetness as to provide weapons for naval auxiliaries and for armed merchantmen. Ultimately, then, all main deck guns (6in and 7in) were removed from the *Virginia* and *Connecticut* classes. The three next earliest classes (*Kearsage, Illinois* and *Maine*) were each reduced to 8 secondary (5in and 6in) guns. Light anti-destroyer guns (3in) were removed (retained only in the *Maine*s, with 6, the *Virginia*s, with 4 or 6, the *Connecticut*s, with 12 and in the four earliest ships, with 4 each on the turret tops), and 2–3in AA mounted aboard most ships. In addition, as in the case of the dreadnoughts, open bridges and torpedo defence (fire control) platforms were finally protected by blast and wind screens, presumably in response to actual steaming experience in very bad weather: the conning towers were just not enough. In the *Virginia* and *Connecticut* classes, as in the dreadnoughts, long-base rangefinders were mounted on forebridges, as an aid to plotting the movement of ships within formations, and as a tactical aid in battle. These changes all corresponded to modifications made in the dreadnoughts.

Note that in 1919 the first four battleships (*Indiana* class and *Iowa*) were all redesignated as numbered Coast Defense Battleships, their names surrendered to new *South Dakota* class ships. *Iowa* became a radio-controlled mobile target.

Huron (ex-*South Dakota*) 3 November 1923 — *CPL*

MONITORS

No	Name	Launched	Disp (normal)	Fate
BM 1	PURITAN	6.12.82	606t	Sold 1922
Amphitrite class				
BM 2	AMPHITRITE	7.6.83	3990t	Sold 1920
BM 3	MONADNOCK	19.9.83	3990t	Sold 1923
BM 4	TERROR	24.3.83	3990t	Sold 1923
BM 5	MIANTONOMOH	5.12.76	3990t	Sold 1922
Monterey				
BM 6	MONTEREY	28.4.91	4084t	Sold 1921

The ancient *Canonicus* of 1863 was also still afloat, but was sold in 1908.

CRUISERS

No	Name	Launched	Disp (normal)	Fate
ACR 2	NEW YORK	2.12.91	8200t	Scuttled 12.41
Brooklyn				
ACR 3	BROOKLYN	2.10.95	9215t	Sold 1921
Pennsylvania class				
ACR 4	PENNSYLVANIA	22.8.03	13,680t	Sold 1931
ACR 5	WEST VIRGINIA	18.4.03	13,680t	Sold 1930
ACR 6	CALIFORNIA	28.4.04	13,680t	Lost 19.7.18
ACR 7	COLORADO	25.4.03	13,680t	Sold 1930
ACR 8	MARYLAND	12.9.03	13,680t	Sold 1930
ACR 9	SOUTH DAKOTA	27.7.04	13,680t	Sold 1930
Tennessee class				
ACR 10	TENNESSEE	3.12.04	14,500t	Wrecked 29.8.16
ACR 11	WASHINGTON	18.3.05	14,500t	Sold 1946
ACR 12	NORTH CAROLINA	6.10.06	14,500t	Sold 1930
ACR 13	MONTANA	15.12.06	14,500t	Sold 1930
Atlanta class				
–	ATLANTA	9.10.84	3189t	Sold 1912
–	BOSTON	4.12.84	3189t	Scuttled 8.4.46
Chicago				
–	CHICAGO	5.12.85	4500t	Foundered 8.7.36
Newark				
C 1	NEWARK	19.3.90	4038t	Sold 1926
Baltimore				
C 3	BALTIMORE	6.10.88	4413t	Sold 1942
Philadelphia				
C 4	PHILADELPHIA	7.9.89	4324t	Sold 1927
San Francisco				
C 5	SAN FRANCISCO	26.10.89	4088t	Sold 1939
Olympia				
C 6	OLYMPIA	5.11.92	5865t	Memorial, extant 1984
Cincinnati class				
C 7	CINCINNATI	10.11.92	3183t	Sold 1921
C 8	RALEIGH	31.3.93	3183t	Sold 1921
Montgomery class				
C 9	MONTGOMERY	5.12.91	2094t	Sold 1919
C 10	DETROIT	20.7.93	2094t	Sold 1910
C 11	MARBLEHEAD	11.8.92	2094t	Sold 1921
Colombia class				
C 12	COLUMBIA	26.7.92	7375t	Sold 1922
C 13	MINNEAPOLIS	12.8.93	7375t	Sold 1921
New Orleans class				
–	NEW ORLEANS	4.12.96	3769t	Sold 1930
–	ALBANY	14.1.99	3769t	Sold 1930
Denver class				
C 14	DENVER	21.6.02	3200t	Sold 1933
C 15	DES MOINES	20.9.03	3200t	Sold 1930
C 16	CHATTANOOGA	7.3.03	3200t	Sold 1930
C 17	GALVESTON	23.7.03	3200t	Sold 1933
C 18	TACOMA	2.6.03	3200t	Wrecked 16.1.24
C 19	CLEVELAND	28.9.01	3200t	Sold 1930
St Louis class				
C 20	ST LOUIS	6.5.05	9700t	Sold 1930
C 21	MILWAUKEE	10.9.04	9700t	Wrecked 13.1.17
C 22	CHARLESTON	17.10.05	9700t	Sold 1930
Chester class				
CS 1	CHESTER	26.6.07	3750t	Sold 1930
CS 2	BIRMINGHAM	29.5.07	3750t	Sold 1930
CS 3	SALEM	27.7.07	3750t	Sold 1930

UNITED STATES OF AMERICA

Armoured cruisers

The ten large (battleship-size) armoured cruisers (ACR 4–ACR 13) were modernised in rough analogy to the pre-dreadnought battleships, with cage foremasts (but not cage mainmasts). In number order they were renamed as follows: *Pittsburgh* (27 August 1912), *Huntington* (11 November 1916), *San Diego* (1 September 1914), *Pueblo* (9 November 1916), *Frederick* (9 November 1916), *Huron* (7 June 1920), *Memphis* (25 May 1916), *Seattle* (9 November 1916), *Charlotte* (7 June 1920), and *Missoula* (7 June 1920). *South Dakota* and *West Virginia* had carried most of 4th US Marine Regiment in the Pacific show-of-force during the 1914 Vera Cruz Incident. *Tennessee* landed 1st Marine Regiment in Haiti, 15 August 1915. *West Virginia* and *California* were flagships for the Nicaragua intervention, *Washington* likewise off Santo Domingo in 1914 and landed marines in Haiti in July 1915. They were scouts; the US Navy very early saw the value of aircraft as an adjunct. Hence the January 1911 experiment in which Eugene Ely landed a Curtiss biplane on a 120ft long platform at the after end of *Pennsylvania*. By 1912 a simple powder catapult had been designed. It was preferable to a flying-off deck because it could be used while the ship was underway. The prototype was installed aboard the *North Carolina* in October 1915, and the first aircraft launched in November 1915. The *Seattle* and *Huntington* were also so fitted, but a fourth installation was cancelled when the United States entered World War One, and the three existing catapults were removed. In each case, the fixed twin-rail catapult ran right aft to the stern, covering the after main battery turret.

As in the case of the pre-dreadnought battleships, war modifications consisted of the removal of main deck secondary weapons and increased bridgework. By the end of the war, the big armoured cruisers had only 4–6in guns (8 in the *Pittsburgh*), 10 or 12 3in/50 single-purpose, and 2–3in AA. *San Diego* (ex-*California*) was mined or torpedoed 10 miles off Fire Island NY by *U 156*, capsizing and sinking in about 20 minutes. Unlike the pre-dreadnoughts, the big armoured cruisers were retained after World War One, in some cases as flagships on foreign stations. *Brooklyn*, for example, was flagship of the Asiatic Fleet in 1917–19, mostly at Vladivostok, while *Pittsburgh* (ACR 4) led a naval detachment off Turkey in 1919. Further modernisation, which might have increased their speed, was considered both in 1922 and in 1929. *Pittsburgh* had her fore funnel removed as flagship of the Asiatic Fleet, 1927–1931.

The older *New York*, the first US armoured cruiser, was renamed *Saratoga* on 16 February 1911 and *Rochester* on 1 December 1917. She survived postwar as Asiatic Fleet flagship and then as station ship in Manila Bay. She had one funnel removed in 1927, four Babcock boilers replacing the original 12. She was stricken in 1938 and laid up in the Philippines until scuttled to avoid capture by the Japanese.

Protected cruisers

The earlier protected cruisers were much less elaborately modified, although most of them were fitted with the characteristic angle-sided windscreens of the period. The big *St Louis* class had 2–6in removed (leaving a total of 12), and their secondary batteries were reduced to 4–3in/50 single-purpose (out of 18) and 2–3in AA. The two fast *Columbia*s had their single 8in guns replaced by single 6in even before the outbreak of war; 4–4in/40 and 2–3in AA were added during the war. Similarly, the *Olympia* had her mixed battery of 8in and 5in guns replaced by a uniform battery of 10–5in/51 in 1917–18. The *New Orleans* class had been rearmed in 1907 with 10–5in/50, although this was reduced to 8 by the end of the war. *Chicago* gave refuge to the defeated Honduran president in 1907 and helped mediate peace with Nicaragua. *Albany* was in the 1909–10 Nicaraguan Expeditionary Squadron. *St Louis* was flagship off Turkey in 1921.

Of the older ships, *Atlanta* served as an accommodation ship from November 1905, and Boston was a TS from June 1911, and a receiving ship from 1918 to 1946, and was renamed *Despatch* in August 1940. *Chicago* served as a TS for naval militia from 1910 and later with submarines; she was classified CA 14 in July 1920, was renamed *Alton* in July 1928, and served as an accommodation ship from 1923 until sold in 1935; she was under tow when lost. *Newark* was stricken in June 1913, but survived as a quarantine and hospital hulk until sold in 1926. *Denver* landed marines at Havana in September 1906. *Des Moines* prevented fighting at Bluefields, Nicaragua, in December 1909.

Baltimore was converted to a minelayer at Charleston N Yd in 1911–12; she was decommissioned in 1922 but survived as a hulk for 20 years. *Philadelphia* was reduced to harbour service in 1904 and was stricken in 1926. *San Francisco* was converted to a minelayer at Norfolk N Yd in 1908–11, armament being reduced to 8–5in/40; she was off Vera Cruz in 1914 and went into reserve in 1921 and was renamed *Tahoe* and then *Yosemite* in 1930–31, and was stricken in 1937.

During the First World War the main armament of the *Cincinnati* class was reduced to 9–5in; similarly the armament of the two surviving *Montgomery* class was reduced to 8–4in by 1919 (*Montgomery* served as a torpedo trials ship 1908–1914 and was renamed *Anniston* in March 1918).

The three *Chester* class ships were the only modern US cruisers of the pre-World War One era. They were designed in response to General Board demands for scouts, arising in large part from the experience of several scouting exercises early in the century. As built, they were used to compare conventional triple-expansion steam engines with the new turbines: *Birmingham* had reciprocating engines, *Chester* had Parsons turbines, and *Salem* had Curtis turbines. In 1917 *Salem* was refitted with General Electric geared turbines of 20,000shp. *Chester* took a battalion of marines from Panama to Vera Cruz in 1914.

The original design called for a uniform-calibre battery of 12–3in/50 guns, sufficient at the time to deal with contemporary destroyers. However, at the same time foreign navies began to build scout cruisers of their own, and it was clear that American scouts would have to break through (or at least fight) screening cruisers. In 1905, therefore, the battery was revised, to 2–5in/50 on the centreline and 6–3in/50; in both cases the ship was to have been armed with two submerged 21in TT. The other major change was in protection. The original design called for conventional cruiser armour, consisting of a 1.5in deck curving down to the waterline. The planned vertical triple expansion engines, however, would have pierced this deck, so some form of vertical protection was needed. A 2in waterline belt was chosen. The deck armour amidships was eliminated as weight compensation.

Both cruiser and destroyer speeds rose so rapidly from 1908 onwards that these ships were never effective scouts; the scouting role passed to the destroyers which, at least in smooth water, were much faster, and which were deliberately increased in size for seakeeping.

The first aircraft take-off from a warship was made by Eugene Ely in a Curtiss Pusher biplane from the bows of *Birmingham* in November 1910. By the end of World War One, all were armed with 4–5in/51, 2–3in/50, 1–3in/50 AA gun, and the original pair of underwater TT.

DESTROYERS

No	Name	Fate
Bainbridge class: launched 1900–1902, 420t		
DD 1	BAINBRIDGE	Sold 1920
DD 2	BARRY	Sold 1920
DD 3	CHAUNCEY	Sunk 19.11.17
DD 4	DALE	Sold 1920
DD 5	DECATUR	Sold 1920
Hopkins class: launched 1902, 408t		
DD 6	HOPKINS	Sold 1920
DD 7	HULL	Sold 1921
Lawrence class: launched 1900, 430t		
DD 8	LAWRENCE	Sold 1920
DD 9	MACDONOUGH	Sold 1920
Paul Jones class: launched 1900–1902, 480t		
DD 10	PAUL JONES	Sold 1920
DD 11	PERRY	Sold 1920
DD 12	PREBLE	Sold 1920
Stewart: launched 1902, 420t		
DD 13	STEWART	Sold 1920
Truxtun class:		
DD 14	TRUXTUN	Sold 1920
DD 15	WHIPPLE	Sold 1920
DD 16	WORDEN	Sold 1920

Chauncey was lost in a Straits of Gibraltar collision with USS *Caya*. *Lawrence* served in the 1914 Mexican crisis, going into reserve 1915–16. *Truxtun* patrolled off Mexico's Pacific coast 1914–16.

TORPEDO-BOATS

No	Name	Fate
Stilleto: launched 1880, 31t		
WTB 1	STILLETO	Sold 1911
Cushing: launched 1890, 116t		
TB 1	CUSHING	Sunk as target 1920
Ericsson: launched 1894, 120t		
TB 2	ERICSSON	Sunk as target 1912
Foote class: launched 1896–97, 142t		
TB 3	FOOTE	*Coast Torpedo-Boat No 1* 8.18, sold 1920
TB 4	RODGERS	*Coast Torpedo-Boat No 2* 8.18, sold 1920
TB 5	WINSLOW	Sold 1911
Porter class: launched 1896–97, 165t		
TB 6	PORTER	Sold 1912
TB 7	DU PONT	*Coast Torpedo-Boat No 3* 8.18, sold 1920
Rowan: launched 1898, 182t		
TB 8	ROWAN	Stricken 29.10.12, sold 1918
Dahlgren class: launched 1899, 146t		
TB 9	DAHLGREN	*Coast Torpedo-Boat No 4* 8.18, sold 1920
TB 10	CRAVEN	Target 1913
Farragut: launched 1898, 279t		
TB 11	FARRAGUT	*Coast Torpedo-Boat No 5* 8.18, sold 1919
Davis class: launched 1898, 155t		
TB 12	DAVIS	Decommissioned 28.3.13, sold 1920
TB 13	FOX	Sold 1916
Morris: launched 1898, 105t		
TB 14	MORRIS	*Coast Torpedo-Boat No 6* 8.18, sold 1924
Talbot class: launched 1897, 46t		
TB 15	TALBOT	Decommissioned 4.14
TB 16	GWIN	Sold 1925
Mackenzie class: launched 1898, 65t		
TB 17	MACKENZIE	Target 1916
TB 18	MCKEE	Target 1912–1920
Stringham: launched 1899, 340t		
TB 19	STRINGHAM	Stricken 20.11.13, sold 1923
Goldsborough: launched 1899, 255t		
TB 20	GOLDSBOROUGH	*Coast Torpedo-Boat No 7* 8.18, sold 1919
Bailey: launched 1899, 235t		
TB 21	BAILEY	*Coast Torpedo-Boat No 8* 8.18, sold 1920

No	Name	Fate
Somers: launched 1897, 143t		
TB 22	SOMERS	*Coast Torpedo-Boat No 9* 8.18, sold 1920
Bagley class: launched 1900–1901, 168t		
TB 24	BAGLEY	*Coast Torpedo-Boat No 10* 8.18, sold 1919
TB 25	BARNEY	*Coast Torpedo-Boat No 11* 8.18, sold 1920
TB 26	BIDDLE	*Coast Torpedo-Boat No 12* 8.18, sold 1920
Blakely class: launched 1900, 196t		
TB 27	BLAKELY	*Coast Torpedo-Boat No 13* 8.18, sold 1920
TB 28	DE LONG	*Coast Torpedo-Boat No 14* 8.18, sold 1920
Nicholson class: launched 1900–1901, 218t–220t		
TB 29	NICHOLSON	Target 1909
TB 30	O'BRIEN	Target 1909
Shubrick class: launched 1899–1900, 200t		
TB 31	SHUBRICK	*Coast Torpedo-Boat No 15* 8.18, sold 1920
TB 32	STOCKTON	Stricken 15.11.13, target 1914–1916
TB 33	THORNTON	*Coast Torpedo-Boat No 16* 8.18, sold 1920
Tingey: launched 1901, 165t		
TB 34	TINGEY	Sold 1920
Wilkes: launched 1901, 175t		
TB 35	WILKES	Sold 1914

Because of their size, *Farragut, Stringham, Goldsborough* and *Bailey* are usually considered prototype TBDs, but they were always part of the TB (and later the CTB series) so are included here.

PATROL GUNBOATS

No	Name	Fate
Dolphin: launched 1884, 1486t		
–	DOLPHIN	Dispatch vessel 1899, sold 1922
Yorktown class: launched 1888–90, 1710t		
PG 1	YORKTOWN	Sold 1921
PG 2	CONCORD	Accommodation ship 1909, sold 1929
PG 3	BENNINGTON	Decommissioned 1905, sold 1910
Petrel: launched 1888, 867t		
PG 2	PETREL	Sold 1920
Bancroft: launched 1892, 839t		
–	BANCROFT	Revenue Cutter *Itasea* 1906
Machias class: launched 1891–92, 1173t		
PG 5	MACHIAS	Mexican *Agua Prieta* 29.10.20
PG 6	CASTINE	Submarine tender 1908–13, sold 1921
Nashville: launched 1895, 1371t		
PG 7	NASHVILLE	Sold 1921
Wilmington class: launched 1895–96, 1397t		
PG 8	WILMINGTON	Renamed *Dover* (IX 30) *c*1942, sold 1946
PG 9	HELENA	Sold 1932
Annapolis class: launched 1896–97, 1000t–1153t		
PG 10	ANNAPOLIS	TS 1920, to Maritime Commission 1940
PG 11	VICKSBURG	Coast Guard Cutter *Alexander Hamilton* 1921
PG 12	NEWPORT	TS 1907–31, for disposal 1934
PG 13	PRINCETON	Sold 1919
Wheeling class: launched 1897, 1000t		
PG 14	WHEELING	Sold 1946
PG 15	MARIETTA	Sold 1920
Topeka: launched 1881 (purchased 1898), 2372t		
–	TOPEKA	Prison ship 1907
Ex-Spanish gunboats: launched 1886–87 (captured 1898), 950t–1020t		
–	ISLA DE LUZON	TS 1903–18, sold 1920
–	ISLA DE CUBA	Venezuelan *Mariscal Sucre* 2.4.12
–	DON JUAN DE AUSTRIA	TS 1907–17, sold 1919
Dubuque class: launched 1904, 1084t		
PG 17	DUBUQUE	TS 1922, sold 1946
PG 18	PADUCAH	TS 1922, sold 1946

Besides the above there were a large number of small gunboats captured from Spain, and recommissioned 1899–1902. In 1906 the most important survivors (and their tonnage and fates) were: *Alvarado* (106t, sold 1912), *Arayat* (243t, sold 1910), *Calamiones* (173t, sold 1907), *Callao* (243t, sold 1923), *Elcano* (620t, target 1928), *Leyte* (151t, sold 1907), *Mariveles* (170t, sold 1909), *Mindoro* (142t, sold 1912), *Pampagna* (243t, target 1928), *Panay* (162t, sold 1920), *Paragua* (243t, sold 1911), *Quiros* (350t, target 1923), *Samar* (243t, sold 1921), *Sandoval* (106t, sold 1919), *Villalobos* (370t, target 1933). *Marietta* (see table) was in the 1914 Dominican Republic intervention. *Paducah* (see table) landed her marines at Bluefields on Nicaragua's Atlantic coast (19 May 1910) where they helped the American supported side win a civil war. *Machias* landed her marines at Port-au-Prince, Haiti, and seized the country's last $500,000 against her foreign debts in December 1914.

MISCELLANEOUS

No	Name	Fate
Vesuvius dynamite-gun cruiser: launched 1888, 929t		
–	VESUVIUS	Experimental vessel, sold 1921
Katahdin armoured ram: launched 1893, 2155t		
–	KATAHDIN	Stricken 9.7.09, sunk as target 1909

A number of armed merchant cruisers taken up during the Spanish-American War were retained in subsidiary capacities: *Buffalo* was a transport 1906–17, a destroyer tender 1918–22, and a barracks ship until sold in 1927; *Dixie* was a destroyer tender from 1909 until sold in 1922; *Panther* was a repair ship 1907–17, and then a destroyer tender until sold in 1923; *Prairie*, after service as a transport, was a destroyer tender from 1917 until sold in 1923; and *Yankee* was a supply ship until stranded and lost in 1908.

A total of 23 armed yachts of a similar vintage also survived in 1906; many saw service in the First World War and were not disposed of until the early 1920s.

CAPITAL SHIPS

The two formative experiences of US battleship design were the World Cruise of 1907–9 and the operations with the Grand Fleet in 1917–18. The cruise tested seakeeping, and demonstrated that American battleships carried their secondary guns much too close to the waterline; correcting this defect would be a continuing theme right to the end of World War One. At the same time, the lessons of the Russo-Japanese War were being digested. They included the dangers presented by tophamper. For example, officers observing the battle while standing outside their conning towers were often killed by shells bursting on the conning tower armour, or else by falling masts and bridges. The solution was to provide large conning towers, and also to discourage officers from standing outside them by eliminating virtually all unprotected bridgework. That gave US dreadnoughts a particularly austere appearance, which did not change until World War One.

The success of long-range gunnery encouraged US attempts to improve fire control, and thus led to the development of the characteristic US cage mast, a fire control support designed to remain standing even after taking multiple hits. The first ships so fitted were the new pre-dreadnoughts *Idaho* and *Mississippi*. The mast was tested in 1908, and ships returning from the World Cruise were refitted with it.

Contact with the Grand Fleet was reflected in battleship refits: the US ships were fitted for director-firing, for secondary battery director fire control (note the small director towers), and for data transmission among ships of a division or squadron, by means of range 'clocks' and turret bearing markings.

The experience of North Sea weather convinced the Navy that weather protection of aloft platforms was essential. Thus the torpedo-defence platforms were plated in with distinctive angled windscreens, reminiscent of the baffles on the bridges of contemporary US destroyers. Similar baffles were applied to the fire control tops surmounting fore and main masts, which were now enclosed and roofed. The light baffles were replaced postwar by large octagonal tops, which were roofed over and glassed in; probably the first ship so fitted was *Mississippi*. Ships prior to *Wyoming* were not fitted with octagonal tops. These torpedo defence positions were shifted to the mast top in the *Tennessee* class, whose heavier cage mast could take the extra weight.

At the same time, ships were fitted with enclosed pilot and chart-houses above their conning towers; they presumably reflect the problems of keeping station in bad weather. Ships from the *Florida* class onwards were refitted with enclosed bridges from 1919 onwards.

Meanwhile, most ships had secondary guns removed for remounting aboard merchant ships and newly-acquired auxiliaries. The *Penn-*

*sylvania*s lost 8 guns each (4 right forward, 4 right aft); the *Nevada*s 9 (the foremost gun on each side forward, and all 7 guns right aft); the *Wyoming* and *New York* classes 5 (one right aft, the foremost gun deck weapon on each side forward; in the *Wyoming*s, the open 5in gun, in the *New York*s, the second gun on each side forward). The *Florida*s and *North Dakota*s lost none, but the *South Carolina*s lost 10 each. Ships serving with the Grand Fleet lost guns only at the end of the war. By the end of the war, Grand Fleet captains were suggesting the removal of *all* gun deck weapons. Later removals, particularly of weapons right aft, reduced most ships to a standard battery of 14–5in/51 by 1921.

By 1918 the standard AA battery was 2–3in/50, generally mounted atop boat cranes in place of searchlights in the dreadnoughts. They were on deck in the *Nevada* and later classes. By 1921 the standard was 8–3in/50, and in ships with 14–5in/51, 2–5in/51 (on the 01 level) were deleted to make room for extra AA guns.

Finally, aircraft appeared aboard the dreadnoughts, on British-type turret top take-off platforms. *Texas* was the first, but in 1919 two platforms each were approved for the three later classes. Within a year work on catapults was far enough advanced to permit abandonment of the platforms, which were not entirely satisfactory. For example, in October 1920 the General Board decided explicitly *not* to fit the *South Dakota*s with flying-off platforms.

Note: In US parlance, battleship side armour for ships prior to the *Nevada* consisted of a main belt (largely underwater) covered by a flat protective deck approximately at the waterline, with a 'lower casemate' above it. The upper casemate covered part or all of the secondary battery in the *Delaware* and later classes. The deck thickness quoted refers to the protective deck over the length of the main belt; there were thicker, curved, decks fore and aft. In the *Nevada* and later ships, the lower casemate and belt were merged, and the main protective deck moved to the top of the belt, well above the waterline. A second (splinter) deck was provided at the waterline, sloping down to meet the lower edge of the belt. Belt thicknesses run from the *upper* to the *lower* edge, so that 10in–8in means a strake 10in thick on top and 8in on the bottom.

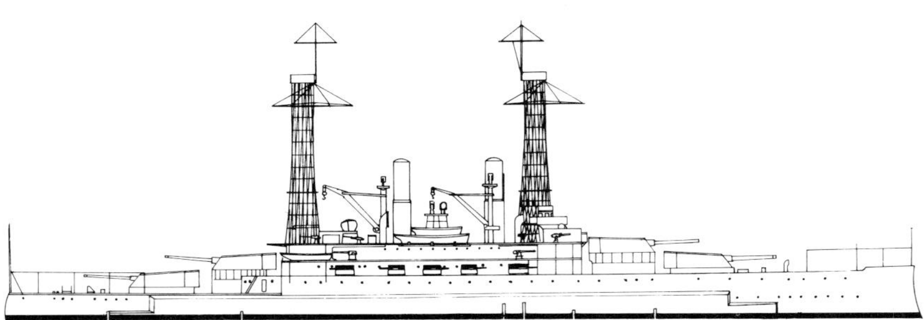

South Carolina as completed

SOUTH CAROLINA class *battleships*

Displacement: 16,000t normal; 17,617t full load
Dimensions: 450ft wl, 452ft 9in × 80ft 5in × 24ft 7in
137.2m, 138.0m × 24.5m × 7.5m
Machinery: 2-shaft VTE, 12 Babcock & Wilcox boilers, 16,500ihp = 18.5kts. Range 5000nm at 10kts
Armour: Belt 10in–8in (254mm–203mm; 12in–10in/305mm–254mm over magazines, 11in–9in/279mm–229mm over machinery), casemate 10in–8in, barbettes 10in–8in, turret faces 12in (305mm), CT 12in, decks 2½in (63mm), 2in–1½in (51mm–38mm)
Armament 8–12in (305mm)/45cal (4×2), 22–3in (76mm)/50cal, 2–21in (533mm) TT sub (beam)
Complement: 869

No	Name	Builder	Laid down	Launched	Comp	Fate
BB 26	SOUTH CAROLINA	Cramp	18.12.06	11.7.08	1.3.10	Stricken 1924
BB 27	MICHIGAN	New York SB	26.5.08	17.12.06	4.1.10	Stricken 1923

The first US single-calibre battleships, they actually preceded HMS *Dreadnought* in design, but not in construction. They were the last American battleships restricted to 16,000t by Congressional mandate, and they conformed to the speed standard of earlier American battleships, 18kts. As a result, they could not operate tactically with the later dreadnoughts, and were often listed with the pre-dreadnoughts. They did not, for example, serve with the later ships in European waters during World War One.

Their concept resulted from gunnery advances, largely due to then-Captain William S Sims. The Bureau of Construction and Repair (C & R) was asked to design a new type of battleship in 1904, and Sims and his colleagues found the bureau much too slow to act; that was probably the origin of the reform movement which, four years later, made the General Board responsible for ship characteristics. Very little of the design background of the class has survived, possibly in part because C&R itself found the episode so embarrassing.

It appears that the bureau's initial approach was a relatively conventional design with twin 12in turrets on the centreline fore and aft, and four single turrets replacing the twin 8in mounts of earlier pre-dreadnoughts. These designs apparently encountered severe structural problems, presumably particularly because Congress limited new battleships to a maximum of 16,000t. Chief Constructor Washington L Capps then chose the radical superfiring arrangement for which the ships were subsequently known. In March 1907 it was tested aboard the monitor *Florida*: one of the two 12in guns in the ship's turret was removed and mounted to superfire above and behind, and a dummy wooden gun mounted in its place; animals and then men were placed in the turret to test the blast effects of superfiring. By this time *South Carolina* could not really have been altered; presumably the issue was whether the ship could fire four guns ahead or astern.

This class also introduced the cage masts characteristics of US dreadnoughts. The original design incorporated a pair of pole masts with a fire control bridge slung between them, but the ships were completed with cages fore and aft on the centreline, and the poles were cut down to serve as kingposts for boat cranes.

South Carolina April 1921
CPL

The cage mast was tested aboard the monitor *Florida* in May 1908, and adopted for the entire fleet that summer. The two ships served in the 1914 Vera Cruz incident.

Both ships were considered heavy rollers. This tendency probably contributed to the collapse of *Michigan*'s foremast in a gale in January 1918. Like the pre-dreadnoughts, *South Carolina* was employed as a convoy escort during 1917–18.

Delaware 1915

DELAWARE class *battleships*

Displacement: 20,380t normal; 22,060t full load (excluding 380t oil fuel)

Dimensions: 510ft wl, 519ft oa × 85ft 4in × 27ft 3in
155.5m, 158.2m × 26.0m × 8.3m

Machinery: 2-shaft Curtis turbines (*North Dakota* VTE), 14 Babcock & Wilcox boilers, 25,000shp = 21kts. Range *c*6000nm at 10kts

Armour: Belt 11in–9in (279mm–229mm), lower casemate 10in–8in (254mm–203mm), upper casemate 5in (127mm), barbettes 10in–4in (254mm–102mm), turret faces 12in (305mm), CT 11½in (292mm), decks 2in (51mm)

Armament: 10–12in (305mm)/45cal (5×2), 14–5in (127mm)/50cal, 2–21in (533mm) TT sub (beam)

Complement: 933

No	Name	Builder	Laid down	Launched	Comp	Fate
BB 28	DELAWARE	Newport News	11.11.07	6.2.09	4.4.10	Stricken 1924
BB 29	NORTH DAKOTA	Fore River	16.12.07	10.11.09	11.4.10	Stricken 1931

The first US battleships to match the standard of the British dreadnoughts, these ships combined the new single-calibre main battery with steam turbines, to achieve the new standard speed of about 21kts. Under the authorising Act, the Navy had to ask for private designs, comparing them with the C&R design. This procedure delayed the ships until late 1907. Although none of the private designs was even remotely satisfactory, it appears that Fore River later developed its version into what became the Argentine battleship *Rivadavia*.

The *Delaware* design was actually completed in 1905–06, the Chief Constructor producing both a 10-gun 20,500t version and a 12-gun 24,000t design. The larger ship was rejected as too expensive for the firepower it provided, even though it was ultimately shaved to 22,000t.

The 20,500t design was severely criticised. Its secondary battery was carried at gun deck (ie below main deck) level, and the two guns sponsoned out in the bows were not only wet, they also broke up the bow wave and thus wasted power. Pre-dreadnought guns similarly situated were so wet that they could not be used effectively in a seaway, as the fleet learned during its World Cruise in 1907–9. Moreover, the secondary guns were entirely unprotected. In addition, steam lines passed around the magazine of No 3 turret. Although magazine refrigeration was fitted, the magazine could not be kept cool enough, and there was a real fear that its powder might become unstable, particularly in the tropics.

In this class the first attempt was made to do away with permanent bridgework; it was hoped that, even in peacetime, the ships could be operated from within their spacious conning towers. As in the *South Carolina*s, plans originally showed a pair of military (pole) masts, with a fire control bridge slung between them, itself between the two funnels. When cage masts were adopted, the poles were relegated to the status of kingposts for boat cranes.

The two ships were competitive sisters, *Delaware* having conventional reciprocating engines, and *North Dakota* Curtis turbines. At this stage of development, the principal effect of the turbine was a sharp *reduction* in fuel economy at cruising speed (estimated at 45 per cent at 14kts). *Delaware*, on the other hand, was the first American battleship that could steam for 24 hours at full speed without needing repairs, even though she had to rely on earlier reciprocating engines. The American reversion to reciprocating engines several classes later is understandable in view of the concentration on very long endurance for Pacific operations. *North Dakota* was re-engined with geared turbines in 1917.

Delaware served with the 6th Battle Squadron of the Grand Fleet in 1917–18.

Delaware about 1913
USN

Florida 16 December 1916

USN

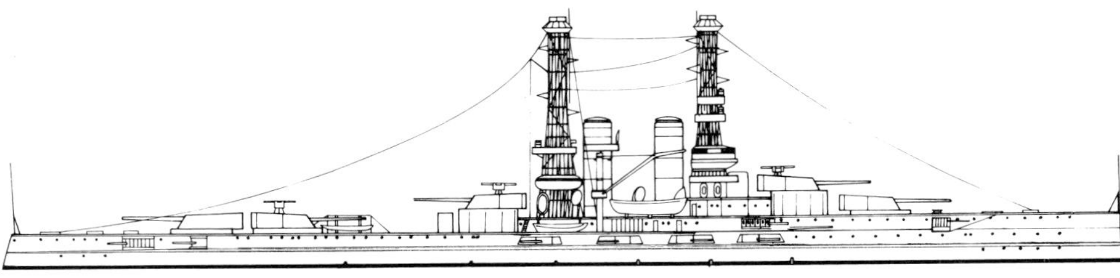

Florida as completed

These were essentially repeat *Delawares*, the major change being enlargement of the machinery spaces to fit either Parsons or Curtis turbines. As a result of criticism of the *Delaware* class at the Newport Conference in 1908, this design was modified to incorporate light armour protection (in the form of an upper casemate) for its secondary battery. By way of weight compensation, the proposed 6in battery was cut back to 5in/51s, very high-powered weapons which replaced the 5in/50s of the previous class.

The two ships were the first battleships off Vera Cruz in the 1914 Crisis, both landing marines and soldiers (1000) under *Florida*'s captain on 21 April for the 3 days fighting that cost 94 US casualties and hundreds of Mexican lives. *Florida* served with 6th Battle Squadron in the Grand Fleet during 1917–18, and from September 1918 *Utah* was based at Bantry Bay, Ireland.

These were the earliest US battleships retained under the Washington Naval Treaty, and both were extensively rebuilt during the 1920s, with oil fuel and blisters. However, both had to be discarded under the terms of the London Treaty of 1930, *Utah* surviving as a remote-controlled target ship from 1931 and then as a fleet AA TS, to be sunk at Pearl Harbor.

FLORIDA class *battleships*

Displacement: 21,825t normal; 23,033t full load
Dimensions: 510ft wl, 521ft 8in × 88ft 3in × 28ft 3in
155.5m, 159.0m × 26.9m × 8.6m
Machinery: 4-shaft Parsons turbines, 12 Babcock & Wilcox boilers, 28,000shp = 20.75kts. Range 6720nm at 10kts
Armour: As *Delaware* class except 1½in (38mm) deck. STS replaced Nickel Steel (NS) for deck and turret protection
Armament: As *Delaware* class except 16–5in (127mm)/51cal
Complement: 1001

No	Name	Builder	Laid down	Launched	Comp	Fate
BB 30	FLORIDA	New York N Yd	9.3.09	12.5.10	15.9.11	Stricken 1931
BB 31	UTAH	New York SB	15.3.09	23.12.09	31.8.11	Sunk 7.12.41

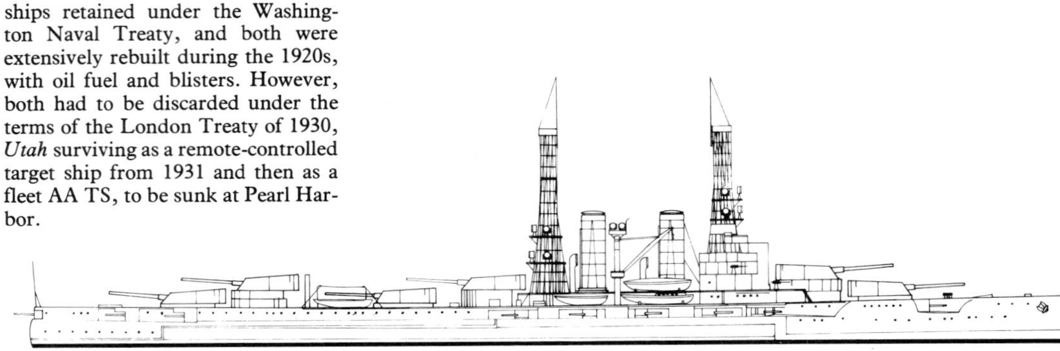

Wyoming as completed

This design was developed as one of three alternatives, after President Theodore Roosevelt asked in 1908 whether the United States should not go from 12in to 14in guns: a 12–12in design, an 8–14in design, and a 10–14in design. At this time there was a widespread feeling that the standard of battleships calibre would soon rise above 12in. For example, there were already reports that Britain had a 13.5in gun under construction. The 12in alternative was chosen in 1909 largely because it entailed the least delay, and because it was the largest ship that could be docked in existing facilities on both coasts, whereas the 10–14in ship could be docked only at Pearl Harbor and Puget Sound, and at New York only if the dock there could be lengthened by 5ft. Therefore the decision was to build and test the 14in gun, and to enlarge docking facilities, so that the more satisfactory ship could be built later. That became the *New York* class, built under the 1910 (FY 11) program. The *Wyoming* design was accepted as an interim solution, particularly after the Bureau of Ordnance had developed a new 50-calibre 12in gun to arm it.

All of these designs were flush-deckers. The World Cruise had already shown the problems of mounting secondary guns too low, and the solution adopted was to slope the main deck from a high bow aft, gaining about 4ft in secondary battery height amidships. *Arkansas* was flagship of the Atlantic Fleet in 1914 and off Vera Cruz landing marines. She served in the 6th Battle Squadron, Grand Fleet, during World War One.

Both ships were rebuilt in the 1920s, with oil fuel and blisters for improved torpedo protection. *Wyoming* was converted into a gunnery TS, her side armour removed, under the London Naval Treaty of 1931. Although reconversion to full battleship configuration was briefly considered early in World War Two, it was never carried out.

WYOMING class *battleships*

Displacement: 26,000t normal; 27,243t full load
Dimensions: 554ft wl, 562ft oa × 93ft 2in × 28ft 7in
168.9m, 171.3m × 28.4m × 8.7m
Machinery: 4-shaft Parsons turbines, 12 Babcock & Wilcox boilers, 28,000shp = 20.5kts. Range 8000nm at 10kts
Armour: Belt 11in–9in (279mm–229mm), lower casemate 11in–9in, upper casemate 6½in (165mm), barbettes 11in, turret faces 12in (305mm), CT 11½in (292mm)
Armament: 12–12in (305mm)/50cal (6×2), 21–5in (127mm)/51cal, 2–21in (533mm) TT sub (beam)
Complement: 1063

No	Name	Builder	Laid down	Launched	Comp	Fate
BB 32	WYOMING	Cramp	9.2.10	25.5.11	25.9.12	Stricken 1947
BB 33	ARKANSAS	New York SB	25.1.10	14.1.11	17.9.12	Target 26.7.46

Arkansas as completed
CPL

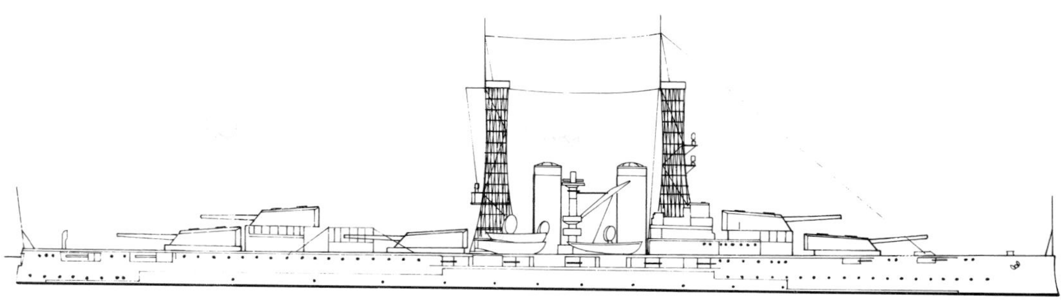

Texas as completed

This was the 10–14in design which had originally been developed in 1908–9 as an alternative to *Wyoming*. The prototype 14in/45 gun was test-fired in January 1910, and this design approved in March. Plans for two-shaft (Curtis) and four-shaft (Parsons) turbine installations were developed, but trials of *North Dakota* appeared to show that turbines were generally unsatisfactory: it was estimated that the new ship would be able to make only about 5605nm at 12kts on turbines, compared to 7060 with reciprocating engines. The former figure would be insufficient to take the ship from the US West Coast to the Philippines. The General Board therefore chose reciprocating engines, even though it was aware that they had no great potential for further development.

The first US battleship AA guns were turret-top 3in guns mounted aboard *Texas* in 1916. *Texas* was also the first US battleship with flying-off platforms for aircraft, fitted in British waters, possibly as early as March 1918. She flew off her first airplane at Guantanamo Bay (Cuba) in March 1919. Both ships served with 6th Battle Squadron, Grand Fleet, during World War One. *New York* went straight to Vera Cruz on commissioning, arriving on 4 May 1914.

NEW YORK class *battleships*

Displacement: 27,000t normal; 28,367t full load
Dimensions: 565ft wl, 573ft oa × 95ft 6in × 28ft 6in
172.3m, 174.7m × 29.1m × 8.7m
Machinery: 2-shaft VTE, 14 Babcock & Wilcox boilers, 28,100ihp = 21kts. Range 7060nm at 10kts
Armour: Belt 12in–10in (305mm–254mm), lower casemate 11in–9in (279mm–229mm), upper casemate 6½in (165mm), armour deck 2in (50mm), turret faces 14in (356mm), top 4in (102mm), side 2in (51mm), rear 8in (204mm), barbettes 10in and 12in, CT 12in, top 4in
Armament: 10–14in (356mm)/45cal (10×2), 21–5in (127mm)/51cal, 4–21in (533mm) TT sub (beam)
Complement: 1042

No	Name	Builder	Laid down	Launched	Comp	Fate
BB 34	NEW YORK	New York N Yd	11.9.11	30.10.12	15.4.14	Sunk 8.7.48
BB 35	TEXAS	Newport News	17.4.11	18.5.12	12.3.14	Memorial 1948

New York as completed
USN

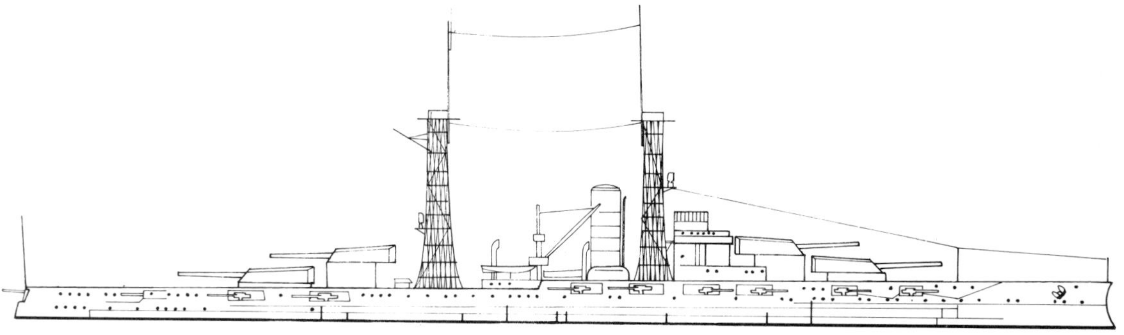

Nevada as completed

This was a revolutionary design, introducing 'all or nothing' protection. Since armour-piercing shells did not burst when penetrating thin plating, the designers reasoned that there was nothing to be gained from using thin armour which would serve only to detonate shells. Better to choose either the thickest armour, which would not be penetrated, or no armour at all; hence the name. The *Nevada*s were the first ships designed to General Board Characteristics (staff requirements), and they reflected the new demands of very long-range battle: heavy deck armour and highly centralised fire control.

NEVADA class *battleships*

Displacement: 27,500t normal; 28,400t full load
Dimensions: 575ft wl, 583ft oa × 95ft 6in × 28ft 6in
175.3m, 177.7m × 29.1m × 8.7m
Machinery: *Nevada* 2-shaft Curtis turbines, 12 Yarrow boilers, 26,500shp = 20.5kts
Oklahoma 2-shaft VTE, 12 Babcock & Wilcox boilers, 24,800ihp = 20.5kts. Range 8000nm at 10kts
Armour: Belt 13.5in–8in (343mm–203mm), deck 3in (76mm), turret faces 18in (457mm) and 16in (406mm), sides 10in–9in (254mm–229mm), top 5in (127mm), rear 9in, barbettes 13in (330mm), CT 16in, top 8in
Armament: 10–14in (356mm)/45cal (2×3, 2×2), 21–5in (127mm)/51cal, 2–21in (533mm) TT sub (beam)
Complement: 864

No	Name	Builder	Laid down	Launched	Comp	Fate
BB 36	NEVADA	Fore River	4.11.12	11.7.14	11.3.16	Sunk 31.7.48
BB 37	OKLAHOMA	New York SB	26.10.12	23.3.14	2.5.16	Sunk 7.12.41

In the previous *New York* class, the central fire control station had to be placed above the relatively thin protective deck, since all of the hull volume below that deck was occupied by machinery and magazines. It was, therefore, enclosed in light splinter armour. In theory, shells would strike the 'lower casemate' and burst before they could reach the 'central', and its thin armour would defeat the splinters. As expected battle ranges increased, however, shells might well pass *over* this upper belt, to strike the 'central' directly. The first step in the *Nevada* design, then, was to move the main armoured deck to the top of the upper belt, with a splinter deck placed below it to protect the machinery and magazines from shells bursting after penetrating the main armoured deck. It followed that the upper and lower belts might as well be merged into a single armour belt. Similarly, the upper casemate armour, which in earlier designs had protected the off-side secondary guns and the uptakes, was abandoned in favour of heavy casemate armour. Armour could also be used more efficiently, because the main battery was concentrated into four rather than five turrets.

At the same time, oil fuel was introduced, after tests in *Delaware*. Its advantages includes a reduction in the engine-room complement, and a consequent saving in berthing. However, there was no longer any coal protection to the machinery spaces, and a new form of underwater protection was required. In fact no truly satisfactory type of underwater protection was developed until 1915, in the *Tennessee* class.

These two ships were built with competitive powerplants, turbine in *Nevada* and reciprocating in *Oklahoma*. Both ships were stationed at Bantry Bay, Ireland, from late August 1918.

Oklahoma about 1930 after modernisation
CPL

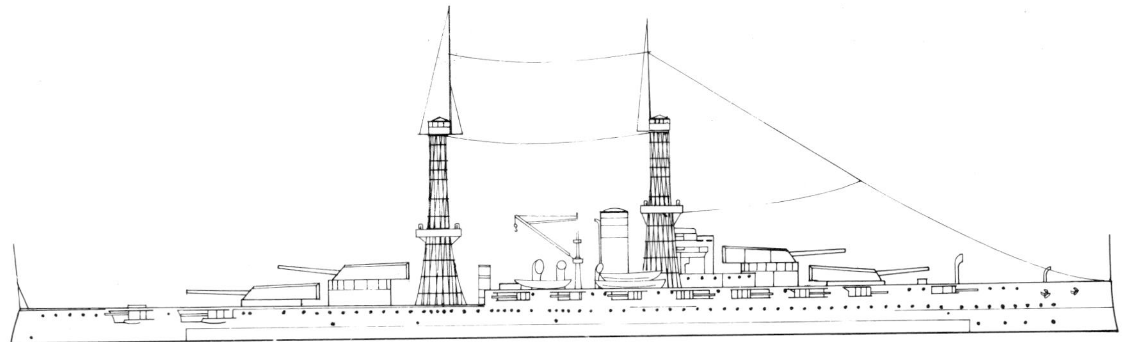

Pennsylvania as completed

PENNSYLVANIA class *battleships*

Displacement:	31,400t normal; 32,567t full load
Dimensions:	600ft wl, 608ft oa × 97ft 1in × 28ft 10in *182.9m, 185.4m × 29.6m × 8.8m*
Machinery:	4-shaft Curtis (*Arizona* Parsons) turbines, 12 Babcock & Wilcox boilers, 31,500shp = 21kts. Range 8000nm at 10kts
Armour:	As *Nevada* class
Armament:	12–14in (356mm)/45cal (4×3), 22–5in (127mm)/51cal, 4–3in (76mm)/50cal, 2–21in (533mm) TT sub (beam)
Complement:	915

No	Name	Builder	Laid down	Launched	Comp	Fate
BB 38	PENNSYLVANIA	Newport News	27.10.13	16.3.15	12.6.16	Scuttled 10.2.48
BB 39	ARIZONA	New York N Yd	16.3.14	19.6.15	17.10.16	Sunk 7.12.41

This was essentially an enlarged *Nevada*, with four triple turrets rather than the previous two twin and two triple mounts. This was what the General Board had originally wanted for the *Nevada* class; Congress had been unwilling to appropriate enough money. In addition, the secondary battery was increased from 21 to 22 5in/51 guns, the weapon right aft being abandoned because it was too difficult to assign for fire control purposes.

This class also incorporated special underwater protection, consisting of a 3in torpedo bulkhead 9ft 6in inboard of the shell plating, with a retaining bulkhead 30in inboard of it. Tests showed that this system could withstand about 300lb of TNT.

Pennsylvania was ordered as a flagship, with a special two-level CT. She was flagship of the Atlantic Fleet 1916–1918, and escorted the liner carrying President Wilson to France for the Peace Conference, arriving in December 1918. *Arizona* joined the 6th Battle Squadron, Grand Fleet, just after the Armistice. She landed marines to guard the US Consulate at Constantinople on 14 May 1919 during the Greek occupation of the Turkish capital. *Pennsylvania* embarked 400 US marines to persuade Panama to accept American mediation in her border dispute with Costa Rica on 18 August 1921.

Pennsylvania 1 January 1920
USN

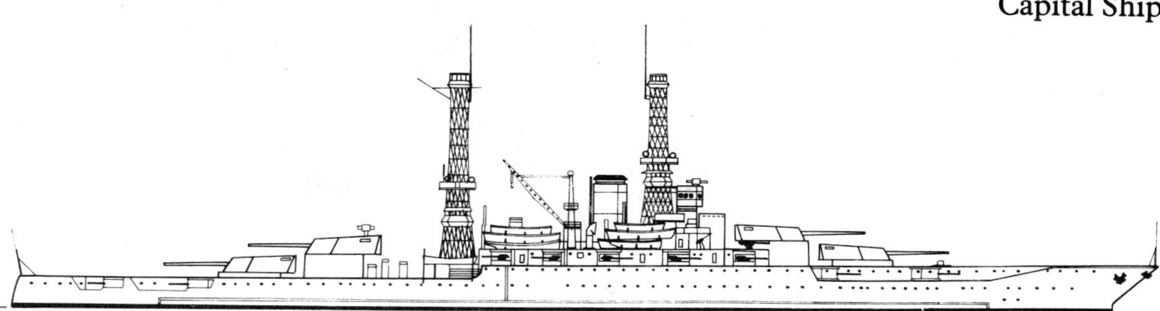
New Mexico as completed

NEW MEXICO class *battleships*

Displacement: 32,000t normal; 33,000t full load
Dimensions: 600ft wl, 624ft oa × 97ft 5in × 30ft
182.9m, 190.2m × 29.7m × 9.1m
Machinery: 4-shaft Curtis (*Idaho* Parsons) turbines, (*New Mexico* General Electric turbo-electric drive), 9 Babcock & Wilcox boilers, 32,000shp (*New Mexico* 27,000shp) = 21kts. Range 8000nm at 10kts
Armour: As *Nevada* class but 3.5in (89mm) armour deck
Armament: 12–14in (356mm)/50cal (4×3), 14–5in (127mm)/51cal, 4–3in (76mm)/50cal, 2–21in (533mm) TT sub (beam)
Complement: 1084

No	Name	Builder	Laid down	Launched	Comp	Fate
BB 40	NEW MEXICO	New York N Yd	14.10.15	23.4.17	20.5.18	Stricken 1947
BB 41	MISSISSIPPI	Newport News	5.4.15	25.1.17	18.12.17	Stricken 1956
BB 42	IDAHO	New York SB	20.1.15	30.6.17	24.3.19	Stricken 1947

In 1913–14 the General Board called for an entirely new battleship design, displacing about 35,500 tons, and armed with ten 16in guns in five twin turrets. Josephus Daniels, the Secretary of the Navy, refused to countenance any substantial increase in tonnage, and decided that the FY 14 battleships would essentially duplicate the *Pennsylvanias*, with whatever improvement that could be incorporated at minimum cost. Two were involved.

First, there was the old complaint of wetness. These ships had a clipper bow, and 12 of their 22 5in/51 guns were mounted in a deckhouse, ie one deck level above the secondaries of the previous class. They still retained 4 guns in the forecastle deck forward, and 4 more right aft, below the main deck; another pair was in the open, atop the deckhouse. One of the three ships was actually completed with all 22 guns, but by that time American experience in the North Sea was showing that only the deckhouse guns would be usable in a seaway. The bow and after positions were soon plated in, reducing the number to 14.

The other major improvement was in main battery gunnery: these ships introduced a new 14in/50 gun, and the weapons elevated independently, in contrast with earlier classes.

A series of detail weight economies permitted the designers to thicken the armoured bulkheads from 13in to 13.5in, and the main armour deck from 3in to 3.5in, both of which figures became standard for later US dreadnoughts.

One ship, the *New Mexico*, tested the turbo-electric drive system advocated by General Electric as an alternative to gearing. The collier *Jupiter*, which became the aircraft carrier *Langley*, had already served as a test platform. The Bureau of Steam Engineering wanted turbo-electric drive for economy, and to do away with astern turbines, which were giving trouble. C&R saw the new system as a means to improve subdivision, and employed it in all of its later dreadnoughts and battlecruisers. It was abandoned after World War One only because of its excessive demands on weight and internal volume.

Two ships were originally planned, but proceeds of the 1914 sale to Greece of the pre-dreadnoughts *Mississippi* and *Idaho* paid for a third ship.

New Mexico in the 1920s

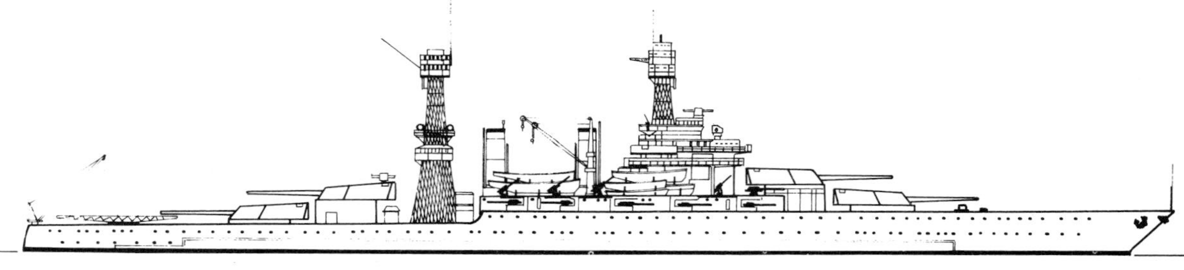
California 1927

TENNESSEE class *battleships*

Displacement: 32,300t normal; 33,190t full load
Dimensions: 600ft wl, 624ft oa × 97ft 5in × 30ft 2in
182.9m, 190.2m × 29.7m × 9.2m
Machinery: 4-shaft Westinghouse (*California* General Electric) turbo-electric drive, 8 Babcock & Wilcox boilers, 26,800shp = 21kts. Range 8000nm at 10kts
Armour: As *New Mexico* class
Armament: As *New Mexico* class
Complement: 1083

No	Name	Builder	Laid down	Launched	Comp	Fate
BB 43	TENNESSEE	New York N Yd	14.5.17	30.4.19	3.6.20	Stricken 1959
BB 44	CALIFORNIA	Mare Island N Yd	25.10.16	20.11.19	10.8.21	Stricken 1959

These two ships were slightly modified *New Mexicos*, the principal changes being major improvements in underwater protection. A series of caisson experiments showed that a series of layers of liquid-filled and void compartments could absorb the explosive energy of even a substantial torpedo warhead; the system in these (and other US battleships of this period) was designed to resist 400lb of TNT. These ships therefore incorporated a series of five bulkheads on either side: the outermost compartment was left void, then there were three liquid-filled ones, and then an inboard void, into which the inner liquid layer could burst in the event of a hit. Inboard of the torpedo protection, each boiler was in a separate compartment, the boilers themselves forming a kind of inner protective layer. Two large turbo-generators were on the centreline. The dispersion of the boilers showed externally in the adoption of two funnels, rather than the previous single trunked one.

The pilothouse and forward superstructure were considerably enlarged,

Tennessee as completed

Maryland in the late 1920s *CPL*

the most prominent feature being a big air intake terminating under the pilothouse. The cage masts were of a new heavier type, and each carried a two-level enclosed top, the upper level of which was for main battery control, the lower for the secondary battery.

In addition, the elevation of the main battery guns was increased from 15 to 30 degrees. Both ships were completed in somewhat modified form, without hull-mounted secondary weapons, and with their hulls faired over the casemates of the original design.

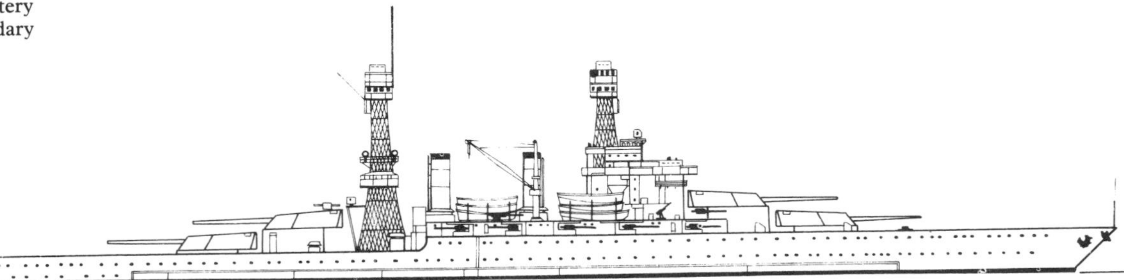

West Virginia as completed

COLORADO class *battleships*

This was a repeat *Tennessee* design with twin 16in/45 guns in place of the earlier triple 14in/50; there was no other substantial change, although for many years there were unofficial claims of a considerable increase in belt armour.

One ship, the *Washington*, was cancelled under the Washington Treaty on 8 February 1922 and sunk as a target in 1924.

Displacement: 32,600t normal; 33,590t full load
Dimensions: As *Tennessee* class
Machinery: 4-shaft turbo-electric drive, 8 Babcock & Wilcox boilers, 28,900shp = 21kts. Range 8000nm at 10kts
Armour: As *New Mexico* class
Armament: 8–16in (406mm)/45cal (4×2), 14–5in (127mm)/51cal, 4–3in (76mm)/50cal, 2–21in (533mm) TT sub (beam)
Complement: 1080

No	Name	Builder	Laid down	Launched	Comp	Fate
BB 45	COLORADO	New York SB	29.5.19	22.3.21	30.8.23	Stricken 1959
BB 46	MARYLAND	Newport News	24.4.17	20.3.20	21.7.21	Stricken 1959
BB 47	WASHINGTON	New York SB	30.6.19	1.9.21		Sunk 25.11.24
BB 48	WEST VIRGINIA	Newport News	12.4.20	19.11.21	1.12.23	Stricken 1959

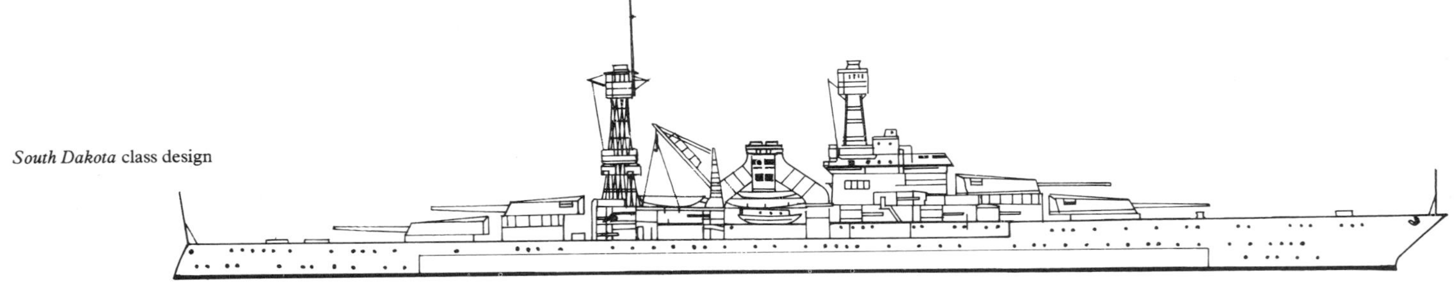

South Dakota class design

SOUTH DAKOTA class *battleships*

With this class the General Board finally achieved what it had wanted since 1914, a jump in battleship capabilities and size. From the start, the board wanted 12–16in guns and a 23kt speed, the latter partly out of fear that Japan would acquire fast battleships (like the British *Queen Elizabeths*) of her own. The board considered a 2kt increase an absolute minimum, given what it supposed was a general tendency towards higher speed. Finally, given a great increase in displacement, it was natural to go from the existing 16in/45 to the much more powerful 16in/50, and from the 5in/51 secondary gun to the new 6in/53. Armour thicknesses did not increase, largely because 13.5in was considered the maximum that could be manufactured with any certainty of consistent quality. Main battery elevation was increased to 40 degrees.

The design, then, amounted to an enlarged *Maryland*, with triple rather than twin turrets, and with all of the secondary battery above the forecastle deck. Visually, the most unusual feature would have been the massive trunked funnel, uniting four smokepipes emerging from the dispensed boiler rooms.

This design was frozen in the summer of 1918. At that time the US naval staff in London was much impressed by HMS *Hood*, and it proposed that the United States develop its own fast battleship, armed with 16in guns. Several sketches were prepared, but the General Board felt that to build them would make existing ships obsolete, and therefore would not be

Displacement: 43,200t normal
Dimensions: 660ft wl, 684ft oa × 106ft × 33ft
201.2m, 208.5m × 32.3m × 10.1m
Machinery: 4-shaft turbo-electric drive, 12 boilers, 50,000shp = 23kts. Range 8000nm at 10kts
Armour: As *New Mexico* class
Armament: 12–16in (406mm)/50cal (4×3), 16–6in (152mm)/53cal, 4–3in (76mm), 2–21in (533mm) TT sub (beam)
Complement: 1191

No	Name	Builder	Laid down	Fate
BB 49	SOUTH DAKOTA	New York N Yd	15.3.20	Cancelled 8.2.22
BB 50	INDIANA	New York N Yd	1.11.20	Cancelled 8.2.22
BB 51	MONTANA	Mare Island N Yd	1.9.20	Cancelled 8.2.22
BB 52	NORTH CAROLINA	Norfolk N Yd	12.1.20	Cancelled 8.2.22
BB 53	IOWA	Newport News	17.5.20	Cancelled 8.2.22
BB 54	MASSACHUSETTS	Fore River	4.4.21	Cancelled 8.2.22

in the US Navy's best interests. It therefore persevered with the much more conventional *South Dakota* design.

Delayed by the emergency ASW program of World War One, the ships were not laid down until after the war, and none was very advanced at the time of the Washington Conference, when all were cancelled.

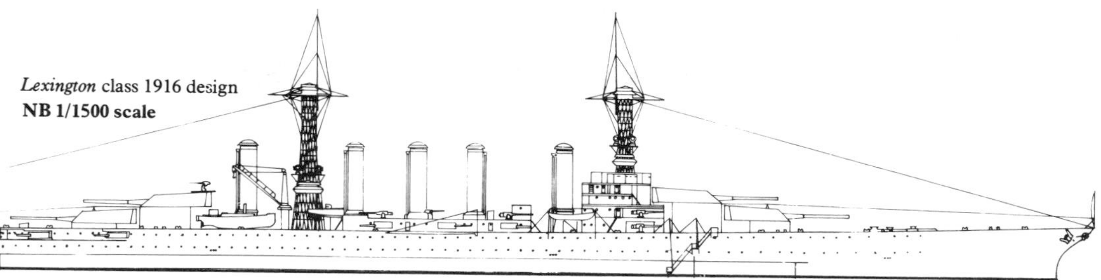

Lexington class 1916 design
NB 1/1500 scale

The General Board considered building battlecruisers in 1912, to counter the four Japanese *Kongos*, but it withdrew them from its proposed programme because Congress was unwilling to buy enough battleships, which it considered a more urgent requirement. The ships contemplated at that time would have been relatively heavily armoured, and as such were much closer to fast battleships than to the 'battle scouts' approved in 1916. The *Lexingtons* were ordered as part of the large 1916 programme, as part of a scouting force to support a large battlefleet. They were, in effect, scaled *up* from a series of designs for cruisers displacing about 10,000 to 14,000 tons, and so would have been much more lightly built than contemporary US battleships. The original 34,800-ton design showed a battery of 10–14in/50 guns, in two twin and two triple turrets; the shift to 16in weapons was not made until 1917. Design requirements included provision for aircraft, which probably explains the break in the main deck right aft: when these ships were designed, the only US catapult was the fixed straight-deck type in the old armoured cruisers. Although trainable catapults were designed immediately after World War One, no later sketches show them in the final design.

These very large ships originated as battle scouts, ie, as ships powerful enough to press home reconnaissance in the face of enemy battlecruisers. They were conceived as part of a 35-knot scouting force, other elements of which were the flush-deck destroyers and the *Omaha* class cruisers. The original design was complicated by the relatively limited steam output of existing boilers: there was not enough space below the armoured deck for the 24 units needed to make 180,000shp. Hence the unusual design initially adopted, in which half the boilers were above the protective deck. It would have been adopted, had not all American capital ship construction been suspended in favour of merchant ship and ASW programmes in 1917. The final, more conventional, boiler arrangement was adopted because, with the appearance of small-tube boilers, their number could be reduced to 16, and all could be fitted below the armour deck.

The final version of the design, presented in the table, owes much to US reactions to HMS *Hood*, even though it was still very lightly armoured, and so still reflected the original operational concept. The Bureau of Ordnance argued, moreover, that on the basis of British analysis of Jutland, the loss of the battlecruisers had been due, not to their lack of armour, but to their poor anti-flash protection: the battle, then, did not imply that more armour was needed, but rather that better magazine arrangements were in order. The choice of a sloping belt owed much to British practice, as (probably) did the decision to provide four abovewater TT to supplement the four underwater ones.

All six were cancelled under the Washington Treaty, two being completed as large aircraft carriers. However, it appears that they were considered obsolescent even before the negotiations, since early in 1921 there were studies of conversions to carriers, and also of the use of material collected for the *Ranger* to build a carrier designed as such from the keel up.

LEXINGTON class *battlecruisers*

Displacement: 43,500t normal; 44,638t full load; 51,217t emergency full load
Dimensions: 850ft wl, 874ft oa × 105ft 4in × 31ft
259.1m, 266.5m × 32.1m × 9.5m
Machinery: 4-shaft turbo-electric drive, 16 boilers, 180,000shp = 33.5kts. Range 12,000nm at 10kts
Armour: Belt 7in (178mm), turret face 11in (280mm), side 6in (152mm), barbette 9in–5in (229mm–127mm), CT 12in (305mm)
Armament: 8–16in (406mm)/50cal (4×2), 16–6in (152mm)/53cal, 4–3in (76mm)/50cal, 8–21in TT (4 aw)
Complement: 1297 (1326 as flagship)

No	Name	Builder	Laid down	Fate
1	LEXINGTON	Fore River	8.1.21	Became carrier CV 2
2	CONSTELLATION	Newport News	18.8.20	Cancelled 17.8.23
3	SARATOGA	New York SB	25.9.20	Became carrier CV 3
4	RANGER	Newport News	23.6.21	Cancelled 17.8.23
5	CONSTITUTION	Philadelphia N Yd	25.9.20	Cancelled 17.8.23
6	UNITED STATES	Philadelphia N Yd	25.9.20	Cancelled 17.8.23

CRUISERS

The US cruiser force of 1917 was largely obsolete, consisting of large armoured cruisers, elderly protected cruisers, and the few modern scouts, the latter already rather slow by modern standards. For some years the General Board had argued the need for new fleet scouts, and sketch designs had actually been developed. However, no ships were authorised until 1916, when a very large naval bill passed just after Jutland. It resulted in the *Constellation* class battlecruisers and the *Omaha* class scouts, both designed to achieve 35 knots. Both designs also incorporated scout aircraft, which before the war had been carried by three armoured cruisers.

Thus the major forms of US cruiser war service were convoy escort, anti-surface raider patrol, and trooping. In rough weather, heavily laden with extra coal, the armoured cruisers took on water through their main deck gun ports, inspiring wartime and postwar proposals that the guns be relocated topside and the ports permanently sealed. In addition, many secondary weapons, of 6in and lesser calibre, were landed for installation aboard armed merchant ships and naval auxiliaries.

Concord about 1935
USN

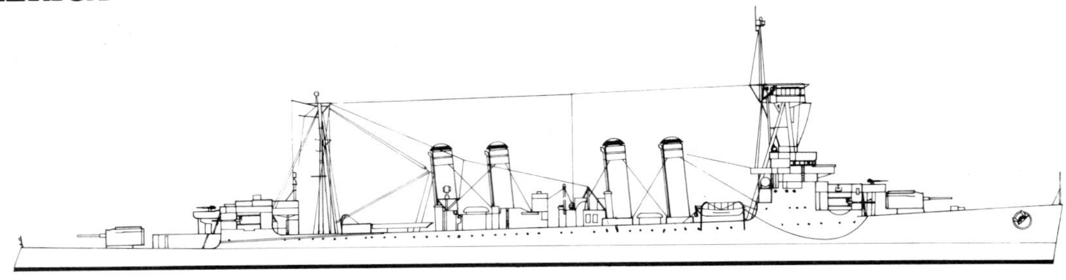

Detroit about 1944

OMAHA class *cruisers*

Displacement: 7050t design normal; 9508t full load (as built)
Dimensions: 555ft 6in × 55ft 5in × 13ft 6in
169.4m × 16.9m × 4.1m
Machinery: 4-shaft Westinghouse turbines, 8 Yarrow boilers, 90,000shp = 34kts. Range 10,000nm at 10kts
Armour: Deck 1½in (38mm), belt 3in (76mm)
Armament: 12–6in/53, 2–3in/50 AA, 10–21in (533mm) TT (2×3, 2×2)
Complement: 458

No	Name	Builder	Laid down	Launched	Comp	Fate
C 4	OMAHA	Seattle	6.12.18	14.12.20	24.2.23	Stricken 1945
C 5	MILWAUKEE	Seattle	13.12.18	24.3.21	20.6.23	To USSR 1944
C 6	CINCINNATI	Seattle	15.5.20	23.5.21	1.1.24	Sold 1946
C 7	RALEIGH	Fore River	16.8.20	25.10.22	6.2.24	Sold 1946
C 8	DETROIT	Fore River	10.11.20	29.6.22	31.7.23	Sold 1946
C 9	RICHMOND	Cramp	16.2.20	29.9.21	2.7.23	Stricken 1946
C 10	CONCORD	Cramp	29.3.20	15.12.21	3.11.23	Sold 1947
C 11	TRENTON	Cramp	18.8.20	16.4.23	19.4.24	Sold 1947
C 12	MARBLEHEAD	Cramp	4.8.20	9.10.23	8.9.24	Stricken 1945
C 13	MEMPHIS	Cramp	14.10.20	17.4.24	4.2.25	Stricken 1946

The first US cruisers authorised since 1904,· despite annual pleas by the General Board for scouts to support US Fleet operations, the *Omaha*s were part of the giant 1916 naval programme. From 1915 on, C&R worked on large, 30kt scouts; the *Omaha* design resulted from a reversion to destroyer rather than classic cruiser practice. The original design called for a battery of 10–6in/53 (4 at each end in casemates, 2 in open mounts in the waist, as well as four 21in TT (2 twin mounts), and 2–3in/50 AA guns. The two waist guns were deleted in the course of preliminary design. Speed was to have matched those of the battlecruisers and destroyers of the 1916 programme, 35kts. In 1917 the Preliminary Design group within C&R argued for an even smaller design, of about 5000t, suggesting that the *Omaha*s carried too little armament on their displacement. This alternative was rejected because it could not be realised by most builders; its margins were much too narrow.

The *Omaha* design reflected prewar US concepts: end-on fire and scouting by aircraft, the latter having been tested aboard the big armoured cruisers in 1915–17. Hence the concentrations of double-storey casemates at each end, permitting 4–6in guns to bear ahead or astern. The quarterdeck was kept clear for a fixed catapult, of the type fitted to the armoured cruisers, and freeboard there was reduced for minelaying. By the time the ships were being completed, however, modern trainable catapults were available, and each was fitted with two, in the waist.

During World War One, the US Navy came into close contact with British cruisers, and the *Omaha* design was severely criticised for its weak broadside and torpedo battery. C&R proposed a stopgap modification, in which two twin 6in/53 mounts, in blast-proof shields, were added, fore and aft, to double the broadside. In addition, a pair of triple 21in TT, taken from destroyers converted to minesweepers, was installed on the forecastle deck abaft the catapults. These additions of weight cost considerable freeboard, so that the original main deck TT (for which ports were cut in the sides of the forecastle) and the lower aft 6in casemates were often quite wet. All ships of the class had their twin TT removed within a few years of completion, but a programme to replace the lower casemates with a single mount on the centreline aft was still incomplete in 1941.

Additional weapons also added personnel, and the ships were considered badly overcrowded as completed, despite some additions of superstructure space. They were, however, well liked as seaboats, and were considered fast and manoeuvrable, even as late as 1940, when there were proposals to convert them to AA cruisers.

Four of the class served in the S Atlantic and off S France (joined by *Marblehead* after repairs to Japanese bomber damage (2 hits, 1 near miss, 49 crew casualties) sustained off Java on 4 February 1942) for all of 1941–45. *Raleigh* was damaged at Pearl Harbor and served in the Aleutians/Kuriles (N Pacific) as did *Richmond*, *Concord* and *Trenton*.

AIRCRAFT CARRIERS

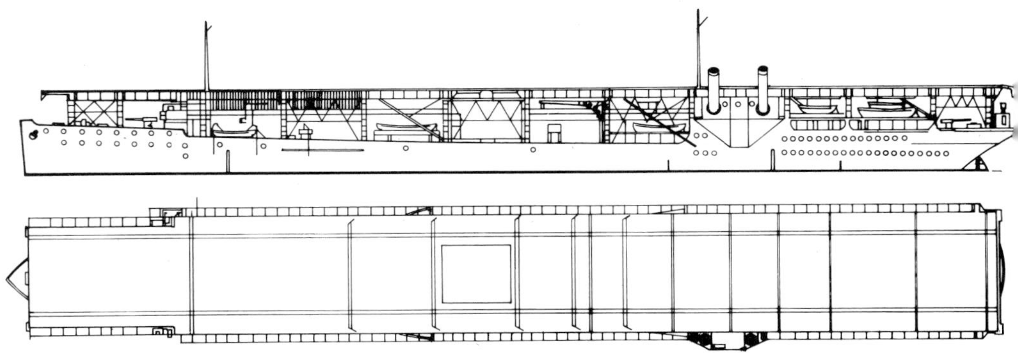

Langley as completed

LANGLEY *aircraft carrier*

Displacement: 13,990t normal
Dimensions: 520ft wl, 542ft 4in × 65ft 3in × 20ft 8in
158.5m, 165.3m × 19.9m × 6.3m
Machinery: 2-shaft General Electric turbo-electric drive, 3 boilers, 6500shp = 15.5kts
Armament: 4–5in (127mm)/51cal, 12 fighters, 12 spotters, 6 torpedo bombers, 6 seaplanes (as in 1924)
Complement: 468

No	Name	Builder	Laid down	Launched	Comp	Fate
CV 1	LANGLEY	Mare Island N Yd	18.10.11	24.8.12	20.3.22	Sunk 27.2.42

The first US aircraft carrier, she was the converted fleet collier *Jupiter*, which in turn had been the test ship for turbo-electric propulsion. *Jupiter* had also carried 300 marines off the W coast of Mexico during the 1914 crisis. Her cranes were removed and her former coal holds converted to take disassembled aircraft. They were hoisted by crane to the former main deck, then loaded on an elevator for transport to the flight deck, which was built atop a light girder structure.

Virtually every feature was experimental, including the arrester gear, and she was far too slow to keep up even with the dreadnoughts. Thus, until full carriers could be built, much of their potential had to be shown in war games ashore; carrier air groups were sometimes simulated by single aircraft catapulted from battleships.

She was converted to an aircraft tender in 1937 because, under the Vinson-Trammell Act, she consumed tonnage which might otherwise have gone into more capable specially-built ships. She was hit 5 times by 9 Japanese level bombers off Java while carrying 32 P40 fighters there and had to be sunk 75nm S of Tjilatjap, Java, by the 4in guns of her escorting destroyer *Whipple;* 16 crew died.

Langley fitting out late in 1921
USN

DESTROYERS AND TORPEDO-BOATS

Although US destroyers were not very heavily modified during World War One, their role did change radically, from fleet surface defence to ASW. That is, the pre-1917 US destroyer force was designed to protect the battleline against torpedo attack by opposing destroyers. Torpedo attack on opposing battleships was a distinctly secondary role, although US destroyers carried very heavy torpedo batteries by world standards. Indeed, the great controversy of pre-1917 destroyer design was whether to emphasise great size, for seakeeping, or to restrict the size of individual destroyers in the hope that they would be more difficult for opposing secondary guns to hit. The General Board ruled in favour of the former view, commenting that, in view of the shortage of cruisers, US destroyers would have to function not merely as battleline escorts but also as scouts.

It must have been clear as early as 1916 that destroyers would have to deal with submarines, and the General Board required that bows be strengthened for ramming. However, the US Navy had no depth charge and, for that matter, no submarine detector prior to entering World War One. Even so, destroyers were considered ASW craft, and their production was accelerated. It was not so much that they were well adapted to this role; rather, it was that they were in production at the outbreak of war, whereas alternative ASW craft, such as the Royal Navy's sloops and P-boats, had to be improvised. Even so, it was immediately evident that prewar destroyer characteristics, such as high speed, greatly exceeded what was needed for U-boat warfare. In 1917, therefore, a special ASW board proposed the construction of special mass-production destroyers capable of about 26kts; they would have foreshadowed the destroyer escorts of a quarter century later.

These special craft were not built, because *any* major change in design would have caused delays. Instead, almost 300 standard fast fleet destroyers of the *Wickes* and *Clemson* classes were built.

At this time submarines generally revealed their location primarily by firing torpedoes. Fast ASW craft could run back down the torpedo tracks, dropping patterns of depth charges around the presumed submarine location. The efficacy of such patterns depended on the area covered; hence the development of Y-guns, which could fire depth charges to each side of a ship, and which therefore could supplement the usual stern racks.

ASW requirements explain the principal destroyer war modifications. All were fitted with depth-charge track aft, and the large wartime loads of such weapons represented considerable top weight. Many destroyers were also fitted with Y-guns aft, sometimes in place of one AA gun. There were also hydrophones, passive submarine detectors. In their most mature form, hydrophones were fitted in 'blisters' on either side of the bow, and their receiving beam turned by a system of electrical compensators similar in principle to that to be found in a modern scanning sonar system. **Note:** In the tables following the data applies to the name ship of the class.

Flusser on trials 1909 *USN*

SMITH class *destroyers*

Displacement: 700t nominal; 900t full load
Dimensions: 289ft wl, 293ft 8in × 26ft × 8ft
88.1m, 89.6m × 7.9m × 2.4m
Machinery: 3-shaft Parsons turbines, 4 Mosher boilers, 10,000shp = 28kts. Range 2800nm at 10kts
Armament: 5–3in (76mm), 3–18in (457mm) TT
Complement: 87

No	Name	Builder	Launched	Fate
DD 17	SMITH	Cramp	20.4.09	Stricken 1919, BU
DD 18	LAMSON	Cramp	18.3.08	Stricken 1919, BU
DD 19	PRESTON	New York SB	14.7.09	Stricken 1919, BU
DD 20	FLUSSER	Bath	20.7.09	Stricken 1919, BU
DD 21	REID	Bath	17.8.09	Stricken 1919, BU

These ships were conceived as fully seagoing destroyers, as compared to the relatively fragile craft of the first US series, ordered in 1898. Hence the high forecastle, and their relatively large size. Ironically, within a few years US practice had jumped once more, to the 'thousand tonners', and these and other smaller destroyers were dismissed as 'flivvers'.

Although the design originally provided for either reciprocating engines or turbines, the turbine bids were much lower. The two Cramp ships had their two amidships funnels closely paired, the New York ship had hers equally spaced, and the two Bath ships had theirs paired fore and aft. All had triple screws driven by Parsons turbines, with the high-pressure unit on the centre shaft, and the two low-pressure turbines (and cruising turbines) on the wing shafts.

The uniform armament of 5–3in/50 guns was a considerable advance on the earlier ships, but, like their predecessors, these destroyers had single TT, with one reload stowed near each tube. By 1916, however, each had three twin tubes, and no reloads. *Smith* was based at Brest 1917–18.

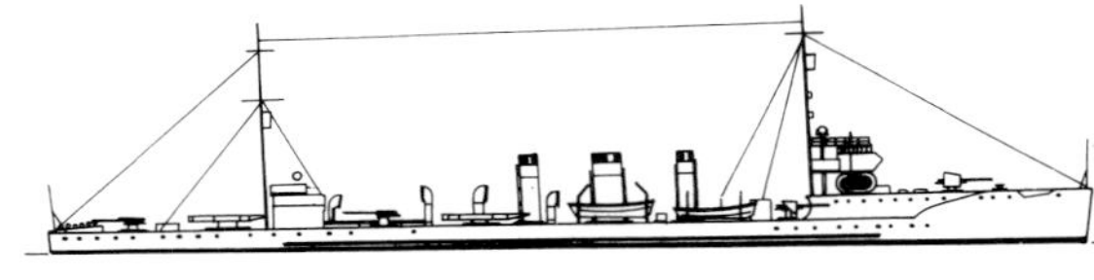
Perkins as completed

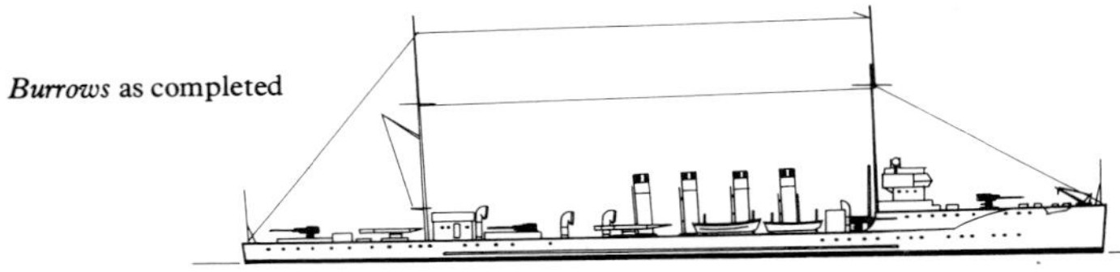
Burrows as completed

PAULDING class *destroyers*

Displacement: 742t normal; 887t full load
Dimensions: 289ft wl, 293ft × 26ft 3in × 8ft
88.1m, 89.6m × 8.0m × 2.4m
Machinery: 3-shaft Parsons turbines, 4 Normand boilers, 12,000shp = 29.5kts. Range 3000nm at 16kts
Armament: 5–3in (76mm), 6–18in (457mm) TT (3×2)
Complement: 86

No	Name	Builder	Launched	Fate
DD 22	PAULDING*	Bath	12.4.10	BU 1934
DD 23	DRAYTON	Bath	22.8.10	BU 1935
DD 24	ROE*	Newport News	24.7.09	BU 1935
DD 25	TERRY	Newport News	21.8.09	BU 1934
DD 26	PERKINS	Fore River	9.7.10	BU 1935
DD 27	STERETT	Fore River	12.5.10	BU 1935
DD 28	McCALL*	New York SB	4.6.10	BU 1935
DD 29	BURROWS*	New York SB	23.6.10	BU 1934
DD 30	WARRINGTON	Cramp	18.6.10	BU 1935
DD 31	MAYRANT	Cramp	23.4.10	BU 1935

These ten improved *Smiths* were authorised in May 1910. The principal change was replacement of the former single tubes by twin tubes. They introduced oil fuel for US destroyers. Most had three shafts, but four ships (DD 26–27 and DD 30–31) had two turbines (Curtis in the Fore River ships, Zoelly in the Cramp ships), with cruising stages incorporated in the main turbines. Cramp, Fore River, and Newport News ships had their two amidships funnels trunked together. *Terry* was in the 1914 Mexican crisis.

Mayrant and *Henley* were fitted with 13,000shp Westinghouse geared turbines in 1915. Four of the class (*) served with the Coast Guard 1924–30.

Tripple 1912 USN

Aylwin about 1916 USN

MONAGHAN class *destroyers*

Displacement: 787t normal; 883t full load
Dimensions: 293ft 8in × 27ft × 8ft 2in
Machinery: 3-shaft Parsons turbines, 4 Thornycroft boilers, 12,000shp = 29.5kts
Armament: 5–3in (76mm)/50 cal (4–3in/50 in DD 40), 6–18in (457mm) TT
Complement: 89

No	Name	Builder	Launched	Fate
DD 32	MONAGHAN*	Newport News	18.2.11	BU 1935
DD 33	TRIPPE*	Bath	20.12.10	BU 1935
DD 34	WALKE	Fore River	3.11.10	BU 1935
DD 35	AMMEN*	New York SB	30.9.10	BU 1935
DD 36	PATTERSON*	Cramp	29.4.11	BU 1935
DD 37	FANNING*	Newport News	11.1.12	BU 1935
DD 38	JARVIS	New York SB	4.4.12	BU 1935
DD 39	HENLEY*	Fore River	3.4.12	BU 1935
DD 40	BEALE*	Cramp	30.8.12	BU 1935
DD 41	JOUETT*	Bath	15.4.12	BU 1935
DD 42	JENKINS	Bath	29.4.12	BU 1935

These were repeat *Pauldings* authorised in March 1909 (DD 32–36) and June 1910. All but the *Walke* (DD 34) had triple screws; six (DD 32, 34, 36, 37, 39, 40) had three funnels. The remaining units (Bath and New York Shipbuilding) all had four funnels. Eight of the class* served in the Coast Guard from 1924. *Jarvis* and *Jenkins* were in the 1914 Mexican intervention. *Fanning* helped sink *U 58* on 17 November 1917.

CASSIN class *destroyers*

Displacement: 1010t nominal; 1235t full load
Dimensions: 300ft wl, 305ft 5in × 30ft 2in
91.5m, 93.1m × 9.2m × 3.0m
Machinery: 2-shaft Parson turbines (plus reciprocating engines for cruising), 4 Normand boilers, 16,000shp = 29kts
Armament: 4–4in (102mm)/50cal (3–4in/50 in DD 43–44), 8–18in (457mm) TT (4×2)
Complement: 98

No	Name	Builder	Launched	Fate
DD 43	CASSIN	Bath Iron Wks	20.5.13	BU 1934
DD 44	CUMMINGS	Bath Iron Wks	6.8.13	BU 1934
DD 45	DOWNES	New York SB	8.11.13	BU 1934
DD 46	DUNCAN	Fore River	5.4.13	BU 1935
DD 47	AYLWIN	Cramp	23.11.12	BU 1935
DD 48	PARKER	Cramp	8.2.13	BU 1935
DD 49	BENHAM	Cramp	22.3.13	BU 1935
DD 50	BALCH	Cramp	21.12.12	BU 1935

These destroyers, authorised in March 1911, were the first whose design was dominated by the General Board, which was above all concerned with the operation of the battlefleet as an integrated formation. It therefore emphasised sea-keeping and range at the expense of the small silhouette which destroyermen regarded as essential for successful torpedo attacks. The board hoped to replace at least one of the 3in/50 guns with a 4in or even a long-recoil 5in; C&R managed to change the gun battery to 4–4in/50, a fourth twin 18in TT replacing the fifth gun. *Cassin* was flagship Atlantic Fleet Torpedo Flotilla 1914–15.

Unlike the 'flivvers', all had twin screws. Two (DD 43 and 44) had a reciprocating engine which could be clutched to one shaft for cruising below 15kts. The remainder had reciprocating engines on both shafts. *Cummings* was based at Brest in 1918. The first 3 ships served with the Coast Guard 1924–1931.

O'BRIEN class *destroyers*

Displacement: 1050t normal; 1171t full load
Dimensions: 305ft 5in × 31ft 2in × 9ft 6in
93.1m × 9.5m × 2.9m
Machinery: 2-shaft Zoelly turbines (plus reciprocating engine for cruising), 4 White Forster boilers, 17,000shp = 29kts
Armament: 4–4in (102mm)/50cal, 8–21in (533mm) TT
Complement: 101

No	Name	Builder	Launched	Fate
DD 51	O'BRIEN	Cramp	20.7.14	BU 1935
DD 52	NICHOLSON	Cramp	19.8.14	BU 1936
DD 53	WINSLOW	Cramp	11.2.15	BU 1936
DD 54	McDOUGAL	Bath Iron Wks	22.4.14	BU 1934
DD 55	CUSHING	Fore River	16.1.15	BU 1936
DD 56	ERICSSON	New York SB	22.8.14	BU 1934

These were improved *Cassins* with 21in TT which had been suggested by the Bureau of Ordnance in May 1912. The first six were authorised in March 1913. The second group of six (DD 57–62), the *Tucker* class, were authorised in 1913. Their General Board characteristics included, for the first time, a call for two AA guns, as well as provision to lay 36 floating mines.

Of this class, DD 51–53 had a reciprocating cruise engine on each shaft; DD 54 and DD 56 had a single reciprocating engine which could be clutched to one shaft for cruising; DD 55 had a pair of cruising turbines; DD 57–59 and DD 61–62 had a single cruising turbine geared to one shaft. *Wadsworth* (DD 60) had the prototype US main turbine geared turbine installation, and so had a considerable effect on destroyer design from 1915 on. *Nicholson* shared the sinking of *U 58* with USS *Fanning* (DD 37) on 17 November 1917.

TUCKER class *destroyers*

Displacement: 1090t (DD 60 1060t, DD 61–62, 1150t) normal; 1205t full load
Dimensions: 315ft 3in × 30ft 6in (29ft 9in in DD 57, 60 and 62) × 9ft 4in (9ft 2in in DD 60, 9ft 8in in DD 61)
96.1m × 9.3m (9.1m) × 2.9m (2.8m, 3.0m)
Machinery: 2-shaft Curtis turbines, 4 Yarrow boilers, 17,000shp (DD 58, DD 59 18,000shp, DD 60 17,500shp) = 29.5kts
Armament: 4–4in (102mm)/50cal, 8–21in (533mm) TT
Complement: 99

No	Name	Builder	Launched	Fate
DD 57	TUCKER	Fore River	4.5.15	BU 1937
DD 58	CONYNGHAM	Cramp	8.7.15	BU 1934
DD 59	PORTER	Cramp	26.7.15	BU 1934
DD 60	WADSWORTH	Bath Iron Wks	29.4.15	BU 1936
DD 61	JACOB JONES	New York SB	29.5.15	Sunk 6.12.17
DD 62	WAINWRIGHT	New York SB	12.6.15	BU 1934

Jacob Jones was torpedoed and sunk by *U 53* off the Scillies. See *O'Brien* class for technical notes. *Wadsworth* was USN destroyer flagship in British waters April 1917.

Sampson as completed

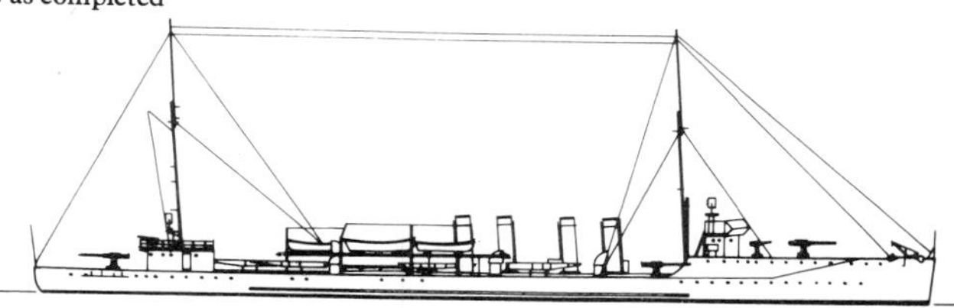

SAMPSON class *destroyers*

Displacement: 1100t normal; 1225t full load
Dimensions: 315ft 3in × 29ft 10in × 9ft 6in
96.1m × 9.1m × 2.9m
Machinery: 2-shaft Curtis turbines, 4 Yarrow boilers, 17,500shp = 29.5kts
Armament: 4–4in (102mm)/50 cal, 2–1pdr AA, 12–21in (533mm) TT (4×3)
Complement: 99

No	Name	Builder	Launched	Fate
DD 63	SAMPSON	Fore River	4.3.16	BU 1936
DD 64	ROWAN	Fore River	23.3.16	BU 1936
DD 65	DAVIS	Bath Iron Wks	15.8.16	BU 1934
DD 66	ALLEN	Bath Iron Wks	5.12.16	BU 1946
DD 67	WILKES	Cramp	18.5.16	BU 1934
DD 68	SHAW	Mare Island N Yd	9.12.16	BU 1934

The last of the 'thousand tonners', these six ships were authorised in June 1914. They incorporated both AA weapons (two 1pdr) and a new triple 21in TT, which had been incorporated in the characteristics for Destroyer 1916, ie for the ships to be authorised in 1915, which became the *Caldwell* class.

DD 66–68 each had a single cruising turbine that could be geared to one shaft. The other ships all had paired cruising turbines. *Shaw* and *Allen* served in European waters 1917–18.

Stockton as completed

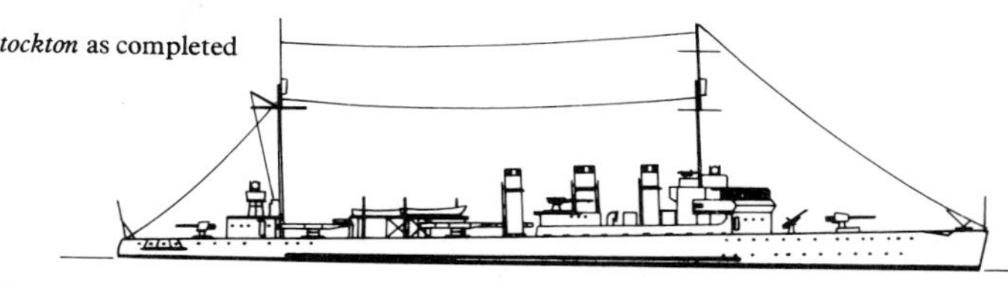

CALDWELL class *destroyers*

Displacement: 1120t normal; 1187t full load
Dimensions: 310ft wl, 315ft 7in × 30ft 6in × 8ft 10in
94.5m, 96.2m × 9.3m × 2.7m
Machinery: 2-shaft turbines (see notes), 4 Thornycroft boilers, 18,500shp = 30kts. Range 2500nm at 20kts
Armament: 4–4in (102mm)/50 cal, 2–1pdr AA, 12–21in (533mm) TT (4×3), 1 Y-gun (in DD 70–71 only)
Complement: 100

No	Name	Builder	Launched	Fate
DD 69	CALDWELL	Mare Island N Yd	10.7.17	BU 1936
DD 70	CRAVEN	Norfolk N Yd	29.6.18	To RN 1940
DD 71	GWIN	Seattle	22.12.17	Sold 1939
DD 72	CONNER	Cramp	21.8.17	To RN 1940
DD 73	STOCKTON	Cramp	17.7.17	To RN 1940
DD 74	MANLEY	Bath	23.8.17	BU 1946

The first of the famous 'flush deckers', these ships were intermediate between the 'thousand tonners' and the mass-production destroyers of World War One. Their characteristics essentially duplicated those of the earlier ships, but C&R proposed a new flush-deck hull form, to reduce rolling and pitching. Beam and midship cross-section both increased slightly, and draft had to be reduced in compensation. That in turn would have reduced hull depth (hence strength) in a conventional broken-forecastle hull; C&R solved the problem by increasing freeboard amidships, so that hull scantlings (hence weight) could be held down. The designers hoped that dryness could be preserved, since the bow freeboard of earlier ships was retained. In practice, however, the flush-deckers were far wetter than their predecessors. Shallow draft also meant that the propellers would not be deep enough, and the ships had to be designed with a drag, ie with a keel sloping aft.

Steam Engineering proposed a new triple-screw powerplant, the centre shaft being driven by the high-pressure turbine, with a geared cruising turbine clutched to it. The sketch design also showed three rather than four funnels, the two inner ones being trunked together. In practice, however, only the two Cramp ships followed the original design. The other four had twin screws (with Curtis geared turbines in DD 69, Parsons geared turbines in the others). Only the two Cramp ships and the *Gwin* had triple funnels. Unlike the mass-production 'flush-deckers', these ships had cutaway (vice cruiser) sterns. During World War One the 1pdr AA guns were replaced by 3in/23s. *Conner* was based at Brest in June 1918. *Manley* bcame the prototype destroyer transport (APD) in 1938.

Jacob Jones on trials 1915
USN

UNITED STATES OF AMERICA

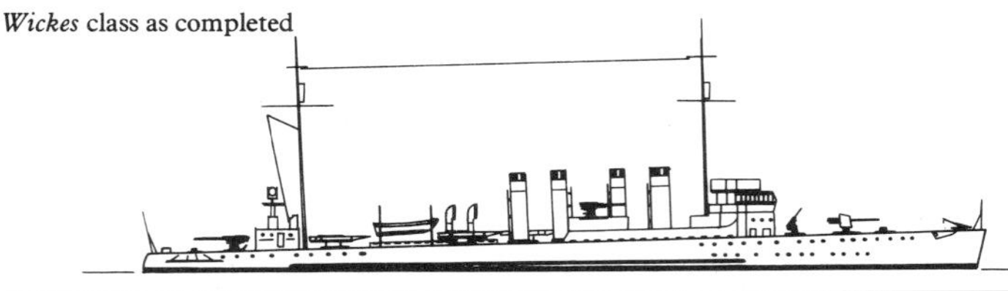

Wickes class as completed

WICKES class *destroyers*

Displacement: 1090t normal; 1247t full load
Dimensions: 310ft wl, 314ft 4in × 30ft 10in × 9ft 2in
94.5m, 95.8m × 9.4m × 2.8m
Machinery: 2-shaft Parsons turbines (with geared cruising turbine on port shaft), 4 White-Forster boilers, 24,200shp = 35kts. Range 2500nm at 20kts
Armament: 4–4in (102mm)/50 cal, 2–1pdr AA or 1–3in (76mm)/23cal, 12–21in (533mm) TT (4×3)
Complement: 114

No	Name	Builder	Launched	Fate
DD 75	WICKES	Bath Iron Wks	25.6.18	To RN 1940
DD 76	PHILIP	Bath Iron Wks	25.7.18	To RN 1940
DD 77	WOOLSEY	Bath Iron Wks	17.9.18	Collision 26.2.21
DD 78	EVANS	Bath Iron Wks	30.10.18	To RN 1940
DD 79	LITTLE	Fore River	11.11.17	Sunk 5.9.42
DD 80	KIMBERLEY	Fore River	14.12.17	BU 1937
DD 81	SIGOURNEY	Fore River	16.12.17	To RN 1940
DD 82	GREGORY	Fore River	27.1.18	Sunk 5.9.42
DD 83	STRINGHAM	Fore River	30.3.18	BU 1946
DD 84	DYER	Fore River	13.4.18	Sold 1936
DD 85	COLHOUN	Fore River	21.2.18	Sunk 30.8.42
DD 86	STEVENS	Fore River	13.1.18	Sold 1936
DD 87	McKEE	Union Iron Wks	23.3.18	Sold 1936
DD 88	ROBINSON	Union Iron Wks	28.3.18	To RN 1940
DD 89	RINGGOLD	Union Iron Wks	14.4.18	To RN 1940
DD 90	McKEAN	Union Iron Wks	4.7.18	Sunk 17.11.43
DD 91	HARDING	Union Iron Wks	4.7.18	Sold 1936
DD 92	GRIDLEY	Union Iron Wks	4.7.18	Sold 1939
DD 93	FAIRFAX	Mare Island N Yd	15.12.17	To RN 1940
DD 94	TAYLOR	Mare Island N Yd	14.2.18	BU 1945
DD 95	BELL	Fore River	14.1.19	Sold 1939
DD 96	STRIBLING	Fore River	29.5.18	Target 1937
DD 97	MURRAY	Fore River	8.6.18	BU 1936
DD 98	ISRAEL	Fore River	22.8.16	Sold 1939
DD 99	LUCE	Fore River	29.6.18	BU 1936
DD 100	MAURY	Fore River	4.7.18	Sold 1931
DD 101	LANSDALE	Fore River	21.7.18	Sold 1939
DD 102	MAHAN	Fore River	4.8.18	Sold 1931
DD 103	SCHLEY	Union Iron Wks	28.3.18	BU 1946
DD 104	CHAMPLIN	Union Iron Wks	7.4.18	Target 1936
DD 105	MUGFORD	Union Iron Wks	14.4.18	BU 1936
DD 106	CHEW	Union Iron Wks	26.5.18	BU 1936
DD 107	HAZELWOOD	Union Iron Wks	22.6.18	BU 1936
DD 108	WILLIAMS	Union Iron Wks	4.7.18	To RN 1940
DD 109	CRANE	Union Iron Wks	4.7.18	BU 1946
DD 110	HART	Union Iron Wks	4.7.18	BU 1932
DD 111	INGRAHAM	Union Iron Wks	4.7.18	Expended 1937
DD 112	LUDLOW	Union Iron Wks	9.6.18	BU 1931
DD 113	RATHBURNE	Cramp	27.12.17	BU 1946
DD 114	TALBOT	Cramp	20.2.18	BU 1946
DD 115	WATERS	Cramp	9.3.18	BU 1946
DD 116	DENT	Cramp	23.3.18	BU 1946
DD 117	DORSEY	Cramp	9.4.18	Lost 1945
DD 118	LEA	Cramp	29.4.18	BU 1945
DD 119	LAMBERTON	Newport News	30.3.18	BU 1947
DD 120	RADFORD	Newport News	5.8.18	Target 1936
DD 121	MONTGOMERY	Newport News	23.3.18	Lost 1944
DD 122	BREESE	Newport News	11.5.18	BU 1946
DD 123	GAMBLE	Newport News	11.5.18	Scuttled 16.7.45
DD 124	RAMSAY	Newport News	8.6.18	BU 1946
DD 125	TATTNALL	New York SB	5.9.18	BU 1946
DD 126	BADGER	New York SB	14.8.18	BU 1945
DD 127	TWIGGS	New York SB	28.9.18	To RN 1940
DD 128	BABBITT	New York SB	30.9.18	BU 1946
DD 129	DeLONG	New York SB	29.10.18	Grounded 1.12.21, stricken 1922
DD 130	JACOB JONES	New York SB	20.11.18	Sunk 28.2.42
DD 131	BUCHANAN	Bath Iron Wks	2.1.19	To RN 1940
DD 132	AARON WARD	Bath Iron Wks	10.4.19	To RN 1940
DD 133	HALE	Bath	29.5.19	To RN 1940
DD 134	CROWNINSHIELD	Bath Iron Wks	24.7.19	To RN 1940
DD 135	TILLMAN	Chesapeake N Yd	7.7.19	To RN 1940
DD 136	BOGGS	Mare Island N Yd	25.4.18	BU 1946
DD 137	KILTY	Mare Island N Yd	25.4.18	BU 1946
DD 138	KENNISON	Mare Island N Yd	8.6.18	BU 1946
DD 139	WARD	Mare Island N Yd	1.6.18	Sunk 7.12.44
DD 140	CLAXTON	Mare Island N Yd	14.1.19	To RN 1940
DD 141	HAMILTON	Mare Island N Yd	15.1.19	BU 1946
DD 142	TARBELL	Cramp	28.5.18	BU 1945
DD 143	YARNALL	Cramp	19.1.18	To RN 1940
DD 144	UPSHUR	Cramp	4.7.18	BU 1947
DD 145	GREER	Cramp	1.8.18	BU 1945
DD 146	ELLIOT	Cramp	4.7.18	BU 1946
DD 147	ROPER	Cramp	17.8.18	BU 1946
DD 148	BRECKINRIDGE	Cramp	17.8.18	BU 1946
DD 149	BARNEY	Cramp	5.9.18	BU 1946
DD 150	BLAKELY	Cramp	19.9.18	BU 1945
DD 151	BIDDLE	Cramp	3.10.18	BU 1946
DD 152	DUPONT	Cramp	22.10.18	BU 1947
DD 153	BERNADOU	Cramp	7.11.18	BU 1945
DD 154	ELLIS	Cramp	30.11.18	BU 1947
DD 155	COLE	Cramp	11.1.19	BU 1947
DD 156	J FRED TALBOTT	Cramp	14.12.18	BU 1946
DD 157	DICKERSON	New York SB	12.3.19	Sunk 4.4.45
DD 158	LEARY	New York SB	18.12.18	Sunk 24.12.43
DD 159	SCHENCK	New York SB	23.4.19	BU 1946
DD 160	HERBERT	New York SB	8.5.19	BU 1946
DD 161	PALMER	Fore River	18.8.18	Sunk 7.1.45
DD 162	THATCHER	Fore River	31.8.18	To RCN 1940
DD 163	WALKER	Fore River	14.9.18	Lost 1941
DD 164	CROSBY	Fore River	28.9.18	BU 1946
DD 165	MEREDITH	Fore River	22.9.18	BU 1936
DD 166	BUSH	Fore River	27.10.18	BU 1936
DD 167	COWELL	Fore River	23.11.18	To RN 1940
DD 168	MADDOX	Fore River	27.10.18	To RN 1940
DD 169	FOOTE	Fore River	14.12.18	To RN 1940
DD 170	KALK	Fore River	21.12.18	To RN 1940
DD 171	BURNS	Union Iron Wks	4.7.18	BU 1932
DD 172	ANTHONY	Union Iron Wks	10.8.18	Target 1937
DD 173	SPROSTON	Union Iron Wks	10.8.18	Target 1937
DD 174	RIZAL	Union Iron Wks	21.9.18	BU 1932
DD 175	MACKENZIE	Union Iron Wks	29.9.18	To RCN 1940
DD 176	RENSHAW	Union Iron Wks	21.9.18	BU 1936
DD 177	O'BANNON	Union Iron Wks	28.2.19	Sold 1936
DD 178	HOGAN	Union Iron Wks	12.4.19	Target 1945
DD 179	HOWARD	Union Iron Wks	26.4.19	BU 1945
DD 180	STANDBURY	Union Iron Wks	16.5.19	BU 1946
DD 181	HOPEWELL	Newport News	8.6.18	To RN 1940
DD 182	THOMAS	Newport News	4.7.18	To RN 1940
DD 183	HARADEN	Newport News	4.7.18	To RCN 1940
DD 184	ABBOT	Newport News	4.7.18	To RN 1940
DD 185	BAGLEY	Newport News	19.10.18	To RN 1940

These were the famous 'flush deckers', mass produced during World War One, which formed the bulk of the US destroyer force nearly until the outbreak of World War Two. They were essentially a 35kt version of the *Caldwell*, the speed matching that of the FY 17 battlecruisers and scouts (*Omaha* class). Higher speed cost nearly 50 per cent more power, and that in turn cost 90 to 100 tons of machinery. The earlier flush-decker hull was, therefore, modified, with a level keel (no drag) and with more nearly horizontal shafting. In arrangement, however, these ships duplicated the first six flush-deckers.

The first 50 were authorised as part of the massive 1916 programme. There were two detail designs, one by Bath and one by Bethlehem Steel, for Fore River and Union Iron Works. Bath employed Parsons or Westinghouse turbines and Normand, Thornycroft, or White-Foster boilers; Bethlehem, Curtis turbines and, in many cases, Yarrow boilers. The latter deteriorated badly in service, and in 1929 the Navy decided to scrap 60 ships with Yarrow boilers. All the non-Bethlehem yards built the Bath design, known unofficially as the 'Liberty' type.

Ships differed radically in performance, particularly in fuel economy, so that although the *Wickes* was credited with about 3178nm at 20kts, Fore River boats were credited with no more than about 3400nm at 15kts, and other Bethlehem ships were credited with only about 2300nm–2400nm at 15kts. The best 107 Bath ships were described as 'Long Radius Boats'. *Little* and *Stevens* were based at Queenstown, Ireland, in 1918.

The design called for two 1pdr AA guns, but in many vessels 3in/23s had to be substituted. Fourteen ships were converted to fast minelayers (DM) in 1920, all of their TT being removed (DD 96–102, 110–112, 171–174). For the new names of vessels transferred to the RN and RCN in 1940, see p47 of the 1922–46 volume. *Little* (APD 4) and *Gregory* (APD 3) were sunk by Japanese destroyers off Guadalcanal while serving as high-speed transports. *Colhoun* (APD 2) was sunk by Japanese aircraft. *Gamble* (DM 15) was damaged by aircraft bombs off Iwo Jima on 18 February 1945 and scuttled off Saipan. *Jacob Jones* was torpedoed and sunk by *U 578* off Cape May, NJ. *Ward* (APD 16) was sunk by Kamikaze attack off Ormoc, Leyte. *Dickerson* (APD 21) was damaged by Japanese aircraft off Okinawa on 2 April 1945 and scuttled. *Leary* was torpedoed and sunk by *U 275* in the North Atlantic. *Palmer* (DMS 5) was sunk by Japanese aircraft in the Lingayen Gulf (Luzon, Philippines).

Fairfax 21 May 1918 USN

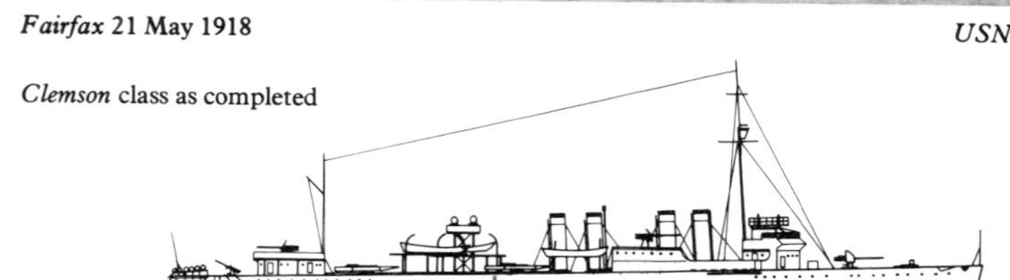

Clemson class as completed

CLEMSON class *destroyers*

Displacement: 1190t normal; 1308t full load
Dimensions: As *Wickes* class except 9ft 10in/*3m* draught
Machinery: 2-shaft Westinghouse geared turbines, 4 White-Forster boilers, 27,000shp = 35kts. Range 2500nm at 20kts.
Armament: 4–4in (102mm)/50cal, 1–3in (76mm)/23cal, 12–21in (533mm) TT (4×3)
Complement: 114

Class (no, launched, fate):
Newport News – *Clemson* (DD 186, 5.9.18, BU 1946), *Dahlgren* (DD 187, 20.11.18, BU 1946), *Goldsborough* (DD 188, 20.11.18, BU 1946), *Semmes* (DD 189, 21.12.18, BU 1946), *Satterlee* (DD 190, 21.12.18, to RN 1940), *Mason* (DD 191, 8.3.19, to RN 1940), *Graham* (DD 192, 22.3.19, collision 16.12.21), *Abel P Upshur* (DD 193, 14.2.20, to RN 1940), *Hunt* (DD 194, 14.2.20, to RN 1940), *Welborn C Wood* (DD 195, 6.3.20, to RN 1940), *George E Badger* (DD 196, 6.3.20, BU 1946), *Branch* (DD 197, 19.4.19, to RN 1940), *Herndon* (DD 198, 31.5.19, to RN 1940), *Dallas* (DD 199, 31.5.19, BU 1945)

Cramp – *Chandler* (DD 206, 19.3.19, BU 1946), *Southard* (DD 207, 31.3.19, stricken 1946), *Hovey* (DD 208, 26.4.19, sunk 6.1.45), *Long* (DD 209, 26.4.19, sunk 6.1.45), *Broome* (DD 210, 14.5.19, BU 1946), *Alden* (DD 211, 7.6.19, BU 1945), *Smith Thompson* (DD 212, 14.7.19, collision 14.4.36, scuttled), *Barker* (DD 213, 11.9.19, BU 1945), *Tracy* (DD 214, 12.8.19, BU 1946), *Borie* (DD 215, 4.10.19, sunk 2.11.43), *John D Edwards* (DD 216, 18.10.19, BU 1945), *Whipple* (DD 217, 6.11.19, BU 1946), *Parrott* (DD 218, 25.11.19, sold 1947), *Edsall* (DD 219, 29.7.20, sunk 1.3.42), *MacLeish* (DD 220, 18.12.19, BU 1946), *Simpson* (DD 221, 28.4.20, BU 1946), *Bulmer* (DD 222, 22.1.20, BU 1947), *McCormick* (DD 223, 14.2.20, BU 1946), *Stewart* (DD 224, 4.3.20, scuttled 2.3.42, see notes), *Pope* (DD 225, 23.3.20, sunk 1.3.42), *Peary* (DD 226, 6.4.20, sunk 19.2.42), *Pillsbury* (DD 227, 3.8.20, sunk 1.3.42), *Ford* (DD 228, 2.9.20, BU 1947), *Truxtun* (DD 229, 28.9.20, grounded 18.2.42), *Paul Jones* (DD 230, 30.9.20, BU 1947)

New York SB – *Hatfield* (DD 231, 17.3.19, BU 1947), *Brooks* (DD 232, 24.4.19, sold 1946), *Gilmer* (DD 233, 24.5.19, BU 1946), *Fox* (DD 234, 12.6.19, BU 1945), *Kane* (DD 235, 12.8.19, BU 1946), *Humphreys* (DD 236, 28.7.19, BU 1946), *McFarland* (DD 237, 30.3.20, BU 1946), *James K Paulding* (DD 238, 20.4.20, BU 1939), *Overton* (DD 239, 10.7.19, BU 1945), *Sturtevant* (DD 240, 29.7.20, sunk 26.4.42), *Childs* (DD 241, 15.9.20, BU 1946), *King* (DD 242, 14.10.20, BU 1946), *Sands* (DD 243, 28.10.19, BU 1946), *Williamson* (DD 244, 16.10.19, BU 1946), *Reuben James* (DD 245, 4.10.19, sunk 31.10.41), *Bainbridge* (DD 246, 12.6.20, BU 1945), *Goff* (DD 247, 2.6.20, BU 1945), *Barry* (DD 248, 28.10.20, sunk 21.6.45), *Hopkins* (DD 249, 26.6.20, BU 1946), *Lawrence* (DD 250, 10.7.20, BU 1946)

Fore River – *Belknap* (DD 251, 14.1.19, BU 1945), *McCook* (DD 252, 31.1.19, to RCN 1940), *McCalla* (DD 253, 28.3.19, to RN 1940), *Rodgers* (DD 254, 26.4.19, to RN 1940), *Ingram* (DD 255, 28.2.19, BU 1946), *Bancroft* (DD 256, 21.3.19, to RCN 1940), *Aulick* (DD 258, 11.4.19, to RN 1940), *Turner* (DD 259, 17.5.19, BU 1947), *Gillis* (DD 260, 29.4.19, BU 1946)

Squantum – *Welles* (DD 257, 8.5.19, to RN 1940), *Delphy* (DD 261, 18.7.18, grounded 8.9.23), *McDermut* (DD 262, 6.7.18, BU 1932), *Laub* (DD 263, 25.8.18, to RN 1940), *McLanahan* (DD 264, 22.9.18, to RN 1940), *Edwards* (DD 265, 10.10.18, to RN 1940), *Greene* (DD 266, 2.11.18, grounded 9.10.45), *Ballard* (DD 267, 7.12.18, BU 1946), *Shubrick* (DD 268, 31.12.18, to RN 1940), *Bailey* (DD 269, 5.2.19, to RN 1940), *Thornton* (DD 270, 22.3.10, BU 1945), *Morris* (DD 271, 12.4.19, BU 1936), *Tingey* (DD 272, 14.4.19, BU 1936), *Swasey* (DD 273, 7.5.19, to RN 1940), *Meade* (DD 274, 24.5.19, to RN 1940), *Sinclair* (DD 275, 2.6.19, BU 1935), *McCawley* (DD 276, 14.6.19, BU 1931), *Moody* (DD 277, 28.6.19, BU 1931), *Henshaw* (DD 278, 28.6.19, BU 1930), *Meyer* (DD 279, 18.7.19, BU 1932), *Doyen* (DD 280, 26.7.19, BU 1930), *Sharkey* (DD 281, 12.8.19, BU 1931), *Toucey* (DD 282, 5.9.19, BU 1931), *Breck* (DD 283, 5.9.19, BU 1931), *Isherwood* (DD 284, 21.9.19, BU 1931), *Case* (DD 285, 21.9.19, BU 1931), *Lardner* (DD 286, 29.9.19, BU 1931), *Putnam* (DD 287, 30.9.19, sold 1931), *Worden* (DD 288, 24.10.19, sold 1931), *Flusser* (DD 289, 7.11.19, BU 1931), *Dale* (DD 290, 19.11.19, sold 1931), *Converse* (DD 291, 28.11.19, BU 1931), *Reid* (DD 292, 15.10.19, BU 1931), *Billingsley* (DD 293, 10.12.19, BU 1931), *Charles Ausburn* (DD 294, 18.12.19, BU 1931), *Osborne* (DD 295, 29.12.19, sold 1931)

Union Iron Wks – *Chauncey* (DD 296, 19.9.19, grounded 8.9.23), *Fuller* (DD 297, 5.12.18, grounded 8.9.23), *Percival* (DD 298, 5.12.18, BU 1931), *John Francis Burnes* (DD 299, 10.11.18, BU 1931), *Farragut* (DD 300, 10.11.18, BU 1931), *Somers* (DD 301, 21.11.18, BU 1931), *Stoddert* (DD 302, 8.1.19, BU 1935), *Reno* (DD 303, 22.1.19, BU 1931), *Farquhar* (DD 304, 18.1.19, BU 1932), *Thompson* (DD 305, 19.1.19, BU 1931), *Kennedy* (DD 306, 15.2.19, BU 1931), *Paul Hamilton* (DD 307, 21.2.19, BU 1931), *William Jones* (DD 308, 9.4.19, BU 1932), *Woodbury* (DD 309, 6.2.19, grounded 8.9.23), *S P Lee* (DD 310, 22.4.19, grounded 8.9.23), *Nicholas* (DD 311, 1.5.19, grounded 8.9.23), *Young* (DD 312, 8.5.19, grounded 8.9.23), *Zeilin* (DD 313, 28.5.19, BU 1931), *Yarborough* (DD 314, 20.6.19, BU 1931), *La Vallette* (DD 315, 15.7.19, BU 1931), *Sloat* (DD 316, 14.5.19, target 1935), *Wood* (DD 317, 28.5.19, BU 1930), *Shirk* (DD 318, 20.6.19, BU 1931), *Kidder* (DD 319, 10.7.19, BU 1930), *Selfridge* (DD 320, 25.7.19, BU 1931), *Marcus* (DD 321, 22.8.19, target 1935), *Mervine* (DD 322, 11.8.19, BU 1931), *Chase* (DD 323, 2.9.19, BU 1931), *Robert Smith* (DD 324, 19.9.19, BU 1931), *Mullany* (DD 325, 9.7.20, BU 1931), *Coghlan* (DD 326, 16.6.20, BU 1931), *Preston* (DD 327, 7.8.20, BU 1932), *Lamson* (DD 328, 1.9.20, BU 1931), *Bruce* (DD 329, 20.5.20, BU 1932), *Hull* (DD 330, 18.2.21, BU 1931), *MacDonough* (DD 331, 15.12.20, BU 1931), *Farenholt* (DD 332, 9.3.21, BU 1931), *Sumner* (DD 333, 24.11.20, BU 1934), *Corry* (DD 334, 28.3.21, BU 1930), *Melvin* (DD 335, 11.4.21, BU 1931)

Mare Island N Yd – *Litchfield* (DD 336, 12.8.19), *Zane* (DD 337, 12.8.19, BU 1946), *Wasmuth* (DD 338, 15.9.20, sunk 29.12.42), *Trever* (DD 339, 15.9.20, BU 1946), *Perry* (DD 340, 29.10.21, sunk 13.9.44), *Decatur* (DD 341, 29.10.21, BU 1945)

Norfolk Navy Yd – *Hulbert* (DD 342, 28.6.19, BU 1946), *Noa* (DD 343, 28.6.19, sunk 12.9.44), *William B Preston* (DD 344, 9.8.19, BU 1946)

Bath Iron Wks – *Preble* (DD 345, 8.3.40, BU 1946), *Sicard* (DD 346, 20.4.20, BU 1946), *Pruitt* (DD 347, 2.8.20, BU 1946)

In an attempt to solve the endurance problem, these ships were provided with about 35 per cent more fuel endurance than the *Wickes* class, so that even the worst of them would equal the best of the earlier ships. Another modification was that the second 3in/23 was moved from a position between the funnels to the after deckhouse. Later this gun was moved to the quarterdeck, the after 4in being moved up, and in many cases it was dispensed with. A similar modification was approved for the *Wickes* class in 1919.

While these ships were being designed, the Germans were reportedly mounting 5.9in guns on their large submarines; the new destroyers were given gun foundations strong enough to take 5in/51 guns, as a counter. Only 5 ships were so fitted (DD 231–235). In addition, DD 208 and 209 had 8–4in/50 in four twin mounts.

USS *Thornton* saved the Mexican port of Manzanillo from bandits on 14 May 1920. *Hovey* (DMS 11) and *Long* (DMS 12) were sunk by Japanese air attack in the Lingayen Gulf (Luzon, Philippines). *Borie* sank after fatally ramming *U 405* in an epic action N of the Azores. *Edsall* was sunk with all hands by the Japanese battleships *Hiei* and *Kirishima* S of Java. *Stewart* was left in Soerabaya drydock (Java) after Japanese bombing but survived demolition efforts to become the Japanese *P 102* and was found in Japanese home waters on 15 October 1945. She was finally expended as a target. *Pope* was sunk by Japanese aircraft in the Java Sea. *Peary* was sunk by the same cause in the Darwin Raid. *Pillsbury* was sunk by Japanese cruisers and destroyers S of Java. *Truxtun* was wrecked in Placentia Bay, Newfoundland. *Sturtevant* was mined and sunk off Marquesas Key, Florida. *Reuben James* was torpedoed and sunk by *U 562*, 600 miles SW of Iceland, the first US warship loss of World War Two. *Barry* (APD 29) took *Kamikaze* damage off Okinawa on 25 May 1945 and was sunk as a decoy the next month. *Belknap* (APD 34) was damaged beyond repair by *Kamikaze* attack in the Lingayen Gulf on 11 January 1945 and scrapped afterward. *Wasmuth* (DMS 15) sank by explosion of her own depth charges in a gale off the Aleutians. *Perry* (DMS 17) was mined and sunk off Palau. *Noa* (APD 24) was sunk in collision with the destroyer USS *Fullam* off Palau. For names of ships transferred to the RN and RCN in 1940, see page 47 of the 1922–1946 volume.

UNITED STATES OF AMERICA

SUBMARINES

The US Navy was John P Holland's first client, and for about a decade the Holland Torpedo Boat Company and its successor, The Electric Boat Company, held a virtual monopoly on US submarine development. At the same time Simon Lake was developing his own type of submarine, attempting to sell it to the Navy. A Lake submarine was tested in 1907, and a contract awarded; from then on the two firms were in competition. Within a few years the Cramp Shipbuilding Company had bought the rights to the Italian Laurenti design, and it formed the American Laurenti Company. However, the latter proved relatively unsuccessful. The next step was for C & R to prepare its own designs. In 1914 it sent sketch designs to bidders, and in 1915 it issued complete designs for a fleet submarine; some of the 'R' class were built to 'bureau' (ie C & R) rather than to private designs. This last followed a Navy decision to develop Portsmouth Navy Yard as a design agency; Portsmouth built the *L 8* and *O 1*. After the failure of Lake's *S 2* design, the Company ceased to develop its own submarine designs. Electric Boat was saved by selling its submarine designs abroad, although from 1919 onwards US submarines were designed by C & R.

During this period, US submarines, like those of other navies, gradually increased in size and in capability, although actual operating experience during World War One tended to show that they were not as capable nor as reliable as had been hoped. Through the 'M' class, American submarines were relatively short for their surface speed, so that they needed relatively large engines, which crowded their pressure hulls. That made for unreliability. At the end of the war, moreover, both the dryness of U-boat bridges and the reliability of their diesel engines were major surprises, the US Navy benefiting greatly from extensive examination of *U 111*, which it obtained at the end of the war.

Holland as completed *USN*

A 2 about 1912 *USN*

Cuttlefish date unknown *CPL*

By 1914 it appeared that a true 'fleet' submarine, capable of accompanying the battlefleet overseas, could be built, and the General Board sought to distinguish between it and a much smaller coastal type. It argued that the latter need not have the speed and size of recent designs, and indeed that any increase in size would keep it from operating in shallow coastal waters.

In theory, coastal submarines were intended for a combination of coast defence and cooperation with the Fleet in home waters; fleet submarines (of which only three, the AA class, were ordered during this period), were to accompany the Fleet overseas. In theory, a coastal submarine would be able to steam, without refuelling, the length of the Atlantic coast and the Caribbean to the Panama Canal, or from Puget Sound to the Canal on the Pacific. In theory, too, it would be able to operate, unaccompanied, 300–500nm offshore, for several weeks at a time. In Fleet manoeuvres in May 1912, for example, the C-in-C sent his entire submarine fleet out of sea, to act as a mobile minefield, directed north or south by radio. He had to recall them when a severe gale rose. At this time, it was expected that the 'K' class would be able to weather such a storm, but the 'E' and lesser craft would not.

War experience in effect reversed the priorities of US submarine design, from underwater to surface performance. Thus the new 'S' class was modified with a much larger bridge and with permanent safety rails on deck, both of which contributed to underwater resistance, and cost about a knot in underwater speed. Note, too, that as built the S-boats were the first US submarines with deck guns too large to be retracted into the casing (for better underwater streamlining). Submarines assigned to overseas (ASW) patrol work had to be provided with enlarged bridges, similar in concept to those of British submarines.

Note: Crescent was Crescent Shipyard, Elizabethport, New Jersey. Applied to submarine diesels, BS is Busch-Sulzer; NLSE was the diesel engine subsidiary of the Electric Boat Company.

HOLLAND *submarine*

Displacement: 64t normal; 74t submerged
Dimensions: 53ft 10in × 10ft 2in × 8ft 6in
16.4m × 3.1m × 2.6m
Machinery: 1 shaft, Otto engine plus electric motor, 45bhp/50shp = 8kts/5kts surfaced/submerged. Diving depth 75ft
Armament: 1–18in (457mm) TT (bow; 3 torpedoes), 1–8in (203mm) dynamite gun
Complement: 7

No	Name	Builder	Launched	Fate
SS 1	HOLLAND	Crescent	17.5.97	Stricken 21.11.10, sold 6.13 for BU

The first modern US submarine, she was also the direct progenitor of modern British and Japanese craft, combining an internal combustion engine (for surface propulsion) with depth control by hydroplane. That is, in contrast to earlier submarines, this one dived with her ballast tanks full, reducing her to neutral or only slightly positive buoyancy. Her stern planes drove her underwater, and kept her down. Earlier submarine designers used partial flooding to dive and also to adjust the angle of dive; as a result, their submarines were unstable underwater, due to free surface effects in the tanks. Another characteristic feature of the Holland submarine was her very limited surface performance, due in part to her lack of reserve buoyancy: it was optimised for underwater performance. John P Holland built his first experimental craft in 1878, and in 1895 won a Navy competition with a design for a steam-powered submarine that was ordered as the USS *Plunger*. However, he believed that steam would never be suitable, and abandoned construction of the craft in favour of the gasoline engine-powered *Holland*, using his own funds. She was purchased by the Navy on 11 April 1900, and commissioned on 12 October. Some accounts claim that there were originally two pneumatic 'dynamite guns', but contemporary cross-sections show only one. She served at the Naval Academy, Annapolis, in a training role until 17 July 1905.

Holland's main American competitor was Simon Lake, who originally developed submarines primarily for underwater (sea-bottom) exploration. Unlike Holland's, his submarines were designed to dive on an even keel, and most of them had external wheels for motion along the seabed. Lake's supporters charged that their product had been rejected unfairly, and Congress for a time forced the Navy to purchase competitive Lake designs; see, for example, the notes on the 'G' class below.

'A' class *submarines*

Displacement: 107t surfaced; 123t submerged
Dimensions: 64ft × 11ft 10in × 10ft 6in
19.5m × 3.6m × 3.2m
Machinery: 1 shaft, Otto engine plus electric motors, 160bhp/150shp (2 hour rate) = 8kts/7kts surfaced/submerged
Armament: 1–18in (457mm) TT (bow; 5 torpedoes)
Complement: 7

No	Name	Builder	Launched	Fate
SS 2	PLUNGER (A 1)	Crescent	1.2.02	Stricken 24.2.13, target, sold 1922
SS 3	ADDER (A 2)	Crescent	22.7.01	Target 1920, stricken 16.1.22
SS 4	GRAMPUS (A 3)	Union Iron Wks	31.7.02	Target, stricken 16.1.22
SS 5	MOCCASIN (A 4)	Crescent	20.8.01	Target, stricken 16.1.22
SS 6	PIKE (A 5)	Union Iron Wks	14.1.03	Target, stricken 16.1.22
SS 7	PORPOISE (A 6)	Crescent	23.9.01	Target 1921, stricken 16.1.22
SS 8	SHARK (A 7)	Crescent	19.10.01	Target, stricken 16.1.22

These developments of the original *Holland* were intended for port defence, the crews living ashore or aboard tenders. All except *Plunger* were shipped to the Philippines (1st Submarine Division, Asiatic Torpedo Fleet off Cavite naval base, Luzon) aboard colliers in pairs 1908, 1909 and 1915, ending their careers in the Far East as targets.

'B' class *submarines*

Displacement: 145t normal; 173t submerged
Dimensions: 82ft 4in × 12ft 6in × 10ft 6in
25.1m × 3.8m × 3.2m
Machinery: 1 shaft, petrol engine plus electric motor, 250bhp/150shp = 9kts/8kts. Range 540nm/12nm at 9kts/4kts surfaced/submerged
Armament: 2–18in (457mm) TT (4 torpedoes)
Complement: 10

No	Name	Builder	Launched	Fate
SS 10	VIPER (B 1)	Fore River	30.3.07	Stricken 1922, target
SS 11	CUTTLEFISH (B 2)	Fore River	1.9.06	Stricken 1922, target
SS 12	TARANTULA (B 3)	Fore River	30.3.07	Stricken 1922, target

Electric Boat design, purchased under Act of April 1904 and commissioned in 1907. All were transferred to the Philippines in 1912 aboard the colliers *Ajax* and *Hector*, spending their remaining service time there. Designed diving depth 150ft.

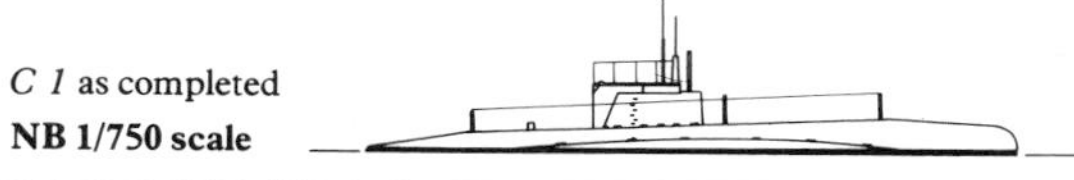
C 1 as completed
NB 1/750 scale

'C' class *submarines*

Displacement: 238t surfaced; 275t submerged
Dimensions: 105ft 4in × 13ft 9in × 9ft 10in
Machinery: 2 shafts, Craig petrol engines plus electric motor, 500bhp/300shp = 10.5kts/9kts. Range 800nm/80nm at 8kts/5kts surfaced/submerged
Armament: 2–18in (457mm) TT (4 torpedoes)
Complement: 15

No	Name	Builder	Launched	Fate
SS 9	OCTOPUS (C 1)	Fore River	4.10.06	Stricken 1920
SS 13	STINGRAY (C 2)	Fore River	8.4.09	Stricken 1920
SS 14	TARPON (C 3)	Fore River	8.4.09	Stricken 1920
SS 15	BONITA (C 4)	Fore River	17.6.09	Stricken 1920
SS 16	SNAPPER (C 5)	Fore River	16.6.09	Stricken 1920

C 1 was bought under the same Act as the B class. The C class was the first considered suitable for operations beyond harbours, and was therefore designated a coast defence type. They operated in local defence of the Panama Canal during World War One. Designed diving depth 200ft.

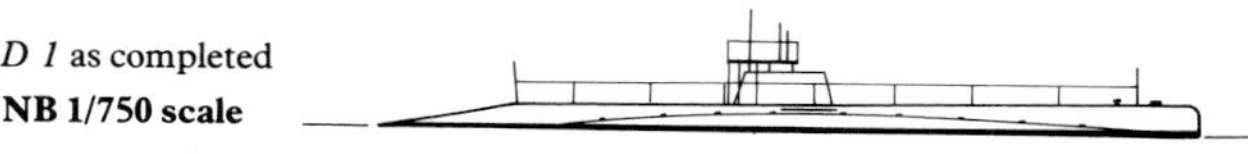
D 1 as completed
NB 1/750 scale

'D' class *submarines*

Displacement: 288t surfaced; 337t submerged
Dimensions: 134ft 10in × 13ft 9in × 11ft 10in
41.1m × 4.2m × 3.6m
Machinery: 2 shafts, NLSE petrol engine, 600bhp/260shp = 12kts/9.5kts. Range 1240nm/9–10kts surfaced
Armament: 4–18in (457mm) TT (4 torpedoes)
Complement: 15

No	Name	Builder	Launched	Fate
SS 17	NARWHAL (D 1)	Fore River	8.4.09	Stricken 1922
SS 18	GRAYLING (D 2)	Fore River	16.6.09	Stricken 1922
SS 19	SALMON (D 3)	Fore River	12.3.10	Stricken 1922

Designed diving depth 200ft. Began their service off the E Coast, *D 3* going to the Caribbean in 1912.

'E' class *submarines*

Displacement: 287t surfaced; 342t submerged
Dimensions: 135ft 2in × 14ft 5in × 11ft 10in
41.2m × 4.4m × 3.6m
Machinery: 2 shafts, diesels plus electric motors, 700bhp/600shp = 13.5kts/11.5kts. Range 2100nm/100nm at 11kts/5kts surfaced/submerged
Armament: 4–18in (457mm) TT (4 torpedoes)
Complement: 20

No	Name	Builder	Launched	Fate
SS 24	SKIPJACK (E 1)	Fore River	27.5.11	Stricken 1922
SS 25	STURGEON (E 2)	Fore River	15.6.11	Stricken 1922

In these submarines the growth in size was reversed; the Submarine Flotilla considered them a 'reversion of type without justification'. They were the first US submarines with diesel engines, which gave considerable trouble; they had to be re-engined in 1915. They also had the first US bow planes, and were the first US submarines with radios. Designed depth 200ft. This class showed a typical pre-1917 American concentration on high underwater speed, which continued through the 'S' class of World War One. *Skipjack* was in the Atlantic 1915–16.

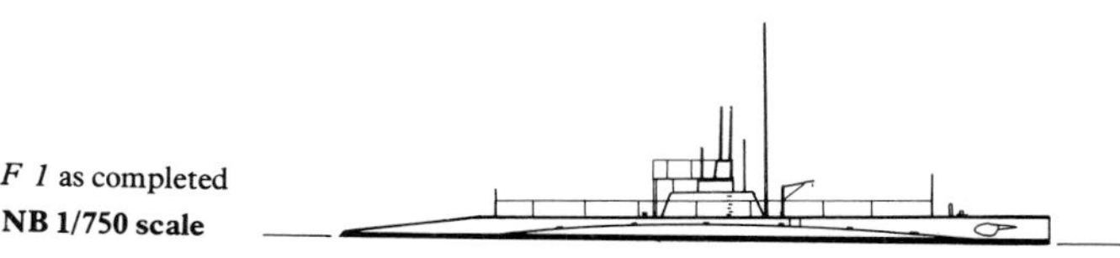
F 1 as completed
NB 1/750 scale

'F' class *submarines*

Displacement: 330t surfaced; 400t submerged
Dimensions: 142ft 9in × 15ft 5in × 12ft 2in
43.5m × 4.7m × 3.7m
Machinery: 2 shafts, diesels plus electric motors, 800bhp (780bhp SS 20–21)/620shp = 13.5kts/11.5kts. Range 2300nm/100nm at 11kts/5kts surfaced/submerged
Armament: 4–18in (457mm) TT (4 torpedoes)
Complement: 22

No	Name	Builder	Launched	Fate
SS 20	CARP (F 1)	Union Iron Wks	6.9.11	Collision 17.12.17
SS 21	BARRACUDA (F 2)	Union Iron Wks	19.3.12	Stricken 1922
SS 22	PICKEREL (F 3)	Moran	6.1.12	Stricken 1922
SS 23	SKATE (F 4)	Moran	6.1.12	Foundered 25.3.15

UNITED STATES OF AMERICA

This design was contemporary with the E class, and used the same type of engine, with the same type of problems. All had to be withdrawn from service in 1915 for re-engining. Designed diving depth 200ft. *Carp* collided on manoeuvres with *Pickerel* during a fog in W Coast waters. *Skate* was salvaged off Pearl Harbor.

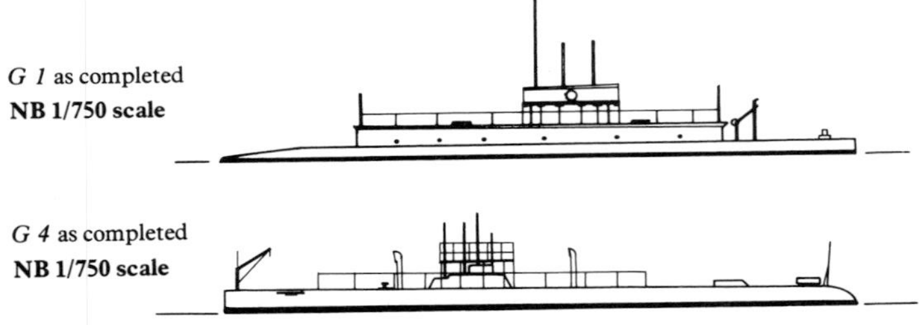
G 1 as completed
NB 1/750 scale

G 4 as completed
NB 1/750 scale

'G' class *submarines*

Displacement:	400t (*Thresher* 360t, *Turbot* 393t) surfaced; 516t submerged (*Thresher* 457t, *Turbot* 460t)
Dimensions:	161ft × 13ft 1in × 12ft 6in *49.1m × 4.0m × 3.8m*
Machinery:	2 shafts, petrol engine, 1200bhp (1000bhp *Thresher*)/520shp (400shp *Thresher*, 600shp *Turbot*) = 14kts/10kts (9.5kts *Thresher* and *Turbot*). Range 2500nm/70nm at 8kts/5kts surfaced/submerged
Armament:	6–18in (457mm) TT (6 torpedoes; 4 TT with 8 in *Tuna*, 10 in *Turbot*)
Complement:	24 (25 *Turbot*)

No	Name	Builder	Launched	Fate
SS 19½	SEAL (G 1)	Newport News	8.2.11	Sunk 21.6.21
SS 26	THRESHER (G 4)	Cramp	15.8.12	Stricken 1920
SS 27	TUNA (G 2)	Lake	10.1.12	Foundered 30.7.19
SS 31	TURBOT (G 3)	Lake	27.12.13	Stricken 1922

This was a group of single designs, out of the mainstream of US submarine development: *G 1*, *G 2* and *G 4* were the last US submarines powered by gasoline engines. All three experienced engine trouble, the Lake craft apparently due to the use of four engines and weak engine foundations, the Cramp boat due to light machinery installation. As a result, the forward engines were removed from *G 1* and *G 2* had to be returned to Lake for further trials.

G 1 was a Lake design, whose contract was awarded parallel to those for *C 2–C 5* and *D 1–D 3*, under the Act of March 1907. She was purchased only after considerable agitation for competition in submarine design, and in fact no submarines were requested at the time she was bought. She was, therefore, essentially a private-venture boat, and she was unique in the US Navy in having a fractional hull number, changed to a whole number only after the ship bearing it had been lost in 1917. The Lake *G 2* was bought the following year (Act of May 1908), with the American Laurenti *G 4*. The Lake *G 3* was bought under the Act of March 1909.

The contract for *G 1* provided that she would be purchased only if she could prove the equal of the best boat then owned by the US government, which, at the time of the agreement, was the *Octopus* (C 1). She was completed in 1912, almost 2½ years overdue; *G 2* was similarly late, apparently due in part to the failure of the original Lake Company, which reorganised in 1915 as the Lake Torpedo Boat Company.

Except for the light construction of the diving plane supports and the stern arrangement, *G 1* was considered satisfactory. She had an unusual feature, a watertight superstructure above the pressure hull. This did not add to sea-keeping abilities, and it was deleted from later Lake-designed craft.

G 4 suffered from both structural and machinery problems, and was almost three years overdue. Her surface range was 1680nm at 8kts and the underwater range was only 40nm at 5kts. Laurenti employed pressure hulls which were not circular in section, and consequently had to use extra framing to brace them; that in turn made his submarines overweight. Their designed diving depth was 200ft. *G 2* was lost in Long Island Sound off New London.

K 8 about 1920 — *USN*

N 1 as completed — *US Naval Institute*

'H' class as completed
NB 1/750 scale

'H' class *submarines*

Displacement:	358t surfaced; 467t submerged
Dimensions:	150ft 3in × 15ft 9in × 12ft 6in *45.8m × 4.8m × 3.8m*
Machinery:	2 shafts, diesel plus electric motor, 950bhp/600shp = 14kts/10.5kts. Range 2300nm/100nm at 11kts/5kts surfaced/submerged
Armament:	4–18in (457mm) TT (8 torpedoes)
Complement:	25

No	Name	Builder	Launched	Fate
SS 28	SEAWOLF (H 1)	Union Iron Wks	6.5.13	Sunk 12.3.20
SS 29	NAUTILUS (H 2)	Union Iron Wks	4.6.13	BU 1931
SS 30	GARFISH (H 3)	Moran	3.7.13	Stricken 1922
SS 147	H 4	Puget Sound N Yd	9.10.18	BU 1931
SS 148	H 5	Puget Sound N Yd	24.9.18	BU 1931
SS 149	H 6	Puget Sound N Yd	26.8.18	BU 1931
SS 150	H 7	Puget Sound N Yd	17.10.18	BU 1931
SS 151	H 8	Puget Sound N Yd	14.11.18	BU 1931
SS 152	H 9	Puget Sound N Yd	23.11.18	BU 1931

This class was considered successful, apart from engine problems; *H 1* and *H 3* failed their first engine endurance runs. *H 4–H 9* were originally ordered by the Czarist Russian government as AG-17-20, 27, and 28, but they were purchased for the US Navy in 1918. This class should not be confused with the Electric Boat-built British and Chilean 'H' class. Designed diving depth 200ft. *H 2* and *H 4–H 9* were stricken in 1930, *H 2* and *H 3* served off the W Coast in 1914–17.

'K' class *submarines*

Displacement:	392t surfaced; 521t submerged
Dimensions:	153ft 7in × 16ft 9in × 13ft 1in *46.9m × 5.1m × 4.0m*
Machinery:	2 shafts, NLSE diesels plus electric motor, 950bhp/680shp = 14kts/10.5kts. Range 4500nm/120nm at 10kts/5kts surfaced/submerged
Armament:	4–18in (457mm) TT (8 torpedoes)
Complement:	28

No	Name	Builder	Launched	Fate
SS 32	HADDOCK (K 1)	Fore River	3.9.13	BU 1931
SS 33	CACHALOT (K 2)	Fore River	4.10.13	BU 1931
SS 34	ORCA (K 3)	Union Iron Wks	14.3.14	BU 1931
SS 35	WALRUS (K 4)	Moran	19.3.14	BU 1931
SS 36	K 5	Fore River	17.3.14	BU 1931
SS 37	K 6	Fore River	26.3.14	BU 1931
SS 38	K 7	Union Iron Wks	20.6.14	BU 1931
SS 39	K 8	Union Iron Wks	11.7.14	BU 1931

As in earlier classes, the diesel engines gave considerable trouble. Three failed to pass their engine tests and, even after overhaul, three of the class failed their final trials. Even so, the class did considerable successful cruising, and the four boats on the West Coast cruised to Hawaii late in 1915. *K 1, 2, 4* and *6* were stationed for anti-U-boat operations in the Azores during World War One. Designed diving depth 200ft.

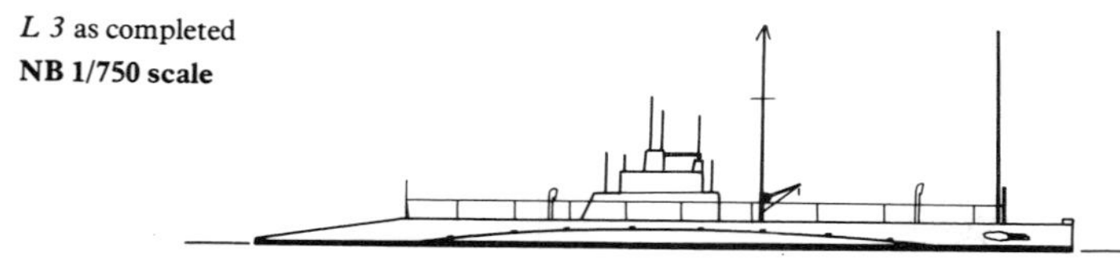
L 3 as completed
NB 1/750 scale

'L' class *submarines*

Displacement: 450t surfaced (*L 5–L 8* 456t); 548t submerged (*L 5–L 8* 524t)
Dimensions: 167ft 4in × 17ft 5in × 13ft 5in
51.0m × 5.3m × 4.1m see notes
Machinery: 2 shafts, BS diesels plus electric motor, 1200bhp/800bhp = 14kts/10.5kts. Range 3300nm/150nm at 11kts/5kts surfaced/submerged
Armament: 4–18in (457mm) TT (8 torpedoes), 1–3in (76mm)/23cal
Complement: 28

No	Name	Builder	Launched	Fate
SS 30	L 1	Fore River	20.1.15	Stricken 1922
SS 41	L 2	Fore River	11.2.15	BU 1932
SS 42	L 3	Fore River	15.3.15	BU 1932
SS 43	L 4	Fore River	3.4.15	Stricken 1922
SS 49	L 9	Fore River	27.10.15	BU 1932
SS 50	L 10	Fore River	16.3.16	Stricken 1930
SS 51	L 11	Fore River	16.5.16	BU 1932
SS 44	L 5	Lake	1.5.16	Sold 1925
SS 45	L 6	Lake	31.8.16	Sold 1925
SS 46	L 7	Lake	28.9.16	Sold 1925
SS 47	L 8	Portsmouth N Yd	23.4.17	Sold 1925

They were the first US submarines with deck guns. Their 3in/23s retracted vertically into a deckhouse until only about half the barrel was extended, to reduce underwater drag.

Of the first four boats, three failed on their surface runs; two failed their submerged battery runs. All required extensive overhauls before they could be accepted. *L 5–L 8* were slightly smaller, measuring 165ft × 14ft 9in × 13ft 1in *(50.3m × 4.5m × 4.0m)*.

During 1917–18, *L 1–L 4* and *L 9–L 11* were stationed at Bantry Bay, Ireland; *L 2* actually attempted to torpedo a U-boat, which reportedly blew up before it could be attacked. In British waters they wore 'AL' numbers on the conning tower to distinguish them from the British 'L' class. Designed diving depth 200ft. *L 7* commissioned at Long Beach, California in December 1917, *L 11* had commissioned in August 1916 with the Atlantic Fleet.

'M' class *submarines*

Displacement: 488t surfaced; 676t submerged
Dimensions: 196ft 3in × 19ft × 11ft 2in
59.8m × 5.8m × 3.4m
Machinery: 2 shafts, NLSE diesels plus electric motors, 840bhp/680shp = 14kts/10.5kts. Range 2750nm at 11kts surfaced, 3hrs endurance submerged
Other particulars: as 'L' class

No	Name	Builder	Launched	Fate
SS 47	M 1	Fore River	14.9.15	Stricken 1922

M 1 was the first US double-hulled submarine. This type of construction was adopted because earlier single-hull types had insufficient reserve buoyancy. *M 1* had the same military characteristics as the 'L' class, but was about 20 per cent larger, with about 27 per cent reserve buoyancy, compared to 11.5 per cent for Lake submarines, and 15.5 in Holland's 'L'. Seaworthiness was satisfactory, but the submarine was too crowded internally; she was considered less habitable than the single-hull types. In addition, when passing from submerged to surfaced condition (or vice versa), she had a considerable negative metacentric height, and tended to take a large list. This problem was solved in the 'T' (AA) class. Designed diving depth 200ft.

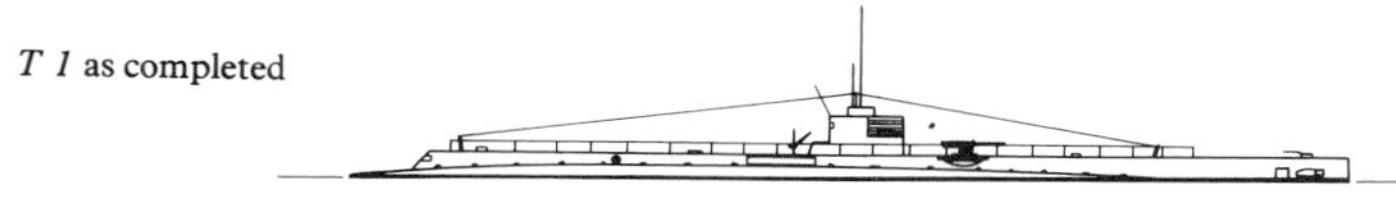
T 1 as completed

'AA' ('T') class *submarines*

Displacement: 1107t surfaced; 1482t submerged
Dimensions: 269ft × 23ft × 14ft 1in
82.0m × 7.0m × 4.3m
Machinery: 2 shafts, NLSE diesels plus electric motors, 4000bhp/1350shp = 20kts/10.5kts. Range 3000nm/100nm at 14kts/5kts surfaced/submerged
Armament: 6–21in (533mm) TT (16 torpedoes), 2–3in (76mm)/23cal
Complement: 38

No	Name	Builder	Launched	Fate
SS 52	SCHLEY (T 1)	Fore River	25.7.18	Also designated *SF 1*; BU 1930
SS 60	AA 2 (T 2)	Fore River	6.9.19	Ex-*SF 2*; BU 1930
SS 61	AA 3 (T 3)	Fore River	24.5.19	Ex-*SF 3*; BU 1930

The first US fleet submarines, they were considered unsuccessful, and were laid up in 1922. They were not fast enough to keep up with the battlefleet, and could dive only to 150ft.

'N' class *submarines*

Displacement: 348t surfaced (*N 4–N 7* 340t); 414t submerged
Dimensions: 147ft 4in × 15ft 9in × 12ft 6in (*N 4—N 7* 155ft × 14ft 5in)
44.9m × 4.8m × 3.8m (47.3m × 4.4m)
Machinery: 2 shafts, NLSE diesels, plus electric motors, 600bhp/300bhp = 13kts/11kts. Range 3500nm/30nm at 5kts submerged
Armament: 4–18in (457mm) TT (8 torpedoes)
Complement: 25 (*N 4–N 7* 29)

No	Name	Builder	Launched	Fate
SS 53	N 1	Seattle	30.12.16	BU 1931
SS 54	N 2	Seattle	16.1.17	BU 1931
SS 55	N 3	Seattle	21.2.17	BU 1931
SS 56	N 4	Lake	27.11.16	Stricken 1922
SS 57	N 5	Lake	22.3.17	Stricken 1922
SS 58	N 6	Lake	21.4.17	Stricken 1922
SS 59	N 7	Lake	19.5.17	Stricken 1922

This class introduced metal bridges into US submarine practice. At the same time, power was actually reduced in the interest of greater engine reliability (to 480 or 600bhp from the previous 800–1200bhp). The success of this step led to a decision to use more moderate power for the 'O', 'R', and 'S' classes, and to the re-engining of many existing submarines. Even so, U-boat type diesels were adopted after World War One. This was the last US class designed without deck guns until 1946. Designed diving depth 200ft. *N 5* was at New York 1918–19.

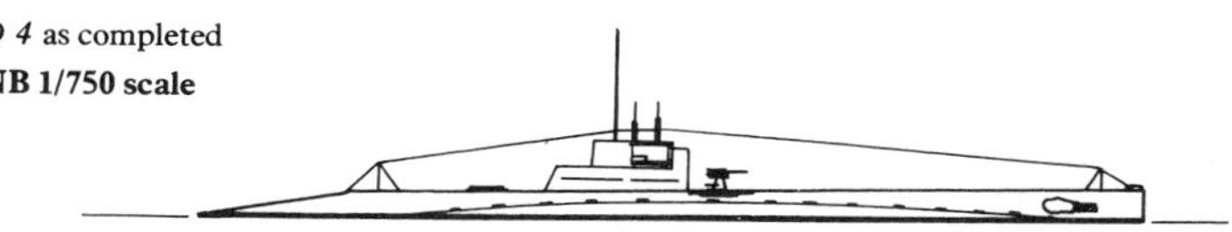
O 4 as completed
NB 1/750 scale

'O' class *submarines*

Displacement: 521t (*O 11–O 16* 491t) surfaced; 629t (*O 11–O 16* 566t) submerged
Dimensions: 172ft 3in × 18ft 1in × 14ft 5in (*O 11—O 16* 175ft 3in × 16ft 9in × 13ft 9in)
52.5m × 5.5m × 4.4m (52.4m × 5.1m × 4.2m)
Machinery: 2 shafts, NLSE (BS in *O 11–O 16*) diesels plus electric motors, 880bhp/740bhp = 14kts/10.5kts. Range 5500nm at 11.5kts
Armament: 4–18in (457mm) TT (8 torpedoes), 1–3in (76mm)/23cal
Complement: 29

No	Name	Builder	Launched	Fate
SS 62	O 1	Portsmouth N Yd	9.7.18	Stricken 1938
SS 63	O 2	Puget Sound N Yd	24.5.18	BU 1945
SS 64	O 3	Fore River	29.9.17	BU 1946
SS 65	O 4	Fore River	20.10.17	BU 1946
SS 66	O 5	Fore River	11.11.17	Sunk 28.10.23
SS 67	O 6	Fore River	25.11.17	BU 1946
SS 68	O 7	Fore River	16.12.17	BU 1946
SS 69	O 8	Fore River	31.12.17	BU 1946
SS 70	O 9	Fore River	27.1.18	Lost 20.6.41
SS 71	O 10	Fore River	21.2.18	BU 1946
SS 72	O 11	Lake	29.10.17	BU 1930
SS 73	O 12	Lake	29.9.17	Sold 1930, BU Norway 1931
SS 74	O 13	Lake	27.12.17	BU 1930
SS 75	O 14	California SB	6.5.18	BU 1930
SS 76	O 15	California SB	12.2.18	BU 1930
SS 77	O 16	California SB	9.2.18	BU 1930

O 7 commissioned in July 1918 and carried out E Coast patrols. Most of the class were used for training from *c*1928. *O 12*, which had been sold out of service, was renamed *Nautilus* and used in 1931 for an attempt to reach the North Pole. Designed diving depth 200ft.

UNITED STATES OF AMERICA

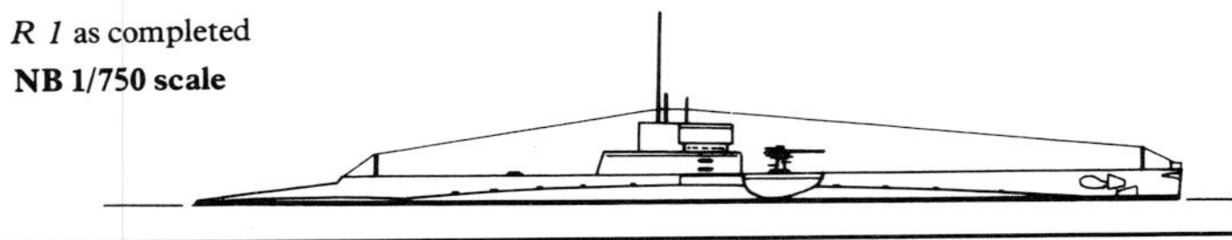
R 1 as completed
NB 1/750 scale

'R' class *submarines*

Displacement: 569t (*R 21–R 27* 510t) surfaced; 680t (*R 21–R 27* 583t) submerged
Dimensions: 186ft 5in × 18ft 1in × 14ft 5in
56.8m × 5.5m × 4.4m
Machinery: 2 shafts, NLSE diesels plus electric motors, 1200bhp/934shp = 13.5kts/10.5kts (1000bhp/800shp = 14kts/11kts in *R 21–R 27*). Range 4700nm at 6.2kts surfaced
Armament: 4–21in (533mm) TT (8 torpedoes, 18in TT in *R 21—R 27*), 1–3in (76mm)/50cal
Complement: 29

No	Name	Builder	Launched	Fate
SS 78	R 1	Fore River	24.8.18	Sold 1946
SS 79	R 2	Fore River	23.9.18	Sold 1945
SS 80	R 3	Fore River	18.1.19	To RN 4.11.41
SS 81	R 4	Fore River	26.10.18	Sold 1946
SS 82	R 5	Fore River	24.11.18	Sold 1946
SS 83	R 6	Fore River	1.3.19	Sold 1946
SS 84	R 7	Fore River	5.4.19	Sold 1946
SS 85	R 8	Fore River	17.4.19	Scuttled 1936
SS 86	R 9	Fore River	24.5.19	Sold 1946
SS 87	R 10	Fore River	28.6.19	Sold 1946
SS 88	R 11	Fore River	12.7.19	Sold 1946
SS 89	R 12	Fore River	15.8.19	Sunk 12.6.43
SS 90	R 13	Fore River	27.8.19	Sold 1946
SS 91	R 14	Fore River	10.10.19	Sold 1946
SS 92	R 15	Union Iron Wks	10.12.17	Str 1946
SS 93	R 16	Union Iron Wks	15.12.17	Sold 1946
SS 94	R 17	Union Iron Wks	24.12.17	To RN 9.3.42
SS 95	R 18	Union Iron Wks	8.1.18	Sold 1946
SS 96	R 19	Union Iron Wks	28.1.18	To RN 9.3.42
SS 97	R 20	Union Iron Wks	21.8.18	Sold 1946
SS 98	R 21	Lake	10.7.18	BU 1930
SS 99	R 22	Lake	23.9.18	BU 1930
SS 100	R 23	Lake	5.11.18	BU 1930
SS 101	R 24	Lake	21.8.18	BU 1930
SS 102	R 25	Lake	15.5.19	BU 1930
SS 103	R 26	Lake	18.6.19	BU 1930
SS 104	R 27	Lake	23.9.18	BU 1930

In this class a non-housing 3in/50 deck gun was adopted, and the hull was lengthened slightly to accommodate 21in torpedoes. Note that the Lake units were scrapped first. Designed dive depth 200ft. *R 19* as HMS *P 514* was rammed and sunk in error by the minesweeper *Georgian*, N Atlantic 21 June 1942. *R 12* was one of only two US submarines lost in the Atlantic during World War Two, being lost on a torpedo practice approach off Key West (Florida) with 42 lives. *R 2* was flagship Sub Div 9 out of San Pedro, California 1921–24. *R 20* was commissioned in October 1918 at San Francisco for two years Pacific service.

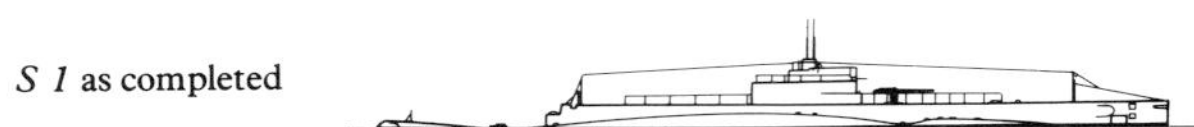
S 1 as completed

'S' class *submarines* (Electric Boat type)

Displacement: 854t surfaced; 1062t submerged
Dimensions: 219ft 5in × 20ft 8in × 15ft 9in
66.9m × 6.3m × 4.8m
Machinery: 2 shafts, BS diesels plus electric motors, 1200bhp/1500shp = 14kts/11kts. Range 3420nm at 6.5kts surfaced
Armament: 4–21in (533mm) TT (12 torpedoes), 1–4in (102mm)/50cal
Complement: 38

No	Name	Builder	Launched	Fate
SS 105	S 1	Fore River	26.10.18	To RN 20.4.42
SS 123	S 18	Fore River	29.4.20	Sold 1946
SS 124	S 19	Fore River	21.6.20	Stricken 1936, scuttled
SS 125	S 20	Fore River	9.6.20	Sold 1946
SS 126	S 21	Fore River	18.8.20	To RN 14.9.42
SS 127	S 22	Fore River	15.7.20	To RN 19.6.42
SS 128	S 23	Fore River	27.10.20	Sold 1946
SS 129	S 24	Fore River	27.6.22	To RN 10.8.42
SS 130	S 25	Fore River	29.5.22	To Poland 11.41
SS 131	S 26	Fore River	22.8.22	Sunk 24.1.42
SS 132	S 27	Fore River	18.10.22	Lost 19.6.42
SS 133	S 28	Fore River	20.9.22	Sunk 4.7.44
SS 134	S 29	Fore River	9.11.22	To RN 5.6.42
SS 135	S 30	Union Iron Wks	21.11.18	Stricken 1946
SS 136	S 31	Union Iron Wks	28.12.18	Stricken 1946
SS 137	S 32	Union Iron Wks	11.1.19	Stricken 1946
SS 138	S 33	Union Iron Wks	5.12.18	Sold 1946
SS 139	S 34	Union Iron Wks	13.2.19	Sold 1946
SS 140	S 35	Union Iron Wks	27.2.19	Target 4.4.42
SS 141	S 36	Union Iron Wks	3.6.19	Sunk 20.1.42
SS 142	S 37	Union Iron Wks	20.6.19	Sunk 20.2.45
SS 143	S 38	Union Iron Wks	17.6.19	Sunk in test, 20.2.45
SS 144	S 39	Union Iron Wks	2.7.19	Sunk 14.8.42
SS 145	S 40	Union Iron Wks	5.1.21	Sold 1946
SS 146	S 41	Union Iron Wks	21.2.21	Sold 1946

Like the flush-deck destroyer, the 'S' class submarine was built in large numbers because it was the design in production when the United States mobilised for World War One. As a result, S (or 'sugar') boats formed the bulk of the submarine force through the 1930s, and fought in substantial numbers in World War Two during which 10 of these obsolete boats sank 14 Japanese warships and merchantmen. Survivors of the earlier 'O' and 'R' classes were relegated to training, although 6 did serve in the British and Polish Navies. Even so, as early as 1925 the 'S' class was officially described as unsatisfactory, partly because it did not have the range necessary for Pacific operations. *S 20* was flagship Sub Div 11 in the Atlantic 1922–23.

S 1, *S 2* and *S 3* were competitive boats, to Electric Boat, Lake, and Bureau designs. *S 2* was considered unsuccessful, and later Lake craft were built to a C & R design. The Electric Boat SS 159–168 and the Lake SS 173–176 were cancelled on 4 December 1918, although Lake actually built SS 159–162; the higher numbers were reassigned to later submarines. Material assembled for the Electric Boat craft was used to build four similar submarines for Peru in 1926–28.

The Bureau-designed 'S' class submarines were double-hulled, and were more crowded in their living spaces than the Electric Boat single-hull types. The sterns of these submarines were similar to those of the Lake type.

As in earlier US submarines, high underwater speed was considered extremely important. As a result, the superstructure and bridge fairwater were carefully steamlined, and appendages above the main deck kept to a minimum (and designed to be stowed when submerged). The first of the Bureau-designed 'S' boats made 12.5kts underwater, compared with 13.3kts for the first Electric Boat unit. However, war experience showed that protection for personnel was more important than even 2–3kts of speed, and a 'chariot-style' bridge, permanent life rails, wood decking, and a non-housing 4in/50 gun were added to most boats before completion. Their speed was, therefore, reduced to 9–10kts underwater.

The Bureau boats were unique among American submarines of their generation in having non-folding bow planes (until about 1923, when they were modified). *S 10* through *S 13* were the first US submarines with stern TT. *S 26* sank in a night collision with *PC 460* in the Gulf of Panama going down in 300ft with all but 2 of her crew. *S 27* grounded on a reef 400 yards off Amchitka in the Aleutians. *S 28* went down in 8400ft with all hands during torpedo exercises off Pearl Harbor. *S 36* grounded on a reef in the Makassar Strait without loss of life. *S 39* grounded on a reef S of Rossel Island (E of New Guinea) on her 5th war patrol and gradually broke up but all her crew were saved. *S 41* served in Chinese waters 1938–41. Designed diving depth 200ft.

'S' class *submarines* (Lake type)

Displacement: 800t surfaced; 977t submerged
Dimensions: 207ft × 19ft 8in × 16ft 1in
63.1m × 6.0m × 4.9m
Machinery: 2 shafts, BS diesels plus electric motors, 1800bhp/1200bhp = 15kts/11kts
Armament: 4–21in (533mm) TT (12 torpedoes), 1–4in (102mm)/50cal
Complement: 38

No	Name	Builder	Launched	Fate
SS 106	S 2	Lake	15.2.19	BU 1931

S 43 in the 1930s — CPL

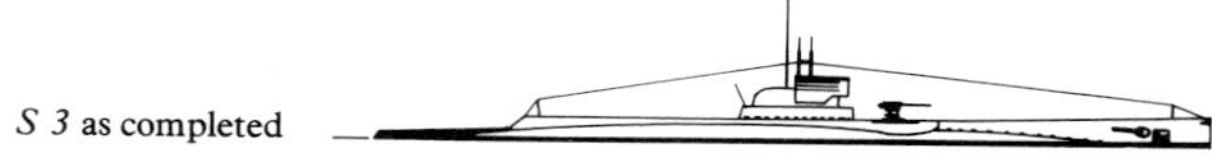
S 3 as completed

'S' class *submarines* (Navy Yard type)

Displacement: 876t surfaced; 1092t submerged (875t and 1088t in *S 3*)
Dimensions: 231ft × 22ft × 13ft 1in
70.4m × 6.7m × 4.0m
Machinery: 2 shafts, NSLE or MAN or BS diesels, 2000bhp (1400bhp in *S 3*/1200shp = 15kts/11kts
Armament: 4–21in (533mm) TT (12 torpedoes), 1–4in (102mm)/50cal
Complement: 38

No	Name	Builder	Launched	Fate
SS 107	S 3	Portsmouth N Yd	21.12.18	BU 1937
SS 109	S 4	Portsmouth N Yd	27.8.19	Sunk 12.7.27
SS 110	S 5	Portsmouth N Yd	10.11.19	Foundered 1.9.20
SS 111	S 6	Portsmouth N Yd	23.12.19	BU 1937
SS 112	S 7	Portsmouth N Yd	5.2.20	BU 1937
SS 113	S 8	Portsmouth N Yd	21.4.20	BU 1937
SS 114	S 9	Portsmouth N Yd	17.6.20	BU 1937
SS 115	S 10	Portsmouth N Yd	9.12.20	BU 1936
SS 116	S 11	Portsmouth N Yd	7.2.21	Sold 1945
SS 117	S 12	Portsmouth N Yd	4.8.21	Sold 1945
SS 118	S 13	Portsmouth N Yd	20.10.21	Sold 1945
SS 119	S 14	Lake	22.10.19	Sold 1945
SS 120	S 15	Lake	8.3.20	Sold 1946
SS 121	S 16	Lake	23.12.19	Target 3.4.45
SS 122	S 17	Lake	22.5.20	Target 5.4.45

S 4 sank off Provincetown, Massachussetts and was raised in spring 1928, finally to be stricken in 1936 and scuttled.

'S' class *submarines* (second group)

Displacement: 906t surfaced; 1126t submerged
Dimensions: 225ft 5in × 20ft 8in × 16ft 1in
68.7m × 6.3m × 4.9m
Machinery: 2 shafts, BS diesels plus electric motors, 1200bhp/1200shp = 14.5kts/11kts. Range 2510nm at 6.5kts surfaced
Armament: 4–21in (533mm) TT (12 torpedoes), 1–4in (102mm)/50cal
Complement: 38

No	Name	Builder	Launched	Fate
SS 153	S 42	Fore River	30.4.23	Sold 1946
SS 154	S 43	Fore River	31.3.23	Sold 1946
SS 155	S 44	Fore River	27.10.23	Sunk 7.10.43
SS 156	S 45	Fore River	26.6.23	Sold 1946
SS 157	S 46	Fore River	11.9.23	Sold 1946
SS 158	S 47	Fore River	5.1.24	Sold 1946

S 44 sank the Japanese heavy cruiser *Kako* on 10 August 1942 off Kavieng after the Battle of Savo Island in the Solomons. She was sunk on her 5th war patrol by gunfire from a Japanese destroyer (mistaken for a merchantman) off Paramushiru in the northern Kuriles, leaving only 2 survivors.

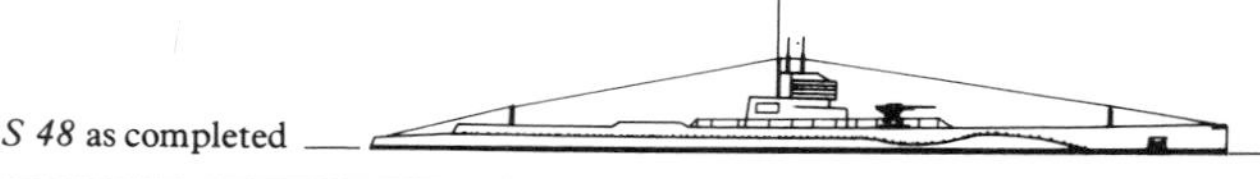
S 48 as completed

'S' class *submarines* (2nd Lake type)

Displacement: 903t surfaced; 1230t submerged
Dimensions: 240ft 2in × 21ft 8in × 13ft 5in
73.2m × 6.6m × 4.1m
Machinery: 2 shafts, BS diesels plus electric motors, 1800bhp/1500shp = 14.5kts/11kts. Range 5900nm at 11kts
Armament: 5–21in (533mm) TT (14 torpedoes), 1–4in (102mm)/50cal
Complement: 38

No	Name	Builder	Launched	Fate
SS 159	S 48	Lake	26.2.21	Sold 1946
SS 160	S 49	Lake	23.4.21	Sold 1931
SS 161	S 50	Lake	18.6.21	BU 1931
SS 162	S 51	Lake	20.8.21	Sunk 25.9.25

S 51 sank in a collision off Black Island (New London, Connecticut) and Summer 1926 salvage attempts failed.

SMALL SURFACE WARSHIPS

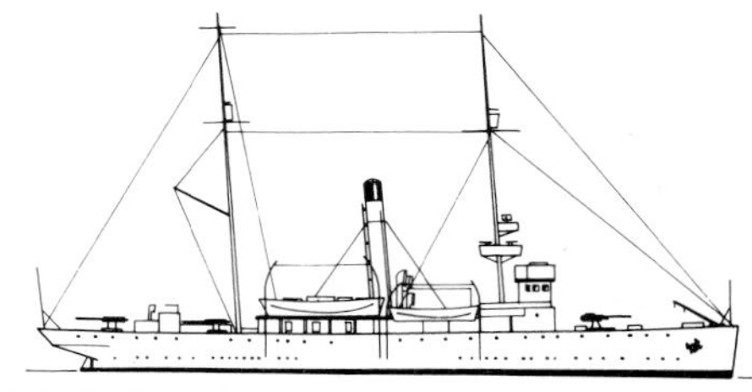
Sacramento as completed

SACRAMENTO *gunboat*

Displacement: 1425t normal; 1592t full load
Dimensions: 210ft wl, 226ft 5in × 41ft × 11ft 6in
64.0m, 69.0m × 12.5m × 3.5m
Machinery: 1-shaft VTE, 2 Babcock & Wilcox boilers, 950ihp = 12.5kts. Coal 428t. Range 4000nm
Armament: 3–4in (102mm)/50cal, 2–3pdr, 2–1pdr
Complement: 163

No	Name	Builder	Launched	Fate
AG 19	SACRAMENTO	Cramp	21.2.14	Sold 1947, merchant ship *Fermina*

This ship was designed as a cheaper alternative to the small cruisers of the *Denver*, *Albany* and *Cincinnati* classes, which in 1914 constituted the US seagoing gunboat force. The General Board observed that the cruisers were comfortable, were good sea boats, were not too fast, and had a fair radius of action, but that they had about twice the complement of a more efficient gunboat, and cost far too much to maintain. In the Asiatic Fleet *c*1923.

MONOCACY class *gunboats*

Displacement: 190t
Machinery: 2-shaft VTE, 2 Babcock & Wilcox boilers, 800shp = 13.25kts. Coal 34t
Armament: 2–6pdr, 6 MG
Complement: 47

No	Name	Builder	Launched	Fate
PG 20	MONOCACY	Mare Island N Yd	27.4.14	Scuttled 1939
PG 16	PALOS	Mare Island N Yd	23.4.14	Sold 1937

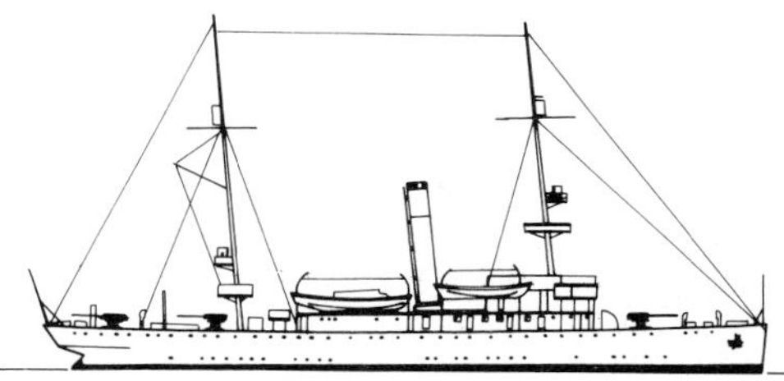
Asheville as completed

ASHEVILLE class *gunboats*

Displacement: 1575t trial; 1760t full load
Dimensions: 225ft wl, 241ft 2in × 41ft 4in × 11ft 2in
68.6m, 73.5m × 12.6m × 3.4m
Machinery: 1-shaft Parsons geared turbine, 3 Thornycroft boilers, 850shp = 12kts. Range 2000nm
Armament: 3–4in (102mm)/50cal
Complement: 159

No	Name	Builder	Launched	Fate
PG 21	ASHEVILLE	Charleston N Yd	4.7.18	Sunk 3.3.42
PG 22	TULSA	Charleston N Yd	25.8.22	*Tacloban* 11.44, sold 10.46

These were the last conventional gunboats built for the US Navy; the later *Erie* and *Charleston* were conceived partly as small cruisers. They were modified *Sacramentos*, the major changes being quarters for about 60 more enlisted men and 4 rather than two boilers. The lines followed those of the earlier ship, but a 15ft section was added amidships. *Asheville* was flagship of the 1923 South China Patrol. Both were in the 1941 Asiatic Fleet, *Asheville* being sunk S of Java with the destroyer *Pillsbury* by Japanese cruisers and destroyers.

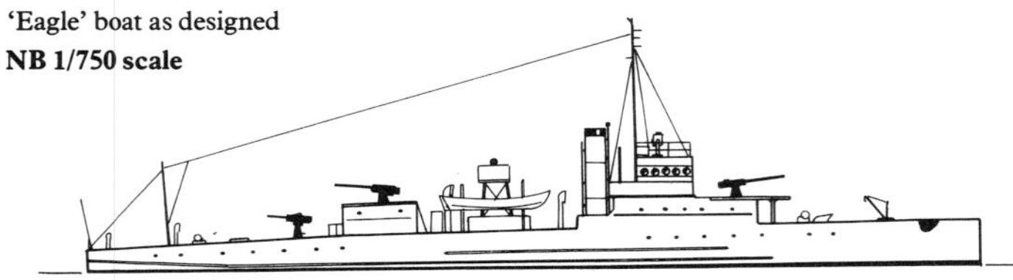

'Eagle' boat as designed
NB 1/750 scale

'EAGLE BOAT' *patrol vessels*

Displacement:	500t normal; 615t full load
Dimensions:	200ft 10in × 33ft 2in × 8ft 6in *61.2m × 10.1m × 2.6m*
Machinery:	1-shaft Poole geared turbine, 2 Bureau Express boilers, 2500shp = 18.3kts. Fuel 105t coal, 45t oil. Range 3500nm at 10kts
Armament:	2–4in (102mm)/50cal, 1–3in (76mm)/50cal, 1 Y-gun
Complement:	61

Class:
PE 1–PE 60

This class was to have comprised *PE 1–PE 112*, 12 of which (including *PE 25, 45, 65, 75, 85, 95, 105* and *112*) were intended for transfer to Italy. However, all but *PE 1–PE 60* were cancelled on 30 November 1918. Eagles *16, 20–22*, and *30* were transferred to the Coast Guard late in 1919. None was actually transferred to Italy. *PE 1* commissioned on 28 October 1918.

These 200ft steel ASW craft were rough US equivalents to the British P-Boat. They were intended for open-water ASW, and as such were effectively substitutes for the more expensive destroyers. Note that a larger austere version of the existing flush-deck destroyer was also proposed in 1917, and came close to production as the DD 181 class.

The destroyers were clearly much more capable, and they had priority; the 200-footer had to be designed for minimum interference with other programmes. So it was built on the Great Lakes or in the Inland Rivers; ultimately the contract was let to Henry Ford, who erected a factory at Highland Park, Detroit, to mass-produce them. As of January 1918 the bureaus hoped that all 100 could be constructed by the end of the year, although in fact most were completed in 1919. The hull was designed specifically for easy assembly, with few curves and a characteristic flat sheer. C & R planned to use diesel engines, but Ford preferred steam turbines; that change was his main contribution to the evolution of the design. The design was also influenced by that of the British P-boat, details of which had been brought from England by Stanley Goodall.

As in other such programmes, the issue was to what extent the destroyer-substitute should approach destroyer performance. The General Board wanted a sustained sea speed of 20kts and a battery of 1–5in and 1–3in gun plus a 6pdr and depth charges. The original bureau proposal of December 1917 envisaged a maximum speed of 18kts, a cruising speed of 10kts, and a battery of 1–3in/50 and 1–3in/50 AA gun. For a time the design also included a twin 21in TT, as in P-boat practice, but a gun replaced it in the final design. In January 1918, the Board reluctantly approved this more austere design, recommending the immediate construction of 100 boats. It went on record that 'as in the case of the 110ft chaser it regards the 200ft boat . . . as an emergency design and not one which should be adopted if time and the submarine situation were not of such seriousness.'

In July 1918 the bureaus suggested a 250ft, 650t patrol boat capable of 25kts, and armed with 2–4in, 1–3in AA, a twin 21in, and a Y-gun. The General Board wanted 5in guns instead, to meet the 5.9in guns of new U-boats; it was willing to sacrifice the TT. It was also willing to accept a reduction to 22kts, since the 25kt of the bureau design exceeded its previous demands. Moreover, 22kts seemed attainable by pairing the turbine plant already in production for the Eagle Boat. However, the Board wanted the radius of action increased from the 3500nm/10kts of the Eagle Boat to 4000nm/10kts. Ultimately the Board backed away from any new programme, for fear that it would delay Eagle production. One of the new boats might be built as an experimental prototype, but nothing more. Secretary Daniels quashed the programme.

Postwar, the Eagle Boats were largely employed in reserve training; some were used for underwater sound experiments. As they wore out, a new austere patrol craft was designed for the reserves; it became the 173ft PC of World War Two.

SC type as designed
NB 1/750 scale

SC (110ft) *submarine-chasers*

Displacement:	77t normal; 85t full load
Dimensions:	110ft oa, 105ft pp × 14ft 9in × 5ft 7in *33.5m × 4.5m × 1.7m*
Machinery:	3 shafts, standard petrol engines, 660bhp = 18kts. Fuel 2400 gals. Range 1000nm at 12kts
Armament:	1–3in (76mm)/23cal, 2 Colt MG, 1 Y-gun
Complement:	27

Class:
SC 1–SC 448

SC 5, 7–16, 28–33, 65–67, 75–76, 140–142, 146, 160–163, 169–176, 243, 249, 313–319, 347–348, 350, and *357–406* were transferred to France upon completion from July 1917 and saw no US service. *SC 408, 409, 411, 417–423, 435, 436*, and *438* were delivered but not commissioned. *SC 413* and *414* were transferred to the War Department (Army) upon completion in 1919. *SC 139, 410, 442*, and *445–448* were cancelled. *SC 22, 68, 153, 155, 183, 197, 199, 268, 333–335, 417, 431, 435* and *438* were transferred to the Coast Guard in 1919–1920. In addition, *SC 233, 234, 267, 275, 276, 279–281*, and *307* were transferred to the War Department in 1919, after Navy service. *SC 274, 302, 311*, and *312* were transferred to Cuba in November 1918. There were 6 war losses: *SC 60, 117, 132, 187, 209* and *219*. They carried K-tube fish hydrophones of 30nm acoustic radius or SC and MB hydrophone tubes in the hull with a 3nm radius.

This wooden boat was developed in 1917 for emergency production. The Elco Company already had built large numbers of 80ft motor launches for the Royal Navy, but the General Board considered them too small for sufficient seakeeping. Wood was used for speed of construction; it was hoped that the entire US order of 345 craft could be ready by 1 January 1918. France was assigned 50 more, and then another 50 to bring the programme up to 448 units. Although they were not delivered on time, the sub-chaser programme was considered one of the triumphs of US World War One mobilisation.

At first it appeared that powerplants would be a bottleneck, and the Navy considered both requisitioning private motor boats and buying the Elco 80-footers. However, three standard heavy-duty gasoline engines (220bhp each) were substituted for the proposed pair of 300bhp units, and the emergency

SC 218 as completed *CPL*

procurement plans were abandoned.

A prominent small-craft designer, Loring Swasey, was retained to design them; he was also responsible for the World War Two SC. The design was approved late in March 1917; by May, the General Board was complaining that so small a boat could not suffice to deal with submarines in the open ocean, and that a much larger steel-hulled type was needed. The latter became the Eagle Boat.

SHAWMUT class *minelayers*

Displacement:	3800t
Dimensions:	395ft oa × 52ft 3in × 16ft *120.4m × 15.9m × 4.9m*
Machinery:	2-shaft VTR, 8 SE boilers, 7000shp = 20kts. Fuel 400t coal, 160t oil
Armament:	1–5in (127mm), 2–3in (76mm) AA, 2 MG
Complement:	314

No	Name	Builder	Launched	Fate
	SHAWMUT (ex-*Bunker Hill*)	Cramp	1907	
	AROOSTOOK (ex-*Massachusetts*)	Cramp	1907	

These two Eastern Steamship Co liners were bought in 1917 for conversion to minelayers. Together with the cruisers *San Francisco* and *Baltimore* as well as the former liners *Canandaigua, Canonicus, Housatonic, Quinnebaug* and *Roanoke* they laid the Northern Mine Barrage from Scotland to Norway in 1918. *Shawmut* was flagship Atlantic Fleet's Mine Squadron One 1921–22. They later served as flying boat tenders for Cross-Atlantic Flights and *Aroostock* became a Pacific aviation tender 1920 to at least 1923.

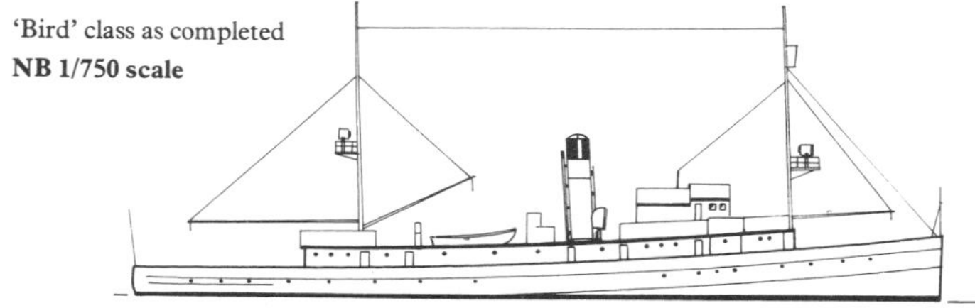

'Bird' class as completed
NB 1/750 scale

'BIRD' class *minesweepers*

Displacement:	950t normal; 1400t full load
Dimensions:	189ft × 35ft 5in × 12ft 6in *57.6m × 10.8m × 3.8m*
Machinery:	1-shaft VTE, 2 Babcock & Wilcox boilers, 1400ihp = 13.5kts. Range 6850nm at 8kts
Armament:	2–3in (76mm)/50cal, 2 MG
Complement:	85

Class:
Todd SB – *Lapwing, Owl, Robin, Swallow, Sanderling, Auk, Chewink, Cormorant, Gannet*
Staten Is SB – *Tanager, Cardinal, Oriole, Curlew, Grebe, Mallard, Ortolan, Peacock*
Gas Engine & Power Co – *Pelican, Falcon, Osprey, Seagull, Tern*
Chester SB – *Turkey, Woodcock, Quail, Partridge*
Philadelphia N Yd – *Sandpiper, Warbler, Vireo, Willet*
Alabama SB & DD Co – *Swan, Whippoorwill, Bittern*
Puget Sound N Yd – *Kingfisher, Rail*
Pusey & Jones – *Eider, Thrush*
Standard SB – *Finch, Heron*
New Jersey DD & T Co – *Flamingo, Penguin*
Builder unknown – *Pigeon*

These 51 ships were designed as dual-purpose minesweeper/fleet tugs, under characteristics approved late in 1916. The following April, with shipyard facilities badly stretched, C & R proposed a dual-purpose design, noting that the only difference between a fleet minesweeper and a tug was that the former was to have a speed of 16kts (to sweep at 10) and a draft of no more than 12ft, whereas the latter was to have a speed of 15kts and a draft of no more than 15ft. Hence a joint design seemed desirable. The Secretary of the Navy approved a 14kt, 950t design in May 1917, and ordered 14 ships built. They were considered very important, and their construction had precedence over that of destroyers. None was built as a tug; the parallel programme of 25 fleet tugs (AT 21–45, of which 40–45 were cancelled), was to a slightly smaller design.

A total of 54 minesweepers was ultimately ordered, and they were designed with an alternative capability to lay mines as well as sweep them. Most were completed in time to help clear the North Sea Barrage, some being damaged by mines. Nine ships were still unfinished on 1 July 1919. Postwar, many were employed as small seaplane tenders (AVP 1–9, ex-AM 1, 10, 18, 19, 23, 27, 34, 41, 51, respectively), and as submarine rescue vessels (ASR 2–6, ex AM 28, 29, 44, 45, 47, respectively). AM 29, 32, and 38 were transferred to the Coast and Geodetic Survey in 1922–23, and AM 48 to the Coast Guard in 1924. AM 53 and 54 were transferred to the Shipping Board in 1920 as salvage tugs. Cancellations: AM 11, 12, 42, 49, 50. In addition, AM 55, 56, and 57, which had been authorised, were not ordered.

US COAST GUARD

This separate force operated a total of 22 cruising cutters, 15 harbour cutters and 11 launches by 1919. During the war most of the big cutters had one or more 3in guns, 2–6pdr and 2 MG. Six had Y-guns fitted for ASW duty. Three were war losses: *McCulloch* (1898, 1280t) by an October 1917 collision in the Pacific; *Tampa* (1912, 1181t) torpedoed and sunk by a U-boat while escorting a convoy in the English Channel, 26 September 1918, *Mohawk* (1902, 980t) was lost in a collision off New York on 1 October 1917.

Shawmut January 1920 *US Naval Institute*

Germany

The Imperial German Navy of the year 1906 was without question the creation of Admiral Alfred von Tirpitz. He became Secretary of State of the *Reichsmarineamt*, the leading administrative office of the Imperial German Navy, on 15 June 1897, and very quickly developed his plans for the future German Navy, getting them approved by the *Reichstag* in two Naval Laws (First German Naval law, 28 March 1898; Second German Naval Law, 12 June 1900). As a philosophical justification for the build-up of a powerful German Fleet he had developed his famous 'Risk Theory', which could be summarised as: 'The German Fleet must be built in such way that her ultimate war aim in a defensive war in the North Sea is a naval battle – what we strive for, is to be as strong, that even for the mighty supremacy of the British Fleet a confrontation might be a certain hazard.' Although innocuously labelled a defensive doctrine, von Tirpitz knew very well that Great Britain must become suspicious sooner or later when the German naval arms race began to threaten Britain's 'Two-Power Standard'. Therefore Captain Carl von Coerper, a man with profound diplomatic and technical knowledge, was established as Naval Attaché in London to report in painstaking detail about Fisher's reforms and the British reactions and countermeasures to Germany's fleet programme. Nevertheless in this first period the question of Germany building up a powerful fleet was more an internal political and financial problem, Britain feeling more piqued than threatened.

THE FIRST NAVAL AMENDMENT OF 1906

To the initiated there was no question that in 1906 a new legislative measure had to be taken which might well result in a Third Naval Law. The *Reichsmarineamt* envisaged 6 additional battleships – a third double squadron – under the plea of asking for the 6 armoured colonial cruisers, which had been postponed in the 1900 Naval Law, concealing the real nature of this request by saying that the international trend was to station more and more powerful ships overseas. However Britain launched the revolutionary *Dreadnought* and to match this ship construction costs would increase so dramatically that there would be definitely no *Reichstag* approval for further battleship squadrons; so von Tirpitz decided to turn back to the original 6 armoured cruisers – in case of war he thought, they could act as an armoured scout squadron. This resulted in the First Amendment of the 1900 Naval Law which asked for 5 armoured cruisers plus one as material reserve, 48 torpedo-boats (*eg* four fiscal year flotillas) and some million Marks for the development of submarines. This Amendment was approved on 19 May 1906 and brought additional ships (as mentioned above) to the regular budget. A more important decision was taken on 26 May when the *Reichstag* approved the regular naval budget including two 18,000-ton battleships and one 15,000-ton armoured cruiser, plus funds to widen the Kaiser Wilhelm Canal, for building larger docks and for enlarging the locks of the main German naval base at Wilhelmshaven. So after long discussions von Tirpitz decided to take up the British challenge of the *Dreadnought* and *Invincible*, which might enable Germany to break Britain's 'Two-Power Standard', because both nations now had to start from scratch, all other battleships becoming obsolete and outclassed over night. The British development of the battlecruiser type was especially convenient, giving von Tirpitz the chance to replace the desired battleships by battlecruisers, which in Germany were still labelled 'armoured cruisers' – at this stage the Imperial German Navy had to take a qualitative step forward rather than a quantitative one.

The opportunity for a British initiative towards halting the incipient arms race occurred in the same year, when Czarist Russia proposed a reassembly of the 1899 Hague Peace Conference to discuss ways of finding peaceful solutions to international disputes. But Germany was convinced that Britain was acting cynically in her own interest and the Conference broke up without any serious discussion of disarmament.

In 1907 the Anglo-French Entente became the Triple Entente on the conclusion of a pact between Great Britain and Czarist Russia, but

the strong diplomatic ring of Britain, France and Russia had a serious effect on the Anglo-German naval arms race: the feeling of encirclement stirred deep fears in the German mind. Von Tirpitz now had one clear objective 'The aim which I had to keep in view . . . for technical and organising reasons as well as reasons of political finance was to build as steadily as possible.' As the tensions increased, Germany became isolated and defensive as she was faced with increasing encirclement brought about as a direct result of the 'Riskflotte'. From this general situation a distinct internal political pressure led to the next Naval Amendment. Also in 1907 the martial-sounding term 'German High Seas Fleet' was introduced instead of the neutral administrative term 'active fleet'.

THE SECOND NAVAL AMENDMENT OF 1908

Favoured by a political situation in which the conservative, liberal and nationalist factions of the *Reichstag* urgently asked for a new Naval Law, von Tirpitz submitted the Second Amendment of the 1900 Naval Law, which asked for a reduction of the 'real lifetime' of the battleships from 25 to 20 years, plus a budget increase of one billion Marks to match the rising building costs and the crash programme of submarine construction. The Second Naval Amendment was approved on 27 March 1908 and had a profound effect on British naval circles.

It was both a military and political *coup*, since the simple reduction of the 'real lifetime' of the battleships meant in consequence that the 8 coast defence battleships of the *Siegfried* class, the obsolete *Oldenburg* class and the 4 units of the *Brandenburg* class had to be replaced quickly. Now von Tirpitz got the required battleship squadrons he had postponed two years earlier, together with the already approved building of 6 armoured cruisers under the 1906 Amendment. In real terms this meant that Germany had switched from building three-ship groups each fiscal year to four-ship groups. However, from 1912 to 1917 this would fall to two ships per year, so the logical step was a further Amendment to the Naval Law.

German industry under the stimulus of the 1908 Second Naval Amendment was developing an impressive capacity for warship construction. Von Tirpitz's policy had been highly successful in bringing into being a large number of commercial shipyards, which now built two-thirds of the new fleet. From the foreign affairs point of view, von Tirpitz's naval policy became more and more autonomous, thus coming into sharp conflict with the political authorities – especially the Imperial Chancellor. Although the *Reichsmarineamt* was *de jure* subordinated to the Chancellor, *de facto* von Tirpitz exceeded the role of a simple adviser of the Chancellor and soon became the decisive force steering the course of foreign policy and Anglo-German relations. It is not surprising that in 1911 the rumour spread that he would become the successor to Bethmann-Hollweg.

To return to the new Amendment: its passage was not as simple as one might guess when considering public opinion and the Emperor's blustering speeches about the German right to outbuild the Royal Navy. When in July 1910 leading German naval officers noted that their nation might soon reach the limits imposed by finances and shipyard capacity, von Tirpitz feared that his whole plan could collapse and that Britain's lead in battleship construction could never be matched if Germany relinquished 6 battleships by falling back to 2 per year in the 1912–17 period. The second Moroccan crisis in 1911 turned out to be the last external assistance for his objectives, but the *Reichsmarineamt* still stood alone in its wish to use the menace of a possible war as an excuse for further naval armament.

The 'Riskflotte' – the pre-war German Fleet at Kiel
CPL

THE THIRD NAVAL AMENDMENT OF 1912

In the preliminary discussions on the Third Naval Amendment apparently the 'doves' got their way and 3 armoured cruisers were deleted from the *Reichsmarineamt's* proposals. The version finally approved on 21 May 1912 was a compromise, providing for 3 additional battleships and 2 additional light cruisers. This meant that at any one time the Imperial German Navy was to have three battle squadrons (instead of two) in commission plus one battlecruiser squadron. Thus the problem of building only 2 capital ships per year could be avoided, and the legal right to build 3 per year could be upheld. So von Tirpitz's aim to build 3 capital ships a year had been finally accepted; this was presented to the German Emperor as means of establishing a permanent 3:2 ratio with Britain.

As approved by the Third Naval Amendment the strength of the Imperial German Navy was to be:

Active fleet:	1 fleet flagship
	3 squadrons of 8 battleships each
	8 battlecruisers
	18 light cruisers
Reserve:	2 squadrons of 8 battleships each
	2 armoured cruisers
	12 light cruisers
Overseas:	8 armoured cruisers
	10 light cruisers
Flotillas:	3 flotilla leaders
	108 torpedo-boats
	54 submarines
Material reserve:	36 torpedo-boats
	18 submarines
	1 flotilla leader

Thus the Imperial German Navy of 1912 had been allowed to build up a powerful naval force that made impossible all attempts from both sides to get to an Anglo-German naval agreement.

THE FINAL CLASH BECOMES INEVITABLE

After the Third Naval Amendment an Anglo-German naval rapprochement was virtually impossible, as had been shown by talks during the second Moroccan crisis and during the Haldane mission. Richard Haldane, British War Minister, had been at Berlin in 1912 for arms reduction talks with high ranking German officers, the Imperial Chancellor Bethmann-Hollweg and even the Emperor himself, but the negotiations led nowhere. Haldane brought back the final draft for the Third Naval Amendment from Berlin: the final clash had become inevitable, the outbreak of war needing only a suitable incident to trigger it. Ironically, the Imperial German Navy had noted that British naval doctrine of 1911 postulated a distant blockade instead of a decisive open battle in Mahan's sense, so that the expensive build-up of a huge battlefleet might show no war-winning advantage; but by this time it had become impossible to stop the inner dynamics of the naval arms race.

PROBLEMS OF POLITICAL LEADERSHIP

Apart from the problems imposed by the encirclement of the German Empire by the Triple Entente, the Imperial German Navy suffered from destructive internal rivalries which were a product of von Tirpitz's struggle for absolute authority in 'his' navy. To understand this we have to go back to 1899 when Alfred von Tirpitz became Secretary of State of the *Reichsmarineamt*. Due to von Tirpitz's persuasion, the

Emperor dissolved the German Naval Supreme Command and reorganised it into several 'departments', and thus three major internal 'pressure groups' were formed. First among these was the German Admiralty which now was reduced to an advisory role. Although they no longer controlled ship design policy, as early as 1907 their study of von Tirpitz's shipbuilding programme forecast a stand-off between the main fleets and emphasised torpedo craft; thus was brought to the fore the battleship-or-submarine question which was never resolved and on which the German war-effort was to founder.

The Fleet Command,with a *Grossadmiral* at its head from 1903 onwards, held more sway and concerned itself more with front-line tactics rather than general policy. In this connection it ran into strong opposition with the *Reichsmarineamt* (third of the 'pressure groups'). The *Reichsmarineamt*, a government authority equal to an Imperial Ministry, was directly responsible to the Imperial Chancellor but took orders from the Emperor. Headed by von Tirpitz, all necessary administrative, technical and training requirements came under its aegis. Less important 'pressure groups' were also to be found in the Naval Cabinet, the cruiser squadron, the home naval bases and the overseas commands.

Although tolerable during peacetime, these departments greatly taxed the judgement and decision-making capacity of the Emperor and during wartime would be counter-productive, proposing as they did diametrically opposed solutions and opinions.

German torpedo-boat crews 1917
CPL

THE BALANCE OF POWER 1914

At the beginning of the First World War Germany had 17 capital ships to Britain's 27; however, this became 19:34 after three months and 21:39 after six months. In the anticipated theatre of operations, the North Sea, the actual balance was 16:24, the average balance for the smaller ships being 3:2 in Britain's favour (with the exception of a parity in older torpedo-boats and a clear German superiority in ocean-going submarines). The strategic situation led to Britain's doctrine of 1911 to trap the High Seas Fleet in the North Sea 'wet triangle' by means of a distant blockade and Germany gaining superiority in the Baltic, where she kept the powerful Czarist Fleet around Petrograd (now Leningrad) at bay.

Although German overseas vessels immediately began commerce warfare (based on a network of coal supplies previously established), they were eventually hunted down and German commerce raiding in its first form vanished from the seas. It was then understood that successful raiding could not be carried out by cruisers and liners, as had been envisaged by pre-war theories, and the second wave consisted of less distinctive vessels.

THE DECISIVE BATTLE FAILS TO APPEAR

Germany had a clear conviction that the land-war on the continent could be won quickly and that Britain would have to accept a final decisive naval battle somewhere between Heligoland and the Thames estuary. Although the rapid decline into a bloody and static land war rendered this naval perspective irrelevant, the German authorities held to it stubbornly. The result on the one hand was increasing pressure on the German C-in-C to lure the Royal Navy into such a battle, and on the other restrictions imposed by Imperial orders, because Wilhelm II did not want to risk the High Seas Fleet preferring to keep it intact as a political pawn for future peace negotiations. German capital ship operations therefore show a steady development of such actions as the shelling of East Coast ports and the Battle of the Dogger Bank.

1915: CRISIS IN THE GERMAN FLEET COMMAND

The Battle of the Dogger Bank had shown up inefficiencies in the German Fleet Command, which was subsequently given a new commander. The Admiralty also was weak: during this year it was lead by a succession of three admirals, von Pohl, Bachmann and von Holtzendorff. Von Tirpitz's role was reduced at the outbreak of the war to an adviser to the Emperor on naval questions, and as his High Seas Fleet failed – having been created by him in the face of heavy opposition – his influence declined further.

One lesson of these first two years of war was that the command structure adopted for the peacetime operation of the High Seas Fleet proved totally ineffective in wartime. The Emperor as supreme commander of the Navy was unable to direct his Fleet in a complex naval war. Furthermore, the powerless Admiralty began once more to issue orders and was responsible for directing the U-boat war. However, by 1915 a clear decision to concentrate on the U-boat war had not been taken and under the energetic command of the new C-in-C Fleet, Admiral Scheer, the High Seas Fleet engaged in new actions which finally culminated in the Battle of Jutland.

Every aspect of this, the largest indecisive sea battle in naval history, is already fully documented and cannot be covered in this brief survey. From the technical point of view both sides claim victory even up to the present day – a senseless dispute since the battle's result for the overall situation was virtually nil. What can be said in one sentence is that Mahan's doctrines – on which the naval armaments race of both sides was essentially based – was simply irrelevant to the present naval war.

DECLINE OF THE HIGH SEAS FLEET

With Germany still eager to fight a final battle, Scheer put his original Jutland plan into operation only four months after Jutland, forming reconnaissance lines with Zeppelins and submarines. Warned by intercepted signals (cipher security as well as excessive radio traffic were major lapses in the Imperial Navy), Jellicoe was at sea in overwhelming strength even before the High Seas Fleet had left the Jade. But by chance Scheer turned away a short time before a possible conflict, and a second Jutland was narrowly avoided.

When German U-boats began the commerce war on 6 October 1916 the role of the High Seas Fleet was reduced from being an aggressive contender for domination in the North Sea to a supporting force of the U-boat campaign. The Fleet's morale, which had been so high after Jutland, now began to collapse disastrously. Tensions between officers and crews arose from badly organised catering – the officers enjoying far better food and separate cooking – and was further expanded into the political sphere by radical socialist and communist agitation. The authorities, fearful of the spread of revolution from Russia, suppressed the resulting mutiny.

It was not until April 1918 that the High Seas Fleet embarked on another sortie north to the Norwegian coast to attack northern convoy routes, which ended without success. But when the crews learned that their admirals planned a last sortie in October 1918 to meet Beatty in a huge final fight to the finish in the southern part of the North Sea, open mutiny broke out on the battleships and Hipper could make no other decision than to call off the operation – called the 'death-ride of the admirals' by the mutineers. The mutiny at Kiel and Wilhelmshaven was a trigger which sparked off the destruction of the German Empire's internal unity; unrest and revolution spread until Germany was on the verge of civil dissension and chaos.

THE SUBMARINE WAR: POLITICAL VERSUS MILITARY NEEDS

To understand the great struggle between the Imperial German Chancellor, Bethmann-Hollweg, and the German Admiralty over whether to use submarines for commerce warfare or not, one must bear in mind that all German discussion was dominated by two political dogmas: first the 'Clausewitz dogma' which decreed that 'Politics has to have primacy over war'; and second, the 'Bismarck dogma' the essence of which was: 'The duty of the military command is the destruction of enemy forces; the aim of the war is to gain by fighting a peace the terms of which correspond with the policy of the state.' During World War One the above mentioned question led to a fierce political discussion that caused even Tirpitz to resign from his job.

German pre-war theory on submarine strategy was very clear: the U-boats should serve as a forward patrolling screen and an integrated part of the High Seas Fleet, while a small part of the submarine arm should carry out offensive operations against hostile warships. As far as the tactics of submarines against merchant shipping were concerned there existed only the rules of the Prize Law (dating back to pre-submarine times) and the Declaration of London of 1909 defining the categories of contraband and the question of neutral shipping.

After the outbreak of the war British authorities decided to reject the London Declaration and to pressurise the German Empire by economic measures declaring a distant blockade by 'Orders in Council'. Germany was virtually cut off from all overseas shipping, including non-contraband and neutral shipping (*eg* raw materials, fertilisers etc) as defined in the terms of the London Declaration.

The possibility of Germany declaring a counter-blockade of the British Isles using U-boats turned out to be a delicate and complex problem under International Law. According to this, a declared blockade had to be consistently enforced. The U-boats had to stop and search a suspicious ship and take care to save the crew if the ship had to be sunk. Unquestionably this kind of warfare conflicted with the very nature of a vulnerable, overcrowded submarine. The essential, but unknown factor was the future behaviour of the neutral nations, especially the United States. Should a total blockade be attempted neutral ships could be treated as blockade-runners. But to declare all the seas surrounding Britain as a blockade zone would be impractical since Germany did not possess enough operational ocean-going submarines.

The standpoint of the German Admiralty was to attack merchant shipping in this blockade zone, although it was never clearly stated that the only way to do so would be to torpedo every vessel encountered there. Tirpitz had a political rather than a military solution resulting in a compromise suggestion: the Thames estuary should be totally blockaded – a practicable proposition – and then Germany would await developments. Germany would have time to gain experience and the neutrals would also have to learn their lesson, or avoid this zone. When Tirpitz gave an interview on this topic to an American journalist, the U-boat war without having even been declared, speedily became an international topic.

The Chancellor agreed that the war had to be brought to an end by military efforts, but declaration of any form of U-boat war might influence neutral nations to join the Allies – at worst the USA, Italy and Rumania would be swayed. This was of course undesirable. The military situation on the continent had to be stabilised in favour of Germany and Austria-Hungary so that no neutral nation – the USA was always regarded as the most prominent one – would risk joining the Allies. For Bethmann-Hollweg it was not a question of whether to start a U-boat war or not, but when to start it.

The German Army tended to the political point of view believing that the war could be won on land, while the Emperor Wilhelm II stood between the four pressure groups and was unable to make a clear decision. Negotiations on this theme continued until January 1915 – under increasing public pressure caused by the food shortages of the first war winter. The Admiralty insisted on starting the U-boat war just as Britain was expecting to receive vital supplies of Argentine food and wheat. When the head of the German Admiralty, von Pohl, became the new C-in-C of the High Seas Fleet, he made a last effort to convince the government, before leaving his old post. Although he had only 13 ocean-going diesel U-boats ready he was convinced that neutral shipping would baulk at entering a declared war zone, thus making for a small-scale U-boat conflict. Bowing to the Admiralty's insistence and public pressure, it was decided to start a U-boat war by declaring a war zone on 1 February 1915.

It must be pointed out that von Tirpitz did not take part in these final negotiations. As mentioned earlier he believed that it was too soon to move and that the Admiralty was going about it in the wrong way by declaring a 'phoney' war zone, which no neutral ship would take seriously: and he was right. The incredible fact that Germany's most prominent naval authority had no influence on this vital decision was a result of the inner rivalries of the Imperial German Navy, which had been split up into several departments by the Emperor to gain power over his navy. In fact Tirpitz's role at this time was reduced to responsibility for naval supply and representing the Navy before Parliament. In his memoirs he states that it was a mistake not to try to convince the Emperor to reverse his decision, because at this time he (Tirpitz) thought that it was better to make a wrong decision than not to make one at all.

As regards the execution of the U-boat war, the situation became ridiculous as von Pohl, previously the most insistent advocate of this kind of war, was informed when he became C-in-C that only three submarines had been sent to patrol off Britain. The German U-boat war had been announced with great publicity to achieve maximum political reaction, and was now based on three boats!

The U-boat war still continued to be a political battle rather than a real one, as the USA submitted a sharp protest note, claiming that each attack on American lives or trade would be seen as an inexcusable breach of neutrality. Under the shadow of this diplomatic threat the Chancellor prevailed upon the Emperor to forbid action against ships under neutral flags. The U-boat war was postponed once more as British ships could easily fly neutral flags. With submarine commanders having no clear orders, and the politicians and military strategists having no clear definition of what they wanted to do – apart from a desire to keep America out of the war – a disaster was almost inevitable. Thus the sinking of the *Lusitania* by *U 20* and the *Arabic* by *U 24* (both carrying US citizens) imposed heavy strains on the conduct of the U-boat war.

In the following clash between the admirals – now headed by Tirpitz – and Bethmann-Hollweg, the Emperor decided in favour of the Chancellor's strategy, which was also backed by the German Army Commander General von Falkenhayn. As a result Tirpitz and the head of the Admiralty backed down. The restriction order of 9 September 1915 stated that attacks were permissible only on undoubtedly British ships, neutral ships were to be treated under the rules of Prize Law and no attacks on passenger liners were permissible at all. With the U-boat war now becoming senseless the new head of the Admiralty, von Holtzendorff, put a stop to it by a secret order of 18 September 1915: the overall war situation demanded that there could be no possibility of orders being misinterpreted. Therefore all boats acting in the Channel and off the British West Coast were recalled; only in the North Sea would the U-boat war be continued, but strictly under the rules of Prize Laws. The U-boat war, which had started with propaganda announcements faded out quietly.

But the political struggle continued. The Fleet command submitted a memo stating that the 'unrestricted U-boat war' was the only way to proceed, while Bethmann-Hollweg was still negotiating with the USA as to which kind of U-boat war they would accept without themselves entering into the war. At the end of 1916 the German Army Commander, von Falkenhayn, entered the discussions now backing an unrestricted U-boat war because the land war could not be won unless England was defeated by having all supplies to her cut off.

This led to the 'intensified U-boat war' the basis of which was that armed merchant ships could be sunk without warning, neutral ships had to be treated as friendly and attacks on passenger liners were strictly forbidden – even when they were armed. For Tirpitz this was a half-hearted compromise and he opted for the 'unrestricted U-boat war', believing now that it was the only way to carry out an offensive war with the aim of blockading Great Britain. The Chancellor, in contrast, still believed that it was possible to reach peace or armistice negotiations with Great Britain without a military victory and voted for a 'restrained U-boat war'. The Emperor could still not decide which course to take and postponed his decision from month to month. In all these meetings Wilhelm II was extremely inconsistent and always inclined to the opinion of the person who was last to report to him.

In March 1916 von Tirpitz finally resigned due to the heavy opposition from those who realised his ambitions were leading in the direction of an unrestricted U-boat war.

The 'intensified U-boat war' was designed to avoid the possibilities of dangerous conflict inherent in an unrestricted U-boat war but nevertheless this kind of warfare resulted in the third U-boat crisis of the war. After the sinking of the French liner *Sussex* by *U 29* the USA threatened to cut off all negotiations with Germany if her submarine commanders continued to break their own rules. Immediately Bethmann-Hollweg asked that the U-boats should act strictly according to the provisions of Prize Laws and an imperial order confirmed this. This kind of warfare being impossible by this stage in the war, the German Admiralty recalled all submarines to avoid conflict of any kind. The U-boat war in British waters was stopped for a second time and the consequences repeated. Von Falkenhayn and von Tirpitz requested the resumption of the U-boat war, while Germany's ambassador in the USA asked for it to be halted as he felt near to bringing about an agreement between Great Britain and Germany through President Wilson. For the Admiralty's part, Admiral Scheer tried to convince the Emperor to allow a U-boat war following the Battle of Jutland. But Bethmann-Hollweg maintained his opinion that the future of the German nation should not be laid in the hands of a few submarine commanders. The next initiative came from the C-in-C of the Flanders submarines, Cdr Bartenbach, who managed to persuade the Fleet Command to reopen the U-boat war – at least in a limited form under the Prize Laws. This resulted in the 6 October 1916 order that the U-boats and the Fleet should begin a prize war against commercial shipping on 15 October. A total of 30 ocean-going, 14 medium and 9 coastal submarines set out, hampered by the heavy autumn gales, achieving good but not remarkable successes until January 1917.

The next steps were taken in the political theatre: because of the catastrophic military situation von Falkenhayn resigned as Head of the Army and von Hindenburg became his successor, Ludendorff becoming his quartermaster-general. Apart from the battles of Verdun and the Russian penetration into Austria-Hungary, Rumania had declared war, and the prestige and authority of these two war-lords drove the decision towards an unlimited U-boat war, their supreme Army command urgently calling for it and rejecting every attempt to interfere with military power for political reasons. For further US developments, Germany had to wait until after the presidential elections. After Wilson had been re-elected in November – campaigning under the slogan 'Keep the United States out of war' – Germany believed that there was an opportunity to enter into preparatory peace negotiations. After the defeat of Rumania the Supreme Army Command asked the Chancellor for his permission for an unlimited U-boat war. The response of the Allies was confusing: Britain, France and Russia asked for reparations and guarantees; Wilson offered mediation. The fierce political struggle between German politicians and generals led to the final conferences of January 1917.

Supreme Army Command succeeded in obtaining the unlimited U-boat war as the last card of the German war effort; the political leaders had to capitulate. The unlimited U-boat war was to begin on 1 February 1917! German guarantees that the U-boat war would be stopped immediately should President Wilson start peace negotiations came too late. Political and diplomatic connections between the German Empire and the USA were cut, and war declared on 4 April with Germany, and with Austria-Hungary the following day.

Commentators in Germany turned now to more propagandist lines, claiming that the US war effort was an unimportant and negligible factor; Germany had to grit her teeth and bear it. But the war was lost and Tirpitz was right in his statement that: 'now it was too late to gain victory; Britain has had three years to prepare against the German U-boat threat, and has developed new tactics, new weapons and a

The submarine war – *U 35* stops a merchantman in the Mediterranean, May 1917
CPL

good convoy system so that our submarines cannot be as successful as they could have been in the first two years.' Although the U-boats achieved remarkable successes they were not capable of cutting off Britain entirely.

One should bear in mind this fatal self-destructive struggle between the advocates of a 'peace-through-victory' and the advocates of a 'peace-by-negotiation' to understand the origins of the thinking behind Hitler and his admirals when they entered World War Two.

THE ACHIEVEMENTS OF THE U-BOAT WAR

From the above one might suspect that the U-boat war did not take place, being constantly constricted. The reason for the German emphasis on submarine-minelaying was one of the results of this constriction, because a mine barrage sinking a neutral ship was not considered to be an attack on the particular nation.

Nevertheless the list of the most successful submarine commanders of both wars is headed by three German First World War aces: Lothar von Arnauld de la Perière, who sank 194 ships totalling 453,718grt with *U 35* and *U 139*; Walter Forstmann who sank 146 ships totalling 384,304grt with *U 12* and *U 39*; and Max Valentiner who sank (probably) 140 ships totalling 310,000grt in command of *U 3, U 38* and *U 157*. By comparison Germany's leading World War Two ace was Otto Kretschmer, who sank 44 ships totalling 266,629grt in command of *U 23* and *U 99*; but it must be pointed out that the First War sinkings occurred mostly in the Mediterranean under extremely 'peaceful' conditions and therefore may not be compared with the Battle of the Atlantic. The actual figures for tonnage sunk in World War One mirror the political stage of the U-boat war: August 1915 to September 1916 – 431 ships of 791,705grt; October 1915 to April 1916 – 359 ships 898,794grt; May 1916 to January 1917 – 1152 ships of 2,099,523grt; February 1917 to December 1917 – 2566 ships of 5,753,751grt; and January 1918 to end – 1046 ships of 2,648,223grt. Unquestionably the U-boats represented a deadly menace to the Allies which led ultimately to the question of what was to become of this powerful force during any future peace.

THE END OF THE U-BOATS

When in autumn 1918 it became clear that the Central Powers could not win the war, the German U-boat force was seen as an important bargaining counter for coming peace negotiations. Admiral Scheer pressed forward his ambitious plans for submarine construction (the so-called 'Scheer programme') until October 1918 with remarkable energy, despite the catastrophic general economic situation of the German Empire.

The Allies, however, insisted that Germany surrender all submarines as an essential prerequisite of any armistice. German politicians in contact with neutral nations such as Denmark and Norway brought home the message that these nations regarded an unlimited German U-boat war as illegal under International Law and that it therefore could form no part of the negotiations.

On 24 October 1918 the German U-boats received the order to cease all attacks and return home. After the breakdown of the German Empire and the abdication of Wilhelm II the German delegations had no hope of countering Allied demands, which exceeded even the worst German fears. Article XII of the stipulations concerning the interning of the German Fleet can be summed up as follows: to the Allies and the United States 160 submarines complete with crew and equipment to be delivered to ports to be named by those powers. All submarine-cruisers and all minelayers have to be included. All other submarines to be demilitarised – this applies to both personnel and equipment – and remain under the control of the Allies and the United States.

The intention was to prevent all possibility of a renewal of the U-boat war. Nevertheless the Germans tried to interpret article XII in a more moderate way to preserve the nucleus of a future U-boat arm, an act which led to rising Allied suspicion. This suspicion finally resulted in the more stringent stipulations requesting delivery of all seaworthy submarines and the destruction of all others in the yards, and the absolute prohibition of any future German submarine construction.

All German submarines affected were transferred or towed to Britain together with their tenders and repair ships in eleven groups; the boats interned in Spain and Norway were also delivered up. Germany even had to forfeit the diesels and electric motors of the incomplete boats lying on the slips.

SCUTTLING AT SCAPA

The Armistice came into effect on 11 November 1918. The British-inspired conditions of the agreement were particularly concerned with the German Navy and stated in article XXIII: two of Germany's three battle squadrons, together with all her 5 battlecruisers, 8 light cruisers and 49 destroyers should be interned; all submarines were to be given up. At dawn on 21 November 1918, 370 ships of the Royal Navy escorted the German Navy to its last anchorage. Lying interned at Scapa Flow, the German ships were gradually demobilised and personnel were subsequently repatriated. When the German officers at Scapa discovered in May 1919 that – as laid before the German delegation at Versailles – the entire fleet interned at Scapa would be handed over to the victorious Allies, with Britain getting the largest share, they were determined to save the honour of their unbeaten fleet.

Misunderstanding the final negotiating position of the German government, secret orders were issued on 17 June for the High Seas Fleet to be scuttled. Taking advantage of the Royal Navy guardships' absence on exercises, Rear-Admiral von Reuter, commanding the German Fleet at Scapa, executed his orders on 21 June. All ships at Scapa were scuttled (listed in order of sinking): the battleships *Friedrich der Grosse, König Albert, Kronprinz Wilhelm, Kaiser, Grosser Kurfürst, Prinzregent Luitpold, König, Kaiserin, Bayern, Markgraf, Baden;* the battlecruisers *Moltke, Seydlitz, Von der Tann, Derfflinger, Hindenburg;* the light cruisers *Brummer, Dresden, Cöln, Bremse, Karlsruhe, Emden, Frankfurt, Nürnberg;* the destroyers (1st flotilla) *G 40, G 86, G 39, G 38, V 129, S 32,* (2nd flotilla) *G 101, G 102, G 103, G 104, V 100, B 110, B 112, B 109, B 111,* (3rd flotilla) *S 54, S 53, S 55, V 70, V 73, V 81, V 82, G 91* (6th flotilla) *S 131, S 132, V 125, V 126, V 127, V 128, V 44, V 43, V 45, V 46, S 49, S 50,* (7th flotilla) *S 56, S 65, V 78, V 83, G 92, S 136, S 135, S 138, H 145, G 89,* (9th flotilla) *V 80, S 36, S 51, S 52, S 60.*

REPARATIONS

According to article XXIII of the armistice the Allies requested the ceding of the following ships and equipment to match the loss of the scuttled High Seas Fleet: 1) the light cruisers *Pillau, Königsberg, Graudenz, Regensburg* and *Strassburg* within 60 days; 2) floating drydocks, cranes, tugs and barges in good condition totalling 400,000t; 3) surrender of all U-boat equipment. However, there were quite a few vessels left which formed the nucleus of the new German Navy, known as the *'vorläufige Reichsmarine'* ('provisional navy'). The naval forces of the new Weimar Republic comprised the elements of a thoroughly antiquated coast defence force: 8 pre-dreadnoughts (including 2 in reserve), 8 light cruisers (2 reserve), 16 destroyers and 16 torpedo-boats (4 of each in reserve); most of these units had been withdrawn from active service during World War One. In the early years a great number of obsolete and worn-out ships were subsequently stricken and scrapped. Much more restricting than the limit on equipment was that on personnel: according to the Versailles Treaty the German Navy was limited to 15,000 officers and men.

But in the first years the problems of the navy were more those of internal politics than those created by the birth of a new navy. The so-called *Marine freikorps* composed of ex-sailors fought in what was virtually a civil war against insurgent Communists and radical Socialists. Later these personnel were concentrated in the *Brigade Erhardt*, which played an unfortunate role in the attempt to rebel against the Versailles Treaty and occupied Berlin during the Kapp-Lüttwitz uprising of 1920. After the suppression of this revolt and the establishment of a Socialist government, the head of the *vorläufige Reichsmarine*, von Trotha, had to leave his post. Under a law of 31 March 1921 the *Reichswehr* was founded, together with the *Reichsmarine*, both services being composed of regular soldiers. For the strength of the German Navy in 1921 see also the 1922–1946 volume in this series.

GERMANY

GERMAN NAVAL GUNS OF DREADNOUGHT PERIOD

German designation	Actual bore diam/length (ins/cals)	Weight incl BM (tons)	Shell (lbs)	MV/59°F (fs)	Range (yds)
38cm SKL/45	14.96/42.4	76.57	1653	2625	22,200/16°, 25,400/20°
35cm SKL/45	13.78/42.4	71.75	1323	2674	25,400/20°
30.5cm SKL/50	12.01/47.4	51.03	893	2805	20,500/13½°, 22,400/16°
28cm SKL/50	11.14/47.4	40.84	666	2887	19,500/13½°, 21,000/16° 25,300/22½°
28cm SKL/45	11.14/42.4	39.17	666	2805	22,400/20°
21cm SKL/45	8.24/42.2	16.14	238	2953	20,900/30°
15cm SKL/45	5.87/42.4	5.63/5.73	99.9	2740	16,350/19°, 17,280/22° 18,510/27°, 19,250/30°
15cm Tbts KL/45 Ubts + Tbts KL/45	5.87/42.2	3.93	99.9	2231	15,850/30° 17,400/40°
10.5cm SKL/45	4.134/42.1	1.43/1.52	38.4	2329	13,900/30°
10.5cm Tbts KL/45	4.134/42.0	1.33			10,350/20°
Ubts + Tbts KL/45	/42.1	1.53	38.4	2133	12,600/30°
Ubts + Tbts Flak L/45	/42.0	1.59			13,400/45°
8.8cm Flak L/45 SKL/45	3.465/42.1	1.14 0.98	22/21.2 22	2461/2510 2461	12,900/45° 11,700/25°
8.8cm Tbts KL/45	3.465/42.4	0.752	22	2133	10,500/25°
8.8cm Tbts KL/30 Ubts KL/30 Ubts + Tbts Flak L/30	3.465/27.1	0.490 0.492 0.634	22	1936	7700/15° 9000/20°, 10,300/30° 10,700/45°

Note: No reliable data has been found for 42cm SKL/45 design.

OLDER GERMAN NAVAL GUNS STILL IN SERVICE

German designation	Actual Bore diam/length (ins/cals)	Weight incl BM (tons)	Shell (lbs)	MV/59°F (fs)	Range (yds)
28cm SKL/40	11.14/36.8	44.58	529	2690	20,600/30°
28cm KL/40	11.14/36.6	43.31	529	2346	16,500/25°
28cm KL/35	11.14/31.7	43.21	529	2247	15,800/25°
24cm SKL/40	9.37/37.3	23.66/25.24	309	2740	18,500/30°
24cm KL/35	9.37/32.3	21.16	309	2264	14,200/25°
21cm SKL/40	8.24/37.3	16.24/19.70	238	2559	13,520/16°, 17,780/30°
17cm SKL/40	6.795/37.1	10.58	141	2789	15,850/22°, 18,500/30°
15cm SKL/40	5.87/37.2	4.60/4.90	88.2	2625	15,200/30°
15cm SKL/35	5.87/32.2	4.43	88.2	2228	13,750/30°
10.5cm SKL/40	4.134/37.1	1.72/1.89	38.4	2264	13,340/30°
10.5cm SKL/35	4.134/32.2	1.25/1.51	38.4	1969	11,800/30°
8.8cm SKL/35	3.465/31.9	0.805	15.4	2526 2264 in older TBD	9940/25° 9610/25°
8.8cm SKL/30	3.465/27.0	0.642	15.4	2198 2021 in older TBD	8000/20° 7530/20°
5.2cm SKL/55	2.047/51.2	0.386	3.86	2789	7770/20°
5.0cm Tbts KL/40 SKL/40	1.969/36.6	0.280 0.236	3.86	2152	6760/20° 5290/12°, 6760/20°

Wörth as rebuilt
CPL

FLEET STRENGTH 1906

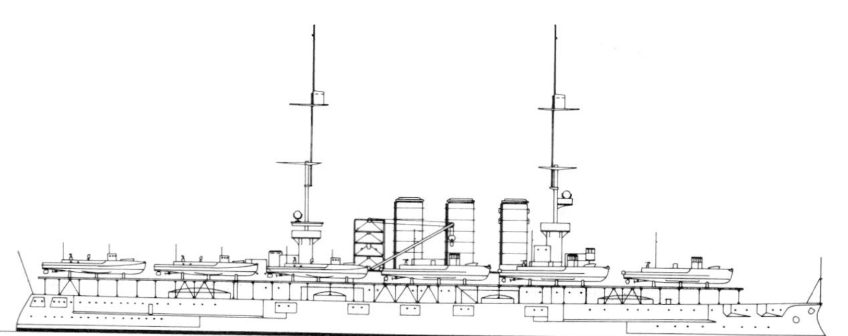
Lothringen 1919 as a minesweeper depot ship

Wittlesbach January 1920 as a minesweeper depot ship
CPL

BATTLESHIPS

Name	Launched	Disp (deep load)	Fate
Brandenburg class			
KURKÜRST FRIEDRICH WILHELM	30.6.91	10,502t	To Turkey 12.9.10
BRANDENBURG	21.9.91	10,502t	Stricken 13.5.19, BU
WEISSENBURG	14.12.91	10,502t	To Turkey 12.9.10
WÖRTH	6.8.92	10,502t	Stricken 13.5.19, BU
Kaiser class			
KAISER FRIEDRICH III	31.7.96	11,599t	Stricken 6.12.19, BU
KAISER WILHELM II	14.9.97	11,599t	Stricken 6.12.19, BU
KAISER WILHELM DER GROSSE	1.6.99	11,599t	Stricken 17.3.21, BU
KAISER KARL DER GROSSE	18.10.99	11,599t	Stricken 6.12.19, BU
KAISER BARBAROSSA	21.4.00	11,599t	Stricken 6.12.19, BU
Wittelsbach class			
WITTELSBACH	3.7.00	12,596t	Stricken 8.3.21, BU
WETTIN	6.6.01	12.596t	Stricken 11.3.20, BU
ZÄHRINGEN	12.6.01	12,596t	Sunk 18.12.44
SCHWABEN	19.8.01	12,596t	Stricken 8.3.21, BU
MECKLENBURG	9.11.01	12,596t	Stricken 25.1.20, BU
Braunschweig class			
BRAUNSCHWEIG	20.12.02	14,167t	Stricken 31.3.31, BU
ELSASS	26.5.03	14,167t	Stricken 31.3.31, BU
HESSEN	18.9.03	14,167t	To USSR 1946
PREUSSEN	30.10.03	14,167t	Stricken 5.4.29, BU
LOTHRINGEN	27.5.04	14,167t	Stricken 31.3.31, BU
Deutschland class			
DEUTSCHLAND	19.11.04	13,994t	BU 1920–22
HANNOVER	29.9.05	13,994t	BU 1944–46
POMMERN	2.12.05	13,994t	Torpedoed 1.6.16
SCHLESIEN	28.5.06	13,994t	Scuttled 5.5.45
SCHLESWIG-HOLSTEIN	7.12.06	13,994t	Bombed 18.12.44

Brandenburg class
Although *Brandenburg* was launched second, the class was named after her in the international naval literature. As the Imperial German Navy's existing ironclads were obsolete, these ships of 1888–89 design mark the first distinct step away from a purely coast defence navy towards a high seas fleet, being clearly intended for the line of battle. For the first time in German shipbuilding they showed extensive water-tight subdivision and employed the latest armour technology. *Kurfürst Friedrich Wilhelm* and *Weissenburg* had Krupp's new nickel steel armour, but the others received compound armour because of delivery shortages. Their layout and the convex main armoured deck reveals strong French influence and the class were nicknamed 'whalers' by the British. On commissioning they formed the 1st division of the 1st Squadron and were detached to China during the 1900 Boxer Rebellion. In 1902–04 they were reboilered and lost their heavy fighting masts. In 1910 the two nickel steel armoured units (giving them effectively twice the protection of the same thickness of compound armour in their sisters) were sold to Turkey and renamed *Heireddin Barbarossa* and *Torgud Reis*. The first was torpedoed and sunk by the British submarine *E 11* in the Dardanelles on 8 August 1915, the other became a training ship in 1924 and was broken up in 1938. The two remaining units served for coastal defence, then as accommodation ships; a planned conversion of *Brandenburg* into a gunnery target ship remained unfinished. Both were stricken on 13 May 1919 and scrapped.

Kaiser class
The ships of the first *Kaiser* class (the second *Kaiser* class being the dreadnoughts of 1911) set a new standard for German pre-dreadnought battleships, although the system of passive protection had been developed in the previous class. Designed in 1892–94, when the main 24cm (9.44in) might seem to be a step backwards after the 11in of the previous classes, it was chosen because of its high rate of fire: 3 rounds of 24cm per minute versus 1 round of 11in. On commissioning they formed the 1st Squadron of the Home Fleet (*Heimatflotte*); after ten years, when new classes were in service, they formed the 3rd Squadron of the High Seas Fleet, which was placed in reserve before the outbreak of the First World War and mobilised as 5th Squadron in 1914. In February 1915 the 5th Squadron was withdrawn from the active fleet. *Kaiser Barbarossa, Kaiser Friedrich III* and *Kaiser Karl der Grosse* served as floating prisons, and *Kaiser Wilhelm II* as a floating HQ for the German C-in-C and *Kaiser Wilhelm der Grosse* as torpedo training ship. All were scrapped in 1920.

Wittelsbach class
Designed in 1897–99 these ships are improved *Kaiser*s with a flush main deck instead of a cut-down quarterdeck. At the outbreak of war they were mobilised as the 4th Squadron, but were soon decommissioned as being too vulnerable. In 1916 they were used as training ships, and *Mecklenburg* became a floating prison. *Schwaben* and *Wittelsbach* were converted to depot ships for shallow draught F-type minesweepers in 1919. All were stricken and scrapped in the early 1920s, except *Zähringen* which was converted to a radio controlled gunnery target ship in 1926–27; she sank after RAF bomb hits on 18 December 1944 at Gotenhafen and was scrapped in 1949–50.

Braunschweig class
Authorised by the 1900 Naval Act these ships were designed in 1900–01. During the war these ships formed the 4th Squadron, which was stationed in the Baltic in 1915. Because of a manpower shortage the 4th Squadron was reduced to harbour guardships by transferring personnel to other ships. Later the ships lost their secondary armament and most of their 88mm AA guns. After the war all five were taken into the *Reichsmarine*'s thoroughly antiquated battleship force, but *Lothringen* and *Preussen* were converted into depot ships for F-type minesweepers, but soon decommissioned: *Preussen* was broken up in 1931 – with the exception of a 63m midship section retained as explosive trials target, nicknamed *Vierkant* (literally 'even keel'). *Lothringen, Braunschweig* and *Elsass* were stricken on 31 March 1931 and subsequently scrapped. *Hessen* was reboilered and converted into a radio-controlled target ship; she was ceded to the Soviet Union in 1946 and renamed *Tsel*, but her further fate is unknown.

Deutschland class
These five ships were the last German pre-dreadnoughts and closely resembled the previous *Braunschweig* class. Being built in a period when the trend towards the all-big-gun battleship was clearly visible, this class was criticised even before its construction. The reason why von Tirpitz insisted on this design was that a future generation of capital ships would require the widening of the Kaiser Wilhelm (Kiel) canal, which would prove an enormous burden on the German naval budget. This decision was short-sighted, as this class did not increase the High Seas Fleet's strength. During the war they formed the 2nd Squadron, took part in the Battle of Jutland, where *Pommern* was sunk. Owing to their obsolescence and vulnerability the remaining ships were withdrawn from the High Seas Fleet at the end of 1916 and withdrawn from active service on 15 August 1917. *Deutschland* served as an accommodation ship at Wilhelmshaven, was condemned on 25 January 1920 and broken up in 1920–22. *Hannover* served as a guardship in the Danish Belt, was condemned in 1935, and a planned conversion to a radio-controlled target ship did not take place; she was scrapped in 1944–46 at Bremerhaven. *Pommern* was torpedoed and sunk during the Battle of Jutland by British destroyers of the 12th Flotilla. *Schlesien* served as a training and accommodation ship at Kiel in 1917 and as a cadet training ship in 1918. In 1936 she was modernised, reboilered and partially rearmed to serve as a cadet training ship. During the last weeks of the Second World War she was once more modernised and up-gunned; returning from a shore bombardment operation in East Prussia she hit a mine and was beached off Swinemünde (Swienouscje) to prevent her from sinking. On 4 May 1945 she was blown up by her crew, the wreck being scrapped *in situ* during 1949–56. *Schleswig-Holstein* was an accommodation ship at Kiel, and from 1918 served with the *Reichsmarine* and was modernised in 1932 as a cadet training ship. She fired the very first shots of the Second World War on 1 September 1939 against the small Polish fortress of Westerplatte, near Danzig.

On 18 December 1944 she was hit by British bombs during a refit at Gotenhafen (Gdynia), and beached and blown up on 21 March 1945; the wreck was broken up *in situ* during 1950–56.

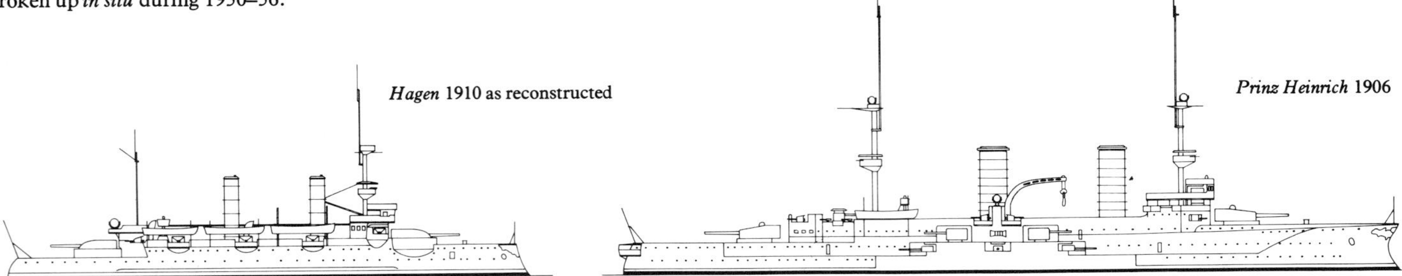
Hagen 1910 as reconstructed

Prinz Heinrich 1906

COAST DEFENCE SHIPS

Name	Launched	Disp* (deep load)	Fate
Siegfried class			
SIEGFRIED	10.8.89	4158t	Stricken 17.6.19, BU
BEOWULF	8.11.90	4158t	Stricken 17.6.19, BU
FRITHJOF	21.7.91	4158t	Stricken 17.6.19, BU
HEIMDALL	27.7.92	4158t	Stricken 17.6.19, BU
HILDEBRAND	6.8.92	4158t	Stricken 17.6.19, BU
HAGEN	21.10.93	4158t	Stricken 17.6.19, BU
Odin class			
ODIN	11.3.94	4224t	Stricken 6.12.19
ÄGIR	3.4.95	4224t	Stricken 17.6.19, sold

Siegfried class
Designed in 1885–89 these small armoured ships were intended to defend the approaches to German harbours. About 1900 this class was rebuilt by cutting them in half, lengthening and reboilering them; they emerged with two funnels. At the outbreak of war they were mobilised and formed the 6th Squadron, which survived until 31 August 1915. After the reduction of their crews they served as accommodation ships, and *Beowulf* as a U-boat practice target; they were all stricken in 1919 and scrapped.

Odin class
Very similar to the previous class these ships were longer because they had a superior boiler arrangement (the *Siegfried*s were lengthened to achieve a similar result) and had the same military career, but not being ready for scrap in 1919 they were sold as merchant ships. The former *Odin* was scrapped in 1935, and the former *Ägir* stranded on 18 December 1929 and was wrecked.

*All tonnages are after reconstruction.

ARMOURED CRUISERS

Name	Launched	Disp (deep load)	Fate
FÜRST BISMARCK	25.9.97	11,281t	Stricken 17.6.19, BU
PRINZ HEINRICH	22.3.00	9652t	Stricken 25.1.20, BU
Prinz Adalbert class			
PRINZ ADALBERT	22.6.01	9719t	Torpedoed 23.10.15
FRIEDRICH CARL	21.6.02	9719t	Mined 17.11.14
Roon class			
ROON	27.6.03	10,104t	Stricken 25.11.20, BU
YORCK	14.5.04	10,104t	Mined 4.11.14
Scharnhorst class			
SCHARNHORST	22.3.06	12,781t	Sunk 8.12.14
GNEISENAU	14.6.06	12,781t	Sunk 8.12.14

Fürst Bismarck
With this ship the Imperial German Navy, against heavy political opposition, took the first step towards a modern armoured, fast and heavily armed unit suitable for overseas duties. In design terms she was an improved *Victoria Luise* – which was an intermediate type between the armoured and protected cruiser – and proved to be highly successful. Because of the 1900 Boxer Rebellion in China she was commissioned with the highest priority and sent to the German Asian station where she proved ideally suited for her duties, therefore setting the trend for the more or less subsequently improved designs of German armoured cruisers. In 1910 she was refitted and modernised to serve as a torpedo training ship; in 1915 she was attached to the torpedo trials command as a target ship, but in 1916 she was reclassified as a training and drill ship. On 31 December 1918 she was decommissioned and served as floating office accommodation. She was stricken in 1919 and scrapped in 1920.

Prinz Heinrich
This was the first of 14 armoured cruisers, envisaged by the Second Navy Law. All these ships were to act as overseas station ships in the colonies, replacing the old cruisers already on station. She served with the fleet until 1902, from 1916 she was a floating office at Kiel, being stricken in 1920 and sold for scrapping.

Prinz Adalbert class
Designed in 1899–1900 these ships had a main armament calibre of 21cm (8.26in) instead of the old, slower firing 24cm (9.44in) of the previous classes. Both served in their intended role as overseas cruisers but were retired as training ships in 1904, and 1908. In 1914 they were both mobilised but lost in the early part of the war: *Friedrich Carl* was sunk on 17 November 1914 in the Baltic on a Russian mine barrage, and *Prinz Adalbert* was torpedoed on 23 October 1915 in the Baltic by the British submarine *E 8*.

Roon class
Designed in 1901, these two armoured cruisers were repeats of the previous design. *Yorck* accidentally ran into two German mines in the Jade estuary on 4 November 1914 and sank. *Roon* was retired from the active fleet in 1916 and served as a guardship and accommodation ship; she was stricken on 25 November 1920 and scrapped.

Scharnhorst class
From the design point of view these armoured cruisers were enlarged and improved *Roons*, having 17cm single turrets in wing arrangement above the casemates. Being too weak for the battle fleet they proved useful on overseas stations. From 1911 onwards they were station ships in Tsingtao (the German colony in China) and formed the nucleus of Admiral Graf Spee's 'East Asian Squadron', which crossed the Pacific, fought the victorious Battle of Coronel and were finally both sunk at the Falklands on 8 December 1914.

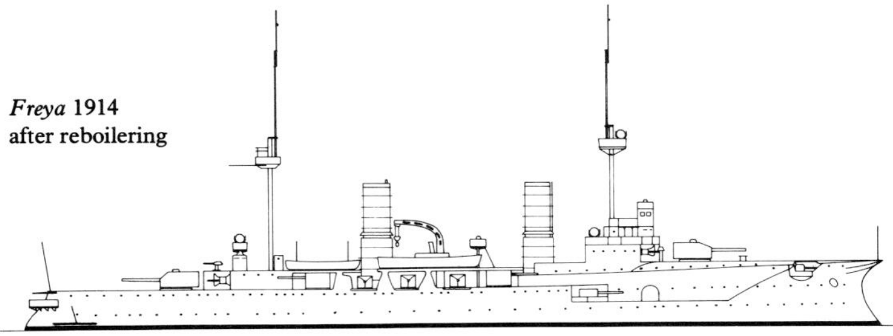
Freya 1914
after reboilering

PROTECTED CRUISERS

Name	Launched	Disp (deep load)	Fate
KAISERIN AUGUSTA	15.1.92	6218t	Stricken 1.10.19, BU
Victoria Luise class			
VICTORIA LUISE	23.8.97	6388t	Stricken 1.10.19, sold
HERTHA	14.4.97	6388t	Stricken 6.12.19, BU
FREYA	27.4.97	6388t	Stricken 25.1.20, BU
VINETA	14.4.97	6599t	Stricken 6.12.19, BU
HANSA	12.3.98	6599t	Stricken 6.12.19, BU

Kaiserin Augusta
Germany, not having the budget funds to build both colonial cruisers and fleet scouts, tried to find a compromise which soon proved to be a miscalculation. *Kaiserin Augusta*'s role was mainly overseas power projection, and she was involved in the first Moroccan crisis in 1895, the international blockade of Crete during the 1897 Greek-Turkish war, and the 1900 Boxer Rebellion. By this time she was obsolete and was therefore modernised in 1903–05 before going into reserve. In 1914 she was mobilised as a gunnery training ship to replace the newer training ships which had now joined the High Seas Fleet. Later she served in the Baltic and was decommissioned on 14 December 1918, stricken and scrapped in 1920.

Victoria Luise class
Designed in 1893–95 these protected cruisers were intended for overseas service and show general similarities in layout to the contemporary German battleships – a fact that applies to all subsequent armoured cruisers too. After their first period of active service they were reboilered in 1905–11, from which they emerged with one funnel less. At the outbreak of the First World War they were mobilised as the 5th Scouting Group (training cruiser division) and served in the Baltic, but were decommissioned by the end of 1914. They then

served as accommodation ships and were stricken and scrapped immediately after the war – with the exception of the *Victoria Luise*, which was sold, converted to a merchant ship and renamed *Flora Sommerfeld*; she was scrapped in 1923.

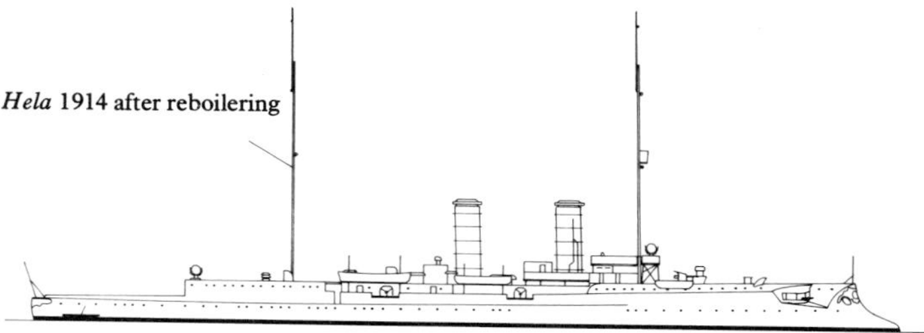
Hela 1914 after reboilering

LIGHT CRUISERS

Name	Launched	Disp (deep load)	Fate
Meteor class			
METEOR	20.1.90	1055t	Stricken 24.6.11, BU
COMET	15.11.92	1093t	Stricken 24.6.11, BU
Bussard class			
BUSSARD	23.1.90	1839t	Stricken 25.10.12, BU
FALKE	4.4.91	1839t	Stricken 25.10.12, BU
SEEADLER (ex-*Kaiseradler*)	2.2.92	1835t	Hulked 1914, sunk 19.4.17
CONDOR	23.2.92	1835t	Stricken 18.11.20, BU
CORMORAN	17.5.92	1835t	Scuttled 28.9.14
GEIER	18.10.94	1888t	Captured by USN in 1917, sunk 21.6.18
HELA	28.3.95	2049t	Sunk 13.9.14
GEFION	31.5.93	4208t	Stricken 5.11.19, sold
Gazelle class			
GAZELLE	31.3.98	2916t	Stricken 28.8.20, BU
NIOBE	18.7.99	2916t	Stricken 24.6.25, sold
NYMPHE	21.11.99	2617t	Stricken 29.8.31, BU
THETIS	3.7.00	2617t	Stricken 27.9.29, sold
ARIADNE	10.8.00	2617t	Sunk 28.8.14
AMAZONE	6.10.00	2617t	Stricken 31.3.13, hulked
MEDUSA	5.12.00	2617t	Stricken 27.3.29, scuttled 3.5.45
FRAUENLOB	22.3.02	2663t	Sunk 31.5.16
ARCONA	22.10.02	2663t	Stricken 15.1.30, scuttled 3.5.45
UNDINE	11.12.02	2663t	Sunk 7.11.15
Bremen class			
BREMEN	9.7.03	3756t	Mined 17.12.15
HAMBURG	25.7.03	3756t	Stricken 31.3.31, hulked
BERLIN	22.9.03	3756t	Hulked 1935, scuttled 1947
LÜBECK	26.3.04	3756t	Stricken 5.11.19, BU
MÜNCHEN	30.4.04	3756t	Stricken 5.11.19, BU
LEIPZIG	21.3.05	3756t	Sunk 8.12.14
DANZIG	23.9.05	3756t	Stricken 5.11.19, BU

Meteor class
These two *avisos* were designed to fight enemy torpedo-boats. They had very short active careers and were reclassified as light cruisers in 1899 although they were in reserve. In 1904 they were reclassified as harbour units, were both stricken on 24 June 1911 and hulked; they were scrapped after the war.

Busssard class
These six 4th class cruisers were especially designed for overseas duties, but in 1899 they were reclassified as light cruisers, and in May 1914 as gunboats. *Cormoran* was at Tsingtao when war broke out and was scuttled on 28 September 1914; *Geier* was interned at Honolulu, captured by the USN in 1917 and, commissioned as the gunboat *Carl Schurz*, she sank on 21 June 1918 after a collision. The other four were in Germany in 1914 but were subsequently decommissioned and hulked. *Seeadler* sank while serving as a mine storage ship after an internal explosion, 19 April 1917.

Hela
The inadequacy of the older *avisos* resulted in a new design approaching that of the modern light cruiser. In 1899 she was reclassified as a light cruiser, and served for two years overseas. Experience showed that ships of this type were too weak to serve as scout cruisers with the Fleet and led to the next design. The *Hela* served as a training ship, was reboilered in 1910, from which she emerged with two funnels. At the outbreak of the First World War she served as a patrol unit and was torpedoed by the British submarine *E 9* off Heligoland.

Gefion
With this ship the German Navy tried to develop a lightly protected cruiser suitable as a scout for the battlefleet and as an overseas cruiser capable of acting as a commerce raider in time of war. During 1897–1901 she was stationed in China, and was reclassified as a light cruiser in 1899. After her return she was modernised and placed in reserve. Owing to personnel shortages she was not mobilised in 1914 and served as an accommodation ship. She was stricken on 5 November 1919, sold and converted to a merchant ship (renamed *Adolf Sommerfeld*), but was scrapped in 1923.

Gazelle class
After the intermediate types of light fighting vessels the *Gazelle* class cruisers, designed in 1895–96, became the basic pattern for German light cruisers, down to the last wartime classes. They were a good compromise between the fleet scout and the overseas cruiser, in which role they served before 1914. Being in reserve at the outbreak of war they were quickly mobilised: *Ariadne* was sunk by British battlecruisers on 28 August 1914 off Heligoland; *Undine* was torpedoed on 7 November 1915 by the British submarine *E 19* in the Baltic; *Frauenlob* was torpedoed during the Battle of Jutland. All the others were subsequently withdrawn from active service in the second half of the war and in 1919 became part of the *Reichsmarine*'s thoroughly antiquated cruiser force. All were stricken in 1929–31 and scrapped, with the exception of *Medusa* and *Arcona*, which were converted into floating batteries in 1942 for the protection of Wilhelmshaven; both were scuttled on 3 May 1945.

Bremen class
This 1901–03 design was an enlarged and improved *Gazelle* and the first class to bear city names. *Lübeck* had the first turbine plant in a German major warship, while her sisters had VTE propulsion. Serving on overseas stations they were up-gunned with the 15cm gun at the beginning of the war. *Leipzig* was sunk at the Battle of the Falklands; *Bremen* was mined in the Baltic, 17 December 1915; *Lübeck*, *München* and *Danzig* became British war reparations after the scuttling of the German Fleet at Scapa Flow and were scrapped immediately. *Hamburg* and *Berlin* served as training cruisers for the *Reichsmarine* and were hulked in 1935. *Hamburg* was sunk by British bombs in August 1944 and broken up 1949–56. *Berlin* was filled with poison gas shells and scuttled by the British in the Skagerrak in 1947.

GUNBOATS

Name	Launched	Disp (deep load)	Fate
ILTIS	1.12.98	1032t	Scuttled 28.9.14
JAGUAR	19.9.98	1032t	Scuttled 7.11.14
TIGER	15.8.99	1091t	Scuttled 29.10.14
LUCHS	18.10.99	1091t	Scuttled 28.9.14
PANTHER	1.4.01	1174t	Stricken 31.3.31, BU
EBER	6.6.03	1174t	Scuttled 26.10.17

Designed especially for colonial service, they were able to operate on the total navigable length of the great Chinese rivers. The first four were on the China station at the outbreak of war and subsequently scuttled at Tsingtao. The other two were station ships at the West African coast. *Panther* became famous for her role in the 1906 Agadir Crisis. *Eber* transferred her guns to the raider *Cap Trafalgar* on the outbreak of war, and sailed under a commercial flag to Bahia in Brazil for interning. On 26 October 1917 she was scuttled when Brazil entered the war. *Panther* served as a coast guard vessel during the war then as a *Reichsmarine* surveying ship, was stricken on 31 March 1931 and scrapped.

TORPEDO-BOATS

Name	Launched	Disp (deep load)	Fate
TAKU	1898	284t	Scuttled 28.9.14
D 3, D 4	1888	300t	Stricken 7.12.20, BU
D 5, D 6	1888	406t	Stricken 7.12.19, BU
D 7, D 8	1890–91	417t	Stricken 7.12.19, BU
D 9	1894	458t	Stricken 7.12.19, BU
D 10	1898	371t	Stricken 28.7.22, BU
S 90–S 101	1899–1900	394t	See below
S 102–S 107	1901	406t	Stricken 1920–21, BU
S 108–S 113	1901–2	440t	Stricken 1920–21, BU
S 114–S 119	1902–3	406t	See below
S 120–S 124	1904	468t	See below
S 125	1904	468t	BU 1921
S 126–S 131	1904–5	468t	See below

Although having the displacement of contemporary destroyers, these boats were classified as torpedo-boats in the Imperial German Navy in 1906 because they were intended to act in this role up until 1914. The gun armament was therefore regarded as merely defensive.

Taku
Built at F Schichau, Elbing, for the Chinese Navy together with four sisters; she was christened *Hai-Ching* but captured together with her sisters on 17 June 1900 by the British destroyers *Fame* and *Whiting* at the Taku yard in the Pei-Ho river. *Hai-Ching* became a German war reparation, was renamed *Taku* and rearmed with 2–5cm/40. She was scuttled at Tsingtao on the outbreak of war.

D 3, D 4
After employment as leaders of torpedo-boat and minesweeping flotillas *D 4* became fishery protection vessel at the end of 1906 and served as a tender from 1910 to 1916, while *D 3* was allocated to the submarine school.

D 5, D 6
Both were reboilered to similar lines as *D 4* and emerged with two funnels. *D 5* served as a fishery protection vessel in 1905–06, both were allocated to the submarine school in 1914 and 1916 respectively.

D 7, D 8
After active service with torpedo-boat and minesweeping flotillas *D 7* was allocated to the submarine school in 1916, while *D 8* was used for trials from 1917.

D 9
Armed with the new 5cm/40 torpedo-boat gun, while the previous boats were up-gunned in 1893. This boat served with a minesweeping flotilla from 1907, then as *D 7*. *D 9* was also reboilered and fitted with two funnels in 1910.

D 10
This Thornycroft boat was ordered to get comparative information on the Royal Navy's '30-Knotters', but showed inferior seakeeping abilities and sustained speed endurance. From 1907 she served as tender, and in 1915 was allocated to the submarine school, and used as an accommodation ship in 1919.

S 90–S 101
S 97 served as dispatch boat for the Emperor under the name *Sleipner*, 1900–14. The first three units served in the colonies, *S 90* was scuttled at Tsingtao, 17 October 1914, *S 100* was lost after a collision on 15 October 1915 in the Baltic; all the others received the new prefix letter T in 1914, served in the war, were stricken after 1918 and scrapped.

S 102–S 107
All boats received the new prefix letter T in 1914 and saw active service in the war with minesweeping flotillas, were taken over by the *Reichsmarine* but cannibalised, stricken and scrapped in the early 1920s.

G 108–G 113
All received the new prefix letter T in 1914 and saw active service during the war; after the war they were stricken and scrapped in the early 1920s.

S 114–S 119
S 116 was torpedoed by the British submarine *E 9* in the North Sea, 6 October 1914; *S 115–S 119* were sunk after a gunnery duel with the British cruiser *Undaunted* and four destroyers in the North Sea, 17 October 1914; the surviving boat was renumbered *T 114* in 1916, stricken on 9 November 1920 and scrapped.

S 120–S 124
S 124 received heavy damage in a collision in the Baltic on 30 November 1914, and was scrapped in 1915; *S 123* was mined in the Baltic, 1 May 1916; those remaining received the new prefix letter T in 1916, *T 122* being mined in the North Sea on 5 October 1918, and the surviving two boats being stricken and scrapped in 1920–21.

S 125
The boat was renumbered *T 125* in 1916 and stricken and scrapped in 1921.

S 126–S 131
S 126 was cut in two after a collision with the light cruiser *Undine* on 17 November 1905; both parts were raised and reconstructed in 1908, the boat surviving the war as a training unit and was scrapped in 1921. *S 129* sank after grounding in the North Sea, 5 November 1915; all the others received the new prefix T in 1916, survived the war, and were stricken and scrapped in the early 1920s.

EARLIER TORPEDO-BOATS
Many of the earlier torpedo-boats were still in service in 1906, many having been rebuilt and reboilered, although some were discarded and others were being relegated to duties as tenders or targets. In 1910 the prefix was changed from S to T. The following boats served during the First World War.
S 7 group: *T 11, T 13, T 14, T 15, T 20, T 23*
S 24 group: *T 24, T 25, T 27, T 28, T 29, T 30* (*T 25* and *T 29* were lost in collisions).
S 33 group: *T 33–T 40*.
S 43 group: *T 43–T 47, T 49–T 57* (*T 43, T 45, T 47, T 50, T 51, T 52, T 54, T 56* and T 57 were war losses).
S 58 group: *T 58–T 65* (*T 58, T 59, T 64* and *T 65* were war losses).
Of the slightly later boats most were still in service in September 1914 when they were also given T prefixes.
S 66/67 groups: *T 66–T 73* (*T 66, T 67, T 68* were mined during the war).
S 74/75 groups: *T 75–T 81* (*T 78* was mined during the war).
S 82 group: *T 82–T 89* (none was lost during the war).
The survivors were sold for breaking up in 1920–21.

MISCELLANEOUS
In 1906 the German Navy also operated the Imperial yacht *Hohenzollern* (ii) (4460t full load, 1892) and its predecessor the paddle yacht *Kaiseradler*, ex-*Hohenzollern* (1962t, 1876). Also in service 1906 were the survey ships *Möwe* and *Planet*, the minelayer *Pelikan* and the fishery protection vessel *Zieten*. There was a squadron of China river gunboats consisting of the *Vorwärts* (406t, 1899), *Tsingtao* and *Vaterland* (495t, 1903). The first was sold in 1911, *Tsingtao* was blown up to avoid capture in 1917, and the other was taken over by the Chinese. Existing old ironclads were used as training and drill vessels: *Moltke, Stosch, Stein, Charlotte, Nixe, Sophie.*

CAPITAL SHIPS

The improvement in fighting power between the series of mediocre pre-dreadnoughts, of which the last were not completed until 1908, and the first German dreadnoughts of the *Nassau* class was remarkable, particularly as there were no intervening ships such as the British *King Edward* and *Lord Nelson*, though they were considered. It cannot be claimed that the *Nassau* was an outstanding design, but the next classes were much improved and in battlecruisers development from the armoured cruisers of the *Scharnhorst* class to the *von der Tann* was even more remarkable, though here the *Blücher* was an intervening ship. The *von der Tann* was a better design than the *Nassau* and later battlecruisers were much improved. Great credit is due to Dr Bürkner and his fellow constructors.

Compared with their British contemporaries German capital ships had lighter hulls of greater beam and a smaller calibre main armament of 11.1in or 12in guns instead of 12in or 13.5in. Only 2 German ships were completed with 15in guns as against 10 British battleships and 4 battlecruisers or large cruisers, and German capital ship construction was greatly delayed or abandoned in 1916–18. Due largely to inferior British APC the disadvantages of a smaller calibre main armament were not as great as they might have been, and the German Navy was far ahead in propellant charges and in freedom from magazine explosions, due in part to the use of brass cartridge cases for part of the charge even in 15in guns; two older ships, the *Pommern* and *Prinz Adalbert*, blew up after torpedo hits, but the cause is thought to have been the detonation of secondary armament shells. It must be noted that the Germans exposed their propellant charges to a far greater extent than did the British, and very serious fires occurred, but they did not develop into explosions.

German dreadnoughts and battlecruisers were well protected between end barbettes against the shells, torpedoes and mines of 1914–18, though armour of 10in or less would have been vulnerable to the later type of 15in and 13.5in APC coming into service late in the war. The forward part was liable to extensive flooding from shell hits and there was often no way to remove this water. The forward broadside 23.6in torpedo flat in the later ships was a particular source of weakness, and shell damage here was the main cause of the loss of the

Lützow, combined with malfunctioning of the complicated drainage and water-tight door system. A mine exploding in this position caused embarassingly serious damage to the *Bayern*. It may be noted that her sister ship *Baden* had a leak pump capacity of 5400 tons per hour, while *Queen Elizabeth* as completed had only 950 tons per hour.

The use of small-tube boilers gave a considerable advantage in machinery weights and volumes, and in addition German engine rooms were decidedly cramped by British standards. Coal supply from some of the bunkers was often difficult and it seems that the quality of the coal was sometimes inferior to British.

In conclusion on the evidence of 1914–18 operations, German battlecruisers were superior North Sea fighting ships to their British contemporaries, but with battleships the difference was less marked, though the indifferent underwater protection of many British ships and their shell and propellant safety deficiencies gave the edge to the German ships in most cases.

Note: All weights in the Capital Ship section are in 'long' tons of 1016kg; thereafter metric tonnes (of 1000kg) are used.

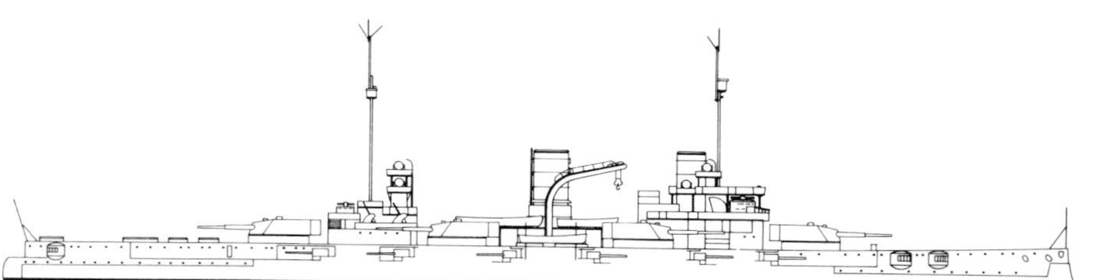

Westfalen 1919

NASSAU class *battleships*

Displacement: 18,570t normal; 21,000t deep load

Dimensions: 451ft 9in pp, 479ft 4in oa × 88ft 5in (*Nassau* 88ft 2in) × 26ft 6in mean, 29ft 3in mean deep load
137.7m, 146.1m × 26.9m × 8.08m, 8.9m

Machinery: 3-shaft 3-cyl VTE, 12 Schulz-Thornycroft boilers, 22,000ihp=19.5kts. Coal 2950t. Range 8000nm/2200nm at 10kts/19kts

Armour: Belt 300mm–80mm (12in–3.2in), bulkheads 210mm–90mm (8.3in–3.5in), battery 160mm (6.3in), barbettes 280mm–50mm (11in–2in), turrets 280–60mm (11in–2.4in), CT 300mm–80mm (12in–3.2in)

Armament: 12–28cm (11.1in) SKL/45 (6×2), 12–15cm (5.9in) SKL/45, 16–8.8cm (3.45in) SKL/45, 6–45cm (17.7in) TT sub

Complement: 1008 (1124–1139 at Jutland)

Name	Builder	Laid down	Launched	Comp	Fate
NASSAU	Wilhelmshaven N Yd	22.7.07	7.3.08	3.5.10	BU 1921
WESTFALEN	Weser, Bremen	12.8.07	1.7.08	3.5.10	BU 1924
RHEINLAND	Vulcan, Stettin	1.6.07	26.9.08	21.9.10	BU 1921
POSEN	Germaniawerft, Kiel	11.6.07	12.12.08	21.9.10	BU 1922

The first German dreadnoughts, built under the 1906–7 programme (and that of 1907–8 for *Rheinland* and *Posen*), were flush-decked ships, easily distinguished by their goose-neck cranes. Freeboard at normal load was about 22ft forward, 17ft 9in midships and 19ft 6in aft with GM 7.65ft, and it was originally thought that bilge keels were not necessary. It was found however that their rolling was synchronous with the North Sea swell and bilge keels had to be fitted. *Nassau*, and particularly *Westfalen*, were not so satisfactory as the other two.

The heavy gun turrets were arranged fore and aft on the centreline with two on either beam, a peculiar distribution which gave a broadside of only 8 guns. The beam turret mountings were Drh LC/1906 in all ships as were the centreline mountings in *Nassau* and *Westfalen*, but the other two had Drh LC/1907 here: C/1906 was a short trunk mounting with fixed working chamber while C/1907 was of long trunk type. Both allowed 20° elevation. Magazines were above shell rooms except for the centreline turrets in *Nassau* and *Westfalen*. The 15cm was on the main deck, and 2–8.8in Flak L/45 eventually replaced the 8.8cm SKL/45 guns.

The TT were located at bow and stern and on either beam forward and abaft the torpedo bulkhead.

The belt was 12in–11½in between end barbettes for about 4ft along the lwl, tapering to 6.3in at the main deck and to 6.7in at the lower edge 63in below lwl. Forward it was 5.5in–3.2in and aft 4.7–3.5in. The barbettes were 11in–8in reduced to 3.2in–2in behind the battery and belt, and the turrets had 11in faces, 8.7in sides, 10.3in rears and 3.5in–2.4in roofs. The armour deck was 1.5in with 2.3in slopes amidships, 2.2in forward and 3.2in–2.2in aft with the upper deck 1.2in–1in over the battery. The torpedo bulkhead ran between end barbettes and was 1.2in–0.8in.

There were 6 boiler and 3 engine rooms and 160 tons of tar oil were later carried for spraying on the coal in the furnaces. Boiler pressure was 235lb/in². Trials were prolonged, the commissioning dates being *Nassau* 1 October 1909, *Westfalen* 16 November 1909, *Rheinland* 30 April 1910, *Posen* 31 May 1910. On the mile all attained 20–20.2kts with 26,244–28,117ihp.

Rheinland ran aground at 15kts on rocks off Lagskär on 11 April 1918 and over 6000t, including belt armour and all guns, had to be removed before she could be got to Kiel; she was never repaired. *Westfalen* was torpedoed amidships by *E 23* on 19 August 1916 and took on 800t of water, but though bulkheads were sagging, she returned to harbour at 14kts.

Posen as completed *CPL*

Helgoland 1914
Navarret Collection

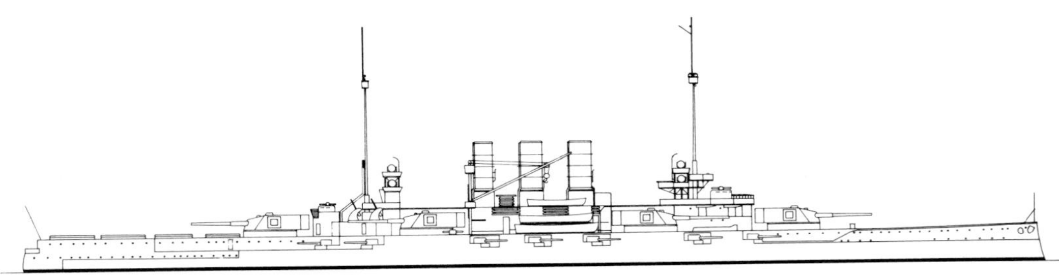

Ostfriesland 1918

HELGOLAND class *battleships*

Displacement:	22,440t normal; 25,200t deep load
Dimensions:	548ft 7in oa × 93ft 6in × 26ft 11in mean, 29ft 6in mean deep load *167.2m × 28.5m × 8.2m, 9.0m*
Machinery:	3-shaft 4-cyl VTE, 15 Schulz-Thornycroft boilers, 28,000ihp = 20.3kts. Coal 3150t. Range 1790nm at 10kts
Armour:	Belt 300mm–80mm (12in–3.2in), bulkheads 210mm–90mm (8.3in–3.5in), battery 170mm (6.7in), barbettes 300mm–60mm (12in–2.4in), turrets 300mm–70mm (12in–2.75in), CT 300mm–100mm (12in–4in)
Armament:	12–30.5cm (12in) SKL/50 (6×2), 14–15cm (5.9in) SKL/45, 14–8.8cm (3.45in) SKL/45, 6–50cm (19.7in) TT sub
Complement:	1113 (1284–1390 at Jutland)

Name	Builder	Laid down	Launched	Comp	Fate
HELGOLAND	Howaldtswerke, Kiel	24.12.08	25.9.09	19.12.11	BU 1924
OSTFRIESLAND	Wilhelmshaven N Yd	19.10.08	30.9.09	15.9.11	Target, sunk 21.7.21
THÜRINGEN	Weser, Bremen	7.11.08	27.11.09	10.9.11	BU 1923
OLDENBURG	Schichau, Danzig	1.3.09	30.6.10	1.7.12	BU 1921

This class, built under the 1908–09 programme (except for *Oldenburg* under that of 1909–10), were a considerable improvement on the *Nassau*. They were easily distinguished by the three funnels arranged close together, and were flush-decked with freeboard at normal load similar to the previous class; GM was 8.53ft.

The turrets were arranged as in *Nassau* with the guns in long trunk Drh LC/1908 mountings with 13½° elevation, increased later to 16°. Magazines were below shell rooms in all turrets. The 15cm battery was on the main deck, and the 8.8cm were eventually replaced by 2–8.8cm Flak L/45. TT were arranged as previously.

The armour belt was 12in between end barbettes for 35in above and 14in below lwl, tapering to 6.7in at the lower edge 63in below lwl and to 6.7in at the main deck but to 10in in way of the wing barbettes. Forward there was 6in–3.2in and aft 5in–3.5in. The barbettes varied with exposure from 12in to 8in, the centreline ones being reduced to 4.7in–3.2in behind side armour while the wing barbettes were 4in–2.4in behind the battery armour and below this protected only by the 10in side. Turrets had 12in faces, 10in sides, 11.5in rears and 4in–2.75in roofs. The armour deck was 1.6in with 2.4in slopes amidships, 2.2in forward and 3.2in–2.2in aft while the upper deck over the battery and the main deck amidships outside the battery, were 1.8in–1in. The torpedo bulkhead was 14¾ft inboard amidships and 1.2in–1.0in.

There were 9 boiler and 3 engine rooms; boiler pressure was 235lb/in² and *c*200 tons tar oil was later carried for spraying on the coal. *Helgoland* was commissioned for trials on 23 August 1911, *Ostfriesland* 1 August 1911, *Thüringen* 1 July 1911, *Oldenburg* 1 May 1912. On the mile 20.8kts–21.3kts was attained with 31,258ihp–35,500ihp, *Oldenburg* being the fastest.

The only serious war damage was to *Ostfriesland* on 1 June 1916 when she struck a mine below the starboard forward wing turret on 1 June 1916. She was able to steam at 15kts, reduced to 10 after the damage had been increased by a sharp turn in avoiding an imaginary submarine.

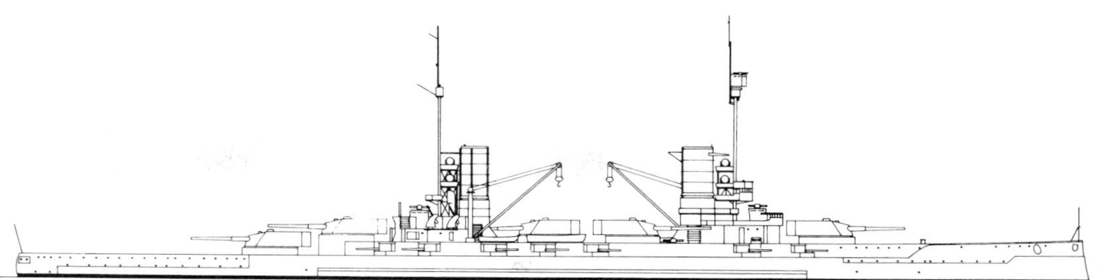

Friedrich der Grosse 1919

KAISER class *battleships*

Displacement: 24,330t normal; 27,400t deep load

Dimensions: 565ft 7in oa × 95ft 2in × 27ft 3in mean, 30ft mean deep load
172.4m × 29.0m × 8.3m, 9.1m

Machinery: 3-shaft Parsons (*F d Grosse* AEG–Curtis, *K Albert* Schichau) turbines, 16 Schulz-Thornycroft boilers, 31,000shp = 21kts. Coal 3540t. Range 6000nm/4000nm at 12kts/19kts
P Luitpold 2-shaft Parsons turbines, 1-shaft Germania diesel (never installed), 14 Schulz-Thornycroft boilers, 26,000shp + 12,000bhp = 22kts. Coal 3150t, diesel oil 395t. Range 7200nm at 12kts (2000nm at 12kts on diesel, as designed)

Armour: Belt 350mm–80mm (14in–3.2in), bulkheads 300mm–130mm (12in–5in), battery 170mm (6.7in), barbettes 300mm–80mm (12in–3.2in), turrets 300mm–80mm (12in–3.2in), CT 350mm–150mm (14in–6in)

Armament: 10–30.5cm (12in) SKL/50 (5×2), 14–15cm (5.9in) SKL/45, 8–8.8cm (3.45in) SKL/45, 4–8.8cm (3.45in) Flak L/45, 5–50cm (19.7in) TT sub

Complement: 1084 (1249–1278 at Jutland)

Name	Builder	Laid down	Launched	Comp	Fate
KAISER	Kiel N Yd	12.09	22.3.11	7.12.12	Scuttled 21.6.19
FRIEDRICH DER GROSSE	Vulcan, Hamburg	26.1.10	10.6.11	22.1.13	Scuttled 21.6.19
KAISERIN	Howaldtswerke, Kiel	11.10	11.11.11	13.12.13	Scuttled 21.6.19
KÖNIG ALBERT	Schichau, Danzig	17.7.10	27.4.12	8.11.13	Scuttled 21.6.19
PRINZREGENT LUITPOLD	Germaniawerft, Kiel	1.11	17.2.12	6.12.13	Scuttled 21.6.19

This class marked a break with previous dreadnoughts. The first two were built under the 1909–10 programme and the others under that of 1910–11. There was a forecastle deck extending to past the mainmast and the boiler rooms and funnels were widely spaced. Freeboard at normal load was about 23ft forward and 13ft aft, with GM 8.50ft.

The arrangement of the main turrets was altered to one forward, two echelonned amidships and two superfiring aft. A 10-gun broadside was practicable as the midships turrets had arcs of 120° on the opposite beam. The mountings were Drh LC/1909, generally similar to C/1908, and with 13½° elevation, later increased to 16°. Magazines in all were below shell rooms. The 15cm guns were in an upper deck battery and the 8.8cm SKL/45 were later removed and the Flak L/45 finally cut to 2. TT were arranged as previously except that there was no stern tube.

The side armour was much improved, the belt between end barbettes being 14in from the main deck 70in–72in above lwl to 14in below lwl, and tapering to 7in at 67in below lwl, with 8in between main and upper decks. Forward there was 7in–3.2in and aft 7in–5in with 6in–3.2in forward and 6in aft in *Kaiserin and Prinzregent Luipold*. Barbettes were 12in–8.7in reduced to 5.5in behind the battery and upper belt armour and to 3.2in behind the main belt, while the turrets had 12in faces, 10in sides, 11.5in rears and 4.3in–3.2in roofs. The armour deck was 1.2in amidships, 2.4in forward and 4.7in–2.4in aft while between end barbettes the upper deck was 1.2in–1.0in outside the battery and the forecastle deck 1.2in over the latter. The torpedo bulkhead was 1.6in with 2in in *Kaiserin* and *Prinzregent Luitpold*, and in all was continued as a 1.2in splinter bulkhead to the upper deck.

There were 10 boiler rooms and 3 sets of turbines in 6 engine rooms – except in *Prinzregent Luitpold* which had 2 sets in 4 – and boiler pressure and tar oil were as in *Helgoland*. Turbines and boilers were noted for giving trouble in *Kaiserin*. Commissioning dates for trials were *Kaiser* 1 August 1912, *Friedrich der Grosse* 15 October 1912, *Kaiserin* 14 May 1913, *König Albert* 31 July 1913, *Prinzregent Luitpold* 19 August 1913. On the mile *Kaiser* was forced to 55,187shp = 23.4kts, while the other 3-shaft ships made 39,813shp–42,181shp = 22.1kts–22.4kts, and *Prinzregent Luitpold* without her diesel 38,751shp = 21.7kts.

None of the class was seriously damaged in 1914–18. They were raised for scrap at Scapa between 1929 and 1937.

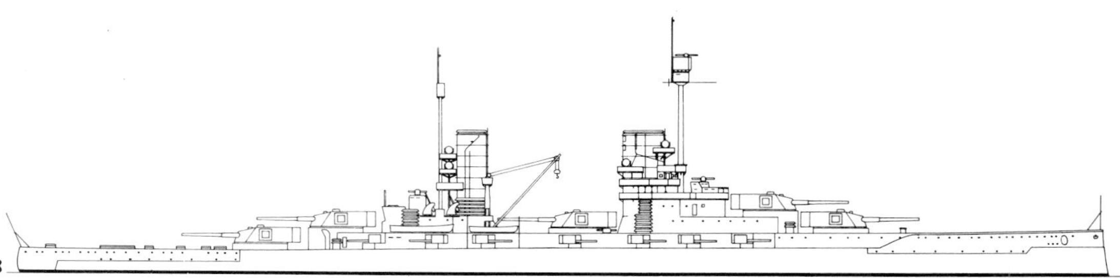

Grosser Kurfürst 1918

KÖNIG class *battleships*

Displacement: 25,390t normal; 29,200t deep load

Dimensions: 575ft 6in oa × 96ft 9in × 27ft 3in mean, 30ft 6½in mean deep load
175.4m × 29.5m × 8.3m, 9.3m

Machinery: 3-shaft Parsons (*G Kurfürst* AEG-Vulcan, *Markgraf* Bergmann) turbines, 15 Schulz-Thornycroft boilers, 31,000shp = 21kts. Coal 3540t, oil 690t. Range 6800nm/4600nm at 12kts/19kts

Armour: Belt 350mm–80mm (14in–3.2in), bulkheads 300mm–130mm (12in–5in), battery 170mm (6.7in), barbettes 300mm–80mm (12in–3.2in), turrets 300mm–80mm (12in–3.2in), CT 350mm–170mm (14in–6.7in)

Armament: 10–30.5cm (12in) SKL/50 (5×2), 14–15cm (5.9in) SKL/45, 6–8.8cm (3.45in) SKL/45, 4–8.8cm (3.45in) Flak L/45, 5–50cm (19.7in) TT sub

Complement: 1136 (1284–1315 at Jutland)

Name	Builder	Laid down	Launched	Comp	Fate
KÖNIG	Wilhelmshaven N Yd	10.11	1.3.13	1.15	Scuttled 21.6.19
GROSSER KURFÜRST	Vulcan, Hamburg	10.11	5.5.13	9.14	Scuttled 21.6.19
MARKGRAF	Weser, Bremen	11.11	4.6.13	1.15	Scuttled 21.6.19
KRONPRINZ	Germaniawerft, Kiel	5.12	21.2.14	2.15	Scuttled 21.6.19

These ships were essentially improved *Kaiser*s with a much better turret distribution. The first three were built under the 1911–12 programme and *Kronprinz* – renamed *Kronprinz Wilhelm* on 27 January 1918 – under that of 1912–13. The run of the forecastle deck and freeboard were similar but the funnels were not so far apart as in *Kaiser*. GM was 8.50ft and fighting draughts apparently varied from 29ft 0½in to 29ft 8¼in (8.85m–9.05m).

The turrets were all on the centreline with superfiring pairs fore and aft and the fifth between the funnels at the same height as the after superfiring one. The mountings were Drh LC/1911, similar to C/1909 and with 13½° elevation, increased to 16°. Magazines were all below shell rooms. The 15cm battery was on the upper deck, and the 8.8cm SKL/45 were later removed and the Flak L/45 reduced to 2. TT were arranged as in *Kaiser*.

The armour was generally as in *Kaiser* but the belt forward was 8in–3.2in and 8in–5in aft. The upper deck amidships was 1.2in outside the battery and 0.8in as the battery floor, while the torpedo bulkhead was 2in and continued as a 1.2in splinter bulkhead to the upper deck.

There were 3 oil-fired and 12 coal-fired boilers, with the oil-fired in the 3 foremost boiler rooms, 6 coal-fired in the next 3 and another 6 in the 3 after boiler rooms. The 3 sets of turbines were in 6 engine rooms, and boiler pressure remained at 235lb/in². Commissioning dates for trials were *König* 10 August 1914, *Grosser Kurfürst* 30 July 1914, *Markgraf* 1 October 1914, *Kronprinz* 8 November 1914, but the deep water mile at Neukrug could not be used and figures were 41,400shp–46,200shp = 21.0kts–21.3kts. In service they were faster than the *Kaiser* class, and *Grosser Kurfürst* was apparently considered the fastest and was said to have touched 24kts, though at Jutland she was outpaced by *König*.

Grosser Kurfürst and *Kronprinz* were both torpedoed by *J 1* on 5 November 1916, respectively right aft (jamming the port rudder) and under the bridge, but both maintained 17kts–19kts. In the Gulf of Riga operations *Grosser Kurfürst* was mined on 12 October 1917 and *Markgraf* on the 29th but the torpedo bulkhead limited flooding in both to 260–280 tons.

At Jutland *König* was hit by 1–15in and 9–13.5in shells, *Grosser Kurfürst* by 5–15in and 3–13.5in, and *Markgraf* by 3–15in, 1–13.5in and 1–12in. The worst damage to *König* was from a 13.5in CPC on the 7in extreme lower edge of the belt which burst about 7ft inboard sending many fragments through 6½ft of coal and the 2in torpedo bulkhead into a 5.9in ammunition room. Sea water flooding in limited the fire to 15 cartridges, but most of the 1630 tons reported after the battle was from this hit. In *Grosser Kurfürst* a 13.5in APC hit the 6in armour forward near the waterline and burst making a hole 51in × 35in. Almost the whole fore part of the ship except the torpedo flats and trimming tanks flooded up to the main deck increasing the draught forward by 5ft.

Grosser Kurfürst was raised at Scapa for scrap in 1936, but salvage rights on the others were not granted until 1962.

Kaiser as completed — *Navarret Collection*

Grosser Kurfürst as completed — *Navarret Collection*

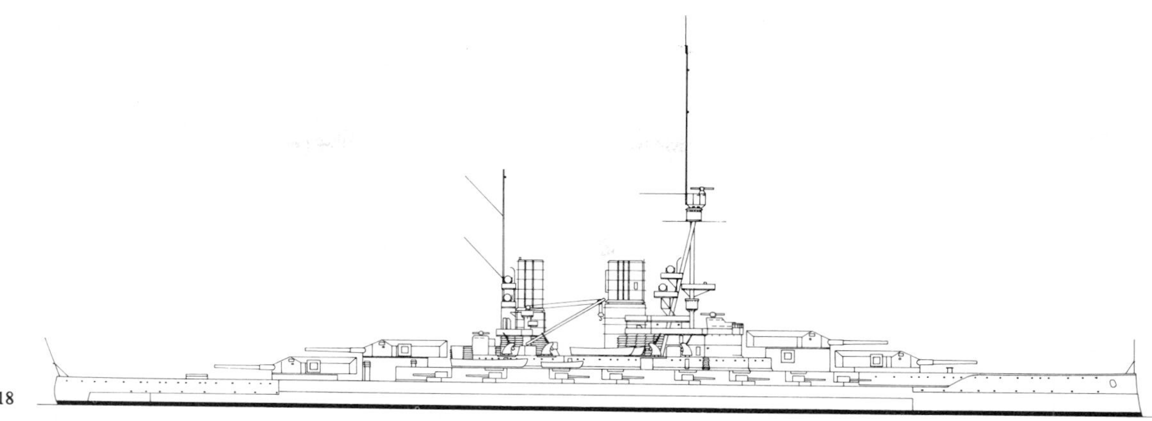

Bayern 1918

In this class the main armament was increased from 12in to 15in without any intervening 13.8in (35cm) as was to have been the case in battlecruisers. Both ships were built under the 1913–14 programme. The forecastle deck extended to the after superfiring turret and freeboard at normal load was 23ft 8in forward and 15ft 1in aft. The funnels were not widely separated and both ships had a tripod foremast with a small mainmast close abaft the after funnel, though initially *Bayern* had none. GM was 8.4ft at 27ft 8in and mean fighting draught 29ft 10in (9.09m). When examined in Britain it was thought that *Baden* was more than 12in over her designed draught at normal load.

The turrets were in superfiring pairs fore and aft and the Drh LC 1913 mountings allowed 16° elevation, later increased to 20° in *Bayern*. There was a 26.9ft rangefinder in each turret. The magazines were all above the shell rooms with crowns formed by the armour deck. The 15cm battery was on the upper deck and the 8 Flak guns were never carried, the number varying from 2 to 4. The TT were arranged as in *Kaiser*, but after *Bayern* was mined the 2 forward broadside tubes were removed in both ships.

BAYERN class *battleships*

Displacement: 28,074t normal; 31,690t deep load

Dimensions: 589ft 10in oa × 98ft 5in × 27ft 8in mean, 30ft 9in mean deep load
179.8m × 30.0m × 8.43m, 9.37m

Machinery: 3-shaft Parsons turbines, 14 Schulz-Thornycroft boilers, 48,000shp = 21kts. Coal 3350t, oil 610t. Range 5000nm/2390nm at 13kts/21.5kts

Armour: Belt 350mm–120mm (14in–4.7in), bulkheads 300mm–140mm (12in–5.5in), battery 170mm (6.7in), barbettes 350mm–25mm (14in–1in), turrets 350mm–100mm (14in–4in), CT 350mm–170mm (14in–6.7in)

Armament: 8–38cm (15in) SKL/45 (4×2), 16–15cm (5.9in) SKL/45, 8–8.8cm (3.45in) Flak L/45, 5–60cm (23.6in) TT sub

Complement: 1187–1271

Name	Builder	Laid down	Launched	Comp	Fate
BAYERN	Howaldtswerke, Kiel	1.14	18.2.15	30.6.16	Scuttled 21.6.19
BADEN	Schichau, Danzig	20.12.13	30.10.15	2.17	Target, sunk 16.8.21

The main 14in belt ran from 70in above lwl to 14in below between end barbettes, tapering to 6.7in at the lower edge 67in below lwl. Between main and upper decks it was 10in. Forward the armour was 8in–6in ending 50ft from the bows and aft 8in–4.7in. The barbettes were 14in–10in reduced to 6.7in behind the battery armour, 8in–3.2in behind the 10in side and 4.5in–1in behind the 14in. The turrets had 14in faces, 10in sides, 11½in rears and 8in–4in roofs. Decks, torpedo and splinter bulkheads were as in *König* except that the forecastle deck was 1.6in near the centreline amidships and the battery floor 1.0in.

There were 3 oil-fired and 11 coal-fired boilers in 9 boiler rooms with the oil-fired in the 3 foremost. Oil fuel sprays could be used in the coal furnaces. The 3 sets of turbines were in 6 engine rooms, and boiler pressure was still 235lb/in². *Bayern* was commissioned for trials on 18 March 1916 and *Baden* on 19 October 1916. On the Belt mile they both recorded 22.0kts with 55,967 and 56,275shp respectively.

Bayern was mined on 12 October 1917 during the Gulf of Riga operations, near the forward broadside torpedo flat beyond the torpedo bulkhead, and flooding was serious, involving the bow torpedo flat and increasing draught forward to 36ft. Temporary patching ran into difficulties and she did not reach Kiel for 19 days. *Bayern* was raised at Scapa for scrap in September 1934 and broken up at Rosyth.

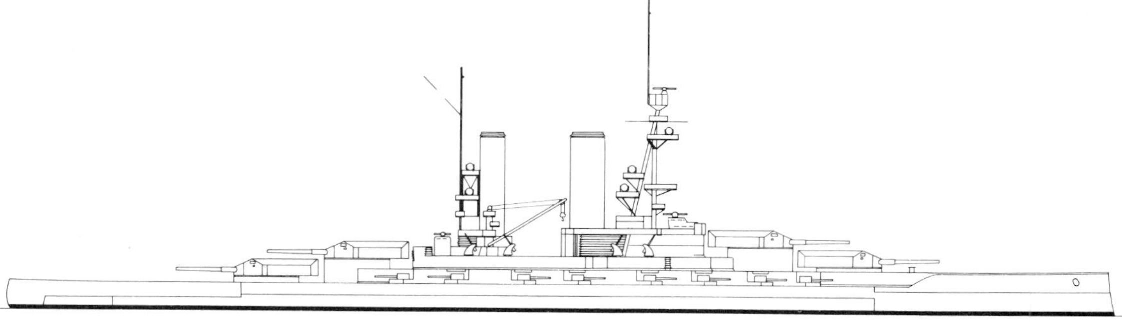

Sachsen design

These ships were slightly lengthened *Bayern*s, *Sachsen* being built under the 1914–15 programme and *Württemberg* under War Estimates, and would have been similar in appearance except for higher funnels in *Sachsen*.

The designed armament was unchanged except that the 38cm mountings were Drh LC/1914 with 20° elevation, and TT would certainly have been reduced to 3. Armour was also as in *Bayern* with a few exceptions. *Sachsen* had a structure protecting the top of the diesel engine for about halfway between armour and main decks. This was 8in–5.5in with 3.2in roof, and both ships are shown with all barbettes 1.6in behind the 14in belt, and with the armour deck

SACHSEN class *battleships*

Displacement: 28,345t normal (*Württemberg* 28,247)t); 31,987t deep load (*Württemberg* 31,700t)

Dimensions: 598ft 5in oa × 98ft 5in × 27ft 8in mean, 30ft 9in mean deep load
182.4m × 20.0m × 8.4m, 9.4m

Machinery: *Sachsen* 2-shaft Parsons turbines, 1-shaft MAN diesel, 9 Schulz-Thornycroft boilers, 31,8000shp + 12,000bhp = 21.5kts. Coal 2660t, oil 1280t
Württemberg 3-shaft AEG – Vulcan turbines, 12 Schulz-Thornycroft boilers, 48,000shp = 22kts. Coal 3050t, oil 890t

Armour: Belt 350mm–120mm (14in–4.7in), bulkheads 300mm–140mm (12in–5.5in), battery 170mm (6.7in), barbettes 350mm–40mm (14in–1.6in), turrets 350mm–100mm (14in–4in), CT 350mm–170mm (14in–6.7in)

Armament: 8–38cm (15in) SKL/45 (4×2), 16–15cm (5.9in) SKL/45, 8–8.8cm (3.45in) Flak L/45, 5–60cm (23.6in) TT sub

Complement: 1165 (*Württemberg* 1196)

Name	Builder	Laid down	Launched	Comp	Fate
SACHSEN	Germaniawerft, Kiel	7.4.14	21.11.16	–	BU 1921
WÜRTTEMBERG	Vulcan, Hamburg	4.1.15	20.6.17	–	BU 1921

2in over some areas amidships.

In *Sachsen* the centre shaft was to be diesel-powered and the two outer steam with 3 oil- and 6 coal-fired boilers and 2 sets of turbines in 4 engine rooms, while in *Württemberg* there were 3 oil- and 9 coal-fired boilers with 3 sets of turbines in 6 engine rooms. Range was to be 2000nm at 12kts on diesel alone.

Baden 1918

Aldo Fraccaroli Collection

L 20 α design *battleships*

Displacement:	*c*43,800t normal; *c*48,700t deep load
Dimensions:	781ft lwl × 110ft × 29ft 6in mean, *c*32ft 6in mean deep load *238.0m × 33.5m × 9.0m, c9.9m*
Machinery:	4-shaft turbines, 22 Schulz-Thornycroft boilers, 100,000shp = 26kts. Coal 2950t, oil 1970t
Armour:	Belt 350mm–130mm (14in–5in), bulkheads 250mm–60mm (10in–2.4in), battery 170mm (6.7in), barbettes 350mm–100mm (14in–4in), turrets 350mm–150mm (14in–6in), CT 350mm–150mm (14in–6in)
Armament:	8–42cm (16.5in) SKL/45 (4×2), 12–15cm (5.9in) SKL/45, 8–8.8cm (3.4in) or 10.5cm (4.1in) Flak L/45, 3–60cm (23.6in) or 70cm (27.6in) TT sub
Complement:	?

This design, dated 2 October 1917, was selected from a number of fast battleship and battlecruiser designs for construction on 11 September 1918, though by this time there was no chance of them ever being built. Outlines show a single trunked funnel with tripod foremast and a forecastle extending to the after superfiring barbette.

The turrets were arranged with superfiring pairs fore and aft, the latter being widely separated by engine rooms. The 15cm were in an upper deck battery. There was a single bow TT and one on either beam abaft the boiler rooms and thus within the torpedo bulkhead, though these would probably have been moved to an above water position behind the forward side armour.

The 14in belt armour extended from a little forward of the fore barbette to a little abaft the after one, and from 77in above lwl to 14in below. It tapered to 6.7in at the lower edge 67in below lwl, and was 10in between the main and upper decks. Forward the armour was 10in with 6in lower edge not extending to the stem, and aft 12in with 5in lower edge. Barbettes are shown as 14in reduced to 10in behind the battery, 10in–6in behind the 10in side and 6in–4in behind the 14in. Turrets had 14in faces, 10in sides, 12in rears and 10in–6in roofs. The armour deck was 2.4in–2in amidships, 2in forward and 4.7in–2in aft, with a 1.6in–0.8in forecastle deck over the battery, apparently 0.8in on most of the upper deck and on the main deck aft. The torpedo bulkhead was 2.4in–2in continued as a 1.2in splinter bulkhead to the upper deck.

There were to be 6 oil-fired and 156 coal-fired boilers but it is not clear whether there were 2 or 4 sets of turbines. They would obviously have been very powerful ships but the decks were thin as was the belt lower edge, and armour of 10in or less would have been vulnerable to later 15in shells.

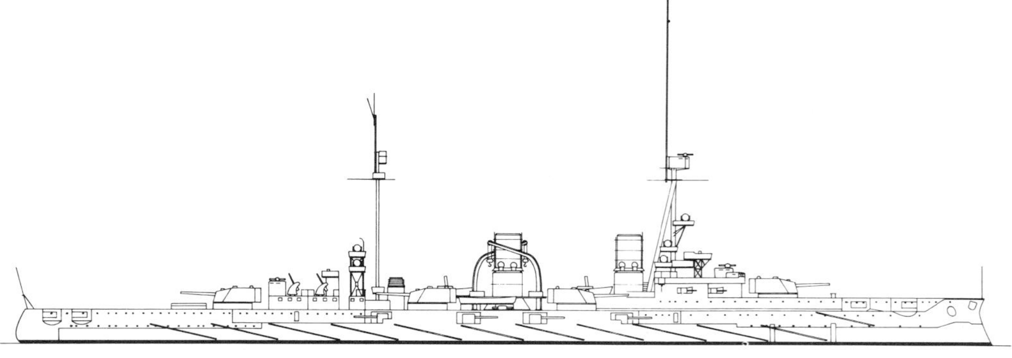

Blücher 1915

BLÜCHER *armoured cruiser*

Displacement:	15,590t normal; 17,250t deep load
Dimensions:	498ft 8in pp, 530ft 6in oa × 80ft 3in × 26ft 3in mean, 28ft 6in mean at deep load *152.0m, 161.7m × 24.5m × 8.0m, 8.7m*
Machinery:	3-shaft 4-cyl VTE, 18 Schulz-Thornycroft boilers, 34,000ihp = 24.25kts. Coal 2260t. Range 6600nm/3520nm at 12kts/18kts
Armour:	Belt 180mm–60mm (7in–2.4in), bulkheads 150mm–80mm (6in–3.2in), battery 140mm (5.5in), barbettes 180mm (7in) max, turrets 180mm–60mm (7in–2.4in), CT 250mm–80mm (10in–3.2in)
Armament:	12–21cm (8.2in) SKL/45 (6×2), 8–15cm (5.9in) SKL/45, 16–8.8cm (3.45in) SKL/45, 4–45cm (17.7in) TT sub
Complement:	847 (1026 at Dogger Bank)

Name	Builder	Laid down	Launched	Comp	Fate
BLÜCHER	Kiel N Yd	21.2.07	11.4.08	24.3.10	Sunk 24.1.15

Built under the 1906–7 programme this armoured cruiser was a development of the *Scharnhorst* class, and although it was known in August 1906 that the British were building the *Invincible* class battlecruisers, matters had gone too far for *Blücher*'s design to be altered. Except for the small turrets, her general appearance was that of a battleship, with two funnels and goose-neck cranes. A tripod mast, the first in any German ship, was fitted in 1913. Freeboard at normal load was approximately 27ft forward, 18ft amidships and 15ft aft and GM is given as 5.35ft.

The main turrets were disposed with 2 on either beam giving an 8-gun broadside and the Drh LC/1906 mountings were of short trunk type with fixed working chambers; elevation was 30°. The two forward beam turrets were supplied by central ammunition rails from magazines below those for the after beam turrets and this arrangement was to prove disastrous. The 15cm guns were in a main deck battery and the TT at bow, stern and forward on either beam.

The belt tapered to 4¾in at the lower edge and main deck with 3.2in–2.4in forward and aft of the end barbettes. The turrets had 7in faces, 5½in sides, 6in rears and 3.2in–2.4in roofs, and the armour deck was 1.2in amidships with 2in slopes, 2in forward and 2.4in–2.8in aft. A 1.2in torpedo bulkhead extended between end barbettes.

There were 5 boiler rooms and on the mile 43,886ihp = 25.86kt was obtained. Legend coal was 885 tons. As usual at that time in German ships trials were lengthy and began on 1 October 1909. The *Blücher* was used for gunnery experiments before 1914. At the Dogger Bank a 13.5in shell from *Princess Royal* at 19,000yds–20,000yds pierced the armour deck and ignited charges on the ammunition rails causing a disastrous fire, while splinters holed the main steam pipe in No 3 boiler room. In spite of much other damage she proved hard to sink and was probably hit by a total of about 50 heavy shells and 2–21in torpedoes.

Blücher as completed
CPL

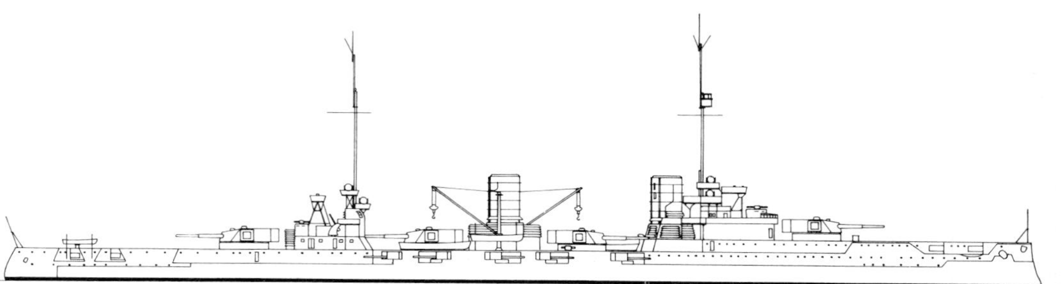

Von der Tann 1918

VON DER TANN *battlecruiser*

Displacement:	19,064t normal; 21,700t deep load
Dimensions:	563ft 4in oa × 87ft 3in × 26ft 6¾in mean, 29ft 8in mean at deep load *171.7m × 26.6m × 8.1m, 9.0m*
Machinery;	4-shaft Parsons turbines, 18 Schulz-Thornycroft boilers, 43,600shp = 24.75kts. Coal 2760t + 200t in Frahm tanks. Range 4400nm at 14kts
Armour:	Belt 250mm–80mm (10in–3.2in), bulkheads 180mm–100mm (7in–4in), battery 150mm (6in), barbettes 230mm–30mm (9in–1.2in), turrets 230mm–60mm (9in–2.4in), CT 250mm–80mm (10in–3.2in)
Armament:	8–28cm (11.1in) SKL/45 (4×2), 10–15cm (5.9in) SKL/45, 16–8.8cm (3.45in) SKL/45, 4–45cm (17.7in) TT sub
Complement:	923, 1174 at Jutland

Name	Builder	Laid down	Launched	Comp	Fate
VON DER TANN	Blohm & Voss, Hamburg	25.3.08	20.3.09	20.2.11	Scuttled 21.6.19

This ship, the first German battlecruiser and built under the 1907–8 programme, was a considerably better fighting ship than any of the 6 British 12in gun battlecruisers. There was a short forecastle extending to the foremast and at normal load freeboard was about 26½ft forward and 19ft amidships and aft. GM is given as 6.92ft and Frahm anti-rolling tanks were fitted during construction, but were later used to take 200 tons of extra coal, and bilge keels fitted instead. Fighting draught was less than deep load and was 28ft 11in (8.8m) with displacement 21,082 tons.

The main turrets were disposed fore and aft with 2 echelonned amidships, the latter being sufficiently far inboard to give a 125° arc on the opposite beam. The long trunk Drh LC/1907 mountings allowed 20° elevation and magazines were above shell rooms except in the after turret. The 15cm were in a main deck battery and the TT at bow, stern and on either broadside forward of the torpedo bulkhead. The 8.8cm SKL/45 guns were later removed and 2–8.8cm Flak L/45 added.

The main belt ran from the forward edge of the fore barbette to a little past the after one and was 10in for 35in above and 14in below lwl, tapering to 6in at the main deck and lower edge 63in below lwl. Forward to the bows it was 4¾in–4in and aft 4in–3.2in. The barbettes were 9in–6¾in above the hull armour but behind the battery and main belt were drastically reduced to 1.2in while the turrets had 9in faces and rears, 7in sides and 3.5in–2.4in roofs. The armour deck was 1in behind the

Von der Tann 1914
CPL

main belt with 2in slopes and 2in forward while aft it was 3.2in with 2in–1in slopes. The main deck was 1in over the belt outside the battery, the upper deck 1in over the battery and the forecastle deck 0.9in round the fore barbette. The torpedo bulkhead was 1.2in–1in and about 13ft inboard amidships, running for the same length as the main belt.

There were 10 boiler rooms and 4 engine rooms with the main high pressure turbines on the wing shafts in the 2 forward rooms and the main low pressure on the inner shafts in the 2 after ones. Boiler pressure was 235lb/in², and about 200 tons tar oil was later carried for spraying on the coal in the boiler furnaces. As usual the boilers were heavily forced on the mile and trial figures were 79,000shp = 27.4kts. She was commissioned for trials on 1 September 1910.

At Jutland she blew up *Indefatigable* in the first 14 or 15 minutes and was later hit by 2–15in and 2–13.5in shells which caused damage aft and put two turrets out of action while troubles in the other two caused the ship to be without any heavy guns for 1¼ hours. The *von der Tann* was raised at Scapa Flow on 7 December 1930 and broken up at Rosyth in 1931–34.

Goeben as completed *CPL*

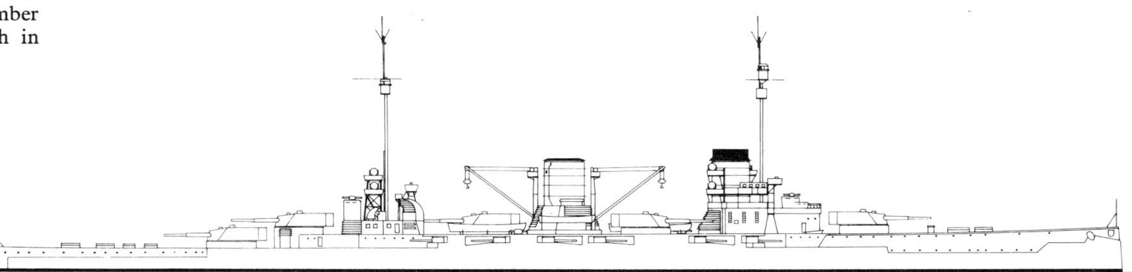

Moltke 1919

MOLTKE class *battlecruisers*

Displacemznt:	22,616t normal; 25,300t deep load
Dimensions:	611ft 11in oa × 96ft 10in × 26ft 11in mean, 29ft 5½in mean at deep load *186.5m × 29.5m × 8.2m, 9.0m*
Machinery:	4-shaft Parsons turbines, 24 Schulz-Thornycroft boilers, 52,000shp = 25.5kts. Coal 3050t. Range 4120nm at 14kts
Armour:	Belt 270mm–100mm (10.7in–4in), bulkheads 200mm–100mm (8in–4in), battery 200mm–150mm (8in–6in), barbettes 230mm–30mm (9in–1.2in), turrets 230mm–60mm (9in–2.4in), CT 350mm–80mm (14in–3.2in)
Armament:	10–28cm (11.1in) SKL/50 (5×2), 12–15cm (5.9in) SKL/45, 12–8.8cm (3.45in) SKL/45, 4–50cm (19.7in) TT sub
Complement:	1053 (1355 at Jutland)

Name	Builder	Laid down	Launched	Comp	Fate
MOLTKE	Blohm & Voss, Hamburg	7.12.08	7.4.10	31.3.12	Scuttled 21.6.19
GOEBEN	Blohm & Voss, Hamburg	28.8.09	28.3.11	28.8.12	BU 1971

This class were a considerable improvement on the *von der Tann* and in addition to increased size, had a different hull form with greater amidships beam and finer ends. The *Moltke* was built under the 1908–9 programme and the *Goeben* under that for 1909–10. The forecastle deck ran to abaft the mainmast and freeboard at normal load was about 24ft forward and 14ft aft. GM was 9.87ft and it was originally intended to use Frahm anti-rolling tanks. Tandem rudders were fitted.

The main turrets were distributed as in *von der Tann* except that the after turret was replaced by a superfiring pair. The Drh LC/1908 mountings were similar to C/1907 but only 13½° elevation was allowed though this was increased to 16° in *Moltke* after Jutland and to 22½° in *Goeben* by the end of the war. All magazines were above shell rooms. The 15cm guns were in an upper deck battery and during the war were reduced to 10, and for a time to 9, in *Goeben*. By the end of 1916 the 3.45in SKL/45 had been replaced in both ships by 4–8.8cm Flak L/45. The TT were located at bow, stern and on either broadside forward of the torpedo bulkhead.

The main belt was 10.7in between the outer edges of the end barbettes and from 55in above to 14in below lwl. It was tapered to 5.1in at the lower edge 69in below lwl, while the upper part was a uniform 8in to the battery port sills or upper deck outside the battery. Forward the belt was 4¾in–4in and aft 4in. The barbettes were 9in–8in but the amidships ones were 3.2in behind the 6in battery armour, and all 1.2in behind the 8in upper belt. The turrets had 9in faces and rears, 7in sides and 3.5in–2.4in roofs, and the armour deck was 1in behind the main belt with 2in slopes, 2in forward and 3.2in with 2in slopes aft. The forecastle deck was 1in over the battery and the upper deck 1in over the main belt outside the battery. The torpedo bulkhead was 2in–1.2in.

There were 12 boiler rooms and 4 engine rooms with main turbines arranged as in *von der Tann*; boiler pressure was also as in this ship, as was the later use of tar oil. On the mile *Moltke* attained 85,780shp = 28.4kts and *Goeben* 85,660shp = 28.0kts. The commissioning dates for trials were respectively 30 September 1911 and 2 July 1912.

In the 1914–18 War *Moltke*, undamaged at Dogger Bank and possibly never fired at, was torpedoed by *E 1* on 19 August 1915 but the hit was right forward and little damage was done. At Jutland she scored 9 hits on *Tiger* in the first 12 minutes and in spite of 4–15in hits and 1–13.5in near miss, was in good fighting order and able to do 25kts at the end of the day. On 24 April 1918 the starboard inner screw fell off and before the turbine could be stopped, the wheel of the engine turning gear disintegrated, wrecking the auxiliary condenser outlet and causing about 2000 tons of water to flood in with salting of all boilers. Emergency repairs enabled her to proceed under own power about 36 hours later, and she was then torpedoed in way of the port engine rooms by *E 42*. Flooding amounted to 1730 tons but no vital damage was caused. The *Moltke* was raised at Scapa Flow in 1927 and broken up in 1927–29.

The *Goeben* was in the Mediterranean in 1914 and was able to outrun the *Indomitable* and *Indefatigable* on 4 August 1914. She entered the Dardanelles on the 10th, was nominally transferred to Turkey as *Yavuz Sultan Selim* and operated with moderate success against the Russian Black Sea Fleet. She struck 2 Russian mines on 26 December 1914 causing about 2000 tons of flood water, and during the sortie from the Dardanelles on 20 January 1918, in which she sank the monitor *Raglan*, struck 3 British mines. None of these 5 mines ruptured the torpedo bulkhead. The two Russian and one of the British mine holes were repaired using coffer-dams.

After the war the *Goeben* became Turkish property and was refitted and the two remaining British mine holes finally repaired in 1926–30. She was laid up in 1948 and decommissioned in 1960.

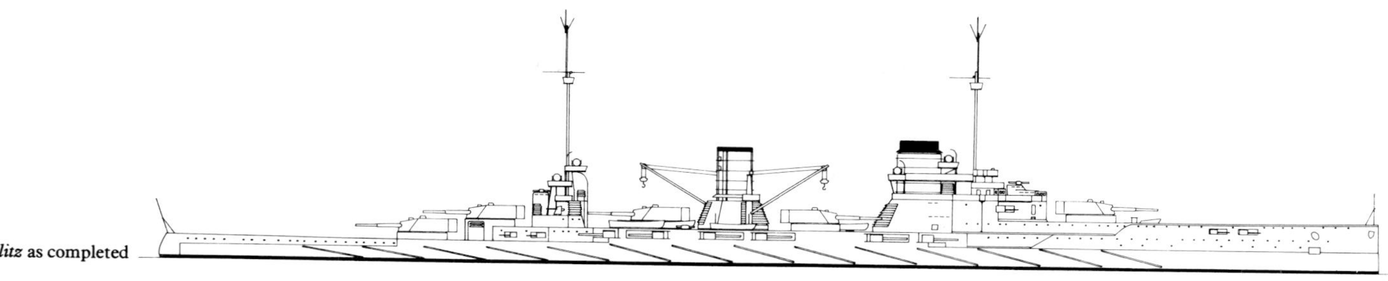
Seydlitz as completed

SEYDLITZ *battlecruiser*

Displacement: 24,594t normal, 28,100t deep load

Dimensions: 657ft 11in oa × 93ft 6in × 26ft 11in mean, 30ft 3in mean at deep load
200.5m × 28.5m × 8.2m, 9.2m

Machinery: 4-shaft Parsons turbines, 27 Schulz-Thornycroft boilers, 63,000shp = 26.5kts. Coal 3540t. Range 4700nm at 14kts

Armour: Belt 300mm–100mm (12in–4in), bulkheads 220mm–100mm (8.7in–4in), battery 200mm–150mm (8in–6in), barbettes 230mm–30mm (9in–1.2in), turrets 250mm–70mm (10in–2.75in), CT 350mm–80mm (14in–3.2in)

Amament: 10–28cm (11.1in) SKL/50 (5×2), 12–15cm (5.9in) SKL/45, 12–8.8cm (3.45in) SKL/45, 4–50cm (19.7in) TT sub

Complement: 1068 (1425 at Jutland)

Name	Builder	Laid down	Launched	Comp	Fate
SEYDLITZ	Blohm & Voss, Hamburg	4.2.11	30.3.12	17.8.13	Scuttled 21.6.19

Built under the 1910–11 programme this ship was in some features an enlarged *Moltke* but the hull form was different and an additional weather deck was added from stem to foremast. Freeboard was 29–30ft forward at normal load and elsewhere slightly less than in *Moltke*. GM was 10.23ft and Frahm anti-rolling tanks were fitted but not so used. There were tandem rudders, the forward one being somewhat ineffective as in *Moltke*, and like all German battlecruisers *Seydlitz* turned slowly and with considerable loss of speed. Full details of her design were obtained by the British but these appear to have had no influence whatsoever on future ships.

The main and secondary armament were arranged as in *Moltke* except that the fore turret was on the weather deck. The Drh LC/1910 mountings were generally similar to C/1908 and the initial 13½° elevation was increased to 16° before Jutland. All turret magazines were above the shell rooms. By Jutland the 8.8cm SKL/45 had been replaced by 2–8.8cm Flak L/45; TT were disposed as in previous battlecruisers.

The main belt was 12in between end barbettes from 55in above to 14in below lwl and was tapered to 6in at the lower edge 67in below lwl. Above it was tapered to 9in at the upper deck and to 8in at the battery port sills. Forward the armour was 4¾in–4in and 4in aft. Barbettes were 9in–8in but the wing barbettes were reduced to 4in behind the battery and all to 1.2in where protected by the 12in–9in belt. The turrets had 10in faces, 8in sides, 8¼in rears and 4in–2¾in roofs. The armour deck was 1.2in amidships, 2in forward and 3.2in with 2in slopes aft, while the forecastle deck was 2.2in–1in over the battery and the upper deck 1in outside. The torpedo bulkhead ran between end barbettes and was 13ft 2in inboard amidships. It was 2in–1.2in and continued as a 1.2in splinter bulkhead to the upper deck.

There were 15 boiler and 4 engine rooms with the main turbines; boiler pressure and later use of tar oil as in the previous ships. She was commissioned for trials on 22 May 1913 and on the mile attained 89,740shp = 28.13kts.

At the Dogger Bank *Seydlitz* was hit by 3–13.5in shells, one of which (from *Lion*) burst as it holed the 9in barbette of the stern turret, and armour fragments caused a fire which spread to the superfiring turret and ignited 62 complete (main and fore) charges. She was mined forward of the torpedo bulkhead on 24 April 1916 and at Jutland was hit by a torpedo from *Petard* or possibly *Turbulent*, and by 8–15in, 6–13.5in and 8–12in shells. The worst damage was from flooding above the armour deck forward, 47in below lwl, caused by 5–15in hits and aggravated by trying to steam too fast after the action of 31 May 1916. She was nearly lost, the flooding at its worst being calculated as 5329 tons with draughts of 46ft 1in forward and 24ft 4in aft and a list of 8° to port.

Seydlitz was raised at Scapa Flow for scrap in November 1928.

Seydlitz November 1918
CPL

Derfflinger 1918 *CPL*

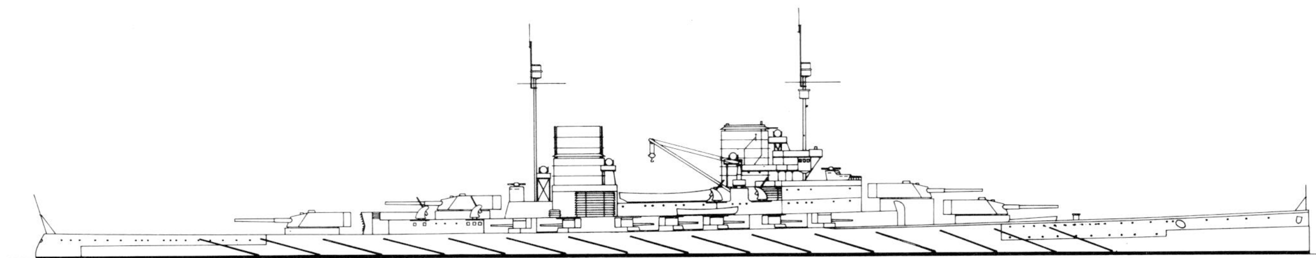

Lützow 1916

DERFFLINGER class *battlecruisers*

Displacement: 26,180t normal (*Lützow* 26,318t); 30,700t deep load

Dimensions: 690ft 3in oa × 95ft 2in × 27ft 3in mean, 31ft mean at deep load
210.4m × 29.0m × 8.3m, 9.5m

Machinery: 4-shaft Parsons turbines, 18 Schulz-Thornycroft boilers, 63,000shp = 26.5kts. Coal 3640t, oil 985t. Range 5600nm at 14kts

Armour: Belt 300mm–100mm (12in–4in), bulkheads 250mm–100mm (10in–4in), battery 150mm (6in), barbettes 260mm–30mm (10.2in–1.2in), turrets 270mm–80mm (10.7in–3.2in), CT 350mm–80mm (14in–3.2in)

Armament: 8–30.5cm (12in) SKL/50 (4×2), 12–15cm (5.9in) SKL/45, 4–8.8cm (3.45in) SKL/45, 4–50cm (19.7in) TT sub (*Lützow* 14–15cm, no 8.8cm, 4–60 (23.6in) TT sub)

Complement: 1112 (1391 at Jutland)

Name	Builder	Laid down	Launched	Comp	Fate
DERFFLINGER	Blohm & Voss, Hamburg	1.12	1.7.13	11.14	Scuttled 21.6.19
LÜTZOW	Schichau, Danzig	5.12	29.11.13	3.16	Sunk 1.6.16

This class was a great improvement on *Seydlitz* and of markedly different design. They were flush-decked with a pronounced sheer giving freeboard at normal load of about 24ft forward and 15ft aft, and an extra deck known as the upper main deck, was worked in forward of the CT. *Derfflinger* was built under the 1911–12 programme and *Lützow* under that of 1912–13. GM is given as 8.53ft and they were accounted excellent seaboats though the casemates were wet. Tandem rudders were fitted and *Derfflinger* had Frahm anti-rolling tanks but they were apparently not used. A heavy tripod foremast was added to her after Jutland.

The 30.5cm turrets were arranged in superfiring pairs fore and aft, the latter being separated by the length of the after engine rooms. The Drh LC/1912 mountings allowed 13½° elevation, increased to 16° after Jutland. Magazines were below shell rooms except for reasons of space in the sternmost turret and this turret also differed in that the shell hoists were not broken at the working chamber. The 15cm were in an upper deck battery and the 8.8cm SKL/45 were later removed in *Derfflinger*, both ships having 8–8.8cm Flak L/45 at Jutland later reduced to 4 in *Derfflinger*. The TT were arranged as in previous battlecruisers.

The main belt ran from the fore barbette to a little past the after one, and was 12in from 55in above to 14in below lwl tapering to 6in at the lower edge 67in below lwl and to 9in at the upper deck. Forward there was 4¾in–4in and 4in aft. The barbettes were 10.2in with the two superfiring ones reduced to 4in behind the battery armour and all to 2.4in behind the main belt with the two forward ones further reduced to 1.2in below the upper main deck. The turrets had 10.7in faces and rears, 8.7in sides and 4.3in–3.2in roofs. The armour deck was 1.2in amidships, 2in forward and 3.2in–2in aft, and the upper deck 1.2in–0.8in outside the battery which had a 2in–1in roof. The torpedo bulkhead ran for the length of the main belt and was 1.8in, continuing to the upper deck as a 1.2in splinter bulkhead.

The boilers were double-ended and there were 12 boiler rooms with the 4 oil-fired boilers in the forward 4. Pressure was still 235lb/in² and oil fuel sprays were later provided for the coal-fired furnaces. The main turbines were arranged in 4 engine rooms as previously. *Derfflinger* was commissioned for trials on 1 September 1914 and *Lützow* on 8 August 1915, but the latter had serious turbine troubles and did not join the fleet until the end of the following March. At Jutland her gunnery was of the highest quality but her watertight integrity was far below normal German standards. The usual deep water mile at Neukrug was considered unsafe in war and the 115ft deep Belt mile was used. At 30ft 6in (9.3m) *Derfflinger* attained 76,600shp = 25.8kts, and *Lützow* at about 29ft 6in (9m) 80,990shp = 26.4kts equivalent to 28.0kts and 28.3kts in deep water at normal load.

At the Dogger Bank *Derfflinger* was hit by 3–13.5in shells with little damage but at Jutland, where she blew up the *Queen Mary* in 11 salvos, she was hit by 10–15in, 1–13.5in and 10–12in shells. Both after turrets were put out of action with serious cartridge fires by 15in shells from *Revenge*, while other 15in hits had earlier caused flooding forward. At the end of the battle 3350 tons of flood water were in her, but 1020 tons of this was in the flooded after turret magazines and 206 tons in the wings to correct a 2° list.

She was raised at Scapa in 1934 for scrap.

At Jutland *Lützow* was hit by at least 24 heavy shells, believed to be 4–15in, 12–13.5in and 8–12in. The worst damage was from 2–12in from *Invincible* which burst below water in or near the broadside torpedo flat and with other shells caused flooding that became uncontrollable, and when the water line forward had reached the upper edge of 'B' barbette, she was sunk in 2 minutes by a torpedo from *G 38*. Her own gunnery was excellent and she blew up *Invincible* and probably *Defence*.

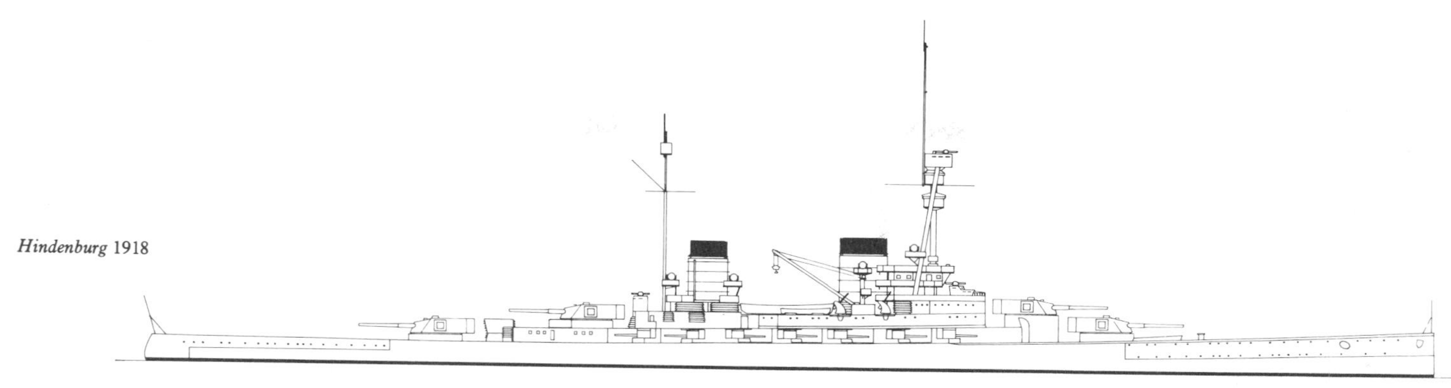

Hindenburg 1918

This ship, built under the 1913–14 programme, was generally similar to the previous class and only the differences are noted. The additional length was mainly due to finer stern lines and a tripod foremast was fitted before completion. She could be distinguished from *Derfflinger* by having shallower funnel caps and the tripod legs less spread.

The armament was arranged as in the previous class but the 30.5cm mountings were Drh LC/1913 allowing 16° elevation and the 10ft turret rangefinders were replaced by 25½ft. In all 4 turrets the magazines were above the shell rooms and the shell hoists were not broken at the working chamber though the cartridge hoists were. It was possible to load the forward and aft superfiring turret shell hoists from depot rooms on the upper main and main (armour) decks respectively.

HINDENBURG *battlecruiser*

Displacement: 26,513t normal; 31,000t deep load

Dimensions: 698ft 2in oa × 95ft 2in × 27ft 3in mean, 30ft 11¼in mean at deep load
212.8m × 29.0m × 8.3m, 9.43m

Machinery: 4-shaft Parsons turbines, 18 Schulz-Thornycroft boilers, 72,000shp = 27.5kts. Coal 3640t, oil 1180t. Range 6800nm at 14kts

Armour: As *Derfflinger* class

Armament: 8–30.5in (12in) SKL/50 (4×2), 14–15cm (5.9in) SKL/45, 4–8.8cm (3.45in) Flak L/45, 4–60cm (23.6in) TT sub

Complement: 1182

Name	Builder	Laid down	Launched	Comp	Fate
HINDENBURG	Wilhelmshaven N Yd	30.6.13	1.8.15	25.10.17	Scuttled 21.6.19

The main belt tapered to 8¾in at the upper deck, and forward there was 4¾in to 54ft from the bows and then 1.2in plating. Aft the side armour ended 24ft from the stern instead of 15ft. The sloping front roof of the turrets was increased to 6in.

The boiler rooms were rearranged with the 4 oil-fired boilers in two groups, one forward and the other separated by 4 coal-fired rooms. The *Hindenberg* was commissioned for trials on 10 May 1917 and attained 95,777shp = 26.6kts at 29ft 6in (9m) on the Belt mile, equivalent to 28.5kts at normal displacement in deep water. She was raised at Scapa for scrap on 22 July 1930 and was still of sufficient interest to be examined in some detail by the Royal Corps of Naval Constructors.

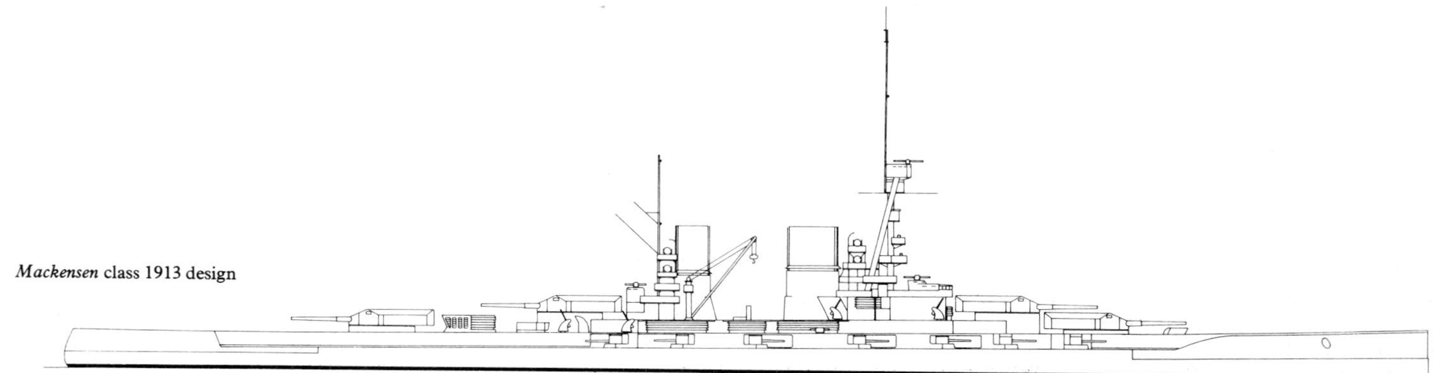

Mackensen class 1913 design

These ships would have differed from previous battlecruisers in having a full length forecastle deck and a return was made to twin instead of tandem rudders. They would have been handsome ships with tripod foremast and 2 funnels. *Mackensen* was laid down under the 1914–15 programme, *Ersatz Freya* under the War estimates and the others were ordered in April 1915. It was originally hoped to complete them from the summer of 1917 to the autumn of 1918, and their 35cm guns would have made them formidable antagonists. *Ersatz Freya* was to have been named *Prinz Eitel Friedrich; Ersatz A*, later known as *Ersatz Friedrich Carl,* was to have been named *Fürst Bismarck*.

The main armament was arranged as in *Hindenburg* and the Drh LC/1914 mountings allowed 20° elevation, while the 15cm were in a long upper deck battery extending from the forward turret to the after superfiring one. The 5 TT would have been arranged with one in the bows and two on either broadside forward and aft of the torpedo bulkhead.

MACKENSEN class *battlecruisers*

Displacement: 30,500t normal, *c*35,500t–36,000t deep load

Dimensions: 731ft 8in oa × 99ft 9in × 27ft 6¾in mean
223.0m × 30.4m × 8.4m

Machinery: 4-shaft Parsons turbines, geared cruising (*Ersatz A* hydraulic drive main turbines), 32 Schulz-Thornycroft boilers, 90,000shp = 28kts. Coal 3940t, oil 1970t. Range 8000nm at 14kts

Armour: Belt 300mm–100mm (12in–4in), bulkheads 250mm–100m (10in–4in), battery 150mm (6in), barbettes 290mm–90mm (11.5in–3.5in), turrets 320mm–110mm (12.8in–4.3in), (*Graf Spee* 300mm–100mm, (12in–4in) CT 350mm–100mm (14in–4in)

Armament: 8–35cm (13.8in) SKL/45 (4×2), 12–15cm (5.9in) SKL/45, 8–8.8cm (3.45in) Flak L/45, 5–60cm (23.6in) TT sub

Complement: 1186

Name	Builder	Laid down	Launched	Fate
MACKENSEN	Blohm & Voss, Hamburg	30.1.15	21.4.17	BU 1923–24
ERSATZ FREYA	Blohm & Voss, Hamburg	1.5.15	13.3.20 to clear slip	BU 1920–22
GRAF SPEE	Schichau, Danzig	30.11.15	15.9.17	BU 1921–23
ERSATZ A	Wilhelmshaven N Yd	3.11.15	–	BU on slip 1922

The 12in main belt ran from 10ft forward of the fore turret to 10ft abaft the after one and tapered to 6in at the lower edge and 9½in at the upper deck. Forward and aft the armour stopped short of the ends and was respectively 4¾in and 4in. The barbettes were reduced to 4¾in (*Ersatz A* 6in) behind the battery armour and to 3½in behind the main belt, while the turrets had 12.8in faces, 8in sides, 8½ rears, 7in–4.3in roofs except that in *Graf Spee* the figures were 12in, 8in, 8¼in, 6in–4in. The armour deck did not extend outboard of the torpedo bulkhead amidships where it was 2.4in–1.2in with 2in forward and 4.3in–3.2in aft. The upper deck was 1in over the main belt and the forecastle deck 2in–1in over the battery. The torpedo bulkhead was 2in increased to 2.4in by the turrets, and continued as a 1.2in splinter bulkhead to the upper deck.

The boilers comprised 24 single-ended coal-fired and 8 double-ended oil-fired and were smaller than in the previous ships. Leak pumps were increased to 8 from 5 in *Hindenburg*.

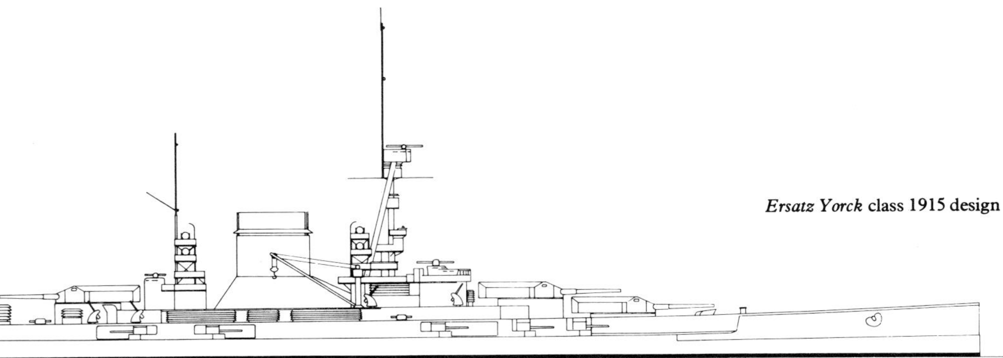

Ersatz Yorck class 1915 design

ERSATZ YORCK class *battlecruisers*

Displacement: 33,000t normal, *c* 38,000t–38,500t deep load

Dimensions: 747ft 5in oa × 99ft 9in × 28ft 6½in mean
227.8m × 30.4m × 8.7m

Machinery: 4-shaft Parsons turbines, hydraulic drive, geared cruising (*Ersatz Scharnhorst* direct drive main turbines), 32 Schulz-Thornycroft boilers, 90,000shp = 27.25kts. Coal 3940t, oil 1970t. Range 8000nm at 14kts

Armour: Belt 300mm–100mm (12in–4in), bulkheads 250mm–100mm (10in–4in), battery 150mm (6in), barbettes 300mm–90mm (12in–3.5in), turrets 300mm–150mm (12in–6in), CT 350mm–100mm (14in–4in)

Armament: 8–38cm (15in) SKL/45 (4×2), 12–15cm (5.9in) SKL/45, 8–8.8cm (3.45in) or 10.5cm (4.1in) Flak L/45, 3–60cm (23.6in) or 70cm (27.6in) TT sub

Complement: 1227

Name	Builder	Laid down	Launched	Comp	Fate
ERSATZ YORCK	Vulcan, Hamburg	7.16			Building stopped
ERSATZ GNEISENAU	Germaniawerft, Kiel	–			
ERSATZ SCHARNHORST	Blohm & Voss, Hamburg	–			

Originally ordered in April 1915 as units of the *Mackensen* class, the design was altered in January 1917 in an attempt to produce a battlecruiser with 8–38cm guns using machinery already ordered. Appearance would have been quite distinct with the uptakes trunked into a single large funnel.

The main armament was arranged as in *Mackensen* but the upper deck 15cm battery was lengthened to 413ft with 6 guns from 'A' barbette to the CT, 4 by the mainmast and 2 by the aftermost barbette. The bow TT was retained with one on either beam aft of the boiler rooms and thus within the area of the torpedo bulkhead.

Armour was generally as in *Mackensen* but the main belt tapered to 9½in–8in at the upper deck and the barbettes were reduced to 7in behind the battery and to 4¾in–3½in behind the belt. The turrets were to have 12in faces, 10in sides, 11½in rears and 10in–6in roofs, while the armour deck was 4in–2.8in aft and the forecastle deck 2in–0.8in.

Construction of *Ersatz Yorck* was halted after 1000–1100 tons of steel had been assembled.

Hindenburg 1918
CPL

CRUISERS

Cruiser development in the nineteenth century divided into two distinct lines: one for commerce destruction or protection; and one for fleet duties such as reconnaissance and acting as leaders for the flotillas. In the Royal Navy there was a clear distinction between both types, but the Imperial German Navy developed a standard cruiser for both duties. However, being a compromise it was bigger, slower and less manoeuverable than its British opponents serving with the battle fleet. The development of German light cruisers through a large number of successive classes shows a steady improvement, in terms of seakeeping abilities, the introduction of turbine propulsion, the introduction of waterline armour as an integrated part of the hull plating, and the disposition of the main armament. Compared with foreign navies, Germany was very late to adopt the more powerful 6in gun, bowing to Tirpitz's pressure in contradiction to the desire of the Fleet.

It must be pointed out that all horsepower figures in the particulars are design requirements: in practice these figures were exceeded in all German light cruisers, which were significantly faster than quoted in the design legend. Builders' trials maximum speeds were: *Königsberg* 24.1kts, *Nürnberg* 23.4kts, *Stuttgart* 24kts, *Stettin* 25.2kts, *Dresden* 25.2kts, *Emden* 24.1kts, *Kolberg* 26.3kts, *Mainz* 27.2kts, *Cöln* 26.8kts, *Augsburg* 26.7kts, *Magdeburg* 27.6kts, *Breslau* 27.5kts, *Strassburg* 28.2kts, *Stralsund* 28.2kts, *Karlsruhe* 28.5kts, *Rostock* 29.3kts and *Graudenz* 29.2kts; for the war-built cruisers no equivalents exist.

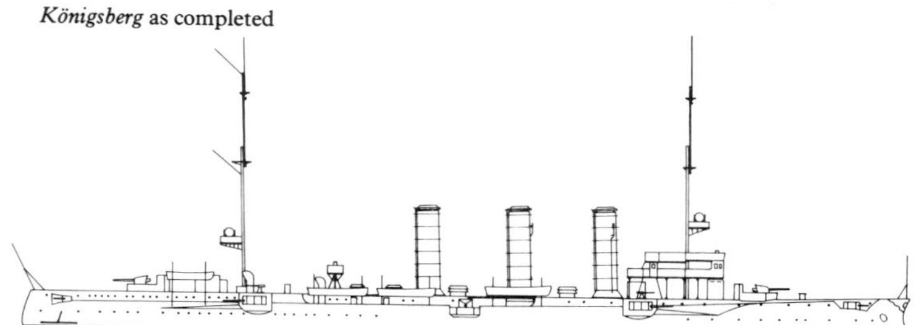

Königsberg as completed

Stuttgart 1918 as a seaplane carrier

KÖNIGSBERG class *light cruisers*

Displacement:*	*Königsberg* 3390t design; 3814t deep load *Nürnberg, Stuttgart* 3469t design; 4002t deep load *Stettin* 3480t design; 3822t deep load
Dimensions:	383ft 2in wl × 43ft 8in × 17ft 5in (*Königsberg* 376ft 8in wl × 43ft 4in × 17ft) *116.8m × 13.3m × 5.3m (114.8m × 13.2m × 5.2m)*
Machinery:	2-shafts 3-cyl VTE, 11 Navy boilers, 12,000ihp = 23kts (*Stettin* 4-shafts, 2 Parsons turbines, 13,500shp = 24kts). Coal 880t (*Königsberg* 820t)
Armour:	Deck 20mm–30mm (¾in–1¾in), CT 100mm (4in), gunshields 50mm (2in)
Armament:	10–10.5cm (4.1in) SKL/40, 8 (*Nürnberg* 10)–5.2cm (2in) SKL/55 QF, 2–45cm (17.7in) TT sub (beam)
Complement:	322

Name	Builder	Laid down	Launched	Comp	Fate
KÖNIGSBERG	Kiel N Yd	1905	12.12.05	6.4.07	Scuttled 11.7.15
NÜRNBERG	Kiel N Yd	1906	29.8.06	10.4.08	Sunk 8.12.14
STUTTGART	Danzig N Yd	1905	22.9.06	1.2.08	BU 1921
STETTIN	Vulcan, Stettin	1906	7.3.07	29.10.07	BU 1921–23

*Displacements in the rest of this section are in Metric Tonnes (of 1000kg) not long tons (of 1016kg).

This class belonged to the 1903–4 (and the later three to the 1904–5) programmes. *Stettin* had 4 shafts and turbines, whereas the others had 2-shaft VTE machinery. Range was originally 4120nm at 12kts in the VTE ships and 4170nm in *Stettin*, but after her 1911–13 refit *Königsberg*'s endurance was increased to 5750nm at 12kts. During the war AA guns were added to the survivors. *Königsberg* was station ship at Dar-es-Salaam in German East Africa at the outbreak of the war, and after a brief commerce raiding career was blockaded in the Rufiji River in October 1914 where she was bombarded by British monitors in July 1915 and finally scuttled by her crew. *Nürnberg* was part of the German East Asian squadron of Admiral Graf Spee and was sunk during the Battle of the Falkland Islands on 8 December 1914. *Stuttgart* served as gunnery training ship and with the German High Seas Fleet. Between February and May 1918 she was converted to a seaplane carrier (armed with 4–10.5cm, 2–8.8cm Flak L/45, 2–45cm TT, 3 aircraft). She was turned over to Great Britain after the war and scrapped in 1921. *Stettin* served with the High Seas Fleet from 1907, with the Submarine school from 1917, was delivered to Great Britain and scrapped in 1921–23 at Copenhagen.

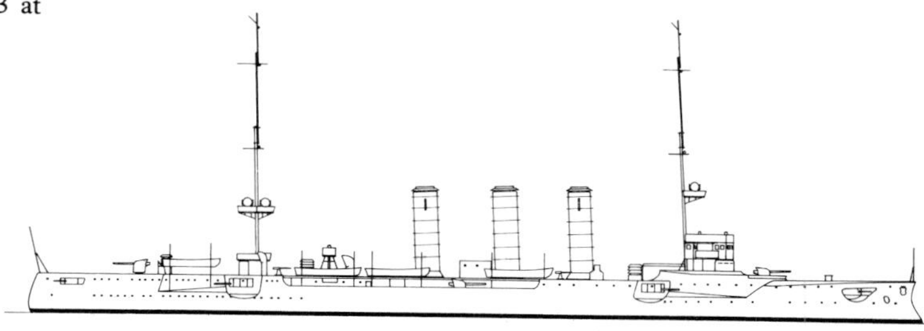

Emden 1914

DRESDEN class *light cruisers*

Displacement:	3664t design; 4268t deep load
Dimensions:	386ft 10in wl × 44ft 4in × 18ft *117.9m × 13.5m × 5.5m*
Machinery:	*Dresden* 2 shafts, 4 Parsons turbines, 12 Navy boilers, 15,000shp = 24kts. Coal 860t max. Range 3600nm at 14kts *Emden* 2-shaft 3-cyl VTE, 12 Navy boilers, 13,500ihp = 23.5kts. Coal 790t max. Range 3760nm at 12kts
Armour:	As *Königsberg* class
Armament:	As *Königsberg* class
Complement:	361

Name	Builder	Laid down	Launched	Comp	Fate
DRESDEN	Blohm & Voss, Hamburg	1907	5.10.07	14.11.08	Scuttled 14.3.15
EMDEN	Danzig N Yd	1906	26.5.08	10.7.09	Sunk 9.11.14

These two cruisers belonged to the 1905–06 programme and had comparative machinery. *Dresden* formed part of the international force which intervened in the Mexican Revolution of 1910. She was in the West Indies when war broke out: to commence her commerce raiding activities she passed into the Pacific via the Magellan Straits, joined the *Leipzig* and finally met Admiral Graf Spee's German East Asian Squadron at Easter Island. Operating with Spee she managed to survive the Battle of the Falklands, escaped once more to the Pacific and was finally trapped by the British cruisers *Kent* and *Glasgow* and the AMC *Orama* at the Chilean island of Mas a Fuera, and shelled into submission on 14 March 1915. During the ceasefire negotiations with British naval officers Lieutenant Wilhelm Canaris, later the Chief of German Counter-intelligence, played an important part during the attempt to reach an armistice between the *Dresden*, which was lying in neutral waters, and her British opponents. She was scuttled to avoid capture.

The famous *Emden* had been in Chinese and Pacific waters since 1909, playing an important role in subduing a rebellion in the German colony of Ponape (in the Carolines). When war broke out she was station ship at the German China colony of Tsingtao. To avoid being trapped there she left immediately and, on the orders of von Spee, started independent commerce raiding. In this role she operated very succesfully in the Indian Ocean until caught by HMAS *Sydney* in the Cocos Islands. Following a gun battle on 9 November 1914 she was beached on the reefs of North Keeling Island; the wreck was partially dismantled by a Japanese firm in the 1950s. The survivors managed to capture a schooner and a steamer and reached Mecca. After an adventurous journey across Saudi Arabia, Syria and Turkey they reached Constantinople and returned to Germany.

Königsberg as completed
Aldo Fraccaroli Collection

Nautilus 1908
Aldo Fraccaroli Collection

Dresden as completed
Navarret Collection

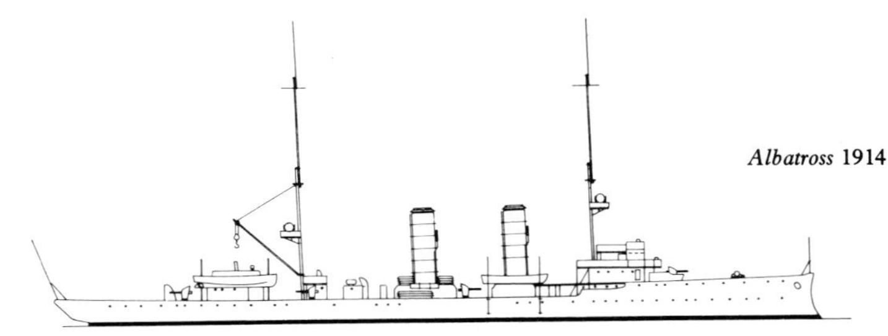

Albatross 1914

Designed as 'Minendampfer A and B' these two cruiser-like units served as minelayers during the war. *Albatross* was beached on the Swedish island of Gotland, 2 July 1915, after an engagement with Russian cruisers; she was refloated and scrapped after the war.

NAUTILUS class *minelayers*

Displacement: 1975t design; 2345t deep load (*Albatross* 2208t design; 2506t deep load)
Dimensions: 315ft 7in wl, 331ft 0in oa × 36ft 9in × 14ft 5in
96.2m, 100.9m × 11.2m × 4.4m
Machinery: 2-shaft VTE, 4 Navy boilers, 6600ihp = 20kts. Coal ?. Range ?
Armour: Nil
Armament: 2–8.8cm (3.45in) SKL/45, 200 mines
Complement: 201 to 208

Name	Builder	Laid down	Launched	Comp	Fate
NAUTILUS	Weser, Bremen	1905	20.8.06	19.3.07	BU 1928
ALBATROSS	Weser, Bremen	1907	23.10.07	19.5.08	Sunk 2.7.15, BU 1921

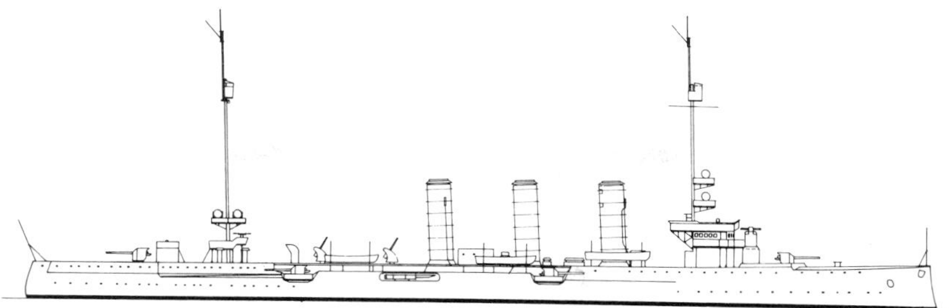

Augsburg 1918

KOLBERG class *light cruisers*

Displacement: 4362t design; 4915t deep load
Dimensions: 426ft 6in wl × 46ft × 17ft 7in
130.0m × 14.0m × 5.4m
Machinery: 4 shafts, 2 sets turbines (see notes), 15 Navy boilers, 19,000shp–20,200shp = 25.5kts–26.7kts. Coal (see notes). Range 3250nm (*Kolberg*), 3630nm (*Mainz*), 3500nm (others) at 14kts
Armour: Deck 20mm–40mm (¾in–1in), CT 100mm (4in), gunshields 50mm (2in)
Armament: 12–10.5cm (4.1in) SKL/45, 2–45cm (17.7in) TT sub (beam), 100 mines
Complement: 367

Name	Builder	Laid down	Launched	Comp	Fate
KOLBERG	Schichau, Danzig	1908	14.11.08	21.6.10	BU 1929
MAINZ	Vulcan, Stettin	1907	23.1.09	1.10.09	Sunk 28.8.14
CÖLN	Germaniawerft, Kiel	1908	5.6.09	16.6.11	Sunk 28.8.14
AUGSBURG	Kiel N Yd	1908	10.7.09	1.11.10	BU 1922

Belonging to the 1906–7 programme these four cruisers marked an important step in the steady development of German light cruisers. Displacement rose about 20 per cent and speed by about 1.5kts compared with the previous *Dresden* class. Speed was bought by a simple increase in displacement to allow for heavier machinery and all four were equipped with competitive turbine systems: *Kolberg* Melms-Pfenninger, *Mainz* AEG-Curtiss, *Cöln* Germania, *Augsburg* Parsons turbines; *Mainz* was the only one to have 2 shafts. Maximum coal capacity varied, being in the above order 970, 1010, 960 and 940 tons.

Augsburg and *Kolberg* were rearmed during 1916–17 with 6–15cm (5.9in) SKL/45, and in 1918 2–8.8cm (3.45in) Flak L/45 AA guns, 2–50cm (19.7in) TT. *Kolberg* served with the High Seas Fleet in the war, after the war she became the French *Colmar* and was condemned in 1927 and broken up in 1929 at Brest.

Mainz and *Cöln* were sunk by British battlecruisers on 28 August 1914 in the North Sea while on patrol duties.

Augsburg was ceded to Japan as war reparations and was scrapped in 1922 at Dordrecht.

Kolberg as completed

Aldo Fraccaroli Collection

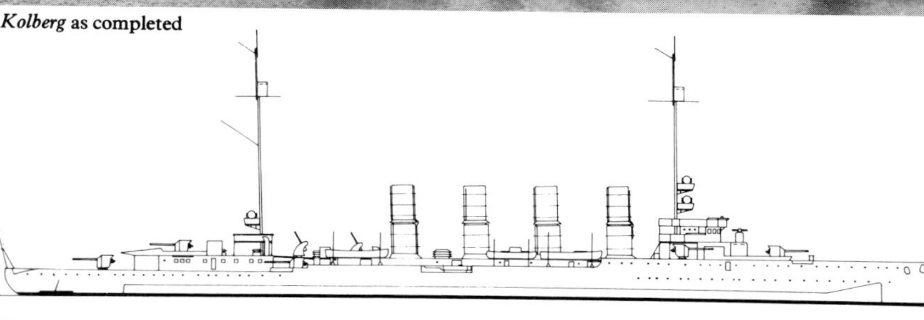

Strassburg 1916

MAGDEBURG class *light cruisers*

Displacement: 4570t design; 5587t deep load
Dimensions: 446ft 2in wl, 455ft oa × 43ft 11in × 16ft 10in
136.0m, 138.7m × 13.4m × 5.1m
Machinery: Comparative turbine arrangements (see notes), 11 Navy boilers (see notes for further details). Coal 1200t, oil 106t max. Range 5820nm/900nm at 12kts/25kts
Armour: Waterline belt 60mm–18mm (2¼in–¾in), deck 40mm–60mm (1½in–2¼in), collision bulkhead 40mm (1½in), CT 100mm (4in), gunshields 50mm (2in)
Armament: 12–10.5cm (4.1in) SKL/45, 2–50cm (19.7in) TT sub (beam), 120 mines
Complement: 354

Name	Builder	Laid down	Launched	Comp	Fate
MAGDEBURG	Weser, Bremen	1910	13.5.11	20.8.12	Sunk 26.8.14
BRESLAU	Vulcan, Stettin	1910	16.5.11	10.5.12	Sunk 20.1.18
STRASSBURG	Wilhelmshaven N Yd	1910	24.8.11	9.10.12	Sunk 23.10.43
STRALSUND	Weser, Bremen	1910	4.11.11	10.12.12	BU 1935

Belonging to the 1908–9 programme, the design of this class shows some important innovations, although these are not obvious at first glance. For the first time a class of light cruisers had an armoured waterline belt consisting of 60mm nickel steel armour reaching about 80 per cent of the length of the hull. To save weight this belt was not bolted on a wooden base – as it was done with the capital ships – but designed as an integral strength member of the hull. The technical problems were very heavy but solved in a manner that became standard practice until recent decades. To save further weight the hull was constructed on a new longitudinal frame system, which took so long to perfect that the design was delayed by 3–4 years. The hull was given entirely new and more hydrodynamically efficient lines. Furthermore a new bow shape improved their seakeeping qualities and kept the forecastle drier. Another new feature was the cut-down quarterdeck, which meant the loss of valuable accommodation, but was necessary in order to provide a mine deck, capable of taking 120 mines. These innovations resulted in a significant increase in battleworthiness without a substantial increase in displacement. All the above-mentioned features became standard in the subsequent classes of German light cruisers.

For comparative purposes, all had different turbine systems, and conse-

quently differed slightly in performance, as follows:
Magdeburg 3 shafts, 3 Bergmann turbines, 29,904shp = 27.6kts
Breslau 4 shafts, 2 AEG-Vulcan turbines, 33,482shp = 27.5kts
Strassburg 2 shafts, 2 Navy turbines, 33,742shp = 28.2kts
Stralsund 3 shafts, 3 Bergmann turbines, 35,515shp = 28.2kts. The middle turbine was removed towards the end of the war reducing power to *c*25,000shp and speed to 27kts.

Strassburg (1915) and *Stralsund* (1916) were rearmed with 7–15cm (5.9in) SKL/45 guns and 2–8.8cm (3.45in) Flak L/45 AA guns and 2–50cm (19.7in) TT extra on deck. *Breslau* received 2 of the new 15cm guns in Turkey in 1916, and in the following year was completely rearmed with 8–15cm.

Magdeburg ran aground on Odensholm Island, 26 August 1914, during a minelaying sortie in the Baltic and was destroyed by Russian cruisers. The Russians were able to recover the German codebooks and passed them on to British intelligence. *Breslau*, with the battlecruiser *Goeben*, formed the German Mediterranean Squadron, and in 1914 was incorporated as *Midilli* into the Ottoman Navy, although still manned by her German crew. She made most of her sorties in company with the *Yavuz Sultan Selim* (ex-*Goeben*) and sank after striking 5 mines during an action against Imbros Island.

Strassburg served with the Scouting Forces of the High Seas Fleet and was handed over to Italy after the war as reparation, becoming the *Taranto*. She was scuttled on 9 September 1943 at La Spezia, refloated and finally sunk by bombs 23 September 1944. *Stralsund* served with the Scouting Force, and was handed over after the war to France, becoming the *Mulhouse;* she was broken up in 1935 at Brest.

Stralsund as completed
CPL

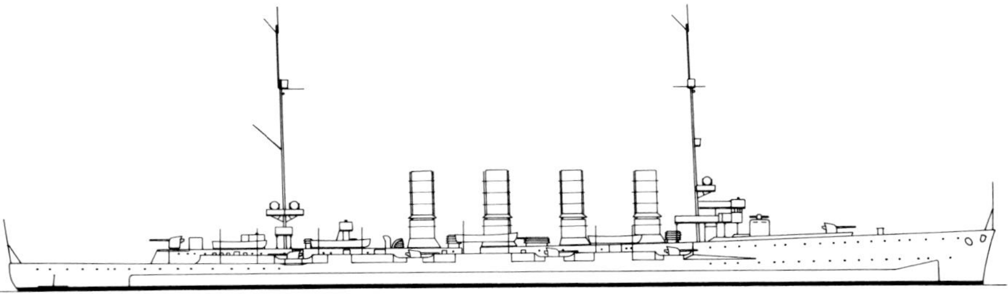

Karlsruhe 1914

KARLSRUHE class *light cruisers*

Displacement: 4900t design; 6191t deep load
Dimensions: 456ft wl, 466ft 6in oa × 44ft 11in × 18ft
139.0m, 142.2m × 13.7m × 5.5m
Machinery: 2-shaft Navy turbines, 14 Navy boilers (10 coal-, 4 oil-fired), 26,000shp = 27kts. Coal 1300t, oil 200t max. Range 5500nm/900nm at 12kts/25kts
Armour: As *Magdeburg* class
Armament: 12–10.5cm (4.1in) SKL/45, 2–50cm (19.7in) TT sub (beam), 120 mines
Complement: 373

Name	Builder	Laid down	Launched	Comp	Fate
KARLSRUHE	Germaniawerft, Kiel	1911	11.11.12	15.1.14	Sunk 4.11.14
ROSTOCK	Howaldtswerke, Kiel	1911	11.12.12	5.2.14	Sunk 1.6.16

These two cruisers were built under the 1910 programme. Trials performances were: *Karlsruhe* 37,885shp = 28.5kts; *Rostock* 43,628shp = 29.3kts. *Karlsruhe* was ear-marked to replace the *Dresden* on the Caribbean Station and to take part in the opening ceremonies of the Panama Canal; but war broke out and she immediately began commerce raiding, sinking 17 merchant vessels totalling 76,609grt. On 4 November 1914 she sank at position 11°07′N, 55°25′W after an accidental internal explosion. The survivors were saved by two German supply ships and managed to reach Germany on board the blockade runner *Rio Negro*.

Rostock served with the Scouting Group of the High Seas Fleet, and took part in the Battle of Jutland where she received a torpedo hit, and was finally sunk by the German torpedo-boats *V 71* and *V 73* on 1 June 1916.

Rostock as completed
CPL

Graudenz 1918
Aldo Fraccaroli Collection

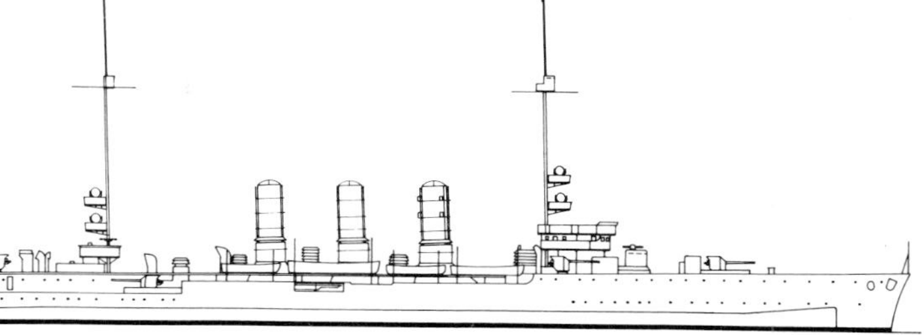

Graudenz 1917

These two cruisers belonged to the 1911 programme. They were rearmed with 7–15cm (5.9in) SKL/45 and 2–8.8cm (3.45in) Flak L/45 guns and 2–50cm (19.7in) TT on deck (*Regensburg*'s submerged TT were also replaced by 2 extra TT on deck). Both were fitted to carry 120 mines.

Graudenz served with the Scouting Group and became Italian after the war under the name *Ancona*; she was broken up in 1938. *Regensburg* served with the Scouting Group during the war and became a French war reparation after the war under the new name *Strasbourg*; she was broken up in 1944.

GRAUDENZ class *light cruisers*

Displacement: 4912t design; 6382t deep load
Dimensions: 465ft wl, 468ft 3in oa × 45ft 3in × 18ft 10in
139.0m, 142.7m × 13.8m × 5.75m
Machinery: 2-shaft Navy turbines, 12 Navy boilers (10 coal-, 2 oil-fired). 29,000shp = 28kts. Coal 1280t, oil 375t max. Range 5500nm/1000nm at 12kts/25kts
Armour: As *Magdeburg* class
Armament: 12–10.5cm (4.1in) SKL/45, 2–50cm (19.7in) TT sub (beam)
Complement: 385

Name	Builder	Laid down	Launched	Comp	Fate
GRAUDENZ	Kiel N Yd	1912	25.10.13	10.8.14	To Italy 1921
REGENSBURG	Weser, Bremen	1912	25.4.14	3.1.15	To France 1920

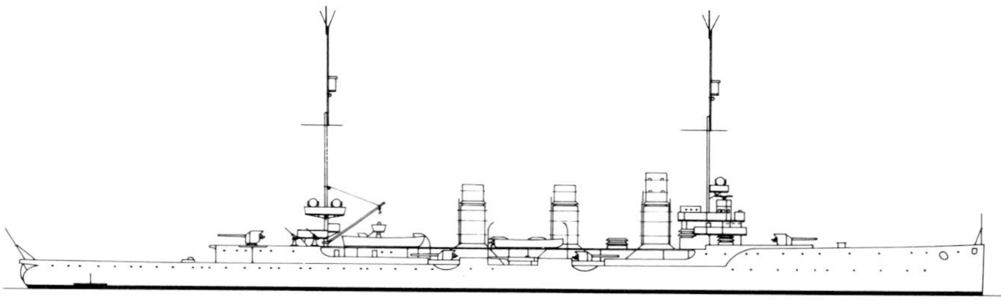

Pillau 1917

In 1912 the F Schichau yard at Danzig (Gdansk) won the contracts for two light cruisers for the Russian Navy against strong international competition. According to Russian practice the two units were named *Muraviev Amurski* and *Admiral Nevelski* when the keels were laid in 1913. When war broke out both units were in the final stages of completion and were taken over by the Imperial German Navy. Originally they were to be armed with Russian weapons: 8–13cm/55 and 4–6.3cm/55 guns. The merits of arming them with the 10.5cm gun – standard for German light cruisers – were discussed, but eventually they received 15cm guns. They were therefore the first German light cruisers with this more powerful calibre, and were a very desirable reinforcement for the German Scouting Forces. They were originally fitted with 4–5.2cm SKL/55 guns but these were soon replaced by the 8.8cm weapons quoted in the table.

Pillau served with the Scouting Forces and went to Italy after the war under the new name *Bari*. She was sunk in September 1943 near Livorno by US aircraft. *Elbing* was so badly damaged in a collision with the battleship *Posen* during the Battle of Jutland that she had to be scuttled.

PILLAU class *light cruisers*

Displacement: 4390t design; 5252t deep load
Dimensions: 440ft 7in wl, 443ft 11in oa × 44ft 7in × 19ft 8in
134.3m, 135.3m × 13.6m × 6.0m
Machinery: 2-shaft Navy turbines, 10 Yarrow boilers (6 coal-, 4 oil-fired), 30,000shp = 27.5kts. Coal 620t, oil 580t max. Range 4300nm at 12kts
Armour: Deck 20mm–80mm (¾in–3in), CT 50mm–75mm (2in–3in)
Armament: 8–15cm (5.9in) SKL/45, 2–8.8cm (3.45in) Flak L/45 AA, 2–50cm (19.7in) TT deck, 120 mines
Complement: 442

Name	Builder	Laid down	Launched	Comp	Fate
PILLAU	Schichau, Danzig	1913	11.4.14	14.12.14	To Italy 1921
ELBING	Schichau, Danzig	1913	21.11.14	1.9.15	Sunk 1.6.16

Pillau 1917
Navarret Collection

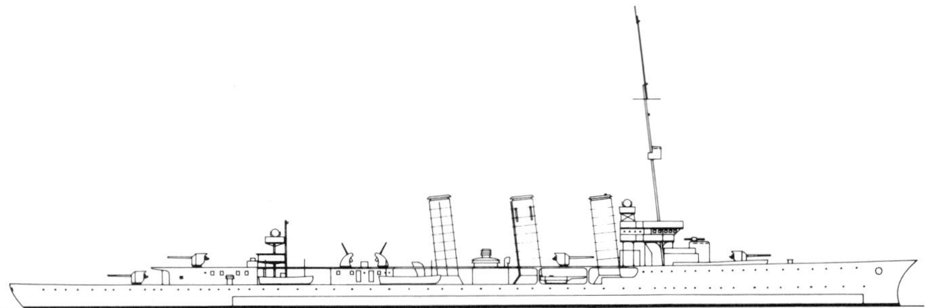

Brummer 1918

The lessons of mine warfare in the Russo-Japanese war of 1904–5 were not really followed up in Germany. When war broke out only the two 'mine-cruisers' *Albatross* and *Nautilus* were purpose-built, although most of the light cruisers were also fitted for minelaying operations. Increasing requests for such vessels led to the decision to build two more, utilising the turbines prepared for the Russian battlecruiser *Navarin*. On trials *Brummer* achieved 42,729shp = 28.0kts and *Bremse* 47,748shp = 28kts. Both units served in their intended role during the war, were interned at Scapa Flow after the armistice, and scuttled on 21 June 1919.

BRUMMER class *cruiser minelayers*

Displacement: 4385t design; 5856t deep load
Dimensions: 442ft 11in wl, 460ft 7in oa × 43ft 4in × 19ft 8in
135.0, 140.4m × 13.2m × 6.0m
Machinery: 2-shaft Navy turbines, 6 boilers (2 coal-, 4 oil-fired), 33,000shp = 28kts. Coal 600t, oil 1000t max. Range 5800nm/1400nm at 12kts/25kts
Armour: Waterline belt 40mm (1½in), deck 15mm (½in), CT 20mm–100mm (¾in–4in)
Armament: 4–15cm (5.9in) SKL/45, 2–8.8cm (3.45in) Flak L/45 AA, 2–50cm (19.7in) TT deck, 400 mines
Complement: 309

Name	Builder	Laid down	Launched	Comp	Fate
BRUMMER	Vulcan, Stettin	1915	11.12.15	2.4.16	Scuttled 21.6.19
BREMSE	Vulcan, Stettin	1915	11.3.16	1.7.16	Scuttled 21.6.19

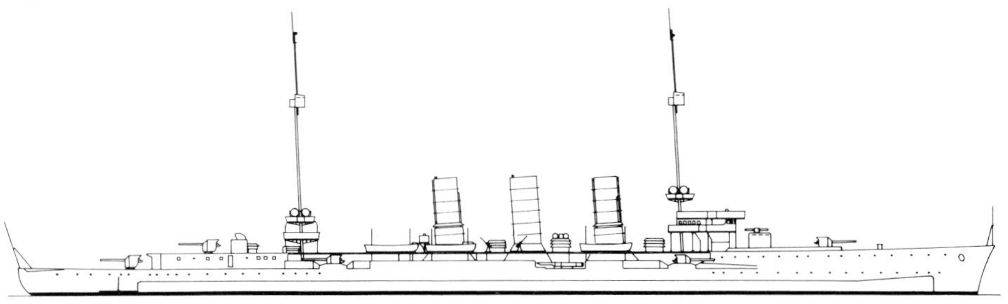

Frankfurt 1916

These two cruisers belonged to the 1912 programme. Their keels were laid at the end of 1913, but completion was delayed when higher priority was given to other work after war broke out. However their working up period was short and they were soon serving with the Scouting Forces. *Wiesbaden* differed in having hydraulic drive on one shaft and a geared cruising turbine on the other. *Wiesbaden* was sunk during the Battle of Jutland, 1 June 1916. *Frankfurt* served with the Scouting Forces and was interned at Scapa Flow after the armistice. The attempt to scuttle her failed, and she was beached. She was handed over to the US Navy and sunk as bombing trials target on 18 July 1921 off Cape Henry, Virginia.

WIESBADEN class *light cruisers*

Displacement: 5180t design; 6601t deep load
Dimensions: 464ft 11in wl, 476ft 9in oa × 45ft 7in × 19ft
141.7m, 145.3m × 13.9m × 5.8m
Machinery: 2-shaft Navy turbines, 12 (*Frankfurt* 14) Navy boilers (10/12 coal- 2 oil-fired), 31,000shp = 27.5kts. Coal 1280t, oil 470t max. Range 480nm/1200nm at 12kts/25kts
Armour: As *Magdeburg* class
Armament: 8–15cm (5.9in) SKL/45, 2–8.8cm (3.45in) Flak L/45 AA, 4–50mm (19.7in) TT (2 beam sub, 2 deck), 120 mines
Complement: 474

Name	Builder	Laid down	Launched	Comp	Fate
WIESBADEN	Vulcan, Stettin	1913	30.1.15	20.8.15	Sunk 1.6.16
FRANKFURT	Kiel N Yd	1913	20.3.15	10.8.15	Sunk 18.7.21

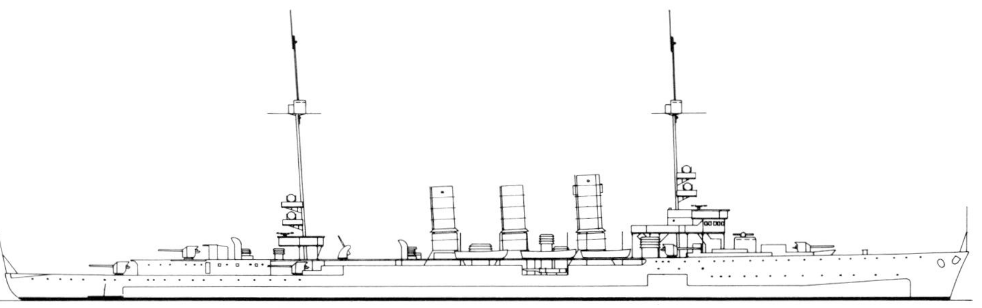

Emden (ii) 1918

Built under the 1913 programme the four units of this class were given the names of the commerce raiding cruisers sunk in the early part of the war. The second *Emden* displayed an Iron Cross on her stemhead in honour of her illustrious predecessor. On trials they all exceeded their designed power by a considerable margin (*Karlsruhe* with geared HP turbines achieved 55,700shp) but it meant only a ½kt above the design speed as the trials were in shallow water. In deep water 29kts would have been exceeded.

Königsberg (ii) served with the Scouting Forces, became a French reparation after the war and was

KÖNIGSBERG (ii) class *light cruisers*

Displacement: 5440t design; 7125t deep load
Dimensions: 478ft 4in wl, 496ft 9in × *46ft 11in* × 19ft 8in
145.8m, 151.4m × 14.3m × 6.0m
Machinery: 2-shaft Navy turbines, 12 Navy boilers (10 coal-, 2 oil-fired), 31,000shp = 27.5kts. Coal 1340t, oil 500t max. Range 4850nm/1200nm at 12kts/27kts
Armour: As *Magdeburg* class
Armament: As *Wiesbaden* class
Complement: 475

Name	Builder	Laid down	Launched	Comp	Fate
KÖNIGSBERG (ii)	Weser, Bremen	1914	18.12.15	12.8.16	To France 1920
KARLSRUHE (ii)	Wilhelmshaven N Yd	1915	31.1.16	23.12.16	Scuttled 21.6.19
EMDEN (ii)	Weser, Bremen	1914	1.2.16	16.12.16	BU 1926
NÜRNBERG (ii)	Howaldtswerke, Kiel	1915	14.4.16	15.2.17	Sunk 7.7.22

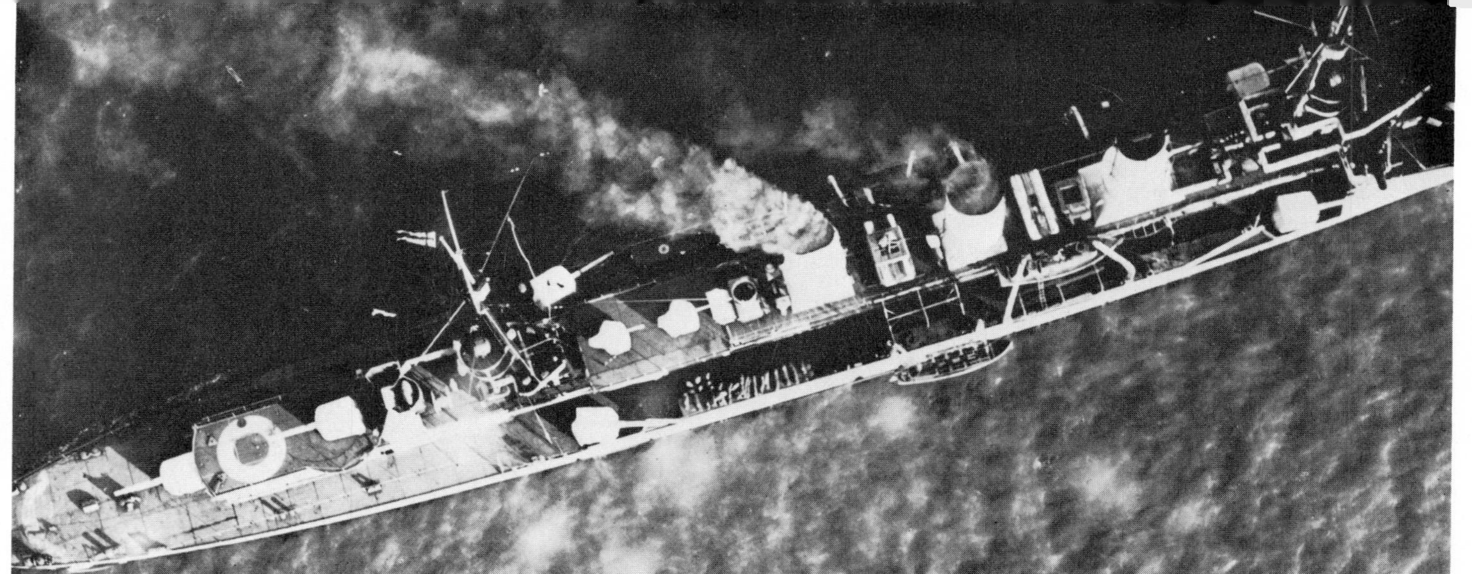

Königsberg (ii) 1917 — *Aldo Fraccoroli Collection*

Bremse 1917 — *CPL*

Wiesbaden as completed — *Aldo Fraccaroli Collection*

renamed *Metz*; she was broken up in 1936 at Brest. *Karlsruhe* (ii) served with the Scouting Forces and was scuttled at Scapa Flow on 21 June 1919. *Emden* (ii) served with the Scouting Forces and was interned at Scapa Flow, where she became flagship of Rear-Admiral Ludwig von Reuter on 25 March 1919. She was beached in a sinking condition after the scuttling of the German High Seas Fleet and finally became a French war reparation. As the damage was too great she did not see active service but was used as an explosive trials target and finally scrapped at Caen in 1926. *Nürnberg* (ii) was beached at Scapa Flow after scuttling and used as a gunnery and explosives target. She was finally sunk on 7 July 1922 off the Isle of Wight.

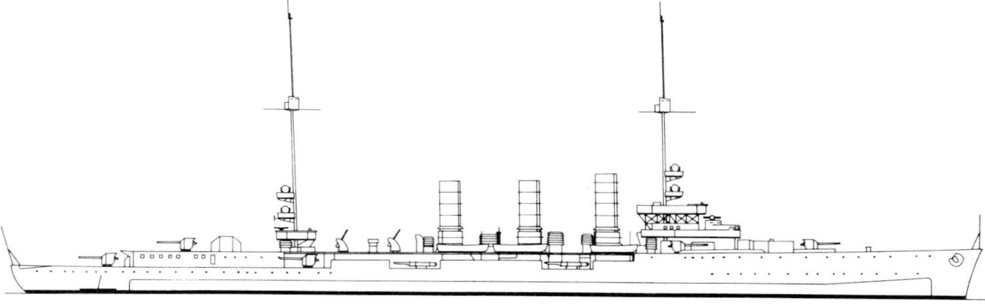

Cöln (ii) 1918

With the outbreak of war the restrictions on numbers imposed by the Naval Act vanished. To replace the war losses of light cruisers the Imperial German Navy began an ambitious programme of ten vessels, but because of manpower and material shortages only two were commissioned, although five more were launched. From the point of view of design they were an improved version of the second *Königsberg* class.

Dresden and *Cöln* (ii) were scuttled at Scapa Flow on 21 June 1919. The others were broken up in the 1920s.

CÖLN class *light cruisers*

Displacement: 5620t design; 7486t deep load

Dimensions: 491ft 6in wl, 510ft 2in oa × 46ft 11in × 19ft 8in
149.8m, 155.5m × 14.3m × 6.0m

Machinery: 2-shaft Navy turbines, 14 Navy boilers (8 coal-, 6 oil-fired), 31,000shp = 27.5kts. Coal 1100t, oil 1050t max. Range 5400nm/1200nm at 12kts/27kts

Armour: As *Magdeburg* class

Armament: 8–15cm (5.9in) SKL/45, 3–8.8cm (3.45in) Flak L/45 AA (only 2 mounted in 1918), 4–60cm (23.6in) TT deck, 120 mines

Complement: 511–552

Name	Builder	Laid down	Launched	Comp	Fate
CÖLN (ii)	Blohm & Voss, Hamburg	1915	5.10.16	17.1.18	Scuttled 21.6.19
WIESBADEN (ii)	Vulcan, Stettin	1915	3.3.17	–	BU 1920
DRESDEN (ii)	Howaldtswerke, Kiel	1916	25.4.17	28.3.18	Scuttled 21.6.19
MAGDEBURG (ii)	Howaldtswerke, Kiel	1916	17.11.17	–	BU 1922
LEIPZIG (ii)	Weser, Bremen	1915	28.1.18	–	BU 1922
ROSTOCK (ii)	Vulcan, Stettin	1915	6.4.18	–	BU 1922
FRAUENLOB (ii)	Kiel N Yd	1915	16.10.18	–	BU 1921
ERSATZ CÖLN	Weser, Bremen	1915	–	–	BU 1921
ERSATZ EMDEN	Weser, Bremen	1915	–	–	BU 1921
ERSATZ KARLSRUHE (A)	Kiel N Yd	1916	–	–	BU 1920

Cöln (ii) November 1918 CPL

DESTROYERS AND TORPEDO-BOATS

In contrast to France and Italy, which favoured small torpedo-boats for coast defence, German torpedo-boat destroyers were always regarded as part of the battle fleet. Officially they were referred to as *Hochseetorpedoboote* (literally, high seas torpedo-boats) to distinguish them from the coastal torpedo-boats, and strictly speaking there were no real destroyers until much later, although they were commonly so called by their crews. The primary function of these craft was not to oppose enemy torpedo-boats – which would have led to an omittance of all torpedo armament, as was done in some foreign navies – but to escort the High Seas Fleet, break through the battle line and attack enemy capital ships with their primary weapon, the torpedo. To engage enemy torpedo-boat forces with gunfire was a secondary consideration.

The size of German torpedo-boat destroyers was determined by Tirpitz's requirement: 'a torpedo-boat has to be big enough to be able to operate in waters beyond our coast together with the High Seas Fleet, but it has to be small enough to be commanded by one single officer.' The latter consideration reflected the personnel situation.

The German Naval Act of 1900 demanded a force of 16 torpedo-boat divisions (later called half-flotillas) with 6 boats each, making a total of 96 units. By the 1906 Amendment this figure was increased to 12 flotillas (24 half-flotillas of 6 boats) totalling 144 units. German practice was to build one flotilla each fiscal (budget) year, so we can speak of the boats *S 13–24* as the fiscal year 1912 flotilla, and so on.

Design and construction of the post 1906 classes meant that a broad degree of practical lessons could be incorporated into each successive design. The boats were built in groups of half-flotillas by different yards, resulting in a surprising number of sub-classes with very slight differences in displacements, dimensions, machinery and small deck details, but following a general layout and with standardised weaponry. The important change over to turbine propulsion was done gradually by fitting the last boat of the fiscal year 1903 (*S 125*), 1905 (*G 137*) and 1907 (*V 161*) flotillas as comparative turbine units to run alongside the conventional VTE-powered units. With the boats of the fiscal year 1908 flotilla the German torpedo-boat force switched to pure turbine propulsion. The request to increase seaworthiness, speed and radius of action resulted in a steady increase in displacement, but the Fleet regarded the newer boats as too big to manoeuvre in a tight battle line of capital ships and asked for smaller boats. Therefore the fiscal year 1911 flotilla – which should have constituted numbers 198–209 – consisted of a scaled-down design, and in consequence the pennant number series was restarted with *V 1–V 6*. Trials showed quickly that this type – nicknamed 'Admiral Lans' cripples' after their protagonist – was inferior especially as regards seaworthiness. Therefore, with the fiscal year 1913 flotilla, Germany returned to the larger design, but keeping the new series pennant numbers *V 25–36*, they being the first pure oil-burning German torpedo-boats.

Until the First World War the standard gun of the German torpedo-boat destroyer was the 8.8cm/30 torpedo-boat gun and in the second part of the pre-war period the more powerful 8.8cm/45. From 1915–16 the new war-built boats received the 10.5cm/45, and most of the older boats were up-gunned. The first real gun-armed destroyers of the German Navy were the former Czarist units *B 97–98, V 99–100* and their follow-ups. Being more seaworthy these big boats convinced the Fleet the advantages of size, and with the 1916 type design, Germany went over to the big-gun destroyer armed with 15cm guns, which would have been a successful match for any enemy units.

Note: All German torpedo-boat destroyers had an auxiliary rudder under the bow. The prefix letters indicate the builder: G for Germaniawerft, Kiel; S for F Schichau, Elbing; V for AG Vulcan, Stettin; H for Howaldtswerke, Kiel; B for Blohm & Voss, Hamburg; and Ww for the Imperial Yard, Wilhelmshaven. Therefore builders are not quoted separately in the tables.

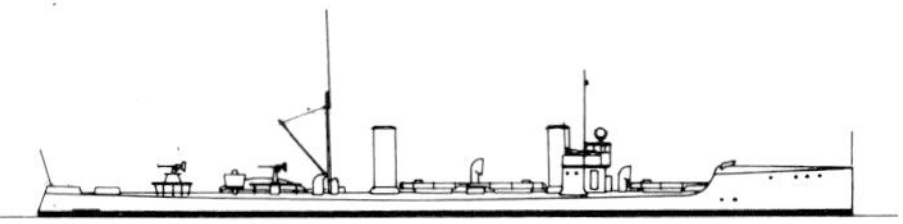
G 132 1908

G 132 class *destroyers*

Displacement:	414t design; 544t deep load
Dimensions:	214ft 3in wl, 215ft 6in oa × 22ft 11in × 8ft 6in *65.3m, 65.7m oa × 7.0m × 2.6m*
Machinery:	2-shaft VTE, 3 Navy boilers, 7000ihp = 28kts. Coal 139t. Range 2000nm/1060nm at 12kts/17kts
Armament:	*G 132–134:* 4–5.2cm (2in) SKL/55 (*G 136, G 135* 1–8.8cm SKL/35, 2–5.2cm SKL/55), 3–45cm (17.7in) TT
Complement:	69 (half-flotilla leaders 84)

Class (launched, fate):
G 132 (12.5.06, sold for BU 28.5.21), *G 133* (30.6.06, sold for BU 28.5.21), *G 134* (23.7.06, sold for BU 13.5.21), *G 135* (7.9.06, sold for BU 10.10.21), *G 136* (25.8.06, sold for BU 20.8.21)

The increased displacement was a result of the strengthened construction, compared with the previous Germania-built *G 108* group, the design now being similar to the Schichau boats in design and construction. All TT were deck-mounted singles as in previous boats. All boats saw active service and were scrapped in 1921.

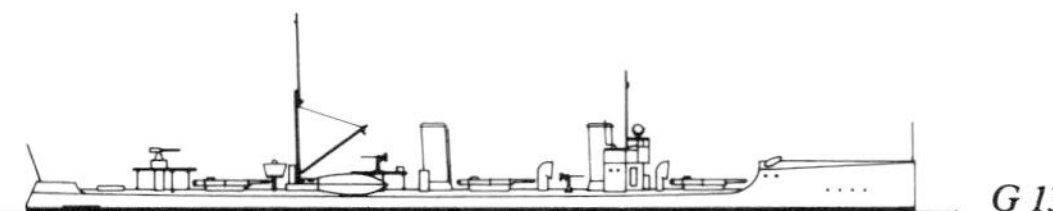
G 137 1908

G 137 *destroyer*

Displacement:	580t design; 693t deep load
Dimensions:	224ft 9in wl, 234ft 7in oa × 25ft 1in × 9ft 2in *68.5m, 71.5m oa × 7.7m × 2.8m*
Machinery:	3 shafts, 6 Parsons turbines, 4 Navy boilers, 10,800shp = 30kts. Coal 168t
Armament:	1–8.8cm (3.45in) SKL/35, 3–5.2cm (2in) SKL/55, 3–45cm (17.7in) TT
Complement:	80

Class (launched, fate):
G 137 (24.1.07, sold for BU 28.5.21)

This last unit of the *G 132* group was propelled by an experimental Parsons turbine set consisting of one high-pressure, two low-pressure, one cruising and two reverse turbines. Hull dimensions were therefore increased compared with the VTE boats, as was speed, armament and crew. Coal consumption was 2 tons per hour higher than in the VTE boats, but 40 tons less than in the following VTE boats *S 138–S 149*. She served as training boat, was renumbered *T 137* in 1916 and finally was ceded to the post-war *Reichsmarine*, but was scrapped in 1921.

S 138 class *destroyers*

Displacement:	533t design; 684t deep load
Dimensions:	230ft 4in wl, 231ft 11in oa × 25ft 7in × 9ft *70.2m, 70.7m × 7.8m × 2.75m*
Machinery:	2-shaft VTE, 4 Navy boilers, 11,000ihp = 30.3kts. Coal 194t. Range 1830nm/390nm at 17kts/24kts
Armament:	1–8.8cm (3.45in) SKL/35, 3–5.2cm (2in) SKL/55, 3–45cm (17.7in) TT
Complement:	80 (half-flotilla leaders 93)

Class (launched, fate):
G 138 (22.9.06, mined in N Sea 7.7.18), *G 139* (12.11.06, stricken 3.8.27, renamed *Pfeil*, BU 1945), *G 140* (22.12.06, sold for BU 8.6.21), *G 141* (7.2.07, stricken 3.8.27, renamed *Blitz*, BU 1933), *G 142* (6.3.07, sold for BU 13.6.21), *G 143* (6.4.07, mined 3.8.14, but raised and repaired; sold for BU 25.3.30), *G 144* 27.4.07, sold for BU 10.4.29), *G 145* (8.6.07, sold for BU 8.6.21), *G 146* (27.6.07, sold for BU 10.4.29), *G 147* (3.8.07, sold for BU 21.5.21), *G 148* (11.9.07, stricken 8.10.28, BU 1935), *G 149* (19.10.07, stricken 16.5.27, BU)

These boats of the 1906 fiscal year were closely modelled on *G 137*. The significant break between bridge and forecastle made the bridge very wet from sea state 6 upwards and hindered the operation of both guns and torpedoes. All boats saw active service in the war: *S 138* and *143* were lost in action, *S 139* and *141* came to the *Reichsmarine* after the war and were converted to remote radio control ships for gunnery target ships, being renamed *Pfeil* and *Blitz*. All the others were part of the torpedo-boat force of the *Reichsmarine*, but were scrapped in two waves in 1920 and 1928.

V 150 class *destroyers*

Displacement:	558t design; 691t deep load
Dimensions:	236ft 10in wl, 237ft 10in oa × 25ft 7in × 9ft 10in *72.2m, 72.5m × 7.8m × 3.0m*
Machinery:	2-shaft VTE, 4 Navy boilers, 10,900ihp = 30kts. Coal 164t. Range 2000nm/890nm at 14kts/20kts
Armament:	2–8.8cm (3.45in) SKL/35 (from *V 156* 2–8.8cm KL/30), 3–45cm (17.7in) TT
Complement:	84 (half-flotilla leaders 97)

Class (launched, fate):
V 150 (1.8.07, sunk in collision with *V 157*, 18.5.15), *V 151* (14.9.07, to USA 1945, BU 1949), *V 152* (11.10.07, stricken 31.3.31, BU 1935), *V 153* (13.11.07, to USA 1945, BU 1949), *V 154* (19.12.07, stricken 8.10.28, BU 1935), *V 155* (28.1.08, scuttled 22.4.45), *V 156* (29.2.08, scuttled 3.5.45), *V 157* (29.5.08, mined 22.10.43), *V 158* (23.6.08, to USSR 1945, BU), *V 159* (18.7.08, BU 1922), *V 160* (12.9.08, BU 1922)

Built by AG Vulcan, Stettin who had a good reputation for its torpedo-boats and destroyers for the export market, they were the first German destroyers to have a single gun in the centreline on the forecastle. All boats saw active service in the First World War: *V 150* sank after a collision in 1915, *V 159* and *V 160* became British war reparations and were scrapped in 1922. The remainder served with the *Reichsmarine* under their new 'T' designation after being refitted for several special duties, and as torpedo recovery vessels or rangefinder training ship.

V 150 and *V 152* August 1913 — CPL

V 161 as completed — BfZ

V 161 *destroyer*

Displacement:	596t design; 687t deep load
Dimensions:	As *V 150* class
Machinery:	2-shaft AEG turbines, 4 Navy boilers, 14,800shp = 33kts. Coal 166t. Range 1520nm at 14kts
Armament:	2–8.8cm (3.45in) KL/30, 3–45cm (17.7in) TT
Complement:	84

Name (launched, fate):
V 161 (21.4.08, BU 1922)

Following standard German practice this twelfth boat of the 1907 fiscal year group was turbine-propelled, on virtually the same dimension as the VTE boats. The boat became a British war reparation and was scrapped in 1922.

S 143 pre-war

BfZ

S 166 as completed *Aldo Fraccaroli Collection*

S 177 as completed *BfZ*

V 164 1910

V 162 class *destroyers*

Displacement: 639t design; 739t deep load
Dimensions: 241ft 6in wl, 242ft 6in oa × 25ft 9in × 9ft 11in
73.6m, 73.9m × 7.9m × 3.0m
Machinery: 2-shaft AEG turbines, 3 Navy boilers (2 coal-, 1 oil-fired), 15,100shp = 32kts. Coal 134t, oil 60t. Range 2140nm/960nm at 12kts/17kts
Armament: As *V 161* class
Complement: 84

Class (launched, fate):
V 162 (9.5.09, mined 15.8.16), *V 163* (24.5.09, BU 1921), *V 164* (27.5.09, BU 1920)

The twelve destroyers of the 1908 fiscal year were distributed amongst three contractors; in this year the Imperial German Navy switched entirely to turbine propulsion for destroyers. The most significant change in the layout was the new position of the three TT, the tube in the prominent break between bridge and forecastle being moved to the after part of the boat. From now on this obvious gap in the boats' silhouettes was narrower. In some boats it was closed off completely during later refits, thus creating more living quarters. *V 162* was lost after hitting a mine in 1916; the two others were scrapped in 1921 and 1920 respectively.

S 165 class *destroyers*

Displacement: 665t design; 765t deep load
Dimensions: 242ft 9in wl, 243ft 5in oa × 25ft 11in × 9ft 11n
74.0m, 74.2m × 7.9m × 3.0m
Machinery: 2-shaft Schichau turbines, 4 Navy boilers, 17,500shp = 32kts. Coal 116t, oil 74t. Range 1050nm/450nm at 17kts/27kts
Armament: As *V 161* class
Complement: 84

Class (launched, fate):
S 165 (26.11.10, BU 1922), *S 166* (27.12.10, BU 1922), *S 167* (15.2.11, sold for BU 3.9.21), *S 168* (16.3.11, stricken 11.1.27, BU)

The original *S 165–168* were sold to the Turkish Navy together with the two pre-dreadnought battleships *Kurfürst Friedrich Wilhelm* and *Weissenburg* before being commissioned for the German Navy, being subsequently renamed *Muavenet-i-Millet, Jadhigar-i-Millet, Numene-i-Hamije* and *Gairet-i-Watanije* (for further details see under Turkey). To maintain the destroyer strength of the 1908 fiscal year Schichau received the order for a replacement group of similar boats, becoming *S 165–S 168* of the Imperial German Navy. *S 165, 166* became British war reparations and were scrapped in 1922, *S 167* was scrapped 1921 at Kiel, *S 168* served with the *Reichsmarine* and was stricken 1927, then scrapped.

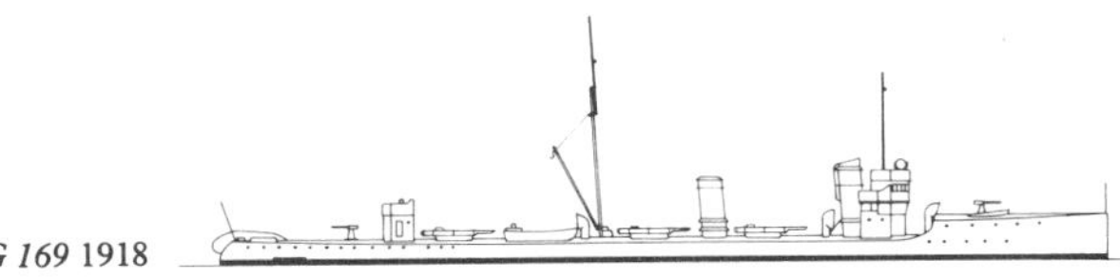
G 169 1918

G 169 class *destroyers*

Displacement: 670t design; 777t deep load
Dimensions: 242ft 9in × 25ft 11in × 9ft 2in
74.0m × 7.9m × 2.8m
Machinery: 3 shafts, 6 Parsons turbines, 4 Navy boilers, 15,000shp = 32kts. Coal 125t, oil 84t. Range 1300nm/460nm at 17kts/30kts (see notes)
Armament: As *V 161* class (except *G 174, G 175* 4–50cm (19.7in) TT)
Complement: 84

Class (launched, fate):
G 169 (29.12.08, BU 1922), *G 170* (3.3.09, sold for BU 27.9.21), *G 171* (28.5.09, sunk in collision with *Zähringen* 4.9.12), *G 172* (10.7.09, mined 7.7.18), *G 173* (28.7.09, BU 1922), *G 174* (8.1.10, BU 1922), *G 175* (24.2.10, stricken 23.9.26, BU)

These Germania boats had the same hull but different turbine systems and therefore different funnel positions. Unusually for German practice they had 3 shafts with the exception of *G 173* which had 2-shaft Zoelly turbines and a range of 1280nm at 17kts. *G 169–G 173* belonged to the last group of the 1908 fiscal year, and the remaining two to the 1909 programme.

G 171 sank after a collision in 1912, all other boats seeing active war service. *G 172* was mined; *G 169, 173, 174* became British war reparations and were scrapped in 1921–22; *G 170* served with the *Reichsmarine*, was stricken in 1921 and broken up; *G 175* served as dispatch vessel *Sleipner*, after the war in the *Reichsmarine*, was stricken in 1926 and broken up.

S 176 class *destroyers*

Displacement: 666t design; 781t deep load
Dimensions: As *S 165* class
Machinery: As *S 165* class, except 17,000shp. Coal 117t, oil 75t. Range 1025nm at 17kts
Armament: As *V 161* class, except 4–50cm (19.7in) TT
Complement: 84

Class (launched, fate):
S 176 (12.4.10, BU 1922), *S 177* (21.5.10, mined 23.12.15), *S 178* (14.7.10, sunk in collision with *Yorck* 4.3.13), *S 179* (27.8.10, BU 1922)

Almost identical to the *S 165–168* group. *S 178* was lost in 1913 after a collision, *S 177* was mined in the Baltic; the two others were British reparations and scrapped in 1922.

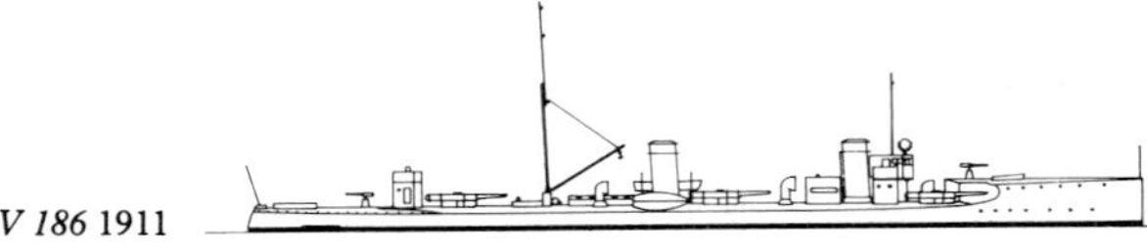
V 186 1911

V 180 class *destroyers*

Displacement: 650t design; 783t deep load (*V 186–V 191* 666t/775t)
Dimensions: 241ft 6in wl, 242ft 6in oa × 25ft 9in × 10ft 3in (*V 186–V 191* 10ft 1in)
73.6m, 73.9m × 7.9m × 3.1m (3.1m)
Machinery: 2-shaft AEG-Vulcan turbines, 4 Navy boilers, 18,000shp = 32kts. Coal 121t, oil 76t (*V 186–V 191* 136t/67t). Range 2360nm/1250nm/480nm at 12kts/17kts/32kts (*V 186–V 191* 1290nm at 17kts)
Armament: As *S 176* class
Complement: 84

Class (launched, fate):
V 180 (15.10.09, BU 1921), *V 181* (6.11.09, BU 1922), *V 182* (1.12.09, BU 1922), *V 183* (23.12.09, BU 1922), *V 184* (26.2.10, BU 1922), *V 185* (9.4.10,

stricken 4.10.32, renamed *Blitz*; to USSR 1945), *V 186* (28.11.10, BU 1922), *V 187* (11.1.11, sunk by gunfire 28.8.14), *V 188* (8.2.11, torpedoed by British submarine 26.7.15), *V 189* (14.3.11, wrecked 12.20), *V 190* (12.4.11, scuttled 1946), *V 191* (2.6.11, mined 17.12.15)

V 180–V 185 belonged to the 1909 fiscal year, the second group to 1910, the hulls being identical with the one exception that the forward TTs could fire straight ahead in the second group. Apparently the boats became so wet through this feature that *V 187* was rebuilt, but the subsequent classes of German destroyers had this feature.

All boats saw active service in the war, *V 180* becoming Brasilian, *V 181* becoming Japanese, *V 182–V 184* becoming British war reparations, but all were broken up in 1921–22. *V 187, 188* and *191* were lost, *V 186* and *189* became British reparations; the first was scrapped, the second ran aground and was broken up in situ. *V 190* became the *Reichsmarine* trials boat *Claus von Bevern*, survived the Second World War, became US and was scuttled with poison gas shells in the Skagerrak in 1946.

G 193 as completed — *Aldo Fraccaroli Collection*

G 192 class *destroyers*

Displacement: 660t design; 810t deep load
Dimensions: 241ft 6in wl, 242ft 9in oa × 24ft 11in × 10ft 3in
73.6m, 74.0m × 7.6m × 3.1m
Machinery: 2-shaft Germania turbines, 4 Navy boilers, 18,200shp = 32kts. Coal 145t, oil 76t. Range 2590nm/1150nm/420nm at 12kts/17kts/30kts
Armament: As *S 176* class
Complement: 84

Class (launched, fate):
G 192 (5.11.10, BU 1922), *G 193* (10.12.10, BU 1922), *G 194* (12.1.11, sunk 26.3.16), *G 195* (8.4.11, BU 1922), *G 196* (24.5.11, to USSR 1945), *G 197* (23.6.11, BU 1921)

Belonged to the fiscal year 1910 and had the same design of the after end of the forecastle for their forward TTs. All boats saw active service in the war: *G 194* was rammed and sunk by the British cruiser *Cleopatra*; *G 192, 193, 195* and *197* became British and were scrapped in 1921–22; *G 196* became a trials vessel of the *Reichsmarine*, survived the Second World and became the Russian *Pronsitelniy*.

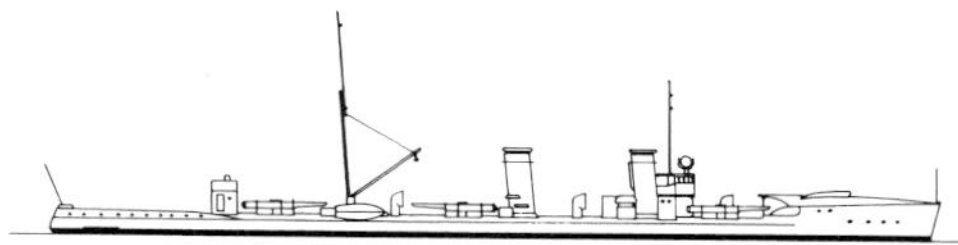

V 1 1913

V 1 class *destroyers*

Displacement: 569t design; 697t deep load
Dimensions: 230ft 4in wl, 233ft 3in oa × 26ft 11in × 10ft 2in
70.2m, 71.1m × 7.6m × 3.1m
Machinery: 2-shaft AEG-Vulcan turbines, 4 Navy boilers, 17,000shp = 32kts. Coal 107t, oil 78t. Range 1190nm/490nm at 17kts/29kts
Armament: 2–8.8cm (3.45in) KL/30, 4–50cm (19.7in) TT
Complement: 74

Class (launched, fate):
V 1 (11.9.11, stricken 27.3.29, BU), *V 2* (14.10.11, sold for BU 25.3.30), *V 3* (15.11.11, sold for BU 25.3.30), *V 4* (23.12.11, torpedoed 1.6.16), *V 5* (25.4.13, sold for BU 25.3.30), *V 6* (28.2.13, stricken 27.3.29, BU)

Originally it was planned to follow on with the traditional torpedo-boat type using the next available numbers (198–209), but the fleet argued for smaller boats which were believed to be more manoeuvrable in the battle line. This resulted in a generation of smaller destroyers (starting in 1911) with new numbers. Trials showed quickly that the reduced displacement caused a remarkable loss of seaworthiness. The original *V 5* and *V 6* were sold to Greece, where they served under the names *Nea Genea* and *Keravnos* until 1927. Two identical replacement boats *V 5* and *V 6* were ordered. *V 3* ran aground in 1911 but was salved; all the class saw wartime service, were transferred to the *Reichsmarine* after the war, but were stricken in 1929 and scrapped.

G 7 class *destroyers*

Displacement: 573t design; 719t deep load
Dimensions: 232ft 11in wl, 234ft 7in × 24ft 10in × 9ft 10in
71.0m, 71.5m × 7.6m × 3.0m
Machinery: 2-shaft Germania turbines, 4 Navy boilers, 16,000shp = 32kts. Coal 110t, oil 80t. Range 1150nm at 17kts
Armament: As *V 1* class
Complement: 74

Class (launched, fate):
G 7 (7.11.11, to USSR 1945), *G 8* (21.12.11, to UK 1945, BU), *G 9* (31.1.12, mined 3.5.18), *G 10* (15.3.12, scuttled 5.5.45), *G 11* (23.4.12, sunk 3.4.45), *G 12* (15.7.12, sunk 8.9.15)

G 8 August 1918 — *Aldo Fraccaroli Collection*

S 14 as completed — *Aldo Fraccaroli Collection*

The second group of the 1911 fiscal year destroyers was built by Germaniawerft, their boats being more stable than the Blohm & Voss design (the old torpedo-boats *S 7–S 57* of the 1885–90 series were in consequence renumbered *T 7–T 57*, most of them then being used as fast minesweepers).

All boats saw wartime service; *G 9* was lost after a mine hit, *G 12* after a collision with *V 1*, all others were transferred to the *Reichsmarine* and served as training vessels, two being lost in the last days of the Second World War; *G 7*, renumbered *T 107*, became the Russian *Porashayushtshiy; G 8*, renamed *T 108*, became a British war reparation and was scrapped.

S 13 class *destroyers*

Displacement: 568t design; 695t deep load
Dimensions: 232ft 11in wl, 234ft 7in oa, 24ft 3in × 9ft 1in
71.0m, 71.5m × 7.4m × 2.8m
Machinery: 2-shaft Schichau turbines, 4 Navy boilers, 15,700shp = 32.5kts. Coal 108t, oil 72t. Range 1050nm/600nm at 17kts/29kts
Armament: As *V 1* class
Complement: 74

Class (launched, fate):
S 13 (7.12.11, blew up 6.11.14), *S 14* (2.3.12, blew up 19.2.15), *S 15* (23.3.12, mined 21.8.17), *S 16* (20.4.12, mined 20.1.18), *S 17* (22.6.12, mined 16.5.17), *S 18* (10.8.12, BU 1935), *S 19* (17.10.12, sold for BU 4.2.35), *S 20* (4.12.12, sunk 5.6.17), *S 21* (11.1.13, sunk 21.4.15), *S 22* (15.2.13, mined 26.3.16), *S 23* (29.3.13, to USSR 1945), *S 24* (28.6.13, wrecked 12.20)

All twelve boats of the 1912 fiscal year were ordered from Schichau, the boats being very similar to the 1911 design and having the same deficiencies. All boats saw active wartime service suffering heavy losses: *S 13* and *S 14* sank after internal explosions; *S 15, S 16, S 17* and *S 22* were lost after mine hits; *S 20* was sunk by gunfire and *S 21* sunk after a collision with the light cruiser *Hamburg; S 18* came to the *Reichsmarine* and was stricken in 1931; *S 23* came to the *Reichsmarine*, served as training vessel and torpedo recovery vessel, was renamed *Komet* in 1939 and served as a remote radio control vessel for the target ship *Hessen* (ex-battleship); both went to the USSR after the Second World War. *S 24* was turned over to Britain, but ran aground and was scrapped in situ.

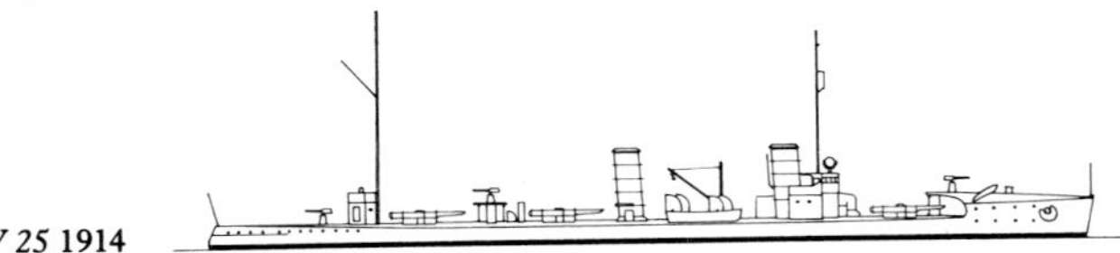
V 25 1914

V 25 class *destroyers*

Displacement: 812t design; 975t deep load
Dimensions: 255ft 3in wl, 257ft 7in oa × 27ft 3in × 10ft 11in
77.8m, 78.5m × 8.3m × 3.3m
Machinery: 2-shaft AEG-Vulcan turbines, 3 Navy oil-fired boilers, 23,500shp = 33.5kts. Oil 225t. Range 1080nm at 20kts
Armament: 3–8.8cm (3.45in) KL/45, 6–50cm (19.7in) TT (2×1, 2×2), 24 mines
Complement: 83

Class (launched, fate):
V 25 (29.1.14, mined 13.2.15), *V 26* (21.2.14, BU 1922), *V 27* (26.3.14, sunk by British cruiser 31.5.16), *V 28* (9.5.14, BU 1922), *V 29* (18.8.14, torpedoed by *Petard* 31.5.16), *V 30* (18.9.14, mined 20.11.18)

With the destroyers of the fiscal year 1913, the German Navy returned – after the unsatisfactory performances of the type 1911–12 boats – to increased dimensions. Considering the general political situation and the performances of foreign destroyers the switch to greater displacement and pure oil-burning produced very desirable results: higher speed, better steaming capabilities and better seaworthiness, increased action radius and increased gun power. Compared with the last big coal-burning destroyers it should be noted that oil-burning meant a remarkable reduction in machinery personnel. These boats were to be armed with a new generation of weapons: the improved 8.8cm KL/45 torpedo-boat gun and the new, more powerful 50cm torpedo.

All boats saw active service during the war, *V 25* being mined, *V 27* and *V 29* being lost in action; *V 26*, *V 28* and *V 30* were surrendered to Great Britain and scrapped; *V 30* was lost after hitting a mine during the transfer to internment at Scapa Flow.

S 31 class *destroyers*

Displacement: 802t design; 971t deep load
Dimensions: 259ft 2in wl, 261ft 2in oa × 27ft 4in × 9ft 2in
79.0m, 79.6m × 8.3m × 2.8m
Machinery: 2-shaft Schichau turbines, 3 Navy oil-fired boilers, 23,500shp = 33.5kts. Oil 220t. Range 1100nm at 20kts
Armament: As *V 25* class
Complement: 83

Class (launched, fate):
S 31 (20.12.13, mined 19.8.15), *S 32* (28.2.14, scuttled 21.6.19, BU 1925), *S 33* (4.4.14, torpedoed by *L 11* 3.10.18), *S 34* (13.6.14, mined 3.10.18), *S 35* (30.8.14, sunk 31.5.16), *S 36* (17.10.14, scuttled 21.6.19, BU 1925)

The second half of the 1913 fiscal year boats were built by Schichau, externally resembling the *V 25*–*V 30* group. *S 35* and *S 36* were to be sold to Greece, but on the outbreak of the war were seized by Germany and commissioned under their original numbers. All boats saw active wartime service: *S 31* was mined in the Baltic, and *S 34* in the North Sea; *S 33* was lost to a British submarine torpedo; *S 35* was lost during the Battle of Jutland; *S 32* and *36* were scuttled at Scapa Flow, raised and scrapped.

S 33 during the war *BfZ*

V 43 as completed *BfZ*

G 37 class *destroyers*

Displacement: 822t design; 1051t deep load (*G 41*, *G 42* 960t/1147t)
Dimensions: 257ft 10in wl, 260ft 10in oa × 27ft 6in × 11ft 4in (*G 41*, *G 42* 269ft 8in wl, 272ft 4in oa × 27ft 6in × 11ft 2in)
78.6m, 79.5m × 8.4m × 3.5m (82.2m, 83.0m × 8.4m × 3.4m)
Machinery: 2-shafts Germania turbines, 3 Navy oil-fired boilers, 24,000shp = 34kts (*G 41*, *G 42* 33.5kts). Oil 299t. Range 1685nm/1300nm at 17kts/20kts (see notes)
Armament: As *V 25* class (*G 42* later 3–10.5cm KL/45)
Complement: 87

Class (launched, fate):
G 37 (12.12.14, mined 4.11.17), *G 38* (23.12.14, scuttled 21.6.19, BU 1924), *G 39* (16.1.15, scuttled 21.6.19, BU 1925), *G 40* (27.2.15, scuttled 21.6.19, BU 1929), *G 41* (24.4.15, scuttled 3.10.18), *G 42* (20.5.15, sunk by gunfire from *Swift* and *Broke* 21.4.17)

1914 type mobilisation destroyers; from *G 41* on the hull was enlarged during construction by 2.5m with oil storage increased to 326t and range extended to 1950nm/1715nm at 17kts/20kts. All boats saw active wartime service: *G 42* was lost in action; *G 37* was mined; *G 41* was scuttled after the German withdrawal from Bruges; *G 38*–*G 40* were scuttled at Scapa Flow, raised and scrapped 1924–25.

V 43 class *destroyers*

Displacement: 852t design; 1106t deep load (*V 47*, *V 48* 924t/1188t)
Dimensions: 258ft 6in wl, 261ft 2in oa × 27ft 3in × 11ft 10in (*V 47*, *V 48* 270ft wl, 272ft 8in oa × 27ft 3in × 11ft 2in)
78.8m, 79.6m × 8.3m × 3.6m (82.3m, 83.1m × 8.3m × 3.4m)
Machinery: 2-shaft AEG-Vulcan turbines, 3 Navy oil-fired boilers, 24,000shp = 34.5kts (*V 47*, *V 48* = 33.5kts). Oil 296t. Range 1750nm/1270nm at 17kts/20kts (see notes)
Armament: As *V 25* class
Complement: 87

Class (launched, fate):
V 43 (27.1.15, sunk as target 15.7.21 by USS *Florida*), *V 44* (24.2.15, BU 1922), *V 45* (29.3.15, scuttled 21.6.19, BU 1924), *V 46* (23.12.14, BU 1924), *V 47* (10.6.15, scuttled 2.11.18), *V 48* (6.8.15, sunk by gunfire 31.5.16)

The second half-flotilla of 1914 mobilisation destroyers. As with the Germania boats, *V 47* and *V 48* were enlarged by 3.5m during construction, increasing oil storage 338t and range to 2050nm at 17kts. From 1916 on they received the new 10.5cm (4.1in) KL/45 instead of the old 8.8cm. All boats saw active wartime service: *V 48* was lost during the Battle of Jutland; *V 47* was scuttled during the German retreat from Belgium; V 43–*V 46* were interned at Scapa Flow and salvaged; *V 43* became US and was sunk in 1921 as target practice; *V 44* and *V 45* were broken up in England; *V 46* became French but was broken up in 1924.

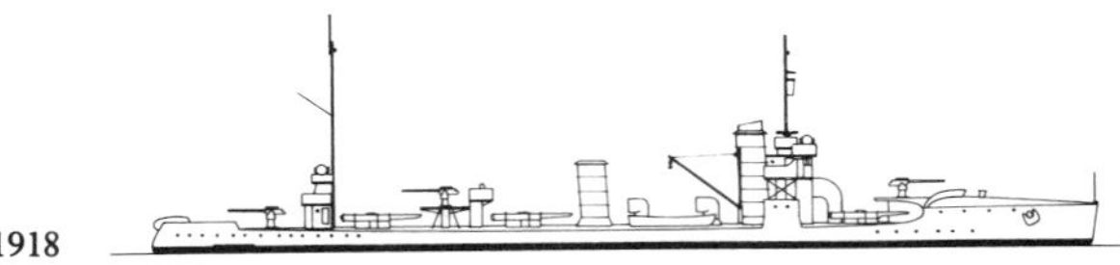
S 49 1918

S 49 class *destroyers*

Displacement: 802t design; 1074t deep load (*S 53*–*S 66* 919t/1170t)
Dimensions: 259ft 2in wl, 261ft 2in × 27ft 7in × 9ft 2in (*S 53*–*S 66* 270ft 8in wl, 272ft 8in oa × 27ft 7in × 11ft 9in)
79.0m, 79.6m × 8.4m × 2.8m (82.5m, 83.1m × 8.4m × 3.6m)
Machinery: 2-shaft Schichau turbines, 3 Navy oil-fired boilers, 24,000shp = 34kts. Oil 252t. Range 1605nm/1270nm at 17kts/20kts (see notes)
Armament: As *V 25* class (except 3–10.cm KL/45 in *S 60* onwards, and replacing 8.8cm in earlier boats from 1916 on)
Complement: 85

Class (launched, fate):
S 49 (10.4.15, scuttled 21.6.19, BU 1924), *S 50* (24.4.15, scuttled 21.6.19, BU 1925), *S 51* (29.4.15, beached 21.6.19, BU 1922), *S 52* (12.6.15, scuttled 21.6.19, BU 1924), *S 53* (18.9.15, scuttled 21.6.19, BU 1927), *S 54* (11.10.15, beached 21.6.19, BU 1921), *S 55* (6.11.15, scuttled 21.6.19, BU 1924), *S 56* (11.12.15, scuttled 21.6.19, BU 1928), *S 57* (8.1.16, mined 10.11.16), *S 58* (5.2.16, mined 11.11.16), *S 59* (16.2.16, mined 11.11.16), *S 60* (3.4.16, BU 1920), *S 61* (8.4.16, scuttled 2.11.18), *S 62* (13.5.16, mined 10.7.18), *S 63* (27.5.16, BU 1937), *S 64* (21.8.16, mined 18.10.17), *S 65* (14.10.16, scuttled 21.6.19, BU 1925), *S 66* (21.11.16, mined 10.7.18)

Belonged to the wartime mobilisation programme, *S 49* and *S 50* being the replacements for *S 35* and *S 36*. The enlarged *S 53*–*S 66* had a cruising turbine on the starboard shaft, carried 305t of oil and had a range of 1960nm at 17kts. All boats saw active wartime service: *S 62* was lost in action; *S 57–S 59*, *S 64* and *S 66* were mined; *S 61* was scuttled during the German retreat from Belgium; *S 49–S 56, and S 65* were interned at Scapa and scrapped; *S 60* which was beached at Scapa Flow became a Japanese war reparation and was scrapped in England in 1920; *S 63* became an Italian war reparation and served under the name *Ardemitoso* until 1937.

V 67 class *destroyers*

Displacement:	924t design; 1188t deep load
Dimensions:	265ft 9in wl, 269ft oa × 27ft 3in × 11ft 2in *81.0m, 82.0m × 8.3m × 3.4m*
Machinery:	2-shaft AEG-Vulcan turbines, 3 Navy oil-fired boilers, 23,500shp = 34kts. Oil 306t. Range 2050nm/1810nm at 17kts/20kts
Armament:	As *S 49* class (including 1916 up-gunning)
Complement:	85

Class (launched, fate):
V 67 (3.8.15, scuttled 2.11.18), *V 68* (24.8.15, mined 8.8.18), *V 69* (18.8.15, scuttled 2.11.18), *V 70* (14.10.15, scuttled 21.6.19, BU 1929), *V 71* (1.9.15, BU 1921), *V 72* (30.12.15, mined 11.11.16), *V 73* (24.9.15, beached 21.6.19, BU 1922), *V 74* (29.10.15, scuttled 3.10.18), *V 75* (15.1.16, mined 10.11.16), *V 76* (27.2.16, mined 11.11.16), *V 77* (28.2.16, scuttled 2.11.18), *V 78* (19.2.16, scuttled 21.6.19, BU 1925), *V 79* (18.4.16, BU 1933), *V 80* (beached 21.6.19, BU 1922), *V 81* (27.5.16, beached 21.6.19, BU 1922), *V 82* (5.7.16, beached 21.6.19, BU 1922), *V 83* (10.6.16, scuttled 21.6.19, BU 1928), *V 84* (17.8.16, mined 26.5.17)

V 82–V 84 were armed with 3–10.5cm KL/45 and the others were similarly up-gunned from 1916. All of these mobilisation destroyers saw active wartime service: *V 68, V 72, V 75, V 76*, and *V 84* were lost on mines; *V 67, V 69, V 74* and *V 77* were scuttled after the German retreat from Belgium; *V 70, V 73, V 78, V 81–V 83* were interned at Scapa and scrapped after their salvage; *V 79* became a French war reparation and served under the name *Pierre Durand* until 1933; *V 80* became a Japanese war reparation but was scrapped in England in 1922.

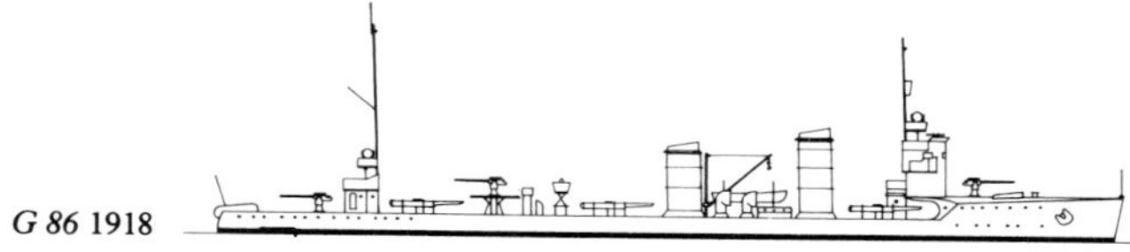
G 86 1918

G 85 class *destroyers*

Displacement:	960t design; 1147t deep load
Dimensions:	269ft 8in wl, 272ft 4in × 27ft 7in × 11ft 2in *82.2m, 83.0m × 8.4m × 3.4m*
Machinery:	2-shaft Germania turbines, 3 Navy oil-fired boilers, 24,000shp = 33.5kts. Oil 326t. Range 1760nm at 20kts
Armament:	3–10.5cm (4.1in) KL/45, 6–50cm (19.7in) TT (2×1, 2×2) 24 mines
Complement:	85

Class (launched, fate):
G 85 (24.7.15, sunk by gunfire from *Swift* and *Broke* 21.4.17), *G 86* (24.8.15, scuttled 21.6.19, BU 1925), *G 87* (22.9.15, mined 30.3.18), *G 88* (16.10.15, torpedoed by CMB 8.4.17), *G 89* (11.12.15, scuttled 21.6.19, BU 1926), *G 90* (15.1.16, mined 11.11.16), *G 91* (16.11.15, scuttled 21.6.19, BU 1924), *G 92* (15.2.16, beached 21.6.19, BU 1921–22), *G 93* (11.7.16, mined 30.3.18), *G 94* (1.8.16, mined 30.3.18), *G 95* (29.8.16, BU 1921–22)

Except for *G 92–G 95* they were armed as the *S 49* class until 1916, but the 10.5cm guns became standard for subsequent war emergency (mobilisation) classes. All of these mobilisation destroyers saw active service in the war: *G 85* and *G 88* were lost in action; *G 87, G 90, G 93* and *G 94* were mined; *G 86, G 89, G 91* and *G 92* were scuttled at Scapa, raised and scrapped, *G 93* became a British war reparation and was scrapped.

G 96 *destroyer*

Displacement:	990t design; 1147t deep load
Dimensions:	270ft wl, 277ft 3in × 27ft 7in × 11ft 2in *82.3m, 84.5m × 8.4m × 3.4m*
Machinery:	2-shaft Germania turbines (plus starboard shaft cruising turbine), 3 Navy oil boilers, 24,000shp = 32kts. Oil 332t. Range 2040nm at 17kts
Armament:	As *G 85* class, except 40 mines
Complement:	105

Class (launched, fate):
G 96 (16.9.16, mined 26.6.17)

G 96, belonging to the 1916 mobilisation type, was an enlarged version of the *G 85* group, the longer forecastle giving better seaworthiness. The boat was lost after hitting a mine off the Flanders coast.

V 67 1917 — *Aldo Fraccaroli Collection*

G 96 as completed — *Aldo Fraccaroli Collection*

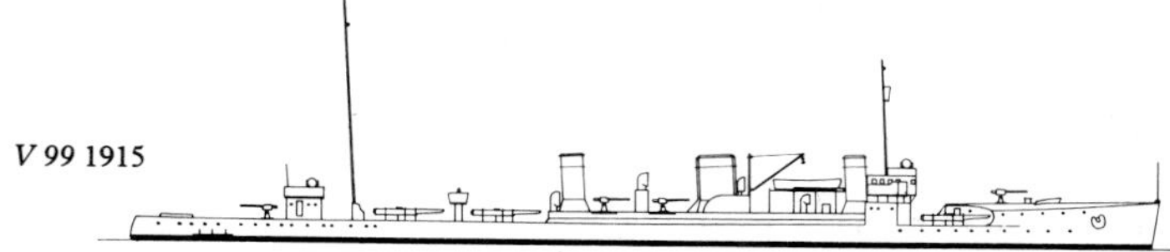
V 99 1915

B 97 class *destroyers*

Displacement:	1374t design; 1843t deep load (*V 99, V 100* 1350t/1847t)
Dimensions:	314ft 11in wl, 321ft 6in oa × 30ft 10in × 11ft 3in (*V 99, V 100* 319ft 11in wl, 324ft 9in oa × 30ft 10in × 11ft 9in) *96.0m, 98.0m × 9.4m × 3.4m (97.5m, 99.0m × 9.4m × 3.6m)*
Machinery:	2-shaft Navy (*V 99, V 100* AEG-Vulcan) turbines, 4 Navy oil-fired boilers, 40,000shp = 36.5kts. Oil 527t (*V 99, V 100* 519t). Range 2600nm
Armament:	4–8.8cm (3.45in) KL/45, 6–50cm (19.7in) TT (2×1, 2×2), 24 mines (all 8.8cm replaced by 10.5cm KL/45 in 1916)
Complement:	114

Class (launched, fate):
B 97 (15.12.14, BU 1939, *B 98* (2.1.15, BU 1919), *V 99* (9.2.15, sunk 17.8.15), *V 100* (8.3.15, BU 1921), *B 109* (11.3.15, BU 1926), *B 110* (31.3.15, BU 1925–26), *B 111* (8.6.15, BU 1926), *B 112* (17.6.15, BU 1926)

One aspect of the Czarist Russian fleet construction programme was the building of a modern yard at St Petersburg, which was undertaken by Blohm & Voss and officially opened on 29 November 1913. When war broke out four powerful destroyers were under construction there: *Leitenant Ilin, Kaptan Kononsotoff, Gavril* and *Mikhail*. Their 40,000shp turbine sets were being built by Blohm & Voss at Hamburg and were seized immediately. The yard proposed to the German Navy the building of destroyers around these sets within six months. Against the opposition of the torpedo authorities – who argued that these boats might not fit into the German flotillas – von Tirpitz pushed through the scheme and they (plus additional boats) were built. They were the first three funnelled boats in the German destroyer arm, and were faster (37.4kts for the *B 109* group on trials) and more heavily armed than contemporary German destroyers and had better seaworthiness. They were referred to as 'destroyers' in German sources, as opposed to the 'high seas torpedo-boats'.

All saw active wartime service, *B 97* becoming an Italian war reparation and serving as *Cesare Rossarol* until 1939; all the others were scuttled at Scapa Flow on 21 June 1919, raised and scrapped, except *V 99* which was sunk after an engagement with Russian surface forces in the Baltic.

GERMANY

G 101 class *destroyers*

Displacement: 1136t design; 1734t deep load
Dimensions: 308ft 5in wl, 312ft 8in × 31ft 1in × 12ft 2in
94.0m, 95.3m × 9.5m × 3.7m
Machinery: 2-shaft Germania turbines, 2 Navy oil-fired boilers, 28,000shp = 33.5kts. OIl 500t. Range 2420nm at 20kts
Armament: As *B 97* class
Complement: 104

Class (launched, fate):
G 101 (12.8.14, BU 1926), *G 102* (16.9.14, sunk as target 13.7.20), *G 103* (14.11.14, foundered November 1925), *G 104* (28.11.14, BU 1926)

Ordered for the Argentine Navy as *Santiago, San Luis, Santa Fé* and *Tucuman* with cruising diesels, 10.2cm guns and 53.3cm torpedoes, they were seized by the Imperial German Navy and commissioned on the outbreak of war. Like the *B 97* class they were referred to as 'destroyers'. All four boats saw active wartime service and were interned and scuttled at Scapa Flow; after their salvaging *G 103* sank in a heavy gale in 1925, *G 102* was ceded to the USA, being sunk as a bombing practice target in 1920; the two others were scrapped in 1926.

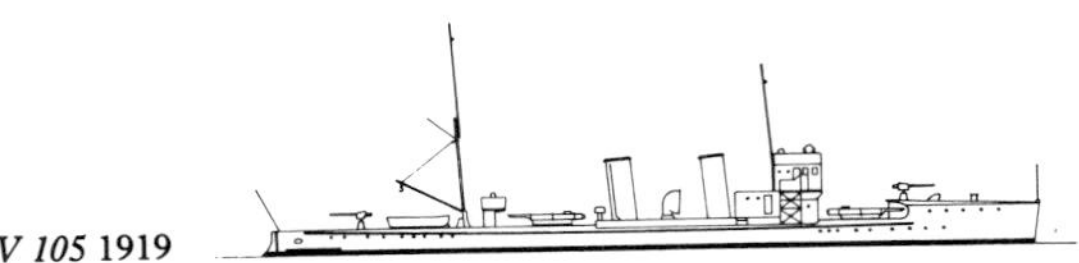
V 105 1919

V 105 class *destroyers*

Displacement: 340t design; 421t full load
Dimensions: 203ft 5in wl, 205ft 5in oa × 20ft 5in × 8ft 2in max
62.0m, 62.6m × 6.2m × 2.5m
Machinery: 2-shaft AEG-Vulcan turbines, 4 Yarrow boilers, 5500shp = 28kts. Coal 60t, oil 16.2t. Range 1400nm/460nm at 17kts/20kts
Armament: 2–8.8cm (3.45in) L/30 (except *V 106* 2–5.2cm L/55; *V 108* 2–8.8cm L/45), 2–45cm (17.7in) TT

Class (launched, fate):
V 105 (26.8.14, to Poland as *Mazur* 1920), *V 106* (26.8.14, BU 1920), *V 107* (12.12.14, mined 8.5.15), *V 108* (12.12.14, to Poland as *Kaszub* 1920)

Originally ordered for the Netherlands as the *Z 1–Z 4*, they were taken over by the German Navy at the builders (Vulcan, Stettin) on 10 August 1914.

G 101 during the war *Aldo Fraccaroli Collection*

V 116 as completed *BfZ*

S 113 1919

S 113 class *destroyers*

Displacement: 2060t design; 2415t deep load
Dimensions: 345ft 9in wl, 347ft 9in oa × 33ft 6in × 11ft 1in
105.4m, 106.0m × 10.2m × 3.4m
Machinery: 2-shaft Schichau turbines, 4 Navy oil-fired boilers, 45,000shp = 36kts. Oil 720t. Range 2500nm at 20kts
Armament: 4–15cm (5.9in) KL/45, 4–60cm (23.6in) TT (2×2), 40 mines
Complement: 176

Class (launched, fate):
S 113 (31.1.18, BU 1936), *S 114* (11.4.18, BU unfinished 1919), *S 115* (20.7.18, BU unfinished 1919)

Genuine torpedo-boat destroyers of the 1916 design type, they represented the new heavily gun-armed type; but they exhibited poor seakeeping capabilities in the rough conditions of the North Sea. They did not become operational, *S 113* running her final trials at the end of the war. *S 113* became a French war reparation, serving under the name *Admiral Sénès* until 1936. The others were 75 and 60 per cent complete in 1918 and were scrapped in 1919.

V 116 class *destroyers*

Displacement: 2060t design; 2360t (*G 119–G 121* 2405t) deep load
Dimensions: 347ft 9in wl, 352ft 8in oa × 33ft 10in × 14ft 9in (*G 119–G 121* 349ft 5in wl × 33ft 9in × 13ft 9in)
106.0m, 107.5m × 10.4m × 4.5m (106.5m × 10.3m × 4.2m)
Machinery: As *S 113* class, except AEG-Vulcan turbines in *V 116–V 118*, and Germania turbines in *G 119–G 121;* oil 660t and 690t respectively
Armament: As *S 113* class
Complement: 176

Class (launched, fate):
V 116 (2.3.18, BU 1937), *V 117* (4.5.18, BU 1921), *V 118* (6.7.18, BU 1921), *G 119* (8.10.18, BU 1921), *G 120* (–, BU 1921), *G 121* (–, BU 1921)

These large destroyers were virtually sister-ships of the *S 113* group, and were in the last stages of completion at the end of the war. *V 116* became an Italian war reparation and served under the name *Premuda* until 1937; all the others were stricken on 3 November 1919 and sold for scrapping on 4 July 1921.

B 122 class *destroyers*

Displacement: 2040t design; 2354t deep load
Dimensions: 352ft 8in wl, 355ft 11in oa × 33ft 9in × 13ft 6in
107.5m, 108.5m × 10.3m × 4.1m
Machinery: As *S 113* class, except oil 716t
Armament: As *S 113* class
Complement: 176

Class:
B 122–B 124

Sister-ships of the *S 113* group; at the end of the war they were 65–40 per cent completed; stricken 3 November 1919 and sold for scrapping in 1921.

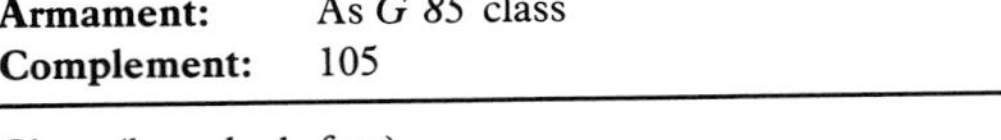

V 125 class *destroyers*

Displacement: 924t design; 1188t deep load
Dimensions: 268ft wl, 269ft oa × 27ft 3in × 11ft 6in
81.7m, 82.0m × 8.3m × 3.5m
Machinery: 2-shaft AEG-Vulcan turbines, 3 Navy oil boilers, 23,500shp = 34kts. Oil 298t. Range 2050nm/1625nm at 17kts/20kts
Armament: As *G 85* class
Complement: 105

Class (launched, fate):
V 125 (18.5.17, BU 1922), *V 126* (30.6.17, BU 1925), *V 127* (28.7.17, BU 1922), *V 128* (11.8.17, BU 1922), *V 129* (19.10.17, BU 1922), *V 130* (20.11.17, BU 1934), *V 140* (–, BU unfinished 1921), *V 141* (–, BU unfinished 1921), *V 142* (25.9.18, BU unfinished 1921), *V 143* (25.9.18, BU unfinished 1921), *V 144* (10.10.18, BU unfinished 1921)

V 125–V 130 were the follow-on boats of the 1916 mobilisation type (the first boat being *G 96*). All boats saw active wartime service: *V 125, V 128* and *V 129* were interned at Scapa Flow and scrapped after salvaging; *V 126* which was

S 134 as completed *BfZ*

V 125 as completed *BfZ*

beached at Scapa Flow and *V 130* became French war reparations, the first being scrapped in 1925, the second serving as *Buino* until 1934; *V 127* which was beached at Scapa Flow became a Japanese war reparation but was scrapped in 1922. A second group of this design, *V 140–V 144*, were about 40–60 per cent finished at the end of the war and were sold on 27.10.21 for breaking up in situ.

S 131 class *destroyers*

Displacement:	919t design; 1170t deep load
Dimensions:	270ft 8in wl, 272ft 8in oa × 27ft 3in × 11ft 10in *82.5m, 83.1m × 8.3m × 3.6m*
Machinery:	2-shaft Schichau turbines, 3 Navy oil-fired boilers, 24,000shp = 34kts. Oil 305t. Range 2450nm/1960nm at 17kts/20kts
Armament:	As *G 85* class
Complement:	105

Class (launched, fate):
S 131 (3.3.17, scuttled 21.6.19, BU 1925), *S 132* (19.5.17, sunk as target by US ships *Delaware* and *Herbert* 15.7.21), *S 133* (1.9.17, BU 1934), *S 134* (25.8.17, BU 1935), *S 135* (27.10.17, BU 1935), *S 136* (1.12.17, scuttled 21.6.19, BU 1928), *S 137* (9.3.18, beached 21.6.19, BU 1922), *S 138* (22.4.18, BU 1926), *S 139* (24.11.17, BU 1934)

S 131–S 139 were the second group of the 1916 mobilisation type, having virtually the same appearance as the *V 125–V 130* group. All saw active wartime service: *S 131, S 136–S 138* were interned at Scapa Flow and scrapped after raising; *S 132* which was beached at Scapa Flow went to the US and was sunk as gunnery practice target in 1921; *S 133–S 135* and *S 139* became French war reparations, serving under the names *Chastang*, *Vesco*, *Mazaré* and *Deligny* until 1934–35.

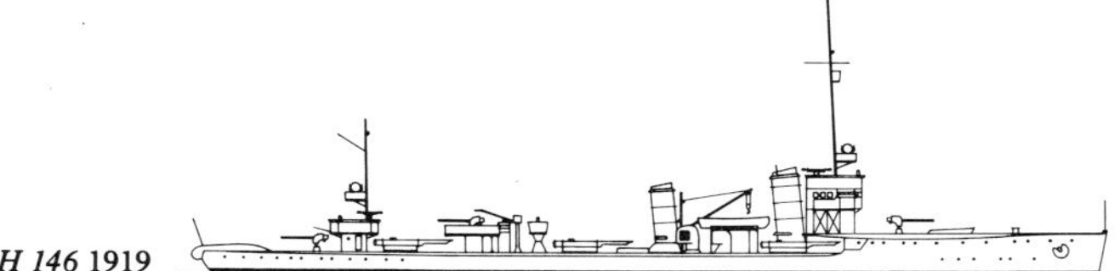

H 146 1919

H 145 class *destroyers*

Displacement:	990t design; 1147t deep load
Dimensions:	271ft 8in wl, 277ft 3in × 27ft 7in × 11ft 2in *82.8m, 84.5m × 8.4m × 3.4m*
Machinery:	2-shaft Germania turbines, plus starboard shaft cruising turbines), 3 Navy oil-fired boilers, 24,000shp = 34kts. Oil 332t. Range 2780nm/2060nm/1840nm at 14kts/17kts/20kts
Armament:	As *G 85* class
Complement:	105

Class (launched, fate):
H 145 (11.12.17, scuttled 21.6.19, BU 1928), *H 146* (23.1.18, BU 1935), *H 147* (13.3.18, BU 1935)

Sister boats to *G 96*, but built by Howaldtswerke, Kiel, and therefore having the prefix letter H. The boats were commissioned immediately before the end of the war; *H 146* and *H 147* became French war reparations; serving under the names *Rageot de la Touche* and *Marcel Delage* until 1935. *H 145* was interned at Scapa Flow and was scrapped after salvaging.

G 148 class *destroyers*

Displacement:	1020t design; 1216t deep load
Dimensions:	274ft 3in wl, 279ft 2in oa × 27ft 7in × 11ft 6in *83.6m, 85.1m × 8.4m × 3.5m*
Machinery:	2-shaft Germania turbines (plus starboard shaft cruising turbine), 3 Navy oil-fired boilers, 24,500shp × 32.5kts. Oil 332t. Range 2170nm/1850nm at 17kts/20kts
Armament:	As *G 96*
Complement:	105

Class:
G 148–G 150, Ww 151

Ww 151, building at the Imperial Yard Wilhelmshaven, was just ready for launching when the war ended and was scrapped; *G 148–G 150* were in the early stages of construction and were scrapped on the slips.

S 152 class *destroyers*

Displacement:	1020t design; 1224t deep load
Dimensions:	269ft wl, 272ft 4in oa × 27ft 3in × 11ft 9in *82.0m, 83.0m × 8.3m × 3.6m*
Machinery:	2-shaft Schichau turbines, 3 Navy oil-fired boilers, 22,000shp = 32.5kts. Oil 324t. Range 1440nm at 20kts
Armament:	As *G 85* class
Complement:	105

Class:
S 152–S 157

These boats were 40–50 per cent complete when the war ended; they were sold in 1920–21 for scrapping.

V 158 class *destroyers*

Displacement:	1030t design; 1236t deep load
Dimensions:	266ft 5in wl, 269ft 8in oa × 27ft 3in × 10ft 5in *81.2m, 82.2m × 8.3m × 3.2m*
Machinery:	2-shaft AEG-Vulcan turbines, 3 Navy oil-fired boilers, 26,500shp = 32.5kts. Oil 360t. Range 1675nm at 20kts
Armament:	As *G 85* class
Complement:	105

Class:
V 158–V 165

The first two were launched on 1 November 1918 but not completed when the war ended while the remainder were about 40 per cent complete. They were all sold on 4 July 1921 and scrapped.

H 166 class *destroyers*

Displacement:	1061t design; 1291t deep load
Dimensions:	273ft 8in wl, 279ft 2in oa × 27ft 7in × 10ft 6in *83.4m, 85.1m × 8.4m × 3.2m*
Machinery:	2-shaft Germania turbines (plus starboard shaft cruising turbine), 3 Navy oil-fired boilers, 26,000shp = 32.5kts. Oil 360t. Range 1895nm at 20kts
Armament:	As *G 85* class
Complement:	105

Class (launched, fate):
H 166 (25.10.19, sold for BU 1920), *H 167* (26.10.18, sold for BU 1920), *H 168* (8.11.19, sold for BU 1920), *H 169* (19.10.18, sold for BU 1920)

None was more than 60 per cent complete at the end of the war, and all were without engines or boilers. They were stricken on 3 November 1919, two still on the stocks were launched to clear the slips, and they were all sold for scrap.

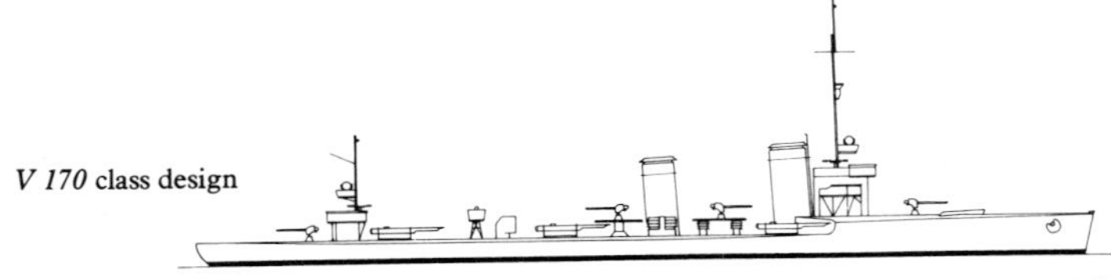
V 170 class design

V 170 class *destroyers*

Displacement: 1268t design; 1563t deep load
Dimensions: 297ft 11in wl, 304ft 6in × 29ft 10in × 10ft 6in
90.8m, 92.5m × 9.1m × 3.2m
Machinery: 2-shaft AEG-Vulcan geared turbines, 3 Navy oil-fired boilers, 36,000shp = 35kts. Oil 330t. Range?
Armament: As rearmed *B 97* class but 40 mines
Complement: 117

Class:
V 170–V 177, V 203–V 210

Large destroyers of the 1917 design type. They were the first German destroyers to have geared turbines. The boats were in the first stages of construction when the war ended; the orders were cancelled.

S 178 class *destroyers*

Displacement: 1268t design; 1523t deep load
Dimensions: 301ft 10in wl, 306ft 6in × 29ft 10in × 10ft 6in
92.0m, 93.4m × 9.1m × 3.2m
Other particulars: As *V 170* class

Class:
S 178–S 185, S 211–S 223

Sister-ships of the *V 170* type. The hulls of *S 178* and *S 179* were converted to sailing ships; *S 180–S 185* were broken up on the slips; the others were never started.

H 186 class *destroyers*

Displacement: 1268t design; 1553t deep load
Dimensions: 298ft 6in wl, 303ft 6in oa × 29ft 10in × 10ft 2in
91.0m, 92.5m × 9.1m × 3.1m
Other particulars: As *V 170* class

Class:
H 186–H 202

Sister-ships of the 1917 type *V 170* class; the orders were cancelled at the end of the war.

A 55 1917 — *Aldo Fraccaroli Collection*

A 1 class *coastal torpedo-boats* (launched 1915)

Displacement: 109t design; 137t deep load
Dimensions: 134ft 6in wl, 136ft 5in oa × 15ft 1in × 3ft 11in
41.0m, 41.6m × 4.6m × 1.2m
Machinery: 1-shaft 3-cyl VTE, 1 Navy boiler, 1200ihp = 20kts. Coal 24.5t. Range 900nm/440nm at 12.5kts/19kts
Armament: 1–5cm (2in) KL/40 (*A 1, A 2, A 17, A 18, A 21–A 25* 1–5.2cm SKL/55), 2–45cm (17.7in) TT, 4 mines
Complement: 28–29

Class:
A 1–A 25

Coastal torpedo-boat 1914 design, A 1 type, built by A G Vulcan, Hamburg (hulls subcontracted to various builders). This was the first design for a small coastal torpedo-boat to be used on the Flanders coast. The boats were commissioned from January 1915 onwards. *A 2, A 4–A 16, A 19* and *A 20* were sent in sections by railway to Antwerp/Hoboken and finished there. Despite being a poor design they saw action in the Channel and suffered heavy losses. Those sunk were: *A 2* (1.5.15), *A 3* (7.11.15), *A 6* (1.5.15), *A 7* (21.3.18), *A 10* (7.2.18), *A 13* (16.8.17), *A 15* (23.8.15), *A 19* (21.3.18). *A 4, A 5, A 8, A 9, A 11, A 12, A 14, A 16* and *A 20* were abandoned in the retreat from Flanders, taken over by Belgium and operated until about 1927 (*A 20* survived to be recaptured in 1940 and was not BU until 1948). The remainder were stricken and/or BU in 1921–22.

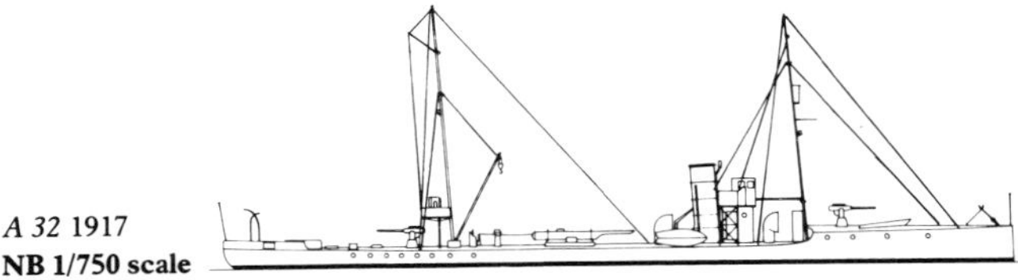
A 32 1917
NB 1/750 scale

A 26 class *coastal torpedo-boats* (launched 1916–17)

Displacement: 227t design; 250t deep load
Dimensions: 160ft 9in wl, 164ft oa × 17ft 6in × 6ft 11in
49.0m, 50.0m × 5.3m × 2.1m
Machinery: 1-shaft Schichau turbine, 1 Navy boiler 3506shp = 25.8kts. Oil 53t. Range 690nm at 20kts
Armament: 2–8.8cm (3.45in) KL/30, 1–45cm (17.7in) TT
Complement: 29

Class:
A 26–A 49

Coastal torpedo-boat/minesweeper 1915 design, A II type, built by Schichau, Elbing. Benefitting from the lessons of war, these boats had better performance characteristics. *A 43, A 44, A 46–A 49* were transferred by railway in sections to Antwerp/Hoboken and finished there. The boats were commissioned from May 1916 onwards and used in the Channel. *A 50* was mined (17.11.17) and only one boat was lost in the Baltic (*A 32*), most of the remainder becoming British war reparations which were broken up in the 1920s; however, *A 30, A 40, A 42, A 43* and *A 47* were taken over by Belgium and operated until about 1927, although *A 43* was not scrapped until 1943.

A 50 class *coastal torpedo-boats* (launched 1917)

Displacement: 229t design; 252t deep load
Dimensions: As *A 26* class, except beam 18ft 5in × 7ft 2in
5.6m × 2.2m
Other particulars: As *A 26* class

Class:
A 50–A 55

Slightly widened version of the 1915 *A II* type. *A 50* was transferred in sections to Antwerp/Hoboken and finished there; *A 51* was transferred by railway

A 8 as completed
BfZ

in sections to Pola and finished there, later serving as tender to the German submarine flotilla in the Mediterranean. *A 50* was mined (17.11.17) and *A 51* was scuttled (29.10.18); the others became British war reparations and were subsequently scrapped in the 1920s.

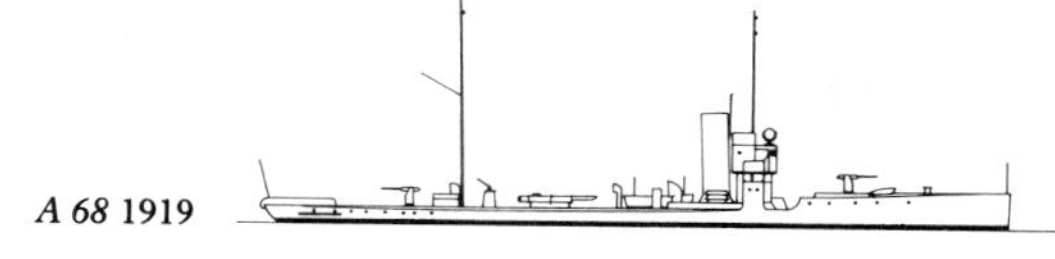

A 68 1919

A 56 class *coastal torpedo-boats* (launched 1917–18)

Displacement:	330t–335t design; 381–392t deep load
Dimensions:	194ft 7in–197ft 6in wl, 198ft 2in–200ft 6in oa × 21ft × 5ft 11in–7ft 6in *59.3m–60.2m, 60.4m–61.1m × 6.4m × 1.8m–2.3m*
Machinery:	2-shaft turbines, 2 Navy oil-fired boilers, 6000shp = 28kts. Oil 82t–92t. Range 800nm at 20kts (see notes)
Armament:	As *A 26* class, except *A 80* 3–8.8cm KL/30, no TT
Complement:	50–55

Class:
Vulcan, Stettin – *A 55–A 67, A 80–A 82, A 86–A 91, A 96–A 113*
Schichau, Elbing – *A 68–A 79, A 92–A 95*
Howaldtswerke, Kiel – *A 83–A 85*

Coastal torpedo-boats of the A III type. Boats built by different builders varied in dimensions, turbines and details such as the shape of funnels. The Schichau boats had geared turbines, the first group reaching only 5800shp = 26.5kts on trials; the remainder had AEG-Vulcan direct drive machinery but only the *A 56–A 67* group made 28kts and the design requirement was reduced to 26kts for later boats.

Only 37 were commissioned, *A 83–A 85* and *A 96–A 113* being incomplete at the end of the war. Nine were mined: *A 56* 12.3.18; *A 57* 1.3.18; *A 58* 16.8.18; *A 60* 23.11.17; *A 71* 4.5.18; *A 72* 14.5.18; *A 73* 20.1.18; *A 77* 20.1.18; *A 79* 10.7.18. *A 82* was transferred to Pola by railway in sections to serve as a tender for the German Mediterranean submarine flotilla and was scuttled there (29.10.18). The surviving boats were broken up in the early 1920s, except for four boats ceded to Poland. *A 59* became *Slazak*, A 64 became *Krakowiak*, *A 68* became *Kujawiak*, *A 80* became *Goral* (later *Podhalanin*).

SUBMARINES

The development history of an autonomous submersible on the Continent dates back to at least 1850 when the Bavarian inventor and engineer Wilhelm Bauer built his *Brandtaucher* at Kiel. It sank during the first diving trial, and Bauer could make no progress in the following years, although he relentlessly tried to convince authorities that his type of submersible would really work.

Until 1902 only two further submersibles were built in Germany, both at the Howaldtwerke: one in 1891 and another in 1897. The next impetus for a German shipyard to build a submarine came in 1902 when the Spanish engineer Raymondo Lorenzo d'Equevilley-Montjustin – a former assistant of the French submarine designer Laubeuf – became employed at Friedrich Krupp's new acquired shipyard, the Germaniawerft at Kiel. His first design was the *Forelle*, which was sold after numerous demonstrations to German authorities to Csarist Russia as part of a submarine export deal also comprising three *Karp* class boats.

Until 1904 von Tirpitz's opinion of submarines was negative, but after the *Forelle*'s success he ordered the *Torpedoinspektion* ('torpedo inspection', a department of the *Reichsmarineamt*, responsible for all development of this new underwater weapon) to design a genuine submarine. The Navy having little experience with this new field of technology, a submarine was ordered from Germaniawerft at the same time for comparative purposes; but important design alterations compared to the boats built for Russia delayed the commissioning of *U 1* until 1906. The Navy-designed boat *U 2* was laid down at the Imperial Yard, Kiel and not launched before 1908. In the following year a certain rivalry grew up between Germaniawerft, which had the better knowledge of submarine technology based on the boats they had already successfully built (*U 3, U 4* for Austria-Hungary and *Kobben* for Norway) and the *Torpedoinspektion*, which had the better design capability. The controversy died down when d'Equevilley left Germaniawerft, and both parties worked well together thereafter. The results of this co-operation were *U 5–8*, the first boats of the Imperial German Navy which were not only trials vessels but had a certain operational value.

In the years 1910–11 the first tactical trials were undertaken, but received a severe setback after the sinking of *U 3* in a diving accident on 17 November 1911. One of the most important problems of this first stage of submarine design was that of propulsion, the first boats having extremely dangerous gasoline and petroleum combustion engines because the development of a reliable lightweight diesel was running into great problems; it was not until *U 19* that the first diesel became operational.

After the first exercises in 1910–11 the *Torpedoinspektion* presented its first scheme for U-boat deployment which would be acceptable to the German High Seas Fleet in 1912. In its major points it asked for:

1 36 U-boats in a perimeter patrol securing the Heligoland Bight, composed of 24 operational boats and 12 boats in reserve.
2 12 U-boats for the defence of Kiel Bay in the Baltic.
3 12 U-boats for offensive operations in the North Sea.
4 10 U-boats as material reserve.

In line with the general emphasis on a surface battleline and the lack of operational experience this was essentially a defensive concept, but nevertheless it requested a total of 70 U-boats to be built by 1919, funded by additional special budgets.

Also in 1912 it was decided to purchase a diesel-propelled submarine from Fiat-Laurenti at La Spezia to gain experiences with foreign diesel technology; delivery was scheduled for 1915 but never took place due to the outbreak of war.

In this first six years of German submarine construction it had shown that the *Torpedoinspektion* was overstrained by handling all aspects of what had grown into an entirely new service with complex needs, so the *Inspektion des U-Bootwesens* (Submarine Inspection) was founded as a new independent administrative body.

The pre-war period of German U-boat development shows a steady improvement in technology. Experience was gained rapidly and the benefits were incorporated into each successive types. Therefore the typology splits up into many different variants depending on the builder and fiscal year whose significant improvements were not apparent in the silhouette but only in internal details. This steady development was abruptly broken when war broke out. In 1914 the submarine arm of the Imperial German Navy comprised 20 battle-ready U-boats, plus a further 15 in commission or under construction, and the Germans immediately switched to a mobilisation programme, the first so called Ms types being *U 51–U 56*. However it was soon evident that completion times of such sophisticated weapons would be too great, considering the expected short duration of this war. Immediately after the outbreak of hostilities the *U-Bootsinspektion* was asked in August 1914 for preliminary studies for a small, single-shaft U-boat capable of railway transportation in sections. Although this concept was rejected at first, the occupation of the Belgian coast quickly led to further pressure to develop both a torpedo and minelaying type. In September 1914 the later UB type was chosen out of a variety of designs, and one week later the first 15 units were ordered, the prototype boat *UB 1* being built within a hundred days. One month later the design for the minelaying UC type had reached a stage where 15 units could also be ordered. The numbers of the first two series were deliberately kept so that the Germans could gain experience under battle conditions and incorporate the lessons into the next series.

To explain German submarine typology it is necessary to note that UA was a submarine under construction for the Norwegians and that the UD types were those under construction for the Austro-Hungarian Navy, all of which were taken over by the Imperial German Navy after their completion. Because of the delicate status of commerce warfare in international law great emphasis was laid on submarine minelayers, and as early as January 1915 the design for the improved UE type was ready. Unlike its rather primitive forerunner, the UC type, it carried its 34 mines in dry stowage and had two TT in the deck structure for active hunting. A further variant (UF) would have had an all-torpedo armament and thus represented the logical approach to a small, quickly built mass-production coastal submarine, but was rejected in favour of ocean-going Ms type U-boats.

Therefore the design and ordering policy for German U-boats also mirrors the frequent changes in administrative direction outlined in the introduction. The German 'war-zone declaration' had been promulgated on 1 February 1915, and consequently some two dozen oceanic Ms type submarines were ordered; but the major bottleneck was the delivery of the diesel engines, so design switched back to the coastal types of which the improved UB II and UC II types emerged in the spring of 1915. The enlarged Ms type 'Project 43' (*U 115, U 116*), with a 20 per cent increase in radius of action was not put forward until the autumn of 1915. The unrestricted U-boat war envisaged in the spring of 1916 nevertheless revealed a shortage of simple, mass-produced boats for torpedo-based commerce warfare around the British Isles. The resulting design was a compromise between the ocean-going Ms types and a scaled-up coastal UB design: the UB III type in which the added offensive component (4 more spare torpedoes) was paid for with decreased speed and endurance compared with the basic *U 19* type. Because of increasing material and manpower shortages the first orders were not placed until May 1916, the boats not being delivered before the summer of 1917.

After the abandonment of the first attempt at unrestricted U-boat warfare in March 1916 for political reasons, the Admiralty ordered designs for large submarine-cruisers with 6in guns capable of commerce warfare according to Prize Laws. Operational and handling experience with such large vessels had already been gained with the clumsy merchant submarines of the *Deutschland* class. The only bottleneck was still the high-power diesels needed to obtain the requested high surface speeds. Nevertheless U-cruisers of the types 46 and 46a were designed, and in August 1916 the first such boats (*U 139–U 141*) were ordered by postponing the Ms types *U 111–U 114* and *U 127–U 130*. The former merchant submarines were also converted into U-cruisers and commissioned as *U 151–U 157*, since their intended role was nullified when the USA entered the war, so in the final analysis of the U-cruisers were merely a design answer to the requirements of a type of warfare that had become obsolescent by the declaration of the unrestricted U-boat war. What Germany needed now were UB III types – for the same reasons as one year previously – and indeed they were ordered in great numbers up to February 1917 (*UB 88–UB 132*). After the highest priority had finally been given to U-boat production in June 1917, a further 95 were ordered: 37 UB III types *UB 133–169*, 39 UC III types (improved minelayer) *UC 80–UC 118*, 10 U-cruisers *U 173–U 182* and 9 Ms types *U 164–U 172*, which were scheduled for completion between the summer of 1918 and January 1919. Because of earlier efforts the number of operational German U-boats in the First World War was at its peak in October 1917 with 140 units, but by then it was too late, as von Tirpitz had foreseen: the Allies had introduced the convoy system in May and had developed new ASW techniques and weapons in the previous years.

After some changes in priorities the programme of June was revised in December 1917 and increased to 120 units, which meant that 11 shipyards had to work around the clock and that all other construction had to be curtailed. Nevertheless increasing material shortages and manpower problems caused by food shortages and a nationwide influenza epidemic in the spring of 1918 proved that the schedules could not be kept in any fashion. The German spring offensive in France finally collapsed in August 1918 and when Admiral Scheer became the new CNS in the same month, he was backed by von Hindenburg and Ludendorff in his insistence that all efforts must be concentrated on U-boat construction and warfare to regain the offensive at sea, since the war could not be won in continental land battles; the necessary material and manpower would be taken from the Army's allocations. This resulted in the ambitious 'Scheer programme' which asked for an increase in the number of completed U-boats by a further third. While exhausting conferences took place on how to ensure the necessary steel production, diesel production, shipyard capacity and manpower, the general situation worsened after the collapse of Bulgaria in September. Without any chance of realisation the preparatory steps of the 'Scheer programme' were pushed forwards because Scheer regarded a strong submarine force as an important bargaining counter in coming peace negotiations. In the meantime German politics had drastically changed with the new Imperial Chancellor Max von Baden, who initiated steps for an armistice. Up to the last moment German naval authorities obviously grossly underestimated the Allied determination to wipe out the German submarine force completely.

During the war the following German submarines were sold to Austria-Hungary: *UB 1* became *Unterseeboot 10, UB 15* became *Unterseeboot 11, UB 43* became *Unterseeboot 43* and *UB 47* became *Unterseeboot 47;* the renumbering of German U-Boats operating in the Mediterranean and the Adriatic is covered in the Austro-Hungarian section. *UB 8* was sold to Bulgaria. Unlike World War Two no intact German U-boat was captured but two sunken coastal submarines were raised and put into commission: Italy raised *UC 12* and renamed her *X 1*; France raised *UB 26*, which was renamed *Lieutenant Morillot*. From 1906 to 1918 the Imperial German Navy ordered a total of 811 U-boats, out of which 343 were commissioned; 134 of them were lost in action, 42 by mines, 17 were lost by accident (some of them raised and recommissioned), 14 were scuttled by their crews, mostly in the Black Sea or in Austrian ports at the end of war, 8 were interned in Sweden and Portugal, but had to be delivered after the armistice, the total of surrendered U-boats making 175, 19 of which were lost by accident during the transfer tow to British ports. Of the nearly completed boats 9 were scrapped in Germany after the war, as were 69 lying unfinished on the slips. Note that these figures cannot be added up to a single total since many of the boats appear in two or three of the above-mentioned fates.

The surrendered U-boats were redistributed amongst the Allies, Britain scrapping its share, the USA getting *U 111, U 117, U 140, UB 88, UB 148* and *UC 97*, which were finally sunk as trials targets. The Netherlands were allowed to retain the raised *UC 8* which was commissioned as *M 1*. Japan received *U 46* (renamed *O 2*), *U 55 (O 3), U 125 (O 1), UB 125 (O 6), UB 143 (O 7), UC 90 (O 4)* and *UC 99 (O 5)*, which were soon scrapped. Italy got *U 54, U 114, U 163, U 120, UB 80, UB 95, UB 102, UC 93, UC 94* and *UC 98* all of which were immediately scrapped. France's share reads as follows, the names of the recommissioned boats being given in brackets (all others were scrapped): *U 25, U 38, U 39, U 57, U 71, U 79 (Victor Réveille), U 91, U 105 (Jean Autric), U 108 (Léon Mignot), U 113, U 157, U 160, U 162 (Pierre Marast), U 166 (Jean Roulier), U 118, U 119 (René Audry), U 121, U 136, U 151, UA, UB 6, UB 8, UB 23, UB 24, UB 73, UB 84, UB 87, UB 94 (Trinité Schillemans), UB 99 (Carrissan), UB 114, UB 121, UB 154, UB 155 (Jean Corre), UC 22, UC 23, UC 27, UC 28, UC 56, UC 58, UC 74, UC 100, UC 103, UC 104, UC 107* and *U 139 (Halbronn)*

U 1 about 1910
NB 1/750 scale

U 1 *submarine*

Displacement:	238t/283t
Dimensions:	138ft 9in × 12ft 6in × 10ft 6in *42.4m × 3.8m × 3.2m*
Machinery:	2 shafts, 2 Körting kerosene engines plus 2 electric motors, 400bhp/400shp = 10.8kts/8.7kts. Oil 20t. Range 1500nm/50nm at 10kts/5kts (surfaced/submerged)
Armament:	1–45cm (17.7in) TT (bow; 3 torpedoes)
Complement:	12

Class (launched, fate):
U 1 (4.8.06, museum exhibit 1921)
Used for trials and training, condemned in 1919, but bought by the builder, Germaniawerft, and donated to the Deutsches Museum, München where it is still exhibited.

U 2 *submarine*

Displacement:	341t/430t
Dimensions:	148ft 11in × 18ft × 10ft 2in *45.4m × 5.5m × 3.1m*
Machinery:	2 shafts, 2 Daimler kerosene engines plus 2 electric motors, 600bhp/630shp = 13.2kts/9kts. Oil 46t. Range 1600nm/50nm at 13kts/5kts (surfaced/submerged)
Armament:	4–45cm (17.7in) TT (2 bow, 2 stern; 6 torpedoes)
Complement:	22

Class (launched, fate):
U 2 (18.6.08, BU 1919)
U 2 (Project 7), built by Kiel N Yd, was used for trials and training, broken up in 1919.

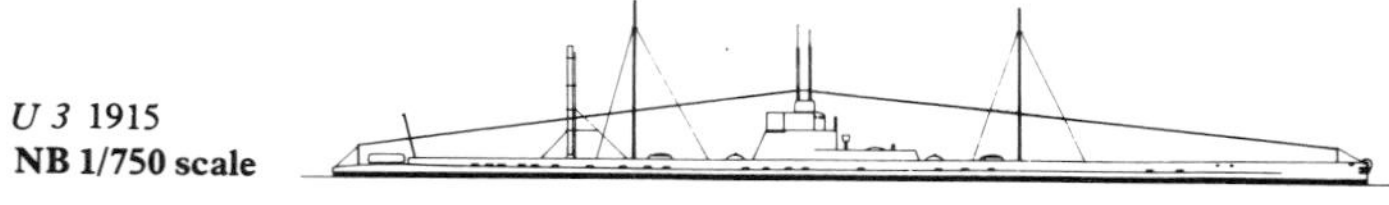
U 3 1915
NB 1/750 scale

U 3 class *submarines*

Displacement:	421t/510t
Dimensions:	168ft 4in × 18ft 4in × 10ft 2in *51.3m × 5.6m × 3.1m*
Machinery:	2 shafts, 2 Körting kerosene engines plus 2 electric motors, 600bhp/1030shp = 11.8kts/9.4kts. Oil 48t. Range 1800nm/55nm at 12kts/4.5kts (surfaced/submerged)
Armament:	As *U 2*
Complement:	22

Class (launched, fate):
U 3 (27.3.09, sunk 1.12.18), *U 4* (18.5.09, BU 1919)
Known as Project 12 these two boats were built at Danzig N Yd. *U 3* served for trials, was raised after a diving accident 1911 and sunk during the transfer tow to England in 1918. *U 4* was broken up after the war.

U 5 class *submarines*

Displacement:	505t/636t
Dimensions:	188ft × 18ft 4in × 11ft 10in *57.3m × 5.6m × 3.6m*
Machinery:	2 shafts, 4 Körting kerosene engines plus 2 electric motors, 900bhp/1040shp = 13.4kts/10.2kts. Oil 54t. Range 1900nm/80nm at 13kts/5kts (surfaced/submerged)
Armament:	As *U 2*
Complement:	29

Class (launched, fate):
U 5 (8.1.10, mined 18.12.14), *U 6* (18.5.10, torpedoed by *E 16* 15.9.15), *U 7* (28.7.10, sunk in error by *U 22* 21.1.15), *U 8* (14.3.11, sunk by *Maori* and *Gurkha* 4.3.15)
All built by Germania, and all lost in the early part of the war.

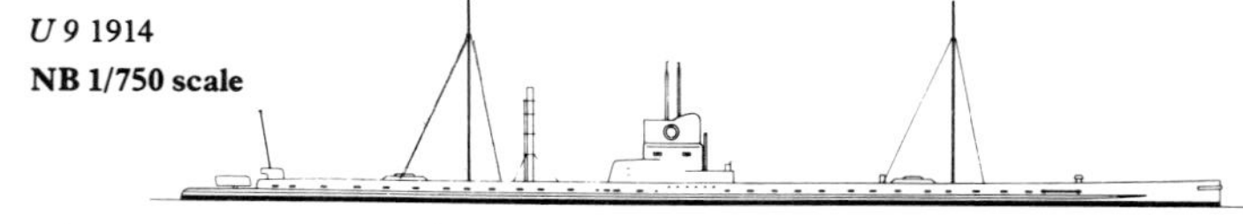
U 9 1914
NB 1/750 scale

U 9 class *submarines*

Displacement:	493t/611t
Dimensions:	188ft 4in × 19ft 8in × 10ft 2in *57.4m × 6.0m × 3.1m*
Machinery:	2 shafts, 4 Körting kerosene engines plus 2 electric motors, 1050bhp/1160shp = 14.2kts/8.1kts. Oil 52t. Range 1800nm/80nm at 14kts/5kts (surfaced/submerged)
Armament:	As *U 2*
Complement:	29

Class (launched, fate):
U 9 (22.2.10, BU 1919), *U 10* (24.1.11, ? mined 5.16), *U 11* (2.4.10, mined 9.12.14), *U 12* (6.5.10, rammed by *Ariel* 10.3.15)
All were built by Danzig N Yd.

U 13 as completed — *Aldo Fraccaroli Collection*

U 2 as completed — *BfZ*

U 7 — *Navarret Collection*

U 16 as completed — *BfZ*

U 13 class *submarines*

Displacement:	516t/644t
Dimensions:	189ft 11in × 19ft 8in × 11ft 2in *57.9m × 6.0m × 3.4m*
Machinery:	2 shafts, 4 Körting kerosene engines plus 2 electric motors, 1200bhp/1200shp = 14.8kts/10.7kts. Oil 64t. Range 2000nm/90nm 14kts/5kts (surfaced/submerged)
Armament:	As *U 2*
Complement:	29

Class (launched, fate):
U 13 (16.12.10, sunk 9.8.14), *U 14* (11.7.11, rammed by trawler *Hawk* 2.6.15), *U 15* (18.9.11, rammed by *Birmingham* 9.8.14)
All built by Danzig N Yd.

U 16 *submarine*

Displacement:	489t/627t
Dimensions:	189ft 8in × 19ft 8in × 11ft 2in *57.8m × 6.0m × 3.4m*
Machinery:	2 shafts, 4 Körting kerosene engines plus 2 electric motors, 1200bhp/1200shp = 15.6kts/10.7kts. Oil 64t. Range 2100nm/90nm at 15kts/5kts (surfaced/submerged)
Armament:	As *U 2*
Complement:	29

Class (launched, fate):
U 16 (23.8.11, foundered 8.2.19)
A Germania-built version of the *U 13* class, *U 16* sank after the war during transfer tow to England in 1919.

U 17 class *submarines*

Displacement: 564t/691t
Dimensions: 204ft 9in × 19ft 8in × 11ft 2in
62.4m × 6.0m × 3.4m
Machinery: 2 shafts, 4 Körting kerosene engines plus 2 electric motors, 1400bhp/1120shp = 14.9kts/9.5kts. Oil 74t. Range 6700nm/75nm at 8kts/5kts (surfaced/submerged)
Armament: As *U 2*
Complement: 29

Class (launched, fate):
U 17 (16.4.12, BU 1919), *U 18* (25.4.12, sunk 23.11.14)

Built by Danzig N Yd. *U 17* served as a TS from 1916; *U 18* was sunk by coastal artillery off Scapa Flow. From 1915 most survivors of *U 3–U 17* classes had 1–5cm (2in) gun added.

U 19 1913

U 19 class *submarines*

Displacement: 650t/837t
Dimensions: 210ft 8in × 20ft × 11ft 10in
64.2m × 6.1m × 3.6m
Machinery: 2 shafts, 2 MAN diesels plus 2 electric motors, 1700bhp/1200shp = 15.4kts/9.5kts. Oil 77t max. Range 7600nm/80nm at 8kts/5kts (surfaced/submerged)
Armament: 4–50cm (19.7in) TT (2 bow, 2 stern; 6 torpedoes), 1–8.8cm (3.45in) KL/30
Complement: 35

Class (launched, fate):
U 19 (10.10.12, BU 1919–20), *U 20* (18.12.12, stranded 5.11.16, BU 1925), *U 21* (8.2.13, foundered 22.2.19), *U 22* (6.3.13, BU 1919–20)

First operational diesel-propelled submarines in the Imperial German Navy, built by Danzig N Yd.

U 23 class *submarines*

Displacement: 669t/864t
Dimensions: 212ft 3in × 20ft 8in × 11ft 6in
64.7m × 6.3m × 3.5m
Machinery: 2 shafts, 2 Germania 6-cyl 2-stroke diesels plus 2 electric motors, 1800bhp/1200shp = 16.7kts/10.3kts. Oil 98t max. Range 7620nm/85nm at 8kts/5kts (surfaced/submerged)
Armament: As *U 19* class
Complement: 35

Class (launched, fate):
U 23 (12.4.13, torpedoed by *C 27* 20.7.15), *U 24* (24.5.13, BU 1922), *U 25* (12.7.13, BU 1921–22), *U 26* (16.10.13, ? mined 9.15)

U 17 embarking torpedoes 1915 — *Aldo Fraccaroli Collection*

U 24 as completed — *Aldo Fraccaroli Collection*

All built by Germaniawerft, Kiel. The *U 23*, *U 27* and *U 31* classes were double-hulled boats with a diving depth of 50m. Diving time for the *U 23* class was 2 minutes 13 seconds. The 8.8cm gun was added in 1915, and they also carried 1 MG; for a time *U 25* had 2–8.8cm fitted.

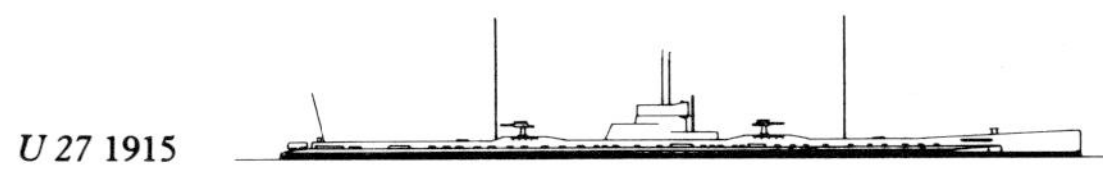
U 27 1915

U 27 class *submarines*

Displacement: 675t/867t
Dimensions: As *U 23* class
Machinery: 2 shafts, 2 MAN 6-cyl 4-stroke diesels plus 2 electric motors, 2000bhp/1200shp = 16.7kts/9.8kts. Oil 104t max. Range 7900nm/85nm at 8kts/5kts (surfaced/submerged)
Armament: As *U 19* class
Complement: 35

Class (launched, fate):
U 27 (14.7.13, sunk by Q-ship *Baralong* 19.8.15), *U 28* (30.8.13, destroyed while sinking munition ship 2.9.17), *U 29* (11.10.13, rammed by *Dreadnought* 18.3.15), *U 30* (15.11.13, BU 1919–20)

Built by Danzig N Yd, diving time in this group was reduced to 80 seconds, *U 29* carried no deck gun at the time of her loss; the others later had 2–8.8cm deck guns, which were exchanged in *U 30* for 1–10.5cm (4.1in) KL/45. All could also carry 1-MG and some had stowage for up to 10 torpedoes.

U 31 class *submarines*

Displacement: 685t/878t
Dimensions: As *U 23* class, except draught 11ft 10in *(3.6m)*
Machinery: As *U 23* class, except 1850bhp/1200shp = 16.4kts/9.7kts. Oil 110t max. Range 7800nm/80nm at 8kts/5kts (surfaced/submerged)
Armament: As *U 19* class
Complement: 35

Class (launched, fate):
U 31 (7.1.14, sunk 1.15), *U 32* (28.1.14, sunk by *Wallflower* 8.5.15), *U 33* (19.5.14, BU 1919–20), *U 34* (9.5.14, sunk by Q-ship *Privet* 9.11.18), *U 35* (18.4.14, BU 1919–20), *U 36* (6.6.14, sunk by Q-ship *Prince Charles* 24.7.15), *U 37* (25.8.14, mined 1.4.15), *U 38* (9.9.14, BU 1921), *U 39* (26.9.14, BU 1923), *U 40* (22.10.14, torpedoed by *C 24* 23.6.15), *U 41* (10.10.14, sunk by Q-ship *Wyandra* 24.9.15)

Germania-built boats, with a diving time of 1 minute 40 seconds. *U 31* had no deck gun when lost; *U 32*, *U 36* and *U 37* had 2–8.8cm for a time; from 1917 *U 32* had a 10.5cm KL/45 on an AA mounting; and the survivors were fitted with 1–10.5cm in lieu of the 8.8cm from 1916–17.

U 35 was the most successful submarine of both wars. Under four renowned commanders (Waldemar Kophamel, Lothar von Arnauld de la Perière, Ernst von Voigt and Heino von Heimburg) she sank 224 ships of 535,900grt. This incredible score was achieved during 25 sorties around England, in the Mediterranean and off the West African coast. Compared with this the most successful submarine of World War Two was the German *U 48*, which sank 51 ships totalling 310,007grt.

U 42 *submarine*

Ordered in Italy this Fiat-Laurenti type was ordered to obtain competitive knowledge especially on Fiat diesel technology. Due to the outbreak of the war the boat was not delivered, but taken over by the Italian Navy under the new name *Balilla*. For particulars and fate see under Italy.

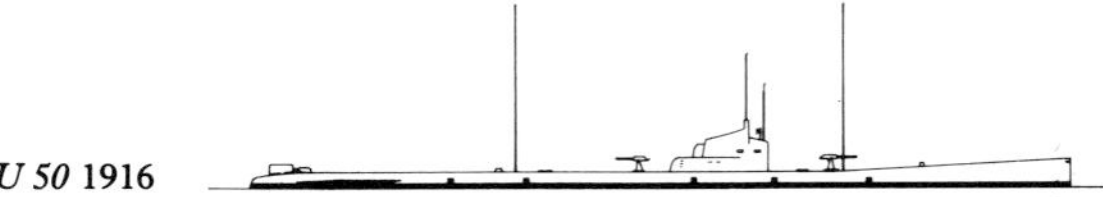
U 50 1916

U 43 class *submarines*

Displacement: 725t/940t
Dimensions: 213ft 3in × 20ft 4in × 12ft 2in
65.0m × 6.2m × 3.7m
Machinery: 2 shafts, 2 MAN 6-cyl 4-stroke diesels plus 2 electric motors, 2000bhp/1200shp = 15.2kts/9.7kts. Oil 110t max. Range 8100nm/51nm at 8kts/5kts (surfaced/submerged)
Armament: 4–50cm (19.7in) TT (2 bow, 2 stern, 6 torpedoes), 2–8.8cm (3.45in) KL/30 (see notes)
Complement: 36

Class (launched, fate):
U 43 (26.9.14, BU 1922), *U 44* (15.10.14, rammed by *Oracle* 12.8.17), *U 45*

U 53 1917 — *Aldo Fraccaroli Collection*

(15.4.15, torpedoed by *D. 7* 12.9.17), *U 46* (18.5.15, Japanese *O 2* 1920, BU 1922), *U 47* (16.8.15, scuttled 28.10.18), *U 48* (3.10.15, stranded and scuttled 24.11.17), *U 49* (26.11.15, rammed by *British Transport* 11.9.17), *U 50* (31.12.15, mined 31.8.17)

Built by Danzig N Yd, these Project 25 boats had a diving time of 1 minute 45 seconds. As with previous classes there was some variation in gun armament: *U 43–U 46* originally had only 1–8.8cm, and from 1916–17, they all received 1–10.5cm KL/45 in lieu of the 8.8cm. From 1916 *U 43* and *U 44* were fitted as minelayers.

U 51 class *submarines*

Displacement: 715t/902t
Dimensions: 213ft 11in × 21ft × 11ft 10in
65.2m × 6.4m × 3.6m
Machinery: 2 shafts, 2 MAN 6-cyl 4-stroke diesels plus 2 electric motors, 2400bhp/1200shp = 17.1kts/9.1kts. Oil 115t max. Range 9000nm/55nm at 8kts/5kts (surfaced/submerged)
Armament: 4–50cm (19.7in) TT (2 bow, 2 stern; 8 torpedoes), 2–8.8cm (3.45in) KL/30 (see notes)
Complement: 35

Class (launched, fate):
U 51 (25.11.15, torpedoed by *H 5* 14.7.16), *U 52* (8.12.15, BU 1922), *U 53* (1.2.16, BU 1922), *U 54* (22.2.16, BU 1919), *U 55* (18.3.16, Japanese *O 3* 1919, BU 1922), *U 56* (18.4.16, sunk by Russian forces 2.11.16)

Built by Germaniawerft, these double-hulled boats were the first of the Mobilisation (Ms) type, and were improved versions of the *U 41*; they had a diving time of 1 minute 45 seconds. Like previous classes there were variations in deck armament throughout the war, some being fitted with 1–10.5cm instead of 2–8.8cm.

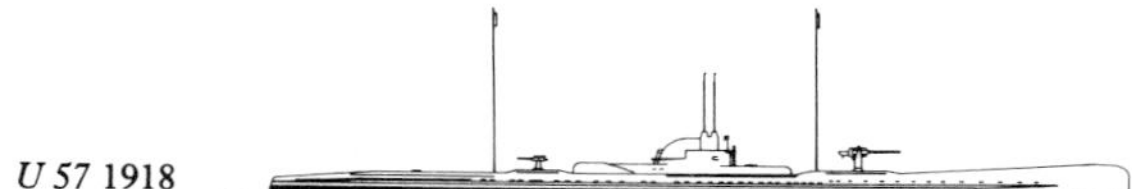

U 57 1918

U 57 class *submarines*

Displacement: 786t/954t
Dimensions: 219ft 10in × 20ft 8in × 12ft 6in
67.0m × 6.3m × 3.8m
Machinery: 2 shafts, 2 MAN 6-cyl 2-stroke diesels plus 2 electric motors, 1800bhp/1200shp = 14.7kts/8.4kts. Oil 119t max. Range 7730nm/55nm and 8kts/5kts (surfaced/submerged)
Armament: As *U 51* class (see notes)
Complement: 35

U 35 June 1916 — *CPL*

Class (launched, fate):
U 57 (29.4.16, BU 1921), *U 58* (31.5.16, sunk by USS *Fanning* and *Nicholson* 17.11.17), *U 59* (20.6.16, mined 15.5.17), *U 60* (5.7.16, stranded 21.11.18, BU 1921), *U 61* (22.7.16, sunk by *PC 51* 26.3.18), *U 62* (2.8.16, BU 1919–20), *U 99* (27.1.17, torpedoed by *J 31* 3.7.17), *U 100* (25.2.17, BU 1922), *U 101* (1.4.17, BU 1922), *U 102* (12.5.17, ? mined 2.9.18), *U 103* (9.6.17, rammed by liner *Olympic* 12.5.18), *U 104* (3.7.17, sunk by *Jessamine* 25.4.18)

Ms type boats built by AG Weser, Bremen. The *U 99* group was an improved version of the *U 27*. Diving time was reduced to 49–52 seconds (depending on group) and from *U 60* they had more powerful 4-stroke diesels of 2400bhp = 16.5kts. Oil was increased to 129t in *U 60–U 62* and surfaced range to 8600nm, although submerged radius was only 49nm. Deck armament varied, some having 1–10.5cm in place of the 8.8cm, and *U 58–U 60* had 1–10.5cm KL/45 on an AA mounting and 1–8.8cm KL/30. *U 57–U 62* could stow only 7 torpedoes, but the *U 99* group could carry 10–12.

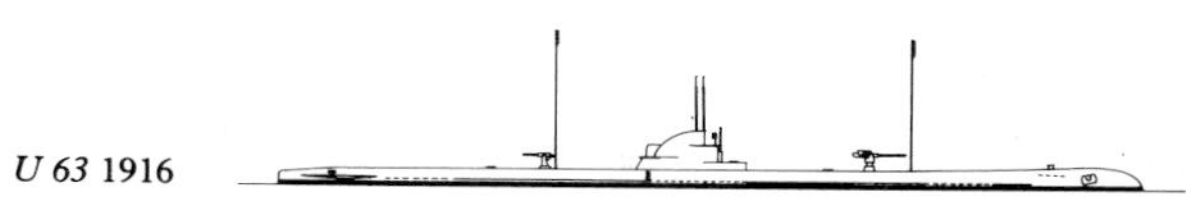

U 63 1916

U 63 class *submarines*

Displacement: 810t/927t
Dimensions: 224ft 5in × 20ft 8in × 13ft 2in
68.4m × 6.3m × 4.0m
Machinery: 2 shafts, 2 Germania 6-cyl 2-stroke diesels plus 2 electric motors, 2200bhp/1200shp = 16.5kts/9.0kts. Oil 118t max. Range 8100nm/60nm at 8kts/5kts (surfaced/submerged)
Armament: As *U 51* class
Complement: 35

Class (launched, fate):
U 63 (8.2.16, BU 1919–20), *U 64* (29.2.16, sunk by *Lychais* and *Partridge II* 17.6.18), *U 65* (21.3.16, scuttled 28.10.18)

Improved *U 51* type Ms boats, built by Germaniawerft, Kiel. Later received 1–10.5cm KL/45. Diving time was 50 seconds.

U 66 class *submarines*

Displacement: 791t/933t
Dimensions: 228ft × 20ft 8in × 12ft 6in
69.5m × 6.3m × 3.8m
Machinery: 2 shafts, 2 Germania 6-cyl 4-stroke diesels plus 2 electric motors, 2300bhp/1260shp = 16.8kts/10.3kts. Oil 89t. Range 6500nm/115nm at 8kts/5kts (submerged/surfaced)
Armament: 5–45cm (17.7in) TT (4 bow, 1 stern; 12 torpedoes), 1–8.8cm (3.45in) KL/30
Complement: 36

Class (launched, fate):
U 66 (22.4.15, sunk by British destroyers 2.10.17), *U 67* (15.5.15, BU 1921), *U 68* (1.6.15, sunk by Q-ship *Farnborough* 22.3.16), *U 69* (24.6.15, sunk by *Patriot* 12.7.17), *U 70* (20.7.15, BU 1919–20)

Originally ordered as *U 7–U 11* for the Austro-Hungarian Navy, these UD type boats were built by Germaniawerft, and were purchased by Germany on 28 November 1914. They had a diving depth of 50m and a diving time of 1 minute 40 seconds. Redesigned and reconstructed to German standards they were commissioned into the Imperial German Navy. Compared with other Austrian submarines of the time, without doubt these units would have been the best. From 1916–17 the deck gun was replaced with a 10.5cm KL/45.

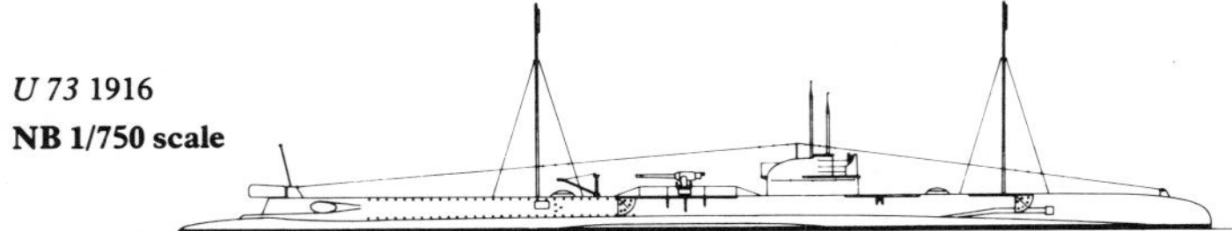
U 73 1916
NB 1/750 scale

U 71 class *submarine minelayers*

Displacement: 755t/832t
Dimensions: 186ft 4in × 19ft 4in × 16ft 1in
56.8m × 5.9m × 4.9m
Machinery: 2 shafts, 2 6-cyl diesels plus 2 electric motors, 900bhp/800shp = 10.6kts/7.9kts. Oil 80t. Range 5800nm/83nm at 7kts/4kts (surfaced/submerged)
Armament: 2–50cm (19.7in) TT (1 port bow, 1 starboard stern, both external; 4 torpedoes), 2–100cm mine tubes (stern; 34 mines), 1–8.8cm (3.45in) KL/30
Complement: 32

Class (launched, fate):
U 71 (31.10.15, BU 1921), *U 72* (31.10.15, scuttled 1.11.18), *U 73* (16.6.15, scuttled 30.10.18), *U 74* (10.8.15, sunk by ASW trawlers 27.5.16), *U 75* (30.1.16, mined 14.12.17), *U 76* (12.3.16, sunk by Russian escorts 27.1.17), *U 77* (9.1.16, sunk by British escorts 7.7.16), *U 78* (27.2.16, torpedoed by *G 2* 28.10.18), *U 79* (9.4.16, BU 1933), *U 80* (22.4.16, BU 1922)

UE and UE I type ocean-going minelayers, built by Danzig N Yd *(U 73, U 74)* and Vulcan, Hamburg. They varied slightly, *U 71, U 72, U 75* and *U 76* having Benz 4-stroke engines, while the rest had Körting 2-stroke diesels of slightly less power and reduced surface speed; range in *U 73* and *U 74* was only 5480nm at 7kts. The deck gun in most was replaced by 1–10.5cm KL/45 from 1916 onwards, and *U 72* carried both from 1917.

U 71 was scrapped in France after the war; *U 79* served as the French *Victor Réveille* until 1933; *U 80* was scrapped in England after the war; *U 72* and *U 73* were scuttled at Cattaro and Pola after the Austrian armistice; the others were lost in action.

U 81 class *submarines*

Displacement: 808t/946t
Dimensions: 230ft × 20ft 8in × 13ft 2in
70.1m × 6.3m × 4.0m
Machinery: 2 shafts, 2 MAN 6-cyl 4-stroke diesels plus 2 electric motors, 2400bhp/1200shp = 16.8kts/9.1kts. Oil 114t max. Range 8100nm/56nm at 8kts/5kts (surfaced/submerged)
Armament: As *U 51* class (see notes)
Complement: 35

Class (launched, fate):
U 81 (24.6.16, torpedoed by *E 54* 1.5.17), *U 82* (1.7.16, BU 1919–20), *U 83* (13.7.16, sunk by Q-ship *Farnborough* 17.2.17), *U 84* (22.7.16, rammed by *P 62* 26.1.18), *U 85* (22.8.16, sunk by Q-ship *Privet* 12.3.17), *U 86* (7.11.16, foundered on way to BU 1921)

Ms type boats based on the *U 65*, and built by Germaniawerft. They had the standard operational depth of 50m and a diving time of 50 seconds. *U 81–U 83* had 1–10.5cm KL/45 in lieu of the 2–8.8cm, and the other boats were so fitted between 1917 and 1918; in 1918 1–8.8cm KL/30 was added in *U 84–U 86*. Maximum torpedo stowage was 10–12 by the end of the war.

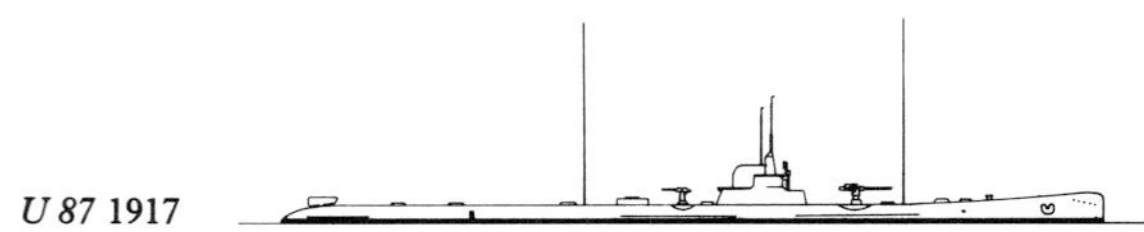
U 87 1917

U 87 class *submarines*

Displacement: 757t/998t
Dimensions: 224ft 9in × 20ft 4in × 12ft 9in
65.8m × 6.2m × 3.9m
Machinery: As *U 81* class, except 15.6kts/8.6kts. Oil 108t max. Range 8000nm/56nm at 8kts/5kts (surfaced/submerged)
Armament: 6–50cm (19.7in) TT (4 bow, 2 stern; 12 torpedoes), 1–10.5cm (4.1in) KL/45 (plus 1–8.8cm KL/30 in *U 87* and *U 89*)
Complement: 36

Class (launched, fate):
U 87 (22.5.16, sunk by *Buttercup* and *PC 56* 25.12.17), *U 88* (22.6.16, sunk by mine 5.9.17), *U 89* (6.10.16, rammed by *Roxburgh* 12.2.18), *U 90* (12.1.17, BU 1919–20), *U 91* (14.4.17, BU 1921), *U 92* (12.5.17, ? mined 9.9.18) mined 9.9.18)

The 'Project 25' boats, based on the *U 50*, were built by Danzig N Yd. They had a diving time of 56 seconds, and in most respects resembled previous classes. The 10.5cm gun on *U 91* and *U 92* were on AA mountings.

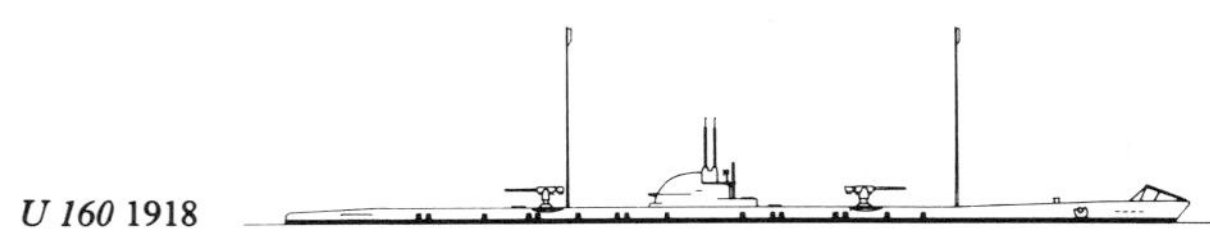
U 160 1918

U 93 class *submarines*

Displacement: 838t (*U 105–U 114* 798t; *U 160* and *U 201* groups 820t)/1000t
Dimensions: 234ft 11in × 20ft 8in × 12ft 9in
71.6m × 6.3m × 3.9m
Machinery: 2 shafts, 2 MAN 6-cyl 4-stroke diesels plus 2 electric motors, 2400bhp/1200shp = 16.8kts/8.6kts. Oil 112t–128t max. Range 8300nm/50nm at 8kts/5kts (surfaced/submerged) (see notes)
Armament: As *U 87* class (see notes)
Complement: 36

Class (launched, fate):
Germaniawerft, Kiel – *U 93* (15.12.16, rammed by SS *Braeneil* 7.1.18), *U 94* (5.1.17, BU 1919–20), *U 95* (20.1.17, 'missing' 1.18), *U 96* (15.2.17, BU 1919–20), *U 97* (4.4.17, foundered 21.11.18), *U 98* (28.2.17, BU 1919–20), *U 105* (16.5.17, BU 1937), *U 106* (12.6.17, mined 8.10.17), *U 107* (28.6.17, BU 1922), *U 108* (11.10.17, BU 1935), *U 109* (25.9.17, sunk by *Beryl III* 26.1.18), *U 110* (28.7.17, sunk by *Moresby* and *Michael* 15.3.18), *U 111* (5.9.17, to USA 1918, sunk as target), *U 112* (26.10.17, BU 1922), *U 113* (29.9.17, BU 1921), *U 114* (27.11.17, BU 1919)

Bremer Vulcan, Vegesack – *U 160* (27.2.18, BU 1922), *U 161* (23.3.18, wrecked en route for BU 1921), *U 162* (20.4.18, BU 1937), *U 163* (1.6.18, BU 1919), *U 164* (7.8.18, BU 1922), *U 165* (21.8.18, sunk in collision 18.11.18, raised and BU 1919), *U 166* (6.9.18, BU 1935), *U 167* (28.9.18, BU 1921), *U 168* (19.10.18, BU incomplete 1919), *U 169–U 172* (only about 75 per cent complete at the end of the war, BU 1919), *U 201–U 209* (BU in 1919 on the slips; little work had been done), *U 210–U 212* (never begun)

Ms type boats subject to continous improvement so differing slightly in details, although based on *U 86*. *U 96–U 98* and *U 111–U 114* had Germania 2-stroke diesels of 2300bhp and the Bremer Vulcan boats had electric motors of 1230shp. Diving time in all groups was 66 seconds. Armament also varied: *U 93–U 95* originally carried 1–8.8cm KL/30, but 1–10.5cm KL/45 on an AA mounting was added in 1918; *U 96–U 98* originally had 1–10.5cm KL/45, but 1–8.8cm was added to *U 96*; the *U 160* group were originally fitted with 1–10.5cm on an AA mounting, but by 1918 most survivors had 1–8.8cm added; some boats could stow 16 torpedoes by the end of the war.

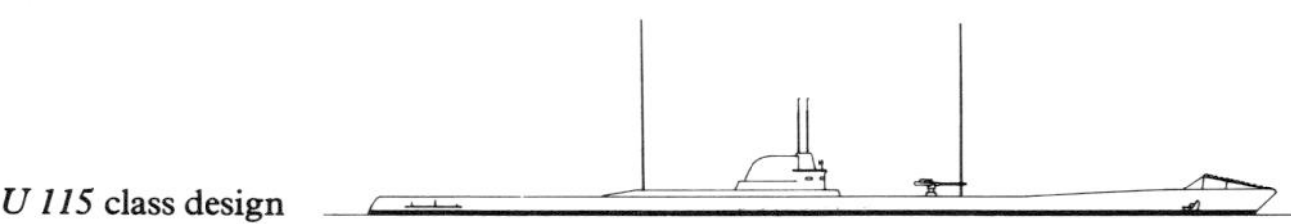
U 115 class design

U 115 class *submarines*

Displacement: 882t/1233t
Dimensions: 237ft 3in × 21ft 4in × 113ft 2in
72.3m × 6.5m × 4.0m
Machinery: 2 shafts, 2 MAN 6-cyl 4-stroke diesels plus 2 electric motors, 2400bhp/1200shp = 16kts/9kts. Oil 136t max. Range 9800nm/60nm at 8kts/4.5kts (surfaced/submerged)
Armament: As *U 87* class
Complement: 36

Class:
U 115–U 116, U 263–U 276

Built by Schichau, Danzig, these 'Project 43' boats were unfinished at the end of war; they were broken up on the slips and the diesels used for merchant ships. The *U 263* group would have had more powerful machinery (2900bhp/1230shp = 16.5kts/9kts), increased bunkerage, and hence range (oil 159t max; range 11,400nm at 8kts).

U 117 class *submarine minelayers*

Displacement: 1164t/1512t (*U 122* group 1468t)
Dimensions: 267ft 4in (*U 122* group 269ft) × 24ft 3in
81.5m (82.0m) × 7.4m × 4.2m
Machinery: 2 shafts, 2 MAN 6-cyl, 4-stroke diesels plus 2 electric motors, 2400bhp/1200shp = 14.7kts/7kts. Oil 167t. Range 9400nm (*U 122* group 163t, 9200nm)/35nm at 8kts/4.5kts (surfaced/submerged)
Armament: 4–50cm (19.7in) TT (4 bow; 12 torpedoes), 2–100cm mine tubes (stern; 42 mines plus 30 in deck stowage), 1–15cm (5.9in) KL/45
Complement: 40

Class (launched, fate):
Vulcan Hamburg – *U 117* (10.12.17, sunk as target 22.6.21), *U 118* (23.2.18), BU 1921), *U 119* (4.4.18, BU 1937), *U 120* (20.6.18, BU 1919), *U 121* (20.9.18, sunk as target 1.7.21)
Blohm & Voss, Hamburg – *U 122* (9.12.17, stranded en route to BU 1921), *U 123* (26.1.18, stranded en route to BU 1921), *U 124* (28.3.18, BU 1922), *U 125* (26.5.18, BU 1922), *U 126* (16.6.18, BU 1923)

UE II type ocean minelayers ('Project 45') with a diving depth of 75m. *U 117* also carried 1–8.8cm KL/30 and *U 123* 2–10.5cm AA instead of the designed armament.

U 117 became US after the war and was sunk during bombing demonstration 1921; *U 119, U 121* and *U 120* became French, the first serving as *René Audry* until 1937; *U 122–U 124, U 126* were scrapped in England; *U 125* became Japanese *O 1* serving until 1922.

U 86 November 1918 after surrendering — *Aldo Fraccaroli Collection*

U 127 class *submarines*

Displacement:	1221t/1649 (*U 131* group 1160t/1527t; *U 135* group 1175t/1534t)
Dimensions:	269ft 4in (*U 131* group 270ft 8in; *U 135* group 273ft 11in) × 24ft 7in × 14ft *82.1m (82.5m, 83.5m) × 7.5m × 4.3m*
Machinery:	2 shafts, 2 diesels (plus 2 diesel generators for surface dash) and 2 electric motors, 3500bhp + 900shp/1690shp = *c*17kts/8.1kts. Oil 167t max. Range 10,000nm/50nm at 8kts/4kts (estimated, surfaced/submerged)
Armament:	6–50cm (19.7in) TT (4 bow, 2 stern; 14 torpedoes), 2–10.5cm (4.1in) KL/45 AA
Complement:	46

Class (launched, fate):
Germaniawerft, Kiel – *U 127–U 130* (–, BU incomplete 1920)
AG Weser, Bremen – *U 131–U 134* (–, BU incomplete 1919–20)
Danzig N Yd – *U 135* (8.9.17, foundered en route to BU 1921), *U 136* (7.11.17, BU 1921), *U 137* (8.1.18, BU incomplete 1919), *U 138* (26.3.18, BU incomplete 1919)

Big Ms type boats built in groups of 4. Most had MAN 6-cyl machinery, but the Germaniawerft group had diesels by the builders, and *U 134* had Körting main engines.

All boats were 80–90 per cent completed at the end of the war; *U 135* sank on the way to the breakers in England, *U 136* became a French war reparation and was scrapped in Cherbourg, 1921; all the others were broken up in Germany, the diesels being used for merchant ships.

U 70 date unknown — *BfZ*

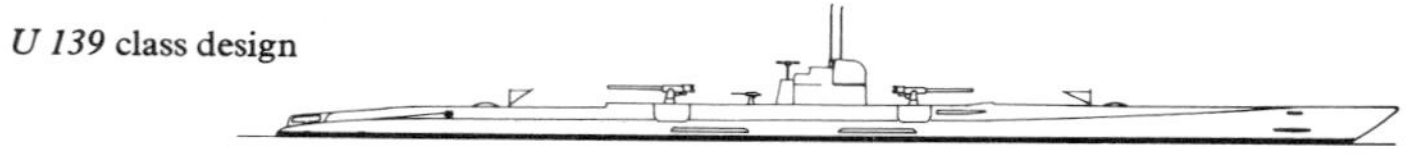
U 139 class design

U 139 class *submarines*

Displacement:	1930t/2483t
Dimensions:	301ft 10in × 29ft 10in × 17ft 4in *92.0m × 9.1m × 5.3m*
Machinery:	2 shafts, 2 MAN (*U 139* Germania) 6-cyl 4-stroke diesels plus diesel generator for dash speed and 2 electric motors, 3300bhp + 450shp/1690shp = 15.3kts/7.6kts. Oil 451t. Range 17,750nm (*U 139* 443t, 12,630nm)/53nm at 8kts/4.5kts (surfaced/submerged)
Armament:	6–50cm (19.7in) TT (4 bow, 2 stern; 19 torpedoes), 2–15cm (5.9in) KL/45
Complement:	66 (plus 20 prize crew)

Class (launched, fate):
U 139 (3.12.17, BU 1935), *U 140* (4.11.17, sunk as target 22.7.21), *U 141* (9.1.18, BU 1923)

These large ocean-going cruiser-type submarines were built by Germaniawerft. They had some protective plating (30mm on the CT and 25mm on the ammunition trunking); diving depth was 75m. These 'Project 46' units were to have the following names: *U 139, Kapitänleutnant Schwieger*, which became a French reparation and served under her new name *Halbronn* until 1935; *U 140, Kapitänleutnant Weddigen*, became a US reparation and was sunk in 1921 as a gunnery target; *U 141* went to Britain and was scrapped in 1923.

U 122 1918 — *Aldo Fraccaroli Collection*

U 151 1917 — *Aldo Fraccaroli Collection*

U 95 as completed — *Aldo Fraccaroli Collection*

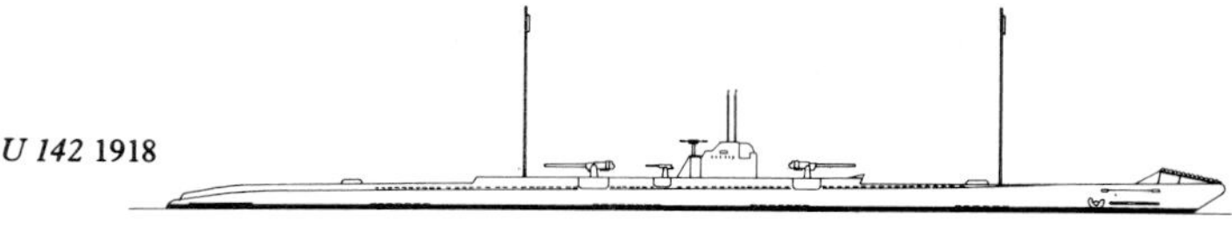
U 142 1918

U 142 class *submarines*

Displacement:	2115t–2175t/2766t–2791t
Dimensions:	319ft 11in × 29ft 10in × 17ft 9in *97.5m × 9.1m × 5.4m*
Machinery:	2 shafts, 2 diesels (plus 2 diesel generators for dash speed) and 2 electric motors, 6000bhp + 900shp/2600shp = 17.5kts/8.5kts. Oil 519t–537t. Range 20,000nm/70nm at 6kts/4.5kts (surfaced/submerged)
Armament:	6–50cm (19.7in) TT (4 bow, 2 stern; 24 torpedoes), 2 (later 3)–15cm KL/45
Complement:	66 (plus 20 prize crew)

GERMANY

Class:
Germaniawerft, Kiel – *U 142–U 144, U 173–U 176, U 183–U 190*
Vulcan, Hamburg – *U 145–U 147, U 177–U 178*
Weser, Bremen – *U 148–U 150, U 179–U 180, U 195–U 200*
Blohm & Voss – *U 181–U 182, U 191–U 194*

'Project 46A' (improved 'Project 46') boats, with increased surface speed. There were slight variations in tonnage and machinery, most having MAN 10-cyl 4-stroke diesels, but licence-built by the builders in the case of some Vulcan and Blohm & Voss boats. Only *U 142–U 144, U 148* and *U 149* had been launched, and none was completed at the end of the war; the orders for *U 195–U 200* were cancelled and they were never laid down. All were broken up in various stages of completion in 1919–20.

U 151 class *submarine cruisers*

Displacement:	1512t/1875t
Dimensions:	213ft 3in × 29ft 2in × 17ft 4in *65.0m × 8.9m × 5.3m*
Machinery:	2 shafts, 2 Germania 6-cyl 4-stroke diesels plus 2 electric motors, 800bhp/800shp = 12.4kts/5.2kts. Oil 328t max. Range 25,000nm/65nm at 5.5kts/3kts (surfaced/submerged)
Armament:	2–50cm (19.7in) TT (2 bow, 18 torpedoes), 2–15cm (5.9in) KL/45, 2–8.8cm (3.45in) KL/45
Complement:	56 (plus 20 prize crew)

Class (launched, fate):
Flensburg – *U 151* (4.4.17, sunk as target 7.6.21), *U 155* (28.3.16, BU 1922)
Reiherstieg, Hamburg – *U 152* (20.5.17, sank en route to BU 1921), *U 153* (19.7.17, sank en route to BU 1921), *U 154* (10.9.17, torpedoed by *E 35* 11.5.18)
Atlas Werke, Bremen – *U 156* (17.4.17, mined 25.9.18
Stülcken Sohn, Hamburg – *U 157* (23.5.17, BU 1921)

This class of submarine cruisers was initially designed as submarine freighters with names. The *Deutschland* made one visit to the USA which was more a propaganda than a commercial success; her sister *Bremen* was lost during her first voyage; the third unit *Oldenburg* was never commissioned as a submarine freighter, since by then the USA had entered the war. From February 1917 they were converted to submarine cruisers, the other units of this type being built as such from keel up. *U 155* had 6 aw TT (3×2) and originally 2–15cm SKL/40 from *Zähringen*. *U 154* and *U 156* were lost in action; *U 152* and *U 153* became British war reparations, but were lost while on tow to the breakers in 1921. *U 155 (ex-Deutschland)* was ceded to Britain and was scrapped in 1922, *U 151* (the original *Oldenburg*) and *U 157* became French war reparations; the first was sunk as a gunnery target in 1921, the second was scrapped in 1921.

U 158 class *submarines*

Displacement:	811t/1034t
Dimensions:	233ft 5in × 20ft 4in × 12ft 10in *71.2m × 6.2m × 3.9m*
Machinery:	As *U 93* class, except 16kts/9kts. Oil 167t max. Range 12,370nm/55nm at 8kts/5kts (surfaced/submerged)
Armament:	As *U 87* class
Complement:	39

Class (launched, fate):
U 158 (16.4.18, BU incomplete 1919), *U 159* (25.5.18, BU incomplete 1919)

Improved 'Project 43' (*U 115*) type boats (themselves known as 'Project 25') of greatly enlarged radius of action, built by Danzig N Yd; they were very nearly finished by the end of the war, but broken up in situ.

U 213 class *submarines*

Displacement:	1335t/1830t
Dimensions:	289ft × 25ft 11in × 13ft 1in *88.1m × 7.9m × 4.0m*
Machinery:	2 shafts, 2 diesels (plus 2 diesel generators for surface dash) and 2 electric motors, 3500bhp + 900shp/1690shp = 18kts/9kts. Oil 250t. Range 12,000nm/90nm at 8kts/4.5kts (surfaced/submerged)
Armament:	6–50cm (19.7in) TT (4 bow, 2 stern; 16 torpedoes), 1–15cm (5.9in) KL/45
Complement:	46

Class:
Danzig N Yd – *U 213–U 218*
Weser, Bremen – *U 219–U 224*
Blohm & Voss, Hamburg – *U 225–U 228*

Large Ms type boats (in effect an enlargement of the 'Project 42' type). From *U 219* they would have displaced slightly more (1400t/1900t). All were broken up incomplete on the slips; none had been launched.

U 229 class *submarines*

Displacement:	908t/1192t
Dimensions:	242ft 9in × 22ft × 14ft 1in *74.0m × 6.7m × 4.3m*
Machinery:	2 shafts, 2 MAN or Germania 6-cyl diesels plus 2 electric motors, 2900bhp/1230shp = 16.5kts/9kts. Oil 159t. Range 11,400nm/50nm at 8kts/5kts (surfaced/submerged)
Armament:	As *U 87* class
Complement:	39

Class:
Germaniawerft, Kiel – *U 229–U 246*
Bremer Vulcan, Vegesack – *U 247–U 262*

An improved Ms type of greater radius. Very little work was done on any of these before the end of the war.

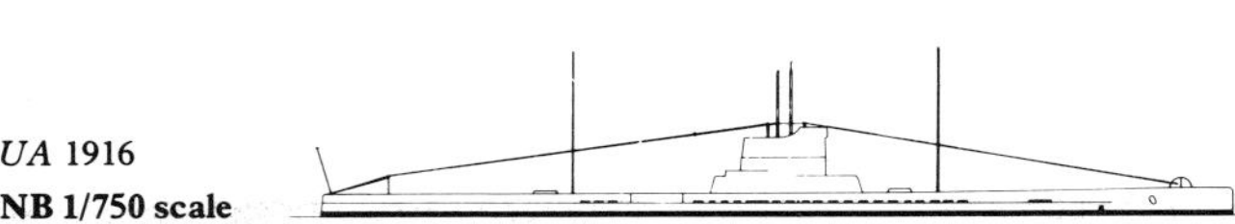

UA 1916
NB 1/750 scale

UA *coastal submarine*

Displacement:	270t/342t
Dimensions:	153ft 3in × 15ft 9in × 9ft 6in *46.7m × 4.8m × 2.9m*
Machinery:	2 shafts, 2 Germania 6-cyl 4-stroke diesels plus 2 electric motors, 700bhp/380shp = 14.2kts/7.3kts. Oil 15t. Range 900nm/76nm at 10kts/3.3kts (surfaced/submerged)
Armament:	3–45cm (17.7in) TT (2 bow, 1 stern; 5 torpedoes), 1–5cm (2in) KL/40 (added in 1917)
Complement:	21

Class (launched, fate):
UA (9.5.14, BU 1919–20)

Ex-Norwegian *A 5* built by Germaniawerft, Kiel and taken over on the outbreak of war. Diving depth was 50m and diving time 75 seconds. She served in a training role from 1916 and was scrapped in Britain after the war.

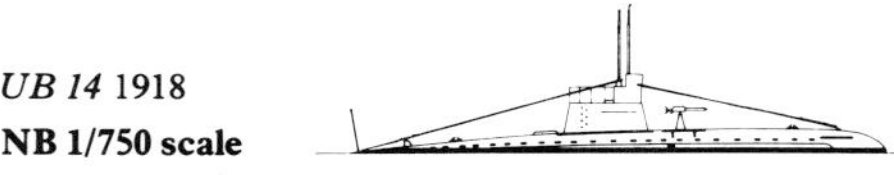

UB 14 1918
NB 1/750 scale

UB 1 class *coastal submarines*

Displacement:	127t/142t
Dimensions:	92ft 2in (*UB 9* group 91ft 6in) × 10ft 6in × 9ft 10in *28.1m (27.9m) × 3.2m × 3.0m*
Machinery:	1 shaft, 1 Daimler (*UB 9* group Körting) 4–cyl diesel plus one electric motor, 60bhp/120shp = 6.5kts/5.5kts. Oil 3.5t. Range 1650nm (*UB 9* group 7.5kts/6.2kts; oil 3t; range 1500nm/45nm at 5kts/4kts (surfaced/submerged)
Armament:	2–45cm (17.7in) TT (2 bow; 2 torpedoes), 1–8mm MG
Complement:	14

Class (fate):
Germaniawerft, Kiel (launched 19.1.15–23.4.15) – *UB 1* (Austrian *U 10*, wrecked 4.6.15 and BU 1918), *UB 2* (BU 1919), *UB 3* ('missing' 5.15), *UB 4* (sunk by Q-ship *Inverlyon* 15.8.15), *UB 5* (BU 1919), *UB 6* (BU 1921), *UB 7* (sunk 10.16), *UB 8* (BU 1921)
Weser, Bremen (launched 6.2.15–21.4.15) – *UB 9* (BU 1919), *UB 10* (scuttled 5.10.18), *UB 11* (BU 1919), *UB 12* (mined 8.18), *UB 13* (caught in mined nets 24.4.16), *UB 14* (BU 1920), *UB 15* (Austrian *U 11* 4.6.15, BU 1919), *UB 16* (torpedoed by *E 34* 10.5.18), *UB 17* (sunk by *Onslow* 11.3.18)

UB I type coastal submarines with a diving depth of 50m; single-hulled type with a diving time of 33 seconds. *UB 10, UB 12, UB 16* and *UB 17* were converted to minelayers in 1918, with the hull lengthened to 105ft (32.0m), tonnage 147t/161t, with TT replaced by 4–100cm mine tubes and 8 mines. Many were transported by rail to Pola and Antwerp. *UB 1* and *UB 15* were so transferred and sold to the Austro-Hungarian Navy, and commissioned at Pola as *U 10, U 11* (see under Austria-Hungary); *UB 8* was sold to Bulgaria and came to France as a war reparation. *UB 3, UB 4, UB 7, UB 16* and *UB 17* were lost in action; *UB 12* and *UB 13* were mined; *UB 2, UB 5, UB 9, UB 11* and *UB 14* were scrapped in Germany 1919; *UB 6* was interned and became French war reparation but was scrapped as were *UB 8* and *UB 15*. *UB 10* was blown up during the German retreat from Flanders.

UB 18 class *coastal submarines*

Displacement: 263t/292t (*UB 30* on 279t/305t)
Dimensions: 118ft 5in (*UB 30* on 121ft) × 14ft 5in × 12ft 2in
36.1m (36.9m) × 4.4m × 3.7m
Machinery: 2 shafts, 2 Daimler, Körting or Benz diesels plus 2 electric motors, 270bhp–284bhp/280shp = 9kts/5.8kts. Oil 32t. Range 6650nm (*UB 20–UB 23* 6450nm; *UB 24–UB 41* 8150nm; *UB 42–UB 47* 6940nm)/45nm at 5kts/4kts (surfaced/submerged)
Armament: 2–50cm (19.7in) TT (2 bow; 4, later 6, torpedoes), 1–5cm KL/40 (see notes)
Complement: 22

Class (fate):
Blohm & Voss, Hamburg (launched 21.8.15–9.10.15; and 16.11.15–6.5.16) – *UB 18* (mined 12.17), *UB 19* (sunk by Q-ship *Penshurst* 30.11.66), *UB 20* (sunk by aircraft 28.7.17), *UB 21* (sank en route to BU 1920), *UB 22* (mined 20.1.18), *UB 23* (BU 1921); *UB 30* (sunk by trawler *John Gillmann* 13.8.18), *UB 31* (sunk by ASW drifters 2.5.18), *UB 32* (sunk by aircraft 9.17), *UB 33* mined 11.4.18), *UB 34* (BU 1922), *UB 35* (sunk by *Leven* 26.1.18), *UB 36* (rammed by French SS *Molière* 21.5.17), *UB 37* (sunk by Q-ship *Penshurst* 14.1.17), *UB 38* (mined 8.2.18), *UB 39* (sunk by Q-ship 17.5.17), *UB 40* (scuttled 1.10.18), *UB 41* (mined 5.10.17)
Weser, Bremen (launched 18.10.15–31.12.15; and 4.3.16–17.6.16) – *UB 24* (BU 1921), *UB 25* (BU 1922), *UB 26* (BU 1931), *UB 27* (sunk by *Halcyon* 29.7.17), *UB 28* (BU 1919), *UB 29* (sunk by *Landrail* 13.12.16); *UB 42* (BU 1920), *UB 43* (BU 1919), *UB 44* (sunk by British escorts 4.8.16, *UB 45* (mined 6.11.16, raised and BU 1936), *UB 46* mined 7.12.16), *UB 47* (BU 1919)

UB II type coastal submarines of single hull construction with saddle tanks. They had a diving depth of 50m and a diving time which varied from 45 seconds in the Blohm & Voss boats to 30 seconds in the *UB 24–UB 29* group. *UB 30–UB 47* had 1–8.8cm KL/30 deck gun, and this weapon replaced the 5cm in *UB 18* and *UB 21–UB 23* in 1916–17. *UB 21, UB 22, UB 27, UB 34, UB 35* and *UB 41* also had 2–50cm rearward-firing external TT when their bow TT were fitted for laying P mines. *UB 43* and *UB 47*, sold to Austria-Hungary in 1917, were commissioned as the Austrian *U 43* and *U 47*, ceded to Italy after the war and scrapped. Of those lost in action *UB 26* was raised, became the French *Lieutenant Morillot*, and was scrapped in 1931. *UB 23* was interned in Spain, but also became a French reparation and was scrapped. *UB 24, UB 25, UB 28* and *UB 42* became British war reparations and were scrapped; *UB 21* sank during transfer to Britain. *UB 40* was scuttled during the German retreat from Flanders.

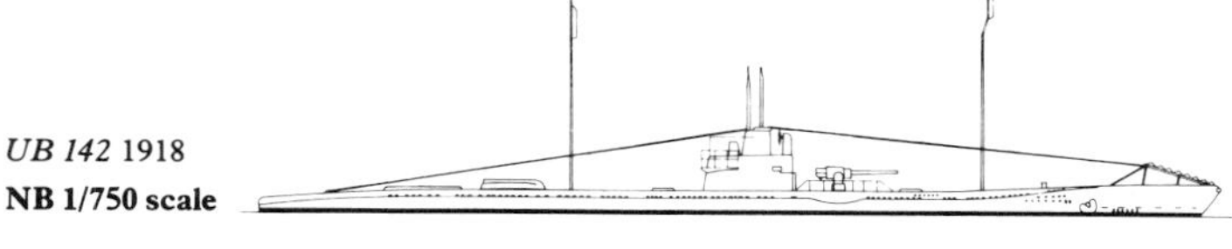
UB 142 1918
NB 1/750 scale

UB 48 class *coastal submarines*

Displacement: 516t/651t (increasing to about 533t/656t in later types)
Dimensions: 181ft 5in (later types 183ft 3in) × 19ft × 12ft 2in (later types 12ft 6in)
55.3m (55.9m) × 5.8m × 3.7m (3.8m)
Machinery: 2 shafts, 2 6-cyl 4-stroke diesels plus 2 electric motors, 1100bhp/788shp = 13.5kts/7.5kts. Oil 78t–86t. Range (see notes)
Armament: 5–50cm (19.7in) TT (4 bow, 1 stern; 10 torpedoes), 1–8.8cm (3.45in) KL/30 (1–10.5cm KL/45 from *UB 88*, and in most surviving earlier boats from 1918)
Complement: 34

Class (fate):
Blohm & Voss, Hamburg (launched 6.1.17–9.3.17; 5.5.17–3.6.17; and 7.7.17–21.11.17) – *UB 48* (scuttled 28.10.18), *UB 49* (BU 1922), *UB 50* (BU 1922), *UB 51* (BU 1922), *UB 52* (torpedoed by *H 4* 25.5.18), *UB 53* (sunk by mine nets 3.8.18); *UB 75* (mined 10.12.17), *UB 76* (BU 1922), *UB 77* (BU 1922), *UB 78* (rammed by SS *Queen Alexandra*), *UB 79* (BU 1922); *UB 103* (sunk by surface forces 16.9.18), *UB 104* (mined 19.9.18), *UB 105* (BU 1922), *UB 106* (wrecked 1921, BU), *UB 107* (sunk by armed yacht *Vanessa* 27.7.18), *UB 108* (? mined 8.18), *UB 109* (mined 29.8.18), *UB 110* (sunk by *Garry* and *ML 23* 19.7.18), *UB 111* (BU 1919–20), *UB 112* (wrecked 1921, BU), *UB 113* (mined 9.10.18), *UB 114* (BU 1921), *UB 115* (sunk by British escorts 29.9.18), *UB 116* (mined 28.10.18), *UB 117* (BU 1919–20)
Weser, Bremen (launched 18.4.17–21.7.17; 4.8.17–10.11.17; 13.12.17–22.6.18; and 23.7.18–19.10.18) – *UB 54* (sunk by British escorts 11.3.18), *UB 55* (mined 22.4.18), *UB 56* (mined 19.12.17), *UB 57* (mined 14.8.18), *UB 58* (mined 10.3.18), *UB 59* (scuttled 5.10.18); *UB 80* (BU 1919), *UB 81* (mined 1.12.17), *UB 82* (sunk by ASW drifters 17.4.18), *UB 83* (sunk by *Orphelia* 10.9.18), *UB 84* (sunk in collision 7.12.17, raised, BU 1921), *UB 85* (sunk by *Coreopsis* 30.4.18), *UB 86* (wrecked 1921, BU), *UB 87* (BU 1921); *UB 118* (wrecked 15.4.19), *UB 119* (? mined 5.18), *UB 120* (BU 1922), *UB 121* (BU 1921), *UB 122* (wrecked 1921), *UB 123* (mined 19.10.18), *UB 124* (sunk by British escorts 20.7.18), *UB 125* (Japanese *O 6* 1918, BU 1921), *UB 126* (BU 1921), *UB 127* (? mined 9.18), *UB 128* (BU 1921), *UB 129* (scuttled 31.10.18), *UB 130* (BU 1921), *UB 131* (BU 1921), *UB 132* (BU 1922); *UB 142* (BU 1921), *UB 143* (Japanese *O 7* 1918, BU 1921), *UB 144* (BU 1922), *UB 145* (BU 1922); *UB 146* (BU incomplete 1919), *UB 147* (BU incomplete 1919), *UB 148* (to USA 1918, sunk as target), *UB 149* (BU 1922), *UB 150* (BU 1922), *UB 151–UB 153* (BU incomplete 1919); *UB 178–UB 187* (little work done, BU); *UB 206–UB 219* (orders cancelled 1919)
Vulcan, Hamburg (launched 14.4.17–26.6.17; 30.7.17–13.9.17; 11.12.17–13.9.18; and 26.10.18) – *UB 60* (wrecked 1921, BU), *UB 61* (mined 29.11.17), *UB 62* (BU 1922), *UB 63* (sunk by ASW trawlers 28.1.18), *UB 64* (BU 1921), *UB 65* (sunk by USS *L 2* 10.7.18); *UB 73* (torpedoed by *D 4* 12.5.18), *UB 73* (BU 1921), *UB 74* (sunk by ASW yacht *Lorna* 26.5.18); *UB 88* (to USA, sunk as target 3.1.21), *UB 89* (sunk in collision with cruiser *Frankfurt* 21.10.18, raised, BU 1920), *UB 90* (torpedoed by *L 12* (16.10.18), *UB 91* (BU 1921), *UB 92* (BU 1919–20), *UB 93* (BU 1922), *UB 94* (French *Trinité Schillemans* 1918, BU 1935), *UB 95* (BU 1919), *UB 96* (BU 1919–20), *UB 97* (wrecked 1921, BU), *UB 98* (BU 1922), *UB 99* (French *Carisson* 1919, BU 1935), *UB 100* (BU 1922), *UB 101* (BU 1919–20), *UB 102* (BU 1919); *UB 154* (never completed, BU 1921), *UB 155* (French *Jean Corre* 1918; BU 1936); *UB 156–UB 169* (BU incomplete 1919); *UB 188–UB 205* (little work done, BU on slips 1919); *UB 220–UB 249* (orders cancelled 1919)
Germaniawerft, Kiel (launched 31.5.17–12.7.17; and 27.9.18) – *UB 66* (sunk by *Campanula* 18.1.18), *UB 67* (BU 1922), *UB 68* (scuttled after action damage 4.10.18), *UB 69* (sunk by *Cyclamen* 9.1.18), *UB 70* (sunk by *Basilisk* and US SS *Lydonia* 8.5.18), *UB 71* (sunk by *ML 413* 21.4.18); *UB 133* (BU 1922), *UB 134* (BU on slips 1919), *UB 135* (BU on slip 1919), *UB 136* (BU 1922), *UB 137–UB 141* (BU on slips 1919); *UB 170–UB 177* (BU on slips 1919)

These UB III type boats in fact constituted many different sub-groups, varying slightly in dimensions and machinery (MAN, AEG, Körting or Benz). Underwater endurance was about 55nm at 4kts in all, but surface range at 6kts varied from about 9040nm (*UB 48, UB 54, UB 66, UB 133* and *UB 170* groups) through about 8500nm (*UB 60, UB 72* and *UB 75* groups) and 8180nm (*UB 80*) to about 7200nm (*UB 88, UB 103, UB 118, UB 142* and later groups). The design was essentially a reduced version of the Ms type, with a double hull and a diving depth of 50m. Most of the survivors were broken up in Britain, but a number were lost en route to the breakers. *UB 73, UB 84, UB 87, UB 142* and *UB 154* were broken up in France; apart from three which saw service in the French Navy, *UB 114, UB 121, UB 126* and *UB 130* were expended in explosive trials in France and the hulks broken up. *UB 59* was scuttled during the German retreat from Flanders, and *UB 48* and *UB 129* likewise at Pola after the Austrian armistice. *UB 80, UB 95* and *UB 102* were broken up in Italy, and *UB 125* and *UB 143* in Japan after brief service in the Japanese Navy.

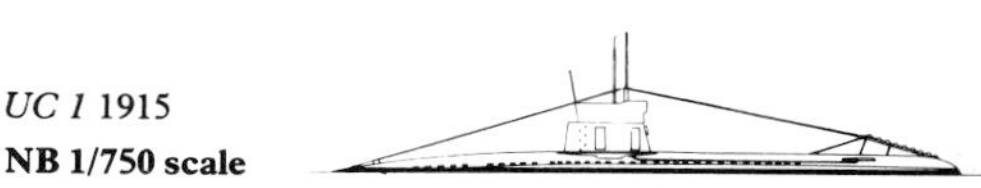
UC 1 1915
NB 1/750 scale

UC 1 class *coastal submarine minelayers*

Displacement: 168t/183t
Dimensions: 111ft 6in × 10ft 4in × 10ft
34.0m × 3.2m × 3.0m
Machinery: 1 shaft, 1 Daimler (*UC 11* Benz) 6-cyl 4-stroke diesel plus one electric motor, 90bhp/175shp = 6.2kts/5.2kts. Oil 3.5t Range 780nm (*UC 11–UC 15* 910nm)/50nm at 5kts/4kts (surfaced/submerged)
Armament: 6–100cm mine tubes (12 UC 120 type mines)
Complement: 14

Class (fate):
Vulcan, Hamburg (launched 26.4.15–15.7.15) – *UC 1* (bombed by 5 British seaplanes 25.7.17), *UC 2* (rammed by SS *Cottingham* 2.7.15), *UC 3* (mined 27.5.16), *UC 4* (scuttled 5.10.18), *UC 5* (stranded and captured 27.4.16, BU 1923), *UC 6* (bombed by British seaplane 28.9.17), *UC 7* (sunk by *Salmon* 6.17.16), *UC 8* (BU 1932), *UC 9* (blown up on own mines 21.10.15), *UC 10* (torpedoed by *E 54* 21.8.16)
Weser, Bremen (launched 11.4.15–19.5.15) – *UC 11* (mined 26.6.18), *UC 12* (blown up on own mines 16.3.16), *UC 13* (stranded and blown up 29.11.15), *UC 14* (mined 3.10.17), *UC 15* (mined 11.16)

Single-hulled UC I type minelayers with a diving depth of 50m. Mines were carried in near-vertical flooded tubes forward; they had no other armament, although *UC 11* was fitted with 1–45cm (17.7in) external tube aft in 1916.

After loss *UC 2* was raised by Britain and put on display; similarly *UC 12* was raised by Italy, rebuilt and commissioned as *X 1* but scrapped in 1919. *UC 13* was lost accidentally after grounding; *UC 4* was scuttled during the German retreat from Flanders, *UC 5* was stranded, captured and put on display by the British. *UC 8* was interned in the Netherlands after grounding and was commissioned as *M 1* between 1915 and 1932.

UB 40 1916 *Aldo Fraccaroli Collection*

UB 68 1917 *Aldo Fraccaroli Collection*

UC 31 surrendering in November 1918 *CPL*

UC 94 being transferred to Italy, February 1919 *CPL*

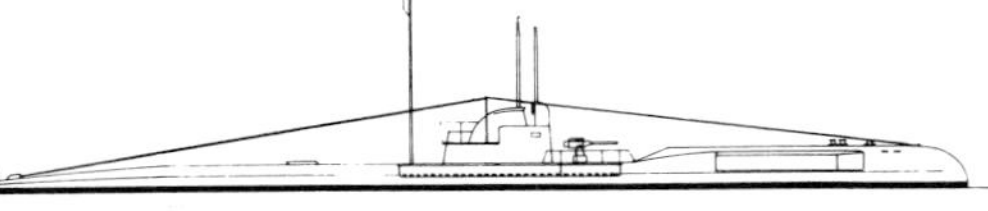

UC 34 1916
NB 1/750 scale

UC 16 class *coastal submarine minelayers*

Displacement:	417t–434t/480t–511t
Dimensions:	162ft–172ft 10in × 17ft 2in × 12ft 2in *49.4m–52.7m × 5.2m × 3.7m*
Machinery:	2 shafts, 2 MAN, Körting or Daimler 6-cyl 4-stroke diesels plus two electric motors, 500bhp/460shp = 11.5kts/7.0kts. Oil 63t. Range (see notes)
Armament:	6–100cm (39.4in) mine tubes (18 UC 200 type mines), 3–50cm (19.7in) TT (2 bow-external in earlier boats, 1 stern; 7 torpedoes), 1–8.8cm (3.45in) KL/30 (few boats 10.5cm KL/45)
Complement:	26

Class (fate):
Blohm & Voss, Hamburg (launched 1.2.16–4.3.16; 6.5.16–25.6.16; and 8.7.16–26.8.16) – *UC 16* (sunk by *Melampus* 23.10.17), *UC 17* (BU 1919–20), *UC 18* (sunk by ASW nets 19.2.17), *UC 19* (sunk by *Ariel* 6.12.16), *UC 20* (BU 1919–20), *UC 21* (mined 27.9.17), *UC 22* (BU 1921), *UC 23* (BU 1921), *UC 24* (torpedoed by French *Circé* 24.5.17); *UC 34* (scuttled 28.10.18), *UC 35* (sunk by French *Ailly* 16.5.18), *UC 36* (bombed by British seaplane 20.5.17), *UC 37* (BU 1920), *UC 38* (sunk by French *Lansquenet* and *Mameluk* 5.6.16), *UC 39* (sunk by *Thrasher* 8.2.17); *UC 65* (torpedoed by *C 15* 3.11.17), *UC 66* (sunk by ASW trawler *Sea King* 12.6.17), *UC 67* (BU 1919–20), *UC 68* (torpedoed by *C 7* 5.4.17), *UC 69* (sunk in collision with *U 96* 6.12.17), *UC 70* (sunk by British monitors 5.6.17, raised and repaired, sunk by *Ouse* and seaplane 28.8.18), *UC 71* (foundered en route to surrender 20.2.19), *UC 72* (bombed by seaplane 9.17), *UC 73* (BU 1919–20)
Vulcan, Hamburg (launched 10.6.16–26.8.16; 5.9.16–20.10.16; and 19.10.16–19.12.16) – *UC 25* (scuttled 28.10.18), *UC 26* (sunk by British destroyers 9.5.17), *UC 27* (BU 1921), *UC 28* (to France 1919, sunk as target), *UC 29* (sunk by Q-ship *Pargust* 7.6.17), *UC 30* (mined 19.4.17), *UC 31* (BU 1922), *UC 32* (blown up by own mines 23.2.17); *UC 40* (sunk en route to surrender 21.2.19), *UC 41* (sunk by ASW trawlers 21.8.17), *UC 42* (blown up on own mines 10.9.17), *UC 43* (torpedoed by *G 13* 10.3.17), *UC 44* (mined 5.8.17), *UC 45* (BU 1919–20); *UC 74* (BU 1921), *UC 75* (sunk by *Fairy* 31.5.18), *UC 76* (BU 1919–20), *UC 77* (sunk by ASW trawlers 10.8.18), *UC 78* (sunk by ASW drifters 2.5.18), *UC 79* (? mined 4.18)
Weser, Bremen (launched 15.7.16–27.9.16; and 11.11.16–27.1.17) – *UC 46* (sunk by *Liberty* 8.2.17), *UC 47* (sunk by *Opossum* 18.11.17), *UC 48* (interned in Spain after action damage 20.3.18, foundered 15.3.19); *UC 61* (wrecked 26.7.17), *UC 62* (torpedoed by *E 45* 10.17), *UC 63* (torpedoed by *E 52* 1.11.17), *UC 64* (mined 20.6.18)
Germaniawerft, Kiel (launched 7.11.16–20.3.17) – *UC 49* (sunk by *Opossum* 8.8.18), *UC 50* (sunk by *Zubian* 4.2.18), *UC 51* (sunk by *Firedrake* 11.17), *UC 52* (BU 1919–20), *UC 53* (scuttled 28.10.18), *UC 54* (scuttled 28.10.18)
Danzig N Yd (launched 2.8.16–8.11.16) – *UC 55* (sunk by British surface forces 29.9.17), *UC 56* (BU 1923), *UC 57* (? mined 11.17), *UC 58* (BU 1921), *UC 59* (BU 1919–20), *UC 60* (BU 1921)

UC II type minelayers; double-hulled boats with improved range and sea-keeping compared with the UC I type. They varied in details (particularly the shape of the bow) and machinery was increased in power in later boats (600bhp/620shp in *UC 34, UC 46* and later groups). Underwater endurance was about 54nm at 4kts, but surface range varied from 7280nm (*UC 46* group) through 8000nm (*UC 61* group) and about 8750nm (*UC 49* and *UC 55* groups) to about 9250nm (*UC 16, UC 25* and *UC 40* groups) to over 10,000nm (in *UC 34, UC 65* and *UC 74* groups).

Lost by accident were *UC 32, UC 40* and *UC 69* as was *UC 45* which was raised and surrendered to Britain. *UC 25, UC 33, UC 53* and *UC 57* were scuttled after the fall of Austria-Hungary, as was *UC 61* which was scuttled by her crew after grounding. *UC 48* was interned at Ferrol in Spain but lost accidentally during the transfer to Britain; *UC 76* was interned in Sweden, ceded to Britain and scrapped. The following boats were ceded to France and scrapped there: *UC 22, UC 23, UC 27, UC 28, UC 56, UC 58, UC 74;* other scrapped boats were broken up in Britain.

UC 80 class *coastal submarine minelayers*

Displacement:	491t/571t
Dimensions:	214ft 10in × 18ft × 12ft 6in *56.5m × 5.5m × 3.8m*
Machinery:	2 shafts, 2 MAN 6-cyl 4-stroke diesels plus 2 electric motors, 600bhp/770shp = 11.5kts/6.6kts. Oil 77t. Range 9850nm/40nm at 7kts/4.5kts (surfaced/submerged)
Armament:	6–100cm (39.4in) mine tubes (14 UC 200 type mines), 3–50cm (19.7in) TT (2 bow external, 1 stern; 7 torpedoes), 1–10.5cm (4.1in) KL/45 (1–8.8cm KL/30 in some)
Complement:	32

Class (fate):
Danzig N Yd – *UC 80–UC 86* (BU on slips 1919), *UC 139–152* (orders cancelled 1919)
Weser, Bremen – *UC 87–UC 89* (BU on slips 1919)
Blohm & Voss, Hamburg (launched 19.1.18–11.8.18) – *UC 90* (Japanese *O 4* 1918, BU 1921), *UC 91* (sank en route to surrender 10.2.19), *UC 92* (BU 1921), *UC 93* (BU 1919), *UC 94* (BU 1919), *UC 95* (BU 1922), *UC 96* (BU 1919–20), *UC 97* (to USA, sunk as target 7.6.21), *UC 98* (BU 1919), *UC 99* (Japanese *O 5* 1918, BU 1920–21), *UC 100* (BU 1921), *UC 101* (BU 1922), *UC 102* (BU 1922), *UC 103* (BU 1921), *UC 104* (BU 1921), *UC 105* (BU 1922), *UC 106* (BU 1921), *UC 107* (BU 1921), *UC 108* (BU 1921), *UC 109* (BU 1921), *UC 110* (sank en route to BU 1921), UC 111 (BU 1921), *UC 112* (BU 1921), *UC 113* (BU 1921), *UC 114* (BU 1921); *UC 115–UC 118* (BU on slips 1918); *UC 119–UC 138* (BU on slips 1919); *UC 153–UC 192* (orders cancelled 1919)

The above data applies to the *UC 90* group which were the only boats completed; lower numbered boats would have been shorter and later boats would have been longer, and would have had Benz or Körting diesels in some cases. These UC III type minelayers were a considerable improvement on their predecessors, and had a diving depth of 75m. Two TT were sited amidships but were forward-firing.

UC 91 was lost after an accident. All other surviving boats were distributed as follows: Britain got *UC 92, UC 95, UC 101–UC 103, UC 105–UC 106* and *UC 108–UC 114* of which *UC 110* was lost by accident during transfer. France got *UC 100, UC 104* and *UC 107* which were scrapped and Italy got *UC 93, UC 94* and *UC 98* which were soon scrapped. Japan got *UC 90* and *UC 99* and commissioned them as *O 4* and *O 5*. The USA got *UC 97* which was sunk as a gunnery practice target after having been put on public display. *UC 80–UC 89* and *UC 115–UC 138* were broken up unfinished on their slips in Germany after the war while the orders for *UC 139–UC 192* were cancelled in 1918–19.

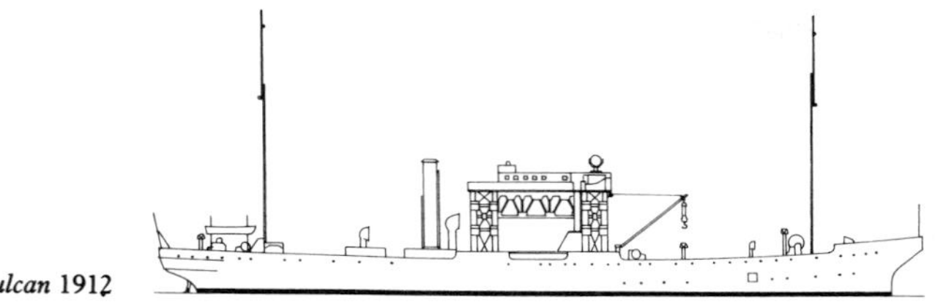
Vulcan 1912

VULCAN *submarine salvage vessel*

Displacement:	2595t deep load
Dimensions:	255ft 11in wl, 279ft 10in oa × 55ft 9in × 12ft 7in *78.0m, 85.3m × 17.0m × 3.9m*
Machinery:	2-shaft turbo-electric (2 turbo-generators, 2 electric motors), 4 boilers, 1340shp = 12kts
Armament:	Nil
Complement:	105

Designed as an integrated part of the German submarine force this salvage and repair vessel was launched in 1907. She had two hulls (a sort of giant catamaran) between which a raised submarine could be docked. Because of the ship's hull form and the large topside area this ship suffered from extremely bad seaworthiness and manoeuvrability. According to the armistice rules both dock ships (including the later *Cyclop*) had to be surrendered with the German submarines. *Vulcan* sank during the transfer to England 26 April 1919.

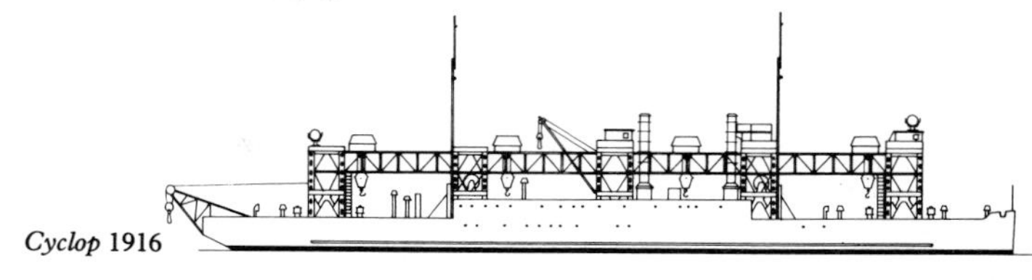
Cyclop 1916

CYCLOP *submarine salvage vessel*

Displacement:	4010t deep load
Dimensions:	282ft 2in wl, 308ft 5in oa × 64ft 4in × 20ft 8in *86.0m, 94.0m × 19.6m × 6.3m*
Machinery:	2-shaft VTE, 4 Navy boilers, 1800ihp = 9kts
Armament:	Nil
Complement:	?

Cyclop was a further development of the *Vulcan* with twice the lifting power (1000t), designed to the same principles. Because her builder, the Imperial Yard at Danzig was overburdened, the unfinished ship was towed after launching in 1916 to the Bremer Vulcan yard at Vegesack and finished there. Because of extensive trials the ship was not commissioned before 1 July 1918. *Cyclop* was also ceded to Great Britain and scrapped in 1923.

AUXILIARY WARSHIPS

Converted commerce raiders had been employed since the American Civil War and auxiliary cruisers (*ie* armed passenger liners) since the Russian 'Volunteer Fleet' of the Russo-Japanese war. In the Second Hague Conference of 1907 one of the declarations referred to the conversion of merchant vessels to auxiliary cruisers. Following this general international acceptance of commerce raiders the Imperial German Government asked prominent German shipping companies to fit their new liners with the necessary preparations (such as strengthened positions for guns) which would allow rapid conversion in wartime.

According to this general belief in the value of converted passenger liners as commerce raiders, we find those ships in action in the opening period of the First World War. Apart from the liners described and listed in this section the liner *Kronprinzessin Cecilie* of the Norddeutscher Lloyd and the Imperial Mail liner *Lützow* were scheduled for conversion, but the first ship returned to New York, where she was interned, and the second was trapped in the Suez Canal when war broke out. Equipment of these liners by overseas cruisers or obsolete station guardships followed a well prepared mobilisation programme. Although a well arranged supply organisation had been prepared and brought into service, the concept of passenger liners as commerce raiders failed: the ships always provoked suspicion and their superior speed was offset by an immense need for coal.

In the second period the Germans started to convert ordinary cargo vessels, but with the principal role of disguised auxiliary minelayers: they were not allowed to start active raiding until they had discharged this duty. By the autumn of 1915 a young Lieutenant, Theodor Wolff, had written a well-considered memorandum that was to presage the most successful aspects of commerce raiding in both world wars. He developed the theory of the disguised freighter acting as a wolf in sheep's clothing – a concept made familiar by the successful later German commerce raiders. The first ship of this second wave was the *Möwe*, although the German Admiralty still insisted that she should lay her mines first.

A more adventurous side issue of German raider warfare was the employment of a full-rigged sailing ship, and post-war publicity and literature mirrors the high public interest in this romantic type of warfare. Comparing the successes of German commerce raiders of both world wars, the only significant point is the growth in size of the average merchant vessel within two decades: First World War, 103 vessels totalling 357,894grt; 129 vessels totalling 772,633grt in the Second.

Kronprinz Wilhelm 1914
Aldo Fraccaroli Collection

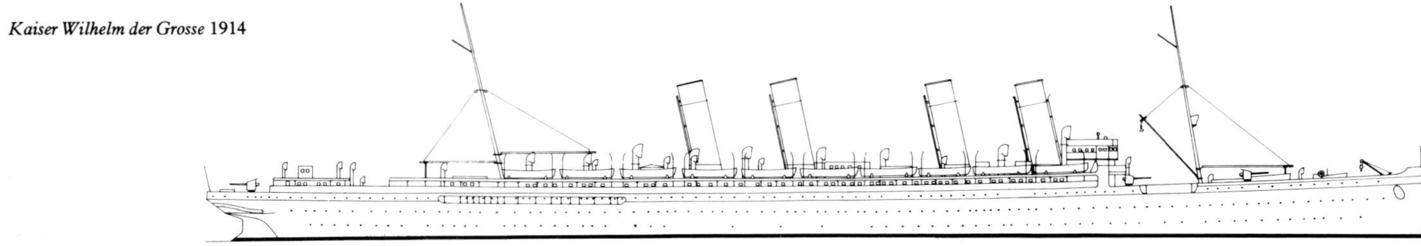
Kaiser Wilhelm der Grosse 1914

KAISER WILHELM DER GROSSE *auxiliary cruiser*

Displacement:	24,300t; 14,349grt
Dimensions:	649ft 7in wl, 654ft 6in oa × 65ft 11in × 27ft 7in *198.0m, 199.5m × 20.1m × 8.4m*
Machinery:	2-shaft VTE, 14 boilers, 28,000ihp = 22.5kts
Armament:	6–10.5cm (4.1in), 2–37mm
Complement:	584

A passenger liner of the Norddeutscher Lloyd and winner of the 'blue ribband' in November 1897, she was launched on 4 May 1897 by Vulcan, Stettin. She commissioned as flagship of the NDL on 9 September 1897 and served on the North Atlantic route. Being in Germany when war broke out she was converted to a commerce raider according to her mobilisation role, was commissioned on 2 August 1914 and operated in the northern and mid-Atlantic. She was attacked during a coaling operation in the neutral waters of the Spanish North African colony of Rio de Oro on 26 August 1916 by the British cruiser *Highflyer*, and was scuttled and capsized. She had captured 3 ships totalling 10,683grt.

PRINZ EITEL FRIEDRICH *auxiliary cruiser*

Displacement:	16,000t; 8797grt
Dimensions:	502ft 11in × 55ft 5in × 23ft 4in *153.3m × 16.9m × 7.1m*
Machinery:	2-shaft VQE, 4 boilers, 7000ihp = 15kts
Armament:	4–10.5cm (4.1in), 6–8.8cm (3.45in), 4–37mm
Complement:	402

Launched 10 June 1904 by Vulcan, Stettin, she was a former passenger liner of the Norddeutscher Lloyd. She served on the Far East route, and when war broke out was en route from Japan to Shanghai, her mobilisation orders sent her to Kiautchou where she received the guns of the obsolete gunboats *Luchs* and *Tiger* and was manned by their crew. On 5 August 1914 she was commissioned in her new role, operating with SMS *Cormoran* in Australian waters. Because of a coal shortage she crossed the Pacific, joined Graf Spee's East Asian Squadron for a short time, rounded Cape Horn and operated in the South Atlantic. She captured 11 ships totalling 33,423grt, but running low on coal and due to the worn out condition of the machinery she entered Newport News, Va, for interning on 9 April 1915. When the USA declared war on Germany the liner was impressed into the US fleet as the troop transport *De Kalb* (7 April 1917); after the war she served under her new name *Mount Clay* for the United America Lines Inc, and was scrapped in 1927.

KRONPRINZ WILHELM *auxiliary cruiser*

Displacement:	24,900t; 14,908t
Dimensions:	663ft 4in × 66ft 3in × 27ft 10in *202.2m × 20.2m × 8.5m*
Machinery:	2-shaft VQE, 16 boilers, 36,000ihp = 23kts
Armament:	2–12cm (4.7in), 2–8.8cm (3.45in)
Complement:	467 + 36

A passenger liner of the Norddeutscher Lloyd, launched by Vulcan, Stettin, on 30 March 1901. She was a near sister of the *Kaiser Wilhelm der Grosse* and won the 'blue ribband' in 1902 while serving on the North Atlantic route. When war broke out she left New York and was armed at sea by the light cruiser *Karlsruhe*, but had no ammunition for her 12cm guns. On 6 August 1914 she was commissioned in her new role. Operating in the Atlantic she captured 15 ships totalling 60,522grt. Running out of supplies and coal she was interned at Newport News, Va, on 26 April 1915. When the USA declared war on Germany the ship was seized (on 7 April 1917) and under the new name *Von Steuben* served as a troop transport in the US Navy. She was scrapped in 1923.

CORMORAN *auxiliary cruiser*

Displacement:	7250t; 3433grt
Dimensions:	341ft 2in × 44ft 11in × 19ft *104.0m × 13.7m × 5.8m*
Machinery:	1-shaft VTE, 4 boilers, 4750ihp = 13kts
Armament:	8–10.5cm (4.1in) SKL/35
Complement:	347

Originally built at Schichau, Elbing for the 'Russian Volunteer Fleet' as the auxiliary cruiser *Rjäsan*, the ship was captured en route to Vladivostok on 4 August 1914 by the German light cruiser *Emden*. Having emplacements for guns she was dispatched to the German colony of Tsingtao to be armed with the guns of the old German cruiser *Cormoran*, also receiving her name and being manned with the *Cormoran*'s crew. She was commissioned in her new role on 7 August 1914. Running out of coal and provisions she was interned at Guam on 13 December 1914; on 7 April 1917 she was scuttled by her crew, before being seized by US forces.

CAP TRAFALGAR *auxiliary cruiser*

Displacement:	23,640t; 18,710grt
Dimensions:	610ft 3in × 71ft 10in × 27ft 3in *186.0m × 21.9m × 8.3m*
Machinery:	2-shaft DE, 14 boilers, ? ihp = 18kts
Armament:	2–10cm (4.1in) SKL/35, 4–37mm
Complement:	319

A liner of the Hamburg Suedamerikanische Dampfschiffahrts-Gesellschaft built by Vulcan, Hamburg and launched in March 1914. The brand new ship served on the South America route and was at Buenos Aires when war broke out. She was armed by the obsolete German gunboat *Eber* which sailed from German South West Africa and then went to Bahîa, Brazil for interning. *Cap Trafalgar* was commissioned in her new role on 31 August 1914 but was intercepted on 14 September 1914, in the vicinity of Trinidad, by the British AMC *Carmania;* she was sunk after an artillery duel.

BERLIN *auxiliary cruiser*

Displacement:	23,700t; 17,324grt
Dimensions:	610ft 3in × 69ft 10in × 28ft 3in *186.0m × 21.3m × 8.6m*
Machinery:	2-shaft VQE, 7 boilers, 14,000ihp = 16.5kts
Armament:	2–10.5cm (4.1in) SKL/40, 6–37mm
Complement:	?

A former passenger liner of Norddeutscher Lloyd, built in 1908 at the AG Weser yard, Bremen, she was converted to a minelayer and auxiliary cruiser and commissioned in her new role on 28 September 1914. The priorities for her first sortie were: 1) laying mines off the British East Coast; 2) the interception and capture of British fishing vessels; and 3) commerce raiding. This unlucky ship, commanded by a captain psychologically unsuited for this job, had only one success in her first role: on 27 October 1914 HMS *Audacious* hit one of *Berlin*'s mines and was lost. The *Berlin* could not fulfil her second duty due to heavy gales. During the attempt to approach a British freighter the German captain decided that the raider had been recognised and cancelled the attack. Believing that he was now hunted by British North Sea Forces and that he had not enough coal to reach Germany he decided to intern the ship in Norway. On 18 November 1914 she entered Trondheim and was interned for the rest of the war. After the war she came to England as a war reparation, served the White Star Line under her new name *Arabic* until 1931, and was then broken up.

VINETA *auxiliary cruiser*

Displacement:	24,500t; 20,576grt
Dimensions:	662ft 1in × 72ft 6in × 27ft 7in *201.8m × 22.1m × 8.4m*
Machinery:	2-shaft VTE, 14 boilers, 16,000ihp = 16.9kts
Armament:	4–15cm (5.9in) SKL/40, 4–8.8cm (3.45in) SKL/45
Complement:	?

Vineta was the former *Cap Polonio*, a passenger liner of the Hamburg Suedamerikanische Dampfschiffahrts-Gesellschaft, built by Blohm & Voss, Hamburg and launched in March 1914. The ship was not commissioned at the outbreak of the war and was to have replaced the *Berlin*, which was now interned in Norway. She had for the first time on a German merchant vessel water-tube boilers with forced draught. To produce enough steam to obtain the desired 18kts or 19kts best British coal would have been necessary, which was of course impossible during wartime. Trials showed that she could make only 16.9kts and was therefore an inferior opponent to the fast British turbine-powered AMCs. During the war she was laid up in Hamburg, then came as a war reparation to Great Britain, was resold to her old owners in 1921, served under her original name *Cap Polonio* on South Atlantic route and was scrapped in 1936.

METEOR *auxiliary minelayer*

Displacement: 3640t; 1912grt
Dimensions: 293ft 4in × 37ft 1in × 16ft 9in
89.1m × 11.3m × 5.1m
Machinery: 1-shaft VTE, 2 boilers, 2400ihp = 14kts
Armament: 2–8.8cm (3.45in) SKL/40, 2–37mm, 347 mines (1–15cm, 2–45cm TT added for second sortie)
Complement: ?

Meteor was the former British merchant vessel *Vienna*, built in 1903 and seized at Hamburg when war broke out. Because of her unsuspicious silhouette and the reduced belief in the efficacy of commerce warfare during this period, she served as a disguised minelayer off British North Sea harbours and never captured any merchant vessel. During her second sortie, on 9 August 1915, she was intercepted by British cruisers and scuttled herself, while the crew returned to Germany on board a Swedish fishing boat.

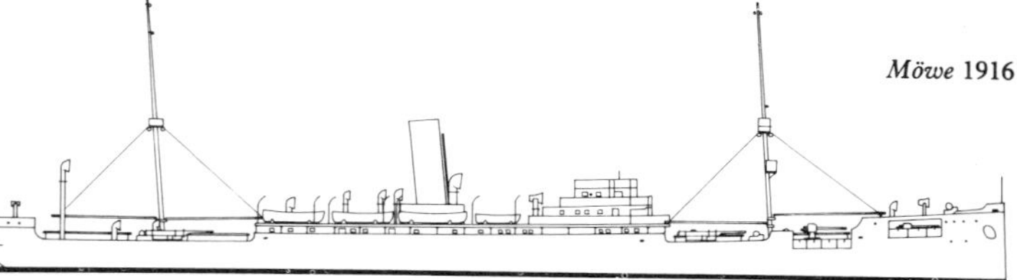
Möwe 1916

MÖWE *commerce raider*

Displacement: 9800t; 4788grt
Dimensions: 405ft 10in × 47ft 3in × 23ft 7in
123.7m × 14.4m × 7.2m
Machinery: 1-shaft VTE, 5 boilers, 3200ihp = 13.3kts
Armament: 4–15cm (5.9in) SKL/45, 1–10.5cm (4.1in) SKL/45, 2–50cm (19.7in) TT
Complement: 234

Möwe was the former banana carrier *Pungo* of the Laeisz Line, built by J C Tecklenborg AG, Wesermünde and launched in 1914. The brand new ship was to become the most successful German raider of the First World War, a role for which she was commissioned on 1 November 1915. She made two sorties, in the first achieving 15 ships sunk (totalling 57,520grt), and in the second 25 ships of 125,265grt. Between these two sorties she saw service as the commerce raider *Vineta* (not to be confused with the ex-*Cap Polonio*) in the Baltic, capturing one ship of 3326grt. After her lucky return she served as the auxiliary mining vessel *Ostsee*, became a British war reparation and served under the name *Greenbeer*. In 1933 she was sold to Germany and renamed *Oldenburg*, on 7 April 1945 she was torpedoed by a British submarine off Norway, beached and BU 1953.

WOLF (i) *commerce raider*

Displacement: 12,900t; 6648grt
Dimensions: 462ft 11in × 53ft 2in × 25ft 7in
141.1m × 16.2m × 7.8m
Machinery: 1-shaft VTE, 4 boilers, 3300ihp = 13kts
Armament: 4–15cm (5.9in) SKL/40, 2–37mm, 2–50cm (19.7in) TT
Complement: 361

Wolf (i) was the former British merchant vessel *Belgravia*, built in 1906 at Workington and seized after the outbreak of war at Hamburg. The ship was commissioned as a raider on 14 January 1916 but ran aground during her first sortie in the Elbe estuary (26 February 1916). She was so heavily damaged that she was decommissioned; she was ceded to France in 1919.

GREIF *commerce raider*

Displacement: 9900t; 4962grt
Dimensions: 432ft × 53ft 10in × 24ft 8in
131.7m × 16.4m × 7.5m
Machinery: 1-shaft VTE, 2 boilers, 3000ihp = 13kts
Armament: 4–15cm (5.9in) SKL/40, 1–10.5cm (4.1in) SKL/40, 2–50cm (19.7in) TT
Complement: 307

Greif was the former mercantile *Guben*, built in 1914 at Neptun, Rostock. She was commissioned on 23 January 1916 but was intercepted during her sortie in the North Sea on 29 February 1916 by the British AMC *Alcantara*. She sank the AMC, but the *Alcantara* had called to her support the AMC *Andes*, the protected cruiser *Comus* and two destroyers, which sank the *Greif*.

WOLF (ii) *commerce raider*

Displacement: 11,200t; 5809grt
Dimensions: 442ft 11in × 56ft 1in × 25ft 11in
135.0m × 17.1m × 7.9m
Machinery: 1-shaft VTE, 3 boilers, 2800ihp = 10.5kts
Armament: 7–15cm (5.9in) SKL/40, 4–50cm (19.7in) TT, 465 mines, 1 seaplane
Complement: 347

Wolf (ii) was the former merchant ship *Wachtfels*, built in 1913 at the Flensburger Schiffbau-Gesellschaft and commissioned in her new role on 16 May 1916. Following German commerce warfare policy she had first to lay her mines before being allowed to start active raiding. As a novelty in raider warfare she was the first such German ship to have a spotting seaplane on board (a Friedrichshafen E 33); she also carried 3–52mm to arm auxiliaries. She laid her first 25 mines off Cape Town on 16 January 1917, and the rest off Colombo. During her active raiding career she captured 14 ships totalling 38,391grt, including the prize *Turritella*, which was temporarily commissioned as the raider *Iltis* to mine Aden. She managed to return unhindered to Gemany, served in the Baltic and was turned over to France in 1919. Renamed *Antinous* she served until 1931 when she was scrapped.

Seeadler 1916 — *Aldo Fraccaroli Collection*

SEEADLER *commerce raider*

Displacement: 4500t; 1571grt
Dimensions: 273ft 11in (excluding bowsprit) × 38ft 9in × 18ft
83.5m × 11.8m × 5.5m
Machinery: 1 auxiliary diesel, 900bhp = 9kts. 27,987sq ft *(2600m²)* sail area
Armament: 2–10.5cm (4.1in) SKL/45
Complement: 64

The *Seeadler*, the only commerce raiding sailing ship of either world war, was the former *Pass of Balmaha*, built in 1878 by R Duncan & Co. She was sold out of British registry to a US owner after the outbreak of the war, and while sailing from Murmansk with a cargo of cotton she was stopped by a British cruiser in the North Sea in 1915 and sent to England with a prize crew on board for further investigation. En route she was stopped on 24 July 1915 by the German submarine *U 36* and sent as a prize to Cuxhaven with the British prize crew still hidden on board. The idea of using a full-rigger as a commerce raider was not, as is commonly supposed, the idea of her publicity-minded skipper, Count Felix von Luckner, but of a junior officer, Alfred Kling. He convinced the German Admiralty to try the ruse, which turned out very successfully. The *Seeadler* duped 16 vessels (totalling 30,099grt) into surrendering before being wrecked through negligence on Mopelia Island in the Societies on 2 August 1917. The place is still on the list of the world's treasure hunters, because Count Luckner said that he had buried the ship's cash-box with its valuable content of gold coins in the sand, and it was never recovered.

GEIER *commerce raider*

Displacement: 9700t; 4992grt
Dimensions: 417ft 4in × 51ft 10in × 21ft
127.2m × 15.8m × 6.4m
Machinery: 1-shaft VTE, 2 boilers, 1800ihp = 12.6kts
Armament: 2–52mm (from *Möwe*)
Complement: 48

Geier was the former British merchant vessel *Saint Theodore*, built in 1913, and captured by the commerce raider *Möwe* on 12 December 1916. She was armed by the *Möwe* and commissioned in her new role on 14 January 1917. She sank two sailing ships totalling 1442grt. On 14 February 1917 she was scuttled by the *Möwe* because of her worn out machinery.

LEOPARD *commerce raider*

Displacement:	9800t; 4652grt
Dimensions:	409ft 1in × 42ft × 24ft 3in *124.7m × 15.8m × 7.4m*
Machinery:	1-shaft VTE, 2400ihp = 13kts
Armament:	5–15cm (5.9in) SKL/40, 4–8.8cm (3.45in) SKL/40, 2–50cm (19.7in) TT
Complement:	319

Leopard was the former British merchant vessel *Yarrowdale*, built in 1912 and captured by the commerce raider *Möwe* on 11 December 1916. She was sent to Germany, equipped as a raider and commissioned in her new role on 9 January 1917. She was sunk during her breakout into the Atlantic, on 16 March 1917, near the Faeroes, after being intercepted by the light cruiser *Dundee* and the armoured cruiser *Achilles*.

ILTIS *commerce raider*

Displacement:	1070t; 5528grt
Dimensions:	443ft 6in × 55ft 6in × 20ft *135.2m × 16.9m × 6.1m*
Machinery:	1-shaft VQE, 2600ihp = 11kts
Armament:	1–52mm, 25 mines (from *Wolf*)
Complement:	74

Iltis was the former British merchant ship *Turritella*, built in 1905 and captured by the German commerce raider *Wolf* on 27 January 1917. The *Turritella* was the former German *Gutenfels*, seized by the British at Alexandria when war broke out. As a ship of the '-fels' type she was a sister-ship of the *Wolf* (ex-*Wachtfels*). She was quickly armed and received some mines and was to be used as a disguised minelayer. She laid her mines in the entrance to the Gulf of Aden and scuttled herself to avoid being captured by the British cruiser HMS *Fox* on 15 March 1917.

SMALL SURFACE WARSHIPS

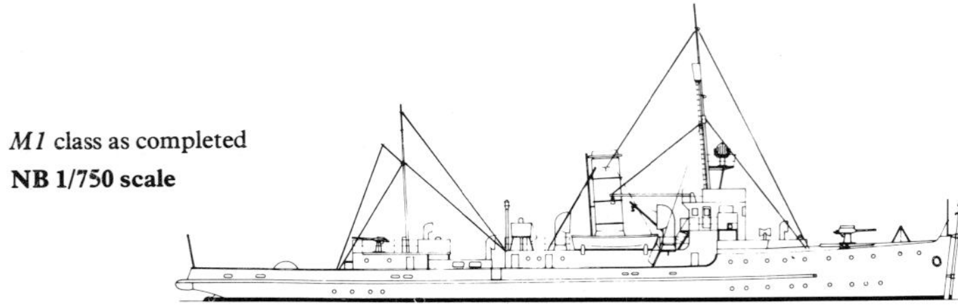

M1 class as completed
NB 1/750 scale

M 1 class *minesweepers* (launched 1915)

Displacement:	425t design; 456t (deep load (*M 7–M 26* 450t; 476t)
Dimensions:	175ft 6in wl, 180ft 9in oa (*M 7–M 26* 179ft 9in, 185ft) × 23ft 11in × 6ft 7in *53.5m, 55.1m (54.8m, 56.4m) × 7.3m × 2.0m*
Machinery:	2-shaft VTE, 2 Navy boilers, 1400ihp = 16.3kts (*M 7–M 26* (1600ihp = 16.2kts)
Armament:	1–8.8cm (3.45in) KL/30, 1–37mm, (later 2–8.8cm KL/30, 30 mines)
Complement:	40

Class:
Seebeck, Geestemünde – *M 1–M 6, M15–M17*
Neptun, Rostock – *M 7–M 12, M 18–M 20*
Nordseewerke, Emden – *M 13, M 14*
Frerichs, Einswarden – *M 21, M 22*
Tecklenborg, Geestemünde – *M 23–M 26*

These Type 1914 fleet minesweepers were seaworthy boats which could make 13kts with sweeping gear deployed. A significant feature of the type was the slight whaleback forecastle. Of the 26 commissioned boats of this group *M 6, M 9, M 11, M 12, M 14, M 15, M 22–M 24* and *M 26* were mined in the North Sea, *M 16* was sunk by a British submarine, and all the others were sold for scrapping in the early 1920s.

M 27 class *minesweepers* (launched 1916)

Displacement:	480t design; 507t deep load (*M 45–M 56* 486t; 513t)
Dimensions:	184ft wl, 191ft 7in oa (*M 45–M 56* 183ft 9in, 191ft 3in) × 23ft 11in × 7ft 4in *56.1m, 58.4m (56.0m, 58.3m) × 7.3m × 2.3m*
Machinery:	2-shaft VTE, 2 Navy boilers, 1800ihp = 16.5kts
Armament:	2–10.5cm (4.1in) KL/45 (*M 43–M 56* 3–8.8cm KL/45), 30 mines
Complement:	40

Class:
Neptun, Rostock – *M 27–M 30, M 45–M 49*
Seebeck, Geestemünde – *M 31–M 34, M 50–M53*
Tecklenborg, Geestemünde – *M 35–M 38*
Vulcan, Bremen – *M 39–M 42, M 54–M 56*
Atlaswerke, Bremen – *M 43, M 44*

Of the 30 commissioned boats of this 1915 Type *M 31, M 36, M 39–M 41, M 47, M 49* and *M 56* were mined, *M 55* was wrecked, and *M 27* was sunk in a collision. *M 28* served with the *Reichsmarine*, was renumbered *M 528* and later named *Pelikan*; *M 50* served with the *Reichsmarine* as R-boat tender *Brommy* (later *M 550*). *M 48, M 51–M 53* were sold to Argentina, serving as *M 1–M 4*, twice renamed and stricken in 1937. *M 42* was converted to a merchant ship, sold to France, but seized by the *Kriegsmarine* in 1944 and converted to the mining vessel *Nymphe*. All the others were sold for scrapping in 1921–22.

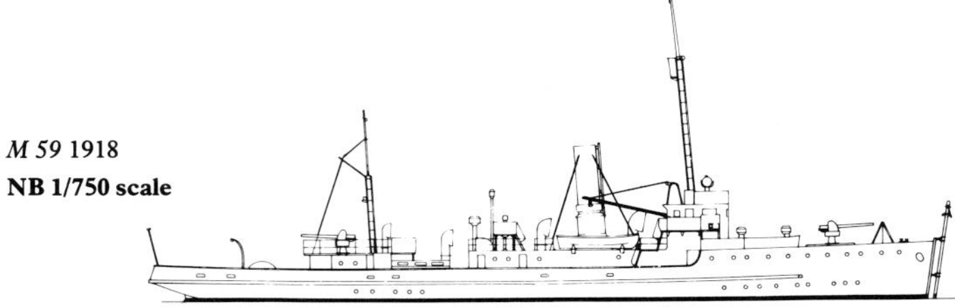

M 59 1918
NB 1/750 scale

M 57 class *minesweepers* (launched 1917–19)

Displacement:	500t design; 539t deep load (*M 71–M 96* 515t; 553t; *M 97–M 176* 525t; 564t)
Dimensions:	183ft 9in wl, 193ft 7in oa × 24ft 3in × 7ft 1in–7ft 6in *56.0m, 59.3m × 7.4m × 2.2m–2.3m*
Machinery:	2-shaft VTE, 2 Navy boilers, 1850ihp = 16kts
Armament:	2–10.5cm (4.1in) SKL/45 (*M 67–M 74, M 85–M 96* 2–8.8cm SKL/45, *M 75–M 84* 3–8.8cm SKL/45), 30 mines
Complement:	40

M 39 as completed — *Navarret Collection*

Seebeck, Geestemünde – *M 57–M 62, M 79–M 82, M 123, M 124;* Tecklenborg, Geestemünde – *M 63–M 66, M 75–M 78, M 87–M 90, M 97–M 100, M 107–M 112, M 137–M 140, M 163–M 166;* Neptun, Rostock – *M 67–M 70, M 91–M 94, M 103, M 104, M 119–M 122, M 144, M 145;* Vulcan, Bremen – *M 71–M 74;* Atlaswerke, Bremen – *M 83, M 84, M 95, M 96, M 101, M 102, M 115–M 118;* Nordseewerke, Emden – *M 85, M 86, M 157, M 158;* Reiherstieg, Hamburg – *M 105, M 106, M 129–M 132, M 161, M 162;* Stülcken, Hamburg – *M 113, M 114, M 141–M 143;* Flensburg – *M 125, M 126, M 146–M 149;* Union, Königsberg – *M 127, M 128, M 159, M 160;* Frerichs, Einswarden – *M 133–M 136, M 153–M 156, M 167, M 168;* Hansawerft, Tonning – *M 150–M 152;* Unterwesen, Lehe – *M169, M 170;* Koch, Lübeck – *M 171, M 172;* Janssen & Schmilinsky, Hamburg – *M 173, M 174;* Nüscke, Stettin – M 175, M 176.

Slightly increased in displacement and dimensions the Type 1916 design was later to become the basis for the German *Kriegsmarine*'s minesweepers of the Type 1935. The orders for *M 159, M 160* and *M 163–M 176* were cancelled; *M 127, M 128, M 141–M 143, M 148, M 149, M 153–M 156* and *M 161, M 162* were unfinished at the end of war and not commissioned. Of the commissioned units *M 62–M 64, M 67, M 83, M 91, M 92* and *M 95* were mined during the war. The surviving boats were taken over by the *Reichsmarine*, converted to merchant ships or sold abroad as follows:

Taken over by the *Reichsmarine: M 60, M 61, M 66, M 72, M 75, M 81, M 82, M 84, M 85, M 89, M 96, M 98, M 102, M 104, M 107–M 111, M 113, M 115, M 117, M 122, M 126, M 129, M 130, M 132–M 136, M 138, M 145, M 146* and *M 157*. Initially they received names and served as auxiliaries, but the surviving boats were redesignated as minesweepers in 1940 adding the prefix '5' to their former numbers. Their later fates are given in the 1922–1946 volume. Sold to Argentina: *M 74, M 79, M 80, M 90, M 101* and *M 105*, serving as *M 5–M 10*, being twice renamed, and stricken in 1937. *M 139* and *M 140* were sold to Colombia as guard vessels, becoming *Bogota* and *Cordova* respectively. *M 59* became the Lithuanian presidential yacht, and *M 68* the Latvian *Virsatis*. *M 97, M 100, M 106, M 112, M 114* and *M 121* were sold to Yugoslavia as minelayers, being renamed *Orao, Galeb, Gavran, Jastreb, Sokol* and *Kobac* respectively. Sold to Italy as minesweepers: *M 119* became *Meteo* and *M 120 Abastro*. The remainder were sold or BU in 1921–22.

FM 28 1918
NB 1/750 scale

FM type *coastal minesweepers* (launched 1918–19)

Displacement: 170t design; 193t deep load (2nd group 185t; 205t)
Dimensions: 137ft 2in wl, 141ft oa (2nd group 145ft, 149ft 3in) × 19ft 8in × 4ft 7in
41.8m, 43.0m (44.2m, 45.5m) × 6.0m × 1.4m
Machinery: 2-shaft VTE, 1 Navy boiler, 600ihp = 14kts (2nd group 750ihp = 14.3kts)
Armament: 1–8.8cm (3.45in) KL/30
Complement: 35

Class:
1st group – *FM 1–FM 36*
2nd group – *FM 37–FM 66*

These small steel-hulled coastal minesweepers (the abbreviation is of *Flachgehende Minensucher*, meaning 'shallow draught minesweepers') were more or less scaled down and austere versions of the ocean-going sweepers of the official Type 1916 design. Because of their intended role they could only operate in open waters to sea state 5 and had inferior manoeuvrability compared with the larger types. Most of the survivors were sold after the war and converted to riverine vessels. Four were sold to Poland, *FM 2* becoming the *Jaskolka*, *FM 27* becoming the *Czaika*, *FM 28* the *Rybita* and *FM 31* the *Mewa*; all were condemned about 1935. *FM 16* became the Albanian gunboat *Sqipnia*, and *FM 23* the *Sqenderbeg*; both were probably condemned about 1935. *FM 19* became the Portuguese fishery protection vessel *Raoul Cascaes* and was condemned in 1936. *FM 24* became the Persian gunboat *Fatiya*, was renamed *Pahlavi* and then *Shanin*, and was scrapped in 1941.

F type *coastal minesweepers* (launched 1915–18)

Displacement: 18t design; 20t–21t deep load
Dimensions: 54ft 2in–57ft 5in × 13ft 2in × 3ft 5in
16.5m–17.5m × 4.0m × 1.1m
Machinery: 2 shafts, 2 petrol engines 120bhp–130bhp = 10kts/11kts
Armament: 1 MG
Complement: 7

Class:
F 1–F 75

These small wooden-hulled minesweepers were used for harbour duties or aboard the especially converted depot ships, the ex-pre-dreadnoughts *Wittelbach, Schwaben, Preussen* and *Lothringen*. One was lost by mine explosion; all others were sold after the war and served in various harbour and riverine duties, most of them as river police launches. *F 16, F 17, F 18, F 20, F 30, F 33, F 35, F 36, F 40, F 48, F 56* and *F 57* became the Belgian *V 1–V 12*.

MOTOR TORPEDO BOATS

The reason for the Imperial German Navy developing fast motor boats was very different from the thinking behind the better known craft of Great Britain or Italy. In the summer of 1916 the German submarine and torpedo-boat base at Zeebrugge was blockaded by British net barrages, and the Navy asked for a fast, low profile net-cutter and a similar boat which could repel British destroyers while these nets were cut loose. Initial tests with adapted civil speedboats were unsatisfactory, so a completely original design was produced. A vital necessity for the success of these tiny vessels were powerful lightweight engines, and Germany was fortunate to be able to fall back on a stock of spare airship motors; but the lack of reversing gearboxes led to rather basic designs. They all had a crew of 7 or 8. The first six boats were ordered in January–February 1917 and were built in groups of two at three different yards to gain experience with the different methods used by the competing manufacturers. The first two groups did not have TT, but were equipped with net-cutters; however, all following boats had a bow tube. By the beginning of 1918 21 LM boats were in service, 7 in the Baltic and 14 in Belgium. The good results with these boats led to the development of a further three competitive types in conjunction with leading engine manufacturers; the plan was that initially one of each type should be worked up and tested, but at the end of the war none of them was ready. The survivors were sold from 1919 onwards, but some that were completed post-war (such as the *Lüsi I*) were repurchased in 1926 by the *Reichsmarine*. They served as an experimental squadron for the development of S-boats and were disguised as *U-boot Zerstörer, Schnellboote* (fast ASW boats) and sold about 1931–33. *Lüsi I*, for example, became UZ(S) 19 and was sold to Colombia as *C* in 1933.

LM 1 class *motor gunboats* (launched 1917)

Displacement: 6m³
Dimensions: 49ft 3in × 7ft 6in × 3ft 7in
15.0m × 2.3m × 1.1m
Machinery: 3 shafts, 3 Maybach petrol engines, 640bhp = 30kts. Petrol 1000 litres. Range 150nm at 30kts
Armament: 1–37mm QF

Class:
LM 1, LM 2

Designed for night operations working as net-cutters off Zeebrugge, they were built by the Lürssen yard. Both were destroyed by fire or explosion in 1918.

LM 6 on trials — *BfZ*

LM 3 class *motor gunboats* (launched 1917)

Displacement: 6m³
Dimensions: 47ft 10in × 7ft 10in × 3ft 7in
14.6m × 2.4m × 1.1m
Machinery: 3 shafts, 3 Maybach petrol engines, 630bhp = 27.8kts. Petrol 1195 litres. Range 180nm at 27.8kts
Armament: 1–37mm QF

Class:
LM 3, LM 4

Competitive design to *LM 1*, to the same specifications, but built by the Naglo yard. Sold in May 1919.

LM 5 class *motor torpedo-boats* (launched 1917)

Displacement: 6m³
Dimensions: 49ft 2in × 7ft 10in × 3ft 7in
15.0m × 2.4m × 1.1m
Machinery: 3 shafts, 3 Maybach petrol engines, 630bhp = 29.5kts. Petrol 1500litres. Range 225nm at 29.5kts
Armament: 1 MG, 1–45cm (17.7in) TT aw (bow)

Class:
LM 5, LM 6

Competitive design to *LM 1* built by the Oertz yard, but first of this type with TT (to ward off destroyers guarding the net barrages). The torpedo was fired from a fixed TT built into the fore deck. Sold in May 1919.

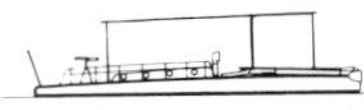

LM 7 class
NB 1/750 scale

LM 7 class *motor torpedo-boats* (launched 1918)

Displacement: 7m³
Dimensions: 52ft 6in × 7ft 10in × 2ft 3in
16.0m × 2.4m × 0.68m
Machinery: 3 shafts, 3 Maybach petrol engines, 720bhp = 31.8kts. Petrol 1500 litres. Range 210nm at 30kts
Armament: 1 MG, 1–45cm (17.7in) TT aw (bow)

Class:
LM 7–LM 10

Built by Lürssen after experience with the three foregoing competitive types. They were ordered in May–June 1917 and were intended for the Baltic. *LM 10* was sold in March 1921, and the others were wrecked on the night of 6/7 November 1921 and the wrecks BU.

LM 11 class *motor torpedo-boats* (launched 1918)

Displacement: 6.5m³
Dimensions: 53ft 4in × 8ft 4in × 2ft 6in
16.3m × 2.6m × 0.76m
Machinery: As *LM 7* class, but 30kts
Armament: 1 MG, 1–45cm (17.7in) TT aw (bow)

Class:
LM 11–LM 13

The alternative type to the new Lürssen *LM 7* design, but built by Naglo; ordered at the same time and also intended for the Baltic. Sold in May 1919.

LM 14 class *motor torpedo-boats* (launched 1918)

Displacement: 6.8m³
Dimensions: 54ft 2in × 7ft 10in × 2ft
16.5m × 2.4m × 0.61m
Machinery: As *LM 7* class, but 31.6kts
Armament: 1 MG, 1–45cm (17.7in) TT aw (bow)

Class:
LM 14–LM 16

In contrast to all earlier LM boats, these were displacement boats (as opposed to planing boats) and could be used up to sea state 3; all later boats similarly adopted a round bilge hull. This group was built by Oertz, and ordered at the same time and for the same purpose as the *LM 7* class. The first two were sold in 1921 and 1919 respectively, but after being sold in 1921, *LM 16* was repurchased by the *Reichsmarine* in 1926 and ordered as the *UZ(S) 20* until sold to Colombia, as motorboat *D* in 1933; BU 1946.

LM 17 class *motor torpedo-boats* launched 1918)

Displacement: 7.3m³
Dimensions: 55ft 9in × 7ft 10in × 1ft 11in
17.0m × 2.4m × 0.6m
Machinery: As *LM 7* class, but 30.8kts
Armament: 1 MG, 1–45cm (17.7in) TT aw (bow)

Class:
LM 17–LM 20

Very similar to the *LM 14* group but built by Roland. This group was ordered at the same time as the *LM 7* class, but *LM 20* was ordered in August and October 1917 (they carried only 1–2cm gun). All sold in 1919, but *LM 20* was repurchased in 1926 and served as the *UZ(S) 13* until sold in 1932.

UNFINISHED MOTOR TORPEDO-BOATS

LM 21–LM 26 were improved versions of the *LM 7* class, the first seeing some Baltic service, but, *LM 22, LM 23* were not completed until 1919 and all were then sold about 1922 (*LM 24–LM 26* were never completed). All were repurchased in 1926, renumbered *UZ(S)21*, *UZ(S)14* and *UZ(S)15*, and served until sold in 1922–23 (*UZ(S)15* became the Colombian *A* and was not BU until 1946).

Of the remaining boats *LM 7–LM 30* were repeats of the *LM 14* class, and *LM 31–LM 33* of the *LM 17* type. Only the first two were completed (too late to see service); were sold in 1922, repurchased in 1926 and served as *UZ(S)16* (sold 1921) and *UZ(S)17* (to Colombia as *B* 1933; BU 1946).

Three more competitive designs were on the slips unfinished, which were each a joint project of one yard with one engine supplier and which were named from the abbreviations of both:

Lüsi 1, Lüsi 2 (Lürssen and Siemens) 10.4m³, 64ft 4in × 9ft 6in × 2ft 8in (*19.6m × 2.9m × 0.82m*), 1200bhp = 32kts, 2–2cm QF, 2–50cm (19.7in) TT
Köro 1, Köro 2 (Körting and Roland) 16m³, 62ft 4in × 9ft 10in × 2ft 7in (*19.0m × 3.0m × 0.79m*), 1350bhp = 31kts, 2–2cm QF, 2–50cm (19.7in) TT
Juno 1–Juno 4 (Junkers and Oertz), 9.3m³, 62ft 4in × 7ft 10in × 2ft 4in (*19.0m × 2.4m × 0.72m*), 1350bhp = 34kts, 2–2cm QF, 2–50cm (19.7in) TT

LM 14, LM 17, LM 15, one unidentified boat and *LM 13* post-war
BfZ

UZ 2
BfZ

An FL type boat
BfZ

Otter 1910
NB 1/750 scale

OTHER COASTAL CRAFT

The German Navy also operated the UZ series of motor anti-submarine boats. These fell into two broad groups: *UZ 1A–UZ 12A*, built 1916–17, were of about 27t and capable of 10kts–17kts; *UZ 1–UZ 22* were larger (40t–44t) and capable of 14kts–15kts. The *FL 1–FL 17* series of 6t motor launches were built in 1915–16; they had 420bhp engines giving a speed of 30kts and were used principally as 'controlled torpedoes', having a charge of 300lb–500lb of explosives in the bow, and being remotely controlled via an umbilical cable.

MISCELLANEOUS

The river gunboat *Otter* of 314t was built by Tecklenborg and launched 15.7.09. She was armed with 2–5.2cm SKL/55 and 3 MG, and her 2-shaft VTE engines of 1300ihp gave a speed of 15.2kts. She was stationed on the Yangtse and interned in China on the outbreak of war, and was later taken over by the Chinese as the *Li Tsieh*; she was BU in 1924.

The Emperor's yacht *Hohenzollern* (iii) was under construction at Vulcan's Stettin yard and was launched shortly after war broke out. The hull was laid up for the duration and when post-war plans to turn her into an exhibition ship collapsed she was sold for BU in 1923.

France

In 1906 France found herself with a navy which consisted of a heterogeneous collection of warships built – in the case of battleships – as prototypes: some damningly called the French Navy 'a navy of prototypes'. It is an established fact however that up to 1909 the Navy faced a period of steady decline in strength and quality and having ranked in 1871 as second in the world shrank to fourth rank among the sea powers. There was no defined naval policy due to frequent changes of Ministers of Marine. Every one of them pursued his own ideas as to how to beat Great Britain at sea – at that time considered France's main enemy. As British industry was stronger, the French tried to build up a navy of small but very numerous coastal combatants such as torpedo-boats and submarines. Thus the big armoured cruisers were intended to act as commerce raiders to destroy British shipping.

Between 1898 and 1909 several politicians of the Charles Pelletan type (considered by some as 'naufrageur de la Marine' or 'Wrecker of the Navy') quite effectively destroyed France as a great sea power. Their chief aim on arriving in office was probably to undo their predecessors's work. They failed to see that France with her extensive coastline and worldwide colonial empire needed a strong navy as an integral part of her armed forces. Instead of building many weak armoured cruisers and small craft it would have been better to launch a few homogeneous classes of seagoing battleships supported by some cruisers and destroyers. French politicians simply had not realised the dangers stemming from the steady growth of German, Italian and Austrian navies. In his report upon the Navy Estimates of 1911 Paul Bénazet adduced the striking fact that, while within 15 years Germany expended £100 million on her fleet and France £152 million, the German Fleet rose to second place among the world's navies and that of France sank to the fourth. He attributed this failure to negligence, neglect and careless maintenance routine.

At the beginning of the First World War the French Navy was able to contain with difficulty the Italian and Austrian navies in the Mediterranean leaving the North Sea and Atlantic to the Royal Navy. Such a solution was possible because of agreements reached between the two countries early in the twentieth century (Entente Cordiale agreement of 1904). There was however much ill feeling in the northern *départements* of France about this where the people living here formed most of the crews and still considered Britain as a threat to their security. When the naval authorities decided to concentrate the French Fleet in the Mediterranean from 1912 there were strong protests.

During the period many new ships were commissioned including 6 *Danton* class semi-dreadnoughts (1906 programme) and 3 big armoured cruisers. The *Danton*s, however, were slow and armed with a mixed battery at a time when other countries had already completed dreadnought-type battleships that were faster, better armoured and armed with a uniform big gun battery. The last French armoured cruisers were a hollow design triumph for, despite their imposing appearance, these ships were relatively weak and were no match for foreign battlecruisers building at that time. As it turned out the French Navy sorely felt the lack of battlecruisers in the Mediterranean (witness the *Goeben* affair in 1914).

From 1909 on Admiral Boué de Lapeyrère who became Minister of Marine took the necessary steps to remedy the sad position of the French Navy. Under his leadership a new Naval Programme was introduced in 1912 and included 28 battleships, 10 scout cruisers, 52 destroyers, 94 submarines and 10 vessels for distant stations all of which were to be completed by 1920. In 1914 the naval staff proposed an addition to the programme that was to include 8 so-called cruiser-battleship *grand eclaireurs d'escadre* designed for a speed of 25 knots inspired by British battleships of the *Queen Elizabeth* class. French Naval Estimates rose steadily from 333 million francs in 1909 to 415 million in 1911, 457 million in 1912 and 567 million in 1913. It was planned to spend over 600 million in 1914.

NAVAL ESTIMATES 1905–14

French Naval Estimates (converted to £s*)

Year	Total expenditure	New construction	% of total budget for armed forces
1905	12,667,856	4,705,295	
1906	12,245,740	4,652,010	26.2
1907	12,486,793	4,138,967	
1908	12,797,308	4,193,544	
1909	13,353,825	4,517,766	
1910	15,023,019	4,977,682	
1911	17,370,960	5,876,659	
1912	18,090,758	6,997,582	
1913	20,847,763	8,893,064	34.7
1914	19,818,052	10,730,520	

*Taken from *Brassey's Naval Annual*, 1914, by Viscount Hythe.

France put considerable effort into submarine development before 1914: *Ventôse* seen here exhibits many features of the early boats, including the external torpedo drop-collars

It is worth noting that while only 6 *Danton* class battleships were approved in the period 1900–9, between 1910 and 1914 16 dreadnoughts were authorised which included seven ships of 23,500t (*Courbets* and *Provences*), 5 of 25,300t (*Normandies*), 4 of 29,500t (*Lyons*). Twelve of them were to be armed with 340mm (13.5in) guns. Battleships were intended to serve in four-ship divisions, hence one *Normandie* class ship was to be attached to three *Provence* class ships to form one division.

The main task of the Navy in event of war in the Mediterranean was to provide escort for troop transports from Algeria to the French mainland. Admiral de Lapeyrère was given command of *I Armée Navale* and proved a competent leader as well as a good administrator. During the years 1912–14 this 'striking force' was well trained and acquired in manoeuvring, tactics, gunnery and torpedo exercises, a proficiency never previously attained; morale also was very good. This was a marked achievement taking into account the Navy's relatively low prestige compared with the Army, a point illustrated by France's Naval League established in 1899 having 28,000 members in 1914.

THE FIRST WORLD WAR

In August 1914 the Navy possessed 690,000 tons of commissioned vessels which included 26 battleships, 19 armoured cruisers, 10 protected cruisers, 85 destroyers, about 100 sea-going and coastal torpedo-boats and 79 submarines. Over 257,000 tonnes of warships were building or on order. Of the above mentioned heavy ships only 19 battleships and 18 armoured cruisers were commissioned together with 34 submarines. All the other vessels were in reserve. Old ships predominated; half of the battleships, cruisers or submarines were elderly or worn out (some of them being old enough to be considered museum pieces). Torpedo-boats were of little fighting value and destroyers were mostly of the 300-tonne type – too small for really effective escort work. During 1914–18 all work on new ships was stopped. Ships scheduled to be laid down in this period were never begun. As the greater part of the French shipbuilding industry was situated in the Eastern and Northern parts of the country, shortly to be occupied by Germans, normal execution of building plans was impossible. Another difficulty stemmed from the Army draft system – many skilled workers were called up into the Army and a depleted shipyard work force was unable to continue work effectively. During the war naval establishments such as Guérigny, Indret and Ruelle were partly converted to work for the Army producing 8500 guns, ammunition and other war equipment.

Under such conditions shipyards were barely able to do repair work and it was not until 1916 that they started to build new ships and only sloops, small gunboats or minesweepers at that. Existing ships were successively modernised and rearmed as the war progressed and were fitted with AA or ASW armament. Older ships were relegated to harbour duty to concentrate seamen in effective units. The Navy also received some foreign-built ships, namely British 'Flower' class sloops, Japanese *Kaba* class destroyers or armed trawlers and patrol boats. In 1914 four large destroyers building in French yards for Argentina were requisitioned as were Greek, Japanese and Rumanian submarines.

French 1914–18 naval operations are generally not well remembered. The battlefleet blockaded the Austrian Navy in the Adriatic and was joined later by the Italian Navy. A major squadron took part in the Dardanelles/Gallipoli campaign. Other ships helped to defend the Suez Canal and blockaded the Syrian coast. The French Navy evacuated 270,000 Serbian troops and 86,000 horses from Albania to Corfu, then to Bizerta and on to Salonika. French warships were the major Allied force in the delicate negotiations with Greece. France's contribution to the Allied ASW effort on 1 November 1918 stood at 111 torpedo-boats, 35 submarines, 63 sloops and gunboats, 153 submarine chasers and 734 armed trawlers. The naval air service comprised 37 airships, 1264 aircraft and over 11,000 men having started with 8 seaplanes in August 1914. U-boats sank 500 French merchant ships totalling 891,000grt. French sailors served as infantry and gunners (*Fusiliers Marins* and *Cannoniers Marins*) on the Western Front, in Serbia and at the Dardanelles.

During the war the French Navy lost the following in action: 4 battleships, 5 cruisers, 23 destroyers and torpedo-boats, 14 submarines, 7 auxiliary cruisers, 49 sloops and patrol vessels and 26 requisitioned transports directly attached to the Fleet. In November 1918 France was left with only 130,000 tons of uncompleted ships still in her shipyards. It was hoped to receive many surrendered German and Austrian ships in 1919 but in the event France was compelled to compete against her Allies for such vessels. Finally 5 light cruisers, 10 destroyers and 10 submarines of Central Powers origin were commissioned.

AFTERMATH

After the First World War there were lengthy discussions in France about the future of her navy. Some argued for the completion of *Normandie* class battleships in a modified form while others suggested building a large fleet of 250–300 submarines and creating a powerful naval air force. However, nothing was done before the Washington Conference limiting naval arms. Early in 1920 it was proposed to build 6 light 5200-ton cruisers capable of over 30 knots and armed with eight 138mm (5.4in) guns and 12 1800-ton destroyers with a speed of 36 knots and armed with 100mm (3.9in) guns. In the end none of these ships were ever authorised although the plan was intended to remedy France's severe shortage of such vessels. Finally the Washington Treaty signed by Great Britain, USA, Japan, France and Italy on 6 February 1922 put an end to the unproductive discussions. France was allotted (as was Italy) 175,000 tons of battleships and 60,000 tons of aircraft carriers. In 1922 a programme was introduced that envisaged series building of light cruisers, destroyers, submarines and eventually heavy cruisers.

FLEET STRENGTH 1906

BATTLESHIPS

Name	Launched	Disp (metric full-load)	Fate
Couronne class			
COURONNE	28.3.61	5983t	Hulked 1910, BU
Redoutable class			
REDOUTABLE	18.9.76	9224t	Stricken 1910, BU
Courbet class			
DÉVASTATION	4.79	10,450t	BU 1922
COURBET	27.4.82	10,450t	Stricken 1910
Amiral Duperré class			
AMIRAL DUPERRÉ	11.9.79	11,030t	Stricken 1909, BU
Terrible class			
TERRIBLE	1881	7530t	Stricken 1911, BU
INDOMPTABLE	18.9.83	7530t	BU 1927
CAÏMAN	21.5.85	7530t	BU 1927
REQUIN	12.6.85	7530t	Stricken 1920, BU
Amiral Baudin class			
AMIRAL BAUDIN	5.6.83	c12,150t	Hulked 1909
FORMIDABLE	16.4.85	c12,150t	Stricken 1911, BU
Hoche class			
HOCHE	29.9.86	c11,050t	Target 25.11.13
Marceau class			
MARCEAU	24.5.87	10,581t	BU 1922
NEPTUNE	7.5.87	10,630t	Stricken 1912, BU
MAGENTA	19.4.90	10,600t	Stricken 1910, BU
Brennus class			
BRENNUS	17.10.91	11,190t	Stricken 1919, BU 1922
Charles Martel class			
CHARLES MARTEL	20.8.93	11,693t	Stricken 1922, BU

Name	Launched	Disp (normal load)	Fate
Carnot class			
CARNOT	12.7.94	11,986t	Stricken 1922, BU
Jauréguiberry class			
JAURÉGUIBERRY	27.10.93	11,824t	BU 1934
Masséna class			
MASSÉNA	24.7.95	11,735t	Hulked 1915
Bouvet class			
BOUVET	27.4.96	12,205t	Sunk 18.3.15
Charlemagne class			
CHARLEMAGNE	17.10.95	11,100t	Stricken 21.6.20, BU
GAULOIS	8.10.96	11,100t	Sunk 27.12.16
ST LOUIS	8.9.96	11,100t	BU 1933
Henri IV class			
HENRI IV	23.8.99	8948t	Stricken 1921, BU
Iéna class			
IÉNA	1.9.98	11,860t	Sunk 12.3.07
Suffren class			
SUFFREN	25.7.99	12,728t	Sunk 26.11.16
République class			
RÉPUBLIQUE	4.9.02	14,605t	Stricken 1921, BU
PATRIE	17.12.03	14,900t	Stricken 1928, BU
Liberté class			
DÉMOCRATIE	30.4.04	14,870t	Stricken 1921, BU
JUSTICE	27.10.04	14,860t	Stricken 1922, BU
LIBERTÉ	19.4.05	14,870t	Sunk 25.9.11
VERITÉ	28.5.07	14,489t	Stricken 1922, BU

Couronne served as gunnery school ship in the 1900s. Her iron hull seems to have lasted well and she remained afloat until 1932. *Jauréguiberry*, although in bad condition, served in the earlier part of the First World War, was stricken on 20.6.20 and condemned in 1932. The hull of *Masséna* was towed from Toulon to Cape Helles to form a breakwater for the January 1916 Gallipoli evacuation (scuttled 9.11.15). *Bouvet* was sunk in under 2 minutes by a Turkish mine with almost all her crew in the Dardanelles operation. *Gaulois* was torpedoed and sunk by the German *UB 47* about 80 miles from Milos Island in the Aegean (Cyclades). *Suffren* was torpedoed and sunk with all hands off Lisbon by the German *U 52* while en route, unescorted, to Brest for repairs. *Iéna* and *Liberté* sank due to internal explosions in Toulon harbour, caused by decomposing shell propellant.

COAST DEFENCE SHIPS

Name	Launched	Disp	Fate
Tonnere class			
FULMINANT	8.77	5871t	Stricken 1908, BU
Tempête class			
TEMPÊTE	8.76	4793t	Stricken 1907, BU
Furieux class			
FURIEUX	7.83	5683t	Stricken 1913, BU
Fusée class			
FUSÉE	7.5.84	1150t	Stricken 1910, BU
FLAMME	8.85	1046t	Stricken 1906, BU
MITRAILLE	3.7.86	1130t	Stricken 1910, BU
GRENADE	18.10.88	1046t	Stricken 1906, BU
Achéron class			
ACHÉRON	23.4.85	1690t	Stricken 1913, BU
COCYTE	13.1.87	1690t	Stricken 1911, BU
PHLÉGÉTON	20.12.90	1767t	Stricken 1910, BU
STYX	22.8.91	1767t	Stricken 1919, BU
Jemmapes class			
JEMMAPES	4.92	6476t	Hulked 1911, BU
VALMY	6.10.92	6476t	Stricken 1911, BU
Bouvines class			
BOUVINES	29.3.92	6681t	Stricken 1920, BU
AMIRAL TRÉHOUART	16.5.93	6681t	Stricken 1922, BU

ARMOURED CRUISERS

Name	Launched	Disp (normal load)	Fate
Dupuy de Lôme class			
DUPUY DE LÔME	27.10.90	6676t	Sold 1920, BU
Amiral Charner class			
AMIRAL CHARNER	18.3.93	4681t	Sunk 8.2.16
BRUIX	3.8.94	4681t	Stricken 1920, BU
CHANZY	24.1.94	4980t	Wrecked 30.5.07
LATOUCHE-TRÉVILLE	8.10.92	4990t	Stricken 21.6.20, BU 1926
Pothuau class			
POTHUAU	19.9.95	5600t	Stricken 3.11.27, BU 25.9.29
Jeanne d'Arc class			
JEANNE D'ARC	8.6.99	11,092t	Stricken 2.2.33, BU 1934
Gueydon class			
DUPETIT-THOUARS	5.7.01	9367t	Sunk 7.8.18
GUEYDON	20.9.99	9548t	Hulked 24.7.35, BU 1942
MONTCALM	27.3.00	9516t	Stricken 28.10.26, BU 1943
Dupleix class			
DESAIX	21.3.01	7604t	Stricken 30.6.21, BU 1927
DUPLEIX	28.4.00	7432t	Stricken 1919, BU 1922
KLÉBER	20.9.02	7730t	Sunk 27.6.17
Gloire class			
AMIRAL AUBE	9.5.02	9534t	Stricken 1922, BU
CONDÉ	12.3.02	10,233t	Stricken 1933, Target
GLOIRE	27.6.00	10,212t	Stricken 1922, BU
MARSEILLAISE	14.7.00	9458t	Stricken 1929, BU
Léon Gambetta class			
LÉON GAMBETTA	26.10.01	11,959t	Sunk 27.4.15
JULES FERRY	23.8.03	12,379t	Stricken 1927, BU
VICTOR HUGO	30.3.04	13,108t	Stricken 20.1.28, BU 26.11.30
Jules Michelet class			
JULES MICHELET	31.8.05	13,105t	Stricken 1931, Target
Ernest Renan class			
ERNEST RENAN	3.6.06	13,504t	Stricken 1931, Target
Edgar Quinet class			
EDGAR QUINET	21.9.07	13,847t	Sunk 9.1.30
WALDECK-ROUSSEAU	4.3.08	13,995t	Stricken 14.6.36, BU 1941–44

Dupuy de Lôme class
Sold to Peru in 1912 as *Commandant Elias Aguirre*, but not delivered and remained in France. In 1914 she was once more renamed *Dupuy de Lôme* but not used during the war because of her poor condition. Sold in 1910 to Belgium and converted into a cargo ship renamed *Peruvier*. Her original building cost was £415,000.

Amiral Charner class
Amiral Charner, after escorting 1914 troop convoys from Morocco to France, with *Desaix* and *Jeanne d'Arc* (see below) rescued 3000 Armenians from the Turks in Antioch Bay, September 1915, and on 28 December, with *Jeanne d'Arc*, occupied Castellorizo Island off the Turkish mainland. *Charner* was torpedoed off Beirut by *U 21* on 8 February 1916 and sank in 4 minutes leaving only 1 survivor. *Bruix* served with *Charner* until sent to the Red Sea in 1915. She then took part in the 1916–17 blockade of Greece and went into reserve at Salonika (1918). *Chanzy* grounded in fog on 20 May 1907 off the Chusan Islands (S of Shanghai). Attempts to refloat her failed and she was lost on 30 May. *Latouche-Tréville*, damaged by Turkish gunfire at Gallipoli, was disarmed on 1 May 1919, and after being stricken in September 1920 was sold to the firm engaged in salvage operations on the blown-up battleship *Liberté* in Toulon. Her hull was used as a caisson. Hulked in 1925, BU 1926. Each ship originally cost 9.2–9.7 million francs (over £353,000).

Pothuau class
Pothuau was regarded as a good sea boat and served in the Mediterranean until sent in 1915 to occupy Krivi in the German Cameroun (W Africa). She served in defence of Egypt 1916–17 before going on to Saigon for a refit and returning to Toulon in 1918. In 1919 the 194mm (7.5in) turrets were removed and replaced by experimental AA guns. She remained a gunnery TS having originally cost 11.2 million francs.

Jeanne d'Arc class
This ship saw varied 1914–18 service, starting with the RN in the Western Channel. She and the battleship *Jauréguiberry* took Ruad Island (1915); she remained off the Levant until finishing the war as a US-France convoy escort. After training midshipmen from 1919 to 1928, she was laid up in 1929–33. Her original building cost was £875,000.

Gueydon class
Gueydon's war service ranged throughout the Atlantic from the West Indies to N Russia (1918 support of the White Russians). She switched to the Baltic in 1918–19 and was refitted in 1923. Employed as a TS in 1928–30, she was hulked in 1935 and used as an accommodation ship in Brest; BU during the German 1940–44 occupation. *Montcalm* joined the Australian Squadron in the 1914 capture of Samoa and after a January–September 1916 refit joined 4th Cruiser Squadron in the West Indies, escorting Atlantic convoys July –November 1918. After being stricken she was used as a barrack ship, renamed *Trémintin* on 1 October 1934 to free her name for the new light cruiser; BU in Brest under German occupation. *Dupetit-Thouars* spent the war in the Channel and the Atlantic. She was torpedoed and sunk by *U 62* 400nm from Brest while escorting 28 merchantmen from New York; US destroyers rescued most of the crew. Each ship originally cost 20.8–22.6 million francs (£817,000–£902,000).

Dupleix class
Desaix patrolled the Channel until December 1914. With *Montcalm* and AMC *Requin* she made the French contribution to the 1915 defence of the Suez Canal.

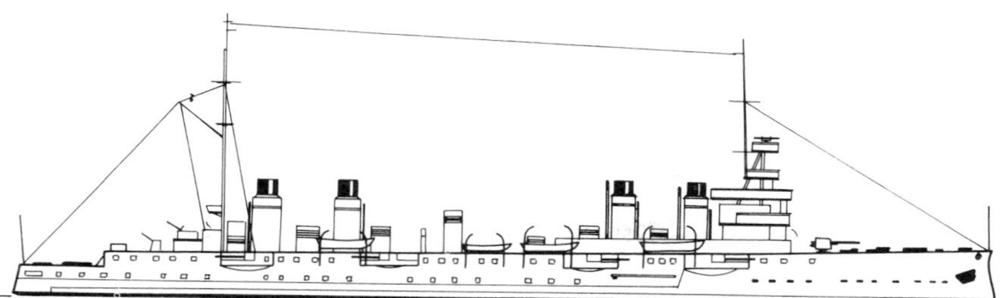

Gueydon 1928

Her 100mm (3.9in) guns were removed to arm merchant ships in 1917 and she received 2–47mm AA guns. In 1918 she relieved *Gloire* in the West Indies and after the war served in the Far East. *Dupleix* saw Far East service from 1910 and on 21 August 1914 captured two German supply ships (*Senegambia* and *Ferdinand Laeisz*) before they could replenish Admiral von Spee's squadron. In May 1915 she shelled Bodrum (Turkey) and saw the war out in the E Mediterranean. *Kléber* served with *Jeanne d'Arc* in the 2nd Light Squadron (Channel and Biscay 1914). She was stranded and refloated under Turkish gunfire off Gallipoli 29–31 May 1915. After repairs at Toulon she continued shore bombardment in the Aegean until a collision with a British cargo vessel (7 July 1915) off Mudros kept her in that island harbour for repairs until October. She left the E Mediterranean for a Bordeaux refit in 1916 before proceeding to Dakar as flagship of 6th Squadron. She was sunk by a mine (laid by *UC 61*) at the entrance of Brest with the lost of 42 crew. The class originally cost 18.9 million francs (£770,000) apiece.

Gloire class
All the class except *Amiral Aube* (E Mediterranean 1915–16) spent the war in the Atlantic, finishing it on convoy escort. *Gloire* was repaired in New York after a collision with the US liner *City of Athens* (May 1918). *Amiral Aube* was probably disarmed after 1916. *Condé* and her sisters formed the 1920 Atlantic Squadron (*Marseillaise* being part of the escort for the US liner *George Washington* taking President Wilson back to America). *Condé* was hulked after 1933 and became an apprentices' barrack ship at Lorient. She was converted into U-boat depot ship there in mid-1940 and was expended as an aircraft target before the Second World War ended. *Marseillaise* served as a gunnery TS in 1925–29 having her 194mm (7.5in) turrets exchanged for 164.7mm (6.4in) ones. Class unit cost was originally £863,000–£883,000.

Léon Gambetta class
All three ships served in the W Mediterranean and Adriatic 1914–15. *Léon Gambetta* was hit by two 18in torpedoes from the Austrian *U 5* in the Strait of Otranto and sank in 10 minutes, only 137 crew surviving. *Victor Hugo* escorted the torpedoed battleship *Jean Bart* to Malta in 1916. She and *Jules Michelet* helped transport the Serbian Army from Corfu to Bizerta. She went into reserve at Toulon in 1923 on return from the Far East and was sold in 1928 for 2.75 million francs having originally cost 29 million francs (£1.2 million).

Jules Michelet class
Jules Michelet spent the whole war in diverse Mediterranean operations. She went into reserve in 1929 being used as an aircraft and submarine target until *Thetis* torpedoed her *c*1937. She originally cost about 29 million francs (£1.2 million).

Ernest Renan class
Ernest Renan also spent the whole war in the Mediterranean. Afterwards her mainmast was removed (for towing a balloon) and the after 164.7mm (6.4in) turrets received AA guns. Her mainmast was put back for gunnery TS duties in 1927–28 and she was sunk as an aircraft and gunfire target in 1931 or after. Her original cost was £1.4 million.

Edgar Quinet class
Edgar Quinet with the two cruisers above formed 1st Light Division hunting *Goeben* and *Breslau* in 1914 and patrolling the Straits of Otranto from Navarino. Her E Mediterranean service culiminated with the rescue of 1200 people from Smyrna (1922). She was converted as a TS in 1925–27 with a modified bridge, four funnels and only 10–194mm (7.6in) and two floatplanes. She went aground on an unmarked rock off Cape Blanc, Algeria, on 4 January 1930 and sank five days later. *Waldeck Rousseau* survived two Austrian U-boat attacks in October-November 1914, cruised the Aegean and Ionian Seas before serving in the Black Sea 1919–20 helping evacuate General Wrangel's White Russian Army. Her active career finished as Far East flagship before going into reserve in 1932. She originally cost £1.3 million.

PROTECTED CRUISERS

Name	Launched	Disp (normal load)	Fate
Sfax class			
SFAX	29.5.84	4561t	Stricken 1906, BU
Tage class			
TAGE	28.10.86	7469t	Stricken 1910, BU
Amiral Cécille class			
AMIRAL CÉCILLE	3.5.88	5839t	BU 1919

Name	Launched	Disp (metric full-load)	Fate
Davout class			
DAVOUT	10.89	3031t	Stricken 1910, BU
Suchet class			
SUCHET	10.8.93	3362t	Stricken 1906, BU
Forbin class			
COËTLOGON	3.12.88	1911t	Stricken 1906, BU
FORBIN	14.1.88	1935t	Stricken 1919, BU 1921
SURCOUF	10.88	2012t	Stricken 1921, BU
Troude class			
COSMAO	8.89	1923t	Stricken 1922, BU
LALANDE	21.3.89	1968t	Stricken 1912, BU
TROUDE	22.10.88	2050t	Stricken 1907, BU 1908
Linois class			
GALILÉE	28.4.96	2318t	Stricken 1911, BU
LAVOISIER	17.4.97	2318t	Stricken 1920, BU
LINOIS	30.1.94	2285t	Stricken 1910, BU
Alger class			
ALGER	23.11.89	4313t	Hulked 1911, BU 1939
ISLY	23.6.91	4406t	Stricken 1914, BU
JEAN BART	11.89	4044t	Wrecked 11.2.07
Friant class			
BUGEAUD	29.8.93	3809t	Stricken 1907, BU
CHASSELOUP-LAUBAT	17.4.93	3824t	Hulked 1913, BU *c*1920
FRIANT	17.4.93	3982t	Stricken 1920, BU
Descartes class			
DESCARTES	27.9.94	3960t	Stricken 10.5.20
PASCAL	26.9.95	3960t	Stricken 1911, BU
D'Assas class			
CASSARD	27.5.96	3890t	Stricken 1924, BU 1925
D'ASSAS	28.3.96	3962t	Stricken 1910, BU 1914
DU CHAYLA	10.11.95	3890t	Stricken 1921, BU 1933
Catinat class			
CATINAT	8.10.96	4048t	Stricken 1911, BU
PROTET	6.7.98	4001t	Stricken 1910, BU
D'Entrecasteaux class			
D'ENTRECASTEAUX	12.6.96	7995t	Stricken 27.10.22, BU
Guichen class			
GUICHEN	15.5.98	8151t	Stricken 1921, BU
Châteaurenault class			
CHÂTEAURENAULT	12.5.98	7898t	Sunk 14.12.17, BU
D'Estrées class			
D'ESTRÉES	27.10.97	2428t	Stricken 1922, BU 1924
INFERNET	7.9.99	2428t	Stranded 22.11.10
Jurien de la Gravière class			
JURIEN DE LA GRAVIÈRE	26.7.99	5595t	Stricken 1922, BU

Friant class
Chasseloup-Laubat was disarmed in 1913 and used during the war as a distilling plant in Corfu. She originally cost *c*£308,000. *Friant* came from Newfoundland to Morocco in 1914 remaining on that station until becoming 3rd Submarine Flotilla tender at Mudros (Aegean) in 1918 (with one funnel).

Descartes class
Descartes remained in the West Indies 1914–17 suffering two collisions, first with the Spanish cargo ship *Telesfora* and then into the British SS *Strathmore*. She came home to Lorient and went into reserve losing her 10–100mm (3.9in) guns to ASW craft and her 4–164.7mm (6.4in) to the Army.

D'Assas class
Cassard spent 1914–18 in the W Mediterranean or Red Sea apart from 1917 detachment to the Indian Ocean. She was attached to the gunnery school in 1922–23 with turrets removed. *Du Chayla* supported the August 1907 Casablanca landing and split her war service between the Atlantic (1914–16) and the Red Sea (1916–18) before operating off the Lebanon at the end and going into

the Black Sea (1918–19). By 1918 most of her gun had gone to the Army leaving her with 2–164.7mm (6.4in), 4–75mm and 4–47mm.

D'Entrecasteaux class
This cruiser was stricken and lent to Belgium in 1923 as a hulk and returned in 1926 when the Belgian Navy was reduced. Sold to Poland for her scrap value on 7 March 1927 and towed to Gdynia as *Król Władysław IV* and renamed *Bałtyk* in 1930. She served as a hulk and was BU *c*1942 by the Germans. Building cost 16,693,000 francs (or £667,000).

Guichen class
Guichen went from the Channel/Biscay to Morocco. She helped in the Armenian rescue operation of September 1915. In 1917 she became a fast transport on the Taranto–Hea (Gulf of Corinth) route. Black Sea operations from 1919 finished her active careet.

Châteaurenault class
Châteaurenault began the war with 2nd Light Squadron in the Channel but from 1915 served in the Mediterranean apart from a February 1916 S Atlantic Sea detachment to search for the raider *Möwe*. She was sunk by two torpedoes from the *UC 38* off Cephalonia (Ionian Sea) while serving as a troop transport (1162 survivors). She cost 19,302,000 francs (or £606,000).

D'Estrées class
D'Estrées moved from the Channel to the Levant (1914–15) and then into the Red Sea (1916–18). Refitted at La Ciotat she served in the Far East until stricken in October 1922.

Jurien de la Gravière class
In company with destroyers this ship chased the Austrian destroyer *Ulan* on 16 August 1914 before patrolling the Otranto Strait. During October 1916 she flew Admiral de Lapeyrère's flag in bombardment operations along the S Turkish coast. Participated in the 1916–17 blockade of Greece. Her active career finished on the Syrian Station.

Note: The unprotected cruiser *Milan* (launched May 1884, 1705t) was the only vessel of her type surviving into this period. She was stricken in 1908 and BU.

TORPEDO CRUISERS

Name	Launched	Disp	Fate
Condor class			
CONDOR	17.5.85	1229t	Stricken 1907, BU
ÉPERVIER	10.86	1268t	Stricken 1911, BU
FAUCON	12.87	1311t	Stricken 1920, BU
VAUTOUR	25.4.89	1266t	Stricken 1908, BU
Wattignies class			
FLEURS	18.3.83	1280t	Stricken 1910, BU
WATTIGNIES	9.4.91	1280t	Stricken 1908, BU
Bombe class			
BOMBE	16.4.85		Stricken 1911, BU
COULEUVRINE	30.6.85		Stricken 1911, BU
DRAGONNE	28.8.85		Stricken 1910, BU
FLÈCHE	8.11.85	369t–418t	Stricken 1912, BU
LANCE	20.4.86		Stricken 1914, BU
SAINTE-BARBE	10.10.85		Stricken 1911, BU
SALVE	6.2.86		Stricken 1906, BU
Lévrier class			
LÉGER	4.8.91	503t	Stricken 1910, BU
LÉVRIER	2.4.91	503t	Stricken 1910, BU
D'Iberville class			
CASABIANCA	21.9.95	970t	Sunk 3.6.15
CASSINI	5.6.94	970t	Sunk 20.2.17
D'IBERVILLE	11.9.92	952t	Stricken July 1919, BU 1920
Dunois class			
DUNOIS	6.10.97	889t	Stricken 1920, BU
LA HIRE	3.11.98	889t	Stricken 31.10.22
Foudre class			
FOUDRE	20.10.95	5994t	Stricken 1.12.21, BU 27.5.22

D'Iberville class
Casabianca and *Cassini* converted to minelayers (97 mines) pre-war. *Casabianca* patrolled in the Otranto Straits and off Corfu 1914–15 and was sunk on one of her own mines. *Cassini* saw much the same service and in turn sank on a mine laid by *UC 35* in the Bonifacio Straits. *D'Iberville* was at Penang in August 1914, unspotted by *Emden*, and steamed to the Mediterranean for service in the Algerian Patrol Division until 1917.

Dunois class
Dunois stayed in the Channel throughout the war, giving gunfire support to the BEF in November 1914 based on Dunkirk. *La Hire* began and ended the war at Toulon Gunnery School. She inspected neutral shipping on the Bizerta-Sardinia route (November 1914), did ASW patrols between Crete and Rhodes (1916) and formed part of the Tunisian Patrol Force (1917–18). Back at Toulon she was fitted with 2–M1917 100mm (3.9in) guns, 6–47mm and depth charges.

Foudre class
Foudre helped build seaplane bases at Port Said and Madros before becoming a submarine tender. She lost some 100mm guns in 1918 receiving modified Army 90mm weapons instead (see also under Aircraft Carriers below).

DESTROYERS

Name	Fate	Name	Fate
Durandal class: launched 1899–1900, 296–306t			
DURANDAL	Stricken 7.6.19, BU	FAUCONNEAU	Stricken 15.1.21, BU
HALLEBARDE	Stricken 4.3.20, BU		
Framée class: launched 1899–1900, 314t			
YATAGAN	Sunk 3.11.16	EPÉE	Stricken 1.10.20, BU
PIQUE	Stricken 28.1.21, BU		
Pertuisane class: launched 1900–1901, 306t			
PERTUISANE	Stricken 16.3.23, BU	FLAMBERGE	Stricken 1.10.20, BU
ESCOPETTE	Stricken 4.4.21, BU	RAPIÈRE	Stricken 27.10.21, BU
Arquebuse class: launched 1902–1904, 298t			
CARABINE	Stricken 8.1.19, BU	FRANCISQUE	Stricken 4.4.21, BU
SARBACANE	Stricken 1.10,20, BU	SABRE	Stricken 5.1.21, BU
ARQUEBUSE	Stricken 10.5.20, BU	DARD	Stricken 3.4.19, BU
ARBALÈTE	Stricken 21.6.20, BU	BALISTE	Stricken 30.10.19, BU
MOUSQUET	Sunk 28.10.14	MOUSQUETON	Stricken 10.5.20, BU
JAVELINE	Stricken 12.1.20, BU	ARC	Stricken 1.10,20, BU
SAGAIE	Stricken 1.10.20, BU	PISTOLET	Stricken 19.9.19, BU
EPIEU	Stricken 28.2.21, BU	BÉLIER	Stricken 25.1.21, BU
HARPON	Stricken 5.3.21, BU	CATAPULTE	Sunk 18.5.18
FRONDE	Stricken 30.10.19, BU	BOMBARDE	Stricken 10.5.20
Claymore class: launched 1905–1908, 350t			
STYLET	Stricken 14.5.21, BU	TRIDENT	Stricken 13.11.31, BU
TROMBLON	Stricken 14.5.21, BU	FLEURET	Stricken 12.1.20, BU
PIERRIER	Stricken 27.7.21, BU	COUTELAS	Stricken 28.1.21, BU
OBUSIER	Stricken 27.5.21, BU	COGNÉE	Stricken 27.7.21, BU
MORTIER	Stricken 30.3.27, BU	HACHE	Stricken 27.2.21, BU
CLAYMORE	Stricken 19.3.26, BU	MASSUE	Stricken 30.3.27, BU
CARQUOIS	Stricken 29.11.30, BU		
Branlebas class: launched 1907–1909, 339t			
GLAIVE	Stricken 13.2.32, BU	FANION	Stricken 27.5.21
POIGNARD	Stricken 3.5.26	SAPE	Stricken 3.5.26
SABRETACHE	Stricken 10.5.20	GABION	Stricken 14.5.21
ORIFLAMME	Stricken 27.5.21	BRANLEBAS	Sunk 30.9.15
ETENDARD	Sunk 25.4.17	FANFARE	Stricken 28.9.25

Durandal class
Durandal saw 1914–18 Channel service mainly based on Dunkirk. She was sold to breakers on 22 February 1921. *Hallebarde* did duty first with 1st Submarine Flotilla and then with 7th (Brindisi) and 8th Destroyer Flotillas. She was sold for scrap 20 April 1920. *Fauconneau* switched from Cherbourg (1st Submarine Flotilla leader) to the Mediterranean, serving off Syria and Salonika (10th Flotilla). She was sold to the breakers with *Hallebarde*.

Framée class
Framée was sunk in collision with the battleship *Brennus* on 11 August 1900. *Yatagan* was in a fatal collision with the British SS *Teviot* off Dieppe during her fishery protection duties. *Pique* operated from Brindisi (1916–17) and S France. In 1916 her bridge was extended round the foremast and first funnel; her stem TT position was replaced by an Army 65mm or 75mm gun and moved between her stern guns. Sold for scrap 28 July 1921. *Epée* saw Mediterranean service and was sold to be BU on 8 January 1921.

Pertuisane class
Also known as 'Rochefortais' class because of the builders (Rochefort DYd).

Pertuisane served in the Channel, vainly seeking *UB 40* on the surface off Le Havre (22 February 1917). She was deleted from the list 16 March 1923 and sold to be BU 20 April 1928. *Escopette* had similar service and was stricken 4 April 1921. *Flamberge* operated in the Mediterranean from 1915 finishing the war at Salonika. She was sold to be BU on 8 January 1921. *Rapière* transferred from 3rd Flotilla (N France) to the Patrol Boat Division off Bizerta.

Arquebuse class
Carabine operated in the Mediterranean until she collided with the British SS *Mentor*. She was towed to Palermo and patched up for a voyage to Bizerta where she was stricken. *Sarbacane* was part of 2nd Flotilla at Brindisi in 1916 and joined South France Patrol Force in 1918. *Arquebuse* moved from the Channel to the Mediterranean, vainly attacking *U 35* on 15 June 1916. She was sold to breakers on 2 March 1921. *Arbalète* took part in the 16 April 1917 bombardment of Gaza and twice vainly attacked *UC 74* that year. She was sold as scrap on 10 May 1921. *Mousquet* was sunk by *Emden* off Penang. *Javeline*, *Sagaie*, *Epieu* and *Harpon* stayed in the Channel. *Sagaie* was sold on 12 April 1921, *Epieu* on 20 May 1922, *Harpon* on 10 July 1922. *Fronde* commissioned from reserve at Saigon in March 1915 and sailed to the Mediterranean. She was sold to breakers on 6 May 1920. *Francisque* was sold to be BU on 10 July 1922 after a war in the Channel. *Sabre* was leader of 1st Submarine Flotilla June 1913 to April 1915, serving in the E Mediterranean for the duration and carrying King Peter I of Serbia from Valona to Corfu in March 1916. *Dard* served in the Mediterranean 1915–18 based on Port Said from 1917. *Baliste* was based at Bizerta and then Salonika. *Mousqueton* was also in the Mediterranean for the duration, finishing with 8th Flotilla at Toulon. *Arc* was attached to 2nd Submarine Flotilla in 1914, spending the rest of the war with 7th and 8th Flotilla in the Mediterranean as was *Pistolet* (sold to be BU 6 May 1920) throughout. *Belier* (sold to be BU 20 May 1922), *Catapulte* and *Bombarde* (sold to be BU 20 April 1921) began the war with 2nd Light Squadron in the Channel before going to the Mediterranean. *Catapulte* was in fatal collision with the British SS *Warrimoo* off Bone.

Claymore class
Romblon, *Obusier*, *Claymore*, *Carquois* and *Fleuret* spent the war in the Channel; *Obusier* being in the British raid on Ostend, 23 April 1918. *Mortier* fought in the Adriatic, colliding there with the liner *Asie*. She served as torpedo school tender June 1919 to October 1923. *Claymore* saw 1920 service in the Baltic. *Carquois* towed a disabled *Obusier* into harbour on 24 May 1916. *Trident* was at the Dardanelles and in the Adriatic, being sold to be BU on 29 November 1932. *Coutelas*, *Cognée* and *Hache* were mainly Adriatic ships though the first two were at the 16 April 1917 bombardment of Gaza. *Massue* was a temporary minesweeper in 1912, spending most of the war at the Dardanelles or in the Adriatic, helping the sinking battleship *Danton* on 19 March 1917. Postwar, she was in the Mediterranean Training Division.

Branlebas class
Glaive served in the Channel, she and *Gabion* escorted the first US troop convoy into Brest 12 August 1917. *Poignard* and *Sabretache* saw 1916 service in the Adriatic. *Oriflamme* (with *Branlebas*) sank the German torpedo-boat *A 15* on 22–23 Augusut 1915 and (with the larger and more modern destroyer *Francis Garnier*) captured a German seaplane off Ostend. *Oriflamme* was in the Baltic in January 1919 capturing the German SS *Elbe* and the tug *Berger I*, taking them through the hostile Kiel Canal to Dunkirk. *Etendard* was sunk with all hands by German destroyers. *Fanion* was based mainly at Brest. *Sape* served at the Dardanelles and Salonika. *Branlebas* was part of the North Sea Flotilla, being mined off Nieuport. *Fanfare*'s war was in the Adriatic and finished with the Algerian Patrol Force.

SEA-GOING TORPEDO-BOATS

Name	Fate	Name	Fate
Balny class: launched 1886, 65t full load			
BALNY	Sold 1913	CAPITAINE CUNY	Sold 1912
DÉROULÉOE	Sold 1907	CAPITAINE MEHL	Sold 1910
DOUDART DE LA GRÉE	Sold 1906	CHALLIER	Sold 1906
Ouragan class: launched 1889, 177t full load			
ALARME	Sold 1906	AVENTURIER	Sold 1910
TÉMÉRAIRE	Sold 1911	DÉFI	Sold 1911
Coureur class: launched 1888, 1891–92, 131t full load			
COUREUR	Sold 1912	GRONDEUR	Sold 1926
VÉLOCE	Sold 1910		
Avant-Garde class: launched 1891–93, 127–129t full load			
ARCHER	Sold 1908	DRAGON	Stricken 8.10.10
TURCO	Sold 1911	GRENADIER	Sold 1919
ZOUAVE	Sold 1908	LANCIER	Sold 1911
Agile class: launched 1889, 1891–92, 119–129t full load			
AGILE	Sold 1912	ORAGE	Sold 1921
ECLAIRE	Sold 1911	SARRAZIN	Sold 1908
KABYLE	Sold 1911	TOURBILLON	Sold 1911
Corsaire class: launched 1892, 168t full load			
CORSAIRE	Sold 1913		

Name	Fate	Name	Fate
Mousquetaire class: launched 1892, 123t			
MOUSQUET-AIRE	Sold 1911		
Chevalier class: launched 1893, 135t full load			
CHEVALIER	Stricken 1.10.19		
Averne class: launched 1893–94, 131t full load			
AVERNE	Stricken 1919, BU 1920	DAUPHINE	Sold 1913
Argonaute class: launched 1893, 129t full load			
ARGONAUTE	Sold 1911	TOURMENTE	Sold 1910
Filibustier class: launched 1895, 123t normal			
ARIEL	Sold 1923	AQUILON	Sold 1919
Forban class: launched 1895, 150t full load			
FORBAN	Stricken 1920		
Mangini class: launched 1896, 140t full load			
MANGINI	Sold 1911		
Cyclone class: launched 1898, 1901, 150–165t full load			
CYCLONE	Stricken 1.10.20	BORÉE	Sold 1921
BOURRASQUE	Stricken 10.21	TRAMONTANE	Sold 1923
RAFALE	Stricken 4.4.21		
Mistral class: launched 1900–1901, 183t full load			
MISTRAL	Stricken 17.5.27, sold 1928	TYPHON	Sold 1928
SIROCCO	Stricken 5.5.25	TROMBE	Sold 1928
SIMOUN	Sold 1924	AUDACIEUX	Stricken 2.23
Takou class: launched 1898, 305t full load			
TAKOU (ex-Chinese *Hai Ching*)	Wrecked 22.2.11		

Chevalier class
This ship served off Provence in 1914–18.

Cyclone class
Cyclone was based at Algiers 1914–18. *Bourrasque* was at Bizerta. *Rafale* was in the Dunkirk Flotilla and sank at Boulogne in an accidental depth charge explosion 1 December 1917. She was raised and repaired. *Borée* served at Brindisi and Toulon. *Tramontane* served in the Dunkirk Flotilla and at Algiers. She was stricken in October 1926 as was *Borée*.

Mistral class
Mistral's war was spent at Brest and she was renamed *Borée* in 1925. *Sirocco* entered Ostend under fire on 15 October 1915 and returned to Dunkirk with the first report of the port's capture. *Trombe* depth charged and shelled *UB 26* off Le Havre when the latter was captured on 5 April 1916. *Audacieux* spent 1914–18 at Brest.

TORPEDO-BOATS

Name	Fate
No 126 class: launched 1889–1890, 78t full load	
Nos 126–129	Stricken 1908–1914
No 130 class: launched 1890–92, 52t	
Nos 130–132, 134–144	Stricken *c*1910
No 133	Stricken 1921
No 145 class: launched 1891–93, 78t	
Nos 145–149, 152–157, 159–171	Stricken *c*1913
No 158	Stricken 1920
No 172 class: launched 1892–95	
Nos 172–200	Stricken *c*1913–14
No 201 class: launched 1897–1904, 83–90t	
Nos 201–292	Some stricken before 1914 and the rest sold 1919 and 1923
No 293 class: launched 1904, 94t	
No 293	Stricken 1910, BU *c*1916
No 294 class: launched 1904, 100t	
No 294	Stricken 1910, BU *c*1914
Libellule class: launched 1905, 39t	
LIBELLULE	Stricken 1911
No 295 class: launched 1905–08, 99–101t	
Nos 300, 317, 319, 325	Mined 1914–18
Nos 295–299, 301–316, 317 318, 320–324, 326–369	Sold 1920

No 201 class
No 225 collided with the destroyer *Oriflamme* and sank on 26 October 1914. *No 289* grounded near Bizerta in late 1918. *Nos 275* and *279* served in the Atlantic Patrol Force (1915–18). *Nos 231, 258, 259, 279, 280* served off Dunkirk and Flanders. *Nos 263, 274* and *289* were in the Tunisian Patrol Force. *Nos 281* and *288* were stationed at Brindisi.

No 295 class
Nos 300 (Le Havre 1 November 1916), *317* (Calais 27 November 1916), *319* (Nieuport 19 January 1915), and *325* (Kerkenah Island, Tunisia, 22 January 1919) were all mined off the ports indicated. *Nos 302, 306, 308, 316, 326, 327, 334* and *340* operated in the Channel, *301* and *307* in the Atlantic. *Nos 305, 314,*

318, 320–323, 341–346, 350–351 and *365* served off Dunkirk and Flanders. *Nos 303, 324, 334, 338* and *367* were in the Bay of Biscay (1916–18). *No 310* was off S France 1916–18 while at the same time *Nos 328–30, 333, 355, 356, 361, 362* and *366* were in the Tunisian Patrol Force. *Nos 349, 360, 368* and *369* were stationed at Brindisi (1915–18). *Nos 309–311, 353, 357* and *359* were at the Dardanelles (1915).

SLOOPS AND GUNBOATS

Name	Fate	Name	Fate
Kersaint class: launched 1897, 1276t			
KERSAINT	Wrecked 5.3.19		
Crocodile class: launched 1882, 492t			
CAPRICORNE	Stricken 1907		
Comète class: launched 1884, 492t			
COMÈTE	Stricken 1909		
Surprise class: launched 1895–1899, 617–637t			
SURPRISE	Sunk by *U 38* 3.12.16	ZÉLÉE	Scuttled 29.9.14
DÉCIDÉE	Stricken 1922		
Gabriel Charmes class: launched 1886, 73t			
GABRIEL CHARMES	Stricken 1907		

Kersaint class
Served 1914–18 in the Far East as a dispatch vessel. Rearmed 19 December 1914 and refitted at Saigon 1916. She helped Allied troops land at Vladivostock 8 December 1918 but struck a coral reef at Moorea (Tahiti) and was declared a total loss 18 July 1919.

Surprise class
Surprise landed armed sailors in the Cameroons and sank the German AMC *Itolo* as well as bombarding shore positions 21–22 September 1914. She was at the October 1914 capture of Victoria (the Cameroun port) with the armoured cruiser *Bruix* and spent 1915–16 on the Morocco Station. *U 38* torpedoed her off Funchal (Madeira). *Décidée* spent 1914–17 on the Indochina Station and 1917–18 with 7th Patrol Division (Syria). *Zélée* had the 1914 Tahiti Station, capturing the German SS *Walkure* at Makatea Island before her guns were landed on Tahiti and she herself was scuttled at Papéete to block the harbour.

CAPITAL SHIPS

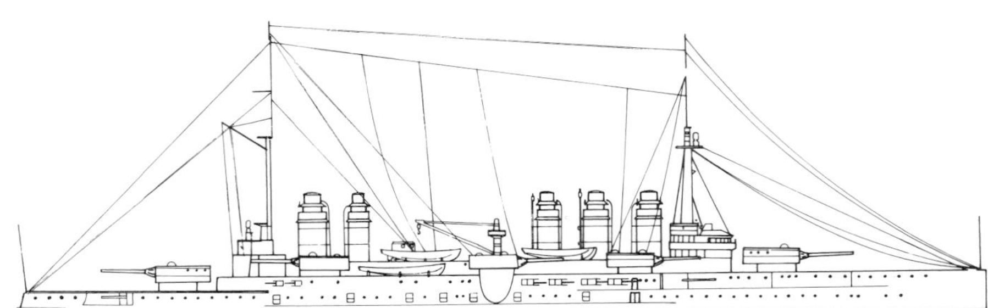
Danton 1911

DANTON class *battleships*

Displacement: 18,318t normal; 19,763t full load

Dimensions: 475ft 5in wl, 481ft oa × 84ft 8in × 30ft 2in
144.9m wl, 146.6m oa × 25.8m × 9.2m full load

Machinery: 4-shaft Parsons turbines, 26 Belleville boilers (*Condorcet, Diderot* and *Vergniaud* fitted with Niclausse), 22,500shp = 19.2kts–19.4kts. Coal 925t/2027t. Range 3370nm/1750nm at 10kts/18kts

Armour: Main belt 270mm (10⅝in) amidships, 150mm (6in) ends, upper deck 48mm (1⅞in), lower deck 45mm (1¾in), torpedo bulkhead 45mm (1¾in), barbettes 280mm (11in), main turrets 300mm (11¾in), secondary turrets 220mm (8⅝in), CT 300mm (11¾in)

Armament: 4–305mm (12in)/45 Mod 06 (2×2), 12–240mm (9.4in)/49.5 Mod 02 (6×2), 16–75mm/65 Schneider Mod 06, 10–47mm Mod 02, 2–450mm (17.7in) TT sub

Complement: 681 (as flagship, 753), later 921–923

Name	Builder	Laid down	Launched	Comp	Fate
CONDORCET	A C de la Loire, St-Nazaire	23.8.07	20.8.09	25.7.11	Deleted 1931, see notes
DANTON	Arsenal de Brest	2.06	4.7.09	1.6.11	Sunk 19.3.17
DIDEROT	A C de la Loire, St-Nazaire	20.10.07	19.4.09	1.8.11	Condemned 1936, BU 1937
MIRABEAU	Arsenal de Lorient	4.5.08	28.10.09	1.8.11	Target 1921/22, BU 1928
VERGNIAUD	C de la Gironde, Bordeaux	7.08	12.4.10	22.9.11	Deleted 27.10, see notes
VOLTAIRE	F C de la Méditerranée, La Seyne	20.7.07	16.1.09	1.8.11	Condemned 1935, BU 1939

France's first large turbine-engined ships, designed by L'Homme for the 1906 programme. Compared with the *Patrie* class battleships which had a displacement of just under 15,000t, the increase to 18,000t in these *Danton* class ships represented a major step forward. The displacement increase was used above all for strengthening the heavy artillery and denoted only a slight increase in speed. Heavy on coal, they were considered unsuccessful ships but were, however, useful in the Mediterranean due to their first-class armament of many rapid-fire guns.

Ships fitted with Belleville boilers made 20.18kts–20.66kts on 3hr trials; those with Niclausse boilers made 19.63kts–19.90kts. Number of rounds carried: 305mm – 75 per gun, 240mm – 100 per gun, 75mm – 500 per gun. In 1918 the 240mm guns had their range increased to 18,000 m from 13,700 m and at the same time they were given a fire control system as fitted to *Dreadnought*. During World War One additional 12–75mm AA were fitted, two each on the 240mm turrets. *Condorcet, Vergniaud* and *Voltaire* had mainmasts shortened in 1918 to enable them to carry kite balloons. *Condorcet, Diderot* and *Voltaire* modernised between 1922 (1923?) and 1925 and fitted with improved underwater protection; from January 1927 they served as TS.

After her deletion *Condorcet* acted as a depot ship for the torpedo school (temporarily carrying a few deck TT but no 75mm AA). Finally she was hulked, and became a barrack ship. Damaged by explosion 27 November 1942 in Toulon, she remained afloat and was used temporarily by the German Navy as a barrack ship. In August 1944 she was seriously damaged by an Allied air raid and sunk in shallow water by Germans. Refloated in September 1944 and sold to be BU 14 December 1945. *Danton* was sunk in the Western Mediterranean (south of Sardinia) by a torpedo from *U 64*. The class spent the entire war in the Mediterranean. All except *Danton* and *Diderot* were off Athens in December 196 as a pro-Allied demonstration, *Mirabeau* fired four rounds, one of which landed near the Royal Palace. The Greek government agreed to Allied proposals. All except *Danton* and *Condorcet* left Corfu for Mudros (Lemnos) to form the main element (with the *Verité* class) of the Aegean Sea Squadron in 1918 barring a feared Central Powers breakout from the Dardanelles. *Voltaire* survived two torpedoings from *UB 48* without significant damage (10–11 October 1918) and her sisters took station with the Allied Fleet off Constantinople on 13 November. *Vergniaud* and *Mirabeau* went into the Black Sea to operate off Sevastopol. *Mirabeau* ran aground in a snowstorm on the Crimean coast on 13 February 1919 and was salvaged April 1919 after the forward 305mm turret (including barbette and side armour) had been removed. Subsequently she was given

over to experimental purposes, having been condemned on 27 October 1921. *Vergniaud* was deleted on 27 October 1921 and until 1926 was a target for explosion and other experiments. Sold on 27 November 1928 for BU, scrapped 1929.

Danton as completed
Navarret Collection

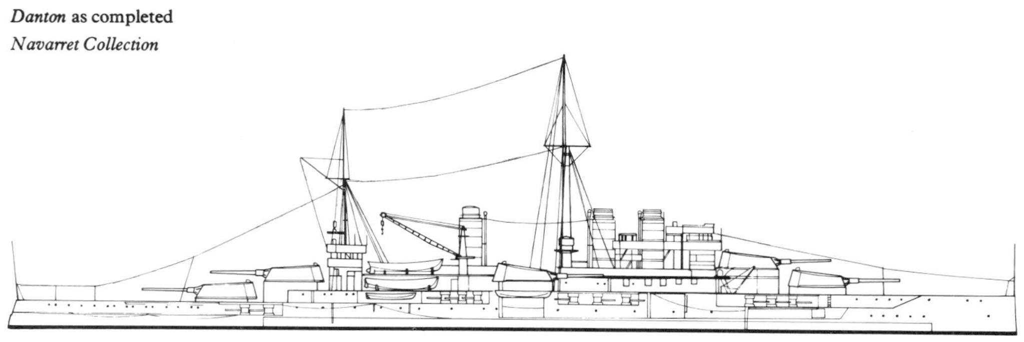

Courbet as completed

COURBET class *battleships*

Displacement: 22,189t normal; 25,000–26,000t full load

Dimensions: 520ft pp, 541ft wl, 551ft 2in oa × 91ft 6in × 29ft 6in
158.5m pp, 165.9m wl, 168.0m oa × 27.9m × 9.0m

Machinery: 4-shaft Parsons turbines, 24 Belleville boilers (*France* and *Paris* fitted with Niclausse), 28,000ship = 20.0kts. Coal 906t plus oil 310t (coal 2706t plus oil 310t). Range 4200nm/1140nm at 10kts/20kts

Armour: Main belt 270mm ($10\frac{5}{8}$in), amidships, 180mm ($7\frac{1}{8}$in) ends, upper belt 180mm ($7\frac{1}{8}$in), main deck 70mm ($2\frac{3}{4}$in), upper deck 50mm (2in), forecastle deck 30mm ($1\frac{1}{8}$in), barbettes 270mm ($10\frac{5}{8}$in), turrets 320mm ($12\frac{5}{8}$in), casemates 180mm ($7\frac{7}{8}$in), CT 300mm ($11\frac{3}{4}$in) with 270mm ($10\frac{5}{8}$in) roof

Armament: 12–305mm (12in)/45 Mod 10 (6×2), 22–138.6mm (5.4in)/55 Mod 10, 4–47mm, 4–450mm (17.7in) TT sub

Complement: 1085–1108

Name	Builder	Laid down	Launched	Comp	Fate
COURBET	Arsenal de Brest	1.9.10	23.9.11	19.11.13	Scuttled 9.6.44
FRANCE	A C de la Loire, St-Nazaire	30.11.11	7.11.12	July or Aug 1914	Foundered 26.8.22
JEAN BART	Arsenal de Brest	15.11.10	22.9.11	5.6.13	Sold for BU 14.12.45
PARIS	F C de la Méditerranée La Seyne	10.11.11	28.9.12	1.8.14	Sold for BU 21.12.55

Authorised under the 1910 (*Courbet* and *Jean Bart*) and 1911 (remainder) programmes, these were the *Marine Nationale*'s first dreadnought-type battleships. Designed by M Lyasse. Although the armour thickness was increased by comparision with the *Danton*s, it was much thinner than was customary practice in the US and even the Royal Navy. The side armour extended comparatively far below the waterline, an arrangement which was due mainly to anxiety about underwater hits. Although the calibre of the medium guns – 138.6mm – was less than the generally prevalent 152mm, the slightly smaller calibre was introduced because these guns had a higher rate of fire, which was important bearing in mind the problems of anti-torpedo-boat defence.

Trials results: *Courbet* 22.0kts, *Jean Bart* 22.6kts and *Paris* 21.7kts. Their 305mm guns were mounted in two pairs of rapid firing twin turrets fore and aft and two twin turrets on the sides on the same frames. Ammunition carried: 100 for each 305mm gun, 275 for each 138.6mm gun together with 12 torpedoes and 30 mines (originally).

During World War One all four ships were employed in the Mediterranean. *Courbet* flew the flag of Vice-Admiral Boué de Lapeyrère and had searchlights added to a platform astern of her second funnel as well as her main mast removed to tow a kite balloon. All of the class had triple 3.6m (12ft) rangefinders installed above their CT. *Jean Bart* took a torpedo hit from the Austrian *U 12* in the Adriatic on 21 December 1914 in her wine store but the forward magazine just aft remained intact. She and *France* rounded off their Great War active service in the 1919 Sevastopol operation. Although the *Courbet*s were considered very carefully constructed and highly detailed in finish, they rapidly became obsolete after 1918 because no thorough modernisation work was carried out. The wetness of foredeck in a rough sea was caused mainly by the effect of the weight of the superimposed turrets (each 561t, of which 234t was armour) and the fact that there were no drydocks long enough to allow their hulls to be lengthened.

Courbet in the 1930s as reconstructed
Navarret Collection

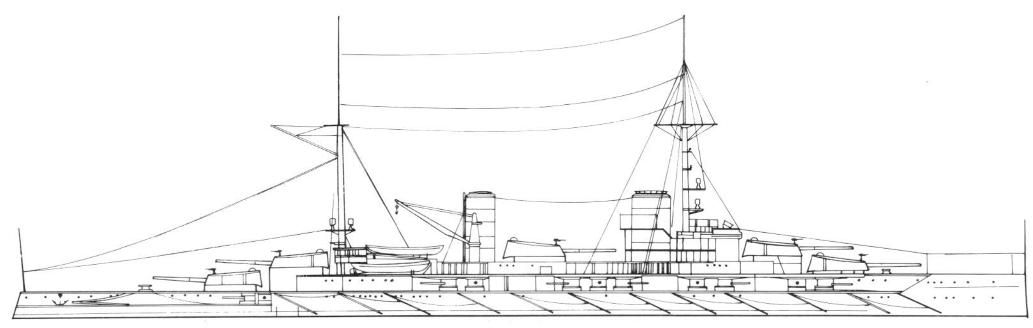

Provence as completed

Provided under the 1912 programme (as replacements for *Carnot, Charles Martel* and *Liberté*) and while they had the same hull and dimensions as the *Courbet* class they had a heavier main armament and a single centreline turret replaced the wing turrets amidships. *Bretagne* class battleships were comparatively well designed although their underwater protection was insufficient. Particular attention was also paid to the weapon and command control equipment. *Bretagne* class battleships were very wet forward and were the only French ship originally fitted with Bullivant net defence, removed in 1917. These ships had the disadvantage of a shorter range than most equivalent ships at that time – the maximum range being 14,500m on the 340mm guns, although in 1917 *Lorraine*'s range was increased to 18,000m by increasing the aftermost turret's elevation (from 12 to 18 degrees). Similar changes to *Bretagne* and *Provence* as well as to *Lorraine*'s remaining turrets were not made before November 1918 due to the amount of work in French dockyards.

All three ships joined the *Armée Navale* in 1916, *Provence* being flagship until 1919 and beginning her service with the Athens and Salamis operations. *Lorraine* was detached to Cattaro in January and March 1919 for repatriating Austrian crews and delivering Austrian ships to France and Italy.

Bretagne sank on 3 July 1940 at Mers-el-Kebir (977 crew killed) due to British action; salvaged in 1952 and BU. *Lorraine* disarmed under French control, July 1940, at Alexandria, but was fighting again by 30 May 1943. She joined the FNFL and served in the Mediterranean. Between 1945 and 1953 used as a TS and finally hulked and stricken on 17 February 1953 and BU in January 1954. *Provence* battle-damaged during British action at Mers-el-Kebir was brought to Toulon for repairs November 1940 and scuttled on 27 November 1942. Raised 11 July 1943 by the Germans and had her 2–340mm guns removed and installed as a coastal battery near Toulon. Scuttled 1944 by the Germans as a blockship and was raised April 1949 and BU.

BRETAGNE class *battleships*

Displacement: 23,230t as designed; *c*25,000t full load

Dimensions: 541ft wl, 544ft 7in oa × 88ft 3in × 29ft 2in, 32ft 2in
164.9m wl, 166.0m oa × 26.9m × 8.9m × 9.8m

Machinery: 4 shafts, 2 Parsons geared turbines, 24 Niclausse boilers (*Provence* 18 Belleville, *Lorraine* 24 Guyot du Temple), 29,000shp = 20kts. Coal 900t plus oil 300t (coal 2680t plus oil 300t). Range 4700nm/2800nm at 10kts/18.75kts

Armour: Main belt 270mm (10⁵/₈in) amidships, 160mm (6¼in) ends, casemates 170mm (6¾in), main deck 30mm–40mm (3¹/₈in–1⁵/₈in), upper deck 40mm (1⁵/₈in), lower deck 40mm (1⁵/₈in) with slopes 70mm (2¾in), barbettes 248mm (9¾in), upper turrets 270mm), centre turret 400mm (15¾in), upper end turrets 250mm (9⁷/₈in), other turrets 340mm (13³/₈in), CT 314mm (13³/₈mm)

Armament: 10–340mm (13.4in)/45 Mod 12 (5×2), 22–138.6mm (5.4in)/55 Mod 10, 4–47mm, 4–450mm (17.7in TT sub (24 torpedoes), up to 30 mines

Complement: 1124–1133

Name	Builder	Laid down	Launched	Comp	Fate
BRETAGNE	Arsenal de Brest	1.7.12	21.4.13	9.15	Sunk 3.7.40
LORRAINE	A C de St-Nazaire-Penhoët	1.8.12	30.9.13	7.16	BU 1954
PROVENCE	Arsenal de Lorient	1.5.12	20.4.13	6.15	See notes

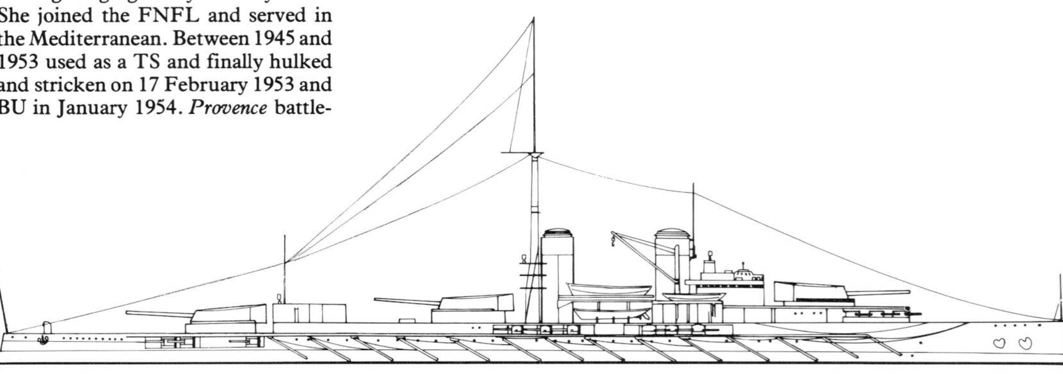

Normandie class design

Normandie and *Languedoc* were ordered on 12 December 1912, *Gascogne* and *Flandre* on 30 July 1913. *Béarn* was approved as a fifth ship on 3 December 1913 to maintain the divisional formation of four battleships with three *Bretagne*s. These ships were fitted with 340mm quadruple turrets which were lighter in total than the *Bretagne*'s 5 double turrets and meant that 2 further guns could be fitted.

The originally proposed double casemate mountings for the 138.6mm guns were not adopted and the conventional single casemate mountings were retained instead. All, except *Béarn*, were designed with 2 4cyl TE on lateral shafts and 2 Parsons (*Gascogne* Rateau-Bretagne, *Languedoc* Schneider-Zoelly) direct action turbines on central shafts without reversing gear.

This class's mixed machinery was considered an unsatisfactory arrangement despite the expected lower fuel consumption than in the

NORMANDIE class *battleships*

Displacement: 25,230t full load

Dimensions: 559ft 9in pp, 576ft 2in wl, 579ft 5in oa × 88ft 7in × 28ft 5in
170.6m pp, 175.6m wl, 176.6m oa × 27m × 8.65m

Machinery: 4-shaft TE and turbines or turbines only (see notes), 21 small tube Guyot du Temple boilers (*Flandre* and *Langeudoc* 28 small tube Belleville, *Béarn* 21 small tube Niclausse), 32,000shp = 21kts (an increase to 45,000hp = 22kts was planned). Coal 900t/2700t plus oil 300t. Range 6500nm/3375nm/1800nm at 12kts/16kts/21kts

Armour: Main belt 300mm (11¾in) amidships, 120mm–180mm (4¾in–7¹/₈in) ends, upper belt 240mm (9½in) amidships, 160mm (6¼in) ends, upper deck 50mm (2in), lower deck 50mm (2in) with slopes 70mm (2¾in), barbettes 284mm (11¹/₈in), turrets 250mm–340mm (9⁷/₈in–13³/₈in), casemates 160mm–180mm (6¼in–7¹/₈in), CT 300mm (11¾in)

Armament: 12–340mm (13.4in)/45 Mod 12 (3×4), 24–138.6mm (5.4in)/55 Mod 10, 6–47mm AA, 6–450mm (17.7in) TT sub

Complement: 1200

Name	Builder	Laid down	Launched	Comp	Fate
BÉARN	F C de la Méditerranée, La Seyne	10.1.14	4.20	See notes	Converted 1923–27 to aircraft carrier
FLANDRE	Arsenal de Brest	1.10.13	20.10.14		BU from 10.24
GASCOIGNE	Arsenal de Lorient	1.10.13	20.9.14		BU 1923–24
LANGUEDOC	F C de la Gironde, Bordeaux	18.4.13	1.5.16		BU from 6.29
NORMANDIE	A C de la Loire	18.4.13	19.10.14		BU 1924–25

Provence after her mid-1930s reconstruction *Navarret Collection*

turbine-driven *Bretagne* class. Reciprocating engines were to be used mainly for cruising. The turbines were designed for steaming ahead only. However, the turbine drive (with 4 Parsons turbines only) was retained for the last of the class – *Béarn*. These ships were left unfinished when war broke out in 1914 as workers joined up and afterwards some of them were left lying incomplete for years. Equipment such as boilers earmarked for the class were fitted to other warships whereas some of the 340mm and 138.6mm guns – in so far as they were completed at all – were placed at the disposal of the Army and were put into action on various fronts. Some of the completed 340mm guns were fitted after 1918 in *Bretagnes* as replacements for their original guns.

Before these battleships were stricken and the orders cancelled, there were discussions as to whether or not they should be completed, bearing in mind recent First World War experience. Considered necessary were: increase in speed from 21–21.5kts to 24kts–25kts, which would have necessitated increasing the propulsive power to 80,000shp (replacing the machinery with new turbines); lengthening the hull and fitting torpedo bulges with a maximum width of 1m each; increasing the range of main guns from 16,000m–16,500m to 25,000m–26,000m; fitting a tripod mast with gunnery control position; improving the internal (mainly horizontal) protection; replacing the 450mm TT by 550mm. For *Béarn* the following alterations were also proposed: replacing the Niclausse boilers by 8 oil-fired boilers of latest design and replacing the turbines with new ones (80,000shp = 24–25kts), and finally an investigation into whether a completely new 340mm quadruple turret with a greater range could be developed and, if not, a discussion on the development of 400mm twin turrets.

Naval specialists were of the opinion that these ships should not be completed and this combined with a shortage of funds meant that the building programme was stopped. France already had 7 dreadnoughts at her disposal, but even so she was now on a par with Italy's navy as far as this class of ship was concerned.

For full details on *Béarn*, as converted to aircraft carrier, see the 1922–1946 volume.

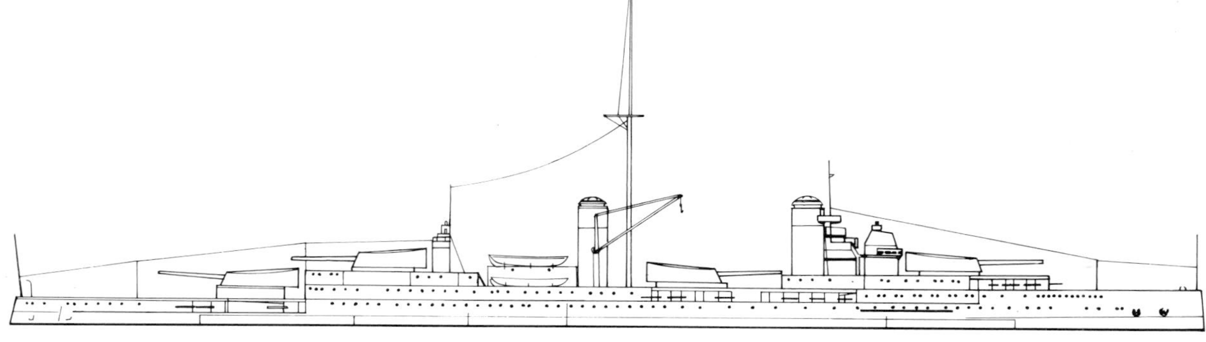

Lyon class design

LYON class *battleships*

Displacement:	29,000t full load
Dimensions:	623ft 4in pp, 638ft 2in oa × 95ft 2in × 28ft 5in, 30ft 2in *190.0m pp, 194.5m oa × 29.0m × 8.65m, 9.2m*
Machinery:	4-shaft turbines and VTE, boilers, 43,000shp = 23kts, see notes
Armour:	See notes
Armament:	16–340mm (13.4in)/45 Mod 12M (4×4), 24–138.6mm (5.4in)/55 Mod 10, or of a new semi-automatic type to be developed, 40mm AA or 47mm AA, 6 TT sub
Complement:	?

Name	Builder	Laid down	Launched	Comp	Fate
DUQUESNE	Arsenal de Brest				
LILLE	F C de la Méditerranée, La Seyne				
LYON	A C de la Loire et Penhoët, St-Nazaire				
TOURVILLE	Arsenal de Lorient				

Authorised under the 1912 programme to a design by M Doyere, none of them were actually started. Orders for *Lille* and *Lyon* were to have been placed on 1 January 1915 and for *Duquesne* and *Tourville* on 1 April 1915, but were not carried out. Had they been built, these ships which were an enlargement of the *Normandies*, but more heavily armed would have been the world's most awesome warships. A few designs had been presented to the naval staff: 27,500t, 14–340mm; 28,500t–29,000t, 16–340mm; 27,000t, 8–380mm, 28,500t–29,000t, 10–380mm or 20–305mm (5×4). The amount of time taken to design a 380mm gun meant that this possibility was rejected as were two 340mm designs, one of which – a 45 calibre gun – was similar to that fitted in *Bretagne* and *Normandie*. Finally a compromise was reached which meant increasing the number of guns while retaining the 340mm calibre: two alternative projects were discussed. The first envisaged 14–340mm and the second 16–340mm. In the case of the ship with 14–340mm guns (three quadruple and one double turret) the displacement was 27,500t on 185m wl × 28m × 8.65m hull. Finally it was decided on 24 November 1913 to adopt the second design (16–340mm/45) envisaging 4 quadruple turrets with hydraulic-electric mountings and all-round loading positions. The outbreak of the First World War put an early end to these designs and construction was not started. The question of propulsion was left undecided: it was proposed to fit combined machinery as in *Normandie* or direct drive turbines as fitted in *Béarn* and the earlier dreadnoughts. Doyere also considered the use of the geared turbines. Trials with *Enseigne Gabolde* had produced favourable results using this type of machinery. It was proposed that the class would have the same type of armour as the *Normandie* class, the difference being slightly thinner upper deck and casemates and stronger submerged sections.

FRANCE

The Naval Law of 30 March 1912 projected for the *Marine Nationale* a strength of 28 capital ships by 1920. Battlecruisers may well have been included in this figure. A specification for battlecruisers was drawn up later by the technical branch of the navy as follows: design displacement 28,000t, speed 27kts, armament 8–340mm, complement was to be no more than 1200 officers and men. Various studies were made by some French naval designers and two of the most complete designs are listed below. These ships were never ordered or even authorised.

This battlecruiser project prepared in 1913 was named after its designer. It could however only be regarded as a starting point for future work, which was never carried out. This project envisaged a fast battleship type (inspired by the British *Queen Elizabeth* class) rather than a true battlecruiser, which would be well armed and relatively lightly armoured. Even the French classification – '*cuirassé-croiseur*' – suggested a new kind of ship, a forerunner of the new, fast capital ships of World War Two.

Gille's battlecruiser design of 1913

Displacement: 28,100t–28,347t
Dimensions: 672ft 7in pp × 88ft 7in × 29ft 6in
205.0m pp × 27.0m × 9.0m
Machinery: 4-shaft geared turbines, 52 Belleville boilers, 80,000shp = 28kts. Coal 2833t plus oil 630t for supplementary burners. Range 6300nm/4240nm/1660nm at 15kts/20.3kts/28kts
Armour: Main belt 270mm (10⁵/₈in) max
Armament: 12–340mm (13.4in) (3×4), 24–138.6mm (5.4in), 6 TT sub
Complement: 1299

Naval designer and later an admiral M Durand-Viel prepared some designs of new capital ships according to the general specification of the 1912 programme. There were three final designs: a slow battleship of 32,000t, 10–380mm (5×2) or 29,000t, 9–380mm (3×3) or 30,000t, 16–340mm (4×4) and a fast battleship of 27,500t, 10–380mm (2×3, 2×2) or 27,500t, 14–340mm (2×4, 3×2) and a battlecruiser in two variants called 'A' and 'B' (for data see above tables).

Durand-Viel's battlecruiser design of 1913 – 'A'

Displacement: 27,065t designed
Dimensions: 689ft wl × 88ft 7in × 28ft 7in
210.0m wl × 27.0m × 8.7m
Machinery: 4-shaft turbines, 21 Belleville boilers, 74,000shp = 27kts. Coal 1810t plus oil 1050t max. Range 3600nm at 16kts
Armour: Very similar to *Normandies*, but main belt 280mm (11¹/₈in) max
Armament: 8–340mm (13.4in) (2×4), 24–138.6mm (5.4in), 4–450mm (17.7in) TT sub
Complement: ?

Durand-Viel's battlecruiser design of 1913 – 'B'

Displacement: As 'A'
Dimensions: As 'A', but 682ft 5in wl (*208.0m*)
Machinery: 4-shaft turbines, 18 Belleville (10 coal, 8 oil), 63,000shp = 26kts or 4-shaft geared turbines, 18 Belleville (10 coal, 8 oil), 80,000shp = 27kts. Range as 'A'
Armour: As 'A'
Armament: 8–370mm (14.6in) (2×4), 24–138.6mm (5.4in) (12×2), 4–450mm (17.7in) TT sub
Complement: ?

CRUISERS

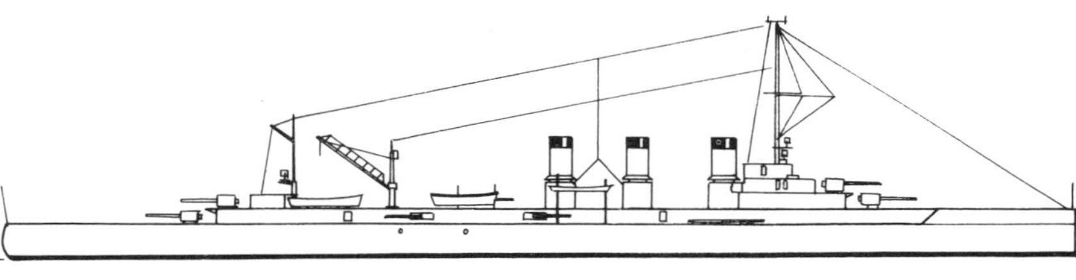

Lamotte Picquet class final design

The French naval programme of 1912 included 10 so-called '*éclaireurs d'escadre*' or fast light scout cruisers to be completed by 1920. Similar ships were already being built for Austrian and Italian navies not to mention the British or German. A sketch design prepared in 1913 was dropped as too large and expensive for their envisaged role. Originally the ships were to have the following specification: 6000t designed, 145.0m (pp) × 15.2m × 6.3m, 2 shafts, 2 sets of geared turbines, 10 boilers, 34,000shp = 27kts, armour – belt 50–100mm, deck 40mm, conning tower 170mm and gun shields 100mm, armament – 10–138.6mm/ 45 Mod 1910, 3–47mm, 2–450mm TT. However in view of foreign developments it was later considered wiser to build smaller and faster ships which would be more flexible so another design was prepared (see above). A smaller 4500t ship was finally authorised and a prototype named *Lamotte Picquet* was to be ordered at Arsenal de Toulon in 1914 and begun in 1915. Two other ships were to be contracted to private yards but these orders were also cancelled in 1915. With the outbreak of war the project was suspended and it was decided to re-examine it and to reorder the cruisers in modified form in the near future. The new cruisers were to be larger and slightly faster (5026t normal, 143.8m × 14.25m × 4.9m, 44,000shp, 29.5kts, range 3800nm/1200nm/700nm at 14kts/25kts/29.5kts). These ships were to have a nearly identical appearance to the 4500t type (slim hull, three funnels, two pairs of superfiring guns fore and aft and two pairs in casemates on each side). Casemate guns on light ships were then obsolete. Submerged TT were a hazard to the watertight integrity of ships. All these plans were dropped as the war progressed. The French Navy got its first real fast light cruisers only in the 1920s – one of them was also named *Lamotte Picquet*.

LAMOTTE PICQUET class (1914 design) *scout cruisers*

Displacement: 4500t (designed); 6000t full load
Dimensions: 452ft 9in × 45ft 3in × 15ft 9in
138.0m × 13.8m × 4.8m
Machinery: 4-shaft turbines, 12 Du Temple-Guyot boilers, 40,000shp = 29kts. Coal 300t. Oil 500t. Range 3300nm/1280nm/775nm at 16kts/26kts/29kts
Armour: Belt 28mm (1¹/₈in) covering vitals only
Armament: 8–138.6mm (5.4in)/45 Mod 1910, 2–47mm, 4–450mm (17.7in) TT (submerged)
Complement: 17 officers, 340 crew

Name	Builder	Laid down	Launched	Comp	Fate
LAMOTTE PICQUET	Arsenal de Toulon	(1915)		(1918–19)	Cancelled 1915

Ex-German KOLBERG class *light cruiser*

Class:
Colmar (ex-*Kolberg*)
Transferred as war reparation as *W* on 28 April 1920 in Cherbourg. Stricken on 21 July 1927 and BU 1929 in Brest.

Ex-German MAGDEBURG class *light cruiser*

Class:
Mulhouse (ex-*Stralsund*)
Transferred as a war reparation as *Z* on 3 August 1920 in Cherbourg. Stricken in 1933 and BU in Brest during 1935. She was refitted in Brest in 1925 but as worn out was little used and soon after placed in reserve.

Ex-German GRAUDENZ class *light cruiser*

Class:
Strasbourg (ex-*Regensburg*)
Transferred as a war reparation as *I* on 4 June 1920 in Cherbourg. Served in French Navy until 1936 and used as a hulk until 1944 in Lorient. Refitted in 1925 when she reached a speed of 26kts on trials.

Ex-German KÖNIGSBERG (ii) class *light cruiser*

Class:
Metz (ex-*Königsberg*)
Transferred 20 July 1920 in Cherbourg as *A* and renamed *Metz*. Served until 1933. BU 1936 in Brest.

Ex-Austrian modified ADMIRAL SPAUN class *scout cruiser*

Class:
Thionville (ex-*Novara*)
Interned at Cattaro in November 1918. Towed to Bizerta in 1920 and under the peace treaty taken over by the French Navy. Refitted at Cherbourg in 1921. Bridge was enlarged. Served as Mediterranean gunnery and torpedo TS. Stricken 1933 and BU 1941. Two other ships of this class served under the Italian flag.

AIRCRAFT CARRIERS

FOUDRE *seaplane carrier*

Originally a cruiser type torpedo-boat depot ship (launched 20 October 1895). She was converted into a repair ship in 1907 and into a minelayer carrying 80 mines in 1910. In 1911 or 1912 she was once more altered into an aircraft depot ship with a hangar being fitted between the third funnel and the mainmast and a crane added. In 1913 she underwent a third conversion into a seaplane carrier capable of carrying 4–8 machines. During 1914–18 she was also used as a submarine tender. Between 10 January 1916 and 21 March 1916 she served as command ship; some of her 100mm guns were disembarked in 1918 and replaced by modified 90mm army guns. After the war she was also used as an aviation school ship for a period before she was stricken on 1 December 1921.

The following vessels also served as aircraft carriers during the war: ex-liner *Campinas* (launched 1896, 3319t, TE-powered, 10kts) converted in 1915 into a seaplane carrier with two hangars for 6–10 flying-boats or float-planes.

The requisitioned Channel packets *Nord* and *Pas-de-Calais* (both launched 1898, 1541grt, paddle-powered, 21kts) used as seaplane carriers 1916–17 returned to owners in 1919.

Rouen (launched 1912, 1656grt, turbine-powered, 24kts), converted into a seaplane carrier in 1917 (classified as a *transport d'aviation*) and returned to her owners in 1919.

DESTROYERS AND TORPEDO-BOATS

French destroyers at the turn of the century were at the same level of development as their foreign equivalents. New ships belonged mainly to the 300 tonner type, but since 1903 they had been outclassed by larger and more heavily armed British ships. French destroyers were simply developed too slowly. Even the first orders for 450 ton *Spahi* class ships did not help very much. Existing ships as well as the ones built prior to the First World War resulted in heterogeneous flotillas and they were not suited for fleet actions. Most of them were too small for effective escort work and their construction (especially of the modern craft) was fragile. It was impossible to maintain high speed in any rougher seas and the fire control system was inferior to that of other big navies.

French Naval Staff realising all these deficiencies planned to launch a new construction programme which by 1920 would provide the French Navy with 32 big 1200–1500 ton destroyers equipped with geared turbines and a main armament of two or three 138.6mm guns and four or more 450mm or 500mm TT in trainable deck mountings. As the Great War broke out the project was stopped and nothing came of it. Only postwar programmes of the early 1920s included bigger and more powerful destroyers. As an interim measure only the four Argentine destroyers then building in French yards were requisitioned. With the progress of war the losses mounted and as French shipyards were unable to continue to build complicated destroyers a decision was reached in 1917 to order 12 such ships of the IJN's *Kaba* class from Japanese yards. French shipyards were at the time overloaded with repair work and were taking part in the general war effort by producing equipment for the Army.

The idea of a big destroyer was revived in France as early as in 1918 when the first preliminary designs were made. It was discussed through 1919–1920 and finally materialised in the 1922 programme which included standard destroyers of 1500t (*Bourrasque* class) and big super-destroyers of 2400t (*Jaguar* class). These designs resulted from

French prewar studies and also from British and German 1914–18 experiences. The French Navy got its first big destroyer in the form of the ex-German *Amiral Sènés* (ex-*S 113*).

Hussard December 1915
CPL

Fantassin as completed *Aldo Fraccaroli Collection*

SPAHI class *destroyers*

Displacement: 530t/550t full load (designed 450t)
Dimensions: 210ft pp × 21ft 8in × 7ft 7in
64.0m (pp) × 6.6m × 2.3m (Lansquenet, Enseigne Henry, Aspirant Herber)
212ft pp × 19ft 10in × 7ft 7in
64.6m (pp) × 6.05m × 2.3m (Spahi)
215ft 11in × 21ft 8in × 4ft 7in
65.8m (pp) × 6.6m × 2.4m (Hussard, Mameluk)
210ft 8in pp × 21ft 4in × 4ft 7in
64.2m (pp) × 6.5m × 2.4m (Carabinier)
Machinery: 2-shaft TE, 4 Normand or Du Temple or Guyot boilers, 7500ihp = 28kts (9000ihp in *Spahi*). Coal 95t (115t in *Lansquenet*). Range 1000nm–1200nm at 10kts (2880nm at 10kts in *Lansquenet*)
Armament: 6–65mm/45 Mod 02, 3–450mm (17.7in) TT
Complement: 77–79

Name	Builder	Launched	Fate
SPAHI	F et Ch de la Méditerranée, La Seyne	3.5.08	Stricken 12.27
HUSSARD	Ch de la Loire, Nantes	12.9.08	Stricken 3.22
CARABINIER	Penhoët, St-Nazaire	10.10.08	Sunk 15.11.18
LANSQUENET	Dyle et Bacalan, Bordeaux	20.11.09	Stricken 12.28
MAMELUK	Ch de la Loire, Nantes	10.3.09	Stricken 2.28
ENSEIGNE HENRY	Arsenal de Rochefort	12.5.11	Stricken 6.28
ASPIRANT HERBER	Arsenal de Rochefort	30.4.12	Stricken 7.30

The first seven ships (named after troop types or naval heroes) of the new 450t class of French destroyers designed to catch up with growth of foreign constructions. All had reciprocating engines, coal-fired boilers and identical armament. They were simply enlarged versions of the earlier 300-tonners. The 65mm guns were of Model 1902 and had 1906 Model torpedoes (2 in single revolving tubes amidships and 1 in bow tube). Ships differed in hull dimensions according to the building yards. They were well built but their sea-going qualities were still insufficient to make them good long range escorts, though they were better than 300-tonners. All ships had 2 groups of stacks placed in pairs before and after the main machinery which was installed amidships. All except *Carabinier* (27kts) exceeded their designed speed on trials reaching 28.25–29.8kts. All the class served in the Mediterranean in 1914–18. *Mameluk* (having rammed and sunk *Fantassin* in a 5 June 1916 night collision) and *Lansquenet* sank *UC 38* and (with *Spahi*) rescued 1162 men from the U-boat and her victim torpedoed cruiser/troopship *Châteaurenault* on 14 December 1917 off Cephalonia (Ionian Sea). *Carabinier* was stranded on 13 November 1918 off Latakieh in Syria and had to be scuttled under Turkish fire two days later, long after formal Ottoman surrender.

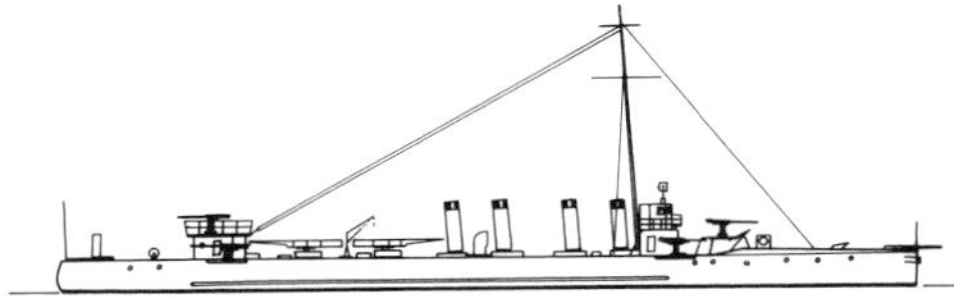

Voltigeur as completed

VOLTIGEUR class *destroyers*

Displacement: 450t designed; 590t full load
Dimensions: 214ft 11in pp × 22ft 4in × 10ft 2in
65.5m pp × 6.8m × 3.1m (Voltigeur)
206ft 8in × 21ft × 9ft 6in
63.0m pp × 6.4m × 2.9m (Tirailleur)
Machinery: 3 shafts, 1 TE set on central shaft and 2 Rateau (*Voltigeur*) or 2 Breguet (*Tirailleur*) turbines on outer shafts, 4 Normand (*Voltigeur*) or Du Temple (*Tirailleur*) boilers, 7500shp = 28kts. Coal 118t. Range 1520nm/5600nm at 10kts/20kts
Armament: 6–65mm/45 Mod 02, 3–450mm (17.7in) TT
Complement: 76–77

Name	Builder	Launched	Fate
VOLTIGEUR	A Ch de la Bretagne, Nantes	23.3.09	Stricken 5.20
TIRAILLEUR	Ch de la Gironde, Bordeaux	27.11.08	Stricken 7.21

Two 450t destroyers of slightly different hull dimensions modelled on the preceeding *Spahi* class were built as an experiment; completed 1908–09. They were fitted with three-shaft machinery – a reciprocating cruise engine in the central shaft and turbines for high speed on the outer shafts. Both proved quite reliable in service but exceeded their designed displacement. However their combined machinery was considered less flexible than the single type of engines in other ships. In this class all four funnels were installed before an engine room.

CHASSEUR class *destroyers*

Displacement: 450t designed, 520t full load
Dimensions: 210ft 8in pp × 21ft 4in × 16ft 2in
64.2m pp × 6.5m × 3.1m (Chasseur)
211ft 8in pp × 21ft 8in × 10ft 2in
64.5m pp × 6.6m × 3.1m (Janissaire)
214ft 7in pp × 22ft × 10ft 2in
65.4m pp × 6.7m × 3.1m (Fantassin)
210ft 8in × 21ft 8in × 10ft 2in
64.2m × 6.6m × 3.1m (Cavalier)
Machinery: 3-shaft Parsons turbines, 4 Normand boilers (3 Foster-Wheeler in *Janissaire*), 7200shp = 28kts. Coal 99t (*Chasseur*) or oil 135t (others). Range 1400nm–1500nm at 10kts
Armament: 6–65mm/45 Mod 02, 3–450mm (17.7in) TT
Complement: 77–79

Name	Builder	Launched	Fate
CHASSEUR	Normand, Le Havre	20.2.09	Stricken 10.19
JANISSAIRE	Penhoët, St-Nazaire	12.4.10	Stricken 10.20
FANTASSIN	F et Ch de la Méditerranée, La Seyne	17.6.09	Sunk 5.6.16
CAVALIER	Normand, Le Havre	9.5.10	TS 1914, stricken 12.27

These ships completed in 1909 and 1911 had their boiler rooms placed before the engine room. They were the first ships in the French Navy to be fitted with oil-fired boilers (not *Chasseur*). On trials they proved successful exceeding their designed power by wide margins (8000–9000shp was reached) with speeds of 28.5kts–31kts. Their main drawback was that their turbines proved less sturdy than had been hoped. All the class served in the Mediterranean 1914–18, *Chasseur* was in 2nd Flotilla at Brindisi (1915–17). *Janissaire* patrolled near Castellorizo Island on the S Turkish coast during 1915–16. *Fantassin* was rammed on 5 June 1916 by *Mameluk* in the Mediterranean and *Fauconneau* subsequently finished off her wreck using her guns. A collision between *Cavalier* and *Fantassin* on 17 August 1914 led to her bow TT being removed during repairs at Malta. She was later used only by mechanics, stokers and divers as a schoolship.

Francis Garnier during the war CPL

Magon during the war CPL

BOUCLIER class *destroyers*

Displacement: 800t designed (*Bouclier* and *Francis Garnier* 692t); 720t–756t normal
Dimensions: 242ft 9in–256ft 1in (*Bouclier* 237ft) oa × 24ft 11in–26ft 3in × 9ft 6in–10ft 10in
74.0m–78.3m (72.3m) × 7.6m–8.0m × 2.9m–3.3m
Machinery: 2-shaft Parsons (a), Zoelly (b), Bréguet (c) or Rateau (d) turbines, 4 Normand, Normand-Sigaudy, Du Temple or Dyle et Bacalan boilers, 13,000shp = 30kts (*Bouclier* and *Casque* had 3-shaft Parsons turbines), oil 120–160t. Range 1200nm/1600nm at 12kts–14kts
Armament: 2–100mm (3.9in)/45 Mod 93, 4–65mm/45 Mod 02, 4–450mm (17.7in) TT (2×2)
Complement: 80–83

Name	Builder	Launched	Fate
BOUCLIER (a)	Normand, Le Havre	29.6.11	Stricken 15.2.33
BOUTEFEU (b)	Dyle et Bacalan, Bordeaux	2.5.11	Sunk 15.5.17
CASQUE (a)	F et Ch de la Méditerranée, Le Havre	25.8.10	Stricken 26.3.26, BU 25.5.27
CIMETERRE (c)	F et Ch de la Gironde, Bordeaux	13.4.11	Stricken 10.7.26
DAGUE (c)	F et Ch de la Gironde, Bordeaux	13.4.11	Sunk 24.2.15
FAULX (d)	De la Brosse et Fouché, Nantes	2.2.11	Sunk 18.4.18
FOURCHE (d)	De la Brosse et Fouché, Nantes	21.10.10	Sunk 23.6.16
CAPITAINE MEHL (a)	A et Ch de la Loire, St-Nazaire	20.4.12	Stricken 10.7.26
COMMANDANT BORY (d)	Dyle et Bacalan, Bordeaux	14.9.12	Stricken 29.7.26
COMMANDANT RIVIÈRE	F et Ch de la Bordeaux	2.10.12	Stricken 6.33
DEHORTER (a)	Penhoët, St-Nazaire	18.4.12	Stricken 1933
FRANCIS GARNIER (a)	Normand, Le Havre	1.10.12	Stricken 10.2.26

These 12 800-tonners were designed by various shipyards to the general specification which included turbines and oil-fired boilers as a requirement – hence many variations from ship to ship. They were however given a uniform armament of 2–100mm 1893 model guns, 4–65mm 1902 model guns and 2 twin trainable 450mm TT. During the war one 45mm or 75mm AA gun was added together with 2–8mm MGs and 8–10 DC of Guiraud type. These ships were laid down in 1909–1910 under 1908 and 1910 programmes and completed in 1911–1913. *Casque* cost 2.96 million francs. They had twin screw machinery – except *Bouclier* and *Casque* which had 3 screws and were the fastest ships of the class, reaching 35.5kts and 34.9kts respectively on trials. *Bouclier* and *Casque* also had the lowest fuel consumption. These 800t destroyers were modified during the war and became overloaded so their top operational sea speed seldom exceeded 26kts. Their hulls showed weakness in a seaway and had to be strengthened and their machinery proved itself to be not very sturdy. Other drawbacks became apparent and needed correcting before the end of the war – armament was thought to be weak, the bridge poorly constructed and the ship's silhouette too high. Ships of this type formed a relatively homogenous class, rare in the French Navy at that time troubled as it was by frequent changes of policy. Four funnels were fitted except in *Casque* which had three. The funnels were stepped in two groups before the engine room (*Boutefeu* and *Cdt Bory* had their stacks spaced equally). The slowest ship of the class was *Bory* which reached only 24kts in service.

All except three of the class spent all of 1914–18 in the Mediterranean. *Bouclier* switched to Dunkirk in December 1916 and was damaged in a 20 May 1917 action with German destroyers. She was an 17 October bombardment of Ostend and lost her poop to one of her own DC while attacking a U-boat on 8 December. She (and *Capitaine Mehl*) sank the German destroyer *A 7* on 21 March 1918, taking part in the Zeebrugge and Ostend raids. *Casque* finished off the mined Austrian destroyer *Triglav* in the Adriatic on 29 December 1915 and was rammed at 31kts by the Italian destroyer *Abba* in the Otranto Strait on 22 December 1916. She was operational by May 1917 but was again rammed by an ally, the minelayer *Pluton*, off the Dardanelles on 29 August 1918. *Commandant Rivière* hit the Austrian *Dinara* in the 22 December 1916 action but had her own boiler room knocked out. *Francis Garnier* carried out 1914 Flanders shore bombardments and gave passage to General Foch on 1 December. She and *Oriflamme* captured a German seaplane off Ostend on 2 March 1916 and took slight damage in the 27 October 1917 action with German destroyers.

Dague had an experimental tripod mast for a time. *Boutefeu* was cut in half and sunk by a mine laid by German *UC 25* off Brindisi, *Dague* sunk by a drifting mine in Antivari Roads, *Faulx* was rammed and sunk by her fellow destroyer *Mangini* in Otranto Strait, *Fourche* was torpedoed and sunk by the Austrian *U 15*.

BISSON class *destroyers*

Displacement: 756t–791t normal; 855t full load; 800t designed
Dimensions: 256ft 2in × 28ft 3in × 10ft 2in (arsenal-built ships)
78.1m pp × 8.6m × 3.1m
Machinery: 2-shaft Bréguet (a), Parsons (b), Zoelly (c) or Rateau (d) turbines, 4 Indret boilers, 15,000shp = 30kts. Oil 165t. Range 1950nm/450nm at 14kts/30kts
Armament: 2–100mm (3.9in)/45 Mod 93, 4–65mm/45 Mod 02, 4–450mm (17.7in) TT (2×2)
Complement: 80–83

Name	Builder	Launched	Fate
BISSON (a)	Arsenal de Toulon	12.9.12	Stricken 6.33
RENAUDIN (a)	Arsenal de Toulon	20.3.13	Sunk 18.3.16
COMMANDANT LUCAS (a)	Arsenal de Toulon	11.7.14	Stricken 6.33
PROTET (b)	Arsenal de Rochefort	15.10.13	Stricken 1933
MANGINI (c)	Schneider, Chalon-sur-Saône	31.3.13	Stricken 1934
MAGON (d)	A et Ch de Bretagne, Nantes	19.4.13	Stricken 16.2.26

Six ships were laid down in 1911–12 under 1910 and 1911 programmes and completed in 1913–14. They had four funnels placed in two distinct pairs; ships constructed in naval dockyards had higher funnels. Building cost was 3.1 million francs. These vessels were quite similar to *Bouclier* class ships. A tripod mast was fitted on *Commandant Lucas*. *Mangini* had to be transported down the Rhone from its builders, Schneider, on a barge specially made for the purpose (in order to clear bridges masts and funnels were removed). All exceeded 30kts on trials, the fastest being *Magon* which reached 32.02kts.

All the class except *Magon* served all of 1914–18 in the Mediterranean. *Bisson* shelled and sank the Austrian *U 3* on 13 August 1915. She was stationed on Mudros in 1918 and went on to the Black Sea in 1919. *Mangini* was (with the destroyer HMS *Shark*) the first Allied warship to anchor off Constantinople on 10 November 1918, before going into the Black Sea. *Magon* went to the Dunkirk Flotilla in December 1916 and fought in four 1917–18 actions with German destroyers. She escorted British monitors in their 14 October 1918 Flanders bombardment. *Bisson* was unlisted from June 1933 and went to the breakers in 1939. *Renaudin* was torpedoed and sunk by Austrian *U 6* off Durazzo, *Protet* was stricken in February 1933 and sold in June 1936 after serving since 1921 as a signal school tender.

ENSEIGNE ROUX class *destroyers*

Displacement: 850t normal; 1075t full load
Dimensions: 271ft oa × 28ft 3in × 9ft 10in
82.6m oa × 8.6m × 3.0m
Machinery: 2-shaft Parsons turbines, 4 Du Temple or Guyot, 17,000shp = 30kts. Oil 175t. Range 1400nm at 14kts
Armament: 2–100mm (3.9in)/45 Mod 93, 4–65mm/45 Mod 02, 4–450mm (17.7in) TT (2×2)
Complement: 76–81

Name	Builder	Launched	Fate
ENSEIGNE ROUX	Arsenal de Rochefort	13.7.15	Stricken 1936
MÉCANICIEN PRINCIPAL LESTIN	Arsenal de Rochefort	15.5.15	Stricken 1935
ENSEIGNE GABOLDE	Normand, Le Havre	–	See notes

All three ships ordered under 1913 programme. The first two of the trio were begun in 1913 and completed in 1916, the third ship was completed after the war to a modified plan (she was planned as an experimental ship). These ships were enlarged versions of the 800 tonners design fitted with tripod masts. Armament of *Enseigne Roux* class was the same as fitted on earlier ships and was augmented during the war with one 75mm AA gun, ten DC of Guiraud type and Pinocchio towed AS torpedo. On trials they reached 30–31kts.

Enseigne Roux served 1915–18 with the Dunkirk Flotilla, fought in the 20 May 1917 action with German destroyers and participated in the 1918 Zeebrugge/Ostend raids as well as the 14 October British monitor bombardment of Flanders. *Mécanicien Principal Lestin* joined the Mediterranean Fleet in March 1916 but went into the Dunkirk Flotilla in April 1918. She was in the 1930 Baltic Division. Both ships were broken up in 1937.

ENSEIGNE GABOLDE *destroyer*

Displacement: 835t standard; 950t normal
Dimensions: 274ft 4in oa, 269ft wl × 26ft 11in × 10ft 2in
83.6m oa, 82.0m wl × 8.2m × 3.1m
Machinery: 2-shaft Parsons geared turbines, 4 Normand boilers, 20,000shp = 31kts. Oil 196t. Range 1300nm at 14kts
Armament: 3–100mm (3.9in)/45 Mod 93, 1–75mm AA, 4–550mm (21.7in) Mod 23 TT (2×2)
Complement: 80

Name	Builder	Launched	Fate
ENSEIGNE GABOLDE	Normand, Le Havre	23.4.21	Stricken 1938

Experimental destroyer *Enseigne Gabolde* was suspended on the slip after the outbreak of war. She was to be fitted with Parsons geared turbines for greater economy. Her building was resumed only shortly before the end of the war and finished in 1923 to a modified design taking into account the lessons of the war. During the war the ex-Argentine *Opiniâtre* and *Téméraire* were fitted with her 4 boilers. She carried 4 funnels (rear pair were shorter than those forward) and had a larger bridge; the forward guns were superimposed (which proved an unsatisfactory arrangement because of the ship's small size). She developed 26,000shp and reached over 33kts on trials.

Téméraire as completed
Aldo Fraccaroli Collection

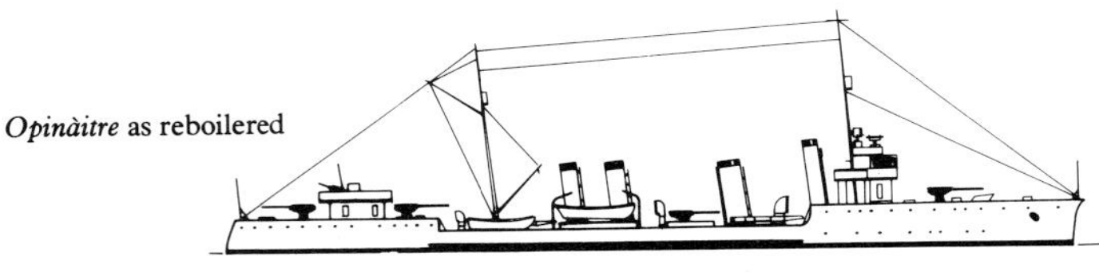
Opinàitre as reboilered

Ex-Argentine AVENTURIER class *destroyers*

Displacement: 930t normal; 1250t full load
Dimensions: 290ft 5in oa, 283ft 2in wl × 28ft 3in × 9ft 10in
88.5m oa, 86.3m wl × 8.6m × 3.1m
Machinery: 2-shaft Rateau turbines, 5 White Foster-Wheeler boilers, 18,000shp = 32kts. Coal 230t. Oil 72t. Range 1850nm at 10kts
Armament: 4–102mm (US 4in pattern), 6–457mm (18in) TT (2×2, 2×1)
Complement: 140

Name	Builder	Launched	Fate
OPINIÂTRE (ex-*Rioja*)	Ch de Bretagne, Nantes	1911	Stricken 1933, BU 1935
AVENTURIER (ex-*Mendoza*)	Ch de Bretagne, Nantes	18.2.11	Stricken 1938, BU 1940
TÉMÉRAIRE (ex-*San Juan*)	Ch de Bretagne, Nantes	8.12.11	Stricken 1936
INTRÉPIDE (ex-*Salta*)	Ch de Bretagne, Nantes	25.9.11	Stricken 1937, BU 1938

Ordered in 1910 by the Argentine Navy and requisitioned on 9 August 1914 while completing. Four other Argentine destroyers were taken over by the German Navy (*G 101* class). French-built ships renamed as *Aventurier* class were armed with 4–100mm/45 Canet guns, one 47mm AA gun and four single 450mm TT (torpedoes Model 1906). Their worn out guns were replaced by new ones in December 1914 (one ship received old guns removed from battleship *Devastation*). *Opiniâtre* and *Téméraire* were repaired at Brest in 1917 after it was discovered that their boilers were leaking badly. Replacement boilers consisted of one oil-fired boiler each (originally earmarked for *Enseigne Gabolde*) and three du Temple type boilers (from *Normandie* and *Gascogne*) as well as reserves (5 in total). They carried four funnels instead of the original three, but could develop only 12,000shp giving just 22kts.

The period 1919–20 saw all four taking part in Baltic operations. Refitting of *Aventurier* and *Intrépide*, took place between 1924–27. *Aventurier* got 2 Schulz-Thornycroft boilers and 1 Du Temple boiler and *Intrépide* received three Schulz-Thornycroft type – all removed from the captured German destroyers *V 100* and *V 126* which were transferred to the French Navy in 1920 and scrapped. After the conversion *Aventurier* and *Intrépide* reached 26kts under full load. From 1927 they had only two funnels. By 1926 all four ships of this class were converted into fast minesweepers.

Enseigne Gabolde as completed
Navarret Collection

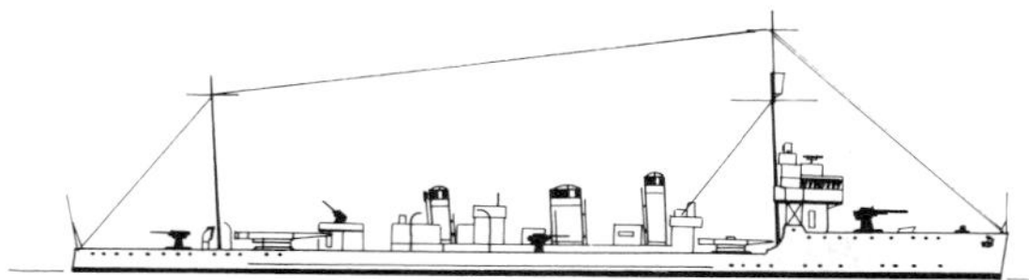
Arabe class

ARABE class *destroyers*

Displacement: 685t
Dimensions: 271ft 11in oa, 260ft 6in wl × 23ft 11in × 7ft 11in
82.9m oa, 79.4m wl × 7.3m × 2.4m
Machinery: 3-shaft VTE, 4 Kampon boilers, 10,000ihp = 29kts. Coal 102t. Oil 118t. Range 2000nm at 12kts
Armament: 1–120mm (4.7in)/40, 3–76mm/40, 1–76mm/40 AA, 4–450mm (17.7in) TT (2×2)
Complement: 86

Name	Builder	Launched	Fate
ALGÉRIEN	Yokosuka DY	1917	Stricken 1936
ANNAMITE	Yokosuka DY	1917	Stricken 1933
ARABE	Kure DY	1917	Stricken 1936
BAMBARA	Kure DY	1917	Stricken 1933
HOVA	Sasebo DY	1917	Stricken 1936
KABYLE	Sasebo DY	1917	Stricken 1936
MAROCAIN	Maizuru DY	1917	Stricken 1935
SAKALAVE	Maizuru DY	1917	Stricken 1936
SÉNÉGALAIS	Kawasaki, Kobe	1917	Stricken 1936
SOMALI	Kawasaki, Kobe	1917	Stricken 1935
TONKINOIS	Mitsubishi, Nagasaki	1917	Stricken 1936
TOUAREG	Mitsubishi, Nagasaki	1917	Stricken 1935

These *Arabe* class destroyers were ordered in Japan in 1917 because it was impossible to get such ships from French, British or US shipyards when they were needed urgently. These ships were built in record time averaging little over 5 months from keel laying to completion. They were modelled on the Japanese *Kaba* type already in service with Japanese Navy and named after the varied peoples of the French Empire. Ships of this class served well under the French flag and were stricken only in the 1930s. Their armament was Japanese and this fact caused some difficulties for supply depots. These ships were used in the Mediterranean and later most of them were based with the Brest North Squadron (7 with 11th Flotilla on Taranto-Hea escort duty and 5 with 3rd Division at Mudros). Others steamed off Morocco during the Riff War (1924–25).

Ex-Greek AETOS class *destroyers*

Class (former names):
Aetos (ex-Argentine *San Luis*), *Ierax* (ex-Argentine *Santa Fé*), *Leon* (ex-Argentine *Tucuman*)
Three destroyers requisitioned and manned by French Navy after the events in Greece. They were seized in December 1916 and served under French colours in 1917–18. *Panther*, fourth in this class was unaccountably not requisitioned.

Ex-Greek NIKI class *destroyers*

Class:
Aspis, Doxa, Niki, Velos
Four coastal 350t destroyers seized by French Navy in the same way as the *Aetos* class. Built 1905–06.

Ex-Greek THYELLA class *coastal destroyers*

Class:
Longhi, Navkratoussa, Sphendoni, Thyella
Four coastal 390t destroyers seized by the French Navy in 1916. Built at Yarrow in 1906.

Ex-Greek DORIS class *torpedo-boats*

Class:
Aigli, Alkyone, Arethousa, Daphni, Doris, Thetis
Six small coastal torpedo-boats of 120t seized in 1916 at Salamis as the *Aetos* class and used for patrols in Aegean in 1917–18, they were returned in 1918. *Thetis* may not have been commissioned.

Ex-Austrian TATRA class *destroyer*

Class:
Matelot Leblanc (ex-*Dukla*)
Incorporated into the French Navy in September 1920 where she served until 1936 when stricken and BU. Seven other ships of the type served in the Italian Navy.

Ex-German V 67 and V 125 class *destroyers*

Class:
Pierre Durand (ex-*V 79*), *Buino* (ex-*V 130*)
Transferred as war reparations on 14 June 1920 in Brest and on 3 August 1920 in Cherbourg respectively. Served in the French Navy until 1933 and 1934 respectively.

Ex-German S 131 class *destroyers*

Class:
Chastang (ex-*S 133*), *Vesco* (ex-*S 134*), *Mazaré* (ex-*S 135*), *Deligny* (ex-*S 139*)
Transferred as war reparations in 1920 and served until 1934, 1935 and 1934 respectively.

Ex-German H 145 class *destroyers*

Class:
Rageot de la Touche (ex-*H 146*), *Marcel Delage* (ex-*H 147*)
Two ships transferred in Cherbourg in 1920 as war reparations. Both BU in 1935.

Ex-German S 113 class *destroyer*

Class:
Amiral Sénès (ex-*S 113*)
Transferred as a war reparation in Cherbourg on 23 May 1920, served in French Navy to 1936 and later BU. She was strengthened and modified in French service and was said to be good for 32kts in the late 1920s.

There were other ex-German destroyers transferred to the French Navy but as they were worn out they were not commissioned but BU and their equipment utilised. These included: *V 100* (BU 1921), *V 126* (BU 1925) and *V 46* (BU 1924).

SUBMARINES

PLONGEUR *submarine*

Displacement: 420t surfaced; 435t submerged
Dimensions: 146ft × 19ft 8in × 9ft 2in
44.5m × 6.0m × 2.8m
Machinery: 1-shaft 4cyl compressed air engine, 80hp = 4.09kts, 23 air reservoirs totalling 128m³ at 12kg/cm². Range 7.5nm/5.7nm at 2.4kts/3.8kts submerged
Armament: 1 spar torpedo
Complement: 13

Name	Builder	Launched	Fate
PLONGEUR	Rochefort	16.4.63	See notes

Cutaway model of *Le Plongeur*
CPL

FRANCE

Designed by Admiral Siméon Bourgois (1815–87) and constructed in collaboration with Charles Brun. This vessel marked a great advance in that she was driven by a compressed-air engine. Although she was provided with horizontal rudders, the problem of maintaining a depth level was never satisfactorily solved, and, as no offensive weapon other than the spar torpedo yet existed, development was halted after a series of trials. Having been disarmed on 20 January 1867 and stricken on 15 February 1872, *Plongeur* served as auxiliary harbour tanker fitted with steam engine between 1872 and 1935 in Rochefort, sold on 26 May 1937.

GYMNÔTE *submarine*

Displacement: 30t surfaced; 31t submerged
Dimensions: 58ft 5in × 5ft 11in × 5ft 6in
17.8m × 1.8m × 1.68m
Machinery: 1-shaft Krebs electric motor, on trials 33.4shp/24.9shp = 7.31kts/4.27kts. Range 65nm/31nm at 5kts/7.3kts surfaced, 25nm/4.27kts submerged
Armament: 2–356mm (14in) torpedoes
Complement: 5

Name	Builder	Launched	Fate
GYMNÔTE (Q 1)	Toulon	24.9.88	Stricken 5.08

Single-hull steel submarine boat designed by Gustave Zédé (1825–91); carried a detachable lead keel. She was ordered on 22 November 1886. Electric power was supplied from battery of 204 cells (total weight 9.5t). *Gymnôte* proved a great success, making some 2000 successful dives during her existence. Incorporation of hydroplanes (three a side) provided the solution which was to become standard in all subsequent submarines. *Gymnôte* could have been inspired by the locomotive torpedo which Robert Whitehead had invented in 1866. *Gymnôte* was essentially an experimental boat. Torpedoes were carried in drop-collars, one on each beam. She was modernised in 1898 with the following changes: displacement 33.2t, length 18.4m, Sautter-Harlé engine 90hp, raised conning tower and new battery. She sank on 19 June 1907 at Toulon in dock and was refloated.

GUSTAVE ZÉDÉ *submarine*

Displacement: 261t–266t surfaced; 270t–272t submerged
Dimensions: 159ft 1in × 10ft 6in × 10ft 7in
48.5m × 3.2m × 3.2m
Machinery: 1-shaft electric motor, 208shp = 9.22kts/6.5kts, see notes. Range 2200nm/5.5kts surfaced, 105nm/4.47kts submerged
Armament: 1–450mm (17.7in) TT (bow; 3 torpedoes)
Complement: 19

Name	Builder	Launched	Fate
GUSTAVE ZÉDÉ (Q 2)	Mourillon, Toulon	1.6.93	Stricken 1909

Gymnôte as modernised
Aldo Fraccaroli Collection

Gustave Zédé date unknown
Aldo Fraccaroli Collection

Originally ordered on 4 October 1890 as *Sirène*, renamed in 1891. Single-hull Roma-bronze submarine boat designed by M Romazotti; carried detachable lead keel. Electric power from battery. Originally fitted with 750shp = 15kts/8kts, but, owing to accident, power reduced to above.

After early difficulties owing to excessive weight and poor design of her electric batteries which had 720 cells, and after additional hydroplanes had been fitted to improve fore-and-aft control, *Gustave Zédé* proved an unqualified success. On trials she travelled the 41nm from Toulon to Marseilles underwater. She made more than 2500 dives without accident and was probably the first submarine with an effective periscope (normally at 5 degrees) as well as a tall conning tower with a platform for surface lookouts.

Morse as completed
NB 1/750 scale

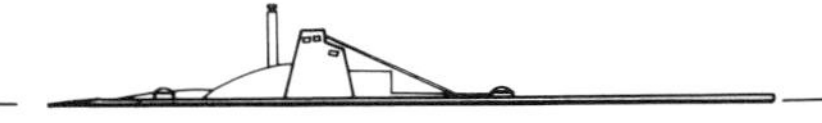

MORSE submarine

Displacement: 143t surfaced; 149t submerged
Dimensions: 119ft 9in × 9ft × 9ft 3in
36.5m × 2.7m × 2.8m
Machinery: 1-shaft electric motor, 284shp = 7.25kts/5.5kts. Range 90nm at 4.3kts surfaced
Armament: 1–450mm (17.7in) TT (bow; 3 torpedoes)
Complement: 13

Name	Builder	Launched	Fate
MORSE (Q 3)	Arsenal de Cherbourg	4.7.99	Stricken 11.09

Single-hull Roma-bronze submarine designed by M Romazotti to combine the best points of *Gymnôte* and *Zédé*. She carried a detachable lead keel. Her initial building cost was £25,920 (648,000 francs). This design was overtaken by *Narval*.

NARVAL *submarine*

Displacement: 117t surfaced; 202t submerged
Dimensions: 111ft 7in × 12ft 6in × 6ft 1in
34.0m × 3.8m × 1.8m
Machinery: 1-shaft TE and Adolphe-Seigle tubular boilers plus electric motor, 220ihp/80shp = 9.88kts/5.30kts. Range 345nm at 8.83kts surfaced, 58nm at 2.83kts submerged
Armament: 4–450mm (17.7in) torpedoes (all Drzewiecki drop-collar)
Complement: 13

Name	Builder	Launched	Fate
NARVAL (Q 4)	Arsenal de Cherbourg	21.10.99	Stricken 1909

Designed by the famous naval constructor Maxime Laubeuf (1864–1939) as a result of an open competition between 29 designs sponsored by the Minister of Marine Lockroy in 1896 for a 200t boat with a 100nm surface range and a 10nm underwater radius. In essence Laubeuf designed an improved torpedo-boat – one which could submerge to make its attack or to avoid detection, but which could at other times be at least as seaworthy as an ordinary torpedo-boat. His other innovation was the provision of the TE engine, driven by steam from an oil-fired boiler for surface operation and for battery charging. *Narval* was the first double-hull French submersible boat: the strongly constructed inner cigar-shaped hull contained all the vital equipment and the thin-plated outer hull had the lines of a torpedo-boat.

Together with the ballast tanks, situated between the two hulls, this gave the ship a 42 per cent coefficient of buoyancy as compared to the 2–3 per cent of the pure submarine. This solution was not only revolutionary but epoch-making in that it led the way to making the submarine a proper warship. With her fixed conning tower, rising from the centre of the flat upper surface of the hull, and a periscope – the first submarine to be so fitted – the *Narval*'s appearance (apart from her funnel!) was the forerunner of all submarines which were to follow her. As much as 21 minutes was needed at first to cool down the boiler and to blow off steam before diving, though this was later reduced to 12 minutes. In all other aspects, her trials, which took place during 1900, proved a complete success.

Narval as completed
CPL

Otarie as completed
Aldo Fraccaroli Collection

SIRÈNE class *submarines*

Displacement: 157t surfaced; 213t submerged
Dimensions: 99ft 3in × 12ft 10in × 8ft 2in
32.5m × 3.9m × 2.5m
Machinery: 1-shaft TE steam engine, 1 boiler plus electric motor, 250ihp/100shp = 9.75kts/5.80kts. Range 600nm/500nm/430nm at 8kts/7kts/7.75kts surfaced, 55nm at 3.75kts submerged
Armament: 4–450mm (17.7in) torpedoes (all Drzewiecki drop-collar)
Complement: 13

Name	Builder	Launched	Fate
ESPADON (Q 13)	Arsenal de Cherbourg	7.9.01	Stricken 11.19
SILURE (Q 14)	Arsenal de Cherbourg	29.10.01	Stricken 11.19
SIRÈNE (Q 5)	Arsenal de Cherbourg	4.5.01	Stricken 11.19
TRITON (Q 6)	Arsenal de Cherbourg	13.7.01	Stricken 11.19

Submersible boats of modified *Narval* type with double hull ordered on 20 May 1899 and 1 May 1900. Designed by Maxime Laubeuf. Initial cost was £24,700 each. They were built like torpedo-boats and submerged by the admission of water into the space between the skins. Machinery generally similar to *Narval*. These boats could dive in 6 minutes *(Espadon)* to 9 minutes *(Triton)*. Based in Cherbourg during 1914–18.

FARFADET class *submarines*

Displacement: 185t surfaced; 202t submerged
Dimensions: 135ft 6in × 9ft 6in × 8ft 9in
41.3m × 2.9m × 2.6m
Machinery: 1-shaft electric motor, 183shp = 6.10kts/4.30kts. Range 115nm at 5.30kts surfaced, 28nm at 4.32kts submerged
Armament: 4–450mm (17.7in) torpedoes (all external cradles)
Complement: 16

Name	Builder	Launched	Fate
FARFADET (Q 7)	Arsenal de Rochefort	17.5.01	Stricken 11.13
GNÔME (Q 9)	Arsenal de Rochefort	24.7.02	Stricken 6.06
KORRIGAN (Q 8)	Arsenal de Rochefort	25.1.02	Stricken 6.06
LUTIN (Q 10)	Arsenal de Rochefort	12.2.03	Stricken 9.07

Single-hull steel submarines designed by M Maugas ordered on 26 September 1899. Initial cost of each boat was £32,000. Electric power supplied from accumulators only. *Farfadet* sank accidentally on 5 July 1905 at Bizerta (14 lives lost) and refloated. Commissioned on September 1909 as *Follet*. *Lutin* also sank accidentally on 16 October 1906 and refloated.

MORSE class *submarines*

Displacement: 147.10t surfaced; 160.06t submerged
Dimensions: 120ft 5in × 9ft × 9ft 2in
36.7m × 2.7m × 2.8m
Machinery: 1-shaft electric motor, 307shp = 10.10kts/8.30kts. Range 135nm at 6kts surfaced, 97nm at 4.30kts submerged
Armament: 1–450mm (17.7in) TT (bow), 2–450mm (17.7in) torpedoes (external cradles)
Complement: 13

Name	Builder	Launched	Fate
ALGERIEN (Q 12)	Arsenal de Cherbourg	25.4.01	Stricken 5.14
FRANÇAIS (Q 11)	Arsenal de Cherbourg	29.1.01	Stricken 5.14

Single-hull steel submarines designed by M Romazotti. Built by national subscription organised by the newspaper *'Le Matin'* at the time of the 1899 Fashoda dispute. Initial cost was £32,972 each.

Triton as completed *Aldo Fraccaroli Collection*

NAÏADE class *submarines*

Displacement: 70.5t surfaced; 73.6 submerged
Dimensions: 77ft 11in × 7ft 5in × 8ft 6in
23.7m × 2.2m × 2.6m
Machinery: 1-shaft Panhard et Levassor petrol engine plus electric motor, 57bhp/95shp = 7.20kts/5.98kts. Range 200nm at 5.5kts surfaced, 30nm at 4.10kts submerged
Armament: 2–450mm (17.7in) torpedoes (all external cradles)
Complement: 12

Name	Builder	Launched	Fate
ALOSE (Q 33)	Arsenal de Toulon	12.10.04	Stricken 5.14
ANGUILLE (Q 32)	Arsenal de Toulon	8.8.04	Stricken 5.14
BONITE (Q 19)	Arsenal de Toulon	6.2.04	Stricken 5.14
CASTOR (Q 26)	Arsenal de Rochefort	5.11.03	Stricken 5.14
DORADE (Q 22)	Arsenal de Toulon	5.11.03	Stricken 5.14
ESTURGEON (Q 18)	Arsenal de Toulon	8.1.04	Stricken 1912
GRONDIN (Q 31)	Arsenal de Toulon	15.7.04	Stricken 1913
LOUTRE (Q 25)	Arsenal de Rochefort	25.8.03	Stricken 5.14
LUDION (Q 24)	Arsenal de Toulon	18.3.04	Stricken 5.14
LYNX (Q 23)	Arsenal de Cherbourg	24.11.03	Stricken 5.14
MÉDUSE (Q 29)	Arsenal de Rochefort	15.6.04	Stricken 5.14
NAÏADE (Q 15)	Arsenal de Cherbourg	20.2.04	Stricken 5.14
OTARIE (Q 28)	Arsenal de Rochefort	16.4.04	Stricken 5.14
OURSIN (Q 30)	Arsenal de Rochefort	26.9.04	Stricken 5.14
PERLE (Q 17)	Arsenal de Toulon	1.11.03	Stricken 5.14
PHOQUE (Q 27)	Arsenal de Rochefort	16.3.04	Stricken 5.14
PROTÉE (Q 16)	Arsenal de Cherbourg	8.10.03	Stricken 5.14
SOUFFLEUR (Q 21)	Arsenal de Toulon	20.4.03	Stricken 5.14
THON (Q 20)	Arsenal de Toulon	18.3.04	Stricken 5.14
TRUITE (Q 34)	Arsenal de Toulon	14.4.05	Stricken 5.14

Single-hull steel submarines, designed by M Romazotti. Provided under the 1900 programme. Small radius of action. Estimated cost: 365,000 francs each.

X *submarine*

Displacement: 168t surfaced; 179t submerged
Dimensions: 123ft 8in × 10ft 2in × 8ft 1in
37.0m × 3.1m × 2.4m
Machinery: 2-shaft Panhard et Levassor engines plus electric motors, 260bhp/230shp = 8.4kts/6.1kts. Range 170nm at 8.37kts surfaced, 60nm at 4.50kts submerged
Armament: 1–450mm (17.7in) TT, 3–450mm torpedoes (2 Drzewiecki drop-collars, 1 external cradle), total 6 torpedoes
Complement: 15

Name	Builder	Launched	Fate
X (Q 35)	Arsenal de Cherbourg	15.11.04	Stricken 5.14

Single-hull steel submarine, designed by M Romazotti. First submarine with two shafts. Estimated cost was 499,400 francs (£19,976). Renamed *Dauphin* on 13 February 1911.

Z *submarine*

Displacement: 202t surfaced; 222t submerged
Dimensions: 135ft 8in × 9ft 10in × 9ft 2in
41.3m × 3.0m × 2.8m
Machinery: 1-shaft diesel engine plus electric motor, 190bhp/?shp = 9kts/7.10kts. Range 500nm at 5kts surfaced, 45nm at 4kts submerged
Armament: 2–450mm (17.7in) TT (fwd)
Complement: 16

Name	Builder	Launched	Fate
Z (Q 36)	Arsenal de Rochefort	28.3.04	Stricken 3.10

Single-hulled steel submarine, designed by Maugas. Improved *Farfadet* class; first French submarine with diesel engine. Diving time 4min 55 sec. Disarmed from 1909. Her estimated building cost was 779,300 francs (£31,172).

Y *submarine*

Displacement: 213t surfaced; 226t submerged
Dimensions: 147ft 4in × 9ft 10in × 9ft 2in
44.9m × 3.0m × 2.8m
Machinery: 1-shaft diesel engine for both surface and submerged motion, 250bhp = 10kts/6kts
Armament: 2–450mm TT (bow), 3–450mm torpedoes (2 Drzewiecki launching systems, 1 aft external)
Complement: 15

Name	Builder	Launched	Fate
Y (Q 37)	Arsenal de Toulon	24.7.05	Stricken 5.09

Single-hulled steel submarine, designed by Émile Bertin. Estimated cost 924,300 francs (£36,972). This boat never completed her trials and was not commissioned. A projected reconstruction (to be completed by the end of 1907) with additional electric motor was abandoned.

Aigrette as completed *Aldo Fraccaroli Collection*

Saphir as completed *Navarret Collection*

Circé as completed *Navarret Collection*

AIGRETTE class

Displacement: 178t surfaced; 253t submerged
Dimensions: 117ft 7in × 13ft 3in × 8ft 7in
35.85m × 4.04m × 2.63m
Machinery: 1-shaft diesel engine plus electric motor, 150bhp/130shp = 9.25kts/6.20kts. Range 1300nm at 8kts surfaced, 65/23nm at 3.8/6.45kts submerged
Armament: 4–450mm torpedoes (2 Drzewiecki launching systems, 2 external cradles)
Complement: 14

Name	Builder	Launched	Fate
AIGRETTE (Q 38)	Arsenal de Toulon	23.1.04	Stricken 11.19
CIGOGNE (Q 39)	Arsenal de Toulon	11.11.04	Stricken 11.19

Twin-hull submersibles, designed by Laubeuf. They were essentially experimental boats and were based on the *Triton* class. *Aigrette*'s diving time was 4 minutes; she played a local defence role during the war, based at Cherbourg while *Cigogne* played a similar role at Brindisi during 1916–18.

Eleven other boats of the *Aigrette* class were planned to be built in Toulon (*Eider, Macreuse, Crèbe, Cygne, Marabout* and *Héron*) and in Cherbourg (*Pluvier, Pingouin, Pélican, Plongeon* and *Vanneau*), but were cancelled in September 1902.

OMEGA *submarine*

Displacement: 306t surfaced; 409t submerged
Dimensions: 160ft 5in × 13ft 9in × 9ft 3in
48.9m × 4.2m × 2.8m
Machinery: 1-shaft reciprocating steam and 2 du Temple boilers plus electric motor, 350ihp/230shp = 10.2kts/6.02kts. Range 1076nm at 8kts surfaced, 45nm at 5kts submerged
Armament: 2–450mm (17.7in) TT (bow), 4–450mm torpedoes (2 Drzewiecki drop-collars, 2 aft trained external cradles), total 6 torpedoes
Complement: 22

Name	Builder	Launched	Fate
OMEGA (Q 40)	Arsenal de Toulon	28.11.05	Stricken 1919

Built to a design by Emile Bertin and Petithomme as experimental twin-hulled submersible. Decision made on 21 May 1907 and completed in 1909 with half of the steam machinery as fitted in the twin screw *Pluviôse* class. Renamed *Argonaute* from 27 September 1910.

ÉMERAUDE class *submarines*

Displacement: 392t surfaced; 425t submerged
Dimensions: 147ft 4in × 12ft 10in × 12ft
44.9m × 3.9m × 3.6m
Machinery: 2-shaft Sautter-Harlé diesels plus electric motors, 600bhp/?shp = 11.5kts/9.2kts. Range 2000nm at 7.3kts surfaced, 100nm at 5kts submerged
Armament: 6–450mm (17.7in) TT (4 fwd, 2 aft; without reloads)
Complement: 21, later 23

Name	Builder	Launched	Fate
ÉMERAUDE (Q 41)	Arsenal de Cherbourg	6.8.06	Stricken 11.19
OPALE (Q 42)	Arsenal de Cherbourg	20.11.06	Stricken 11.19
RUBIS (Q 43)	Arsenal de Cherbourg	26.6.07	Stricken 11.19
SAPHIR (Q 44)	Arsenal de Toulon	6.2.08	Sunk 15.1.15
TOPASE (Q 45)	Arsenal de Toulon	2.7.08	Stricken 11.19
TURQUOISE (Q 46)	Arsenal de Toulon	3.8.08	See notes

Single-hull type boats to a design by Maugas, they were all built under the 1903 programme. Although proper submarines their surface buoyancy was not good; similarly their diesels were poorly designed which meant that trials were delayed and fraught with problems. In August 1915 *Topase* and *Turquoise* were fitted with 1–37mm, the first French submarines to receive them. *Topase* was given a lengthened conning tower. *Saphir* sank in the Dardanelles after hitting a mine in January 1915. *Turquoise* was damaged by Turkish gunfire and consequently beached on 30 October 1915. The Turks changed her name to *Mustadieh Ombashi* (or *Müstecip ombasi*) after refloating her but she was not commissioned. She was condemned shortly after being returned to the French in 1919.

CIRCÉ class *submarines*

Displacement: 351t surfaced; 491t submerged
Dimensions: 154ft 6in × 16ft 1in × 9ft 10in
47.1m × 4.9m × 3.0m
Machinery: 2-shaft MAN diesels plus electric motors, 630bhp/460shp = 11.9kts = 7.7kts. Range 2160nm at 8kts surfaced, 98nm/44nm at 3.5kts/5.1kts submerged
Armament: 6–450mm (17.7in) torpedoes (2 Drzewiecki drop-collars, 4 external cradles), 1–47mm
Complement: 22

Name	Builder	Launched	Fate
CALYPSO (Q 48)	Arsenal de Toulon	22.10.07	Collision 7.7.14
CIRCÉ (Q 47)	Arsenal de Toulon	13.9.07	Sunk 20.9.18

Twin-hull submersibles designed by M Laubeuf. Ordered 8 October 1904 under the 1904 programme. *Calypso* was sunk in collision with *Circé* off Toulon. On 25 May 1917 in the Mediterranean *Circé* torpedoed the German submarine minelayer *UC 24*. She was later sunk in the Adriatic by *U 47*.

Vendémiaire June 1912
CPL

GUÊPE 1 class *submarines*

Displacement: 45t surfaced; 50t submerged
Dimensions: 67ft 3in × 6ft 11in × ?
20.5m × 2.1m × ?m
Machinery: 1-shaft diesel for both surface and submerged propulsion, 240bhp = 10.5kts/9kts. Range 128nm at 10.5kts surfaced, 80nm at 6kts submerged
Armament: 2–450mm (17.7in) torpedoes (Drzewiecki drop-collar)
Complement: 7

Name	Builder	Launched	Fate
GUÊPE 1 (Q 49)	Arsenal de Cherbourg	–	–
GUÊPE 2 (Q 50)	Arsenal de Cherbourg	–	–

Single-hull submarines designed by M Petithomme. Ten planned in the 1904 programme (first 4 have been built in Cherbourg, 3 in Rochefort and last 3 in Toulon), but only first two were ordered on 8 October 1904 and laid down. Construction stopped in March 1908. Numbers Q 51–Q 58, reserved for *Guêpe 3* to *Guêpe 10*, were assigned later to the *Pluviôse* class (1905 programme).

PLUVIÔSE class *submarines*

Displacement: 398t surfaced; 550t submerged
Dimensions: 167ft 4in × 16ft 4in × 16ft 3in
51.1m × 4.9m × 3.0m
Machinery: 2-shaft reciprocating steam and 2 du Temple boilers plus electric motors, 700ihp/450shp = 12kts/8kts. Range 1500nm/900nm at 9kts/12kts surfaced, 50nm at 5kts submerged
Armament: 1–450mm (17.7in) TT (bow, see notes), 6–450mm torpedoes (2 Drzewiecki drop-collars, 2 external cradles abeam CT trained fwd, 2 external cradles trained aft), total of 8 torpedoes
Complement: 24

Name	Builder	Launched	Fate
AMPÈRE (Q 68)	Arsenal de Toulon	30.10.09	Stricken 1919
BERTHELOT (Q 66)	Arsenal de Rochefort	19.5.09	Stricken 1919
CUGNOT (Q 76)	Arsenal de Rochefort	14.10.09	Stricken 1919
FLORÉAL (Q 54)	Arsenal de Cherbourg	18.4.08	Collision 2.8.18
FRESNEL (Q 65)	Arsenal de Rochefort	16.6.08	Sunk 5.12.15
FRUCTIDOR (Q 58)	Arsenal de Cherbourg	13.11.09	Stricken 1919
GAY-LUSSAC (Q 69)	Arsenal de Toulon	17.3.10	Stricken 1919
GERMINAL (Q 53)	Arsenal de Cherbourg	7.12.07	Stricken 1919
GIFFARD (Q 77)	Arsenal de Rochefort	10.2.10	Stricken 1919
MESSIDOR (Q 56)	Arsenal de Cherbourg	24.12.08	Stricken 1919
MONGE (Q 67)	Arsenal de Toulon	31.12.08	Sunk 29.12.15
PAPIN (Q 64)	Arsenal de Rochefort	4.1.08	Stricken 1919
PLUVIÔSE (Q 51)	Arsenal de Cherbourg	27.5.07	Stricken 1919
PRAIRIAL (Q 55)	Arsenal de Cherbourg	26.9.08	Collision 29.4.18
THERMIDOR (Q 57)	Arsenal de Cherbourg	3.7.09	Stricken 1919
VENDÉMIAIRE (Q 59)	Arsenal de Cherbourg	7.7.07	Collision 8.6.12
VENTÔSE (Q 52)	Arsenal de Cherbourg	15.9.07	Stricken 1919
WATT (Q 75)	Arsenal de Rochefort	18.6.09	Stricken 1919

Constructed under the 1905 programme, laid down in 1906 and completed between October 1908 and January 1911. These 18 twin-hulled submarines (named after scientists and the Revolutionary months) were built to a design by Laubeuf. Their steam propulsion prevented them from submerging very quickly although in fact they were good sea boats. Despite their one main drawback the class were almost constantly employed during the war. Only *Floreal, Germinal, Monge* (sometimes referred to instead as *Prairial*) and *Ventôse* retained in 1914 a bow TT which had been fitted originally; they were removed from the others. *Pluviôse* was rammed and sunk near Calais by the cross-channel steamer *Pas-de-Calais* 26 May 1910 when surfacing with the loss all hands. She was refloated and returned to service.

Floréal was sunk in a collision with the British armed boarding steamer *Hazel* off Mudros. Fresnel was torpedoed off Durazzo by Austro-Hungarian destroyers and blew up. *Monge* was sunk in the south Adriatic by the Austro-Hungarian cruiser *Helgoland*. *Vendémiaire* collided with French battleship *St Louis*. *Prairial* collided off Le Havre with the British SS *Tropic* off Le Havre.

Modified ÉMERAUDE class *submarines*

Displacement: 425t surfaced
Dimensions: 193ft 7in × 12ft 10in × ?
54.9m × 3.9m × ?m
Machinery: 2-shaft diesels plus electric motors, 600bhp/?shp
Armament: ?
Complement: ?

Name	Builder	Launched	Fate
(Q 59)	Arsenal de Rochefort	–	–
(Q 60)	Arsenal de Rochefort	–	–

Single-hulled submarines designed by Petithomme under the 1904 programme. Construction started on 18 October 1905 and 21 December 1905. Cancelled *c*1908. Numbers Q 59 and Q 60 were later assigned to *Vendémiaire* and *Brumaire*.

Q 61 *submarine*

This small (21t displacement) experimental submarine, designed by Marquis de Dion (famous automobile designer), were a derivation from *Goubet*. Classified as *sous-marin vedette* or *immersible vedette*. Planned for handling on one of the battleships. Construction started on 18 October 1904, but was later cancelled. Uncompleted hull used for experiments.

BRUMAIRE class *submarines*

Displacement: 397t surfaced; 551t submerged
Dimensions: 170ft 11in × 17ft 9in × 10ft 2in
52.1m × 5.14m × 3.1m
Machinery: 2-shaft 4-stroke 6cyl diesels plus electric motors, 840bhp/660shp = 13kts/8.8kts. Range 1700nm at 10kts surfaced, 84nm at 5kts submerged
Armament: 1–450mm (17.7in) TT (bow), 6–450mm torpedoes (4 Drzewiecki drop-collars, 2 external cradles abeam CT, total of 8 torpedoes)
Complement: 29

Name	Builder	Launched	Fate
ARAGO (Q 86)	Arsenal de Toulon	29.6.12	Stricken 1921
BERNOUILLI (Q 83)	Arsenal de Toulon	1.6.11	Mined 13.2.18
BRUMAIRE (Q 60)	Arsenal de Cherbourg	29.4.11	Stricken 1930
COULOMB (Q 85)	Arsenal de Toulon	13.6.12	Stricken 1919
CURIE (Q 87)	Arsenal de Toulon	18.7.12	Stricken 3.28
EULER (Q 71)	Arsenal de Cherbourg	12.10.12	Stricken *c*1923 (or 1927–29?)
FARADAY (Q 78)	Arsenal de Rochefort	27.6.11	Stricken 1921
FOUCAULT (Q 70)	Arsenal de Cherbourg	15.6.12	Sunk 15.9.15
FRANKLIN (Q 72)	Arsenal de Cherbourg	22.3.13	Stricken 1922
FRIMAIRE (Q 62)	Arsenal de Cherbourg	26.8.11	Stricken 1923
JOULE (Q 84)	Arsenal de Toulon	7.9.11	Mined 1.5.15
LE VERRIER (Q 88)	Arsenal de Toulon	31.10.12	Stricken 1925
MONTGOLFIER (Q 81)	Arsenal de Rochefort	18.4.12	Stricken 1921
NEWTON (Q 80)	Arsenal de Rochefort	20.5.12	Stricken Dec 1925
NIVÔSE (Q 63)	Arsenal de Cherbourg	6.1.12	Stricken 1921
VOLTA (Q 79)	Arsenal de Rochefort	23.9.11	Stricken 22.10.22

Curie after the war
CPL

Provided under the 1906 programme. Double-hull submersibles designed by Laubeuf – they were a diesel-powered version of *Pluviôse* class. MAN type diesels produced by A C Loire, Sautter-Harlé, Normand, Indret and Sabathé.

Some (*eg Arago, Faraday, Le Verrier*) were fitted in 1916 with 1–75mm or 1–47mm. All the class spent 1914–18 in the Mediterranean. *Bernouilli* broke into Cattaro on 4 April 1916 and blew the stern off the Austrian destroyer *Csepel*. *Le Verrier* rammed the German *U 47* by accident, each firing torpedoes without hitting on 28 July 1918. *Fourcault* was sunk off Cattaro by Austrian aircraft. *Curie* was captured on 20 December 1914 at Pola after getting into the base and commissioned by the Austrians (radius 6500nm surfaced), with a new battery and a 1–88mm and renamed *U 14*. She was recovered by the French after the First World War. *Joule* was mined in the Dardanelles.

It was planned in 1917 to convert six boats of the *Brumaire* class into minelaying submarines following the example of *Amarante* and *Astrée* but the project was abandoned.

Archimède as completed
NB 1/750 scale

ARCHIMÈDE *submarine*

Displacement: 598t surfaced; 810.5t submerged
Dimensions: 197ft × 18ft 5in × 13ft 7in
60.5m × 5.6m × 4.1m
Machinery: 2-shaft reciprocating steam and 2 boilers plus electric motors, 1700ihp/1230shp = 14.92kts/10.95kts (max 11.25kts). Range 1160/680nm at 10kts/14.9kts surfaced, 100nm at 4.5kts submerged
Armament: As *Brumaire* class
Complement: 26

Name	Builder	Launched	Fate
ARCHIMÈDE (Q 73)	Arsenal de Cherbourg	4.8.09	Stricken 11.19

Authorised under the 1906 programme and designed by M Hutter. She was essentially an improved version of the *Pluviôse* class having superior machinery. Twin-hull type, fitted with three horizontal and one vertical rudder. She attained 15.2kts on the surface and sank 4 transports in her 1914–18 service.

MARIOTTE *submarine*

Displacement: 530.7t surfaced; 627t submerged
Dimensions: 210ft 3in × 14ft 1in × 12ft 6in
64.7m × 4.3m × 3.8m
Machinery: 2-shaft Sautter-Harlé 6cyl 4-stroke diesels plus electric motors, 1400bhp/1000shp = 14.26kts/11.66kts. Range 1050nm at 10kts surfaced, 100nm at 5kts submerged
Armament: 4–450mm (17.7in) TT, 2–450mm torpedoes (Drzewiecki drop-collars), total 8 torpedoes
Complement: 29

Name	Builder	Launched	Fate
MARIOTTE (Q 74)	Arsenal de Cherbourg	2.2.11	Sunk 27.7.18

Authorised under the 1906 programme, this single-hulled submarine was designed by Radiguer and was similar to the *Émeraude* design. Trials took place between March 1910 and November 1912; she attained a high submerged speed at that time. However, all but two of her buoyancy tanks were moved forward to improve sea-keeping. *Mariotte* sank in the Dardanelles in July 1915 after having been caught in Turkish net defences and fired on.

AMIRAL BOURGOIS *submarine*

Displacement: 555.6t surfaced; 735.2t submerged
Dimensions: 184ft 5in × 18ft 1in × 12ft
56.2m × 5.5m × 3.6m
Machinery: 2-shaft Schneider 4-stroke diesels plus electric motors, 1400bhp/1000shp = 13.85kts/8.65kts. Range 2500nm at 10kts surfaced, 100nm at 5kts submerged
Armament: 4–450mm (17.7in) TT (2 fwd, 2 aft)
Complement: 25

Name	Builder	Launched	Fate
AMIRAL BOURGOIS (Q 82)	Arsenal de Rochefort	25.11.12	Stricken 11.19

Authorised under the 1906 programme. Twin-hulled submersible designed by M Bourdelle. She served in the Channel during 1914–18.

CHARLES BRUN *submarine*

Displacement: 355.6t surfaced; 450t submerged
Dimensions: 144ft 4in × 13ft 1in × 10ft 10in
44.0m × 4.0m × 3.3m
Machinery: 2-shaft Schneider accumulators and alternators, 1300shp = 13.54kts/7.25kts
Armament: 2–450mm (17.7in) TT (bow), 4–450mm torpedoes (2 Drzewiecki drop-collar abeam CT, 2 external cradles aft)
Complement: 24

Name	Builder	Launched	Fate
CHARLES BRUN (Q 89)	Arsenal de Toulon	14.9.10	Condemned 6.20

Experimental boat ordered on 31 December 1906 which never officially entered service. Trials of her experimental propulsion system were conducted between October 1910 and October 1913.

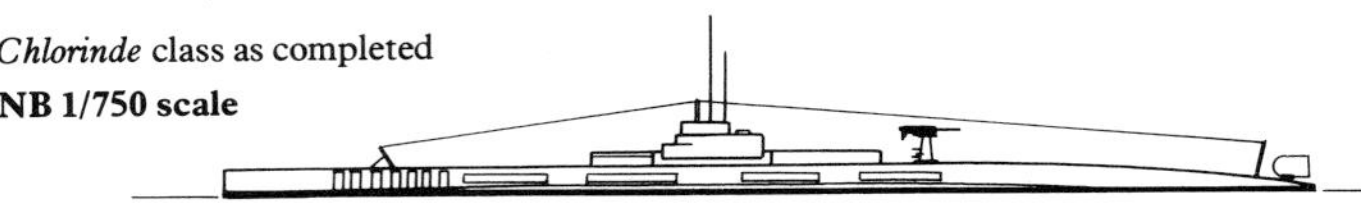

Chlorinde class as completed
NB 1/750 scale

CLORINDE class *submarines*

Displacement: 413t surfaced; 567t submerged
Dimensions: 176ft 10in × 16ft 9in × 11ft 2in
53.9m × 5.1m × 3.4m
Machinery: 2-shaft MAN-Loire 2-stroke diesels plus electric motors, 800 (1300 designed) bhp/700shp = 13 (15 designed)kts/9 (9.5 designed)kts. Range 1300nm at 10kts surfaced, 100nm at 5kts submerged
Armament: 8–450mm (17.7in) torpedoes (6 Drzewiecki drop-collars, 2 fwd external cradles), later 1–75mm
Complement: 29

Name	Builder	Launched	Fate
CLORINDE (Q 90)	Arsenal de Rochefort	2.10.13	Stricken 1.26
CORNÉLIE (Q 91)	Arsenal de Rochefort	29.10.13	Stricken 12.26

Authorised under the 1909 programme, designed by M Hutter and was a derivation of the Laubeuf type submersibles (*eg Brumaire* class). Employed in the Atlantic during 1917–18.

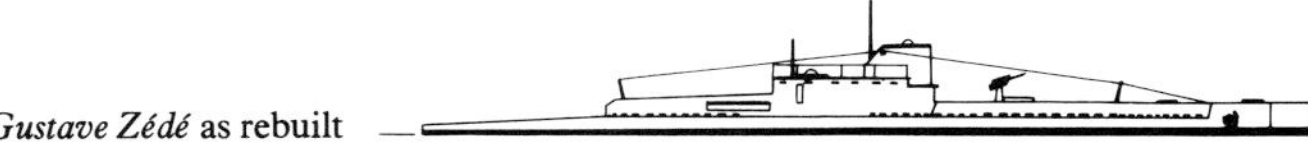

Gustave Zédé as rebuilt

GUSTAVE ZÉDÉ class *submarines*

Displacement: 849t (*Nereide* 820t) surfaced; 1098t (*Nereide* 1047t) submerged
Dimensions: 242ft 9in × 19ft 8in × 12ft 2in
74.0m × 6.0m × 3.7m
Machinery: 2-shaft Delaunay-Belleville 3cyl reciprocating steam engines and 2 return-flame du Temple boilers plus electric motors, 3500 (4000 designed) ihp/1640shp = 17.57kts/11.44kts. Range 1400nm at 10kts surfaced, 135nm at 5kts submerged (*Néréide*: Schneider-Carels diesels plus electric motors, 2400 (4800 designed) bhp/1640shp = 17.3kts/10.5kts. Range 3120nm/1550nm at 10kts/16kts surfaced, 90nm at 4kts submerged)
Armament: 8–450mm (17.7in) TT (2 bow, 4 inboard, 2 external cradles; 10 torpedoes), 1–75mm, 1–47mm
Complement: 47

Name	Builder	Launched	Fate
GUSTAVE ZÉDÉ (Q 92)	Arsenal de Cherbourg	20.5.13	Stricken 1937
NÉRÉIDE (Q 93)	Arsenal de Cherbourg	9.5.14	Stricken 2.35

Authorised under the 1911 programme to a design by Simonot. *Gustave Zédé* was equipped in 1912 with steam propulsion while *Néréide* was fitted with the originally specified diesel motors which were only half as powerful as was first envisaged. Both originally designed with 2–65mm. *Gustave Zédé* was reconstructed in 1921–22 and was fitted with diesels from an ex-German submarine (2 MAN Q 6 type diesels from *U 165* with a total of 2400bhp = 15kts). She also received a replacement bridge and conning tower and her fuel capacity was increased as two ballast tanks were converted to carry diesel. After the war *Néréide* also received a new bridge and was fitted with more air vents, a twin revolving periscope and a new periscope. *Néréide* served in the Atlantic during the war while *Gustave Zédé* was employed in the Adriatic.

AMPHITRITE class *submarines*

Displacement: 414t surfaced; 609t submerged (except *Amarante* and *Astrée*)
Dimensions: 176ft 10in × 17ft 9in × 10ft 10in
53.9m × 5.4m × 3.3m
Machinery: 2-shaft MAN-Schneider (except *Andromaque* and *Ariane* MAN-Loire, *Amphitrite* MAN-Chaléassière, *Astrée* and *Amarante* MAN-Indret) 2-stroke diesels plus electric motors, 800 (designed 1300) bhp/700shp = 12–13 (designed 15)kts/9.5kts. Range 1300nm at 10kts surfaced, 100nm at 5kts submerged
Armament: As *Clorinde* class
Complement: 29

Name	Builder	Launched	Fate
AMARANTE (Q 99)	Arsenal de Toulon	11.11.15	Stricken 1925
AMPHITRITE (Q 94)	Arsenal de Rochefort	9.6.14	Stricken 9.35
ANDROMAQUE (Q 101)	Arsenal de Cherbourg	13.2.15	Stricken 1931
ARÉTHUSE (Q 97)	Arsenal de Toulon	20.4.16	Stricken 1927
ARIANE (Q 100)	Arsenal de Cherbourg	5.9.14	Sunk 19.6.17
ARTÉMIS (Q 96)	Arsenal de Toulon	14.10.15	Stricken 1927
ASTRÉE (Q 95)	Arsenal de Rochefort	6.12.15	Stricken 1928
ATALANTE (Q 98)	Arsenal de Toulon	14.4.15	Stricken 1931

Authorised under the 1909 programme these boats were laid down between 1911 and 1912. Designed by Hutter as an improved *Clorinde* class. *Astrée* and *Amarante* were taken to Le Havre under tow after their launch where they were completed as minelaying submarines (1918) with the Normand-Fenaux system. Their displacement at 440t surfaced and 610t submerged was slightly more than their sisters. *Amphitrite* and *Atalante* were renamed *Amphitrite II* and *Atalante II* on 20 April 1928, their names being transferred to new units. *Ariane* was sunk by a torpedo from the German *UC 22* during trials. Tests were carried out with the Walser hydrophone using *Amarante* together with the sloop *Engageante*.

BELLONE class *submarine*

Displacement: 523t surfaced; 788t submerged
Dimensions: 216ft 6in × 17ft 9in × 11ft 6in
60.6m × 5.4m × 3.5m
Machinery: 2-shaft Sabathé (*Gorgone* Sulzer) 2-stroke diesels plus electric motors, 1640 (originally designed 1800)bhp/800shp = 14.7kts/9kts (never achieved designed 17kts/9.5kts). Range 2300nm at 10kts surfaced, 100nm at 5kts submerged
Armament: 8–450mm (17.7in) TT, 1–75mm
Complement: 38

Name	Builder	Launched	Fate
BELLONE (Q 102)	Arsenal de Rochefort	8.7.14	Discarded July 1935
GORGONE (Q 104)	Arsenal de Toulon	23.12.15	Discarded July 1935
HERMIONE (Q 103)	Arsenal de Toulon	15.3.17	Discarded July 1935.

Authorised under the 1912 programme, designed by M Hutter. Twin-hull coastal type. Known also as *Gorgone* class; derived from the *Clorinde* class. Modernised postwar with improvements to reduce diving time and a 24ft 7in (7.5m) periscope installed in the conning tower. *Bellone* served in the Atlantic 1917–18 and the other two in the Adriatic.

Artémis after the war
Aldo Fraccaroli Collection

Sané as completed *Aldo Fraccaroli Collection*

DUPUY DE LÔME class *submarines*

Displacement: 833t surfaced; 1287t submerged
Dimensions: 246ft 1in × 21ft × 11ft 10in
75m × 6.4m × 3.6m
Machinery: 2-shaft Delaunay-Belleville 3cyl reciprocating steam engines and 2 return-flame du Temple boilers plus electric motors, 3500ihp/1640shp = 17kts/11kts. Range 2350nm/1350nm at 10kts/14kts surfaced, 120nm at 5kts submerged
Armament: 8–450mm (17.7in) TT (10 torpedoes), 1–47mm AA (only projected, later mounted 2–75mm or more probably 1–75mm and 1–47mm)
Complement: 43

Name	Builder	Launched	Fate
DUPUY DE LÔME (Q 105)	Arsenal de Toulon	9.9.15	Discarded July 1935
SANÉ (Q 106)	Arsenal de Toulon	27.1.16	Discarded July 1935

Authorised under the 1913 programme and designed by M Hutter. They were enlargements of Hutter's very successful design for the *Archimède*. Greater buoyancy coefficient as *Gustave Zédé* class, machinery also as *Gustave Zédé*. On trials *Dupuy de Lôme* achieved 19kts on reciprocating steam engine. From 1917 to the close of World War One both boats served in the Morocco Flotilla based on Gibraltar. After World War One they were reconstructed. Their steam engines was replaced by two 1200bhp diesels (*Dupuy de Lôme* Krupp, *Sané* Körting) taken from ex-German submarines with greatly increased radius; they also had new equipment as fitted in the *Gustave Zédé* class.

Daphné as completed

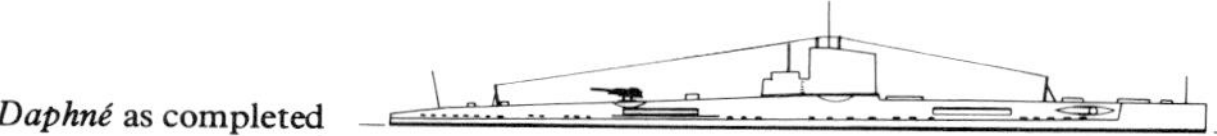

DIANE class *submarines*

Displacement: 633t surfaced; 891t submerged
Dimensions: 223ft 1in × 18ft 1in × 12ft 2in
68m × 5.5m × 3.7m
Machinery: 2-shaft Vickers 4-stroke (*Daphné* Sulzer 2-stroke) diesels plus electric motors, 1800bhp/1400shp = 17kts/11.5kts. Range 2500nm at 10kts surfaced, 130nm at 5kts submerged
Armament: 10–450mm (17.7in) TT, 1–75mm (except *Diane*)
Complement: 43

Name	Builder	Launched	Fate
DAPHNÉ (Q 108)	Arsenal de Cherbourg	25.10.15	Stricken Feb 1935
DIANE (Q 107)	Arsenal de Cherbourg	30.9.16	Sunk 11.2.18

Authorised under the 1912 programme, designed by M Simonot, twin-hull type. An enlarged *Archimède* class and derivation from *Gutave Zédé* class with dimensions reduced to 92 per cent. Submerged speed and range and armament were better than in *Bellone* class. *Diane* was lost with all hands, by explosion off La Pallice. After the war *Daphné* was modernised on the lines of the *Amphitrite* and *Bellone* classes.

JOESSEL/FULTON class *submarine* (first series)

Displacement: 870t surfaced; 1247t submerged
Dimensions: 242ft 9in × 21ft × 11ft 10in
74m × 6.4m × 3.6m
Machinery: 2-shaft Schneider-Carels 8cyl diesels plus electric motors, 2700bhp/1640shp = 16.5kts/11kts. Range 4300nm at 10kts surfaced, 125nm at 5kts submerged
Armament: 8–450mm (17.7in) TT (10 torpedoes), 2–75mm
Complement: 47, later 53

Name	Builder	Launched	Fate
FULTON (Q 110)	Arsenal de Cherbourg	1.4.19	Stricken July 1935
JOESSEL (Q 109)	Arsenal de Cherbourg	21.7.17	Stricken Apr 1935

Joessel as reconstructed
Aldo Fraccaroli Collection

Amazone after the war
Aldo Fraccaroli Collection

Henri Fournier as completed
Aldo Fraccaroli Collection

Maurice Callot being launched
Aldo Fraccaroli Collection

Authorised under the 1914 programme. Designed by M Simonot as steam submarines with two geared turbines (4000shp = 20kts and range 2400nm at 10kts surfaced), but changed to diesel propulsion during construction. Their turbines were used for two *Aigrette* class sloops. *Fulton* and *Joessel* achieved on surface trials 17.5kts. After completion a new high conning tower was fitted with a bridge and new periscopes, one of 24ft 7in (7.5m) in the conning tower and one of 31ft (9.5m) in the central operation room.

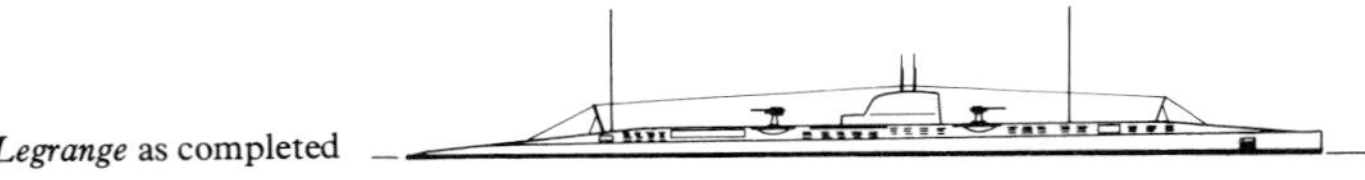

Legrange as completed

LAGRANGE class *submarines*

Displacement: 920t surfaced; 1318t submerged
Dimensions: 246ft 9in × 20ft 8in × 11ft 10in
75.2m × 6.3m × 3.6m
Machinery: 2-shaft Sulzer diesels plus electric motors, 2600bhp/1640shp = 16.5kts/11kts. Range 4300nm at 10kts surfaced, 125nm at 5kts submerged
Armament: 8–450mm (17.7in) TT (10 torpedoes), 2–75mm
Complement: 47

Name	Builder	Launched	Fate
LAGRANGE (Q 112)	Arsenal de Toulon	31.5.17	Stricken July 1935
LAPLACE (Q 111)	Arsenal de Rochefort	12.8.19	Stricken 1937
REGNAULT (Q 113)	Arsenal de Toulon	25.6.24	Stricken 1937
ROMAZOTTI (Q 114)	Arsenal de Toulon	31.3.18	Stricken July 1937

Authorised under the 1913 (first three) and 1914 (*Romazotti*) programmes. Completed between February 1918 and 1924. Designed by M Hutter and were to have been steam driven (4000bhp = 19kts surfaced, range 2075nm at 10kts surfaced) as the *Joessel/Fulton* class, but completed with diesels; were reconstructed postwar. Parsons steam turbines were later mounted in the *Marne* class sloops. The class had 440 rounds of ammunition for their 75mm guns.

JOESSEL/FULTON class *submarines* (second series)

Particulars: As first series

Name	Builder	Launched	Fate
Q 115	Arsenal de Cherbourg	–	–
Q 116	Arsenal de Cherbourg	–	–
Q 117	Arsenal de Toulon	–	–
Q 118	Arsenal de Toulon	–	–
Q 119	Arsenal de Rochefort	–	–
Q 120	Arsenal de Rochefort	–	–

Provided under the 1915 Programme. Planned to be laid down from 1 May 1915. Cancelled in the First World War.

ARMIDE class *submarines*

Displacement: 457t surfaced; 670t submerged
Dimensions: 184ft 5in × 17ft 1in × 9ft 10in
56.2m × 5.2m × 3.0m
Machinery: 2-shaft Schneider-Carels 2-stroke diesels plus electric motors, 2200bhp/900shp = 17.46kts/11kts. Range 2600/900nm at 11/13kts surfaced, 160nm at 5kts submerged
Armament: 4–450mm (17.7in) TT (except *Armide* 6 TT), 1–47mm (except *Amazone* 1–75mm)
Complement: 31

Name	Builder	Launched	Fate
AMAZONE (SD 4)	Schneider, Chalon-sur-Saône	8.16	Stricken 7.32
ANTIGONE (SD 3)	Schneider, Chalon-sur-Saône	10.16	Stricken 8.35
ARMIDE (SD 2)	Schneider, Chalon-sur-Saône	7.15	Stricken 7.32

Requisitioned 3 June 1915 and 30 May 1917, first two were ex-Greek, third ex-Japanese *No 14*. Double-hulled of Laubeuf type. *Amazone* renamed *Amazone II* on 20 April 1928.

O'BYRNE class *submarines*

Displacement: 342t surfaced; 513t submerged
Dimensions: 172ft × 15ft 5in × 8ft 10in
52.4m × 4.7m × 2.7m
Machinery: 2-shaft Schneider-Carels 4-stroke diesels plus electric motors, 1020bhp/400shp = 14kts/8kts. Range 1850nm/875nm at 10/12kts surfaced, 55nm at 5kts submerged
Armament: 4–450mm (17.7in) TT, 1–47mm
Complement: 25

Name	Builder	Launched	Fate
HENRI FOURNIER (SC 6)	Schneider, Chalon-sur-Saône	30.9.19	Discarded 7.35
LOUIS DUPETIT-THOUARS (SC 7)	Schneider, Chalon-sur-Saône	5 or 6.20	Discarded 11.28
O'BYRNE (SC 5)	Schneider, Chalon-sur-Saône	22.5.19	Discarded 7.35

Requisitioned while building for the Rumanian Navy. Double-hull boats of Laubeuf type.

Pierre Chailley about 1930
CPL

MAURICE CALLOT *submarine*

Displacement: 931t surfaced; 1298t submerged
Dimensions: 247ft 9in × 22ft × 11ft 8in
75.5m × 6.7m × 3.5m
Machinery: 2-shaft Schneider 2-stroke diesels plus electric motors, 2900bhp/1640shp = 16.5kts/10.5kts
Armament: 6–450mm (17.7in) TT (4 fwd, 2 aft; 8 torpedoes), 1–75mm, 27 mines
Complement: 48

Name	Builder	Launched	Fate
MAURICE CALLOT	F C De la Gironde, Bordeaux	26.3.21	Discarded 1936

Minelaying submarine of Schneider-Laubeuf type (double-hull design). Begun under 1917 programme (without Q number). Laid down May 1917 and completed 1921. The mines were fitted in the superstructure being laid by the Laubeuf system. This was superseded by the more efficient Fenaux system in which mines were directly released from wells in the outer ballast tanks.

PIERRE CHAILLEY *submarine*

Displacement: 884t surfaced; 1191t submerged
Dimensions: 229ft 8in × 24ft 7in × 13ft 1in
70m × 7.5m × 4.0m
Machinery: 2-shaft Sulzer 2-stroke diesels plus electric motors, 1800bhp/1400shp = 13.75kts/8.5kts. Range 2800nm at 11kts surfaced, 80nm at 5kts submerged
Armament: 4–450mm (17.7in) TT (2 bow, 2 trainable), 1–100mm, 40 mines (200kg/441lb type)
Complement: 44

Name	Builder	Launched	Fate
PIERRE CHAILLEY	Normand, Le Havre	19.12.21	Stricken 1936

Provided under the 1917 programme (without Q number). This twin-hull submarine of the Normand-Fenaux type was the prototype for the successful minelaying submarines of the *Saphir* class (launched 1928–35). The simple and safe Nomand-Fenaux system has vertical external mine-tubes. Sometimes referred to by old, reliable, sources incorrectly as *Paul Chailley*.

The *Marine Nationale* seized and operated the Greek submarines *Delphin* and *Xiphias* from 1916 to 1917, but they were returned in 1918. For full details see under Greece.

EX-ENEMY SUBMARINES

The German *UB 26* scuttled off Le Havre 5.4.16, was refloated and incorporated in the French Navy on 30.8.17 as *Roland Morillot*; discarded in January 1925. For full details see under Germany.

After the war 10 ex-German U-boats were commissioned in 1918 – 19 for further service as: *Victor Réveille* (ex-*U 79*, stricken 29.7.35), *Jean Autric* (ex-*U 105*, stricken 1937), *Léon Mignot* (ex-*U 108*, stricken July 1935), *René Audry* (ex-*U 119*, stricken 1937), *Halbronn* (ex-*U 139*, stricken July 1935), *Pierre Marrast* (ex-*U 162*, stricken 1936), *Jean Roulier* (ex-*U 166*, stricken July 1935), *Trinité-Schillemans* (ex-*UB 94*, stricken 1935), *Carissan* (ex-*UB 99*, stricken 1935), *Jean Corre* (ex-*UB 155*, stricken 1937). Nominally these submarines were awarded to the French Navy as a result of the Conference of Ambassadors on 25 June 1920.

The following 36 ex-German U-boats were awarded to the French for BU: *U 25, U 38, U 39, U 57, U 71, U 91, U 113, U 118, U 121, U 136, U 151* (sunk 1921), *U 157, UB 23, UB 24, UB 73, UB 84, UB 87, UB 114, UB 118* (sunk 15.4.19), *UB 121, UB 126, UB 130, UB 142, UB 154, UC 22, UC 27, UC 28, UC 56, UC 58, UC 74, UC 100, UC 103, UC 104* and *UC 107*.

For full details see under Germany.

SMALL SURFACE WARSHIPS

British 'FLOWER' class *escort sloops*

Class (launched, fate):
Barclay Curle – *Aldébaran* (19.5.16, stricken 1934), *Algol* (17.6.16, stricken 1935), *Cassiopée* (10.2.17, stricken 1933), *Régulus* (19.3.17, stricken 1935)
Hamilton – *Altair* (6.7.16, stricken 1940), *Antarés* (4.9.16, stricken 1936)
Henderson – *Bellatrix* (29.5.16, stricken 1933), *Rigel* (6.7.16, sunk 2.10.16)

Built in pairs in British yards under the 1916 War Programme. Virtually identical with British ships but armed with 2–138.6mm/45 guns and 4–47mm guns. The 47mm guns were later replaced by 2–75mm during the war. *Aldebaran* damaged *U 23* on 8 August 1917 in the Mediterranean where all except *Cassiopëe* and *Regulus* spent the war. *Antares* rammed and damaged *U 39* on the surface, 5 August 1917. In 1920s and early 1930s employed on colonial service. All stricken between 1933–40. *Rigel* torpedoed and sunk by German *U 35* off Algiers. In the 1920s some ships got shields for their 138.6mm guns.

Ex-British AUBRIETIA class *sloop*

Class (launched, fate):
Ville d'Ys (June 1916, stricken 1947)

Former British decoy sloop *Andromeda* bought in 1917 while building to replace the lost *Rigel* of 'Flower' class. Renamed *Andromédé*, later changed to *Ville d'Ys*. After the war used on fishery protection duties. Armament reduced to 1–100mm, 3–76mm AA, 2–47mm guns. In appearance resembled small merchant vessel. Built by Swan Hunter.

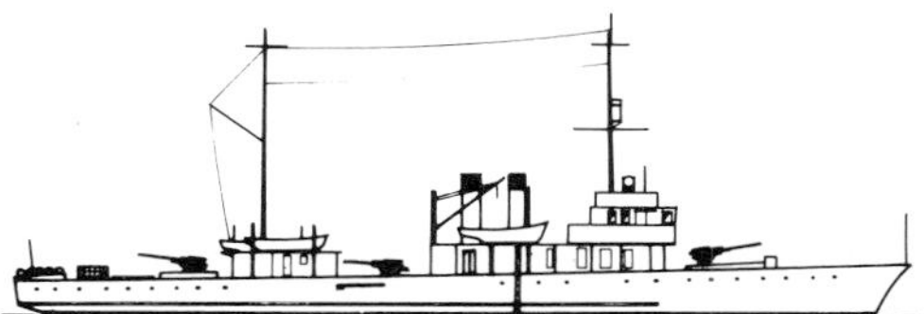

Marne class after the war

MARNE class *sloops*

Displacement: 570t (*Marne* 601t)
Dimensions: 255ft 11in oa × 29ft 2in × 11ft 2in
78.0m oa × 8.9m × 3.4m
Machinery: 2-shaft Parsons geared turbines, 2 Normand or Du Temple boilers, 4000shp = 20kts (*Marne* 5000shp = 21kts). Oil 143t. Range 4000nm at 11kts
Armament: 2–65mm
Complement: 113

Class (launched, fate):
Arsenal de Lorient – *Aisne* (7.17, BU 1939), *Marne* (25.11.16, scuttled 10.3.45)
Arsenal de Rochefort – *Meuse* (6.17, BU 1938), *Yser* (1.17, scuttled 27.11.42)
Arsenal de Brest – *Oise* (12.10.17, BU 1938), *Somme* (3.17, sold for BU 14.10.41)

All six vessels were built in the 1916 War Programme. Ships built by the same yard had the same appearance. *Marne* and *Aisne* had two funnels, the others one. Completed in 1917–18. Original weak armament was altered after the war to 4–100mm/40 guns and 1–75mm, some retained 2–65mm or received 2–47mm in addition to 4–100mm guns. Their machinery was initially intended for the *Joessel* and *Lagrange* classes of steam submarines. During the war (all six vessels served in the Atlantic Patrol Force) all except *Marne* were fitted with hydrophones. *Marne* sunk at Can Tho, Indochina was raised and scrapped on 19.6.57, *Yser* scuttled in Toulon and raised in 1943 as German *SG 37* was BU in 1946.

Cassiopée as completed *Aldo Fraccaroli Collection*

Calais as completed *Aldo Fraccaroli Collection*

AMIENS class *sloops*

Displacement: 850t normal
Dimensions: 245ft 8in oa × 236ft 3in × 28ft 7in × 10ft 6in
74.9m oa, 72.0m pp × 8.7m × 3.2m
Machinery: 2-shaft Parsons geared turbines, 2 Normand or Du Temple boilers, 5000shp = 20kts. Oil 200t or coal 185t. Range 3000nm at 11kts
Armament: 2–138.6mm (5.4in)/45, 1–75mm AA, 4 MG, DCT, 20 DC, other ASW gear
Complement: 103

Class (launched, fate):
Ch de la Méditerranée, La Seyne – *Amiens* (5.19, sold for BU 13.10.49), *Calais* (11.19, sold for BU 25.11.46), *Craonne* (1.20, BU 1935), *Épernay* (9.19, BU 1934), *Liévin* (3.20, BU 1935), *Lunéville* (1.20, BU 1935), *Montdement* (1.20, BU 1935), *Montmirail* (9.20, BU 1933), *Péronne* (3.20, BU 1935, built in Le Havre).
Arsenal de Brest – *Arras* (7.18, BU 2.46), *Dunkerque* (7.18, BU 4.42), *Reims* (7.18, BU 1938), *Verdun* (11.18, BU 1938)
Ch de Provence – *Baccarat* (1.18, BU 1933), *Béthune* (7.21, BU 1934)
Arsenal de Lorient – *Bapaume* (8.18, BU 1937), *Bar-le-Duc* (1918, stranded 13.12.20), *Belfort* (3.19, sold for BU 22.11.46)
Penhoët, St-Nazaire – *Coucy* (6.19, sold for BU 25.2.46), *Épinal* (8.19, BU 12.46)
Ch de Bretagne – *Lassigny* (7.19, stricken 21.10.41), *Les Éparges* (9.19, scuttled 27.11.42)
Arsenal de Cherbourg – *Nancy* (3.19, BU 1938)
F et Ch de la Gironde – *Remiremont* (7.20, BU 1936), *Revigny* (9.20, BU 1937)
Ch de la Loire – *Tahure* (3.18, sunk 24.9.44), *Toul* (4.19, BU 1935), *Vauquois* (8.19, mined 18.6.40), *Vimy* (12.19, BU 1935), *Vitry-le-François* (3.20, BU 1935)

A total of 30 fast sloops or escort ships built under the 1916 and 1917 Programmes and completed mostly in 1919–21 (*Mondement* in 1922 and *Reims* in 1924). They resembled three-island type merchant vessels in layout and were considered very roomy and comfortable ships for their size. Their high bows made them dry in head seas, but rolled heavily because of the topweight of guns and superstructure. For a time some were armed with 2–145mm guns (Army pattern). Oil-fired ships reached speeds of 22kts in good weather, coal-fired were slightly slower. Following ships used coal as fuel: *Craonne, Liévin, Montmirail, Mondement, Béthune, Baccarat.*. A total of 13 ships were ordered but never laid down: *Betheny, Chalons, Château-Thierry, Compiègne, Douaumont, Fère Champenoise, Gerbeviller, Noyon, Roye, Saint Die, Senlis, Soissons* and *Souchez*. *Dunquerque* and *Verdun* were respectively renamed *Ypres* and *Laffaux* in 1928. *Amiens* and some other ships got steel shields for their 138.6mm guns. In 1940 *Amiens* was fitted with experimental twin 37mm AA Mk 33 mounting destined for the new battleships. Some of this class had their masts stepped aft of the funnel. They had varied careers: *Bar-le-Duc* was stranded near Lesbos while escorting the White Russian General Wrangel's ships to Bizerta; *Bapaume* was fitted with temporary flight deck (from bow to bridge) after the war for tests conducted by Lt Teste; *Les Eparges* and *Ypres* served as surveying vessels (armament removed); *Belfort* as a seaplane tender and *Vauquois* with *Remiremont* were used for training cadets. *Les Eparges* was German manned in 1943 as a minesweeper *M 6060, Arras* was cannibalised for spares for *Amiens, Lassigny* was hulked in Bizerta, abandoned in December 1942, scuttled July 1943 by Italians in Bizerta Lake; *Tahure* was torpedoed by the US submarine *Flasher*; *Vauquois* mined off Brest.

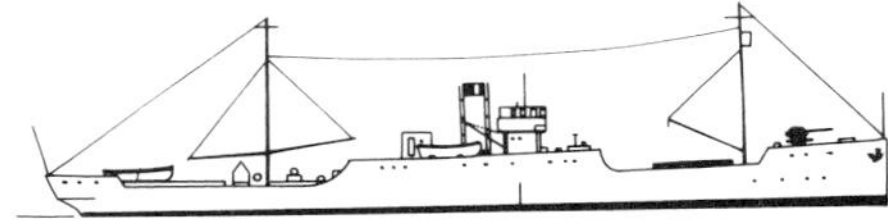

Ailette class as completed

AILETTE class *sloops*

Displacement: 492t
Dimensions: 229ft 4in oa × 27ft 3in × 9ft 10in
69.9m oa × 8.3m × 3.0m
Machinery: 2-shaft Parsons geared turbines, 2 Du Temple boilers, 4000shp = 20kts. Oil 143t. Range 4000nm at 11kts
Armament: 4–100mm (3.9in)/40, 2–65mm
Complement: 107

Class (launched, fate):
Arsenal de Brest – *Ailette* (3.18, sold for BU 14.10.41), *Escaut* (3.18, stricken 1934)
Built under 1917 War Programme and externally disguised as mercantile vessels (three island type with straight stem). In these sloops 100mm guns were concealed behind shields fore and aft of the superstructure. Completed in 1918, served in the Atlantic.

SCARPE class *sloops*

Displacement: 604t
Dimensions: 250ft oa × 28ft 7in × 10ft 10in
76.2m oa × 8.7m × 3.3m
Machinery: 2-shaft Parsons geared turbines, 2 Du Temple boilers, 5000shp = 20kts. Oil 143t. Range 4000nm at 11kts
Armament: 4–100mm (3.9in)/40, 1–65mm, DC
Complement: 107

Class (launched, fate):
Arsenal de Lorient – *Ancre* (4.18, stricken 1940), *Scarpe* (31.10.17, stricken 1938)
Arsenal de Brest – *Suippe* (4.18, BU 1953)

Small escort sloops built under 1917 War Programme and completed in 1918. Flushdecked ships with single funnel and straight bows (*Scarpe* had a clipper bow). *Suippe* was seized by Royal Navy in June 1940 and on 14 April 1941 was bombed by German aircraft off Falmouth, salved later and BU 1953.

Ancre between the war

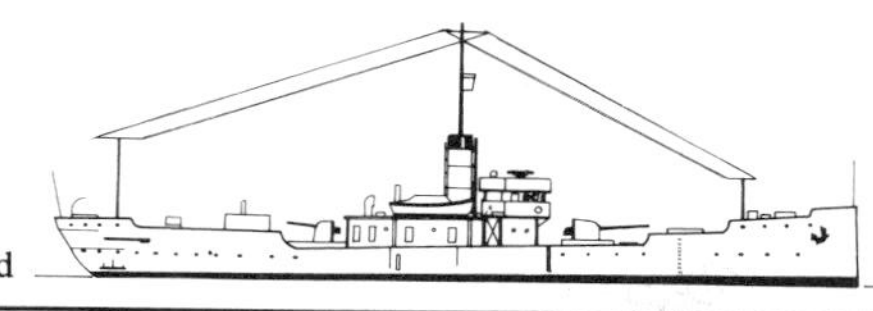
Dubourdieu as completed

DUBOURDIEU class *sloops*

Displacement: 453t
Dimensions: 212ft 11in oa × 26ft 11in × 16ft 2in
64.9m oa × 8.2m × 3.1m
Machinery: 2 shafts, 3 Breguet geared turbines, 2 Du Temple boilers, 2000shp = 16.5kts. Oil 140t. Range 2000nm at 15kts
Armament: 1–138.6mm (5.4in)/45; 1–100mm (3.9in)/40, DC
Complement: 74

Class (launched, fate):
Arsenal de Lorient – *Dubourdieu* (4.18, sunk 8.11.12), *Du Chaffault* (9.18, stricken 1938), *Dumont D'Urville* (6.11.18, stricken 1933), *Du Couëdic* (7.19, stricken 1939), *Duperré* (12.18, stricken 1933), *Decres* (cancelled)

Six sloops or *avisos* built under the 1917–18 War Programmes and completed June 1919–1May 1920. Sixth ship cancelled with the end of the war. *Dumont D'Urville* was renamed *Enseigne Henry* on 19.10.29 to make her name available for a new colonial sloop ordered in 1930. Resembled merchant vessels with superstructure amidships. *Dubourdieu* sunk at Casablanca; *Enseigne Henry* scuttled at Lorient on 18 June 1940, but later salved and hulked, stricken on 25 June 1941.

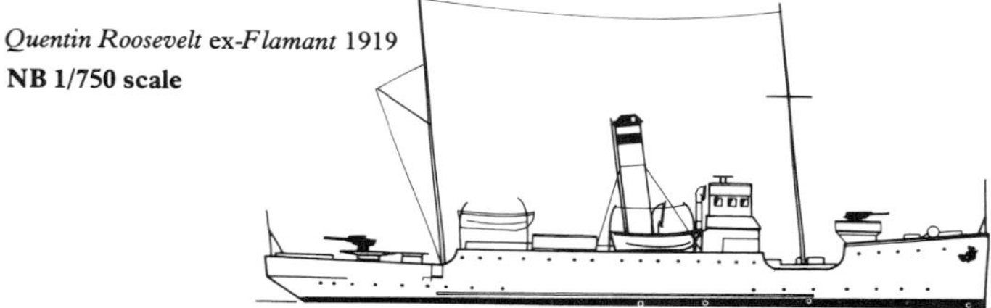
Quentin Roosevelt ex-*Flamant* 1919
NB 1/750 scale

FLAMANT *sloop*

Displacement: 585t
Dimensions: 164ft 1in oa, 153ft 10in pp × 27ft 7in × 19ft
50.0m oa, 46.9m pp × 8.4m × 5.8m
Machinery: 1 shaft, reciprocating engine, 2 cylindrical boilers, 1200ihp = 14.5kts. Coal 105t. Range 1200nm at 10kts
Armament: 1–75mm, 1–47mm
Complement: 53

Class (launched, fate):
Arsenal de Rochefort – *Flamant* (12.16, BU 1955)

Fishery protection vessel *Flamant* was begun in 1913, stopped 1914–17, completed in April 1918 and later named *Quentin Roosevelt* to commemorate one of President Theodore Roosevelt's sons, who had joined French Air Force and was killed in action on 14 July 1918. Used for fishery protection duties. Seized by British on 3 July 1940 was used for AS training, returned in 1945, stricken 1947.

ARDENT class *gunboats*

Displacement: 310t (except *Agile, Ardent, Inconstant, Espiègle, Eveille, Emporte, Etourdi, Sans Souci* 266t), 400–410t full load
Dimensions: 203ft 5in oa × 23ft 8in × 9ft 6in
60.2m oa × 7.2m × 2.9m
Machinery: 2 shafts (one shaft in 266-tonne ships), reciprocating engines, Du Temple or Normand boilers, 1500–2200ihp = 14–17kts. Coal 85t. Range 2000nm at 10kts
Armament: 2–100mm (3.9in)/40 (*Ardent, Etourdi, Sans Souci* 2–145mm, 5.7in), DC
Complement: 55

Class (launched, fate):
Arsenal de Brest – *Agile* (1916, stricken 1933), *Ardent* (5.3.16, stricken 1936), *Inconstant* (6.3.16, stricken 1933)
Arsenal de Rochefort – *Alerte* (1916, stricken 1936), *Courageuse* (1916, stricken 1920), *Espiègle* (1916, stricken 1920)
Ch de Provence – *Audacieuse* (1917, BU 1.40), *Batailleuse* (1917, sunk as target 1938), *Malicieuse* (1916, stricken 1939), *Railleuse* (1916, stricken 1.3.20), *Tapageuse* (1917, BU 1944)
Ch de la Gironde – *Belliqueuse* (1916, stricken 1928), *Dedaigneuse* (1916, scuttled 27.11.42), *Impetueuse* (1917, stricken 1938)
Ch de la Méditerranée – *Boudeuse* (1916, sold to Rumania 1920), *Eveille* (1917, stricken 1928)
Ch de la Loire – *Capricieuse* (1916, stricken 1934), *Emporté* (1916, unlisted 1927)
Arsenal de Lorient – *Curieuse* (1916, stricken 1926), *Etourdi* (21.3.16, scuttled 19.6.40, BU 6.41), *Moqueuse* (1916, wrecked 1923), *Sans Souci* (1916, stricken 1936), *Gracieuse* (1916, stricken 1938)

This class of 23 ships was built under the 1916 and 1917 War Programmes. They all had clipper bow but varied a little in the shape of the superstructure and equipment. Their masts were well stepped to the starboard off the centreline. As there was a shortage of labour and materials, some of these ships were fitted with reciprocating machinery stripped from the old coastal torpedo boats stricken from the list. At least 9 spent 1916–18 in the Mediterranean, the rest served in the Bay of Biscay. Some were converted for minesweeping at the end of the war or shortly after. After the war they were classed and used as minesweepers. *Boudeuse* was sold to Rumania to provide spares for the four *Friponne* class gunboats also sold to that country. *Dedaigneuse* scuttled at Toulon was later refloated in 1943 by Italians and repaired as *FR 56*, captured in turn by Germans was renamed *M 6020* in September 1943 and used as minesweeper.

Courageuse June 1919
Aldo Fraccaroli Collection

***Diligente* after the war**
Aldo Fraccaroli Collection

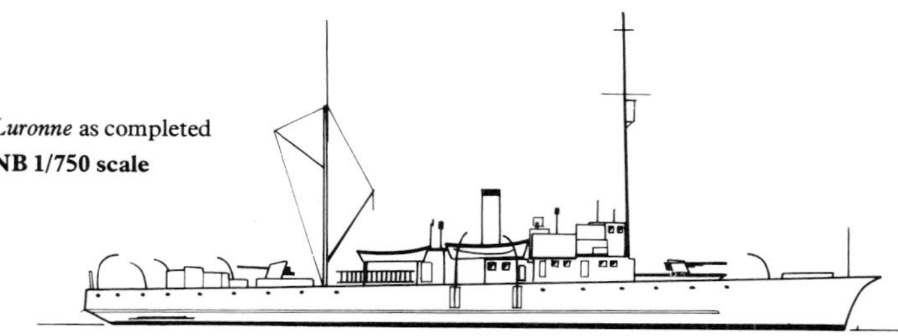
Luronne as completed
NB 1/750 scale

LURONNE *gunboat*

Displacement: 266t
Dimensions: 203ft 5in oa × 23ft 8in × 9ft 6in
60.2m oa × 7.2m × 2.9m
Machinery: 2 shafts, 2 Fiat diesels, 630bhp = 13.7kts. Oil 30t. Range 3000nm at 10kts
Armament: 2–100mm (3.9in)/40, DC
Complement: 54

Luronne was a diesel powered version of the preceeding *Ardent* class of steam ASW gunboats built on the same hull by Arsenal de Brest in 1917 under 1916 War Programme. Fitted with only one small and thin stack for diesel exhaust. Mined off Lorient and BU April 1941.

FRIPONNE class *gunboats*

Displacement: 315t
Dimensions: 217ft 10in oa × 23ft × 8ft 10in
66.4m oa × 7.0m × 2.8m
Machinery: 2 shafts, 2 Sulzer diesels, 900bhp = 14.5kts. Oil 30t. Range 3000nm at 10kts
Armament: 2–100mm (3.9in)/40
Complement: 54

Class (launched, fate):
Arsenal de Lorient – *Bouffonne* (1916, stricken 1925), *Chiffonne* (1917, sold in 1920 to Rumania and renamed *Locotenant Lepri Remus*), *Friponne* (1916, sold in 1920 to Rumania and renamed *Locotenant-Comandor Stihi Eugen*)
Arsenal de Brest – *Diligente* (1916, BU 12.46), *Engageante* (1712.16, stricken 1944, BU 3.12.45), *Impatiente* (1916, sold in 1920 to Romania and renamed *Capitan Dumitrescu C), Mignonne* (1917, sold in 1920 to Rumania as *Sublocotenant Ghiculescu*), *Surveillante* (1917, stricken 1938)

Eight ASW gunboats generally similar to steam *Ardent* class but fitted with diesels for lower speed and greater range. Built under the 1916 War Programme. The class was to include *Coquette, Heroine, Joyeuse, Guerriere* and *Mutine* which were ordered but cancelled in 1918–19. They had no funnels except *Chiffonne, Engageante* and *Mignonne*. Six of the ships served in the Mediterranean, two in the Atlantic. *Surveillante* rammed and sank the Italian torpedo boat *Scorpione* by mistake 15 May 1917. All had clipper bows except *Diligente* which had a straight stem. Ships sold to Rumania gave useful service even after World War Two. *Mignonne, Friponne* and *Impatiente* are still in service in Rumania as auxiliaries (1984).

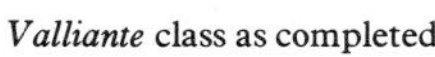
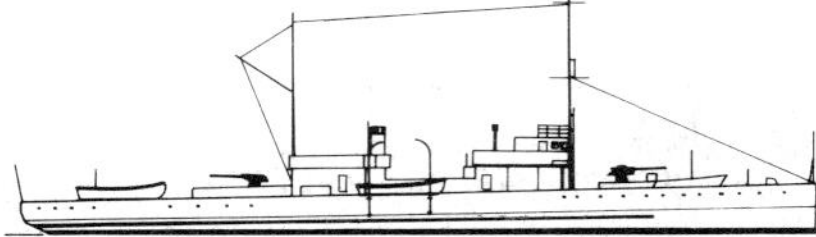
Valliante class as completed

VALLIANTE class *gunboats*

Displacement:	457t
Dimensions:	217ft 10in × 25ft 11in × 8ft 10in *66.4m oa × 7.9m × 2.8m*
Machinery:	2 shafts, 2 Sulzer diesels, 1800bhp = 17kts. Oil 30t. Range 3000nm at 10kts
Armament:	2–100mm (3.9in)/40, DC
Complement:	54

Class (launched, fate):
Conquerante (1917, sunk 14.4.41), *Valliante* (1917, stricken 1932)

Two gunboats built by the Arsenal de Brest under the 1917 War Programme as a modified version of *Friponne* class but with straighter bows. *Conquerante* was seized by the British on 3 July 1940 and sunk by German aircraft at Falmouth the next year.

There were also four Greek gunboats of *Achelaos* class seized by the French in December 1916 and armed under the French flag. These were *Achelaos, Alpheos, Eurotas* and *Peneios* completed in 1885 and refitted in 1895. They were returned to Greece in 1918 and served until 1928–30.

PLUTON class *minelayers*

Displacement:	660t (full load); 566t (normal)
Dimensions:	193ft 7in oa × 27ft 3in × 10ft 10in *59.0m oa × 8.3m × 3.3m*
Machinery:	1 shaft, reciprocating engine, ? boilers, 3000ihp = 20kts. Coal 150t.
Armament:	2–100mm (3.9in)/45 Mod 91, 1–75mm/65 Mod 06, 120 mines
Complement:	65

Class (launched, fate):
A Normand, Le Havre – *Pluton* (10.3.13, stricken 1921, BU 1923)
Nantes – *Cerbère* (13.7.12, stricken 1923)

During 1911–12 two torpedo-cruisers *Cassini* and *Casabianca* were converted into minelayers; however they proved unsatisfactory (too big, too slow and carried too few mines – 97) and so in 1911 two purpose-built ships were ordered. These become *Pluton* and *Cerbère* completed respectively in 1913 and 1912. They were small, handy ships with good turn of speed and good mine capacity (120 mines). In appearance they resembled small merchant ship with straight stem, counter stern and superstructure and funnel amidships. Armament reduced to 1–75mm AA. Both began the war with 2nd Light Squadron in the Channel. *Pluton* captured the German SS *Porto* there on 5 August 1914. Both ships laid mines off Flanders. *Cerbère* went to the Mediterranean in 1915, laying mines off Castellorizo, Beirut, Salonika and the Dardanelles.

HERSE class *minesweepers*

Displacement:	255t
Dimensions:	111ft 7in × 22ft 8in × 7ft 11in *34.0m × 6.8m × 2.4m*
Machinery:	1-shaft TE, 600ihp = 12kts
Armament:	2–47mm
Complement:	?

Class (fate):
Charrue (unlisted 1923), *Herse* (unlisted 1919), *Pioche* (unlisted 1923), *Rateau* (unlisted 1923)
Built by F C de la Méditerranée, La Seyne; laid down 1913, launched 1913–14 and completed 1914.

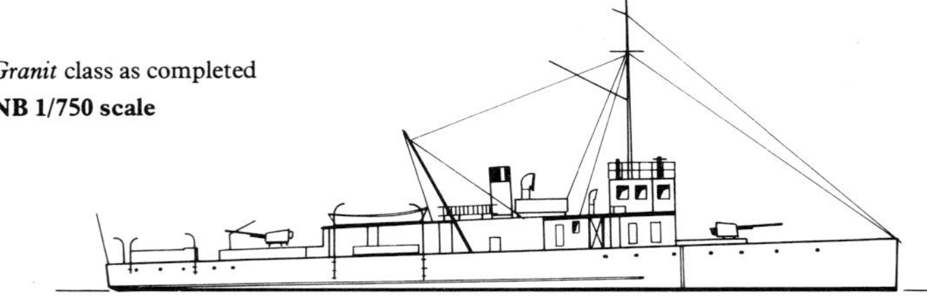
Granit class as completed
NB 1/750 scale

GRANIT class *minesweepers*

Displacement	360t
Dimensions:	189ft × 25ft 11in × 7ft 7in *57.6m × 7.9m × 2.3m*
Machinery:	1-shaft Cochot reciprocating steam engine, 1 Belleville boiler, 600ihp = 12.5kts
Armament:	1–65mm
Complement:	63

Class (fate):
Granit (see notes), *Gres* (condemned 1920), *Marbre* (condemned 1920), *Mica* (condemned 1938), *Porphyre* (condemned 1932)

Gres and *Mica* built by St Nazaire; others by C de la Loire, Nantes. Launched and completed in 1918. Boilers from uncompleted battleship *Flandre. Granit* flew a kite-balloon in 1918. Again commissioned in 1939, she was scuttled on 27 November 1942 at Toulon. Refloated and used by Germans as *SG 26*, her further fate is unknown.

ALBÂTRE class *minesweepers*

Displacement:	380t
Machinery:	1-shaft Cochot reciprocating steam engine, 1 cyl boiler, 500ihp = 10.5kts
Other particulars:	As *Granit* class

Class (fate):
Albâtre (sold 1920 as coaster of the same name), *Basalte* (unlisted 1919), *Gypse* (unlisted 1919), *Meulière* (stranded 24.5.41), *Pyrite* (lost 1926), *Quartz* (unlisted 1939), *Silex* (sold 1920)

Basalte, Meulière and *Silex* built by C de la Loire, St Nazaire; other four by C de la Loire, Nantes. Provided under the 1917 Programme, launched and completed in 1919. *Basalte* and *Gypse* probably not completed. *Meulière* lost off Corsica, *Pyrite* off Madagascar.

Ex-American SC type *submarine chasers*

The US Navy transferred 50 (?48) of these vessels to France from July 1917 and further 50 by October 1918 (see US section for details). They became *C 1–C 100 (?C 98((ex-SC 5, SC 7–SC 16, SC 28–SC 33, SC 65–SC 67, SC 75, SC 76 SC 140–SC 142, SC 146, SC 160–SC 163, SC 170–SC 177, SC 243, SC 249, SC 313–SC 319, SC 347, SC 348, SC 350, SC 357–SC 404, SC 406*). Armed with 1–75mm army gun and 1 Y-gun DC thrower. Ex-US *SC 141* (French number unknown) was lost with all her crew on 15 December 1917 in collision in the Atlantic on passage to France. *C 27* and *C 80* were sold in 1922 to Bulgaria as *Belomorec* and *Chernomorec* respectively. *C 43* collided with the destroyer *Fronde* and sank on 3 July 1918 (sometimes credited with other fate; lost by fire on 2 June 1918 at Dunkirk). *C 31* renamed 1925 *Colonel Casse* (VP 107) and served as *vedette de patrouille auxiliaire* (unlisted 1947). SC type ships were hurriedly constructed, most of them lasted for only a short time in service. In 1939 only eight were in commission: *C 25* (scuttled 27.11.42 at Toulon), *C 51* (BU 10.11.39), *C 56* (BU 29.12.39), *C 58* (BU 10.10.39), *C 74* (fate unknown), *C 81* (seized by the Germans 8.12.42 at Bizerta) and scuttled in this port 6.5.43), *C 95* (BU 10.10.39) and *C 98* (seized by the British in June 1940 at Dunkirk).

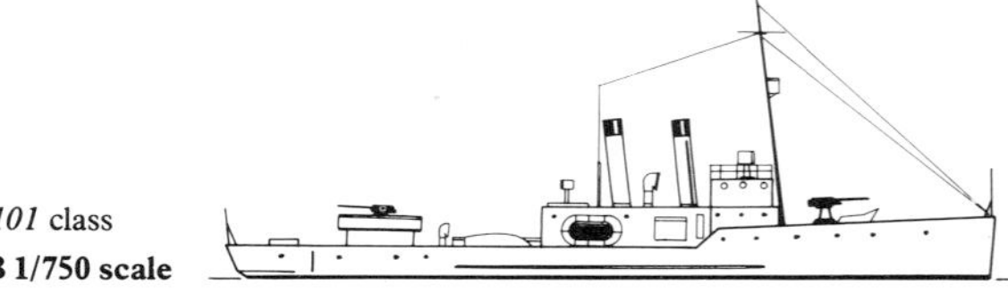
C 101 class
NB 1/750 scale

C 101 class *submarine chasers*

Displacement:	128t–133t; 150t full load
Dimensions:	135ft 10in pp, 142ft 5in oa × 17ft 1in × 7ft 11in *41.4m pp, 43.4m oa × 5.2m × 2.4m*
Machinery:	2-shafts TE, 2 Normand or du Temple boilers; 1300ihp = 16.5kts. Coal 32t
Armament:	1–75mm army gun, 1 MG, 8 DC (75kg), 1 Pinocchio towed torpedo
Complement:	31

Class:
C 101–C 117 (?C 116)
Originally 37 units were ordered in March and April 1918 from Normand, Le Havre (8 boats), La Loire, Nantes (10), Dubigeon, Nantes (7), Arsenal de Lorient (8) and Dyle et Baccalan, Bordeaux (4). By September 1918 their construction had hardly started and by the end of 1918 *c*20 boats had been cancelled. Only Le Havre and Nantes (probably 6 plus 10) boats were completed in 1919–20. Sometimes given 2–14pdr and 2 MG only. They had steel hulls and the funnels set to port and starboard of the centre line. All had the 'C' prefix altered to 'Ch' after the war. Only three or four were in commission in 1939: *C 106* (probably), *C 107* (collided and sunk 12.4.40), *Commandant Bourdais* (ex-*C 111*, renamed in 1928, scuttled 9.3.45 at Haiphong), and *Avalanche* (ex-*C 112*, renamed in 1928, sank 9 or 10.3.45).

NAVARIN class *patrol vessels*

Displacement:	640t
Dimensions:	?
Machinery:	1-shaft reciprocating steam engine, 500ihp = 11kts
Armament:	1–100mm, see notes
Complement:	?

Class:
Bautzen, Cerisoles, Inkermann, Leoben, Lutzen, Malakoff, Mantoue, Navarin, Palestro, Sebastopol, Senef, St-George
Launched between 29 January and 3 October 1918, completed between 20 September and 21 September 1918. These 12 trawlers, built by Canadian Car Co, Fort Willian, and mainly named after French battles or sieges, suffered from very bad stability. *Cerisoles* and *Inkermann* were lost on 24 November 1918 in Lake Superior while on passage to Boston – hence it was decided to disarm the rest of class at Boston.

BOUVINES class *patrol vessels*

Displacement:	684t
Dimensions:	147ft 8in × 25ft 7in *45.0m × 7.8m*
Machinery:	1-shaft reciprocating engine, 500ihp = 9.5kts
Armament:	2–100mm (3.9in)
Complement:	?

Class:
Austerlitz, Bouvines, Fleurus, Jemmapes, Lodi, Magenta, Marengo, Valmy
A total of 38 trawlers (rest see below) were ordered in 1918 and the Foundation Co, Savannah (USA) had decided to build a special yard for their construction. No ship was complete by November 1918 due to the great delay in building this shipyard and other reasons. Finally only the first eight were dispatched to Franch where they were soon placed on the sale list. The others, also named after French land battles, (*Alma, Arcole, Auerstaedt, Bassano, Castiglione, Dego, Denain, Eckmuhl, Essling, Hohenlinden, Hondschoote, Isly, Lens, Les Dunes, Les Pyramides, Lonato, Marignan, Minciao, Mondovi, Montebello, Montenotte, Poitiers, Rocroi, Sambre-et-Meuse, Solferino, Steinkerque, Tagliamento, Tilsitt, Wattignies, Zurich*), completed in 1919, were sold in the USA. At least nine ships of this class served in World War II.

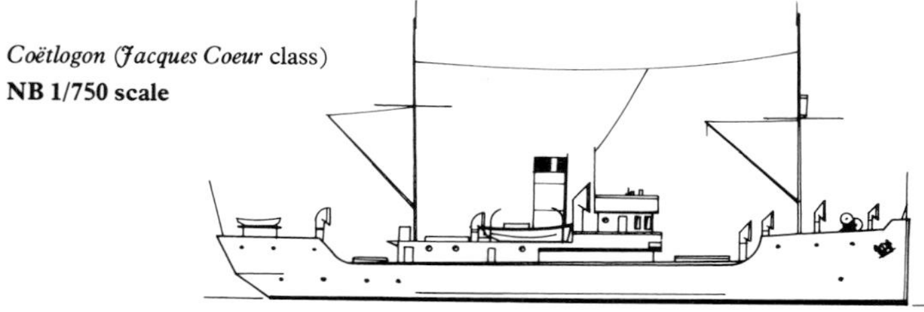

Coëtlogon (*Jacques Coeur* class)
NB 1/750 scale

JACQUES COEUR class *patrol vessels*

Displacement:	700t
Dimensions:	167ft 6in × 25ft 11in × 13ft 11in *51.2m × 7.9m × 4.2m*
Machinery:	1-shaft reciprocating steam engine, 2 cyl boilers, 1100ihp = 12kts
Armament:	2–100mm (3.9in), 1 MG
Complement:	?

Class (fate):
Arsenal de Brest – *Champlain, Châteaurenault* (cancelled), *D'Estaing* (unlisted 1937), *Jacques Coeur, Laperouse* (converted 1920 as *D'Estaing*, scuttled 13.5.45 in Indochina), *Primauguet* (renamed *Allier* 1922, unlisted 1938), *Seignelay* (cancelled)
Arsenal de Lorient – *Kerguelen* (cancelled), *La Clocheterie* (cancelled)
C de la Loire, Nantes – *Coëtlogon, Forfait, Hamelin, Lamotte-Picquet* (renamed *Adour* 1922, *Alfred de Courcy* 1924, unlisted 1937)

All except two survey ships and cancelled units were used as transports *c*1922. *D'Estaing* (renamed *Beautemps-Beaupré* 1920), lengthened by 12m and tonnage increased to 781t, became a survey ship.

GARDON class *patrol vessels*

Displacement:	665t
Machinery:	1-shaft diesel = 10kts (see notes)
Armament:	1–100mm (3.9in), 1–47mm, ASW equipment
Complement:	?

Class:
Normand – *Equille, Gardon, Goujon, Lamproie, Murene*
Port de Bouc – *Cigale, Coccinelle, Libellule*
Le Troit – *Cinquet*
These nine trawler type ships were built 1917–18 and all were unlisted in 1919 except *Criquet* which served as transport in 1920 and unlisted 1921. *Equille, Lamproie* and *Murene* had reciprocating steam engine with Belleville boiler from the uncompleted battleship *Flandre*.

BARBEAU class *patrol vessels*

Displacement:	315t
Machinery:	1-shaft reciprocating steam engine, 365ihp = 9kts
Armament:	1–90mm (3.5in) army gun, 1–47mm
Complement:	?

Class:
Ablette, Anguille II, Barbeau, Breme, Brochet, Perche, Tanche, Truite
These eight trawler type ships, similar type to *Barbeau*, were built by various yards and were all unlisted in 1919.

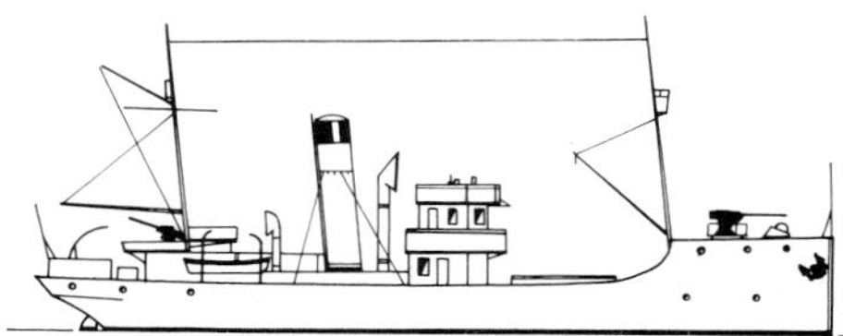

Passereau (*Mauviette* type)
NB 1/750 scale

MAUVIETTE type *patrol vessels*

Displacement:	420t–460t
Dimensions:	142ft 9in × 23ft 11in × 11ft 2in–13ft 9in *43.5m × 7.3m × 3.4m–4.2m*
Machinery:	1-shaft reciprocating steam engine, 1 cyl boiler, ?ihp = 10kts. Coal 120t
Armament:	1–90mm (3.5in) army gun, 1–47mm

Class (fate):
Alouette II (unlisted 1919), *Bec Figue* (unlisted 1919), *Bergeronnette* (unlisted 1919), *Caille II* (unlisted 1919), *Canard* (fate unknown), *Chardonneret II* (unlisted 1919), *Colibri* (unlisted 1919), *Corneille II* (unlisted 1919), *Engoulevent* (unlisted 1919), *Etourneau* (unlisted 1919), *Fauvette II* (unlisted 1919), *Grive II* (unlisted 1919), *Linotte III* (unlisted 1919), *Loriot* (unlisted 1919), *Martinet* (unlisted 1919), *Martin-Pêcheur* (1919 converted into survey ship *Alidade*, foundered 12.12.31), *Mauviette* (1919 converted into survey ship *Astrolabe*, bombed 26.2.44), *Merle II* (unlisted 1919), *Moineau II* (unlisted 1919), *Ortolan* (1920 converted into survey ship *Gaston Rivier*, BU 1946), *Passereau II* (unlisted *c* 1945–46), *Perruche II* (1920 converted into survey ship *Sentinelle*, BU 14.11.47), *Pie II* (1920 converted into survey ship *Estafette*, sunk 8.11.42), *Pierrot II* (unlisted 1919), *Pinson II* (1919 converted into survey ship *Bousolle*, unlisted 1932), *Pivert* (1919 converted into survey ship *Octant*, bombed 12.1.45), *Roitelet II* (stricken 1920), *Rossignol II* (stricken 1920), *Rouge-Gorge II* (unlisted 1919), *Sansonnet* (unlisted 1919)
These trawler type patrol vessels were completed *c*1918. Built by C de la Méditerranée, La Seyne and Normand, Le Havre. *Passereau II* fitted as minesweeper.

LOUP class *patrol vessels*

Displacement:	285t
Machinery:	1-shaft reciprocating steam engine, 1 Belleville boiler, 600ihp = 10kts
Armament:	1–75mm

Class (fate):
Loup (see notes), *Marcassin* (see notes), *Renard I* (mined 19.10.17), *Sanglier* (unlisted 1940)
Patrol tugs built by C de la Méditerranée, La Seyne (commissioned 1917). Boilers were from uncompleted battleship *Flandre*. *Loup* and *Marcassin* were scuttled on 27.11.42 at Toulon, the second being refloated and sunk here 5.7.44 by Allied aircraft.

HIPPOPOTAME class *patrol vessels*

Displacement: 970t
Machinery: 1-shaft reciprocating steam engine, 2 d'Allest boilers, 1800ihp = 12kts
Armament: 2–75mm

Class (fate):
C de Normandie, Rouen – *Mammouth* (unlisted 1963), *Mastodonte* (unlisted 1952)
Penhoët, St-Nazaire – *Hippopotame* (unlisted 1952), *Rhinoceros* (sunk 25.3.43)

These patrol tugs were completed in 1917–19 and served in World War II.

PLUVIER class *patrol vessels*

Displacement: 680t–780t
Machinery: 1-shaft reciprocating steam engine, 750ihp = 11kts

Class (fate):
C de la Loire, Nantes – *Heron* (scuttled 27.11.42, refloated 1946, unlisted 1949), *Pigeon* (unlisted 1945), *Pingouin II* (unlisted 1949), *Pintade* (unlisted 1945), *Pluvier* (unlisted 1920), *Perdreau II* (collision 14.8.18), *Tourterelle* (scuttled 9.11.42, refloated 1943, condemned 1956), *Vanneau II* (unlisted 1920)
C de la Loire, St Nazaire – *Canari* (unlisted 1919), *Colombe* (unlisted 1922), *Coq* (unlisted 1919, requisitioned 1939–45), *Faisan* (unlisted 1945), *Gelinotte* (unlisted 1951), *Paon* (sunk 2.10.44), *Ramier* (unlisted 1949)

All these tugs, used as patrol boats, were completed early in 1918.

AUROCHS class *patrol vessels*

Displacement: 290t
Machinery: 1-shaft reciprocating steam engine, 1 d'Allest boiler, 650ihp = 10kts
Armament: 1–90mm (3.5in), 1–47mm

Class:
Aurochs, Elan, Renne, Zebu

Built by C de Bretagne and completed before 1918. These tugs, used as patrol vessels, were in service in World War Two (2 lost).

CLAMEUR class *patrol vessels*

Displacement: 370t
Machinery: 1-shaft reciprocating steam engines (2 sets), 2 cyl boilers, 720ihp = 12kts
Armament: 1–90mm (3.5in) army gun

Class (fate):
C de la Ciotat – *Clameur* (unlisted 1940), *Fracas* (probably scuttled May 1943), *Vacarme* (foundered 6.8.42)
C de la Gironde – *Tapage* (unlisted 1925), *Tintamarre* (unlisted 1931), *Tumulte* (bombed 21.5.40)

Tugs used as patrol boats, completed after the Armistice.

ATHLETE class *patrol vessels*

Displacement: 585t
Machinery: 2-shaft Sisson reciprocating steam engines, 1 Belleville boiler, 500ihp = 12kts
Armament: 2–120mm (4.7in)

Class (fate):
Athlete (scuttled 18.6.40), *Gladiateur V* (unlisted 1920), *Lutteur* (scuttled 18.6.40, see notes)

These tugs were bı ilt by Arsenal de Brest and were completed in 1918–19. *Athlete* and *Lutteur* wc·e scuttled at Brest, second refloated by the Germans.

CRABE class *patrol vessels*

Displacement: 360t–370t
Machinery: 1-shaft Fraser and Chulner reciprocating steam engine, 1 Belleville boiler, 400ihp = 9kts–10kts
Armament: 1–90mm (3.5in)

Class:
Arsenal de Brest – *Calmar, Crabe, Homard, Tourteau*
Arsenal de Lorient – *Cedre, Chene, Erable, Frêne, Hetre, Orme, Peuplier, Platane*

All these 12 tugs were completed in 1918–20 and served in the Second World War (6 lost). Boilers were from old cruiser *Descartes*.

VIGILANTE class *river gunboats*

Displacement: 123t
Dimensions: 145ft × 23ft 11in × 2ft
44.2m × 7.3m × 0.6m
Machinery: 2 shafts, reciprocating engines, 2 boilers, 500ihp = 13kts. Coal *c*20t
Armament: 2–90mm (3.5in), 4–37mm
Complement: 30 (53?)

Class (launched, fate):
Argus (17.2.00, stricken 1920), *Vigilante* (1900, stricken 1920)

Steel river gunboats of the British *Woodlark* type with one funnel and pole mast. Built by Thornycroft of Chiswick for service in China. Laid down in 1899 and completed in 1900. The ships' vital spaces were covered with bullet-proof plating.

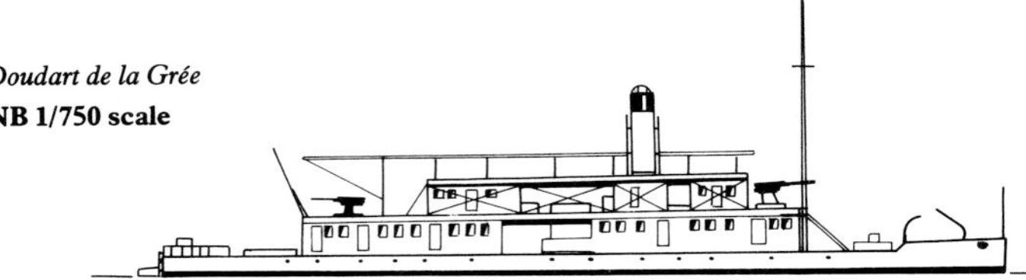

Doudart de la Grée
NB 1/750 scale

DOUDART DE LA GRÉE *river gunboats*

Displacement: 183t normal
Dimensions: 178ft 6in oa × 171ft 7in pp × 22ft × 3ft 3in
54.4m oa, 52.3m pp × 6.7m × 1.0m
Machinery: 2 shafts, 2 reciprocating engines, 2 Fouché boilers, 900ihp = 14kts. Coal 45t
Armament: 6–37mm
Complement: 57 (+7 Chinese)

A flushdecked, one funnelled river gunboat built by Chantiers de Bretagne in Nantes for service in China. Ordered on 11 March 1908, launched on 5 January 1909, completed on 4 February 1909. She spent 1917–18 in the Far East and was laid up at Shanghai in 1939 and BU in 1941. The ship was rearmed with 1–75mm (army pattern), 2–37mm, 4 MG.

Argus as completed
Navarret Collection

BALNY *river gunboat*

Displacement: 201t normal; 226t full load
Dimensions: As *Doudart de la Grée*
Machinery: As *Doudart de la Grée* but coal 27t
Armament: 6–37mm
Complement: 61

A near sister to the *Doudart de la Grée* but fitted with two funnels, built by the same yard Ch de la Bretagne, Nantes. Work stopped during 1914–1918. Launched in June 1914 and completed in 1920. Rearmed with 2–75mm and 2–37mm guns. Laid up in Chungking 1940, presented to China and BU 1944. One of her engines was transferred in World War One to the Q-ship *Meg*.

VIGILANTE (ii) class *river gunboats*

Displacement: 178t normal; 218t full load
Dimensions: 170ft oa × 25ft 3in × 3ft 11in
51.8m oa × 7.7m × 1.2m
Machinery: 2 shafts, 2 reciprocating engines, 2 boilers, 600ihp = 12kts. Oil fuel
Armament: 2–75mm, 2–37mm, 4–8mm MG
Armour: Bullet-proof plating
Complement: 42

Class (launched, fate):
Argus (ii) (1923, stricken 1941), *Vigilante* (ii) (1923, scuttled 9.3.45)
Two river gunboats built for service by Arsenal de Toulon in China. *Argus* laid up in Haiphong 1940, transferred to China as *San-Min*. *Vigilante* scuttled in Haiphong, later salved in June 1946 and sold as mercantile ship (in 1946). These ships were given the names of the earlier Thornycroft-built vessels.

OTHER RIVER GUNBOATS
The French Navy operated in 1906 a number of river gunboats in China and Indochina. These included: *Peï-Ho* ex-*Lieutenant Contal* (123t, 2–90mm, 4–37mm, 13kts, built 1901); *Doucet* and *Rollandes* (120t, 8.8kts, 1–47mm, 4–37mm, built 1886); *Berthe-de-Villers* and *Jasquin* (200t, 9kts, 2–100mm, 4–37mm, built 1884), and other small boats such as *Javelot, Estoc, Henri Rivière, Jacques d'Uzes, Leon Blot, Boeni, Onyx, Opale, Fourmi, La Grandière, Massie, Ham-Luong, Corail, Jules-Davoust, Mage, Diamant, Eméraude, Etincelle, Rubis, Surveillant, Saphir, Turquoise, Mirmidon, Pygmée* and *Niger*.

There were also river gunboats for French mainland rivers (floating batteries). These river gunboats were designed by French naval constructors for service with the Army in France. Their construction was decided in 1915 when three types were designed. However only two of them were built. The first type armed with an M1893 138.6mm (5.4in) gun and second type armed with 2–100mm guns. Both had 2–47mm AA guns. Officially they were designated by letters (A, B, C, *etc*). The ships' companies gave them unofficial names such as *Ardente, Brutale, Cruelle* or *Decidée*. Of the first type eight boats were ordered in May 1915 and delivered in July by Arsenal de Brest and Arsenal de Lorient. The same yards built four boats of the second type between July 1915 and September 1915. Gunboat C was lost on the Somme on 16 July 1916 by a 150mm shell but was soon refloated. Two other boats sank in bad weather on 4 October 1918 while on tow to Cherbourg. Between July 1915 and December 1917 these three batteries of gunboats (12 boats) fired 40,524rds of 138.6mm shell, 16,628rds of 100mm and 4961rds of 47mm in Belgium, on the Somme, in Champagne, on the Oise and the Aisne. They were decommissioned in 1917 but four of the first type (C, G, H, I) joined the Rhine Flotilla in 1918 and renamed *Aisne, Marne, Oise* and *Somme* (armament was changed to only one 75mm army gun). Beside these regular river gunboats there were in service about 10 improvised gunboats made from requisitioned canal boats or barges (armed with 138.6mm, 164.7mm, 194mm or 240mm guns). These gunboats were manned by the Navy but operated under Army control on canals around Verdun and also in Flanders or Champagne. Some of them joined the Rhine Flotilla after the Armistice.

MOTOR BOATS
After a study of several ASW-boat designs, the *Marine Nationale* finally purchased four class of *vedettes à moteur* with the following 73 units. All, except two, were disposed of before 1925.

V 1 class *motor boats*

Displacement: 40t
Dimensions: 78ft 9in × 12ft 6in × 3ft 3in
24.0m × 3.8m × *1.0m*
Machinery: 2 Standard petrol engines, 440bhp = 20kts max
Armament: 1–75mm army gun, 1–2 MG, 1 Y-gun DC thrower, 1 'C' tube ASW system
Complement: ?

Class:
V 1–V 40
Forty units had been originally ordered by the Royal Navy from Elco of Bayonne, USA, through Vickers of Montreal, Canada and were part of the British *ML 114–ML 548* series. Delivered 1916–17. *V 1–V 4* reached Cherbourg in May 1916 to serve in the Dunkirk Torpedo Flotilla and on the Rhine as did *V 32–V 35*. *V 5–V 28* served in the Mediterranean. *V 21* was lost in a fire on 4 May 1917 at Algiers, *V 23* grounded on 23 August 1917 near Cape Bouragoni (Algeria), and *V 37* was lost on 24 November 1917 by explosion at Les Sables D'Olonne on the Atlantic coast.

V 41 class *motor boats*

Displacement: 40t
Dimensions: 82ft × 12ft 2in × 3ft 3in
25.0m × 3.7m × 1.0m
Machinery: 2 Panhard petrol motors, 20kts max
Armament: 1–75mm army gun, 1–2 MG, 1 Y-gun DC thrower, 1 'C' tube ASW system

Class (fate):
V 41–V 53 (paid off 11.19)
Designed by M Despujols and built in his yard at Neuilly-sur-Seine. First four boats had engine difficulties which delayed delivery until September 1917 when they were assigned to the Biscay Patrol Division while the next six went to Dunkirk. Three were cancelled.

V 54 class *motor boats*

Displacement: 40t–41t
Dimensions: 86ft 11in × 13ft 1in × 4ft 3in
26.5m × 4.0m × 1.3m
Machinery: 2 American Wolverine petrol motors, 3600bhp = 16.5kts (designed, 14.5kts only in service)
Other particulars: not available

Class:
V 54–V 61
Ordered in August 1916 from the Gustave Cornilleau yard near Marseilles. Delivered between January and June 1917.

V 62 class *motor boats*

Displacement: 41t (?32t)
Dimensions: 76ft 9in × 12ft 2in
23.4m × 3.7m
Machinery: =19kts
Other particulars: not available

Class:
V 62–V 73
Built by Vickers, Montreal to be delivered in May 1918, but because of delayed trials *V 62–V 65* were not in service until two days after the Armistice.

AUXILIARY WARSHIPS

AUXILIARY CRUISERS
During 1914–18 the French Navy employed a number of armed merchant ships as auxiliary cruisers for patrol duties when and where the true cruisers were scarce. These ships were used as cruisers mainly in 1914 and later alternatively as auxiliary cruisers or as troopers (mostly for trooping to the Dardanelles and Macedonian fronts). The force of auxiliary cruisers consisted mainly of fast passenger ships requisitioned from the merchant navy. The following is a list of the 23 most important ships of this category.
Amazone II (6007t gross/built 1897, 19kts); 1919 unlisted.

Burdigala (12,000t/1897, 18kts); in Mediterranean; mined (from *U 73*) off Zea Island, Aegean on 14 November 1916.
Caledonien (4130t/1832, 15kts); 1914–17 cruiser in the Mediterranean; mined (from *UC 34*) off Port Said on 30 June 1917.
Carthage (5275t/1910, 19kts); 1914–15 cruiser in Mediterranean, torpedoed by German *U 21* off Gallipoli on 4 July 1915.
Djemnah (3716t/1875, 13kts); used as trooper 1915–18, torpedoed and sunk by German *UB 105* on 14 July 1918 off Cyrenaica.
Europe (4838t/1906, 14kts); used as cruiser 1914–15 and 1915–18 as trooper, 1919 unlisted.
Flandre (8450t/1914, 17kts); 1914–17 cruiser and trooper, 1919 unlisted.
Gallia (14,900t/1913, 21kts); 1914–1915 cruiser, 1916 trooper, torpedoed and sunk by German *U 35* on 4 October 1916 off Cape Matapan.
Gange (6876t/1905, 13.5kts); 1914–17 trooper, mined and sunk off Bizerte on 14 April 1917.
Golo II (1380t/1903, 18kts); used as small cruiser, torpedoed and sunk by German *UC 22* on 22 August 1917 off Corfu.
Himalaya (5620t/1902, 14kts); used as trooper, torpedoed and sunk by German *U 63* on 23 June 1917 off Marrittimo, Sicily.
Italia (1305t/1904, 17kts); used as trooper and torpedoed by Austrian *U 4* on 30 May 1917 30nm off Taranto.
Lorraine II (11,146t/1899, 21.5kts); 1914 cruiser, 1915–18 belonged to the Levant Squadron, 1919 unlisted.
Lutetia (14,654t/1913, 20.5kts); 1916–18 cruiser.
Newhaven (1656t/1910, 24kts); 1914 cruiser 2nd Light Squadron, 1915–18 patrols in Channel, unlisted in 1919.
Niagara (8590t/1890, 16kts); 1914 cruiser 2nd Light Squadron, 1915–18 patrol and trooping, 1919 unlisted.
Polynesien (6363t/1890, 17kts); 1914–18 trooper, torpedoed by German *UC 22* on 10 August 1918 in Malta Channel.
Provence II (13,753t/1906, 22.5kts); 1914–15 cruiser, patrols and shore bombardment, 1915–16 trooper, torpedoed by German *U 35* on 26 February 1916 W of Cerigo (Kithira) Island.
Savoie (11,168t/1900, 21kts); 1914 cruiser, 1915–18 trooper, 1919 unlisted.
Santa Anna (9350t/1910, 16.5kts); 1914–15 cruiser, 1915–18 trooper, torpedoed and sunk by German *UC 54* on 11 May 1918 between Bizerta and Malta.
Sontay (7236t/1907, 15kts); 1914–17 trooper, torpedoed on 16 April 1917 by German *UC 54* off Tunisia.
Timgad (1911); 1914 cruiser, 1915 hospital ship, 1916–18 trooper, 1919 unlisted.
Touraine (9429t/1891, 19kts); 1914 cruiser, 1915–18 trooper, 1919 unlisted.

All these ships were armed as cruisers with various combinations of guns according to their size and envisaged role; for example *Provence II* as a cruiser was armed with 5–138.6mm (5.4in) guns and 4–47mm guns and smaller *Golo II* got only 2–65mm guns and 2–47mm guns.

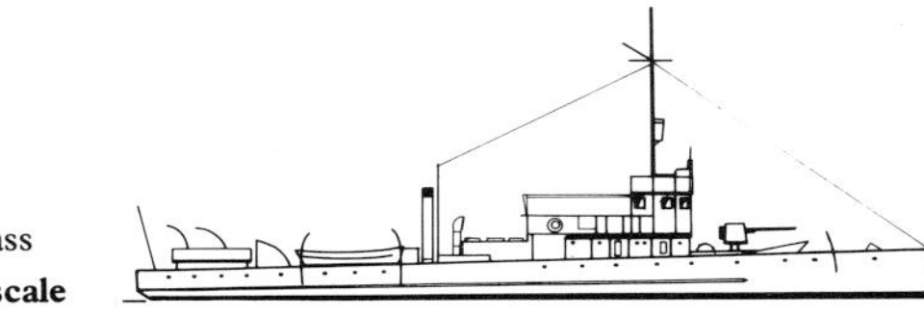

Briscard class
NB 1/750 scale

AUXILIARY MINESWEEPERS

The 10-ship trawler type *Camelia class* (124t, 170ihp/9kts, 1–75mm) also included *Datura, Francoa, Fresia, Godetia, Ipeca, Magnolia, Paulownia, Reseda* and *Zinnia*. Built by C de Bretagne, Nantes and powered by reciprocating steam engine with 1 cyl boiler. Provided under the 1917 Programme, and completed 1918. Most were paid off after postwar mine clearance and sold to fishery owners. *Camelia* and *Datura* served as harbour tugs postwar and both were scuttled at Toulon, the first on 27 November 1942 by the French, the second in August 1944 by the Germans. The 10-ship *Ajonc* class (112t, 220bhp/9.5kts, 1–75mm) also included *Aster, Chardon, Genet, Jasmin, Lilas, Lupin, Mugnet, Myosotis* and *Nenuphar*. Provided under the 1917 Programme and built by C Baudouin, Marseilles. Four of these ships were completed before the Armistice. Powered by oil engine and had been designed with the view to transform them into 140t trawlers with a gas engine, hulls being strengthened for this purpose. Fates as *Camelia* class.

The 10-ship trawler type *Fanfaron* class (C Niclausse, Paris, 154t, 300bhp/9kts, 1–90mm or 1–75mm) also included *Fantasque, Farouche, Favori, Flambant, Fougueux, Forrageur, Frondeur, Fulgurant* and *Furieux*. Provided under the 1917 Programme; all were completed 1919 (except *Flambant* 1918) – this later renamed *Maréchal Foch* and became a Rhône tug. Powered by 1-shaft reciprocating steam engine with 1 Niclausse boiler. Fates as *Camelia* class.

The 6-ship *Amandier* class (C Bocanini, Cannes, 78t, 160bhp/9kts, 1 light gun) also included *Bananier, Cocotier, Dattier, Murier* and *Palmier*. Provided under the 1917 programme; only *Amandier* and *Bananier* were completed.

The 12-ship *Campanule* class (80t, 325bhp/13kts) also included *Clematite, Jacinthe, Jonquille, Lavende* and *Marjolaine* built by Arsenal de Lorient and *Paquerette, Perce-Neige, Renoncule, Sauge, Tulipe* and *Vilette* built by Arsenal de Rochefort. Provided under the 1917 Programme. Ten were completed before the Armistice. Powered by 1-shaft Fiat oil engine. *Clematite* unlisted 1922, *Perce-Neige* in 1934, other fates as *Camelia* class.

The 16-ship *Briscard* class (370t, 131ft 3in × 23ft 11in × 10ft 6in, *41m × 7.3m × 3.2m*) also included *Chevronne, Franc-Tireur, Fusilier, Grognard, Mathurin, Poilu, Rengage, Sapeur, Troupier, Veteran* and *Volontaire* built by Sud-Ouest, Bordeaux and *Bombardier, Canonier, Mitrailleur* and *Pionnier* built by Baudouin, Marseilles. Provided under the 1917 Programme. Powered by reciprocating steam engine, 425ihp = 11kts except *Mathurin* and *Troupier* petrol engine, 420bhp = 11kts and Marseilles-built ships reciprocating engine, 500ihp = 11.5kts. *Grognard, Poilu* and *Rengage* were sold in 1922 to the Spanish Navy and renamed *Tetuan, Larache* and *Alcazar* respectively. *Bombardier* was sold in 1922 and became a tug, *Veteran* was sold in 1920 as a pilot boat.

There were also five trawler minesweepers bought in 1910–11: *Alcyon I* (300t, 320ihp/8.5kts); *Damier* (155t, 340ihp/9kts); *Ivoise* (built 1907, 240t, 430ihp/10kts); *Lorientais* (433t, 370ihp/9.7kts); *Orient* (385t, 565ihp/10kts). All except *Damier* (1923) were unlisted in 1919.

AUXILIARY TRAWLERS

A total of 250 trawlers were requisitioned during the First World War (45 lost) and many trawlers etc were purchased abroad: 8 in Belgium (1916–17), 4 in Brazil (1916–17); 23 in Great Britain (2 lost); 8 in Greece (1917); 10 in Iceland (1917); all fitted as 600t minesweepers, 1 in Italy (1915, lost); 34 in Japan (1916, 3 lost); 11 in the Netherlands (1916); 43 in Norway (6 lost); 3 in Sweden (1916–17); 98 in Spain (1915 and later, 4 lost); 13 in USA and 8 elsewhere.

Japan

Like the US Navy, its future adversary, the modern Japanese Navy was still, in 1906, a recent development. It had also just triumphed over the Russian Imperial Navy in a war that climaxed in the Battle of Tsushima, an event seen at the time as a twentieth century Trafalgar. Like the United States, too, Japan had an intense drive to be accepted as an equal by the advanced (Western) powers. In her case, this was at least partly a response to the humiliations of the decade of her opening, in the mid-nineteenth century. This factor explains, for example, the demands for parity at naval arms limitation conferences. Manifest Western anti-Japanese racism also fed Japanese demands for equal treatment.

Japan's energies were concentrated on expansion on the mainland of Asia, partly (at least in theory) to overcome the crowding of her population, and partly to obtain markets for her growing industries. The corollary was that she wished, throughout the period prior to 1945, to exclude economic and political rivals from East Asia. Another consistent element of Japanese policy was the attempt to gain control over the sources of raw materials and energy, such as Manchuria, with its iron and coal deposits.

Although in theory a maritime nation, Japan had throughout this period a very powerful Army, which derived its importance at least partly from its role in maintaining internal order, ie from the feudal past. Until the end of World War Two, rivalry between Army and Navy was a major issue in Japanese strategy and also in the allocation of what were, often, relatively scarce resources. At least through the late nineteenth century, the Army was dominant, the Navy forming its own general staff largely in order to maintain its own power in the face of the Army's. The strategic split between the two services can be traced to the end of the nineteenth century when the United States displaced Spain in the Philippines.

Until that time there had been only two major Far Eastern powers, China (clearly in decline) and Tsarist Russia. Japanese ambitions for great power status therefore required the defeat, first of China (in 1894–95) and then of Russia (in 1904–5). After Russia had been defeated, the Japanese Navy argued that the United States remained a bar to Japan's hegemony in the area. It was the United States which, mediating at Portsmouth (Virginia), convinced the Japanese government to settle for less than what many in Japan considered her due. The United States also consistently opposed Japanese attempts to gain control over China, albeit relatively ineffectively. In 1907 Japanese Fleet strength was formally set at 8 battleships and 8 large cruisers and the list of probable enemies was formalised, with Russia in first place, followed by two major Far Eastern colonial powers, the United States and France; Britain was an ally.

Aki on trials
Aldo Fraccaroli Collection

BRITISH INFLUENCE

The other major factor in Japanese naval development during this period was Great Britain, which succeeded France as the dominant foreign supplier in the 1890s. France supplied the large *Matsushima* class cruisers, the most powerful Japanese units engaged against China in 1894, as well as parts for many torpedo-boats; Emile Bertin, a well-known French naval architect, introduced the Japanese Navy to steel construction while serving as director of the Yokosuka naval shipyard, 1886–90. British technicians served in Japan at this time, but British influence really became prominent when the Japanese Navy decided to purchase battleships, which had to be built abroad. Cruisers were built in Japan, but their performance was disappointing, and foreign yards predominated until well into the first decade of this century.

On a more subtle note, while the Japanese Army turned to Germany as its model, the Navy turned to the Royal Navy; its academy, Eta Jima, was modelled on Dartmouth. Firms such as Vickers supplied first the ships and then the designs for the modern fleet. Japanese carrier aviation can be traced back to the British Semphill Mission of 1921, and through the early post-World War One period British designers were seconded to several Japanese aircraft manufacturers, developing, among others, specialised naval types. British naval influence was so strong that, until the 1930s, bridge commands such as helm orders were typically given in English. Japanese warships were designed in English units of measurement, metric units becoming predominant only after 1921.

WORLD WAR ONE

In 1902, as part of her strategy of concentration in the North Sea, Britain signed a mutual defence treaty with Japan, in effect awarding her responsibility for Far Eastern waters. That was why Japan entered World War One on the Allied side, on 23 August 1914. At that time there were virtually no other Allied naval forces in the Pacific. Thus, as part of the operation against Vice-Admiral Graf von Spee's East Asiatic Squadron, Japan seized the German colony of Tsingtao in China, which was the main German Pacific base. This was an elaborate amphibious operation by Vice-Admiral Baron Kamimura's Second Fleet to land 22,980 Japanese and 1369 British troops; Tsingtao did not fall until 7 November 1914. The Japanese cruiser *Takachiho*, the destroyer *Shirotaye*, and *Torpedo Boat No 33* were all torpedoed or mined in its course. The ex-freighter *Wakamiya* functioned as a seaplane carrier during the siege, her aircraft making a bombing run over the city before it was invested, but it was the Fleet's gunfire that proved decisive in the capture of the outer defences on Prince Heinrich Hill.

At the outset of the war, the Japanese Navy's First Fleet occupied the German Pacific islands (Marshall and Caroline groups) to deny these bases to von Spee. Under provisions of secret treaties with Britain, Japan retained these islands after 1918. Japanese warships of the Third Fleet also helped convoy Australian and New Zealand troops to the Middle East. The trade protection role in the Pacific effectively ceased with the fall of Tsingtao and the destruction of the German raiding cruiser *Emden* in November 1914. However, Japanese warships remained active, for example helping Britain to suppress a rebellion in Singapore in February 1915.

By 1917 Allied naval strength in European waters, particularly for ASW, had been so stretched that in January Britain asked Japan to assign destroyers to the Mediterranean. The cruiser *Akashi* and the 10th (*Katsura, Kaede, Kusunoki,* and *Ume*) and 11th (*Matsu, Kashiwa, Sakaki,* and *Sugi*) Destroyer Divisions arrived in Malta on 13 April 1917, joined that autumn by the cruiser *Nisshin* and the new 15th Destroyer Division (*Momo, Kashi, Hinoki*, and *Yanagi*). To replace these ships 6 more second class destroyers of an improved *Momo* class were ordered (Extraordinary War Expenditures, 1917). However, Japan refused Admiral Jellicoe's 1917 request to buy the *Kongo* class battlecruisers outright.

World War One was also an opportunity for Japan to realise her goals in East Asia. In 1915 she pressed China for special status. On 4 April 1918 Admiral Kato landed 500 marines from two cruisers in Vladivostok to help protect Allied interests threatened by the Bolshevik Revolution. On 3 August the Japanese 12th Infantry Division began going ashore. Those troops (70,000 by October 1918) remained in place after the end of hostilities (in fact until October 1922), and some suggested that Japan hoped to seize Siberia (and its resources) for herself, as a kind of ultimate settlement of the Russo-Japanese War. The United States strongly resisted both the 1915 demands and the Siberian operation, and it can be argued that American policy generally was to deny Japan either hegemony over East Asia or the close connection with Britain which would have presented difficulties in the event of US-Japanese hostilities. Thus the Anglo-Japanese Treaty was dissolved as part of a multilateral series of guarantees negotiated in tandem with the Washington Treaty limiting warship construction, in 1921-22. Henceforth British naval planners had to consider the possibility that Japan would attempt to seize the major British colonies in the East, to the extent that war with Japan became a major British naval planning consideration. Even so, the close relationship between the two navies persisted for many years.

ECONOMIC WEAKNESSES

The other major factor in Japanese naval development during this period was the relative weakness of the Japanese economy. Given the unsatisfactory conclusion of the Sino-Japanese War, the Government began an expensive military and naval expansion programme, which weakened the country prior to the Russo-Japanese War, even though some of this expansion was funded by the Chinese war indemnity. Japanese participation in the suppression of the 1900 Boxer Rebellion was also costly, although it had the considerable appeal of placing Japan clearly among the major powers in the Far East. These strains exacerbated the effects of the Russo-Japanese War itself. Thus, in 1905, although Russia was severely damaged by revolution, she could still have supplied more troops. Japan was bankrupt and had no Army reserves; she had to settle. That she did well was a measure of how successful she had been with such limited means. As Japan emerged from her war debts, she fell victim to a world economic depression (about 1910).

Naval construction itself was extremely expensive. In 1904 it was reported that, relative to her national income, Japan was spending five times as much on the Imperial Navy as Britain was spending on the Royal Navy. Much of this money, moreover, was spent abroad, so that it could not be considered a means of expanding Japanese industry – as US naval expansion might be considered. Finally, unlike Britain and the United States, Japan maintained a very large active army.

An undeveloped Japanese industrial base could not supply sufficient high-quality steel or ordnance or, later, turbines. Thus, 61 per cent of the material for the 1906 battleship *Satsuma* had to be imported. At the time of the Russo-Japanese War only the Kure Arsenal built 12in guns. Because production was limited, battleships designed to mount uniform batteries of such weapons could not be built; some units ran their trials without guns aboard, waiting considerable periods for them. For instance the armoured cruiser or battlecruiser *Ikoma* ran her trials as early as November 1907, but was not completed until February 1911. Similarly, 27,000shp Curtis turbines were ordered in the spring of 1906 for the battleship *Aki* and the battlecruiser *Ibuki*. They were delivered only in October 1908, delaying both ships very considerably. Delays were bad enough: during the Russo-Japanese War deliveries of foreign war material and warships had been embargoed altogether. A Japanese Government bent on pursuing an independent foreign policy (some would say, pursuing hegemony in the Far East) could not allow the instrument of that policy, its navy, to be subject to foreign veto.

Industrial independence thus became a major Japanese objective, reflected in the Mitsubishi (Parsons) and Kawasaki (Curtis) licences to build turbines in Japan, and in the determination to use Japanese-produced material after about 1913, as in the later ships of the *Kongo* class. On another level, during the Russo-Japanese War capital ships were ordered from the two major naval shipyards, which previously had built only small protected cruisers. Full independence in design came later; it appears, for example, that all battleships prior to the 1919 *Nagato* were essentially British designs, and even that ship is often described as a Japanese version of the *Queen Elizabeth*. Japanese warships began to take on a distinctive form only about the end of World War One, as naval architects trained abroad, largely in Britain, reached maturity.

NAVAL BUILDING PROGRAMMES 1896–1920

In the summary of Japanese naval programme which follows, it is

The launch of *Tosa* 18 December 1921 *Aldo Fraccaroli Collection*

important to distinguish between statutory approval of Fleet strength and actual appropriation of funds, a distinction parallelling US practice. Although the Japanese 1903 programme included two battleships, one of them, which became the super-dreadnought *Fuso*, was not funded until 1911. Note, too, that Japan was not alone in its series of statutory fleet programme. They were similar in spirit to the German Navy Laws; and France had her equivalent. In this sense, the United States and Britain may have been almost unique for their time in *not* having legislated ultimate levels of naval strength. The Japanese concept was that ships passed through three periods of life: one in the first line, one operational but ageing, and one in reserve. At first each was ten years, but during the period of interest here each was eight years. Thus the '8-8' programme ultimately called for two eight-ship squadrons each unit of which would be less than eight years old, backed by other modern ships in their second period of life.

The Japanese naval staff first developed a long-range fleet programme after the victory over China in 1894–95. Previous Japanese naval construction had been limited to cruisers. As tension with China rose in 1892, the Japanese Government decided to order its first two battleships, to balance the two Chinese units. They were ordered in Britain in 1893, and delivered postwar. By that time, analysis suggested that, better handled, the two Chinese battleships might well have been decisive.

As a result, a Naval Expansion Plan of March 1896 called for the construction of 4 more modern battleships (for a total of 6), as well as 4 large cruisers (of the British *Edgar* type, 7500 tons) and 3 smaller ones. However, the naval staff argued that a single (6-ship) armoured squadron would not suffice to execute an offensive while protecting the Japanese coast; it would be necessary to build two armoured squadrons. As a result, a Second Naval Extension Programme, passed in September 1896, replaced the cruisers of the original programme with 6 armoured cruisers (comparable to the British *Cressy*). The armoured cruisers were clearly a compromise, half battleship, half cruiser. The balance set at this time, between squadrons of battleships and large cruisers, continued to characterise the Japanese Navy until the end of World War One. Note that the big cruisers did not replace smaller protected cruisers, which might be envisaged as scouts; the ten year programme of 1896 included 3 second and 3 third class protected cruisers (4800 and 3200 tons, respectively).

The 1896 programme might be characterised as a '6-6' plan. It was essentially complete by 1903, when a new programme was approved, authorising construction of 3 battleships, 3 armoured cruisers, and 2 protected cruisers. However, actual construction was predicated on replacement of over age units. Thus, given the advanced age of the first two modern Japanese battleships, two new ones, *Kashima* and *Katori*, were ordered in Britain prior to the outbreak of war with Russia. By late 1903 the Japanese Government expected to fight. In expectation of an arms embargo, it sought ships in Europe, buying 2 Italian armoured cruisers, which became *Kasuga* and *Nisshin*. They replaced the 2 protected cruisers of the programme. In Japanese parlance, the armoured cruisers were to be semi-battleships. Thus this authorisation was used to build *Ibuki*, later classed as a battlecruiser due to her 12in main battery.

A new expansion programme was approved soon after the outbreak of war, and 2 battleships (which became *Aki* and *Satsuma*) were added after 2 older ships had been lost in May 1904. The other units were 4 armoured cruisers (*Tsukuba*, *Ikoma*, and *Kurama*); 1 second class cruiser (*Tone*); 2 dispatch boats (*Mogami* and *Yodo*); 31 small destroyers; and 13 submarines (of which only 6 were ordered at once). A second programme (1905) included an armoured cruiser and 3 destroyers.

By this time there was little hope of further funding, and no new programme was passed until 1907. It included 2 more battleships, 1 big armoured cruiser, 3 smaller cruisers, 1 large destroyer, and 2 submarines. However, HMS *Dreadnought* had appeared, and much of the Japanese Navy was too clearly on the edge of obsolescence, with little hope of matching the Western Powers. The situation was particularly ironic in that Japan had considered all big-gun ships somewhat earlier than others, and that she had decided to build such ships well before she was able to do so. The battleship planned for 1907 was to have been propelled by turbines and armed with 10–12in guns, just like *Dreadnought*.

Russo-Japanese War experience convinced the Naval Staff that each squadron should be expanded to eight. This is the origin of the '8-8 Fleet Plan' which was stopped only by the Washington Treaty. The Imperial Defence Council formally approved the 8-8 policy on 4 April 1907. By the standards of the time, it represented an unusual emphasis on fast heavy ships; by the end, the Japanese had largely abandoned the distinction between battleship and battlecruiser in favour of the fast capital ship concept advocated by the Royal Navy, and exemplified by HMS *Hood*. In neither case, 6-6 or 8-8, was there the implication that earlier ships would be discarded, only that a modern first-line fleet (initially up to 10 years old, later up to 8 years old) be maintained.

Given Japanese economics and the enormous strain of building up to the Russo-Japanese War, the advent of HMS *Dreadnought* was a real disaster. In 1907, after losing 2 battleships early in the war, Japan had 2 newly-delivered replacements, with 2 more (plus 4 big armoured cruisers) either under construction or authorised; she was half-way to the 8-8 fleet. Moreover, existing authorisations covered 3 battleships and 4 more armoured cruisers, although they had not been funded.

Thus, as of 1910, there still remained authorisations for 1 battleship and 4 armoured cruisers, as well as lesser craft. Naval technology was changing extremely rapidly, and in December 1909 the Navy proposed that Japan order 2 battlecruisers, one to be built in Britain and one in Japan (from British plans), as a means of gaining access to the latest ideas. These ships became the *Kongos*; the battleship became the first Japanese super-dreadnought, *Fuso*, which is sometimes described as a battleship version of the battlecruisers. All five ships represented a new level of naval strength; previous Japanese capital ships and battlecruisers had to be considered obsolescent. As of 1910, then, any 8-8 planner had to contemplate the authorisation of 7 more battleships and 4 more battlecruisers. The Navy actually sought 7 battleships and 3 large cruisers (as well as 4 light cruisers, 1 scout, 26 destroyers, and 18 submarines) in the spring of 1910, but it was rejected. Instead, the 1911 Fleet Replenishment Programme included only funds to build ships already authorised.

Even so, the Navy Minister asked for a large new programme in fiscal year 1912, including 7 battleships and 2 battlecruisers. This was too much, and the Cabinet had to compromise down to a 4-4 standard: 3 new battleships (which became the balance of the *Fuso* and *Ise* classes) and no new battlecruisers. The Navy did not retreat this far, calling for an '8-4' Fleet, which would have included 4 more new battleships. Moreover, the Imperial Defence Council pressed for an 8-8 Fleet, on the basis of its 1907 decision. By July 1914, then, the decision had been made to proceed to 8-8 status, going first for an 8-4 fleet and then building four more battlecruisers. The 8-4 programme was presented to the Diet in the spring of 1915. In theory, it would have provided the full 8-4 Fleet by 1923, including four new battleships: the two *Nagato*s and the two *Kaga*s. However, the earliest of them, *Fuso*, would be eight years old that year, so new construction would be needed to replace her. Similarly, the first two *Kongo*s would have reached replacement age. Although it was approved in principle, the Diet was unable to vote on it before July 1917. The very large US three-year programme of 1916 (10 battleships, 6 battlecruisers, and lesser craft) may have acted as a stimulus, as since 1907 the United States had been considered one of three major enemies.

Funds for all 4 battleships and 2 battlecruisers were provided during the Diet sessions of 1916 and 1917, as was money for additional cruisers, destroyers, and submarines. Note that, although nominally equivalent to the earlier 14in gun super-dreadnoughts, these new ships, with their 16in guns, represented an entirely new level of firepower. It might, then, legitimately be supposed that they represented the initial (4-2) stage of a new 8-8 Fleet, just as the *Kongo*s and *Fuso* had, about four years earlier. In any case, the Navy proposed expansion to an 8-6 standard late in 1917, and 2 more battlecruisers were ordered, sisters of the two ordered under the original 8-4 programme.

At this point, then, there were 4 16in battleships and 4 16in battlecruisers on order. Meanwhile, with the end of the war tension between the United States and Japan increased with the United States attempting to prevent Japan from occupying Eastern Siberia. Although Russia still preceded the United States in the theoretical order of enemies, the collapse of Tsarist Russia must have emphasised problems with the United States. The United States recognised that Japan was her own most likely future enemy, transferred the bulk of her battlefleet into the Pacific in 1919. Finally, with the end of the war, Japan received mandates over the former German Pacific possessions, through which any US fleet proceeding to the Philippines would have to pass. The Navy goal became '8-8-8', a pair of underage squadrons backed by a third, the 14in ships which would be in its second 8-year period of life. That also translated to construction of 4 more battleships and 4 more battlecruisers by 1928. This programme was approved in 1920, and was aborted by the Washington Conference of 1921.

By this time Japan was in severe economic trouble. She was spending almost a third of her national budget on the Navy. Moreover, because her resources were limited, the sheer size of her naval programme was forcing a rapid inflation in naval construction and armament costs, which in turn was increasing the burden. Although many in Japan seem to have resented Japanese agreement to the Washington Treaty, it seems unlikely in retrospect that the 8-8 programme could have been realised. Like Britain, Japan was fortunate to have the status quo ante fixed.

In any case, unlike Britain and the United States, Japan was able to continue to build the unregulated classes of ships. She also found herself in an approved strategic position, at least with respect to the United States, since she retained control over the ex-German island chains through which any US fleet would have to steam en route to the decisive battle zone in the Far East. Although the treaty forbade the fortification of these islands, nothing could prevent Japan from basing submarines and naval aircraft on them.

Despite Japan's relative economic weakness her merchant marine grew from just over a million gross tons in 1905 (1309 steamers and 3564 sailing ships) to 1,770,000 tons in 1914 and to 3,350,000 in 1921 when the First World War building programme came to fruition.

The Imperial Japanese Navy which numbered 35,000 sailors in 1906 grew to 63,225 all ranks in 1916. The yearly intake of 5000-6000 conscripts and the same number of volunteers served for 4 years on the active list and 7 years in reserve (35,000 plus by 1919). Their bases (at home) were Yokosuka (one slip in 1906 became 6 by 1919), Kure, Sasebo (at least 4 docks built there 1906–19) and Maizuru (3 docks completed by 1913) and Ominato (N Honshu). Overseas there was Ryojun (Port Arthur), Daison (Dalny), Chinkai (Korea), and Bako in the Pescadores.

FLEET STRENGTH 1906

BATTLESHIPS

Name	Launched	Disp (normal)	Fate
Chin Yen			
CHIN YEN	28.11.82	7200t	TS 1908, BU 1914
Fuji class			
FUJI	31.3.96	12,533t	TS 1922, BU 1948
Shikishima class			
SHIKISHIMA	1.11.98	14,850t	TS 1923, BU 1947
ASAHI	13.3.99	15,200t	TS 1923, sunk 25.5.42
Mikasa			
MIKASA	8.11.00	15,140t	Disarmed 1922, museum ship
Central battery ironclad			
FUSO	14.4.77	3117t	BU 1910

Chin Yen
Refloated at Wei-Hai-Wei and towed to Port Arthur, arriving there 27 February 1895. Renamed and placed on Navy List 16 March, refitted and rearmed at Port Arthur 4 April–1 June. Sailed to Japan 4 July. Rerated second class battleship 21 March 1898 and as first class coast defence ship 11 December 1905. Served in the international force against the Boxer Rebellion 1900. Non-combat role mainly as convoy escort and blockader in the Russo-Japanese War. Designated TS 1 May 1908. Stricken 1 April 1911, used as target for battleship *Kurama*'s 8in guns among other shell/torpedo tests. Sold 6 April 1912 and scrapped at Yokohama. Her preserved CT burnt out in World War Two air attack. Anchor still survives in Okayama Prefecture near Kobe. *Chin Yen* means 'striking from a long way off'.

Fuji class
Reboilered with 10 Miyabara boilers and armed with 4 Japanese Model 41 12in 40cal guns in 1910, being reclassed as a coast defence ship. Named after the famous mountain Fuji-Yama, she was disarmed in 1922–23 as a hulk TS at Yokosuka (9179t, 21ft 10in draught) with deckhouses of wood and no propellers.

Shikishima class
Named after an old poetical name for Japan, *Shikishima* was rerated (with *Asahi*) as a first class coast defence ship on 1 September 1921 and used as a TS for submariners. Stricken and disarmed in 1923, rated as transport from 1 April. Remained as hulk at Sasebo until BU.
Asahi ('the Morning or Rising sun') became a gunnery TS in 1914. On 1 April 1923 she was designated as a submarine/repair ship, disarmed in July and converted (1 funnel and heavy beam lifting frames). She was torpedoed and sunk by the US submarine *Salmon* 100nm SW of Cape Paderas (Vietnam).

Mikasa class
This flagship named after a mountain sank at Sasebo on the night of 11–12 September 1905 after an ammunition and torpedo explosion, but was raised on 7 August 1906 and re-entered service on 24 August 1908. Rerated as a first class coast defence ship in September 1921 but ran aground near Askold Island off Vladivostock on 17 September 1921. Refloated and stricken 20 September 1923. Opened as a memorial by Prince (later Emperor) Hirohito and Admiral Tojo at Yokosuka on 12 November 1926. Restored in 1960 and extant in 1985.

Central battery ironclad
Fuso (='Japan') had a reduced armament of 2–6in QF and 4–4.7in/40 QF from 1903, being stricken in 1908. Her name was passed on to the 1914 battleship.

ARMOURED CRUISERS

Name	Launched	Disp	Fate
Asama class			
ASAMA	22.3.98	9700t	TS 1922, BU 1947
TOKIWA	6.7.98	9700t	Sunk 9.8.45, BU
IDZUMO	19.9.99	9700t	TS 1922, sunk 7.45, BU 1947
IWATE	29.3.00	9700t	TS 1922, sunk 7.45, BU 1947
Yakumo			
YAKUMO	8.7.99	9646t	TS 1920, BU 1947
Adzuma			
ADZUMA	24.6.99	9307t	TS 1921, BU 1946
Kasuga class			
KASUGA	22.10.02	7628t	BU 1948
NISSHIN	9.2.03	7628t	Target 1936

Asama class
Asama (named after a sacred volcanic island) refitted with 16 Miyabara boilers December 1915–March 1917. As TS in 1922 she carried 8–3in/40 and 1–3in/40.
Tokiwa (='Evergreen') was a TS from 1920 and rerated a first class coast defence ship in 1921. Recommissioned as a minelayer (300 mines) on 1 April 1922.
Idzumo served in the 1914 hunt for von Spee off the American West Coast. She sailed on a 7-month world training cruise in 1921–22, arriving at New York during the Washington Conference. Rerated a first class coast defence ship in 1921 as was *Iwate*.

Yakumo
She sailed with *Idzumo* on the 1921–22 world training cruise for 150 cadets. Rerated a first class coast defence ship in 1921.

Kasuga class
Kasuga grounded off Tandjon Delar (Banka Straits) on 13 January 1918 and was refloated by June 1918. She sailed to Siberia in 1922. *Nisshin* served in the Mediterranean for the last year of World War One.

PROTECTED CRUISERS

Name	Launched	Disp (normal)	Fate
Naniwa class			
NANIWA	18.3.85	3650t	Sunk 26.7.12
TAKACHIHO	16.5.85	3650t	Sunk 17.10.14
Matsushima class			
MATSUSHIMA	22.1.90	4217t	TS 1906, sunk 30.4.08
ITSUKUSHIMA	11.7.89	4217t	TS 1906, BU 1922
HASHIDATE	24.3.91	4217t	TS 1906, BU 1927
Akitsushima			
AKITSUSHIMA	6.7.92	3100t	Stricken 1921, BU 1927
Suma class			
SUMA	9.3.95	2657t	Disarmed 1921, BU 1928
AKASHI	18.12.97	2756t	Target 8.30
Chitose class			
CHITOSE	23.1.98	4760t	Target 19.7.31
KASAGI	20.1.98	4900t	Sunk 13.8.16
Tsushima class			
TSUSHIMA	15.12.02	3366t	Stricken 1936, BU 1947
NIITAKA	15.11.02	3366t	Sunk 26.8.22
Otowa			
OTOWA	2.11.03	3000t	Sunk 1.8.17

Naniwa class
Naniwa (= name of an imperial palace) was wrecked off Uruppa Islands in the Kuriles. *Takachiho* (= sacred place in Japan), acting as a minelayer, was torpedoed (271 dead) by the German TB *S 90* off Tsingtao.

Matsushima class
Matsushima (named after an island) was lost by magazine explosion (141 dead) in Makung harbour in the Pescadores.
Itsukushima was a TS 1906–18. Stricken in 1919 and used as a submarine tender until 1922. *Hashidate* (named after a port) TS until stricken in 1923 and after.

Suma class
Named after neighbouring places in Japan, *Suma* was stricken in 1923 while *Akashi* was a TS after repairs by April 1905 and led 8 destroyers to the Mediterranean in April 1917. Stricken in 1923 she was hulked and renamed *Hai Kan No 2* on 6 July 1928.

Chitose class
Kasagi (named after a mountain) was a TS from 1910 and was wrecked in Tsugaru Strait. *Chitose* ('long life') was disarmed in 1922 and rerated as a second class coast defence ship. Stricken and renamed *Hai Kan No 1* on 6 July 1928. Expended as aircraft/gunnery target in Saeki Bay, Bungo Straits.

Tsushima class
Rerated second class coast defence ships on 1 September 1921. *Niitaka* foundered off Kamchatka in a typhoon (284 dead). *Tsushima* was disarmed in 1930.

Otowa
Wrecked near Daio Saki, Mieken Shima Harito.

DESTROYERS

Name	Launched	Disp	Fate
Ikazuchi class (Yarrow built)			
AKEBONO	25.4.99	363t	Tender 1918, BU 7.21
IKAZUCHI	15.11.98	363t	Sunk 10.10.13, BU
INAZUMA	28.1.99	363t	Sunk 12.09, BU
OBORO	5.10.99	363t	Tender 1918, stricken and BU 1921
SAZANAMI	8.7.99	363t	Sunk 10.11.13
Murakumo class (Thornycroft built)			
MURAKUMO	16.11.98	275t	Depot ship 1921
KAGERO	23.8.99	275t	BU 1923
SHINONOME	14.12.98	275t	Sunk 20.7.13
SHIRANUI	14.3.99	275t	BU 1923
USUGUMO	16.10.00	275t	BU 1927
YUGIRI	26.1.99	275t	Stricken 1921, depot ship
Akatsuki class (Yarrow built)			
KASUMI	23.1.02	360t	BU *c* 1920
Shirakumo class (Thornycroft built)			
SHIRAKUMO	1.10.01	340t	BU 1923
ASASHIO	10.1.02	340t	BU 1923
Harusame class (*Kure, Yokosuka)			
HARUSAME	31.10.02	375t	Sunk 24.11.11
ASAGIRI	4.03	375t	Stricken 1922, target, BU
MURASAME	11.03	375t	Stricken 1922, target, BU 1923
ARIAKE*	7.12.04	375t	Stricken 1925, BU 1926
ARARE*	5.4.05	375t	Stricken 1924, BU 1926
FUBUKI*	21.1.05	375t	Stricken 1925, BU 1926

Ikazuchi class
Niji (launched 16 December 1899) was wrecked on 29 July 1900 in home waters. *Ikazuchi* badly damaged by Russian gunfire at Tsushima was lost by boiler explosion. *Inazuma* sank in collision with a schooner 30nm S of Hakodate. *Akabono* means 'dawn', *Niji* 'thunder', *Inazuma*, 'lightning' and *Sazanami* 'the pretty, small waves raised by a zephyr'.

Murakumo class
Murakumo was wrecked 10 May 1909 in a typhoon but salvaged and repaired at Toba DYd. *Shinonome* suffered the same fate, being repaired at Yokosuka before succumbing to another typhoon off Formosa. *Usugumo* was stricken in 1922. *Yugiri* was badly damaged by Russian gunfire at Tsushima. *Murakumo* means 'cloud cluster', *Kagero* the 'shimmering mist that rises from the earth on a hot day', *Shinonome* means 'daybreak cloud'.

Akatsuki class
Akatsuki was mined and sunk 8nm SSW off Cape Liao Ti Chan, Port Arthur on 17 May 1904. *Kasumi* was stricken in 1913 and served as a target until 1920 or later.

Shirakumo class
Both ships were stricken in April 1922 and disarmed at Kure in 1923.

Harusame class
Harusame was badly damaged by Russian gunfire at Tsushima on 27 May 1905 but repaired. She was stranded in a Sea of Japan storm (45 dead). *Hayatori* (launched at Yokosuka in March 1902) was mined during the Russo-Japanese War on 3 September 1904, 2nm S of Lun Wan Tan on Port Arthur blockade duty.

PRIZES SEIZED IN THE RUSSO-JAPANESE WAR

Note: In the list which follows, the refitting yard and the date refit as completed are listed.

BATTLESHIPS

Name	Refitted	Disp	Fate
Ex-Borodino class			
IWAMI (ex-*Orel*)	Uraga 6.07	13,500t	Disarmed 1922, target 1924
Ex-Peresviet class			
SAGAMI (ex-*Peresviet*)	Yokosuka 4.08	12,700t	Russian *Peresviet* 5.4.16
SUWO (ex-*Pobieda*)	Yokosuka 10.08	12,700t	Disarmed 1922, BU 1946
HIZEN (ex-*Retvizan*)	Sasebo 11.08	12,700t	Disarmed 1922, target 1924
Ex-Petropavlovsk class			
TANGO (ex-*Poltava*)	Maizuru 11.11	10,960t	Russian *Poltava* 5.4.16
Ex-Imperator Alexander II class			
IKI (ex-*Nikolai I*)	7.05	9700t	Stricken 1915, target 1915

The Russian battleships were generally considered topheavy, and their high superstructures were cut down in Japanese service. In many cases Russian guns were replaced by Japanese or Armstrong weapons of similar calibre, and 47mm and 37mm guns were removed altogether, generally replaced by 2 or 3 6.5mm MGs. The details which follow apply to individual ships.

Iwami Twin 6in turrets replaced by 6–8in/45 (2 Japanese, 4 Armstrong) at level of after 12in turret. Russian 3in cut from 20 to 16. The aw TT were removed, only 2 submerged tubes being retained.

Sagami class Main guns (4–10in/45) retained, but 11–6in/45 replaced by 10–6in/45 Armstrong and Japanese; bow gun removed. The 20 Russian 3in replaced by 16–3.1in Model 41; 2 submerged 18in TT retained.

Hizen Kept main guns (12in and 6in), but 20–3in replaced by 14–3.1in Type 41 (1908). Only 2 submerged 18in TT were retained. She was deployed to the US West Coast in the 1914 hunt for von Spee's squadron.

Tango No armament change except 47 and 37mm removed; 6–3.1in Model 41 added, 4 surface 15in TT kept but 2 submerged removed. Cylindrical boilers replaced by 16 Miyabara large-tube.

Iki Her 4–9in/35 (old Russian) were replaced by 4–6in/45 Japanese or Armstrong, other 6in/45 (8 fitted 1.05) retained.

CRUISERS

Name	Refitted	Disp	Fate
ASO (ex-*Bayan*)	Maizuru 1906	7800t	Minelayer 1920, stricken 1930, target 1932
TSUGARU (ex-*Pallada*)	Sasebo 5.10	6600t	Minelayer 1920, stricken 1922, target 1924
SOYA (ex-*Varyag*)	Yokosuka 1907	6500t	Russian *Varyag* 5.4.16
SUZUYA (ex-*Novik*)	Yokosuka 12.08	3000t	Stricken 1913, BU

Aso 2–8in/45 Russian retained, replaced in March 1913 by 2–6in/50 Armstrong; 8–6in/45 Vickers, 3in reduced to 16 Armstrong; 2–6.5mm MG; TT removed.

Tsugaru 6in/45 Russian replaced by 8 (later 7) 6in/45 Armstrong; 3in reduced to 12–3.1in Model 41; 2–6.5mm MG; TT removed. In March 1913 by 2–6in/50 Armstrong; 8–6in/45 Vickers, 3in reduced to 12–3.1in Model 6 41; 2 6.5mm MG; TT removed. This ship was a sister of the *Aurora* of Russian Revolution fame.

Soya Russian 6in retained; 3in cut to 10; 2 side TT above water retained. Although handed over to Russian control April 1916 this ship was disarmed at Liverpool June 1917. She was stranded in tow off the Irish Coast 2.18, then salved and used as a depot ship for the RN 1918–19, then BU 1922.

Suzuya Fore funnel removed, fore boiler room and lateral engines removed; cut to 6000ihp = 20kts. Russian guns replaced by 2–6in (fore/aft) and 4–4.7in/45 in sponsons; TT removed. As completed, the German-built *Novik* was extremely fast, making 25.6kts on trials.

COAST DEFENCE SHIPS

Name	Refitted	Disp	Fate
Ex-Admiral Ushakov class			
MISHIMA (ex-*Admiral Senyiavin*)	Maizuru 7.05	4200t	Stricken 1928, submarine tender, target 1936
OKINOSHIMA (ex-*General Admiral Apraksin*)	9.05	4200t	Stricken 1922, BU 1939

Mishima 4–9in/45 retained, but Russian 4.7in, 47mm and 37mm replaced by 4–4.7in/45 Armstrong, 4–3.1in Armstrong, 2–2in (50mm) Yamaguchi; TT removed.

Okinoshima Russian 3–9in guns were retained but 2–4.7in were added.

DESTROYERS

Name	Disp	Fate
Puilki class		
FUMIZUKI (ex-*Silny*)	240t	Stricken 1913
YAMABIKO (ex-*Riechitelny*)	240t	Stricken 1913
Boiki class		
SATSUKI (ex-*Biedevoi*)	356t	BU 1922

Fumizuki was scuttled at Port Arthur, but raised by the Japanese.

Yamabiko was captured in 1904, and fought at Tsushima as *Akitsuki*. She was renamed against after battle damage repairs. Both refitted 1905–6 with Miyabara boilers and Japanese weapons (3–47mm, 2–18in TT); were considered good for 3800ihp = 27kts.

Satsuki was refitted 1905–6 with Miyabara boilers and Japanese weapons (5–47mm, 3–18in TT); was considered good for 5700ihp = 26kts. Admiral Rozhestvenski, the Russian commander, was captured aboard this ship after Tsushima.

CAPITAL SHIPS

Japan led the world in two aspects of capital ship design during the period of this book. She appears to have considered an all-big-gun design even before the experience of the Russo-Japanese War made a case for such ships. She also appears to have appreciated, more than others, the value of speed in conventional battleships. The *Kongo*s were, for their time, unusually well-protected battlecruisers, perhaps more nearly fast battleships, and from the *Fuso* onward, Japanese battleships (always named after provinces) were designed for higher speeds. This trend culminated in the ships of the final '8-8' programme. It was little known outside Japan. Thus the US Navy did not learn that the *Nagato*s were capable of over 26 knots until the 1930s. On the other hand, Japan was relatively slow to shift to total dependence on oil fuel (perhaps due in large part to the absence of oil reserves in the home islands). Nor was she quick to adopt US-style 'all-or-nothing' protection. Note, however, that Japanese battleships showed what was, for their time, unusual attention to the requirements of splinter (internal) protection, based, perhaps, on British World War One experience. In the final pre-Washington Treaty designs, an internal splinter bulkhead, an upward continuation of the torpedo bulkhead, was led behind the main armour belt.

Up to and including the *Ise* class the battleships were essentially British designs, similar in general appearance to British dreadnoughts. However, *Nagato* was designed by Captain (later Rear Admiral) Hiraga Yuzuru, who at the time was head of the Fundamental Design unit of the Shipbuilding Section of the Naval Technical Department. She had a unique hectapodal mast carrying numerous platforms, a forerunner of the later characteristic 'pagodas'. Hiraga was also responsible for the revolutionary cruiser *Yubari*, which had an undulating deckline, for maximum girder strength (ie avoiding breaks in the ship girder) while avoiding excessive deck heights (for minimum weight).

As early as 1903 the Japanese Navy Technical Board drew up a design for a ship with cruiser (as in *Tsukuba*) armour and 8–12in/45 guns, on a displacement of 17,000 tons. It became the basis for the *Satsuma* design, which initially called for 12–12in/45 (4 twin and 4 single mounts) on 19,300 tons. The ship was actually ordered in this form late in 1904, but it had to be revised because there were insufficient 12in guns in Japan. Hence the mixed battery actually fitted. Similarly, a shortage of 50-calibre 12in guns explains the mixed armament of the next, all-big-gun *Settsu* class.

The experience of the first major action of the Russo-Japanese War, the Battle of the Yellow Sea on 10 August 1904, tended to confirm the wisdom of the all-big-gun choice. At the same time it was decided that armoured cruisers would be armed with 12in guns. The failure of Russian 3in guns against Japanese torpedo attacks led to a decision to use 4.7in guns instead, which was well ahead of other navies.

Japanese ideas of this period can be gauged from a series of design proposals preserved in the Vickers archives. In October 1905 the company offered both Russia and Japan 14,500 ton armoured cruisers carrying 16–10in guns, capable of about 22 knots. Japan was also offered a 25 knot cruiser armed with 12–12in guns. In January 1907 She was offered a variety of battleships with large numbers of 12in guns. For a 23,500 ton battleship (560ft × 85ft × 44ft hull depth), 18 guns could be fitted in triple turrets (with 24–4in and 4 TT). Alternatively, 10–12in (2 triple and 2 twin) could be carried on 18,750 tons. Armoured cruiser designs offered at this time included both an equivalent to the ten-gun battleship and a much smaller ship, of 13,500 tons (480ft × 73ft × 40ft × 24ft), driven at 23 knots by 23,000shp turbines, and armed with 3 twin 12in, 20–4in, and 4TT. There was also a much larger ship, of 25,000 tons (580ft × 86ft × 44ft × 27ft), carrying the extraordinary battery of 20–12in guns, in 4 triple and 4 twin mounts, with 24–4in and 4 TT.

The 1907 programme called for 2 battleships and 1 armoured cruiser of 18,500 tons. The battleship was to have been armed with 10–12in guns, the cruiser with 4–12in and 8–10in (later 8–12in), and both were to be powered by turbines. Presumably the Vickers designs described above provided part of the basis for these figures. In any case, within a few years the 12in gun was no longer the most powerful. Thus Vickers Design 538 of August 1909 shows 8–13.5in in 4 twin turrets, all on the same deck level, on 21,500 tons (530ft × 83ft × 26ft), with 12–6in and 8–4.7in. The mixed secondary battery presumably reflects Japanese thinking of the time.

The existing battleships and battlecruisers (apart from the *Nagatos*) had many platforms added to their tripod foremasts after World War One, so that even before the major reconstructions of the 1930s these masts were said to resemble pagodas. Torpedo nets, which had been retained through World War One, were removed by 1926.

The major reconstructions of the interwar period are all described in detail in *Conway's All the World's Fighting Ships 1922–1946*. In general, ships were blistered for better torpedo protection, and deck armour was increased. They were also reboilered (for oil fuel only), re-engined, and lengthened (for decreased wave-making resistance), so that the high speed of the Japanese battleline was preserved. As in other navies, heavy anti-aircraft guns (in this case 5in) were fitted. Main battery elevation was considerably increased, as noted below on a class by class basis. Visually, the major change was installation of tower ('pagoda') foremasts, which provided a stabler foundation for the numerous control and observation platforms. Smoke interference was clearly a problem, as witness the installation of smoke hoods (and the trunking of the forefunnel in the *Nagato* class) in the 1920s; with the advent of larger oil-burning boilers the forefunnel could be eliminated altogether.

The battleships saw little World War Two combat because it was Japanese policy to husband them for a decisive engagement with the United States Fleet. Thus they were involved in the Midway operation, which was to have been such a battle, and also in the various phases of the Battle of Leyte Gulf. The four *Kongos* were different: they were considered less valuable than pure battleships, hence somewhat more expendable. They were also the only Japanese capital ships that could keep up with fast carriers. Hence their much more active careers.

Katori as completed
CPL

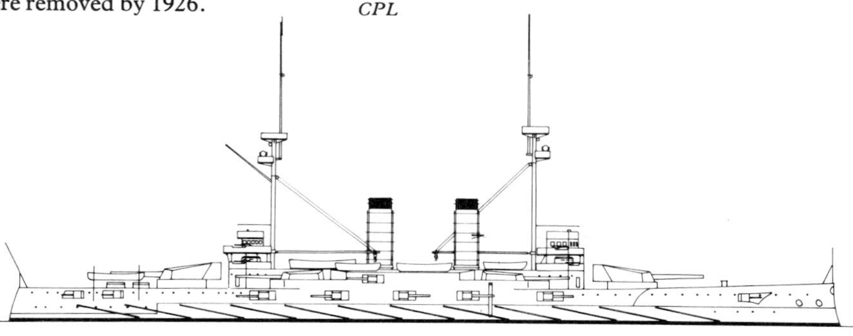

Kashima as completed

KASHIMA class *battleships*

Displacement: 16,400t normal (*Katori* 15,950t); 17,200t full load (*Katori* 16,663t)

Dimensions: 473ft 7in oa, 420ft pp × 78ft 2in × 26ft 4in (*Katori* 456ft 3in oa, 425ft pp × 78ft × 27ft)
129.6m, 128.0m × 23.8m × 8.1m (139.0m, 129.5m × 23.8m × 8.2m)

Machinery: 2-shaft 4cyl VTE, 20 Niclausse boilers, 15,800shp (*Kashima* 16,600shp) = 18.5kts. Coal 2007t (*Kashima* 1857t). Range 10,000nm at 10kts

Armour: Belt 9in (229mm) belt (4in forward, 2½in aft), upper belt 6in (152mm), barbettes 12in–5in (305mm–127mm, 6in barbettes for 10in guns), turrets 9in (8in or 203mm for 10in guns), CT 9in, deck 2in (50mm) with 3in slopes

Armament: 4–12in (305mm)/45 (2×2), 4–10in (254mm)/45, 12–6in (152mm)/45, 14–3.1in/40, 2–3.1in/28, 5–18in (457mm) TT sub

Complement: 864

Name	Builder	Laid down	Launched	Comp	Fate
KASHIMA	Armstrong	29.2.04	22.3.05	23.5.06	BU 1924
KATORI	Vickers	27.4.04	4.7.05	20.5.06	BU 1924–5

Ordered on the eve of the Russo-Japanese War, these were the last foreign-built Japanese battleships, approximately equivalent to the contemporary British *King Edward VII* class, except that the 9.2in guns of the former were replaced by 10in weapons. They had two more 6in guns than the British ships, but somewhat less armour (eg 6in rather than 7in over the 6in battery). They were the last Japanese capital ships with ram bows.

Katori made 20.22kts on 18,500ihp on 8 hour full-power trial. Her funnels were closer together than those of *Kashima*, and her after funnel was oval rather than round. Each was fitted with two 3.1in AA guns during World War One (probably 1916): those of *Kashima* were forward of her second funnel, those of *Katori* abaft it. The single-purpose 3.1in battery was reduced to ten guns. Both ships were disarmed at Maizuru in April 1922. Mitsubishi scrapped *Kashima* at Nagosaki and *Katori* BU at Maizuru.

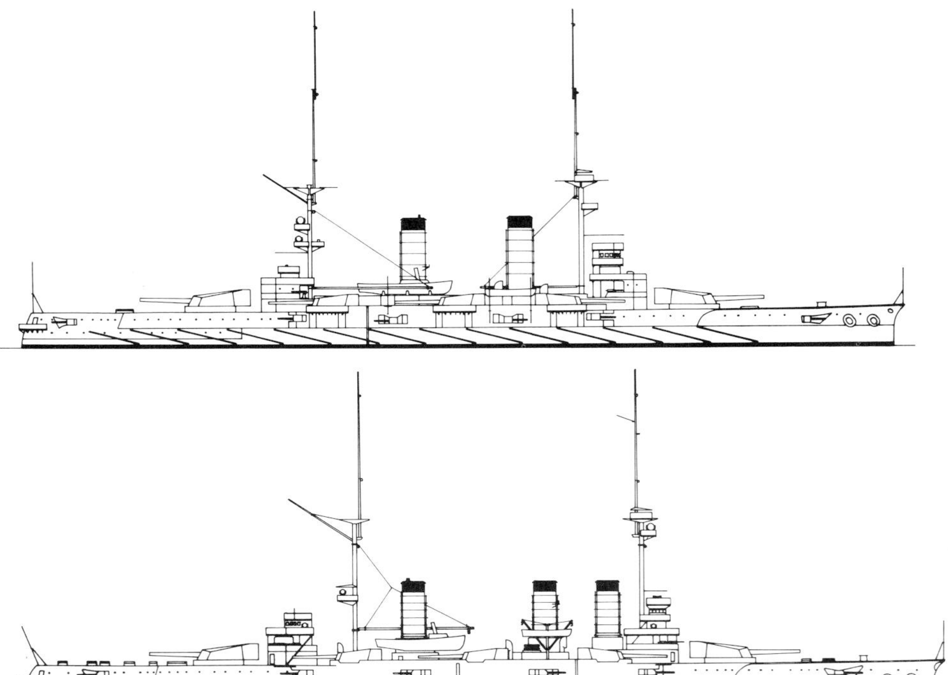

Satsuma as completed

Aki as completed

These were to have been the first Japanese all-big-gun battleships, but 10in guns had to be substituted for single 12in due to shortages in Japan. Thus the planned 12–12in/45 (4×2, 4×1) were replaced by 4–12in and 12–10in (6×2). Both units were ordered from the two main Navy yards (Yokosuka and Kure) late in 1904, but *Aki* could not be laid down until her slip was vacated by the armoured cruiser *Tsukuba*. The delay allowed the Japanese Navy to decide to fit her with turbines (which were Curtis units built by the Fore River Yd in the United States), and to replace her 4.7in secondary battery with 6in guns. *Aki* also differed visually from her near sister. She had three unequally spaced funnels (the third further apart than the other two). By way of contrast, the next ship, the *Kawachi*, had her *last* two funnels closer together.

Satsuma made 18.95kts on 18,507ihp on trials; *Aki*, 20.25kts on 27,740shp. Each was fitted with 2–3.1in AA guns during World War One; that reduced the 3.1in battery of *Aki* to 8 guns. *Satsuma* was disarmed at Yokosuka in 1922, towed to Kure and stricken on 20 September 1923. She was sunk in Tokyo Bay by the battleships *Mutsu* and *Nagato*. *Aki* underwent the same procedure being sunk 5 days earlier by the battlecruisers *Kongo* and *Hyuga*.

SATSUMA class *battleships*

Displacement: 19,372t normal (*Aki* 20,100t); 19,700t full load (*Aki* 21,800t)

Dimensions: 482ft oa, 479ft wl × 83ft 6in × 27ft 6in (*Aki* 492ft oa, 482ft wl × 83ft 7in × 27ft 6in)
146.9m, 146.0m × 25.4m × 8.4m (150.0m, 146.9m × 25.5m × 8.4m)

Machinery: 2-shaft VTE, 20 Miyabara boilers, 17,300ihp = 18.25kts. Coal 2860t, oil 377t (*Aki* 2-shaft Curtis turbines, 15 Miyabara boilers, 24,000shp = 20kts. Coal 3000t, oil 172t)

Armour: Belt 9in–4in (229mm–102mm), barbettes 9⅛in–7in (234mm–178mm), turrets 8in–7in (203mm–178mm; *Satsuma* 9in–7in), CT 6in (152cm), decks 2in (50mm)

Armament: 4–12in (305mm)/45 (2×2), 12–10in (254mm)/45 (6×2), 12–4.7in (120mm)/40, (*Aki* 8–6in/45), 4 (*Aki* 12)–3.1in/40, 4–3.1in/28, 5–18in (457mm) TT sub

Complement: 887 (*Aki* 931)

Name	Builder	Laid down	Launched	Comp	Fate
SATSUMA	Kure N Yd	15.5.05	15.11.06	25.3.10	Target 7.9.24
AKI	Yokosuka N Yd	15.3.06	15.4.07	11.3.11	Target 2.9.24

Satsuma December 1915

Aldo Fraccaroli Collection

Settsu about 1918

CPL

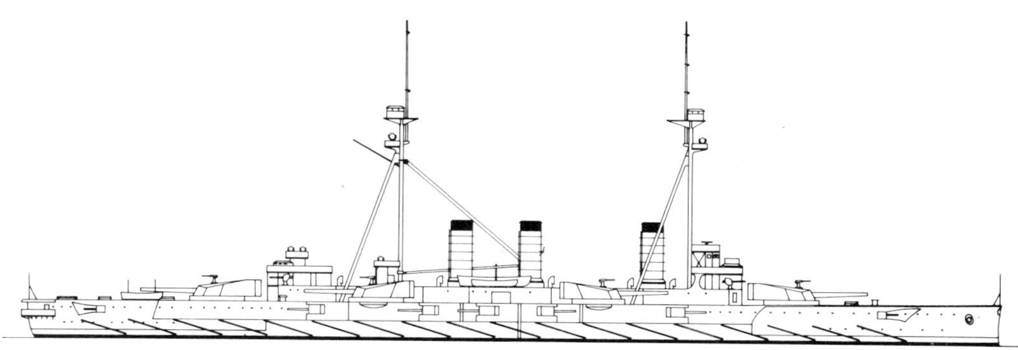

Kawachi 1917

This was a modified *Aki* type, designated Design A-30 by the Japanese Navy. Construction was delayed by a severe world depression. The 12in guns were ordered in England, but the 25,000shp Brown-Curtis turbines were built under license by Kawasaki. Note that only about 20 per cent of the material was imported, compared to about 60 for the *Satsuma*. *Kawachi* had a straight stern and *Settsu* a clipper bow. Although nominally dreadnoughts, these ships did not have a really uniform main battery, since the guns differed in length, and therefore in performance, particularly at very long range. *Kawachi* sank by magazine explosion (700 dead) in Tokuyama Bay. She was stricken on 2 September 1918 and later BU.

Settsu had 4–3.1in AA guns (and no single-purpose 3.1in) in 1921, mounted in pairs atop her end turrets. By this time, too, 2–18in TT had been removed.

SETTSU class *battleships*

Displacement: 21,443t normal (*Kawachi* 20,823t)

Dimensions: 526ft oa, 500ft pp × 84ft 2in × 27ft 10in (*Kawachi* 27ft)
160.6m × 25.7m × 8.5m (8.2m)

Machinery: 2-shaft Curtis turbines, 16 Miyabara boilers, 25,000shp = 20kts. Coal 2300t, oil 400t. Range 2700nm at 18kts

Armour: Belt 12in–4in (305mm–102mm), barbettes and turrets 11in (280mm), CT 10in (254mm), deck 1⅕in (30mm)

Armament: 4–12in (305mm)/50 (2×2), 8–12in (305mm)/45 (4×2), 10–6in (152mm)/45, 8–4.7in (120mm)/40, 12–3.1in/40, 4–3.1in/28, 5–18in (457mm) TT

Complement: 986 (*Kawachi* 999)

Name	Builder	Laid down	Launched	Comp	Fate
SETTSU	Kure N Yd	18.1.09	30.3.11	1.7.12	Sunk 24.7.45
KAWACHI	Yokosuka N Yd	1.4.09	15.10.10	31.3.12	Sunk 12.7.18

Settsu was disarmed at Kure in 1922 (stricken 1 October 1923) under the terms of the Washington Treaty, but in 1924 she was armoured as a light bombing target. Her middle funnel was removed, as was her belt armour, and her speed reduced to 16kts (16,130t). She was converted to radio control (with the destroyer *Yukaze* as control ship) and armoured against 8in shell fire (and 10kg bombs dropped from 12,000ft) in 1937–8; one boiler was removed. However, in 1940 a new boiler and engines were installed and the former second funnel replaced while her forefunnel was considerably reduced. She was used to train carrier pilots and sunk in shallow water by US TF 38 aircraft. Salvaged and BU at Harima.

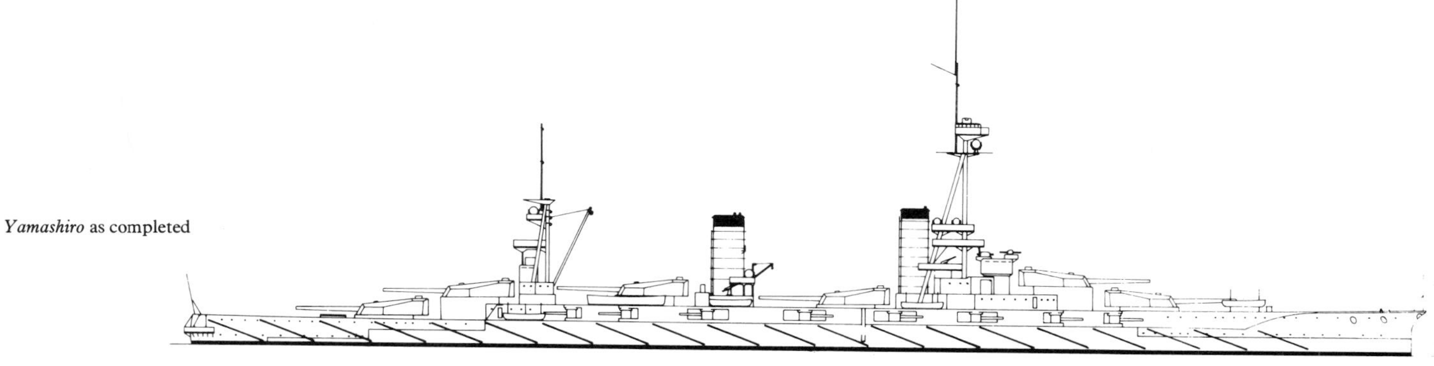

Yamashiro as completed

This was a battleship version of the *Kongo* design; it was designated A-64 by the Japanese Navy. Relatively great length was needed to accommodate 6 twin 14in turrets; the Vickers files show that designs for triple turrets (at least in 12in calibre) were available to the Japanese, so that the choice of twins must have been deliberate. A postwar Japanese account suggested that it was superior in attack, whereas the US triple system was superior in defence. That may mean that a ship with six individual turrets would be better able to deal with multiple targets.

By 1923 both had increased numbers of foremast platforms, and forefunnel caps to reduce smoke interference. *Yamashiro* alone was fitted with a large searchlight platform forward of her second funnel; 6–3.1in AA were later fitted. *Yamashiro* had the prototype Japanese flying-off platform, atop her No 2 turret; later she carrier her airplane atop her No 4 turret (each carried 3 aircraft from 1927 onwards).

They were the first ships reconstructed during the 1930s with new

FUSO class *battleships*

Displacement: 30,600t normal (*Yamashiro* 34,700t); 35,900t (*Yamashiro* 39,154t)

Dimensions: 665ft oa, 630ft pp × 94ft × 28ft 6in
202.7m, 192.1m × 28.7m × 8.7m

Machinery: 4-shaft Brown-Curtis turbines, 24 Miyabara boilers, 40,000shp = 22.5kts. Coal 5022t, oil 1026t. Range 8000nm at 14kts

Armour: Belt 12in–4in (305mm–102mm), casemate 6in (152mm), barbettes and turrets 12in–8in (305mm–204mm), CT 12in, director tower 6in, deck 3in–1⅕in (76mm–30mm)

Armament: 12–14in (356mm)/45 (6×2), 16–6in (152mm)/50, 4–3.1in/40 AA, 6–21in (533mm) TT sub

Complement: 1193

Name	Builder	Laid down	Launched	Comp	Fate
FUSO	Kure N Yd	11.3.12	28.3.14	18.11.15	Sunk 25.10.44
YAMASHIRO	Yokosuka N Yd	20.11.13	3.11.15	31.3.17	Sunk 25.10.44

oil-burning boilers and tower (pagoda) foremasts (completed 12 May 1933 and 30 March 1935); however, *Fuso* needed a second reconstruction, which was completed on 19 February 1935. Her 14in gun elevation was increased from 30 to 43 degrees (range 25,000 metres or 13.5nm rather than 20,000 metres or 10.8nm) and 6in elevation from 15 to 30 degrees. Power was increased to 75,000shp; on post-reconstruction trial *Fuso* made 24.682kts on 76,889shp at 38,368.6t displacement. This compared to *Yamashiro*'s August 1915 performance of 23.3kts on 47,730shp at 30,577t. *Fuso* was initially fitted with a catapult atop her No 3 turret, but it was relocated to her quarterdeck during her second reconstruction, presumably to reduce topweight. Her sister's catapult was always on the quarterdeck. With the removal of her forefunnel and the addition of numerous platforms around the base of the remaining funnel, *Fuso*'s No 3 14in turret trained forward (rather than aft) on the centreline. *Yamashiro*'s trained aft.

Like the *Ises*, both saw little action during World War Two prior to their loss at Surigao Strait.

Fuso 1927
CPL

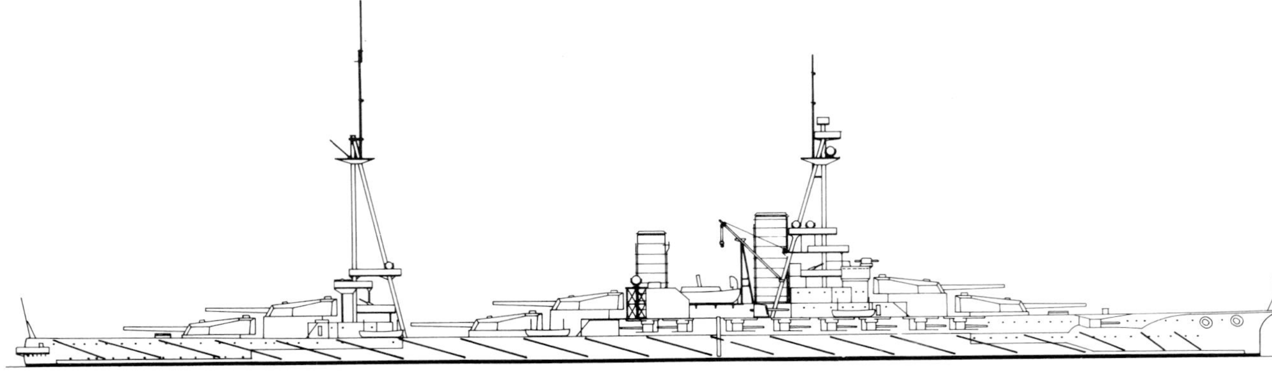

Ise 1918

ISE class *battleships*

Displacement:	31,260t normal; 36,500t full load
Dimensions:	675ft oa, 640ft × 94ft × 209ft 1in *205.8m, 195.1m × 28.7m × 8.8m*
Machinery:	4-shaft Curtis (*Hyuga* Parsons) turbines, 24 Kampon boilers, 45,000shp = 23kts. Coal 4706t, oil 1411t. Range 9680nm at 14kts
Armour:	Belt 12in–4in (305mm–102mm), barbettes and turrets 12in–8in (305mm–203mm) forward CT 12in, aft CT 6in (152mm) decks 2⅕in–1⅓in (55mm–34mm)
Armament:	12–14in (356mm)/45 (6×2), 20–5.5in (140mm)/50, 4–3.1in/40 AA, 6–21in (533mm) TT sub
Complement:	1360

Name	Builder	Laid down	Launched	Comp	Fate
ISE	Kawasaki, Kobe	10.5.15	12.11.16	15.12.17	Sunk 28.7.45
HYUGA	Mitsubishi, Nagasaki	6.5.15	27.1.17	30.4.18	Sunk 24.7.45

Design A–92. a modified *Fuso*, slightly lengthened, with rearranged main turrets, concentrated in pairs for better fire control and protection. The secondary battery was to have been the 6in/50 of the *Fuso*, but a new Japanese 5.5in/50 was substituted. Contemporary accounts suggest that its somewhat lighter shell was better adapted to the smaller stature of the average Japanese seaman: the secondary gun was generally defined as the largest weapon the shell for which could be carried by a single man, for maximum rate of fire. Moreover, casemate protection was reduced, and 4 of the guns were entirely unarmoured.

Protection was generally similar to that of the *Fuso*, but the middle (protective) deck sloped down to meet the lower edge of the belt armour over both boiler rooms and magazines; in the earlier ships it was flat over the boiler rooms. Splinter protection was considerably increased, at a cost of about a thousand tons. Small-tube Kampon boilers were adopted for greater steaming efficiency. On trials in September 1917 *Ise* made 23.64kts on 56,498shp at 31,153t.

Both were fitted with numerous foremast platforms and then with forefunnel smoke hoods in 1926–7, and 3 aircraft were added, with a flying-off platform atop No 5 turret (superfiring aft); 4–3.1in AA guns were fitted about 1921.

Both ships were reconstructed prior to World War Two (completed, respectively, 23 March 1937 and 7 September 1936). Gun elevation was increased as in the *Fusos*, and both were fitted with quarterdeck catapults. On post-reconstruction trial, *Hyuga* made 25.264kts on 81,050shp at 40,706t.

After the Battle of Midway they were again modified as semi-aircraft carriers (completed, respectively, 5 September 1943 and 30 November 1943), their aftermost pair of turrets covered by a short flight deck (actually an aircraft handling deck); aircraft were to have been launched from powerful catapults. The entire 6in secondary battery was removed; the ships were armed with 8–14in guns, 16–5in AA, and 6–4.7in rocket launchers. Their air group was initially to have consisted of 22 dive bombers ('Judy'), later changed to floatplane dive bombers ('Paul'). In fact no aircraft appear to have been carried. In this guise both served as decoys at Leyte Gulf. The two *Fusos* were also to have been converted but they were withdrawn after the Battle of the Philippine Sea.

Ise May 1918
Aldo Fraccaroli Collection

Nagato as completed

NAGATO class *battleships*

Displacement:	33,800t normal; 38,500t full load
Dimensions:	700ft oa, 660ft 4in pp × 95ft × 30ft *213.4m, 201.4m × 29.0m × 9.1m*
Machinery:	4-shaft geared Gihon turbines, 15 oil-burning and 6 mixed-firing Kampon boilers, 80,000shp = 26.5kts. Oil 3400t, coal 1600t. Range 5500nm at 16kts
Armour:	Belt 12in–4in (305mm–102mm), turrets and barbettes 12in, CT 12in, deck 3in–1½in (76mm–38mm)
Armament:	8–16in (406mm)/45 (4×2), 20–5.5in (140mm)/50, 4–3.1in/40 AA, 8–21in (533mm) TT (4 sub, 4 aw)
Complement:	1333

Name	Builder	Laid down	Launched	Comp	Fate
NAGATO	Kure N Yd	28.8.17	9.11.19	25.11.20	Sunk 19.7.46
MUTSU	Yokosuka N Yd	1.6.18	31.5.20	22.11.21	Sunk 8.6.43

Design A-102, the first purely Japanese battleships, designed by Capt Y Hiraga. Hiraga's originality showed, for example, in the unusual bow profile, similar to that adopted in contemporary light cruisers. The design was completed in the spring of 1916, the Japanese claiming later that it antedated the US *Maryland* by four months. Thus, these can be considered the first battleships in the world to mount 16in guns; the decision in favour of this weapon over the existing 14in/50 was made by the Navy Minister, Admiral Tomosaburo Kato.

They were also extremely fast, and were, in effect, Japanese equivalents of the British *Queen Elizabeth*s. It is not clear whether this was merely a continuation of the long-standing Japanese policy of high battleship speed though wartime British battleship designs to which the Japanese probably had access, called for relatively high speed. What was remarkable was how well the speed of these ships were concealed; for years they were generally described as capable of 23kts. The US Navy apparently learned of their higher speed (as reconstructed) only in 1937, one immediate result being the redesign of the new *South Dakota*. On trials in October 1920 *Nagato* made 26.7kts on 95,500shp at 34,000t.

Visually they were dominated by the uniquely Japanese heptapodal mast, with two legs sloping forward, two aft, one to either beam, and a thick central leg containing an elevator connecting the main director position in the foretop to the upper deck. This structure was adopted for maximum steadiness and survivability under shellfire, after a series of experiments; it was described by the Japanese as virtually shellproof. The heptapod, then, may be considered, along with the US cage, an alternative to the more conventional tripod. Note that, although their legs were sometimes shot through, no British tripod fell in wartime. It is, then, somewhat surprising that the Japanese, who probably had access to this data, chose so heavy an alternative. When completed, these ships already showed numerous foremast platforms (for heavy and light directors, lookouts, and searchlights), the lineal ancestors of the 'pagodas' soon installed on the tripods of the other ships.

As might have been expected, the intermediate platforms experienced smoke interference. A smokehood was installed on the forefunnel in 1921 (*Mutsu* 1923), and in 1924 the forefunnel was bent aft.

The armour arrangement resembled that of contemporary US 'all or nothing' battleships, and so represented a break with previous Japanese (and British) practice: the ends were 'soft' and there was no side armour above the main belt. However, unlike US ships, they continued to devote considerable armour to the lower deck, which in American practice was a relatively thin splinter deck. Moreover, they had both a flat protective deck over the belt *and* an upper armoured deck over the otherwise unprotected lower secondary guns. The arrangement of the torpedo bulkhead was also unusual: its upper end sloped up and out to meet the lower edge of the downward-sloping armour deck. This complete armoured enclosure of the vitals was typical of all later Japanese capital ship designs of this period. The armoured citadel was 440ft long.

Both were reconstructed (completed 31 January and 30 September 1936) during which time the elevation of the main battery was increased to 43 degrees (range increased from 20,000 to 28,000 metres, but one source claims 37,000m maximum range). On post-reconstruction trial, *Nagato* made 25.8kts on 83,445shp at 43,473t. Unlike the four earlier ships, these two had their catapults on their weather decks just forward of No 3 turret, which in *Mutsu* carried an aircraft crane. *Nagato* survived the war and was expended in the atomic bomb test at Bikini; her sole major wartime engagement was the unsuccessful battle against the US escort carriers off Samar in the Philippines. She had been torpedoed near Truk by the US submarine *Skate* on 25 December 1943.

Nagato 1920
Aldo Fraccaroli Collection

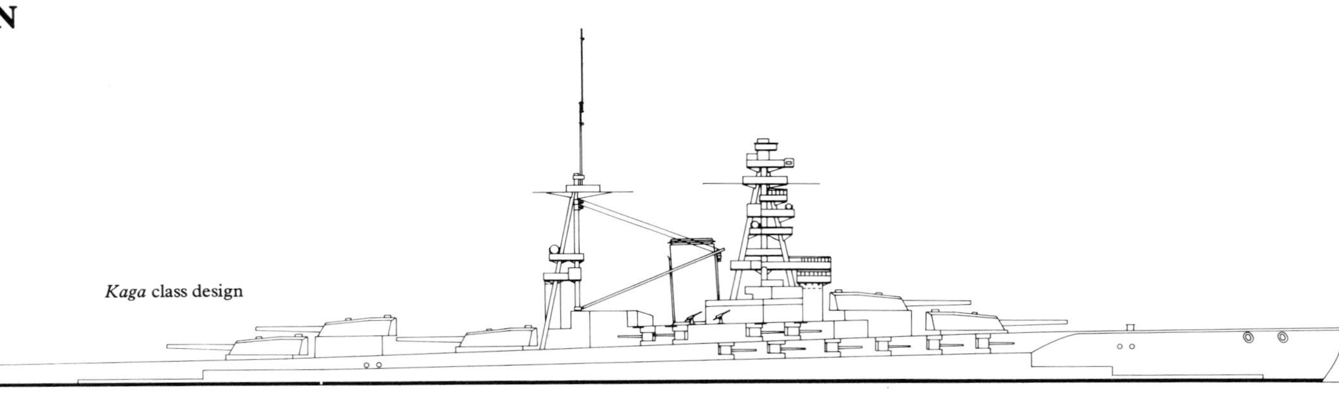
Kaga class design

Design A-127, designed by Y Hiraga, essentially an enlarged *Nagato* with a flush deck for maximum girder strength. Note the adoption of 24in torpedo tubes, all above water; the design initially called for 4 submerged and 4 above water tubes, but the former were dropped due to problems of firing at high speed. The Japanese also considered turbo-electric drive after American announcements of success with the plant in *New Mexico*, estimating 70,000shp = 25.25kts, 2500nm endurance at full speed, 7800nm at 14kts. It was rejected, but the turbo-electric oiler *Kamoi* was ordered in 1921 from the US to test it.

Hiraga adopted sloping belt armour to resist 16in shells between 12,000 and 20,000 metres. The lower armour deck, which had been the main protective deck in earlier ships, was virtually eliminated in this class, in favour of a heavy flat deck covering the belt, as in contemporary US battleships. Below these was a 1½in splinter deck. The former heavy lower armour deck was reduced to an almost vertical inward-sloping continuation of the 3in torpedo bulkhead, connected to the lower edge of the belt proper by a short upward-sloping deck. The upper end of this torpedo-bulkhead/splinter bulkhead was a short vertical 1⅛in splinter bulkhead above the splinter deck, which was itself above the waterline. This system was repeated in slightly modified form in the *Amagi* and *Kii* classes.

KAGA class *battleships*

Displacement: 39,900t normal; 44,200t full load
Dimensions: 760ft oa, 715ft pp × 100ft × 30ft 10in
231.7m, 218.0m × 30.5m × 9.4m
Machinery: 4-shaft geared Curtis turbines, 12 Kampon (8 oil-firing, 4 mixed firing) boilers, 91,000shp = 26.5kts. Oil 3600t, coal 1700t. Range 6500nm/14kts, 5500nm/16kts, 2250nm/26.5kts
Armour: Belt 11in (280mm) sloped at 15 degrees, bulkhead 11in–9in, barbettes and turrets 12in–9in (305mm–229mm), CT 14in (356mm), deck 4in (102mm)
Armament: 10–16in (406mm)/45 (5×2), 20–5.5in (140mm)/50, 4–3.1in AA, 8–24in (610mm) TT aw
Complement: 1333

Name	Builder	Laid down	Launched	Comp	Fate
KAGA	Kawasaki, Kobe	19.7.20	17.11.21	(25.12.22)	Completed as carrier
TOSA	Mitsubishi, Nagasaki	16.2.20	18.12.21	(3.23)	Sunk 9.2.25

Both ships were cancelled as a result of the Washington Treaty (building stopped on both 5 February 1922), *Tosa* (stricken 1 April 1924) being expended as a target in the Bungo Straights. Accounts of tests against her show shells striking below the waterline; the Japanese interest in internal armour may correspond to this threat. She was also tested against mines and torpedoes. *Kaga* was to have been scrapped, but was completed as a carrier after the *Amagi* was damaged in the Tokyo earthquake of 1923. The completion dates in parentheses are those originally planned. It was planned to replace the 3.1in AA with a new 4.7in/45.

These ships mark the decision of the Naval Staff to merge the battleship and battlecruiser categories; they were designated simply 'High Speed Battleships'. Designed by Y Hiraga, they were based on *Amagi* class with slightly thicker belt and deck armour, the latter 4.675 rather than 3¾in. All were cancelled (under the Washington Treaty). The first two were ordered on 12 October 1921; stopped 5 February 1922, and cancelled 14 April 1924. Second pair cancelled 19 November 1923. None were laid down.

KII class *battleships*

Displacement: 42,600t normal; 48,500t full load
Dimensions: 820ft oa, 770ft pp × 101ft × 31ft 9in
250.0m, 234.8m × 30.8m × 9.7m
Machinery: 4-shaft geared Gihon turbines, 19 Kampon boilers, 131,200shp = 29.75kts. Oil 3900t, coal 2500t. Range 8000nm at 14kts
Armour: Belt 11½in (292mm) sloped 12 degrees, barbettes 11in–9in (280mm–229mm), bulkheads 2⅞in (73mm), CT 14in (356mm), deck 4⅝in (120mm)
Armament: 10–16in (406mm)/45 (5×2), 16–5.5in (140mm)/50, 4 (later 6)–4.7in/45 AA, 8–24in (610mm) TT aw
Complement: ?

Name	Builder	Laid down	Launched	Comp	Fate
KII	Kure N Yd				
OWARI	Yokosuka N Yd				
No 11	Kawasaki, Kobe				
No 12	Mitsubishi, Nagasaki				

Tsukuba as completed
USN

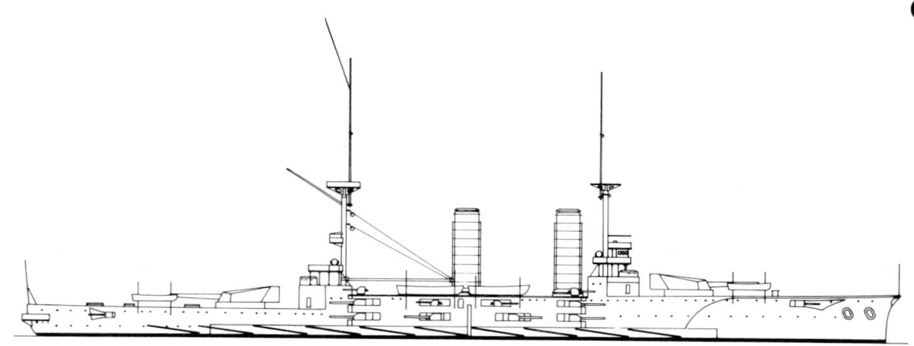

Ikoma 1912

These two armoured cruisers were ordered in June 1904 to replace the battleships *Hatsuse* and *Yashima*, both mined off Port Arthur in May. The decision to arm them with 12in guns was made on the basis of experience at the Yellow Sea battle of 10 August 1904, when the Russians successfully opened fired at 19,000 yards. By the time they were completed, they were already obsolescent, since the new battlecruisers were both faster and better armed. However, both were reclassified as battlecruisers in 1912, then de-rated to first class cruisers in 1921. In 1919 *Ikoma* was rearmed with 10–6in, 8–4.7in, 6–3.1in to be gunnery TS. *Tsukuba* reportedly had many defects, perhaps due to her rapid construction.

On trials *Tsukuba* made 20.5kts on 20,736ihp. *Ikoma* made 21.9kts on 22,670ihp. *Tsukuba* blew up in a Yokosuka Bay magazine explosion (305 dead), but was later raised and BU. *Ikoma* was disarmed under the Washington Treaty in 1922 and scrapped by Mitsubishi at Nagasaki.

TSUKUBA class *battlecruisers*

Displacement: 13,750t normal; 15,400t full load

Dimensions: 450ft oa, 440ft pp × 75ft 5in (*Ikoma* 74ft 8in) × 26ft 1in
137.1m, 134.1m × 23.0m (22.8m) × 8.0m

Machinery: 2-shaft VTE, 20 Miyabara boilers, 20,500ihp = 20.5kts. Coal 2000t (*Ikoma* coal 1911t, oil 160t)

Armour: Belt 7in–4in (178mm–102mm), barbettes and turrets 7in, CT 8in (203mm), deck 3in (76mm)

Armament: 4–12in (305mm)/45 (2×2), 12–6in (152mm)/45, 12–4.7in (120mm)/40, 4–3.1in/40, 2–40mm MG, 3–18in (457mm) TT sub

Complement: 879

Name	Builder	Laid down	Launched	Comp	Fate
TSUKUBA	Kure N Yd	14.1.05	26.12.05	14.1.07	Sunk 14.1.17
IKOMA	Kure N Yd	15.3.05	9.4.06	24.3.08	BU 13.11.24

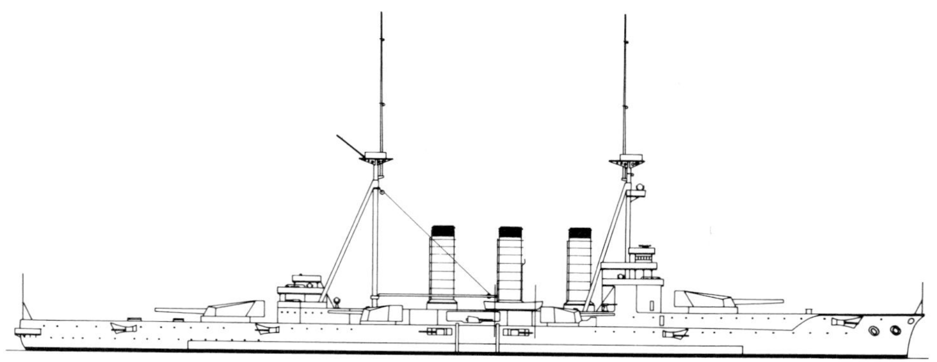

Kurama 1912

These were improved and slightly enlarged *Tsukuba*s. The second ship, *Ibuki*, was delayed by other construction at Yokosuka, and as a result her design was recast (1906–7) to fit her with turbines. She was the first Japanese warship so fitted. Note that she was launched less than six months after she was laid down. *Kurama* had tripod masts and slightly taller funnels. On trials *Ibuki* made 21.16kts on 28,977shp, compared to 21.5kts on 23,081ihp for *Kurama*. *Ibuki* was one of the ships hunting for von Spee's squadron in 1914 and escorted the ANZAC troop convoy from Australia on 1 November.

IBUKI class *battlecruisers*

Displacement: 14,636t normal; 15,595t full load

Dimensions: 485ft oa, 451ft wl × 75ft 4in × 26ft 1in
137.2m × 23.0m × 8.0m

Machinery: 2-shaft VTE, 22,500ihp = 20.5kts (*Ibuki* 2-shaft turbines, 24,000shp = 21.5kts). Coal 1868t, oil 200t (*Ibuki* coal 2000t, oil 218t)

Armour: Belt 7in–4in (178mm–102mm), barbettes and turrets 7in–5in (178mm–127mm), CT 8in (203mm), deck 3in (76mm)

Armament: 4–12in (305mm)/45 (2×2), 8–8in (203mm)/45 (4×1, 2×2), 14–4.7in (120mm)/40, 4–3.1in/40, 3–18in (457mm) TT sub

Complement: 844

Name	Builder	Laid down	Launched	Comp	Fate
IBUKI	Kure N Yd	22.5.07	21.11.07	1.11.09	BU by 9.12.24
KURAMA	Yokosuka N Yd	23.8.05	21.10.07	28.2.11	BU 1924–5

Ibuki as completed
USN

Kongo as completed
CPL

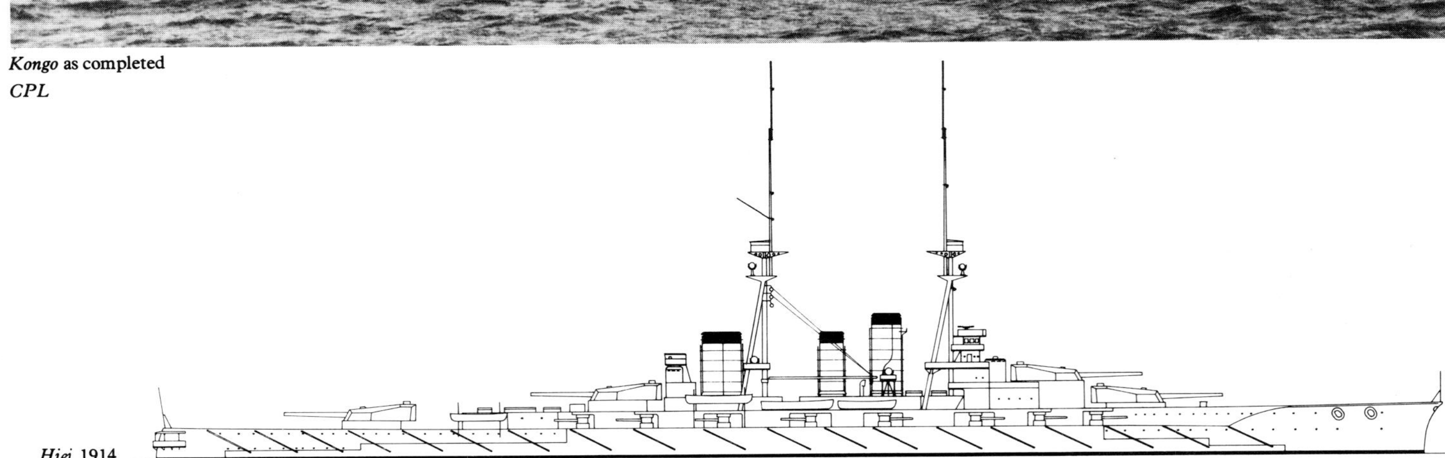

Hiei 1914

KONGO class *battlecruisers*

Displacement: 27,500 normal; 32,200t full load
Dimensions: 704ft oa, 659ft 4in wl × 92ft × 27ft 7in
214.5m, 211.0m × 28.0m × 8.4m
Machinery: 4-shaft Parsons (*Haruna* Brown-Curtis) turbines, 64,000shp = 27.5kts. Coal 4000t (1100t normal load), oil 1000t. Range 8000nm at 14kts
Armour: Belt 8in–3in (203mm–76mm), barbettes 10in (254mm), turrets 9in (227mm), CT 10in, decks 2¼in–1⅝in (57mm–41mm)
Armament: 8–14in (356mm)/45 (4×2), 16–6in (152mm)/50, 8–3.1in/40, 8–21in (533mm) TT sub (16 torpedoes)
Complement: 1221 (*Kongo* 1201)

Name	Builder	Laid down	Launched	Comp	Fate
KONGO	Vickers	17.1.11	18.5.12	16.8.13	Sunk 21.11.44
HIEI	Yokosuka N Yd	4.11.11	21.11.12	4.8.14	Sunk 13.11.42
HARUNA	Kawasaki, Kobe	16.3.12	14.12.13	19.4.15	Sunk 28.7.45
KIRISHIMA	Mitsubishi, Nagasaki	17.3.12	1.12.13	19.4.15	Sunk 15.11.42

All four ships named after mountains. *Kongo* was the last Japanese capital ship constructed outside the country; the design, which the Japanese Navy designated B-46, was Vickers Design 472C, by Sir George Thurston. It appears that earlier versions of the design, sketched in the summer of 1910, showed a main battery of 8–12in guns (plus 16–6in and 8–21in TT), but otherwise corresponded roughly to the design as completed; an alternative battery was 10–12in. The contract, signed in November 1910, stipulated protection against 14in fire between 20,000 and 25,000 metres. The design is usually described as a battlecruiser version of the contemporary Turkish *Reshadieh*, which became HMS *Erin* during World War One. They were the first ships in the world to be armed with the new 14in/45 gun, and their 32,200t full load displacement made them quite large for their time. Protection consumed 23.3 per cent of their displacement. Due to lack of slips, the last two ships were ordered from private yards, the first Japanese capital ships to be so constructed. Much of the material was supplied by Vickers, amounting to 31 per cent of *Haruna*, for instance.

Kongo was the only ship to mount paired 12pdr guns atop her turrets, and she and *Hiei* were the only two ships with 'knuckled' 14in turrets. In addition, *Kongo* differed from her sister ships in having her forefunnel closer to the foremast. In the other ships the forefunnel was much closer to the second funnel, and in *Haruna* and *Kirishima* it was also taller. In all but *Kongo* the second funnel was also considerably thinner than the others.

The machinery of *Hiei* was delivered by Vickers; she was the first ship fitted with the Japanese Kampon watertube boilers. *Haruna* was unique in having Curtis turbines. On trial, in May 1913, *Kongo* made 27.54kts on 78,275shp at 27,580t. *Kongo* tested the prototype Japanese flying-off platform in September 1917. That year *Haruna* was damaged by a mine laid in the S Pacific by the German auxiliary cruiser *Wolf*.

In common with other Japanese capital ships of this period, these ships received massive new tops (incorporating director fire controls) after World War One, as well as forefunnel smoke hoods to reduce smoke interference. At this time a mainmast fighting top was removed from *Hiei*.

The ships then underwent two separate series of reconstructions. In the first, the number of boilers was reduced from 36 to 16 (6 all-oil and 10 mixed-firing), coal bunkerage being reduced to 3292t and oil fuel stowage increased to 2661t for an endurance of 9500nm at 14kts; 787 tons were saved on boiler weights. Deck armour and bulges were fitted, and speed was reduced to 25.95kts due to the net addition of 3913t. The forefunnel was removed and the bridge structure built up. Four torpedo tubes were removed, and the elevation of the 14in guns increased from 33 to 43 degrees (range from 20,000 to 25,000 metres). Three aircraft were carried between Nos 3 and 4 turrets. However, no catapult was fitted. Reconstructions were carried out at Yokosuka (*Haruna*, March 1924–31 July 1928), Kure (*Kirishima*, March 1927–31 March 1930), and Yokosuka (*Kongo*, September 1929–31 March 1931). At this time the AA battery was increased from 4 to 7–3.1in.

At this time *Hiei* was demilitarised under the London Treaty of 1930, as were the USS *Wyoming* and the British *Iron Duke*. She was the only one of the three to be returned to duty as a battleship, work beginning in November 1936.

All four ships were rebuilt as fast battleships during the 1930s. Like the battleships, they were lengthened and re-engined, the new 136,000shp plant driving them at 30.5kts. Endurance increased to 10,000nm at 18kts (6330 tons of oil fuel, 11 Kampon boilers). On trials *Hiei* made 29.9kts on 137,970shp at 36,332t. *Kongo* made 30.27kts on 137,188shp at 37,003t.

They were also fitted with a new fire control system and with catapults between Nos 3 and 4 turrrets. The remaining 14–6in guns had their elevation raised from 15 to 30 degrees, and the AA battery was increased to 8–5in, 4–40mm, and 8–13mm (both MG types were replaced by 20–25mm soon after completion). *Hiei*, the last to be rebuilt, was used to test the bridge structure designed for *Yamato*. Reconstructions were carried out at Kure (*Haruna*, August 1933–30 September 1934 and *Hiei*, November 1936–31 January 1940), Sasebo (*Kirishima*, June 1934–8 June 1936), and at Yokosuka (*Kongo*, June 1935–8 January 1937).

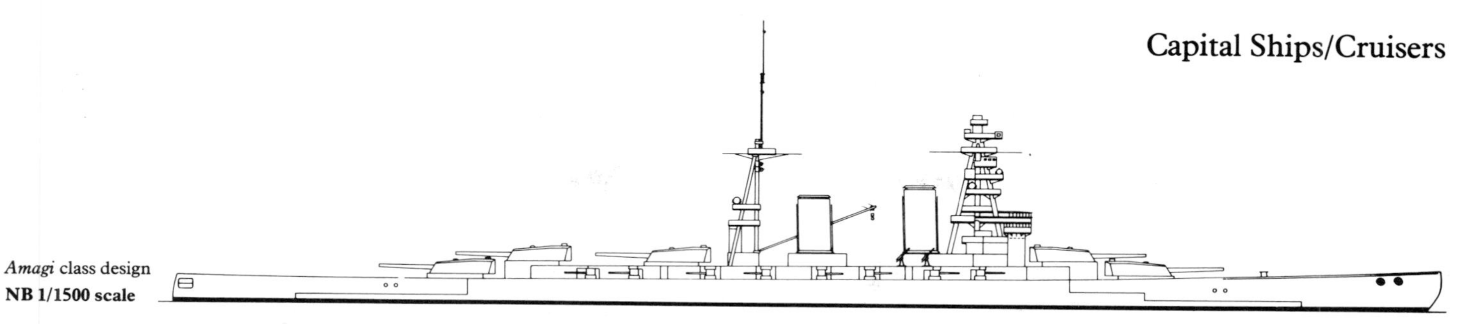

Amagi class design
NB 1/1500 scale

This design B-64 of 1919, by Y Hiraga, was an enlarged *Kaga* with thinner belt and deck. Although 16in/45 was planned, they might have been armed with a 16in/50 tested in 1920. The secondary battery was reduced to 16 guns; note the use of a new AA gun. Hiraga considered turbo-electric drive (105,000shp = 28kts, 9600nm at 14kts). All construction as battlecruisers ceased on 5 February 1922 under the Washington Treaty when *Amagi* was 40 per cent complete. Planned completion dates in parentheses.

Both *Akagi* and *Amagi* were to have been completed as aircraft carriers, corresponding to USS *Lexington* and *Saratoga*, but the latter was destroyed in the Tokyo earthquake and the fast battleship *Kaga* substituted. Conversion work had already begun, but the hull structure was too badly strained to be usable. She was stricken 31 July 1922 and BU began on 14 April 1924. *Atago* and *Takao* were cancelled 31 July 1922, stricken 14 April 1924 and BU on the slip. All named after mountains except *Takao*, a town.

AMAGI class *battlecruisers*

Displacement: 41,217t normal; 47,000t full load
Dimensions: 826ft 1in oa, 820ft 3in wl × 101ft × 31ft
251.8m, 250m × 30.8m × 9.5m
Machinery: 4-shaft geared Gihon turbines, 19 Kampon boilers (11 oil firing, 8 mixed firing), 131,200shp = 30kts. Oil 3900t, coal 2500t. Range 8000nm at 14kts
Armour: Belt 10in (254mm) sloped 12 degrees, bulkhead 2⅞in (73mm), barbettes 11in–9in (280mm–229mm), CT 14in–3in (356mm–76mm), decks 3⅞in (98mm)
Armament: 10–16in (406mm)/45 (5×2), 16–5.5in (140mm)/50, 4 (later 6)–4.7in (120mm)/45 AA, 8–24in (610mm) TT aw
Complement: ?

Name	Builder	Laid down	Launched	Comp	Fate
AMAGI	Yokosuka N Yd	16.12.20		(11.23)	Wrecked 1.9.23
AKAGI	Kure N Yd	6.12.20		(12.23)	Completed as carrier
ATAGO	Kawasaki, Kobe	22.11.21		(before 12.24)	BU 1924
TAKAO	Mitsubishi, Nagasaki	19.12.21		(before 12.24)	BU 1924

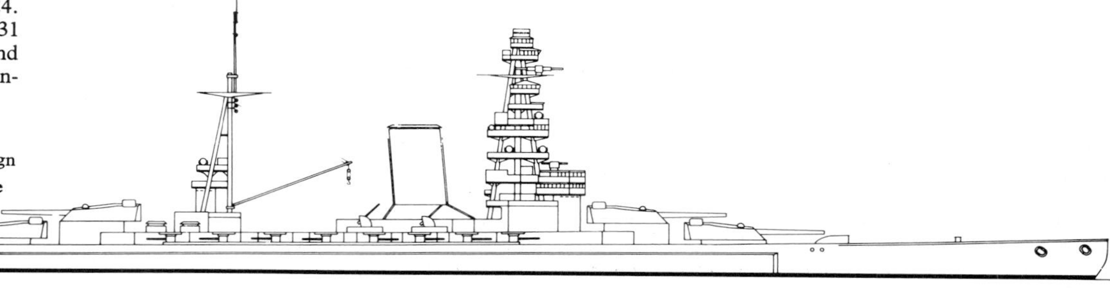

No 13 class design
NB 1/1500 scale

This Y Hiraga 1921 design was based on *Amagi/Kii*, but scaled up to take the new 18in gun. They were to have been rated 'fast battleships'. The first ship would have been laid down mid-1922. The class was scheduled for completion by 1927. Protection was scaled up to match the new gun, hence the thicker side and deck. Note that the 18in gun was not available in 1921, although a 19in gun had been tested at Kure in 1916–17.

No 13 class *battlecruisers*

Displacement: 47,500t normal
Dimensions: 900ft oa, 850ft pp × 101ft × 32ft
274.4m, 259.1m × 30.8m × 9.8m
Machinery: 4-shaft geared Gihon turbines, 22 Kampon boilers, 150,000shp = 30kts
Armour: Belt 13in (330mm) sloped at 15 degrees, deck 5in (127mm)
Armament: 8–18in (457mm)/45 (4×2), 16–5.5in (140mm)/50, 8–4.7in (120mm)/45 AA, 8–24in (610mm) TT aw
Complement: ?

Name	Builder	Laid down	Launched	Comp	Fate
No 13	Yokosuka N Yd				Cancelled 19.11.23
No 14	Kure N Yd				Cancelled 19.11.23
No 15	Mitsubishi, Nagasaki				Cancelled 19.11.23
No 16	Kawasaki, Kobe				Cancelled 19.11.23

CRUISERS

The first modern Japanese cruisers (always named after rivers) were designed as scouts, in accordance with the experience of the Russo-Japanese War. Tsushima in particular emphasised the importance of distant scouts in bringing an enemy fleet to action. These ships, then, correspond to the US *Chesters*. The Japanese Navy considered building more modern equivalents later, but in fact all of its later light cruisers (of the period covered by this book) were conceived basically as destroyer leaders. Some were later used as flagships of submarine formations.

Through the interwar period the Japanese Navy developed an emphasis on night torpedo attacks, ultimately leading to its great successes in the Solomons Campaign of 1942–43. The motive was a need to wear down a numerically superior US battlefleet before it could engage the Japanese battleline. There were two complementary programmes. Several cruisers were modified to lead special night-attack destroyer squadrons, the major change being a heavier catapult to launch a special night reconnaissance floatplane, the Aichi E11A1, which had a 15-hour endurance. In addition, in 1937 three ships, the *Kitakami*, *Kiso* and *Oi*, were ordered to be rebuilt as torpedo cruisers, each armed with 40–24in torpedo tubes (10 quadruple mounts), to form a special night attack division. In the event only two were completed in this form.

In addition, between 1935 and 1939 the Japanese Navy planned to modify the two *Tenryus* and several 5500 ton cruisers as anti-aircraft ships, in analogy to contemporary British conversions. They would have been armed with new 3.1in/65 (*Tenryus*) or 3.9in/65 (5500 ton ships) Model 98 guns. However, new *Akitsuki* class anti-aircraft destroyers (similar in size to small cruisers) were built instead; there was also a proposed class of AA cruisers that would have been armed with 6 twin 3.9in guns (versus 4 in the destroyers).

During the 1930s these ships' 3.1in/40 AA guns were replaced by twin 25mm mounts on a one-for-one basis.

Tone as completed
CPL

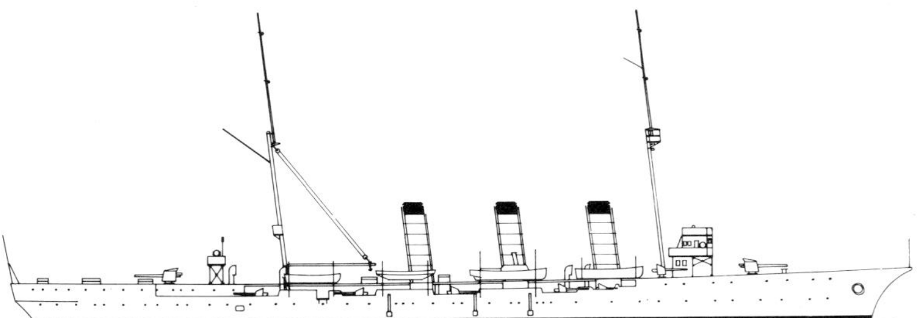

Tone 1919

A second class cruiser laid down under the Third Fleet Law of 1903, the Diet rejected a Navy request for a sister ship. Soon after completion No 2 4.7in gun was removed from each broadside, and later two 3.1in AA were added. The clipper bow was the first in Japanese service. On trials she made 15,215ihp = 23.368kts at 4103t. Stricken on 1 April 1931, she was sunk by aircraft off Amami-O-Shima.

TONE *light cruiser*

Displacement: 4113t normal; 4900t full load
Dimensions: 373ft 4in wl, 359ft 10in pp × 47ft 3in × 16ft 9in
113.8m, 109.8m × 14.4m × 5.1m
Machinery: 2-shaft 4cyl VTE, 16 Miyabara boilers, 15,000ihp = 23kts. Coal 900t, oil 124t. Range 7340nm at 10kts
Armour: Deck 3in–1½in (76mm–38mm), CT 4in (102mm)
Armament: 2–6in (152mm)/45, 10–4.7in (120mm)/40, 4–3.1in/40, 3–18in (457mm) TT aw
Complement: 370

Name	Builder	Laid down	Launched	Comp	Fate
TONE	Sasebo N Yd	17.11.05	24.10.07	15.5.10	Target 4.33

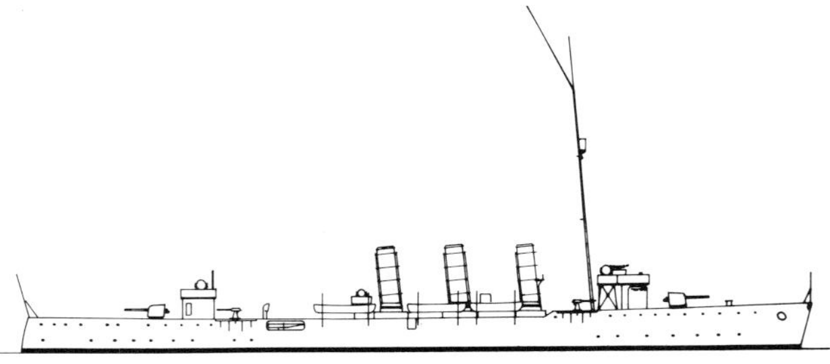

Mogami as completed

Essentially small cruisers although rated as dispatch boats, these craft became obsolete with the advent of radio communitions. Because they had to be very fast, *Mogami* was the first turbine ship in the Japanese Navy, and also the first with three shafts. Although their particulars were similar, *Yodo* had a clipper bow and two funnels, whereas *Mogami* had a straight raked bow and three funnels. Both were delayed in construction, although officially laid down on 11 December 1905.

Both were reclassified as gunboats in 1912. *Yodo* became a survey ship in 1927, and was removed from the effective list only on 1 April 1940. *Mogami* was stricken in 1928.

YODO class *cruisers*

Displacement: 1250t normal (*Mogami* 1350t)
Dimensions: 305ft 5in oa (*Mogami* 315ft 11in), 280ft pp (*Mogami* 300ft) × 32ft 1in × 9ft 9in
93.1m (96.3m), 85.3m (91.4m), 9.8m × 3.0m
Machinery: 2-shaft 4cyl compound (*Mogami* 3-shaft Parsons turbines), 4 Miyabara boilers (6in *Mogami*), 6500ihp = 22kts (*Mogami* 8000shp = 23kts). Coal 339t, oil 76t. Range 3600nm at 10kts (*Mogami* 3300nm)
Armour: Deck 2½in (63mm), CT 2in (51mm)
Armament: 2–4.7in (120mm)/50, 4–3.1in/40, 1 MG, 2–18in (457mm) TT aw
Complement: 180

Name	Builder	Laid down	Launched	Comp	Fate
YODO	Kawasaki, Kobe	2.10.06	19.11.07	10.7.08	BU *c*1945
MOGAMI	Mitsubishi, Nagasaki	3.3.07	25.3.08	16.9.08	BU 1931

Yodo July 1908
USN

Yahagi between the wars
USN

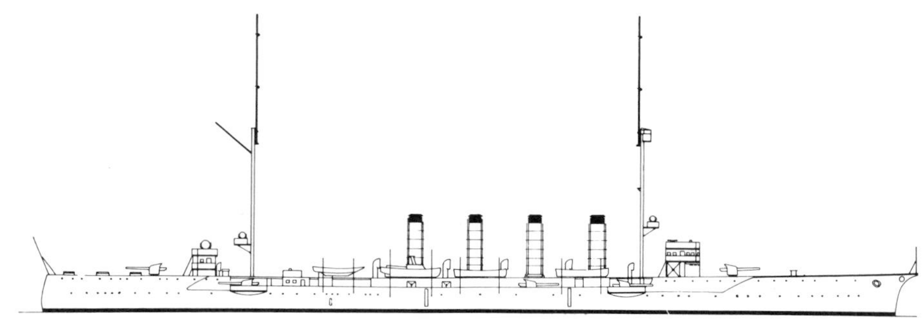

Chikuma 1915

These improved *Tone* class light cruisers were built under the 1907 programme. Their single-calibre main battery was unusual at this time, although it was adopted in 1909 in the British *Dartmouth* class. Two additional 6in guns (for the total of 8) were mounted in the waist soon after completion, replacing 4–3.1in. *Chikuma* took part in the 1914 hunt for von Spee. Two 3.1in/40 AA were added abeam the fourth funnel in 1924, the single-purpose 3.1in being retained until about 1932, when the aftermost pair was removed, leaving 2 guns in *Hirado*, one in the others. By 1924 they had 4–21in TT. *Yahagi* was training ship at Eta Jima (Japanese Naval Academy) 1940–45.

Their turbines were Mitsubishi-built Parsons in *Yahagi*, Kawasaki-built Curtis in other two. Trials: *Yahagi*: 29,536shp = 27.140kts at 4998t. *Hirado*: 26,149shp = 26.786 at 4970t. *Chikuma*'s final fate is unknown.

CHIKUMA class *light cruisers*

Displacement: 5000t normal; 5040t full load
Dimensions: 475ft oa, 440ft pp × 46ft 7in × 16ft 9in
144.8m, 134.1m × 14.2m × 5.1m
Machinery: 2-shaft Curtis (*Yahagi* Parsons) turbines, 16 Kampon boilers, 22,500shp = 26kts. Coal 1128t, oil 300t (*Chikuma*). Range 10,000nm at 10kts
Armour: Belt 3½in–2in (89mm–50mm), deck 2¼in–1½in (57mm–38mm), CT 4in (102mm)
Armament: 8–6in (152mm)/45, 4–3.1in/40, 2 MGs, 3–18in (457mm) TT aw
Complement: 414

Name	Builder	Laid down	Launched	Comp	Fate
CHIKUMA	Sasebo N Yd	1.4.09	1.4.11	17.5.12	Stricken 1.4.31
YAHAGI	Mitsubishi, Nagasaki	20.6.10	3.10.11	27.7.12	Stricken 1.4.40, BU by 8.7.47
HIRADO	Kawasaki, Kobe	10.8.10	29.6.11	17.7.12	Stricken 1.4.40, BU 7.47

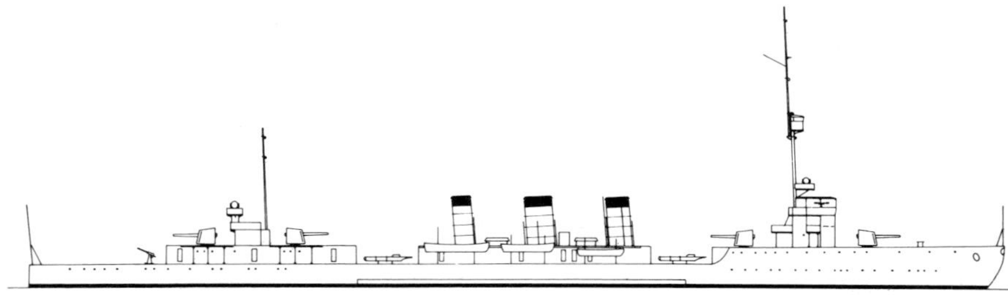

Tatsuta as completed

This design C-33 was essentially an enlarged destroyer, inspired by the British *Arethusa* and 'C' classes. To lead the new destroyer squadrons it had to have the very high designed speed of 33kts. Note the use of single-reduction geared turbines. New 5.5in guns, as in the battleship *Ise*, replaced the earlier and heavier 6in guns. They also had the first Japanese triple 21in TT. *Tenryu* was fitted with a tripod foremast between April 1927 and January 1928, and her sister similarly in 1931; both ships were fitted with 2–13mm AA MG in 1939. Before the start of the Pacific War, a twin 25mm AA mount replaced the old single 3.1in AA in *Tenryu*, and 4 more twin 25mm were fitted on either side abeam the funnels. However, in March 1944, *Tatsuta* had 4–5.5in, 1–3.1in AA and 4 twin 25mm.

Tenryu made 59,844shp = 34.206kts at 3530t on trial. *Tenryu* was torpedoed and sunk by the US submarine *Albacore* 10nm E of Madang while US submarine *Sandlance* torpedoed and sank *Tatsuta* 145nm SSW of Yokosuka.

Three 6000-ton cruisers (presumably ocean scouts) armed with 4–8in guns were proposed during the formulation of the 1916 programme but these ships were built instead.

TENRYU class *light cruisers*

Displacement: 3948t normal; 4350t full load
Dimensions: 468ft 11in oa, 440ft pp × 40ft 6in × 13ft
142.9m, 134.1m × 12.3m × 4.0m
Machinery: 3-shaft Brown-Curtis geared turbines, 10 Kampon boilers (8 oil, 2 mixed), 51,000shp = 33kts. Oil 920t, coal 150t. Range 5000nm at 14kts
Armour: Belt 2in (51mm), deck 1in (25mm)
Armament: 4–5.5in (140mm)/50, 3–3.1in/40 AA, 6–21in (533mm) TT (2×3; 12 torpedoes)
Complement: 327

Name	Builder	Laid down	Launched	Comp	Fate
TENRYU	Yokosuka N Yd	17.5.17	11.3.18	20.11.19	Sunk 18.12.42
TATSUTA	Sasebo N Yd	24.7.17	29.5.18	31.3.19	Sunk 13.3.44

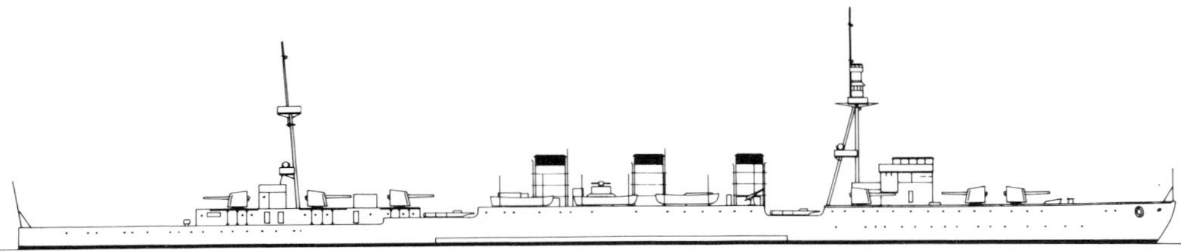

Oi 1922

This design was adopted in place of a combination of a larger ocean scout and an improved *Tenryu*: as of July 1917 the 8–4 programme provided for 6 improved 3500t *Tenryu* and 3 7200t 'scouting cruisers'. All were to be 35kt units (36kt max), with 12 5.5in/50 (4 twin, at least 4 single); alternative battery 8in; 4 twin 24in TT; 3in belt over vitals.

At the end of 1917 it was decided to postpone these ships, and instead built an intermediate class of 5500 tonners, for both scouting and flotilla work. They were conceived as an improved *Tenryu* with greater speed, radius, and battery. Note the reversion to twin 21in TT. On trials *Kitakami* made 91,100shp = 35.4kts at 5499t.

Kiso was temporarily fitted with a rotating take-off platform aft in 1922, and then, as in later ships of this type, with a flying-off platform and hangar below her bridge. Her two forward funnels were later fitted with anti-flare tops. Even after the hangar had long since been removed, *Kiso* retained her distinctive tall flat-faced forward superstructure, similar to that of later classes. The flying-off platform was never used.

Kuma was fitted with funnel caps (June 1929–March 1930). Only she (August–December 1934) and *Tama* (1935) were rebuilt with catapults aft and tripod mainmasts supporting plane-handling cranes. Their hulls (and those of their sister ships) were strengthened, and their bridges and foremast tops enlarged. *Kitakami* had her forefunnel raised in 1934. In 1938 the two 3.1in/40 AA were replaced with 2 twin 25mm MG. By this time maximum speed had fallen to 33.6kts. All were fitted with 24in TT in 1940, their displacement rising to 5610t. A twin 5in AA mount replaced 2–5.5in guns at this time. Note that *Kuma* was not so fitted, retaining 6–5.5in until she was sunk.

Typical wartime light batteries as of early 1944: *Kuma* 2 triple, 2 twin 25mm; *Tama* 4 triple, 2 twin 25mm; *Kiso* 3 triple and 1 twin 25mm. In July 1944 *Tama* 5 triple, 4 twin, 18 single 25mm (41), 6 single 13mm. *Kiso* 4 triple, 4 twin, 18 single 25mm (38), 1 twin, 8 single 13mm.

Oi and *Kitakami* were converted to torpedo cruisers (completed September and December 1941), with 4–5.5in guns (forward mounts only) and 40–24in TT (10×4) mounted five on either beam, the hull being sponsoned out for 200ft. The AA battery was 8–25mm MG. In both, the 5.5in were replaced by 5in DP (two twin mounts) guns and the 25mm battery increased to 36 by 1943. In 1942–3, 8 quadruple 24in TT were removed from *Kitakami* so that she could carry 14m landing craft. Four for these mounts were replaced in January 1944, for a total of 24 TT. She was severely damaged by HM submarine *Templar* (25 February 1944), and had to be again reconstructed, this time as a human torpedo (*Kaiten*) carrier. The turbine was removed from her damaged engine room, and it was converted to store Kaiten equipment and spares, her power falling to 30,000shp = 23kts. All TT were removed, and she carried 8 *Kaiten* (4 on each side), with a 20-ton crane aft.

As of March 1944, each had 4–5.5in guns, plus: *Kitakami* 2 triple and 2 twin 25mm, 1 twin 13mm; *Oi* 2 triple and 2 twin 25, 1 twin 13mm. As of January 1945, *Kitakami* had 2 twin 5in AA guns, 12 triple and 27 single 25mm (63), no 13mm.

On trials in December 1941 *Kitakami* made 77,989shp = 31.67kts at 7041t; in January 1945 she made only 35,110shp = 23.81kts at 7009t.

KUMA class *light cruisers*

Displacement: 5500t normal; 5832t full load

Dimensions: 532ft oa, 520ft 1in wl × 46ft 6in × 15ft 9in
162.1m, 158.6m × 14.2m × 4.8m

Machinery: 4-shaft Gihon geared turbines, 12 Kampon boilers (10 oil, 2 mixed), 90,000shp = 36kts. Oil 1260t, coal 350t. Range 5000nm at 17kts, 9000nm at 10kts

Armour: Belt 2½in (63mm), deck 1¼in (32mm)

Armament: 7–5.5in (140mm)/50, 2–3.1in/40 AA, 8–21in (533mm) TT aw (4×2; 16 torpedoes), 48 mines

Complement: 450

Name	Builder	Laid down	Launched	Comp	Fate
KUMA	Sasebo N Yd	29.8.18	14.7.19	31.8.20	Sunk 11.1.44
TAMA	Mitsubishi, Nagasaki	10.8.18	10.2.20	29.1.21	Sunk 25.10.44
KITAKAMI	Sasebo N Yd	1.9.19	3.7.20	15.4.21	BU by 31.3.47
OI	Kawasaki, Kobe	24.11.19	15.7.20	3.10.21	Sunk 19.7.44
KISO	Mitsubishi, Nagasaki	10.6.19	14.12.20	4.5.21	Sunk 13.11.44

Tenryu about 1926
CPL

Kuma about 1935
CPL

Yura August 1937
USN

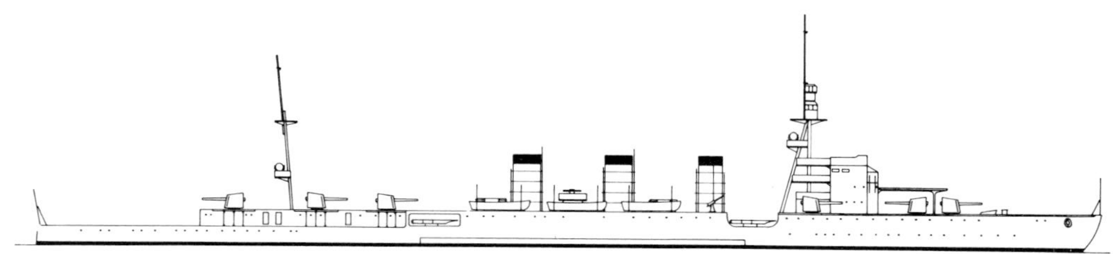

Kinu 1926

Nagara was the first ship in the Japanese Navy to carry 24in torpedo tubes. The last three ships were named *Suzuka, Otonase* and *Minase* until November 1921. All the ships of this class had fixed flying-off platforms over their Nos 1 and 2 gun mounts, forward of their bridges, with hangars in their bridgework, as in contemporary British cruisers. As a result, they had tall slab-sided forward superstructures even after the removal of the flying-off platforms. It appears that the platforms were never used. On trials, *Natori* made 91,100shp = 34.94kts at 5532t.

Abukuma collided with *Kitakami* on 20 October 1930 and was fitted with a yacht-type bow, like that of *Naka* in the next class at Kure.

Catapults (15 metre powder type) were installed on the take-off platforms of *Yura* (1929) and *Kinu* (1931), and *Jintsu* (1930). They were removed after accidents during trials, and the decision made to mount revolving catapults aft in these and the other 5500-ton cruisers. The standard refit involved installation of the catapult and also fitting of a tripod mainmast. Dates of refit: *Nagara* (October 1932–September 1933), *Isuzu* (May 1932–1933), *Natori* (July 1931–September 1932), *Kinu* (November 1933–August 1934).

In *Nagara*, *Isuzu* and *Abukuma* the take-off platform was removed in refit, and quad 13mm fitted forward of the bridge. In the others, the take-off platform was removed later (1936 in *Natori* and *Kinu*); they too received the 13mm mount after removal of the platform. Two twin 25mm replaced the two 3.1in AA in 1938. By 1938 maximum speed had fallen to 34.5kts.

During a second refit (April 1937–February 1938) *Abukuma* was altered as flagship of destroyer squadrons trained for night attacks. See the *Jintsu* class in the 1922–46 volume.

During World War Two *Isuzu* was converted into an anti-aircraft cruiser, armed (March 1944) with 3 twin 12.7mm, 11 triple and 6 single 25mm AA machine guns.

The other ships all had 2–5.5in replaced by 1 twin 5in AA mount. As of March 1944 light AA batteries were: *Nagara* 2 triple 25mm, 2 twin 25mm, 4 single 25mm, 1 quad 13mm; *Natori* 4 triple and 2 twin 25mm, 1 quad 13mm; *Kinu* 2 triple and 2 twin 25mm, 1 quad 13mm; *Abukuma* 4 triple and 2 twin 25mm and 1 quad 13mm. Batteries were very rapidly augmented after that. As of July 1944: *Nagara* 2 triple, 6 twin, 14 single 25mm (32), 1 twin, 8 single 13mm; *Isuzu* 11 triple, 5 single 25mm (38), no 13mm; *Abukuma* 4 triple, 2 twin, 14 single 25mm (30), 1 twin, 5 single 13mm MG.

NAGARA class *light cruisers*

Displacement: 5570t normal
Dimensions: 532ft oa, 520ft 1in wl × 46ft 6in × 15ft 9in
162.1m, 158.6m × 14.2m × 4.8m
Machinery: 4-shaft Gihon geared turbines, 12 Kampon boilers (10 oil, 2 mixed), 90,000shp = 36kts. Oil 1260t, coal 350t. Range 5000nm/14kts
Armour: Belt 2½in (63mm), deck 1¼in (32mm)
Armament: 7–5.5in (140mm)/50, 2–3.1in/40 AA, 8–24in (610mm) TT aw (4×2; 16 torpedoes), 48 mines
Complement: 450

Name	Builder	Laid down	Launched	Comp	Fate
NAGARA	Sasebo N Yd	9.9.20	25.4.21	21.4.22	Sunk 7.8.44
ISUZU	Uraga Dock, Tokyo	10.8.20	29.10.21	15.8.23	Sunk 7.4.45
NATORI	Mitsubishi, Nagasaki	14.12.20	16.2.22	15.9.22	Sunk 18.8.44
YURA	Sasebo N Yd	21.5.20	15.2.22	20.3.23	Sunk 25.10.44
KINU	Kawasaki, Kobe	17.1.21	29.5.22	10.11.22	Sunk 26.10.44
ABUKUMA	Uraga Dock, Tokyo	8.12.21	16.3.23	26.5.25	Sunk 25.10.44

AIRCRAFT CARRIERS

British 1914–18 carrier experience had a considerable impact on the Imperial Japanese Navy, which retained close ties with Britain. The Imperial Navy established its first Flying Corps *(Kokutai)* at Yokosuka in April 1916, and its second at Sasebo in 1917; they were reformed in 1920 into groups of 3 squadrons: 2 combat (each with 6 aircraft) and one training (with 18).

A British naval aviation mission, headed by Captain Sir William Semphill RN, arrived in September 1921. Note that flying-off experiments (aboard the *Wakamiya*) preceded its arrival. However, the Semphill mission must have provided much detailed knowledge. The first take-off and landing aboard the *Hosho* were carried out by a British ex-service pilot, William Jordan, acting as a Mitsubishi test pilot in a Sopwith Pup; a Japanese pilot followed him a month later. Training for carrier operations began at the end of 1923, and the *Hosho* joined the main fleet in 1926.

It was reported in 1921 that two large and fast carriers were to be embodied in the battlefleet by 1924, one to carry torpedo bombers, the other spotters and reconnaissance aircraft. Presumably these were the ships cancelled under the Washington Treaty.

WAKAMIYA *seaplane carrier*

This war prize of the Russo-Japanese conflict (captured W of Okinawa by *TB No 72*), the British-built 4421grt *Lethington* of W R Rea Shipping Co, Belfast, was initially used as a transport. In 1914 she became the first Japanese air-capable ship, flying her Farman biplanes from September to November in support of the assault on Tsingtao. Her aircraft reportedly sank one German minelayer and damaged shore installations; they arguably therefore made the first successful carrier air raid in history. They also dropped leaflets urging surrender.

The aircraft were carried in her holds, and by the end of World War One both well decks were covered by canvas shelters. In 1920 she was reclassified as an aircraft carrier (1 April) fitted with a take-off deck (for Sopwith Pups) over her forecastle, presumably as an experiment during the design of *Hosho*. The first take-off was made in June 1920.

Wakamiya served as a seaplane carrier until 1924, when she was replaced by the converted tanker *Notoro*.

Displacement: 5895t normal; 7720t standard
Dimensions: 365ft pp × 48ft 2in × 19ft
111.3m × 14.7m × 5.8m
Machinery: 1-shaft VTE, 3 cylindrical boilers, 1591ihp = 10kts. Coal 851t
Armament: 2–3.1in/40, 2–47mm; 2 Farman floatplanes and 2 reserve
Complement: 234

Name	Builder	Laid down	Launched	Comp	Fate
WAKAMIYA	Duncan, Port Glasgow	21.9.01	12.1.05	17.8.14	Stricken 1.4.31

Hosho on trials December 1922
Aldo Fraccaroli Collection

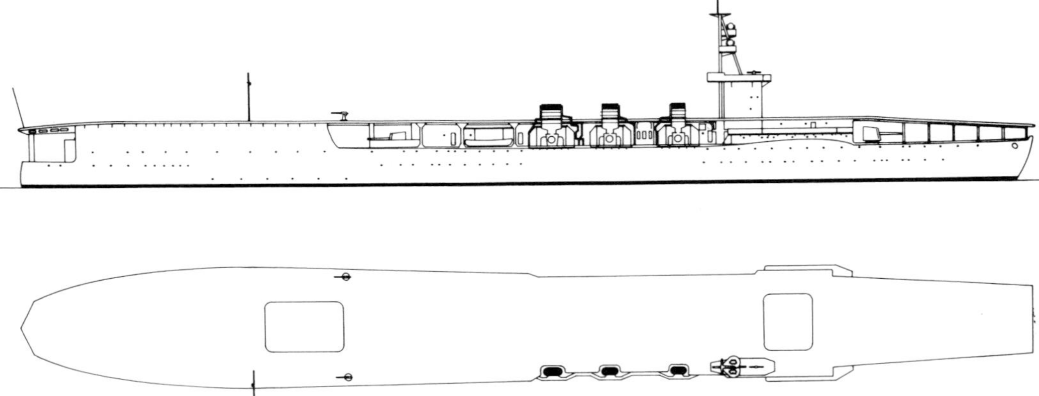

Hosho as completed

HOSHO *aircraft carrier*

Initially to have been named *Hiryu*, she was one of six specialised transports ordered under the 8-6 Fleet plan, and the first carrier designed as such to be completed in the world. It is sometimes suggested that she was either designed as a tanker or based on a tanker design, and that the early postwar British Semphill Mission was largely responsible for the form she took. *Hosho* ('Soaring Phoenix') was stabilised by a Sperry Gyroscope. Her flightdeck was 519t × 74ft 6in; it was lengthened to 593ft (extended fore and aft) in 1944. The initial air group consisted of 21 aircraft (6 bombers plus 4 reserve; 5 fighters plus 2 reserve; 4 reconnaissance). The first aircraft to take off from her was a Mitsubishi Type 10, on 22 February 1923. On trials (14 December 1922) she made 26.66kts on 31,117shp at 9510t.

Displacement: 9499t normal; 7470t standard
Dimensions: 541ft 4in wl, 510ft pp × 59ft × 20ft 3in
165m, 155.5m × 14.7m × 6.2m
Machinery: 2-shaft Parsons turbines, 8 Kampon boilers (4 oil-firing, 4 mixed-firing), 30,000shp = 25kts. Oil 2700t, coal 940t. Range 10,000nm at 14kts
Armament: 4–5.5in (140mm)/50, 2–3.1in/40 AA, 21 aircraft
Complement: 550

Name	Builder	Laid down	Launched	Comp	Fate
HOSHO	Asano, Tsurumi	16.12.19	13.11.21	27.12.22	BU 1947

In 1923 the island was replaced by a bridge on the starboard side forward under her flight deck, making her a flush-decker; the folding funnels were made fixed in 1934. *Hosho* was recommissioned in February 1936 with her 2–3.1in AA guns replaced by 3 quadruple 13mm MGs. By 1944 her 5.5in guns had been removed, and she had 10 triple 25mm, as well as twin and single mounts; 8 of the triple 25mm were removed, apparently for installation aboard other ships, later in the war, and by summer 1945 she had only two triple mounts.

Hosho was used for training in 1933–1940, then operated off the Chinese coast (1940). She operated with the battleship group at Midway, seeing no action, and served as a training carrier through 1944. Although damaged in the air attacks at Kure in 1945, she was used as a repatriation ship postwar.

SHOKAKU class *aircraft carriers*

This new 12,500-ton type was projected for the 1922 and 1923 programmes under the 8–8 Fleet plan. It was cancelled after Japan signed the Washington Treaty in favour of capital ship conversions.

DESTROYERS AND TORPEDO-BOATS

Like the US Navy, Japan moved very rapidly from small destroyers, like the 'emergency' class which begins this section, to large oceangoing types. However, she could not afford large numbers of such craft, and therefore developed a medium (second class) destroyer.

Japanese destroyers appear to illustrate a shift in function, from the defence of the battlefleet towards an emphasis on offensive torpedo tactics, as in the contemporary Imperial German Navy. That is, early post-Russo-Japanese War designs show relatively powerful gun batteries, well beyond British or American practice; for example, small second class destroyers carried the 4.7in gun while British and US fleet destroyers were limited to 4in weapons. However, during and after the First World War the balance apparently shifted towards the torpedo, as illustrated first in more numerous tubes and then in the shift to the 24in calibre (which was not, incidentally, the oxygen-fuelled 'Long Lance' of World War Two; that came later).

The Japanese Fleet would always have to fight outnumbered. Destroyer torpedoes were a valued equaliser, particularly after the advent of the 24in torpedo in the early 1920s. That was very clearly the case on the eve of World War Two, but a British naval expert, Hector Bywater, saw much the same attitudes when attending Japanese naval manoeuvres in 1919. At that time, the flotillas carried out frequent night exercises with masked lights. They had just been reorganised: a full flotilla consisted of 2 first class boats as leader and half-leader, and 10 second class boats. The flotilla commander was generally a torpedo specialist; his second-in command was usually a commander who had specialised in navigation. By way of contrast, the navigator would have commanded in the British or US navies, where the primary role of the destroyer was defence of the battle line against torpedo attack.

Bywater also considered Japanese complements unusually large. In the 1919 manoeuvres, when *Amatsukaze* was serving as a leader, she had 200 on board, including 9 commissioned officers. Second class boats of 835 tons averaged 140 officers and men at that time.

Japanese destroyers were initially named (first class after types of weather, especially winds, in poetic style; second class after trees, flowers and fruits), but on 12 October 1921 it was decided to number them instead, their names being dropped formally on 1 April 1922. Names, which did not match the original ones, were revived on 1 August 1928. Under the numbering scheme, odd numbers were allocated to first, even to second class units. However, *Nos 14* and *20* had already been laid down when it was decided to abandon construction of further second class destroyers (July 1922) as a result of the Washington Treaty. Ten first class destroyers (odd numbers from *35* to *53*) and 13 second class destroyers (even numbers from *28* to *54*) were reordered to new designs, the first three of the even numbers being built as first class destroyers. The others became the 'Special Type' or *Fubuki* class (which was numbered from *35* through *54*).

Note that two British *Acorn* class destroyers, HMS *Minstrel* and HMS *Nemesis*, were lent to Japan for escort work in June 1917 (returned 1919), becoming HIJMS *Sendan* and *Kanran*, respectively.

Asakaze class as completed

ASAKAZE class *destroyers*

Displacement: 381t normal; 450t full load
Dimensions: 236ft 2in oa × 21ft 7in × 5ft 11in
72.0m × 6.6m × 1.8m
Machinery: 2-shaft 4cyl VTE, 4 Kampon boilers, 6000ihp = 29kts. Coal 150t, oil 20t. Range 12nm at 15kts
Armament: 2–3.1in/40, 4–3.1in/28, 2–18in (457mm) TT
Complement: 70

Class (builder, launched, completed, fate):
Asakaze (Kawasaki, Kobe, 28.10.05, 1.4.06, minesweeper 1923, BU 1928), *Kamikaze* (Yokosuka N Yd, 15.7.05, 16.8.05, minesweeper 1923, BU 1928), *Hatsushio* (Yokosuka N Yd, 13.5.05, 18.8.05, minesweeper 1923, BU 1928), *Yayoi* (Yokosuka N Yd, 7.8.05, 23.9.05, stricken 1925, target, BU 1926), *Kisaragi* (Yokosuka N Yd, 6.9.05, 19.10.05, minesweeper 1923, BU 1928), *Shiratsuyu* (Mitsubishi, Nagasaki, 12.2.06, 23.8.06, stricken 1928, BU), *Shirayuki* (Mitsubishi, Nagasaki, 19.5.05, 6.8.06, stricken 1928, BU), *Matsukaze* (Mitsubishi, Nagasaki, 23.12.06, 15.3.07, stricken 1925, target, BU 1926), *Harukaze* (Kawasaki, Kobe, 25.12.05, 14.5.06, minesweeper 1923, BU 1928), *Shigure* (Kawasaki, Kobe, 12.3.06,?, stricken 1925, BU), *Asatsuyu* (Osaka IW, Osaka, 2.4.06, 16.11.06, wrecked 10.11.13 off Schichi Towan, Noto Hanto), *Hayate* (Osaka IW, Osaka, 22.5.06, 13.6.07, stricken 1925, BU), *Oite* (Maizuru N Yd, 10.1.06, 21.8.06, stricken 1925, hulked 1926), *Yunagi* (Maizuru N Yd, 22.8.06, 25.12.06, stricken 1925, BU), *Yugure* (Sasebo N Yd, 17.11.05, 26.5.06, minesweeper 1923, BU 1928), *Yudachi* (Sasebo N Yd, 26.3.06, 16.7.06, minesweeper 1923, BU 1928), *Mikazuki* (Sasebo N Yd, 26.5.06, 12.9.06, stricken 1928, BU), *Nowaki* (Sasebo N Yd, 25.7.06, 1.11.06, stricken 1924, BU), *Ushio* (Kure N Yd, 30.8.05, 1.10.05, minesweeper 1923, BU 1928), *Nenohi* (Kure N Yd, 30.8.05, 1.10.05, minesweeper 1923, BU 1928), *Hibiki* (Yokosuka N Yd, 31.3.06, 6.9.06, minesweeper 1923, BU 1928), *Shirotaye* (Mitsubishi, Nagasaki, 30.7.06, 21.1.07, sunk 3.9.14), *Hatsuharu* (Kawasaki, Kobe, 21.5.06, stricken 1925, BU), *Wakaba* (Yokosuka N Yd, 25.11.05, 28.2.06, minesweeper 1923, BU 1928), *Hatsuyuki* (Yokosuka N Yd, 8.3.06, 17.5.05, minesweeper 1923, BU 1928), *Uzuki* (Kawasaki, Kobe, 20.9.06, 6.3.07, stricken 1925, BU), *Minazuki* (Mitsubishi, Nagasaki, 5.11.06, 14.2.07, minesweeper *No 10* 1926, BU 2.30), *Nagatsuki* (Uraga Dock, Tokyo, 15.12.06, 31.7.07, minesweeper *No 11* 1926, BU 1930), *Kikuzuki* (Uraga Dock, Tokyo, 10.4.07, 20.9.07, minesweeper *No 12* 1926, BU 2.30), *Uranami* (Maizuru N Yd, 8.12.07, 2.10.08, minesweeper *No 8* 1926, BU 2.30), *Isonami* (Maizuru N Yd, 21.11.08, 2.4.09, minesweeper *No 7* 1926, BU 2.30), *Ayanami* (Maizuru N Yd 20.3.09, 26.6.09, minesweeper *No 9* 1926, BU 2.30)

These 32 ships were built under the 1904 and special war programmes. The first were ordered in June 1904, others following that September and in 1905. They were an improved version of the existing *Harusame*, itself a Thornycroft design. The large number could not be built in naval dockyards, and for the first time commercial builders had to be employed. That was the opposite of most foreign practice, in which one or more commercial yards first developed the delicate techniques of destroyer construction. As a result, construction stretched over several years, many being completed after the design was quite obsolete.

As compared to the earlier design, they had short 3.1in (80mm) guns in place of 60mm (2.4in) guns, for uniform calibre. Boats converted to minesweeping in the 1920s were rearmed with 2–4.7in/45 and 2–3.1in/40 (1922–26) weapons from earlier classes. *Hatsuyuki* means 'First Snow'.

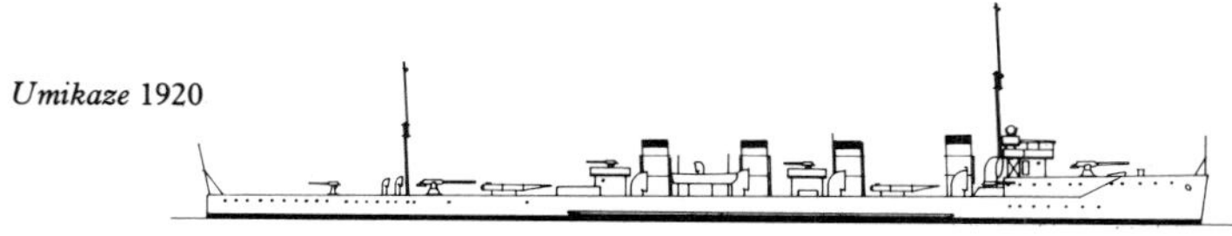
Umikaze 1920

UMIKAZE class *destroyers*

Displacement: 1030t normal; 1150t full load
Dimensions: 323ft 3in oa, 310ft 1in pp × 28ft 1in × 9ft
98.5m, 94.5m × 8.5m × 2.7m
Machinery: 3-shaft Parsons turbines, 8 Kampon boilers, 20,500shp = 33kts. Coal 250t, oil 178t. Range 2700nm at 15kts
Armament: 2–4.7in (120mm)/40, 5–3.1in/40, 4–18in (457mm) TT (2×2; *Yamakaze* 3×1)
Complement: 140

Class (builder, launched, completed, fate):
Umikaze (Maizuru N Yd, 10.10.10, 28.9.11, minesweeper *No 8* 1930, stricken 1936, BU), *Yamakaze* (Mitsubishi, Nagasaki, 21.1.11, 21.10.11, minesweeper *No 7* 1930, stricken 1936, BU)

Design F-9, the first Japanese ocean-going destroyers. Both were ordered in 1907, but laid down only in 1909, after their plans had been much modified. Their Parsons turbines, built by Mitsubishi, were delivered only in March 1910, which accounts for part of the delay. Ships this large were relatively expensive, hence the reversion to a much smaller design in the next (*Sakura*) class.

Note the adoption of the 4.7in gun, which was quite powerful by contemporary standards. When they were converted for minesweeping, armament was reduced to 1–4.7in and 4–3.1in and power to 11,000shp = 24kts.

Kaba about 1919
USN

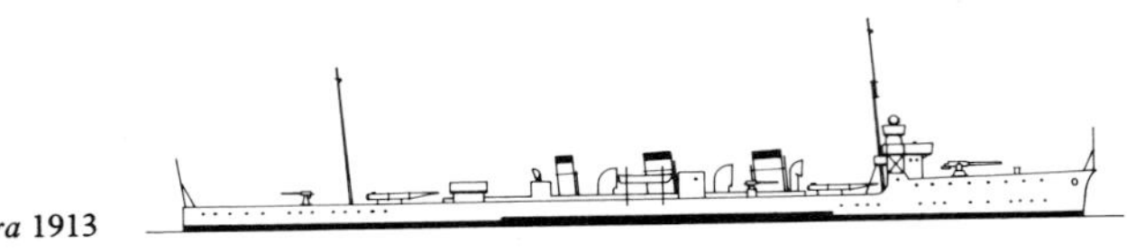
Sakura 1913

SAKURA class *destroyers*

Displacement: 605t normal; 830t full load
Dimensions: 274ft oa, 260ft pp × 24ft × 7ft 3in
83.6m, 79.2m × 7.3m × 2.2m
Machinery: 3-shaft 4cyl VTE, 5 Kampon boilers, 9500ihp = 30kts. Coal 228t, oil 30t. Range 2400nm at 15kts
Armament: 1–4.7in (120mm)/40, 4–3.1in/40, 4–18in (457mm) TT (2×2)
Complement: 92

Class (launched, completed):
Sakura (20.12.11, 21.5.12), *Tachibana* (27.1.12, 25.6.12)

Although the destroyers of the 1910 Programme (Fleet Replenishment) were to have been of the large ocean type, they had to be reduced to a medium coastal type (second class) because of fiscal problems. The result was the first Japanese-designed destroyer. Note the reversion to reciprocating engines in this F-10 design. Both ships were built by Maizuru N Yd, stricken in 1931 and BU 1933. *Sakura* means 'Cherry'.

KABA class *destroyers*

Displacement: 665t normal; 850t full load
Dimensions: As *Sakura* class except 7ft 9in/*2.3m* draught
Machinery: 3-shaft 4cyl VTE, 4 Kampon boilers, 9500ihp = 30kts. Coal 100t, oil 137t. Range 1600nm at 15kts
Other particulars: as *Sakura* class

Class (builder, launched, completed):
Kaba (Yokosuka N Yd, 6.2.15, 5.3.15), *Kaede* (Maizuru N Yd, 20.2.15, 25.3.15), *Katsura* (Kure N Yd, 4.3.15, 31.3.15), *Ume* (Sasebo N Yd, 27.2.15, 31.3.15), *Kusunoki* (Kawasaki, Kobe, 5.3.15, 31.3.15), *Kashiwa* (Mitsubishi, Nagasaki 14.2.15, 4.4.15), *Matsu* (Mitsubishi, Nagasaki, 5.3.15, 6.4.15), *Sugi* (Mitsubishi, Yokohama, 16.2.15, 7.4.15), *Kiri* (Uraga Dock, Tokyo, 28.2.15, 22.3.15), *Sakaki* (Susebo N Yd, 15.2.15, 26.3.15)

These 10 destroyers were built under the 1914 War Programme to redress the serious shortage of modern destroyers. *Kaba* means 'Birch'. Their F-23 design was adapted from that of the *Sakura*; 12 more were built in Japan for France as the *Algerien* class. The hull was the same as that of the *Sakura*, but displacement was increased as shown. *Kaede, Katsura, Ume, Kusonoki* and *Sakaki* served in the Mediterranean in 1917–18, the last being torpedoed by the Austrian submarine *U 27* on 11 June 1917. All 5 returned to Japan in December 1919. The class was stricken in November 1931 and BU.

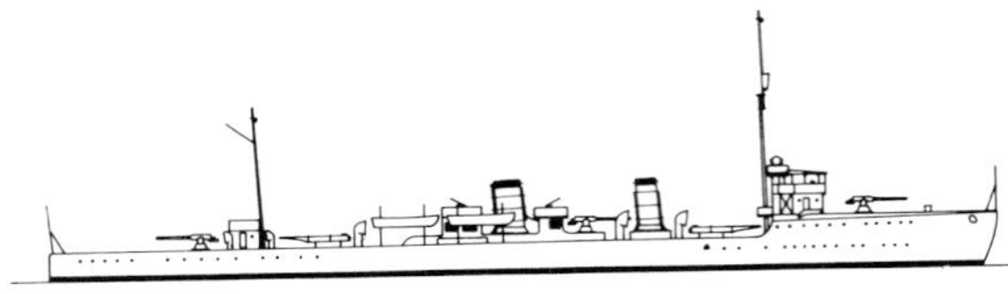
Momo 1917

MOMO class *destroyers*

Displacement: 835t normal; 1080t full load
Dimensions: 281ft 8in wl, 275ft pp × 25ft 4in × 7ft 9in
85.8m, 83.8m × 7.7m × 2.3m
Machinery: 2-shaft Curtis geared turbines, 4 Kampon boilers, 16,000shp = 31.5kts. Oil 212t, coal 92t. Range 2400nm at 15kts
Armament: 3–4.7in (120mm)/45, 2–7.7mm MG, 6–18in (457mm) TT (2×3)
Complement: 110

Class (builder, launched, completed, fate):
Momo (Sasebo N Yd, 12.10.16, 23.12.16, stricken 1940 and BU), *Kashi* (Maizuru N Yd, 1.12.16, 31.3.17, sunk 10.10.44), *Hinoki* (Maizuru N Yd, 25.12.16, 31.3.17, stricken 1940 and BU), *Yanagi* (Sasebo N Yd, 24.2.17, 5.5.17, stricken 1.4.40, BU 1.4.47)

This F-27 design parallelled the first class *Isokaze* in having a new hull design with a curved (rather than straight) bow and a single-calibre main battery. It also had the first geared turbines and the first triple TT in the Japanese Navy. All served in the Mediterranean during World War One, returning to Japan in February 1919.

Kashi was transferred to the Manchukuo Navy in 1937 and renamed *Hai Wei*; she was returned to Japan in 1943 and renamed *Kali*. Sunk off Okinawa by US TF 38 carrier aircraft. *Yanagi* became a training hulk and was BU at Ominato.

ENOKI class *destroyers*

Displacement: 850t normal; 1100t full load
Machinery: As *Momo* class except 17,500shp, coal 98t
Other particulars: As *Momo* class

Class (builder, launched, completed):
Enoki (Maizuru N Yd, 5.3.18, 30.4.18), *Nara* (Yokosuka N Yd, 28.3.18, 30.4.18), *Kuwa* (Kure N Yd, 23.2.18, 31.3.18), *Tsubaki* Kure N Yd 23.2.18, 30.4.18), *Maki* (Sasebo N Yd, 28.12.17, 7.4.18), *Keyaki* (Sasebo N Yd, 15.1.18, 20.4.18)

The construction of these ships, which were very similar to the *Momo* class, marked a decision to build two categories of destroyer, first and second class, to achieve large numbers at an affordable price. *Nara* and *Enoki* became minesweepers (*Nos 9* and *10*) on 1 June 1930, armed with 2–4.7in and 2 MG. They were stricken in 1938 and BU, their sisters being deleted on 1 April 1932.

Amatsukaze 1921
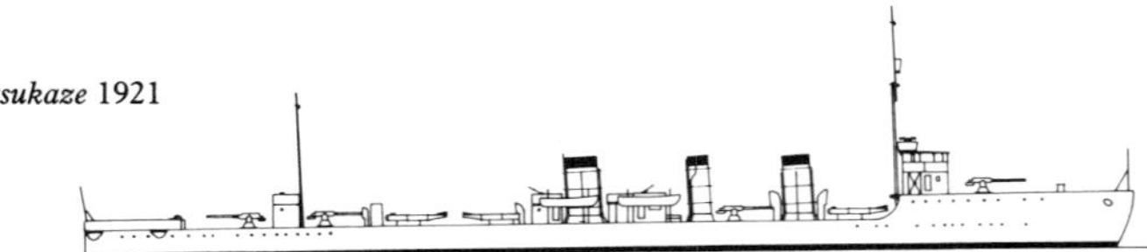

ISOKAZE class *destroyers*

Displacement: 1227t normal; 1570t full load
Dimensions: 318ft 1in oa, 309ft 9in pp × 27ft 11in × 9ft 3in
96.9m, 94.5m × 8.5m × 2.8m
Machinery: 3-shaft Parsons (Curtis in *Tokitsukaze* and *Amatsukaze*) turbines, 5 Kampon boilers
Armament: 4–4.7in (120mm)/40, 6–18in (457mm) TT (3×2)
Complement: 128

Kuwa about 1929
USN

Class (builder, launched, completed, fate):
Isokaze (Kure N Yd, 5.10.16, 28.2.17, BU 1935), *Amatsukaze* (Kure N Yd, 5.10.16, 14.4.17, BU 1935), *Hamakaze* (Mitsubishi, Nagasaki, 30.10.16, 28.3.17, BU 1935), *Tokitsukaze* (Kawasaki, Kobe, 27.12.16, 31.5.17, BU 1.3.48)

This design F-24 had the same general hull design as *Umikaze*, but was slightly larger. It had increased power and speed, and introduced a single-calibre main battery, three instead of two twin TT. These were the first Japanese destroyers rated as first class, but that was only in comparison with the second class units which followed *Umikaze*. They had three funnels in place of the four of the *Umikaze* class. *Amatsukaze* means 'Heavenly Wind'. All four were stricken on 1 April 1935. *Tokitsukaze* broke in half off Kyushu on 25 March 1918, was raised, repaired at Maizuru by February 1920. For many years she served as TS at Eta Jima (Japanese Naval Academy).

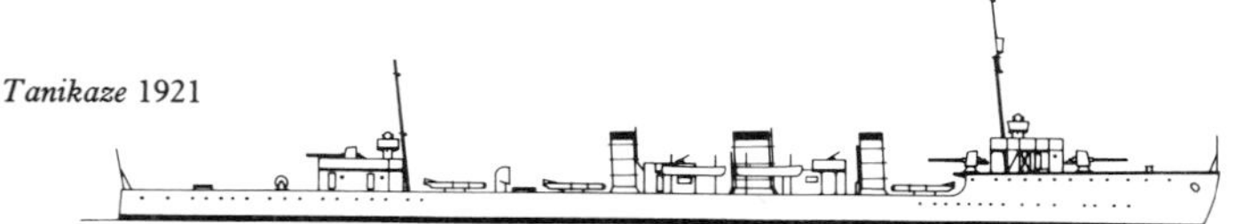
Tanikaze 1921

TANIKAZE class *destroyers*

Displacement:	1300t normal; 1580t full load
Dimensions:	336ft 6in oa, 320ft pp × 29ft × 9ft 3in *103.6m, 97.6m × 8.8m × 2.8m*
Machinery:	2-shaft Curtis (Parsons in *Kawakaze*) geared turbines, 4 Kampon boilers 34,000shp = 37.5kts. Oil 380t. Range 4000nm at 15kts
Armament:	3–4.7in (120mm)/45, 6–21in (533mm) TT (3×2)
Complement:	128

Class (builder, launched, completed, fate):
Tanikaze (Maizuru N Yd, 20.7.18, 30.1.19, stricken 1.4.35), *Kawakaze* (Yokosuka N Yd, 10.10.17, 11.18, stricken 1.4.34, BU)

These ships, Design F-30, were an improved *Isokaze*, slightly longer and beamier, with more powerful engines and oil fuel only. The gun battery was reduced to 3–4.7in (but 45 rather than 40 calibre), but at the same time they had 21in rather than 18in TT. They were later re-armed with two triple tubes. *Tanikaze* became a Kaiten TS in 1944 and was later scuttled as a breakwater at Kure before being BU.

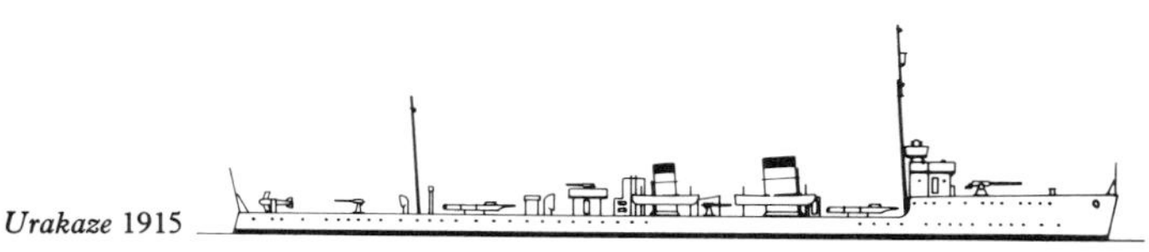
Urakaze 1915

URAKAZE class *destroyers*

Displacement:	907t normal; 1085t full load
Dimensions:	286ft 3in oa, 275ft 3in × 27ft 7in × 8ft *87.2m, 83.9m × 8.4m × 2.4m*
Machinery:	2-shaft Curtis turbines, 3 Yarrow boilers, 22,000shp = 30kts. Oil 248t. Range 1800nm at 15kts
Armament:	1–4.7in (120mm)/45, 4–3.1in/40, 4–21in (533mm) TT (2×2)
Complement:	120

Class (builder, launched, completed, fate):
Urakaze (Yarrow, 16.2.15, 14.10.15, BU 9.9.48), *Kawakaze* (Yarrow, 27.9.15, 23.12.16, to Italy 7.16)

Urakaze was the last destroyer built abroad for the Japanese Navy, ordered from Yarrow in November 1912. Short cruising range was a common problem, since high-speed turbines were inefficient at low power. She was, therefore, to have had cruising diesels, in analogy with modern CODOG diesel-gas turbine plants: 22,000shp Brown-Curtis turbines on 2 shafts, with 2–1200bhp Burmeister & Wain diesels for cruising at 12kts. The diesels were to have been coupled to the main shafts through German-built Fottinger transformers, which could also reverse the propellers, as diesels could not run in reverse. The transformers were tried in Germany in July 1914, but could not be delivered due to the outbreak of war. Instead a temporary oil tank was fitted.

Urakaze was the first Japanese destroyer with 21in TT tubes, and also the first to be all oil-fired. She made 30.26kts on trials. One source suggests that her combined-plant concept was due, not to the Japanese Navy, but to Yarrow. As a unique unit, she was used for many years as a guard ship in China, rather than as a unit of a squadron.

Kawakaze was delivered to Italy, a replacement being authorised under the 8–4 plan of 1917. She was replaced by a unit of the *Tanikaze* class (see above). *Urakaze* was completed on 14 October 1915, but was not delivered to Japan until 1919. She was stricken in 1936 and hulked at Yokosuka in 1936, being sunk there by aircraft of US TF 38 on 18 July 1945.

Nokaze about 1935
Aldo Fraccaroli Collection

MINEKAZE class *destroyers*

Displacement:	1345t normal; 1650t full load
Dimensions:	336ft 6in oa, 320ft pp × 29ft 8in × 9ft 6in *102.6m, 97.5m × 9m × 2.9m*
Machinery:	2-shaft Parsons geared turbines, 4 Kampon boilers, 38,500shp = 39kts. Oil 395t–400t. Range 3600nm at 14kts
Armament:	4–4.7in (120mm)/45, 2–7.7mm MG, 6–21in (533mm) TT (3×2), 20 mines
Complement:	148

Class (launched, completed, fate):
Maizuru N Yd – *Minekaze* (8.2.19, 29.5.20, sunk 10.2.44 by US submarine *Pogy* 85nm NNE of Formosa); *Okikaze* (launched 3.10.19, 17.8.20, stricken 1938 but operational 1941, sunk 10.1.43 by US submarine *Trigger* 35nm SE of Yokosuka); *Shimakaze* (31.3.20, 15.11.20, *Patrol Boat No 1* 1939, sunk 21.1.43 by US submarine *Guardfish* 65nm WSW of Kavieng); *Nadakaze* (26.6.20, 30.9.21, *Patrol Boat No 2* 1.4.40, sunk 25.7.45 by British submarine 175nm E of Soerabaja, Java); *Shiokaze* (22.10.20, 29.7.21, badly damaged 31.1.45 by US air attack off Formosa, towed to Japan and BU 1948); *Hokaze* (12.7.21, 22.12.21, sunk 6.7.44 by US submarine *Paddle* 105nm NNE of Menado, Celebes Sea); *Tachikaze* (31.3.21, 5.12.21, sunk 17.2.44 by US TF 38 carrier aircraft at Truk Atoll); *Nokaze* (1.10.21, 31.3.22, sunk 20.2.45 by US submarine *Pargo* near Cape Varella); *Namikaze* (24.6.22, 11.11.22, badly damaged 8.9.44 by US submarine in Sea of Okhotsk, transferred to China 3.10.47 renamed *Shen Yang* disarmed and BU); *Numakaze* (25.2.22, 24.7.22, sunk 19.12.43 by US submarine *Grayback* 50nm ENE of Naha, Okinawa)
Mitsubishi, Nagasaki – *Sawakaze* (7.1.19, 16.3.20, aircraft rescue ship 1939, patrol vessel 1941, surrendered at Yokosuka, BU 1948); *Yakaze* (10.4.20, 19.7.20, target ship 20.7.42, badly damaged 18.7.45 by US TF 38 carrier aircraft at Yokosuka, BU 1948); *Hakaze* (21.6.20, 16.9.20, sunk 23.1.43 by US submarine *Guardfish* 15nm SSW of Kavieng); *Akikaze* (14.12.20, 1.4.21, sunk 3.11.44 by US submarine *Pintado* 160nm W of Cape Bolinao); *Yukaze* (28.4.21, 24.8.21, to Britain 14.8.47, towed to Singapore and BU)

This design F-41 (1345t type) was designed for high speed in rough weather. It represented a break with previous Japanese practice (which had followed pre-1914 British concepts), in favour of German pre-1914 destroyer practice. That is, the forecastle was extended and the bridge set well back from its break, with a bank of torpedo tubes in the well thus created. In theory, the bridge would thus be freed from the pounding of heavy seas, which would break up on the forecastle. The guns were also raised well above the main deck, both amidships and aft. Geared turbines were adopted for higher speed. In all, 36 ships of this type were built, forming the Combined Fleet destroyer flotillas until the completion of the even larger *Fubuki* class in the late 1920s and 1930s. There was also a parallel second class destroyer design, the *Momi* class (see below).

On trials *Shimakaze* ('Island Wind') made 40,652shp = 40.65kts at 1379t in October 1920; *Sawakaze* (March 1920) made 42,742shp = 38.13kts at 1386t; *Nadakaze* (September 1921) made 40,511shp = 39.81kts at 1358t. They were considered good for 36kts in service.

The last three ships (*Nokaze* class, or Type F-41A) differed from F-41 in gun arrangement, to improve ammunition supply and fire control. No 3 gun was mounted with No 4 on the after deck house instead of abaft the second funnel; the searchlight platform was fitted abaft the second funnel instead of between No 2 and No 3 TT mounts. *Numakaze* made 38,000shp = 38.7kts at 1373 on trial.

Yakaze was refitted as radio control ship for the ex-battleship *Settsu* in 1937, her armament reduced to one or two 4.7in guns. She became an aircraft bombing target in September 1942 (11,260shp = 24kts, 1–50mm gun).

In 1937–8 the others had their hulls strengthened and their funnels raised and fitted with rain-proof caps. Fuel capacity was reduced: *Minekaze, Okikaze* 275t; *Shimakaze, Akikaze, Shiokaze, Yukaze, Nadakaze* 230t; *Hakaze, Hokaze, Tachikaze* 295t. Displacement rose to 1552t, and maximum speed fell to 36kts. In 1939 *Kamikaze, Nokaze, Numakaze,* and *Namikaze* were refitted: ballast was added, hulls strengthened, and rain-proof funnel tops added, displacement rising to 1692t, maximum speed falling to 34.5kts. *Kamikaze* displaced 1784t and could make only 34kts. They were recommissioned in May 1940.

Minekaze and *Okikaze* were removed from the effective list in 1938 but rearmed in 1941. Others were withdrawn for escort duties, beginning with *Nadakaze* and *Shimakaze* in 1939. Two of their four boilers were removed (leaving them 19,250shp = 20kts), and the 4–4.7in guns replaced by 2–4.7in/50 DP guns (fore and aft) and 10–25mm MG replaced the two after banks of TT. They carried 16 DCs at this time. By the end of 1941 they had been converted to destroyer transports, with only 1–4.7in DP gun, but two *Daihatsu* landing craft and 250 troops (plus 18 DCs).

The remaining ships were similarly converted to escorts in 1941–42, but no boilers were removed; they were considered good for 35kts at 1350t. These conversions roughly parallelled the contemporary British AA escort conversion of the 'V' and 'W' class destroyers of slightly earlier vintage. As in the case of other Japanese warships, the surviving escorts were fitted with extra AA weapons in the summer of 1944: their batteries then consisted of 13 to 20–25mm and 5–13mm MG (*Akikaze, Nadakaze, Namikaze, Nokaze, Sawakaze, Shiokaze, Yukaze*). As escorts, they carried 4 DC throwers and 36 DCs.

Sawakaze had been reconstructed as an aircraft rescue ship in 1940, but became a patrol vessel (as above) in 1941; she had no TT. Towards the end of the war her remaining (forward) 4.7in gun was replaced by an experimental ASW weapon, a nine-barrelled 5.9in RL.

Namikaze was torpedoed in September 1944, and then reconstructed at Maizuru as a *Kaiten* (human torpedo) carrier, her stern rebuilt. One (of three) boilers was removed (22,000shp = 28kts), and she carried 2 *Kaitens*. She then carried only 1–4.7in DP gun, 20–25mm, and 8–13mm. *Shiokaze* was severely bombed in January 1945, and was also reconstructed as a *Kaiten* carrier, in her case with 4 human torpedoes. She also stowed 7 *Kaiten* hulls in No 1 boiler room. Her light battery consisted of 11–25mm AA.

Hishi about 1925
CPL

No 12 (later *Yugao*) about 1926
CPL

Yunagi August 1928
CPL

MOMI class *destroyers*

Displacement:	850t normal; 1020t full load
Dimensions:	280ft wl, 275ft pp × 26ft × 8ft *85.3m, 83.8m × 7.9m × 2.4m*
Machinery:	2-shaft Curtis (Parsons in *ships) geared turbines, 3 Kampon boilers, 21,500shp = 36kts. Oil 240t. Range 3000nm at 15kts
Armament:	3–4.7in (120mm)/45, 2–7.7mm MG, 4–21in (533mm) TT (2×2)
Complement:	110

Class (builder, launched, completed, fate):
Momi (Yokosuka N Yd, 10.6.19, 27.12.19, stricken 1.4.32, kept as experimental hulk in Yokosuka, BU later); *Kaya* (Yokosuka N Yd, 10.6.19, 28.3.20, stricken 1939 and BU); *Nashi* (Kawasaki, Kobe, 26.8.19, 10.12.19, stricken 1939 and BU); *Take* (Kawasaki, Kobe, 26.8.19, 25.12.19, disarmed 1939; tender 1940, BU 1947 at Maizuru); *Kaki** (Uraga Dock, Tokyo, 20.10.19, 8.8.20; disarmed 1939, tender 1940, TS *OSU* 23.2.45, BU 1947 at Kure); *Tsuga** (Ishiwakajima, Tokyo, 17.4.20, 20.7.20, sunk 15.1.45 by US TF 38 carrier aircraft in Makung harbour, Pescadores Is); *Nire** (Kure N Yd, 22.12.19, 31.3.20, disarmed 1939, tender 1940, TS *Tomariura No 1* 15.12.44, BU by 15.8.45 at Uraga); *Kuri* (Kure N Yd, 19.3.20, 30.4.20, sunk 8.10.45 by mine off Pusan, Korea)

Kiku (Kawasaki, Kobe, 13.10.20, 10.12.20, *PB No 31* 1939, sunk 30.3.44 by US TF 38 aircraft off Palau); *Aoi* (Kawasaki, Kobe, 9.11.20, 20.12.20, *PB No 32* 1939, beached and sunk 23.12.41 at Wake Island after damage from US coastal batteries); *Hagi** (Uraga Dock, Tokyo, 29.10.20, 20.4.21, *PB No 33* 1939 fate as *Aoi*); *Fuji* (Fujinagata, Osaka, 27.11.20, 31.5.21, *PB No 36* 1939, damaged 17.5.45 at Soerabaja, Java, by aircraft from carriers HMS *Illustrious* and USS *Saratoga*, ceded to Netherlands 7.46, BU 1947), *Susuki** (Ishiwakajima, Tokyo, 21.2.21, 5.5.21, *PB 34* 1939, badly damaged 6.3.43 in collision with target ship *Yakaze*, sunk 3.7.44 by air attack while in Truk for repairs); *Hishi** (Uraga Dock, Tokyo, 9.5.21, 3.3.22, *PB 37* 1939, badly damaged 24.1.42 by US destroyers *Pope* and *Parrott* off Balikpapan, raised and BU); *Hasu** (Uraga Dock, Tokyo, 8.12.21, 31.7.22, badly damaged 16.1.45 by US TF 38 carrier aircraft, BU 1946 at Sasebo), *Warabi* (Fujinagata, Osaka 28.9.21, 19.12.21, originally to be named *Toko*, sunk 24.8.27 in collision with cruiser *Jintsu*, 107 dead); *Tade* (Fujinayata, Osaka, 15.3.22, 31.7.22, originally to be named *Fuyo*, *PB 39* 1939, sunk 23.4.43 by US submarine *Seawolf* 150nm NE of Formosa); *Sumire* (Ishiwakajima, Tokyo, 14.12.21, 30.3.23, disarmed 1939, tender 1940, TS *Mitaka*, BU 3.48 at Harima)

Tsuta (Kawasaki, Kobe, 9.5.21, 30.6.21, originally to be named *Tsuru*, *PB 345* 1939, sunk 2.9.43 by USAAF aircraft at Lae, New Guinea); *Ashi* (Kawasaki, Kobe, 3.9.21, 29.10.21, disarmed 1939, tender 1940, TS *Tomiura No 2* 15.12.44, BU 1947), *Yomogi* (Ishikawajima, Tokyo, 14.3.22, 9.8.22, *PB 38* 1939, sunk 25.11.44 by US submarine *Atule* 100nm N of Cape Engano)

This F-37 design of 21 ships parallelled the larger *Minekaze* (F-41), introducing the German-style forecastle with a TT in a well forward of the bridge. They were also the first second class destroyers armed with 21in TT.

For comaprison, Uraga units were to have been powered by Rateau, and Ishikawajima with Zoelly turbines, but except for *Sumire* and *Yomogi* with Zoelly (which in *Sumire* gave much trouble), the Uraga and Ishikawajima ships had Parsons. *Nire* made 34.35kts on 23,165shp at 893t in March 1920. They were considered good for 31kts in service.

Kiku group was Design F-37A, with a larger and longer bridge, searchlight abaft second funnel instead of atop the bridge, and foremast separated from bridge. *Tsuta* group was classed as Design F-37B.

In 1937 *Fuji, Susuki, Hishi, Hasu, Tsuka, Yomogi* and *Tade* had their funnels raised and capped. Reconstructions for escort work began in 1939, when *Fuji, Kiku, Aoi, Susuki, Hishi, Yomogi*, and *Tade* had their after 4.7in guns and their TT (and one boiler) removed, for a battery of 2–4.7in, 6–25mm AA, and 60 DCs. They then displaced 935t, 12,000shp = 18kts. They were then redesignated in a numbered Patrol Boat series, as noted above. *Nire, Take, Kake, Ashi* and *Sumire* were similarly modified in 1940, with one or two 4.7in guns and 2–21in TT (9000shp = 14kts). They served as tenders. That left only *Hasu, Kuri* and *Tsuga* as destroyers. During 1942–43 their amidships 4.7in guns were replaced by 2 triple 25mm AA.

The patrol boats (less *Kiku, No 31*) were rebuilt as fast transports in 1941, their sterns modified to launch a 46ft Daihatsu landing craft with 150 troops. By 1942 they were armed with 2–4.7in and 6–25mm AA. *No 31*, the only remaining patrol boat, had 2–4.7in, 8–25mm, and 60 DCs. *Osu* and *Mitaka* were disarmed and fitted with wooden deckhouses for accommodation and training in 1944.

Due to their shallow draft, they were much used in Chinese waters. They were used for amphibious fire support and escort during World War Two.

WAKATAKE class *destroyers*

Displacement:	900t normal; 1100t full load
Dimensions:	as *Momi* class except 8ft 3in/*2.5m* draught
Machinery:	as *Momi* class except Zoelly turbines*, = 35.5kts. Oil 244t
Other particulars:	as *Momi* class

Class (builder, launched, completed, fate):
Kikyo (Kawasaki, Kobe, 24.7.22, 30.9.22 as *No 2*, renamed *Wakatake* 1928, sunk 30.3.44 by US TF 58 carrier aircraft 60nm N of Palau); *Yuri* (Kawasaki, Kobe, 21.10.22, 21.12.22 as *No 4* renamed *Kuretake* 1928, sunk 30.12.44 by US submarine *Razorback* 65 miles SE of Formosa); *Ajisai* (Fujinagata, Osaka, 23.9.22, 16.3.23 as *No 16*, renamed *Fuyo* 1928, sunk 20.12.43 by US submarine *Puffer* 60nm W of Manila); *Kakitsubata** (Ishikawajima, Tokyo, 4.11.22, 10.5.23 as *No 10*, renamed *Asagao* 1928, badly damaged 22.8.45 by mine in Shimonoseki Straits, BU 10.6.48 at Yoshimi); *Karukaya* (Fujinagata, Osaka, 19.3.23, 20.8.23 as *No 18*, sunk 10.5.44 by US submarine *Cod* 35nm WNW of Iba, Luzon); *Ayame** (Uraga Dock, Tokyo, 15.2.23, 5.11.23 as *No 5*, renamed *Sanae* 1928, sunk 18.11.43 by US submarine *Bluefish* 90nm S of Basilan Island); *Tsutsuji** (Ishikawajima, Tokyo, 14.4.23, 31.5.24 as *No 12*, renamed *Yugao* 1928, *PB 46* 1942, sunk 10.11.44 by US submarine *Greeling* 75nm SW of Yokosuka); *Kaido** (Uraga Dock, Tokyo, 1.9.23, 24.7.24 as *No 8*, renamed

Sawarabi 1928, foundered 5.12.32 in storm 100nm NE of Keelung in Formosa Straits); *Shian* and *Omodaka* (*No 14* and *No 20* ordered from Kawasaki, Kobe and BU on slip 1922); *Nadeshiko** (*No 22* cancelled from Fujinagata, Osaka); *Botan** (*No 24* cancelled from Uraga Dock, Tokyo); *Basho* (*No 26*) cancelled from Ishihawajima, Tokyo)

This F-37C or No 2 type, later the 8-ship *Wakatake* class, was the last second class destroyer type. Four units were cancelled, followed by *No 14* in 1922. All were rated as minelayers and sweepers. *Sawarabi* capsized and sank due to poor stability. However, of the entire class, only *Sanae* ('Rice Seedling') and *Wakatake* were refitted and ballast added (1938); their forefunnels were fitted with rain-proof caps. They emerged displacing 1131t and capable of 31kts.

Yugao was refitted as a patrol boat in 1939–40, her horsepower reduced to 10,000 (18kts) and her armament to 2–4.7in, 8–25mm AA and 60 DCs. The others were refitted in 1941–42, the after 4.7in being removed and six 25mm plus several 13mm AA fitted; they carried 36 or 48 DCs, with throwers aft. *Asagao* had her forward bank of TT removed at this time.

KIYOKAZE (KAMIKAZE) class *destroyers*

Displacement: 1400t normal; 1720t full load
Dimensions: 336ft 6in oa, 320ft pp × 30ft × 9ft 7in
102.6m, 97.5m × 9.1m × 2.9m
Machinery: 2-shaft Parsons geared turbines, 4 Kampon boilers, 38,500shp = 37.2kts. Oil 420t. Range 3600nm at 14kts
Other particulars: as *Minekaze* class

Class (builder, launched, completed, fate):
Kiyokaze or *Shirushikaze* (Mitsubishi, Nagasaki, 25.9.22, 19.12.22 as *Destroyer No 1*, renamed *Kamikaze* 1928, wrecked 7.6.46 near Omaezahi, BU by 31.10.47 at Suruga Wan); *Karuikaze* or *Suzukaze* (Mitsubishi, Nagasaki, 8.12.22, 16.6.23 as *No 3*, renamed *Asakaze* 1928, sunk 23.8.44 by US submarine *Haddo* 20nm SW of Cape Bolinao); *Makaze* (Maizuru N Yd 18.12.22, 31.5.23 as *No 5*, renamed *Harukase* 1928, badly damaged by mine 4.11.44 and by air attack 21.1.45 by US TF 38 carrier aircraft near Makung, Formosa, towed to Japan. BU 1947); *Okaze* (cancelled 3.22); *Tsumujikaze* (cancelled 3.22); *No 7* (Maizuru N Yd, 30.10.23, 5.4.24, renamed *Matsukaze* 1928, sunk 9.6.44 by US submarine *Swordfish* 70nm SE of Chichijima, Bonin), *No 9* (Maizuru N Yd, 15.3.24, 30.8.24, renamed *Hatakaze* 1928, sunk 15.1.45 by US TF 38 carrier aircraft at Takao harbour, Formosa); *No 11* (Uraga Dock, Tokyo, 27.11.24, 30.10.25, renamed *Oite* 1928, sunk 17.2.44 by US TF 38 carrier aircraft while carrying cruiser *Agano* survivors at Truk); *No 13* (Ishikawaijima, Tokyo, 23.3.25, 21.11.25, renamed *Hayate* 1928, sunk 11.12.41 by US coastal batteries 2nm SW of Wake Island); *No 15* (Fujinagata, Osaka, 21.4.24, 29.12.25, renamed *Asanagi* 1928, sunk 22.5.44 by US submarine *Polluck* 200nm WNW of Chichijima); *No 17* (Sasebo N Yd, 23.4.24, 24.5.25, renamed *Yunagi* 1928, sunk 25.8.44 by US submarine *Picuda* 20nm NNE of Cape Bojeador)

This Type F-41B or *No 1* type was designated the *Kamikaze* class when the 9 destroyers were renamed in 1928. The hull was slightly beamier to compensate for a gradual increase in topweight, eg due to the use of steel protection in the bridge structure for the first time. They also introduced a new model 4.7in/50 DP gun. Speed was lost: on trials in December 1922, *Kiyokaze* reached 38.67kts on 40,312shp at 1443t. *No 7* (*Matsukaze*) made 41,202shp = 39.2kts at 1459t. They were considered good for 34kts in service.

They were refitted in 1941–42, when No 4 4.7in gun was replaced by light AA guns, No 3 TT mount was removed, and 6 to 10–25mm were fitted; they then carried 18 DCs. Normal displacement rose to 1523t. By June 1944 light armament was 13 to 20–25mm and 4–13mm, and maximum speed had fallen to 35kts.

Hayate was sunk by a shore battery at Wake Island, the first Japanese naval casualty of the Pacific War. *Kamikaze* grounded and sank near Cape Omaezaki while salvaging the stranded repatriation ship *Kunashiri*.

SUBMARINES

As in the case of destroyers, Japanese submarine policy changed radically towards the end of the period covered by this book. It appears that attention turned from the area immediately around Japan to the East, amid the former German Pacific islands, an area through which the US Fleet would have had to pass en route to any decisive engagement closer to Japan. Thus large numbers of medium submarines were cancelled in 1922 in favour of smaller numbers of much longer-range submarine cruisers of the KD and J types. The coincidence in dates suggests that the change in strategy was due to the numerical inferiority in capital ships which Japan had to accept as part of the Washington Treaty. Submarines, like destroyers armed with 24in torpedoes, became valuable equalisers.

Thus, it was reported in 1921 that future Japanese policy would be to build only two types: very large ocean-going cruisers (some minelayers) and smaller ocean boats of up to 1000t and moderate speed, some of which would be minelayers. Construction of 500t coastal boats would be abandoned. In effect the *definition* of coastal v ocean changed. In 1921 the existing 'K' and 'L' boats were considered good for 5000 to 6000nm, which in other navies might be considered ocean range. Now the requirement rose to 10,000 to 20,000nm, as the expected operational area moved well to the East.

Note, too, that even before this shift the Japanese Navy emphasised long endurance, which was partly a function of the ability of crews to adapt to cramped conditions. It was reported in 1919 that *No 16*, a small coastal boat, made a three week cruise, only touching at three ports for a few hours during that period. During World War One, crews of Western ocean submarines found a three week cruise the limit of their endurance. That must have been partly a function of the strain of constant danger in a war zone, but a British observer, Hector Bywater (who published *Sea Power in the Pacific* in 1921), concluded that, given two submarines of identical type, tonnage, and fuel capacity, one manned by a Japanese crew and the other by a Western crew, the boat with the Japanese complement could stay at sea 30 per cent longer.

In the notes which follow, submarine classes are distinguished by standard letter-number combinations, eg *C 3* for Vickers 'C' class Model 3; *S 1–S 2* Schneider-Laubeuf (2 models); *F 1–F 2* Fiat-Laurenti class (Kawasaki licence); *L 1–L 4* Vickers 'L' class (Mitsubishi licence); Mitsubishi K – Mitsubishi Kobe, *K 1—K 4* and *KT* were Navy medium classes; *KD 1* was a large class based on British practice, *KD 2* a large submarine based on the German *U 139*.

The submarine numbering system was changed (effective from 1 November 1924) to reflect the new priorities. The smallest boats were classified as *Ha*; the newly coastal ones as *Ro*, and the largest were numbered in a new *I* series. Formerly all submarines had been numbered in a single sequence. Note, too, that the *I* numbers *were not sequential* but were issued in blocks. Thus the J-type cruisers were assigned *I-1* through *I-4*; the minelayers, the *I-20* series, the KD-type cruisers the *I-50* series and above. That left the numbers through *I-50* blank (the minelayers were later renumbered to remove them from the original sequence), and the result is somewhat confusing, the most modern pre-1941 submarines falling into this series. Early boats were renumbered in 1942, the digit 100 being added to their numbers, to remove them from the lower-numbered parts of the series.

HOLLAND type *submarines*

Displacement: 103t/124t
Dimensions: 67ft oa, 60ft pp × 11ft 11in × 10ft 3in
20.4m, 18.3m × 3.6m × 3.1m
Machinery: 1-shaft 4cyl gasoline engine plus electric motor, 180bhp/70hp = 8kts/7kts. Oil 2t. Range 184nm/21nm at 8kts/7kts
Armament: 1–18in (457mm) TT (2 torpedoes)
Complement: 13

Class (launched, completed):
No 1 (20.3.05, 1.8.05), *No 2* (2.5.05, 5.9.05), *No 3* (16.5.05, 5.9.05), *No 4* (27.5.05, 1.10.05), *No 5* (13.5.05, 1.10.05)

The first Japanese submarines, they were ordered from the Fore River Co (Holland company design) in 1902, after a Japanese naval mission visited Britain, France, and the United States. Built in great secrecy, they were sent by rail (in knocked-down condition) to Seattle, thence by ship to Yokosuka, where they arrived 12 December 1904. Assembly was delayed; they were launched only in March and May 1905, the first being ready in June 1905. They differ from contemporary boats in greater hull strength, reinforced by a broad strip of bronze plating. Two bilge keels, 24.5ft × 9.5in, also stiffened the hull to resist pressure at a maximum diving depth of 125ft. All were stricken in 1921 and BU. *No 4* sank at Kure by petrol explosion on 14 November 1916 but was raised and repaired.

The launch of submarine *No 1*
Aldo Fraccaroli Collection

No 6 February 1916
Aldo Fraccaroli Collection

No 9 about 1911
Aldo Fraccaroli Collection

No 12 October 1915
Aldo Fraccaroli Collection

KAIGUN-HOLLAND type *submarines*

Displacement: 57t/63t (see notes)
Dimensions: 73ft 10in oa, 69ft 4in pp × 7ft × 6ft 8in
22.5m × 2.1m × 2.0m (see notes)
Mahcinery: 1-shaft gasoline engine/electric motor, 300bhp/22hp = 8.5kts/4kts. Oil 1.4t. Range 184nm/12nm at 8kts/4kts
Armament: 1–18in (457mm) TT (1 torpedo)
Complement: 14

Class (launched, completed):
No 6 (28.9.05, 30.3.06), *No 7* (28.9.05, 30.3.06)

Nos 6 and 7 (Kaigun-Holland type) were built at Kawasaki, Kobe under Holland supervision between November 1904 and March 1906. Compared to the first Holland submarines, they displaced less, but were longer and stronger, with greater engine power, 300hp gasoline v 180hp Otto in the first boats. *No 7* displaced 78t/95t and measured 84ft 3in oa, 80ft 1in pp × 7ft 11in × 7ft 8in *(25.7m, 24.4m × 2.4m × 2.3m)*. The Japanese Navy reportedly considered them experimental units for material and tactical trials, hence the single torpedo. Note also the change in emphasis compared to the original Holland concept, surface speed being much greater than submerged. This was typical of other navies at the time, as boats were expected to cruise out to their operating areas on the surface, diving largely to attack.

No 6 sank in about 10 fathoms on 15 April 1910 after the ventilator valve flooded in Hiroshima Bay off Kure, the fortitude of Lt Sakuma's crew (16 dead) becoming famous. She was raised the next day and became a memorial at Kure after being stricken in 1920.

C 1 VICKERS class *submarine*

Displacement: 286t/321t
Dimensions: 142ft 3in oa, 131ft 6in pp × 13ft 7in × 11ft 3in
43.3m, 40.1m × 4.1m × 3.4m
Machinery: 1 shaft, 16cyl Vickers diesel/electric motor, 600bhp/300hp = 12kts/8.5kts. Oil 15t. Range 660nm/60nm at 12kts/4kts
Armament: 2–18in (457mm) TT (2 torpedoes), 1 MG
Complement: 26

Class (launched, completed, fate):
No 8 (19.5.08, 26.2.09, *Ha 1* 1924, stricken 1928 and BU), *No 9* (19.5.08, 9.3.09, *Ha 2* 1924, stricken 1928 and BU)

The two 1907 submarines (built under the 1904 programme) were identical to the Royal Navy 'C' class. Built by Vickers, Barrow, they were shipped to Japan after completion aboard a specially-built cargo ship. In the RN, the 'C' class was considered the first type suitable for overseas, as opposed to coastal, operation. However, the IJN had to operate over much greater distances, as witness its search for much longer-range submarines (Schneider-Laubeuf and Fiat-Laurenti, below).

C 2 VICKERS class *submarines*

Displacement: 291t/326t
Dimensions: As *C 1* type
Machinery: As *C 1* type except oil 15.5t
Armament: As *C 1* type
Complement: 25

Class (launched, completed):
No 10 (4.3.11, 12.8.11), *No 11* (18.3.11, 26.8.11), *No 12* (27.3.11, 3.8.11)

A slightly modified version of the C 1 type, these submarines (ordered under the 1910 Programme) were shipped in sections to Kure for reassembly. Renamed *Ha 3*–*Ha 5* respectively in 1924 before being stricken on 1 December 1928 and BU.

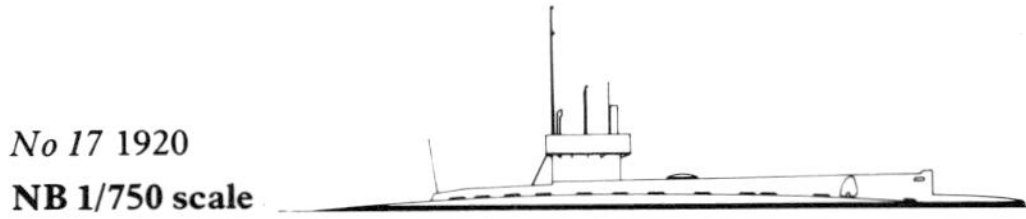

No 17 1920
NB 1/750 scale

C 3 VICKERS class *submarines*

Particulars: As C 1 type (see notes)

Class (launched, completed, fate):
No 16 (15.3.16, 1.11.16, *Ha 7* 1924, stricken 1.12.28 and BU), *No 17* (15.3.16, 2.2.17, *Ha 8* 1924, stricken 1.12.28 and BU)

As in the case of the second class destroyers, this was a repeat version of an obsolete design, chosen for rapid construction under the 1915 programme and both built by Kure N Yd.

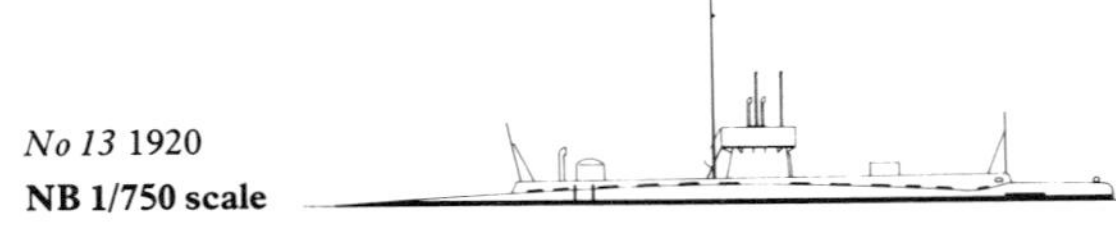

No 13 1920
NB 1/750 scale

VK type *submarine*

Displacement: 304t/340t
Dimensions: 126ft 9in oa, 125ft pp × 12ft 7in × 10ft
38.6m, 38.1m × 3.8m × 3.1m
Machinery: 1-shaft gasoline engine/electric motor, 1000bhp/300hp = 10.8kts/8kts. Oil 17.8t
Armament: 2–18in (457mm) TT (2 torpedoes)
Complement: 26

Class (builder, launched, completed, fate):
No 13 (Kawasaki, Kobe, 18.7.12, 30.9.12, *Ha 6* 1924, stricken 1.12.28 and BU)

This Vickers-Kawasaki submarine was an experimental type based on the 'C' class, just as the Holland-Kaigun boats had been based on the original Holland design. It was ordered under the 1910 Programme.

No 15 1919
NB 1/750 scale

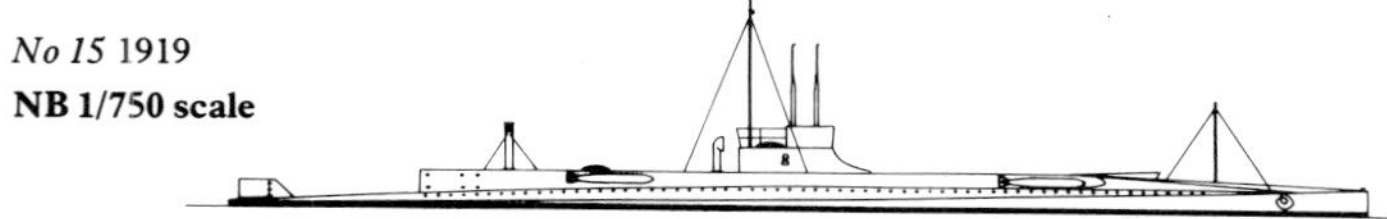

S 1 class *submarines*

Displacement: 418t/665t
Dimensions: 186ft 1in oa, 184ft 4in pp × 17ft 1in × 10ft 2in
56.7m, 56.2m × 5.2m × 3.1m
Machinery: 2-shafts, Schneider diesels, 2 electric motors, 2000bhp/850hp = 17kts/10kts. Oil 32t. Range 2050nm/60nm at 10kts/4kts
Armament: 4–18in (457mm) TT (8 torpedoes), 1–2pdr AA
Complement: *c*30

Class (launched, completed, fate):
No 14 (7.15, 6.16, French *Armide* 6.15), *No 15* (7.4.11, 20.7.17, *Ha 10* 1924, stricken 1.12.18 and BU)

The first really long-range submarines ordered by the Japanese Navy, they were ordered from Schneider-Creusot in December 1911 under the 1912 Programme. Unlike the Vickers craft, they were double-hulled, hence their greater fuel capacity. Only *No 15* was delivered. *No 14* was commissioned in June 1916 as the French *Armide*. A replacement, which became *No 14(ii)*, was authorised in 1915. This design is significant as the basis for the first truly Japanese submarine design, the *Kaigun* (K) class.

Both *No 15* and *No 14(ii)* were armed with 1–3.1in/40 deck gun in 1919.

S 2 class *submarine*

Displacement: 480t/737t
Dimensions: 192ft 3in oa × 17ft × 10ft 8in
58.6m × 5.2m × 3.3m
Machinery: 2 shafts, Schneider diesels, 2 electric motors, 1800bhp/850hp = 16.5kts/9.5kts. Oil 35t. Range 2050nm/60nm at 10kts/4kts
Armament: 6–18in (457mm) TT (8 torpedoes), 1–7.7mm MG
Complement: *c*30

Class (builder, launched, completed, fate):
No 14 (ii) (Kure N Yd, 28.3.18, 30.4.20, *Ha 9* 1924, stricken 1.12.28 and BU)

This replacement for the French *Armide* was a modified Schneider-Laubeuf design, slightly longer than *No 15* with only 2 torpedoes in dropping cradles, as compared to 4 in *No 15*. The Schneider-Carels diesels were imported from France.

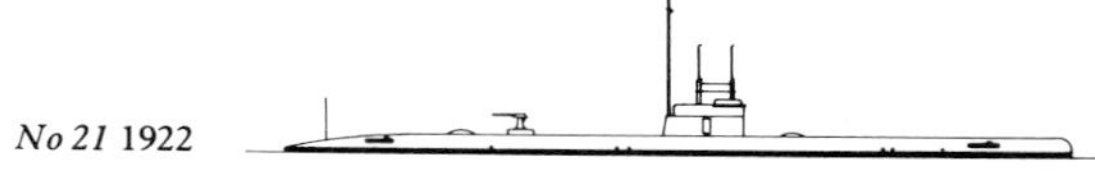
No 21 1922

F 1 class *submarines*

Displacement: 689t/1047t
Dimensions: 215ft 1in oa, 198ft 7in pp × 19ft 11in × 13ft 9in
65.6m, 60.5m × 6.1m × 4.2m
Machinery: 2 shafts, Fiat diesels, 2 Savigliano electric motors, 2800bhp/1200hp = 13kts/8kts. Oil 58.4t. Range 3500nm/75nm at 10kts/4kts
Armament: 5–18in (457mm) TT (8 torpedoes), 1–7.7mm MG
Complement: 43

Class (builder, launched, completed, fate):
No 18 (Kawasaki, Kobe, 28.7.19, 31.3.20, *Ro 1* 1924, stricken 1930), *No 21* (Kawasaki, Kobe, 22.11.19, 20.4.20, *Ro 2* 1924, stricken 1930)

These Italian-designed submarines were the first truly ocean-going units of the Japanese Navy. However, their non-cylindrical single hulls (for extra internal volume) were considered relatively weak, to the extent that extra scantlings were worked into their hulls during construction. They did not form the basis of any later classes. They were credited with a diving depth of 130ft; 2 were ordered under the 1915–16 programme, and 3 more in 1918. They were armed with 3.1in/28 deck guns shortly after completion. Note that they were the earliest boats numbered in the postwar medium (*Ro*) series.

No 29 as completed
Aldo Fraccaroli Collection

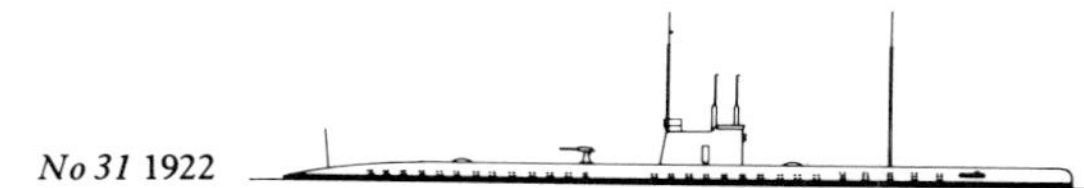
No 31 1922

F 2 class *submarines*

Dimensions: As F 1 type except 13ft 3in/*4.1m*
Machinery: As F 1 type except 2600bhp = 14kts
Other particulars: As F 1 class

Class (launched, completed, fate):
No 31 (10.3.21, 17.7.22, *Ro 3* 1.11.24, stricken 1930); *No 32* (22.6.21, 5.5.22, *Ro 4* 1.11.24, stricken 1930); *No 33* (17.9.21, 9.3.22, *Ro 5* 1.11.24, stricken 1930)

This improved *No 18* type had a modified bridge. After completion a 3.1in/28AA gun was fitted in addition to the 7.7mm MG. The Fiat engines were unsatisfactory, the boats making only 14kts rather than the expected 17kts. They were also unreliable. Units planned for the 1919 Programme (8-6 Fleet plan) were replaced by 'K' and 'L' boats (*Nos 48—50, 60, 61*).

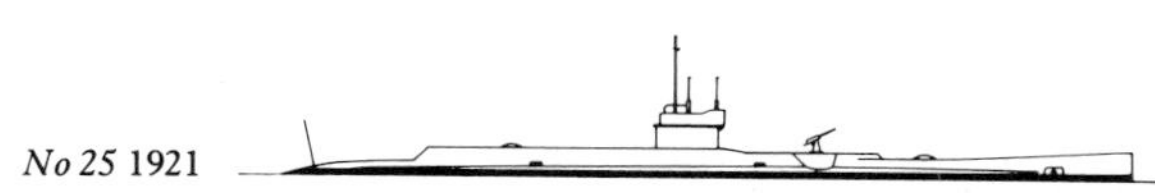
No 25 1921

L 1 class *submarines*

Displacement: 893t/1195t
Dimensions: 231ft 7in oa, 220ft 3in pp × 23ft 6in × 12ft 11in
70.6m, 67.1m × 7.2m × 3.9m
Machinery: 2 shafts, 4 cycle Vickers diesels, 2 electric motors, 2400bhp/1600hp = 17kts/8kts. Oil 75t. Range 5500nm/80nm at 10kts/4kts
Armament: 6–18in (457mm) TT (bow and 2 beam; 10 torpedoes), 1–3.1in/28 AA, 1–7.7mm MG
Complement: 48

Class (builder, launched, completed, fate):
No 25 (Mitsubishi, Kobe, 10.10.19, 30.6.20, *Ro 51* 1.11.24, stricken 1940), *No 26* (Mitsubishi, Kobe, 9.3.20, 30.11.20, *Ro 52*, 1.11.24, stricken 1.4.32)

This Mitsubishi-Vickers type was similar to the early British 'L' class of 1916, the standard British 'overseas' patrol submarine of its period, and thus the lineal successor to the earlier 'C' class. It was a single-hull submarine with saddle tanks, like the earlier 'C', and unlike the Schneider type. The Japanese Navy contracted with Vickers late in 1917, ordering the first unit from Mitsubishi (Kobe) in March 1918. Diesel engines were imported from England or built in Japan. *No 26* sank on 29 October 1923 at Kure due to a flooding error but was raised on 17 November.

L 2 class *submarines*

Particulars: As L 1 class (see notes)

Class (launched, completed, fate):
No 27 (6.7.20, 10.3.21, *Ro 53* 1.11.24, stricken 1938), *No 28* (13.10.20, 10.9.21, *Ro 54* 1.11.24, stricken 1939), *No 29* (10.2.21, 15.11.21, sunk 29.10.23 in accident off Kobe, raised to be *Ro 55*, 1.11.24, stricken 1939), *No 30* (11.5.21, 16.1.22, *Ro 56* 1.11.24, stricken 1940)

Slightly modified L type built by Mitsubishi, Kobe under the the 1918 Programme. The principal difference was omission of the two beam TT and 5t more oil fuel.

L 3 class *submarines*

Displacement: 897t/1195t
Dimensions: 250ft oa, 242ft 9in × 23ft 6in × 13ft
76.2m, 74m × 7.2m × 4.0m
Machinery: As L 1 type except oil 98t. Range 7000nm/85nm at 10kts/4kts
Other particulars: As L 2 type (see notes)

Class (launched, completed, fate):
No 46 (3.12.21, 30.7.22, *Ro 57* 1.11.24, stricken 1.5.45, BU 1946), *No 47* (2.3.22, 25.11.22, *Ro 58* 1.11.24, stricken 1.5.45, BU 1946), *No 57* (28.6.22, 20.3.23, *Ro 59* 1.11.24, stricken 1.5.45, BU), *Nos 48–50* were cancelled in 1920 and replaced by minelayers (KRS type).

These submarines were similar to the L 2 type but had 21in TT tubes, and carried their 3.1in guns atop their fairwaters instead of on deck forward of them. A minelaying version, similar to British mining submarines, with mines carried in tubes in the saddle tanks, was planned in 1921 but not built, as L(M). Oil tankage was later increased to 117t. All 3 still existed in 1941 as training boats; *No 46* was used to train midget submarine crews at Shodojima in 1945 and *No 57* likewise at the Submarine School, Otake.

No 57 as completed
Aldo Fraccaroli Collection

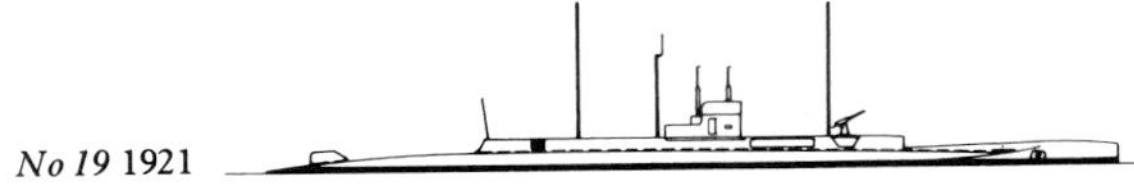

No 19 1921

K 1 class *submarines*

Displacement:	735t/1030t
Dimensions:	227ft oa × 20ft 10in × 11ft 3in *69.2m × 6.4m × 3.4m*
Machinery:	2 shafts, 2 Sulzer diesels, 2 electric motors, 2600bhp/1200hp = 18kts/9kts. Oil 60t. Range 4000nm/85nm at 10kts/4kts
Armament:	6–18in (457mm) TT (4 bow, 2 on deck in cradles; 10 torpedoes), 1–3.1in/28 AA
Complement:	44

Class (builder, launched, completed, fate):
No 19 (Kure N Yd, 15.10.17, 31.7.19, *Ro 11* 1924, stricken 1931), *No 20* (Kure N Yd, 1.12.17, *Ro 12* 1924, stricken 1931)

This S 7 or *Kaigun* (Navy) medium design, derived from the Schneider-Laubeuf type, was the first fully Japanese boat, the various foreign designs having been found deficient in hull strength. Work on this class, specially adapted to Far Eastern rather than to European conditions, began in 1916. The principal difference was that Japanese and Pacific waters were much deeper than the North Sea and the Mediterranean, so that submarines could not expect to lie on the bottom very often. Thus reliable depth control was extremely important.

Moreover, powerful and erratic sub-surface currents tend to drive submarines off their course and produce sudden changes of trim, hence involuntary dives below operating depth. Thus the emphasis on hull strength. In 1921 it was claimed that the 'K' class, with its beamy but enormously strong hull, was therefore more capable of resisting depth charge attacks than any other type extant. These boats were said to have been dived to depths at which European submarines would collapse; to have survived groundings, collisions, and other accidents that would have been fatal to foreign boats. For example, Nos *19* and *20*, the first of the Kaigun type, rammed one another in the 1919 manoeuvres. Although seriously injured, they both returned to port safely. Besides being exceptionally strong in framing and plating, the Kaigun boats were said to have an abnormal amount of internal sub-division and bulkheading. This rendered them very cramped and uncomfortable internally. The Sulzer diesels were Swiss-built.

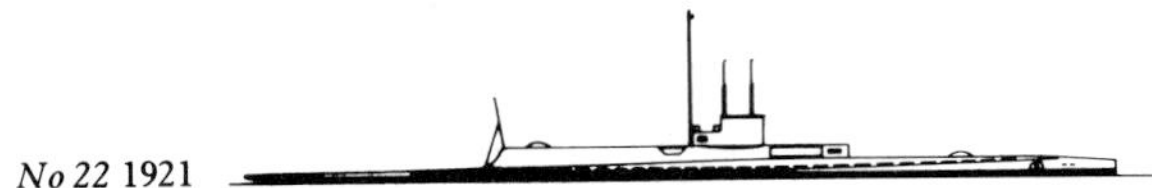

No 22 1921

K 2 class *submarines*

Displacement:	755t/1050t
Dimensions:	230ft oa × 20ft × 12ft 1in *70.1m × 6.1m × 3.7m*
Other particulars:	As K 1 class except 17kts surfaced, oil 75t. Range 6000nm at 10kts
Complement:	45

Class (launched, completed, fate):
No 22 (31.3.19, 17.2.21, *Ro 14* 1.11.24, stricken 1931, training hulk 1940, BU 9.48 at Harima); *No 23* (26.8.19, 30.9.20, *Ro 13* 1.11.24, stricken 1.4.32), *No 24* (14.10.20, 30.6.21, *Ro 11* 1924, stricken 1931)

This Navy (*Kaigun*) design, type S 18 built by Kure N Yd, was a modified K 1, with the same powerplant, hence a slightly lower speed. The bow, fairwater, and stern differed in shape, the latter overhanging.

K 3 class *submarines*

Particulars:	As K 2 class

Class (launched, completed, fate):
Kure N Yd – *No 34* (24.2.21, 20.10.21, *Ro 17* 7.11.24, stricken 1.4.32),

No 41 as completed
Aldo Fraccaroli Collection

No 35 (25.3.21, 15.12.21, *Ro 18* 1.11.24, stricken 1.4.36), *No 36* (28.12.20, 15.3.22, *Ro 19* 1.11.24, stricken 1.4.36, BU 1948 at Naniwa); *No 37* (22.4.21, 29.4.22, *Ro 16* 1.11.24, stricken 1.4.36)
Yokosuka N Yd – *No 38* (26.10.20, 1.2.22, *Ro 20* 1.11.24, stricken 1.4.32 and sold), *No 39* (26.10.20, 1.2.22, *Ro 21* 1.11.24, stricken 1.4.32 and sold), *No 40* (15.10.21, 10.10.22, *Ro 22* 1.11.24, stricken 1.4.32), *No 41* (25.10.21, 28.4.23, *Ro 23* 1.11.24, stricken 1.4.32)
Sasebo N Yd – *No 42* (8.12.19, 30.11.20, *Ro 24* 1.11.24, stricken 1.4.32), *No 43* (17.7.20, 25.10.21, *Ro 25* 1.11.24, stricken 1.4.36 and BU)

A slightly improved version of the 1917 K 2 class, built by Kure N Yd under the 1918 Programme. Up to this time this was the most numerous single class (9 boats), marking the development of what must have appeared to be a satisfactory design. *Nos 38* and *39* were sold to Kanagawa Prefecture in 1932 for 5000 yen each and scuttled to act as breeding grounds for fish. *No 43* sank on 19 March 1924 in collision with the light cruiser *Tatsuta* off Sasebo, was raised on 25 April and used for trials.

K 4 class *submarines*

Displacement:	770t/1080t
Dimensions:	As K 2 class except 243ft 6in oa, *74.2m*
Machinery:	As K 2 class
Armament:	4–21in (533mm) TT (8 torpedoes), 1–3.1in/28 AA, 1–7.7mm MG
Complement:	45

Class (builder, launched, completed, fate):
No 45 (Sasebo N Yd, 18.10.21, 25.1.23, *Ro 26* 1.11.24, stricken 1.4.40 and BU 4.48 at Kanagawa), *No 58* (Yokosuka N Yd, 22.7.22, 13.7.24, *Ro 27* 1.11.24, stricken, 1.1.40 and BU 10.47 at Iwakuni), *No 62* (Sasebo N Yd, 13.4.22, 30.11.23, *Ro 28* 1.11.24 and BU 5.48 at Kumagaya Gumi)

This Design S 18A was slightly larger than K 3, with 21in rather than 18in TT, and the 3.1in gun forward of the fairwater instead of abaft it. *Nos 44* and *51* reordered to new (large) designs. Note that a K 5 design (*Ro 33–34* of 1933) was not related to this one; it was a mobilisation design for a medium submarine. *Ro 26* refitted 1932, *Ro 27* and *Ro 28* in 1934.

Cancellations (1922): *Nos 48–50* were reordered as minelayers (KRS) in May 1923; *Nos 53–56, 60—61, 63—67* were cancelled. Of the last group, all but *No 67* had been ordered.

In addition, *Nos 74–83, 85–87*, which would have been of 'K' and 'L' types, were cancelled. The 8-8 plan envisaged another 28 submarines (*Nos 88–116*), but plans were redrafted following the Washington Conference.

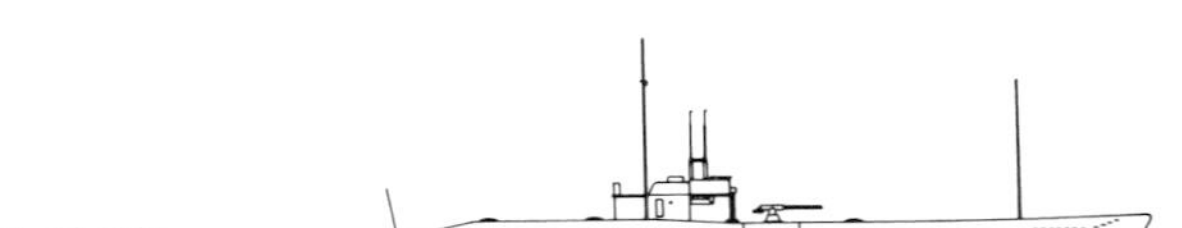

No 68 1926

KT class *submarines*

Displacement:	665t/1000t
Dimensions:	As K 4 class
Machinery:	2 shafts, 2 Sulzer diesels, 2 electric motors, 1200bhp/1200bhp = 13kts/8kts. Oil 113t–116t. Range 8000nm/85nm at 10kts/4kts
Armament:	4–21in (533mm) TT (8 torpedoes), 1–4.7in (120mm)/45, 1–7.7mm MG
Complement:	43

Class (launched, completed, fate):
No 68 (5.12.22, 15.9.23, *Ro 29* 1924, stricken 1.4.36), *No 69* (18.1.23, 29.4.24, *Ro 30*, 1.11.24, stricken 1.4.42 and training hulk at Submarine School, Otake, BU fter 8.45), *No 70* (2.23, sunk 21.8.23 during trials off Kobe. Salvaged 11.24 and returned to service as 25.9.26, renamed *Ro 31* 10.5.27, stricken 5.5.45, scuttled 5.4.46 at Sasebo by USN), *No 71* (19.3.23, 31.5.24, *Ro 32* 1.11.24, stricken 1.4.42 becoming submarine school hulk, BU after 8.45).

This was a 'Navy Medium Special Type' ordered under the 1918 Programme, and based (like the K class) on the Schneider-Laubeuf double-hull design. Note the heavier surface armament (a 4.7in gun). Although sometimes described as minelayers, they carried no mines. They were fitted with Sulzer diesels, rather than with the Fiat engines often listed.

SUBMARINES: WAR PRIZES
2 Mittel-U: *O 3* (ex-*U 55*), *O 2* (ex-*U 46*)
2 small ocean-going boats (UB III type): *O 6*, (ex-*UB 125*), and *O 7* (ex-*UB 143*)
3 minelayers: UE type: *O 1* (ex-*U 125*)
O 4 and *O 5*, UC III type, *O 4* (ex-*UC 90*), *O 5* (ex-*UC 99*)

The Japanese also obtained plans of the German *U-kreuzers*, which were adapted both for the KD 2 class and for a larger cruiser called the *Junsen* (J 1). The UE II minelayer was adapted as the KRS. The J-class, *I 1* to *I 4*, were identical to the wartime German *U 142* except for their armament and the shape of their bridge. They were built under the 1922–28 and 1923–28 Fleet Laws, constructed under the supervision of Dr Ing H Techel, formerly of the Krupp Germania yard. Normal displacement was 2791t, and they were powered by 2 MAN diesels (4 cycle, 10 cylinder) of 3000bhp each, for a designed speed of 17.5kts. However, they reached 18.8kts (*I 1*) or 19.1kts (*I 2*, *I 3*) on trial). Radius (on the surface) was 24,400nm/10kts or 17,500nm/12kts with 545–558t oil. Their armament was projected as 3–5.9in/45 as in *U 142*, but was changed to 2–5.5in/40, a new and shorter version of the cruiser gun, the 5.5in/50. They carried 20–21in torpedoes (6 tubes), and had 60mm armour over their conning towers.

SMALL SURFACE WARSHIPS

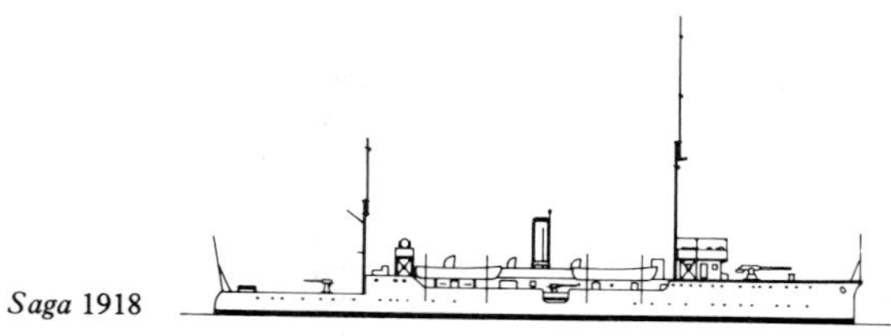
Saga 1918

SAGA *gunboat*

Displacement: 785t normal; 885t full load
Dimensions: 226ft 3in oa, 208ft 8in × 29ft 6in × 7ft 3in
69.0m, 63.6m × 9.0m × 2.3m
Machinery: 2-shaft VTE, 2 Kampon boilers, 1600ihp = 15kts. Coal 190t
Armament: 1–4.7in (120mm)/45, 3–3.1in/40, 3 MG
Complement: 98

Name	Builder	Launched	Fate
SAGA	Sasebo N Yd	27.9.12	Sunk 22.1.45

A first class steel gunboat. Completed 16 November 1912. By 1941 3 MG were added. Sunk by USAAF aircraft at Hong Kong.

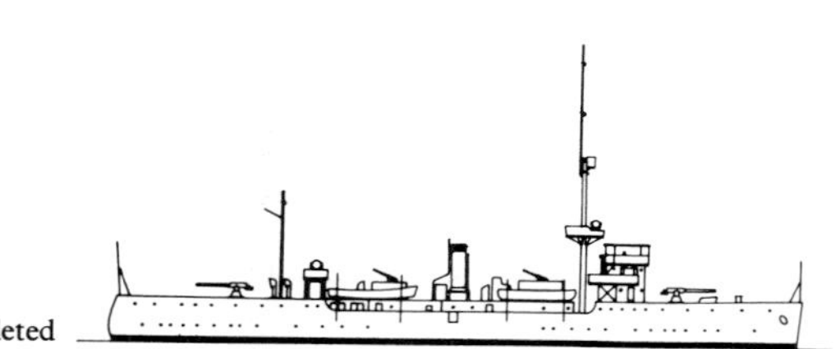
Ataka as completed

ATAKA *gunboat*

Displacement: 880t normal; 1133t full load
Dimensions: 222ft pp × 29ft 6in × 7ft 5in
67.1m × 9.0m × 2.3m
Machinery: 2-shaft VTE, 2 Kampon boilers, 1700ihp = 16kts. Coal 235t
Armament: 2–4.7in (120mm)/45, 2–3.1in/40, 6 MG
Complement: 118

Name	Builder	Launched	Fate
ATAKA	Yokohama Dock	11.4.22	Chinese *An Tung* 8.45

Part of the 1920 Fleet Construction Programme as gunboat and submarine tender. Higher freeboard than customary in Japanese warships. Completed 12 August 1923 and served as flagship of the Yangtze Flotilla.

Ataka was refitted April–July 1937 at Kure and blistered (beam increased about 2.6 feet, displacement 1094t) for increased stability; her pole foremast with fighting top for MG was replaced by a tripod. Her after 4.7in gun was replaced by a 3.1in/40 AA gun (formerly mounted forward of her funnel), and she had twin 13mm MG to port and starboard of her bridge, as well as 4 Vickers 7.7mm MG in single mounts. Later, probably in 1939, 2 twin 13mm MG were added on her poop deck and before her funnel. Surrendered at Singapore in August 1945.

SUMIDA *river gunboat*

Displacement: 126t normal; 105t light
Dimensions: 145ft pp × 23ft 7in × 1ft 11in
44.2m × 7.2m × 0.6m
Machinery: 3-shaft VTE, Thornycroft boilers, 550ihp = 13kts. Coal 40t
Armament: 2–47mm/40, 4 MG
Complement: 40

Name	Builder	Launched	Fate
SUMIDA	Thornycroft, Woolston	26.6.03	Stricken 1935, BU

Built in England in sections under the 1896–97 postwar programme. Reassembled October 1903 to April 1906.

FUSHIMI *river gunboat*

Displacement: 180t normal; 150t light
Dimensions: 159ft 9in pp × 24ft 3in × 2ft 3in
48.7m × 7.4m × 0.7m
Machinery: VTE, Yarrow boilers, 900ihp = 14kts. Coal 25t
Armament: 2–57mm/40, 3 MG
Complement: 45

Name	Builder	Launched	Fate
FUSHIMI	Yarrow, Scotstown	5.8.06	Stricken 1935 and BU

Last gunboat built outside Japan, sent to Japan in sections in October 1906. At the end of the year Kawasaki stripped her for reassembly at Shanghai.

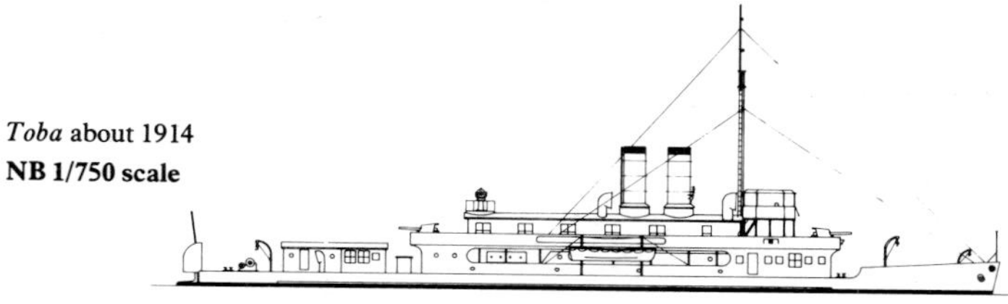
Toba about 1914
NB 1/750 scale

TOBA *river gunboat*

Displacement: 250t normal; 291t full load
Dimensions: 183ft 4in oa × 27ft × 2ft 7in
55.9m × 8.3m × 0.8m
Machinery: 3-shaft, 3 cyl VTE, 2 cyl boilers, 1400ihp = 15kts. Coal 80t
Armament: 2–3.1in/28, 6 MG
Complement: 59

Name	Builder	Launched	Fate
TOBA	Sasebo N Yd	7.11.11	Chinese *Yangi Ch'i* 8.45

Built under the 1910 budget, additional cabins were added aft. Completed 17 November 1911. Surrendered at Shanghai.

Seta about 1936
Aldo Fraccaroli Collection

SETA class *river gunboats*

Displacement: 338t normal; 400t full load
Dimensions: 184ft oa, 180ft pp × 27ft × 3ft 4in
56.1m, 54.9m × 8.2m × 1.0m
Machinery: 2-shaft 2 cyl compound, 2 Kampon boilers, 2100ihp = 16kts. Coal 74t, oil 25t. Range 1750nm at 10kts
Armament: 2–3.1in/40, 3 or 6 13mm MG
Complement: 62

Name	Builder	Launched	Fate
SETA	Harima	30.6.22	Chinese *Chang Teh* 8.45
KATATA	Harima	16.7.22	BU post 8.45
HIRA	Mitsubishi, Kobe	14.3.23	BU 1945
HOZU	Mitsubishi, Kobe	9.4.23	BU 1945

These gunboats were built on the same dimensions as the *Toba* under the 1920–28 Replenishment Programme, for service on Chinese rivers. They were built in sections and assembled at Shanghai (*Seta, Katata*) and Hankow (on the Yangtze). *Seta* was completed on 6 October 1923 and damaged on 6 June 1943 on the Yangtze by Chinese aircraft. She surrendered at Shanghai. *Katata* was completed on 20 October 1923 and badly damaged by USAAF aircraft on the Yangtze at Kiukiang (12 December 1944). She was towed to Shanghai and further damaged on 2 April 1945 by USAAF aircraft. *Hira* (completed 24 August 1923) and *Hozu* (7 November 1923) were wrecked near Anking on 26 November 1944 by Chinese aircraft and BU in place.

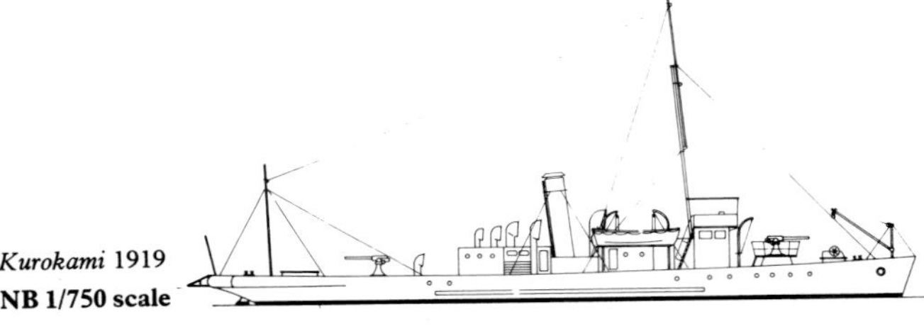

Kurokami 1919
NB 1/750 scale

NATSUSHIMA class *minelayers*

Displacement: 420t normal; 405t standard
Dimensions: 149ft 11in × 24ft 11in × 7ft 7in
45.7m × 7.6m × 2.3m
Machinery: 1-shaft VTE (2 propellers), 1 boiler, 600ihp = 12.8kts. Range 600nm at 10kts
Armament: 2–3.1in/40, 2 MG, 45 mines
Complement: ?

Class (builder, launched, completed, fate):
Natsushima (Yokosuka N Yd, 3.11.11, 1911, BU 1932), *Sokuten* (Maizuru N Yd, 3.13, 1913, BU 1937); *Toshima* (Maizuru N Yd, 10.14, 1914, sunk 30.7.45 at Maizuru by Allied carrier aircraft); *Kuroshima* (Maizuru N Yd, 10.14, 1914, Repatriation Service 1945–47, to China 14.11.47 renamed *Chein 29); Ashizaki* (Maizuru N Yd, 10.15, completed 1915, wrecked 17.11.45 at Hayakawa in storm and abandoned); *Katoku* (Maizuru Yd, 10.15, 1915, Repatriation Service 1945–47, to Japan 1948, MSDF *PS 29*, stricken 1953–54 and BU); *Kurokami* (Kure N Yd, 2.17, 1917, Allied Minesweeping Service 1945–47, to Britain 4.11.47, BU in Japan); *Katashima* (Maizuru N Yd, 2.17, 1917, Allied Minesweeping Service 1945–47, to USSR 3.10.47); *Ento* (Maizuru N Yd, 3.17, 1917, severely damaged 15.1.45 at Fangliao, Formosa by US TF 38 carrier aircraft, BU 1945); *Enoshima* (Maizuru N Yd, 1917, severely damaged 14.10.44 in Takao, Formosa by US TF 38 carrier aircraft, BU 1945); *Kurosaki* (Yokosuka N Yd, 1918, wrecked 18.11.45 off Hachinohe); *Ninoshima* (Kure N Yd, 1918, captured 1945 in Formosa and BU); *Washizaki* (Yokosuka N Yd, 1920, Repatriation Service 1945–47, to Britain 24.11.47, BU 1948 at Sasebo)
1948 at Sasebo).

A class of 13 coastal and harbour minelayers also fitted for minesweeping. In 1941–42 refits they were reduced to 1–80mm (3.1in) but a capacity of 120 Type 4 mines with 1 or 2–13mm MG being added 1944–45.

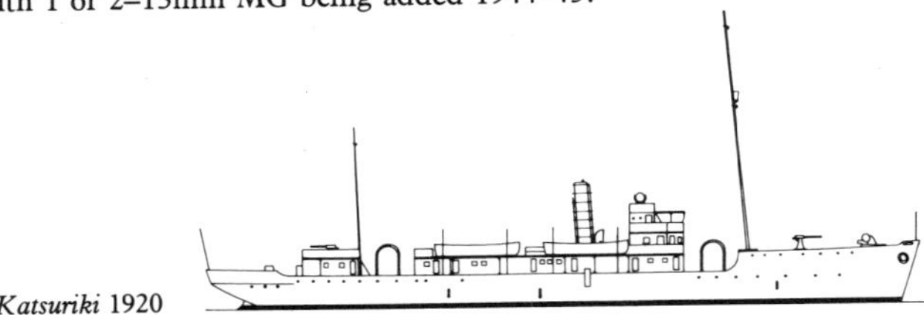

Katsuriki 1920

KATSURIKI *minelayer*

Displacement: 2000t normal; 1540t standard
Dimensions: 240ft wl × 39ft × 14ft
73.1m × 11.9m × 4.3m
Machinery: 2-shaft VTE, 2 Kampon boilers, 1800ihp = 13kts. Coal 449t. Range 1800nm/10kts
Armament: 3–3.1in/40, 150 mines
Complement: ?

Name	Builder	Launched	Fate
KATSURIKI	Kure N Yd	5.10.16	Sunk 21.9.44

Part of the 1915–16 Programme and completed in January 1917 with 4 wooden minewarfare gallows, she was employed as a survey vessel from 1936 and rerated as such in July 1942. Sunk by US submarine *Haddo* 80nm SW of Manila.

Thornycroft type *coastal motor boats*

Displacement: 14t normal
Dimensions: 55ft oa × 11ft 1in × 3ft 3in
16.8m × 3.4m × 1.0m
Machinery: 2-shaft petrol engines, 1000bhp = 40kts. Range 200nm at 40kts
Armament: 2–.303in MG, 2–18in (457mm) TT, 2 DC
Complement: 5

Class (fate):
Naikatei No 615 (stricken by 1938), 2nd boat No unknown (stricken by 1938), 3rd boat (unknown), *Naikatei No 1149* (TRV and dispatch boat at Kure, extant 1945)

Launched by Thornycroft of Southampton in 1920 and bought by Japan as her first MTBs. First boat later attached to Yokosuka engineering school.

AUXILIARY MINELAYERS

A large total of steam trawlers were requisitioned for the 1914–18 war, 33 remaining in the Fleet List 1920–44 with the numbers *1–44* (except *10, 12, 16–20, 34* and *38–40*). Only 9 can be definitely identified. *No 1* (ex-*Shinten Maru No 7*, 1901, 320grt), *No 5* (ex-*Ominato Maru No 2*, 1900, 302grt), *No 11* (ex-*Takeshiki Maru*, 1899, 366grt), *No 12* (ex-*Nasami Maru*, 1899, 366grt), *No 21* (ex-*Shinten Maru No 3*, 1888, Mitsubishi, 295grt), *No 24* (ex-*Keikan Maru No 2*, 1900, 284grt), *No 26* (ex-*Keikan Maru*, 135grt), *No 29* (ex-*Shinten Maru No 5*, 1898, 315grt), *No 41* (ex-*Tenkyo Maru No 1*, 1899, 304grt)

ARMED MERCHANT CRUISERS

The following 10 merchant vessels were requisitioned for the Russo-Japanese War (1904–5):
America Maru (1898, 6069grt, sunk 6.3.44 by US submarine *Nautilus* S of Iwo Jima); *Bingo Maru* (1897, 6242grt, BU 1934); *Hong Kong Maru* (1896, 6169grt); *Kasuga Maru* (1898, 3819grt); *Kumano Maru* (1901, 5076grt, sunk 10.6.27 off Takamatsu by collision); *Nikko Maru* (1903, 5823grt, wrecked 14.5.05 off Pusan but salvaged for commercial use until sunk 9.4.45 by US aircraft in Manila Bay); *Nippon Maru* (1818, 6168grt, became Chilean *Renaico*); *Taichu Maru* (1897, 3320grt, rerated as minelayer 1905, sunk 12.4.44 in E China Sea by US submarine *Halibut); Yawata Maru* (1898,

3817grt, rerated as transport and returned); *Yobo* (3435grt taken 9.2.04 as Russian prize at Inchon)

AUXILIARY GUNBOATS

The following 12 merchant vessels were requisitioned for the Russo-Japanese War (1904–5):

Fuso Maru (1895, 319grt, BU 21.9.34 at Osaka); *Heiju Maru* (1903, 1201grt, renamed *Shohei Maru* 1936 and sunk 6.2.45 S of Lushun by US submarine *Spadefish*); *Kagawa Maru* (1903, 613grt); *Kaijo Maru* (1902, 284grt); *Kikawa Maru* (1892, 209grt, requisitioned 2.05); *Manda Maru* (1900, 248grt); *Miyoshima Maru* (1902, 273grt); *Otagawa* (1893, 498grt, mined 8.8.04 E of Port Arthur); *Ryojun Maru* (1897, 499grt); *Sabagawa Maru* (1890, 313grt, requisitioned 2.05); *Yehime Maru* (1903, 623grt, requisitioned 2.05); *Yoshidagawa Maru* (ex-*Inegawa Maru*, 1890, 310grt)

Ataka at Hankow 1935
USN

Italy

The first twenty years of the present century represent one of the most interesting periods in the Italian Navy's history, both from historical and technical viewpoints. The climax in historical terms occurred in 1919; by this time the war against Austria-Hungary, Germany and Turkey had ended in victory for Italy, and on 24 March that year much of the formerly Austrian fleet steamed from Pola to Venice in Italian hands. These ships, consisting of the dreadnought *Tegetthoff*, the pre-dreadnought *Erzherzog Franz Ferdinand* and numerous scouts, destroyers, torpedo-boats and submarines, were devoid of flags, while the escorting Italian ships were dressed overall. When this mass of ships caught sight of the destroyer *Audace* (with King Vittorrio Emanuele III on board) and the other Italian units which had sailed from Venice to meet them, Vice-Admiral Cagni, Commander of the formation, ordered the flag signal 'Peace to the dead of Lissa' to be raised on the ex-enemy ships, as a signal that the Italian defeat of 20 July 1866 had been avenged. On that occasion the fleet commanded by Admiral Count Carlo Persano had lost two ships before being defeated by the numerically inferior Austrian squadron led by Rear Admiral Wilhelm Tegetthoff. As the formation arrived at San Marco dock, the sun emerged from behind the clouds and lit the scene brilliantly. For the Italian National Navy, which had been formed on 17 March 1861 with the unification of the various regional navies, this was its finest hour.

TECHNICAL INNOVATIONS

From the technical viewpoint, the Italian Navy showed great enterprise during this period, four examples being the following:

– the concept of a battleship with principal armament of a single calibre (all big gun ship). See the study 'An ideal battleship for the British Fleet', by Engineer Commander Vittorio Cuniberti, which was published in *Jane's Fighting Ships* of 1903, after the Italian Navy Minister had judged it to be over-ambitious for his own country.

– the concept of the Mas boat (a lightweight, fast motor launch, armed with two torpedoes and/or a small gun and depth charges) – one of which, *Mas 15*, sank the Austrian dreadnought *Szent István* in the open sea on 10 June 1918, in spite of the vessel's strong escort.

– the climbing boats (virtually a naval tank, equipped with two lateral caterpillar tracks and armed with two torpedoes); one of these machines attempted to force the barrages of the naval base of Pola in May 1918.

– the frogmen, two of whom piloted a self-propelled mine, forced the barrages of Pola at the end of October 1918 and sank the Austrian dreadnought *Viribus Unitis*.

Italian naval aviation had also been developed during these years, and proved to be a bold and efficient weapon. In 1923 the new air force or *Regia Aeronautica* was formed under the Commission for Aeronautics, subsequently becoming the Ministry of Aeronautics in August 1925; many naval officers who had already become pilots and observers during the 1915–1918 war, now hastened to join the new force.

In 1906, the year in which this volume starts, Vice-Admiral Carlo Mirabello was Navy Minister, and he remained in office for six years – from December 1903 to December 1909. This relatively long period allowed him to set up and proceed with a rational naval programme following the moral and material crisis that had followed the East African campaign of 1895–96. The Army had emerged from this campaign discouraged, but the Navy had also been involved, and parliamentary deputies subsequently criticized the Naval administration (1900–1903). However, the inquiry (1904–05) concluded in favour of the Navy.

The budget figures were always rather modest, certainly insufficient for Italy's ambitious aims and in every case low enough to ensure that vessels would be under construction for so long that they were bound to be outdated at completion. In fact, with the naval budget set at 121 million lire per annum for the period 1901–1906, the construction of important ships simply took too long; for example a good seven years for the pre-dreadnought battleship *Vittorio Emanuele*. This ship, laid down in September 1901, finished fitting out in August 1908. (Perhaps the Navy was overstretching itself; perhaps it should have devoted its energies to building fewer ships, but more rapidly). One result was that the *Dante Alighieri*, the first Italian dreadnought, entered service after the Austrian battleship *Viribus Unitis*, and thus Austria could claim to have the first battleship in service in the world fitted with triple turrets, although the Italian ship had been designed, laid down and launched earlier than the Austrian vessel, which was fitted out more rapidly.

Vice-Admiral Mirabello's ministry will be remembered not only for the ordering of *Dante Alighieri*, but also for the construction of four armoured cruisers, one of which, the *San Marco*, featured numerous world firsts. The *San Marco* was the first turbine-driven ship with four screws, the first fitted with a gyroscopic compass, the first to have an anti-roll system (Frahm water tanks), and the first in which the use of timber had been eliminated, since even the furniture was made of metal. Finally, with her sister ship *San Giorgio*, *San Marco* was the first ship fitted with electric gun mounting machinery.

In 1907 a Central Naval Staff was set up, led by Vice-Admiral Giovanni Bettòlo. During this early period, training of personnel for war was intensified, the fruits of which were evident in the 1911–12 Libyan War and the war of 1915–1918 (Italy entered the war on 24 May 1915). A vast programme of equipment renewal included the ordering of numerous series of open sea torpedo-boats, destroyers, 5 dreadnoughts (the *Cavour* and *Doria* classes), 14 submarines, but unfortunately only 3 scouts, only one of which was really successful (*Quarto*, one of the best ships ever to be designed and built in Italy). From this time on, all the ships were built wholly in the national dockyards, and the former dependence on foreign industry came to an end.

Even the guns were produced in Italian factories, although the main weaponry had their origin on foreign drawing boards (principally British), and the gun designs were often foreign (French and British). In the area of arms and munitions the results were not always identical to those obtained with the foreign originals. This was evident when the original munitions ran out for the cruisers and scouts of German origin transferred to Italy as war reparations in 1919–20. With the original German shells, the results were very good, but with the shells subsequently produced in Italy the targets were hit much less fre-

The Italian battlefleet in the Adriatic in 1918, led by the *Giulio Cesare*.
All photographs in the Italian section: Aldo Fraccaroli Collection

quently, even though the Italian gun direction equipment was of ingenious design and technically well made.

Italy showed an enterprising spirit in the area of mine warfare, inventing and perfecting a system of automatic depth-setting for moored mines (credited to Lieutenant Giovanni Elia), and making good use of them in wartime.

The war against Turkey declared on 29 September 1911 gave the Italian Fleet the task of transporting 30,000 troops in 55 transports from the peninsula to Libya. The Italian ships had their chance to prove their aggressive spirit in actions fought at Prevesa (29–30 September 1911) and Santa Maura (Ionian Sea), on the Syrian coast, in the Dardanelles (demonstration 16–19 April 1912), in the Red Sea (6 cruisers and 6 torpedo-boats), and also in the naval bombardments against Tripoli which was seized by a naval landing party on 5 October 1911 after the garrison of 7000 Turks evacuated as was Tobruk the day before. Troops landed at Tripoli on 11 October and also at Homs, Derna and Benghazi. Naval operations finished with the May 1912 occupation of Rhodes and the other Dodecanese islands which became Italian naval bases.

Since 1882 Italy had been a partner in the Triple Alliance with Germany and Austria-Hungary, and, in spite of ups and downs in the relations between Italy and Austria, a Naval Convention was signed in June 1913 by Italy, Austria and Germany, providing for the three fleets to collaborate in the Mediterranean in the case of war, with an Austrian admiral designated combined commander. Bearing in mind this convention, one might have thought that the design characteristics of the Italian ships would have taken account of the alliance. Instead, strange as it may seem, Italy and Austria competed amongst themselves; Italy designed ships to rival those of Austria, rather than ships suitable for fighting France and England. Apart from the fact that Austria had been considered the national enemy since 1848, Italy was extremely anxious to seize from Austria the areas of Trieste and Trentino, which were geographically Italian; for her part the Hapsburg Empire was obliged to prepare to stop such claims from her ally and rival.

THE FIRST WORLD WAR

In 1915 Italy had a numerous fleet at her disposal (active personnel numbered 40,000) the purpose of which was, in part, to make up for the geo-strategic inferiority in which she found herself in the Adriatic. The Italian Adriatic coast is flat and has few ports; from Venice it was necessary to sail as far as Ancona and then directly to Taranto to find ports suitable for large vessels. During the First World War vast projects were carried out to make Brindisi capable of accepting large ships. These ports were vulnerable to attack from the sea, as was confirmed in the very first hours of the war (24 May 1915), when the entire Austro-Hungarian Fleet bombarded many coastal areas. The Adriatic east coast features innumerable islands, and the waters are deep, so that the Austrian ships were easily able to shelter in secluded refuges, and then appear unexpectedly on the open sea.

Although Italy had laid down good, modern destroyer classes since 1910 (the 6 *Indomito* in 1910–11, the 4 *Ardito* and *Animoso* in 1912, the 8 *Pilo* in 1913–14), and the 39 very successful coastal torpedo-boats of the PN, OS, AS and RM types, the Italian Navy found itself short of light warships in the surface war with Austria and against the U-boats in the Mediterranean. The Italian battlefleet, to which had been added a few obsolescent British battleships, did gain supremacy in the Adriatic and Ionian Seas, so Italy did not continue building the 4 *Caracciolo* class super-dreadnoughts, instead devoting her shipyards to building scouts, destroyers, torpedo-boats and submarines.

This construction programme was, unfortunately, restricted by the scarcity of steel, bronze and other materials. As partial compensation for the lack of light ships, the 4 scouts of the *Vifor* class (building or completing at Naples for the Rumanian Navy) were requisitioned. The 4 *Leone* class ships were ordered, but could not be laid down, apparently for the lack of steel, while the 4 *Sirtori* class destroyers were laid down along with the 8 *La Masa* types. The 4 *Palestro*, the 4 *Curtatone*, the 6 *Generali* and a further 6 destroyers were also ordered, not one of which (of these 20 destroyers) could be laid down during hostilities. Precedence was given to smaller vessels: a further 30 coastal torpedo-boats were built, while work on a further 10 had to be abandoned. During hostilities no fewer than 63 submarines were made ready (9 of large displacement), along with 3 minelayers and 9 midget craft for harbour defence. A few submarines were acquired from Great Britain or Canada, and another was ex-Austrian, rebuilt after sinking.

But the most characteristic Italian vessel of this period was the Mas boat, of which as many as 299 were built, designed to act as torpedo-boats and for attacking submarines. Up to the end of the war, a further 50 USA-built Mas boats also entered service; these were larger but slower. Dozens more were commissioned after the Armistice, both of the Italian type (fast and light) and of the American type, built in US and Italian yards. Equally indispensable for escorting merchant traffic (Italy had 684 steamers worth 1,035,815 tons net and 517 sea-going sailing ships of 210,814 tons in 1916) were the 47 fishing boats, built in Japan and acquired and armed in 1916–17; they were classified as vedette boats, and distinguished by a number preceded by the letter 'G' (for '*Giappone*').

To aid in operations against enemy land positions (Carso, Hermada and others) a number of monitors and self-propelled floating batteries were built or converted, armed with medium and large-calibre guns (up to 15in, they were the big guns built for the *Caracciolo* class super dreadnoughts). To defend Venice, threatened by the Austro-German advance in October/November 1917, numerous lighters and barges (even ex-Austrian captured boats), several self-propelled and even unpowered floating batteries were converted and armed – in particular in Venice Navy Yard. These vessels fought gallantly in the canals and in the lagoon east of Venice. Of the 57 minesweepers laid down, a large number were commissioned in wartime. Furthermore, as was to be expected, the Italian Navy requisitioned many merchant ships, some of which were armed as cruisers (16 ships), and others (13) converted to hospital and ambulance ships. Finally there were the scrapings of the naval barrel: tugs, fishing boats, patrol boats, small steamers; all requisitioned and armed for naval purposes as auxiliary escorts, minesweepers, and gunboats.

The 1915–1918 war cost Italy 3 battleships; 2 armoured cruisers; 2 small cruisers (plus 2 flotilla leaders sunk by mines after hostilities); 8 destroyers; 6 torpedo-boats; 12 submarines; and 12 assorted ships, operating as monitors and gunboats. In addition, the Navy lost 267 aircraft and 7 airships.

With the end of the war and from 1921 onward, the Navy demobilised, although it did proceed with ships already building (1 scout, 6 destroyers, 5 submarines, as well as lesser craft) as well as 2 flotilla leaders and 10 destroyers which, although ordered, it had not been possible to lay down because of steel shortages etc, were also begun.

WAR PRIZES

As compensation for her own war losses, Italy demanded a *Tegetthoff* class battleship and one of the *Radetsky* class to replace the sunken battleships *Leonardo da Vinci* and *Benedetto Brin*. The Italian Navy did not obtain the two battleships, but was able to get 3 ex-German light cruisers, 3 ex-German and 9 ex-Austrian destroyers, while 2 small ex-Austrian torpedo-boats (110 tons) joined the Italian Customs Guard. In addition, 62 ex-Austrian and 17 ex-German auxiliaries and minor vessels were commissioned in the Italian Navy. One oiler, of the 17 German ships, was built under the War Reparatiôns account, laid down after the war (in 1922) and commissioned in the Italian Navy as *Urano*; 2 tugs of the 62 Austrian ships found incomplete at Trieste were completed after the war for the Italian Navy. No former U-boats were maintained in working order: in fact, all the U-boats (13 ex-Austrian and 10 ex-German) allotted to Italy after the end of the war were scrapped.

Italy reached the end of the war with about 450,000 metric tonnes of naval ships, while France had about 700,000 tonnes. In the international Washington treaties of 1921/1922, Italy obtained parity with France in battleships (total standard displacement: 175,000 tons) and aircraft carriers (total: 60,000 tons) with an enforced break of six years before further battleships could be laid down. In the meantime Italy was authorised to maintain in service the dreadnoughts *Doria, Duilio, Cavour, Cesare, Leonardo da Vinci* (sunk in 1916, recovered, but never actually recommissioned), *Dante*; and the four obsolete ships *Napoli, Regina, Elena, Roma, Vittorio Emanuele*, which were allowed to remain in service indefinitely, but not to be replaced by newly built vessels. In light forces and submarines, Italy did not obtain parity with France, even though at first France appeared willing to agree to this. In 1922 the destroyer *Quintino Sella* was laid down, the first unit of the 1922/1923 naval programme; the first since the end of the war.

ITALIAN NAVAL GUNS 1906–1921

Official designation (calibre in mm and length in calibres)	Calibre in inches	Builder and year of introduction	Weight (metric tonnes)	Weight of projectile (kg) AP/HE	Muzzle velocity (m/sec)	Range (metres)	Rate of fire (rpm)	Remarks
381/40	15	A,S,V 1914	83.6	../875	770	24,000	1.2	for the not completed *Caracciolo* class super-dreadnoughts
305/46	12	A, V 1909	64.1	417/404.6	860	12,000 from 1916: 18,000	2	*Dante, Cavour* and *Doria* classes
305/40	12	A 1904	50.65	../385.6	780	11,600	2.1	*Regina Elena* class
254/45	10	A, V 1907	36.8	227/221.9	853–870		2.6	*Pisa* and *San Giorgio* classes
190/45	7.5	A, V 1906–08	14.52	90.9/90.05	864		3.2	*Pisa* and *San Giorgio* classes
152/50	6	V 1913, A 1917–18	8.1	50.0/45.4	870		3.5	
152/45	6	S 1911	7.025	47.0/..	830		3.3	*Doria* class
120/50	4.7	A, V 1909	3.35	22.5	860		6	*Dante, Cavour* class, *Quarto, Bixio* class
120/45	4.7	A 1913, A 1918	4.0	22.0	750	15,400	7	
102/45	4	S, A 1917–19	2.35	16.0	840	14,600	7	Late destroyers
102/35	4	A 1914–15	1.22	15.0	755	11,700	7	*Pilo* and *Sirtori* classes
76/50	3	V 1908, A, V 1909	1.14	5.6/7.0	815		15	*Dante, Cavour* classes
76/45	3	S 1911	0.704	6.5	760		15	*Doria* class
76/45 AA	3	S 1911–14	0.71	6.075	760		14	*Doria* class
76/40	3	A 1912	0.625	5.9	680	9850	15	*Regina Elena* class, destroyers
76/40 AA	3	A 1917	0.66	6.0	680	9675	14	
EX-AUSTRIAN and EX-GERMAN GUNS								
149/47	5.9	Sk 1910	6.3	45.5	880		10	
149/43	5.9	K 1914–17	5.88	45.3	890	17,600	7	*Ancona, Bari, Taranto*
149/42	5.9	K 1916	3.985	45.3/44.9	840		7	*Premuda*
105/45	4.1	K 1913	1.755	16	890	12,200		
100/47	3.9	Sk 1911	2.02	13.75	880		15–20	*Venezia* class ex-Austrian *Tatra* class
66/47	2.6	Sk 1910–14	0.52	4.5	830		20	ex-Austrian *Tatra* class

Notes: A = Armstrong, K = Krupp, S = Schneider, Sk = Skoda, V = Vickers.

ITALIAN TORPEDOES 1906–1921 Official designation	Firm and year of introduction	Calibre (inches)	Explosive charge (kg)	Max length (cm)	Range (metres)/ speed (kts)	Ships so armed
Cold air						
A 90/450	W 1910	17.7	90	483.3	800/34 1000/31 2000/24	
A 95/450	W-SB 1910	17.7	95	520.3	800/34 1000/32.5 2000/36	submarines of *F*, *N*, *H*, *X*, *Micca* and *Pacinotti* classes
A 100/450	W-SB 1914	17.7	100	483.3	800/34 1000/31 2000/24	Mas boats
A 100/450	W-SB 1914	17.7	100	520.3	800/34 1000/32.5 2000/26	submarines
Hot air (with heaters)						
A 100/450	W 1921	17.7	100	414.2	2000/38.5	Mas boats
A 100/450	W 1914	17.7	100	525	1000/42 2000/38	high seas torpedo-boats, *OS*, *AS*, *PN*, *RM*, *CP*, *OL* classes
A 110/450	W 1913	17.7	110	528	2000/38 4000/30 6000/26	All the dreadnoughts, *Regina Elena* class, *San Giorgio* and *Pisa* classes, *Falco* class and more recent destroyers
A 115/450	W 1910	17.7	115	5237	1000/41 2000/36 3000/30	
A 145/450	W 1916	17.7	145	5064	1365/41 3185/29	submarines, *H*, *X*, *W* classes
Ex-AUSTRIAN and EX-GERMAN TORPEDOES						
A 191-e/500	Sch 1917–18	19.7	191	611.9	5000/27	*Ancona*, *Bari*, *Taranto*, *Premuda*, *Ardimentoso*, *Rossarol*
A 191-e/500	Sch 1917–18	19.7	191	7021	5000/35 10,000/28.5	
A 180/533	W 1914	21	180	630 and 637.5	2000/33.7–34.5 6000/30–31.5 7000–28.5–29	*Venezia* class
A 180-bis/533	W 1914	21	180	630 and 637.5	9000/25–27	*Venezia* class

Notes: A before the official designation means Acciaio (= Steel). Firms: Sch = Schwarzkopf, W = Whitehead, W-SB = Whitehead type, built by the Royal Italian Navy at San Bartolomeo (La Spezia).

FLEET STRENGTH 1906

BATTLESHIPS

Name	Launched	Disp (full load, in metric tonnes)	Fate
Duilio class			
DUILIO	8.5.76	12,071t	Stricken 27.6.09
DANDOLO	10.7.78	12,037t	Stricken 23.1.20
Italia class			
ITALIA	29.9.80	15,407t	Stricken 16.11.21
LEPANTO	17.3.83	15,649t	Sold for BU 27.3.15
Ruggiero di Lauria class			
ANDREA DORIA	21.11.85	11,027t	Stricken 25.5.11, BU 1929
FRANCESCO MOROSINI	30.7.85	11,145t	Sunk 15.9.09
RUGGIERO DI LAURIA	9.8.84	10,997t	BU 1946–47
Re Umberto class			
RE UMBERTO	17.10.88	15,454t	Stricken 4.7.20
SARDEGNA	6.7.91	15,426t	Stricken 4.1.23
SICILIA	20.9.90	14,842t	Stricken 4.3.23
Ammiraglio di Saint Bon class			
AMMIRAGLIO DI SAINT BON	29.4.97	10,531t	Stricken 18.6.20
EMANUELE FILIBERTO	29.9.97	9,940t	Stricken 29.3.20
Regina Margherita class			
BENEDETTO BRIN	7.11.01	14,737t	Sunk 27.9.15
REGINA MARGHERITA	30.5.01	14,093t	Sunk 11.12.16
Regina Elena class (Not yet in service in 1906)			
NAPOLI	10.9.05	13,995t	Stricken 3.9.26
REGINA ELENA	19.6.04	14,028t	Stricken 16.2.23
ROMA	21.4.07	13,992t	Stricken 1.9.27
VITTORIO EMANUELE	12.10.04	14,137t	Stricken 1.4.23

Duilio class
Duilio, after having been discarded, was numbered *GM 40* and used as a floating dock for coal and oil, for several years. *Dandolo*, after her rebuilding of 1895–98, had some slight alterations in her armament, which from 1915 (when she served as a local defence ship, first at Brindisi, later at Valona) was: 4–10in/40, 7–6in/40, 5–4.7in/40, 2–3in/40, 16–57mm/43, 2 MGs and 4–17.7in TT.

Italia class
In 1905–06 *Italia*'s six original funnels were reduced to four, and the single central mast was replaced by two separate ones, placed forward of the first funnel and aft the fourth one; 1–5.9in/26, 6–57mm and 8–37mm guns were removed, but two more TT were added. In 1909–10 she served as a torpedo TS, in 1912 as a TS for petty officers, and in 1914 she became the central ship for the defence at Taranto. She was laid up on 1 June 1914 and on 4 June 1914 removed from the Naval List, but on 20 April 1915 towed to Brindisi and on 23 May 1915 reinstated in the Naval List as '*nave sussidiaria di l^classe*'(first class auxiliary ship). She served as a floating battery in the outer harbour of Brindisi (her armament having been reduced to 4–17in guns) until 16 December 1917. In December 1917 she reached La Spezia for her conversion to a cereal carrier, armed with 2–4.7in/32 guns. From 1 June 1919 she served as a cereal carrier under the authority of the Ministry of Transport, and on 27 July 1919 transferred to the State Railways. She was returned to the Navy on 13 January 1921 and finally discarded. *Lepanto* served as a TS for gunners from 1902, her armament having been altered to: 4–17in/27, 4–4.7in/32, 9–57mm/40, 6–37mm/25, 2 MGs, no TT. Discarded on 26 May 1912. Reinstated as a first class auxiliary ship on 13 January 1913, but was eventually discarded on 15 January 1914 and sold for scrap on 27 March 1915.

Ruggiero di Lauria class
Andrea Doria, after having been discarded, was used as a depot ship at Taranto, and later – numbered *GR 104* converted to a floating battery, served in the harbour of Brindisi from 7 April 1915 for the defence of that base. After World War One her hulk was used as a floating oil tank. Scrapped in 1929.

Francesco Morosini, less than one month after being discarded, was used for torpedoing experiments and was sunk on 15 September 1909 at La Spezia. Her wreck was scrapped. *Ruggiero di Lauria*, after having been stricken on 11 November 1909, was numbered *GM 45*, and served at La Spezia as a floating oil depot, and her hull was sunk there by an air raid in World War Two in shallow waters and was scrapped afterwards.

Re Umberto class
Re Umberto was laid up at Genoa in October 1912 and used as a depot ship. Removed from the Naval List on 10 May 1914, she was towed to La Spezia in June 1915 and employed as a depot ship for *Andrea Doria*, the new dreadnought then being completed. She was reinstated in the Naval List on 9 December 1915 as an auxiliary ship and became a floating battery for the defence of Brindisi (March 1916–November 1917) and later of Valona (November 1917–April 1918), her armament having been reduced to 4–13.5in/30. From April to October 1918 she was modified, in Taranto Navy Yard, as an assault ship for the task of forcing the Austrian main base of Pola; her armament consisted of eight shielded 3in guns, and a number of 240mm trench mortars, and she was fitted also with special saws and cutters for use against boom and net defences. About 40 Mas-boats would have followed her. In October 1918 she was transferred to Venice for the raid, but the war ended. *Sardegna* was wartime flagship of the Northern Adriatic Naval Forces until 15 November 1917, then she went to Brindisi as local defence ship with armament reduced to 4–13.5in/30, 4–3in/40, 2 AA MGs; and from 10 July 1918 with the same task at Taranto. Stationary ship at Constantinople 7 November 1919–5 April 1922. *Sicilia* used as depot ship at La Spezia for the dreadnought *Giulio Cesare* then being completed. She was discarded on 9 July 1914, but reinstated on 16 August as an auxiliary ship and used as a depot ship at Taranto for sailors and ammunition, without any armament.

Re Umberto as converted for the attack on Pola

Emmanuele Filiberto during the war

Marco Polo as the troop transport *Cortellazzo* 1918

Ammiraglio di Saint Bon class
In 1911–13 both *Saint Bon* and *Emanuele Filiberto* were fitted with 6 searchlights in newly mounted tops abreast the funnels and the mast; and a rangefinder was mounted on the conning tower. *Emanuele Filiberto* also had her funnels remarkably shortened. The war saved the class from being scrapped in 1914–15. From April 1916 till November 1918 *Saint Bon* served as AA ship for the defence of Venice.

Regina Margherita class
In 1912 the number of 3in guns was increased from 20 to 24. *Benedetto Brin* was sunk in the harbour of Brindisi as a result of Austrian sabotage: the casualties were 595, including 456 dead, among them Rear-Admiral Baron Ernesto Rubin de Cervin. *Regina Margherita* was sunk off Valona by two mines laid by the German submarine *UC 14*.

Regina Elena class
This class formed the 1st Division of the Italian Fleet in the war with Turkey, bombarding Tripoli and seizing Rhodes.

ARMOURED CRUISERS

Name	Launched	Disp	Fate
Marco Polo class			
MARCO POLO	27.10.92	4820t	Stricken 5.1.22, BU
Vettor Pisani class			
CARLO ALBERTO	23.9.96	7057t	Stricken 12.6.20
VETTOR PISANI	14.8.95	7128t	BU 13.3.20
Garibaldi class			
FRANCESCO FERRUCCIO	23.4.02	8100t	Stricken 1.4.30, BU
GIUSEPPE GARIBALDI	29.6.99	8100t	Sunk 18.7.15
VARESE	6.8.99	8100t	Stricken 4.1.23, BU

Marco Polo class
In 1911 her armament was reduced to 6–6in/40, 4–4.7in/40, 6–57mm/40, 2–37mm/20, 1 MG, 4–17.7in TT and 2–75mm field guns. In 1917–18 she was converted in Venice Navy Yard to a troop-transport with her armament removed, and on 4 April 1918 was renamed *Cortellazzo*. Again renamed *Europa* on 1 October 1920 and discarded 16 January 1921, but in the same time reinstated in the Naval List with the name *Volta*.

Vettor Pisani class
Carlo Alberto in 1907–10 used as a TS for torpedo ratings and gunners. In 1917 she began conversion, in Venice NYd, to a troop-transport, and the works were completed in 1918 in Taranto NYd. Recommissioned as a transport on 4 April 1918, receiving the new name *Zenson*. *Vettor Pisani* was at Brindisi and later Taranto, during 1915–18 except for 20 January–18 September 1916 when at Valona. Used as repair-ship from 1 November 1916 to 27 November 1918. Discarded 2 January 1920 and sold for scrapping.

Garibaldi class
All 3 ships helped bombard Tripoli in 1911 and they sank 2 Turkish warships at Beirut on 23 February 1912. *Ferruccio* in 1919 was employed as TS for naval cadets, and in 1924 was actually converted for that task. From 1919 to 1929 (when discarded) she carried out 11 naval training campaigns. *Garibaldi*, flagship of the 5th Battle Squadron (Rear-Adm Trifari), was bombarding enemy railways between Ragusa and Cattaro (Dalmatian coast), when hit by one or two torpedoes fired by the Austrian submarine *U 4* and sunk off Gravosa. *Varese* was employed as a TS for naval cadets from 1920–22.

PROTECTED CRUISERS

Name	Launched	Disp	Fate
Bausan class			
GIOVANNI BAUSAN	15.12.83	3277t	Stricken 15.1.20
Etna class			
ETNA	26.2.85		Stricken 15.5.21
ETTORE FIERAMOSCA	30.8.88	3737t–	Stricken 15.7.09
STROMBOLI	4.2.86	3888t	Stricken 10.3.07
VESUVIO	21.3.86		Stricken 11.5.11
Dogali class			
DOGALI	23.12.85	2050t	BU 1931
Piemonte class			
PIEMONTE	23.8.88	2639t	Stricken 15.5.20
Umbria, or Regions, class			
ELBA	12.8.93		Stricken 5.1.20
ETRURIA	23.4.91		Sunk 13.8.18
LIGURIA	8.6.93	2411t–	Stricken 15.5.21
LOMBARDIA	12.7.90	3110t	Stricken 4.7.20
PUGLIA	22.9.98		Stricken 22.3.23
UMBRIA	23.4.91		Sunk ?1911
Calabria class			
CALABRIA	20.9.94	2660t	Stricken 13.11.24

Bausan class
Giovanni Bausan, after 1913 was employed as a distilling ship and at the same

time as HQ for the Tobruk Naval Command. From 1 July 1916 she was a depot ship for submarines at Brindisi.

Etna class
Etna was converted to a TS in 1905–07, her armament altered to: 4–6in/40, 2–4.7in/40, 2–3in/40, 4–57mm, 2–47mm, 2–37mm, 1 MG and 1–75mm field gun. She was used as a TS until September 1914, but took part in the Libyan War. During 1915–18 she was employed as harbour HQ ship at Taranto, later as a harbour defence ship and lastly as a depot ship and HQ for the Commander-in-Chief, Italian Fleet, at Taranto. *Vesuvio* had her armament altered to: 8–6in, 5–57mm, 6–37mm, 2–57mm revolvers, 3 MGs plus one 75mm field gun.

Dogali class
Dogali, when in Montevideo, was sold on 16 January 1908 to the Uruguayan Government and was renamed *24 de Agosto* and again renamed *Montevideo* in 1910. Stricken in 1914, she was scrapped in 1931.

Piemonte class
In 1906 *Piemonte*'s armament comprised: 2–6in/40, 10–4.7in/40, 10–57mm, 6–37mm, 4–10mm MGs, 2–14in TT. From 1913: 10–4.7in/40, 6–57mm/40, 2–37mm/20, 2–14in TT. In the Italo-Turkish war, after having taken part in it in the Mediterranean, she distinguished herself in the Red Sea, in the action off Kunfida (7 January 1912) against 8 Turkish gunboats and one armed yacht.

Umbria class
The armament of these cruisers was several times altered. In 1906 it comprised 2–6in/40, 8–4.7in/40 plus lesser guns, and 2–17.7in TT (not in *Puglia*). From 1915 *Lombardia* and *Etruria* carried: 6–4.7in/40, 8–57mm/40 (*Etruria*: 6–57mm/40), 2–37mm/20 and 2–17.7in TT; from 1914 *Liguria* had 8–4.7in/40, 8–57mm/40, 2–37mm/20, 2 MGs and 2–17.7in TT. In 1917 *Liguria* was fitted for minelaying with only 6–4.7in/40 and 2–37mm/20. *Elba* from 1907 fitted as a balloon ship and in 1914–15 used as a depot ship for 3 seaplanes. From 1915 she had 6–4.7in/40, 2–37mm/20, 1 MG and 2–17.7in TT. *Liguria* in 1908–11 fitted as balloon ship. *Lombardia* used as a depot ship for submarines from 1908. *Puglia* from 1 July 1916 served as a minelayer, her gun armament having been reduced to 7–3in/45, 1–37mm/43 and 1-40mm/39 MG. *Etruria* was sunk in Leghorn harbour by the explosion of an ammunition barge. *Umbria*, sold to Haiti in 1911, and renamed *Ferrier*, sank because of her new crew's inexperience.

Calabria class
Calabria had her armament altered in 1914 to 6–4.7in/40, 6–57mm/40, 2–37mm/20, 1 MG and 2–17.7in TT. Reclassed as a gunboat in 1921: 1–6in/40, 6–4.7in/40, 8–57mm/40, 2–37mm/20 and 1–40mm/39 MG. In 1924 she served for some months as a TS for gunners before her deletion from the Naval List.

TORPEDO CRUISERS

Name	Launched	Disp	Fate
Tripoli class			
TRIPOLI	25.8.86	952t	Stricken 4.3.23
Goito class			
GOITO	6.7.87	974t	Stricken 15.3.20
MONTEBELLO	14.3.88	955	Stricken 26.1.20
Partenope class			
ARETUSA	14.3.91	833t	Stricken 14.11.12
CALATAFIMI	18.3.93	839t	Stricken 10.3.07
CAPRERA	9.5.94	846t	Stricken 18.5.13
EURIDICE	22.9.90	904t	Stricken 10.3.07
IRIDE	20.7.91	931t	Stricken 6.12.20
MINERVA	27.2.92	846t	Stricken 15.5.21
PARTENOPE	23.12.89	821t	Sunk 23.3.18
URANIA	18.6.91	931t	Stricken 14.1.12
Agordat class			
AGORDAT	11.10.99	1340t	Stricken 4.1.23
COATIT	15.11.99	1292t	Stricken 11.6.20

Tripoli class
Fitted for minelaying in 1897, she was so employed during World War One and was officially classed as a minelayer only on 1 July 1921. Her armament was altered several times: from 1904 to 1909 she had: 1–3in/40, 6–57mm/40, 1–47mm/40 and 3–14in TT; from 1910: 2–3in/40, 4–57mm/40 and 64 mines, no TT.

Goito class
For some time, *Goito* had a fore 4.7in gun mounted experimentally. Since 1897 she was fitted for minelaying. In 1906 *Goito*'s armament consisted of: 7–57mm guns and 4–14in TT; *Montebello*'s: 4–57mm, no TT. *Montebello* employed as a TS for mechanics, at Venice, having been fitted with different types of boilers (2 Pattisons, 2 Yarrows, 2 Thornycrofts), coal and oil burning.

Partenope class
Partenope (1906–08) and *Minerva* (1909–10) were reboilered and converted to minelayers, their armament having been reduced to 2–3in/40, 4–57mm/43 and 2–37mm/20, plus 20 mines each. *Partenope*, after having gallantly fought till her last shot against the German submarine *UC 67*, was sunk by enemy gunfire and torpedo off Tunisia.

Agordat class
Built as protected cruisers, they were reclassed (as scouts) on 4.6.14, but they were slow ships (actually, less than 20 knots) and had a poor endurance. *Agordat*'s armament altered to 2–4.7in/40 and 8–3in/40 guns in 1921, when reclassed as a gunboat. *Coatit* fitted for minelaying in 1919, with armament modified to: 2–4.7in/40 and 4–3in/40.

DISPATCH VESSELS

Name	Launched	Disp	Fate
Folgore class			
SAETTA	30.5.87	401t	Stricken 14.5.08
Rapido class			
RAPIDO	16.11.76	1433t	Stricken 8.9.07
Barbarigo class			
AGOSTINO BARBARIGO	23.1.79	805t	Stricken 5.1.13
MARCANTONIO COLONNA	6.8.79	770t	Stricken 5.1.13
Messaggero class			
MESSAGGERO	13.7.85	1005t	Stricken 11.3.07
Archimede class			
ARCHIMEDE	8.3.87	950t	Sold for BU 22.2.15
GALILEO GALILEI	3.5.87	886t	Stricken 14.12.13

Folgore class
Saetta, only survivor of this class after deletion (12.4.00) of *Folgore*, was used as a TS for gunners. In 1906 she was armed with: 1–3in, 4–57mm, 2–47mm, 1–37mm, 1 revolver 37mm; no TT.

Rapido class
Rapido's armament in 1906 was of 4–57mm. From 1907 to 1912 she served as a harbour hulk at Genoa.

Barbarigo class
In 1906 their armament consisted of 5–57mm and 2 MGs.

Messaggero class
In 1906 *Messaggero*'s armament consisted of 4–57mm and 4–37mm. After deletion, her hulk was employed for several years as a depot ship at Panigaglia (La Spezia).

Archimede class
Archimede in 1906 was armed with: 4–4.7in, 2–57mm, 2–37mm revolvers. After having been discarded, her hulk served for some years as a powder hulk at La Spezia. *Galilei*'s armament was reduced, in 1906, to only 4–57mm, when the ship was modified for being used as a stationary ship at Constantinople, where she remained from July 1907 till September 1911.

***Tripoli* as a minelayer**

***Nembo* as reboilered**

ITALY

DESTROYERS

Name	Fate	Name	Fate
Fulmine class: launched 1898, 342t (full load metric)			
FULMINE	Stricken 15.5.21		
Lampo class: launched 1899–1900, 354t (full load metric)			
DARDO	Stricken 18.3.20	LAMPO	Stricken 18.3.20
EURO	Renamed *Strale* 9.9.24 Stricken 13.11.24	OSTRO	Stricken 30.9.20
FRECCIA	Beached 12.10.11	STRALE	Stricken 13.1.24
Nembo class : launched 1901–1904, 386t (full load metric)			
AQUILONE	Stricken 1923	NEMBO	Sunk 17.10.16
BOREA	Sunk 15.5.17	TURBINE	Sunk 24.5.15
ESPERO	Stricken 1923	ZEFFIRO	Stricken 1924

Fulmine class
Fulmine used 1906–11 for naval cadet training, except for a period (November 1911–May 1912) when she took part in the Italo-Turkish war.

Lampo class
In 1915–18 they were fitted for minelaying (12 or more mines). *Euro* was used as a target 1922–24. On 9 September 1924 she was renamed *Strale. Freccia* lost on 12 October 1911, during the Italo-Turkish war, having been beached at the entrance to Tripoli harbour. Survivors reclassed as torpedo-boats, 1 July 1921.

Nembo class
From 1908–12 all were reboilered for burning fuel oil and the two funnels were increased to three. From 1909 their armament was altered to: 4–3in/40 and 2–17.7in TT. In 1915–18 fitted for minelaying (10–16 mines). After World War One the forward boiler and its funnel were removed together with a 3in gun, and 1 MG was added. *Borea* was sunk off the Albanian coast in action against the Austrian destroyers *Csepel* and *Balaton. Espero* discarded on 16 January 1921 but the same day reinstated with the new name *Turbine*. Finally discarded on 5 April 1923. *Nembo* sunk in the Southern Adriatic by two torpedoes from the Austrian submarine *U 16*, which was herself sunk, probably by the explosion of *Nembo*'s depth charges, when they reached the preset depth. *Turbine* sunk on 24 March 1915 in the Southern Adriatic, in action against the Austrian scout *Helgoland* and the destroyers *Csepel, Tatra* and *Lika*.

TORPEDO-BOATS

Name	Fate	Name	Fate
FIRST CLASS TORPEDO-BOATS			
Aquila class: launched 1888, 150t (full load metric)			
AQUILA	Stricken 1912–14	NIBBIO	Stricken 1912–14
AVVOLTOIO	Stricken 1912–14	SPARVIERO	Stricken 1912–14
FALCO	Stricken 1912–14		
Condore class: launched 1898, 154t			
CONDORE	Stricken 1920		
Pellicano class: launched 1899, 184t			
PELLICANO	Stricken 1920		
Sirio class: launched 1905, 210 metric tonnes			
SAFFO	Grounded 1920	SERPENTE	Sunk 1916
SAGITTARIO	Stricken 1923	SIRIO	Stricken 1923
SCORPIONE	Sunk 1917	SPICA	Stricken 1923
Pegaso class (Perseo group): launched 1905–06, 210 metric tonnes			
PALLADE	Stricken 1923	PERSEO	Sunk 1917
PEGASO	Stricken 1923	PROCIONE	Stricken 1924
SECOND CLASS TORPEDO-BOATS			
Schichau class: launched 1898, 79t			
60 S, 61 S, 62 S, 65 S, 68 S, 70 S, 71 S, 73 S, 75 S, stricken 1907–19			
Yarrow class: launched 1887–95, 119t			
76 YA, 77 YA, 78 YA, 79 YA, stricken 1907–10			
Schichau class: launched 1886–94, 86t			
80 S–92 S, 95 S–98 S, 100 S–109 S, 112 S–153 S, stricken 1907–23			
THIRD CLASS TORPEDO-BOATS			
T class: launched 1882–87, 35–44t			
23 T, 24 T, 26 T, 28 T–32 T, 34 T–38 T, 40 T–46 T, 59 T all discarded 1907–14.			

First class torpedo-boats
All obsolete and with a low naval value in 1906, with some exceptions: *Condore*, in 1912–14 used as a TS for naval cadets, and during 1915–18 used as an ASW escort. *Pellicano* used as TS for naval cadets in 1912–13. *115 S* during the First World War allotted to the Submarine School of the Italian Navy.

GUNBOATS

Name	Launched	Disp	Fate
Guardiano class			
GUARDIANO	1874	271t	Stricken 1923
Curtatone class			
CURTATONE	1888	1292t	Stricken 1913
VOLTURNO	1887	1174t	Stricken 1914
Governolo class			
GOVERNOLO	1894	1203	Stricken 1912

Guardiano class
In 1906 *Guardiano*'s armament comprised only 2–37mm guns.

Curtatone class
Curtatone's armament in 1906 consisted of: 6–57mm, 2–37mm, 2 MGs; *Volturno* retained her original armament, apart from the TT, which was removed.

SUBMARINES

Name	Launched	Disp	Fate
DELFINO	1890	95/107t	Stricken 1918
Glauco class			
GLAUCO	1905	157/161t	Stricken 1916
SQUALO	1906	157/161t	Stricken 1918

MINELAYERS

There was one specialist minelayer: *Castore* (launched 1888, 530 metric tonnes). In the Navy List from 18 July 1891. Originally classed as a gunboat, but in 1898–99 reclassed as a *betta* (= barge) and again reclassed in 1904 as a minelayer. From November 1915 used as a floating torpedo testing craft. Discarded on 8 October 1925.

Of the ships in service in 1906, the following were fitted for minelaying and were eventually classed as minelayers: the cruisers *Liguria, Puglia, Tripoli, Goito, Partenope, Minerva;* all *Lampo* and *Nembo* class destroyers.

Dante Alighieri 29 March 1914

CAPITAL SHIPS

Dante Alighieri 1926

The first Italian dreadnought type battleship, designed by Eng Admiral Edoardo Masdea and Eng Commander Antonino Calabretta. She was the first ship in the world with triple large calibre turrets and the first with medium calibre guns (partially) in turrets, instead of side batteries; and the first Italian capital ship with four propellers. In 1913 she received a 'Curtiss' reconnaissance seaplane. In 1915 her 13–3in/40 guns were replaced by 16–3in/50 guns plus 4–3in/50 AA guns. First Italian dreadnought to be stricken from the Navy List, excluding the sunken *Leonardo da Vinci* (qv).

DANTE ALIGHIERI *battleship*

Displacement: 19,552t normal; 21,600t full load

Dimensions: 518ft 5in wl, 551ft 6in oa × 87ft 3in × 28ft 10in
158.4m, 168.1m × 26.6m × 8.8m

Machinery: 4-shaft Parsons geared turbines, 23 Blechynden boilers (7 oil, 16 mixed), 35,350 projected hp, max 32,190hp = 22.83kts. Range 4800nm/1000nm at 10kts/22kts

Armour: Terni KC. Side 254mm (10in), deck 38mm (1½in), CT 305mm (12in), main turrets 254mm (10in), 4.7in gun turrets and battery 98mm (3⅞in)

Armament: 12–305mm (12in)/46 (4×3), 20–120mm (4.7in)/50 (4×2, 12×1), 13–76mm (3in)/40, 3–450mm (17.7in) TT sub

Complement: 31 + 950

Name	Builder	Laid down	Launched	Comp	Fate
DANTE ALIGHIERI	Castellammare RN Yd	6.6.09	20.8.10	15.1.13	Stricken 1.7.28

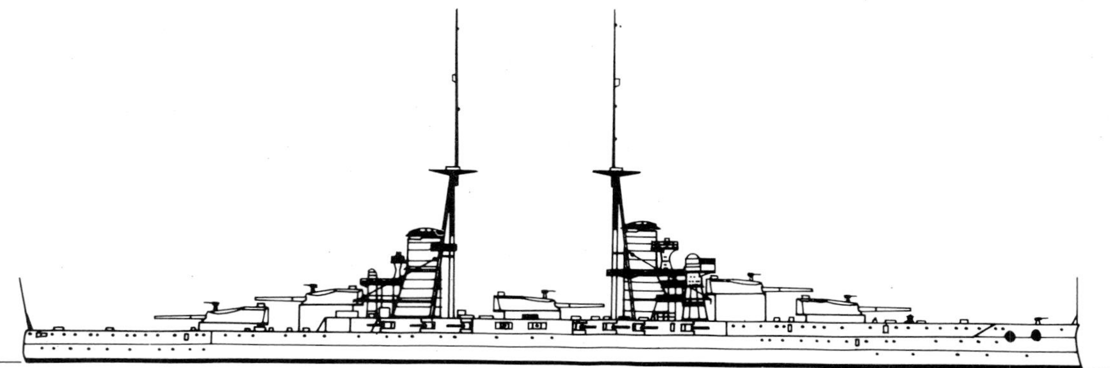

Leonardo da Vinci 1914

First group of Italian dreadnoughts, designed by Eng Adm Edoardo Masdea. During World War One, 4–76mm (3in)/50 AA guns were added, on the top of the main turrets. *Leonardo da Vinci* was sunk on 2 August 1916 at Taranto, by an Austrian sabotage explosion. She was refloated on 17 September 1919 upside down. It was planned to refit her, with the main armament reduced to 10–305mm (12in)/46 (suppressing the amidships turret) and mounting, as AA armament, 6–102mm (4in)/35 guns. But the project was not carried out and the ship was discarded from the Navy List and sold for scrapping on 26 March 1923 at Taranto. In 1921–22 *Cavour*'s and *Cesare*'s fore tripod masts were replaced by quadripod ones, placed forward of the first funnel, for protecting the gun directors from smoke and heat from the boilers. In 1925 both *Cavour* and *Cesare* were provided with an M 18 reconnaissance seaplane, on the top of the central 12in turret. In 1926 *Cavour* was fitted with a catapult, on the fore part of her deck, for launching the seaplane. Reconstruction and modernisation took place from October 1933 to June 1937 *(Cavour)* and from October 1933 to October 1937 *(Cesare)* in CRDA Trieste Yd and Cantieri del Tirreno, Genoa respectively.

CAVOUR class *battleships*

Displacement: 22,992t normal; 24,250t full load (*Cesare* 23,193t–24,801t; *Leonardo* 23,087t–24,677t)

Dimensions: 554ft 1in wl, 557ft 5in oa × 91ft 10in × 30ft 6in (*Cesare* 30ft 10in)
168.9m, 176.0m × 28.0m × 9.3m (9.4m)

Machinery: 4-shaft Parsons geared turbines, 8 oil and 12 mixed Blechynden boilers (*Cesare* 12 and 12 Babcock & Wilcox), 31,278hp = 22.2kts (*Cesare* 30,700hp = 21.56kts; *Leonardo* 32,300hp = 21.6kts. Range 4800nm/1000nm at 10kts/22kts

Armour: Terni KC. Side 254mm (10in), deck 111mm (4½in), CT 279mm (11in), turrets 254mm (10in), MC battery 127mm (5in). Total weight of armour 5150t

Armament: 13–305mm (12in)/46 (3×3, 2×2), 18–120mm (4.7in)/50, 13–76mm (3in)/50 (*Leonardo* 14–76mm (3in)/50, 3–450mm (17.7in) TT sub

Complement: 35 + 1197–1200

Name	Builder	Laid down	Launched	Comp	Fate
CONTE DI CAVOUR	La Spezia RN Yd	10.8.10	10.8.11	1.4.15	Sunk 12.11.40, BU 1947–52
GIULIO CESARE	Ansaldo, Genoa	24.6.10	15.10.11	14.5.14	To USSR 1948
LEONARDO DA VINCI	Odero, Sestri Ponente	18.7.10	14.10.11	17.5.14	Sunk 2.8.16

Giulio Cesare 18 March 1914

Andrea Doria 1 May 1916

Duilio as completed

This class was an improvement of the *Cavour* class. Its construction, the work of Eng Vice-Admiral Giuseppe Valsecchi, involved a larger medium calibre, and the medium guns were disposed in a better arrangement against destroyer and torpedo-boat attacks. The central 12in turret was lowered (in comparison with the *Cavours*) by one deck level and the foremast was placed ahead of the fore funnel, after *Cavour* class experience. While completing, *Doria*'s two funnels were slightly lengthened for improving the draught of the boilers. After World War One the 6–3in/50 AA guns were replaced with 6–3in/40 AA guns plus 2–40mm/39 Vickers MGs. In 1925 both were fitted with an M 18 reconnaissance seaplane, and one year later both were provided with a catapult for the seaplane. Modernisation and reconstruction took place from 8 April 1937 to 26 October 1940 *(Doria)* and from 1 April 1937 to 15 July 1940 in CRDA Trieste Yd and Cantieri del Tirreno, Genoa respectively.

DORIA class *battleships*

Displacement: 22,956t normal; 24,729t full load (*Duilio* 22,994t–24,715t)

Dimensions: 554ft 1in wl, 557ft 5in oa × 91ft 10in × 30ft 10in (*Duilio* 577ft 1in × 91ft 10in × 30ft 10in)
168.9m, 176.0m × 28.0m × 9.4m (176.0m × 28.0m × 9.4m)

Machinery: 4-shaft Parsons geared turbines, 8 oil and 12 mixed Yarrow boilers, 30,000hp = 21kts (*Duilio* 31,009hp = 21.3kts). Range 4800nm at 10kts and about 1000nm at full speed

Armour: Terni KC (*Duilio* Carnegie). Side 254mm (10in), deck 98mm (3⅞), CT 280mm (11in), turrets 280mm (11in), battery 130mm (5⅛in)

Armament: 13–305mm (12in)/46 (3×3, 2×2), 16–152mm (6in)/45, 13–76mm (3in)/50, 6–76mm (3in)/50 AA, 3–450mm (17.7in) TT sub

Complement: 35 + 1198

Name	Builder	Laid down	Launched	Comp	Fate
ANDREA DORIA	La Spezia RN Yd	24.3.12	30.3.13	13.3.16	Stricken 1.11.56
DUILIO	Castellammare RN Yd	24.2.12	24.4.13	10.5.15	Stricken 15.9.56

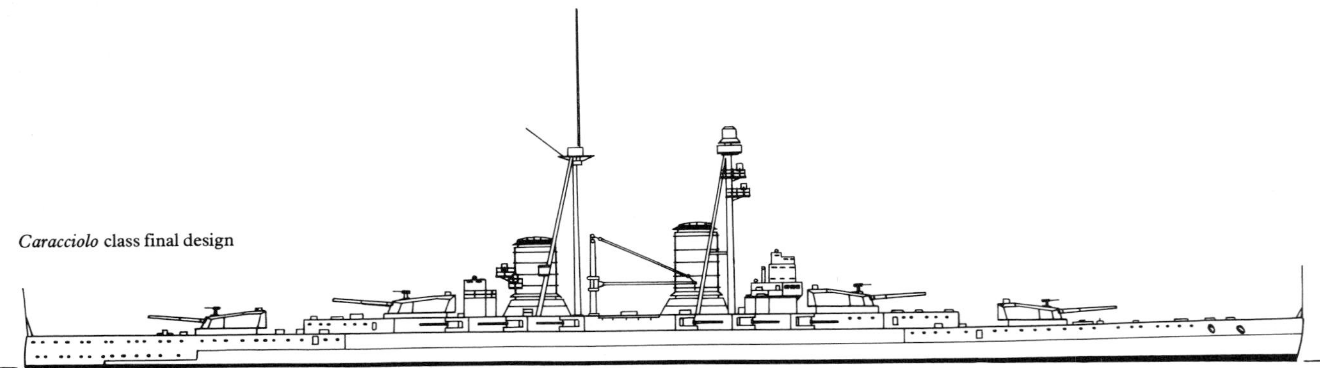

Caracciolo class final design

Designed by Eng Rear-Admiral Edgardo Ferrati. The original plan for these four super-dreadnoughts (the first in the Italian Navy) was for ships armed with 12–15in guns and with 20–6in guns for the medium calibre. The final project provided for battleships similar to the British *Queen Elizabeth* class, with the above armament (8 HC guns, 12 MC guns). But for lack of steel and other materials, and, on the other side, for the need of destroyers, submarines and light craft, the Italian Navy was compelled to abandon the completion of these powerful battleships. *Caracciolo:* construction was suspended in March 1916 when about 9000 tonnes of the hull had been built. Work resumed in October 1919 and the ship was launched, but the hull was sold, on 25 October 1920, to the 'Navigazione Generale Italiana' shipping company, which intended to convert her to a merchant ship. But the hull was dismantled and scrapped *Colombo:* work was suspended in March 1916, when about 12.5 per cent of the hull had been built, 5 per cent of the machinery finished: total construction about 5.5 per cent. *Colonna* and *Morosini*: work suspended soon after beginning. The ships were planned to be commissioned: the first three in 1917, the fourth in 1918.

CARACCIOLO class *battleships*

Displacement: 31,400t normal; 34,000t full load

Dimensions: 661ft 5in wl, 695ft oa × 97ft 1 in × 31ft 2in
201.6m, 212.0m × 29.6m × 9.5m

Machinery: 4-shaft Parsons geared turbines, 20 oil Yarrow boilers, 105,000hp = 28kts. Range 8000nm at 10kts

Armour: Terni KC. Side 303mm (11 15/16in), decks (50mm (2in), CT 400mm (15¾in), turrets 400mm (15¾in), battery 220mm (8⅝in)

Armament: 8–381mm (15in)/40, 12–152mm (6in)/45, 8–102mm (4in)/45, 12–40mm/39 MG, 8–450mm (17.7in) or 533mm (21in) TT

Name	Builder	Laid down	Launched	Comp	Fate
FRANCESCO CARACCIOLO	Castellammare RN Yd	16.10.14	12.5.20		Stricken 2.1.21
CRISTOFORO COLOMBO	Ansaldo, Genoa	14.3.15			Stricken 2.1.21
MARCANTONIO COLONNA	Odero, Sestri Ponente	3.3.15			Stricken 2.1.21
FRANCESCO MOROSINI	Orlando, Leghorn	27.6.15			Stricken 2.1.21

CRUISERS

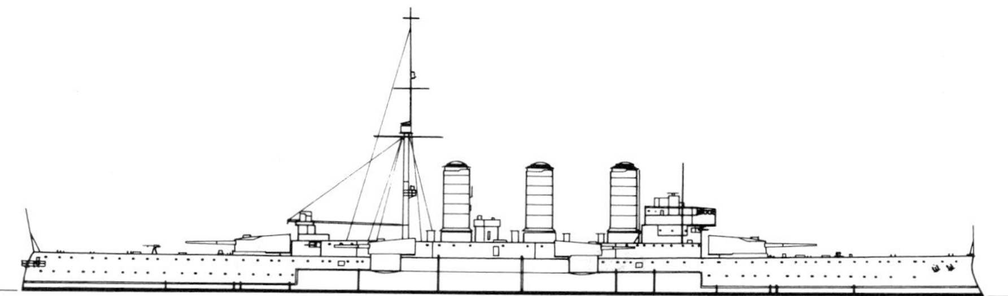

Amalfi 1912

Designed by Eng Giuseppe Orlando, who, within limits, repeated the main data of the *Regina Elena* class of battleships, with minor calibre guns and so on. Work began in August 1904, several months before the keels were laid down. In comparison with their displacement, they were heavily armed ships, but quite inferior to battlecruisers, originated only during the lengthy *Pisa* class construction period. Originally classed as second class battleships, according to Italian classification of that time. *Amalfi* was sunk on 7 July 1915 in the Northern Adriatic by a torpedo from the Austrian submarine *U 26*, which actually was the German *UB 14* (with a German crew), but inscribed in the List of the Austrian Navy, because at that time Italy and Germany were not at war. During World War One a foremast was added to *Pisa* and the 3in and 47mm guns were replaced with 14–3in/40 and 6–3in/40 AA guns. On 1 July 1921 *Pisa* was reclassed as a coastal battleship and employed as a TS. In 1925 she received a M 7 reconnaissance seaplane aboard. During 1925–30 *Pisa* was employed as a TS for naval cadets and special courses for lieutenants.

PISA class *armoured cruisers*

Displacement: 9832t normal; 10,600t full load (*Amalfi* 10,401t)

Dimensions: 426ft 6in wl, 461ft oa × 68ft 11in × 23ft (*Amalfi* 22ft 8in)
130.0m, 140.5m × 21.0m × 7.1m (6.9m)

Machinery: 2-shaft VTE, 22 coal Belleville boilers, projected 20,000ihp, *Pisa* 20,808ihp = 23.47kts, *Amalfi* 20,260ihp = 23.6kts. Range *c*2500nm/*c*1400nm at 12kts/21kts

Armour: Vickers. Side 200mm (7⅞in), deck 130mm (5⅛in), CT 180mm (7⅞in), 10in gun turrets 160mm (6⅜in), 7.5in gun turrets 130mm (5¼in)

Armament: 4–254mm (10in)/45 (2×2), 8–190mm (7.5in)/45 (4×2), 16–76mm (3in)/40, 8–47mm/50, 4 MG, 3–450mm (17.7in) TT sub

Complement: 32 + 652–655

Name	Builder	Laid down	Launched	Comp	Fate
PISA	Orlando, Leghorn	20.2.05	15.9.07	1.9.09	Stricken 28.4.37
AMALFI	Odero, Sestri Ponente	24.7.05	5.5.08	1.9.09	Sunk 7.7.15

Amalfi 30 August 1909

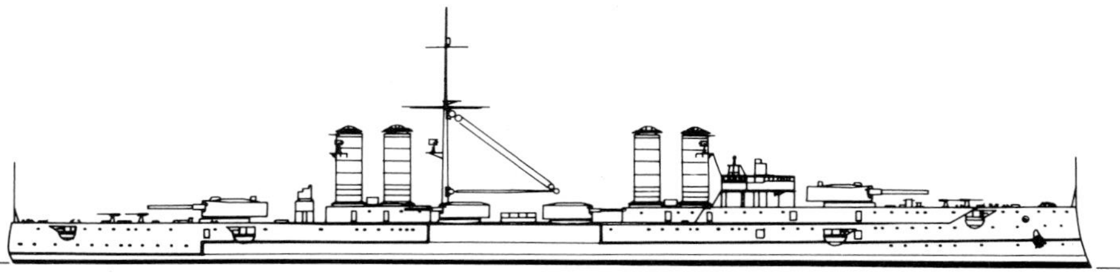

San Marco as completed

The *San Giorgio* class was ordered immediately after the *Pisa* class – *San Giorgio* on 3 August 1904, and *San Marco* on 18 September 1905. The design was the work of Eng VA Edoardo Masdea, who improved on the *Pisa* class. The same armament was employed but with a different disposition of armour, a long forecastle for better seaworthiness, altered machinery distribution and improved habitability. The *San Marco* was experimentally fitted with turbines, which were more powerful than the VTE of the *San Giorgio*. The height of the funnels was shortened after sea trials. Originally fitted with only the mainmast, they were provided also with a foremast in 1916. During World War One the light armament

SAN GIORGIO class *armoured cruisers*

Displacement: 10,167t normal; 11,300t full load (*San Marco* 10,969t–11,900t)

Dimensions: 429ft 9in pp, 462ft 2in oa × 68ft 11in × 24ft (*San Marco* 25ft 3in)
131.0m, 140.8m × 21.0m × 7.3m (7.7m)

Machinery: 2-shaft VTE, 14 mixed Blechynden boilers, designed 19,500ihp, max 19,595ihp = 23.2kts (*San Marco* 4-shaft Parsons turbines, 14 mixed Babcock & Wilcox boilers, 23,000shp projected, max 23,030shp = 23.75kts). Range 6270nm/2640nm at 10kts/20kts (*San Marco* 4800nm/2480nm at 10kts/21.25kts)

Armour: Terni (*San Marco* Midvale). Side 200mm (7⅞in), deck 50mm (2in), CT 254mm (10in), 10in gun turrets 200mm (7⅞in), 7.5in gun turrets 160mm (6¼in)

Armament: 4–254mm (10in)/45 (2×2), 8–190mm (7.5in)/45 (4×2), 18–76mm (3in)/40, 2–47mm/50, 2 MG, 3–450mm (17.7in) TT sub

Complement: 32 + 666–673

Name	Builder	Laid down	Launched	Comp	Fate
SAN GIORGIO	Castellammare RN Yd	4.7.05	27.7.08	1.7.10	Stricken 18.10.46
SAN MARCO	Castellammare RN Yd	2.1.07	20.12.08	7.2.11	Stricken 27.2.47, BU 1949

San Marco on sea trials 18 August 1910

was so modified: 10–3in/40 and 6–3in/40 AA. *San Giorgio* was reconstructed at La Spezia N Yd in 1937–38 as a TS, with light armament modified to 8–3.9in/47 AA (later: 10–3.9in/47 AA), 6–37mm/54 MGs, 12–20mm/65 MGs, 4 (later 14)–13.2mm MGs. No more TT. In World War Two she was used as a floating battery for the defence of Tobruk, where she was scuttled on 22 January 1941 by her commanding officer and some of her crew. Refloated in 1952, she was being towed to Italy when, about 100 miles off Tobruk, having broken the tow-ropes with the tug, she sank in heavy seas.

San Marco was converted in 1931–35 to a radio-controlled (by torpedo-boat *Audace*) target-ship. The boilers were replaced with 4 Thornycroft type (oil) and the machinery capacity was reduced to 13,000hp giving 18kts. This resulted in the following displacement: 8953t normal, 9110t full load. Captured by the Germans at La Spezia on 9 September 1943, she was found sunk, at the end of the war, in La Spezia Navy Yd and was scrapped in 1949.

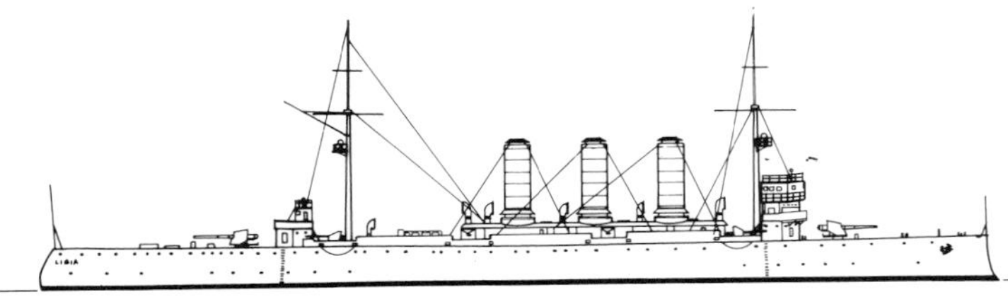
Libia as completed

LIBIA *protected cruiser*

Displacement: 3760t normal; 4466t full load
Dimensions: 339ft 11in wl, 366ft 10in oa × 47ft 7in × 18ft 1in
103.6m, 111.8m × 14.5m × 5.5m
Machinery: 2-shaft VTE, 16 coal Niclausse boilers, projected 12,500ihp, max 11,530ihp = 22.9kts. Range 3150nm/2700nm/1260nm at 10kts/12kts/18kts
Armour: Deck 100mm (3⅞in), CT 100mm (3⅞in), gunshields 76mm (3in)
Armament: 2–152mm (6in)/50, 8–120mm (4.7in)/45, 8–47mm/50, 6–37mm/20, 2–450mm (17.7in) TT aw
Complement: 14 + 300

Name	Builder	Laid down	Launched	Comp	Fate
LIBIA (ex-Turkish *Drama*)	Ansaldo, Genoa	1907	11.11.12	25.3.13	Stricken 11.3.37

Ordered by Turkey from Ansaldo of Genoa in 1910, the plans were very similar to those of the Turkish Elswick-built cruiser *Hamidieh* (built 1902–04). Designed by Elswick-Ansaldo. When Italy declared war on Turkey, the ship was taken over by Italy, her name having been changed to *Libia*. Originally classed, according to Italian naval classification, '*nave da battaglia di 4^ classe*' (fourth class battleship), later '*esploratore*' (scout), notwithstanding her rather low speed, and finally '*incrociatore*' (cruiser) from 1 July 1929. During World War One she received 3–3in/40 AA guns. In 1925 her 6in guns were removed, so her chief armament became the 4.7in guns.

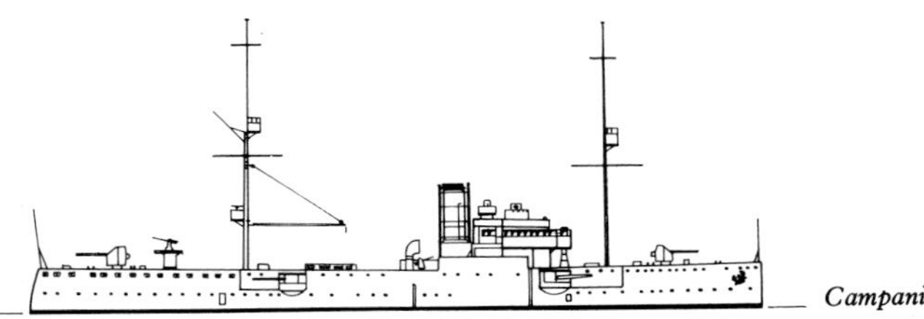
Campania 1918

CAMPANIA class *protected cruisers*

Displacement: 2483t normal; 3187t full load
Dimensions: 252ft wl, 272ft 4in oa × 41ft 8in × 16ft 7in
76.8m, 83.0m × 12.7m × 5.0m
Machinery: 2-shaft VTE, 4 coal cylindrical boilers, 5001ihp = 15.7kts (*Basilicata* 4129ihp = 15.5kts). Range 1850nm at 10kts
Armour: Deck 25mm (1in), CT 50mm (2in)
Armament: 6–152mm (6in)/40, 2–76mm (3in)/40, 3–76mm (3in)/40 AA, 2–47mm/50, 2 MG
Complement: 11 + 193

Name	Builder	Laid down	Launched	Comp	Fate
CAMPANIA	Castellammare RN Yd	9.8.13	23.7.14	18.4.17	Stricken 11.3.37
BASILICATA	Castellammare RN Yd	9.8.13	23.7.14	1.8.17	Sunk 13.8.19,

Designed by Eng Captain Giuseppe Rota, reproducing the old *Calabria* (built 1892–97), for colonial service and with the capability to embark 100 naval cadets each, with all their officers, petty officers, attendants, cooks and equipment. *Basilicata* sank on 13 August 1919, at Tewfik (near Port Said), due to the explosion of one of her boilers. Refloated on 12 September 1920, discarded 15 May 1921 as she was not worth repairing, and sold at Suez for scrapping on 1 July 1921. *Campania*'s armament was reduced to 4–6in guns in 1921–22, plus the lesser guns, and from 1 July 1921 she was reclassed as a gunboat. In 1932 she served as a TS for naval cadets.

Libia 4 June 1914

Campania 20 September 1922

Quarto as completed

One of the more successful ships of the Italian Navy, the *Quarto* was designed by Eng Lt Commander Giulio Truccone, the same who 20 years later, out of service, projected the very fine *Maestrale* class destroyers of 1931, from which all the *Oriani* class (built 1935–37) and *Soldati* class destroyers (built 1937–42) derived. *Quarto*'s draught was so shallow that several times she escaped torpedoes fired from enemy submarines during the 1915–18 war. Their captains had wrongly estimated her real speed, mismeasuring the waves raised by her hull. Until her last days, she could sail at nearly 28kts. Shortly after being commissioned, her aw TTs were converted to sub. In 1926–27 she received a M 18 AR reconnaissance seaplane; and in 1936 three of her 3in were replaced by 13.2mm MGs. In August 1938 one of her boilers blew up. On 5 September 1938 she was reclassed as a cruiser. After being discarded, her hull was towed from La Spezia to Leghorn, for experiments.

QUARTO *scout cruiser*

Displacement: 3271t normal; 3442t full load
Dimensions: 413ft 5in wl, 439ft 9in oa × 42ft × 13ft 5in
126.0m, 131.6m × 12.8m × 4.1m
Machinery: 4-shaft Parsons turbines, 8 oil and 2 mixed Blechynden boilers, projected 25,000hp, max 29,215shp = 28.61kts. Range 2300nm/15kts, 588nm/28kts
Armour: Deck 38mm (1½in), CT 100mm (3⅞in)
Armament: 6–120mm (4.7in)/50, 6–76mm (3in)/50, 2–450mm (17.7in) TT aw, 200 mines
Complement: 13 + 234

Name	Builder	Laid down	Launched	Comp	Fate
QUARTO	Venice RN Yd	14.11.09	19.8.11	31.3.13	Stricken 5.1.39

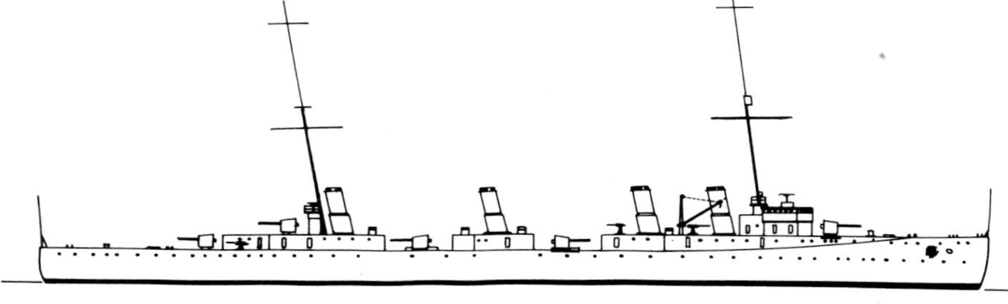

Marsala as completed

Designed by Eng Captain Giuseppe Rota, they had the same armament (but differently arranged) as the *Quarto*. Nevertheless their displacement was greater and, on the contrary, their performance was less good. Only *Marsala* reached the contractual speed (27.5kts) and they were discarded many years earlier than the *Quarto*, because their machinery never ran well. The official publications of the Italian Navy did not state the actual maximum power developed by their machinery and the maximum attained speed. They limited themselves to saying that the contractual power was 22,500hp. In 1915–16 *Marsala*'s boilers were modified, for burning oil only in 12 of them. But *Marsala* was the first to be discarded, two years earlier than her sister ship and more than 11 years earlier than *Quarto*.

BIXIO class *scout cruisers*

Displacement: 3575t normal; 4141t full load
Dimensions: 431ft 1in wl, 160ft 4in oa × 42ft 8in × 13ft 5in
131.4m, 140.3m × 13.0m × 4.1m
Machinery: 3-shaft Curtiss turbines, 14 mixed Blechynden boilers, designed 22,500hp, max *c*23,000shp = 26.82kts (*Marsala* 27.66kts). Range 1400nm at 13kts
Armour: Deck 38mm (1½in), CT 100mm (3⅞in)
Armament: 6–120mm (4.7in)/50, 6–76mm (3in)/50, 2–450mm (17.7in) TT sub, 200 mines
Complement: 13 + 283

Name	Builder	Laid down	Launched	Comp	Fate
NINO BIXIO	Castellammare RN Yd	15.2.11	30.12.11	5.5.14	Stricken 15.3.29
MARSALA	Castellammare RN Yd	15.2.11	24.3.12	4.8.14	Stricken 27.11.27

ITALY

Nino Bixio 23 June 1914

Ex-German MAGDEBURG class *light cruiser*

Displacement: 4570t normal; 5587t full load (German); 5933t full load (Italian)
Dimensions: 427ft 10in wl, 455ft oa × 44ft 0in × 16ft 5in German (18ft 8in Italian)
130.4m, 138.7m × 13.4m × 5.0m (5.7m)
Machinery: 2-shaft Parsons turbines, 16 mixed Thornycroft-Schultz boilers, as designed 25,000hp, max 33,742shp = 28.2kts, Italian, 27,000shp = 27.5kts. Range 5820nm/900nm at 12kts/25kts
Armour: Side 60mm (2⅜), deck 50mm (2in), CT 100mm (3⅞in), gunshields 50mm (2in)
Armament: 7–150mm (5.9in)/43, 2–76mm (3in)/40 AA, 4–500mm (19.7in) TT aw, 120 mines
Complement: 18 + 468

Name	Builder	Laid down	Launched	Acquired	Fate
TARANTO (ex-*Strassburg*)	Kaiserliche Werft, Wilhelmshaven	4.10	24.8.11	20.7.20	Stricken 27.3.47

Designed by Chief Eng Hans Bürkner, she was originally armed with 12–10.5cm/45 (after the German standard of denomination of calibre in centimetres) and 2–19.7in TT sub. From 1915 her armament consisted of: 7–15.0cm/45, 2–8.8cm AA guns and 4–19.7in TT (2 sub, 2 aw). At the same time the boilers, originally burning only coal, were converted for burning oil and coal (*viz* mixed). When commissioned in the Royal Italian Navy on 2 June 1925 she had received some modifications, and her main armament, after the Italian system, was called 7–149mm/43; the two 8.8cm German AA guns were replaced by two Italian built 3in/40 AA guns. In 1926 *Taranto* was fitted with an M7 reconnaissance seaplane; on 19 July 1929 she was reclassed as a cruiser; and in 1931 she received aboard a Cant 24 R reconnaissance seaplane. In 1936–37 the *Taranto* was converted for colonial service; two boilers were removed together with her fore funnel. The resulting speed was of no more than 21kts, which lowered to about 18kts in World War Two. During World War Two her armament consisted of: 7–5.9in/43, 2–3in/40 AA, 8–20mm/65 MGs, 10–13.2mm MGs. She was always able to carry 120 mines. Scuttled by the Italians immediately after the armistice, on 9 September 1943, in La Spezia Navy Yd; refloated by the Germans, sunk by aircraft bombs on 23 October 1943; again refloated but again sunk, 23 September 1944, by aerial bombs in La Spezia roads and broken up in 1946–47.

Quarto about 1914

Ex-Austrian Modified ADMIRAL SPAUN class *scout cruisers*

Displacement: 3500t normal; 4327t full load (*Brindisi* 4375.5t)
Dimensions: 410ft 1in, 428ft 6in oa × 42ft 0in × 14ft 9in normal, 17ft 1in full load
125.0m, 130.6m × 12.8m × 4.5m, 5.2m
Machinery: 2-shaft Melms Pfenninger turbines (*Brindisi* 2-shaft AEG turbines), 16 coal Yarrow boilers, as designed 25,600shp = 27kts: as *Saida*, on 15.4.14, 29,619shp = 27.1kts, as *Helgoland*, on 22.8.14, 29,565shp = 27.3kts. Range 1600nm/860nm at 24kts/27kts
Armament: 9–100mm (3.9in)/47, 1–37mm AA, 4–533mm (21in) TT aw, 120 mines
Complement: 15 + 346–353

Name	Builder	Laid down	Launched	Acquired	Fate
BRINDISI (ex-*Helgoland*)	Danubius Yd, Fiume	28.10.11	23.11.12	19.9.20	Stricken 11.3.37
VENEZIA (ex-*Saida*)	Cantiere Navale Triestino, Monfalcone	9.9.11	26.10.12	19.9.20	Stricken 11.3.37

Fast scouts which were an improvement of the *Admiral Spaun* (built 1908–10) with two more 3.9in guns. Their armament, similar to the Austrian system, was 9–10.0cm/50 which in the Italian Navy were called 9–100mm/47. In 1917 the two scouts were provided also with 1–6.6cm/50 AA gun, which was replaced by a 37mm in the Italian Navy. Their original torpedo armament consisted of 6–17.7in TT aw, which were replaced, during World War One, by 4–21in TT. In the Italian Navy (to which they were transferred under the peace treaty) their machinery attained the following during sea trials: *Brindisi*, 25,600shp and *Venezia* 24,619shp. *Brindisi* was commissioned on 7 June 1923 under the Italian colours, and *Venezia* on 5 July 1921. In her last years, *Brindisi* (1929–37) served as an accommodation ship at Ancona, Pola and at last at Trieste; *Venezia* was used as an accommodation ship 1930–37 at Genoa and finally La Spezia.

Ex-German GRAUDENZ class *light cruiser*

Displacement: 6396t normal; 7486t full load
Dimensions: 438ft 4in wl, 468ft 2in oa (before lengthening of forecastle) × 45ft 3in × 19ft 4in
133.6m, 142.7m × 13.8m × 5.89m
Machinery: 2-shaft Navy turbines, 10 coal and 2 oil Thornycroft-Schultz boilers, 26,000shp = 27.5kts. Range 4500nm/1000nm at 12kts/25kts
Armour: Side 60mm (2⅜in), deck 60mm (2⅜in), CT 100mm (3⅞in), gunshields 50mm (2in)
Armament: 7–150mm (5.9in)/43, 3–76mm (3in)/40 AA, 3–6.5mm MG, 4–500mm (19.7in) TT aw, 120 mines
Complement: 15 + 427

Name	Builder	Laid down	Launched	Acquired	Fate
ANCONA (ex-*Graudenz*)	Kiel N Yd	1912	25.10.13	1.6.20	Stricken 11.3.37

An improved *Madgeburg* class, the *Graudenz* class consisted of two light cruisers. *Graudenz*'s original displacement was 4912t normal, 6382t full load, draught 5.75m (max 6.0m). Originally armed with: 12–10.5cm/45, 2–19.7in TT sub. Rearmed in 1915 with 7–15.0cm/45, 2–8.8cm/45 AA, 4–19.7in TT (2 aw, 2 sub). Complement: 21 + 364. Under Italian colours, she underwent important changes between 1921–24 in Taranto RN Yd. The coal capacity was augmented from normal 380t (max 1280t) to 750t (900t max); fuel oil capacity which had been 100t (375t max) was increased to 580t (1520t max). She was commissioned into the Italian Navy on 6 May 1925. In 1926 *Ancona* was provided with an M7-ter reconnaissance seaplane. Between 1928 and 1929 the forecastle was extended and the bows lengthened for mounting a catapult for the seaplane. Reclassed as a cruiser on 19 July 1929.

Ex-German PILLAU class *light cruiser*

Displacement: 5155.5t normal; 5305.2t full load
Dimensions: 419ft 11in wl, 443ft 11in × 44ft 7in × 18ft 4in
128.0m, 135.3m × 13.6m × 5.6m
Machinery: 2-shaft Parsons-Schichau turbines, 6 coal and 4 oil Yarrow boilers, 28,000hp = 28kts. Range 2600nm at 14kts
Armour: Deck 40mm (1½in), CT 76mm (3in), gunshields 50mm (2in)
Armament: 8–150mm (5.9in)/43, 3–76mm (3in)/40 AA, 2–500mm (19.7in) TT, 120 mines
Complement: 21 + 418

Name	Builder	Laid down	Launched	Acquired	Fate
BARI (ex-*Pillau*)	F Schichau Yd, Danzig	1913	11.4.14	20.7.20	BU 1948

Light cruiser of a class of two ordered by Russia from the German Schichau yard under the name of *Muraviev Amurski*. Her scheduled armament was: 8–130mm (5.1in)/55, 4–63mm/55 AA guns. No side armour. At the outbreak of war with Russia, Germany seized her (and her sister ship *Admiral Nevelskoy*, which was also in the Danzig Schichau Yd) on 5 August 1914 and completed her for its Navy, renaming her *Pillau*. Transferred to Italy under the Peace Treaty and commissioned on 21 January 1924. On 19 July 1929 reclassed as a cruiser. Transformed and rebuilt more times, chiefly in 1934–35 for colonial service: the six coal fore boilers and the fore funnel were removed, widening the oil tanks, so endurance was raised to 4000nm (at 14kts). The power was reduced to 21,000shp with about 24.5kts. The remaining two funnels were shortened. In World War Two her armament of MGs was: 6–20mm/65 and 6–13.2mm. In Spring 1943 *Bari* was to be converted to an all AA escort: probably 6–90mm/50, 8–37mm/54 MGs and 8–20mm/65 or 70 cal. MGs. But she was severely damaged at Leghorn by US bombing on 28 June 1943 and sank in shallow waters two days later. On 8 September she was again damaged by the Italians to avoid the capture of her hull by the Germans. Partially broken up by the Germans at Leghorn 1944. Hull refloated 13 January 1948 and sold to scrappers. Officially discarded 27 February 1947.

DESTROYERS AND TORPEDO-BOATS

In the Italian Navy the following ships were classed as *esploratori leggieri* (light scouts), but actually they were flotilla leaders, as they are classed here.

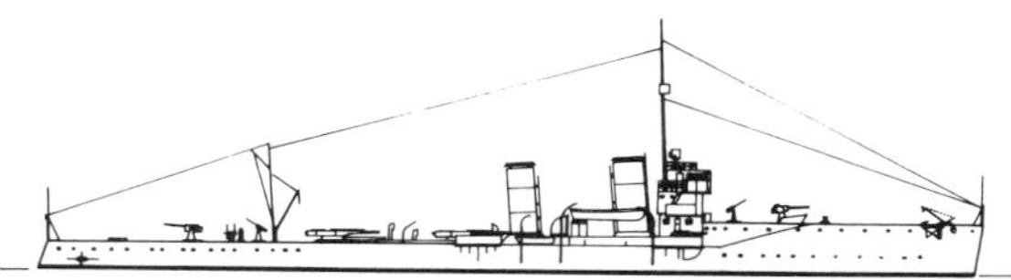
Guglielmo Pepe 1916

POERIO class *flotilla leaders*

Displacement: 1028t normal; 1216t full load
Dimensions: 272ft 8in wl, 278ft 10in oa × 26ft 3in × 9ft 3in normal, 10ft 2in full load
83.1m, 85.0m × 8.0m × 2.8m, 3.1m
Machinery: 2-shaft Belluzzo turbines, 3 Yarrow boilers; 20,000hp designed = 31.5kts. (*Pepe* 24,115shp max = 32.6kts, *Poerio* 32.3kts, *Rossarol* over 31.5kts). Range *c*2100nm/13kts, *c*740nm/31.5kts
Armament: 6–4in (102mm)/35, 4–450mm (17.7in) TT (2×2), 42 mines
Complement: 5 + 124

Name	Builder	Laid down	Launched	Comp	Fate
ALESSANDRO POERIO	Ansaldo, Genoa	25.6.13	4.8.14	25.5.15	Stricken 6.38
GUGLIELMO PEPE	Ansaldo, Genoa	2.7.13	17.9.14	20.8.15	Stricken 6.38
CESARE ROSSAROL	Ansaldo, Genoa	30.6.13	15.8.14	6.8.15	Sunk 16.11.18

Designed by Society Gio Ansaldo & Co, of Genoa, to be armed with a powerful torpedo armament, consisting of 8–17.7in TT (4×2), and 4–4in/35 guns (4×1). Actually the three ships were completed with 6–4in/35 guns and only 4–17.7in TT (2×2). In 1916 *Pepe* was armed also with 2–3in/40 AA guns, but in 1917 these two guns were removed and all three ships were armed with 2 additional 40mm/39 Vickers MGs. In 1918 the 6–4in/35 guns were replaced by 6–4in/45 guns (only 5 guns aboard *Poerio*) *Rossarol* sunk on 16 November 1918 by a mine off Punta Merlera (Istrian coast, Northern Adriatic). On 1 July 1921 the two remaining ships were reclassed as destroyers. For several years following 1924, *Pepe* was provided with a Sperry gyro-stabiliser. In 1927 one out of the two *Poerio*'s 40mm MGs was removed. In June 1938 *Pepe* and *Poerio* were removed from Italy's Naval List and transferred to Nationalist Spain, changing their names respectively to *Teruel* and *Huesca*. Discarded respectively 1947 and 1949.

MIRABELLO class *flotilla leaders*

Displacement: 1784t normal; 1972t full load
Dimensions: 331ft 4in wl, 339ft 5in oa × 10ft 10in normal, 12ft full load
101.1m, 103.75m × 9.7m × 3.3m, 3.6m
Machinery: 2-shaft Parsons turbines, 4 Yarrow boilers. Designed 44,000hp = 35kts (*Mirabello* 44,026shp max = 33.74kts; *Racchia* 43,190shp = 35.4kts; *Riboty* 38,962shp = 35.03kts). Range 2300nm/12kts, 500nm/32kts
Armament: 8–4in (102mm)/35 (*Racchia* and *Riboty* 1–6in/40, 7–4in/35), 2–3in/40 AA, 2–6.5mm Colt MG, 4–450mm (17.7in) TT (2×2), 100 mines (*Riboty* 120)
Complement: 8 + 161

Name	Builder	Laid down	Launched	Comp	Fate
CARLO MIRABELLO	Ansaldo, Genoa	21.11.14	21.12.15	24.8.16	Sunk 21.5.41
CARLO ALBERTO RACCHIA	Ansaldo, Genoa	10.12.14	2.6.16	21.12.16	Sunk 21.7.20
AUGUSTO RIBOTY	Ansaldo, Genoa	27.2.15	24.9.16	5.5.17	BU 1951

First plans, in 1913, provided for 5000-ton ships, lightly armoured. Designed by Eng Capt Nabor Soliani and Society Gio Ansaldo & C, Genoa. Commissioned into the Royal Italian Navy as scouts, they were reclassed as light scouts on 1 July 1921 and reclassed as destroyers on 5 September 1938. In 1917 *Mirabello*'s fore 4in gun was replaced by 1–6in/45, but in 1919 the fore 6in guns were removed from all three ships, because the gun was too heavy, it stressed the hull too much and was too slow in firing. During 1920–22 the class's armament was 8–4in/45 guns, 2–3in/40 AA (replaced, a few months later, by 2–40mm/39 Vickers

MGs) and 2–6.5mm MGs, plus the 4–17.7 in TT. In 1925 *Mirabello* was provided, experimentally and for a short time, with a reconnaissance seaplane. *Racchia* sank, by a mine, off Odessa. *Mirabello* sank by a mine off Cape Dukato (Albania). In 1942 *Riboty*'s 2–4in guns were removed and one more 40mm/39 MG added; and 2–8mm Breda MGs replaced the old 6.5mm Colts. In 1943 the armament was again modified and it was: 4–4in/45, 6–20mm/70 Oerlikon MGs, 2–8mm Breda MGs; no more TT. Allotted to Soviet Russia after World War Two and renumbered *F 3* for her delivery, *Riboty* actually remained in Taranto because she was too old and was scrapped.

Alessandro Poerio on trials 1915

Augusto Riboty about 1919

Nibbio about 1919

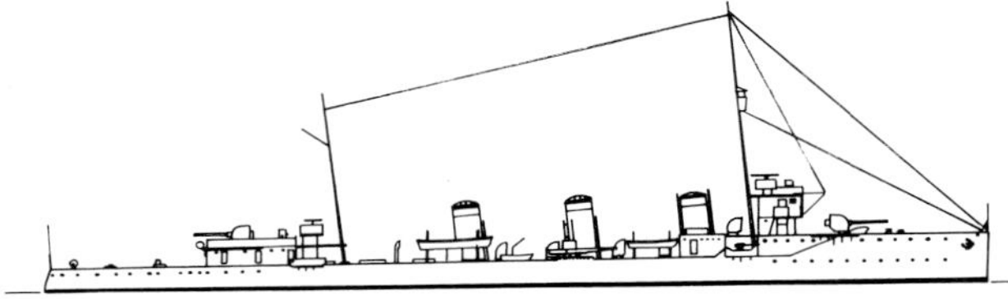

Aquila 1921

AQUILA class *flotilla leaders*

Displacement:	1594t normal; *Aquila* 1733t full load (*Falco, Nibbio, Sparviero* 1760t)
Dimensions:	309ft 5in wl, 310ft 9in oa × 11ft 2in–11ft 10in *94.3m, 94.7m × 9.5m × 3.5m–3.6m*
Machinery:	2-shaft Tosi turbines, 5 Thornycroft boilers, designed 40,000hp = 34kts (*Aquila* 38,925shp max = 36.44kts, *Falco* 35.2kts, *Nibbio* 39,500shp = 37.4kts, *Sparviero* 48,020shp = 38.04kts). Range *c*1700nm/15kts, 380nm/34kts
Armament:	3–6in (152mm)/40, 4–3in/40 (*Falco* 5–4.7in (120mm)/45, 2–3in/40), 2–6.5mm MGs, 4–450mm (17.7in) TT (2×2), 44 (*Nibbio* 24, *Falco* 38) mines
Complement:	9 + 137

Name	Builder	Laid down	Launched	Comp	Fate
AQUILA (ex-*Vifor*)	Pattison, Naples	11.3.14	26.7.17	8.2.17	To Spain 6.1.39
FALCO (ex-*Viscol*)	Pattison, Naples	19.8.16	16.8.19	20.1.20	To Spain 6.1.39
NIBBIO (ex-*Vartez*)	Pattison, Naples	15.7.14	30.1.18	15.5.18	To Rumania 1.7.20
SPARVIERO (ex-*Vijelie*)	Pattison, Naples	29.1.14	25.3.17	15.7.17	To Rumania 1.7.20

The above ships had been ordered in 1913 by Rumania from Pattison Yds of Naples. Designed by Eng Luigi Scaglia, they had to be armed with 3–4.7in/45, 4–75mm/50 and 5 TT, with an endurance of 10 hours at full speed, as they had to operate in the limited waters of the Black Sea. Some few days after Italy entered the war, the four ships were requisitioned (5 June 1915) by the Italian Government when they were complete respectively 60 per cent, not yet laid down, 20 per cent, and 50 per cent. They were entered on the Italian Naval List on 27 July 1916 as scouts and with the above Italian names. The first projected Italian armament was of 7–4in/35 guns and 4–17.7in TT (2×2), but for outgunning the Austrian *Admiral Spaun* class scouts (armed with 3.9in guns), the first three Italian ships were armed with 3–6in/40, 4–3in/40 (plus the TT). However, negative experience with the old and obsolete 3–6in/40 guns (see *Mirabello* class), persuaded the Italian Navy to mount the new 4.7in/45 guns in the fourth ship, *Falco*. After the transfer of *Nibbio* and *Sparviero* to Rumania, *Aquila*'s three 6in guns were replaced by 4–4.7in/45 (2×2), and the fifth 4.7in gun of *Falco* was removed, so the two ships which kept the Italian colours were both armed with 4–4.7in/45 and 2–3in/40 AA guns, plus the 2–6.5mm MGs and the 4–17.7in TT. *Aquila* and *Falco* were reclassed as destroyers on 5 September 1938. Transferred on 11 October 1937 to Nationalist Spain (officially 6 January 1939), and renamed *Melilla*, and *Ceuta* respectively. Definitively discarded 1948.

Nibbio re-transferred to Rumania and renamed *Marasesti*; seized by Soviet Russia (8.44) and renamed *Logkiy*; returned to Rumania and deleted *c*1965. *Sparviero* re-transferred to Rumania and renamed *Marasti*; seized by Soviet Russia (8.44) and renamed *Lovki*; returned to Rumania and deleted *c*1964.

Premuda about 1922

One of the 13 heavy and powerful *Grosse Torpedoboote V 116* had a short life in the Imperial German Navy, and was transferred at Cherbourg to the Italian Navy as a war reparation. *V 116*'s gun armament was differently measured and it resulted as written above. Under the new colours 2 + 2 MGs were added, and the 60cm TT were replaced with 4–500mm (German built). The original number of mines carried was 40. Entered in the Italian Naval List on 1 August 1920 and classed as a scout she was commissioned on 1 June 1921 and reclassed as a destroyer on 15 September 1938. In 1929–30 she was used as a TS for naval cadets. In 1932 all her German TT were removed and replaced by 2–17.7in Italian TT and by 1–4.7in/15 light howitzer.

Ex-German V 116 class *flotilla leader*

Displacement: 2302t normal; 2555t full load
Machinery: 2-shaft Parsons turbines, 4 Thornycroft-Speedy boilers, designed 45,000hp = 34.5kts, max in the Italian Navy 53,975shp = 33.75kts. Range 1900nm/16kts
Armament: 4–149mm (5.9in)/42, 2–40mm/39 and 2–6.5mm MG, 4–500mm (19.7in) TT
Complement: 9 + 153

Name	Builder	Laid down	Launched	Acquired	Fate
PREMUDA (ex-*V 116*)	Vulcan Yd, Stettin	1916	2.3.18	23.5.20	Stricken 1.1.39

Cesare Rossarol about 1930

One of an 8-strong class, *B 97* served in the German Navy from February 1915 until transferred at Cherbourg as a war reparation. She was entered in the Italian Naval List on 19 September 1920 and classed as a scout. Reclassed on 2 June 1921 as a light scout, she was commissioned in the Royal Italian Navy on 1 December 1924 and again reclassed on 1 October, as a destroyer. In summer 1916 4–10.5cm/45 guns replaced the earlier 8.8cm. Her maximum power under German colours was 36,727shp = 35.5kts and designed range was 2600nm at 20kts. In the Italian Navy the armament was modified as written above; her fore funnel was raised *c*4ft. During sea trials (21 December 1923) at 60 per cent of her maximum power, she reached 26.3kts. Probably her top sea speed was then of no more than 29–30kts. In 1931 the 4–500mm German-built TT were replaced by 4–17.7in Italian TT; and her aft boiler was removed to be replaced by a Sperry gyro-stabiliser. From 1932 *Rossarol* was used as an experimental ship and was deprived of all weapons (including minelaying rails), except the fore 4.7in mounting (1×2), but in 1935 the ship was again rearmed

Ex-German B 97 class *flotilla leader*

Displacement: 1655t normal; 1756t full load
Machinery: 2-shaft Parsons turbines, 4 Navy boilers, as designed 40,000hp = 36.5kts (see notes). Range 2600nm/14kts, 780nm/28kts
Armament: 3–4.7in (120mm)/45 (1×2, 1×1), 2–3in/40 AA, 2–6.5mm MG, 4–500mm TT (2×2), 29 mines
Complement: 6 + 144

Name	Builder	Laid down	Launched	Acquired	Fate
CESARE ROSSAROL (ex-*B 97*)	Blohm & Voss, Hamburg	1914	15.12.14	16.9.20	Stricken 17.1.39

Leone as completed

An improvement of the already good *Mirabello* class, the *Leone* class was designed by Society Gio Ansaldo & Co, of Genoa. Five ships were ordered from Ansaldo Yds on 18 January 1917, but for lack of steel and other materials the ships could not be laid down in wartime. A new order, on 30 October 1920, provided for three ships, the other two having been cancelled. Classed as light scouts, and reclassed as destroyers on 5 September 1938. In 1931–32 2–40mm/39 MGs were added and the 6–17.7in TT were replaced by 4–21in TT (2×2). In 1936 the three ships were fitted for colonial service (Red Sea) and the 2–3in guns were removed. In 1938 six MGs were added: 4–13.2mm (2×2) and 2–6.5mm. The complement resulted of 16 + 190 and the displacement at full load was 2648–2691 metric tonnes. *Leone* sank in the Red Sea off Massawa, after striking an uncharted rock while *Pantera* and *Tigre* were scuttled there two nights later.

LEONE class *flotilla leaders*

Displacement: 2195t normal; 2289t full load
Dimensions: 359ft 7in wl, 372ft 1in oa × 33ft 10in × 10ft 8in normal, 11ft 10in full load
109.6m–113.4m × 10.3m × 3.2m, 3.6m
Machinery: 2-shaft Parsons turbines, 4 Yarrow boilers. Designed 42,000hp = 34kts. Maximum *Leone* 45,667shp = 33.7kts, *Pantera* 48,705shp = 34.3kts, *Tigre* 46,272shp = 33.5kts. Range 2000nm/530nm at 15kts/28kts
Armament: 8–4.7in (120mm)/45 (4×2), 2–3in/40 AA, 2–6.5mm MG, 6–17.7in TT (2×3), 60 mines
Complement: 10 × 194

Name	Builder	Laid down	Launched	Comp	Fate
LEONE	Ansaldo, Genoa	23.11.21	1.10.23	1.7.24	Sunk 1.4.41
LEOPARDO	Ansaldo, Genoa				Construction cancelled
LINCE	Ansaldo, Genoa				Construction cancelled
PANTERA	Ansaldo, Genoa	19.12.21	18.10.24	28.10.24	Scuttled 3/4.4.41
TIGRE	Ansaldo, Genoa	23.1.22	7.8.24	10.10.24	Scuttled 3/4.4.41

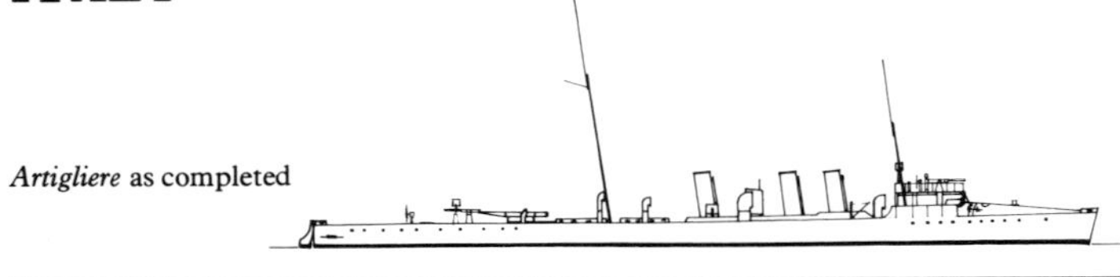
Artigliere as completed

'SOLDATI' class, 1st group (*Artigliere* group) *destroyers*

Displacement: 395t–412t
Dimensions: 211ft 4in wl, 213ft 3in oa × 20ft × 6ft 11in
64.4m, 65.0m × 6.1m × 2.1m
Machinery: 2-shaft VTE, 3 Thornycroft boilers, 6000ihp designed = 28.5kts; max 6392ihp = 28.78kts. Range 1500nm/12kts, 400nm/23.5kts
Armament: 4–3in/40, 3–17.7in (450mm) TT, 10 mines
Complement: 3 + 52

Name	Builder	Launched	Fate
ARTIGLIERE (AR)	Ansaldo, Genoa	18.1.07	Stricken 14.6.23
BERSAGLIERE (BG)	Ansaldo, Genoa	2.10.06	Stricken 5.7.23
CORAZZIERE	Ansaldo, Genoa	11.12.09	Stricken 1.6.28
GARIBALDINO	Ansaldo, Genoa	12.2.10	Sunk 16.7.18
GRANATIERE (GR)	Ansaldo, Genoa	27.10.06	Stricken 3.11.27
LANCIERE	Ansaldo, Genoa	28.2.07	Stricken 4.3.23

Designed by Society Gio Ansaldo & Co, these destroyers were known, when projected and when laid down, as *Nembo* modified type of 28½kts (referring to the *Nembo* class of 1901–04). All the six ships of this group were coal burners. When the W/T was mounted aboard (1910–12), the originally short fore mast was raised to the same height as the main mast. *Garibaldino* sank at night off Villefranche (S France), after collision (ramming) with the destroyer HMS *Cygnet*. All reclassed as torpedo-boats on 1 July 1921. Distinctive letters are given where known.

Pontiere 23 May 1910

Ascaro under construction 1912

Animoso 18 May 1914

'SOLDATI' class, 2nd group (*Alpino* group) *destroyers*

Displacement: 407t–424t
Dimensions: As 1st group
Machinery: 2-shaft VTE, 3 Thornycroft boilers, 6000ihp designed = 28.5kts; max 6911ihp = 29.11kts. Range 1600nm/12kts, 400nm/24kts
Armament: 4–3in/40, 3–17.7in (450mm) TT, 10 mines
Complement: 3 + 47

Name	Builder	Launched	Fate
ALPINO (AP)	Ansaldo, Genoa	27.11.09	Stricken 1.6.28
FUCILIERE (FC and FL)	Ansaldo, Genoa	21.8.09	Stricken 15.12.32
PONTIERE (PN)	Ansaldo, Genoa	3.1.10	Stricken 1.7.29

All the above ships were oil burners and were practically identical to the *Artigliere* group. *Pontiere* was damaged 14 September 1911 by running aground on a rock off Sardinia; partially rebuilt and relaunched on 1 November 1913. All were reclassed as torpedo-boats on 1 July 1921.

ASCARO *destroyer*

Displacement: 396t–414t
Dimensions: As 'Soldati' class
Machinery: 2-shaft VTE, 3 Thornycroft boilers, 6000ihp designed = 28.5kts; max 6416ihp = 28.62kts. Range 1000nm/12kts, 400nm/24kts
Armament: 4–3in/40, 3–17.7in (450mm) TT, 10 mines
Complement: 3 + 52

Name	Builder	Launched	Fate
ASCARO (ex-*Ching Po* or ex-*Tsing Po*)	Ansaldo, Genoa	6.12.12	Stricken 31.5.30

Ordered by the Chinese Government from Ansaldo about 1910, but acquired by the Italian Government in 1912, after agreement with China. The fore boiler burnt oil, the other two boilers, coal. The original projected armament, for China, provided for 2–3in and 4–47mm guns, but it was modified when the ship passed to Italy, in order to have another 'Soldati' class destroyer. Her distinctive letters were AS and AO.

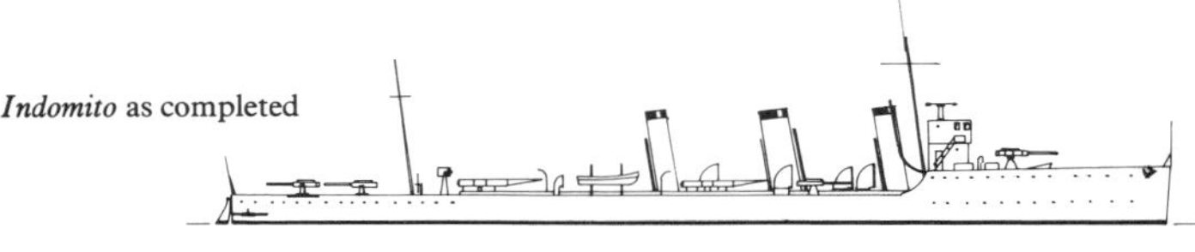
Indomito as completed

INDOMITO (or 'I') class *destroyers*

Displacement: 672t–770t
Dimensions: 237ft 11in wl, 239ft 6in oa × 24ft × 7ft 11in
72.5m, 73.0m × 7.3m × 2.4m
Machinery: 2-shaft Tosi turbines, 4 Thornycroft boilers, 16,000hp designed = 30kts, max 17,620shp = 35.79kts. Range *c*1200nm/14kts, 500nm/25kts, 350nm/30kts
Armament: 1–4.7in (120mm)/40, 4–3in/40, 2–17.7in (450mm) TT
Complement: 4–5 + 65–74

Name	Builder	Launched	Fate
INDOMITO (ID)	Pattison, Naples	10.5.12	Stricken 11.7.37
IMPAVIDO (IV)	Pattison, Naples	22.3.13	Stricken 1.9.37
IMPETUOSO	Pattison, Naples	23.7.13	Sunk 10.7.16
INSIDIOSO (IS)	Pattison, Naples	30.9.13	Sunk 5.11.44
INTREPIDO	Pattison, Naples	7.8.12	Sunk 4.12.15
IRREQUIETO (IR)	Pattison, Naples	12.12.12	Stricken 11.10.37

The first large Italian destroyers and the first fitted with turbines. Designed by Eng Luigi Scaglia of Society Pattison of Naples. In the Italian Navy, from this class onwards all 3-funnelled destroyers (viz till *Generali* class destroyers launched in 1921–22) were commonly known as the 'tre pipe' or 'tre canne', from the number of their funnels. Their armament was modified in 1914, adding two more 17.7in TT; during World War One when guide rails for minelaying were ordered (10 mines); and in 1918–19, when the original guns were replaced by 5–4in/35 plus 1–40mm/39 MG. During World War One their oil capacity was augmented from 100 to 128 tonnes, with an expected greater endurance, but full load displacement reached nearly 900 tonnes so speed and endurance were reduced. All were reclassed as torpedo-boats on 10 October 1929. *Intrepido* sank off Valona by a mine laid from the German submarine *UC 14*. *Impetuoso* sank in the Otranto Straits, by torpedoes from the Austrian submarine *U 17*. *Insidioso* was discarded on 18 September 1938 but reinstated in the Naval List from 1 March 1941: only two funnels, about 24kts and the following armament: 1–4in/45, 4–20mm/70 and 2–13.2mm MGs, 2–21in TT; complement 5 + *c*70. She served as a target ship for the submarine school at Pola, as an escort ship in Adriatic and as an AS craft. Scuttled by her own crew on 10 September 1943 at Pola, she was repaired by the Germans and was commissioned by them on 8 November as *TA 21* = *Wildfang* armed with 2–4in/35, 9–20mm MGs, 2 TTs. Damaged by British aircraft MG fire on 9 August 1944, repaired and definitively sunk at Fiume by torpedo from a US plane.

ARDITO class *destroyers*

Displacement: 695t–790t
Dimensions: As *Indomito* class
Machinery: 2-shaft Parsons turbines, 4 Thornycroft boilers, designed 16,000hp = 30kts, max 15,733shp = 33.4kts. Range *c*1200nm/14kts, 350nm/29kts
Armament: As *Indomito* class
Complement: 4 + 65

Name	Builder	Launched	Fate
ARDITO (AI, AO, AT)	Orlando, Leghorn	20.10.12	Stricken 2.10.31
ARDENTE (AE and AR)	Orlando, Leghorn	15.12.12	Stricken 11.3.37

Nearly identical to the *Indomitos*, but designed by Orlando Yd, Leghorn. They too had alterations in armament: in 1915 their single 17.7in TT were replaced by two twin mountings, and guide rails were set up for minelaying (10 mines). In 1918–20 the original guns were replaced by 5–4in/35, 1–40mm/39 and 2–6.5mm MGs. Both reclassed as torpedo-boats on 1 October 1929.

AUDACE (i) class *destroyers*

Displacement: 750t–840t
Dimensions: 245ft 5in wl, 247ft 9in oa × 24ft 7in × 8ft 6in
74.8m, 75.5m × 7.5m × 2.6m
Machinery: 2-shaft Zoelly turbines, 4 White-Forster boilers, designed 16,000hp = 30kts, max under 15,000shp = 36.1kts. Range *c*950nm/14kts, 300nm/27kts
Armament: As *Indomito* class
Complement: 4–5 + 65–74

Name	Builder	Launched	Fate
AUDACE	Orlando, Leghorn	4.5.13	Sunk 30.8.16
ANIMOSO (AN)	Orlando, Leghorn	13.7.13	Stricken 5.4.23

Orlando Yds modified the Pattison's *Indomitos*, and put in Swiss-built (by Escher-Wyss) turbines that did not reach the performance of the Parsons type turbines built by Ansaldo, Orlando and Tosi. *Audace* sank during the night in the Ionian Sea, after a collision with SS *Brasile* in the convoy which she was escorting. In 1919–20 *Animoso*'s gun armament was modified as for the *Indomitos* and *Arditos*, but with 2–40mm/39 MGs while her torpedo armament remained the original one (2 TT). After a boiler explosion (29 July 1921), *Animoso* was paid off while waiting to be stricken.

Audace (ii) 10 November 1918

Rosolino Pilo as completed

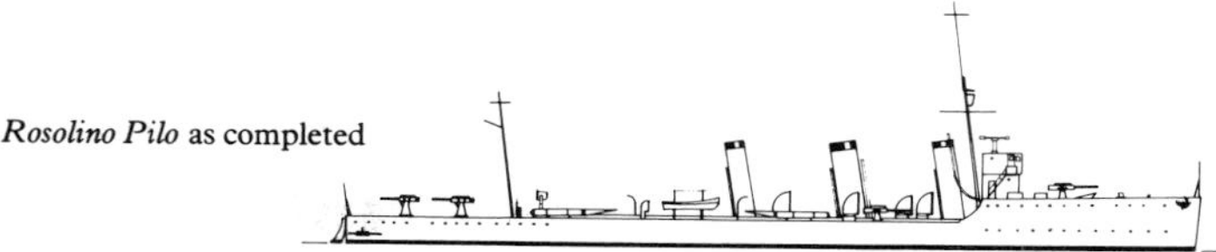

PILO class *destroyers*

Displacement: 770t–*c*850t
Dimensions: 237ft 11in wl, 239ft 6in oa × 24ft × 8ft 1in
72.5m, 73.0m × 7.3m × 2.72m
Machinery: 2-shaft Tosi turbines, 4 Thornycroft boilers, designed 16,000hp = 30kts, max *c*17,000shp for Odero boats, *c*14,800shp for Pattison boats = 33.8–30.4kts. Range 200nm/12kts, 370nm/28kts
Armament: 4–3in/40, 2–3in/40 AA, 4–17.7in (450mm) TT, 10 mines
Complement: 4–5 + 65–74

Name	Builder	Launched	Fate
ROSOLINO PILO (PL)	Odero, Sestri	24.3.15	Stricken 1.10.54
GIUSEPPE CESARE ABBA (AB)	Odero, Sestri	25.5.15	Stricken 1.9.58
PILADE BRONZETTI (BR)	Odero, Sestri	26.10.15	Sunk 3.5.45
GIUSEPPE MISSORI (MS)	Odero, Sestri	20.12.15	Scuttled 3.5.45
ANTONIO MOSTO (MO and MT)	Pattison, Naples	20.5.15	Stricken 15.12.58
IPPOLITO NIEVO (NV)	Odero, Sestri	24.7.15	Stricken 25.4.38
FRANCESCO NULLO	Pattison, Naples	24.7.15	Sunk 23.12.40
SIMONE SCHIAFFINO (SF and SH)	Odero, Sestri	11.9.15	Sunk 24.4.41

An improvement on the *Indomito* class, this class had a single calibre gun armament, stronger torpedo armament, larger tank capacity for fuel oil (150 tonnes instead of 100), more economical turbines for cruising speed, and the guide rails for minelaying set up from the outset. After the First World War the 6–3in guns were replaced by 5–4in/35 guns, 2–40mm/39 and 2–6.5mm MGs. All reclassed as torpedo-boats on 1 October 1929. During 1940–45 the armament was modified to: 2–4in/35, 6–20mm/65, 2 or more 8mm MGs, plus the TT. *Giuseppe Dezza* (*Pilade Bronzetti* was renamed on 16 January 1921) was scuttled on 16 September 1943 in Fiume harbour; seized and repaired by the Germans, who recommissioned her as *TA 35* on 9 June 1944. Sunk by mine in Fasana Channel off Pola on 17 August 1944 but refloated. *Giuseppe Missori* captured by the Germans on 10 September 1943, in Durazzo harbour. Designated *TA 22* under German colours and recommissioned on 3 December. Damaged by the Italian part of her crew (11 August 1944) and towed to Trieste for repair. Scuttled by the Germans in Muggia Bay (near Trieste). Scrapped 1949. *Mosto* and *Cesare Abba* became minesweepers in 1953. *Nullo* and *Schiaffino* were mined off Libya and Cape Bon respectively.

AUDACE (ii) *destroyer*

Displacement: 922t–1170t
Dimensions: 275ft 3in wl, 287ft 1in oa × 27ft 3in × 8ft 2in
83.9m, 87.5m × 8.3m × 2.5m
Machinery: 2-shaft Brown-Curtis turbines, 3 Yarrow boilers, designed 22,000hp = 30kts, max 34.5kts. Range 2180nm/15kts, 560nm/30kts
Armament: 7–4in (102mm)/35, 2–40mm/39 and 2–6.5mm MG, 4–17.7in (450mm) TT (2×2)
Complement: 5 + 113

Name	Builder	Launched	Fate
AUDACE (ii) (ex-*Intrepido*, ex-*Kawakaze*) (AU and AD)	Yarrow, Scotstoun	27.9.16	Sunk 1.11.44

Ordered by the Japanese Navy from Yarrow, together with sister ship *Urakaze*. Under an agreement of 3 July 1916 between the Japanese and Italian navies, transferred to Italy, when still incomplete, with only a part of her armament. Her original Japanese name was changed to *Intrepido* on 5 July 1916, and again 25 September 1916, to *Audace*. The specified 2 diesel engines for cruising speed, with Föttinger hydraulic transmission to the turbines, were not delivered by the builders (German), because of the war. The designed armament consisted, for the Japanese Navy, of 1–4.7in/40 or 45, 4–3in/30 AA, 2–40mm/39 MGs, 4–21in TT. The lateral position of the twin TT was later repeated in Italian-built destroyers. On 1 September 1929 reclassed as a

Generale Achille Papa about 1922

torpedo-boat. In 1937–40 used as the radio-control-ship for the target-ship *San Marco*. From 1942 her armament changed to 2–4in/35, 20–20mm/65 (10×2), no more TT (removed in 1938), and complement of 7 + 120. Seized by the Germans 12 September 1943 in Venice harbour, when not operational, recommissioned under German colours on 21 October with the number *TA 20*. Sunk off Zara (Yugoslavia) by gunfire, in action with two escort destroyers HMS *Avon Vale* and *Wheatland*.

SIRTORI class *destroyers*

Displacement: 790t–*c*850t
Dimensions: 237ft 11in wl, 241ft 2in × 24ft × 9ft 4in
72.5m, 73.5m × 7.3m × 2.8m
Machinery: 2-shaft Tosi turbines, 4 Thornycroft boilers, designed 15,500hp = 30kts, max *c*17,000shp = 33.6kts. Range *c*2000nm/14kts, *c*400nm/29kts
Armament: 6–4in (102mm)/35, 2–40mm/39 and 2–6.5mm MGs, 4–17.7in (450mm) TT (2×2), 10 mines
Complement: 4–5 + *c*80

Name	Builder	Launched	Fate
GIUSEPPE SIRTORI (SR)	Odero, Sestri	24.11.16	Scuttled 25.9.43
GIOVANNI ACERBI (AC)	Odero, Sestri	14.2.17	Sunk 4.4.41
VINCENZO GIORDANO ORSINI (OR)	Odero, Sestri	23.4.17	Scuttled 8.4.41
FRANCESCO STOCCO (ST)	Odero, Sestri	5.6.17	Sunk 24.9.43

An improvement of the *Pilo* class with a higher calibre gun armament and twin TT side mountings. From 1920 the 4in/35 calibre guns were replaced with the more modern 45 calibre guns. All reclassed as torpedo-boats on 1 October 1929. In 1940 their full load displacement nearly reached 900 metric tonnes. *Acerbi* was sunk by a British air attack on Massawa (Eritrea) and *Orsini* scuttled off the port. *Giuseppe Sirtori* severely damaged by German bombs at Corfu on 14 September 1943; she was grounded and scuttled, on the 25th by her crew, in Corfu Straits, to avoid German capture. *Stocco* sunk by German aircraft attack off Corfu.

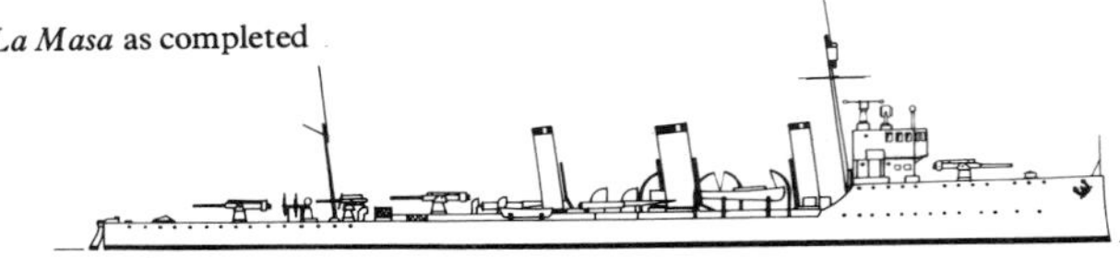

Giuseppe La Masa as completed

LA MASA class *destroyers*

Displacement: 785t–851t
Dimensions: As *Sirtori* class
Machinery: As *Sirtori* class. Range 2230nm/12.5kts, 410nm/28.5kts
Armament: See notes
Complement: 4 + 74

Name	Builder	Launched	Fate
GIUSEPPE LA MASA (LM)	Odero, Sestri	6.9.17	Scuttled 11.9.43
ANGELO BASSINI	Odero Sestri	28.3.18	Sunk 28.5.43
AGOSTINO BERTANI	Odero Sestri	6.6.19	Scuttled 27.9.43
BENEDETTO CAIROLI	Odero, Sestri	28.12.17	Sunk 10.4.18
GIACINTO CARINI (CA and CR)	Odero, Sestri	7.11.17	Stricken 31.12.58
NICOLA FABRIZI	Odero, Sestri	8.7.18	Stricken 1.2.57
GIUSEPPE LA FARINA	Odero, Sestri	12.3.19	Sunk 4.5.41
GIACOMO MEDICI (MD)	Odero, Sestri	6.9.18	Sunk 16.4.43

This class, designed by Odero Yards of Sestri Ponente, was also known as the third series of the improved *Indomito*s, and repeated the *Sirtori* class with some alterations: only 4–4in guns, but 45 calibres long and differently placed; 2–3in/40 AA guns instead of the 2–40mm/39 MGs. *Benedetto Cairoli* sank, at night, in the Ionian Sea, after colliding with her sister ship *Giacinto Carini*. *Agostino Bertani* was renamed *Enrico Cosenz* on 16 January 1921. The ships were reclassed as torpedo-boats on 1 October 1929. *La Farina* sunk near buoy no 4 off Kerkennah Is (Tunisia), probably by mine. During the Second World War the armament was modified: *Bassini*, *Cosenz*, *Fabrizi* and *Medici* had 3 or 2–4in/45 guns, 6–20mm/65 MGs and 2 or 4–17.7in TT; *Carini* and *La Masa* had 1–4in/45, 8–20mm/65 MGs, 3–21in (1×3) and 2–17.7in (1×2) TT. *Bassini* sunk in Leghorn harbour by bombing. *Cosenz* (ex-*Bertani*) damaged in collision with SS *Ulisse*, on 25 September 1943 off Lagosta; severely damaged by German bombs; scuttled by her crew at Lagosta. *Carini* converted to minesweeper in 1953; stricken from the Naval List, but used for several years as a training hulk for schools (distinctive letters: *GM 517*) at La Maddalena, Sardinia. *Fabrizi* converted to minesweeper in 1952. *La Masa* scuttled in Naples harbour, where she was under repair. *Medici* sunk in Catania harbour, by aircraft bomb; her wreck refloated in 1952 and scrapped.

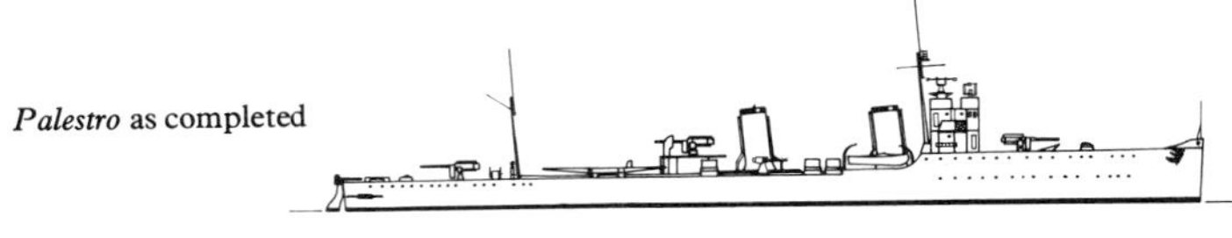

Palestro as completed

PALESTRO class *destroyers*

Displacement: 875t–1076t
Dimensions: 262ft 6in wl, 268ft 8in oa × 26ft 3in × 8ft 10in normal, 9ft 2in full load
80.0m, 81.9m × 8.0m × 2.7m, 2.8m
Machinery: 2-shaft Zoelly turbines, 4 Thornycroft boilers, designed 18,000hp = 32kts, (max *Confienza* 33.2kts, *Palestro* 32.4kts, *San Martino* 31.1kts, *Solferino* 31.9kts). Range 1970nm/15kts, 370nm/27kts
Armament: 4–4in (102mm)/45, 2–3in/40 AA, 2–6.5mm MG, 4–17.7in (450mm) TT (2×2), 10–38 mines
Complement: 5–6 + 112

Name	Builder	Launched	Fate
PALESTRO (PT)	Orlando, Leghorn	23.3.19	Sunk 22.9.40
CONFIENZA (CF)	Orlando, Leghorn	18.12.20	Sunk 20.11.40
SAN MARTINO (SM)	Orlando, Leghorn	8.9.20	Sunk 12.10.44
SOLFERINO (SL)	Orlando, Leghorn	28.4.20	Sunk 19.10.44

This class was an enlargement and improvement of the *Audace* (i) class, laid down in 1912 and launched in 1913. Eight destroyers were ordered by the Italian Navy from Orlando on 31 December 1915, but owing to lack of steel and other materials only the first four (*Palestro* class) could be laid down in wartime, late in April–May 1917, and completed after the end of the war (from January 1921 to April 1923). In 1930 their fore funnel was remarkably lengthened. On 1 October 1938 the ships were reclassed as torpedo-boats. Immediately before World War Two, it was projected to replace the central 4in gun and the two 3in AA guns with 4–20mm MGs (1×2, 2×1), but this plan was not carried out. *Confienza* sank in collision with the AMC *Capitano A Cecchi* off Brindisi. *Palestro* sank off Durazzo by a torpedo from HM Submarine *Osiris*. *San Martino* captured by the Germans in the Piraeus on 9 September 1943, recommissioned under German colours on 28 October with the designation *TA 18*, changed on 16 November to *TA 17*. Her German armament was: 3–4in/45, 6–20mm/65 MGs, 4–17.7in TT. Severely damaged at Piraeus 18 September 1944 by British bombing and sunk there by another British air raid. *Solferino* captured by the Germans in Suda Bay (Crete) on 9 September 1943, recommissioned 25 July 1944 under their colours as *TA 18*, with 4–4in/45, 2–20mm/65 MGs, no TT. Sunk off Volos (Greece) in action with the British destroyers *Termagant* and *Tuscan*.

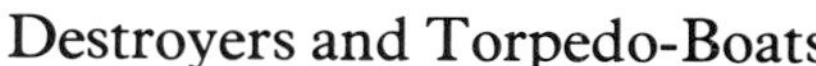

Giovanni Acerbi November 1917

'GENERALI' or CANTORE class *destroyers*

Displacement: 810t–870.4t
Dimensions: 236ft 5in wl, 239ft 8in × 23ft 11in × 8ft 10in normal, 9ft 10in full load
72.5m, 73.5m × 7.3m × 2.7m, 3.0m
Machinery: 2-shaft Tosi turbines, 4 Thornycroft boilers, designed 15,500hp = 30kts (max *Cantore* 33.20, *Cascino* 32.71, *Chinotto* 32.31, *Montanari* 32.70, *Papa* 32.32, *Prestinari* 32.71kts). Range 1995–2237nm/14kts, 400nm/30kts
Armament: 3–4in (102mm)/45, 2–3in/40 AA, 4–17.7in (450mm) TT (2×2)
Complement: 6 + 100

Name	Builder	Launched	Fate
GENERALE ANTONIO CANTORE (CE)	Odero, Sestri	23.4.21	Sunk 22.8.42
GENERALE ANTONINO CASCINO (CI)	Odero, Sestri	18.3.22	Scuttled 9.9.43
GENERALE ANTONIO CHINOTTO (CH)	Odero, Sestri	7.8.21	Sunk 28.3.41
GENERALE CARLO MONTANARI (MN)	Odero, Sestri	4.10.22	Scuttled 4.10.44
GENERALE ACHILLE PAPA (PP later PA)	Odero, Sestri	8.12.21	Sunk 25.4.45
GENERALE MARCELLO PRESTINARI (PR)	Odero, Sestri	4.7.22	Sunk 31.1.43

An improvement of the *La Masa* class and therefore the 4th series of improved *Indomito*s, with only 3–4in guns, but placed in the centre line, so the broadside firepower was the same. All reclassed as torpedo-boats on 1 October 1929. From 1939 the 2–3in/40 AA guns were replaced by 4–20mm/65 and from 2 to 4–8mm MGs. *Cantore* sunk by mine off Ras-el-Tin (Libya). *Cascino* scuttled at La Spezia. *Chinotto* sunk by mines, off Palermo. *Montanari* scuttled at La Spezia, by her own crew on 9 September 1943; rescued by the Germans, but not employed by them, and again scuttled. Wreck refloated 1949 and scuttled. *Papa* scuttled at La Spezia by her crew, captured by the Germans who recommissioned her on 17 October 1943 as *TA 7*, but next day renamed again as *SG 20*. New German armament: 2–37mm/54, 16–20mm/65 or 70 MGs. Damaged by mine 1 November 1943; sunk 6 January 1944 in Genoa harbour and towed to beach on 12 January. Hit by aircraft bombs. Wreck towed to Oneglia for blocking that harbour and sunk at its entrance, *Prestinari* sunk by mine off Sicily.

Improved 'INDOMITO' (5th series) class *destroyers*

The Italian Navy ordered another class of six-700 metric tonnes destroyers from Pattison Yards, of Naples (names not yet allotted), but cancelled it by the end of the 1914–18 war.

Ex-German S 49 class *destroyer*

Displacement: 1050t–1130t
Machinery: See notes. Range 1960nm/17kts, 616nm/26kts
Armament: 3–3.9in (100mm)/47, 2–40mm/39, 2–6.5mm MG, 4–500mm (19.7in) TT (2×2), 24 mines
Complement: 5 + 106

Name	Builder	Acquired	Fate
ARDIMENTOSO (AM) (ex-*S 63*)	Schichau, Elbing	23.5.20	Stricken 4.2.39

Transferred at Cherbourg as a war reparation and renamed *Ardimentoso*. Commissioned on 1 October 1925. Modified and partially rebuilt 1921–25 in Taranto Navy Yd. The Italian displacement resulted as above specified. During sea trials, with 60 per cent power, the attained speed was 25.6kts. Probably, at full power, the speed would have been of *c*30kts. In 1933 the two twin 500mm TT centre line mountings were removed and replaced by two Italian-built 17.7in twin side mountings. From 1931 *Ardimentoso* was used as a TS for gunners and rangetakers at Pola.

Ex-Austrian TÁTRA class *destroyers*

Displacement: 847t–908t normal; 1035.6t–1070t full load
Machinery: 2-shaft AEG Curtis turbines, 6 Yarrow boilers (2 coal burners, 4 oil burners), designed 20,600hp = 32.5kts (*Csepel* 23,398shp = 32.9kts, *Orjen* 23,700shp = 33.46kts, *Lika* (ii) 21,300shp = 33.6kts, *Uzsok* 22,500shp = 33.6kts). Range 1600nm/12kts, 360nm/30kts
Armament: 2–3.9in (100mm)/47, 4–66mm/47 and 2–66mm/47 AA, 2–6.5mm MG, 4–17.7in (450mm) TT (2×2)
Complement: 5 + 114

Name	Builder	Acquired	Fate
FASANA (ex-*Tátra*)	Danubius Yd, Porto Rè	26.9.20	Stricken 5.7.23
MUGGIA (MG) (ex-*Csepel*)	Danubius Yd, Porto Rè	26.9.20	Lost 25.3.29
POLA (PA) (ex-*Orjen*)	Danubius Yd, Porto Rè	26.9.20	Stricken 1.5.37
ZENSON (i) (ZS and ZN) (ex-*Balaton*)	Danubius Yd, Porto Rè	26.9.20	Stricken 5.7.23
CORTELLAZZO (CZ) (ex-*Lika* (ii)	Danubius Yd, Porto Rè	26.9.20	Stricken 5.1.39
GRADO (GD) (ex-*Triglav* (ii)	Danubius Yd, Porto Rè	26.9.20	Stricken 30.9.37
MONFALCONE (MF) (ex-*Uzsok*)	Danubius Yd, Porto Rè	26.9.20	Stricken 5.1.39

Best and strongest destroyers of the Austro-Hungarian Navy, transferred to Italy as war reparations. *Fasana* and *Zenson* (i) were neither refitted nor commissioned into the Italian Navy because of their poor condition. The original Austrian armament consisted of 2–10cm/50 and 6–6.6cm/45 guns and 4–53.3cm TT (2×2). When refitted in Italian hands, the 21in TT were replaced by 4–17.7in TT (2×2), and 2–6.5mm MGs were added. *Muggia* was lost after grounding in fog and at night, on a rock off Hea Chu Is (China). *Pola* was renamed *Zenson* (ii) on 9 April 1931. The remaining ships reclassed as torpedo-boats 1 October 1929. Maximum speed attained under Italian colours: *Pola* 33.5kts, *Cortellazzo* 32.9kts.

Grado 16 May 1932

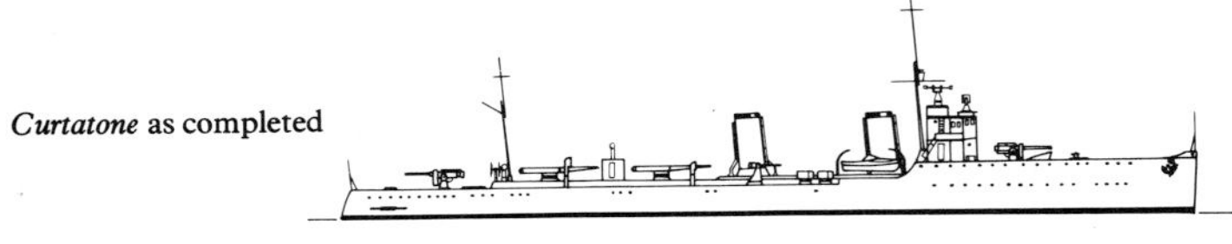
Curtatone as completed

CURTATONE class *destroyers*

Displacement: 1107t–1214t
Dimensions: 277ft 7in wl, 278ft oa × 26ft 3in × 9ft 6in normal, 9ft 10in full load
84.6m, 84.7m × 8.0m × 2.9m, 3.0m
Machinery: 2-shaft Zoelly turbines, 4 Thornycroft boilers, designed 22,000hp = 32kts. (*Calatafimi* 33.3kts, *Castelfidardo* 33.5kts, *Curtatone* 33.6kts, *Monzambano* 33.54kts). Range *c*2200nm/15kts, 460nm/28kts
Armament: 4–4in (102mm)/45 (2×2), 2–3in/30 AA, 6–17.7in (450mm) TT (2×3), 16 mines
Complement: 6–7 + *c*110

Name	Builder	Launched	Fate
CALATAFIMI (CM)	Orlando, Leghorn	17.3.23	Sunk 9.8.44
CASTELFIDARDO (CD)	Orlando, Leghorn	4.6.22	Sunk 2.6.44
CURTATONE (CT)	Orlando, Leghorn	17.3.22	Sunk 20.5.41
MONZAMBANO (MB)	Orlando, Leghorn	6.8.23	Stricken 15.4.51

Ordered by the Italian Navy on 31 December 1915, at the same time as the 4 *Palestros*, but, owing to lack of steel, their construction was postponed and their design – originally identical to the *Palestros* – was modified on the basis of the experience gained with the name ship of that class. So the *Curtatones* were 4.51m longer also for attaining a higher speed, and were fitted with twin mountings for the 4in guns and triple mountings for the TT: these were respectively the first twin gun mountings and the first TT triple mounting aboard Italian destroyers. The first ship, *Curtatone*, was laid down on 3 January 1920. As for the *Palestros*, their fore funnel was considerably lengthened *c*1930–32. Reclassed as torpedo-boats 1 October 1938. During World War Two the 2–3in guns were replaced by 2–20mm/70 MGs and 2–8mm MGs were added. *Curtatone* sunk by explosion of one or two mines in Saronikos. In 1942–43 *Calatafimi*'s and *Monzambano*'s aft twin gun mounting was replaced by one single gun, and *Calatafimi*'s 6–17.7in TT were replaced by 2–21in TT (1×2). *Calatafimi* was captured on 10 September 1943 by the Germans at the Piraeus and recommissioned by them on the 13th, renamed *Achilles*. Her armament under German colours was: 2–4in/45, 1–35mm AA, 5–20mm MGs, 2–21in TT. On 28 October she was renamed *TA 15* and again renamed on 16 November *TA 19*. Sunk by torpedo from the Greek submarine *Pipinos*, near Vathi. *Castelfidardo* captured by the Germans in Suda Bay on 9 September 1943 and recommissioned by them on 14 October with name *TA 16* and armament: 4–4in/45, 4–20mm MGs, 6–17.7in TTs. Sunk at Heraklion (Crete) by British aircraft rockets. There was an abortive attempt to refloat her on 13 June. *Monzambano* in 1946–47 had her armament altered to: 2–4in/45, 6–20mm/65 MGs (3×2), 2–21in TT (1×2).

Albatros date unknown

Orsa date unknown

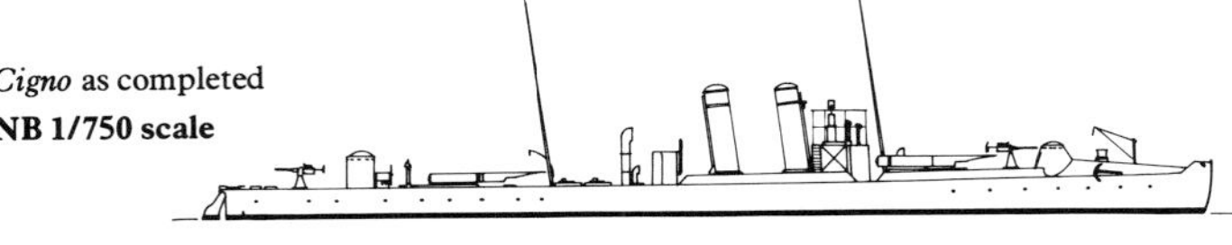
Cigno as completed
NB 1/750 scale

PEGASO class (*Cigno* group) *torpedo-boats*

Displacement: 216.5t (*Calipso* and *Climene* 208.1t)
Dimensions: 164ft 1in wl, 173ft 11in oa × 17ft 5in × 5ft 10in (*Calipso* and *Climene* 5ft 7in)
50.0m, 50.3m × 5.3m × 1.7m (1.72m)
Machinery: 2-shaft VTE, 2 coal Thornycroft boilers (see notes), designed 2900ihp = 25kts, max 3255ihp = 26.5kts for coal *c*330nm/25kts
Armament: 3–47mm/53, 3–17.7in (450mm) TT
Complement: 3 + 35 (*Calipso* and *Climene* 3 + 32)

Name	Builder	Launched	Fate
CALIPSO	Pattison, Naples	26.4.09	Stricken 1927
CALLIOPE	Pattison, Naples	27.8.06	Stricken 1924
CANOPO (CN)	Pattison, Naples	28.2.07	Stricken 1923
CASSIOPEA	Pattison, Naples	5.7.06	Stricken 1927
CENTAURO (CT)	Pattison, Naples	20.12.06	Sunk 5.11.21
CIGNO	Pattison, Naples	9.5.06	Stricken 1923
CLIMENE	Pattison, Naples	15.5.09	Stricken 1926
CLIO	Pattison, Naples	20.10.06	Stricken 1927

Good and seaworthy boats, built to a Thornycroft design. Their displacement was slightly heavier than in *Perseo* group, as plates were thicker; yet *Calipso* and *Climene*, were *c*8t lighter, since their completion, fitted with oil burning boilers; and had a greater endurance. In 1917–20 the armament of all boats was replaced by 2–3in/40, 1–13.2mm MG, 2–17.7in TT (2×1, but one boat or more 1×2). *Cassiopea* and *Climene* employed as fast minesweepers in 1915–18. *Centauro* grounded at night in the Gulf of Adalia (Turkey) and sank.

PEGASO class (*Alcione* group) *torpedo-boats*

Particulars: As *Cigno* group

Name	Builder	Launched	Fate
AIRONE (AI)	Odero, Sestri	13.5.07	Stricken 1923
ALBATROS (AB)	Odero, Sestri	22.1.07	Stricken 1923
ALCIONE	Odero, Sestri	13.9.06	Stricken 1923
ARDEA	Odero, Sestri	10.1.07	Stricken 1923
ARPIA	Odero, Sestri	22.8.07	Stricken 1923
ASTORE	Odero, Sestri	22.6.07	Stricken 1923

Practically identical to *Cigno* group. In 1910–13 *Airone*, *Alcione* and *Ardea* were converted to oil burners. In World War One armament altered to 1–3in/40, 1–3in/30 AA, 1–13.2mm MG, 2–17.7in TT. From 1918 *Airone*, from 1917 *Alcione* and *Arpia* converted to fast minesweepers. *Arpia* severely damaged on 17 January 1918 off Porto d'Ascoli in the Adriatic having struck the uncharted wreck of the Neapolitan frigate *Torquato Tasso* (grounded 10 January 1860 and sunk 21 February 1860). *Arpia* sank in shallow water between Porto d'Ascoli and San Benedetto del Tronto, was refloated, towed to Ancona, put again on slip and repaired. Returned to service on 25 July 1918.

ORIONE class *torpedo-boats*

Displacement: 220t
Dimensions: 167ft 4in wl, 172ft 7in oa × 19ft 8in × 4ft 11in
52.6m, 51.0m × 6.0m × 1.5m
Machinery: 2-shaft VTE, 2 coal burning Blechynden boilers, designed 2900hp = 25kts, max 3246ihp = 25.4kts. Range *c*300nm/24kts
Other particulars: As *Pegaso* class

Name	Builder	Launched	Fate
OLIMPIA	Odero, Sestri	17.7.06	Stricken 1920
ORFEO	Odero, Sestri	23.4.07	Stricken 1923
ORIONE	Odero, Sestri	29.3.06	Stricken 1923
ORSA	Odero, Sestri	5.5.06	Stricken 1921

Designed by Odero they had the same displacement and armament as the *Pegaso* class, but were different in the shape of their hulls and bottoms, and in their machinery. They were not so good and seaworthy as the *Pegaso* class and in few years they lost 5kts of speed. In 1915–18 their armament was modifed to: 2–3in/30 AA, 1–13.2mm MG, 2–17.7in TT.

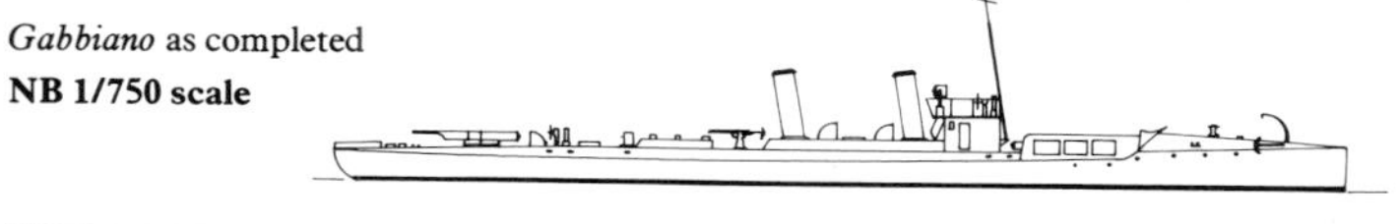
Gabbiano as completed
NB 1/750 scale

GABBIANO *torpedo-boat*

Displacement: 161.8t normal; 174t full load
Dimensions: 159ft 1in wl × 162ft 9in oa × 19ft 4in × 5ft 7in
48.5m, 49.6m × 5.9m × 1.7m
Machinery: 2-shaft compound, 2 oil modified Normand boilers, designed 2200hp = 22kts, max *c*23kts. Range 2440nm/10kts, 750nm/17kts
Armament: 2–47mm/40, 3–14in (356mm) TT, 14 mines
Complement: 2 + 30

Name	Builder	Launched	Fate
GABBIANO	La Spezia NY	9.4.07	Stricken 1921

Planned by the Direction of La Spezia R Naval Yd, an experimental type projected for re-using the Schichau-built machinery of the discarded *110 S* and *111 S* torpedo-boats (both launched in 1888). But this economy did not give good results; and, as the armament was weaker than in the *Pegasos* (only two small guns; the calibre of the TT lowered to 14in from the 17.7in of contemporary boats), this prototype was not repeated, even though *Gabbiano* gave reliable service.

'PN' class *torpedo-boats* (series I)

Displacement: 120t normal; 134t–143t full load
Dimensions: 139ft 5in × 15ft 1in × 4ft 7in–4ft 11in
42.5m × 4.6m × 1.4m–1.5m
Machinery: 2-shaft VTE (except *31 AS* and *32 AS*, see notes), 2 oil Thornycroft boilers, designed 3200hp = 27kts, max 3705ihp = 30.5kts. Range *c*175nm at full speed
Armament: 1–57mm/43, 2–17.7in (450mm) TT
Complement: 1 + 22–29

Class (launched, fate):
Pattison, Naples – *1 PN* (18.1.11, stricken 1925), *2 PN* (3.2.11, stricken 1929), *3 PN* (24.4.11, stricken 1928), *4 PN* (29.6.11, stricken 1928), *5 PN* (5.9.11, sunk 27.6.15), *6 PN* (6.11.11, stricken 1925), *7 PN* (18.4.12, stricken 1932), *8 PN* (14.5.12, stricken 1925), *9 PN* (26.7.12, stricken 1932), *10 PN* (18.9.12, stricken 1925), *11 PN* (21.11.12, stricken 1925), *12 PN* (1.1.13, stricken 1932)
Odero, Sestri – *13 OS* (16.11.11, stricken 1927), *14 OS* (5.12.11, stricken 1925), *15 OS* (27.1.12, stricken 1930), *16 OS* (28.3.12, stricken 1929), *17 OS* 16.4.12, sunk 2–3.7.15), *18 OS* (7.5.12, stricken 1927), *19 OS* (8.6.12, stricken 1930), *20 OS* (29.6.12, stricken 1925), *21 OS* (25.7.12, stricken 1925), *22 OS* (17.8.12, stricken 1925), *23 OS* (12.9.12, stricken 1924), *24 OS* (13.9.12, stricken 1927)
Ansaldo, Sestri – *25 AS* (15.5.12, stricken 1925), *26 AS* (6.7.12, stricken 1928), *27 AS* (5.8.12, stricken 1925), *28 AS* (17.8.12, stricken 1925), *29 AS* (14.9.12, stricken 1932), *30 AS* (12.10.12, stricken 1925), *31 AS* (4.1.13, stricken 1923), *32 AS* (17.6.13, stricken 1923)
Pattison, Naples – *33 PN* (2.5.13, stricken 1931), *34 PN* (1.5.13, stricken 1932), *35 PN* (22.5.13, stricken 1932), *36 PN* (7.6.13, sunk 10.11.18), *37 PN* (29.7.13, stricken 1925), *38 PN* (25.8.13, stricken 1932)

The best class of Italian coastal torpedo-boats, strong, low silhouette (and therefore suitable for night operations), sufficiently fast and provided with good endurance in narrow seas. Designed by Pattison Yards of Naples, they were built by them and by Ansaldo of Sestri (*AS* boats); Odero of Sestri (*OS* boats); Orlando of Livorno = Leghorn (*OL* boats); by the Navy itself (*RM Regia Marina*, one only, in La Spezia N Yd); by CNR of Palermo (*CP* boats); plus a third series provided with turbines (*OLT*, Orlando, Livorno, with turbines). *31 AS* was fitted with 3-shaft Parsons turbine machinery, and *32 AS* with a 2-shaft Bergmann turbines, but these powerplants did not prove successful and required a very long period of trials for adjustment. In wartime, *1 PN–4 PN, 7 PN, 8 PN, 26 AS–30 AS* were fitted for minelaying (with 8–10 mines): and armament altered to: 1–3in/40 or 1–3in/30 AA plus 1–6.5mm MG (*6 PN:* 1–3in/40 and 1–3in/30 AA), plus, of course, the TT. *5 PN* sank in the Gulf of Venice by torpedo from the German submarine *UB 1*, disguised as the Austrian *U 10* (because Germany and Italy were not then at war); *17 OS* sank off the Istrian coast on one of her own mines, while laying a minefield; *36 PN* sank off Cape Rodoni, by mine.

39 RM *experimental torpedo-boat*

Displacement: 140.1t normal; 157.9t full load
Dimensions: As 'PN' class except *1.59*m/5ft draught
Machinery: 3 sets: 2-shaft vertical double expansion + 1-shaft turbines, 2 super-heated steam boilers, designed 2700hp = 27kts. Range 185nm at full speed
Other particulars: As 'PN' class (series I)

Name	Builder	Launched	Fate
39 RM	La Spezia N Yd	12.8.15	Stricken 1923

Experimental torpedo-boat, designed by Eng Lt Commanders Eugenio De Vito and Marcello Boella for machinery. She could not perform all the necessary trials, owing to war demands for ships. In wartime the gun armament was altered to: 1–3in/40. In 1918 the original super-heated boilers were replaced by two Thornycroft type oil boilers, as in the other PN boats. The top speed reached with the new boilers was 26kts, while with the original was 30.72kts, yet with a lesser displacement.

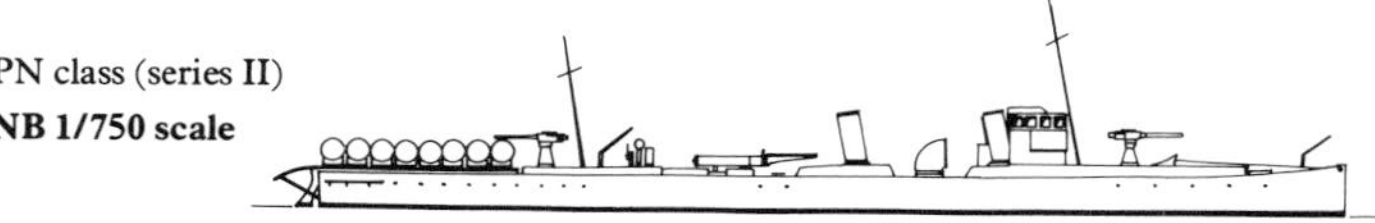
PN class (series II)
NB 1/750 scale

'PN' class *torpedo-boats* (series II)

Displacement: 129.3t normal; 156.7t–167.9t full load (max 173.9 with 10 mines aboard)
Machinery: 2-shaft VTE, 2 oil burning Thornycroft boilers, designed 2700hp = 27kts, max 4134ihp = 29.8kts. Range *c*170nm at full speed
Armament: 2–3in/30 AA (but *46–51 PN, 52 AS, 54 AS, 58 OL–60 OL* also 1–37mm AA; or *64 PN–69 PN* 1–6.5mm MG), 2–17.7in (450mm) TT (1×2), fitted 10 mines
Complement: 1 + 29

Class (launched, fate):
Pattison, Naples – *40 PN* (25.3.16, stricken 1927), *41 PN* (12.5.16, stricken 1932), *42 PN* (7.6.16, stricken 1930), *43 PN* (15.7.16, stricken 1930), *44 PN* (30.8.16, stricken 1930), *45 PN* (16.9.16, stricken 1932)
Odero, Sestri – *46 OS* (17.3.16, stricken 1930), *47 OS* (27.4.16, stricken 1932), *48 OS* (17.4.16, stricken 1931), *49 OS* (17.6.16, stricken 1932), *50 OS* (16.5.16, stricken 1932), *51 OS* (1.7.16, stricken 1932)
Ansaldo, Sestri – *52 AS* (1.7.16, stricken 1932), *53 AS* (29.7.16, stricken 1932), *54 AS* (27.8.16, stricken 1932), *55 AS* (17.9.16, stricken 1932), *56 AS* (11.10.16, stricken 1934), *57 AS* (13.11.15, stricken 1934)
Orlando, Leghorn – *58 OL* (9.4.16, stricken 1932), *59 OL* (28.5.16, stricken 1931), *60 OL* (25.6.16, stricken 1932), *61 OL* (30.7.16, stricken 1932), *62 OL* (27.8.16, stricken 1932), *63 OL* (16.2.16, stricken 1932)
Pattison, Naples – *64 PN* (19.11.17, stricken 1932), *65 PN* (22.12.17, stricken 1932), *66 PN* (30.3.18, renamed *70 PN* on 16.1.21; stricken 1932), *67 PN* (8.6.18, stricken 1929), *68 PN* (20.7.18, renamed *71 PN* on 16.1.21, stricken 1932), *69 PN* (25.9.18, stricken 1932)

8 PN as completed

60 OL about 1930

Cantieri Navali Riuniti, Palermo – *70 CP, 71 CP, 72 CP, 73 CP*

The torpedo-boats of this second series were slightly heavier than those of the first series: the bows structure was strengthened in order to allow better ramming of submarines; a stronger gun armament (2–3in guns instead 1–57mm); the rails for minelaying; the larger tank capacity: oil fuel from 15.5t (first series) to 23t, reserve water for boilers: from 2.6t (first series) to 4.1t. The TT were in a twin mount, instead of singles. The last 4 were ordered on 30 October 1917, but laying down delayed for lack of steel. Their construction was actually begun in June 1918 (first pair) – August 1919 (second pair), but with numbers changed to *76 CP, 77 CP, 78 CP, 79 CP* and suspended in the second half of 1920, when hulls were *c*38 (first pair) or 31 per cent (second pair) complete.

74 OLT 1928
NB 1/750 scale

'PN' class *torpedo-boats* (series III)

Displacement: 194.6t full load (201.1t with 7 mines aboard)
Dimensions: 149ft 11in oa, 146ft × 15ft 4in × 5ft 7in (5ft 9in with mines)
45.7m, 44.5m × 4.6m × 1.7m (1.78m)
Machinery: 2-shaft Orlando turbines, 2 oil Thornycroft boilers, designed 3500hp = 27kts, max *c*4500shp = 28.9kts. Range 864nm/14.4kts, 175nm at full speed
Armament: As series II except 7 mines
Complement: 1 + 30

Class (builder):
70 OLT–75 OLT (Orlando, Leghorn)

Practically identical to the torpedo-boats of the 2nd series, except for machinery, which, after an Orlando design, was composed of turbines instead of VTE. All 4 laid down 1916–17 but construction was slow for lack of materials, and was suspended in 1919. Only two ships (*74 OLT*, launched 25.10.17, stricken 1934; and *75 OLT* launched 12.1.18, stricken 1937), out of six, were completed and commissioned.

Ex-Austrian Tb VII class *coastal torpedo-boat*

Displacement: 110t
Dimensions: 142ft 1in × 14ft 1in × 4ft 7in
43.3m × 4.3m × 1.4m
Machinery: 2-shaft VTE, 2 oil White-Forster boilers; designed 2400hp = 28kts, max 2676ihp = *c*29kts
Other particulars: As Austrian Tb VII class

Name	Builder	Acquired	Date
FRANCESCO RISMONDO (ex-*TB 11*, ex-*TB XI*)	Danubius Yd, Porto Rè	5.10.17	BU 1925

One of the six ships of the 2nd group of 110t class Austrian coastal torpedo-boats, the first Austrian Navy ships fitted with oil-burning boilers only. Delivered to the Italian Navy after the mutiny of her crew. Under Italian colours, renamed 20 October 1917 and recommissioned on 28 October. In wartime she served as an escort vessel. After war, she was used by the Permanent Board for testing war materials. In February 1920 her weapons were removed and she was used for lighthouse service. Scrapped 1925.

SUBMARINES

MICCA class *large submarines*

Displacement: 842t/1244t
Dimensions: 207ft 6in × 20ft 4in × 14ft
63.2m × 6.2m × 4.2m
Machinery: 2-shaft Fiat (*Torricelli* Tosi) diesels plus 2 Ansaldo (some boats Savigliano) electric motors, 2600–2900bhp/1300hp–1800hp = 11kts/10.9kts. Oil 60t
Armament: 1–3in/40, 1–3in/30 AA, 6–17.7in (450mm) TT (4 bow, 2 stern; 8 torpedoes)
Complement: 4 + 36

Name	Builder	Launched	Fate
PIETRO MICCA	La Spezia N Yd	3.6.17	Stricken 2.6.30
ANGELO EMO	La Spezia N Yd	23.2.19	Stricken 1.10.30
LUIGI GALVANI	La Spezia N Yd	26.1.18	Stricken 1.1.38
LORENZO MARCELLO	La Spezia N Yd	29.9.18	Stricken 21.1.28
LAZZARO MOCENIGO	La Spezia N Yd	26.7.19	Stricken 10.4.37
TORRICELLI	La Spezia N Yd	16.6.18	Stricken 1.10.30

Designed by the Committee for new ships with the co-operation of Eng Lt Virginio Cavallini, these large boats, even though ordered in 1914, took no part in World War One. *Emo*, *Marcello* and *Mocenigo* were laid down in Venice NY, *c* June 1914; and construction continued until the autumn. Then this order was passed, together with the order for the other three boats to the La Spezia N Yd; and the hulls begun in Venice were dismantled. Two other TT were planned, aw, on the deck, rotating, but they were not actually mounted. Frequent breakdowns in the Fiat diesels and poor manoeuvrability made these boats unreliable, despite their great endurance. From 1923 they were partially rebuilt. After being discarded *Galvani* was towed from La Spezia to Leghorn (summer 1941).

Balilla as completed

Angelo Emo date unknown

BALILLA *medium submarine*

Displacement: 728t/875t
Dimensions: 213ft 3in × 19ft 8in × 13ft 5in
65.0m × 6.0m × 4.1m
Machinery: As *Micca* class, except 2600–1600bhp/900hp = 14kts/9kts
Armament: 2–3in/30 AA, 4–17.7in (450mm) TT (2 bow, 2 stern; 6 torpedoes)
Complement: 4 + 34

Name	Builder	Launched	Fate
BALILLA (ex-German *U 42*)	Fiat-San Giorgio, La Spezia	4.8.15	Sunk 14.7.16

Designed by Fiat-San Giorgio Yards, this boat had been ordered in 1913 by the German Navy and her name was to be *U 42*, but her hull, not yet launched, was requisitioned by the Italian Navy in June 1915. Renamed *Balilla* under Italian colours. Sunk in the Adriatic, NW of Lissa Island, by gunfire and torpedoes from the Austrian torpedo-boats *65 F* and *66 F*.

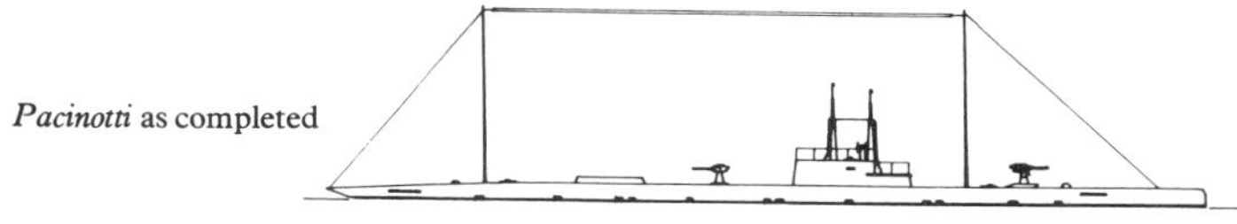

Pacinotti as completed

PACINOTTI class *medium submarines*

Displacement: 710t/868.9t
Dimensions: As *Balilla*
Machinery: As *Micca* class = 1100bhp/900hp = max 14.6kts/10.24kts. Range *c*3000nm/12kts
Armament: 2–3in/30, 5–17.7in (450mm) TT (3 bow, 2 stern, 7 torpedoes)
Complement: 4 + 35

Name	Builder	Launched	Fate
PACINOTTI	Fiat-San Giorgio La Spezia	13.3.16	Stricken 1921
GUGLIELMOTTI	Fiat-San Giorgio, La Spezia	4.6.16	Sunk 10.3.17

Very similar to the ex-*U 42* ordered by the German Navy, but this class had 3 bow TT, the only Italian class of submarines so armed, excepted the 'CC' class laid down in 1943. *Guglielmotti*, during her maiden voyage, was mistaken for a U-boat by the sloop HMS *Cyclamen*, NW of Capraia Is, and sunk by gunfire and ramming. Although fast and rather good, her sister boat was stricken less than 3 years after the war ended, and the class was not repeated.

PROVANA class *medium submarines*

Displacement: 762t/924t
Dimensions: 219ft 10in × 19ft 4in × 12ft 6in
67.0m × 5.9m × 3.8m
Machinery: 2-shaft Fiat diesels plus 2 Ansaldo electric motors, 2600bhp/1400hp = 16kts/9.8kts
Armament: 2–3in/40, 6–17.7in (450mm) TT (4 bow, 2 stern; 8 torpedoes)
Complement: 4 + 36

Name	Builder	Launched	Fate
ANDREA PROVANA	Fiat-San Giorgio, La Spezia	27.1.18	Stricken 21.1.28
AGOSTINO BARBARIGO	Fiat-San Giorgio, La Spezia	18.11.17	Stricken 1.5.28
GIACOMO NANI	Fiat-San Giorgio La Spezia	8.9.18	Stricken 1.8.35
SEBASTIANO VENIERO	Fiat-San Giorgio, La Spezia	7.7.18	Sunk 6.8.25

Designed by Eng Cesare Laurenti and Eng Lt Cdr Virginio Cavallini, the boats of this class were laid down in October 1915, but were only completed after the Armistice. New, in them, was the position of the electric batteries, placed in four watertight compartments under a horizontal deck that ran all along the length of the boats, excluding the TT compartments. Their machinery was powerful, so the speeds, both on surface and submerged, were rather high. They enjoyed good manoeuvrability but could not submerge more than 50m. They were not repeated. The central part of *Provana*, with her conning tower, was exhibited at the Turin Navy show of 1928 (10th anniversary of victory in the First World War). *Veniero* sunk off Cape Passero (Sicily) by collision with the Italian SS *Capena*.

Delfino as modified
NB 1/750 scale

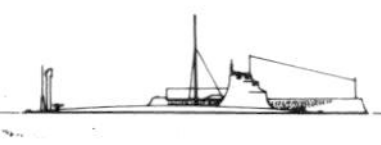

DELFINO *small submarine*

Displacement: 102.1t/113t after 1902–4 rebuilding (till 1902 95t/107t)
Dimensions: 80ft 9in × 9ft 5in × 9ft 2in (originally 78ft 9in × 9ft 5in × 8ft 4in)
24.6m × 2.8m × 2.7m (24.0m × 2.8m × 2.5m)
Machinery: 1-shaft petrol motor plus 1 electric motor, 130bhp/65hp = 6kts/5kts (originally only the electric motor)
Armament: 1–17.7in (450mm) TT (originally 2–14in (356mm) TT)
Complement: 2 + 9 (originally 1 + 7)

Name	Builder	Launched	Fate
DELFINO	La Spezia N Yd	1892 (?)	Stricken 26.9.18

First submarine boat of the Italian Navy, obviously experimental. Designed by Eng Inspector Giacinto Pullino, she was known also as *Delfino-Pullino* or *Pullino* for short. The dates of her construction are not certain. In official sources she was built between 1892 and 1895, but others say she was laid down in autumn 1889, launched in 1890 (or 1892) and completed 1892. First sea trials may have been made on 29 April 1892 and she may have been commissioned on 1 April, but official sources say 1896 (no day). This uncertainty may be explained by *Delfino*'s experimental construction. To the original electric motor (with 3 propellers, two of which had vertical axis, for diving and surfacing) a petrol motor was added during the rebuilding of 1902–04, for surface navigation; her turret was enlarged and 1–17.7in TT replaced the 2–14in TT. Discarded after having taken part in World War One.

Glauco as completed
NB 1/750 scale

GLAUCO class *small submarines*

Displacement: 157t–161t/240t–244t
Dimensions: 120ft 9in × 14ft 1in × 8ft 8in
36.8m × 4.3m × 2.6m
Machinery: 2-shaft Fiat (*Otaria* and *Tricheco* Thornycroft) petrol motors plus 2 Savigliano electric motors, 600bhp/170hp = 13kts/6kts. Range 900nm/8kts, 40nm/5kts
Armament: 2–17.7in (450mm) TT (*Glauco* 3–17.7in TT)
Complement: 2 + 13

Name	Builder	Launched	Fae
GLAUCO	Venice N Yd	9.7.05	Stricken 1916
NARVALO	Venice N Yd	21.10.06	Stricken 1918
OTARIA	Venice N Yd	25.3.08	Stricken 1918
SQUALO	Venice N Yd	10.6.06	Stricken 1918
TRICHECO	Venice N Yd	6.6.09	Stricken 1918

Designed by Eng Lieut Cesare Laurenti, this class may be considered an experimental one, even though it was the first mass-produced class. There were some differences among the boats, eg the TT, three for *Glauco* reduced to two in the rest. Their motors were not reliable and the petrol aboard was a continuous source of danger (see *Foca*). During the war they were employed for harbour defence at Brindisi and Venice.

Andrea Provana as completed

Foca date unknown

FOCA *small submarine*

Displacement: 185t/280t
Dimensions: 139ft 5in × 14ft × 5ft 3in
42.5m × 4.2m × 2.6m
Machinery: 2-shaft Fiat petrol motors plus 2 Siemens electric motors, 600bhp/160hp = 16kts/6kts. Range 875nm/8kts (see notes)
Armament: 2–17.7in (450mm) TT
Complement: 2 + 15

Name	Builder	Launched	Fate
FOCA	Fiat-San Giorgio, La Spezia	8.9.08	Stricken 1918

Medusa as completed

Designed by Fiat-San Giorgio Yards, the *Foca* was a development of the *Glauco* class and was the only Italian submarine provided with 3 shafts and 3 propellers, operated by three sets of Fiat petrol motors for a total of 800bhp. On 26 April 1909 an internal petrol explosion set fire to her fuel, in Naples harbour so it was necessary to sink the boat. Refloated and towed to La Spezia, she was repaired, and the central motor with its shaft and propeller were removed. After this accident, the Italian Navy gave up building petrol-powered submarines.

MEDUSA class *small submarines*

Displacement: 248t–252t/*c*305t
Dimensions: 147ft 8in × 13ft 9in × 9ft 6in–9ft 8in
45.1m × 4.2m × 2.9m–3.0m
Machinery: 2-shaft Fiat (*Velella* MAN) diesels plus 2 Savigliano (*Velella* Siemens) electric motors 650bhp/300hp = 12kts/8kts
Armament: 2–17.7in (450mm) TT (bow; 4 torpedoes)
Complement: 2–3 + 19

Name	Builder	Launched	Fate
ARGO	Fiat-San Giorgio, La Spezia	14.1.12	Stricken 1918
FISALIA	Orlando, Leghorn	25.2.12	Stricken 1918
JALEA	Fiat-San Giorgio, La Spezia	3.8.13	Sunk 17.8.15
JANTINA	Riuniti Yds, Muggiano	20.11.12	Stricken 1918
MEDUSA	Fiat-San Giorgio, La Spezia	30.7.11	Sunk 10.6.15
SALPA	Riuniti Yds, Muggiano	14.5.12	Stricken 1918
VELELLA	Fiat-San Giorgio, La Spezia	25.5.11	Stricken 1918
ZOEA	Orlando, Leghorn	2.3.13	Stricken 1918

Designed by Fiat-San Giorgio and Eng Lt Cdr Cesare Laurenti, they were the first Italian submarines to have diesel motors. These required long trials and time for adjustment. They were very good boats when submerged, with good manoeuvrability and stability. *Jalea* sunk in the Gulf of Trieste by an Austrian mine. *Medusa* sunk off Porto di Piave Vecchia (N Adriatic), torpedoed by the German submarine *UB 15*, disguised as the Austrian *U 11*. *Zoea* beached on 26 November 1917, by storm, at Rimini; salvaged by tug *Ciclope* and some torpedo-boats, and towed to Venice on 1 December for repairs. That month Venice N Yd began work to convert *Argo* into an assault submarine for forcing the Austrian main base of Pola, with the aid of frogmen for breaking the harbour barrages.

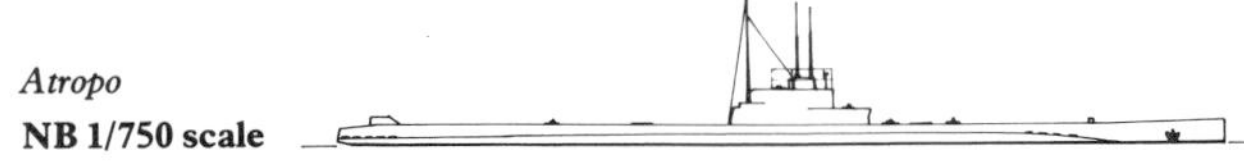

Atropo
NB 1/750 scale

ATROPO *small submarine*

Displacement: 231t/320t
Dimensions: 146ft × 14ft 5in × 8ft 10in
44.5m × 4.4m × 2.7m
Machinery: 2-shaft Krupp diesels plus 2 AEG electric motors, 700bhp/200hp = 14.75kts/8kts. Range *c*1300nm/12.5kts, *c*40nm/8kts
Armament: 2–17.7in (450mm) TT (bow; 4 torpedoes)
Complement: 2 + 12

Name	Builder	Launched	Fate
ATROPO	Germania-Werft, Kiel	22.3.12	Stricken 1919

Ordered by the Italian Navy from a yard of her then ally Germany. Her German data were 237t/318t; contractual speed 12kts/7.3kts. Her pressure hull was very strong, and the boat reached a high surface speed thanks to the shape of her outer casing, with lines similar to those of a torpedo-boat, so modified by the Italian Navy.

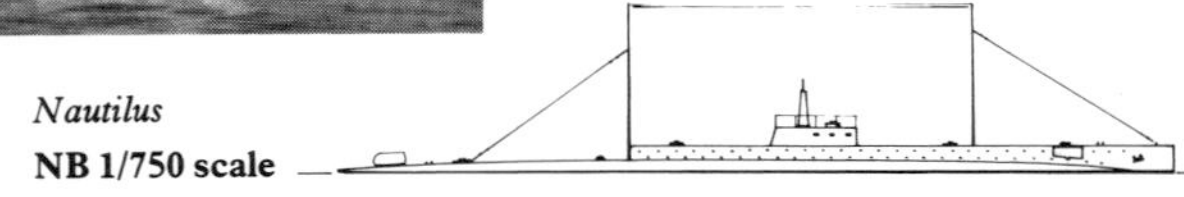

Nautilus
NB 1/750 scale

NAUTILUS class *small submarines*

Displacement: 225t/320t
Dimensions: 134ft 4in × 14ft 1in × 9ft 4in
40.9m × 4.3m × 2.8m
Machinery: 2-shaft Sulzer diesels plus 2 Ansaldo electric motors, 600bhp/320hp = 13.2kts/8kts
Armament: 2–17.7in (450mm) TT (bow; 4 torpedoes)
Complement: 2 + 17

Name	Builder	Launched	Fate
NAUTILUS	Venice N Yd	25.4.13	Stricken 1919
NEREIDE	Venice N Yd	12.7.13	Sunk 5.8.15

First class of submarines designed by Eng Lt Commander Curio Bernardis, who became a well-known submarine designer. Their hulls were similar to those of a torpedo-boat. Originally it was planned to have a third TT on the deck, but this was not mounted. *Nereide* sunk, near Pelagosa Is (Adriatic), by torpedoes of the Austrian submarine *U 5*.

PULLINO class *small submarines*

Displacement: 345t/405t
Dimensions: 138ft 5in × 13ft 5in × 12ft 4in
42.2m × 4.1m × 3.7m
Machinery: 2-shaft Fiat diesels plus 2 Savigliano electric motors, 1460bhp/520hp = 14kts/9kts
Armament: 1–57mm, 1–37mm, 6–17.7in (450mm) TT (2 bow, 2 stern, 2 in exterior cages, upon the deck; 8 torpedoes)
Complement: 2 + 19

Name	Builder	Launched	Fate
GALILEO FERRARIS	La Spezia N Yd	9.11.13	Stricken 1919
GIACINTO PULLINO	La Spezia N Yd	21.7.13	Sunk 1.8.17

Double hull submarines, designed by Eng Lt Cdr Virginio Cavallini, able to bear the maximum projected pressure (50m), provided with the strongest yet TT armament (in the Italian Navy) and also the first deck guns. *Ferraris* beached, night of 27–28 November 1917, at Magnavacca (now Porto Garibaldi), by storm. Salvaged in January 1918, but she was too damaged to serve any longer, and was stricken 1919. *Pullino* ran aground on the night of 30–31 July 1916, at Galiola Is (Quarnaro); was damaged by her crew; captured by the Austrians and sank while being towed to Pola. Raised on 28 February 1931 by the Italian Navy and scrapped in 1931.

ARGONAUTA *small submarine*

Displacement: 255t/306t
Dimensions: 148ft × 13ft 9in × 9ft 10in
45.1m × 4.2m × 3.0m
Machinery: 2-shaft Fiat diesels plus 2 Savigliano electric motors, 700bhp/450hp = 13.5kts/8.8kts. Range 950nm/12kts, 100nm submerged
Armament: 2–17.7in (450mm) TT (bow; 4 torpedoes)
Complement: 2 + 22

Name	Builder	Launched	Fate
ARGONAUTA (ex-*Svyatoy Georgi*)	Fiat-San Giorgio, La Spezia	5.7.14	Stricken 1928

Designed by Fiat-San Giorgio Yards and Eng Lt Cdr Cesare Laurenti, she was an improved version of the *Medusa* class, with some additions requested by the Russian Imperial Navy, which had ordered her in 1912: these included a second periscope, better motors, retractable horizontal rudders and submarine signalling gear. A short time after the outbreak of war, when Italy was still neutral, a young Italian lieutenant took possession of her (known, after her yard number, *N 43*) in an attempt to sail the boat into the Adriatic for attacking Austrian ships, so forcing Italy to war. But in Corsica *N 43* was stopped by the French authorities and given back to Italy, which bought her from Russia in 1915.

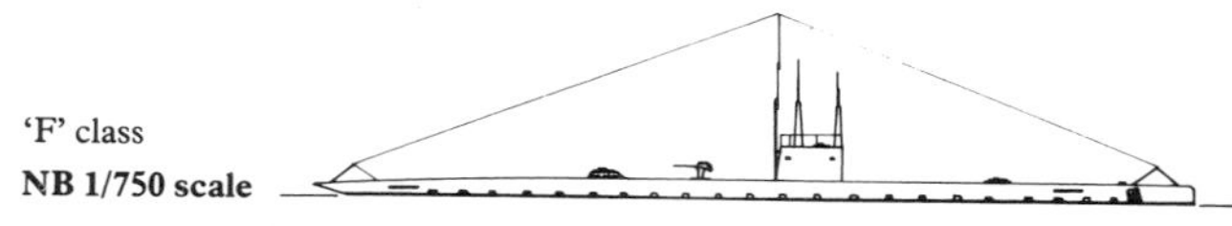
'F' class
NB 1/750 scale

'F' class *small submarines*

Displacement: 262t/319t
Dimensions: 149ft 7in, 148ft × 13ft 9in × 10ft 2in
45.6m, 45.1m × 4.2m × 3.1m
Machinery: 2-shaft Fiat diesels plus 2 Savigliano electric motors, 670bhp/500hp = 12.5kts/8.2kts. Oil 12t. Range c1600nm/8.5kts, c80nm/4kts
Armament: 1–3in/30 AA gun, 2–17.7in (450mm) TT (bow; 4 torpedoes)
Complement: 2 + 24

Name	Builder	Launched	Fate
F 1	Fiat-San Giorgio, La Spezia	2.4.16	Stricken 2.6.30
F 2	Fiat-San Giorgio, La Spezia	4.6.16	Stricken 1.2.29
F 3	Fiat-San Giorgio, La Spezia	6.7.16	Stricken 1919
F 4	Orlando, Leghorn	19.11.16	Stricken 1919
F 5	Fiat-San Giorgio, La Spezia	12.8.16	Stricken 20.7.29
F 6	Orlando, Leghorn	4.3.17	Stricken 1.8.35
F 7	Fiat-San Giorgio, La Spezia	23.12.16	Stricken 1.2.29
F 8	Fiat-San Giorgio, La Spezia	13.11.16	Stricken 1919
F 9	Fiat-San Giorgio, La Spezia	24.9.16	Stricken 1.8.28
F 10	Fiat-San Giorgio, La Spezia	19.10.16	Stricken 2.6.30
F 11	Fiat-San Giorgio, La Spezia	17.9.16	Stricken 1919
F 12	Fiat-San Giorgio, La Spezia	30.11.16	Stricken 20.7.29
F 13	Orlando, Leghorn	20.5.17	Stricken 1.8.35
F 14	Odero, Sestri	23.1.17	Sunk 6.8.28
F 15	Orlando, Leghorn	27.5.17	Stricken 28.5.29
F 16	Odero, Sestri	19.3.17	Stricken 1.5.28
F 17	Orlando, Leghorn	3.6.17	Stricken 1.11.29
F 18	Odero, Sestri	15.5.17	Stricken 1.10.30
F 19	Fiat-San Giorgio, La Spezia	10.3.18	Stricken 2.6.30
F 20	Fiat-San Giorgio, La Spezia	17.3.18	Stricken 1.7.35
F 21	Fiat-San Giorgio, La Spezia	19.5.18	Stricken 1.10.30

Designed by Fiat-San Giorgio Yards and Eng Lt Cdr Cesare Laurenti. Three forerunners of this class were the Brazilian *F 1, F 3, F 5*, built by the Italian Fiat-San Giorgio Yards and launched in 1913–14. These were improved *Medusas* faster in diving, provided with two periscopes, a gyrocompass and a Fessenden submarine signalling gear, and armed with a 3in gun. They had good manoeuvrability both on surface and when submerged. The original orders (1915) were for 24 boats for the Italian Navy (*F 1* to *F 24*), but three (*F 19–F 21*) were sold to Portugal and became *Foca, Golfinho, Hidra;* and three others (*F 22–F 24*) were sold to Spain, and became *A 1 – Monturiol, A 2 – Garcia, A 3* (no name). Nevertheless the Italian Navy ordered three other boats for itself, which were the above mentioned *F 19* (ii), *F 20* (ii), *F 21* (ii). *F 8* sunk on 14 February 1917 off La Spezia, during a trial. Refloated, was put back into service in September. *F 14* sunk by the destroyer *Giuseppe Missori*, which rammed the boat while she was surfacing during an exercise off Pola. Raised on 7 August 1928 and scrapped.

Ex-British 'S' class *small submarines*

Class (transferred):
S 1 (15.9.15), *S 2* (20.9.15), *S 3* (26.9.15)

This class repeated the Italian *Argonauta*, and its three boats were built in Great Britain, the design being by Fiat-San Giorgio Yards and Eng Lt Cdr Cesare Laurenti, modified by Scott's Shipbuilding and Engineering Co Ltd, of Greenock. When they were transferred to the Italian Navy, *S 1* had been serving with the Royal Navy for one year, *S 2* had just passed trials with the Royal Navy, *S 3* was about to begin sea trials. All were stricken in 1919.

Galileo Ferraris 1915

Argonauta 1916

Ex-British 'W' class *small submarines*

Class (transferred):
W 1 (23.8.16), *W 2* (23.8.16), *W 3* (23.8.16), *W 4* (7.8.16)

Designed by Armstrong, the four boats had been built in Armstrong-Whitworth Yards, at Newcastle-upon-Tyne, for the Royal Navy, and were later sold to the Italian Navy. When transferred to the Italian Navy, a 3in/30 AA gun was added to *W 1* and *W 2*. They had poor manoeuvrability and often suffered diesel breakdowns. The second pair were more successful and made several war cruises and attacks against Austrian ships. *W 4* probably sunk by an Austrian mine off Cape Rodoni on 4–6 August 1917. The others were stricken in 1919.

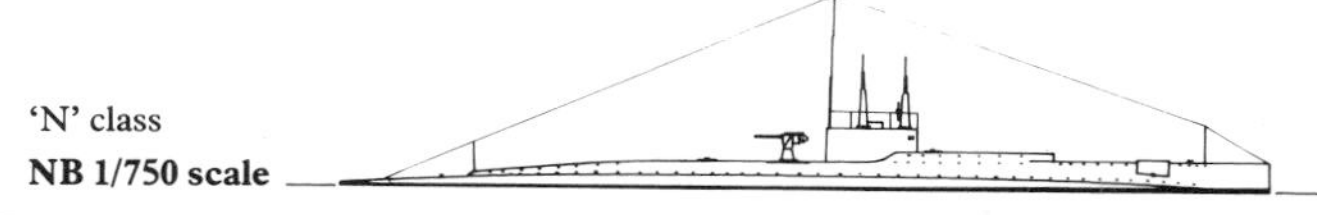
'N' class
NB 1/750 scale

'N' class *small submarines*

Displacement: 277t/363t
Dimensions: 150ft 6in × 14ft × 10ft 2in
45.8m × 4.2m × 3.1m
Machinery: *N 1* to *N 4* 2-shaft Sulzer diesels plus 2 Ansaldo electric motors, 650bhp/400hp = 12.5kts/7.6kts
N 5 and *N 6* 2-shaft Tosi diesels plus 2 Ansaldo electric motors, 700–820bhp/400–450hp = 13.5kts/7.9kts. Oil 9t–10t
Armament: 1–3in/30 AA, 2–17.7in (450mm) TT (bow; 4 torpedoes)
Complement: 2 + 21

Name	Builder	Launched	Fate
N 1	Ansaldo, Sestri	6.9.17	Stricken 1.10.30
N 2	Ansaldo, Sestri	26.1.18	Stricken 1.5.28
N 3	Ansaldo, Sestri	27.4.18	Stricken 1.8.35
N 4	Ansaldo, Sestri	6.10.18	Stricken 1.8.35
N 5	Tosi, Taranto	18.11.17	Stricken 10.7.29
N 6	Tosi, Taranto	20.9.18	Stricken 1.8.35

These boats designed by Eng Cdr Curio Bernardis, were an improvement of the *Nautilus* class, with a greater displacement, a better powerplant and the addition of a 3in gun. The two Tosi built boats gave better results in speed (13.56kts/7.94kts instead of 12.5kts/7.6kts) and endurance (on surface: 750nm at 12.5kts, instead of 508nm at the same speed; 1485nm at 9kts, instead of 1300nm at 9kts; submerged: 17nm at 7.5kts, instead of 15nm at 7.5kts; 120nm at 2 kts, instead of 80nm at 2kts) than those built by Ansaldo. Their construction was slow because of lack of materials in wartime; and likewise after the war because there was no more necessity to employ them in naval operations.

British 'H' class *small submarines*

Class (launched, fate):
Canadian Vickers, Montreal – *H 1* (16.10.16, stricken 23.3.47), *H 2* (19.10.16, stricken 23.3.47), *H 3* (26.4.17, stricken 10.4.37), *H 4* (17.4.17, stricken 23.3.47), *H 5* (25.4.17, sunk 16.4.18), *H 6* (23.4.17, sunk 14.9.43), *H 7* (24.5.17, stricken 1.10.30), *H 8* (24.5.17, sunk 5.6.43)

An excellent class of handy and reliable boats, designed and built for several navies by the Electric Boat Co, and assembled at Montreal. Remarkable for the power of their electric motors, which exceeded the diesels. The depth acceptance test was of 80m, higher than that of other Italian submarines (for Italian-built boats, it did not exceed 50m). They could fire a couple of torpedoes and, after about 5 seconds another two. A 3in deck gun was added after 1920. *H 5* sunk in error, in the South Adriatic, by torpedo fired by the British submarine *H 1*, called in the Adriatic, by the Italians and by the French, *HB 1*, to avoid confusion with the Italian 'H' boats. *H 6* sunk after Italy's armistice at Bonifacio (Corsica), by the Germans. *H 8* sunk by air bombs at La Spezia; refloated and converted to hull for charging batteries.

Ex-German UC 1 class *coastal submarine minelayer*

Displacement:	171.2t/184.2t
Dimensions:	110ft 3in oa, 108ft 7in wl × 10ft 4in × 5ft 10in *33.6m, 33.1m × 3.1m × 2.7m*
Machinery:	1-shaft Sulzer diesel plus 1 Siemens-Schuckert electric motor, 80–90bhp/175hp = 6kts/4.5kts
Armament:	1–3in/30 AA, 6 mine tubes (12 mines)
Complement:	1 + 15

Name	Rebuilder	Relaunched	Fate
X 1 (ex-Austrian *U 24*, ex-German *UC 12*)	Taranto N Yd	9.12.16	Stricken 1919

Originally built as the German minelayer submarine *UC 12*, launched in A G Weser Yards, of Bremen, on 29 April 1915; nominally transferred to the Austrian Navy under the Austrian number *U 24* (but she continued to have a German crew). *U 24* sank on 16 March 1916 off Taranto on one of her own mines. Raised by the Italian Navy, the wreck was rebuilt under the control of Eng Cdr Curio Bernardis, renumbered *X 1* with the above particulars. Commissioned at the end of March 1917.

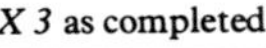

X 3 as completed

Alfa 25 July 1913

A 5 1916

X 2 class *coastal submarine minelayers*

Displacement:	403.3t/467.7t
Dimensions:	139ft 9in × 18ft 1in × 10ft 2in *42.6m × 5.5m × 3.1m*
Machinery:	2-shaft Sulzer diesels plus 2 Ansaldo electric motors, 650bhp/325hp = 8.2kts/6.3kts
Armament:	1–3in/30 AA, 9 mine tubes (18 mines)
Complement:	2 + 20 to 23

Name	Builder	Launched	Fate
X 2	Ansaldo, Sestri	25.4.17	Laid up 16.9.40
X 3	Ansaldo, Sestri	29.12.17	Laid up 16.9.40

The letter 'X' was adopted, in the Italian Navy, to mean 'minelayer' (submarine). This class was designed by Eng Commander Curio Bernardis, who had rebuilt the ex-*UC 12* as *X 1*; and he followed the German system for the embarking and laying equipment, enlarging the room for mine compartments, to allow the mounting of nine mine tubes for a total of 18 mines of the Italian AE1916/125t type. One 3in gun was also mounted, after the Italian use, and, some years after 1918, two cage TTs (for 17.7in torpedoes) were mounted in the main flooding trunk. The two boats were slow and had poor manoeuvrability.

ALFA class *experimental midget submarines*

Dimensions:	19ft 8in × ? × 2ft 6in *6.0m × ? × 76cm*
Machinery:	1-shaft electric motor = *c*8kts on surface

Name	Builder	Built	Fate
ALFA	Venice N Yd	1912–13	Stricken *c*1915–16
BETA	Venice N Yd	1912–13	Stricken *c*1915–16

These two boats, of submarine or semi-submarine type, were built in secret in Venice N Yd with the task of surveillance and defence of the harbour entrance. They were not entered in the Naval List, not having passed armament trials.

'A' class *midget submarines*

Displacement:	31.2t/36.7t
Dimensions:	44ft 3in pp × 7ft 3in × 7ft 5in *13.5m × 2.2m × 2.3m*
Machinery:	1-shaft electric motor, 40–60hp = 6.8kts/5.08kts
Armament:	2–17.7in (450mm) torpedoes, in exterior cages, upon the deck
Complement:	1 + 3

Class (launched):
A 1 (17.10.15), *A 2* (15.12.15), *A 3* (29.12.15), *A 4* (31.12.15), *A 5* (15.1.16), *A 6* (11.2.16)

These very small boats, designed by Eng Vice Admiral Edgardo Ferrati and built at La Spezia N Yd, were conceived for the defence of some Adriatic harbours, such as Venice, Ancona, Brindisi. They were transportable by railway. They were not successful, had a very low endurance and their periscope was not retractable. All stricken in 1918.

'B' class

NB 1/750 scale

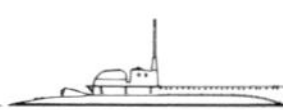

'B' class *midget submarines*

Displacement:	40t/46t
Dimensions:	49ft 7in × 7ft 7in × 8ft 2in *15.1m* × 2.3m × 2.5m
Machinery:	1-shaft Itala petrol motor plus 1 Savigliano electric motor, *c*85bhp/40–60hp = 6.9kts/5kts. Range *c*128nm/6.9kts, 9nm/5kts
Armament:	2–17.7in (450mm) TT (bow; 2 torpedoes)
Complement:	1 + 4

Class (launched):
B 1 (8.7.16), *B 2* (1.10.16), *B 3* (25.11.16)

An enlargement and an improvement of the 'A' class, these boats, also designed by Eng Vice Admiral Edgardo Ferrati, were provided with two different kind of motors, having a petrol motor for surface navigation and a greater endurance. Their torpedoes were in real tubes. They too had been conceived for harbour defence and were transportable by railway. *B 1–B 3* stricken in 1919. *B 4–B 6* construction suspended in 1917, discarded 1919, scrapped 1920.

SMALL SURFACE WARSHIPS

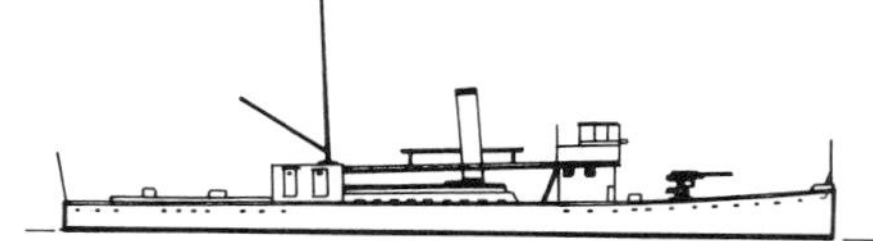

Brondolo as completed
NB 1/750 scale

BRONDOLO class *gunboats*

Displacement: *c*115t
Dimensions: 124ft 8in × 20ft 8in × 2ft 6in
38.0m × 6.3m × c0.74m
Machinery: 2-shaft VTE, *c*500ihp = *c*13kts
Armament: 1–3in/40, could carry mines
Complement: 18

Name	Builder	Launched	Fate
BRONDOLO	Venice N Yd	4.12.09	Stricken 1934
MARGHERA	Venice N Yd	29.3.09	Stricken 1934

Originally classed as lagoon gunboats; reclassed as minelayers on 1 July 1921. First name of *Marghera* was *Malghera* (till 2 May 1909). They had a small draught, for operating in shallow waters near Venice.

SEBASTIANO CABOTO *gunboat*

Displacement: 877t–1050t
Dimensions: 208ft × 31ft 10in × 9ft 10in
63.4m × 9.7m × 3.0m
Machinery: 2-shaft VTE, 1203ihp = 13.2kts
Armament: 6–3in/40, 4–6.5mm MG
Complement: 6 + 101

Name	Builder	Launched	Fate
SEBASTIANO CABOTO	CNR, Palermo	20.7.12	Sunk 9.43

Designed by Eng Cdr Ettore Berghinz, served during World War Two at Rhodes. Scuttled by her own crew after Italy's armistice; captured by the Germans on 12 September 1943, who tried to recommission her. Sunk off Rhodes by British aircraft bombs.

ABISSO (ex-French) *gunboat*

Displacement: 295t–400t
Dimensions: 131ft 3in pp × 22ft × 9ft
40.0m × 6.7m × 2.7m
Machinery: 1-shaft VTE, 550ihp = 12kts
Armament: 2–3in/40, 4–6.5mm MG

Name	Builder	Launched	Fate
ABISSO (ex-*Falco II*, ex-*Petrel*)	Duthie Torry & Co, Aberdeen	1912	Sunk 24.8.41

Ex-French merchant vessel *Petrel*; Italian gunboat *Falco II* from 1 July 1915 to 2 January 1917; renamed *Abisso*. From 1 July 1921 renamed *Riccardo Grazioli Lante*. Sunk off Libyan coast by British aircraft bombs.

CIRENAICA (ex-Dutch) *gunboat*

Displacement: 305t
Dimensions: 136ft 6in pp × 18ft 10in × 9ft 4in
41.5m × 5.7m × 2.8m
Machinery: 1-shaft VTE, 308ihp = 10.4kts
Armament: 2–3in/40 AA

Name	Builder	Launched	Fate
CIRENAICA (ex-*Leda*)	Scotland	1885	Stricken 1924

The ex-Dutch yacht *Leda* was bought in 1916 and commissioned in 1917.

Sebastiano Caboto pre-war

LINOSA (ex-Spanish) *gunboat*

Displacement: 388t
Dimensions: 111ft 7in pp × 21ft × 9ft 10in
34.1m × 6.4m × 3.2m
Machinery: 1-shaft VTE = 10kts
Armament: 2–3in/40, 4–6.5mm MG

Name	Builder	Launched	Fate
LINOSA (ex-*Maria Isabel*)	Cochrane & Cooper, Beverley	1898	Stricken 1923

The ex-Spanish merchantman *Maria Isabel* was bought and commissioned in 1916. Renamed *Bumeliana* on 21 July 1921.

PALMAIOLA (ex-Spanish) *gunboat*

Displacement: 562t
Dimensions: 131ft 3in × 19ft 8in × 11ft 10in
40m × 6m × 3.6m
Machinery: 1-shaft VTE, 374ihp = 8.5kts
Armament: 1–3in/40 AA
Complement: 8

Name	Builder	Launched	Fate
PALMAIOLA (ex-*Mary*)	Cook Welton, Hull	1902	Sunk 27.2.43

The ex-Spanish merchantman was bought and commissioned in 1916. Served as a minesweeper in 1916–18. Sunk in Syracuse harbour by Allied bombing.

GENERALE ARIMONDI (ex-French) *gunboat*

Displacement: 580t
Dimensions: 135ft 2in × 23ft × 13ft
41.2m × 7.0m × 3.9m
Machinery: 1-shaft VTE, 540ihp = 9kts
Armament: 1–3in/40 AA, 2–6.5mm MG
Complement: 2 + 27

Name	Builder	Launched	Fate
GENERALE ARIMONDI (ex-*Gorgo*, ex-*Pelican*)	Mackie & Thomson, Glasgow	1910	Stricken 1934

The ex-French merchantman was bought in 1915 and commissioned in 1917.

BOEO (ex-Dutch) *gunboat*

Displacement: 235t
Dimensions: 98ft 9in × 19ft 2in × 6ft 11in
30.1m × 5.8m × 2.1m
Machinery: 1-shaft VTE, 415ihp = 10.5kts
Armament: 1–3in/40 AA
Complement: 4 + 8

Name	Builder	Launched	Fate
BOEO (ex-*Tromp*)	Y Constant Lievits & Co, Dordrecht	1916	Sunk 15.8.43

ITALY

The Dutch SS *Tromp* was bought and commissioned in 1917. Mined and sunk on 18 November 1918, she was raised and recommissioned. Sunk by aircraft bombs at Vibo Valentia.

CAPITANO SAURO (ex-Austrian) *gunboat*

Displacement: 320t
Dimensions: 151ft 7in × 20ft 8in × 6ft 8in
46.2m × 6.3m × 2.04m
Machinery: 2-shaft steam engines, 700ihp = 11kts
Armament: 1–4.7in/40, 2–3in/40 AA, 2–37mm/25

The ex-Austrian merchant vessel *Timavo* was modified and armed in Venice N Yd, and commissioned in the First World War. Stricken *c*1919.

SCAPARRO *gunboat*

Displacement: 160t
Dimensions: 62ft 4in × 20ft 8in × 5ft 3in
19.0m × 6.3m × 1.6m
Machinery: 2-shaft Peter motors, 152bhp = kts
Armament: 2–5in/51

The ex-lighter *Gina-Ida* was armed at Venice for the port's defence. Converted to a water carrier, stricken 1922.

Ape as completed

APE class *canal gunboats*

Displacement: 30t–*c*50t
Dimensions: 65ft 9in pp × 11ft 2in × 2ft 11in
20.5m × 3.4m × 0.9m
Machinery: 2-shaft Buffalo cruiser motors, 80–120bhp = 9.4kts
Armament: 1–3in/17 Army gun, on a two-wheel carriage, 11–6.5mm MG

Name	Builder	Launched	Fate
APE	Venice N Yd	29.6.18	Stricken 1924
VESPA	Venice N Yd	22.6.18	Stricken 1924

Built for riverine operations around Venice.

ERMANNO CARLOTTO *gunboat*

Displacement: 218t
Dimensions: 160ft 1in × 24ft 7in × 2ft 11in
48.8m × 7.5m × 0.91m
Machinery: 2-shaft VTE, 1100ihp = 14kts
Armament: 2–3in/40, 4–6.5mm MG
Complement: 4 + 40

Name	Builder	Launched	Fate
ERMANNO CARLOTTO	Shanghai Dock & Engineering Co, Shanghai	19.6.18	Stricken 1960s

Commissioned 1921, scuttled by her own crew on 9 September 1943 at Shanghai. Refloated by the Japanese in November 1943 and commissioned by them with the new name *Narumi*. After July 1945 transferred to China (later Communist China) and renamed *Kiang Kun*.

MARECHIARO (ex-Austrian) *gunboat*

Displacement: 1327t
Dimensions: 219ft 10in wl, 261ft 2in oa × 29ft 10in × 15ft 9in
67.1m, 79.6m × 9.1m × 4.8m
Machinery: 2-shaft VTE, 3255ihp = 14.7kts
Armament: 4–3in/40
Complement: 4 + 64

Name	Builder	Launched	Fate
MARECHIARO (ex-*Taurus*, ex-*Nirvana*)	William Henderson, Glasgow	1904	Sunk 11.9.43

Built as the British merchant vessel SS *Nirvana*. Purchased by the Austrian Navy in 1909. Transferred to the Italian Navy on 4 March 1923 and renamed *Marechiaro*. Renamed *Aurora* on 15 April 1928 and became the presidential yacht (viz used as the yacht of the President of the Italian Cabinet [Prime Minister]). Sunk by torpedoes fired by German *S 64* and *S 61* off Ancona.

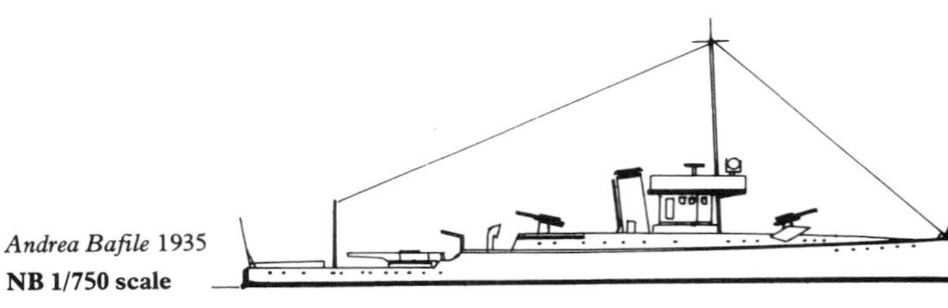

Andrea Bafile 1935
NB 1/750 scale

BAFILE class *gunboats*

Displacement: 260t normal; 284t full load (with mines)
Dimensions: 170ft 7in pp × 18ft 10in × 5ft 11in
52.0m × 5.7m × 1.8m
Machinery: 2-shaft VTE, 2 Thornycroft boilers, designed 2400hp, max 3462ihp = 25.3kts–3331ihp = 25.8kts. Range 1100nm/11kts, 675nm/15kts
Armament: 2–4in (102mm)/35, 2–6.5mm MG, 2–17.7in (450mm) TT (1×2), 12 mines
Complement: 3 + 50

Class (launched, fate):
Andrea Bafile (8.12.21, stricken 1939), *Carlo del Greco* (9.9.22, stricken 1939), *Tolosetto Farinati* (16.5.22, stricken 1939), *Ernesto Giovannini* (11.3.22, stricken 1950), *Emanuele Russo* (26.1.22, lost 29.3.23), *Alessandro Vitturi* (27.6.22, stricken 1939)

An improved version of the 'PN' torpedo-boats built 1910–18 by Pattison of Naples, as escort-gunboats for coastal convoys. *Russo* sunk by fire in Naples harbour.

BETTA N 3 *minelayer*

Displacement: 580t
Dimensions: 131ft 3in × 23ft 8in × 10ft 6in
40.0m × 7.2m × 3.2m
Machinery: 1-shaft VTE, 277ihp = 8.6kts
Armament: 1–3in/40

Name	Builder	Launched	Fate
BETTA N 3	Cravero, Genoa	1891	Stricken 13.3.24

Originally classed as a harbour craft; then converted to minelayer.

Ex-Austrian MT class *minelayers*

Displacement: 128t (145t with mines)
Dimensions: 96ft 5in × 21ft 4in × 5ft 7in
29.4m × 6.5m × 1.7m
Machinery: 2 VC engines, 1 Yarrow oil boiler, 280ihp = *c*11kts
Armament: 1–3in/40, 34 mines
Complement: 27

Class (former no, launched, fate):
RD 58 (ex-*MT 130*, 20.7.18, transferred to Italy 3.1.20, renamed *Albona* 1921. Sunk 31.10.44), *RD 59* (ex-*MT 131*, 24.8.18, transferred to Italy 7.2.20, renamed *Laurana* 1921. Sunk 20.2.45), *RD 60* (ex- *MT 132*, 28.9.18, transferred to Italy 16.7.20, renamed *Rovigno* 1921. Sunk 31.10.44).

Light minelayers built by Danubius, Porto Ré, for the Austrian Navy, but fitted also as minesweepers. *Laurana* fitted in 1941 with smoke apparatus for the defence of Venice. *Albona* and *Rovigno* captured by the Germans at Syros on 10 September 1943; renamed respectively *Netztender 57* and *Netztender 56* and armed more powerfully. Scuttled by the Germans at Salonika. *Laurana* captured on 11 September 1943 by the Germans at Venice; commissioned by them on 30 September keeping her name. Served as a minelayer in the Adriatic. Sunk at Trieste by aircraft bombs.

RONDINE *minesweeper*

Displacement:	400t
Dimensions:	128ft × 22ft × 11ft 2in *39.0m × 6.7m × 3.4m*
Machinery:	1-shaft VTE, 540ihp = 11.5kts
Armament:	1–3in/40

The ex-French SS *Thaïs*, launched by I Duthie, Aberdeen. Served as minesweeper in Italian Navy from 1 July 1915. Stricken 5 July 1923.

RD class *minesweepers*

Number (builder, disp, dimensions, machinery, launched):
RD 1–RD 6 (Castellammare di Stabia N Yd; 196t; 116ft × 19ft × 6ft 11in/*35.3m × 5.8m × 2.1m;* 1 VTE, 800ihp = *c*13kts; 1916)
RD 7–RD 12 (Tosi, Taranto; 215.7t; 116ft 6in × 19ft × 6ft 11in/*35.5m × 5.8m × 2.1m;* 1 VTE, max 1014ihp = 13.8kts; 1916–17)
RD 13–RD 14 (Poli, Chioggia; 196t; as *RD 1–RD 6;* 1 VTE, max 807ihp = 13kts; 1917)
RD 15–RD 20 (Castellammare di Stabia N Yd; 200.82t; 116ft × 19ft × 7ft 1in/*35.3m × 5.8m × 2.1m*; 1 VTE, *c*800ihp = 13.5kts; 1916–17)
RD 21–RD 26 (Castellammare di Stabia N Yd; 201t; 119ft 9in × 19ft × 7ft/*36.5m × 5.8m × 2.1m*; 1 VTE, max 881ihp = 13.3kts; 1917–18)
RD 27–RD 30 (Tosi, Taranto; 200t; 119ft 9in × 19ft 2in × 6ft 7in/*36.5m × 5.8m × 2m*; 1 VTE, max 970ihp = 13–14kts; 1918)
RD 31–RD 37 (Catellammare di Stabia N Yd; 207.3t; 119ft 9in × 19ft × 7ft 3in/*36.5m × 5.8m × 2.2m;* 1 VTE, max 864ihp = 12–14kts; 1917–19)
RD 38 (Naples N Yd; 200.1t; 118ft 1in × 19ft × 6ft 1in/*36.0m × 5.8m × 2.1m*; 1 VTE max 823ihp = 12.4kts; 1919)
RD 39–RD 44 (Tosi, Taranto; 203t; as *RD 31–RD 37*; 1 VTE, 750ihp = 13.6kts; 1919–20)
RD 45–RD 49 (Pattison, Naples, 211.9t; 124ft 8in × 19ft 8in × 6ft 3in/*38.0m × 6.0m × 1.9m*; 1 VTE, 816ihp–1155ihp = *c*12.5kts; 1920–21)
RD 50–RD 52, wooden hulls, (Costruzioni Navali di Voltri; 302t; 111ft 7in × 23ft 8in × 8ft 2in/*34.0m × 7.2m × 2.5m;* 1 VTE, max 588ihp = *c*10kts; 1919)
RD 55–RD 57 (Migliardi, Savona; 212t; 116ft 6in × 19ft × 7ft 3in/*35.5m × 5.8m × 2.2m*; 1 VTE, max 872ihp = 12.9kts, 1923)

RD means *Rimorchiatore Dragamine* (Tug minesweeper), later modified to *Regio Dragamine* (HM Minesweeper). They were all armed with 1–3in/40 or 1–3in/40 AA gun, plus, added later, 2–6.5mm MG. *RD 7*'s 3in/40 gun was later replaced by a longer 3in/50 gun. The complement of each boat was 22 men. *RD 53–RD 54* (290t) were laid down in 1918 by Cantieri Navali Riuniti, Palermo, but construction was suspended. *RD 58–RD 69* ordered from Ansaldo-San Giorgio of Muggiano (La Spezia), but not laid down. The numbers *RD 58, RD 59, RD 60* were later given to the ex-Austrian minelayers-minesweepers *MT 130, MT 131, MT 132*, but on 2 July 1921 the boats were reclassed as minelayers and renamed respectively *Albona, Laurana, Rovigno* (see under *minelayers*).

RD 7 5 October 1940

Fates
RD 1, RD 3, RD 5, RD 8, RD 15, RD 19, RD 45, RD 50, RD 52 stricken 1921, *RD 46, RD 47, RD 48* stricken 1923. *RD 2* capsized on 16 July 1919 off Ancona, *RD 6, RD 16, RD 21, RD 25* (after been salvaged, because damaged on 16 August 1943 near Messina), *RD 27, RD 28, RD 29* all transferred to Yugoslavia in 1947–48 and renamed, respectively, *ML 301, ML 302, ML 303, ML 304, ML 305, ML 306, ML 307. RD 7* sunk 15 June 1942, Saronikos, by a mine (?). *RD 9, RD 17, RD 26* abandoned on 9 September 1943 at Piraeus and captured by the Germans; *RD 35* captured 13 September 1943 by the Germans at Syros (Aegean Sea); *RD 49* captured by the Germans at La Spezia on 9 September 1943 and sunk by them 1945. *RD 10* sunk on 29 October 1918 off Cape Rodoni by a mine. *RD 11* transferred to the Revenue Cutter service, lost 1931, grounded near Porto Palo (Sicily). *RD 12* transferred to the Revenue Cutter service, sunk 2 May 1943 off Cape Bon (Tunisia) by aircraft. *RD 13* scuttled 9 September 1943 at Viareggio. *RD 14* capsized and sank on 3 January 1918 between Porto Corsini and Ancona, when being towed to Ancona for completion. *RD 18* transferred to the Revenue Cutter Service, sunk, 6 May 1943 off Cape Zebib (Tunis) by aircraft. *RD 20* sunk on 11 April 1943 in Trapani (Sicily) by aircraft bombs. *RD 22* sunk 25 October 1943 off Brindisi, probably by a mine. *RD 23, RD 42, RD 57* sunk on 5 May 1943 at La Goulette (Tunis), by aircraft bombs. *RD 24* capsized on 18 February 1943, W of Sicily. *RD 30* sunk on 26 December 1942 in Bizerta by aircraft bombs. *RD 31, RD 39* sunk, night of 20 January 1943, off Zuara by British destroyers *Kelvin* and *Javelin* as were *RD 36* and *RD 37* (which had transferred to the Revenue Cutter Service). *RD 32* discarded 1956. *RD 33* capsized on 22 January 1943, Gulf of Tunis. *RD 34* discarded in 1965. *RD 38* sunk 18 May 1943 at Trapani by aircraft. *RD 40* discarded 1955. *RD 41* discarded 1953. *RD 43* transferred to the Revenue Cutter service, capsized 22 January 1943 in the Gulf of Tunis. *RD 44* sunk off Bizerta on 5 May 1943, by enemy aircraft. *RD 55* sunk 25 May 1943 off Messina, by aircraft bombs. *RD 56* sunk on 9 January 1943 at Bizerta by aircraft bombs; refloated but definitively sunk on 24 March while being repaired there.

Ex-German M 57 class *minesweepers*

Displacement:	365t normal; 515t full load, 606t with the mines
Machinery:	2-shaft VTE, 2 Thornycroft coal boilers, 1600ihp = 14kts
Armament:	2–4in (102mm)/35, 42 mines (as minelayer)
Complement:	4 + 49

Name	Builder	Launched	Fate
ABASTRO (ex-*M 120*)	Neptun Yards, Rostock	24.7.18	Extant 1984
METEO (ex-*M 119*)	Neptun Yards, Rostock	22.6.18	Sunk 23.9.43

Both transferred to Italy on 9 March 1921, and both commissioned on 15 December as minesweepers, renamed respectively *Abastro* and *Meteo*. Both converted 1922–25 to minelayers, *Abastro* renamed *Cotrone* on 4 June 1925 and *Grotone* by 1931. Seized by the Germans at La Spezia on 9 September 1943, damaged by fire and grounded there in May 1944. Refloated again, sunk 1945 and again refloated 1949. She became the merchant TS *Garaventa* from 1949 without engines. *Vieste* seized by the Germans at Naples on 11 September 1943 and sunk by them 12 days later.

Mas 2 1915

MAS 12 ton type ('A' group) *experimental motor boats*

Displacement:	12.5t
Dimensions:	52ft 6in × 8ft 6in × 3ft 3in *16.0m × 2.6m × 1.0m*
Machinery:	2-shaft Isotta Fraschini petrol engines, 450hp = 23kts, plus 2-shaft Rognini electric motors (installed 1917), 10hp = 4kts
Armament:	2–17.7in (450mm) internal stern TT, 3–6.5mm MG (from Dec 1916, converted to minelayers: 4 mines, 1–47mm gun, 2–6.5mm MG)
Complement:	8

Two prototype MAS boats, designed by Eng Attilio Bisio of the SVAN yards, modified by the Royal Italian Navy and launched by SVAN, Venice in 1915. MAS or Mas originally meant *Motobarca armata SVAN*, from the name of the yards, *SVAN* = *Società Veneziana Automobili Nautiche*, Venetian Motor Boat Company. Later MAS meant *Motorbarca anti-sommergibile* (anti-submarine motor launch) and also *Motobarca armata silurante* (torpedo-armed motor launch), and at last *Motoscafo anti-sommergibile* (anti-submarine motorboats, ie subchaser). The electric motors were mounted in these and in several other Mas-boats for a silent approach of the Mas to the submerged submarine, during the attack. After World War One *Mas 1* was fitted with 2–17.7in exterior tubes, experimentally. *Mas 1* commissioned 1 December 1916, sunk 25 April 1917 off Caorle after collision with *Mas 9*; refloated 1 May and recovered; stricken 1 April 1928. *Mas 2* sunk on 29 October 1917 off Venice in bad seas; refloated and recovered in November. Stricken 1922.

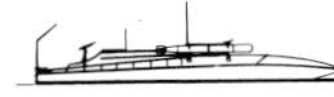

Mas 3 (SVAN type)
NB 1/750 scale

SVAN 12 ton type ('A' group 1st series) *motor boats*

Displacement: 16t
Dimensions: 52ft 6in × 8ft 7in × 3ft 11in
16.0m × 2.6m × 1.2m
Machinery: 2-shaft Isotta Fraschini (*Mas 11* Sterling) petrol engines, 450hp = max 22.3kts–25.2kts, plus (*Mas 9, 10, 12, 13, 14, 15, 18, 20, 21, 22*) 2-shaft Rognini electric motors, 10hp = 4kts
Armament: 2–17.7in (450mm) torpedoes or 1–47mm/40 gun, 1 to 3–6.5mm MG, 4–6 DC
Complement: 8

Class (launched):
Mas 3–Mas 22 (1916–17)

All boats designed by Eng Bisio and Italian Navy, all built by SVAN, Venice. *Mas 3* sunk on 20 November 1917 by hurricane. *Mas 7* sank on 4 November 1916 off Durazzo after collision with *36 PN*. *Mas 9* (Lt Luigi Rizzo) penetrated Trieste during the night of 9 December 1917 and sank the Austrian battleship *Wien*. *Mas 10* sank on 17 March 1918 in Lake Garda after a fire. *Mas 14* sank on 5 February 1918 off Venice in a collision with *Mas 13*. *Mas 15* sank the Austrian dreadnought *Szent István* on 10 June 1918, off Premuda Island and she has been preserved as a relic in Rome since 16 June 1936. *Mas 16* sunk on 18 December 1917 on the River Sile by enemy gunfire. *Mas 18* sunk on 17 September 1918 off Venice, refloated and repaired; stricken 1928. *Mas 22* renumbered *Mas 16* on 1 February 1921. All the other boats stricken 1920–27.

SVAN-Ansaldo 12 ton type ('A' group, 1st series) *motor boats*

Displacement: 11.8t
Dimensions: 52ft 6in × 8ft 7in × 4ft 3in
16.0m × 2.6m × 1.3m
Machinery: 2-shaft Sterling petrol engines, 400hp = *c*18–23.5kts
Armament: *Mas 23–44* 1–47mm/40 AA gun, 1–6.5mm MG, 4 DC
Mas 45 (prototype) 2–14in (356mm) internal bow TT, 1–37mm/20 gun (later converted as *Mas 23–44*)
Mas 46–52 designed armament as *Mas 45*, but were completed as *Mas 23–44*
Complement: 8

Class (launched):
Mas 23–Mas 52 (1916–17)

Designed by Eng Bisio, modified by the Italian Navy and Ansaldo Yards. All 30 boats built by Ansaldo. *Mas 25* sank on 2 May 1917 at Sanremo, after fire as did *Mas 28* on 27 December 1916 off Cape Kefali. *Mas 33* sank on 2 December 1917 off Massalubrense; refloated and repaired. *Mas 34* sank 27 April 1925 in the Northern Adriatic in heavy seas. *Mas 49* wrecked on 28 February 1917 at Brindisi. All the other boats stricken 1920–29.

SVAN 12 ton type ('A' group, 2nd series) *motor boats*

Displacement: 11.4t
Dimensions: As 1st series
Machinery: *Mas 53* 2-shaft Isotta Fraschini petrol engines, 450hp = 24.6kts
Mas 54–57 2-shaft Sterling petrol engines, 400hp = 25.2kts
Armament: 1–47mm/40, 1–6.5mm MG, 6 DC; from 1918 *Mas 53* 2–17.7in (450mm) torpedoes, 1–6.5mm MG, 6 DC
Complement: 8

Class (launched):
Mas 53–Mas 57 (1917)

Designed by Eng Attilio Bisio and built by SVAN, Venice. All 4 stricken 1926–29.

SVAN 12 ton type (modified 'A' group) *motor boats*

Displacement: 11.9t–12.5t
Dimensions: 52ft 6in × 9ft 10in × 3ft 11in
16.0m × 3.0m × c1.2m
Machinery: *Mas 58* 3-shaft Sterling petrol engines, 600hp = *c*25kts
Mas 59–62 2-shaft Sterling petrol engines, 400hp = *c*22–23kts
Other particulars: As *Mas 53–Mas 57*

Class:
Mas 58–Mas 62 (1917)

Designed by Eng Attilio Bisio (SVAN) and Eng Luigi Orlando (Orlando Yards, Leghorn). All 5 boats built by SVAN, Venice. Stricken 1921–26.

ELCO 44 ton type ('C' group, 1st series) *motor boats*

Displacement: 40.6t–43.8t
Dimensions: 80ft 1in × 12ft 2in × 3ft 11in
24.4m × 3.7m × 1.2m
Machinery: 2-shaft Standard petrol engines, 460hp = 15kts–17kts
Armament: 1–3in/40, 1–6.5mm MG, 10 DC
Complement: 15

Class (launched):
Mas 58–Mas 90 (1917)

All 43 boats built by Electric Boat Company, Bayonne, NJ (USA), ordered by the Italian Government. The boats were carried, unarmed, from America to Italy aboard merchant transport ships and were armed in Italy. *Mas 66* wrecked 19 September 1923 en route from Gallipoli (Italy) to Corfu. *Mas 77* and *87* were commissioned about a year after the other boats (17 June 1918) having been loaned to the US Navy from April to December 1917. *Mas 79* sank on 4 July 1918 off Ponza Island after collision with *22 OS*; rescued and scrapped. *Mas 82* reclassified *ME 61* after having been discarded. *Mas 87* transferred 1923 to R Guardia di Finanza (= Italian revenue cutters). *Mas 88* renumbered *Mas 89* (ii) on 1 February 1921. *Mas 89* (i) lost in an October 1917 gale in the Mediterranean from the deck of SS *Maine*, en route from America to Italy. All other boats stricken 1920–28.

Orlando 12 ton type ('A' group, 1st series) *motor boats*

Displacement: 11.5t (armed with gun); 12.4t (with torpedoes) + *c*1t for boats also fitted with electric engines
Dimensions: 52ft 10in × 9ft 2in × 4ft 3in
16.1m × 2.8m × c1.3m
Machinery: 2-shaft Isotta Fraschini petrol engines, 500hp (450hp for *Mas 91*) = 29.5kts, plus (only *Mas 92, 94, 95, 96, 100, 101, 102*) 2-shaft Rognini electric engines, 10hp (for silent approach) = 4kts
Armament: As MGB 1–47mm/40, 1–6.5mm MG, 2 DC
as MTB 2–17.7in (450mm) torpedoes, 2 to 3–6.5mm MG, 4 DC
Complement: 8

Class (launched):
Mas 91–Mas 102 (1917–18)

Designed by Eng Luigi Orlando and built by Orlando Yards, Leghorn. The electric motors were for a silent approach during an antisubmarine chase. *Mas 93* capsized on 26 December 1919 off Rovigno. *Mas 94* preserved till summer 1946 as a relic in La Spezia Naval Museum; damaged by explosion in the N Yd. *Mas 96* taken to Gardone (Lake Garda) and offered as a gift to Gabriele d'Annunzio; since April 1958 preserved as a relic in the Vittoriale at Gardone. *Mas 99* sank on 9 December 1926 off Elba after fire. *Mas 100* transferred on 26 April 1937 to Nationalist Spain, and renamed *Napoles* (later *LT 17*); definitely stricken 1941 and scrapped. All the other boats stricken 1921–34.

Mas 95 20 October 1917

ELCO 44 ton type ('C' group, 2nd series) *motor boats*

Particulars: As *Mas 58–Mas 90*

Class (launched):
Mas 103–Mas 114 (1917–18)

All 12 boats built by Electric Boat Company, Bayonne, NJ (USA) and carried, without armament, from America to Italy aboard merchant transports. *Mas 104* lost on 8 May 1918 at Naples, after fire. *Mas 105* reclassified *ME 62* on 31 October 1929 after having been stricken as was *Mas 113* becoming *ME 77*. *Mas 108* sunk on 18 November 1925, off Cape Ferro, by an exercise torpedo fired from *Mas 422*. *Mas 109* renumbered *Mas 104* (ii) and *Mas 112* renumbered *Mas 264* (ii) 1 February 1921. *Mas 110* reclassified *ME 63* on 31 October 1929 after having been discarded. All other boats stricken 1922–28.

Mas 120 (SVAN, 'B' group, 1st series) 1918

SVAN 19 ton type ('B' group, 1st series) *motor boats*

Displacement: 19t
Dimensions: 59ft 1in × 10ft 6in × 3ft 11in
18.0m × 3.2m × 1.2m
Machinery: 2-shaft Isotta Fraschini petrol engines, 500hp = *c*23kts
Armament: 1–3in/30, 1–6.5mm MG, 20 DC
Complement: 12

Class (launched):
Mas 115–Mas 139 (1918)

Boats from *Mas 115* to *128* laid down and launched in Venice SVAN Yards; *Mas 129* to *139* laid down and launched in La Spezia SVAN Yards. Nearly all were completed in the new SVAN factory at Piacenza, where they were carried by rail; and eventually armed in Venice N Yd. *Mas 125* sank on 9 August 1918 off Civitavecchia, after fire. *Mas 133* sunk on 1 June 1927 at Torre del Greco by a torpedo fired on exercise by the submarine *H 8*. *Mas 135* sank 22 April 1919 in the Tyrrhenian Sea, by collision with *Mas 270*. All the other boats stricken 1921–28.

SVAN 12 ton modified type ('A' group) *motor boats*

Displacement: 12t
Dimensions: 52ft 6in × 8ft 6in × 3ft 7in
16.0m × 2.6m × 1.1m
Machinery: 2-shaft Sterling petrol engines, 400hp = 24kts (*Mas 143–147* and *Mas 153* Fiat 480hp = 25kts)
Armament: 1–57mm/43, 1–6.5mm MG, 6 DC
Complement: 8

Class (launched):
Mas 140–Mas 157 (1917–19)

All 18 boats built by Maccia Marchini Yards, Carate Lario (Lake Como). *Mas 140* sank on 3 August 1918 at Porto Corsini, after fire. *Mas 144* sank 17 April 1918 in Lake Como, after fire during trials. *Mas 151* wrecked on 27 May 1927 on Elba. *Mas 152* sank on 27 June 1922 in Tyrrhenian Sea, in heavy sea, while being towed by *59 OL*. All other boats stricken 1922–34.

SVAN 12 ton modified type ('A' group) *motor boats*

Displacement: 12.2t (*Mas 166–175, 201–202* 12.1t)
Dimensions: As *Mas 140–Mas 157*
Machinery: 2-shaft Fiat petrol engines, 480hp (*Mas 158, 159, 164* Sterling 400hp) = 25kts (Sterling engined 23kts, *Mas 166–175* 480hp = 24.5kts–26.5kts)
Armament: As *Mas 140–Mas 157* (*Mas 158–160* 2–17.7in torpedoes, 2–6.5mm MGs, 6 DC)
Complement: 8

Mas 230 (Orlando, 'A' group, 2nd series) 1919

Class (launched):
Mas 158–Mas 202 (1917–18)

Mas 158–Mas 165 were built by Picchiotti of Limite sull'Arno. *Mas 160* sank, night of 22 May 1927, off Venice, by collision with *Mas 190*. Refloated 26 June but stricken that year. The other boats stricken 1925–29. *Mas 166–Mas 175* built by Gallinari, Leghorn in 1917–18. *Mas 166* sank on 12 November 1918 in Brindisi harbour after collision with *67 PN*. The other boats were stricken 1921–25. *Mas 176–Mas 200* built in 1918 by Piaggio of Sestri Ponente. *Mas 178* lost on 12 September 1930 after grounding because of fire. The other boats stricken 1922–1938. *Mas 201* and *202* built by Foggi & Agretti of Leghorn, stricken 1922.

Baglietto 12 ton *experimental motor boat*

Displacement: 12t (as MGB)–12.9t (as MTB)
Dimensions: 52ft 6in × 5ft 3in × 2ft 10in (2ft 11in as MTB)
16.0m × 2.6m × 0.8m (0.9m)
Machinery: 2-shaft Fiat petrol engines, 460hp = 26.4kts, plus 2 Rognini electric motors, 10hp = 4kts
Armament: As MGB 1–47mm/40 (as MTB 2–17.7in torpedoes) 1–6.5mm MG, 10 DC
Complement: 8

Prototype built experimentally, as a private venture, by Baglietto of Varazze. The design and the boat were accepted as *Mas 203* by the Italian Navy. Commissioned 10 August 1917. Stricken 1922.

Baglietto 12 ton type ('A' group) *motor boats*

Displacement: 13.4t (as MGB)–13.9t (as MTB)
Dimensions: 52ft 6in × 5ft 3in × 3ft 3in (3ft 7in as MTB)
16.0m × 2.6m × 1.0m (1.1m)
Machinery: 2-shaft Fiat petrol engines, 480hp = 23kts–24.5kts, plus (all but *Mas 217*) 2 Rognini electric engines, 10hp = 4kts
Armament: As MGB 1–57mm/43, 1–6.5mm MG, 10 DC
As MTB 2–17.7in (450mm) torpedoes, 1–6.5mm MG, 10 DC
Complement: 7

Class (launched):
Mas 204–Mas 217 (1918)

Designed by Baglietto and built by them at Varazze. After 1926 the gun and the electric engines were removed, and the Fiat engines were replaced by Isotta Fraschini ones, with a max speed of *c*27kts. The five *Mas* (*204, 206, 210, 213* and *216*) carried to Massawa in 1936 did not exceed 10–15kts during World War Two, and for no longer than one hour. *Mas 204, 206, 210, 213* and *216* scuttled on 8 April 1941 at Massawa. *Mas 208* sunk 15 April 1934 off Unie Is after collision. Refloated 22 April, stricken in August. The other boats were stricken 1922–35.

Orlando 12 ton type ('A' group, 2nd series) *motor boats*

Displacement: 12t (as MGB)–12.9t (as MTB)
Dimensions: 53ft 10in × 9ft 6in × 4ft 5in (4ft 7in as MTB)
16.4m × 2.8m × 1.3m (1.4m)
Machinery: 2-shaft Isotta Fraschini petrol engines, 500hp = 28kts, plus (only aboard *Mas 218–222* and *228*) 2 Rognini electric engines, 10hp = 4kts
Armament: As MGB 1–57mm/43, 1–6.5mm MG, 2 DC
As MTB 2–17.7in (450mm) torpedoes, 2 to 3–6.5mm MG, 4 DC
Complement: 8

Class (launched):
Mas 218–Mas 232 (1918)

Designed by Eng Luigi Orlando, all 15 boats built in 1918 by Orlando Yards, Leghorn. *Mas 220* and *221* sold 1920 to the Finnish Navy, where they were renamed *MTV 1* and *MTV 2* respectively, and later *Sisu II* and *Hurja*; both lost in World War Two. *Mas 223* used as a radio-controlled boat (June–November 1924), during trials with destroyer *Cosenz*. Transferred 26 April 1937 to Nationalist Spain and renamed *Sicilia*, later *LT 18*. Definitively stricken March 1941. *Mas 226* and *227* sold 1921 to China. *Mas 231* and *232* sold to Swedish Navy in 1921 and renumbered respectively *N 1* and *N 2*. Both stricken 1927. The other boats stricken 1926–37.

SVAN 19 ton type ('B' group, 2nd series) *motor boats*

Displacement: 19.4t
Dimensions: 59ft 1in × 10ft 10in × 3ft 11in
18.0m × 3.3m × 1.2m
Machinery: 2-shaft Isotta Fraschini petrol engines, 500hp = *c*20.5kts
Armament: 1–3in/40, 1–6.5mm MG, 20 DC
Complement: 12

Class (launched):
Mas 233–Mas 252 (1918–19)

Designed by SVAN and built by Ducrot yard of Palermo, these 20 boats were more powerful than the 1st series (*Mas 115–139*) and better able to chase submarines. They were provided with 2 'C tubes' (AS detectors). The Ducrot yard specialised in seaplane construction but had no experience of boats, so works went slowly. *Mas 237* reclassified *ME 78* in 1929. *Mas 240* sank SW of Sardinia on 28 October 1918 after fire. *Mas 243* reclassified *ME 79* in 1929. *Mas 249* reclassified *ME 76* in 1929. All the remaining boats were stricken in 1922–29.

Mas 260 (ELCO, 'C' group, 3rd series) 1918

ELCO 44 ton type ('C' group, 3rd series) *motor boats*

Displacement: 40.6t–43.8t
Dimensions: 80ft 1in pp × 12ft 2in × 3ft 11in
24.4m × 3.7m × 1.2m
Machinery: 2-shaft Standard petrol engines, 460hp = 17kts
Armament: 1–3in/40, 1–6.5mm MG, 10 DC
Complement: 15

Class:
Mas 253–Mas 302

All 50 boats built in 1918 by Electric Boat Company, Bayonne, NJ (USA). They were transported to Italy without armament, and completed in Italian yards. They had a good endurance: *c*900 miles at 14kts, and *c*700 miles at full speed (*c*17kts). They too were provided with two 'C tubes', for detecting submerged submarines. *Mas 253* and *Mas 254* sank on 3 June 1918 in Civitavecchia harbour, after fire. Refloated and restored. *Mas 256* reclassified *ME 64* in 1929. *Mas 259* lost on 2 January 1921 in N Adriatic, after having gone aground as was *Mas 261* near Veglia Island. *Mas 260* reclassified in ME category in 1929. *Mas 262* sank on 28 September 1927 off La Maddalena, Sardinia, by exercise torpedo from *Mas 418*. Lifted and discarded 1927. *Mas 264* lost on 4 July 1918 off Porto Maurizio (now Imperia) together with SS *Napoli* (sunk by collision) which carried her from the USA to Italy. *Mas 265* reclassed 1929 in ME category. *Mas 266* blew up in Taranto while refuelling on 14 September 1927. *Mas 268* and 273 sold to Rumanian Navy, renumbered respectively *M 1* and *M 2*, later *VAS 1* and *VAS 2*; finally discarded *c*1932. *Mas 270* and *271* in 1929 reclassified respectively *ME 65* and *ME 66*. *Mas 280, 289* and *292*, in 1928, reclassified respectively *ME 55, ME 56, ME 57*. *Mas 293* mined and sank on 25 March 1919 off Cape Rodoni. *Mas 297* and *298*, in 1929, reclassified respectively *ME 68* and *ME 69*. *Mas 302*, in 1927, reclassified *ME 47*. All the other boats stricken 1919–29.

Mas 303 (ELCO type, 'C' group, 1st series)
NB 1/750 scale

ELCO 44 ton modified type ('C' group, 1st series) *motor boats*

Displacement: 42.8t–44.6t
Dimensions: 66ft 11in pp × 12ft 4in × 4ft 3in
24.4m × 3.7m × 1.3m
Machinery: 2-shaft Standard petrol engines, 460hp = 19kts
Armament: 1–3in/40, 1 to 2–6.5mm MG, 10 DC
Complement: 15

Class (launched):
Mas 303–Mas 317 (1918–19)

These 15 boats were of ELCO type and design known as 'May 1917' type, but modified by the Italian Navy (Castellammare Di Stabia NY). Built in Italian yards: *Mas 303–Mas 311*, by Castellammare di Stabia N Yd; *Mas 312* and *313* built by Cosamati of Naples; *Mas 314* and *315*, by Bonifacio, Castellammare di Stabia; *Mas 316* and *317*, by Amendola, Naples. *Mas 307* transferred 1923 to Italian Revenue cutter service; *Mas 308* sank in Tripoli harbour on 31 December 1918, refloated but unable to be restored, so stricken 1919. *Mas 310* renumbered *Mas 296* (ii) on 1 February 1921. *Mas 312* in 1929 reclassified as *ME 70*. The remaining boats all stricken in 1919–25.

Mas 318 *motor boat*

Displacement: 19.9t
Dimensions: 57ft 5in × 10ft 2in × 3ft 11in
17.5m × 3.1m × 1.2m
Machinery: 2-shaft Isotta Fraschini petrol engines, 500hp = 20kts
Armament: 1–3in/40, 1–6.5mm MG, 20 DC
Complement: 10

This boat, designed by Baglietto, had been ordered by a private person, who did not buy her, so the boat, without engines, remained at Baglietto. She was offered to the Italian Navy in 1916 and again in 1917, and the Navy accepted her in October 1917. Commissioned on 14 December she served for training purposes at La Spezia; and in 1918 the 3in gun was replaced by 1–57mm/43. Stricken in 1926.

SVAN 12 ton modified type ('A' group, 1st series) *motor boats*

Displacement: 14.2t
Dimensions: 52ft 6in × 9ft 2in × 3ft 11in
16.0m × 2.8m × 1.2m
Machinery: 2-shaft Isotta Fraschini petrol engines, 700hp = 28kts
Armament: 2–17.7in (450mm) torpedoes, 2 to 3–6.5mm MG, 4 DC
Complement: 8

Class (launched):
Mas 319–Mas 323 (1919)

Designed by SVAN and built in La Spezia SVAN yards. The designed Isotta Fraschini 500hp engines were actually replaced by 700hp engines. *Mas 319, 320* and *321* commissioned in September 1919, while for *Mas 322* and *323* construction was suspended on 19 June 1920. The first three boats were stricken in 1920–31.

SVAN 12 ton modified Pecoraro *experimental motor boat*

Displacement: 12t
Dimensions: 52ft 6in × 10ft 8in × 3ft 11in
16.0m × 3.2m × 1.2m
Machinery: 2-shaft Sterling petrol engines, 400hp = more than 23kts as designed
Armament: 2–17.7in (450mm) torpedoes or 1–57mm/43 gun, 1 to 2–6.5mm MG, 4 DC
Complement: 10

Mas 324 was designed by Eng Captain Nino Pecoraro, modifying the 12 ton SVAN boat. The construction was slow, because the SVAN yards were full of work. So, the boat, even if ordered on 1 September 1917, was perhaps not laid down, and the order was cancelled on 19 June 1920.

SVAN 12 ton modified type ('A' group, 2nd series) *motor boats*

Displacement: 13t (as MGB)–13.6t (as MTB)
Dimensions: As 1st series except *c*1.18m draught
Machinery: 2-shaft Sterling petrol engines, 440hp = 23kts
Armament: As MGB 1–57mm/43 AA, 1–6.5mm MG, 4 DC
As MTB 2–17.7in (450mm) torpedoes, 2–6.5mm MG, 4 DC
Complement: 8

Class (launched):
Mas 325 and *Mas 326* (1918)

Designed by SVAN Yards. Both boats built by Picchiotti, Limite sull'Arno. Launched 1918 and commissioned immediately after the end of World War One, they were stricken respectively in 1926 and 1929.

ELCO 44 ton modified type ('C' type group, 2nd series) *motor boats*

Displacement: 42.8t–44.6t
Dimensions: As 1st series except 4ft 3in/*1.3m* draught
Other particulars: As 1st series

Class (launched):
Mas 327–Mas 376 (1918–20)

Like the 1st series these 50 boats were ELCO type modified by the Italian Navy and built in Italian yards: *Mas 327–338* by Castellammare di Stabia N Yd; *339* and *340* by Bonifacio of Castellammare di Stabia; *341* and *342* by Donnarumma, Castellammare di Stabia; *343–345* by Marinelli, San Giovanni a Teduccio (Naples); *345–351* Pattison, Naples; *352–363* by Gallinari, Leghorn; *364–367* by Picchiotti, Limite sull'Arno; *368–371* by Guastavino, Varazze; *372–376* by La Spezia N Yd. *Mas 327–334*, all commissioned 1919. *Mas 332* sank on 23 March 1929 at Torre del Greco, after fire. Refloated the same day but discarded 1929. Building of *Mas 335–338*, *340* and *342*, suspended in March 1919. *Mas 339* completed 1920 by Castellammare di Stabia N Yd, but without armament and stricken 1920. *Mas 341* completed as a fishing boat in 1920. *Mas 343* hull damaged by fire, on slip; converted to a fishing boat and sold. *Mas 345* converted to a fishing boat and sold. *Mas 348, 349, 350* and *351* were sold in 1921 to the Rumanian Navy, renumbered respectively *M 3, M 6, M 4, M 7*, later *VAS 3, VAS 6, VAS 4, VAS 7* and definitely stricken *c*1932. *Mas 354* sank on 19 May 1925 at Portoferraio (Elba) by fire. *Mas 355* and *356* reclassified 1928 as, respectively, *ME 48* and *ME 49*. *Mas 358–363* suspended on 24 December 1919 and hulls converted to fishing boats, sold 1921. *Mas 364–367* hulls delivered to the Navy, converted 1922 in La Spezia N Yd to fishing boats and sold. *Mas 373* sold 1921 to the Rumanian Navy, renumbered *M 5*, later *VAS 5*; definitively stricken *c*1931. All remaining boats discarded 1920–29.

ELCO 44 ton type ('C' group, 4th series) *motor boats*

Displacement: 40.6t–43.8t
Machinery: As 1st series = *c*17kts
Other particulars: As 1st series

Class (launched):
Mas 377–Mas 396 (1918–19)

All 20 built by Electric Boat Company, Bayonne, NJ (USA) and commissioned 1918–19. *Mas 378* stricken 1919 and converted 1919–20 to an experimental fishing boat. *Mas 384* transferred 1923 to Revenue Cutters service. *Mas 387, 389, 390, 391, 392* and *396* reclassified 1928–29 respectively as *ME .., ME 71, ME 72, ME 73, ME .., ME 75*. *Mas 395* from 29 August 1926 till 20 June 1927 renamed *Roma* and put at the Governor of Rome's disposal; reclassified in 1929 as *ME 74*. All the others stricken 1920–28.

Baglietto veloce type ('D' group) *motor boats*

Displacement: 30t
Dimensions: 69ft 7in × 13ft 11in × 3ft 11in
21.2m × 4.2m × 1.2m
Machinery: 2-shaft Isotta Fraschini main petrol engines, 1600hp, and 1-shaft (central) Isotta Fraschini auxiliary petrol engine, 300hp = 28.2kts, 2 Rognini electric engines, 10hp, for silent approach = 4kts
Armament: 1–3in/40, 1–6.5mm MG, 4–17.7in (450mm) torpedoes, 4 DC
Complement: 12

Class (launched):
Mas 397–Mas 400 (1918–20)

In order to attain high speed, SVAN and Baglietto yards studied new hull shapes and the mounting of more powerful engines. This type, called 'veloce' (fast), was to attain 33kts, but actually it reached 28.2kts with all three petrol engines, 7.5kts with the central engine. Their names were to be, respectively, *Cingallegra, Cutrettola, Procellaria* and *Scricciolo* (names of birds), but in March 1918 they reverted to the usual Mas numbers. In 1924 the already commissioned *Mas 397* and the other three not yet completed boats were modified, reducing their armament. After this, with a reduced armament (no gun; 2–17.7in torpedoes, 2–6.5mm MG, 10 DC), the highest speed attained was *c*33kts, and a sea speed of *c*30kts was normal. All four boats reclassified *ME*, respectively *83, 84, 85* and *86* in 1935.

SVAN veloce type ('D' group) *motor boats*

Displacement: 27.5t–29.4t
Dimensions: 72ft 2in × 13ft 1in × 3ft 11in
22.0m × 4.0m × 1.2m
Machinery: 4-shaft Isotta Fraschini petrol engines, 1600hp = 28.6kts, plus 2 Rognini electric engines, for silent approach, 10hp = 4kts
Armament: 2–17.7in (450mm) torpedoes, 2–6.5mm MG, 20 DC
Complement: 10

Class (launched):
Mas 401–Mas 410 (1922–23)

These boats were also designed for a higher speed; their powerplant changed from a 3-shaft arrangement to four engines in series on 2 shafts, but as built there were 4 propellers and a reduced armament, omitting the designed 3in/30 gun and 1–6.5mm MG. The designed speed of 30kts was not reached, their top speed being of 28.6kts, and best sea speed of *c*27.5kts. They too were to have bird names (*Capinera, Usignolo, Pettirosso, Allodola, Fringuello, Balestruccio, Picchio, Passero* and *Stornello*), but from March 1918 they were given the usual numbers. All boats designed and built by SVAN, some at Venice, some others at La Spezia, but all completed by Venezia SVAN Yards. All stricken in 1928.

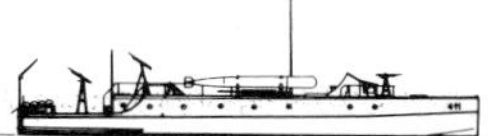
Mas 411 (SVAN type, 'D' group, 1st series)
NB 1/750 scale

SVAN velocissimo type ('D' group, 1st series) *motor boats*

Displacement: 18t–*c*22.5t
Dimensions: 59ft 1in × 11ft 10in × 3ft 11in
18.0m × 3.6m × 1.2m
Machinery: 2-shaft Isotta Fraschini petrol engines, 1600hp = *c*25kts, plus 2 Rognini electric engines, 16hp = 5kts
Armament: 2–17.7in (450mm) torpedoes, 3–6.5mm MG, 4 DC
Complement: 10

Class (launched):
Mas 411–Mas 414 (1919)

This type, called *'velocissimo'* (very fast), only had an offensive role, being armed with torpedoes, and no gun. All boats built by SVAN at La Spezia and carried by rail to Venice for completion. The designed speed of 35kts was never attained. They were modified more times, in propellers and so on. Their best sea speed was *c*23.5kts. All stricken in 1921.

Mas 401 (SVAN, 'D' group) as completed

Grillo as completed

SVAN velocissimo type ('D' group, 2nd series) *motor boats*

Displacement: 18t–21.2t
Machinery: 3-shaft Isotta Fraschini petrol engines, 1200hp = 25.5kts–28kts, plus 2 Rognini electric engines, 16hp = *c*5kts
Armament: 2–17.7in (450mm) torpedoes, 3–6.5mm MG, 6 DC
Other particulars: As 1st series

Class (launched):
Mas 415–Mas 422 (1922–23)

These second series *'velocissimo'* (very fast) boats awaited, for their completion, the results of the first series (*411–414*), which were not good. Anyhow, this second series reached, during sea trials, 9 speed of 28kts. All 8 boats, designed and built by SVAN were launched in La Spezia and were completed in Venice. *Mas 415* and *417* were reclassified respectively *ME 58* and *ME 59* in 1929; *Mas 416* was reclassisfied *ME 60* in 1928. The other five boats were stricken from 1927–38.

CANCELLED CONSTRUCTION

Apart from the already mentioned incomplete Mas-boats (*322–323, 324, 335–338, 339, 340, 342, 343, 345, 358–363, 364–367*) some series were cancelled: 30 boats of ELCO 44-ton modified type ('C' group), which, together with another 20 as yet unordered boats, were to form the 3rd series of that type, as follows: 10 boats ordered from Gallinari of Leghorn, 6 boats ordered from Picchiotti of Limite sull'Arno, 14 boats ordered from Castellammare di Stabia N Yd; 11 boats of SVAN 19-ton type ('B' group), which were to form the 3rd series of that type, numbers being 423–433, to be ordered from Ducrot of Palermo.

GRILLO class *climbing boats*

Displacement:	8t
Dimensions:	52ft 6in × 10ft 2in × 2ft 4in *16.0m × 3.1m × 0.7m*
Machinery:	1-shaft two Rognini & Balbo electric engines, 10hp = 4kts. Range *c*30nm/4kts
Armament:	2–17.7in (450mm) torpedoes
Complement:	1 + 3

Class:
Grillo, Cavalletta, Pulce, Locusta

These boats, designed by Eng Attilio Bisio (of SVAN Yards) and the Navy, were 'naval tanks', provided with two lateral caterpillar chains for overcoming harbour barrages. They were designed to force the main Austrian naval base of Pola. All four built in Venice NY and commissioned in March 1918. *Cavalletta* was scuttled on 13 April 1918 off Pola, together with *Pulce, Grillo* damaged by Austrian gun fire, was scuttled on night of 14 May 1918 while forcing the barrages of Pola. She was raised by the Austrian Navy, which tried to copy her. *Locusta* stricken 1921.

'MIGNATTA' *self-propelled mine*

A special self-propelled weapon, consisting of an old 14in Mark B 57 torpedo (B = bronze), fed by compressed air at 205 atmospheres, and in two mines containing totally 340kg of TNT. The weapon could reach *c*3–4 knots of speed and had an endurance of *c*10 miles. It was controlled by two men, both in the water. The two mines were provided with electro-magnets for their application to enemy keels (limpet mines), and there was a timer for their explosion. The design was due to Eng Lt Cdr Raffaele Rossetti, and the weapon, called 'S 1' was built in Venice N Yd in 1918. Eng Rossetti and Doctor Lt Raffaele Paolucci led the 'S 1', forced the barrages of the naval base of Pola and, during the night of 31 October–1 November 1918, sank the Austrian dreadnought *Viribus Unitis*, which – but the Italian Navy and the two officers in particular did not know this – had been transferred a few hours earlier to the newly formed Yugoslav Navy. Another part of the charges damaged the Austrian steamer *Wien*.

VEDETTE BOATS

A total of 47 Japanese fishing boats (built 1909–13) was bought by the Italian Navy in 1916. Their naval displacement was between 280 and 500 metric tonnes, their speed from 8kts to 12.5kts. All commissioned in the Italian Navy in 1917 with one or two 3in guns. In the Italian Navy they were numbered *G 1–G 47* (G = *Giappone*).

G 1 renamed *Berenice* in 1922 and stricken 1929. *G 3* renamed *Maggiore Toselli* in 1920, lost 1930, grounded near Ras-el-Tin (Libya).

G 4 sunk night 28–29 October 1918 off Elba, after collision with British transport *Cycle*.

G 5 renamed *Frigido* in 1919 and converted to water-carrier, stricken 1975.

G 6 sunk 12 August 1918, off Cape Passero (Sicily), by torpedo from *U 63*.

G 13 renamed *Cirene* in 1922, sunk on 11 June 1941 in Benghazi by RAF bombs.

G 15 renamed *Porto Corsini* in 1923, captured on 8 April 1941 at Massawa by the British.

G 16 renamed *Rimini* 1923, captured on 9 September 1943 by the Germans at La Spezia, scuttled May 1945.

G 19 transferred 1919 to the Italian Fishery Commission and renamed *Sardegna*, repurchased 1922 by the Italian Navy and renamed *Tritone*, used as a survey ship till 1934, stricken 1934.

G 21 renamed *Cariddi* 1923, served as survey ship, sunk on 6 April 1923 at Trapani, by Allied bombing.

G 23 renamed *Alula* 1923, captured by the Germans on 9 September 1943 and commissioned by them as the coastal defence boat *GA 77*, sunk October 1944 harbour of Salonika.

G 24 renamed *Mario Bianco* 1921, used as a survey ship after 1928, later as a lighthouse tender, sunk on 11 June 1941 in Benghazi by RAF bombs.

G 25 converted to a water-carrier and renamed *Zuara*, stricken 1921.

G 31 renamed *Gallipoli* 1923, used as a netlayer in World War Two, captured by the Germans at Syra Is, and commissioned by them as *GA 79*, sunk in 1944 at Salonika.

G 32 sunk 7 February 1918, W of Portoferraio (Elba) by torpedo from *UB 49*.

G 34 renamed *Dante de Lutti* 1921 and used as a survey ship, sunk 6 July 1941 off Benghazi by British submarine *Triumph*.

G 36 renamed *Otranto* 1923, used as a netlayer in WW 2, captured by the Germans at Syra Island and commissioned by them as *GA 78*, sunk in 1944 at Salonika.

G 37 renamed *Augusta* 1923, stricken 1932.

G 45 recommissioned as a survey ship and renamed *Luigi Garavoglia* in 1919, lost 21 August 1921 near Derna, grounded. All the others stricken 1921–23.

AUXILIARY VEDETTE BOATS

During the period 1906–21 the Italian Navy commissioned 85 fishing boats, tugs or small steamers, for escort duty, minesweeping and other similar services. Their displacement was between 107 and 615 metric tonnes, their speed between 8kts and 12kts, they were armed with 1 to 4–57mm or 3in guns and 1 to 2–6.5mm MGs. They were all discarded in 1919–21, and returned to their owners or sold for scrapping, with the exception mentioned as below. Here are their names:

Alessandro, Alfredo Cappellini (sunk 1917), *Aliseo, America 2, Anatra, Argentario; Aventino* (converted to a water-carrier after World War One, stricken 1935); *Baia, Baiardo* (renamed *Valoroso* 1918, sunk 1941), *Balena* (renamed *Palmaria* 1933, sunk 1945); *Basiluzzo* (stricken 1949 and transferred 1949 to Yugoslavia); *Bengasi II, Bufera, Burrasca* (discarded after 1938); *Candiano, Capodoglio, Cerboli, Ciclone, Cicogna, Costa Azzurra, Cuma, Favignana, Filicudi* (sunk 1917), *Flutto, Folaga, Fortunale, Friuli, Gaeta* (stricken 1951), *Gaiola, Iberia, Lampedusa* (stricken 1951), *Lampedusa II, Lavezzi, Leopardo* (renamed *Voragine* 1917), *Levanzo* (used as a lighthouse tender after World War One, sunk 1943); *Lido* (ex-Italian naval tug *N 27*, launched 1908, used in peace as a lighthouse tender, in wartime as a minesweeper, captured by the Germans 1943); *Lilibeo* (stricken 1958); *Liscabianca, Liscanera* (captured by the Germans 1943 and scuttled by them; refloated after 1945 and recommissioned in the Italian Navy, stricken 1963); *Maestrale, Marmarica, Maroso, Meloria* (sunk 1916); *Monsone I* (sunk 1916), *Monsone II, Montecristo, Nembo* (between the wars used as a transport, again a gunboat in World War Two, sunk 1943); *Ogliastra, Onda, Palatino* (sunk 1915), *Panaria* (renamed *Scilla* 1923 and reclassed as a survey ship, *c*1935 reclassed as a lighthouse tender, captured 1943 by the Germans and sunk by them); *Pantera* (renamed *Vortice* 1917); *Pelago, Peloro* (sunk 1916); *Piombino* (reclassed as a tug after 1919, stricken after 1946); *Porto Ercole, Portofino* (wrecked 1946), *Principessa Mafalda 2) Procella, Quirinale, Ravenna 2, Razzoli, Regina Elena 2, Salina, San Francesco* (renamed *Selinute* 1918); *Scirocco, Scolta* (stricken 1929), *Serpentara, Sirena, Spartivento, Stella, Stromboli, Talamone* (stricken 1946 and transferred to USSR 1949), *Tempesta, Terracini* (lost 1943); *Tifone, Tigre* (renamed *Vigilante* 1917, stricken 1932); *Tramontana, Tuono, Uragano, Vortice, Zannone, Zelina*.

MISCELLANEOUS

CUNFIDA (ex-Turkish) *armed yacht*

The Turkish armed yacht *Cipka* was captured by Italian warships on 7 January 1912 in the Red Sea action near Kunfida. Armed with 3–47mm and given a crew of 35. Later rearmed with 2–3in/40. Stricken on 13 November 1924.

CAPITANO VERRI (ex-Turkish) *armed yacht*

The scuttled Turkish armed yacht *Tarablus*, was captured on 30 September 1911 at Preveza (Ionian Sea) by the Italian destroyers *Artigliere* and *Corazziere*. She was refloated and commissioned on 6 May 1912 into the Italian Navy. Stricken on 19 December 1926.

GIULIANA (ex-British) *armed yacht*

Displacement: 1050t
Dimensions: 250ft 2in oa, 221ft 6in wl × 27ft 11in × 12ft 10in
76.2m, 67.5m × 8.5m × 3.9m
Machinery: 1-shaft VTE, 700ihp = 11.9kts
Armament: 4–57mm
Complement: 2 + 46

Name	Builder	Launched	Fate
GIULIANA (ex-*Rhouma*)	Napier & Company, Glasgow	6.93	Stricken 1928

The ex-British SS *Rhouma* commissioned into the Italian Navy on 19 July 1912. Later 1915–18 rearmed with 2–3in/40.

ARCHIMEDE (ex-British) *armed yacht*

Displacement: 815t–900t
Dimensions: 228ft 1in × 26ft 7in × 12ft
69.8m × 8.1m × 3.6m
Machinery: 1-shaft VTE, 800ihp = 13kts
Armament: 4–57mm/43
Complement: 2 + 46

Name	Builder	Launched	Fate
ARCHIMEDE (ex-*Homs*, ex-*Capercailzie*)	Barclay Curle Company, Glasgow	4.92	Stricken 1928

The former British yacht was commissioned into the Italian Navy on 28 July 1912; captured on 25 March 1918 by the Austro-Germans at Odessa; recaptured by the Italians on 29 November at Sevastopol. Rearmed with 2–3in/40 and 1–6.5mm MG.

TOBRUK (ex-British) *armed yacht*

Displacement: 700t–850t
Dimensions: 200ft 2in oa, 183ft 9in × 24ft 11in × 11ft 10in
61.0m, 56.0m × 7.6m × 3.6m
Machinery: 1-shaft VTE, 554ihp = 11.5kts
Armament: 3–47mm
Complement: 2 + 38

Name	Builder	Launched	Fate
TOBRUK (ex-*Evona*)	Ailsa Shipbuilding Company, Troon	12.97	Stricken 1925

Commissioned into the Italian Navy on 3 August 1912. During 1915–18 rearmed with 3–3in/40 and 1–6.5mm MG.

MISURATA (ex-British) *armed yacht*

Displacement: 700t–880t
Dimensions: 207ft oa, 191ft 3in × 25ft 3in × 11ft 10in
63.1m, 58.3m × 7.7m × 3.6m
Machinery: 1-shaft VTE, 781ihp = 12.5kts
Armament: 2–47mm
Complement: 2 + 38

Name	Builder	Launched	Fate
MISURATA (ex-*Arrow*)	W Hamilton & Co, Glasgow	6.94	Stricken 1924

Former British yacht. Commissioned into the Italian Navy 5 September 1912. During 1915–18 rearmed with 2–3in/40 AA, 1–6.5mm MG.

EUROPA (ex-British) *seaplane carrier*

Displacement: 6400t–8805t
Dimensions: 403ft 7in oa, 392ft 1in wl × 46ft × 19ft, 24ft 11in
123.1m, 119.5m × 14.0m × 5.8m, 7.6m
Machinery: 1-shaft VTE, 2594ihp = 12.2kts
Armament: 2–3in/30 AA, 8 seaplanes
Complement: ?

Name	Builder	Launched	Fate
EUROPA (ex-*Quarto*, ex-*Salacia*, ex-*Manila*)	Chas Connell Co, Scotstoun, Glasgow	4.8.95	Stricken 1920

Built as the British SS *Manila* (4134grt, net 2636t); in 1898 renamed *Salacia*. She kept her name in 1911, becoming German. In 1913 she became the Italian merchant ship *Quarto*. Bought by the Italian Navy on 6 February 1915 and converted to a seaplane transport, commissioned on 6 October and renamed *Europa*. Her capacity was 8 seaplanes, but usually carried 2 reconnaissance and 2 fighters. Fitted also as a depot ship for submarines.

ARMED DHOWS

Name	In Italian Navy	Disp	Armament
ANTILOPE (ex-*Nutcohill*)	1902–14	60t	1–75mm, 1–37mm
CAMOSCIO (i)	1903–07	22t	2–75mm
CAMOSCIO (ii)	1907–14	70t	2–75mm
CAPRIOLO	1903–11	35t	2–75mm
CERVO (ii) (ex-*Amber*)	1909–13	30t	1–75mm, 2–37mm
DAINO	1910–14	86t	2–75mm, 1–37mm
GAZZELLA (ii) (ex-*Sahada*)	1902–09	56t	2–75mm, 1–37mm
GAZZELLA (iii) (ex-*Sultani*)	1909–14	60t	2–75mm, 1–37mm
ZEBRA	1903–12	30t	2–75mm

All sailing ships (*Sambuchi* in Italian), equipped with native seamen, commanded by Italian officers or petty officers, served in Red Sea and along the coast of Italian Somaliland. Complement varied from 18 to 28 men.

ALFREDO CAPPELLINI *monitor*

Displacement: 1452t
Dimensions: 118ft 1in × 59ft 1in × 7ft 11in
36.0m × 18.0m × 2.4m
Machinery: 1-shaft VDE, 265ihp = 3.5kts
Armament: 2–15in (381mm)/40

Name	Builder	Launched	Fate
ALFREDO CAPPELLINI (ex-*GA 53*)	Orlando, Leghorn	1915	Sunk 16.11.17

The hull, originally built for a crane, was altered and strengthened, fitted with two large guns destined for the battleship *Francesco Morosini* (construction suspended during 1915–18), protected by two anti-torpedo nets. Commissioned on 28 April 1916. The guns had 20° of max elevation and could be trained 15° to right and to left. Wrecked off Ancona.

Europa about 1918

Alfredo Cappellini as completed

Faà di Bruno date unknown

FAA' DI BRUNO *monitor*

Displacement: 2854t
Dimensions: 182ft 1in × 88ft 7in × 7ft 3in
55.5m × 27.0m × 2.2m
Machinery: 2 old Thornycroft engines, from discarded torpedo-boats, 2-shaft, 465ihp = *c*3kts
Armament: 2–15in (381mm)/40, 4–3in/40 AA, 2–40mm/39 MG

Name	Builder	Launched	Fate
FAA' DI BRUNO (ex-*GA 43*)	Venice N Yd	30.1.16	Stricken 1924

Designed by Eng Rear-Admiral Giuseppe Rota. The two large guns were destined for the battleship *Cristoforo Colombo* (construction suspended during 1915–18). Max elevation of the 15in guns 15°; the turret could be trained 30° to right and to left. Hull protected all around by a 2.9m concrete cofferdam. Armour of 40mm for deck, 60mm for barbette, 20 + 20 + 70mm for turret. Commissioned on 23 July 1917. Again in service as *GM 194*, used as a floating battery for the defence of Genoa in World War Two.

MONFALCONE *monitor*

Displacement: 525t
Dimensions: 78ft 9in × 46ft 3in × 6ft 7in
24.0m × 14.1m × 2m
Machinery: 2 Polar diesels, 400bhp = 6kts
Armament: 1–12in (305mm)/46

Monfalcone, ex-Austrian barge of the same name, refloated by the Italians on the Isonzo river in June 1915. Rebuilt in SAVINEM Yards, Venice, and commissioned on 11 June 1917 into the Italian Navy. The gun was mounted over an old 17in mounting of a discarded battleship, and had a max elevation of 30°. Stricken 1921.

MONTE SANTO class *monitors*

Displacement: 570t
Dimensions: 121ft 5in × 28ft 3in × 6ft 6in
37.1m × 8.6m × 1.9m (Sabotino: 37.5m × 8.6m × 1.9m)
Machinery: 1-shaft Tosi diesel, 350bhp = 6kts
Armament: 1–15in (381mm)/40

Name	Builder	Launched	Fate
MONTE SANTO (ex-*Jella*)	SAVINEM, Venice and Venice N Yd	24.3.18	Stricken 1924, see notes
SABOTINO or MONTE SABOTINO (ex-*Tina*)	SAVINEM, Venice, and CNR, Ancona	20.2.18	Stricken 1924

Originally two Austrian barges, captured on the Isonzo river by the Italians, who rebuilt them (their original displacements were 62t and 66t respectively) and rearmed with the 15in guns, originally intended for the *Caracciolo* class battleships, whose construction had been suspended. Rebuilding design by Eng Rear-Admiral Giorgio Pruneri. In 1928–9 *Monte Santo* was converted to AA floating battery with 6–3in/40 AA guns.

MONTE CUCCO *monitor*

Displacement: 440t
Dimensions: 110ft 7in × 28ft 7in × 4ft 9in
33.7m × 8.7m × 1.4m
Machinery: 1 Fiat diesel, 250bhp = 6kts
Armament: 1–12in (305mm)/40

Name	Builder	Launched	Fate
MONTE CUCCO or CUCCO (ex-*Nedda*)	SAVINEM, Venice	30.7.17	Stricken 1924

Originally the Austrian barge *Nedda*, captured by the Italians at Monfalcone 1915. Totally rebuilt and modified by the Italian Navy, entered service 11 September 1917.

VODICE *monitor*

Displacement: 440t
Dimensions: 109ft 11in × 28ft 7in × 4ft 7in
33.5m × 8.7m × 1.4m
Machinery: 1 Fiat diesel, 250bhp = *c*6kts
Armament: 1–12in (305mm)/40
Complement: 2 + 28

Name	Builder	Launched	Fate
VODICE (ex-*Ena*)	Venice N Yd	9.9.17	Stricken 1924

Ex-Austrian lighter captured by the Italians at Monfalcone 1915. Totally rebuilt (design by Eng Rear-Adm Giorgio Pruneri) and converted.

CARSO *monitor*

Displacement: 360t
Dimensions: 118ft 1in × 31ft 2in × 4ft
36.0m × 9.5m × 1.2m
Machinery: 2 Polar diesels, 300bhp = *c*7kts
Armament: 2–7.5in (190mm)/45

Name	Builder	Launched	Fate
CARSO	SAVINEM, Venice	8.6.17	Stricken 1924

Ex-Austrian barge captured by the Italians at Monfalcone 1916, and totally rebuilt. The 7.5in guns had 28° of max elevation. Completed 3 August 1917.

PASUBIO *monitor*

Displacement: 225t
Dimensions: 67ft 3in × 21ft 8in × 5ft 7in
20.5m × 7.6m × 1.7m
Machinery: 1 Fiat diesel, 250bhp = 7kts
Armament: 1–6in (152mm)/50
Complement: 2 + 43

Name	Builder	Launched	Fate
PASUBIO (ex-*Ostrica*)	Venice N Yd	10.3.18	Stricken 1924

Ex-Austrian lighter, captured by the Italians at Monfalcone and completely rebuilt, to a design of Eng Rear-Adm Giorgio Pruneri. Max elevation of the 6in gun was 25°.

MONTE GRAPPA class *monitors*

Displacement: 575t–633t
Dimensions: 131ft 3in pp × 32ft 10in × 5ft 10in
40.0m × 10.0m × 1.7m
Machinery: 2-shaft Fiat-San Giorgio diesels, *c*700bhp = 7kts
Armament: 1–15in (381mm)/40

Class (launched):
Monte Cengio (10.12.19), *Monte Grappa* (21.9.18), *Montello* (31.12.18), *Monte Novegno* (31.5.19)

First monitors designed originally as such (not rebuilding, as all the other preceding ones). All built by Castellammare di Stabia N Yd and armed with the large guns destined for the *Caracciolo* class battleships, whose construction had been suspended. They were not completed in time for taking part in the First World War. All stricken in 1924 but first and last ship converted to torpedo-testing barges.

PADUS *monitor*

Displacement: 95.5t
Dimensions: 91ft 10in × 15ft 9in × 3ft 1in
28.0m × 4.8m × 0.9m
Machinery: 2-shaft Fiat diesels, 200bhp = 8.5kts
Armament: 1–6in (152mm)/50

Name	Builder	Comm	Fate
PADUS	SAVINEM, Venice	1917	Lost 7.11.17

Ex-Austrian barge captured by the Italians at Monfalcone June 1915, and converted. She went aground near Caorle.

ARMED MERCHANT CRUISERS

Name	Gross tons/ built	Number propellers/ power in hp or ihp/ speed in kts	Armament	Fate
AMERICA	8996/1909	2/7648/18	4–4.7in	BU 1928
ANCONA	8188/1907	2/7100/18	4–4.7in	Sunk 7.11.15 by German *U 38*
BOSNIA	2503/1898	1/1638/12	2–57mm, 4–37mm	Sunk 10.11.15
BULGARIA	2503/1898	1/1667/12	2–57mm, 2–37mm	
CANDIA	1046	1/1393/11.5	2–57mm, 4–37mm	
CAPRERA	1825/1910	2/3800/14	2–4.7in/40, 4–3in/40	Sunk 5.2.18, W Med by German *U 64*
CITTA' DI BENGASI	3052/1913	2/3697/14	4–4.7in/40	Sunk 8.9.43, Naples
CITTA' DI CAGLIARI	2161/1910	2/3850/14	2–4.7in/40, 2–3in/40	Returned to owner 1919
CITTA' DI CATANIA	3261/1910	3/13,620/20	4–4.7in/40, 2–3in/40	Sunk 3.8.43 off Brindisi, by British submarine
CITTA' DI MESSINA	3495/1910	3/12,500/20	4–4.7in/40, 2–3in/40	Sunk 23.6.16, Straits of Otranto by Austrian *U 15*
CITTA' DI PALERMO	3414/1910	3/12,000/19.5	4–4.7in/40 2–3in/40 AA	Sunk 8.1.16, off Brindisi, by mine
CITTA' DI SASSARI	2167/1910	2/4500/14	2–4.7in/40 2–3in/40	Sunk 1.12.17, off Cape Mele by German *U 65*
CITTA' DI SIRACUSA	3497/1910	2/12,000/19.5	2–4.7in/40 6–3in/40	Distilling ship in the 1930s
DOMENICO BALDUINO (ex-*China*)	4580/1882	1/2849/15	2–57mm, 4–37mm	
DUCA D'AOSTA	8169/1909	2/8500/16	4–4.7in/40	BU 1929
DUCA DEGLI ABRUZZI	8249/1907	2/8400/16	4–4.7in/40	BU 1929
DUCA DI GENOVA	7600/1907	2/7200/16.5	4–4.7in/40	Sunk 6.2.18
F D GUERRAZZI	637/1912	1/708/12	2–3in/40	Returned to owner 1919; sunk 26.4.45 Genoa, scuttled by Germans
MEMFI (ex-*Gottardo*)	2853/1883	1/1170/13	2–57mm, 4–37mm	
MISURATA	2690/1888		2–57mm, 4–37mm	Sunk 3.5.17
MONTENEGRO	2450/1898	1/1600/14	2–57mm, 4–37mm	
OCEANIA	8996/1909	2/7000/16.5	4–4.7in/40	
ORIONE	4141/1883	1/5219/13	2–57mm, 4–37mm	
PERSEO	4158/	1/4871/12.5	2–57mm, 4–37mm	
PORTO DI SUEZ (ex-*Oasis*)	1320/1883	1/1000/13	1–4.7in/40 2–3in/40	Returned to owner 1919
PORTO MAURIZIO (ex-*Ville de Bastia*)	848/1885	1/892/12	1–4.7in/40 1–3in/40	
PORTO TORRES (ex-*Helen*)	1163/1901	1/1140/13	1–4.7in/40 2–3in/40	Returned to owner 1918
PRINCIPE DI UDINE	7828/1908	2/8569/16.5	4–4.7in/40	BU 1929
PRINCIPESSA MAFALDA	9210/1908	2/10500/16	4–4.7in/40	Sunk 25.10.27
PRINCIPE UMBERTO	7838/1909	2/7200/16	4–4.7in/40	Sunk 8.6.16 by torpedo
REGINA ELENA	7940/1907	2/7200/16	4–4.7in/40	Sunk 4.1.18 by torpedo
REGINA MARGHERITA	3577/1884	1/5720/16	2–57mm, 4–37mm	
RE VITTORIO	7847/1907	2/7200/16.5	4–4.7in/40	BU 1928
ROMANIA	2450/1898	1/1700/12	2–57mm, 4–37mm	Sunk 16.4.18
SASSARI	1489/	1/1760/11		Used also as a decoy ship (see Q-ship section)
SERBIA	2564/1898	1/1650/11	2–57mm, 4–37mm	Sunk 27.6.18
TAORMINA	8921/1908	2/7430/16.5	2–4.7in	BU 1929
TEBE (ex-*Indipendente*)	2852/1883	1/2623/14	2–57mm, 2–37mm	
TOLEMAIDE	2690/1899	1/2500/14		Returned to owner 1919
TOMASO DI SAVOIA	7914/1907	2/8568/16.5	4–4.7in/40	BU 1928
UMBERTO I	2821/1878	1/2257/12	2–57mm, 4–37mm	Sunk 14.8.17 by German *UC 35*
VERONA	8886/1908	2/7200/16.5	4–4.7in/40	Sunk 11.5.18 by torpedo

Carso as completed

FOLGORE

Displacement: 107.8t
Dimensions: 90ft 7in × 17ft 5in × 5ft 9in
27.6m × 5.3m × 1.7m
Machinery: 2-shaft Sulzer diesels, 200bhp = 9.5kts
Armament: 1–4.7in (120mm)/50

Ex-Italian merchant-ship, ex-Austrian SS *Zeta* launched 1914. Commissioned on 1 July 1917 as a decoy (Q ship). Sunk November 1917 on Piave river by Austrian gunfire. Refloated, discarded 1919.

GALLINARA

Ex-motor schooner *Nostra Signora del Boschetto*, built 1908, commissioned 1 July 1915 as a decoy ship with 1–47mm gun and 8 men as complement. Sunk, night 22–23 November 1915, by gunfire from Austrian destroyer *Lika*.

GIANICOLO

Displacement: 262.3t; 139.9t net
Dimensions: 139ft 1in × 24ft 7in × 7ft 7in
42.4m × 7.5m × 2.3m
Machinery: 2-shaft 4-cylinder steam engines, 300ihp = 8kts
Armament: 2–57mm, 2–25mm four-barrel Nordenfelt MG
Complement: 2 + ?

Ex-river steamer of Società Marittima e Fluviale, of Rome; launched 1908. Commissioned by the Italian Navy on 16 May 1915 and armed as a decoy ship against U-boats. Stricken 1918.

MALAMOCCO

Motor schooner of 300grt, commissioned by the Italian Navy in 1916, not armed, which operated in 1917 as a decoy ship together with the submarine *Pacinotti*. Stricken 1920.

PANTELLERIA

Ex-motor schooner *Cuore di Gesù*, 204grt, commissioned by the Italian Navy on 1 July 1915. Armed with 2–47mm guns and a complement of 16 men. Engaged Austrian submarine *U 4*, which sank her with one torpedo S of Taranto, 14 August 1916.

SAETTA

Displacement: 107.8t
Dimensions: 91ft 10in × 17ft 5in × 5ft 9in
28.0m × 5.3m × 1.7m
Machinery: 2-shaft Sulzer diesels, 200bhp = 9.5kts
Armament: 1–4.7in (120mm)/50

Ex-Austrian SS *Lowcen* (launched 1915). Commissioned 1 July 1917 by the Italian Navy as a decoy ship. Sunk by Austrian gunfire on 17 December, but refloated, repaired and used again. Stricken 1919.

SASSARI

See in Armed Merchant Cruisers section. She was used for some months in 1916 as a decoy ship.

USTICA

Ex-motor schooner *Raffaele Padre*, 198grt, commissioned 1 July 1915 as a decoy ship. She was armed with 2–47mm guns and a complement of 16 men. Later used as a searchlight-ship in Valona harbour. Stricken 1919.

SORRENTO *depot ship*

Displacement: 989t–1052t
Dimensions: 261ft 6in oa, 229ft 4in wl × 27ft 7in × 15ft 1in
79.7m, 69.9m × 8.4m × 4.6m
Machinery: 2-shaft MAN diesels, 3255bhp = 14.7kts
Armament: 4–3in/40 AA, see notes
Complement: 3 + 42

Name	Builder	Launched	Fate
SORRENTO (ex-*Lussin*)	STT 'San Rocco', Muggia	22.12.83	Stricken 1928

Built as a torpedo-gunboat for the Austrian Navy and completed 1884. She originally had a 2-shaft compound reciprocating engines with 4 boilers. Used as a TS from 1889. In 1911–14 she was converted to a yacht and her machinery was replaced by the diesels. In 1915 disarmed and employed as an accommodation ship at Pola for German U-boat crews. Allocated to Italy 1920 and commissioned on 11 September 1924. Under Italian colours used as a depot ship for Mas boats after being commissioned.

Russia

Increasingly, under the impact of the humiliating Russo-Japanese War, various Russian social groups had been demonstrating their discontent with both the social and political systems. The massacre of peaceful demonstrators at St Petersburg on 'Bloody Sunday' sparked off a wave of revolt that swept through the whole Empire during 1905/7. The magnitude of revolt forced Czar Nicholas II to act and he issued the manifesto which effectively promised some form of constitution and establishment of an elected legislature (Duma). The regime which followed was however substantially different from that before 1905. Although the principle of autocracy was officially upheld and the bureaucratic system remained almost intact, political parties were allowed as were public meetings and open political debate in the Duma, while the workers were able to form trade unions.

Improvements in agriculture and progress in industry, backed by a marked tendency towards the formation of large concentrations of capital, caused an economic boom after 1909. The total grain output reached 93 million tons in 1913 while that of pig iron was 5.2 million tons and of coal was 40 million tons. The 1914 census recorded a population of 169 million with the urban part rising to 15 per cent. The railway mileage reached 43,700 miles in 1913 while those of suitable standard roads did not exceed 11,000 miles. But despite unquestionable progress made in many fields after the Russo-Japanese War, the Russian Empire remained economically backwards as compared with the other European powers.

THE NAVAL SHIPBUILDING PROGRAMMES OF 1908–1914

From the third naval power in the world – a position held for many years – Russia fell to the sixth place after the Russo-Japanese War. In the wake of defeat the Czar replaced the Naval Authority with the Naval Ministry in June 1905 and the Naval General Staff was formed in April 1906. At first the Russian admirals aimed at the rebuilding of her traditional naval power in the Baltic and the Far East, believing that a renewal of war against Japan was inevitable. So the 1907 Naval Shipbuilding Estimate called for two squadrons for both the Baltic and the Far Eastern stations and one for the Black Sea Fleet (a squadron was to comprise 8 dreadnoughts, 4 battlecruisers, 9 cruisers and 36 destroyers), but succumbed after voting in the Duma which allowed construction of one squadron for the Baltic Fleet but in the end did not award any funds for it. The aspirations of naval planners were cooled but even the moderate 1908 Estimate (4 dreadnoughts, 3 submarines for the Baltic Fleet and 14 destroyers and 3 submarines for the Black Sea Fleet) did not win the approval of the Duma. Only the Bosnian crisis, in which Russia was publicly humiliated by Germany, enabled the Czar to release 127 million roubles to build 4 dreadnoughts for the Baltic Fleet. This crisis marked the end of a transitional period in Russian policy towards the Central Powers and drove Russia into the anti-German camp. The strong position of Japan forced the Russians to abandon their plans for revenge in the Far East and after conflicts with Britain in Persia, Afghanistan and Tibet were mitigated by the 1907 Convention, Russian foreign policy became absorbed by European affairs.

By that time the Russian Navy was fed with leftovers from the pre-1903 programmes, ships ordered on the score of the 1903–23 Naval Estimate and those completed from the 1904 Emergency Programme and the Public Subscription Fund which amounted to 4 battleships, 1 armoured cruiser, 5 cruisers, 51 destroyers, 16 submarines and 25 gunboats completed between 1906–1911. This period was utilised for reconstruction of the state-owned shipbuilding industry and investments totalling 30 million roubles were made mainly in the Baltic and the Admiralty Yards at St Petersburg and the Nikolayev Admiralty Yard on the Black Sea. But these funds were not effectively spent, which, together with the inertia of a state bureaucracy, caused prolonged building times and financial conditions far worse than those offered by more efficient private enterprises. They, thanks to foreign assistance, were able to gain most of the further orders.

After abandonment of support for Serbia, Russian diplomacy tried to organise an anti-Austrian block of Balkan states. The cold reaction of Turkey, and plans for rebuilding of her battlefleet, softened opinion in the Duma which in 1911 authorised 150 million roubles to build 3 battleships, 9 destroyers and 6 submarines for the Black Sea Fleet by 1915. After a further straining of relations with Germany, when Russia gave support to France in the conflict over Morocco, the Navy Minister tried to persuade the Duma to pass the Naval Law known as the Great Shipbuilding Programme which planned three squadrons for the Baltic Fleet by 1930, as an attempt to counter the German programmes. But the Duma was as cautious about spending massively as it was with the 1909–19 Estimates and the reduced Small Shipbuilding Programme for 1912–16 was authorised instead (433 million roubles assigned to build 4 battlecruisers, 4 cruisers, 36 destroyers, 12 submarines for the Baltic Fleet; 2 cruisers for the Black Sea Fleet as well as 2 cruisers and 6 submarines for the Siberian Flotilla). Moreover another 92 million were designated in 1913 for construction of the central mine-artillery position on the Reval-Porkkala-Udd line

When Turkey purchased the Brazilian dreadnought *Rio de Janeiro* (under construction in Britain) the 1914 Increased Shipbuilding Programme for the Black Sea was approved by the Duma. A sum of 110 million roubles was assigned for construction of 1 battleship, 2 cruisers, 8 destroyers and 6 submarines during 1914–17. Also the Russian Government negotiated with Brazil about the possibility of buying two *Sao Paulo* class dreadnoughts for some time before August 1914 to prevent similar Turkish intentions.

The total naval expenditures made during 1906–13 amounted to the equivalent of 519 million US dollars which placed Russia in fifth place behind the British Empire, US, Germany and France.

RUSSIA IN THE FIRST WORLD WAR 1914–1917

The Austrian ultimatum to Serbia after the Archduke Ferdinand's murder put Russia in a terrible dilemma. If she abandoned Serbia, thus evading the war for which she was not yet prepared, the whole of the Balkans would be lost, raising doubts about her usefulness as an ally of France. In that event Russia was likely to drift into the status of a mere satellite of Germany. But in 1914 the Franco-Russian alliance proved its value, as the German Army could have crushed either France or Russia alone, but not together. The outbreak of hostilities found the Imperial Navy in the midst of the rearmament programmes which were to be finished by 1917 and only 4 battleships, 4 destroyers and 1 submarine were completed by the end of 1914. The operational plans were therefore of a defensive nature, those for the Baltic Fleet being confined to protecting the seaward flank of the Army fronts and defence of the Imperial capital – renamed Petrograd after August 1914. The Black Sea Fleet was entrusted with defence of its main base, Sevastopol, and mining waters off the Bosphorus.

In February 1915 the Naval Ministry issued the Submarine Programme which added 23 boats for the Baltic, 22 for the Black Sea and 40 boats for the Siberian Flotilla, to be built on top of the existing programmes. But only 18 boats were ordered (17 in US, 1 in Italy) in 1915 while the Far Eastern boats were cancelled after the Russians became sure about Japan's friendly intentions. With the considerable number of ships on order in Russian yards, priorities had to be set in July 1915 for the reduced manpower and material available. Thus only 1 battlecruiser, 4 cruisers, 13 destroyers and 6 submarines of the Baltic Fleet as well as 2 battleships, 5 destroyers and 6 submarines of the Black Sea Fleet were given top priority. The 6 submarines ordered originally for the Siberian Flotilla were reassigned to the Baltic Fleet.

In September 1915 the Emergency Shipbuilding Programme authorised construction of 4 mine cruisers and 24 torpedo boats for the Baltic as well as 12 torpedo boats for the Black Sea Fleet, but the whole programme remained a paper one. These programmes were supplemented by the end of 1915 with 50 landing craft ordered for the Black Sea Fleet to assist the successful operations on the Caucasian front. With this exception the 1914–15 campaign was disastrous for the Russian Army as the invasion of East Prussia was a failure while the advance into Galicia was stopped by the offensive of the Central Powers in Poland and resulted in enormous losses of territory. These disasters aroused bitter discontent as well as demands in both the Duma and the press for a government commanding the confidence of the nation. The Czar ignored these demands and insisted on assuming the supreme command of the armies in the field. Economic conditions deteriorated, the mobilisation of manpower disorganised both industry and agriculture while transport was overloaded. Prices rose much faster than wages and there were serious shortages of goods, even food. In 1915 two battleships, 8 destroyers and 8 submarines were completed while in 1916 the shipbuilding programmes delivered 8 destroyers, 13 submarines, 50 landing craft and 3 guard ships. The steady build up of the Russian Navy had a marked influence on its efficiency.

Arguably Russia's most important naval contribution to the Allied war effort came in the very first month when the Baltic cruisers *Pallada* and *Bogatyr* not only sank the grounded German cruiser *Magdeburg* off Estonia but also recovered from her the German Navy's most secret *Signalbuch der Kaiserlichen Marine* codebook, their gridded chart of the Baltic, the ship's log and war diary. Captain Kredoff and Commander Smirnoff sailed in the cruiser HMS *Theseus* from Alexandrovsk to Scapa Flow and handed these priceless documents to Winston Churchill on 13 October. For the rest of the war the Admiralty's Room 40 organisation was to read German naval and diplomatic codes and ciphers. The Naval Staff in St Petersburg received its intelligence right up to the 1917 October Revolution and not until mid-1918 did the Germans learn of the *Magdeburg* coup. The SKM codebook was not replaced until May 1917 despite the repeated urgings of the German Baltic C-in-C, Prince Henry of Prussia and brother to the Kaiser.

Gangut and *Petropavlovsk* during the Bolshevik Revolution
Twardowski Collection

By the time the Russian Baltic Fleet's C-in-C Admiral Nicholas Otto von Essen died in mid-1915, offensive minelaying operations and sorties by the Russian light forces (invariably conducted with strict radio silence) forced the Germans to abandon their offensive plans. The Russian submarines backed by a British flotilla of modern boats hampered German supplies of iron ore and food from Sweden.

The Black Sea Fleet under Admirals Eberhard and Alexander V Kolchak (after July 1915) showed more vigour throughout the war, mainly thanks to its supremacy over the Turkish Fleet. Its heavy ships not only foiled Admiral Souchon's moves but also escorted Russian troop convoys to Caucasian harbours, while the light and submarine forces successfully fought Turkish shipping and laid offensive minefields as far as the Bosphorus. Persistent Russian measures against the submarine base at Varna drove German U-boats out of the Black Sea in 1916. The new Arctic Ocean Flotilla was formed in 1916 to sweep German mines and screen Allied supplies transferred via Romanovo (Murmansk) and Arkhangelsk. Because of the scant forces available, the flotilla was made up of old Russian ships bought back from the Japanese as well as mercantile conversions and was backed by British and French ships.

The year 1916 saw an improved military situation (successful offensives in Galicia and on the Caucasian front) and industrial production peak with over 120,000 tons of warships launched. The shipyards were so overloaded that the Naval Ministry did not place many orders for the larger surface ships, only 14 guardships, 11 minesweepers and 30 landing ships being ordered by Febraury 1917. The gigantic 1916 Submarine Programme was launched instead and the sum of 298 million roubles was authorised in May 1916 for construction of 55 boats (supplemented by 4 minelaying submarines later on). The second half of 1916 with no military victories brought increased public discontent. By January 1917 the food supply in the capital worsened so that at the beginning of March 1917 (February in the old style) strikes, demonstrations and food queues filled the streets with aimless crowds. Mutinies took place in some barracks and the Czar left Petrograd. The Imperial Government was replaced by the Provisional Government and the Czar abdicated. The new Government pledged itself to continue the war and was therefore rapidly recognised by the Allied powers. To improve the war effort numerous moves were undertaken to make industrial production more efficient. The less advanced warship construction was cancelled or suspended and work concentrated on the most suitable ships. Moreover, 6 guardships, 22 minesweepers and 24 minelayers were authorised by October 1917 for the Baltic Fleet. During 1917 one battleship, 9 destroyers, 9 submarines and 6 guard ships were completed before the next revolution paralysed the country.

Despite growing popular sentiment for peace, the offensive was launched in June 1917 but the Russians were routed by the counter-attacking Germans. Russian discipline and morale then began to disintegrate rapidly as a result of both military failure and growing Communist propaganda. Desertion mounted and by the time of the Bolshevik Revolution the Army was scarcely a fighting force.

THE BOLSHEVIK REVOLUTION AND THE CIVIL WAR 1917–1921

Following a failed counter-revolutionary coup by the Army's chief of staff, popular support for the Provisional Government fell away rapidly and the country polarised toward the extremes of left and right. The revolutionary mood of the masses, accentuated by rampant inflation and food shortages, was channelled into direct action by the Bolshevik Party. After the February Revolution it was led by Lenin whose return to Russia was facilitated by the Germans in the hope that he would undermine the war effort of the Provisional Government. The Bolshevik coup of 7 November 1917 (25 October in the old style) at Petrograd succeeded thanks to popular support and the participation of the Baltic Fleet. This was quickly followed by more coups in most other parts of Russia. However the Communist takeover was resisted in the south by Ukrainian nationalists who established an autonomous regime.

The Bolshevik appeal for peace, sincerely invited by the Russian masses, was rejected by the Allies and considered a betrayal of the war effort. The Central Powers quickly took advantage of it and began peace negotiations at Brest-Litovsk. After Commissar Trotsky refused to sign the treaty in February 1918, the Germans resumed their offensive towards Petrograd and the Ukraine. Then the Soviets had to accept heavy German conditions, surrendering the Baltic Provinces, Poland, Ukraine, Finland and the Caucasus to the Central Powers but they won a breathing space for consolidation of their rule. The Soviet warships if not evacuated to bases in Russian territory had to be disarmed and the Germans had the secret hope of seizing these ships which could, once in their hands, constitute a serious threat toward the Allies. Thus most of the Baltic Fleet left Reval (Tallinn) and Helsingfors (Helsinki) and 211 vessels finally reached Kronstadt after a really heroic voyage through heavy ice, bearing in mind the appalling condition of most of the ships and their reduced crews. But 171 lesser ships were not able to leave the wartime Baltic bases. The Black Sea Fleet remained at Sevastopol as the Soviets created the nominally independent Tauridian Republic in the Crimea, but the Germans claimed that the Crimea belonged to the Ukrainian mainland and demanded that ships should be disarmed according to the Brest-Litovsk treaty. Thus the most modern units (some against the will of their crews) were evacuated to Novorossisk, while the elderly or unfit ones (6 battleships, 2 cruisers, 12 destroyers and 14 submarines) were seized by the Germans in May 1918.

With the Germans advancing on Novorossisk, the dreadnought *Volya* and 6 destroyers returned to Sevastopol while *Svobodnaya Rossiya* and 10 destroyers were scuttled to prevent capture. Thus almost all the Black Sea Fleet fell into German hands and some ships were commissioned before being surrendered to the Allies in November 1918. The Arctic Ocean Flotilla, the Siberian and Caspian Flotillas were seized in March, April and August 1918 by the Allies who intervened with the intention of getting Russia back into the war and of suppressing the Communist revolution. The collapse of Germany in November 1918 ended their original excuse but the British and the French in European Russia as well as the Japanese and Americans in Asiatic Russia landed additional forces and stepped up their support for the anti-Communist Russians – the Whites. Backed by their foreign supporters they launched offensives toward Moscow in 1919 from Siberia, the Don and Estonia.

The Communist Russians – the Reds – were able to reactivate only part of the Baltic Fleet and they formed the Active Squadron of 1 dreadnought, 1 battleship, 1 cruiser, 5 destroyers and 4 submarines. This was largely neutralised by the British raid on Kronstadt in July 1919. But numerous river and lake flotillas were improvised from local merchant craft and Black Sea Fleet small craft as well as ships transferred from the Baltic. On the other hand the Whites were given support from Allied squadrons and locally formed flotillas. The Black Sea Fleet's most valuable ships were evacuated by the Allies from Sevastopol to Izmid in April 1919, when the Crimea was temporarily occupied by the Reds, and handed over to the Whites under General Wrangel who reactivated the Black Sea Fleet in the shape of 1 dreadnought, 2 battleships, 2 cruisers, 10 destroyers and 4 submarines. Though militarily formidable the Whites were weakened politically by their authoritarian tendencies and unwillingness to leave the peasants in possession of land given already by the Reds, while the Allied intervention was not sufficiently massive or resolute. One by one the White thrusts (including the one on Petrograd where 11,000 Red sailors fought on land) were turned back and by late 1920 the serious challenge of counter-revolution was at an end. Wrangel's fleet was evacuated to Constantinople, then to Bizerta and interned there by the French. The ships remaining from other waters (with the exception of the Baltic Fleet which remained in the Soviet hands) were distributed between the intervening powers or damaged and disarmed to prevent further use by the Reds. By that time only the Japanese and the Whites in Siberia remained with which Moscow dealt through a nominally independent Far Eastern republic that was absorbed into Soviet Russia after the Japanese withdrew in 1922.

The passions and desperation of the Civil War rapidly transferred the Communist regime into a tyrannical one-party dictatorship. Suppression of opposition parties was paralleled by the development of authoritarian practices within the Bolshevik Party. After an attempt was made to transform the Russian society directly into the classless Communist ideal by the sweeping nationalisation of industry and the introduction of War Communism, instead of an open market, the country was brought almost to a standstill. The countryside was seething with unrest over the requisitioning of food and strikes, although outlawed by the Soviet Government, erupted in the major cities. The 1921 Kronstadt mutiny of sailors in the heart of the Bolshevik Revolution made the party leaders realise that a continuation of War Communism would endanger the Soviet regime and forced them to begin a strategic retreat from the ideals of the revolution.

RUSSIAN NAVAL SHIPBUILDING YARDS, 1906–21

BALTIC

Admiralty Yd, St Petersburg (formerly Galernyj Isl Yd and New Admiralty Yd united in 1908, stated owned, 5 slips)
Baltic Yd, St Petersburg (state owned, 4 slips)
Nevskij Yd, St Petersburg (8 slips)
Metal Wks, St Petersburg (4 slips)
Putilov Yd, St Petersburg (6 slips)
Russo-Baltic Yd, Reval (Estonia, 8 slips)
Bekker and Co Yd, Reval (Estonia, 7 slips)
Noblessner Yd, Reval (Estonia, 6 slips)
Mühlgraben Yd, Reval (Estonia, founded 1913)
Crichton Yd, Abo (Finland)
Crichton Yd, St Petersburg
Maskin Brobygnack Yd, Helsingfors (Finland, 2 slips)
Sandvikens Yd, Helsingfors (Finland)

BLACK SEA

Nikolayev Admiralty Yd, Nikolayev (state owned)
Russud Yd, Nikolayev (5 slips)
Naval Yd, Nikolayev (8 slips)
Ropit Yd, Odessa

INLAND WATERWAYS

Sormovo Wks, N Novgorod

RUSSIAN NAVAL EXPENDITURES 1906–1914 (million roubles)

	1906	1907	1908	1909	1910	1911	1912	1913	1914
Planned	142	90	92	90	110	110	159	228	250
Actual	112	80	87	91	113	136	165	247	

RUSSIAN NAVAL GUNS 1906–1921

Bore/Cal/Model	Weight (t)	Projectile (kg)	Muzzle velocity (fs)	Range (m)
14in/52/1912*	80.3	747.7	823	
12in/52/1910	50.6	470.3	823	25,000
130mm/55/1913	55	36.8	814	
4in/60/1913	2.9	14.1	914	
75mm/30.5/1914**	0.7	5.5	2.5	1000
2.5in		2.5		

*Designed for the *Borodino* class, did not enter service.
**AA

RUSSIAN TORPEDOES 1906–1921

Torpedo/Model	Weight (kg)	Explosive (kg)	Range (m/kts)
18in/1912		99.8	1000/43 6000/28
18in/1910		99.8	1000/39 5200/24
18in/1908		38.5	1000/38.5 3600/29
18in/1906	640	27.0	1000/32 2000/26

RUSSIAN NAVAL MINES 1906–1921

Mine	Weight (kg)	Diameter (cm)	Explosive (kg)	Length of mineline (m)
River type 1			8	11
Model 1912	609	87.5	100	132
Model 1909	480	77.5	130	
Model 1908	582	87.5	115	110
Model 1906	450	77.5	55	110

FLEET STRENGTH 1906

BATTLESHIPS

Name	Launched	Disp	Fate
Petr Veliki class			
PETR VELIKI	27.8.72	9790t	BU 1959
Ekaterina II class			
TCHESMA	18.5.86	10,930t	Stricken 1907
EKATERINA II	22.5.86	11,084t	Stricken 1907
GEORGI POBIEDONOSETS	9.3.92	11,940t	Sold 1924
SINOP	1.6.87	10,181t	BU 1922
Imperator Alexander II class			
IMPERATOR ALEXANDER II	26.7.87	9672t	Stricken 1925
Dvienadtsat Apostolov class			
DVIENADTSAT APOSTOLOV	13.9.90	8433t	Hulked 1912
Tri Svititelia class			
TRI SVITITELIA	12.11.93	13,318t	BU 1922
Rostislav class			
ROSTISLAV	1.9.96	10,140t	Scuttled 16.11.20
Kniaz Potemkin-Tavricheski class			
PANTELIMON	26.9.00	12,480t	BU 1922
Tsesarevich class			
TSESAREVICH	23.2.01	13,110t	BU 1924
Borodino class			
SLAVA	29.8.03	13,516t	Scuttled 17.10.17
Ioann Zlatoust class			
EVSTAFI	3.11.06	12,840t	BU 1922
IOANN ZLATOUST	14.5.06	12,840t	BU 1922
Imperator Pavel I class			
ANDREI PERVOZVANNY	20.10.06	17,400t	Stricken 1924
IMPERATOR PAVEL I	7.9.07	17,600t	Sold 11.23

Petr Veliki class
Converted into the Baltic Fleet gunnery TS during 1905/6. Reconstruction included plating up of the hull to the boat deck level, reboilering and fitting of two funnels and two military masts. She was rearmed with 4–8in/50 in sponsons on the new upper deck, 12–6in/45 in casemates on the original upper deck, 12–75mm, 4–57mm, 8–47mm, 2–37mm. Renamed *Respublikanets* in 1917, hulked in October 1918 and converted to the mine depot ship *Barrikada* later on.

Ekaterina II class
All with the Black Sea Fleet in 1906. *Tchesma* used as a target for experimental purposes after 1908 and had a section modelled on those of the dreadnought type battleship built in her hull in 1913. *Sinop* was converted to the minefield runner for the Battleship Brigade in 1914 by the addition of large bulges. With armament reduced and TT removed *Sinop* and *Ekaterina II* were relegated to coast defence ships during the First World War. *Sinop* being disarmed at Sevastopol in June 1917, flew the Ukrainian colours in April 1918, was captured by the Germans and transferred to the British in November 1918, who wrecked her machinery on 6 April 1919 to prevent use by the Reds. *Georgi Pobiedonosets* raised the Ukrainian flag in April 1918, was captured by the Germans at Sevastopol in May 1918 and surrendered to the British in November 1918. Transferred to Wrangel's fleet in September 1919.

Imperator Alexander II class
She was with the Baltic Fleet in 1906. Relegated to the gunnery TS in 1914 with armament changed to 2–12in/30, 1–8in/45, 10–6in/45, 4–120mm, 4–48mm, 8 MG. Rearmed with 2–12in/40, 6–6in/45, 4–120mm, 1–75mm AA, 2–47mm by 1917. Renamed *Zarya Svobody* on 22 May 1917, participated in the Bolshevik Revolution, hulked in May 1918.

Petr Veliki after 1906 reconstruction
Lemachko Collection

Dvienadtsat Apostolov class
Deleted 1911 and converted to the Black Sea mine depot ship *Hulk No 8* in 1914. In 1925 she was used as a dummy battleship *Kniaz Potemkin-Tavricheski* in Sergei M Eisentein's famous film. BU late 1920s.

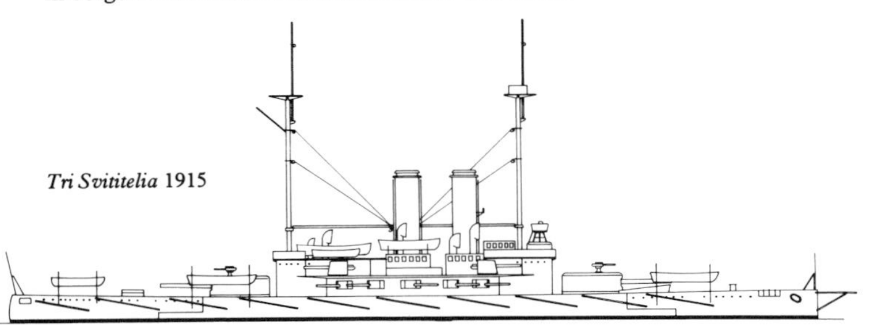

Tri Svititelia 1915

Tri Svititelia class
Remained in front line service until commissioning of the Black Sea dreadnoughts, being modernised during 1911–12. Her superstructure was cut down by one deck and replaced by deckhouses, while the military masts were removed and substituted by the light pole rig. In place of the old 120mm battery, 4–6in shields were mounted, one on either corner of the superstructure deck. An extra 6in was added on the main deck on both sides at the middle of the existing battery and the TT removed. Later during the First World War 4–57mm AA were placed on the turret crowns. Shifted to secondary duties in 1915 she raised the Ukrainian colours at Sevastopol in April 1918 where she was captured by the Germans and surrendered by them to the British in November 1918. Her machinery and armament were wrecked to prevent use by the Reds.

Rostislav class
Served with the Black Sea Fleet and virtually unchanged by 1914 she had TT removed and light guns replaced by 4–75mm AA later during the First World War. Being in reserve in August 1914 she was reactivated afterwards and by 1917 had taken part in numerous operations against *Goeben* and Turkish shore installations. Raised the colours of independent Ukraine in April 1918 at Sevastopol but captured by the Germans and used as an accommodation hulk until seized by the British in November. With her machinery wrecked on 9 April 1919 to prevent her use by the Reds she was used as a floating battery by the Whites after the Bolshevik retreat from the Crimea. Scuttled off Kerch to avoid recapture by the Red Army.

Kniaz Potemkin-Tavricheski class
Renamed *Pantelimon* on 12 May 1905 to expunge the record of the crew's mutiny and became the flagship of the Black Sea Fleet. During 1910–11 she had her bow TT and fighting tops with 4–47mm removed. Active throughout the First World War she had 2–75mm AA mounted on the spar deck in 1915 and remaining TT removed in 1916. All her old 75mm were probably removed by 1917. Renamed *Potemkin-Tavricheski* on 13 April 1917 as a democratic gesture by the Provisional Government, once again she changed her name to *Borets za Svobodu* on 11 May. Raised the Ukrainian colours in 1918 and captured by the Germans at Sevastopol in May 1918. Surrendered to the British in November 1918 and had her machinery wrecked by them on 9 April 1919 to prevent use by the advancing Reds.

Tsesarevich class
Transferred to the Baltic Fleet after the Russo-Japanese War she had her heavy masts replaced by the pole rig with the light guns and surface TT removed. Fitted with 2–1.45in AA during the First World War and renamed *Grashdanin* on 13 April 1917. She was hit twice by the German dreadnought *Kronprinz* off Moon Sound (Gulf of Riga) on 17 October 1917 but escaped. Hulked in May 1918 and her guns were landed during the Civil War. Sold to German breakers.

Borodino class
The sole survivor of the ill-fated class by virtue of being with the Baltic Fleet, she had her 75mm guns and TT removed after the Russo-Japanese War. She received 2–37mm AA placed on the main turrets during the First World War. Scuttled by a torpedo from the destroyer *Turkmenets-Stavropolski* after being damaged on 17 October 1917 by the German dreadnought *König* in the entrance to Moon Sound. The wreck was broken up by the Estonians in 1935.

Ioann Zlatoust class
Part of the Black Sea Fleet from 1910. Bow TT removed and 2–75mm AA added during the First World War. Possible the remaining light guns were landed later on. Both raised colours of the Independent Ukraine at Sevastopol in 1918 but were seized there by the Germans in May and surrendered in

November to the British who wrecked their machinery on 9 April 1919 to prevent use by the Reds.

Imperator Pavel I class
With the Baltic Fleet from 1910. During 1916–17 both had their cage masts replaced by pole ones, the battery of 47mm removed and replaced by 2–75mm AA and torpedo nets added. *Imperator Pavel I* renamed *Respublika* on 29 April 1917 and laid up at Kronstadt in September 1918. *Andrei Pervozvanny* taken over by the Bolsheviks in October 1917, participated in the October Revolution and the Civil War. Torpedoed and seriously damaged by the British *CMB 88* at Kronstadt 18 August 1919. Her 120mm guns were landed afterwards and she was laid up in September 1920.

COAST DEFENCE BATTLESHIPS

Name	Launched	Disp	Fate
Admiral Spiridov class			
ADMIRAL CHICHAGOV	13.10.68	3630t	Stricken 1907
ADMIRAL SPIRIDOV	28.8.68	3797t	Stricken 1907
Admiral Lazarev class			
ADMIRAL GREIG	30.10.67	3807t	Stricken 1909
ADMIRAL LAZAREV	21.9.67	3779t	Stricken 1907
Charodeika class			
CHARODEIKA	12.9.67	2100t	Stricken 1907

ARMOURED CRUISERS

Name	Launched	Disp	Fate
Kniaz Pozharski class			
KNIAZ POZHARSKI	12.9.67	4137t	Stricken 1911
Minin class			
MININ	12.9.67	6136t	Mined 15.8.15
General-Admiral class			
GENERAL-ADMIRAL	8.10.73	4480t	Expended *c*1959
GERZOG EDINBURGSKI	10.9.75	4525t	Hulked 1915
Pamiat Azova class			
PAMIAT AZOVA	1.7.88	6734t	Sunk 18.8.19
Rossia class			
ROSSIA	12.5.96	12,195t	Sold 1922
GROMOBOI	20.5.99	12,395t	Sold 1922
Bayan class			
ADMIRAL MAKAROV	28.5.06	7835t	Sold 1922
BAYAN (ii)	15.8.07	7835t	Sold 1922
PALLADA	10.11.06	7835t	Sunk 11.10.14
Rurik class			
RURIK	17.11.06	15,544t	BU 1923

Kniaz Pozharski class
Her 8in and 6in guns were removed around 1904 and after 1906 she served as a TS. Hulked 1909.

Minin class
Converted to minelayer in October 1909 armed with 4–47mm and mine capacity up to 1200. Renamed *Ladoga*, lost on a mine laid by *UC 4* off Oro Island in the Baltic.

General Admiral class
Both converted to minelayers in 1909 with 600 mines each and armed with 4–75mm, 4 MG. Renamed *Narova* and *Onega* respectively. The latter was seized by Finland in 1918 and scrapped afterwards. *Narova* served during the Civil War and was renamed *25 Oktyabrya* in 1922. Hulked in 1938 she was expended as a breakwater in the Neva river.

Pamiat Azova class
Relegated to Baltic training duties after 1904 and her crew mutinied in 1906. Became the torpedo TS afterwards with armament reduced to 4–47mm. Renamed *Dvina* on 25 February 1909 and returned to her old name on 13 April 1917, she served as a submarine depot ship until sunk by the British *CMB 79* at Kronstadt.

Rossia class
After damage sustained from Japanese armoured cruisers at Ulsan in 1904 both received additional 6–6in sponsons on the upper deck while the bow 6in was remounted on the forecastle. The 1906–9 modernisation of *Rossia* included removing the centre cruising engine and shaft as well as the mizzen mast. Her additional 6in were covered with 5in casemates, sights in the CT reduced in size and rangefinders armoured. The 1913 modernisation of *Gromoboi* included addition of armoured casemates for the 8in and 6in (except the two foremost 6in pieces), fitting of new 2–15in TT (sub). Her rig and CT was altered similarly to *Rossia*. In 1914 *Rossia* had mine rails for 100 mines added and she became the flagship of the Baltic Fleet's Second Cruiser Brigade. It was planned to rebuild her in 1915 by cutting down the forecastle deck and adding 4–8in in pairs at both ends, but these plans failed and in October 1915 she appeared with 2–8in added at bow and stern and 6in reduced to 14 though the casemate mountings remained. The light armament comprised 4–48mm and 3 MG. *Gromoboi* was rearmed with 2–8in replacing 6in at bow and stern, 2–75mm remained in the stern casemates and 2 MG added. In July 1917 *Gromoboi* came under Bolshevik control and was followed in September 1917 by *Rossia*. Both were laid up in 1918 and sold to German breakers.

Evstafi as completed — *Lemachko Collection*

Imperator Pavel I 1916 — *Lemachko Collection*

Rossia 1916 — *Micinski Collection*

Admiral Makarov 1914 — *Author's Collection*

Rurik 1917 — *Author's Collection*

RUSSIA

Bayan class
Admiral Makarov was ordered in 1905 as the repeated *Bayan* class when news about the lead ship's fighting value reached Russia. To replace cruisers lost in Port Arthur two additional ships were laid down in St Petersburg. The three repeated *Bayans* incorporated numerous changes from the lessons of the Russo-Japanese War, such as lowering of the deckhouses, reduction of armour and replacing wooden furniture with steel. *Admiral Makarov* joined the Baltic Fleet in 1908, followed by her sisters in 1911. It was planned in 1913 to fit *Pallada* with a seaplane but this was abandoned after August 1914. The cruisers served with the Cruiser Brigade (First Cruiser Brigade since 1915). After the loss of *Pallada* which exploded and vanished with all hands after being torpedoed by *U 26*, the remaining pair was fitted with rails for 150 mines each and participated in minelaying actions as far as Gotland. During 1916–17 both had their 75mm removed and 1–8in covered with shield mounted on the main deck abaft the fore funnel and 4–6in added by two on each side – by the second funnel and between the third and fourth one. *Bayan* (ii) was in the 17 October 1917 Moon Sound action when one 12in hit from *König* caused a serious fire. They were fitted with 2 light AA guns each: *Admiral Makarov* 75mm, *Bayan* 48mm. Laid up in 1918, sold for scrap to Germany.

Rurik class
After completion in August 1908 she underwent firing practice in Russian waters when the stiffenings and rivetting of her 10in barbettes and starboard bow 8in barbette were found to be too light. After some improvements she finally entered service in July 1909 and participated in that year's Spithead Review. She became the flagship of the Baltic Fleet being shifted to the First Cruiser Brigade in 1915. After being fitted with rails for 400 mines she participated in the minelaying operation off Gotland where she was badly damaged by grounding on 13 February 1915 and reached Reval with 2400t of water inside. During the gun duel with German cruisers off Gotland on 2 July 1915 she received light damage and on 19 November 1916 her bow was again holed after being mined. She appeared back in service early in 1917 being fitted with a tripod foremast and 1–40mm AA. Laid up at the end of 1918.

CRUISERS

Name	Launched	Disp	Fate
Yaroslavl class			
PAMIAT MERKURIA	22.5.80	2997t	Stricken 1907
Admiral Kornilov class			
ADMIRAL KORNILOV	9.4.87	5840t	Stricken 1911
Pallada class			
AURORA	24.5.00	6731t	Preserved 1948
DIANA	12.10.99	6731t	Sold 1922
Askold class			
ASKOLD	2.3.00	5905t	Sold 1922
Bogatyr class			
BOGATYR	30.1.01	6645t	Sold 1922
KAGUL	2.6.02	6645t	Sold 1924
OLEG	27.8.03	6645t	Sunk 17.6.19
OCHAKOV	1.10.02	6645t	Constructive total loss 16.7.42
Almaz class			
ALMAZ	2.6.03	3285t	Sold 1924
Zhemchug class			
ZHEMCHUG	27.8.03	3080t	Lost 28.10.14

Pallada class
Unlike her sisters *Aurora* had 6in guns with shields upon completion. During 1906–8 her military mast was removed together with 4–75mm and TT while 2–6in were added instead on the main deck by the mainmast. The sighting hood was removed from the CT and sights reduced here. *Diana* was laid up at that time and was recommissioned in August 1914 with 10–130mm/55 (5.1in), 4–75mm while the TT were removed. The light guns were replaced by 2–75mm AA later on. Both served with the Baltic Fleet's Second Cruiser Brigade throughout the First World War and during autumn 1916–February 1917 *Aurora* was rearmed with 4 additional 6in and 1–75mm AA instead of the older light mounts. After emerging from the Franco-Russian Works her crew, being influenced by Bolshevik agitation, mutinied giving support for the February Revolution. She participated in the Bolshevik Revolution firing from her bow 6in on 7 November 1917 as a signal for it to start. *Aurora* and *Diana* were laid up in 1918, the former being recommissioned in 1923 with 10–130mm/55 instead of 6in, while the latter was sold for scrap in Germany.

Almaz as a seaplane carrier during the war — *Twardowski Collection*

Komintern (ex-*Pamiat Merkuria*, ex-*Kagul*) about 1923 — *Lemachko Collection*

Askold class
Interned at Shanghai after the Round Island action. In 1906 she became the flagship of the Siberian Flotilla. She steamed 55,000nm while serving in the Far East and then the Mediterranean during 1914–16 participating in the Dardanelles operation during which she was nicknamed 'Packet of Woodbines' by her British allies. Being designated for the Arctic station on 21 October 1916 she was overhauled in Toulon and Britain during 1916–17 when 2 bow 75mm and all the 47mm and 30mm were replaced by 2–47mm AA, old TT replaced by 4–18in TT, mine rails and DC racks fitted. Arrived in the Arctic in September 1917 where her crew came completely under Bolshevik influence in December 1917. Seized by the British on 14 July 1918 and commissioned as *Glory IV* on 3 August. Returned to the Reds in 1921 and sold for scrap to Germany.

Bogatyr class
Bogatyr and *Oleg* returned to the Baltic Fleet after the end of the Russo-Japanese War and had their torpedo nets and 4–75mm, 4–47mm removed during 1906–8. During the First World War both served with the Baltic Fleet's First Cruiser Brigade and in 1916 were rearmed with 16–130mm (5.1in)/55 (4 in turrets, 4 in casemates, 8 in single mountings on the main deck), 4–75mm AA and received rails for 100 mines. In August 1917 both ships went over to the Bolshevik's and *Oleg* participated in the October Revolution. She remained in service with the Soviet Active Squadron during 1919 until sunk at night by a torpedo from the British *CMB 4* off Kronstadt. She went down in 12 minutes but all but 5 of her crew were rescued.

Ochakov, far from being completed, was commissioned on 9 November 1905 and 3 days later her crew mutinied being followed by 6 other ships anchored off Sevastopol. *Ochakov* was shelled by the loyal battleships and damaged by a fire. Renamed *Kagul* on 7 April 1907 while the first *Kagul* was renamed *Pamiat Merkuria* instead. During 1913–14 she received 4–6in additionally while the old 75mm battery was replaced by 2–75mm AA in singles on both turrets. Similar reconstruction of *Kagul* was cancelled because of the war and it was possible only to add 4–6in in 1915. In 1916 all her 6in were removed and replaced by 14–130mm/55 in single mountings. Armoured turrets were removed as well as the lesser guns which were replaced by 2–75mm AA. After the February Revolution *Kagul* was renamed *Ochakov* on 13 April 1917. Both flew the Independent Ukraine colours in April 1918 and were seized by the Germans at Sevastopol. Surrendered to the Allies in November 1918, *Ochakov* was transferred to Wrangel's fleet in September 1919 and renamed *General Kornilov*. *Pamiat Merkuria* came briefly into Red hands after their 1919 seizure of Sevastopol, she finally was recaptured by them in November 1920 and renamed *Komintern* on 6 March 1923. She carried 4–6in in 2 twin turrets and 8–130mm/55 in single mountings on the main deck sponsons. The 6in turrets were replaced by 2 single 130mm (5.1in) mountings and her final armament consisted of 10–130mm, 6–75mm, 3–3in AA in 1940.

Almaz class
Rearmed at Vladivostok in summer 1905 with 3–120mm, 10–75mm, 2–47mm but only 6 light guns were retained before her return to the Baltic Fleet in 1906. Rerated as dispatch vessel in 1906, she was classed as an armed yacht after 1908. Transferred to the Black Sea Fleet in 1911 she was converted into a seaplane carrier during the First World War with a large boom carried to operate her 4 seaplanes. Rearmed with 7–120mm, 4–75mm AA. Raised the Independent Ukraine colours in April 1918 but seized by the Germans at Sevastopol who surrendered her to the British in November 1918. Transferred to Wrangel's fleet in September 1919.

Zhemchug class
Remained with the Siberian Flotilla after the Russo-Japanese War and rebuilt with the forward and mizzen masts removed. After being shelled and torpedoed by the German cruiser *Emden* in Penang she was destroyed by internal explosion. Some of her 120mm guns were removed from the wreck in December 1914 and mounted on some ships of the Baltic and the Black Sea Fleets.

TORPEDO GUNBOATS

Name	Launched	Disp	Fate
Leitenant Ilin class			
LEITENANT ILIN	24.7.86	714t	Stricken 1911
KAPITAN SAKEN	12.5.89	742t	Hulked 1909
Kazarski class			
GRIDEN	12.11.93	400t	Stricken 1907
KAZARSKI	1889	411t	BU 1927
POSADNIK	13.4.92	393t	BU 1938
VOEVODA	8.12.92	415t	BU 1938
Abrek class			
ABREK	23.5.96	535t	BU *c* 1946

Leitenant Ilin class
Leitenant Ilin rerated in September 1907 as a dispatch vessel while *Kapitan Saken* was renamed *Bombory* when hulked.

Kazarski class
Posadnik and *Voevoda* became Baltic Fleet dispatch vessels in 1907 with 2–57mm/40 replacing the 47mm gun. In 1910 they were rearmed with 2–75mm, 2–57mm, 2 MG while the bow TT was removed. In 1911 *Posadnik* received the new model 4in/60 in place of the bow 75mm one and in 1917 she received another 4in piece. In March 1918 together with *Voevoda* she was taken over by the Finnish. *Kazarski* reboilered in 1906 and rearmed with 3–75mm became a Black Sea dispatch vessel in 1907, as well as *Griden*.

Abrek class
Rerated as dispatch vessel in 1907 and disarmed. During 1908–14 in the Coast Guard armed with 2–75mm, became dispatch vessel again in 1914. During 1918–21 served as a survey ship but laid up afterwards and reactivated as the dispatch vessel in 1926. Became a depot ship by the late 1930s.

DESTROYERS

Name	Launched	Fate
Pruitki class: 220t–240t		
PRUITKI	10.8.95	BU 1922
PODVIZHNI	3.6.01	BU 1930
PORAZHAYUSHCHI	12.12.98	BU 1922
POSLUSHNI	5.98	BU 1925
PROCHNI	1.10.98	BU 1922
PRONZITELNI	29.6.99	Stricken 1911
PROZORLIVI	3.7.99	Foundered 2.10.25
PYLKI	28.5.98	Stricken 1911
RETIVI	23.6.00	BU 1922
REZVI	31.8.99	BU 1925
RYANI	6.7.00	BU 1930
SERDITI	3.11.01	BU 1923
SKORI	17.5.03	BU 1923
SMYELI	10.2.03	BU 1923
SMYETLIVI	2.8.01	Scuttled 18.6.18
STATNI	21.11.03	BU 1923
STREMITELNI	1.10.01	Scuttled 18.6.18
STROGI	2.8.01	Stricken 1929
SVIRYEPI	7.9.01	Stricken 1927
Bditelni class: 350t		
BEZPOSHCHADNI	25.10.99	BU 1923
BEZSHUMNI	17.3.00	BU 1924
BEZTRASHNI	12.8.99	BU 1924
Boiki class: 350t		
BODRI	17.5.02	BU 1923
BOIKI	24.8.01	BU 1925
BRAVI	12.10.01	BU 1925
VIDNI	1905	BU 1922
Vnimatelni class: 312t		
GROZOVOI	11.3.02	BU 1921
VLASTNI	28.11.01	Sold 1921
Grozni class: 350t		
GROMYASCHI	1904	BU 1924
GROZNI	19.7.04	BU 1923
Z-ZH classes: 350t		
ZADORNI	11.04	Sunk 10.3.16
ZAVETNI	1903	Scuttled 1.5.18
ZAVIDNI	1903	BU 1923
ZORKI	10.04	Sold 1924
ZVONKI	11.04	Sold 1924
ZHARKI	1904	Sold 1924
ZHIVOI	10.4.04	Stranded 16.11.20
ZHIVUCHI	1904	Sunk 25.4.16
ZHUTKI	1904	BU 1923
Tverdi class: 297t full load		
INZHENER-MEKHANIK ANASTASOV	19.8.07	Scuttled 1921
LEITENANT MALEEV	18.9.07	BU 1923
TOCHNI	10.12.06	Stricken 4.27
TREVOZHNI	6.06	BU 1923
TVERDI	2.10.06	Stricken 4.27
Lovki class: 402t–420t		
ISKUSNI	11.7.05	BU 1922
ISPOLNITELNI	30.7.05	Sunk 12.12.14
KREPKI	24.8.05	BU 1924
LEGKI	27.9.05	BU 1924
LEITENANT BURAKOV	19.6.05	Sunk 12.8.17
LETUCHI	16.11.05	Sunk 12.12.14
LIKHOI	13.12.05	BU 1922
LOVKI	15.10.05	BU 1924
METKI	24.6.05	BU 1922
MOLODETSKI	15.9.05	BU 1923
MOSHCHNI	3.10.05	BU 1925
Bditelni class: 355t		
BDITELNI	17.3.06	Sunk 27.11.17
BOEVOI	9.1.06	BU 1925
BURNI	7.2.06	BU 1929
INZHENER-MEKHANIK DMITRIEV	4.11.05	BU 1929
INZHENER-MEKHANIK ZVEREV	7.10.05	BU 1930
KAPITAN YURASOVSKI	1907	BU 1924
LEITENANT SERGEEV	1907	BU 1924
VNIMATELNI	20.2.06	Stricken 1922
VNUSHITELNI	5.4.06	BU 1940
VYNOSLIVI	31.3.06	BU 1947
Storozhevoi class: 380t (D-boats 390t)		
DYELNI	21.5.07	BU 1925
DYEYATELNI	20.7.07	BU 1923
DOSTOINI	20.7.07	BU 1922
RASTOROPNI	21.5.06	BU 1922
RAZYASHCHI	17.9.06	BU 1922
SILNI	5.9.06	BU 1922
STOROZHEVOI	24.8.06	BU 1925
STROINI	2.1.07	Sunk 21.8.17
Ukraina class: 580t normal		
DONSKOI KAZAK	10.3.06	BU 1922
KAZANETS	11.5.05	Sunk 28.10.16
STEREGUSHCHI	1905	BU 1922
STRASHNI	1905	BU 1922
TURKMENETZ-STAVROPOLSKI	18.2.05	Stricken 1958 (?)
UKRAINA	3.10.04	Stricken 1958 (?)
VOJSKOVOI	26.11.04	Stricken 1958 (?)
ZABAJKALETZ	27.4.06	BU 1922
Emir Bukharski class: 570t normal		
DOBROVOLETZ	12.6.05	Sunk 21.8.16
EMIR BUKHARSKI	12.1.05	BU 1925
FINN	1905	BU 1925
MOSKVITYANIN	1905	Sunk 21.5.19
Gaidamak class: 570t		
AMURETZ	1905	BU 1950
GAIDAMAK	7.05	BU 1927
USSURIETZ	1907	BU 1927
VSADNIK	7.05	BU 1929
General Kondratenko class: 615t		
GENERAL KONDRATENKO	1906	BU 1924
OKHOTNIK	1906	Sunk 26.9.17
POGRANICHNIK	1906	BU 1924
SIBIRSKI STRYELOK	1906	Stricken *c* 1957
Leitenant Shestakov class: 605t		
KAPITAN-LEITENANT BARANOV	5.11.07	Scuttled 18.6.18
LEITENANT PUSHCHIN	14.9.07	Sold 1924
LEITENANT SHESTAKOV	28.7.07	Scuttled 18.6.18
LEITENANT ZATSARENNI	22.10.07	Sunk 30.6.17

Puitki class
Pylki and *Pronzitelni* were transferred from the Baltic to the Caspian in 1907 and served until being sold to merchant owners in 1911. In 1914 *Porazhayushchi* and *Prozorlivy* became dispatch vessels detached to the Submarine Forces, while the other 8 boats of the Baltic Fleet were converted to fast minesweepers and commissioned with the 2nd Minesweeping Flotilla. *Ryani, Prozorlivi, Poslushni, Rezvi* and *Podvizhni* abandoned at Helsingfors were taken over by the Finnish Navy in April 1918 and commissioned as *S 1–S 5* respectively. *S 3* and *S 4* were returned to the Soviet Union in 1922. The remaining Baltic boats were transferred to the Caspian in 1918.

Of the 4 Black Sea boats *Smyetlivi* and *Stremitelni* were scuttled off Novorossiysk to avoid capture by the Germans, while *Strogi* and *Sviryepi* were recommissioned by the Reds after hostilities ceased and renamed *Marti* (changed to *Badina* later on) and *Leitenant Schmidt* respectively. *Smyeli, Statni, Serditi* and *Skori* were based at Vladivostock during World War I.

Bditelni class
Rearmed in 1912 with 2–75mm and 6 MG they attained no more than 22 knots at that time. *Bezposhchadni* was laid up in 1916 because of lack of boiler tubes while the remaining pair was transferred to the Arctic Ocean Flotilla in October 1917. Captured by the British in March 1918, *Beztrashni* was laid up because of her bad condition while *Bezhumni* was transferred to the Whites. She was seized by the Reds in March 1920 but not recommissioned by them.

Boiki class
Vidni served with the 5th, then 9th Destroyer Flotilla in the Baltic and was laid up in May 1918. The others (based at Vladivostock) were rearmed before the First World War with 2–75mm and 6 MG with the bow TT removed. *Boiki* was laid up in 1916 because of lack of spares, while *Bodri* was destroyed by the Whites in 1922 to prevent capture by the Soviets who were able to restore *Bravi* only in November 1922 (renamed *Anisimov* on 19 September 1923), but she had to be laid up in December 1923 because of her bad condition.

Vnimateli class
Rearmed during 1912–13 with 2–75mm, 6 MG and rebuilt with a bridge in place of the searchlight platform. Both transferred from Vladivostock to the Arctic Ocean Flotilla in 1916 and *Grozovoi* was credited with sinking *U 56*. Both sailed to Britain in February 1917 to refit and were sold in May 1918 in exchange for coal but seized by the RN and from August were operational at Archangelsk. *Vlastni* returned in May 1921 and sold to Germany for scrap while *Grozovoi* was scrapped by the British.

Grozni class
Rearmed in 1909 and 1913 respectively with 2–75mm, 6 MG and fitted with mine rails for 20 mines. *Grozni* was laid up at Vladivostock in 1916 and destroyed by the retreating White Forces in October 1922. *Gromyaschi* served in the Baltic with the 9th Destroyer Flotilla and was laid up in 1918.

Z-ZH classes
All served in the Black Sea. *Zadorni* renamed *Leitenant Pushchin* on 8 April 1907. Modernised during 1909–13 with 47mm gun removed and second 75mm mounted instead, mine rails for 18 mines fitted and oil fuel capacity enlarged. *Leitenant Pushchin* was seriously damaged by two 150mm projectiles from *Goeben* in August 1914 but repaired within 20 days. *Zhivuchi*, damaged by a boiler explosion in January 1916, broke in half 3 months later when striking a mine laid by *UC 15* off Sevastopol, while *Leitenant Pushchin* was lost on a mine off Varna. *Zavetni* was scuttled by her crew at Sevastopol to prevent capture by the Germans, raised by the Soviets in August 1921 and scrapped. The remaining ships were seized by the Germans in May 1918 and *Zorki* was commissioned as *R 10* on 7 May 1918, *Zvonki* as *R 11*, *Zhivoi* as *R 12*(ii) on 22 October 1918. *Zhutki* was designated *R 12*(i) at first but recommission plans were abandoned because of her bad condition. *Zavidni* was designated *R 13* but did not enter service. All of them were transferred to the Allies in November 1918. *Zorki*, *Zvonki*, *Zharki* and *Zhivoi* were transferred to Wrangel's fleet in September 1919 while the remaining pair was destroyed by the British in April 1919. *Zhivoi* was lost in a gale during Wrangel's evacuation to Constantinople. The other three reached Bizerta while *Zavidni* was renamed *Marti* in 1920 but not rebuilt.

Tverdi class
All 5 assembled in sections sent to Vladivostock from 1906–8 and modernised during 1910–11 being rearmed with 2–75mm and 2 MG. Seized by the Whites in 1918 and transferred to the Japanese later on. *Inzhener-Mekhanik Anastasov* was scuttled to prevent use by the Reds while *Leitenant Maleev* and *Trevozhny* were wrecked in October 1922. *Tverdi* and *Tochni* were recommissioned by the Soviets in November 1922 and renamed *Lazo* and *Potapenko*.

Lovki class
All 11 stationed in the Baltic. *Ispolnitelni* capsized during a gale after one of her own mines exploded on deck when participating in a minelaying operation off Gotland. *Letuchi* during crew salvage attempts capsized too and vanished with all hands. *Leitenant Burakov* (dispatch vessel since 1912) was lost on mines laid by *UC 78* off the Aaland Islands. *Metki* participated in the Bolshevik Revolution and was laid up at Helsingfors but was able to reach Kronstadt in April 1918. The remaining boats were laid up there at the end of 1918. After 1920 *Likhoi*, *Metki*, *Lovki* and *Krepki* (renamed *Roshal* on 31 December 1922) served with the Frontier Guard.

Amuretz as rearmed — *Author's Collection*

Bditelni class
Kapitan Yurasovski and *Leitenant Sergeev* transferred from Vladivostock to the Arctic Ocean Flotilla in 1917 and were manned by the Allies in July 1918. Abandoned in 1920 they were taken over by the Soviets and formed the backbone of the White Sea Flotilla formed in 1920. All the others were Baltic boats forming the 3rd and then the 7th Destroyer Flotilla, *Bditelni* was lost on mines laid by *UC 78* off the Aaland Islands. Except for *Boevoi* and *Burni* (laid up in 1918), the others were converted to minesweepers during 1920–21. They were laid up during 1924–25 and renamed on 5 May 1928 as *Martinov* (ex-*Vnushitelni*), *Artemev* (ex-*Vynoslivi*), *Roshal* (ex-*I-M Dmitriev*) and *Zhemchuzhin* (ex-*I-M Zverev*). *Martinov* was reactivated in 1928, became a TS and then a guard ship 1934. *Artemev* served as dispatch vessel during 1926–28, transferred to the Ossoaviachim in 1932, sunk during the Second World War but raised later and scrapped.

Storozhevoi class
All 8 served in the Baltic from 1907–8. They formed the 5th, then the 9th Destroyer Flotilla during the First World War being detached to the Mine Arm. *Dyeyatelni* was shelled by the German dreadnought *König* off Moon Sound in October 1917 and participated in the Bolshevik Revolution soon after. After February 1917 *Silni* was armed with additional 1–37mm AA while *Stroini* grounded in the Gulf of Riga and was so badly damaged by a 130lb bomb from a seaplane that she was abandoned. With exception of *Silni* and *Razyashchi* (laid up at Kronstadt in May 1922 finally) the remaining boats were transferred to the Caspian Flotilla during 1918–19.

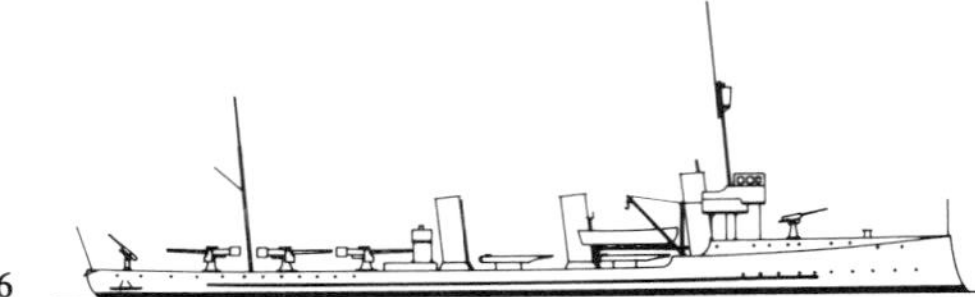
Donskoi Kazak 1916

Ukraina class
Being discovered top heavy after completion, all 8 were fitted with 20t of pig iron but this was found not satisfactory and an additional 35t was added. Rearmed with 2–4in/60 during 1909–10 and the main mast was restepped farther aft. Formed the 2nd and then the 6th Destroyer Flotilla during the First World War and participated in operations off Gotland in July 1914, off Riga in 1915 and the defence of Moon Sound in October 1917. *Donskoi Kazak* was damaged on mines in the Iber Straits (entrance to the Gulf of Riga) while *Kazanetz* sunk on the minefield laid by *UC 27* off Odensholm. *Ukraina* and *Vojskovoi* as well as *Turkmenetz Stavropolski* later on were transferred to the Caspian early in 1920. Between June and August 1920 they were called *Karl Marx*, *Fridrich Engels* and *Mirza Kuchuk*. Renamed *Bakinski Rabochi*, *Markin* and *Alvater* (changed to *Sovetski Dagestan* in 1945) respectively between June–August 1920. They became TS after 1949.

Emir Bukharski class
During the First World War they served in the Baltic with the 1st and then the 5th Destroyer Flotilla together with ships of the *Gaidamak* class. *Dobrovoiletz* was lost on a Russian minefield in the Irben Straits while the remaining boats were transferred to the Caspian in May 1918. *Moskvityanin* was sunk by the 6in and 4in gunfire of the improvised British Caspian Squadron off Alexandrovsk. The other two were renamed *Yakov Sverdlov* (ex-*Emir Bukharski*) and *Karl Liebknecht* (ex-*Finn*) in 1920.

Gaidamak class
Amuretz was damaged by a mine during a minelaying operation in the Ibern Straits on 12 August 1915 but repaired. Except for *Gaidamak* (laid up 1918) the others served with the Active Squadron in 1919 and the Onega Flotilla during the Civil War. Renamed *Zhelesniakov*, *Roshal* and *Sladkov* respectively in 1922. The first served as a dispatch vessel until hulked in 1933.

General Kondratenko class
During the First World War they formed the Half-Flotilla for Special Purposes being the best Russian destroyers in the Baltic by 1915, then shifted to 4th Destroyer Flotilla. *Okhotnik* was damaged by a German mine in the Iber Straits but repaired and once again mined here and sunk. *General Kondratenko* and *Pogranichnik* mined the entrance to Riga being the last Russian ships to leave this base on 3 September 1917 until 1940. *Sibirski Stryelok* was renamed *Konstruktor* in 1926.

Leitenant Shestakov class
The first Russian destroyers that reflected lessons of the Russo-Japanese War before completion. All served in the Black Sea from 1909. The designed armament of 6–75mm, an unusual battery for destroyers of the day, was augmented by replacing the forward 75mm with a 120mm (4.7in) gun. *Leitenant Pushchin* was renamed *Kapitan Saken* on 8 April 1907 and she alone of this class remained at Sevastopol in April 1918 with the Ukrainian colours raised. *Leitenant Zatsarenni* sank on a mine. Seized by the Germans and commissioned as *R 04* on 12 October but could not reach anything above 18kts at that time. Surrendered to the Allies in November 1918 and transferred to Wrangel's fleet in September 1919. She escaped to Bizerta in 1920.

TORPEDO-BOATS

Name	Fate	Name	Fate
Vzryv class: launched 12.8.77, 160t (Baltic)			
VZRIV	Stricken 1907		
Batum class: launched 12.6.80, 43t (Black Sea)			
251 (ex-*Batum*)	Stricken 1908		
Improved Batum class: launched 1883–84, 63t–78t (Black Sea)			
254 (ex-*Gagry*)	Stricken 1907	*256* (ex-*Sukhum*)	Stricken 1908
255 (ex-*Gelendzhik*)	Dispatch vessel 1916	*258* (ex-*Poti*)	Dispatch vessel 1916
Kotlin class: launched 1885, 67t (Baltic)			
101 (ex-*Kotlin*, ex-*1*)	Stricken 1906		
Izmail class: launched 1886–87, 73t–76t (Baltic)			
105 (ex-*Lakhata*, ex-*2*)	Stricken 1906	*107* (ex-*Narva*, ex-*4*)	Stricken 1910
106 (ex-*Luga*, ex-*3*)	Stricken 1910	*267* (ex-*Izmail*, ex-*17*)	Stricken 1913
Sveaborg class: launched 1886, 103t designed (Far East)			
205 (ex-*Sveaborg*, ex-*5*)	Stricken 1913	*206* (ex-*Revel*, ex-*6*)	Stricken 1913
Viborg class: launched 6.7.86, 106t (Baltic)			
102 (ex-*Viborg*, ex-*7*)	Stricken 1910		
Abo class: launched 1886, 87t full load			
108 (ex-*Abo*, ex-*8*)	Stricken 1910	*263* (ex-*Novorossisk*, ex-*12*)	Stricken 1913
109 (ex-*Vindava*, ex-*9*)	Stricken 1910	*254* (ex-*Reni*, ex-*16*)	Stricken 1911
110 (ex-*Libava*, ex-*10*)	Stricken 1910	*265* (ex-*Chardak*, ex-*13*)	Stricken 1911
261 (ex-*Kodor*, ex-*14*)	Stricken 1911	*266* (ex-*Yalta*, ex-*11*)	Stricken 1911
262 (ex-*Kiliya*, ex-*15*)	Stricken 1911		
Yanchikhe class: launched 1887, 76t (Far East)			
201 (ex-*Yanchikhe*)	Stricken 1911	*202* (ex-*Suchene*)	Stricken 1911
Ussuri class: launched 1889, 175t (Far East)			
203 (ex-*Ussuri*, ex-*Nargen*)	Stricken 1907		
Adler class: launched 4.9.90, 164t (Black Sea)			
259 (ex-*Adler*)	Deleted 1917		
Anakria class: launched 1889, 1893–95, 85t–100t			
115 (ex-*Tosna*)	Stricken 1910	*126* (ex-*Tranzund*)	Stricken 1910
116 (ex-*Domesnes*)	Stricken 1910	*131*	Stricken 1910
121 (ex-*Nargen*)	Stricken 1910	*132*	Stricken 1917?
122 (ex-*Gogland*)	Stricken 1910	*260* (ex-*Anakriya*)	Stricken 1917
125 (ex-*Aspe*)	Stricken 1910	*268*	Stricken 1911
Borgo class: launched 1890, 106t (Baltic)			
117 (ex-*Ekenes*)	Stricken 1910		
Bierke class: launched 1890–92, 81t designed			
111 (ex-*Bierke*)	Stricken 1910	*114* (ex-*Moonzund*)	Stricken 1910
112 (ex-*Rochensalm*)	Stricken 1910	*252* (ex-*Anapa*)	Stricken 1917?
113 (ex-*Gapsal*)	Stricken 1910	*253* (ex-*Aj-Todor*)	Stricken 1917?
Dago class: launched 1891, 100t–101t			
118 (ex-*Dago*)	Stricken 1910	*124* (ex-*Seskar*)	Stricken 1910
123 (ex-*Kronshlot*)	Stricken 1910	*256* (ex-*Kotka*)	Stricken 1925
Pernov class: launched 1892–99, 120t			
103 (ex-*Pernov*)	Sold 1922	*138*	Stricken 1911
119 (ex-*Polangen*)	Sold 1922	*139*	Stricken 1911
120 (ex-*Pakerort*)	Sold 1922	*140*	Stricken 1914
127	Stricken 1911	*141*	Stricken 1914
128	Sold 1922	*142*	Sunk 5.23
129	Sold 1922	*209*	Stricken 1911
130	Stricken 1911	*210*	Stricken 1911
133	Stricken 1911	*211*	Stricken 1915
134	Stricken 1914	*270*	Scuttled 4.19
135	Stricken 1911	*271*	Scuttled 4.19
136	Stricken 1913	*272*	Sunk 28.8.14
137	Stricken 1911	*273*	Stricken 1924
Sestroretsk class: launched 3.94, 79.5t (Baltic)			
104 (ex-*Sestroretsk*)	Sold 1922		
Improved Ussuri class: launched 1902, 186t (Baltic)			
212	BU 1922	*213*	BU 1926
Cyclone class: launched 1902–04, 150t (Baltic)			
214	Sold 1922	*219*	Sold 1922
215	Sold 1922	*220*	Sold 1922
216	Sold 1922	*222*	Sold 1922
217	Sold 1922	*223*	Stricken 1911
218	Sold 1922		

Improved Batum class
255 and *258* deleted and hulked in 1908 but recommissioned as minesweepers during 1910–13 but disarmed in 1916 and employed as dispatch vessels *9* and *10* respectively.

Izmail class
267, the only boat in the Black Sea, mutinied in 1905 to support the crew of the battleship *Potemkin*. Deleted in 1907 but recommissioned as minesweeper 9 in 1908.

Sveaborg class
Converted to dispatch vessels in 1911.

Abo class
The first 3 were in the Baltic, the rest in the Black Sea. Crew of *265* mutinied in 1907 to support the mutinied cruiser *Ochakov, 261* served as hulk *Sanitar* during 1914–17.

Adler class
Rearmed in 1914 with 2–47mm, 2–37mm, 1 MG and became dispatch vessel *Letuchi* (renamed *8* in 1916).

Anakria class
All except the last 2 (Black Sea) were in the Baltic. *132* deleted in 1910 but reactivated in 1914 as the minesweeper *Cheka* and armed with 1–47mm, stranded August 1916 off Hangö but refloated later and served until laid up in 1918. *260* rearmed with 3–47mm, 1–37mm, 2 MG in 1915 and became dispatch vessel *Miner*, renamed *2* in 1916.

Bierke class
All except the last 2 (Black Sea) were in the Baltic. *252* and *253* have had 1 TT removed and 1–47mm, 1 MG mounted instead in 1915 and became dispatch vessels *Uchebnyj* and *Provodnik* (renamed *1* and *3* respectively in 1916).

Dago class
All except *256* (Black Sea) were in the Baltic. *256* reboilered in 1908 and became dispatch vessel *Lotchik* in 1915 armed with 2–47mm, 2–37mm, 1 MG, 1 TT. Renumbered *4* in 1916, then *11* in 1918 and scuttled by the Reds in Novorossisk 18 June 1918. Raised later on and recommissioned as TS.

Pernov class
All served in the Baltic except *209–211* (Far East) and *270–273* (Black Sea). *103, 119, 120, 128, 129, 142* rearmed in 1912 only 1–47mm retained and reclassed as dispatch vessels (*119* renamed *Periskop*). Hulked at Helsingfors in December 1917 with exception of *142* and seized by the Finns there in April 1918. Returned to the Soviets in 1922 but sold to the local breakers because of bad condition. *142* converted to minesweeper during the First World War, sunk at Kronstadt because of a machinery room leak, wreck raised and BU. *136* was beached off the Finnish coast in December 1912. Except for *272* (lost in collision with auxiliary minesweeper *T 247*) the other Black Sea boats became minesweepers *5* (ex-*273*), *6* (ex-*270*), *7* (ex-*271*) in 1915 and were rearmed with 2–37mm, 1 MG, 2TT. Rerated as dispatch vessels in 1916 and renumbered *7*, *5* and *6* respectively. Seized by the Germans at Sevastopol they were wrecked by the British in April 1919 but *7* was repaired by the Soviets and recommissioned as *Razvedchik*.

Sestroretsk class
Became a Baltic dispatch vessel after 1912 being rearmed with 1–30mm. Captured by the Finns in 1918, returned to the Soviet Union in 1922 but sold to the local breakers.

Improved Ussuri class
Converted to minesweepers in 1914 and rearmed with 2–47mm, 2 MG, 2 TT. *212* seized by the Finns in 1918 and commissioned as *S 6* but returned to the Soviet Union in 1922.

Cyclone class
Converted to minesweepers in 1914, hulked by the end of 1917 at the Finnish bases and seized here by the Finns in April 1918. Returned to the Soviet Union in 1922 but sold to local breakers.

SMALL TORPEDO-BOATS (MINONOSKI)

The Russian Navy with its 1877 small torpedo-boat programme became the first to use the torpedo on a mass scale. This decision was motivated by the successful use of a torpedo during the early stages of the Russo-Turkish War of 1877–78 and the lack of a powerful battlefleet to defend the approaches to St Petersburg. At a cost equivalent to one battleship a huge flotilla of 110 small torpedo-boats was created during 1877–79. This numerous force of dubious fighting value became obsolete with the development of more modern torpedo craft. The typical Russian small torpedo-boat *(mininoska)* was *c*25t, one shaft boat with a locomotive boiler forward and manned by 9 men. Only 26 of them (3 Bellino-Fenderich type, 23 Yarrow type) had tubes for Whitehead torpedoes when completed, the others being equipped with spar torpedoes. They were replaced with droppable torpedoes just after 1879 in some boats. In January 1886 the newly introduced numeral system of names was changed to reflect the type of weapon carried: those armed with tubes for Whitehead torpedoes received numbers 50–100 while those fitted with spare torpedoes and droppable ones were numbered from 101 upwards. If a boat later received the Whitehead tube she was given a corresponding number in 1889.

From 1886 onwards the lightweight pneumatic or gunpowder fired 14in torpedoes (7kts) were fitted to the remaining spar torpedo-boats. At first the *minonoski* did not carry any guns but 1–37mm Hotchkiss gun was fitted in 1878 in *Sudak*, *Raketa*, *Shtyk* and later on the boats equipped with the above mentioned 14in TT.

Note: In the following tables the stations for the ships are abbreviated thus: B (Baltic), BS (Black Sea) and FE (Far East).

RUSSIA

Luk as completed
NB 1/750 scale

Thornycroft types
Builder: Thornycroft
Displacement: 24.5t
Dimensions: 75ft × 9ft 3in × 3ft 3in
22.9m × 2.8m × 1.0m
Machinery: High pressure, 114ihp = 14kts

Name: early 1877	July 1877	1885	1886	1895	Station/Fate
1	–	–	–	–	BS/Lost 1877
2	SULIN	*123*	*92*	*88*	BS/Stricken 1904

Builder: Thornycroft
Displacement: 12.5t
Dimensions: 62ft 8in × 7ft 6in × 3ft 6in
19.1m × 2.3m × 1.1m
Machinery: High pressure, 112ihp = 12kts

Name	1885	1886	1895	Station/Fate
KEFAL	*160*	*160*	*90*	BS/Harbour service 1900

Builder: Ropit Yd, Sevastopol
Displacement: 24.4t
Dimensions: 71ft 6in × 8ft 10in × 6ft 3in
21.8m × 2.7m × 1.9m
Machinery: High pressure, 200ihp = 12.5kts

Name	1885	1886	1895	Station/Fate
SHSHEGLENOK	*161*	*85*	*83*	BS/Stricken 1905
SHCHUKA	*163*	*86*	*84*	BS/Stricken 1902
YASHCHERITSA	*165*	*87*	*85*	BS/Stricken 1902

Bychok class
Builder: Baird, St Petersburg
Displacement: 16t
Dimensions: 60ft × 7ft 6in × 3ft 6in
18.3m × 2.3m × 1.1m
Machinery: Compound, 220ihp = 11.5kts

Name	1885	1886	1895	Station/Fate
BYCHOK	–	–	–	BS/To Bulgaria 1884
CHEREPAKHA	–	–	–	BS/To Bulgaria 1884

Schichau types
Builder: Schichau Yd, Elbing
Displacement: 23t
Dimensions: 65ft 3in × 8ft 3in × 4ft
19.9m × 2.5m × 1.2m
Machinery: Compound, 220ihp = 16kts

Name	1885	1895	Station/Fate
BOMBA	*108*	*77*	B/Stricken 1900
BULAVA	*110*	–	B/Harbour service 1895
KOPE	*102*	–	B/Harbour service 1895
LUK	*104*	*75*	B/Harbour service 1900, *Shlem*
MECH	*106*	*76*	B/Harbour service 1900
PALITSA	*112*	*78*	B/Harbour service 1900
PRASHCH	*114*	*79*	B/Stricken 1897
SHTYK	*118*	*80*	B/Harbour service 1897, *Pika*
STRELA	*116*	–	B/Harbour service 1895, *Strelka*
YADRO	*120*	*81*	B/Harbour service 1900

Builder: Schichau Yd, Elbing
Displacement: 11.3t
Dimensions: 65ft × 8ft 6in × 2ft
19.8m × 2.6m × 0.6m
Machinery: 3 cyl, 120ihp = 13kts

Name	1885	1895	Station/Fate
KARABIN	*124*	*89*	BS/Harbour service 1900, *25*

Yarrow types
Builder: Baird, St Petersburg
Displacement: 25t
Dimensions: 71ft 6in × 8ft 10in × 6ft 6in
21.8m × 2.7m × 1.9m
Machinery: Compound, 220ihp = 13kts

Name	1885	1886	1895	Station/Fate
VOROBEY	*78*	*144*	–	B/Stricken 1889
VORONA	*86*	*151*	–	B/Sunk as target 1892

Builder: Baltic Yd, St Petersburg

Name	1885	1886	1895	Station/Fate
ALBATROS	*31*	*71*	*26*	B/Stricken 1908
BEKAS	*10*	*101*	*43*	B/Stricken 1906
GLUKHAR	*146*	*146*	*64*	FE, 1904/Stricken 1907
VORON	*12*	*103*	*50*	B/Stricken 1908

Builder: New Admiralty Yd, St Petersburg

Name	1885	1886	1895	Station/Fate
AIST	*144*	*144*	*63*	B/Stricken 1908
AKULA	*142*	*142*	*62*	B/Stricken 1908

Builder: Baltic Yd, St Petersburg
Displacement: 23t
Dimensions: 71ft 6in × 8ft 10in × 5ft 6in
21.8m × 2.7m × 1.7m
Machinery: Compound, 220ihp = 14kts

Torpedo-boat *61* (ex-*141*, ex-*74*, ex-*Konoplyanka*) about 1904 *Lemachko Collection*

Name	1885	1886	1895	Station/Fate
CHAJKA	*27*	*68*	*18*	FE, 1904/Stricken 1907
CHIZHIK	*45*	*78*	*93*	FE/Stricken 1907
DELFIN	*13*	*54*	*12*	B/Stricken 1908
DRAKON	*15*	*56*	*11*	*B*/Stricken 1908
FAZAN	*24*	*115**	*35*	B/Stricken 1908
FILIN	*33*	*72*	*20*	B/Stricken 1908
FOREL	*49*	*80*	*95*	FE/Stricken 1907
KHAMELEON	*25*	*66*	*17*	B/Stricken 1908
OREL	*50*	*117*	*49*	B/Stricken 1908
PODORO-ZHNIK	*47*	*79*	*94*	FE/Stricken 1908
SUDAK	*14*	*105*	*46*	B/Stricken 1908
SVIRISTEL	*19*	*60*	*15*	B/Stricken 1908
TETEREV	*16*	*107*	*47*	FE, 1904/Stricken 1907
TRESKA	*35*	*73*	*42*	B/Stricken 1908
TSAPLYA	–	–	–	B/Sunk as target 1885
UDAV	*18*	*109*	–	B/Lost 1886
UGOR	*20*	*111***	*36*	B/Stricken 1908
UTKA	*22*	*113*	*48*	FE, 1904/Stricken 1907
UZH	*37*	*74*	*37*	B/Stricken 1908
YASTREB	*39*	*70*	*19*	B/Stricken 1908

*after 1889 numbered *49*
**after 1889 numbered *50*

Builder: Baird, St Petersburg

Name	1885	1886	1895	Station/Fate
DROZD	*82*	*147*	–	B/Stricken 1895
DYATEL	*51*	*51*	*1*	B/Stricken 1908
INDYUK	*70*	*137*	*55*	B/Stricken 1908
IVOLGA	*62*	*129*	*53*	B/Stricken 1908
KAKADU	*69*	*69*	*29*	B/Stricken 1908
KAMBALA	*72*	*139*	*56*	B/Stricken 1908
KANAREJKA	*80*	*145*	–	B/Stricken 1895
KARAS	*60*	*127**	*27*	B/Stricken 1908
KOLIBRI	*54*	*121*	*51*	B/Stricken 1908
KONOPL-YANKA	*74*	*141*	*61*	B/Stricken 1907
KOPCHIK	*56*	*123***	*28*	B/Stricken 1908
KORYUSHKA	*53*	*53*	*2*	B/Stricken 1908
KRECHET	*61*	*61*	*6*	FE, 1904/Stricken 1907
KROKODIL	*63*	*63*	*7*	FE, 1904/Stricken 1907
KUKUSHKA	58	125	52	B/Stricken 1908
KURITSA	*65*	*65*	*8*	B/Stricken 1908
ZMEYA	*84*	*149*	—	B/Stricken 1895
ZYABLIK	*67*	*67*	*9*	FE, 1904/Stricken 1907
ZHAVORON-OK	*76*	*143*	*98*	FE/Stricken 1908
ZHURAVL	*52*	*119*	*45*	B/Stricken 1908

*After 1889 numbered *47*
**After 1889 numbered *48*

Builder: Harbour Workshops, St Petersburg

Name	1885	1886	1895	Station/Fate
NALIM	*98*	*162*	*69*	B/Stricken 1908
NYROK	*100*	*163*	*70*	B/Stricken 1907
OSETR	*64*	*131**	*30*	B/Stricken 1906
PAVLIN	*66*	*133*	*60*	B/Stricken 1908
PELIKAN	*68*	*135*	*54*	B/Stricken 1908
PEREPEL	*59*	*59*	*5*	B/Stricken 1908
PESKAR	*55*	*55*	*3*	FE, 1904/Stricken 1907
PLOTVA	*91*	*91*	*10*	B/Stricken 1908
POPUGAJ	*57*	*57*	*4*	B/Stricken 1908

*after 1889 numbered *96*

Builder: Izhora Wks, St Petersburg

Name	1885	1886	1895	Station/Fate
BELUGA	*95*	*95*	*40*	B/Stricken 1908
KUROPATKA	*90*	*153*	*67*	B/Stricken 1908
LASTOCHKA	*92*	*157*	*68*	B/Stricken 1908
LEBED	*94*	*159*	*25*	B/Stricken 1908
LESHCH	–	–	–	B/Sunk as target 1885
LOSOS	*96*	*161*	*73*	B/Stricken 1908
MALINOVKA	*93*	*93*	*22*	B/Stricken 1908

Builder: Crichton Yd, Abo

Name	1885	1886	1895	Station/Fate
PETUKH	*140*	*140*	*72*	B/Stricken 1908
RYABCHIK	*132*	*132*	*97*	FE/Stricken 1908
SALAMANDRA	*134*	*97*	*34*	B/Stricken 1908
SARDINKA	*131*	*82*	*39*	B/Stricken 1908
SELD	*138*	*138*	*71*	B/Stricken 1908
SIG	*136*	*136*	*58*	B/Stricken 1908

Builder: Nevskij Yd, St Petersburg

Name	1885	1886	1895	Station/Fate
DROKHVA	*126*	*126*	–	BS/Stricken 1895
GOLUB	*121*	*81*	*21*	BS, 1896/Stricken 1902
GORLITSA	*128*	*128*	*59*	B/Stricken 1908
GRACH	*130*	*94*	*33*	B/Stricken 1908
GUS	*122*	*122*	*57*	B/Stricken 1908

Builder: Britnev Wks, Kronshtadt

Name	1885	1886	1895	Station/Fate
SNIGIR	*150*	*98*	*38*	B/Lost 1900
SOKOL	*154*	*154*	*66*	B/Stricken 1908
SOLOVEJ	*156*	*99*	*31*	B/Stricken 1908
SOM	*158*	*100*	*32*	B/Stricken 1908
SOVA	*152*	*152*	*65*	B/Stricken 1906

Name	1885	1886	1895	Station/Fate
SKVORETS	*148*	*148*	*44*	B/Stricken 1908

Modified Yarrow types
Builder: Baltic Wks, St Petersburg
Displacement: 24.3t
Dimensions: 75ft × 9ft 10in × 3ft 6in
22.9m × 3.0m × 1.1m
Machinery: Compound, 220ihp = 13kts

Name	1885	1886	1895	Station/Fate
SOROKA	*39*	*75*	*82*	BS/Stricken 1904
STERLYAD	*41*	*76*	*91*	FE/Stricken 1907
STRAUS	*43*	*77*	*92*	FE/Stricken 1907

Builder: Baltic Wks, St Petersburg
Displacement: 33.45t
Dimensions: 74ft 6in × 11ft 3in × 5ft
22.7m × 3.4m × 1.5m
Machinery: Compound, 220ihp = 13kts

Name	1885	1886	1895	Station/Fate
GALKA	*11*	*52*	*13*	B/Stricken 1908
SELEZEN	*23*	*64*	*41*	BS, 1896/Stricken 1902

Builder: Baltic Wks, St Petersburg
Displacement: 29t
Dimensions: 89ft 10in × 8ft 10in × 5ft 10in
27.4m × 2.7m × 1.8m
Machinery: Compound, 220ihp = 13kts

Name	1885	1886	1895	Station/Fate
SIRENA	*21*	*62*	*16*	B/Stricken 1908

Vulkan type
Builder: Vulkan, Stettin
Displacement: 33t
Dimensions: 79ft × 10ft 10in × 5ft 6in
24.1m × 3.3m × 1.7m
Machinery: Compound, 250ihp = 13kts

Name	1885	1886	1895	Station/Fate
RAKETA	*133*	*83*	*23*	B/Experimental ship 1908
SAMOPAL	*135*	*84*	*24*	B/Stricken 1908

Bellino-Fenderich type
Builder: Bellino-Fenderich Yd, Odessa
Displacement: 25.4t
Dimensions: 61ft 4in × 10ft × 5ft
18.7m × 3.0m × 1.5m
Machinery: High pressure, 220ihp = 12kts

Name	1885	1886	1895	Station/Fate
SKORPION	*171*	*90*	*96*	FE/Sunk as target 1896
SKUMBRIYA	*169*	*89*	*87*	BS/Stricken 1906
SULTANKA	*167*	*88*	*86*	BS/Stricken 1904

Streamlined hull type
Builder: Baltic Yd, St Petersburg
Displacement: 24t
Dimensions: 72ft × 10ft × 6ft 3in
21.9m × 3.0m × 1.9m
Machinery: Compound 220ihp = *13kts*

Name	1885	1886	1895	Station/Fate
KASATKA	*17*	*58*	*14*	B/Stricken 1908

1889 Thornycroft type
Builder: Thornycroft
Displacement: 17t
Dimensions: 60ft × 8ft 6in × 4ft 3in
18.4m × 2.6m × 1.3m
Machinery: Compound, 220ihp

Number	1895	Station/Fate
46	*74*	B/Stricken 1900

GUNBOATS

Name	Launched	Disp	Fate
Ersh class (Baltic)			
ERSH	17.8.74	321t	Stricken 1907
Burun class (Baltic)			
BURUN	24.9.79	379t	Hulked 1908
DOZHD	21.10.79	450t	Stricken 1907
GROZA	17.7.80	416t	Stricken 1907
VIKHR	6.11.79	390t	Hulked 1908
Korietz class (Far East)			
MANDZHUR	12.86	1418t	BU 1923
Kubanetz class (Black Sea)			
CHERNOMORETZ	29.8.87	1299t	Stricken 1911
DONETZ	30.11.87	1224t	Sunk 5.19
KUBANETZ	9.4.87	1284t	Stricken *c* 1941
TERETZ	29.8.87	1284t	Stricken *c* 1941
URALETZ	8.12.87	1227t	Sunk 1.12.13
ZAPOROZHETZ	4.6.87	1224t	Stricken 1911
Grozyashchi class (Baltic)			
GROZYASHCHI	31.5.90	1627t	BU 1922
Khrabri class (Baltic)			
KHRABRI	21.11.95	1735t	BU *c* 1962
Khivinets class (Baltic)			
KHIVINETZ	11.5.05	1340t	BU *c* 1946
Gilyak class (Baltic)			
BOBR	8.07	960t	BU 1927
GILYAK	27.10.06	960t	BU 1922
KORIETZ	5.07	960t	Scuttled 20.8.15
SIVUCH	1.8.07	960t	Sunk 19.8.15

SUBMARINES

Name	Fate	Name	Fate
Delfin class: launched 1903, 113t surfaced			
DELFIN (ex-*150*, ex-*113*)	Sunk 5.9.17		
Kasatka class: launched 1904, 140t surfaced			
FELDMARSHAL GRAF SHEREMETEV	BU 1922	NALIM	Scuttled 26.4.19
KASATKA	BU 1922	OKUN	BU 1922
MAKREL	BU 1922	SKAT	Scuttled 26.4.19
Holland type: launched 1904–07, 105t surfaced			
BELUGA	Scuttled 25.2.18	SOM (ex-*Fulton*)	Lost 23.5.16
LOSOS	Scuttled 26.4.19	STERLYAD	Scuttled 25.2.18
PESKAR	Scuttled 25.2.18	SUDAK	Scuttled 26.4.19
SHCHUKA	Scuttled 25.2.18		
Lake type: launched 1905, 153t surfaced			
BYCHOK	Stricken 1913	PALTUS	Stricken 1913
KEFAL	Stricken 1915	PLOTVA	Stricken 1913
OSTER (ex-*Protector*)	Stricken 1913	SIG	Stricken 1914
Forel class: launched 1902, 16t surfaced			
FOREL	Stricken 1911		
Karp class: launched 1907, 207t surfaced			
KAMBALA	Lost 11.6.09	KARP	Scuttled 26.4.19
KARAS	Scuttled 26.4.19		
Keta class: converted 1905, 3t			
KETA	Stricken 1908		

MINELAYERS

Name	Launched	Disp	Fate
Amur (ii) class			
AMUR	6.07	2926t	Scuttled 27.8.41
YENISEI	18.7.06	2926t	Sunk 4.6.15
Volga class			
VOLGA	1905	1711t	Expended *c*1959

Volga about 1910
Twardowski Collection

CAPITAL SHIPS

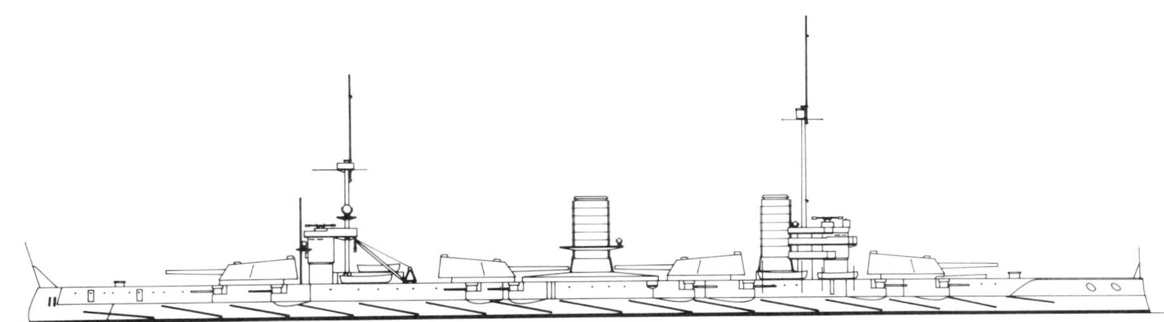

Gangut as completed

GANGUT class *battleships*

Displacement:	23,360t normal; 25,850t full load
Dimensions:	590ft 6in wl, 549ft 6in oa × 87ft 3in × 27ft 6in mean, 30ft 2in max *180.0m, 181.2m × 26.6m × 8.4m, 9.2m*
Machinery:	4-shaft Parsons turbines, 25 Yarrow boilers, 42,000shp = 23kts. Oil fuel 1170t max, coal 3000t max
Armour:	Belt 9in–4in (229mm–102mm), turrets 8in–5in (203mm–127mm), barbettes 8in (203mm), CT 10in (254mm), decks 3in–1.5in (76mm–38mm)
Armament:	12–12in (305mm)/52 (4×3), 16–4.7in (120mm)/50, 4–47mm, 4–18in (457mm) TT (sub)
Complement:	1126

Name	Builder	Laid down	Launched	Comp	Fate
GANGUT	Admiralty Yd, St Petersburg	16.6.09	7.10.11	12.14	BU 1959
PETROPAVLOVSK	Baltic Yd, St Petersburg	16.6.09	9.9.11	12.14	Constructive total loss 23.9.41
POLTAVA	Admiralty Yd, St Petersburg	16.6.09	10.7.11	17.12.14	Stricken 1925
SEVASTOPOL	Baltic Yd, St Petersburg	16.6.09	27.6.11	17.11.14	BU 1957

Despite strong opposition from the Duma, the first Russian dreadnoughts were authorised at the end of 1908 by the Czar Nicholas II. Their principal characteristics were worked out during 1906–7 by the Naval Staff and provided for 21.5kt battleships armed with 12–12in in triple turrets and 16–120mm in casemates. Because of lack of experience, tenders for the design were invited in early 1908. In response 6 Russian and 21 foreign yards and designers presented a total of 51 designs. The German Blohm and Voss Yd design was considered the best one by the Naval Technical Committee while the Naval General Staff preferred that presented by Cuniberti. The latter was rejected however on the grounds that the 120mm guns were placed in turrets and not in casemates as had been required.

The prospects of an order for battleships from Germany attracted political opposition in both Russia and France. The Russian Prime Minister decided to purchase the German drawings while the battleships themselves were to be built in Russia according to a design of the Baltic Yd. The design had to be re-worked completely and the assistance of the British John Brown Yd was utilised together with design material received from abroad as far as possible. Finally the compromise between battleship and battlecruiser (called Baltic-dreadnought at that time) was achieved, strongly reflecting Cuniberti's ideas in the general layout.

The four triple turrets with the excellent Obukhov 12in pieces placed on the centreline, gave an effective broadside a third heavier than in contemporary British and German capital ships. Positioning of the 120mm battery was not so successful as the casemates had been arranged immediately below the 12in muzzles.

The powerplant consisted of two groups of boiler rooms separated by B turret, while the machinery room was placed abaft the Y mounting. Introduction of the light Yarrow boilers instead of the Belleville ones, in common use in the Russian battlefleet, allowed an increase of speed of 1.5kts this giving 2kts–3kts margin above other dreadnoughts. The high speed achieved (*Poltava* developed 52,000shp = 24.3kts on 24,000t displacement during trials) involved substantial weight penalties for the power and sacrifices had to be made in the armour.

As a result of Russo-Japanese War experience it was decided to extend the armour over the whole hull area as it was done in the *Andrei Pervozvanni* class. Because of this assumption the belt thickness had to remain correspondingly thinner by 1in – 3in than in the other 12in gun capital ships building at that time. The belt covered the hull from the level of the main deck to 5½ft below the normal load waterline where it tapered to 6in. At the ends after the outermost turrets the belt was reduced to 4in–5in. The sides above the main deck were given 5in armour (reduced to 3in forward of the bow casemates), while additional side protection was provided by the longitudinal 1½in–2in bulkhead placed 11ft from the outer plating. The horizontal armour consisted of 1in–1½in armoured deck, inclined to the lower edge of the main belt. The main deck was covered with 1in plates while the upper deck reached 1½in. The funnel uptakes received 3in armour while the turret roofs and both CTs 3in and 4¾in respectively. The bow 4in armoured bulkhead was placed immediately forward the bow turret while the after 4in–5in bulkhead was positioned abaft the rudders. The underwater protection was provided by the 4ft double bottom which reached as far as the armoured deck. The 1½in torpedo bulkheads were constructed as extensions of the longitudinal ones.

The longitudinal construction of the main members of the hull and use of high tensile steel throughout caused many inconveniences for the designers. In the summer of 1910 doubts had arisen about the hull's general strength and building had to be stopped for a time to introduce necessary corrections. The other unusual features included provision of the ice-breaking bow and cage masts. The latter were abandoned during construction in favour of the pole ones after excessive vibrations had been experienced during trials of the *Andrei Pervozvanni* class.

The design faults and shipyard shortcomings as well as inertia in the state bureaucracy delayed completion of the ships by 2 years which made the class obsolescent and outclassed by the advent of 13.5in gun battleships. Building costs soared to 29 million roubles for each ship, sufficient to obtain 2 similar ships from abroad in 1912. After completion the four ships formed the First Battleship Brigade operating from Helsingfors (Helsinki). They were not to be rushed unnecessarily and the strategic plans proposed employment of the capital ships on defence of the Nargen-Porkalla-Udd position at the entrance to the Gulf of Finland. Subsequently their service was restricted to confined waters, only *Gangut* and *Petropavlovsk* ventured as far as Gotland when screening minelaying forces there.

The *Gangut* class did not incorporate numerous changes during the First World War. The most noticeable was omission of 4–47mm, one planned atop each turret, and only during 1917 did all ships receive 4 light AA guns placed in pairs on the outermost turrets (*Poltava* and *Sevastopol* 75mm ones, the others 63mm pieces). The torpedo nets were removed by the end of 1916 and at that time the director control of the Geisler system was introduced for the main guns and placed on both CTs instead of the large rangefinders.

After the February Revolution the crews succumbed to Bolshevik agitation and during July/August 1917 the First Battleship Brigade came under Bolshevik control. With other ships stationed in Helsingfors the dreadnoughts were demobilised in January 1918 and three months later they were evacuated to Kronstadt. Only *Petropavlovsk* re-entered service and participated in the Civil War with the Active Squadron of the Baltic Fleet. Her 12in gunfire covered the retreat of Soviet minesweepers into Kronstadt, forcing British destroyers to break off their pursuit on 31 May 1919. On 17 August she was sunk in shallow water by three torpedoes from the British *CMB 31* and *CMB 88*. The remaining three were laid up at the end of 1918. Because of total negligence the fire which had broken out in *Poltava*'s forward boiler room on 24 November 1919 damaged the ship so severely that she was found not worth repairing. It was decided in 1925 to disarm her and expend her for experimental purposes, but she was renamed *Frunze* on 7 January 1926 instead and 2 years later the intentions were changed again and repairs begun. Work proceeded slowly however and after reconstruction of the new battleships had been decided in the mid-1930s, *Frunze* once again was hulked. She was sunk in Leningrad in 1941 but raised in 1944 and BU by the mid-1950s.

After the Civil War the remaining ships were in desperate need of repair and only *Petropavlovsk* (renamed *Marat* 31 May 1921) was recommissioned in 1922 with 6–75mm AA mounted in threes on the foremost turrets and a light rangefinder platform added on the foremast. *Sevastopol* was renamed *Parizhkaya Kommuna* on 31 March 1921 while *Gangut* surrendered her name to become *Oktyabrskaya Revolyutsiya* 27 May 1925.

Marat (ex-*Petropavlovsk*) about 1923 — *Author's Collection*

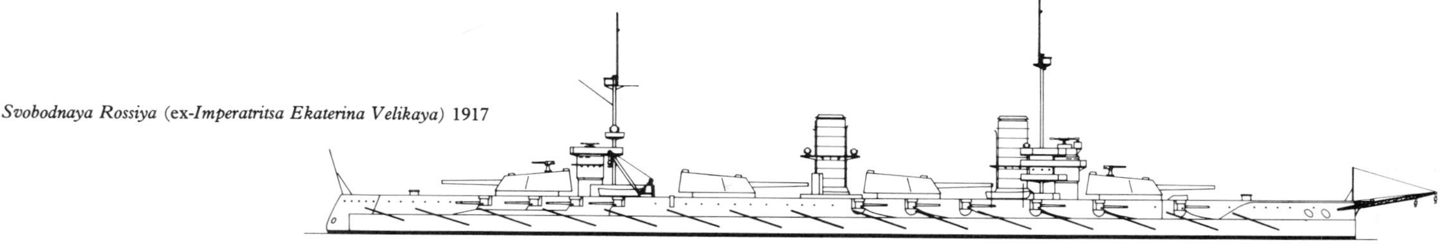

Svobodnaya Rossiya (ex-*Imperatritsa Ekaterina Velikaya*) 1917

IMPERATRITSA MARIYA class *battleships*

Displacement:	22,600t normal (*Ekaterina II* 23,783t); 24,000t full load (24,960t)
Dimensions:	550ft 6in oa (*Ekaterina II* 557ft) × 89ft 6in (91ft 6in) × 27ft 6in *167.8m (169.8m) × 27.3m (27.9m) × 8.4m*
Machinery:	4-shaft Parsons (*Volya* Brown-Curtiss) turbines, 20 Yarrow boilers, 26,500shp (*Ekaterina II* 27,000shp) = 21kts. Oil fuel 720t, coal 3000t max
Armour:	Belt 10.5in–4in (267mm–102mm), turrets 12in (305mm), barbettes 8in (203mm), CT 12in (305mm), decks 3in (76mm)
Armament:	12–12in (305mm)/52 (4×3), 20 (*Volya* 18)–5.1in (130mm)/55, 8–75mm, 4–47mm, 4 MG, 4–18in (457mm) TT (sub)
Complement:	1220

Name	Builder	Laid down	Launched	Comp	Fate
IMPERATRITSA MARIYA	Russud Yd, Nikolayev	30.10.11	1.11.13	6.7.15	Lost 20.10.16
VOLYA (ex-*Imperator Alexander III*)	Russud Yd, Nikolayev	30.10.11	15.4.14	28.6.17	Sold 1924
IMPERATRITSA EKATERINA VELIKAYA (ex-*Ekaterina II*)	Naval Yd, Nikolayev	30.10.11	6.6.14	18.10.15	Sunk 18.6.18

Authorised under the 1911 Programme. The preliminary characteristics issued by the Technical Committee provided for 20,000t, 20.5kts battleships armed with 12in guns. The Naval Staff rejected this idea and demanded 14in, 22kt ships to follow development trends of the day and to counter the *Resadiye* class battleships ordered by Turkey. Unfortunately for the Russians the 14in guns were then only in the earliest stage of development in the Obukhov Works at that time and it was therefore decided to mount 12in to avoid delays. The general layout was modelled on the *Gangut* class but the new capital ships were to be pure battleships unlike the previous class and with protection substantially improved. The 10.5in belt was backed by a 2in longitudinal bulkhead extended down to form the armoured torpedo bulkhead. The horizontal armour remained the same as in the previous class while special attention was paid to turret protection. The medium battery of the newly introduced 130mm/55 guns was placed in the casemates covered with 5in armour. Disposition of casemates showed signs of improvement as compared with the *Gangut* class but interference with the main calibre guns was not avoided in all cases.

Financial problems hampered Naval Staff requirements and the speed was reduced to 21kts and the displacement limited to 21,500t normal. The same reason caused abandonment of the 1911 proposals for 24kts and increased protection. The authorised displacement was increased by 1100t to fulfil requirements already settled on, while *Imperatritsa Ekaterina* exceeded twice this figure. Such a divergence between her and the remaining pair was due to the various supervisory firms of the Russud Yd and Naval Yd, backed by John Brown Yd and Vickers Yd respectively. Initially cage masts were planned but pole ones were fitted instead.

The first pair was completed in 1915 (*Ekaterina II* was renamed on 27 June 1915) with their light guns outfit varying from the designed one in the light of war experience. *Imperatritsa Mariya* received only 4–75mm AA mounted one atop each turret while *Imperatritsa Ekaterina Velikaya* had one 75mm AA mounted atop the forward turret with 2 other pieces placed atop the after turret, one on each side of the roof. Commissioning of 2 dreadnoughts shifted the balance of power in the Black Sea to the Russian side and enabled the Black Sea Fleet to bombard the Turkish and Bulgarian shore installations. *Imperatritsa Mariya* capsized at Sevastopol as a result of internal explosion caused by unstable propellant. The wreck was raised in 1918 and broken up in 1922.

Despite being given top priority in July 1915 *Imperator Alexander III* entered service only after the February Revolution being renamed *Volya* on 29 April 1917 while *Imperatritsa Ekaterina Velikaya* became *Svobodnaya Rossiya* on the same day. *Volya* varied from the prototype in details, having an AA armament consisting of 4–75mm placed one by one atop the foremost turrets on the centreline, while the forward casemate hole on either side was plated out. This was introduced when it became evident that *Imperatritsa Mariya* had a tendency when in a seaway to ship a large amount of water through her forward casemates. The hull of *Svobodnaya Rossiya* being 7ft longer presented no such problems so the forward 130mm guns were retained. After the October Revolution *Svobodnaya Rossiya* went over to the Bolshevik side and she followed the order to leave Sevastopol for Novorossisk in April 1918 to escape the advancing Germans. When Novorossisk fell the destroyer *Kerch* sank her with torpedoes. *Volya* on the contrary flew the Independent Ukraine colours from 29 April 1918 but being forced by the Bolshevik ships to leave Sevastopol she returned there two weeks later being seized by the Germans who commissioned her on 15 October 1918 as *Volya* (not *Wolga* as was erroneously stated by most sources). She was able to perform only one trial cruise off the Bosphorus and in November 1918 she passed under British control. In April 1919 she was sent to Izmid in Turkey to prevent capture by the Reds. She was transferred to Wrangel's fleet on 17 October and commissioned as *General Alekseev* performing well until the capitulation of the Crimea. Broken up by 1936 by the French.

Imperatritsa Mariya as completed
Lemachko Collection

IMPERATOR NIKOLAI I battleship

Displacement: 27,300t normal
Dimensions: 616ft 9in oa, 597ft wl × 94ft 9in × 29ft 6in
188.0m, 182.0m × 28.9m × 8.0m
Machinery: 4-shaft Brown Curtiss turbines, 20 Yarrow boilers, 27,3000shp = 21kts. Oil fuel 720t, coal 2300t
Armour: Belt 10.5in–4in (267mm–102mm), turrets 12in (305mm), barbettes 8in (203mm), decks 4in (102mm), CT 16in (406mm)
Armament: 12–12in (305mm)/52 (4×3), 20–5.1in (130mm)/55, 8–75mm, 4–47mm, 4–18in (457mm) TT
Complement: 1252

Name	Builder	Laid down	Launched	Comp	Fate
IMPERATOR NIKOLAI I	Russud Yd, Nikolayev	28.1.15	18.10.16	–	BU incomplete 1923/4

Authorised in June 1914 to counter the additional Turkish battleship purchased from Brazil. She was practically a repeat of the *Imperatritsa Mariya* class with the protection increased by 50 per cent in weight proportions. The main belt was backed by a 3in longitudinal bulkhead that was extended down to form a torpedo bulkhead. The 1½in armoured deck was overhung by 2½in battery deck while the casemates had 3in protection only. At an early stage a changeover to 14in guns was considered but abandoned for the same reasons as with the previous class. Later during the war even 8–16in in four turrets was speculated about but it was not certain where such guns would be obtained. As a result of war experience the light guns outfit was changed to 4–4in AA. Being known under the false name *Ivan Grozni* to confuse the enemy she received secondary priority in July 1915 when the failure of Turkish plans to strengthen their battlefleet became evident. She was renamed *Demokratiya* on 29 April 1917 and her incomplete hull fell into German hands in February 1918 and was destroyed by the Allies in 1919 to prevent completion by the Reds.

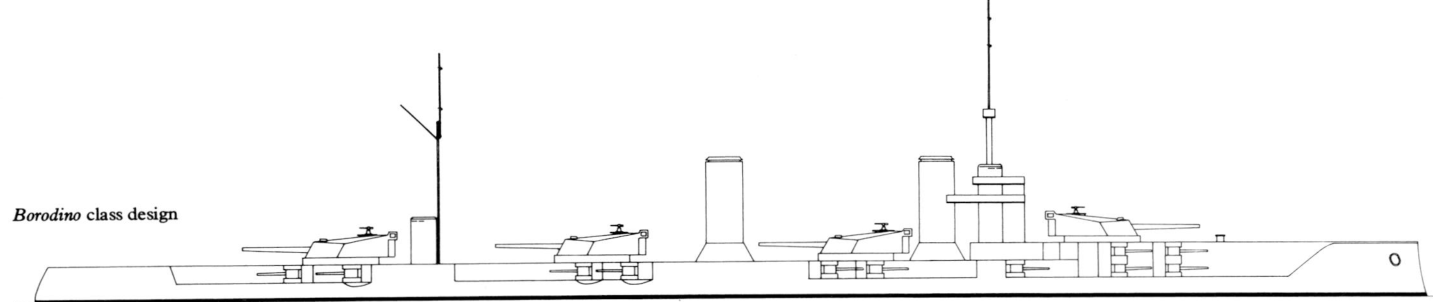

Borodino class design

BORODINO class *battlecruisers*

Displacement: 32,500t normal; 38,000t full load
Dimensions: 728ft pp, 750ft oa × 100ft × 33ft 6in
221.9m, 228.6m × 30.5m × 10.2m
Machinery: 4-shaft Parsons turbines, 25 Yarrow boilers, 68,000shp = 26.5kts. Oil fuel 1575t max, coal 1950t max.
Armour: Belt 9⅜in–4in (238mm–102mm), turrets 9⅜in–6in (238mm–152mm), decks 2½in (63mm)
Armament: 12–14in (356mm)/52 (4×3), 24–5.1in (130mm)/55, 8–75mm, 4–63mm AA, 4 MG, 6–21in (533mm) TT (sub)
Complement: *c*1250

Name	Builder	Laid down	Launched	Comp	Fate
BORODINO	Admiralty Yd, St Petersburg	19.12.13	1.7.15	–	BU incomplete 1923
IZMAIL	Baltic Yd, St Petersburg	19.12.13	27.6.15	–	BU incomplete 1931
KINBURN	Baltic Yd, St Petersburg	19.12.13	30.10.15	–	BU incomplete 1923
NAVARIN	Admiralty Yd, St Petersburg	19.12.13	9.11.16	–	BU incomplete 1923

Authorised under the 1912 Programme for deployment with the Baltic Fleet. The preliminary characteristics provided for 28kt battlecruisers armed with 9–14in guns in 3 triple turrets. The increased main armament calibre stemmed from rumours about the same move in the German Navy. In 1912 the fourth triple turret was added and speed reduced by 1.5kts to the same as the German battlecruisers. At that time emphasis was laid on standardisation of silhouette with the *Gangut* class dreadnoughts. The latter's flush deck hull had to be abandoned in favour of the raised forecastle for higher speed. Although designated battlecruisers the new ships were better armoured than the *Gangut* class, but were still inferior to the contemporary German battlecruisers. The designers did not avoid repeating the *Gangut* class error of placing 130mm casemates directly below the heavy turrets.

Unfortunately for themselves, the Russians tried to expedite construction of the *Borodino* class by ordering turbines abroad, those of *Navarin* from Vulkan, Germany and those of *Kinburn* (?) from Parsons, England. After August 1914 they had to be re-ordered from the Franco-Russian Works as had been done originally for the remaining pair. The shortage of materials and labour problems forced the Russians to concentrate on construction of *Izmail* only after June 1915, while the others were given lower priority. Development and introduction of 14in/52 Model 1912 guns in the Obukhov Works caused numerous problems despite Vickers' assistance. Later during the First World War proposals were made to replace them with the well-proven 12in/52 apparently because of delays in completing the 14in pieces.

At the beginning of 1917 construction of the less advanced trio was suspended while *Izmail* was scheduled for completion at the beginning of 1918. Because of the Bolshevik Revolution, work on *Izmail* practically stopped and she was laid up. Her three sisters were sold to Germany in 1922 while concrete plans about completion and modernisation of *Izmail* were considered (completion as an aircraft carrier was proposed also) in the late 1920s but were not carried out finally.

CHESMA *battleship*

The former Russian battleship *Poltava* salvaged by the Japanese after the fall of Port Arthur in 1905 was commissioned by them as *Tango*. Returned to Russia at Vladivostok on 5 April 1916 and renamed *Chesma*, designated for the Arctic station. She was transferred there via the Indian Ocean and Suez Canal and commissioned with the Arctic Ocean Flotilla on 3 February 1917. At that time she was armed with 4–12in, 8–6in, 2–75mm AA. Seized by the Allies in March 1918, disarmed, immobilised and hulked by them subsequently. Scrapped by the Soviets in 1923.

CRUISERS

MURAVEV AMURSKI class *cruisers*

Displacement: 4500t normal
Dimensions: 440ft 6in wl, 443ft 10in oa × 44ft 6in × 18ft 4in
134.3m, 135.3m × 13.6m × 5.6m
Machinery: 2-shaft Navy turbines, 10 Yarrow boilers, 30,000shp = 27.5kts. Oil fuel 580t, coal 620t
Armour: Deck 3in (76mm), CT 3in (76mm), gunshields 2in (51mm)
Armament: 8–5.1in (130mm)/55, 4–63mm AA, 5–18in (457mm) TT, 150 mines
Complement: 359

Name	Builder	Laid down	Launched	Comp	Fate
MURAVEV AMURSKI	Schichau, Danzig	9.13	11.4.14	14.12.14	Sunk 8.9.43
ADMIRAL NEVELSKOI	Schichau, Danzig	9.13	21.11.14	1.9.15	Sunk 1.6.16

Authorised under the 1912 Programme for the Far Eastern station, they reflected the Russian view on the light type of protected cruiser, in common use in these waters before the Russo-Japanese War. In all respects they were a reduced version of the *Svetlana* class being built in home yards at that time. Their silhouettes were standardised with those of the mentioned cruisers and 35kts destroyers. Both ships were requisitioned by the German Government on 5 August 1914 and completed for the Kaiserliche Marine as *Elbing* and *Pillau* respectively. See under Germany.

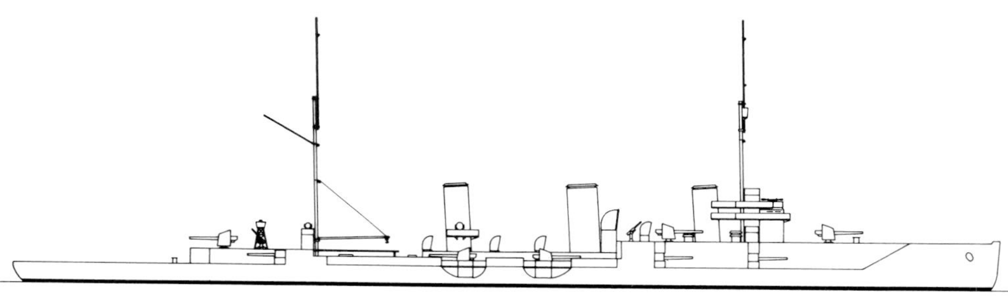

Svetlana class 1913 design

SVETLANA class *cruisers*

Displacement: 6750t normal
Dimensions: 507ft 10in wl, 519ft 8in oa × 50ft 2in × 18ft 3in
154.8m, 158.4m × 15.3m × 5.6m
Machinery: 4-shaft Brown-Curtiss (*Adm Butakov, Adm Spiridov* Parsons) turbines, 13 Yarrow boilers, 50,000shp = 29.5kts. Fuel 1167t
Armour: Belt 3in (76mm), deck 1½in (38mm), CT 3in (76mm), gunshields 1in (25mm)
Armament: 15–5.1in (130mm)/55, 4–63mm AA, 4 MG, 2–18in (457mm) TT (sub), 100 mines
Complement: *c*630

Name	Builder	Laid down	Launched	Comp	Fate
SVETLANA	Russo-Baltic Yd, Reval	7.12.13	27.11.15	1.7.28	BU 1960
ADMIRAL BUTAKOV	Putilov Yd, St Petersburg	29.11.13	5.8.16	–	BU incomplete 1956/7
ADMIRAL SPIRIDOV	Putilov Yd, St Petersburg	29.11.13	9.9.16	24.12.26	Hulked 1947
ADMIRAL GREIG	Russo-Baltic Yd, Reval	7.12.13	9.12.16	24.12.26	Stranded 23.12.38

Authorised under the 1912 Programme for deployment with the Baltic Fleet. The preliminary studies initiated in 1907 resulted in the characteristics of a 4500t, 28kt cruiser armed with 1–8in, 6–120mm (3×2) in turrets. There were several designs and requirements evaluated in June 1911 extending to 30kt ships armed with 12–6in/50 in 4 triple turrets. Their silhouettes were similar to those of *Gangut* class dreadnoughts. In February 1912 when it was learned that those demands could be fulfilled within a 10,000t hull, the Naval Staff issued in May 1912 tenders for 6500t, 30kt ships armed with 12–130mm/55 in single shield mountings and armoured with a 3in belt. Because of the abandonment of turrets it was decided to standardise silhouettes with those of the 35kt destroyers being designed at the same time. To save money for the enlarged battlecruiser programme the Naval Ministry decided in February 1913 to reduce speed by half a knot and on 14 February 1913 orders were placed for 4 ships. The side protection of the hull comprised 1in armour between the main and lower deck and 3in belt on the whole length from the lower deck down to 3ft below the waterline. The main and lower decks had 20mm (¾in) of armour each and funnel uptakes had 1in.

In 1913 one seaplane was introduced and at the end of 1917 it was decided to increase their number to 2, together with the crane added to handle them. *Svetlana* had her 63mm AA replaced by 75mm ones, the others were to get 4in AA guns.

The contracted completion dates of June–October 1915 were rescheduled because of shortage of material and manpower and difficulties with replacing of orders for equipment placed in Germany.

RUSSIA

Completion of the most advanced *Svetlana* was planned for the beginning of 1918. She was evacuated with the other incomplete ships from Reval to Petrograd in December 1917 but the Reds were not able to complete her for service with the Active Squadron in 1919. Renamed *Profintern* on 7 December 1922. *Admiral Greig* and *Admiral Spiridov* were completed as mercantile motor tankers *Azneft* and *Grozneft* by the Baltic Yd and Northern Yd respectively and transferred to the Black Sea. The former was stranded in a gale off Tuapse. The hull of *Admiral Butakov* had been laid up after the Bolshevik Revolution and was renamed *Voroshilov* in 1928.

Profintern (ex-*Svetlana*) in the early 1930s
Author's Collection

Chervona Ukraina (ex-*Admiral Nakhimov*) in the late 1920s
Lemachko Collection

ADMIRAL NAKHIMOV class *cruisers*

Displacement: 7600t normal
Dimensions: 535ft 6in wl × 51ft 6in × 18ft 3in
163.2m × 15.7m × 5.6m
Machinery: 4-shaft Brown-Curtiss turbines, 14 Yarrow boilers, 55,000shp = 29.5kts. Fuel 1230t
Armour: Belt 3in (76mm), deck 1.5in (38mm), gunshields 1in (25mm), CT 3in (76mm)
Armament: 15–5.1in (130mm)/55, 4–63mm AA, 4 MG, 2–18in (457mm) TT (sub), 100 mines, 1 seaplane
Complement: 630

Name	Builder	Laid down	Launched	Comp	Fate
ADMIRAL NAKHIMOV	Russud Yd, Nikolayev	31.10.13	6.11.15	27.2.27	Foundered 13.11.41
ADMIRAL LAZAREV	Naval Yd, Nikolayev	31.10.13	21.6.16	25.1.32	Sunk 1950s
ADMIRAL KORNILOV	Russud Yd, Nikolayev	7.14	1922	–	BU incomplete 1922
ADMIRAL ISTOMIN	Naval Yd, Nikolayev	7.14	–	–	BU incomplete 1938

Authorised under the 1912 (first pair) and 1914 Programmes for deployment with the Black Sea Fleet. The Naval Staff decided to build these cruisers as the repeated *Svetlana* class and appropriate drawings were presented to the Russud and Naval Yards. The design was critically reviewed and John Brown Yd consulted to help the Russians to rework these with the general layout retained but displacement enlarged by 1000t and speed increased. The Naval Staff approved the modified design and the first pair of ships was ordered in March 1914, followed by the second one in October 1914. The yards made an agreement giving hull construction to Russud while the Naval Yd was to fit them out. In 1917 the Naval Staff decided to add the second seaplane and a crane to handle it. At that time it was decided to equip *Admiral Nakhimov* with 75mm AA instead of 63mm while the other ships were to be fitted with 4in AA. The completion of this cruiser was delayed from autumn 1916 to December 1917 because of wartime difficulties and her sister ships were far less advanced at that time. The Bolshevik Revolution prevented completion of *Admiral Nakhimov* which together with incomplete hull of *Admiral Lazarev* was seized by the Germans in 1918. Both of them were handed over to the Allies in November 1918 and transferred to Wrangel's fleet in 1919. Still incomplete in 1920 *Admiral Nakhimov* was scheduled for evacuation but the Whites were forced to abandon her in Odessa. She was seized there by the Reds and renamed *Chervona Ukraina* in December 1926. *Admiral Lazarev* was completed to the modified design in 1932 and entered service under the name *Krasni Kavkaz*. *Admiral Kornilov* was launched to clear the slipway in 1922 and BU while *Admiral Istomin* was dismantled *in situ*.

Ex-Turkish MEDJIDIEH *protected cruiser*

The Turkish protected cruiser *Medjidieh* (*Mecidiye*) was mined 15 miles off Odessa on 3 April 1915 and sunk on an even keel. She was raised by the Russians and docked in the Ropit Yd, Odessa on 31 May 1915. Under the name *Prut* she was placed on the List 26 June and re-armament as well as reconstruction begun. She was to be armed with 6–130mm, 4–75mm AA, 2 MG but this was supplemented by additional 4–130mm in midship sponsons. The works were completed in January 1917 and she reached 17.9kts during sea trials. Seized by the Germans in Sevastopol and returned to Turkey on 12 May 1918.

PERESVIET *cruiser*

The Russian battleship sunk at Port Arthur during the Russo-Japanese War and salvaged by the Japanese after fall of the fortress. Reconstructed during 1908–9 and commissioned as the coast defence battleship *Sagami*. Returned to Russia at Vladivostok on 5 April 1916, returned to her old name and rerated as cruiser. Designated for the Arctic Ocean Flotilla, she was armed with 4–10in, 10–6in, 2–75mm AA. Stranded off Vladivostok on 23 May 1916 she was not refloated before July. During the transfer to the Arctic she was sunk on 4 January 1917 on 2 mines laid by *U 73* off Port Said.

VARIAG *protected cruiser*

The Russian cruiser scuttled after action against Japanese cruisers off Chemulpo on 9 February 1904. Raised by the Japanese and commissioned by them as the training ship *Soya*. Returned to the Russians at Vladivostok on 5 April 1916 she reverted to her old name while the armament was augmented by mounting forecastle and quarterdeck 6in guns on the CL thus enlarging the broadside to 8 pieces. In June 1916 she sailed for the Arctic being armed at that time with 12–6in, 4–75mm, 2 MG, 3 TT. Arrived Liverpool in February 1917 for repairs and rearmament with 10–130mm but these were never carried out. Seized by the British on 8 December 1917 and beached off the Irish coast while under tow but raised later and hulked. Sold for scrap 1920 but stranded again off Scotland and scrapped there during 1923–25.

4000t *cruiser-minelayer design*

Displacement: 4000t–5000t
Armament: 6 or 8–130mm/55, 350–450 mines

Four such cruisers were authorised under the 1915 Emergency Programme for deployment with the Baltic Fleet. Their characteristics were worked out by the Naval Staff under the influence of successful minelaying offensive operations by the Russian light forces. Not one of these cruisers was even ordered.

Prut (ex-*Medjidieh*) 1917
Lemachko Collection

AIRCRAFT CARRIERS

ORLITSA *seaplane carrier*

Displacement: 3800t
Dimensions: 300ft × 40ft × 17ft
91.5m × 12.2m × 5.2m
Machinery: 1-shaft VTE, 2200ihp = 12kts
Armament: 8–75mm, 2 MG, 5 seaplanes

Name	Builder	Launched	Comp	Fate
ORLITSA	Caledon, Dundee	1903	20.2.15	Mercantile 1923

*All completion dates in this section are actually commissioning dates.

Converted during 1913–15 from a freighter (ex-*Imperatritsa Alexandra*, ex-*Vologda*). Fitted with 2 hangars that housed 4 seaplanes and the fifth one was carried in the hold. She was commissioned on 20 February 1915. At first FBA flying boats were carried being substituted by the Russian M 9 type ones in 1916. *Orlitsa* participated in action against the German-held shore in Courland and Gulf of Finland during the First World War. Returned to mercantile service in 1923 and renamed *Sovet*.

Orlitsa during the war
Lemachko Collection

IMPERATOR ALEXANDER I class *aviation cruisers*

Liners purchased in Britain in 1913, converted during 1914–16 for seaplane carriers and both commissioned on 29 November with the Black Sea Fleet. Fitted with a large hangar and a flight deck aft. In 1916 their seaplanes sank the German coaster *Irmingard*. *Alexander I* renamed *Respublikanets* on 11 May 1917 and the other became *Aviator* a week later. Seized by the Germans in Sevastopol in April 1918 and surrendered to the British in November 1918.

Displacement: 9240t
Dimensions: 384ft × 50ft × 20ft 6in
117.0m × 15.4m × 6.2m
Machinery: 1-shaft VTE, 5100ihp = 15kts
Armament: 6–120mm (4.7in), 6–75mm (*Nikolai I* 2.25in) AA, 7–9 seaplanes

Name	Launched	Comp	Fate
IMPERATOR ALEXANDER I (ex-*Imperator Alexander III*)	1913	29.11.16	Scuttled 1919
IMPERATOR NIKOLAI I	1913	29.11.16	Scuttled 1919

Imperator Alexander I during the war
Lemachko Collection

REGELE CAROL I *aviation cruiser*

Loaned in 1916 by Rumania and converted into a seaplane carrier. Commissioned with the Black Sea Fleet.

Displacement: 2368t
Dimensions: 350ft × 42ft × 18ft 6in
106.7m × 12.8m × 5.6m
Machinery: 2-shaft VTE, 6500ihp = 18kts
Armament: 4–6in (152mm), 4–75mm AA, 4 seaplanes

Name	Builder	Launched	Comp	Fate
REGELE CAROL I	Fairfield, Glasgow	1898	1916	Returned 1918

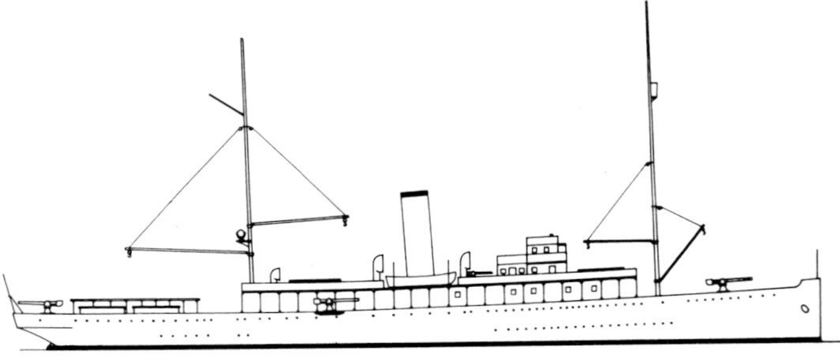

Rumynia 1917

RUMANIA class *aviation cruisers*

Loaned in 1916 from the Rumanian Government and converted to seaplane carriers for the Black Sea Fleet. Fitted with a flight deck aft. Captured by the Germans in Sevastopol and Novorossik in April 1918. Surrendered to the Allies in November 1918 and returned to the owners.

Displacement: 4500t full load
Dimensions: 356ft 10in × 41ft 10in × 27ft 6in
109.0m × 12.8m × 8.4m
Machinery: 2-shaft VTE, 6500ihp = 18kts
Armament: 4–6in (152mm), 1 to 4–75mm AA, 4–7 seaplanes

Name	Builder	Launched	Comp	Fate
DAKIA (ex-*Dacia*)	Ch de la Loire, St Nazaire	1907	1916	Returned 1918
IMPERATOR TRAJAN (ex-*Imparator Traian*)	Ch de la Loire, St Nazaire	1907	1916	Returned 1918
RUMYNIYA (ex-*Rumania*)	Ch de la Loire, St Nazaire	1904	1916	Returned 1918

DESTROYERS AND TORPEDO-BOATS

NOVIK *destroyer*

Displacement: 1280t normal
Dimensions: 336ft 3in × 31ft 3in × 9ft 10in
102.5m × 9.5m × 3.0m
Machinery: 3-shaft AEG turbines, 6 Vulkan boilers, 40,000shp = 36kts. Oil fuel 450t
Armament: 4–4in (102mm)/60, 2MG, 8–18in TT (4×2), 60 mines
Complement: 130

Name	Builder	Launched	Fate
NOVIK	Putilov Yd, St Petersburg	4.7.11	Mined 28.8.41

Ordered on 11 August 1909 for 2 million roubles which remained the budget after 18 destroyers and 4 submarines had been ordered thanks to the funds earned by public subscription. The principal dimensions were decided at the end of 1905 and aimed at a 36kt, turbine-driven, oil-fired 1400t destroyer. Design tenders were invited from Russian yards in 1908 and the contract was awarded to the Putilov Yd which supplied a design prepared with the help of the German Vulkan Yd, Stettin; the latter was also subcontractor for the machinery plant and much of the fittings. The original design called for 2–4in guns but this was augmented in 1912 as was done on the other 35kt designs. This and other additions as well as weight miscalculations caused a displacement increase of 140t and increased the draught by 1ft which was concealed by the yard simply by putting the draught marks up. The speed trials of 30 May 1912 achieved 35.8kts and were repeated twice after a changeover of propellers and *Novik* was able to attain 35.97kts at best. The Vulkan Yd unaware of the draught excess, committed itself to improve the boiler output by lengthening the water tubes which was done by August 1913. *Novik* reached 37.2kts max and 36.86kts in a 3hr run which earned her the status of then being the fastest ship in the world. Commissioned with the Cruiser Brigade on 4 September 1913 she became a flagship of the Destroyer Division in 1915. Laid up in 1918 she was converted to the 1717t (normal) flotilla leader during 1916–31 and recommissioned as *Yakov Sverdlov*. This conversion was reversed in December 1940 when she returned to the fleet destroyer role.

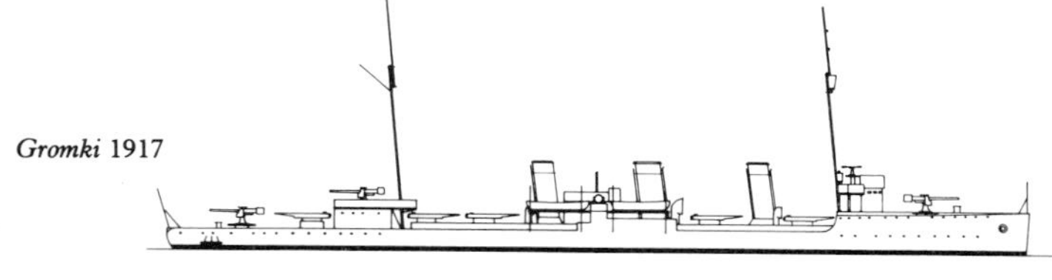
Gromki 1917

BESPOKOINY class *destroyers*

Displacement: 1100t (1088t Nevski Yd boats) normal; 1320t (1460t) full load
Dimensions: 321ft 6in × 30ft 6in × 10ft 6in
98.0m × 9.3m × 3.2m
Machinery: 2-shaft Brown-Boveri turbines (AEG in Nevski Yd and Putiliv Yd boats), 5 Thornycroft (Vulkan) boilers, 25,500shp = 34kts. Oil fuel 350t
Armament: 3–4in (102mm)/60, 2–47mm AA, 4 MG, 10–18in (457mm) TT (5×2), 80 mines
Complement: 125

Name	Builder	Launched	Fate
BESPOKOINY	Naval Yd Nikolayev	31.10.13	Sold 1924
DERZKI	Naval Yd, Nikolayev	15.3.14	Sold 1924
GNEVNY	Naval Yd, Nikolayev	31.10.13	Sold 1924
PRONZITELNY	Naval Yd, Nikolayev	15.3.14	Scuttled 18.6.18
BYSTRY	Metal Wks, St Petersburg	7.6.14	Lost 21.9.41
GROMKI	Nevski Yd, St Petersburg	18.12.13	Scuttled 18.6.18
POSPESHNY	Nevski Yd, St Petersburg	4.4.14	Sold 1924
PYLKI	Metal Wks, St Petersburg	28.7.14	Sold 1924
SCHASTLIVY	Putilov Yd, St Petersburg	29.3.14	Stranded 24.10.19

Novik on trials — *Lemachko Collection*

Part of the 1911 Programme, intended for the Black Sea Fleet. Design studies for a 35kt destroyer had begun however just after the issue of the 1907 Naval Shipbuilding Estimate. The preliminary characteristics of this class were influenced by those decided for *Novik*. Tenders for the design having been invited, the one prepared by the Metal Wks was regarded as the best (1025t, 35kts, 2–4in/60, 4–18in TT). The contract was not signed however as the existing 1908 Programme did not provide new destroyers, so the Naval General Staff changed the requirements by adding 1–4in, 6–18in TT and pressed for use of AEG or Parsons turbines, instead of Rateau ones fitted in the awarded design.

Tenders for the design were invited once again and a displacement increase of 50t was accepted to house the additional armament, which would cost a knot of speed. It was stipulated that these ships had to be built on the Black Sea coast. This time the Putilov Yd, backed by the Vulkan Yd, and the Naval Yd, backed by Vickers, were awarded design contracts, the former one became obligatory for the other Baltic coast yards which were to deal with the order. Externally both design variations could be recognised by shape of the funnels – round section in the Putilov Yd design and the oval one of the Naval Yd design. A small assembly yard was erected at Vadona off Kherson to lay down the hulls of *Bystry*, *Pyliki* and *Schastlivy* (sections for the former pair were subcontracted to the Putilov Yd). The hulls of *Gromki* and *Pospeshny* were laid down in the Admiralty Yd, Nikolayev. Except for the Nevski Yd, the other Baltic coast yards subcontracted the turbines to the German Vulkan Yd. Because of labour and transportation problems the Nevski and Putilov orders were taken over by the Naval Yd.

The first 4 were commissioned on 29 October 1914 while the Baltic boats entered service in summer 1915 – over a year behind schedule. Not one of this class attained the contracted speed during trials, the best one, *Bespokoiny,* was able to develop 32.7kts while the slowest of them *Pylki* attained 28.9kts only.

Derzki was damaged slightly during the gun duel with the Turkish cruiser *Hamidiye* in January 1915 while *Pospeshnyi* sustained damage from German aircraft on 25 August 1916 during action against the U-boat base at Varna. Except for *Bystry* and *Schastlivy* which raised the Ukrainian colours, the others left Sevastopol for Novorossisk on 30 April 1918 (*Gnevny* damaged by a German shore battery was beached en route) but returned except for *Pronzitelny* and *Gromki* which were scuttled there (the wrecks were located in 1947).

All seized by the Germans who commissioned *Schastlivy* in October 1918 as *R 01* while *Bystry* and *Gnevny* were designated *R 02* and *R 03*, but did not enter service. Handed over to the Allies in November 1918 and with the exception of *Bystry* (scuttled by the British on 6 April 1919 to avoid capture by the Reds, refloated later on and commissioned by the Soviets as *Frunze* on 2 December 1927) and *Schastlivy* (stranded in a gale while under British tow to Malta) transferred to Wrangel's fleet in September 1919. *Bespokoiny* was damaged by a mine on 15 September 1920 off Kerch when proceeding to the Sea of Azov.

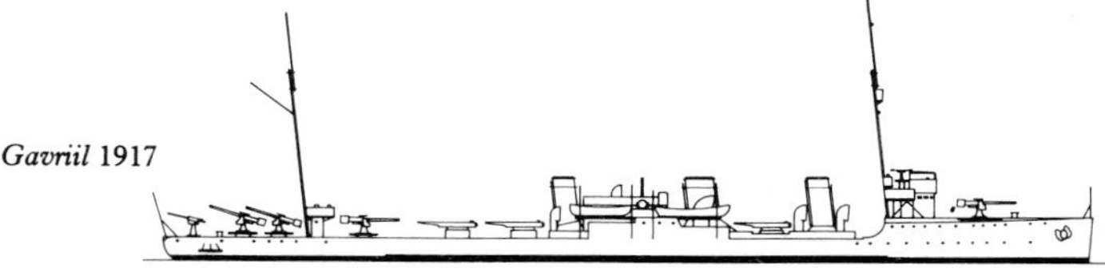
Gavriil 1917

LEITENANT ILIN/ORFEJ/GAVRIL classes *destroyers*

Displacement: 1260t normal
Dimensions: 321ft 6in × 30ft 6in × 9ft 10in
98.0m × 9.3m × 3.0m
Machinery: 2-shaft AEG turbine, 4 Vulkan boilers, 30,000shp (*Leitenant Ilin* class 31,500shp) = 32kts. Oil fuel 400t
Armament: 4–4in (102mm)/ 60, 1–40mm AA, 2 MG, 9–18 (457mm) TT (3×3), 50 mines
Complement: 150

Grom as completed
Lemachko Collection

Class (launched, fate):
Putilov Yd, Petrograd – *Kapital Belli* (29.10.15, BU 1950s), *Kapitan Izylmetev* (4.11.14, scuttled 24.6.41), *Kapitan Kern* (27.8.15, BU 1950s), *Kapitan Konon-Zotov* (23.10.15, BU incomplete 1923), *Kapitan Kroun* (5.8.16, BU incomplete 1923), *Kapitan I Ranga Miklucha-Maklai*, ex-*Kapitan Kingsbergen* 27.6.15 (27.8.15, BU *c* 1954), *Leitenant Dubasov* (9.9.16, BU incomplete 1923), *Leitenant Ilin* (28.11.14, BU 1950s)
Metal Wks, Petrograd – *Orfei* (5.6.15, BU 1929), *Azard* (5.6.16, lost 28.8.41), *Desna* (4.11.15, lost 24.8.41), *Grom* (5.6.15, lost 14.10.17), *Letun* (4.11.15, BU 1925), *Pobeditel* (5.11.14, lost 28.8.41), *Samson* (5.6.15, BU *c* 1953), *Zabijaka* (5.11.14, BU *c* 1953)
Russo-Baltic Yd, Reval – *Gavriil* (5.1.15, lost 21.10.19), *Konstantin* 12.6.15, lost 21.10.19), *Mikhail* (1916, BU incomplete 1923), *Mechislav* (ex-*Leitenant Lombard* 27.6.15, 1917, BU incomplete 1923), *Sokol* (1917, BU incomplete 1923), *Vladimir* (18.8.15, lost 21.10.19)

Part of the 1912 Programme, designated for the Baltic Fleet. The preliminary characteristics aimed at a modified *Bespokoiny* class with an armament of 2–4in/60, 12–18in TT (6×2). The existing Putilov Yd design for the Black Sea destroyer was duly changed and offered as the common enterprise by the Putilov Yd, Metal Wks and Russo-Baltic Yd. This was accepted by the Naval Staff after double TT sets were replaced by 4 triple ones to avoid a blast effect from the after 4in gun on the aftermost TT. The orders were placed in December 1912 for 22 boats that were to be identical in appearance as the three yards decided to go on with the common working design. In August 1915 when some of the boats were fairly advanced the gun armament was enlarged by the Naval Staff simply by replacing one TT mounting with one (later 2) 4in/60 as a temporary measure to increase the firepower of the light forces until the *Svetlana* class cruisers were completed.

A total of 14 destroyers in these 3 classes were completed during 1915–17 and they formed the 1st, 2nd and 3rd Destroyer Flotillas (renumbered 11th, 12th and 13th later on) during most of the war. *Kapitan Izylmetev* served with the Active Squadron in 1919, and was renamed *Lenin* on 31 December 1922. *Kapitan I Ranga Miklucha-Maklai* (renamed *Spartak* 18 December 1918) served with the Active Squadron and was captured off Reval by 2 British destroyers and 2 cruisers after running aground during an escape attempt on 26 December 1918, presented to Estonia in February 1919 and commissioned as *Wambola* (see under Estonia). *Leitenant Ilin* served with the Active Squadron in 1919, being renamed *Garibaldi* on 3 July 1919, then *Trotski* 31 December 1922 and finally *Voikov* on 14 February 1928. The boats ordered in the Metal Works were launched in the Izhora Yd, a branch of this enterprise established in 1912. The hulls of *Pobeditel* and *Zabijaka* had to be towed to Petrograd for completion while the others were fitted locally.

Azard distinguished herself during sorties with the Active Squadron in 1919 encountering the British destroyer *Walker* (31 May) and helping sink the British submarine *L 55*. In October 1919 she steered clear of a minefield where 3 of her sisters were lost. Renamed *Zinoviev* on 31 December 1922 and again *Artem* in 1934. *Samson* participated in the Bolshevik Revolution and together with *Desna* and *Pobeditel* was laid up in 1919. The three were renamed *Stalin*, *Engels* and *Volodarski* on 31 December 1922 and were reactivated by 1925. *Letun* and *Orfei* were damaged on mines (7 November 1916) and autumn 1917 respectively) and laid up subsequently. *Zabijaka* was damaged on a mine on 24 December 1915 off Dagerort during a Baltic minelaying operation but was soon repaired and took part in the Bolshevik Revolution. Laid up in 1919 and renamed *Uritski* on 31 December 1922 she was reactivated in 1925. *Gavriil*, *Konstantin* and *Vladimir* (renamed *Svoboda* on 12 September 1917) served with the Active Squadron in 1919. The first one successfully escaped the British cruiser *Cleopatra* when screening 4 escaped minesweepers on 17 May 1919 out from Kronstadt. On 2 June her gunners hit the pressure hull of the British submarine *L 55* and she sank with all hands in Petrograd Bay after her torpedoes had missed the destroyer. Once again she had luck being missed by a torpedo from *CMB 24* and *CMB 62* off Kronstadt, sinking her assailants a few minutes later. *Svoboda* was damaged by the British aircraft in Kronstadt later on. These three ships met a cruel end, being lost on a British minefield off Kronstadt with a total of only 25 survivors. *Kapitan Belli* and *Kapitan Kern* were completed by the Soviets in October 1927 and commissioned as *Karl Libknecht* and *Rykov* respectively, the latter became *Valeryan Kuibyshev c* 1937. The 90 per cent complete *Mechislav*, *Mikhail* and *Sokol* were towed to Petrograd in October 1917 to avoid capture by the advancing Germans. Completion of the last pair was contracted to the Baltic Wks but did not happen.

Avtroil as completed *Lemachko Collection*

IZYASLAV class *destroyers*

Displacement:	1350t normal
Dimensions:	351ft 6in × 31ft 3in × 9ft 10in *107.1m × 9.5m × 3.0m*
Machinery:	2-shaft Brown-Boveri turbines, 5 Normand boilers, 32,700shp = 33kts
Armament:	5–4in (102mm)/60, 1–40mm AA, 2 MG, 9–18in (457mm) TT (3×3), 80 mines
Complement:	150

Class (launched, fate):
Avtroil (13.1.15, BU *c* 1947), *Bryachislav* (1.10.15, BU incomplete 1923), *Fedor Stratilat* (1915 ?, BU incomplete 1923), *Izyaslav* (ex-*Gromonosets* 27.6.15, 22.11.14, lost 8.8.41), *Pryamyslav* (9.8.15, lost 28.8.41)

In the 1912 Programme for the Baltic Fleet. The design was prepared with the French Normand Yd helping and much of the fittings were ordered there. The composition and distribution of armament underwent frequent changes, ranging from 2–4in/60, 12–18in TT as contracted in 1913 with one triple TT mount added in 1914, 2 triple TT mounts surrendered to 2 additional 4in/60 in 1915 and the fifth 4in gun added abaft the bridge finally. The embargo set up by the Swiss Government after August 1914 meant that only *Avtroil* and *Izyaslav* received their designed turbines. The new orders for *Pryamyslav* had to be placed in Britain while the remaining ones were made in the USA. Thus only the above mentioned pair was completed by Böcker and Lange of Reval (the class builders) before the Bolshevik Revolution and they served with the 3rd (later 13th) Destroyer Flotilla. *Izyaslav* was laid up during 1918–22 and renamed *Karl Marx* (31 December 1922). *Avtroil* was captured by 3 British destroyers and 2 cruisers off Reval on 27 December 1919 and handed over to Estonia she became *Lennuk* (see under Estonia). The remaining ships were towed to Petrograd to avoid capture by the Germans in September 1917 and work proceeded on *Pryamyslav* for some time (she was completed finally in 1927 as *Kalinin*).

GOGLAND class *destroyers*

Displacement:	1350t normal
Dimensions:	325ft × 30ft 10in × 8ft 10in *99.1m × 9.4m × 3.0m*
Machinery:	2-shaft Schichau turbines, 5 Schichau boilers, 32,000shp = 33kts. Oil fuel 400t
Armament:	4–4in (102mm)/60, 2 MG, 9–18in (457mm) TT (3×3), 80 mines
Complement:	150

Class (fate):
Gogland, *Grengamn*, *Khios*, *Kulm*, *Patras*, *Rymnik*, *Smolensk*, *Strisuden*, *Tenedos* (all cancelled 14.10.17)

Ordered under the 1912 Programme for the Baltic Fleet in the German Schichau Yd in spite of growing tensions between these Powers, simply because that yard was able to offer a price 25 per cent lower than the Russian ones. The condition was raised however that these ships had to be assembled in Russia, so a Schichau subsidiary yard was founded in 1913 at Reval. The contract design provided 2–4in/60, 12–18in TT and this was changed in 1915 to 4–4in, 6–18in TT but finally one triple TT set was added. The hulls of *Gogland, Grengamn, Patras* and *Strisuden* were laid down in December 1913 but work on them practically stopped after August 1914. In June 1915 the yard was taken over by the Russian Government and Metal Wks were ordered to complete the 4 ships mentioned above in 1918 as Fleet Minesweepers armed with 5–4in/60, 1–40mm AA, 6–18in TT. The others were re-ordered to be built according to the *Orfei* class design. The Fleet Minesweepers, being 18 per cent ready in February 1917, were subsequently cancelled with the others which had not been laid down by that date.

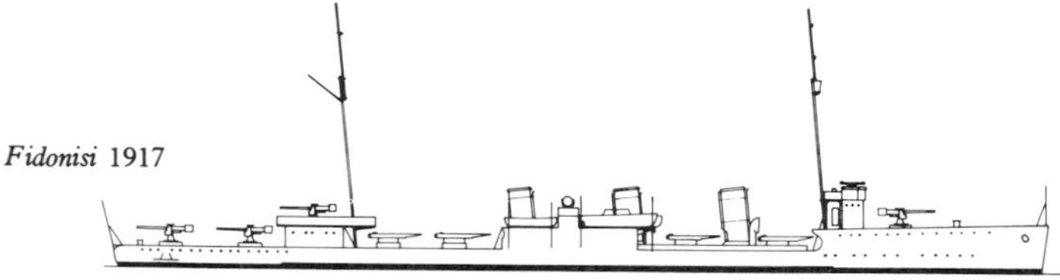

Fidonisi 1917

KERCH class *destroyers*

Displacement: 1326t normal
Dimensions: 334ft 6in × 31ft 4in × 10ft 6in
102.0m × 9.5m × 3.2m
Machinery: 2-shaft Parsons turbines, 5 Thornycroft boilers, 29,000shp = 33kts. Oil fuel 390t
Armament: 4–4in (102mm)/60, 1–40mm AA, 12–18in (457mm) TT (4×3), 80 mines

Class (launched, fate):
Fidonisi (31.5.16, sunk 18.6.18), *Gadzhibei* (27.8.16, scuttled 18.6.18), *Kaliakriya* (27.8.16, lost 13.5.42), *Kerch* (31.5.16, scuttled 19.6.18), *Korfu* (1924, BU 1956), *Levkas* (1924?, BU 1950s), *Tserigo* (1917, sold 1924), *Zante* (1917, lost 10.4.42)

In the 1914 Programme for deployment with the Black Sea Fleet. This class was previously planned as an enlargement of the standard 35-knotter design with 1570t displacement, armed with 4–3in/60, 1–47mm, 2–40mm AA, 2 MG, 12–18in TT (4×3). To keep costs as low as possible an improved *Bespokoiny* class was finally decided on with one 4in added. Only 4 of them, namely *Fidonisi, Gadzhibei, Kaliakriya* and *Kerch* were completed by 1917 and formed the 3rd Destroyer Flotilla but only the first of them saw any action. Influenced by the Bolsheviks they left Sevastopol on 30 April 1918 and arrived at Novorossisk where *Gadzhibei* was scuttled and *Fidonisi* sunk by a torpedo from *Kerch*. The latter after sinking the battleship *Svobodnaya Rossiya* was scuttled off Tuapse. *Tserigo* was completed by the Whites in 1919 and commissioned with Wrangel's fleet. The remaining incomplete ships were seized by the Germans then transferred to the Allies in November 1918 and handed by them to Wrangel's fleet in February 1919. They were not able to launch or complete these destroyers and *Zante* was stranded off Odessa during attempts to evacuate her to prevent seizure by the Reds in April 1919. Refloated by the Soviets and commissioned on 7 November 1923 as *Nezamozhnyi* (renamed *Nezamozhnik* on 29 April 1926). *Korfu* and *Levkas* were launched by the Soviets and commissioned on 10 May 1925 as *Petrovski* (renamed *Zheleznyakov* on 23 June 1939, served with the Bulgarian Navy during 1949–56) and 12 December 1926 as *Shaumyan* respectively. *Kaliakriya* was raised in 1925 and commissioned on 24 August 1929 as *Dzerzhinski*. *Gadzibei* was raised in 1926 and scrapped but her turbines were fitted on *Petrovski* during 1930s. The wreck of *Kerch* was raised in November 1926 but sunk again and excavated in parts by December 1932.

Repeat KERCH class *destroyer*

Ordered in November 1916 from the Naval-Russud Yd, Nikolayev instead of a dozen 500t torpedo-boats which had been authorised under the 1915 Emergency Programme for the Black Sea Fleet. Their armament was changed to 4–4in/60, 1–75mm AA, 12–18in TT (4×3), as compared with the original *Kerch* class. Four cancelled on 14 October 1917 while some of the remaining 8 were laid down that month but their construction was abandoned after the Bolshevik Revolution.

2500t *destroyers*

Five of these super-destroyers, presumably inspired by the German *S 113* class, were ordered in 1916 from the Russo-Baltic Yd, Reval instead of 24 500t torpedo-boats which had been authorised under the 1915 Emergency Programme for the Baltic Fleet. The order was confirmed in October 1917 but work probably did not go beyond the design stage.

500t *torpedo-boats*

Displacement: 500t normal
Speed: 30kts
Armament: 3–4in (102mm)/60, 4–18in (457mm) TT (2×2)

Authorised under the 1915 Emergency Programme for deployment with the Black Sea Fleet (12) and the Baltic Fleet (24). These plans were soon abandoned in favour of 12 *Kerch* class destroyers and five 2500t ones respectively for the two fleets.

SUBMARINES

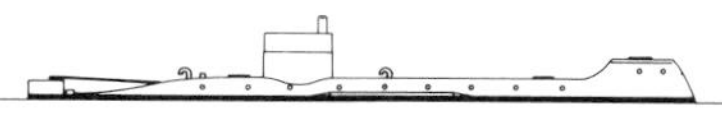

Alexsandrovski's submarine as completed
NB 1/750 scale

ALEKSANDROVSKI type *submarine*

Displacement: 355t
Dimensions: 110ft × 13ft × 12ft (depth)
33.5m × 4.0m × 3.6m
Machinery: 2-shaft compressed air engines = 1.5kts
Armament: 2 mines
Complement: 22

Name	Builder	Launched	Fate
–	Baltic Yd, St Petersburg	1865	BU 1873

Ordered on 30 June 1863 and completed May 1866. She had an iron hull of oval triangle section and a forecastle fitted with a chamber to embark divers when submerged. The supply of 220 cu ft of air at 850psi–1500psi was enough for 2.5 mile radius. Her diving limit was 30ft, maximum depth attained 60ft. The hull was crushed during 100ft trials in 1871. The wreck was raised in 1873 and scrapped.

Drzewiecki Type I submarine
NB 1/200 scale

Drzewiecki Type III submarine
NB 1/200 scale

DRZEWIECKI *midget submarines*

Type I (built 1877, Odessa)
Dimensions: 15ft × 5ft × 5ft
4.5m × 1.5m × 1.5m
Machinery: 1-shaft treadle driven = *c*1.5kts
Armament: 2 mines
Complement: 1

Type II (built 1879, Nevski Yd, St Petersburg)
Displacement: *c*2.5t
Dimensions: *c*20ft × 5ft × 3ft 6in
c6.0m × 1.5m × 1.0m
Machinery: 2 shaft, 1 bow, 1 stern treadle driven = *c*2kts
Armament: 2 mines

Type III (built 1878–1881, Nevski Yd, St Petersburg)
Displacement: *c*2.5t
Dimensions: 20ft × 5ft × 3ft 6in
6.0m × 1.5m × 1.0m
Machinery: 1-shaft treadle driven = 2kts–3kts
Armament: 2 mines
Complement: 4

This midget submarine series of 52 boats were built to 3 designs by the Polish engineer Stefan Drzewiecki. The prototype boat was of twin hull construction (upper part housed the operator, the lower one – ballast tank) and built as one of the Russian measures to counter the Turkish Fleet during the 1877–78

Russo-Turkish War. The armament of 2 dynamite mines was to be fixed to the bottom of a target ship with a rubber suction cup in the operator's hands which were covered with watertight rubber sleeves. After successful trials in which a lighter was destroyed, the Naval Authority refused to fund further experiments after the conclusion of hostilities with Turkey. The idea was however approved by the Army Authority which ordered the Type II boat. After a series of successful trials and presentation to the Czar an order was placed for 50 boats (Type III) with some changes incorporated. The iron hull of oval section had a small bridge positioned centrally, 2 pockets (one forward, one aft) for stowage of mines and 2 hook eyes at both ends to hoist the boat ashore or on to the davits of a mother vessel. The mines were operated with the help of air-filled rubber cushions. The whole series was built in great secrecy and the boats were to be used in the close defence of coastal fortresses; 16 boats were attached to Kronstadt while the remainder were divided between Sevastopol and Odessa.

Two Type III boats were converted in 1884 for experiments with electric propulsion. One was fitted with 1hp motor and water jet propeller thus enabling her to develop 3kts while the second one received a 1.8hp electric motor and 1 screw which gave a speed of 4kts and battery capacity enough for 10 hours.

When defence of coastal installations became a responsibility of the Naval Authority in 1886 all the Drzewiecki boats were deleted and most of them converted to buoys later on. See also *Keta* – submersible.

Delfin 1905
NB 1/750 scale

DELFIN *submarine*

Displacement: 113t/124t
Dimensions: 64ft 3in × 10ft × 9ft 6in
19.6m × 3.3m × 2.9m
Machinery: 1 shaft, gasoline engine/electric motor, 300bhp/120hp = 9kts/4.5kts. Range 243nm surfaced, 35nm/2.5kts submerged
Armament: 2 Drzewiecki torpedo drop-collars, 1 MG
Complement: 22

Name	Builder	Launched	Fate
DELFIN (ex-*150*, ex-*113*)	Baltic Wks, St Petersburg	1903	Sunk 5.9.17

The first combat submarine ordered by the Imperial Russian Navy in July 1901 to the design of the engineer Bubnov. A single hull type with saddle tanks, the outer plating was covered with teak to prevent damage when grounding. When completed in 1904 she carried a number instead of a name, being officially rated as a torpedo-boat. The first trials discovered faulty venting in the ballast tanks and diving took 12 minutes. The diving limit was 25 fathoms. While doing a practice dive she sank accidentally in the Neva on 29 June 1904 (21 lives lost, 11 survivors) but was raised four days later and transferred to Valdivostok in November 1904, becoming operational in February 1905. Once again sunk by an explosion of petrol vapours in May 1905 she was recommissioned after the conclusion of hostilities against Japan. Transferred to the Arctic in October 1916 but proved unsuitable for modern warfare and was deleted in August 1917. She was sunk while abandoned in Murmansk.

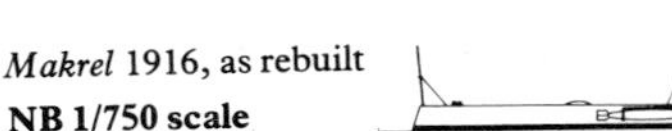
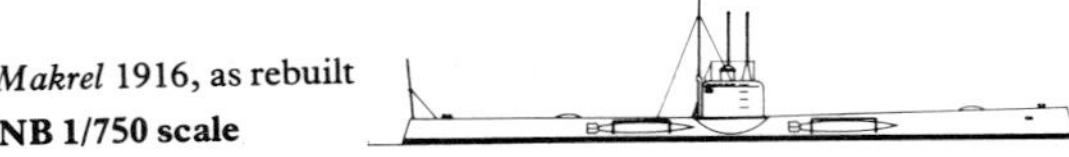

Makrel 1916, as rebuilt
NB 1/750 scale

KASATKA class *submarines*

Displacement: 140t/177t
Dimensions: 110ft × 11ft 6in × 11ft 3in
33.5m × 3.5m × 3.4m
Machinery: 1 shaft, kerosene engine/electric motor, 200bhp/100hp = 8.5kts/5.5kts. Range 700nm/8kts surfaced, 50nm/3kts submerged
Armament: 4 Drzewiecki torpedo drop-collars, 1 MG
Complement: 24

Name	Builder	Launched	Fate
FELDMARSHAL GRAF SHEREMETEV	Baltic Wks, St Petersburg	1904	BU 1922
KASATKA	Baltic Wks, St Petersburg	1904	BU 1922
MAKREL	Baltic Wks, St Petersburg	1907	BU 1922
NALIM	Baltic Wks, St Petersburg	8.9.04	Scuttled 26.4.19
OKUN	Baltic Wks St Petersburg	1904	BU 1922
SKAT	Baltic Wks, St Petersburg	1904	Scuttled 26.4.19

Katsatka as completed
Lemachko Collection

Peskar date unknown *Lemachko Collection*

A Bubnov design prepared after experience with *Delfin*. *Kasatka* was ordered under the 1903 Programme, the 4 following boats under the 1904 Emergency Programme while *Sheremetev* came from the Public Subscription Fund being named after a major contributor. Because of lack of time to supply enough engines, the designed 3-shaft power plant was replaced by 1-shaft one and only *Kasatka* ran trials in the Baltic before transfer to the Far East. She experienced troubles when filling ballast tanks, operating steering gear, and shipped water through the main hatchway when in a seaway and heavily trimmed aft when submerged. To overcome the latter trouble 2 floats were added to the after part of the casing on *Kasatka* first and then on the others. Except for *Makrel* and *Okun* (designated for evaluation of the type) they transferred to Vladivostok during September–December 1904 and became operational in March 1905 (*Kasatka*, *Skat*) and May 1905 (*Sheremetev*, *Nalim*). After the Russo-Japanese War all 6 of this type were rebuilt with diesel-electric power plant (120bhp diesel engine) and a large bridge amidships. Their displacement reached 153t/186t and the diving limit 25 fathoms.

Nalim and *Skat* were transferred to the Black Sea Fleet in 1915 (carried 1–47mm gun at that time) and deleted in March 1917. Both flew the Ukrainian colours in April 1918 but were seized by the Germans and transferred to the British in November 1918 being scuttled by them to prevent capture by the Reds advancing on Sevastopol. The remaining Far East boats were transferred to the Baltic Fleet in 1915 (*Sheremetev* renamed *Keta* on 17 August 1917). *Kasatka*, *Makrel* and *Okun* were shipped to the Caspian in 1918.

HOLLAND type *submarines*

Displacement: 105t/122t
Dimensions: 65ft 6in × 11ft 6in × 9ft 6in
20.0m × 3.5m × 2.9m
Machinery: 1-shaft gasoline engine/electric motor, 160bhp/70hp = 8.5kts/6kts. Range 585nm surfaced, 42nm submerged
Armament: 1–15in (381mm) TT, 1 MG
Complement: 22

Name	Builder	Launched	Fate
BELUGA	Nevski Yd, St Petersburg	1905	Scuttled 25.2.18
LOSOS	Nevski Yd, St Petersburg	1907	Scuttled 26.4.19
PESKAR	Nevski Yd, St Petersburg	1905	Scuttled 25.2.18
SHCHUKA	Nevski Yd, St Petersburg	4.05	Scuttled 25.2.18
SOM (ex-*Fulton*)	Nevski Yd, St Petersburg	1904	Scuttled 25.2.18
STERLYAD	Nevski Yd, St Petersburg	1905	Scuttled 25.2.18
SUDAK	Nevski Yd, St Petersburg	1907	Scuttled 26.4.19

Six ordered under the 1904 Emergency Programme while *Fulton* was purchased a month later and delivered in sections to facilitate assembly of the whole series. Only *Som* ('Sheath fish') and *Shchuka* were delivered by rail to Vladivostok in time and became operational in April and November 1905 respectively. The former boat was the most active submarine of the Siberian Flotilla as she covered over 1300 miles during her war patrols. *Losos* and *Sudak*

The three *Karp* class boats as completed *Author's Collection*

transferred to the Black Sea in 1907, the others remained on the Baltic. Re-engined with diesels later on (only *Sudak* had one upon completion). The diving limit was 16 fathoms.

Som and *Shchuka* transferred to the Black Sea Fleet in 1915 but finally reached the Baltic the same year. Of little fighting value at that time, the Baltic boats were fitted with 1–47mm gun and except for *Som* (lost in collision with SS *Angermanland* off the Aaland Islands) the remaining boats were deleted during 1916–17 and hulked in Reval and Sevastopol. The 4 Reval boats were scuttled by the Russians to prevent capture by German troops while *Losos* and *Sudak* flew Ukrainian colours at Sevastopol in April 1918, but were seized by the Germans and surrendered to the British in November. Scuttled off Sevastopol to prevent capture by the Reds.

LAKE type *submarines*

Displacement: 153t/187t
Dimensions: 72ft × 12ft × 12ft 3in
22.0m × 3.6m × 3.7m
Machinery: 2 shafts, 2 gasoline engines/2 electric motors, 240bhp/120hp = 8.5kts/4.5kts. Range 385nm surfaced, 35nm submerged
Armament: 3–15in (381mm) TT (2 bow, 1 stern)
Complement: 24

Name	Assembly	Launched	Fate
BYCHEK	Arsenal, Libau	1905	Stricken 1913
KEFAL	Arsenal, Libau	1905	Stricken 1915
OSETR (ex-*Protector*)	Arsenal, Libau	1905	Stricken 1913
PALTUS	Arsenal, Libau	1905	Stricken 1913
PLOTVA	Arsenal, Libau	1905	Stricken 1913
SIG	Arsenal, Libau	1905	Stricken 7.14

Five ordered on 10 May 1904 from the Simon Lake Wks under the 1904 Emergency Programme, while *Protector* was bought to lead assembly of the whole series and arrived at Kronstadt on 15 June. Renamed *Osetr* ('Sturgeon'), she had hydraulically operated wheels (stowed within the keel) to allow the submarine to move on the sea bed and was fitted with a chamber to embark divers when submerged. The diving limit was 16 fathoms.

Osetr and *Kefal* became operational at Vladivostok in September and October 1905 while the others were also transferred there by rail, except for *Sig*, but were not completed before 1906.

Forel as completed
NB 1/750 scale

FOREL *midget submarine*

Displacement: 16t/17t
Dimensions: 43ft × 7ft × 7ft
13.1m × 2.1m × 2.1m
Machinery: 1-shaft electric motor, 60hp = 4kts. Range 20nm
Armament: 2 torpedoes

Name	Builder	Acquired	Fate
FOREL	Krupp Wks	6.5.04	Stricken 1911

Bought from the German Krupp Wks who built her as a private venture to attract the attention of the German Admiralstab towards underwater warfare. Arrived Vladivostok in August 1904 and operational from September but did not venture on any patrol.

Keta as completed
NB 1/200 scale

KETA *submersible*

Displacement: 3t
Dimensions: 21ft × 5ft × 3ft 6in
6.4m × 1.5m × 1.0m
Machinery: 1-shaft gasoline engine
Armament: 2 Drzewiecki torpedo drop-collars, 1 MG

Paltus about 1907 *Lemachko Collection*

One of the Type III Drzewiecki midget submarines converted into a low profile patrol submersible by the Lessner Wks, St Petersburg in 1905 and transferred to the Far East. Employed in the Amur estuary she even had the opportunity of attacking a Japanese destroyer but beached when approaching the target. She was deleted on 19 June 1908.

KARP class *submarines*

Displacement: 207t/235t
Dimensions: 130ft oa × 9ft × 8ft
39.6m × 2.7m × 2.5m
Machinery: 2 shafts, 2 kerosene engines/2 electric motors, 400bhp/200hp = 10kts/8.5kts. Range 1250nm surfaced, 50nm submerged
Armament: 1–18in (457mm) TT, 2 Drzewiecki torpedo drop-collars
Complement: 28

Name	Builder	Launched	Fate
KARP	Germaniawerft, Kiel	1907	Scuttled 26.4.19
KAMBALA	Germaniawerft, Kiel	1907	Lost 11.6.09
KARAS	Germaniawerft, Kiel	1907	Scuttled 26.4.19

Ordered on 6 June 1904 under the 1904 Emergency Programme, this class was a D'Equevilley design, twin hull type with 7 ballast and trimming tanks and diving limit of 16 fathoms. The kerosene engines were much safer than gasoline. The first German submarine *U 1* was derived from the *Karp* class design and was built in record time in contrast to the Russian trio which were only delivered in 1907. Transferred by rail to the Black Sea in 1908, *Kambala* was lost in collision with battleship *Rostislav* off Sevastopol, the parts of wreck were raised and scrapped that year. The remaining boats were deleted in March 1917 and hulked at Sevastopol. They flew the Ukrainian colours in April 1918 but were seized by the Germans in May and surrendered to the British in November. Scuttled to prevent capture by the Reds.

Krokodil about 1914 *Lemachko Collection*

RUSSIA

KAIMAN class *submarines*

Displacement: 409t/482t
Dimensions: 132ft × 14ft × 16ft
40.2m × 4.3m × 4.9m
Machinery: 2 shafts, 2 gasoline engines/2 electric motors, 1200bhp/400hp = 10.5kts/7kts. Range 1050nm/8kts surfaced, 40nm/5kts submerged
Armament: 4–18in (457mm) TT (2 bow, 2 stern)
Complement: 34

Name	Builder	Launched	Fate
KAIMAN	Crichton Yd, St Petersburg	11.07	Scuttled 25.2.18
ALLIGATOR	Crichton Yd, St Petersburg	1908	Scuttled 25.2.18
DRAKON	Crichton Yd, St Petersburg	1908	Scuttled 25.2.18
KROKODIL	Crichton Yd, St Petersburg	1908	Scuttled 25.2.18

Ordered in 1906 this Lake design was developed from that of *Protector* with displacement enlarged to house a more powerful armament and to increase the radius of action so that the boats could operate off the Japanese coast. Completed in December 1910 they were not accepted because of numerous design and working faults as well as exceeding the displacement by *c* 12t. To anticipate the builder's intentions of selling the boats abroad the Russian Naval Ministry decided to take them over without paying the final price. The funds spared were utilised on a conversion that took place during 1911 and included removal of one 3-cylinder section from each gasoline engine (800bhp remained to give 8.4kts on surface) and placing new ballast pumps in their place. This reduced diving time from 10 to 3 minutes. Moreover 2 Drzewiecki drop-collars for 18in torpedoes were added.

Commissioned at the end of 1911 the class formed the Baltic Fleet's 2nd Submarine Flotilla from 1913 (renumbered the 3rd in 1915). Armed with 1–47mm, 1 MG (1–37mm on *Drakon*) later on. Quite active during the early stages of the First World War (*Alligator* and *Kaiman* seized German prizes in October 1915) they were deleted on 15 November 1916 to release experienced crews for the *AG* class. *Krokodil* became a charging plant. All 4 scuttled at Reval to avoid capture by the Germans.

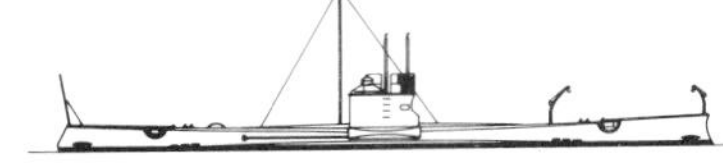
Minoga 1910
NB 1/750 scale

MINOGA *submarine*

Displacement: 123t × 155t
Dimensions: 107ft × 9ft × 9ft
32.6m × 2.8m × 2.8m
Machinery: 1 shaft, 2 diesel engines/1 electric motor, 240bhp/70hp = 11kts/5kts. Oil fuel 11t. Range 600nm/10kts surfaced, 50nm/3.5kts submerged.
Armament: 1–37mm, 1 MG, 2–18in (457mm) TT (bow)
Complement: 22

Name	Builder	Launched	Fate
MINOGA	Baltic Wks, St Petersburg	24.10.08	BU 1922

***Akula* as completed**
Lemachko Collection

Pochtovy as completed *Twardowski Collection*

A Bubnov design ordered in February 1906. Single hull type with saddle tanks, diving limit 16 fathoms. The first submarine designed in the light of experience gained by the Russian submarine arm off Vladivostok. She marked a big step forward in Russian submarine construction having diesel propulsion, but the diesels were not reliable, and a single screw power plant with various powers to transmit needed control pitch propellers to be fitted. In consequence the boat was too complex and too cramped to be wholly successful. Served with 1st Submarine Flotilla after completion, then the 4th in 1913. Transferred to the Caspian in October 1918.

AKULA *submarine*

Displacement: 370t/475t
Dimensions: 184ft × 12ft × 11ft
56.0m × 3.7m × 3.4m
Machinery: 3 shafts, 3 diesel engines/1 electric motor, 900bhp/300hp = 10.6kts/6.6kts. Range 1900nm surfaced, 38nm/4.75kts submerged
Armament: 1–47mm, 2 MG, 4–18in (457mm) TT (2 bow, 2 stern), 4 Drzewiecki torpedo drop-collars, 4 mines
Complement: 34

Name	Builder	Launched	Fate
AKULA	Baltic Yd, St Petersburg	4.9.07	Sunk 28.11.15

Ordered in December 1906 as a Bubnov's version of the 400t Lake type submarines (*Kaiman* class). In many respects she represented the enlarged *Minoga* design with a more reliable powerplant. She experienced serious teething problems, the most troublesome being replacement of 225hp electric motor by a 300hp one and triple changing of propellers. She was a single hull type with saddle tanks and a diving limit of 25 fathoms. Undoubtedly the most successful of the pre-war Russian submarines, she near missed the German coastal battleship *Beowulf*. Lost on a mine off Windau in the Baltic.

POCHTOVY *submarine*

Displacement: 134t/146t
Dimensions: 113ft × 10ft × 9ft 3in
34.4m × 3.0m × 2.8m
Machinery: 1 shaft, 2 gasoline engines, 260hp = 10.5kts/6.2kts
Armament: 4 Drzewiecki torpedo drop-collars

Name	Builder	Launched	Fate
POCHTOVY	Metal Wks, St Petersburg	1908	Stricken 1913

Drzewiecki design, construction funded by public subscription. The chief aim of the design was to provide a submarine with a single diesel propulsion when surfaced and submerged. Because of the lack of a suitable diesel engine in 1905 gasoline ones were fitted instead. These were supplied with oxygen from 45 air cylinders (350 cu ft of air under 2500psi was carried) when submerged. Exhaust gases were ejected overboard by compressor jointed to a perforated pipe under the keel. With only 1 engine running she was able to cover 28 miles when submerged and 350 miles on both engines when on the surface. The whole system proved reliable enough but further refinement was abandoned because of steam collecting inside the hull when the boat was submerged and the bubble wake on the surface.

KRAB *minelaying submarine*

Displacement: 512t normal; 560t full load/740t full load
Dimensions: 173ft 3in × 14ft × 12ft 9in
52.8m × 4.3m × 3.9m
Machinery: 2 shafts, 4 gasoline engines/2 electric motors, 1200bhp/400hp = 11.8kts/7.1kts. Range 1700nm/7kts surfaced, 82nm/4kts submerged
Armament: 1–75mm, 2 MG, 2–18in (457mm) TT, 2 Drzewiecki torpedo drop-collars, 60 mines
Complement: 50

Name	Builder	Launched	Fate
KRAB	Naval Yd, Nikolayev	1.9.12	Scuttled 26.4.19

Naletov design, ordered in 1908 she was the world's first submarine minelayer but not being completed until July 1915 was overtaken by the German UC-boats. Single hull type, diving limit 25 fathoms. The mines were stowed horizontally in two tubes within the hull casing and were transported aft by electrically-powered chain conveyor.

On her first war cruise she sailed under commercial colours, laying a minefield off the Bosphorus in which the Turkish gunboat *Isa Reis* was damaged. She participated in a second mining of the Bosphorus in 1916 and later in that year laid a minefield off Varna which cost the Bulgarians the torpedo-boat *Shumni* lost and *Strogi* damaged. She flew the Ukrainian colours in April 1918 but was seized by the Germans and surrendered by them to the British in November. Scuttled off Sevastopol to avoid capture by the Reds. The wreck was raised in 1935 and scrapped.

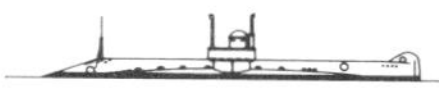
Holland type midget submarine *2*
NB 1/750 scale

HOLLAND type *midget submarines*

Displacement: 33t normal; 35t full load/44t
Dimensions: 67ft 4in × 7ft 6in × 6ft
20.5m × 2.3m × 1.8m
Machinery: 1-shaft, diesel-electric, 50bhp/35hp = 8kts/6kts
Armament: 2–18in (457mm) TT (bow)
Complement: 4

Class (fate):
Nevski Yd, St Petersburg, – *1* (launched 1913, transferred to the Arctic 1916, sunk in collision with submarine *Delfin* off Murmansk 26 April 1917), *2* (transferred to the Arctic 1915, stranded in a gale off Svjatoi Nos 15.10.1915), *3* (transferred to the Duna River, captured by Austro-Hungarian forces at Reni 12.3.1918 but abandoned later).

Ordered by the Army Ministry for local defence on the Black Sea coast, they reflected positive experience with the Drzewiecki boats of the 1870s. Transferred to Navy control in August 1914.

Krab during the war *Micinski Collection*

Morzh 1915

MORZH class *submarines*

Displacement: 630t (*Nerpa* 645t)/760t
Dimensions: 220ft × 15ft × 13ft
67.0m × 4.5m × 3.9m
Machinery: 2 shafts, 2 diesel engines/2 electric motors, 500bhp/800hp = 10.8kts/8kts. Range 2500nm surfaced, 120nm submerged
Armament: 1–57mm, 1–47mm (*Tyulen* 1–75mm, 1–57mm), 4–18in (457mm) TT (2 bow, 2 stern), 8 Drzewiecki drop-collars
Complement: 47

Name	Builder	Launched	Fate
MORZH	Baltic Yd, Nikolayev	28.9.13	Lost May 1917
NERPA	Baltic Yd, Nikolayev	28.9.13	Stricken 1931
TYULEN	Baltic Yd, Nikolayev	1.11.13	Sold 1924

In the 1911 Programme for the Black Sea Fleet. Bubnov design, single hull type, diving limit 25 fathoms, diving time 3.5 minutes. Design developed from *Akula* but incorporated numerous structural faults: lack of watertight compartments, power consuming body lines and ballast tanks venting being the most troublesome ones. The order for diesels had been placed in the German Krupp Wks and these were not delivered by August 1914 so had to be replaced by engines removed from the Amur Flotilla river gunboats. Because the designed 2280bhp was not attained, not one of the class attained the planned 16kts on surface while a badly shaped hull prevented them from developing the designed 12kts under water.

Commissioned during 1914–15 they became the most active of the Black Sea submarines being credited with 16 merchantmen sunk. *Morzh* narrowly missed *Goeben* in November 1915 and was damaged by a Turkish aircraft in May 1916. She sailed on her last patrol on 11 May 1917 being mined a few days later or sunk by Turkish aircraft off the Bosphorus. *Tyulen*, after sinking the 1545t Turkish steamer *Zorgouldak* with gunfire on 10 August 1915, was captured by the Germans in Sevastopol, then surrendered to the British in November 1918 and transferred by them to Wrangel's fleet in September 1919. She reached Bizerta in 1920. *Nerpa* remained inoperational in Nikolayev and was recommissioned by the Reds on 3 June 1922 (renamed *Politruk* in January 1923).

SVYATOI GEORGI *submarine*

Fiat-Laurenti design, ordered in 1913 in Italy for comparision purposes. Designated for the Black Sea Fleet and completed in 1915 she was taken over by the Royal Italian Navy on 18 February 1915 and commissioned as *Argonauta* (see under Italy).

NARVAL class *submarines*

Displacement: 621t/994t (*Narval* 673t/1045t)
Dimensions: 230ft × 21ft 6in × 11ft 6in
70.1m × 6.5m × 3.5m
Machinery: 2 shafts, 4 diesel engines/2 electric motors, 640bhp/900hp = 9.6kts (*Narval* 10.5kts)/11.5kts. Range 400nm surfaced, 120nm submerged
Armament: 1–75mm, 1–63mm (except *Narval*), 2 MG (*Kashalot* 1 MG, *Kit* none), 4–18in (457mm) TT (2 bow, 2 stern), 8 (*Narval* 4), Drzewiecki torpedo drop-collars
Complement: 47

Name	Builder	Launched	Fate
KASHALOT	Nevski Yd, Nikolayev	1914	Scuttled 26.4.19
KIT	Nevski Yd, Nikolayev	1914	Scuttled 26.4.19
NARVAL	Nevski Yd, Nikolayev	1914	Scuttled 26.4.19

Part of the 1911 Programme, designated for the Black Sea Fleet. Holland design (Type 31A), double hull type, diving limit 25 fathoms, diving time 1 minute. Unlike contemporary Russian submarines these were fitted with a crash diving tank, gravitionally filled ballast tanks and watertight bulkheads built in. Undoubtedly the best submarine type ever built for the Imperial Russian Navy. The original design provided 2 diesels 850bhp each and 16kts surface speed but these were not fitted because of the notorious shortage of diesels. The class accounted for 8 merchantmen and 74 coasters sunk. *Kit* and *Narval* flew the Ukrainian colours for some time but were captured by the Germans together with *Kashalot* and surrendered to the Allies in November 1918. Scuttled off Sevastopol to prevent capture by the advancing Reds.

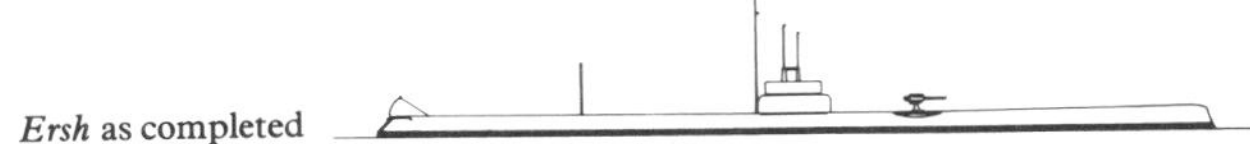
Ersh as completed

BARS class *submarines*

Displacement: 650t × 780t
Dimensions: 223ft × 15ft × 13ft
68.0m × 4.5m × 3.9m
Machinery: 2 shafts, 2 diesel engines/2 electric motors, 2640bhp/900hp = 18kts/10kts (see notes). Oil fuel 40t. Range 400nm/17kts surfaced, 25nm/9kts submerged
Armament: 1–63mm, 1–37mm AA, 4–18in (457mm) TT (2 bow, 2 stern), 8 Drzewiecki torpedo drop-collars (see notes)
Complement: 33

Name	Builder	Launched	Fate
BARS	Baltic Yd, Petrograd	2.6.15	Sunk 28.5.17
EDINOROG	Baltic Yd, Petrograd	1916	Sunk 25.2.18
GEPARD	Baltic Yd, Petrograd	2.6.15	Sunk 28.10.17
KUGUAR	Noblessner Yd, Reval	1916	Hulked 1922
LEOPARD	Noblessner Yd, Reval	1916	Hulked 1936
LVITSA	Noblessner Yd, Reval	23.10.15	Sunk 11.6.17
PANTERA	Noblessner Yd, Reval	26.4.16	BU 1955
RYS	Noblessner Yd, Reval	1916	Sunk 13.9.35
TIGR	Noblessner Yd, Reval	18.9.15	BU 1936
TUR	Noblessner Yd, Reval	1916	Sunk 25.7.35
UGOR	Baltic Yd, Petrograd	1916	Sunk 27.3.20
VEPR	Baltic Yd, Petrograd	1915	Hulked 1922
VOLK	Baltic Yd, Petrograd	1915	Stricken 1936
YAGUAR	Noblessner Yd, Reval	1916	Stricken 1936
YAZ	Noblessner Yd, Reval	1917?	Deleted 5.22
ZMEYA	Baltic Yd, Petrograd	1916	Sunk 5.9.34
ERSH	Baltic Yd, Petrograd	1917?	Lost 22.5.31
FOREL	Baltic Yd, Petrograd	1916	Stricken 5.22
BURVESTNIK	Naval Yd, Nikolayev	1916	Sold 1924
GAGARA	Baltic Yd, Nikolayev	7.10.16	Scuttled 26.4.19
LEBED	Naval Yd, Nikolayev	1917	Scuttled 26.4.19
ORLAN	Naval Yd, Nikolayev	1916	Scuttled 26.4.19
PELIKAN	Naval Yd, Nikolayev	Sept 1917	Scuttled 26.4.19
UTKA	Baltic Yd, Nikolayev	1916	Sold 1924

Bars as completed — *Lemachko Collection*

Narval at launch — *Lemachko Collection*

Part of the 1912 Programme, 12 authorised for the Baltic Fleet, 6 for the Siberian Flotilla (reassigned to the Baltic in March 1915) and 1914 Programme, 6 for the Black Sea Fleet. A Bubnov design, based on the *Morzh* class with a 3ft section added amidships. Single hull type, diving limit 25 fathoms. This new class incorporated all the shortcomings of the previous Bubnov designs: no watertight bulkheads were fitted while the ballast tanks were filled by pumps which resulted in a diving time exceeding 3 minutes. The unfortunate venting of the foremost tanks resulted in two 10ft vertical fountains of blue water appearing off both ends when submerging. Increased hull resistance prevented the boats attaining the designed underwater speed; instead 8.5kts–9kts were developed at best. The shortage of diesels hampered construction of the whole class as only *Kuguar* and *Zmeya* received the designed sets. The others were fitted with 2 sets of 250bhp removed from Amur Flotilla gunboats, 240bhp of local production or imported 420bhp diesels which gave surface speeds of 11.5kts and 13kts respectively with ranges of 2500 miles and 1700 miles.

Ersh, Forel and *Ugor* were originally ordered from the Noblessner Yd, Reval but re-ordered in August 1915 and the former pair was converted to minelayers with niches for drop-collars removed and 2 tubes for 21 mines each placed under the casing aft. The minelaying system was based on that in *Krab*. The gun armament varied as *Bars, Vepr* and *Volk* carried additional 63mm instead of 37mm one, *Leopard, Pantera, Rys* and *Tigr* received an additional 75mm gun, the Black Sea boats were fitted with 1–75mm, 1–37mm AA (*Gagara* and *Utka* had 2–75mm only) while the minelaying boats received 1–63mm, 1 MG.

The first trials of *Bars* and *Vepr* (completed in summer 1915) disclosed the vulnerability of drop-collars placed in the hull niches low above the waterlines. Thus all the Noblessner Yd boats had the niches reduced and torpedoes placed higher up while the Baltic Yd introduced this change after the fourth boat completed while *Bars* and *Gepard* were reconstructed in this manner during 1916. The drop-collars were abandoned later on and niches were plated up, while the Black Sea boats retained them in their original configuration. Although the most numerous class of Russian submarines in the First World War they were not very effective vessels because of their unreliable surface propulsion. Thus their war successes totalled only 8 merchantmen sunk (4 by *Volk* during 1915–17) and the British destroyer *Vittoria* sunk at anchor by *Pantera* east of Seiskar Island in the Baltic on 31 August 1919. She remains the largest warship ever sunk by a submarine of the Red Navy.

Bars sailed for her last patrol on 16 May 1917 and was mined off Norrköping (Sweden) or sunk after depth charging. *Gepard* was damaged by the German Q-ship *K* in May 1916 and was probably lost on mines off Luzerort a year later. *Edinorog* was stranded on 25 September 1917 off Ere Island but refloated in October 1917 and temporarily repaired at Reval, was lost when towed to Helsingfors. *Lvitsa* was lost from an unknown cause off Gotland. Except for *Ugor* (sunk in Petrograd because of negligence, raised later and scrapped), *Forel* and *Yaz* (both deleted incomplete) as well as *Kuguar* and *Vepr* (designated as stationary training units) the other Baltic boats were commissioned by the Soviets and changed their names to those connected with the Soviet regime in January 1923, then changes once again to numbers in October 1934. *Leopard* became *Krasnoarmeets* then *B 4*, *Pantera* became *Komissar* then *B 2* (modernised 1934–35 with 2 watertight bulkheads fitted, 2 additional TT mounted in bow and bridge enlarged) and reverted to her old name in 1935, deleted in August 1941 became charging plant after April 1942); *Rys* became *Bolshevik* then *B 7* (lost in an accident in Finnish Bay, refloated and scrapped later); *Tigr* became *Kommunar* then *B 6*; *Tur* became *Tovarishch* then *B 3* (sunk in collision with battleship *Marat*, raised and scrapped in 1936). *Volk* became *Batrak* then *B 1* (sunk in 1927 during exercises, refloated and recommissioned later); *Zmeya* became *Proletari* then *B 5* (lost during exercises, refloated and scrapped); *Yaguar* became *Krasnoflotets* then *B 8*, *Ersh* became *Rabochi* (sunk in collision with *Krasnoarmeets* in Finnish Bay, raised later and scrapped).

All of the Black Sea Fleet boats were captured by the Germans at Sevastopol in May 1918 and only *Utka* was commissioned by them as *US 3* on 1 August 1918, while *Gagra*, designated *US 4* performed only 2 trial cruises. Possibly *Burvestnik* and *Orlan* were also redesignated to *US 1* and *US 2* respectively. All 6 were surrendered to the British in November 1918 and except for *Burvestnik* and *Utka* (transferred to Wrangel's fleet in September 1919) they were scuttled off Sevastopol to prevent capture by the Reds. *Lebed* and *Pelikan* were still incomplete at that time.

Commissioning of *F 1* 1917 *Lemachko Collection*

AG 14 date unknown *Twardowski Collection*

F 1 *submarine*

Displacement: 260t/305t
Dimensions: 147ft 6in × 14ft × 10ft
45.0m × 4.3m × 3.1m
Machinery: 2 shafts, 2 Fiat diesel engines/2 electric motors, 700bhp/500bhp = 13kts/8.5kts
Armament: 1–75mm, 2–18in (457mm) TT (bow)

Name	Builder	Launched	Fate
F 1	Ansaldo-San Giorgio, Spezia	1916	Stricken 1925

Laurenti-Ansaldo design, ordered in Italy under the 1915 Emergency Programme as a replacement for *Svyatoi Georgi* requisitioned by the Italian Navy. Commissioned on 20 May 1917 in Spezia and name changed to *Svyatoi Georgi (ii)*. During June–September 1917 she covered over 5000 miles being transferred to the Arctic Ocean Flotilla via Gibraltar, Lisbon and Plymouth. Renamed *Kommunar* by the Reds in 1918 she was beached in the Dvina during the summer of 1918 to avoid capture by the Allies.

AG class *submarines*

Displacement: 355t/433t
Dimensions: 151ft × 16ft × 12ft 6in
46.0m × 4.9m × 3.8m
Machinery: 2 shafts, 2 NELESCO diesel engines/2 electric motors, 960bhp/640hp = 12kts/10kts. Oil fuel 16.5t
Armament: 1–47mm, 4–18in (457mm) TT (bow)
Complement: 30

Class (launched, fate):
Baltic Yd, Petrograd – *AG 11* (1916, scuttled 3.4.18), *AG 12* (1916, scuttled 3.4.18), *AG 13* (1916, scuttled 3.4.18), *AG 14* (1916, mined 6.7.17), *AG 15* (1916, scuttled 3.4.18), *AG 17* (became US *H 4*), *AG 18* (became US *H 5*), *AG 19* (became *US H 6*), *AG 20* (became US *H 7*)
Baltic Yd, Nikolayev – *AG 21* (1917, stricken 1948), *AG 22* (1919, sold 1924), *AG 23* (1.6.20, scuttled 6.42), *AG 24* (1921, stricken autumn 1942), *AG 25* (1921, sunk 4.11.43), *AG 26* (*c*1921, stricken autumn 1943), *AG 27* (became US *H 8*), *AG 28* (became US *H 9*)

Part of the 1915 Emergency Programme, assigned to the Baltic and the Black Sea Fleets (from *AG 21* onwards). Holland design (*AG* stands for Amerikanskij Golland = American Holland), identical with the H-boats built for the Royal Navy, US Navy and Italian Navy. Delivered to Petrograd and Nikolayev in sections for assembly there. *AG 11–AG 15* commissioned during the autumn and winter of 1916 and formed the 4th Submarine Flotilla. *AG 13* lost accidentally but raised and recommissioned as *AG 16* on 21 July 1917. *AG 15* lost accidentally on 18 June 1917 but raised and recommissioned. Except for *AG 14* (mined off Libau, Latvia) the other Baltic boats were scuttled at Hango (Finland) to avoid capture by the Germans. Not one of the Black Sea boats entered service under the Imperial Russian Navy colours. *AG 21*, completed in 1918, was seized by the Germans in April at Sevastopol and transferred to the Allies in November and scuttled by them to prevent capture by the Reds on 26 April 1919. Raised by the Soviets in 1928 she was recommissioned on 30 November 1930 as *16*, then *Metallist* and *A 5* finally after September 1934. *AG 22* commissioned with Wrangel's fleet in 1919. *AG 23–AG 26* were assembled by the Reds after the seizure of Nikolayev and commissioned as following: *AG 23* in September 1920, became *Nezamozhny* after February 1923 and *Shakhter* after July 1923, *Lunacharski* (ex-*AG 24*) in July 1921, became *Kommunist* after February 1923, *AG 25* in May 1922, became *Marksist* after February 1923, *Polirabotnik* (ex-*Kamenev*, ex-*AG 26*) in July 1923. They were renumbered *12–15* respectively in 1929 and once again to *A 1–A 4* in September 1934. *A 1* hulked in spring 1941 was scuttled at Sevastopol to avoid capture by the Germans, *A 3* was sunk by the German *UJ 117* off the Tendra Peninsula. *AG 17–AG 20, AG 27, AG 28* were never delivered to Russia because of the Bolshevik Revolution.

B class *submarines*

Displacement: 971t/1264t
Dimensions: 265ft × 23ft × 13ft
80.0m × 7.0m × 4.0m
Machinery: 2 shafts, diesel engines/electric motors, 17kts/9kts. Range 1200nm surfaced, 22.5nm submerged
Armament: 2–75mm, 2 MG, 10–18in (457mm) TT, 6 Drzewiecki torpedo drop-collars, 10 mines

Class (fate):
Baltic Yd, Petrograd – *B 1–B 4* (cancelled)
Russo-Baltic Yd, Reval – *B 5–B 10* (cancelled)

Part of the 1916 Submarine Programme, designated for the Baltic Fleet. Bubnov design, influenced by the Holland ones and therefore included such innovations as a double hull and subdivision into 8 watertight compartments. Four of her TT were transversally sited. Ordered 1916, construction begun 1916–17 but abandoned after the Bolshevik Revolution.

G class *submarines*

Displacement: 952t/1289t
Dimensions: 265ft × 23ft × 13ft
80.0m × 7.0m × 4.0m
Machinery: 2 shafts, diesel engines/electric motors, 16kts/9kts
Armament: 2–75mm, 2 MG, 10–18in (457mm) TT, 6 Drzewiecki torpedo drop-collars, 10 mines

Class (fate):
Noblessner Yd, Reval – *G 1–G 10* (cancelled)
Russud Yd, Nikolayev – *G 11–G 14* (cancelled)
Builder and station unknown – *G 14–G 28* (cancelled)

Part of the 1916 Submarine Programme, designated for the Baltic (*G 1–G 10*) and the Black Sea Fleets (*G 11–G 14*). Holland design, double hull type, 7 watertight compartments. Ordered 1916, construction of the first 14 begun 1916–17 but abandoned after the Bolshevik Revolution.

V class *submarines*

Displacement: 920t/1140t
Dimensions: 265ft × 23ft × 13ft
80.0m × 7.0m × 4.0m
Machinery: 2 shafts, diesel engines/electric motors, 13kts/10.5kts
Armament: 2–75mm, 2 MG, 10–18in (457mm) TT, 6 Drzewiecki torpedo drop-collars, 10 mines

Class (fate):
Russud Yd, Nikolayev – *V 1–V 4* (cancelled)
Builder unknown – *V 5–V 7* (cancelled)

In the 1916 Submarine Programme, designated for the Black Sea Fleet. Fiat design, double hull type, 7 watertight compartments. Ordered in 1916 and construction of the first 4 begun 1916–17 but abandoned after the Bolshevik Revolution.

Z class *minelaying submarines*

Displacement: 230t/368t
Machinery: Diesel-electric, 10kts/5kts. Range 2000nm surfaced, 90nm submerged
Armament: 20 mines

Class (fate):
Russo-Baltic Yd, Reval – *Z 1–Z 2* (cancelled)
Baltic Yd, Petrograd – *Z 3–Z 4* (cancelled)

Part of the 1916 Submarine Programme, designated for the Baltic Fleet. Ordered 1917 but construction abandoned after the Bolshevik Revolution.

SMALL SURFACE WARSHIPS

ARDAGAN class *gunboats*

Displacement: 623t
Dimensions: 200ft × 28ft × 8ft
61.0m × 8.5m × 2.4m
Machinery: 2 shafts, diesel engines, 1000bhp = 14kts. Oil fuel 30t
Armament: 2–4.7in (120mm), 4–75mm, 4 MG
Complement: 128

Class (launched, fate):
Admiralty Yd, St Petersburg – *Ardagan* (25.9.09, deleted 1950s), *Kars* (1909, deleted 1950s)

The first diesel-engined surface ships ever built, transferred to the Caspian Flotilla in July 1911. Surrendered to the British at Baku 1 March 1919 but recaptured by the Soviets in the following year. Renamed *Trotski* and *Lenin* respectively 19 May 1920. The 75mm guns were replaced by 2–4in later on. *Trotski* renamed *Krasny Azerbaidzhan* in 1927. Both served during the Second World War being armed with 3–100mm AA, 2–45mm AA, 2–37mm AA, 4–.5in MG, 2–.3in MG. Training ships afterwards.

***Kars* and *Ardagan* as completed** *Lemachko Collection*

***Shtorm* as completed** *Lemachko Collection*

***Zyryanin* (ex-*Armurets*) as completed** *Lemachko Collection*

GROZNYI class *gunboats*

Displacement: 1120t
Speed: 10kts
Armament: 2–4.7in (120mm), 2–4in, 1–47mm AA (*Strazh* 2–6in, 1–45mm AA)

Class (completed, fate):
Groznyi (1918, Wrangel's fleet 1919, sold to Italy 1923)
Strazh (1920, Wrangel's fleet 1919, sold to Italy 1923)

SHKVAL class *armoured turret river gunboats*

Displacement: 946t
Dimensions: 233ft × 42ft × 4ft 6in
70.9m × 12.8m × 1.4m
Machinery: 4 shafts, 4 diesel engines, 1000bhp = 11kts. Oil fuel 127t
Armour: Belt 4.5in (114mm), turrets 4.5in (114mm), CT 2in (50mm)
Armament: 2–6in (152mm)/50, 4–4.7in (120mm)/50 (2×2), 7 MG
Complement: 117

Class (fate):
Groza (hulked 1914–15, stranded off Khabarovsk autumn 1921); *Shkval* (one engine removed *c*1914, in Japanese hands 1920–25, recommissioned 16.6.27 as *Sun Yat Sen*, deleted 1950s); *Shtorm* (hulked 1914–15, recommissioned May 1921 as *Lenin*, deleted 1950s); *Smerch* (one engine removed *c*1914, hulked *c*1920, recommissioned 24.7.32 as *Triandafilov*, renamed *Kirov*, deleted 1950s); *Taifun* (hulked 1914–15, scuttled 1921, refloated and recommissioned 24.7.32 as *Vostrietsov*, then *Dzherzhinski*, deleted 1950s); *Uragan* (hulked 1914–15, re-engined 1917, recommissioned May 1921 as *Trotski*, renamed *Krasnyi Vostok* *c*1928, deleted 1950s); *Vikhr* (hulked 1914–15, aviation vessel *Amur* with 5 seaplanes carried during 1928–32, recommissioned 24.6.34 as the river monitor *Dalnevostochny Komsomolets*, deleted 1950s); *Vyuga* (hulked 1914–15, recommissioned 1923 as *Sverdlov*, deleted 1950s).

A class of 8 powerful riverine warships designed and sectioned by the Baltic Yd, St Petersburg, and assembled at Khabarovsk-Ossipovski, Amur River in 1911 for Far East Service.

KALMYK class *armoured river gunboats*

Displacement: 244t
Dimensions: 179ft × 27ft × 3ft 4in mean
54.5m × 8.2m × 1.0m
Machinery: 2 shafts, 2 VTE, 2 boilers, 480shp = 10kts. Coal 45t, oil fuel 36t
Armour: Belt 1in, deck 1in
Armament: 2–4.7in (120mm)/45, 1–47mm howitzer, 4 MG
Complement: 63

Class (fate):
Sormovo Yd, Volga River, assembled 1908 at Khabarovsk-Ossipovski, Amur River – *Kalmyk* (hulked 1914, recommissioned *c*1919, in Japanese hands 1920–25, recommissioned 15.5.27 as *Proletari*, deleted 1950s); *Kirgiz* (hulked 1914, BU *c*1922); *Korel* (hulked 1914, scuttled 23.9.20 by the Japanese); *Sibiryak* (hulked 1914, recommissioned 1921 with machinery removed from *Orochanin*, renamed *Krasnaya Zvezda*, deleted 1950s); *Vogul* (ex-*Zabaikalets*, hulked 1914, recommissioned 1921 as *Bednota*, renamed *Krasnaya Zvezda* 1939, rebuilt 1941–42, deleted 1950s); *Votyak* (ex-*Ussuriets*, hulked 1914, in Japanese hands 1920–25, BU late 1920s ?); *Zyryanin* (ex-*Amurets*, hulked 1914, BU *c*1922).

BURYAT class *river gunboats*

Displacement: 193t
Dimensions: 179ft × 27ft × 2ft 4in mean
54.5m × 8.2m × 0.7m
Machinery: 2 shafts, 2 VTE, 2 boilers, 480shp = 11kts. Coal 45t, oil fuel 36t
Armament: 2–75mm/50, 4 MG
Complement: 66

Class (fate):
Sormovo Yd, Volga River, assembled 1907 at Khabarovsk-Ossipovski, Amur River – *Buryat* (in Japanese hands 1920–25, deleted 1950s), *Mongol* (in Japanese hands 1920–25, repaired and recommissioned 1932, deleted 1950s), *Orochanin* (BU *c*1922)

Orochanin as completed *Lemachko Collection*

KOPCHIK class *guard ships*

Displacement: 450t normal
Dimensions: 168ft × 26ft × 10ft 6in
51.2m × 7.9m × 3.2m
Machinery: 2 shafts, 2 VTE, 3 Yarrow boilers, 1350shp = 15.3kts. Coal 38t
Armament: 2–4in (102mm), 1–47mm, 1 MG, 70 mines
Complement: 48

Class (launched, fate):
Sandvikens Yd, Helsingfors – *Kopchik* (1916, deleted *c*1940), *Korshun* (1916, renamed *Pioner* 1920s, sunk in Kronstadt 21.9.41, refloated April 1942, deleted 1950s)

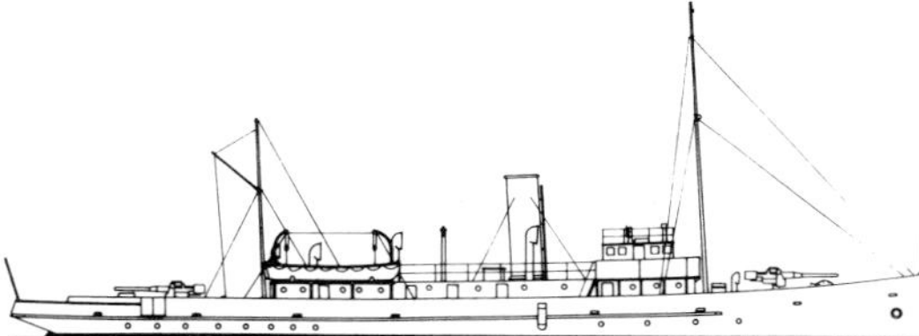

Pingvin 1918
NB 1/750 scale

GOLUB class *guard ships*

Displacement: 400t normal; 530t full load
Dimensions: 170ft 6in × 24ft 6in × 11ft
52.0m × 7.5m × 3.4m
Machinery: 2 shafts, 2 VTE, 3 boilers, 1400shp = 15kts. Coal 70t
Armament: 2–4in (102mm), 1–40mm AA, 3 MG
Complement: 54

Class (launched, fate):
Maskin-Brobygnack Yd, Helsingfors – *Bekas* (1919, 1920 sold to Chile, *Orompello*), *Golub* (1917, captured by the Germans 4.18, commissioned as *Beo*, 11.18 to Finland, (Uusimaa, Kulik (1919, 1920 sold to Chile, *Elicura), Pingvin* (1917, taken over by the Red Finns 3.18, captured by the Germans 4.18 commissioned as *Wulf*, 11.18 to Finland, *Hameemaa)*
Sandvikens Yd, Helsingfors – *Chibis* (1919, 1920 sold to Chile, *Colocolo*), *Strizh* (1919, 1920 sold to Chile, *Leucoton*)

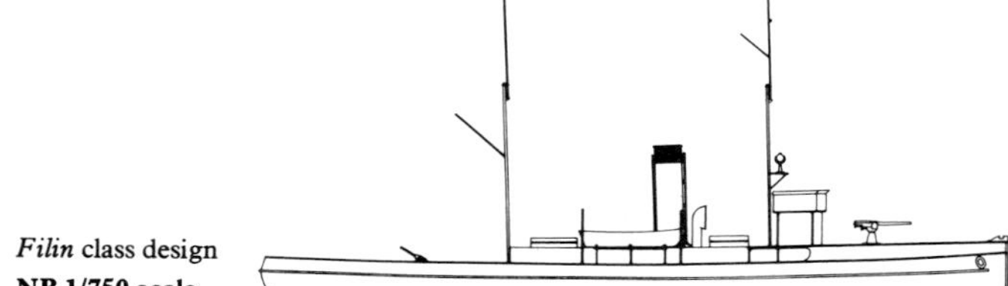

Filin class design
NB 1/750 scale

FILIN class *guard ships*

Displacement: 342t
Dimensions: 164ft × 23ft × 9ft 6in
50.0m × 7.0m × 2.9m
Machinery: 2 shafts, VTE, 2 boilers, 1150ihp = 15kts. Coal 50t
Armament: 1–75mm, 1–40mm AA

Class (launched, fate):
Crichton Yd, Abo – *Chirok* (1918, 1918 to Finland, *Turunmaa*), *Filin* (1918, 1918 to Finland, *Kariala*), *Gorlitsa* (BU incomplete), *Lun* (1919, 1921 sold to Poland, *Komendant Pilsudski*), *Sova* (BU incomplete), *Vodorez* (1919, 1921 sold to Poland, *General Haller*)

Dunai in her early years *Lemachko Collection*

BUG class *minelayers*

Displacement: 1380t
Dimensions: 204ft × 34ft × 16ft
62.2m × 10.4m × 4.9m
Machinery: 2 shafts, VTE, 4 boilers, 1400ihp = 13kts. Coal 265t
Armament: 6–47mm, 4–37mm, 250 mines
Complement: 238

Class (launched, fate):
Lindholmen Yd – *Bug* (1891, transport after 1907), *Dunai* (1891, BU 1940s)

Mine transports built for experiments with minelaying. Deployed with the Black Sea Fleet, rated as minelayers after 1907. *Bug* scuttled at Sevastopol in 1905 during the mutiny aboard *Potemkin* to prevent an accidental explosion of mines, raised in 1907. *Dunai* rearmed with 2–75mm, 4–47mm, 4 MG during the First World War. Renamed *1 Maya c*1922.

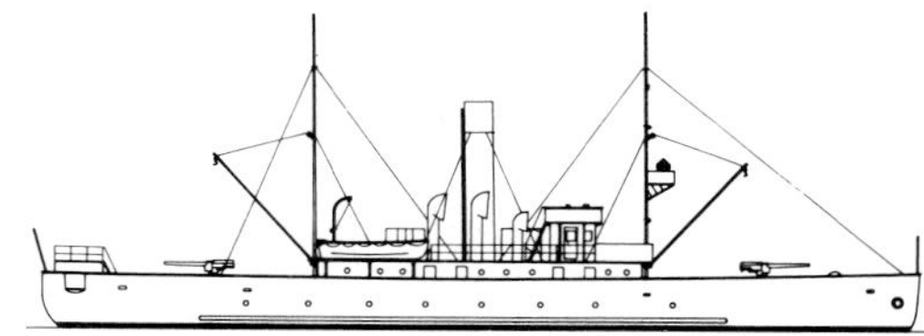

Voin 1918
NB 1/750 scale

VOIN *minelayer*

Displacement: 640t
Dimensions: 164ft × 26ft × 9ft
50.0m × 8.0m × 2.7m
Machinery: 800ihp = 10kts
Armament: 2–75mm, 150 mines
Complement: 47

Class (launched, fate):
Kolomna Yd, Moscow – *Voin* (launched 1916, 1918 to Finland, *M 1* then *Louhi*, mined 21.1.45)

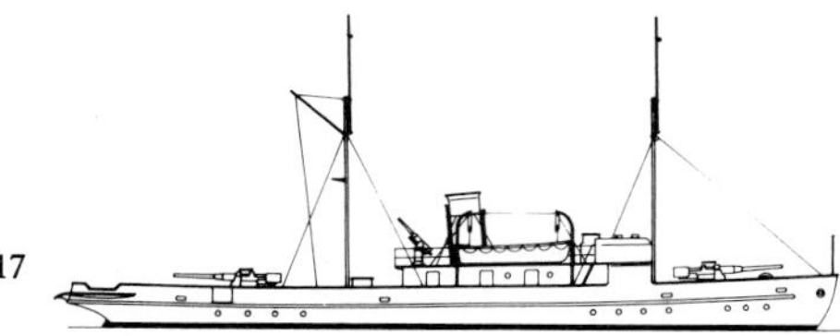

Prypyet (ex-*Demosfen*) 1917
NB 1/750 scale

DEMOSFEN class *netlayers*

Displacement: 320t–338t
Machinery: Diesel engine, 8kts–11kts
Armament: 1–75mm (*Pripyat* 2–4in), 1–75mm AA, 90–100 mines

Class (fate):
Iset, Kivach, Klyazma, Kuban, Luga (1918 to Finland), *Pripyat* (ex-*Demosfen*, 1902 – converted merchantmen), *Sejm, Selenga, Terek*

A class of 8 netlayers all launched in 1917 for service with the Baltic Fleet.

BEREZINA class *netlayers*

Displacement: 380t normal; 450t full load
Dimensions: 165ft 6in × 54ft 9in × 6ft 6in
50.5m × 16.7m × 2.0m
Machinery: Diesel engines, 600bhp = 8.5kts
Armament: 2–4in (102mm), 1–75mm AA, 2 MG, 100 mines

Class (launched):
Kolomenskaya Yd, Kolomna – *Berezina* (1917), *Yauza* (1917)

Baltic Fleet ships, fates unknown.

Gruz during the war *Author's Collection*

INDIGIRKA class *netlayers*

Displacement: 220t
Machinery: Diesel engine, 9kts
Armament: 2–75mm, 85 mines

Class (launched, fate):
Nizhnegorodski Teplokhod Wks – *Mologa* (1917, 1918 to Finland), *Indigirka* (1917).
Baltic Fleet

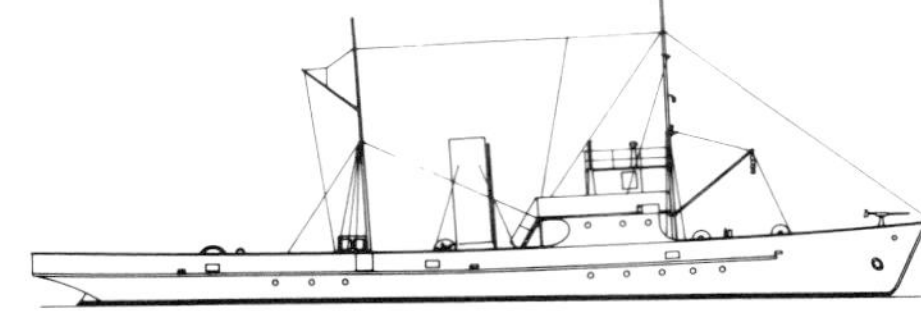

Vzryv about 1915
NB 1/750 scale

FUGAS class *minesweepers*

Displacement: 150t
Dimensions: 148ft × 20ft × 6ft 3in
45.1m × 6.1m × 1.9m
Machinery: 2 shaft, 2 DE, 2 boilers, 400ihp = 11.5kts
Armament: 1–63mm, 50 mines
Complement: 33

Class (launched, fate):
Fugas (1910, mined 22.11.16 off Suurop), *Minrep* (1910, deleted 1930s), *Provodnik* (1910, mined 27.8.14 off Takhora), *Vzryv* (1910, mined 26.5.16 off Russarö Island), *Zapal* (1910, mined 8.40 off Cape Juminda).

Baltic Fleet. The first minesweepers of the world built by Izhora Yd, St Petersburg especially for experiments. Fitted with a main mast during the First World War. *Zapal* was rebuilt at Kronstadt Drydock in 1932 and rearmed with 1–3in, 1–45mm AA, 2 MG.

ALBATROS class *minesweepers*

Displacement: 106t
Dimensions: 85ft × 17ft 6in × 5ft
25.9m × 5.3m × 1.5m
Machinery: 1 shaft, steam engines, 2 boilers, 137ihp = 8.7kts
Armament: 2–37mm
Complement: 31

Patron as completed *Lemachko Collection*

T 13 in British service *Twardowski Collection*

Class (launched):
Bellino-Fenderich Yd, Odessa – *Albatros* (1910), *Bakan* (1910)
Black Sea Fleet ships, fates unknown.

GRUZ class *minesweepers*

Displacement: 248t
Draught: 4ft 6in
1.4m
Machinery: 2 shafts, 2 TE, 2 boilers, 650ihp = 9kts
Armament: 1–75mm, 1–37mm, 64 mines

Class (launched, fate):
Putilov Yd, Petrograd – *Gruz* (1916, 1918–22 Finnish *MP 7*, returned, BU 1930s), *Kapsyul* (1916, 1918–1922 Finnish *T 14*, returned, BU 1930s)
Russo-Baltic Yd, Reval – *Krambol* (1916, 1918–22 Finnish *MP 11*, returned, BU 1930s), *Shchit* (1916, mined 6.12.16 off Ozylia on mines of *UC 25*)

Part of the 1912 Programme for the Baltic Fleet.

PATRON class *minesweepers*

Displacement: 445t normal; 500t full load
Dimensions: 140ft × 24ft 6in × 13ft
42.7m × 7.5m × 3.9m
Machinery: 1 shaft, TE, 2 boilers, 520ihp = 11.5kts
Armament: 1–75mm

Class (launched, fate):
Smith Dock, Middlesborough – *Iskra* (1913, mined 6.10.16 off Hangö), *Patron* (1913, BU 1930s), *Plamya* (1913, 1918–22 Finnish *Altair*, returned, renamed *Izhora*, 1925 mercantile)

Tugs designated for the Siberian Flotilla but they remained in the Baltic. Converted to minesweepers in 1915.

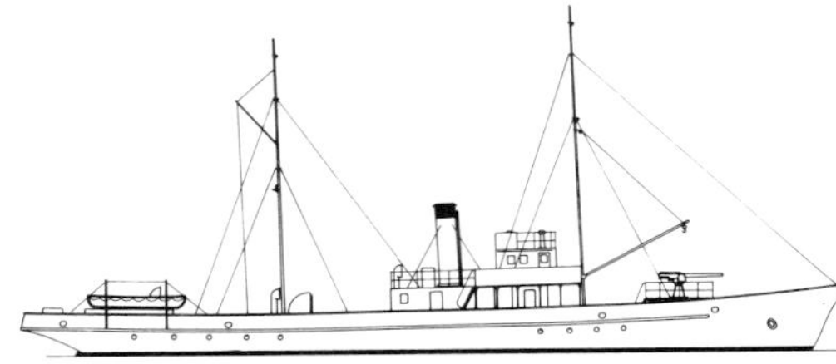

Fortral 1918
NB 1/750 scale

ZASHCHITNIK class *minesweepers*

Displacement: 190t
Dimensions: 147ft 6in × 20ft 4in × 5ft 6in
45.0m × 6.2m × 1.7m
Machinery: TE, 550ihp = 12kts
Armament: 1–75mm, 30 mines
Complement: 35

Class (launched, fate):
Putilov Yd, Petrograd – *Udarnik* (1916, mined 2.10.42), *Zashchitnik* (1916, 1918 to Finland, *T 2*, then *Vilpula*)
Ahlström Yd, Björneberg – *Fortral* (1917, 1918 to Finland, *Rautu*), *Klyuz* (1916, mined 24.11.42)

Part of the 1912 Programme for the Baltic Fleet. Further boats of this type were ordered in the Metal Wks, Petrograd and Russo-Baltic Yd, Reval. *Klyuz* and *Udarnik* rebuilt at Kronstadt Drydock in 1937, rearmed with 1–3in, 1–45mm AA, 2 MG.

T 13 class *minesweeping trawlers*

Displacement: 520t (*T 19* (ii) 540t)
Dimensions: 130ft pp (*T 19* (ii) 135ft 6in) × 23ft 6in × 12ft
39.6m (41.1m) × 7.2m × 3.7m
Machinery: 1 shaft, VTE, 1 boiler, 490ihp = 10.5kts. Coal 180t
Armament: 1–3in, 1 MG
Complement: 32

Class (launched, fate):
Smith Dock, Middlesborough – *T 13* (1916, 1918 to Britain, *Goldaxe*), *T 14* (1916, 1918 to Britain, *Stoneaxe*), *T 15* (1916, sunk 2.8.18, raised, deleted 1923), *T 16* (1916, 1918 to Britain *Battleaxe*), *T 17* (1916, 1918 to Britain, *Iceaxe*), *T 18* (1916, lost 18.3.17), *T 19* (i) (1916, stranded before commissioning 3.10.16), *T 20* (1916, 1918 to France, *T 20*), *T 21* (1916, deleted 1923), *T 22* (1916, 1918 to France, *Commandant Vergoignan*), *T 23* (1916, deleted 1923), *T 24* (1916, deleted 1923)
Cochrane Yd, Selby – *T 19* (ii) (1917, replacement for *T 19* (i), 1918 to Britain, *Poleaxe*)

Britain built 13 trawler minesweepers for Russia's Arctic Ocean Flotilla.

Nikolson type MTB 1906
NB 1/750 scale

NIKOLSON type *MTBs*

Displacement: 35t
Dimensions: 90ft × 12ft × 5ft
27.4m × 3.7m × 1.5m
Machinery: 2 shafts, 2 gasoline engines, 600bhp = 20kts
Armament: 1–47mm, 2 MG, 1–18in (457mm) TT
Complement: 11

Class (fate):
No 1 (deleted *c*1950), *No 2* (deleted 1940), *No 3* (deleted 1924), *No 4* (deleted 1929), *No 5* (deleted 1940), *No 6* (deleted 1929), *No 7* (deleted 1940), *No 8* (deleted 1924), *No 9* (deleted 1940), *No 10* (deleted 1924).

Ordered in August 1904 from the US firm Flint and Co, assembled by the Sevastopol Admiralty Drydock in 1905. Designated for the Far Eastern station but transferred to the Baltic Fleet after conclusion of the Russo-Japanese War. *No 2–No 10* laid up during 1911–14 because of shortage of petrol. Once again laid up in 1921 some of them were reactivated in 1937, re-engined and rearmed as submarine chasers. *No 1* served during the Second World War as *MO 312*.

SKA 1 type motor launch in the Baltic *Lemachko Collection*

SK 311 and *SK 318* during the war *Lemachko Collection*

SKA series *motor launches*

Class (fate):
SKA 1–SKA 12

A 35t series by Zolotov Yd, Petrograd delivered 1916 to the Baltic Fleet. *SKA 10* (lost 1.12.16), *one* (number unknown, 1918 to Finland).

SK series *motor launches*

Displacement: 14t
Speed: 24kts
Armament: 1–47mm, 2 MG

Class (fate):
SK 311–317, SK 321–SK 327, SK 331–337, SK 341–SK 347

Total of 18 delivered by US firms, (assembly Revenski Yd, Odessa) in 1915 for the Black Sea Fleet, further batch ordered 1916. *SK 313* was lost in July 1917. *SK 324* converted to a MTB in summer 1917 with 1–15in (381mm) TT firing diagonally to port.

MN 1–MN 18 *motor launches*

Ordered in US, delivered for the Arctic Ocean Flotilla.

No 511 series *motor launches*

Displacement: 20t
Dimensions: 60ft × 10ft × 4ft
18.3m × 3.1m × 1.2m
Machinery: 2 shafts, 2 gasoline engines, 250bhp = 12kts
Armament: 2 MG

Class:
511–518, 521–528, 531–538, 541–547

Ordered 1916 from US firms, assembly contracted to the Revenski Yd, Odessa. Designated for the Black Sea Fleet, unknown number completed for the Imperial Russian Navy. One seized by the Austro-Hungarian forces in 1918.

BK series *motor launches*

Displacement: 25t
Dimensions: 50ft × 10ft × 2ft 6in
15.3m × 3.1m × 0.8m
Machinery: 2 shafts, 2 gasoline engines, 200bhp = 10kts
Armament: 2 MG

Class:
BK 1–BK 12

Ordered 1916 for the Black Sea Fleet and built by Revenski Yd, Odessa – *BK 7* (lost July 1917), two seized by the Autro-Hungarian forces in 1918 and two completed for Austria-Hungary, 1918.

TEPLOKHOD class *motor minelayers*

Displacement: 80t
Dimensions: 68ft 9in × 15ft 3in × 4ft
22.0m × 4.6m × 1.2m
Machinery: 1 shaft, diesel engine, 80bhp = 9kts. Oil fuel 1.25t
Armament: 1–47mm, 80 mines
Complement: 10

Class, fate):
Pori Yd, Finland – *T 1* (1918 to Finland, *T 22*, to be returned 1922), *T 2* (1918 to Estonia), *T 3* (1918 to Estonia), *T 4–T 7* (1918 to Finland, *T 21, T 15, T 16, M 7* respectively, then *Loimu, Paukku, Leska* and *Pommi*), *T 8* (1918 to Estonia, *Kalev* then *Vaindlo*, 1940 seized by the Soviets, became dispatch vessel 1942), *T 9* (1918 to Estonia), *T 10* (1918 to Estonia, *Olev* then *Keri*, 1940 seized by the Soviets, scuttled 27.8.41).

Ten small minelayers launched 1914–16.

MT type motor minesweeper as completed
NB 1/750 scale

MT series *motor minesweepers*

Displacement: 25t (29t, *M 10* on)
Dimensions: 50ft pp × 11ft 6in
15.3m × 3.5m
Machinery: 1 shaft, gasoline engine, 50bhp = 9kts (12.5kts *M 10* on)
Armament: 1 MG
Complement: 8

Class (fate):
Andre Rozenkvist Yd, Abo – *MT 1* (lost 30.11.17), *MT 2* (1918 to Finland, *AF 2*), *MT 3* (1918 to Finland, *AF 3*), *MT 4* (1918 to Finland), *MT 5–MT 9* (incomplete seized 1918 by the Finns).
Botnia Yd, Abo – *MT 10* (1918 to Finland), *MT 11* (lost 7.17), *MT 12–MT 13* (1918 to Finland), *MT 14* (lost 30.11.17), *MT 15–MT 18* (1918 to Finland).

Ordered in 1917 for the Baltic Fleet.

A class *motor minesweepers*

Displacement: 13t–21t

Class:
Crichton Yd, Abo – *A 10–A 45*

Ordered 1916–17 for the Baltic Fleet. *A 11, A 12, A 19–A 21, A 37–A 45* remained in Finland in 1918 and commissioned under the same numbers.
Note: There was also a class of 12 50t motor minesweepers, ordered from the Krogius Yd, Helsingfors, designated for the Baltic Fleet. Only 4 completed for the Whites in 1919.

Pika 1918
NB 1/750 scale

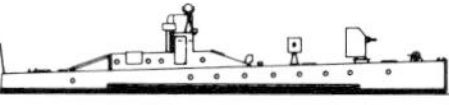

PULYA class *river motor gunboats*

Displacement: 23.5t normal; 25t full load
Dimensions: 72ft × 10ft 6in × 2ft 4in
22.0m × 3.2m × 0.7m
Machinery: 2 shafts, 2 gasoline engines, 200bhp = 14.5kts
Armament: 1–75mm, 2 MG
Complement: 10

Class (fate):
Kope (deleted 1940s), *Pika* (deleted 1940s), *Kindzhal, Rapira, Sablya, Shtyk* (the 4 latter were transferred to the Black Sea, 1915), *Palash, Pistolet, Pulya, Shashka* (the 4 latter were transferred to the Baltic, 1916, to Finland 1918, became *BVA, BVB, BVC, BVD*).

Built by Putilov Yd, St Petersburg, launched 1910 and transferred to the Amur Flotilla.

1915 PROGRAMME ARMY RIVER CRAFT
At the beginning of 1915 the River Shipbuilding Programme was authorised and provided for completion of 3 fast armoured river flotillas by 1917 to support Army Units. The programme was to be financed by the Army and the boats manned by troops.

The following types were taken under consideration and ordered shortly afterwards: 9 24t AMGBs, 18 15t AMBs and 18 6.5t AMBs which formed the backbone of these flotillas. This was supplemented by 18 16t dispatch MBs, 12 MSBs, 750 motor pontoons and 30 24ft armoured LCs. Draught of these vessels was not to exceed 2ft and their dimensions had to allow transportation by railroads.

Unlike the Naval Programmes, this one was completed promptly by early 1917 and the boats distributed between Army flotillas on the Pripet Marshes, Lakes Onega and Ilmen, and the Duma and Volga rivers. Most of those remaining in the hands of the Reds were transferred to naval control during the Civil War.

Model 1916 armoured motor gunboat as completed
NB 1/750 scale

Model 1916 *river armoured motor gunboats*

Displacement:	24t
Dimensions:	67ft oa, 66ft lw × 10ft 6in × 2ft *20.4m, 20.2m × 3.2m × 0.6m*
Machinery:	2 shafts, 2 Bufallo gasoline engines, 150bhp = 12.5kts
Armament:	2–75mm, 2 MG
Complement:	*C*12

Nine completed by 1917, builder Bekker and Co Yd, Reval.

Model 1916 armoured motor boat 1917
NB 1/750 scale

Model 1916 *river armoured motor boats*

Displacement:	15t
Dimensions:	52ft 6in oa × 10ft × 2ft *16.0m × 3.1m × 0.6m*
Machinery:	2 shafts, 2 Stirling gasoline engines, 100bhp = 11.5kts
Armament:	2 MG

Four completed by Bjoneborg Wks, Borgo and 14 by Revenskij Yd, Odessa.

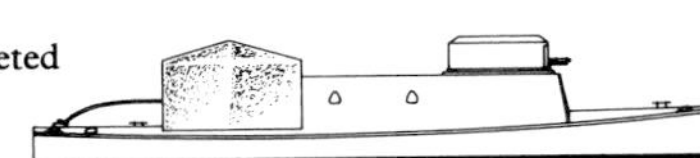
N type armoured motor boat as completed
NB 1/200 scale

N type *river armoured motor boats*

Displacement:	6.5t
Dimensions:	30ft × 8ft × 2ft *9.2m × 2.4m × 0.6m*
Machinery:	1 shaft, 1 Stirling gasoline engine, 97.5bhp = 11kts
Armament:	1 MG

Eighteen delivered from USA by 1917.

MISCELLANEOUS

ELPIDIFOR type *landing ships* (built 1917–27)

Displacement:	1050t
Dimensions:	250ft × 34ft × 6ft *74.6m × 10.4m × 1.8m*
Machinery:	2 shafts, 2 VTE, 600ihp = 10kts
Armament:	2–4.7in (120mm), 250 mines

Class (fate):
Naval-Russud Yd, Nikolayev – *No 410–No 412* (captured by the Germans 4.18), commissioned as *FD 20, FD 25, FD 26*, surrendered to the Allies 11.19, transferred to Wrangel's fleet 11.19, sold 1924), *No 413* (*Krasnaya Abkhaziya* since 1921, damaged 12.43, became survey vessel *Kursograf*), *No 414* (*Krasnayi Adzaristan* since 1921, deleted late 1940s), *No 415* (beached 9.1.21 after shelled by French destroyers), *No 416* (*Krasnyi Krym* since 1921, renamed *Krasnaya Armeniya* 1930, lost 22.9.41), *No 417* (*Krasnaya Gruziya* since 1921, lost 28.2.43), *No 418* (1921 mercantile tanker *Vasili Fomin*), *No 419* (1921 mercantile tanker *Aleksandr Emshanov*), *No 420* (mercantile tanker *Berezan*), *No 421* (mercantile tanker *Tendra*), *No 422* (naval oil barge *Krasnaya Moldaviya*), *No 423* (general cargo *Volgo-Don*), *No 424–No 427* (completed 1927 as mercantile coal carriers), *No 428–No 429* (BU incomplete 1920s), *No 430–No 439* (cancelled 9.17).

Authorised in 1917 for the Black Sea Fleet. A total of 30 were ordered 23.2.17 to a design based on a typical coastal Azov Sea lighter *Elpidifor*. Four holds were arranged and two 20ft booms as well as minesweeping gear was fitted. Their chief role was to land troops on beaches. This was done with help of 2 gangplanks overhung above the bow and operated by the bowsprit boom. Moreover they could be employed as minesweepers, minelayers, cargo transports, rescue vessels, etc. The 4 renamed by the Soviets in 1921 were rearmed later and served during the Second World War as gunboats with 3–130mm, 2–3in AA, 2–45mm AA, 2–37mm AA, 5 MG.

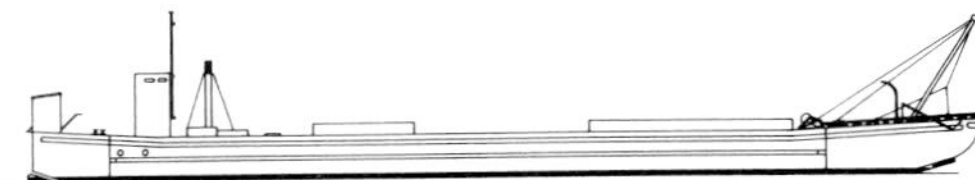
Russud type landing craft as completed
NB 1/750 scale

RUSSUD type *landing craft*

Displacement:	225t
Dimensions:	179ft 6in oa × 140ft wl × 21ft 6in × 4ft *54.7m, 42.7m × 6.6m × 1.2m*
Machinery:	2 shafts, 2 diesel engines, 80bhp–100bhp = 5.5kts
Armament:	None (see notes)
Complement:	8

Class (built):
Russud Yd, Nikolayev – *No 1–No 50* (1915–16)

In the 1915 Emergency Programme, designated for the Black Sea Fleet. Ordered on 2 December 1915, could carry 520 men in hold and 240 on the deck. They were embarked on beach by the bow ramp lowered with help of a pair of bow booms. Because of lack of diesels the craft numbered *No 11–No 24, No 27, No 30, No 33–No 36, No 41–No 50* were not fitted with any propulsion. Most of them were fitted later with MG mountings while 6 were fitted with 1–6in and lesser guns and served as the river gunboats with Danube Flotilla being renumbered *K 1–K 6*.

Served on both sides during the Civil War, *No 4–No 7* converted by the Reds into floating batteries and renamed *Revolyutsiva*, *25 Oktyabrya*, *Sverdlov* and *Marat* respectively. Converted to mercantile service after hostilities.

Krasnaya Abkhaziya (ex-*No 413*) in the 1920s
Lemachko Collection

Kommuna (ex-*Volkhov*) *Twardowski Collection*

VOLKHOV *submarine salvage vessel*

Displacement: 2400t
Dimensions: 315ft × 43ft 4in × 12ft
96.0m × 13.2m × 3.7m
Machinery: 2 shafts, 2 diesel engines, 1200bhp = 10kts

Name	Builder	Launched	Fate
VOLKHOV	Putilov Yd, St Petersburg	30.11.13	Extant 1982

Design based on the German *Vulkan* built in 1907. Catamaran hull type with 4 lifts of total capacity of 1000t. Commissioned on 27 July 1915, renamed *Kommuna* in 1923, modernised after the Second World War and transferred to the Black Sea Fleet.

DOZORNY class *dispatch vessels*

Displacement: 100t
Dimensions: 101ft × 16ft 6in × 5ft 6in
30.8m × 5.0m × 1.7m
Machinery: 1 shaft, VTE, 600ihp = 16kts
Armament: 1–37mm, 1 MG
Complement: 23

Class (built, fate):
Crichton-Vulkan Yd, Turku – *Dozorny* (1904, deleted 1950s), *Razvedchik* (1904, ?lost 1942).

Razvedchik as completed *Lemachko Collection*

KONVOIR class *dispatch vessels*

Displacement: 211t
Dimensions: 121ft × 20ft × 6ft
37.0m × 6.1m × 1.8m
Machinery: 1 shaft, VTE, 1 boiler, 500ihp = 12kts. Coal 80t
Armament: 1–75mm
Complement: 20

Class (launched, fate):
Crichton Yd, St Petersburg, taken over by Kronstadt Drydock for completion – *Konvoir* (6.7.12, sunk 5.17), *Sputnik* (11.7.12, captured by the Germans 2.18, commissioned as *Lauterbach*, 11.18 to Estonia, *Laine*)

BARSUK class *dispatch vessels*

Displacement: 168t
Dimensions: 100ft × 19ft × 6ft 10in
30.5m × 5.8m × 2.7m
Machinery: 1 shaft, VTE, 1 boiler, 350ihp = 11kts
Armament: 1–75mm, 1–40mm AA

Class (launched, fate):
Lehtonemi Yd, Finland – *Barsuk* (ex-*O 1*, 1915, stranded 19.10.17); *Gronostaj* (ex-*O 4*, 1916, to Caspian 1918, mercantile tanker since 1924); *Khorek* (ex-*O 6*, 1916, to Caspian 1918, deleted 1930s); *Kunitsa* (ex-*O 2*, 1916, Onega Flotilla 1919, to Caspian 1920, renamed *Mogilevski*, deleted 1950s); *Laska* (ex-*O 5*, 1916, Onega Flotilla 1919, to Caspian 1929, deleted 1930s); *Sobol* (ex-*O 6*, 1916, to Caspian 1918, mercantile tanker since 1924); *Vydra* (ex-*O 7*, 1916, Onega Flotilla 1919, to Caspian 1920, deleted 1930s)

AUXILIARY WARSHIPS

AUXILIARY MINELAYERS/NETLAYERS

THE BALTIC FLEET 1914–1917
Name (launched/displacement/speed/armament, commissioned/fate):
Bureya (ex-*Matros*, 1915/250t/12kts/95 mines, 10.16/1918 to Germany).
Dyuna (1868/594t/8kts, 5.16).
Ilmen (ex-*Sofia Scharlotta*, 1912/2160t/12kts/2–3in, 400 mines, 7.15/1918 German *Preussen*).
Irtysh (ex-*Konovod*, 1916/230t/12kts/95 mines, 10.16).
Khoper (ex-*Konstantin*, 1866/1100t/11kts, 5.16).
Lena (2400t/12kts/370 mines).
Lovat (ex-*No 3*, ex-*Runo*, 1912/600t/9kts/80 mines, 10.15).
Msta (ex-*Russland*, 1883/1955t/8kts/360 mines, 6.16/1918 German *Russland*).
Mologa (ex-*No 21*, ex-*Sinemorets*, 1903/450t/11kts/80 mines; 8.15/lost 14.6.16).
Ob (ex-*Orion*, 1905/780t, 1918 to Finland).
Sheksna (ex-*No 20*, ex-*Anastasiya*, 1904/450t/12kts/80 mines, 7.15/1918 to Germany).
Svir (ex-*Virgilia*, 1911/1800t/10kts/2–3in, 550 mines, 6.16/1918 to Germany).
Terek (ex-*Oranienbaum*, ex-*Olivia*, 5.16).
Ural (ex-*Fert*, ex-*Etel Frederich*, 2400t/10.5kts/4–3in, 360 mines, 6.15).
Zeya (ex-*Burlak*, 1915/250t/12kts/95 mines, 10.16/lost 1918).

THE BLACK SEA FLEET 1914–1917
Name (launched/displacement/speed/armament, commissioned/fate):
Ayu-Dag (1898/1765t/9kts, 1.16).
Beshtau (1907/1120t/10kts/2–3in, 100 mines, 9.14/1916 became transport).
Dikhtau (1907/1110t/7.5kts/2–3in, 120 mines, 9.14/1916 became transport).
Elborus (1893/1050t/9kts, 1.16/1917 renamed *Chorokh*).
General Brusilov (11.16).
General Ruzitski (1916/400grt/11kts, 9.16).
Gidra (1889/300t/9kts, 12.16).
Kiev (1.17).
Mina (1913/180t/10kts/80 mines, 6.16),
Oleg (11.14/lost 24.12.14).
Penaj (Nov 1914).
Titaniya (1879/128t/9kts, 9.16).
Tsesarevich Georgi (1896/1130t/14kts/1–6in howitzer, 3–75mm, 1–37mm AA, 280 mines, 9.14).
Velikaya Knyazinyà Kseniya (1895/2700t/14kts/1–6in howitzer, 3–75mm, 2–37mm AA, 160 mines, 8.14).
Veliki Knyaz Aleksei (1890/2400t/14kts/1–6in howitzer, 3–75mm, 1–37mm AA, 200 mines, 8.14).
Veliki Knyaz Konstantin (1891/2500t/13kts/1–6in howitzer, 3–75mm, 1–37mm AA, 200 mines, 9.14/sold 1924).

THE SIBERIAN FLOTILLA 1911–1917
Name (launched/displacement/speed/armament, commissioned/fate):
Monogugai (ex-*Prouto*, 1891/2500t/9kts/7–47mm, 310 mines, 1911/transport 1916).
Shika (ex-*Erika*, 1897/3500t/11kts/4–4.7 (120mm), 8–75mm, 4 MG, 500 mines, 1911).
Ussuri (ex-*5*, ex-*Lyutsun*, 1901/3200t/10.5kts/3–4.7in (120mm), 4–47mm, 2 MG, 500 mines, 1911/1916 transferred to Arctic, lost 1.8.18).

Irtysh during the war *Lemachko Collection*

AUXILIARY MINESWEEPERS

THE BALTIC FLEET 1914–1917

Name (launched/displacement/speed, fate):
No 1 (ex-*Linnea*, 1892/450t/10kts, mined 16.9.15).
No 2 (ex-*Van Doebbeln*, 570t/11kts, 1918 to Finland).
No 3 (i) (ex-*Runo*, 1912/600t/9kts, 10.15 minelayer *Lovat*).
No 3 (ii) (ex-*Rus*, 1875/245t, 1918 to Finland).
No 4 (i) (ex-*Dagoe*, 600t/9kts, lost 23.10.15).
No 4 (ii) (ex-*Ajax*, 1894/1100t/10kts).
No 4 (iii) (ex-*Miner*, 1914/200t, 1918 to Estonia).
No 5 (ex-*Ryurik*, 580t/10kts, mined 27.5.16).
No 6 (ex-*Stella*, 1889/700t/8kts, lost 22.8.15).
No 7 (i) (ex-*No 10*, ex-*Triton*, 1890/590t/9kts, mined 22.9.14).
No 7 (ii) (ex-*Vulkan*, 1904/700t/8.5kts, 1918 German *Vulkan*).
No 8 (i) (ex-*No 2*, ex-*Moon*, 600t/9kts, mined 22.9.14).
No 8 (ii) (ex-*Andromeda*, 1910/700t/8.5kts, 1918 German *Andromeda*).
No 9 (ex-*Ceres*, 1911/700t/9kts).
No 10 (ex-*Priamus*, 1911/700t/8.5kts, 1918 German *Priamus*).
No 11 (ex-*Bolid*, ex-*Fedra*, 1898/800t/8.5kts).
No 12 (ex-*Diana*, 1901/600t/8.5kts).
No 14 (ex-*Lebedyank*, 140t/10kts).
No 15 (ex-*Volsk*, 140t/13kts, 1918 to Finland).
No 16 (ex-*Gruzin*, 140t/8.8kts, 1918 to Finland).
No 17 (ex-*Amerikanets*, 140t/10.5kts, 1918 to Finland).
No 18 (ex-*Apostol Petr*, 1906/499t/13.5kts, 1918 Estonian *Ristna*).
No 19 (ex-*Apostol Pavel*, 1906/501/13kts, 1918 Estonian *Suurop*).
No 20 (ex-*Anastasiya*, 1904/450t/12kts, 7.15 minelayer *Sheksna*).
No 21 (ex-*Sinemorets*, 1903/450t/11kts, 8.15 minelayer *Mologa*).
No 22 (ex-*Aleksej*, 750t/12kts, stranded 11.17).
No 23 (ex-*Vaza*, 1882/800t/10kts).
No 24 (ex-*Adolf Age*, 150t/9kts, renamed *Shchit* 1920).
Alesha Popovich (1913/350t/8kts, 1918 to Finland).
Dobrynya (1911/325t/11kts, 1918 to Finland).
Dulo (1915/100t/9.5kts, 1918 to Finland).
Garpun (ex-*Ronashill*, 1915/310t/10kts).
Ilya Muromets (1910/330t/12.5kts, mined 23.8.17).
Kitoboj (ex-*Erris*, 1915/310t/10kts, fleed to Allies 13.6.19).
Kometa (ex-*Ebba Munck*, 1888/322t, 1918 to Finland).
Mikula (1911/300t/11kts, 1918–1922 Finland).
Namet (ex-*Mäy*, 1915/310t/10kts).
Nevod (ex-*Carsten Bury*, 1915/310t/10kts).
Planeta (i) (ex-*Aura I*, 1858/287t, patrol ship *Pregrada*).
Planeta (ii) (ex-*Yakor*, ex-*Aura II*, 1893/134t, 1918 to Finland).
Potok Bogatyr (1913/370t/11kts, 1918 to Finland).
Stvol (1915/100t/9.5kts, 1918 to Finland).
Svyatogor (1911/400t/11.8kts, 1918 to Latvia).
Tsapfa (1915/145t/9.5kts, 1918 to Finland).
Tumba (1915/145t/9.5kts, 1918 to Finland).
Yakor (ex-*Rio Cunene*, 1915/400t/10kts).

THE BLACK SEA FLEET 1914–1917

Name (launched/displacement/speed, fate):
T 211 (ex-*Dunaj*, 682t).
T 220 (ex-*Anna D*, 1100t).
T 221 (ex-*Kefaloniya*, 1904/894t/9kts).
T 222 (ex-*Helvetia*, 1905/623t/9kts).
T 223 (ex-*Giuseppe*, 1905/776t/8.5kts).
T 224 (ex-*Aspaziya*, 1896/783t/8kts).
T 225 (ex-*Lela*, 1897/783t/11kts, became gunboat *III Internatsional* 1919).
T 226 (ex-*T 249*, ex-*Trud*, 1914/613t/8kts).
T 227 (ex-*Vanya*, 1904/644t/7.5kts).
T 228 (ex-*Energiya*, 1891/690t/8kts).
T 229 (ex-*Diamantidi*, 1895/650t/9kts).
T 230 (ex-*Elpidifor*, 1905/671t/10kts).
T 231 (ex-*Volga*).
T 232 (ex-*Sosiek*, 1910/579t/10kts).
T 231 (i) (ex-*Enriketta*, stranded 1916).
T 233 (ii) (ex-*T 294*, ex-*Julia*, 1883/426t/7.5kts).
T 234 (ex-*Roza*, 1910/510t/8kts).
T 235 (ex-*Prorok Iona*, 1896/472t/8.5kts).
T 236 (ex-*Fedor Fedofani*, 1904/537/8kts).
T 237 (ex-*Afanasi Fedofani*, 1904/530t/8kts).
T 238 (ex-*Janetta*, 1915/519t/9kts).
T 239 (ex-*Olimpiada*, 1911/551t/9kts).
T 240 (ex-*Mariya*, 295t/9kts).
T 242 (ex-*Poleznyi*, 1887/800t/10kts).
T 246 (ex-*Danaj*, 215t, became dispatch vessel).
T 247 (ex-*Uspekh*, 1872/400t).
T 248 (ex-*Yakov*, 1883/800t/7.5kts).
T 249 (ex-*T 295*, ex-*Sofiya*, 800t).
T 250 (ex-*Sofiya Pustovojtova*, 515t, lost 10.3.16).
T 251 (ex-*Victoria*, 1891/510t/7.5kts).
T 252 (i) (ex-*Berdyanik*, lost 1916).
T 252 (ii) (ex-*Olga*).
T 253 (ex-*Marietta*, 500t).
T 254 (ex-*Churubash*, 100t).
T 255 (ex-*Borisfen*, 200t).
T 256 (ex-*Berezan*, 100t).
T 257 (ex-*Skif*, 100t).
T 258 (ex-*Jazon*, 100t/9kts).
T 259 (ex-*Ueri*, 1877/180t/9kts).
T 260 (ex-*Adolf*, 1910/590t/9.5kts).
T 261 (ex-*Georgij*, 1910/453t/9kts).
T 262 (ex-*Edvard*, 1896/328t/8kts).
T 263 (i) (ex-*Fani Kuppa*, 1895/328t/4kts, deleted 1917).
T 263 (ii) (ex-*Amalia*, became gunboat *Chervonyj Kazak*).
T 264 (ex-*Sofia Kuppa*, 1890/281t/7.5kts).
T 265 (ex-*Elena Kuppa*, 1893/318t/7.5kts).
T 266 (ex-*Khorlynets*, 1902/225t/10kts).
T 272 (ex-*Nikolai*).
T 273 (ex-*Dobrovolets*, 1913/102t/10kts).
T 274 (ex-*Kafa*, 82t).
T 280 (ex-*T 282*, ex-*Anna*, 201t).
T 281 (ex-*Anatra*, 1871/100t/8kts).
T 282 (ex-*Test*, 1883/173t/7kts).
T 283 (ex-*Pandiya*, 1874/500t/7kts).
T 290 (ex-*T 241*, ex-*Smelyj*, 1895/470t/12kts).
T 291 (ex-*T 243*, ex-*Delfin*, 1895/490t/8kts).
T 292 (ex-*T 244*, ex-*Rabotnik*, 1896/300t/9kts).
T 293 (ex-*T 245*, ex-*Dmitrij Geroj*, 1901/480t/10kts).
Batum (1273t), *Kharaks* (1324t), *Khersonets* (1324t), *Mechta* (2792t), *Rossiya* (1573t), *Truvor* (2629t), *Vesta* (ex-*Amalia*, 1273t), *Vityaz* (1845t).

THE ARCTIC OCEAN FLOTILLA 1914–1917

Name (launched/displacement/speed, fate):
T 1 (ex-*Fisk 1*, 1909/219t/10kts, 1918 to Britain, returned).
T 2 (ex-*Fisk 2*, 1907/215t/10kts, 1918 to Britain, returned).
T 3 (ex-*Russel*, 1912/242t/10kts, 1918 to Britain, returned).
T 4 (ex-*Hubro*, 1912/320t/8kts, 1920 surveying ship *Mezen*).
T 5 (ex-*Sprät*, 1912/225t/10kts, deleted 1923).
T 6 (ex-*Vostok*, 1899/220t/11kts, 1918 British *Greataxe*).
T 7 (ex-*Velmozha*, 1908/104t/9.5kts, deleted 1923).
T 8 (i) (ex-*Antoni*, 1894/351t/8.5kts, became transport 6.16).
T 8 (ii) (ex-*Skum*, 1912/158t/10.5kts, deleted 1940s).
T 9 (ex-*Emma*, 1894/208t/8kts, 1918 to Norway.
T 10 (ex-*Opyt*, 1890/170t/9kts, lost 14.10.17).
T 11 (ex-*Nikolai*, 1908/300t/9kts, lost 12.17).
T 12 (ex-*Zapad*, 1908/332t, 1918 British *Steamaxe*).
T 13–T 24 (see *T 13* class minesweeping trawlers).
T 25 (ex-*Villa de Cee*, 1905/500t, deleted 1923).
T 26 (ex-*Santiago*, 1905/500t, deleted 1923).
T 27 (ex-*Erla*, 1908/500t, deleted 1923).
T 28 (ex-*Avispa*, 1908/500t, deleted 1923).
T 29 (ex-*Habana*, 1904/500t, deleted 1920).
T 30 (ex-*Once*, 1906/261t, deleted 1920).
T 31 (ex-*Uno*, 1907/195t, 1918 British *Sureaxe*).
T 32 (ex-*Dos*, 1907/195t, deleted 1920).
T 33 (ex-*Tres*, 1908/270t, 1918 British *Silveraxe*).
T 34 (ex-*Cautro*, 1908/270t, 1918 British *Firmaxe*).
T 35 (ex-*Cinco*, 1908/181t, deleted 1923).
T 36 (ex-Seis, 1910/263t, 1918 British *Coalaxe*).
T 37 (ex-*Siete*, 1911/276t, deleted 1923).
T 38 (ex-*Ocho*, 1911/275t, deleted 1922).
T 39 (ex-*Nueve*, 1907/270t, deleted 1923).
T 40 (ex-*Diez*, 1909/251t, deleted 1923).
T 41 (ex-*Atlas*, 1899/191t, 1918 British *Frostaxe*).
T 42 (ex-*Albatros*, 1899/187t, deleted 1923).
T 43 (ex-*Spy*, 1905/283t, did not reach Russian waters).
T 44 (ex-*Riple*, 1910/244t, see *T 43*).
T 45 (ex-*Foam*, 1911/244t, see *T 43*).
Aleksandra (ex-*Eos*, 1886/288t, became transport 1916).
Avans (ex-*Avance*, 1884/263t/8kts, patrol boat *Olen* 1916).
Kovda (ex-*Taurus*, 1902/1225t, dispatch vessel 7.16).
Orezund (ex-*Oresund*, 1908/195t, lost 20.12.15).
Sever (ex-*Niagara*, ex-*Satanick*, 1894/179t, lost 20.12.15).
Svyatoi Nikolai (ex-*Skandinavien*, ex-*Union*, 1858/141t/7kts, lost 20.12.15).
Vera (1903/360t/10kts, lost 20.12.15).
Yug (ex-*Teesmouth* 1906/191t, lost 10.12.15).

THE SIBERIAN FLOTILLA 1914–1917
Name (displacement, fate):
Ayaks (ex-*Nakhodka*, 190t, 1922 to Japan); *Paris* (1922 to Japan), *Patroki* (ex-*Fedrya*, 200t, 1922 to Japan), *Uliss* (1922 to Japan).

DISPATCH VESSELS/AUXILIARY DESPATCH VESSELS

THE BALTIC FLEET 1914–1917
Name (launched/displacement/speed/armament, commissioned/fate):
Abrek (1896/650t/21kts).
Astarta (1899/220t/14kts, 5.16).
Berkut (1904/325t/14.5kts, scuttled 1918).
Borivoi (August 1916).
Chajka (ex-*Regina*, 1903/1300t/12kts, 6.15).
Dyuna (1868/594t/8kts, Aug 1915/became minelayer May 1916).
Eros (1892/444t/8kts).
Gelsingfors.
Grif (ex-*Bore II*, 1898/723t, Nov 1916/scuttled 1918).
Ilza (i) (1872/588grt, Oct 1914/hulked 12.15).
Ilza (ii) (ex-*Riga*, 10.15).
Imperator Nikolai II (1898/915t/12kts, 8.15).
Kondor (1904/325t/14.5kts, scuttled 1918).
Konstantin (1866/1100t/11kts, 8.15/became minelayer 5.16).
Krechet (ex *Polaris*, 1898/2800t/12.5kts, 1915/deleted 1920s).
Kronstadt (8.14).
Luna (8.14).
Neptun (ex-*Peks*, 10.14).
Nevka (8.14).
Okhranny (ex-*Merkur*, 1897/235t, 1915/1918 to Estonia).
Oranienbaum (ex-*Olivia*, 12.15/became minelayer 5.16).
Orel (1896/126t).
Pregrada (ex-*Planeta* (i), ex-*Aura I*, 1858/287t).
Roksana (1893/95.5t.
Skatudden (1901/251t/10kts, 1907).
Ruslan (Dec 1916).
Slavnyi (Aug 1914).
Sneg (ex-*Dnestr*, 1914/248t, 1917/1918 German *Reval*).
Strazh (1874/207t/8.5kts, 1914/stranded 9.16).
Ust Narova (ex-*Gugenberg*, 1895/716grt/11kts, 10.14/1918 to Estonia).
Viola.
Voron (ex-*Ledokol No 2*).
Yastreb (ex-*Bore*, 1916/1150t/12kts/2–4in, 1916/deleted 1920s).
Zarnitsa (ex-*Foros*, 1891/1086t/14.7kts/2 guns, 6.15.
Zarya (8.14/deleted 1914).

THE BLACK SEA FLEET 1914–1917
Name (launched/displacement/speed/armament, commissioned/fate):
Graf Ignatev (510t/10kts, 9.17).
Kolchida (ex-*Tamara*, 1897/990t/14kts/3–75mm, 1913).
Nagentor (ex-*Fratelli Mendel*, 1894/200t/9kts, 7.17).
Sulin (ex-*Rumyniya*, 1898/510t/10kts, 9.17).
Odessa (202t, 10.17).
Yastreb (1911/390t/14.5kts/4–47mm).

THE ARCTIC OCEAN FLOTILLA 1914–1917
Name (launched/displacement/speed/armament, commissioned/fate):
Bakan (1898/885t/11kts/2–47mm, 2–37mm, 1914/deleted 1950s).
Edinenie (ex-*Ciprus*, 1913/914t/16kts, 6.16/lost 30.8.17).
Gorislavna (ex-*Josephine*, 1898/1650t/15kts/1–100mm, 8.16).
Inej (ex-*Chalden*, 1909/220t/11.5kts, 1.17).
Kolguchev (5.16).
Kovda (ex-*Taurus*, 1902/1225t, 1916/mined 7.8.16).
Kupava (ex-*Surendols-Fiord*, 1915/450t/12kts/1–75mm, 9.16/deleted 1950s).
Ludmila (ex-*Lady Gvendolen*, 1911/3817t/15kts/2–120mm, 7.17/1918 to Britain).
Mlada (ex-*Semiramida*, 1900/1792t/15kts/2–120mm, 1.17/1918 to Britain).
Olen (ex-*Avans*, ex-*Avance*, 1884/263t/8kts, 1916).
Orlik (ex-*Ganzen*, 3.17).
Pechenga (ex-*Angara*, ex-*Moskva*, 1889/12050t/20kts, 11.16).
Poryv (ex-*Vanadis* (1908/852t/15kts, 6.17).
Rassvet (ex-*Alberta*, 1896/1164t/14kts, 7.16/1918 to Britain).
Rogdaj (ex-*Nevada*, 1915/3600t, 8.17/sold 1920s).
Snezhinka (ex-*Tekla*, 1916/180t/16kts/1–47mm, 8.16).
Sokolitsa (ex-*Alvinia* 3.17/1918 to Britain).
Strepet (450t/7kts, 1916).
Tajmyr (1908/1500t/12.5kts/2–75mm, 1916/extant 1950s).
Voskhod (ex-*Diana*, 1896/751t/14kts, 6.16).
Yaroslavna (ex-*Lizystrada* 1900/1940t/20kts/2–120mm, 4–47mm, 2 MG, 7.15/renamed *Vorovski* 1920s, deleted 1950s).
Zlata (ex-*Petalina*, 900t/14kts, 5.17/did not reach Russian waters).

THE CASPIAN FLOTILLA 1914–1917
Name (launched/displacement/speed/armament, commissioned/fate):
Araks (1901/740t/12.5kts/4–47mm, 1901).
Astrabad (1900/326t/12kts/5–47mm, 3.11).
Geok-Tepe (1882/1100/11.5kts/4–47mm).
Krasnovodsk (ex-*General Skobelev*, 1882/214t/7kts/2–75mm).

Austria-Hungary

In 1906 Austria-Hungary was a huge multi-national empire in the heart of Europe which faced geo-political problems very similar to those of Russia. Although she enjoyed some 370 miles of Adriatic coastline this could very quickly be blockaded – and indeed this happened in the war – since she had no port in the open Mediterranean. In the south Austria-Hungary bordered on the recently independent states released by the gradually weakening Ottoman Empire.

European foreign policy, which was in this period inevitably a policy of colonialism, developed some distinctive geographical axes which crossed in the Balkan peninsula and the Near East, thus creating a potentially dangerous zone.

Austria-Hungary had a very unfortunate policy of expansion in the direction of Greece, after determined Italian efforts had opposed the conquest of Valona (now Vlore in Albania) for the Hapsburg Empire. Following this an attempt was made to provide a land connection with Salonica (Thessaloniki) and a railway was planned from Belgrade to that port. The occupation of the three regions of Bosnia, Herzegovina and the Sandchakof Novi Pazar in 1878 were the first attempts to build this link, but after the failure of Austrian Mediterranean policy only Bosnia and Herzegovina were formally occupied under a military government in 1908, the Sandchakof Novi Pazar being released to the Kingdom of Serbia.

When Italy's attempts to conquer colonies in Abyssinia or Tunisia led to both a military and political debacle, Italy focused her attention on the opposite shore of her *'mare nostro'*, on Albania and Montenegro, thus interfering with the Austrian line of expansion to the south east. The relationship of these two nations was therefore contradictory: on the one hand they were in strong competition for the same areas in the Balkans, resulting in increasing rivalry; on the other hand they were trading partners linked by many bilateral agreements. When the eastward direction of Italian expansionism culminated in the Italo-Turkish war of 1911, Austria could have exploited the conflict for her own ends, but stayed loyal to her agreements and so prevented the conflict from spreading throughout the peninsula and involving proud and sensitive new nations like Serbia, Montenegro, Albania and Greece.

Czarist Russia also traditionally focussed its claims on this area, firstly for free access to the Mediterranean, secondly for economic and imperialist reasons, and thirdly from religious motives – it was always felt that the old centre of Orthodox Christianity, Byzantium (then Constantinople, today Istanbul), should be reconquered from the Muslim Turks.

What looked like an area of interest for three surrounding empires was also of importance to other major European nations. Great Britain was about to secure her vital routes to India and East Africa by increasing her influence in Iraq and southern Persia and was merely interested in preserving a *status quo* which would gradually lead to a 'fading away' of the Ottoman Empire without Czarist Russia conquering the Dardanelles. France for her part tried to gain influence in Syria and the German Empire tried to obtain similar influence in Asia Minor. Germany's most ambitious project was to build a railway from Berlin to Baghdad and indeed her influence led to a restoration of confidence within Turkey which collided with British and French interests.

The Austro-Hungarian fleet at Pola some time after 1916
Unless otherwise credited, all photographs in this section: G Pawlik Collection

Within this delicate network of economic interests, political influence and counter-influence, treaties and power politics, Austria-Hungary adopted a highly unfortunate foreign policy which cost her the sympathies of all the opposing powers: France never forgave Austria for backing Germany in the Agadir crisis, while Great Britain signed the treaty of Reval with Russia in 1908 to establish non-conflicting policies in the East and in Macedonia; and Czarist Russia left no doubt that she was the only legitimate leader of the Slavic nations, which sooner or later had to be freed from the regimes at Vienna and Budapest.

THE TRIPLE ALLIANCE

In the light of this complex and delicate background the Triple Alliance between Austria-Hungary, Germany and Italy was an unnatural combination. Although enjoying short interior lines of communication, the alliance faced naval threats at each corner of its sea boundaries: the Russians in the Baltic, the British in the North Sea, and the joint French and British in both halves of the Mediterranean, plus the Russian Black Seas Fleet.

Nevertheless two secret naval treaties were drawn up (the first dating from 1900, the second from 1913), to ensure a strong joint command of the Central Powers' forces in the Mediterranean (composed of the Italian and the Austro-Hungarian fleets, and the Imperial German Mediterranean Squadron). As with Italian-Austrian foreign relations, the value of this treaty was ambiguous.

One group in Austria-Hungary sincerely believed in the loyalty of the Italians to the Alliance, especially as the head of the Italian General Staff, General Pollio, was said to be an absolute believer in the Alliance's aims; the other group, led by the head of the Austrian General Staff, Conrad von Hötzendorf, and the Crown Prince, Archduke Franz Ferdinand, did not trust Italy's long-term aims and predicted an Austro-Italian war for several reasons.

WAR GAMES

Because of rising tensions in foreign affairs and the Italo-Austrian problems in the Triple Alliance, the Austrian General Staff under the command of General Conrad von Hötzendorf developed a number of

possible war scenarios. It was significant that the impulse came from the Army: the Austro-Hungarian Navy was then involved in an exhausting basic debate about whether she should build up 'blue water' Mahan-style fleet or a *Jeune École* type of coast defence fleet, and although the Navy made its own independent studies of the same problems, it only presented insufficient solutions with no consequences for design policy. The Army scenarios were:

War Case I assumed a war with Italy, Germany and Russia remaining neutral.

War Case B assumed a war against Serbia and Montenegro, all other nations remaining neutral. Reserves had to be kept back in case Italy and/or Russia entered this war.

War Case R assumed an armed conflict in alliance with Germany and Rumania against Russia, plus a secondary action against Serbia and Montenegro.

For each war situation a series of possible chain reactions in the light of existing European treaties were analysed and it transpired that the worst case would be I and R. Nevertheless no clear naval construction policy emerged out of these discussions.

THE MONTECUCCOLI ERA

Austria-Hungary as a continental power always concentrated its main interest and resources on the Army. For decades the Navy faced an exhausting internal debate about whether it should restrict itself purely to coast defence – which would be cheaper and more logical, given Austria-Hungary's geographical situation – or whether she should enter the group of major naval powers by building dreadnoughts, which would be capable of power-projection and might be a powerful tool for a more active foreign policy.

In the period between the Battle of Lissa in 1866 and 1904 the naval share of the total defence budget was very small and only rose from 7.7 per cent to 15.7. Because modern warships had become more and more expensive this meant that obsolete warships were replaced by scarcely less outdated ones – 'too good to die and too bad to fight with', as cynical contemporary critics expressed it.

In 1900, when virtually every nation calling herself a naval power, had presented long-term naval building programmes and adopted them in the form of Naval Acts or Naval Laws, Austria-Hungary still lacked such a policy for reasons of domestic politics. Perhaps the greatest single obstacle to the plans of Austrian navalists was the stubborn Hungarian opposition to any increase in naval expenditure. It must be explained that a consequence of the dual status of the Hapsburg Empire was that two independent delegations (of Austria and of Hungary) had to reach a mutual approval of the defence budget, and that the Hungarian delegation therefore opposed large naval expenditure, which brought no tangible benefits to the Hungarian part of the Dual Monarchy.

A unique clash occurred in 1904 when the then C-in-C of the Austro-Hungarian Navy, Admiral Spaun, presented a fleet expansion programme to counter Italian plans. He was forced by the Imperial Minister of war, General of Ordnance Pitreich, to reduce the special budget requirement by half (from 50 to 25 million crowns), while the Army was only to cut its provision by 5 million crowns. After protesting Spaun resigned and was succeeded by Vice-Admiral County Rudolf von Montecuccoli.

The unfortunate legacy of this affair was that absolutely no special provision for new construction appeared in the budgets from 1905 to 1909. By 1910 even the few new ships approved within the regular budgets of recent years could not be finished. However, from 1907 onwards the Crown Prince increased his influence on the Navy and as early as 1908 plans for dreadnought construction were announced. Therefore the budget of 1910 also included two retrospective instalments to amortize old debts, but no funds for the new dreadnoughts, scout cruisers and destroyers. All this was approved – the details concerning the *Tegetthoff*s are described in the class notes below – in the 1911 budget. From this programme emerged – with the addition of 12 torpedo-boats and 4 submarines approved in the next budget – nearly all the modern warships which fought the First World War. When Montecuccoli resigned on 22 February 1913 on his 70th birthday, he left his successor the nucleus of a modern fleet with a promising future.

THE HAUS ERA

On becoming the new C-in-C of the Austro-Hungarian Navy, Admiral Anton Haus faced exactly the same problems as his predecessor, but he had more luck and as early as May 1914 his second building programme was approved: this included another 4 dreadnoughts, 3 more scout cruisers, and 6 destroyers. Unfortunately war broke out some weeks later, all major units were postponed, and only some destroyers were built to replace war losses.

THE FIRST WORLD WAR

In May 1914 the C-in-C, Admiral Haus, finally obtained funds for a remarkable build-up of the Austro-Hungarian fleet. However, the Austrian Crown Prince and his wife were assassinated at Sarajevo on 28 June 1914 and this sparked off a chain of events leading to the First World War. The Navy had to postpone its fleet expansion and entered the war with a mixed force of modern and antiquated ships.

Both periods of the naval war in the Adriatic opened with large scale fleet operations. Immediately after the outbreak of hostilities the entire Austrian battle fleet went south to escort the German Mediterranean Squadron to Pola, but the German Admiral Souchon had decided to make for Constantinople. The daring idea of sending the Austro-Hungarian battle fleet to the Dardanelles and into the Black Sea to help its Turkish ally was rejected by the fleet command because it probably would have ended in a one-way sortie, leaving the domestic coast unprotected. The second phase of the war in the Adriatic was when Italy switched to the Entente and declared war on Austria-Hungary (23 May 1915). The Austrian Fleet immediately left Pola harbour for a big shore bombardment.

However, the everyday war was less spectacular, due to the remote geographical situation of the Adriatic, where Austria-Hungary soon found her naval forces bottled up. It was possible, nevertheless, to ensure Austrian pre-eminence in the Adriatic by repelling intruding enemy forces. This resulted in some minor naval engagements with no benefits for either side. Apart from the two above-mentioned sorties, the modern capital ships stayed inactive at Pola during the war, with one exception. When Admiral Horthy, later the Imperial Administrator of Hungary, became the new C-in-C of the Navy, the Adriatic U-boat bases were blockaded by the Otranto barrage; so for the second time a raid on the net lines in the Otranto Straits was planned, the four *Tegetthoff* class dreadnoughts providing the backbone of the force. However, the *Szent István* was torpedoed and sunk during the sortie and the whole operation was cancelled.

The naval war in the Adriatic mainly involved the patrolling destroyers and torpedo-boats, leaving this force in a badly worn-out condition after four years of combat with few opportunities for refits. Another distinctive feature of the war in the Adriatic was the extensive use of aircraft, the Austro-Hungarian Navy being one of the few fleets that had developed its own genuine air arm.

AUSTRO-HUNGARIAN NAVAL AVIATION

As early as 1910 Austrian naval authorities recognised the particular advantages of naval aircraft for reconnaissance and hoped for a powerful supplement of the weak torpedo-boat force. Although this first generation of flying boats were very fragile and vulnerable the type was assumed to have operational advantages in a good weather area like the Adriatic. It must be pointed out that Austrian naval aviation developed along its own technical lines in parallel to Army aviation. The reason for the Navy developing its own flying boats was the simple fact that a wheeled aircraft was inevitably lost when forced to land in the sea after a defect or battle damage while a flying boat could probably be towed in and repaired. Another remarkable fact is that Austro-Hungarian naval aviation was never placed under the command of another service and on its own responsibility made reconnaissance flights, bombing missions and fighter interceptions not only over the sea but also deep into enemy territory. Although it was heavily outnumbered by the British, French and Italian flying corps from 1917 there is no doubt that this inferior force tied up a three-fold number of enemy aircraft which otherwise could have been employed on the Italian-Austrian front.

During the war 570 Austrian flying boats entered service: 56 were lost in action; 151 by accidents or crash landings; 80 were deleted in a worn out or obsolete condition.

One of the outstanding successes of Austro-Hungarian naval aviation was the first sinking of a submarine by an aircraft. On 15 September 1916 the flying boats *L 132* and *L 135* bombed the French submarine *Foucault*, sank her and saved the crew by landing and taking them aboard until a torpedo-boat arrived.

AUSTRO-HUNGARIAN RIVERINE FORCES

Although this book does not include riverine vessels in detail, it should be mentioned that the Hapsburg Empire, whose main river was the Danube, possessed a strong force of riverine vessels. This consisted of the ten Danube monitors *Maros, Leitha* (310t, launched 1871, reconstructed 1893–94), *Körös, Szamos* (448t, launched 1892), *Temes, Bodrog* (440t, launched 1904), *Enns, Inn* (540t, launched 1914 and 1915), *Sava, Bosna* (580t, launched 1914 and 1915); two large monitors, *No XI* and *XII* (1240t) were intended to be laid down in 1917, but apart from some preliminary orders no work took place because of the acute steel shortage of that year. The force also consisted of the 60t river patrol craft *Fogas, Csuka* (60t), the 133t *Wels, Barsch, Compó, Viza,* the 140t *Stör* and *Lachs*, the 36.5t *b* and the 39t *c* and *d*. All units were extremely useful in riverine warfare against Serbia and later proceeded to the Danube estuary.

UNIQUE PROBLEMS OF A MULTI-NATIONAL NAVY

The Hapsburg Empire was a multi-national empire formed by about 20 different nationalities under the hegemony of German-speaking Austrians as well as Hungarians. Unlike the Army, where national groups formed homogeneous regiments and battalions, each ship of the Austro-Hungarian Navy could represent a microcosm of the Hapsburg Empire with a mixed crew of a dozen nationalities speaking different languages. The percentages for non-commissioned personnel are: 34.1 Croats and Slovenians, 20.4 Hungarians, 16.3 Austrians, 14.4 Italians, 11 Czechs and Slovakians, and 4.6 Poles, Ruthenians and Rumanians. Because of the rising tension between Germans, Slavs, Hungarians, Slovenians and Italians, the Navy faced substantial problems, which in their political dimensions later resulted in the break-up of the Empire into independent nations. Furthermore the rise of political consciousness culminated in strong socialist and communist opposition to the Monarchy, and the old forces of conservativism and feudalism.

It is hardly surprising that an Italian-speaking subject felt more in common with his 'brothers' living a few miles away across the Italian border, although he felt more personal loyalty to the old Emperor Francis Joseph I than to the authorities in Vienna or Budapest situated some hundred miles away; similarly it seems no wonder that Croatians and Slovenians felt closer related to their 'Slavic brothers' in Serbia than to their Hungarian government.

As long as 'the old Emperor at Vienna' was alive (he died on 21 November 1916) there is no doubt that everybody felt himself as 'his' subject despite all national differences – as expressed in the Emperor's personal motto 'Viribus Unitis' ('with common effort'). Francis Joseph I himself held this Empire together purely by the strength of his personality.

After his death, with the war situation becoming so bad that many believed it could not be won, rising nationalism and socialist movements led to the point where nobody believed in the future existence of the Empire, so that the war was pointless even if it could have been won. This led to a series of incidents which are at first glance extremely dishonourable for the Navy but must be understood in the light of the above-mentioned problems and tensions. On 5 October 1917 the officers of *Tb 11* were imprisoned by the crew, which had been persuaded by a Slovenian and a Czech member to desert to Italy; the boat left Sebenico, crossed the Adriatic and surrendered (see torpedo-boat section below). On 11 May 1918 two crew members of *Tb 80* were executed for making a similar attempt. On 3 June 1918 two naval airmem of Italian extraction deserted to Italy with the flying boat *L 127*.

Other mutinies had political causes but were at least aggravated by the poor food and supply situation. On 22 January 1918 the civilian workers of the Naval Arsenal at Pola went on strike and on 1 February the spirit of revolution reached the naval units in Cattaro Bay (Boka Kotorska), where the crews of the armoured cruiser *Sankt Georg*, the torpedo depot ship *Gäa*, the harbour guardship *Kronprinz Erzherzog Rudolf* and some destroyers rose in a communist-inspired mutiny. On the other units – especially the cruisers – the officers were able to persuade the wavering mutineers to stay loyal. After being shelled by land batteries authority was restored in the fleet, 800 mutineers were landed, and in the final court-martial four leaders of the mutiny were sentenced to death. However, in Yugoslavia they are now regarded as heroes of the struggle to establish the independence of their nation.

After the armistice and the subsequent breakdown of the Hapsburg monarchy, the Austro-Hungarian Navy disintegrated in an incredible way within a few days. Its ships became a bone of contention between the new SHS state (the state of the Slovenians, Croates and Serbs in Slavic abbreviation – later Yugoslavia), which wanted to keep it for military reasons, and Italy, which wanted to take it over in order to dominate the Adriatic. After a period of uncertainty of more than two years, when British, US and French naval forces occupied parts of the Dalmatian coast to separate both hostile parties, the former Austro-Hungarian ships were distributed or sold. For political reasons most of the units were immediately scrapped, but by the time this happened, former Austro-Hungarian naval personnel had long since been dispersed to their new states, becoming by the provisions of a treaty Austrians, Czechoslavakians, Hungarians, Italians and so on. Unlike other countries, where at least the veterans could indulge their nostalgia at the ports where they had served, the veterens of the Austro-Hungarian Navy had become subjects of new nations far from the sea and had to struggle for economic survival against their former comrades-in-arms.

THE AUSTRIAN REPUBLIC

With the armistice of Villa Giusti, signed on 3 November 1918, the Hapsburg monarchy found itself one of the losing powers of the First World War, and further developments resulted in the Empire being completely expunged from the political map of postwar Europe. The

Demobilised river patrol craft at Linz during the winter of 1921–22. They are *Barsch* (foreground), *Compó, Stör* and *Fogas*
Baumgartner Collection

AUSTRIA-HUNGARY

Emperor Charles I (who was also King Charles IV of Hungary) abdicated on 1 November 1918. Amidst a chaotic situation, close to civil war, the 'provisional national assembly' tried to establish governmental power in what was then called the 'Republic of German-Austria' (*Republik Deutschösterreich*). With all the former Hapsburg-ruled states becoming independent nations only the nucleus of the German-speaking former Austrian half of the Dual Monarchy was left to form a tiny state. Doubts about its economic viability were so strong that a union with Germany was suggested. Following secret talks with German politicians, the national assembly declared on 12 March 1919, 'German-Austria is a part of the Republic of Germany', but three days later the Commission for territorial peace regulations at Paris decided that Austria was to remain an independent state. On 10 September 1919 the Austrian State Chancellor, Dr Karl Renner, signed the Peace Treaty of St Germain-en-Laye and in accordance with this on 21 November the national assembly revoked the decision of 12 March and the new state was henceforth called the 'Republic of Austria'.

With regard to the seapower of the former Austro-Hungarian Empire, which also possessed a powerful riverine force, the naval forces of the Republic of Austria were reduced to nearly zero. Three days after the declaration of the Republic of German-Austria her provisional volunteer army was founded. Called the *Volkswehr* ('People's Defence'), it also contained a naval branch, the *Volkswehr-Marinewehr*, which consisted mainly of naval infantry and operated only a few riverine launches.

The Treaty of St Germain, coming into force on 16 July 1920, marked the period the Austrians call the 'St Germain Army ' (1920–32). According to the terms of St Germain 4 former Austro-Hungarian Danube patrol craft of different classes were allocated to Austria and handed over on 15 November 1920 by the NACDEV at Novisad. These were the 60t *Fogas*, the two 128t *Wels* class vessels *Barsch* and *Compó*, and the 140t *Stör* (ii).

The nearly disarmed and cannibalised boats were towed to Budapest where they were forced to remain during the winter because of low water in the Danube. They arrived at Vienna on 14 May 1921 and finally at their base at Linz on 1 September 1921. Given the poor condition of the boats and the adverse economic situation it was decided on 15 March 1922 only to fit out the *Barsch*, and if possible the *Fogas*. On 6 October 1927 *Fogas*, *Compó* and *Stör* (ii) were sold to Hungary and renamed *Gödöllö*, *Györ* and *Pozsony* respectively.

Gödöllö was never put into service and was scrapped in 1945 after heavy bomb damage. *Györ* was rearmed subsequently and saw service during the war until 1945 when she was in action against the Soviet siege of Vienna; she was scrapped in 1949. *Pozsony* was renamed *Sopron* in 1930, saw active service during the war; in 1950 she was converted to a merchant vessel and renamed *Hertha*, in 1953 she was transferred to the Rhine for her new Swiss owner, and in 1962 renamed *Irene* and finally scrapped in 1966.

The only operational Austrian unit of the period covered in this volume was the *Barsch*, which is detailed at the end of the class tables.

NOTES

Although all contemporary sources and literature refer to the standard anti-torpedo-boat gun as the 7cm Skoda gun, the actual calibre was 66mm, which produced some confusion. For reasons of clarity the various models of 7cm guns are always given their real calibre of 66mm in the tables below.

Metric tonnes of 2204.6lb (as opposed to 'long tons' of 2240lbs) are used throughout the class lists.

The main builders are abbreviated STT (Stabilimento Tecnico Triestino), Trieste, and CNT (Cantiere Navale Triestino), Monfalcone.

FLEET STRENGTH 1906

BATTLESHIPS

Name	Launched	Disp (design)	Fate
Habsburg class			
HABSBURG	9.9.00	8232t	BU 1921
ÁRPÁD	11.9.01	8232t	BU 1921
BABENBERG	4.10.02	8232t	BU 1921
Erzherzog Karl class			
ERZHERZOG KARL	4.10.03	10,472t	BU 1920
ERZHERZOG FRIEDRICH	30.4.04	10,472t	BU 1920
ERZHERZOG FERDINAND MAX	21.5.05	10,472t	BU 1920

Habsburg class
In 1910–11 *Habsburg* and *Árpád* had one superstructure deck removed to save topweight. During the war the ships formed the 4th Division; later in the war they were decommissioned and served as harbour guardships. After the war all three were allocated to Great Britain, but were sold and broken up in Italy in 1921.

Erzherzog Karl class
During the war the ships formed the 3rd Division. After the war all three were taken over by the new Yugoslavian Navy but were ceded as war reparations to France and Great Britain, sold and scrapped.

COAST DEFENCE SHIPS

Name	Launched	Disp (design)	Fate
KRONPRINZESSIN ERZHERZOGIN STEPHANIE	14.4.87	5075t	BU 1926
KRONPRINZ ERZHERZOG RUDOLF	6.7.87	6829t	BU 1922
Monarch class			
MONARCH	9.5.95	5547t	BU 1920–21
WIEN	6.7.95	5547t	Sunk 10.12.17
BUDAPEST	27.4.96	5547t	BU 1920–21

Kronprinzessin Erzherzgin Stephanie
In 1910 she was hulked and in 1914 she became an accommodation ship to the mine warfare school. In 1920 she was ceded to Italy as a war reparation and scrapped there in 1926.

Kronprinz Erzherzog Rudolf
From 1906 she was classified as a local defence ship and spent the war in Cattaro Bay. In 1919 she was ceded to Yugoslavia, renamed *Kumbor*, but scrapped in 1922.

Monarch class
At the beginning of the war the ships formed the 5th Division, but remained in reserve. *Wien* was preparing for a shore bombardment when she was sunk on 10 December 1917 at Muggia in the Bay of Trieste by the Italian *MAS 9* under the command of Luigi Rizzo, the Italian officer who would later also sink the *Szent István*. *Budapest* was decommissioned in March 1918 to serve as an accommodation ship for the Pola submarine base. In May–June 1918 a 38cm/17 howitzer was installed instead of No 1 turret for a planned shore bombardment which never took place. Both survivors of this class were allocated to Great Britain, sold and scrapped in Italy 1920–21.

ARMOURED CRUISERS

Name	Launched	Disp (design)	Fate
KAISERIN UND KÖNIGIN MARIA THERESIA	24.9.93	5330t	BU *c*1920
KAISER KARL VI	4.10.98	6166t	BU *c*1920
SANKT GEORG	8.12.03	7289t	BU *c*1920

These three ships do not form a homogeneous class, the later two being improved versions of the first cruiser.

Kaiserin und Königin Maria Theresia was modernised and completely rearmed in two stages 1906–8 and 1909–10: the heavy tubular fighting masts were removed, the 24cm were replaced by 19cm in single turrets and the 15cm were redistributed on the main deck level. The new armament was then: 2–19cm (7.5in)/42, 8–15cm (5.9in)/35, 12–47mm/44 QF, 2–47mm/33 QF, 4–37mm revolving guns, 2–66mm/18 landing guns. 4–45cm (17.7in) TT aw (1 bow, 1 stern, 2 beam). Although technically part of the 1st Cruiser Division, she was stationed as harbour guardship at Sebenico from 1914 to 1916; disarmed and decommissioned in 1917 she served as an accommodation ship for German submarine personnel at Pola, while her guns were transferred to the Italian front.

The other two took part in some cruiser actions as supporting units. All three were allocated to Great Britain in 1920, then sold to Italy and scrapped there.

PROTECTED CRUISERS

Name	Launched	Disp	Fate
Kaiser Franz Joseph I class			
KAISER FRANZ JOSEPH I	18.5.98	3967t	Sunk 10.19
KAISERIN ELISABETH	25.9.90	3967t	Scuttled 2.11.14

At the outbreak of World War One both ships were obsolete. *Kaiserin Elisabeth* was station in China in 1914 and took part in the defence of the German naval base at Tsingtao. Her 15cm and 47mm guns were removed and mounted ashore in the 'Elisabeth' battery. She was scuttled on 2 November 1914, 5 days before the base surrendered to the Japanese. *Kaiser Franz Joseph I* served with the 2nd Cruiser Division at the outbreak of war and took part in the shelling of French naval batteries on Mount Lovcen, but was soon relegated to the role of harbour defence ship at Cattaro. In 1917 she was completely disarmed and became a floating HQ. She was ceded to France as a war reparation, was over-laden with dismantled machinery and sank in a heavy gale off Kumbor in Cattaro Bay in 1919.

LIGHT CRUISERS

Name	Launched	Disp (design)	Fate
Panther class			
PANTHER	13.6.85	1557t	BU 1920
LEOPARD	10.9.85	1557t	BU 1920
Tiger			
TIGER	28.6.87	1657t	BU 1920
Zenta class			
ZENTA	18.8.97	2313t	Sunk 16.8.14
ASPERN	3.5.99	2313t	BU 1920
SZIGETVÁR	29.10.00	2313t	BU 1920

Panther class
Designed and constructed in Great Britain as so called 'torpedo ram cruisers', both units were obsolete and their main armament was removed in 1909–10. *Leopard* was decommissioned on 15 May 1914 and used as a harbour defence ship at Pola; in 1917 *Panther* was attached to the submarine commanders' school as a seagoing TS. Both were allocated to Great Britain as war reparations, but sold to Italy and scrapped there in 1920.

Tiger
This ship was an enlarged and improved version of her British-built forerunners. In 1905–6 she was partially disarmed and converted into an admiralty yacht, and renamed *Lacroma*. In 1915 she was completely disarmed, and in 1919 she became Yugoslavian; in 1920 she was ceded to Italy and scrapped there.

Zenta class
Although obsolete these three light cruisers saw active service with the 1st Cruiser Division at the beginning of World War One. *Zenta* was sunk on 16 August 1914 in a one-hour naval action with French battleships when patrolling off the Montenegran coast. *Aspern* was disarmed in 1918 and served as an accommodation ship at Pola, as was *Szigetvár* which served the torpedo warfare school as an accommodation and target ship. Both were allocated to Great Britain, but sold to Italy in 1920 and scrapped there.

TORPEDO WARFARE VESSELS

The Austro-Hungarian Navy like other navies tried to develop different types of torpedo-carrying units: the 'torpedo ships' were to act as flotilla leaders (for a period the light cruisers *Panther, Tiger* and *Leopard* were also classified as torpedo ships); the next largest type was the 'torpedo vessel' which was in fact a torpedo-boat destroyer; and the smallest type was to be the torpedo-boat. As in other navies all attempts to use larger ships as torpedo carriers failed and the existing torpedo ram cruisers, torpedo cruisers and torpedo ships were soon withdrawn from active service and modified for other purposes. Following the international trend only the destroyer and the different types of torpedo-boats survived.

Sebenico about 1900 CPL

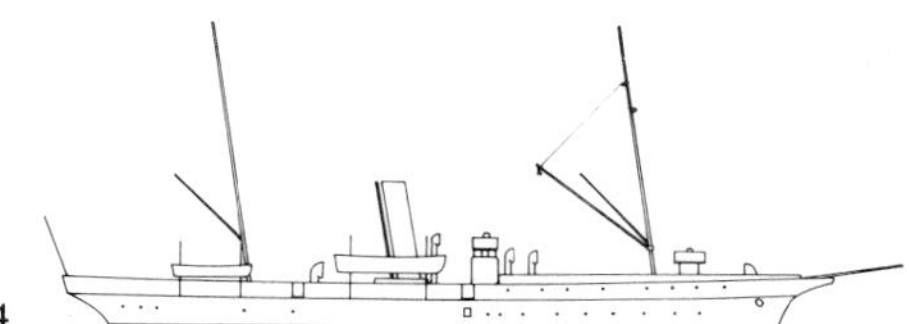
Zara about 1914

TORPEDO SHIPS

Name	Launched	Disp (design)	Fate
Zara class			
ZARA	13.11.79	838t	BU 1920
SPALATO	30.8.79	838t	BU 1920
SEBENICO	28.2.82	882.6t	BU 1920
LUSSIN	22.9.83	995.25t	BU 1920

With their elegant lines and barquentine rig these torpedo ships looked more like contemporary steam yachts than warships. As fighting ships they turned out to be misconstrued and did not suit any requirements: as scout cruisers and flotilla leaders they were too slow and poorly armed to protect torpedo-boats against enemy destroyer attacks. Therefore they were modified for other duties immediately after commissioning.

Zara class
Launched at the Pola N Yd and STT respectively, they had the following particulars: 205ft 9in × 27ft × 12ft *(62.7m × 8.2m × 3.7m)*; 2600ihp = 14.29kts; armament as built 4–9cm (3.5in) BL, 1–7cm (2.75in) BL, 2–25cm revolving guns, 3–35cm (13.8in) TT (2 bow, 1 trainable); added in 1887: 4–47mm/33, 1–47mm revolving gun, 2–35cm TT on deck instead of one; in 1906 the two deck TT were replaced by one stern TT; from 1917: 2–66mm/45, 4–47mm/44, TTs as above. *Zara* became a torpedo training vessel, and in 1906 cadet instruction vessel; in 1920 she was ceded to Italy and scrapped there in 1920. *Spalato* served from 1910 as a gunnery TS, was ceded to Italy and scrapped there in 1920.

Sebenico
Although referred to in the literature as belonging to the *Zara* class, she was an enlarged and modified version, built at the Pola N Yd; she differed from her sisters in having only one (main) mast, sponsons for her guns and decreased speed. Her particulars were: 228ft 8in × 27ft × 11ft 2in *(69.7m × 8.2m × 3.4m)*; 1344ihp = 12.8kts; armament as built 4–9cm (3.5in) BL, 1–66mm/18 landing gun, 2–25mm revolving guns, 1–35mm (13.8in) TT sub (bow); from 1903 2–12cm (4.7in)/40, 1–66mm/15, 4–47mm/44 QF, 4–47mm/33 QF, 4–37mm QF, 2–8mm MG; crew 135. From 1903 *Sebenico* served with the gunnery training school; from 1914 as a guardship at Sebenico (Sibenik); and from 1918 as tender of the torpedo traning school at Pola. She was ceded to Italy and scrapped there in 1920.

Lussin
Built by the STT to the particulars: 262ft 1in × 27ft 8in × 12ft 6in *(79.9m × 8.4m × 3.8m)*; armament as built 2–15cm (5.9in)/21, 1–66mm/18 landing gun, 1–35cm (13.8in) TT sub (bow); in 1887 4–47mm/44 QF were added. Since she suffered from same deficiencies as her sisters, she was disarmed completely in 1890 and served as machinery TS and from 1891 as a stoker TS; in 1910 she was converted into an admiralty yacht, receiving two MAN diesels (1800bhp = 14kts). In 1916 she became an accommodation ship for German submarine personnel at Pola, and was ceded to Italy in 1920, renamed *Sorrento*, and probably scrapped.

AUSTRIA-HUNGARY

DESTROYERS

Name	Launched	Disp (design)	Fate
METEOR	16.6.87	428.15t	BU *c* 1920
Blitz class			
BLITZ	7.7.88	418.3t	BU *c* 1920
KOMET	8.8.88	418.3t	BU *c* 1920
PLANET	25.6.89	498.23t	BU *c* 1920
TRABANT	21.5.90	531.5t	BU *c* 1920
SATELLIT	21.9.92	606.3t	BU *c* 1920
MAGNET	21.3.96	477.27t	BU *c* 1920
HUSZÁR	31.5.05	383.3t	Sank 12.12.08

Komet was reboilered in 1914, with two funnels. Apart from *Meteor*'s 47mm/33 QF, the guns in all boats were 66mm/45 and 47mm/44 QF weapons. *Satellit* had an extra 45cm TT added in 1913, and after reboilering in 1912–13 had three funnels instead of one. *Huszár*'s gun armament was 1–66cm/45, 7–47mm/44 QF.

Of the survivors, *Satellit* was ceded to France in 1920 and BU; the rest went to Italy in 1920 and were also scrapped.

HIGH SEAS TORPEDO-BOATS

Name	Launched	Disp (design)	Fate
VIPER *(Tb 17)*	16.12.95	124t	BU *c* 1920
NATTER *(Tb 18)*	1.96	166.2t	BU *c* 1920
Python class			
PYTHON *(Tb 13)*	11.4.99	132t	BU *c* 1920
KYGYO *(Tb 14)*	11.4.99	132t	BU *c* 1920
BOA *(Tb 15)*	8.98	132t	BU *c* 1920
COBRA *(Tb 16)*	9.98	132t	BU *c* 1920

Viper (17): launched 16 December 1895 at Yarrow, London; it had the particulars: 124t; 44.96m × 4.5m × 2.3m; 1900ihp = 25kts; 2–47mm QF, 3 TT; crew 21.

In 1910 Austro-Hungarian torpedo-boats were given arabic numbers, *Viper*, for example, becoming *Tb 17*. During the war *Viper* saw active service on convoy and minesweeping duties, and 1920 she was allocated to France and scrapped there.

Natter (18)
Launched January 1896 at Schichau, Elbing, it had the particulars: 166.2t; 47.3m × 5.3m × 2.8m; 2200ihp = 24kts; 2–47mm QF, 3 TT; crew 21.

Due to strong vibration at high speeds *Natter* was never fully operational. In 1910 she was renamed *Tb 18* and was designated a floating mobile torpedo-battery at Pola. The torpedo armament was changed twice: in 1910–11 she received a single tube on the centreline instead of the sided pair, and in 1917 this was replaced by a twin mounting. The boat served during the war as a training and exercise ship and was allocated to Great Britain; she was sold to Italy in 1920 and scrapped there.

Competitive trials with the *Viper* and *Natter* had shown that there was little to chose between them in terms of stability and seaworthiness, but the Schichau design was inferior in longitudinal stability and suffered from propeller vibration at high speeds. Therefore it was decided to order another Yarrow type (the *Python* class) from England. The boats were launched in 1898–99. In 1910 they were given arabic numbers (quoted in brackets above). *Tb 14* served from 1914 as a salvage vessel at the Pola naval air base, and then at Sebenico. The others served as convoy escorts and minesweepers during the war and were allocated to Great Britain and scrapped in 1920; *Tb 14* was allocated to France and also scrapped in 1920.

FIRST CLASS TORPEDO-BOATS

These were *Kibitz (Tb 19), Kukuk (Tb 20), Star (Tb 21), Krähe (Tb 22), Rabe (Tb 23), Elster (Tb 24), Gaukler (Tb 25), Flamingo (Tb 26), Sekretär (Tb 27), Weihe (Tb 28), Marabu (Tb 29), Harpie (Tb 30), Sperber (Tb 31), Habicht (Tb 32), Bussard (Tb 33), Condor (Tb 34), Geier (Tb 35), Uhu (Tb 36), Würger (Tb 37), Kranich (Tb 38), Reiher (Tb 39), Ibis (Tb 40)*. Launched between 1886 and 1892 at the Pola N Yd and STT these boats were built along the lines of the Schichau prototypes *Sperber* and *Habicht*. From 1 April 1910 all torpedo-boats in service were given new arabic numbers (quoted here in brackets after the original name). At the beginning of World War One these boats were obsolete. *Tb 26* sank on 23 August 1914 after hitting a mine; *Tb 28* was sold to the Army in 1912 and served as *Tender 28*; all the others were converted to minesweepers and survived the war to be ceded to Italy and Yugoslavia. Italy scrapped her boats in 1920, while Yugoslavia kept them in service until 1927–29, *Tb 19* becoming *D 1*, *Tb 21* becoming *D 4*, *Tb 36* becoming *D 2* and *Tb 38* becoming *D 3*.

The old first class torpedo-boats *Adler (Tb 41)* and *Falke (Tb 42)* served from 1905 as harbour guard boats. On 22 July 1899 the boiler of *Falke* exploded, damaging the boat so heavily that she had to be rebuilt, which included a straight vertical stem instead of the distinctive ram bow; *Adler* also received this feature during a refit.

They were launched in 1885 at Yarrow's London yard. Although not serving with the torpedo-boat force they received arabic numbers in 1910 but were stricken in 1911 and scrapped.

SECOND CLASS TORPEDO-BOATS

The survivors in 1906 were: (B type) *Tb XI, Tb XIII, Tb XV–Tb XVIII, Tb XX–Tb XXIV, Tb XXVI*; (C type) *Tb XXVII, Tb XXX–Tb XXXII*; (D type) *Tb XXXIII–Tb XXXIX*.

The B type torpedo-boats were built between 1883 and 1886 at the Pola N Yd based on the Yarrow prototypes *IX* and *X*. By 1900 they were obsolete and worn-out, and all were stricken in the years up to 1909 and sold for scrapping; except that *Tb XXIII* was converted and served as *Tender 55*.

The C type were launched between 1886 and 1888 at the Pola N Yd and had the same particulars as the B type but with a vertical bow. All were stricken by 1909 and sold for scrapping.

The D type were launched between 1887 and 1891 at the Pola N Yd and were based on the Schichau prototype *Tb XXXIII*. On 1 April 1910 they were given the new designations *Tb 44–Tb 49* but were at the end of their useful lives. They were stricken and sold for scrapping with the exception of three boats which were sold to the Army and served as tenders in Cattaro Bay, *Tb 44* becoming *Mamula*, *Tb 45* becoming *Obostnik* and *Tb 48* becoming *Arsa*.

HARBOUR DEFENCE SHIPS

Name	Launched	Disp (design)	Fate
ERZHERZOG ALBRECHT	24.4.72	5980t	BU *c* 1947
CUSTOZA	20.8.72	7609t	BU *c* 1920–21
KAISER MAX	28.12.75	3548t	BU *c* 1920–21
PRINZ EUGEN	7.9.77	3548t	BU *c* 1920–21
TEGETTHOFF	15.10.78	7431t	BU 1920

These obsolete centre battery ships were immobilised and used as harbour defence ships, tenders, hulks and finally as floating barracks. When their names were needed for new units they were renamed: *Erzherzog Albrecht* in 1908 became *Feuerspeier*; *Prinz Eugen* was converted to a repair ship and renamed *Vulkan*; *Tegetthoff* was renamed *Mars* in 1912. All were scrapped after the war with the exception of the *Feuerspeier* which was renamed *Buttafuoco* by Italy and served as a hulk until 1947.

Erzherzog Franz Ferdinand 1917

CAPITAL SHIPS

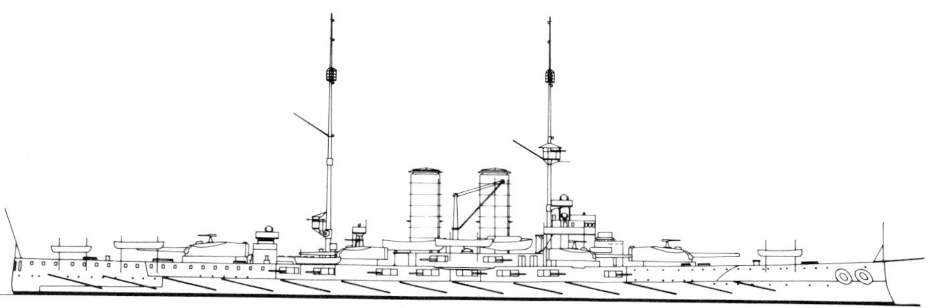

Zrinyi as completed

RADETZKY class *battleships*

Displacement: 14,508t design; 15,845.5t (*Zrinyi* 15,847t) deep load
Dimensions: 450ft 11in wl, 455ft 4in oa × 80ft 8in × 26ft 9in deep load
137.5m, 138.8m × 24.6m × 8.1m
Machinery: 2 shafts, 4-cyl VTE, 12 Yarrow boilers, 19,800ihp = 20.5kts. Coal 1350t max. Range 4000nm at 10kts
Armour: Belt 230mm–100mm (9in–4in), deck 48mm (2in), slopes 48mm (1¾in), torpedo bulkhead 54mm (2⅛in), main turrets 250mm–60mm (9¾in–2¼in), secondary turrets 200mm–50mm (7¾in–2in), casemates 120mm (4¾in), CT 250mm–100mm (9¾in–4¼in)
Armament: 4–30.5cm (12in)/45 (2×2), 8–24cm (9.4in)/45 (4×2), 20–10cm (3.9in)/50, 2–66mm/18 (landing guns), 4–47mm/44 QF, 1–47mm/33 QF, 3–45cm (17.7in) TT (2 beam, 1 stern)
Complement: 876 (890 in 1913–14)

Name	Builder	Laid down	Launched	Comp	Fate
ERZHERZOG FRANZ FERDINAND	STT	12.9.07	30.9.08	5.6.10	1926
RADETZKY	STT	26.11.07	3.7.09	15.1.11	1920–21
ZRINYI	STT	20.1.09	12.4.10	15.9.11	1920–21

About two weeks after the launching of the *Erzherzog Friedrich* the Austro-Hungarian Naval Section ordered the start of design work for the next generation of battleships. Six weeks after the launching of the *Erzherzog Ferdinand Max* the Austrian C-in-C, Admiral Montecuccoli, presented his plans for the future build-up of the fleet, envisaging a full strength of 12 battleships, 4 armoured cruisers, 8 scout cruisers, 18 ocean-going destroyers, 36 ocean-going torpedo-boats and 6 submarines. Between 25 and 29 September 1905 a design board evaluated five preliminary designs with similar dimensions and displacements, their armament variants reading dimensions and displacement, their armament variants reading as follows:

A 4–28cm (11in)/45 in centreline twin turrets, 4–24cm (9.4in)/45 in four wing single turrets, 8–19cm (7.5in)/45 in casemates
B main and intermediate battery as above, but tertiary battery 12–10cm (3.9in)/45 in casemates
C 8–28cm/45 in two centreline and two wing twin turrets, 16–10cm/45 in casemates
D 6–30.5cm (12in)/45 in two centreline twins and two wing single turrets, 16–10cm/45 in casemates
E 4–30.5cm/45 in two centreline twin turrets, 8–19cm/45 in four wing twin turrets, 12–10cm/45 in casemates.

Although the naval architects, headed by Siegfried Popper, and the gunnery technicians voted for the all-big-gun design (pre-project D) the board finally decided in favour of pre-project E. However, even Popper himself stated that a genuine all-big-gun battleship was impracticable as it would require a displacement of at least 16,000t, which meant not only increased building costs but also providing a new floating drydock. At a later stage of the design the intermediate calibre was raised from 19cm to 24cm; and 30.5cm was chosen as the main calibre because the wedge breech of the 28cm gun was unreliable. Although the main and intermediate calibre guns were nearly identical from the technical point of view, a comparison of performances shows that the decision was unwise: the 30.5cm gun had nearly double the armour penetration power and a 25 per cent greater range than the 24cm.

Another factor emphasised by Popper was underwater protection. In August and November 1906 explosive trials were held against the hulked centre battery ship *Kaiser Max*. The tests were held with a 10kg payload but brought no useful results – it had originally been intended to show blast damage on a 1:10 scale representing the standard 100kg mine charge. Bearing in mind these poor results Popper's development of an armoured double bottom anti-mine protection scheme, as it was first incorporated in the *Radetzky* design, was based entirely on mathematical hypothesis rather than on practical scientific experiment.

As a result of their small displacement the *Radetzkys* proved to be over-armed and suffered from structural weakness in the hull around the forward CT and magazines resulting in serious deformations. However they were not entirely unsuited for the special circumstances of Adriatic warfare; and again, for the displacement allotted, a very powerful design was achieved. Following the international design practice of the pre-dreadnought period, the choice of an intermediate battery was not unusual. The armament was excellent, and the armour not far below that of the British dreadnoughts – but some protection had been sacrificed to speed, it seems, which now approached that of the *Regina Elena* class.

Radetzky participated in the British Coronation Review of 1911, and all three units of the class made two training cruises in the eastern Mediterranean in 1912; in spring 1914 *Zrinyi* made a training cruise together with the two new dreadnoughts *Viribus Unitis* and *Tegetthoff* in the eastern Mediterranean, also visiting Malta. During the First World War they formed the 2nd Division of the 1st Battle Squadron. *Radetzky* was part of the bombardment group that knocked out the Montenegran batteries dominating Cattaro Bay from their positions at Mount Lovcen. All three units took part in the bombardment of the Italian coast in May 1915. For the rest of the war the 2nd Division remained inactive as a fleet in being at Pola harbour, and fell into Italian hands there after the end of the hostilities.

Radetzky and *Zrinyi* were put under US Navy command and transferred to a berth at Castelli Bay near Spalato (Split) to keep them out of the political quarrel between Italy and Yugoslavia. After the Treaty of St Germain all three *Radetzkys* were ceded to Italy; *Radetzky* and *Zrinyi* were handed over to the Italians by the US Navy outside the 3-mile zone and were scrapped in Italy in 1920–21; *Erzherzog Franz Ferdinand* was scrapped in Italy in 1926.

Tegetthoff May 1914
CPL

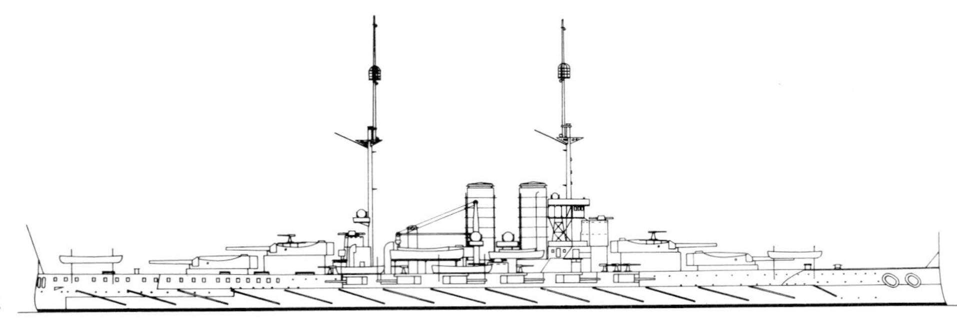

Viribus Unitis 1914

TEGETTHOFF class *battleships*

Displacement:	20,013.5t design; 21,595t deep load (*Szent István* 20,008t; 21,689t)
Dimensions:	495ft 5in wl, 499ft 3in oa × 89ft 8in × 29ft deep load *151.0m, 152.2m × 27.3m × 8.9m*
Machinery:	4-shaft Parsons geared turbines, 12 Yarrow boilers, 27,000shp = 20.3kts (*Szent István* 2-shaft AEG-Curtiss turbines, 12 Babcock & Wilcox boilers, 26,400shp = ?kts; no official trials due to war). Coal 2000t max. Range 4200nm at 10kts
Armour:	Belt 280mm–150mm (11in–6in), deck 48mm–30mm (1¾in–1¼in), slopes 48mm (1¾in), torpedo bulkhead 50mm (2in), main turrets 280mm–60mm (11in–2¼in), casemates 180mm (4¾in), CT 280mm–60mm (11in–2¼in)
Armament:	12–30.5cm (12in)/45 K 10 (4×3), 12–15cm (5.9in)/50 K 10, 18–66mm/50 K 10 (from 1914 3–4 on AA mountings on turret roofs), 2–66mm/18 (landing guns), 4–53.3cm (21in) TT (1 bow, 1 stern, 2 beam)
Complement:	1087 (*Szent István* 1094)

Name	Builder	Laid down	Launched	Comp	Fate
VIRIBUS UNITIS	STT	24.7.10	24.6.11	5.12.12	Sunk 1.11.18
TEGETTHOFF	STT	24.9.10	21.3.12	21.7.13	BU 1924–25
PRINZ EUGEN	STT	16.1.12	30.11.12	17.7.14	Sunk 28.6.22
SZENT ISTVÁN	Danubius, Fiume	29.1.12	17.1.14	13.12.15	Sunk 10.6.18

Influenced by the impending construction of the first Italian dreadnought, the Austrian C-in-C, Montecuccoli, announced on 20 February 1908 that Austria-Hungary would build a new generation of battleships displacing 18,000t–19,000t. In March 1908 Germany launched her first dreadnought *(Nassau)* and took the next step in the naval arms race by approving the Second Naval Amendment. Italy therefore postponed the keel laying of her first dreadnought obviously because Cuniberti and his chief naval engineer Edoardo Masdeo had to rethink the parameters of their design. In October 1908 the Austrian Naval Section issued orders for preliminary design studies and furthermore offered a prize in a design competition open to Austro-Hungarian naval architects. The results of both were to be overtaken by events during the next half-year. When in March 1909 the STT yard presented five different design studies, it had just become public that the Italians had gone their own way by adopting triple turrets for their *Dreadnought A* (later the *Dante Alighieri*). The further development of the new Austrian battleship became problematical for the naval authorities, so they decided to adopt the triple turret as well, at the same time asking their German ally for information on the design of their newest type, the *Kaiser* class. This they duly received in April 1909 by special permission of the German Emperor. Nevertheless it seems that Austria-Hungary did not take into consideration German design philosophy and experience, since the basic *Tegetthoff* design had been accepted on 27 April 1909.

Italy had begun construction of *Dreadnought A* by 6 June 1909, so the Austrian C-in-C believed that obtaining the necessary funds in the 1910 budget (to be discussed in November 1909) would not be difficult. Two of the *Radetzky* class pre-dreadnoughts had already been launched and STT urgently needed follow-up contracts to maintain their force of skilled workers, so Montecuccoli lost no time and suggested as early as August 1909 that both STT and Skoda should start construction at their own risk until the budget was approved. To everyone's surprise the funds were refused for political reasons, and Montecuccoli was forced to embark on an elaborate campaign of deception and propaganda to disguise the fact that the ships were being built without parliamentary approval. He claimed that industry was financing construction on speculation, but it certainly was not, and was very uneasy with the situation. Not until Montecuccoli took an expensive 32 million crowns credit on his own responsibility were the keels of dreadnoughts IV and V laid, on 24 July and 24 September 1910. In the meantime Italy had launched the *Dante Alighieri* and started construction of her second dreadnought and France had laid the keel of her first *(Courbet)* to match the Central Powers' dreadnought superiority in the Mediterranean. Therefore the two Austrian dreadnoughts were already in the early stages of construction when the mutual parliamentary delegations met in March 1911 to discuss the 1911 budget.

From the technical point of view the *Tegetthoff*s were very compact and powerful ships and the first dreadnoughts in service with 12in triple turrets, although Italy was the first naval power to design a triple turret and lay down a triple-turreted ship. Obviously German design theories about underwater protection came too late, so once again the *Tegetthoff*s had Popper's underwater protection scheme incorporating a double bottom. Although the Austro-Hungarian Naval Technical Committee had organised a design competition for this type, it was entirely Popper's brainchild because he had been consultant to the main contractor, STT, since his retirement in 1907.

In spring 1914 *Viribus Unitis* and *Tegetthoff* made their only training cruise in the eastern Mediterranean. During the war they formed the 1st Division of the 1st Battle Squadron and participated in the shore bombardment of the Italian coast in May 1915 (with the exception of *Szent István*, which was nearing completion at the Pola N Yd where she had been towed after launching). In June 1918 all four were to form the backbone of a raiding force which was to attack the Otranto barrage, but *Szent István* was torpedoed and sunk off Premuda Island on 10 June 1918 by the Italian *MAS 15* during the sortie, causing the whole operation to be cancelled. *Viribus Unitis* was sunk in Pola harbour on 1 November 1918 by a limpet mine laid by two Italian frogman, after she had been handed over to the Yugoslav National Council. *Tegetthoff* was ceded to Italy in 1919 and scrapped in 1924–25 at La Spezia. *Prinz Eugen* was ceded to France in 1919, towed to Toulon and completely disarmed and stripped of her interior fittings. She was used as an explosives target for underwater shock tests and aircraft bombs. She was finally sunk as a gunnery target on 28 June 1922 by the French battleships *Bretagne*, *Jean Bart*, *Paris* and *France*. Whether some of her guns were used in coastal batteries by the French or the Germans (Atlantic Wall) is not known.

Admiral Spaun 1917

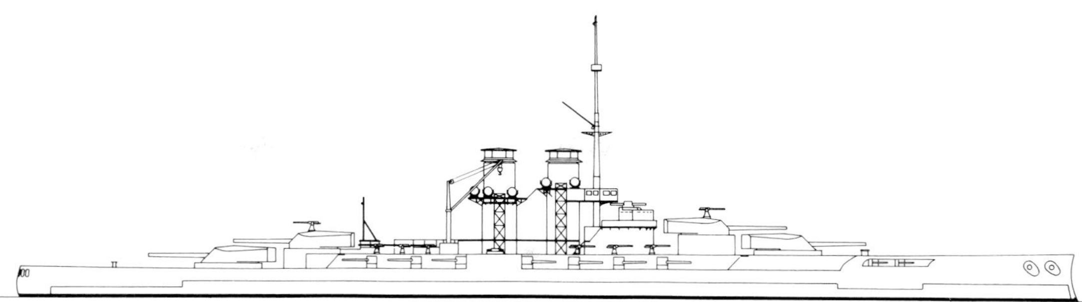

Improved *Tegetthoff* class July 1914 design

Improved TEGETTHOFF class *battleships*

Displacement: 24,500t design

Dimensions: 564ft 3in wl, 568ft 3in oa × 93ft 6in × 27ft 5in (design)
172.0m, 173.2m × 28.5m × 8.4m

Machinery: 4-shaft steam turbines, 15 Yarrow boilers (9 coal-, 6 oil-fired), 31,000shp = 21kts (design). Coal 1425t, oil 1425t max. Range 5000nm at 10kts

Armour: Belt 310mm–140mm (12¼–5½), deck 36mm (1½in), slopes 36mm (1½in), torpedo bulkhead 85mm (3¼in), main turrets 340mm–80mm (13¼in–3¼in), casemates 150mm (6in), CT 320mm

Armament: 10–35cm (13.8in)/45 (2×2, 2×3), 15–15cm (5.9in)/50, 20–90mm/45 (12 on AA mountings), 2–47mm/47, 2–66mm/18 (landing guns), 6–53.3cm (21in) TT (2×1, 2×2, bow, stern and beam)

Complement: No figures available

Name	Builder	Laid down*	Launched	Comp*	Fate
BATTLESHIP VIIII	STT	1.7.14	–	30.6.17	Never laid down
BATTLESHIP IX	Danubius, Fiume	1.1.15	–	31.12.17	Never laid down
BATTLESHIP X	STT	1.6.16	–	31.5.19	Never laid down
BATTLESHIP XI	Danubius, Fiume	1.6.16	–	31.5.19	Never laid down

*As proposed in secret schedule of 12.1.14

International naval literature always refers to the projected battleships VIII-XI as the 'Ersatz *Monarch* class', but in official files these ships were given only project numbers (project I, II, III and so on) or tonnage designations (22,000t battleships, 23,400t battleship and the final variant 24,500t battleship); they were finally referred to as the 'Improved *Tegetthoff* class'. Initially the pressure for a new group of dreadnoughts came from the Skoda Works and not from the Navy. While completing the 12in triple turrets for the *Tegetthoffs* Skoda requested follow-up business, arguing for the necessity to maintain highly skilled jobs and to ensure design continuity. Therefore on 18 April 1911 Skoda submitted to the Naval Section detailed plans for 13.6in (345mm) twin and triple turrets. They had anticipated the naval architects' requirements and proposed triple turrets and superimposed twins – which had a strong resemblance to contemporary British turrets – to be fitted on the centreline.

The Naval Section rejected this design for minor technical reasons, and to counter Skoda's dominating influence, on 3 June 1911 the naval authorities ordered preparatory designs for the next generation of dreadnoughts to the following alternative particulars: A 23,000t, 10–30.5cm/45, 18–15cm, 24–66mm QF; and B 24,600t, 10–34.5cm/45, 18–15cm, 24–66mm QF. The displacement limit was the result of the need to fit the future ship (with half consumable stores and full ammunition load) into floating drydock No 1, which had a lifting power of 23,800t. It was believed, nevertheless, that such a design could match contemporary opponents by cutting down the cruising radius – *ie* saving fuel weight – because of the geographical position of the Hapsburg Empire. The most remarkable requirement was for alternative designs for both diesel and turbine propulsion; but diesel was soon rejected in favour of conventional coal- and oil-burning boilers.

In December 1911 the Naval Technical Committee presented its design studies for 'A' and 'B', which had the following particulars: A – 22,000t, 12–30.5cm/45, 22–15cm/50, 24–75cm/50 QF, 5 TT, and B – 23,400t, 10–34.5cm/45, 22–15cm/50, 24–75mm/50. The demand for more secondary armament was solved by using twin casemates. The Skoda 75mm/50 (3in) QF was a further development of the standard 66mm/45 (2.6in) and was offered to the Austro-Hungarian Navy in 1911. After detailed calculations had been done it became clear that the strict tonnage limit had been exceeded so sub-variants (with a cut-down quarterdeck) were presented in February 1912.

In December 1911 private industry once again tried to demonstrate their predominance in design matters and Danubius, STT, CNT and the naval architect Silvius Morin presented no less than 26 alternative designs. However, Popper's successor, Pitzinger, did not want to be overruled a second time and all other designs were rejected. In the meantime Skoda was asked to work out new designs for the 34.5cm/45 turrets. A board meeting of 12 May 1912 increased the final calibre to 35cm (13.8in) to balance the loss of penetration power in the standard shell to be developed. A second reason might have been the compatibility with German ammunition (compare the calibre of the German battlecruisers of the *Mackensen* class). In January 1913 the Naval Technical Committee presented its next design: 24,500t, 10–35cm, 18–15cm. The strict weight limit forced the designers to save every possible ton and therefore they reduced the secondary armament, omitted the aft CT and the mainmast and designed the heavy guns in triple turrets superimposed over twins. As this obviously affected stability, ammunition stowage was reduced and in July 1913 exactly the same design was presented with superimposed twin mountings.

Apparently Austrian naval architects felt that such an austere design would not be well balanced and presented two enlarged alternative designs in January 1914, showing that more displacement was necessary, also allowing a speed increase of 2kts: pre-project I – 29,600t, 23kts, 12–35cm, 18–15cm; and pre-project II – 32,000t, 23kts, 13–35cm, 18–15cm. However the tonnage limit was upheld, so in July the last design variant was presented; for weight reasons the number of secondary guns was reduced to 14–15cm. This is the last design variant, to which the 'Improved *Tegetthoffs*' obviously would have been built.

From the political point of view the history of this design was not a repeat of the *Tegetthoffs*, although for a second time industry wanted to begin construction on credit. In March 1913 the Crown Prince urged the new C-in-C, Admiral Haus, to order the new dreadnoughts, because the last of the STT-built *Tegetthoffs* had been launched 4 months previously and the yard urgently needed follow-up orders. But the Hungarian authorities stubbornly refused to allow construction on credit, arguing that the only legal way would be by providing funds in the 1914–15 budget. Even the Emperor himself could not persuade the Hungarian ministry of finance to acquiesce, resulting in a one-year delay in dreadnought construction. The 1914–15 budget – including the new battleships VIII–IX – was not approved until 28 May 1914. At the end of June 1914 STT was ordered to build No VIII and Danubius to build No IX, but due to the outbreak of the First World War the keel laying was postponed and never took place.

Skoda, which had already begun to manufacture the 35cm guns and turrets, delivered a trial barrel for first tests in November 1914 and completed guns No 1 and 2. No 1, dubbed 'Georg', was used for a mixed long-range battery (together with a 38cm/17) operating in Northern Italy which first fired on 25 May 1916. Guns No 2 and 3 were also completed but never saw front-line action; at the end of war gun No 4 was ready for delivery at Skoda and guns No 5–11 were in different stages of production.

A last attempt to build at least one unit of the 'Improved *Tegetthoff*' class in an austere version under the limitations of war was made in May 1915. The use of armour plate already manufactured for the triple turrets was discussed, with a view to building twin mountings for one ship with 8–35cm guns in four twin turrets; but the idea was dropped when Italy declared war.

AUSTRIA-HUNGARY

CRUISERS

Admiral Spaun as completed

After an eight-year gap the Austro-Hungarian Navy re-entered the field of cruiser construction when the Naval Technical Committee was ordered to design a 3500t cruiser on 1 May 1906. In the previous period the complex typology of cruisers, avisos, scouts, flotilla leaders and torpedo cruisers had become somewhat simplified in the world's navies. What was asked for in Austria-Hungary was a turbine-powered ship which would be faster than contemporary cruisers such as the British *Adventure*, the US *Chester* and the German *Emden*), with slightly better armour protection; therefore armament had to be sacrificed. *Admiral Spaun* and her successors were designed as typical fast scouts, able to employ hit-and-run tactics to disrupt enemy communications and shipping routes and to dominate an engagement by the use of speed – and indeed they were used in this role during the war.

ADMIRAL SPAUN *scout cruiser*

Displacement: 3500t design; 4000t deep load
Dimensions: 425ft 4in wl, 428ft 8in oa × 41ft 11in × 17ft 4in deep load
129.7m, 130.6m × 12.8m × 5.3m
Machinery: 4 shafts, 6 Parsons turbines, 16 Yarrow water-tube boilers, 25,130shp = 27.07kts max
Armour: Side 60mm (3¹/₃in), deck 20mm (¾in), CT 50mm (2in)
Armament: 7–10cm (3.9in)/50, 1–47mm/44 (landing gun), 1–8mm MG, 2–45cm (17.7in) TT (1×2, added in 1916)
Complement: 327

Name	Builder	Laid down	Launched	Comp	Fate
ADMIRAL SPAUN	Pola N Yd	30.5.08	30.10.09	15.11.10	BU 1920–21

Admiral Spaun was the first major turbine-powered unit of the Austrian-Hungarian Navy; she had a 4-shaft arrangement, 2 of her 6 turbines being cruising turbines on the inner shafts. Nevertheless her propulsion system must be seen as an experimental prototype, and the ship suffered so many teething troubles with her engines that she never participated in the cruiser operations of her successors, although she saw wartime service in minor and less dangerous roles. In 1917 it was planned to up-gun her by replacing the 2–10cm on the forecastle by 1–15cm/50, but this was never executed. In 1920 she was ceded to Britain and immediately sold to Italy for scrapping.

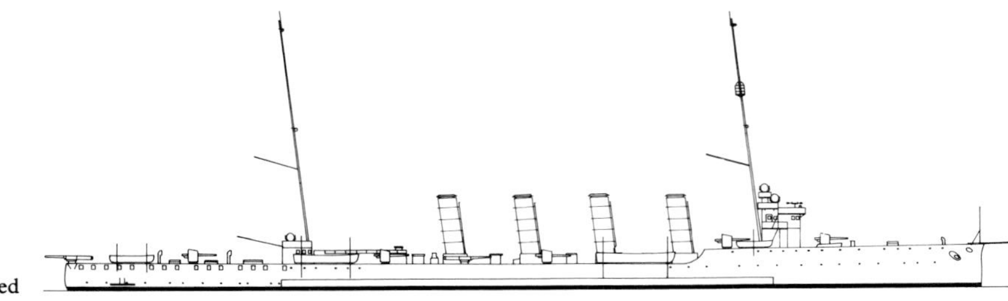
Novara as completed

The three 'modified *Spauns*' were approved in the same budget as the *Tegetthoffs*. Basically they had the same dimensions and displacement as *Admiral Spaun*, but with the rapid development of turbines 52t machinery weight could be saved by using a simpler 2-shaft arrangement. Of this 21t were used to strengthen the hull and the bulkheads, the remaining 21t being used to increase the armament. Of the two proposed alternatives (adding 1–15cm gun or 2–10cm), the second was chosen. The 'modified *Spauns*' therefore were a real improvement, enjoying reliable machinery and two more guns, although still being inferior in armament when compared with their contemporary opponents. As Fred T Jane stated in 1912, the period of the scout was over, and these units were very rapidly obsolescent. For reasons of equal distribution of armament contracts, two of them were to be built at the new Hungarian shipyard of Danubius at Fiume (Rijeka), while the name-ship was the first major warship built at the privately owned Cantiere Navale Triestino. In contrast to her Hungarian sisters she had a different type of turbine which gave her a slightly lower speed.

Modified ADMIRAL SPAUN class *scout cruisers*

Displacement: 3500t design; 4010t deep load
Dimensions: As *Admiral Spaun*
Machinery: 2-shaft AEG (*Saida* Melms-Pfenniger) turbines, 16 Yarrow boilers, 30,178shp = 27kts
Armour: Side 60mm (2³/₈in), deck 20mm (¾in), turrets 40mm–8mm (1⁵/₈in–³/₈in), CT 50mm (2in)
Armament: 9–10cm (3.9in)/50, 1–47mm/44 (landing gun)
Complement: 340

Name	Builder	Laid down	Launched	Comp	Fate
SAIDA	CNT	9.9.11	26.10.12	1.8.14	To Italy 1920
HELGOLAND	Danubius, Fiume	28.10.11	23.11.12	29.8.14	To Italy 1920
NOVARA	Danubius, Fiume	9.12.12	15.2.13	10.1.15	To France 1920

The three cruisers saw extensive wartime service, participating in several cruiser actions. Like their predecessor it was planned to up-gun them in 1917 by removing 3–10cm on the forecastle and 2–10cm on the quarterdeck and replacing them by 1–15cm/50 on the forecastle and another on the quarterdeck, but this was also never executed. However, 1–66mm/50 AA and 6–53.3cm (2in) TT (3×2) were added in 1917. In 1920 *Saida* and *Helgoland* were ceded to the Italian Navy and commissioned as *Venezia* and *Brindisi* respectively. Both were discarded on 11 March 1937. *Novara* was ceded to France in 1920, commissioned as *Thionville* and served as a gunnery and torpedo TS in the Mediterranean until 1932. She was then disarmed and served as a stationary accommodation ship at the naval arsenal of Toulon; in 1941 she was sold for scrapping.

In 1913 the Chinese government ordered four light cruisers of two different designs from Cantiere Navale Triestino, Monfalcone. Preparatory work began in December 1914, the keel of the large Chinese cruiser being laid in March 1915. When Italy declared war on Austria-Hungary on 23 May 1915 only parts of the keel and some frames were erected.

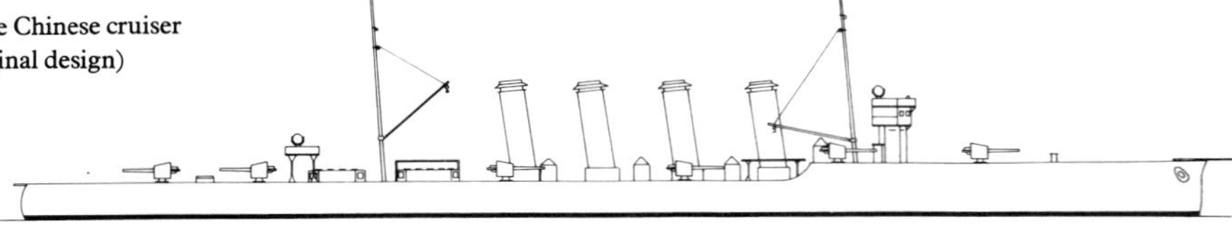
1917 modification of large Chinese cruiser (see under China for original design)

Ex-Chinese *light cruisers*

Unfortunately the battle line virtually ran across the shipyard area, resulting in damage beyond repair to most of the ships under construction there. When Austrian troops re-captured the area on 27 October 1917 during the 12th battle of the Isonzo, the four cruisers for China showed remarkably little damage because construction was so little advanced.

The design of the large Chinese cruiser could be easily reworked to Austro-Hungarian standards, the 37,000shp turbine set and the entire boiler system were ready for delivery, and 31 per cent of the hull material was already stockpiled, so plans were drawn up in April 1918 to restart work on at least the large cruiser. Proposed armament was 8–15cm (5.9in)/50, 9–90mm/50 AA, 4–45cm (17.7in) TT (2×2). However, during the discussions the war reached a point where it became impossible to restart construction.

Helgoland early in the war

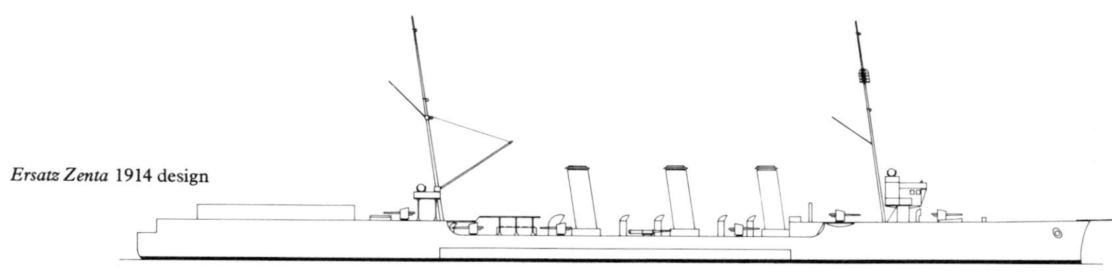

Ersatz Zenta 1914 design

Approved on 28 May 1914 in the same 1914–15 naval budget as 'Improved *Tegetthoffs*', these three fast light cruisers were a continuation of and improvement on previous designs, showing a clear switch from the scout to the better armed fleet cruiser. Of the designs submitted by the naval architects Pitzinger, Morin and Fiala, apparently Fiala's designs were taken into consideration, but before a clear decision in favour of any one was taken war broke out and the laying down of the first unit was postponed.

In December 1915, although Italy had now entered the war, the Naval Command demanded changes in the cruiser design which clearly reflected the lessons of the first year of war and also the urgent need for fast but better armed cruisers for Adriatic warfare: 19cm and 15cm main armament plus powerful AA guns and more than trebled belt armour. However, most skilled shipyard workers had been conscripted into the Army, leaving the building yards with an insufficient number of experienced shipwrights, so all wartime projects must be considered as pure design studies without any serious possibility of completion.

Ersatz ZENTA type *light cruisers*

Displacement: 4950t design; 5611t deep load
Dimensions: 496ft wl, 502ft 3in oa × 44ft 11in × 20ft 11in deep load
151.2m, 153.1m × 13.7m × 6.4m
Machinery: 2-shaft AEG turbines, ? boilers, 38,000shp = 30.1kts
Armour: Original design, side 20mm (¾in), deck 38mm (1½in)
1915 redesign, belt 150mm–120mm (6in–4¾in)
Armament: Original design 14–12cm (4.7in)/45, 1–47mm/44, 2–45cm (17.7in) TT, 1–66mm/18 (landing gun)
1915 redesign 2–19cm (7.5in)/45, 6–15cm (5.9in)/50, 4–90mm/45 AA, 2–53.3cm (21in) TT
Complement: ?

Name	Builder	Laid down*	Launched	Comp*	Fate
CRUISER K	–	1.7.14	–	31.12.16	Never laid down
CRUISER L	–	1.7.15	–	31.12.17	Never laid down
CRUISER M	–	1.7.15	–	31.12.17	Never laid down

*As proposed in secret schedule of 12.1.14

DESTROYERS AND TORPEDO-BOATS

The introduction of destroyers and the various types of torpedo-boats into the Austro-Hungarian Navy clearly shows two distinct stages, a third stage of development based on the wartime lessons, being confined to the drawing board. After an international period of rethinking the tactics and size of torpedo-carrying craft, in 1904 Austria-Hungary introduced its new types, when a displacement of 400t was regarded as sufficient for a destroyer, 200t for a sea-going torpedo-boat and 110t for a coastal torpedo-boat. Only 6 years later rapid technological development required turbine propulsion for all types except the coastal torpedo-boat. With the introduction of the later types in 1910 the displacement of Austrian destroyers doubled to 800t, and the displacement of sea-going torpedo-boats rose nearly one-third to 275t. Only the coastal torpedo-boat was adequate in its old dimensions.

Thus at the outbreak of the First World War the *Huszár* class – formerly the backbone of the Austrian destroyer force – was little more than an old but reliable sea-going torpedo-boat. Because of the particular geographical situation of the Dual Monarchy (being bottled up in the Adriatic), the main wartime duties of the Austro-Hungarian destroyer and torpedo-boat force were patrol, escort and minesweeping, offensive action being reserved for the few modern units.

Although of largely academic interest, it is worth looking at the wartime lessons as seen in the 1918–20 naval budget. What was envisaged was a big flotilla leader (2400t; 4–15cm, 4–90m DP) replacing the under-gunned scouts and destroyers; a 1000t destroyer (2–12cm, 2–90mm DP) replacing the series from *Tb 74* onward; and 50 MTBs and MGBs replacing all torpedo-boats, while all obsolete torpedo-boats would have been converted to minesweepers.

Ulan as completed

Tátra as completed

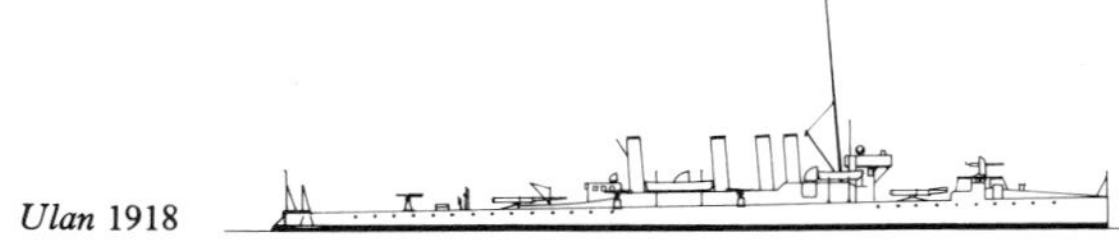
Ulan 1918

HUSZÁR class *destroyers*

Displacement:	389.4t design; 414t deep load
Dimensions:	220ft 3in wl, 224ft 4in oa × 20ft 6in × 6ft 3in deep load *67.1m, 68.4m × 6.3m × 1.9m*
Machinery:	2-shaft 4-cyl VTE, 4 Yarrow water-tube boilers, 6000ihp = 28.43kts
Armament:	1–66mm/45, 7–47mm/44 (from 1912–13 1–66mm/45, 5–66mm/30), 2–45cm (17.7in) TT
Complement:	65–70

Name	Builder	Launched	Fate
HUSZÁR (i)	Danubius, Fiume	31.5.05	Wrecked 3.12.08
ULAN	STT	8.4.06	To Greece 1920
STREITER	STT	16.6.06	Sunk in collision 16.4.18
WILDFANG	STT	29.8.06	Mined 4.6.17
SCHARFSCHUTZE	STT	5.12.06	To Italy 1920, BU
USKOKE	STT	20.7.07	To Italy 1920, BU
HUSZÁR (ii)	Pola N Yd	20.12.10	To Italy 1920, BU
TURUL	Danubius, Fiume	9.10.08	To Italy 1920, BU
PANDUR	Danubius, Fiume	25.10.08	To France 1920, BU
CSIKÓS	Danubius, Fiume	24.1.09	To Italy 1920, BU
REKA	Danubius, Fiume	28.4.09	To France 1920, BU
DINARA	Danubius, Fiume	16.10.09	To Italy 1920, BU
VELEBIT	Danubius, Fiume	24.7.09	To Italy 1920, BU

In 1904 the Austro-Hungarian Navy ordered a prototype 400t destroyer from Yarrow, together with a 200t torpedo-boat. A further 11 units of the Yarrow destroyer type were built at the above mentioned domestic yards. By 1910 advances of international destroyer development had left this type under-armed, so they were up-gunned in 1912–13. The first *Huszár* ran aground near Traste and sank, so a replacement unit was built at the Pola N Yd to maintain the full dozen.

Although obsolete at the outbreak of war these boats saw extensive wartime service: *Wildfang* was mined west of Peneda Island; *Streiter* sank off Laurana after a collision with SS *Petka*. All the others were ceded to Italy or France and were scrapped immediately, except *Ulan*, which went to Greece as the *Smyrni*, and was discarded in 1928.

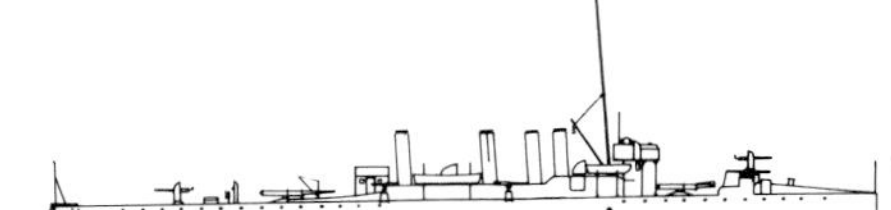
Warasdiner 1915

WARASDINER *destroyer*

Displacement:	As *Huszár* class
Dimensions:	As *Huszár* class
Machinery:	2-shaft VTE,4 Yarrow water-tube boilers, 6000ihp = 30kts
Armament:	As built 2–3in (76mm)/50 Armstrong, 4–3pdr (47mm)/50 Armstrong, 2–45cm (17.7in) TT (1×2) As rearmed 2–66mm/45, 4–66mm/30, 4–45cm (17.7in) TT (2×2)
Complement:	75

Originally ordered from STT by the Chinese government as *Lung Tuan* in 1911, and intended to be the prototype of a class of 12 boats. Launched in 1912 the *Lung Tuan* was taken over by the Austro-Hungarian Navy on 28 August 1914, renamed *Warasdiner* and rearmed to Austrian standards. None of her sister-ships was ever laid down. *Warasdiner* saw active wartime service, was ceded to Italy in 1920 and scrapped.

TÁTRA class *destroyers*

Displacement:	850t design; 1000t deep load
Dimensions:	273ft 11in oa × 25ft 7in × 9ft 10in deep load inc propeller *83.5m × 7.8m × 3.0m*
Machinery:	2-shaft AEG-Curtiss turbines, 6 boilers (4 oil-, 2 coal-fired), 20,640shp = 32.6kts
Armament:	2–10cm (3.9in)/50, 6–66mm/45, 4–45cm (17.7in) TT (2×2)
Complement:	105

Name	Builder	Launched	Fate
TÁTRA	Danubius, Porto Ré	5.11.12	To Italy 1920
BALATON	Danubius, Porto Ré	16.11.12	To Italy 1920
CSEPEL	Danubius, Porto Ré	30.12.12	To Italy 1920
LIUA (i)	Danubius, Porto Ré	15.3.13	Mined 29.12.15
TRIGLAV (i)	Danubius, Porto Ré	22.12.13	Mined 29.12.15
ORJEN	Danubius, Porto Ré	26.8.13	To Italy 1920

In May 1910 the Austrian Naval authorities asked the Danubius, Stabilimento Tecnico Triestino, Cantiere Navale Triestino and Vulcan, Stettin, shipyards to tender for six 800t turbine-powered destroyers capable of 32.5kts. Ultimately the Hungarian Danubius yard was awarded the contract for political reasons – to ensure Hungarian approval of the 1911 naval budget containing funds for the *Tegetthoffs*, two of which were already under construction. The boats were built at Danubius' subsidiary at Porto Ré (Kraljevica) and saw active wartime service.

Lika and *Triglav* were lost after striking mines off Durazzo. All others were ceded to Italy in 1920 and renamed as follows: *Tátra* and *Balaton* became *Fasana* and *Zenson* respectively and were discarded in 1923; *Csepel* was recommissioned as *Muggia* and was lost on 25 March 1929 off Amoy during a typhoon; *Orjen* was renamed *Pola* and then *Zenson* in 1931 and discarded in 1937.

Ersatz TÁTRA class *destroyers*

Displacement:	880t design; 1045t deep load
Dimensions:	277ft 6in wl, 279ft 9in × 25ft 7in × 7ft 10in hull, deep load *84.6m, 85.4m × 7.8m × 2.4m*
Machinery:	2-shaft AEG-Curtiss turbines, 6 boilers (4 oil-, 2 mixed oil/coal-fired), 22,360shp = 32.6kts
Armament:	2–10cm (3.9in)/50, 6–66mm/45 (2 on AA mountings), 1–8mm MG, 4–45cm (17.7in) TT (2×2)
Complement:	114

Name	Builder	Launched	Fate
TRIGLAV (ii)	Danubius, Porto Ré	24.2.17	To Italy
LIKA (ii)	Danubius, Porto Ré	8.5.17	To Italy 1920
DUKLA	Danubius, Porto Ré	18.7.17	To Italy 1920
UZSOK	Danubius, Porto Ré	26.9.17	To France 1920

Six further *Tátra* type destroyers had been authorised on 28 May 1914 from the 1914–15 naval budget but they were never started due to the outbreak of war. To replace wartime losses and to increase the number urgently needed modern destroyers, four replacement units of this type were authorised in 1916. Because of their relatively late completion they did not see much wartime service and were ceded to Italy and France in 1920. *Triglav* (ii) became *Grado* and was discarded in 1937; *Lika* (ii) and *Uzsok* became *Cortellazzo* and *Monfalcone* respectively and were discarded in 1939. France renamed *Dukla* the *Matelot Leblanc*, which was discarded in 1936.

Improved TÁTRA class *destroyers*

Displacement: As Ersatz *Tátra* class
Dimensions: As Ersatz *Tátra* class
Machinery: As Ersatz *Tátra* class, but Danubius turbines
Armament: 2–12cm (4.7in)/45, 2–90mm/45 AA, 4–45cm (17.7in) TT (2×2)
Complement: –

Four units of this up-gunned version of the Ersatz *Tátra* class were ordered on 22 December 1917, but the steel shortage prevented their being laid down.

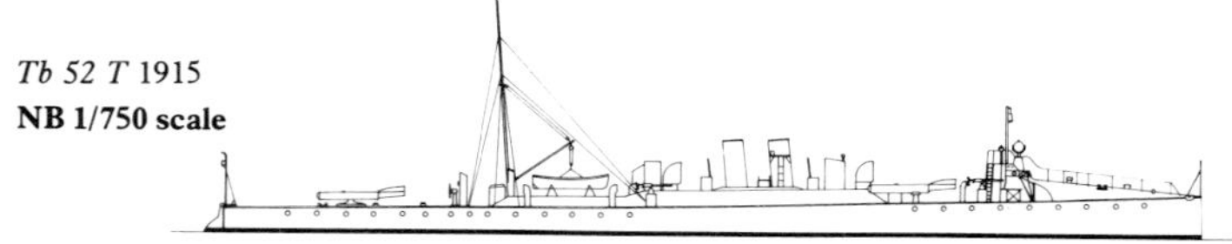
Tb 52 T 1915
NB 1/750 scale

KAIMAN class *sea-going torpedo-boats*

Displacement: 210t design; 203.3t deep load
Dimensions: 186ft 8in × 17ft 9in × 4ft 5in
56.9m × 5.4m × 1.4m
Machinery: 1-shaft 4-cyl VTE, 2 boilers, 3000ihp = 26.2kts
Armament: 4–47mm/33, 3–45cm (17.7in) TT (1–8mm MG added 1915)
Complement: 38

Class (launched, renumbered 1913):
Kaiman (2.6.05, *Tb 50 E*), *Anaconda* (7.5.06, *Tb 51 T*), *Alligator* (30.6.06, *Tb 52 T*), *Krokodil* (25.7.06, *Tb 53 T*), *Wal* (10.9.06, *Tb 54 T*), *Seehund* (15.9.06, *Tb 55 T*), *Delphin* (29.11.06, *Tb 56 T*), *Narwal* (17.12.06, *Tb 57 T*), *Hai* (23.3.07, *Tb 58 T*), *Möve* (30.3.07, *Tb 59 T*), *Schwalbe* (9.4.07, *Tb 60 T*), *Pinguin* (18.4.07, *Tb 61 T*), *Drache* (13.7.07, *Tb 62 T*), *Grief* (8.7.07, *Tb 63 T*), *Triton* (18.7.08, *Tb 64 F*), *Hydra* (11.10.08, *Tb 65 F*), *Skorpion* (15.11.08, *Tb 66 F*), *Phönix* (10.1.09, *Tb 67 F*), *Krake* (7.2.09, *Tb 68 F*), *Polyp* (17.4.09, *Tb 69 F*), *Echse* (8.5.09, *Tb 70 F*), *Molch* (14.7.09, *Tb 71 F*), *Kormoran* (31.7.09, *Tb 72 F*), *Alk* (2.10.09, *Tb 73 F*)

After the commissioning of the four *Cobra* class boats there was a break of four years in Austrian torpedo-boat and destroyer construction. In 1904 a prototype boat was ordered from Yarrow, which was christened *Kaiman*. Both Stabilimento Tecnico Triestino (representing the Austrian half of the domestic yards) and the new Danubius, Fiume yard (representing the Hungarian part) received British plans and engineering assistance and eventually built 23 units of this class. By an order of 19 November 1913 all torpedo-boats in service gave up their names and were given arabic numbers instead. This was carried out by 1 April 1910. *Kaiman* became *Tb 50 E* (the suffix letter denoting 'England', since she was the Yarrow-built unit) and locally-built boats became *Tb 51 T*—*Tb 63 T* (T denoting Trieste, for the STT-built units) and *Tb 64 F*–*Tb 73 F* (F meaning Fiume, for the Danubius boat). This suffix letter was omitted by the order of 21 May 1917, so from this time on all Austrian torpedo-boats had only numbers. The *Kaiman* class proved to be a very successful design, all boats seeing extensive active service during World War One. All survived, although some boats were badly damaged after collisions or mining. After the war they were distributed between Great Britain and Yugoslavia, Great Britain scrapping her boats in 1920 in Italy. Yugoslavia kept her boats in service until 1927–28 under the following new names: *Tb 54*, as *T 12*, *Tb 60* as *T 9*, *Tb 61* as *T 10*, *Tb 69* as *T 11*.

Tb 74 T class *sea-going torpedo-boats*

Displacement: 262t design; 267.3t deep load
Dimensions: 189ft 9in × 18ft 10in × 5ft 1in
57.8m × 5.8m × 1.5m
Machinery: 2-shaft Parsons turbines, 2 Yarrow water-tube boilers, 5000shp = 28kts
Armament: 2–66mm/30 (on AA mountings from 1917), 2–45cm (17.7in) TT (1–8mm MG added 1914)
Complement: 41

Class (launched):
Tb 74 T (28.8.13), *Tb 75 T* (20.11.13), *Tb 76 T* (15.12.13), *Tb 77 T* (30.1.14), *Tb 78 T* (4.3.14), *Tb 79 T* (30.4.14), *Tb 80 T* (3.8.14), *Tb 81 T* (6.8.14)

In 1910 the Naval Technical Committee ordered the development of a 275t coastal torpedo-boat, capable of sustaining 30kts for 10 hours (this being the duration of a passage from Cattaro to the Otranto Straits, time to gain contact and attack before morning, and return at full speed – four years before the war such torpedo-boat attacks on enemy forces blockading the Otranto Straits were clearly predicted). Turbines, diesel and turbo-electric propulsion were discussed, but the decision was quickly made: diesels in the necessary dimensions were not available; and turbo-electric propulsion would not be advisable without the practical experience gained by running a test vessel. Of the two yards competing, STT won the contract for eight boats. Although their particulars were very nearly those requested by the Navy for the coastal torpedo-boat, they were classified as sea-going boats. Being the first Austrian turbine-powered small units, it is not surprising that the first boats experienced constant troubles with their machinery. Initially they were to be armed with 3–66mm/30 guns and 3 TT (1×2, 1×1) but for reasons of standardisation they received the same armament as the following Danubius-built class.

All boats saw active service on convoy, submarine hunting, escort and minesweeping duties, and all survived the war. *Tb 74*, *Tb 75*, *Tb 80* and *Tb 81* were allocated to Rumania in 1920 and renamed *Viforul*, *Virtej*, *Vijelia* and *Zborul*, the first three being stricken in 1927, but *Zborul* was in service until 1958. *Tb 76*–*Tb 79* were allocated to Yugoslavia and renamed *T 1*–*T 4*: *T 4* was lost after stranding in 1932; *T 2* was stricken in 1939; *T 1* and *T 2* were incorporated into the Italian Navy in April 1941, under their old designations. After the collapse of Mussolini's empire, the former *T 1* was returned to the navy of the independent Croatian state on 7 December 1943 renamed *Golesnica* and served with the later Yugoslavian Navy until 1959. The former *T 2* also became part of the navy of independent Croatia in 1943, but served as the German *TA 48* with an exclusively Croatian crew; she sank after suffering bomb hits on 20 February 1945 at Trieste.

Dukla April 1918

Tb 81 T before May 1917

Tb 89 after May 1917

Tb 82 F class *sea-going torpedo-boats*

Displacement: 244t design; 267t deep load
Dimensions: 192ft 9in × 19ft 2in × 5ft 1in
58.8m × 5.8m × 1.5m
Machinery: 2-shaft AEG-Curtiss turbines, 2 Yarrow water-tube boilers, 5000shp = 28kts
Armament: 2–66mm/30 (on AA mountings from 1917), 1–8mm MG, 4–45cm (7.7in) TT (2×2)
Complement: 41

Class (launched):
Tb 82 F (11.8.14), *Tb 83 F* (7.11.14), *Tb 84 F* (21.11.14), *Tb 85 F* (5.12.14), *Tb 86 F* (19.12.14), *Tb 87 F* (20.3.15), *Tb 88 F* (24.4.15), *Tb 89 F* (12.5.15), *Tb 90 F* (28.5.15), *Tb 91 F* (21.6.15), *Tb 92 F* (29.9.15), *Tb 93 F* (25.11.15), *Tb 94 F* (8.3.16), *Tb 95 F* (24.6.16), *Tb 96 F* (8.7.16), *Tb 97 F* (8.7.16)

Built at the Danubius yards in Porto Ré (Kraljevica) and Bergudi (Brgud), these boats were the Danubius version of the STT 250t boats and differed in the make of turbines and in having two funnels instead of one. Originally Danubius were to have built only four boats, but after having reduced their price by about 10 per cent 16 boats were ordered. Commissioned between July

1915 and December 1916, they saw active service in the war and all boats survived. *Tb 82–Tb 84* were allocated to Rumania in 1920 and renamed *Naluca, Zmeul* and *Fulgerul*. The *Fulgerul* capsized and sank on 8 February 1922 in a heavy gale in the Black Sea during her transfer to Rumania. *Naluca* was sunk by Soviet bombers in the harbour of Constanza in 1944 and the *Zmeul* was in service until 1958. *Tb 85–Tb 86* and *Tb 88–Tb 91* were sold to Portugal in 1920 and renamed *Zezere, Ave, Cavado, Sado, Liz* and *Mondego*. *Zezere* and *Cavado* ran aground between Tunis and Algier on 29 December 1921 while being towed to Portugal. *Liz* was stricken in 1934, *Mondego* in 1938, *Sado* in 1940, while *Ave* ran aground and was lost in the same year. *Tb 92* was sold to Greece in 1920 and renamed *Panormos*, as were *Tb 94* and *Tb 95*, which were renamed *Proussa* and *Pergamos*. *Panormos* was stranded in 1928 and sunk; *Proussa* was hit by German bombs on 4 April 1941 and scuttled, while *Pergamos* was scuttled on 25 April 1941 when laid up for repairs in the Greek Navy yard at Salamis. *Tb 87* was allocated to Yugoslavia in 1920 and was renumbered *T 5*, as were *Tb 93* which became *T 6*, *Tb 96* which became *T 7* and *Tb 97* which became *T 8*. All were taken over without changing their designations by the Italian Navy in April 1941; *T 6* was scuttled on 11 September 1943; *T 8* was sunk on 10 September 1943 by German bombers; the other two became part of the navy of the independent Croatian state; *T 7* stranded after a naval action with a British MTB on 25 June 1944 and was lost, while *T 5* served as *Cer* in the Yugoslavian Navy until 1963.

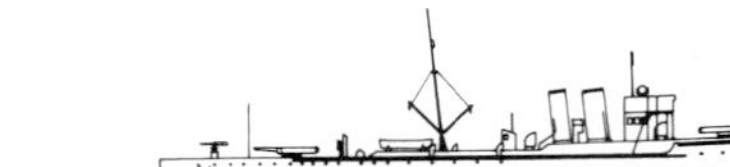

Tb 98 M 1917

Tb 98 M class *sea-going torpedo-boats*

Displacement:	250t design; 265t deep load
Dimensions:	198ft × 18ft 4in × 5ft 1in *60.4m × 5.6m × 1.5m*
Machinery:	2-shaft Melms-Pfenniger turbines, 2 Yarrow water-tube boilers, 5000shp = 29.5kts
Armament:	2–66mm/30, 1–8mm MG, 4–45cm (17.7in) TT (2×2)
Complement:	41

Class (launched):
Tb 98 M (18.11.14), *Tb 99 M* (17.12.14), *Tb 100 M* (15.1.15)

Built by Cantiere Navale Triestino at Monfalcone. Initially only the numbers 82–85 should have been built by Danubius, with the series 86–100 allocated to the Pola N Yd, but when Danubius was ordered to build 16 units after the intervention of the Hungarian Ministry of Commerce, the remaining units were ordered from Cantiere Naval Triestino. They were commissioned in 1915–16 and saw active service during the war. All three survived and they were sold to Greece in 1920 and renamed *Kyzikos, Kios* and *Kidoniai*. *Kios* was damaged by German bombs on 23 April 1941 and scuttled; *Kyzikos* was scuttled on 25 April 1941 at the Greek Navy yard at Salamis; and *Kidoniai* sank after German bomb hits on 26 April 1941.

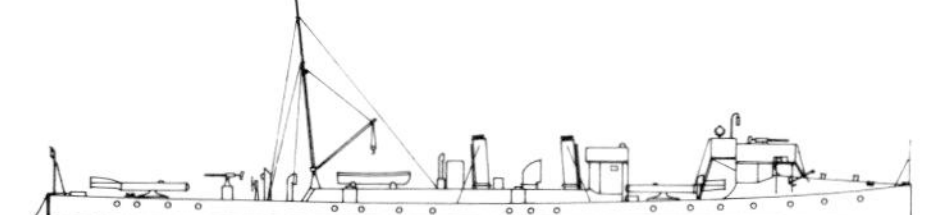

Tb I class
NB 1/750 scale

Tb I class *coastal torpedo-boats*

Displacement:	116t design
Dimensions:	144ft 10in × 14ft 2in × 3ft 11in *44.2m × 4.3m × 1.2m*
Machinery:	1-shaft 3-cyl VTE, 2 Yarrow water-tube oil-fired boilers, 2500ihp = 28kts
Armament:	2–47mm/44, 2–45cm (17.7in) TT
Complement:	20

Class (launched):
Tb I (12.8.09), *Tb II* (27.9.09), *Tb III* (8.11.09), *Tb IV* (2.12.09), *Tb V* (30.12.09), *Tb VI* (1.10)

In 1905 the Austrian Naval Technical Committee presented three different designs for a 110t coastal torpedo-boat, mainly differing in the propulsion system (VTE or turbines). Having insufficient experience with turbines, a final VTE-propelled design with oil-firing was presented in 1907. To compare it with foreign technology, Krupp, Schichau and Yarrow were asked for competitive designs, all of which turned out to be inferior. Initially STT was ordered to build 8 such boats, but this was reduced to 6, because Danubius had to participate. When the older torpedo-boats lost their names in 1910 in favour of arabic numbers, these units became in consequence *Tb 1–Tb 6*. The boats were surprisingly seaworthy up to sea state 5–6, and during the war they saw active service on escort, minesweeping and anti-submarine duties. All survived and were allocated to Italy in 1920 and scrapped there, with the exception of *Tb 3* which served with the Italian customs until 1925.

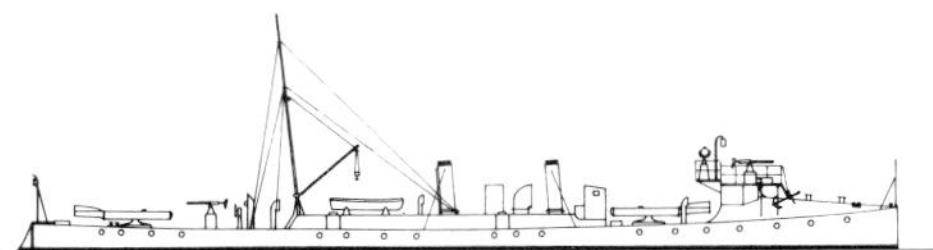

Tb XII 1911
NB 1/750 scale

Tb VII class *coastal torpedo-boats*

Displacement:	131.5t design
Dimensions:	145ft × 14ft × 4ft 9in *44.2m × 4.3m × 1.5m*
Machinery:	1-shaft 3-cyl VTE, 2 White-Forster water-tube oil-fired boilers, 2400ihp = 26.5kts
Armament:	2–47mm/47, 2–45cm (17.7in) TT
Complement:	20

Class (launched):
Tb VII (30.1.10), *Tb VIII* (24.2.10), *Tb XI* (22.3.10), *Tb X* (14.5.10), *Tb XI* (24.5.10), *Tb XII* (31.5.10)

Built by Danubius, Fiume, they were virtually the same type as the *Tb I* class, the only external difference being the searchlight platforms situated on the CT, while the STT boats had their searchlight fitted before the forward funnel. Much more significant was the fact that the Danubius units had a different boiler system, different main and auxiliary machinery, shafts and propellers. It was necessary for reasons of internal politics to let Hungarian industry (represented by Danubius and its Hungarian subcontractors) participate, but from the point of view of spare part standardisation and supply it was without question an unfortunate solution. Another deficiency of this group was the heavy angle of heel which developed at high speed caused by the turning moment of the single propeller; through inexperience the yard was unable to anticipate this and take steps to counter it in the design. All boats survived active war service and were allocated to Italy and scrapped in 1920 (with the exception of *Tb 7* which served the Italian customs until 1926). *Tb 11* suffered a mutiny and was hijacked by her crew on 5 October 1917 after the crew had imprisoned the two officers. The boat crossed the Adriatic and surrendered to the Italians, who commissioned her as *Francesco Rismondo*; she was stricken in 1925.

SUBMARINES

PRE-WAR DEVELOPMENT

Like the Imperial German Navy the Austro-Hungarian Navy awaited developments in the submarine field, leaving other navies to do the pioneering work. It was not until 1904 that the Austrian Naval Technical Committee (MTK) was ordered to produce a design for a genuine Austrian submarine. For reasons of competition this was put out to public tender, but nothing was achieved, since neither the MTK design of January 1905 nor the private projects were considered practicable. Therefore it was decided to buy three different foreign types (two boats of each), which were to be competitively evaluated, to formulate the particulars of a submarine suitable for the special needs of the Austrian Navy. This resulted in the orders for Lake, Germania and Holland boats. All three types were about 100ft long, had a very similar displacement, but showed significantly different capabilities: the single-hulled Lake type had the best diving and steering qualities, but was hampered by her gasoline engines, which were unable to reach even contract power; the double-hulled Germania type had the worst diving abilities, produced much exhaust smoke, but was the most reliable design with the best living conditions; and the single-hulled Holland type also suffered from a gasoline engine, resulting in frequent intoxication of the crew. Based on these trials results, a double-hulled submarine of about 500 tonnes displacement, diesel propulsion and 16–18kts surface speed and 3 to 5–45cm (17.7in) TT was envisaged for the next generation of Austro-Hungarian U-boats.

After a series of design presentations one Whitehead and one Germania design reached the final round, after which the Germania design 506d (German designation UD) was ordered because a better price was offered. Laid down in 1913 they were to become *U 7–U 11*, but were sold back to Germany and commissioned as *U 66–U 70* (see German section), as a transfer to Pola by sea was considered to be impossible given the war situation.

THE WAR

The Austro-Hungarian submarine force entered war with six more or less experimental boats, of which *U 1* and *U 2* were not operational, because they were drydocked to receive diesels instead of their dangerous gasoline engines. Therefore it is not surprising that immediate steps were taken to build up the Austrian U-boat force to real operational strength. As a first measure the improved Holland boat *SS 3* – which had been built by Whitehead on speculation in 1911 and been offered twice to the Austrian Navy but rejected – was bought and finally commissioned as *U 12*. A severe setback for the desire to strengthen the U-boat force was the re-sale of *U 7–U 11* to Germany in November 1914, which, in the light of later events, proved a hasty measure, because these boats could have reached Austrian ports and would have been the best of the tiny Austro-Hungarian U-boat force. Nevertheless the Austrian Navy fought the U-boat war during 1914 with an inferior number of boats while ways were sought to build them up.

Another type of submarine thought to be readily available was the Whitehead-designed *Havmanden* type, 3 of which had been built for the Royal Danish Navy before the war, while 6 further boats had been built under Whitehead's supervision in Danish yards. Although the Austrian Navy was not happy with this design, it was the only one for which plans could be obtained and which could be built in domestic yards immediately. Although their deficiencies were known, 4 of these boats were eventually ordered and built. Due to technical problems and those imposed by the need to divide the orders between Austrian and Hungarian contractors, this turned out to be an unreliable, unfortunate type which did not come into service before the end of 1917 and achieved absolutely no successes, while in contrast two of them were lost.

The first significant wartime strengthening of the U-boat force was the raising of the French *Curie*, which had been trapped in the outer net barrage of Pola harbour. She was commissioned as *U 14* (the number *U 13* was never allocated for reasons of superstitition). During the war this boat was to become one of the most successful Austrian submarines. The other, more promising, way was to buy German UB-types, especially considering the advantages of short construction time and railway transportability. The first contracts of February 1915 quickly led to the purchase of the German coastal submarines *UB 1* and *UB 15* (renamed *U 10, U 11*) and the ordering of *U 15–U 17* from AG Weser's Bremen yard. The performance of this type was well known in Austria, as the German U-boats *UB 3, UB 8* and *UB 9* had been sent by railway to Austria to begin operations off the Dardanelles; although manned by German crews they were temporarily commissioned for security reasons under the Austrian numbers *U 7–U 9*. Having satisfied the most urgent needs for more Austrian submarines by buying and receiving the above-mentioned boats, for the next step it was decided to negotiate construction licences for German UB II types to be modified to Austrian needs. These were to become *U 7-U 32* and *U 40* and *U 41*, while *U 43* and *U 47* were genuine German boats sold to Austria.

GERMAN U-BOATS UNDER THE AUSTRIAN FLAG

The Austrian U-boat force being too weak for offensive high-seas operations, from the beginning of the allied landings at the Dardanelles the Germans showed a keen interest in assisting their treaty partner. On one hand, Hersing with his *U 21* had demonstrated that a German ocean-going submarine was able to reach Pola, and even operated off the Dardanelles with tremendous success; on the other hand, Germany sent coastal types via the railways to be assembled at Pola for operations in Adriatic and Turkish waters.

This led to an increasing number of German submarines operating in the Mediterranean. Initially for security reasons, and later with an eye to international law, most of these boats operated under the Austro-Hungarian flag and were – at least temporarily – commissioned with Austrian numbers in the Austrian Navy. This was done after long bilateral discussions following Italy's declaration of war on Austria-Hungary (but not on Germany) on 23 May 1915. However, Germany regarded herself as treaty-bound to Austria against Italy, although war between both nations was not declared before 28 August 1916. The distribution of Austrian numbers for German submarines fills the gaps in the sequence of genuine Austrian submarines which otherwise looks illogical. This reads as follows (first number is Austrian, the second German, and some allocations were duplicated): *U 7–U 9 = UB 7–UB 9; U 18, U 19 = UC 14, UC 15; U 24, U 25 = UC 12, UC 13; U 26 = UB 14; U 33–U 35 = U 33–U 35; U 36 = U 21* and *U 47; U 37 = U 32; U 38, U 39 = U 38, U 39; U 42–U 47 = UB 42–UB 47; U 54–U 58 = UB 128–UB 132; U 60 = UC 20; U 62 = UC 22; U 63 = UC 23* and *U 63; U 64, U 65 = U 64, U 65; U 66 = UB 66* and *UC 66; U 67, U 68 = UB 67, UB 68; U 69 = UB 69* and *UC 69; U 70, U 71 = UB 70, UB 71; U 72, U 73 = U 72, U 73; U 74, U 75 = UC 34, UC 35; U 77 = UC 37; U 78 = UC 38* and *UC 116; U 79–U 82 = UB 48–UB 51; U 83 = U 63* and *UC 23* and *UB 52* and *UC 120; U 84 = UB 53* and *U 121; U 88, U 89 = UC 24, UC 25; U 90 = UC 27; U 91 = UC 67; U 92, U 93 = UC 73, UC 74; U 94–U 96 = UC 52–UC 54; U 97 = UB 105; U 99 = UC 103; U 110 = UC 108; U 133–U 135 = UB 133–UB 135; U 146, U 147 = UB 146, UB 147.*

After the declaration of war between Germany and Italy this was not changed, in order to avoid retrospective arguments about 'flag misuse', but on 1 October 1916 it was decided that only the German *U 35, U 38* and *U 39* should continue to operate under the Austrian flag; all others were to use the German flag. When in March 1917 the German Admiralty started 'unrestricted U-boat warfare' and issued orders to attack enemy hospital ships too, this was deplored by the Austrian authorities, perhaps not so much out of respect for international law but because they feared allied retaliation on Austrian hospital ships, which up to now had been unhindered. Although in the last two years of the war submarines of both Central powers operated in the Mediterranean and even after the USA had entered the war, a final settlement of this delicate question was never achieved and all sinkings were officially announced: 'U-boats of the Central Powers have sunk in the Mediterranean . . .'

German U-boats in the Adriatic used Pola and Cattaro as bases where they were given the Austrian torpedo depot ship *Gäa* as an accommodation and repair ship. The Germans also transferred the coastal torpedo-boats *A 51* and *A 82* to Pola by rail where they served under the German flag with German crews as dispatch vessels and tenders for the German Mediterranean submarine flotilla. Social contact between Austrian and German submarines can be described as the well known love-hate relationship; the Germans were a homogeneous ethnic group with harsh discipline and superior equipment, while the Austrians were a multi-national force suffering from insufficient material resources, but were able to show that they could fight on equal terms.

PROJECTS

During the war three interesting projects were under consideration, but soon dropped. The first was to arm the private scientific mini-submarine *Loligo* (44.1t/50t; 40ft 4in × 8ft 10in × 7ft 6in, *12.3m × 2.7m × 2.3m;* 1 electric engine, 30shp = 4kts) and use it against Italy on the Lake Garda. The second project was proposed by the Austrian Naval League, influenced by the German mercantile submarine *Deutschland*: for trade with Spain and other neutral Mediterranean nations an Austrian merchant submarine would be financed by private funds and contributions. The Austrian Fleet Command rejected this because shipyard capacity was needed for fighting units. The Austrian Naval League was so enamoured of this project that it next proposed to use this merchant submarine as an ammunition transport to Turkey, but the project had to be dropped definitively in August 1916.

In the autumn of 1916 the Austrian Army asked the Navy to design a river submarine for operations on the Serbian and Bulgarian stretches of the Danube. The required capabilities were comprehensive: destruction of bridges and port facilities, anti-shipping operations, mine location, and the demolition of sunken ships and underwater obstacles; it was therefore not practicable with contemporary technology.

EXPANSION DURING THE WAR

To build up the Austrian U-boat force no less than 18 submarines were under construction in 1916: 8 UB II licensed types, 4 *Havmanden* class boats, and the 6 ocean-going boats *U 48–U 53*, which belonged to three different types built at three different yards.

The launch of *U 27*, Austria's most successful submarine, in 1917

Because of the material shortage and manpower problems construction times were so elongated that in 1917 only 14 Austrian U-boats were operational – some in badly worn-out condition – the others being used for training. When the medium-range UB II licensed types and the *Havmandens* were nearing commissioning all efforts were thrown into ocean-going types, 6 of which were ordered in December 1917. The last plan of the Austro-Hungarian U-boat arm of 1918 envisaged 21 operational submarines in the Mediterranean: allowing a 2:1 ratio of boats in harbour to those on operation, this would require 63 ocean-going types, while the 12 boats requested for local defence in the Adriatic were already in existence. Of the planned 63 ocean-going types, 22 were under construction (*U 54–U 59* and *U 101–U 110*), but of the 41 missing boats only *U 111–U 120* were ordered before the end of the war. None of these types was commissioned during the war due to material shortages and a much reduced labour force.

WAR SUCCESSES

The Austro-Hungarian Navy commissioned a total of 27 boats which gained some remarkable successes, although overshadowed by their German comrades operating in the Mediterranean. The top scores were achieved by Lt (sen) Georg Ritter von Trapp, in command of *U 5* and *U 14*, who sank 1 armoured cruiser, 1 submarine and 12 freighters totalling 45,668grt, and Lt (sen) Zdenko Houdecek, in command of *U 17* and *U 28*, who sank 1 destroyer and 11 freighters totalling 47,726grt; the highest score by a single boat was achieved by *U 27*, which sank 1 destroyer and 35 merchant vessels (mostly coastal schooners) totalling 18,145grt. The list of enemy warships sunk by Austro-Hungarian U-boats is as follows: the French armoured cruiser *Léon Gambetta*, the Italian armoured cruiser *Giuseppe Garibaldi*, the British destroyer *Phoenix*, the French destroyers *Renaudin* and *Fourche*, the Italian destroyers *Impetuoso* and *Nembo*, the Italian submarine *Nereide* and the French submarine *Circe*. The list of damaged major enemy warships is: the French battleship *Jean Bart*, the British light cruisers *Dublin* and *Weymouth*, and the Japanese destroyer *Sakaki*. During World War One the 27 Austro-Hungarian submarines sank or captured 108 merchant vessels totalling 196,102.5grt (the greatest percentage coastal sailing vessels); the probable sinking of a further 11 steamers totalling 41,000grt is unconfirmed, since they may have reached harbour in damaged condition.

U 4 as completed

U 2 1915
NB 1/750 scale

U 1 class *submarines*

Displacement:	229.7t/248.9t (223t/277.5t after modernisation)
Dimensions:	100ft (100ft 11in after modernisation) × 15ft 9in × 12ft 8in *30.5m (30.8m) × 4.8m × 3.9m*
Machinery:	2 shafts, petrol (diesel after modernisation) engines plus 2 electric motors, 720bhp/200shp = 10.3kts/6kts. Range 950nm/40nm at 6kts/2kts surfaced/submerged
Armament:	3–45cm (17.7in) TT (2 bow, 1 stern; 5 torpedoes), 1–37mm MG
Complement:	17

Class (launched, fate):

U 1 (10.2.09, BU 1920), *U 2* (3.4.09, BU 1920)

Built to the design of the American Simon Lake at the Pola N Yd and had the features typical of this submarine designer: two retractable wheels for movement over the seabed, a diving chamber under the bow and variable pitch propellers. The diving tanks were situated on top of the cylindrical single hull, above the waterline, which meant that a heavy ballast keel was necessary to provide vertical stability, and had to be flooded by pumps, the whole operation totalling 8 minutes. Furthermore the gasoline engines could not be considered effective under war conditions and did not reach the contract power, so the Austro-Hungarian Navy only paid for the hulls and armament. Thereafter new diesels were ordered in Austria and until their delivery the original engines were employed on lease. *U 2* was given a small conning tower in 1915. During the war both units served as training boats and were declared obsolete on 11 January 1918; both were ceded to Italy as war reparations in 1920 and scrapped at Pola.

U 3 class *submarines*

Displacement:	240t/300t
Dimensions:	138ft 9in × 14ft × 12ft 6in *42.3m × 4.5m × 3.8m*
Machinery:	2 shafts, 2 kerosene engines plus 2 electric motors, 600bhp/320shp = 12kts/8.5kts. Range 1200nm/40nm at 12kts/3kts surfaced/submerged
Armament:	2–45cm (17.7in) TT (bow, 3 torpedoes)
Complement:	21

Class (launched, fate):
U 3 (20.8.08, sunk 13.8.15), *U 4* (20.11.08, BU 1920)

Built by Germaniawerft at Kiel and towed to Pola via Gibraltar, they were of a double-hull type with internal saddle tanks. Although the German designers had evaluated the best hull-shaped in extensive model trials, these boats had constant troubles with their diving planes. The fins were changed in size and shape, and finally the bow planes were removed and a fixed stern flap was installed. Because of their greater displacement these boats had better seakeeping qualities and living conditions than their competitors. Considering that this was one of the first Germaniawerft designs, produced without extensive practical experience, these boats showed a high degree of effectiveness, and *U 4* had the longest operational history of all Austrian submarines. Both saw action during the war. *U 3* made an unsucessful attack on the Italian armed merchant cruiser *Città di Catania*, was rammed and damaged, and when surfacing was hit by the French destroyer *Bisson* and sunk. *U 4* was ceded as a war reparation to France and scrapped in 1920, her greatest success being the sinking of the Italian armoured cruiser *Giuseppe Garibaldi* on 18 July 1915.

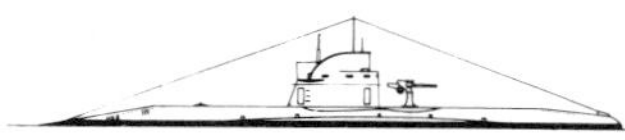
U 5 1917 **NB 1/750 scale**

U 5 class *submarines*

Displacement:	240t/273t
Dimensions:	105ft 4in × 13ft 9in × 12ft 10in *32.1m × 4.2m × 3.9m*
Machinery:	2 shafts, 2 petrol engines plus two electric motors, 500bhp/230shp × 10.75kts/8.5kts. Range 800nm/48nm at 8.5kts/6kts surfaced/submerged
Armament:	2–45cm (17.7in) TT (2 bow; 4 torpedoes)
Complement:	19

Class (launched, fate):
U 5 (10.2.09, BU 1920), *U 6* (12.6.09, scuttled 13.5.16), *U 12* (14.3.11, mined ? 12.8.16)

These boats were built by the Fiume-based firm of Whitehead which had bought a licence from the Irish-American John Philip Holland to build his submarines. The first two boats were partially assembled in the United States and assembled at Whitehead's, which caused a lot of trouble. The third boat was built on speculation and featured improvements in all the mechanical and electrical systems. Named *SS 3* this unit was offered to the Austrian Navy too, but she was refused because the trials programme was not yet completed. Whitehead then offered the boat to the navies of Peru, Portugal, Netherlands, Brazil, Bulgaria and again to the Austro-Hungarian Navy. When war broke out Austria bought the unsold boat and provisionally commissioned her as *U 7*, but by the end of August 1914 she was definitely commissioned as *U 12*. The single-hulled Holland type featured a distinctive tear-drop hull and an interesting design of the TT hatches: these were clover-leaf shaped and rotated on a central axis. All three saw active war service. *U 5*, sunk after hitting a mine during trials on 16 May 1917, was raised and rebuilt with a conning tower and a 7.5cm/30 gun; she was ceded as a war reparation to Italy in 1920 and scrapped. *U 6* was trapped in submarine nets during an attempt to break through the Otranto barrage and scuttled by the crew. *U 12* was sunk with the loss of all hands by a mine when trying to penetrate the harbour of Venice, about 12 August 1916. Raised by Italy at the end of 1916 she was scrapped in the Venice N Yd.

U 7 class *submarines*

Displacement:	695t/885t
Dimensions:	228ft oa × 20ft 8in × 12ft 5in *69.5m × 6.3m × 3.9m*
Machinery:	2 shafts, 2 diesels plus two electric motors, 2300bhp/1240shp = 17kts/11kts
Armament:	5–45cm (17.7in) TT (4 bow, 1 stern; 9 torpedoes), 1–66mm/26
Complement:	?

Class:
U 7–U 11

After the first Austrian trials a 500t submarine with 12kts submerged speed was requested. Of the submitted designs the final choice came down to the Whitehead Type 48 and the Germania Type 506d, and the German type was adopted because of its low price. The five boats were to be an improved *U 3* type, and the particulars given in the table relate to the original design for Austrian requirements. Ordered on 1 February 1913 the construction time was scheduled to be 29–33 months. Because of the war situation the transfer of the completed boats via Gibraltar to Pola was believed to be impossible. Therefore they were sold to Germany on 28 November 1914, and commissioned as *U 66–U 70* (see under Germany). When the German Lieutenant (sen) Hersing brought his boat, *U 21*, into the Mediterranean a few months later (in April 1915), it was obvious that sea-going U-boats could reach the Adriatic without trouble. In the light of this event a transfer to Austria-Hungary would have been possible and the re-sale of the boats must be seen as a severe setback for Austrian U-boat warfare.

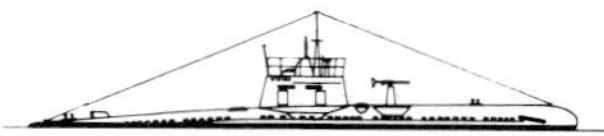
U 17 1916 **NB 1/750 scale**

U 10 class *coastal submarines*

Displacement:	125.5t/140.25t
Dimensions:	91ft 6in × 16ft 10in × 8ft 11in *27.9m × 5.2m × 2.7m*
Machinery:	1 shaft, 1 diesel plus one electric motor, 60bhp/120shp = 6.5kts/5.5kts
Armament:	2–45cm (17.7in) TT (2 bow, 2 torpedoes) (see notes)
Complement:	17

Class (launched, fate):
U 10 (ex-German *UB 1*, 22.1.15, BU 1920), *U 11* (ex-German *UB 15*, BU 1920), *U 15* (4.15, BU 1920), *U 16* (26.4.15, sunk 17.10.16), *U 17* (21.4.15, BU 1920)

At first the Austrian Navy planned only to purchase plans or building licences (and some sub-assemblies) of German coastal submarines of the UB I type to build up the U-boat force. However it transpired that AG Weser (Bremen) was able to deliver complete boats within five months; transport to Pola could be effected in sections by railway, so that the units had only to be riveted together. The order was placed on 1 April 1915, the first two boats being commissioned for the Imperial German Navy as *UB 1* (built by Germaniawerft) and *UB 15* (Austrian numbers *U 10, U 11*) and operated with a German commander and crew but an Austrian officer for pilotage and training reasons until 4 July and 14 June 1915 respectively; they were then taken over by Austrian crews. The three other units were ordered from the beginning as Austrian submarines and never operated under a German crew. All boats differed in their conning tower configuration and some minor layout details and were up-gunned during the war as follows: in October 1916 all boats received a 37mm/23 QF, with the exception of *U 11*, which was given the 66mm/18 planned for *U 14* (which received a 88mm instead); the 37mm was replaced by a 47mm/23 QF in November 1917.

U 16 was rammed by the convoyed freighter *Borminda*, during an attack in which she had torpedoed the escorting Italian destroyer *Nembo*; she was scuttled after heavy damage. *U 10* hit a mine on 9 July 1918 off Caorle and was beached with heavy damage. After having been plundered by Austrian Army troops she was towed to Trieste for repair but this was not finished until the end of war. She was ceded with all her sisters to Italy as war reparations in 1920 and scrapped at Pola.

U 14 *submarine*

Displacement:	397t/551t
Dimensions:	171ft 1in × 17ft 1in × 10ft 6in *52.2m × 5.2m × 3.2m*
Machinery:	2 shafts, 2 diesels plus 2 electric motors, 480bhp (after modernisation 840bhp)/660shp = 12.2kts (12.6kts (12.6kts))/9kts. Range 1700nm (6500nm)/84nm at 10kts/5kts surfaced/submerged
Armament:	1–53.3cm (21in) TT (bow), 6–53.3cm TL (7 torpedoes), 1–88cm/30 (after modernisation), 1–47mm
Complement:	28

The French submarine *Curie* (launched in 1912) was trapped on 20 December 1914 in the net barrage of Pola harbour during an attempt to penetrate, was forced to the surface and sunk by gunfire. Raised in February 1915, she was refitted and commissioned as *U 14*. She was originally armed with 1 TT, 4 trainable Drzewiecki TL systems sided fore and aft and 2 fixed TL abreast the CT, firing forward but angled outward from the centreline. From February to November 1916 she was re-engined, rearmed and was given a German-style conning tower instead of her small, wet lookout platform, all of which improved her fighting potential significantly. In 1918 2 of the Drzewiecki TL were replaced with 2 fixed aft-firing TL. Operating under the command of Lieutenant (sen) Georg Ritter von Trapp (whose postwar career was made famous by the film 'The Sound of Music'), *U 14* achieved one of the highest scores of all Austrian U-boats. On 17 July 1919 she rejoined the French Navy under her old name, served until 1928 and was scrapped in 1929.

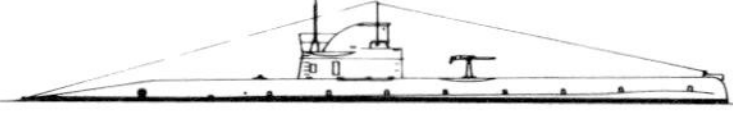
U 23 1918 **NB 1/750 scale**

U 20 class *coastal submarines*

Displacement:	173t/210t
Dimensions:	127ft 2in × 13ft × 9ft *38.8m × 4.0m × 2.8m*
Machinery:	1 shaft, 1 diesel plus one electric motor, 450bhp/160shp = 12kts/9kts
Armament:	2–45cm (17.7in) TT (2 bow, 2 torpedoes), 1–66mm/26, 1–8mm MG
Complement:	18

Class (launched, fate):
U 20 (18.9.16, sunk 6.7.18), *U 21* (15.8.16, to Italy 1920, BU), *U 22* (27.1.17, to France 1920, BU), *U 22* (5.1.17, sunk 21.2.18)

AUSTRIA-HUNGARY

Between 1911 and 1912 the Royal Danish Navy ordered 3 single-hulled *Havmanden* class (A type) boats from Whitehead's Fiume yard, and the Austro-Hungarian Navy seized the plans after the outbreak of war and ordered 4 boats on 27 March 1915. Following the pattern of the Dual Monarchy, construction was divided between the Austrian Pola N Yd (*U 20* and *U 21*) and the Hungarian UBAG yard. The subcontracts were also divided up, which led to a lot of technical troubles, later modifications and modernisations during construction, finally resulting in an unfortunate and long-delayed type. They were not commissioned until the end of 1917 and operated without success. *U 23* was sunk on 21 February 1918 with an explosive paravane, when she attacked a convoy in the Otranto straits. *U 20* was torpedoed by the Italian submarine *F 12* off the Tagliamento estuary; raised in 1962 she was scrapped. The CT plus a small midships section of this boat is now exhibited in the Heeresgeschichtliches Museum in Vienna. *U 21* was ceded to Italy in 1920, *U 22* to France, and both were scrapped.

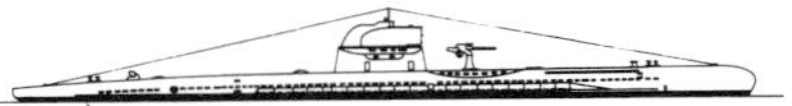

U 29 1917 **NB 1/750 scale**

U 27 class *coastal submarines*

Displacement:	264t/301t
Dimensions:	121ft 1in × 14ft 4in × 12ft 2in *36.9m × 4.4m × 3.7m*
Machinery:	2 shafts, 2 diesels plus two electric motors, 270bhp/280shp = 9kts/7.5kts
Armament:	2–45cm (17.7in) TT (bow; 4 torpedoes), 1–75mm/30, 1–8mm MG
Complement:	23–24

Class (launched, fate):
U 27 (19.10.16, BU 1920), *U 28* (8.1.17, BU 1920), *U 29* (21.10.16, BU 1920), *U 30* (27.12.16, lost 1 or 2.4.17), *U 31* (28.3.17, BU 1920), *U 32* (11.5.17, BU 1920), *U 40* (21.4.17, BU 1920), *U 41* (11.11.17, BU 1920)

Modified Austrian licence-built variant of the German UB II type. Ordered on 12 October 1915, they were built at the Pola N Yd, except *U 29–U 32* which were built by Danubius, Fiume; the boats were commissioned between 14 February 1917 and 19 February 1918. The hull of *U 41* was lengthened by 77cm, to take the already delivered diesel built for *U 6*, which had been lost. All saw active service in the latter part of the war: *U 30* was lost by unknown cause in the Otranto Straits; *U 31* and *U 41* were allocated to France in 1920 and scrapped, while all the others were allocated to Italy; *U 27* was scrapped at Fiume, and all the others at Venice.

U 43 class *coastal submarines*

Displacement:	263t/292t
Dimensions:	118ft 5in × 14ft 4in × 12ft 2in *36.1m × 4.4m × 3.7m*
Machinery:	2 shafts, 2 diesels plus two electric motors, 284bhp/280shp = 9.2kts/5.8kts
Armament:	2–50cm (19.7in) TT (bow, 4 torpedoes), 1–88mm/30, 1–8mm MG
Complement:	22

U 43 and *U 47* were both built in Germany by AG Weser in 1916, transferred to Pola by railway and commissioned as the German *UB 43* and *UB 47*; after one year's service both were decommissioned on 21 June 1917 and sold in a worn-out condition to the Austro-Hungarian Navy which commissioned them as *U 43* and *U 47* on 30 July 1917. After active service they were ceded as war reparations to France and scrapped in 1920.

U 48 class *submarines*

Displacement:	818t/1183.5t
Dimensions:	240ft 4in × 21ft 11in × 10ft 10in *73.3m × 6.7m × 3.3m*
Machinery:	2 shafts, 2 diesels plus two electric motors, 2400bhp/1200shp = 16.25kts/8.5kts
Armament:	6–45cm (17.7in) TT (4 bow, 2 stern; 9 torpedoes), 2–90mm/35 (*U 58, U 59* 2–12cm/35)
Complement:	32

Class:
U 48–U 49, U 58–U 59

Built by CNT Pola using a German AG Weser design, none was ever launched. *U 48* was 70 per cent complete, and *U 49* 55 per cent complete at the end of the war; all were broken up in 1920. *U 58* and *U 59* were never laid down.

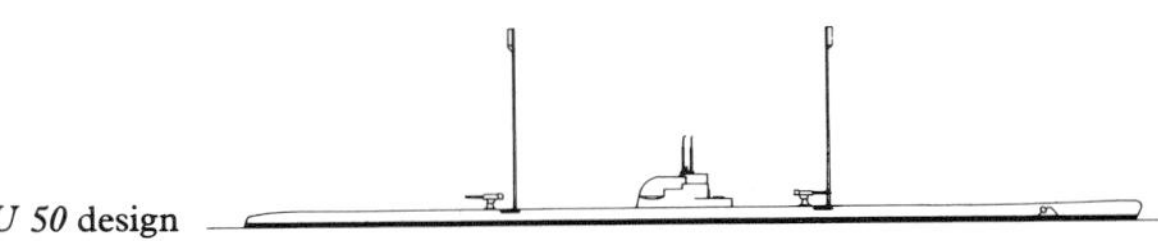

U 50 design

U 50 class *submarines*

Displacement:	840t/1100t
Dimensions:	*c*241ft × 20ft 8in × 12ft 11in *73.5m × 6.3m × 4.0m*
Machinery:	2 shafts, 2 diesels plus 2 electric motors, 2300bhp/1200shp = 16.5kts/9kts
Armament:	6–45cm (17.7in) TT (4 bow, 2 stern; 9 torpedoes), 2–10cm (3.9in)/35 (*U 56, U 57* 2–12cm/35)
Complement:	33

Class:
U 50, U 51, U 56, U 57

All built by Danubius Fiume (Project 835, Germania type licence-built). *U 50* was 90 per cent complete at the end of the war, and *U 51* 60 per cent; they were broken up in 1920. *U 56* and *U 57* were never laid down.

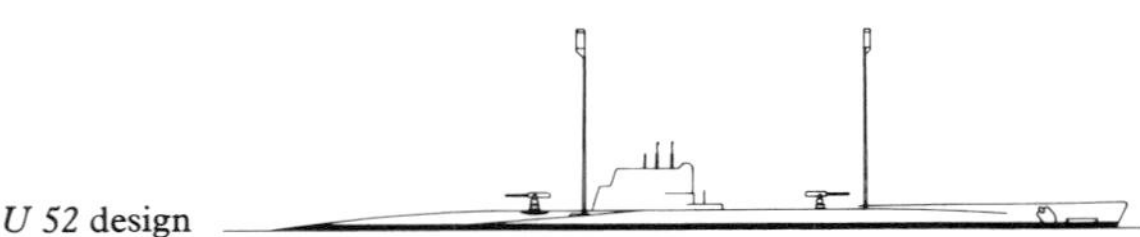

U 52 design

U 52 class submarines

Displacement:	849t/1200t
Dimensions:	249ft 3in × 22ft 10in × 11ft 6in *76.0m × 7.0m × 3.5m*
Machinery:	2 shafts, 2 diesels plus 2 electric motors, 2400bhp/1480shp = 15.75kts/9kts
Armament:	6–45cm (17.7in) TT (4 bow, 2 stern; 9 torpedoes), 2–10cm (3.9in) 35 (*U 54, U 55* 2–12cm/35), 1–8mm MG
Complement:	40

Class:
U 52–U 55

This design was the winner of a competition between the submarine yard of Stabilimento Tecnico, the newly named Austriawerft, and UBAG. The A 6 type designation indicates that the previous projects A 1–A 5 were rejected. *U 52* was about 25 per cent complete at the end of the war, *U 53* about 10 per cent; both were broken up in 1919; *U 54–U 55* were never laid down.

U 14 March 1917

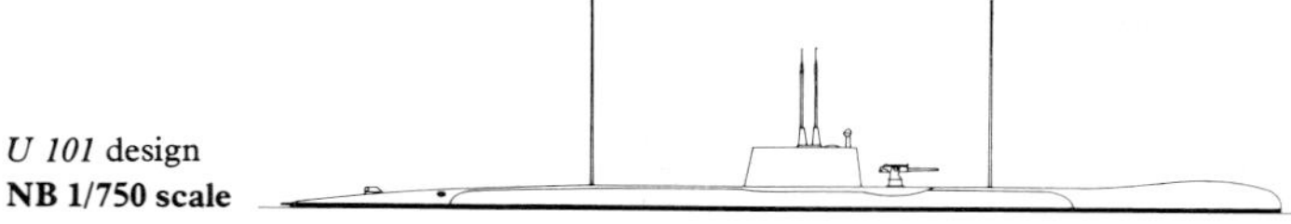
U 101 design
NB 1/750 scale

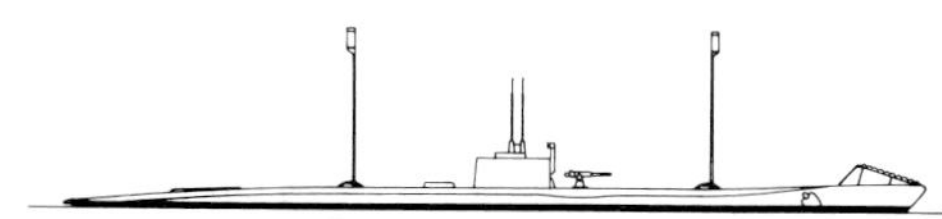
U 107 design

U 101 class *submarines*

Displacement: 428t/620t
Dimensions: 175ft 6in × 19ft × 11ft 10in
53.5m × 5.8m × 3.6m
Machinery: 2 shafts, 2 diesels plus two electric motors, 1060bhp/788shp = 13.25kts/8.25kts
Armament: 5–45cm (17.7in) TT (4 bow, 1 stern, 10 torpedoes), 1–10cm (3.9in/35), 1–8mm MG
Complement: 26

Class:
U 101–U 106, U 118–U 120

To be built by the Austriawerft Trieste. When the question arose as to whether German UB III type boats should be built under licence, the Austrian UBAG company presented its Type 1916 S 1 design, and it was decided to build both types. The UB III for Adriatic use, and the Austrian design for employment further afield. Numbers over 100 were allocated as it was intended to scrap the obsolete boats *U 1–U 6* and in future to omit the first two ciphers, *U 101* becoming the new *U 1* and so on. The first three boats were laid down at the end of 1917/beginning of 1918, and were respectively 47 per cent, 30 per cent and 15 per cent complete at the end of the war. The other boats were never laid down.

U 107 class *submarines*

Displacement: 791t/933t
Dimensions: 228ft × 23ft × ?
69.5m × 7.0m
Machinery: 2 shafts, 2 diesels plus 2 electric motors, 2300bhp/1260shp = ?/?kts
Armament: 5–45cm (17.7in) TT (4 bow, 1 stern; ?12 torpedoes), 1–10cm (3.9in)/35
Complement: 36

Class:
U 107–U 141

To have been constructed by Danubius, Fiume, and very similar to the design of the Germania UD type, of which the Austro-Hungarian Navy had ordered *U 7–U 11* which were sold back to the Imperial German Navy. The particulars are very unclear as only *U 107* and *U 108* were laid down in March and May 1918 respectively, but only completed to 35 per cent and 30 per cent at the end of the war; for *U 109* and *U 110* 25 per cent and 20 per cent of the material had been stockpiled.

SMALL SURFACE WARSHIPS

From 1904 onwards the Austro-Hungarian received various offers to design MTBs, the most important coming from Yarrow and Thornycroft, and even the Austrian Naval Technical Committee presented design studies. None of them was considered with the exception of a 12t Yarrow boat, two of which were ordered, but as patrol craft for the Danube flotilla. Immediately after the start of the war, when the British and the Italian Navies began to pursue MTB development with great energy, Austria-Hungary responded with an entirely private, but nevertheless innovative effort.

The 'Versuchsgleitboot' 1915 *Bilzer Collection*

'VERSUCHSGLEITBOOT' *experimental air-cushion boat*

Displacement: 7.6t
Dimensions: 42ft 8in oa × 13ft 1in × 1ft 2in
13.0m × 4.0m × 0.4m
Machinery: 2 shafts, 2 Austro-Daimler aircraft petrol engines, plus 1 Austro-Daimler aircraft petrol engine for hovering 480bhp + 65bhp = 32.3kts. Range 120nm at 30kts
Armament: 2–45cm (7.7in) TL, 1–8mm MG (later 3 DCs)
Complement:

The origin of the *Versuchsgleitboot* goes back to a private proposal of Lt Cdr Müller-Thomamuehl concerning a hovercraft, the actual experimental prototype being a modified design with a wooden rectangular hull of spindle-shaped design, with the bottom divided, by a vertical step, into planing and hover sections. To ensure eddyless air-injection a swallowtail-shaped duct was situated at the vertical step. The fan was situated in the forward section of the rectangular hull and produced an air-cushion under the hovering part of the bottom. Skirts at both sides prevented the air from escaping but there were no skirts at stem and stern. The main armament consisted of two torpedoes, each in an open chute arranged for launching over the stern by means of compressed air. Three small 6kg (13lb) DCs were added later. Launched on 2 September 1915 it underwent extensive trials with different propeller types but was considered unworthy of further development due to a number of technical deficiencies. What really was needed was a fast, armoured MTB, so the *Versuchsgleitboot* was cannibalised and finally scrapped during the following years.

Mb 107 class *armoured motor torpedo-boats*

Displacement: 26t full load
Dimensions: 80ft 9in × 15ft 1in × 2ft
24.6m × 4.6m × 0.6m
Machinery: 3 shafts, 3 6-cyl petrol engines, 600bhp = 24kts
Armament: 1–66mm/45 AA, 2–8mm MG, 2–45cm (17.7in) TT (bow)
Complement: 12

Class:
Mb 107–Mb 115

Ordered 9 December 1916 to a design submitted by naval constructor Eckert von Labin, only 3 of the projected 9 boats were launched, between July 1917 and August 1918 at the Pola N Yd; the 6 further boats ordered from Austriawerft were never launched due to material and manpower shortages. They were designed to carry 40mm armour, and to make 26.5kts at 24t or 24.5kts at 26t; range was to be 450nm at 12.5kts. *Mb 107* was ceded to Italy in 1920 and was used by the Italian Customs Service until 1925; the two other boats were probably scrapped immediately.

GLEITBOOT No I class *motor torpedo-boat/gunboat*

Displacement: 6.65t
Dimensions: 44ft 1in × 9ft 7in × 1ft 5in
13.5m × 2.9m × 0.4m
Machinery: 4 shafts, 4 petrol engines, 600bhp = 33.8kts. Range 200nm at 20kts
Armament: *No I* design – 1–66mm/18, 2–8mm MG, 4 DCs
No II design – 1–35cm (13.8in) TT, 4–8mm MG
Complement: 7

Gleitboot No 1 on trials 11 May 1918
Bilzer Collection

Class:
Gleitboot No I, Gleitboot No II

In January 1917 the naval architect Max Szombathy, who had already participated in the design of Müller's hovercraft, presented the design of a 4-shaft hydroplane in both a torpedo-boat and gunboat configuration. On 2 February the Naval Section ordered two trials units to be built, after the supply of obsolete 150bhp aircraft engines was cleared. *No I* was to be built in the gunboat configuration, *No II* as a torpedo-boat. One year later *No I* was 95 per cent ready, but *No II* was only 30 per cent complete. The slow progress in construction was caused by the acute shortage of manpower, as every hand was needed for repairs to the fighting units.

On 15 April 1918 *No 1* was launched, and on 11 May a first trials run was held; a second trial held on 13 June was cut short when four clutches broke down. Further trials in June 1918 achieved speeds of 33.6kts–33.8kts. On 7 September 1918, the boat was handed over to the submarine chaser flotilla, her armament consisting of 4 DCs and 4 MG; her 66mm gun had not been installed. Boat *No II* was probably launched in September 1918, but was never completed. Four further boats, *No III–No VI*, of this 6t Szombathy type were in the early stages of construction at the end of the war. All boats fell into Italian hands after the war, and their fate is unknown.

Mb 164 class *assault craft*

Displacement:	10.5t
Dimensions:	43ft 6in × 7ft 10in × 2ft 9in *13.3m × 2.4m × 0.9m*
Machinery:	1 shaft, 1 electric cruising engine, 2shp = 4kts; 2 tracks, 1–13shp electric engine
Armament:	2–45cm (17.7in) TL
Complement:	3

Class:
Mb 164, Mb 165

The Austrian Navy was deeply impressed by the Italian tracked MTB *Grillo* (this was not an amphibious tank, as might be expected, the tracks being designed only to negotiate floating barricades) which was captured on 14 May 1918 after an unsuccessful attempt to penetrate into Pola harbour, the Vienna-based boatyard of Fritz Eppel Jr was ordered to design and built two austere versions of such a vessel. *Mb 164* was intended to attack Ancona, and her sister *Mb 165* to penetrate into Chioggia harbour. On 12 October 1918 test runs were held with *Mb 164* in a tributary of the Danube at Vienna, in the presence of high-ranking Austro-Hungarian naval officers, but when the unit was ready for railway delivery to Pola, the war was over. Both units were scrapped after the war.

Ex-German LM type *motor torpedo-boats*

Originally called L-boats because of their airship *(Luftschiff)* engines, this type of German 7t MTB was later reclassified as LM boats to avoid confusions with the L-numbered Zeppelins. The Austrian Navy showed keen interest in obtaining German MTBs and an agreement of 20 August 1918 ordered that out of the 6 boats *(LM 3–LM 6, LM 11, LM 12)* which were to be sent to Pola via railway for employment by the German C-in-C of the Mediterranean U-boats, all were to be handed over to the Austro-Hungarian Navy. Also *LM 13* was to be sold to the Austrians after her completion; but none of these boats reached Pola before the end of the war.

NOTE
A remarkable attempt to capture Italian MTBs failed in April 1918. The raid was carried out against the Italian MTB base at Ancona by 60 Austro-Hungarian soldiers, but probably through treachery no Italian MTB was present when the raiding group went ashore and the Austrians were taken prisoner.

MISCELLANEOUS

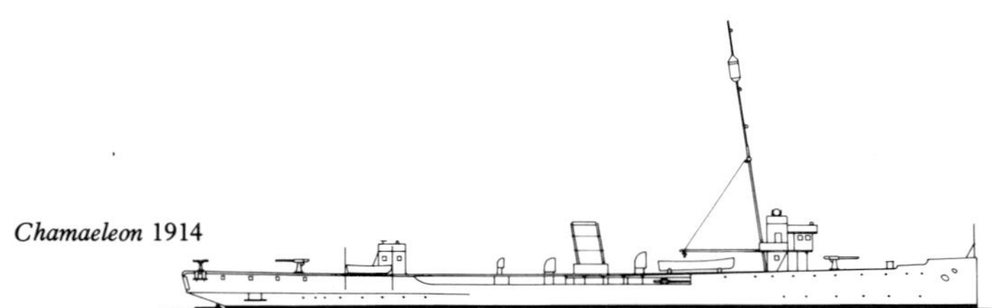

Chamaeleon 1914

CHAMAELEON *minelayer* (launched 1913)

Displacement:	1100t design; 1165t deep load
Dimensions:	285ft 9in × 30ft 2in × 8ft 10in *87.1m × 9.2m × 2.7m*
Machinery:	2-shaft 4-cyl VTE, 4 Yarrow boilers, 5500ihp = 20.8kts
Armament:	2–90mm/45 AA, 2–90mm/45 QF, 300 mines (C 12 type)
Complement:	154

Chamaeleon was built at the Pola N Yd and was the most modern Austrian minelayer. She served in this role during the war, was ceded to Great Britain after the war, but was sold to an Italian shipbreaker in 1920.

GÄA *torpedo depot ship* (launched 1890)

Displacement:	12,130t
Dimensions:	502ft 8in × 57ft 9in × 24ft 11in *153.2m × 17.6m × 7.6m*
Machinery:	2-shaft VTE, 9 boilers, 14,743ihp = 18.7kts
Armament:	4–12cm (4.7in)/35, 4–66mm/44
Complement:	?

The Austrian Navy wanted a fast ship that could follow the torpedo-boats into battle, refuel and replenish them and defend herself and her torpedo-boats. As there were insufficient funds for a purpose-built vessel of the requested type, a fast passenger liner was regarded as the best conversion for this role. Originally the *Gäa* was the German HAPAG liner *Fürst Bismarck*, which made her maiden voyage in April 1890 on the North Atlantic route. In 1904 she was bought by the Czarist Navy and transformed into the auxiliary cruiser *Don*, in 1906 she was handed over to the Russian Voluntary Fleet and renamed *Moskva*.

In 1909 she was bought by the Austrian Navy, renamed *Gäa* and adapted: her 12cm guns were from the disarmed light cruisers *Leopard* and *Panther*, and her gooseneck cranes from the battleships *Erzherzog Karl* and *Erzherzog Friedrich*. She could stow 81 torpedoes and 100 mines. In 1914 she was sent to

Cattaro Bay, serving as a maintenance, repair and accommodation ship for Austrian and German submarines. After the war she was ceded to the Italian Railways, leased to Cosulich Shipping Co, renamed *San Giusto* and made one trip to New York but was damaged by a heavy gale on the way back. She was laid up and scrapped in Italy in 1923–24.

BARSCH *river patrol craft*

Displacement:	128.9t standard; 133t deep load
Dimensions:	144ft 4in × 19ft 8in × 3ft 3in *44.0m × 6.0m × 1.0m*
Machinery:	2-shaft Curtiss-AEG turbines, 2 Yarrow boilers, 1100shp = 18kts
Armour:	Sides 7.5mm, deck 6mm, CT and turrets 10mm
Armament:	4–70mm/26 (2×2), 3 MG
Complement:	42

The former Austro-Hungarian *Wels* class vessel, launched in 1915 by Danubius, Budapest as patroler *m* and renamed *Barsch* in 1916. Commissioned on 14 March 1916, she saw active war service. In 1919 she was seized by the SHS Navy (Kingdom of the Serbs-Croats-Slovenians, the predecessor of Yugoslavia) as *Bregalnica*. During 1922–28 she was commissioned as *Barsch* in Austria, until sold to Hungary (on 30 November 1928) in exchange for the 60t patrol craft *Siofok* (ex-Austro-Hungarian *k*, later *Csuka*; commissioned in Austria as *Birago*, scrapped 1939). In Hungary renamed *Baja* but never in service, laid up decommissioned until 1945 then probably scrapped.

Gäa during the war

Norway

The Union between the Kingdoms of Sweden and Norway came to an end in 1905. Earlier Norway – like Sweden – had built up a navy of some coastal battleships and a lot of torpedo-boats. From monitors – one built in Sweden – the 1890s saw the building of 4 coastal battleships at British yards and 4 gunboats of varying types, 1 destroyer and 12 small torpedo-boats. In the last years of the Union only some torpedo-boats were added.

From 1906 Norway did not do much to modernise her navy which was manned by about 1000 regulars and 1000 annual conscripts under a rear-admiral despite having 13,000 miles of coastline and 150,000 islands to protect: 3 small destroyers, 3 large and some smaller torpedo boats as well as 4 submarines were all the warships built before the First World War broke out. But Norway, like the other two Scandinavian countries, decided to complete her division of coastal battleships. Two such with lighter armament than the contemporary Swedish and Danish vessels were ordered in England in 1912. Launched in 1914 they were both seized by the British government as war broke out and never reached the Horten naval base on Oslofjord. During and after the war the Navy was busy minesweeping and recovering 222 dead bodies washed up on the coast.

Norway's neutrality veered towards the Allies. In 1916, tipped off by the Admiralty's Room 40, the Government seized a German diplomatic bag in Kristiania (Oslo) and found glanders germs intended to infect the reindeer pulling sledges of British arms from North Norway to Russia. In January 1918 it was abortively suggested that a coastwatching service be established to monitor U-boats in return for the Navy receiving the latest British hydrophones and other equipment. German efforts to cut cable links between the two countries were always short-lived.

From 1919 Norway trusted in the everlasting peace and the League of Nations and only some submarines, voted in 1914, were built and completed during the 1920s.

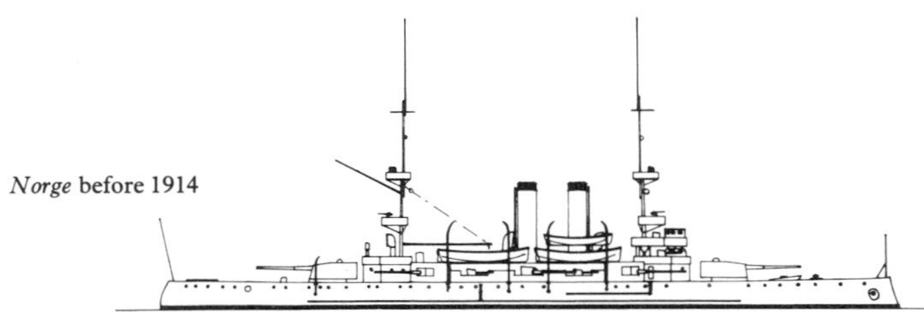
Norge before 1914

COASTAL BATTLESHIPS

Name	Launched	Disp (std)	Fate
Norge class			
NORGE	31.3.00	3645t	Sunk 9.4.40
EIDSVOLD	14.6.00	3645t	Sunk 9.4.40
Haarfagre class			
HARALD HAARFAGRE	4.1.97	3380t	BU 1947
TORDENSKJOLD	18.3.97	3380t	BU 1948

MONITORS

Name	Launched	Disp	Fate
Thor class			
THOR	5.6.72	2035t	Stricken 1918, sold
Mjölner class			
MJÖLNER	2.5.68	1539t	Stricken 1908, sold
TRUDVANG	3.5.69	1539t	Stricken 1918, sold
Skorpionen class			
SKORPIONEN	30.10.66	1470t	BU 1908

The original armament of all four monitors was 2–21.6cm (10.5in) guns. In 1897 it changed to 2–12cm (4.7in), 2–65mm (6pdr) and 2–37mm (1pdr) guns.

PROTECTED CRUISERS

Name	Launched	Disp	Fate
FRITHJOF	15.11.95	1427t	Stricken 1928
VIKING	2.4.91	1120t	Stricken 1920

Frithjof was rebuilt in 1908 as a cadet TS. *Viking* originally had 2–15cm, 2–75mm, 4–65mm (6pdr) and 4–37mm (1pdr) guns and 1–35.6cm (16in) bow TT. In 1904 she was rearmed with 1–15cm, 1–12cm, 4–76mm, 2–75mm and 6–47mm guns and the same TT. From 1924 she sailed as a hospital ship for the Norwegian Red Cross.

DESTROYER

Name	Launched	Disp	Fate
VALKYRJEN	1896	415t	Stricken 1922

This vessel was officially called Division torpedo boat. She was ordered from the German Schichau yard at Elbing with money collected by patriotic Norwegian ladies.

GUNBOATS

Name	Launched	Disp	Fate
ÆGER	1.7.93	316t	Stricken 1932, BU
Gor class			
GOR	7.5.84	290t	Stricken 1945
TYR	16.3.87	278t	Sold 1945
Ellida class			
ELLIDA	25.8.80	1045t	Stricken 1925
Vale class			
VALE	14.4.74	200t	BU 1945
ULLER	21.7.76	200t	Sunk 30.4.40
NOR	23.10.78	200t	Sold 1949
BRAGE	1.11.78	200t	BU 1945
VIDAR	3.1.82	200t	Sold 1947
Rjukan class			
RJUKAN	22.11.60	220t	Stricken *c*1918
SARPEN	8.12.60	220t	Stricken *c*1918

Gor class
The first warships built of steel in Norway. *Tyr* was laid up from 1900 till the 1905 mobilisation. She served as tender to the first Norwegian submarine *Kobben* from 14 April 1910 until 31 December 1913. She and *Gor* were converted to minelayers in 1914 receiving rails to take 55 contact mines. The 26cm (10.5in)/30cal Krupp BL was replaced by a Belgian 12cm (4.7in) Cockerill QF. *Tyr* spent 1914–18 in the Hvaler Division farthest out in Oslofjord. She was laid up after minesweeping duties on 1 April 1919.

Ellida
A wooden-hulled ship which also had the designation steam corvette. Dimensions: 190ft 3in × 32ft 6in × 14ft 5in/*58m × 9.9m × 4.4m*. Armament: 5–15cm, 1–12cm and 2–37mm guns, 1–35.6cm bow TT. In 1898 rearmed as cadet TS with 2–76mm, 1–75mm, 2–65mm and 2–37mm guns, no TT. During 1914–18 used as barrack and repair ship for submarines.

Vale class
All 4 originally had 1–27cm (10.6in) and 3–37mm (1pdr) guns. In 1911–12 rebuilt as minelayers with 1–15cm, 1–47mm and 2–37mm guns (*Vidar, Brage* and *Nor*) and 1–12cm and 3–37mm guns (*Uller* and *Vale*). All had a capacity of 50 mines.

Rjukan class
Originally had 1–17cm (6.7in) and 1–16cm (6.3in) gun. In 1893 modified to command vessels with 2–65mm and 2–37mm guns. *Sarpen* spent her last years as a submarine salvage vessel.

Garm date unknown *Author's Collection*

TORPEDO-BOATS

Name	Launched	Disp (full load)	Fate
Ravn class			
RAVN	18.12.03	73t	Scuttled 17.4.40
ÖRN	8.12.03	73t	Stricken 1945, sold 1946
GRIB	26.1.05	74.5t	Scuttled 17.4.40
JO	10.7.05	73.5t	Scuttled 17.4.40
LOM	14.9.05	73.5t	Sold 1946
Hvas class			
HVAS	1900	75t	Stricken 1945, sold 1946
KJÆK	1900	75t	Stricken 1945, sold 1946
HAUK	3.6.02	75t	Stricken 1945
FALK	26.6.02	75t	Stricken 1945, sold 1946
Hval class			
HVAL	1896	102t	Stricken 1931
DELFIN	1896	102t	Stricken 1927
HAI	1896	102t	Stricken 1920
TRODS	14.3.98	107t	Stricken 1931, sold
STORM	1.6.98	107t	Sunk 13.4.40
BRAND	22.9.98	107t	Stricken 1945, BU
LAKS	12.7.00	107t	Stricken 1945, sold
SILD	30.7.00	107t	Scuttled 5.5.40
SÆL	25.9.01	107t	Damaged 18.4.40, lost
SKREI	31.10.01	107t	Scuttled 8.5.40
Myg class			
MYG	29.8.99	27t	Stricken 1920
Varg class			
KVIK	1898	70t	Stricken 1945, sold 1947
DRISTIG	1898	70t	Scuttled 3.5.40
DJERV	29.5.97	70t	Scuttled 3.5.40
GLIMT	29.5.97	65t	Stricken 1920
BLINK	1896	65t	Stricken 1945, BU
LYN	1896	65t	Stricken 1945, BU
RAKET	17.5.94	65t	Stricken 1920, sold 1923
VARG	17.5.94	65t	Stricken 1920
Snar class			
OTER	13.12.88	55t	Stricken 1920
ORM	28.4.88	55t	Stricken 1920
SNAR	25.7.87	50t	Stricken 1920
Od class			
PIL	16.1.86	45t	Stricken 1920
RASK	31.10.85	45t	Stricken 1920
SPRINGER	3.9.83	45t	Stricken 1920
OD	14.3.82	42t	Stricken 1920
Ulven class			
ULVEN	1878	16t	Stricken 1920
Rap class			
RAP	1872	10t	Stricken 1920

Hvas class
All four classified as patrol boats in 1931, without TT, and with minesweeping capacity.

Myg class
Myg was Norway's sole 'torpedo-boat 3rd class'.

Varg class
Kvik was from 1931 classified as patrol boat, without TT, *Dristig* and *Djerv* formally stricken 1927 but laid up as reserve patrol boats. *Blink* and *Lyn* from 1931 patrol boats.

Ulven class
Ulven was a spar torpedo-boat.

Stegg date unknown — *Author's Collection*

Rap class
Rap, built at Thornycroft, was the first real torpedo-boat in the world. She originally had a Harvey towed torpedo. From 1875 a spar torpedo, from 1879 two 35.6cm (14in) torpedoes in immersion davits. In 1900–1920 she was used as a patrol boat without torpedoes. With her last armament she now is a museum boat at the naval museum in Horten.

MAJOR SURFACE SHIPS

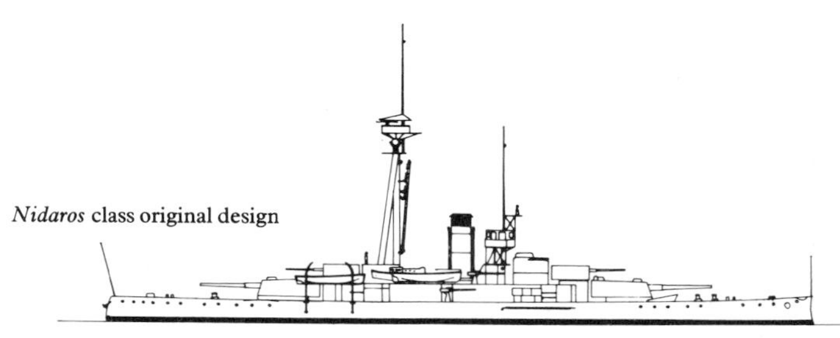

Nidaros class original design

NIDAROS class *coastal battleships*

Displacement: 4900t
Dimensions: 310ft oa × 55ft 1in × 17ft 9in
94.5m × 16.8m × 5.4m
Machinery: 2-shaft VTE, 4 boilers, 4500ihp = 15kts
Armour: See *Gorgon* class (British section)
Armament: 2–240mm (9.4in), 4–152mm (5.9in) (2×2), 6–100mm (3.9in), 2–457mm (18in) TT sub

Name	Builder	Launched	Fate
NIDAROS	Elswick	9.6.14	To RN 1914
BJÖRGVIN	Elswick	8.8.14	To RN 1914

Voted in 1912 and ordered from Armstrong Elswick in January 1913 they were to complete the coastal battleship division of only four ships. They carried the ancient Norwegian names for the cities of Bergen and Trondheim. As the First World War broke out building was stopped. Bought by Britain for £370,000 each, they were taken over by the Royal Navy in 1915 and modified as the monitors *Gorgon* and *Glatton* respectively. See British *Gorgon* class.

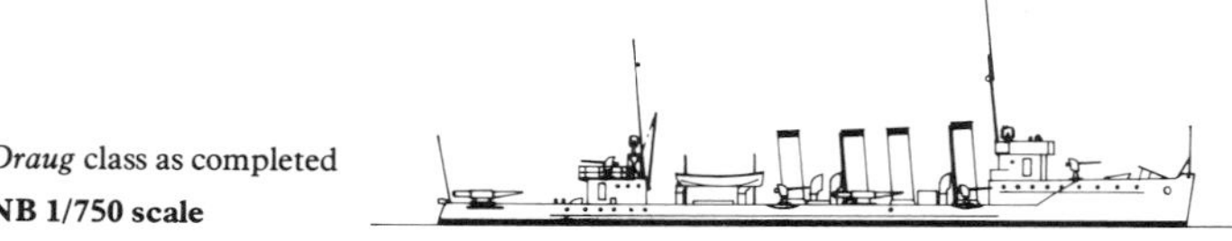

Draug class as completed
NB 1/750 scale

DRAUG class *destroyers*

Displacement: 578t (*Garm* 597t)
Dimensions: 226ft 7in × 23ft 11in × 9ft 6in
69.2m × 7.3m × 2.9m
Machinery: 2-shaft VTR (*Draug* and *Troll*), Germania turbines in *Garm*, 8000ihp = 26.5kts (*Draug*), 27kts (*Troll*), 27.4kts (*Garm*). Coal 105t
Armament: 6–76mm, 3–457mm (18in) TT
Complement: 76

Name	Builder	Launched	Fate
DRAUG	Horten N Yd	18.3.08	BU 1940s
TROLL	Horten N Yd	7.7.10	Sold 1947, BU
GARM	Horten N Yd	27.5.13	Sunk 26.4.40

Norway's only home-built destroyers until the *Aalesund* class were laid down in April 1939.

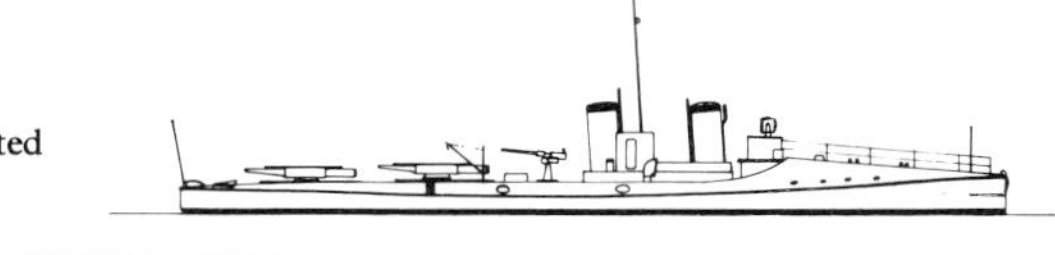

Teist class as completed
NB 1/750 scale

TEIST class *torpedo-boats*

Displacement: 108t (*Kjell* 125t)
Dimensions: 134ft 10in × 15ft 5in × 7ft 7in, 7ft 11in
41.1m × 4.7m × 2.3m, 2.4m (Kjell)
Machinery: 1-shaft VTE, 2 boilers, 1700ihp = 25kts. Coal 15.4t
Armament: 2–47mm (*Kjell* 1–76mm), 3–457mm (18in) TT (1 bow, 2 deck)
Complement: 21

Class (launched, fate):
Teist (14.12.06, scuttled 14.4.40), *Skarv* (18.2.07, BU 1940), *Kjell* (12.3.12, BU after 1945)

Built by Horten N Yd. *Teist* achieved 1767ihp and 25.2kts, *Skarv* 1741ihp and 25.9kts, *Kjell* 1864ihp and 25.8kts.

TRYGG class *torpedo-boats*

Displacement: 256t
Dimensions: 173ft 11in × 18ft 1in × 5ft 11in
53.0m × 5.5m × 1.8m
Machinery: 2-shaft VTE, 2 boilers, 3500ihp = 25kts (*Stegg* 24kts). Oil 33t
Armament: 2–76mm, 4–457mm (18in) TT (2×2), mines
Complement: 33

Class (launched, fate):
Trygg (31.5.19, sunk 23.10.44), *Snögg* (2.9.20, BU 1945), *Stegg* (16.6.21, sunk 20.4.40)

Moss Yd built the lead boat, Horten N Yd the other two from a 1916–17 design. Often called the *Snögg* class.

SUBMARINES

KOBBEN *submarine*

Displacement: 206t/259t
Dimensions: 128ft 11in × 12ft 2in × 9ft 10in
39.3m × 3.7m × 3.0m
Machinery: 2 shafts, Körting diesels plus 2 electric motors, 440bhp/250ihp = 11.9kts/8.9kts. Range 1450nm at 9kts, 45nm at 6.5kts
Armament: 3–457mm (18in) TT (2 bow, 1 stern deck; 4 torpedoes)
Complement: 14

Name	Builder	Launched	Fate
KOBBEN	Germaniawerft, Kiel	5.5.09	Sold 1933

Her name was changed to *A 1* in 1913. First exported U-boat similar to *U 1*.

A 2 date unknown — *Author's Collection*

Glommen date unknown — *Author's Collection*

A 2 class *submarines*

Displacement: 268t/355t
Dimensions: 152ft 7in × 15ft 9in × 8ft 10in
46.5m × 4.8m × 2.7m
Machinery: 2 shafts, Germania diesels plus 2 electric motors, 700bhp/380shp = 14.5kts/9kts
Armament: 3–457mm (18in) TT (2 bow, 1 stern; 5 torpedoes)
Complement: 17

Class (fate):
A 2 (BU 1940), *A 3* (scuttled 16.4.40), *A 4* (scuttled 16.4.40)

All 3 launched by Germaniawerft, Kiel, in 1913. *A 5* (launched 9.5.14) became the German *UA* at the outbreak of war.

SMALL SURFACE WARSHIPS

ORKLA class *gunboats*

Displacement: 270t
Dimensions: 124ft 8in × 23ft × 5ft 9in
38m × 7m × 1.7m
Machinery: 360ihp = 10kts
Armament: 2–120mm (4.7in)

Class:
Orkla, Rauma

Both launched in 1917 and stricken *c*1923.

FRÖYA *minelayer*

Displacement: 870t
Dimensions: 247ft 1in × 26ft 11in × 9ft 2in
75.3m × 8.2m × 2.8m
Machinery: 2 shafts, 7000ihp = 21.8kts. Coal 165t
Armament: 4–102mm (4in)/40, 2–457mm (18in) TT, 180 mines
Complement: 78

Name	Builder	Launched	Fate
FRÖYA	Horten N Yd	20.6.16	Sunk 4.40

A large minelayer built during the First World War. She was beached by her own crew on 13 April 1940, being torpedoed and blown up by a U-boat some days later.

GLOMMEN class *minelayers*

Displacement: 351t (*Laugen* 357t)
Dimensions: 137ft 10in × 27ft 11in × 6ft 11in
42.0m × 8.5m × 2.1m
Machinery: 340ihp = 9.9kts (*Laugen* 9.8kts). Coal 21kts
Armament: 2–76mm, 120 mines
Complement: 35

Name	Builder	Launched	Fate
GLOMMEN	Akers mekaniske verksted, Oslo	1917	Sunk 1944
LAUGEN	Akers mekaniske verksted, Oslo	1918	Sold 1950

MISCELLANEOUS
In addition the Coast Guard operated an armed whaler, the patrol boat *Morelos*, 6 armed auxiliaries and 3 armed trawlers in 1914–18.

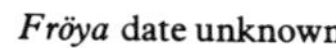

Fröya date unknown — *Author's Collection*

Denmark

After Prussia and Austria had deprived Denmark of her German provinces of Lauenburg, Holstein and Slesvig in 1864 (the last-mentioned with a big Danish population) and with an ever more powerful German Empire as neighbour, Denmark was in a very difficult strategic situation.

From the first years of this century the defence budget only permitted small expenditures on new warships. Between 1897 and 1911 not one torpedo-boat was built in spite of the Navy's earlier emphasis on this type. All the money was spent on the third ship of the *Herluf Trolle* class, the monitor-like *Peder Skram*, and the first small submarines. Personnel remained at 4000 in this period.

The First World War meant hard neutrality watching for all ships and boats. The only coastal battleship, *Niels Iuel*, could not be delivered – no heavy guns, no armour etc – and only 10 small torpedo-boats and some submarines could be delivered from the Naval Yard in Copenhagen, whose main drydock (out of 3) was lengthened in 1912. Private yards were much enlarged in 1915–17.

After Germany's defeat Denmark got back the northern part of the Slesvig province (referendum 1920 under international control). As in the other Nordic countries most people counted on the 'eternal peace' with the establishment of the League of Nations.

FLEET STRENGTH 1906

COASTAL BATTLESHIPS

Name	Launched	Disp (metric)	Fate
Herluf Trolle class			
HERLUF TROLLE	2.9.99	3735t	Stricken 30.4.32, BU 1934
OLFERT FISCHER	9.5.03	3650t	Sold 10.36
Skjold class			
SKJOLD	8.5.96	2195t	Stricken 21.5.29, BU
Iver Hvitfeldt class			
IVER HVITFELDT	14.4.86	3478t	Stricken 26.2.19, BU
Tordenskjold class			
TORDENSKJOLD	30.9.80	2534t	Stricken 13.3.08, BU
Helgoland class			
HELGOLAND	9.5.78	5480t	Stricken 29.6.07, BU
Odin class			
ODIN	12.12.72	3232t	Stricken 12.6.12, BU
Gorm class			
GORM	17.5.70	2350t	Stricken 12.6.12, BU
Lindormen class			
LINDORMEN	8.8.68	2100t	Stricken 29.6.07, BU

Herluf Trolle class
Officially the same class these ships were built over a period of more than ten years (*Peder Skram* launched 1908) and differed in many details from each other: armour type and thickness, gun range, rate of fire and so on. *Olfert Fischer* ended her career as a very special target ship. Minus all material not necessary for steaming at 9kts and with extra protection of wood and armour for a skeleton crew she steamed up and down in the Faxe Bugt for 12 days in October 1936 as a target for Army and Navy bombers; of 386 small (12kg) bombs only 12 hit the ship.

Skjold class
Skjold was rated as 'armoured battery'. Her very low freeboard made her more of a monitor than a seagoing ship.

Iver Hvitfeldt class
Iver Hvitfeldt was a real coastal battleship with two Krupp 26cm (10.2in) guns in two well armoured turrets.

Tordenskjold class
Tordenskjold was also an 'armoured ship' and not of monitor type.

Helgoland class
Helgoland (named after the 1864 battle against the Austro-Hungarian squadron), was throughout her career the biggest and heaviest gunned coastal battleship of the Scandinavian countries. Also internationally with her 5480t she was a real battleship ie over 5000t.

Odin class
Odin was classified as an armoured ship, not a battery ship.

Gorm and Lindormen classes
Gorm and *Lindormen* were designated armoured batteries. *Lindormen* was the first big iron construction at Copenhagen N Yd and a development of the earlier armoured battery *Rolf Krake*. She was the first Danish warship with two screws.

CRUISERS

Name	Launched	Disp	Fate
Hekla class			
HEIMDAL	30.8.94	1342t	Stricken 22.10.30, BU
GEISER	5.7.92	1282t	Stricken 29.3.28, BU
HEKLA	28.11.90	1322t	Stricken 1913, BU 1955
Valkyrien class			
VALKYRIEN	8.9.88	3020t	Stricken 5.10.23, BU 1924
Fyen class			
FYEN	27.9.82	2737t	Stricken 1907, barrack ship, BU 1962

Hekla class
With the same dimensions these three ships had different and varying armament. One of *Hekla*'s 15cm guns was taken away in 1901. She served without guns from 1913 as a submarine depot and barrack ship. Towed to Isefjorden by the Germans in 1943. In 1945 towed back to Copenhagen and sold 1955, 65 years old.

Valkyrien class
Valkyrien was totally rearmed in 1915 with 2–15cm/50, 6–75mm/55, 2–57mm, 2–37mm and 5 TT were reduced to 3.

Fyen class
In 1900 it was decided to remove *Fyen*'s 15cm guns, but 2 of the 18 remained until 1907. As barrack ship she served in World War Two with the rooms below the armour deck used as air raid shelters!

Olfert Fischer at the Coronation Review 1911 — *Author's Collection*

TORPEDO-BOATS

Name	Launched	Disp	Fate
Hajen class			
SÖBJÖRNEN	1898	142t	Stricken 1928
HAVÖRNEN	1897	142t	Stricken 1928
HAJEN	1896	139t	Stricken 1928
Makrelen class			
NORDKAPEREN	1893	128t	Stricken 1920
MAKRELEN	1893	128t	Stricken 1920
Springeren class			
SPRINGEREN	1891	89t	Stricken 1919
P 8 class			
P 9	1895	48t	Stricken 1927
P 8	1894	48t	Stricken 1930

Name	Launched	Disp	Fate
P 4 class			
P 7	1890	20t	Stricken 1927
P 6	1890	20t	Stricken 1927
P 5	1890	20t	Stricken 1927
P 4	1889	20t	Stricken 1927
Tb 2 kl nr 12 class			
Tb nr 13	1889	25t	Stricken 1919
Tb nr 12	1889	25t	Stricken 1919
Tb 2 kl nr 10 class			
Tb nr 11	1888	17t	Stricken 1917
Tb nr 10	1888	17t	Stricken 1917
Stören class			
NARHVALEN	1888	115t	Stricken 1919
HAVHESTEN	1888	115t	Stricken 1919
SÖLÖVEN	1887	115t	Stricken 1919
STÖREN	1887	115t	Stricken 1919
Tb 2 kl nr 6 class			
Tb nr 9	1886	16t	Stricken 1916
Tb nr 8	1886	16t	Stricken 1916
Tb nr 7	1884	15t	Stricken 1916
Tb nr 6	1884	15t	Stricken 1916
Delfinen class			
HVALROSSEN	1884	74t	Stricken 1919
DELFINEN	1883	74t	Stricken 1919
Tb 2 kl			
Tb nr 4	1882	33t	Stricken 1910
SVÆRDFISKEN	1880	38t	Stricken 1919
SÖULVEN	1881	59t	Stricken 1911
HAJEN	1879	33t	Stricken 1916

The Danish torpedo-boats have always given confusion to the naval annuals with their repeated changes of names and numbers. In 1920 the earlier mast and funnel markings were changed to numbers in so curious a manner, that the youngest got No 1 and the oldest vessel then existing, the *Hajen* of 1896, got No 23. Three years later all the numbers were again changed: *Hajen* became *A 1*, *Havörnen* A 2 and *Söbjörnen* A 3. The *Springeren* class received numbers earlier: *Springeren* T 1 from 1916, *Makrelen* T 6 from 1918 and P 2 from 1920, *Nordkaperen* T 7 from 1918 and P 3 from 1920. From 1912 *Tb nr 10–Tb nr 13* became P 10–13. From 1916 the *Stören* class got following numbers: *Narhvalen* T 5, *Havhesten* T 4, *Sölöven* T 3 and *Stören* T 2. *Tb 8* and 9 from 1912 had the numbers P 14 and P 15, changed in 1916 to Pa and Pb. *Tb 6* and 7 from 1912 got the numbers P 2 and P 3, changed in 1916 to Pc and Pd. From 1912 *Hvalrossen* and *Delfinen* were numbered T 5 and T 4, changed in 1916 to P 3 and P 2. The three oldest boats originally had only numbers: *Sværdfisken* was named *Tb nr 6*, got her name in 1882, from 1912 T 3 and from 1916 P 1, *Söulven* originally *Tb nr 5*, from 1882 named, from 1894 *Tb 2 kl nr 3*, *Hajen* originally *Tb nr 4*, from 1882 named, from 1894 *Tb 2 kl nr 2* and from 1912 P 1.

MISCELLANEOUS

There was also the 283t minelayer *Hjælperen* (launched by Copenhagen N Yd in 1890, armed with 3 MG and stricken 1928)

Other ships of little fighting value: minelayer *Beskytteren* (300t, 2–3pdr), corvette *Dagmar* (1861, 1200t) and TS *Ingolf* (1876, 1000t), brig *Örnen* (300t), the 119ft long, 11.6kt gunboats *Grönsund* (1883, rebuilt 1905–6, 260t, 2 MG, 49 crew) and *Guldborgsund* (1884, rebuilt 1903, 270t, 2–3pdr, 4 MG, 46 crew), the 250t gunboat *Little Belt* (1875, rebuilt 1894, 7.6kts, 2–3pdr, 4 MG, 30 men). There was also the Royal Yacht *Dannebrog* (1879, 1190t, 13kts, 2 small guns) and 15 patrol boats *No 1–15* (1879–95, 16–47t, 12–20kts, 1–3pdr or 2 MG or 1–1pdr and 14in TT).

Peder Skram 1923 — *Author's Collection*

MAJOR SURFACE SHIPS

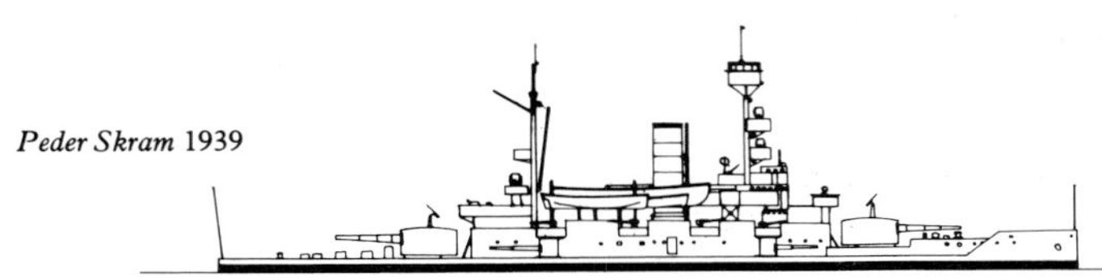

Peder Skram 1939

HERLUF TROLLE class *coastal battleships*

Displacement: 3735t normal; 3785t full load
Dimensions: 275ft 7in, 286ft 9in × 51ft 6in × 16ft 5in
84.0m, 87.4m × 15.7m × 5.0m
Machinery: 2-shaft VTE, 2 Thornycroft boilers, 5400ihp = 16kts. Coal 245t
Armour: Belt 195mm–155mm (7⅝in–6⅛in), turret faces 190mm (7½in), sides 175mm (6⅞in), rear 160mm (6¼in), barbettes 185mm (7¼in), casemate face 140mm (5½in), rear 75mm, deck 65mm–45mm (2½in–1¾in, CT 190mm
Armament: 2–240mm (9.4in)/43, 4–150mm (5.9in)/50, 10–75mm/55, 2–37mm/38, 4–457mm (18in) TT sub (1 bow, 2 beam, 1 stern)
Complement: 257–258

Name	Builder	Launched	Fate
PEDER SKRAM	Copenhagen N Yd	2.5.08	Sold for BU 1.5.49

Peder Skram was the third ship of the *Herluf Trolle* class, built nine years after the first and in some details improved. Her original light armament was changed many times. The 57mm guns were changed to fewer 75mm and 40mm and 20mm were added in 1934. In 1939–40 the ship got 4–40mm Bofors AA. As a German seizure of the Danish Fleet was expected, the ship was scuttled on 29 August 1943 at the Copenhagen N Yd. The Germans salvaged her, placed the 15cm guns in a coastal battery at Fanö and rebuilt the ship as an AA and training vessel, renamed *Adler*. Sunk by Allied bombers at Kiel-Friedrichsort in April 1945, she was salvaged and brought to Copenhagen. After three years at the Naval Yard as a wreck *Peder Skram* was sold to be BU at Odense.

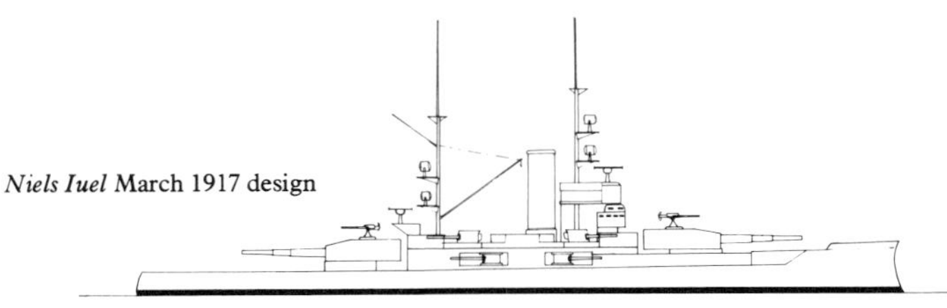

Niels Iuel March 1917 design

NIELS IUEL *coastal battleship*

Displacement: 3800t standard; 4100t full load
Dimensions: 295ft 3in oa, 285ft 5in × 53ft 6in × 16ft 5in
90.0m, 87.0m × 16.3m × 5.0m
Machinery: 2-shaft VTE, 4 Yarrow boilers, 5800ihp = 16kts. Oil 240t, coal 250t
Armour: Belt 195mm–155mm (7⅝in–6⅛in), deck 55mm (2⅛in), 150mm gunshield 50mm (2in), CT 170mm (6¾in), roof 40mm (1⅝in)
Armament: 10–150mm (see notes)
Complement: 310–369

Name	Builder	Launched	Fate
NIELS IUEL	Copenhagen N Yd	3.7.18	Sunk 3.5.45

Niels Iuel is the correct name of the ship (after the famous seventeenth century Danish admiral) but sometimes in Denmark and more often abroad the name is spelt with a 'J'. Originally planned as a coastal battleship with two 30.5cm guns in two turrets the ship was laid down on 21 September 1914. Through the years 1914–18 the Navy yard had so much work with the active ships on neutrality watch that *Niels Iuel* made little progress. Krupp could not deliver the planned guns and after the Armistice the Allies forbad delivery. After long discussions Bofors got the contract for 15cm guns in 1922. *Niels Iuel* became a hybrid between an armoured ship and a light cruiser. The 10–15cm guns were placed behind shields in very curious positions: 2 side by side at the bow, 3 starboard and 3 port of the deck and the 2 last at stern, the X gun over the Y. The ship was rebuilt many times, receiving a heavy pole mast and modern AA in 1935–36. During the German capture of the Danish Fleet *Niels Iuel* first tried to escape to Sweden, then grounded in Nyköbing Bugt on 29 August 1943. Scuttling failed. The Germans placed her guns in coastal batteries, rebuilt the ship as the cadet ship *Nordland* with 3–10.5cm, 3–37mm and 16–20mm AA and 4–8mm AA MG. Used as a refugee ship for officers and their families the ship was bombed at Eckernförde, NW of Kiel. The wreck rests at 30m in the fjord.

Ormen 1909 *Author's Collection*

ORMEN *torpedo-boat*

Displacement: 97t standard; 105t full load
Dimensions: 124ft 8in × 14ft 1in × 8ft 6in
38.0m × 4.3m × 2.6m
Machinery: 1-shaft VTE, 2100ihp = 26.2kts. Coal 11t
Armament: 2–37mm, 3–457mm (18in) TT
Complement: 21

Name	Builder	Launched	Fate
ORMEN	Copenhagen N Yd	1907	Stricken 1932

After a ten year pause in torpedo-boat building plans were purchased from Normand and a unit built. The TT were curiously arranged: one bow tube and a double deck tube with its tubes in contrary directions. Pennant numbers: from 1920 20, from 1923 B 1, from 1929 R 1.

TUMLEREN class *torpedo-boats*

Displacement: 249t
Dimensions: 185ft 1in × 19ft × 6ft 3in
56.4m × 5.8m × 1.9m
Machinery: 1-shaft turbine, Normand boilers, 500ihp = 27.5kts
Armament: 2–75mm, 5–457mm (18in) TT (1 bow, 2 on each beam)
Complement: 33

Name	Builder	Launched	Fate
TUMLEREN	Schichau, Elbing	1911	Stricken 1935
VINDHUNDEN	Copenhagen N Yd	1911	Stricken 1935
SPÆKHUGGEREN	Copenhagen N Yd	1911	Stricken 1935

After the Normand boat *Ormen* it was decided to buy plans from Germany and England and build two more of both types in Denmark. The German type was lower and one-funnelled and was so successful, that the German Navy in 1914–18 built about 90 similar, the so-called A type torpedo-boats, used in the Baltic and off Flanders. Pennant numbers: from 1919 19, 18 and 17, from 1921 1, 2 and 3, from 1929 N 1, 2 and 3.

SÖRIDDEREN class *torpedo-boats*

Displacement: 240t
Dimensions: 181ft 9in × 18ft 1in × 6ft 7in
55.4m × 5.5m × 2.0m
Machinery: 1-shaft Curtis *(Söridderen)* or Burmeister & Wain turbine, Yarrow boilers, 5000ihp = 27.5kts
Other particulars: As *Tumleren* class

Name	Builder	Launched	Fate
SÖRIDDEREN	Yarrow, Glasgow	1911	Stricken 1937
FLYVEFISKEN	Burmeister & Wain, Copenhagen	1911	Stricken 1937
SÖULVEN	Burmeister & Wain, Copenhagen	1911	Stricken 1937

This English type had a higher freeboard and was more seaworthy than the German. Pennant numbers: from 1920 16, 15 and 14, from 1923 D 1, 2 and 3, from 1929 O 1, 2 and 3.

HVALROSSEN class *torpedo-boats*

Displacement: 182t
Dimensions: 148ft 4in × 17ft 1in × 6ft 11in
45.2m × 5.2m × 2.1m
Machinery: 2-shaft VTE, 3500ihp = 26.3kts
Armament: 1–75mm, 4–457mm (18in) TT (1 bow, 1 twin and 1 single on deck)
Complement: 30

Class (fate):
Hvalrossen (scuttled 29.8.43, BU 1945), *Delfinen* (stricken 1932), *Svaerdfisken* (stricken 1932)

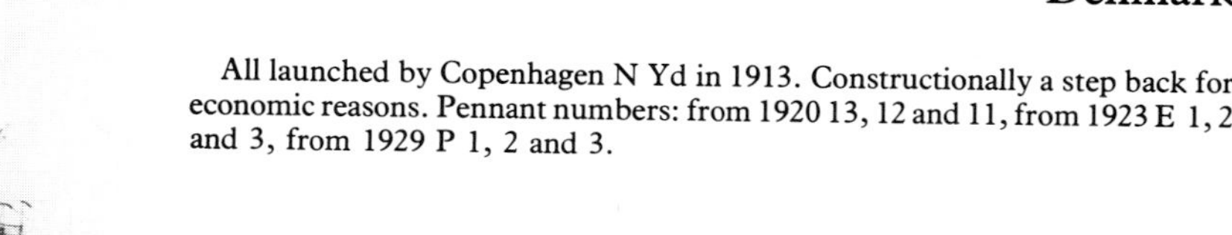

All launched by Copenhagen N Yd in 1913. Constructionally a step back for economic reasons. Pennant numbers: from 1920 13, 12 and 11, from 1923 E 1, 2 and 3, from 1929 P 1, 2 and 3.

Spaekhuggeren 1930 *Twardowski Collection*

Söulven as completed *Author's Collection*

Svaerdfisken 1923 *Author's Collection*

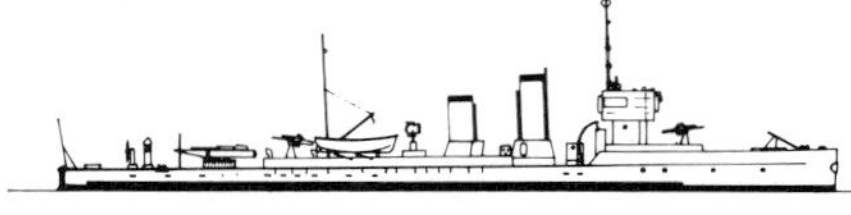

Spingeren class as completed
NB 1/750 scale

SPRINGEREN class *torpedo-boats*

Displacement: 108t
Dimensions: 126ft 4in × 14ft 1in × 8ft 10in
38.5m × 4.3m × 2.7m
Machinery: 1-shaft VTE, 2000ihp = 24.6kts
Armament: 2–75mm, 2–457mm (18in) TT (1 bow, 1 deck)
Complement: 24

Class (launched, fate):
Springeren (1916, stricken 1946), *Stören* (1916, stricken 1940), *Sölöven* (1916, stricken (1945), *Söhunden* (1917, stricken 1940), *Havhesten* (1917, blown up by own crew 29.8.43 at Stammenakke), *Narhvalen* (1917, stricken 1949), *Makrelen* (1918, blown up by own crew 29.8.43 at Copenhagen N Yd), *Nordkaperen* (1918, sunk by own crew 29.8.43, salvaged by the Germans, BU), *Havkatten* (1919, stricken November 1948), *Saelen* (1919, sunk by own crew 29.8.43, salvaged by the Germans, BU)

A World War One construction of a more simple type by Copenhagen N Yd, with the *Ormen* as general design. *Havkatten* – together with some small minesweepers – escaped to Sweden on 29 August 1943, modernised at Karlskrona N Yd and together with the minesweepers first Danish naval units home again at liberation May 1945. Pennant numbers: from 1920 10 to 1 respectively, from 1923 B 2–11, from 1929 S 1–6 and R 2–5. *Sölöven* from 1937 named *Söridderen*, stricken 1940, returning for service 1943 with the name *Hajen*. *Havhesten* changed name to *Havörnen* in 1938.

SUBMARINES

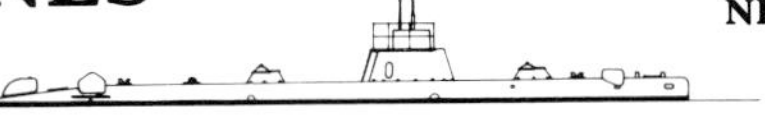

Dykkeren as completed
NB 1/750 scale

DYKKEREN *submarine*

Displacement: 105t/132t
Dimensions: 113ft 10in × 10ft 10in × 7ft 3in
34.7m × 3.3m × 2.2m
Machinery: 2 shafts, Fiat petrol engines plus 2 electric motors, ?/210hp = 12kts/7.5kts. Range 24nm/100nm at 12kts/8kts
Armament: 2–457mm (18in) TT (bow)
Complement: 9

Name	Builder	Launched	Fate
DYKKEREN	Fiat-San Giorgio, La Spezia	18.6.09	Sunk 9.10.16

Accepted 3 October 1909. Many teething troubles but improved at Copenhagen N Yd. From April 1913 carried the pennant number 1. Sunk in collision with the Norwegian steamer *Vesla* of Bergen. Salvaged, stricken June 1917 and BU 1918.

Havfruen (foreground) and *Najaden* about 1914 — *Author's Collection*

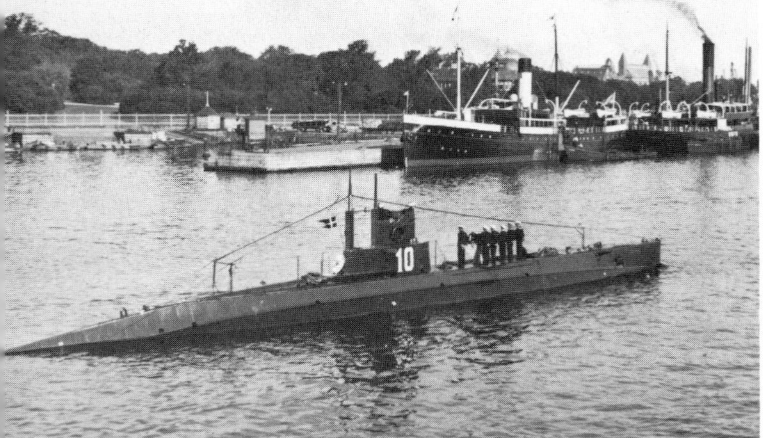

Triton after the war — *Author's Collection*

Rota date unknown — *Author's Collection*

HAVMANDEN class *submarines*

Displacement: 164t/204t
Dimensions: 127ft 8in × 11ft 10in × 7ft 7in
38.9m × 3.6m × 2.3m
Machinery: 1 shaft, 6 cyl, 2-stroke Fiat or MAN diesel plus 2 electric motors, 450bhp/275hp (430bhp/270hp *Havmanden*, *Thetis* and *Triton*) = 13kts/10kts. Range 1400nm/23nm at 10kts/8kts
Armament: 2–457mm (18in) TT (bow), 1–8mm MG (from 1917)
Complement: 10 (later 14)

Name	Builder	Launched	Fate
HAVMANDEN	Whitehead, Fiume	23.12.11	Stricken 26.4.28
HAVFRUEN	Copenhagen N Yd	31.8.12	Stricken 3.5.32
THETIS	Whitehead, Fiume	19.6.12	Stricken 26.4.28
TRITON	Whitehead, Fiume	31.3.13	Stricken 15.1.29, target, BU 1932
NAJADEN	Copenhagen N Yd	9.7.13	Stricken 9.9.31
NYMFEN	Copenhagen N Yd	10.2.14	Stricken 11.3.32

The Whitehead Yard at Fiume was contracted in 1910 for the *Havmanden* and sold plans for *Havfruen*. Two more were ordered from the Austrian yard in May 1911 and licence for the last two. A fund-raising drive obtained a sum for a new submarine, the fund bought *Triton* and changed her name to *2den April* as commemoration of the Nelson battle in the Copenhagen Roads 1801. And so the government could order a new submarine. Initially the *Havfruen* had the pennant number H 1, *Havmanden* H 2 and *Thetis* T 1. In April 1913 the submarines got new numbers: 2 = *Havfruen*, 3 = *Havmanden*, 4 = *Thetis*, 5 = *2den April* (ex-*Triton*), 6 = *Najaden* and 7 = *Nymfen*. Later these submarines were called the 'A' class but never had an A on their tower.

ÆGIR (or B) class *submarines*

Displacement: 185t/235t
Dimensions: 133ft 2in × 12ft 2in × 7ft 11in
40.6m × 3.7m × 2.4m
Machinery: 1 shaft, 2 diesels plus 2 electric motors, 450bhp/340hp = 13.5kts/9.8kts
Armament: 3–457mm T (18in) TT (2 bow, 1 stern), 1–57mm AA (from 1917)
Complement: 11 (later 14)

Name	Builder	Launched	Fate
ÆGIR	Copenhagen N Yd	8.12.14	Stricken 26.4.33
RAN	Copenhagen N Yd	30.5.15	Stricken 1940, BU 1946
TRITON	Copenhagen N Yd	29.7.15	Stricken 1940, BU 1946
NEPTUN	Copenhagen N Yd	22.12.15	Stricken 26.4.33
GALATHEA	Copenhagen N Yd	15.4.16	Stricken 1940, BU 1946

After the sinking of *Dykkeren* a sixth boat of the B class was ordered and got the new building no 131 at the Copenhagen N Yd. Material was collected but this submarine never was laid down. The building stopped in 1922. Pennant numbers respectively: 8, 9 (later B 9), 10 (later B 10), 11 and 12 (later B 12). The sixth boat should have had no 13.

ROTA (or C) class *submarines*

Displacement: 301t/369t
Dimensions: 155ft 10in × 14ft 5in × 8ft 10in
47.5m × 4.4m × 2.7m
Machinery: 2 shafts, 2 diesels plus 2 electric motors, 900bhp/640ihp = 14.5kts/10.5kts
Armament: 4–457mm (18in) TT (3 bow, 1 stern), 1–57mm AA
Complement: 17 (later 24)

Name	Builder	Launched	Fate
ROTA	Copenhagen N Yd	16.8.18	Scuttled 29.8.43, BU 1952
BELLONA	Copenhagen N Yd	14.3.19	Scuttled 29.8.43, BU 1952
FLORA	Copenhagen N Yd	23.4.20	Scuttled 29.8.43, BU 1952

Originally all three should have had a 5th deck TT but because it worked badly on *Rota* the two later boats never got it. *Bellona* got special radio equipment and *Flora* installations for laying mines.

SMALL SURFACE WARSHIPS

LOSSEN *minelayer*

Displacement: 628t
Dimensions: 149ft 3in × 28ft 3in × 9ft 6in
45.5m × 8.6m × 2.9m
Machinery: 900ihp = 13kts. Coal 20t
Armament: 2–75mm, 180 mines
Complement: 53

Name	Builder	Launched	Fate
LOSSEN	Copenhagen N Yd	1910	Scuttled 29.8.43

Salvaged by the Germans, sunk off Rostock in 1945 but salvaged by E Germany and repaired as tug *Wismar*.

Lossen as completed *Author's Collection*

KVINTUS class *minelayers*

Displacement: 186t
Dimensions: 88ft 3in × 20ft 4in × 6ft 7in
26.9m × 6.2m × 2.0m
Machinery: 2 shafts, Bergsund surface-ignition heavy-oil motors, electric drive, 290ihp = 9.5kts
Armament: 2–37mm
Complement: 53

Name	Builder	Launched	Fate
KVINTUS (Minekran V)	Copenhagen N Yd	1917	Scuttled 29.8.43
SIXTUS (Minekran VI)	Copenhagen N Yd	21.12.18	Scuttled 29.9.43

Salvaged by the Germans, *Kvintus* sunk in 1945 as guardship *Fürstenberg* at Warnemünde, *Sixtus* sunk off Rostock in 1945.

MISCELLANEOUS
The Coast Guard added *Islands Falk* (1906, 760t, 13kts, 52 men), *Diana* (1916, 260t, 10.5kts, 27 men), and *Fenris* (1915, 190t, 12kts, 18 men), the latter both Dutch-built, to *Absalon* (1877, 292t, 10kts, 26 men) and *Saltholm* (Copenhagen 1882, 300t). All were armed with 2–3pdr.

Sweden

The union between Sweden and Norway (forced in 1814 by Sweden's crown prince, the former French marshal Bernadotte) had after years of Norwegian obstruction been peaceably ended in 1905. But the two '*Förenade Konungadömena*' (United Kingdoms) together had a strong defence position between the Baltic and the North Sea. From 1905 Sweden had a real coastline of 7624km (4116nm), most of that on the Baltic and only the smaller part to the west: Kattegat and Skageraak, the passages to the North Sea.

From the 1860s and especially from the 1890s into the new century Sweden had built up a modern navy, stronger than any comparable nation. A very strong naval wind blew over the country. In 1900, for example, the Navy Minister asked for only small sums to complete one coastal battleship but a single member of the First Chamber of the Parliament moved for funds to begin three more – and parliament approved. This trend continued some years, but, after its election victory in 1911, the liberal government, in accordance with the growing social democratic party, reversed that year's decision to start building a new class of much heavier coastal battleships of the F type (later *Sverige* class). In response a popular movement in a few months collected 15 million Swedish crowns – for that time an incredibly big sum – more than the cost of the first battleship.

THE FIRST WORLD WAR
Sweden was lucky enough to stand neutral throughout the First World War and the Navy carried most of the burden of maintaining her neutrality. During 1914–18 3 coastal battleships were built in spite of material shortages, 2 destroyers and 7 submarines also, but not enough to maintain the fleet of 1906. After the 1918 Armistice the people were war-weary, the economy poor and most of the nation thought that the everlasting peace had begun with the League of Nations. By 1922 all the services had lost their 1919 quality and three years later the left-wing majority in the Parliament took a decision for one of the greatest voluntary acts of disarmament that any nation has taken in history until the Nazi threat turned the trend.

Sweden's navy had been built up first of all to keep the country outside a war and, if this was not possible, fight against a Baltic enemy, Russia or Germany. Since Viking days the Swede has been a good sailor and industrial capacity was sufficient to provide all the ships and arms needed. Only sometimes has a prototype vessel been acquired from a major foreign naval power. During the period 1906–21 only one submarine was imported: *Hvalen* from Fiat-Laurenti and two Italian MAS boats in 1921.

SUBMARINES
As the naval budgets were trimmed and surface ship construction became more and more expensive, the submarine was seen as a form of 'democratic' vessel – the small navy's weapon against the big Baltic powers' battleships. So Sweden's parliament has always voted for submarines, but never as many at the naval authorities have found necessary. But up to the 1970s most technical particulars have been top secret. Even today it is difficult to reconstruct some details – even launching dates!

Probably from the eighteenth century, the National Maritime Museum in Stockholm has a wooden model of a vessel 'to go under the water' from the Model Chamber of the Karlskrona Naval Yard. There were some later projects made but the first real submarine, built in Sweden, was the 60t Nordenfelt submarine of 1885, 19.5m length and a diameter of 2.7m. It had a steam engine of 100hp and two steam accumulators for underwater operation and a complement of 3 men. Most of this submarine was produced at Bolinders Mekaniska Verkstad in Stockholm but the vessel was put together and completed by Nordenfelt's weapon factory at Karlsvik, Kungsholmen in Stockholm. In the summer of 1885 the submarine was demonstrated for a Swedish and international public off Landskrona in the Sound. This submarine was sold to Greece. Nordenfelt's next three boats were built in England.

BASE AND ORGANISATION
The main base for the active fleet since 1680 has been Karlskrona (fortified, 6 drydocks and the submarine station) with Stockholm (fortified, 3 drydocks, mining and torpedo craft station) and Göteborg as complements. The biggest yards – civil and naval – were also located at these ports. Smaller bases were Fårösund at the northern end of the big Baltic island of Gotland and Hemsö in the middle of the Gulf of Bothnia, north of the Baltic. Regular personnel numbered 3500–4000 in the period with 23,000 annual conscripts, including Coastal Artillery.

The '*Marinen*', under an admiral as commander-in-chief, has been divided in two branches since 1902: the Navy and the Coastal Artillery. This last is not only a coast artillery but also an amphibious organisation with minelayers, marine infantry, heavy and light artillery in fortifications in the Swedish granite, mobile guns and so on. For a country with a very long coastline and thousands of islands covering more than half of her borders, a coast artillery of that type remains indispensable for defence.

FLEET STRENGTH 1906

COASTAL BATTLESHIPS

Name	Launched	Disp	Fate
Svea class			
SVEA	12.12.86		Stricken 1940, BU 1944
GÖTA	30.9.89	3097t	Stricken 1923, BU 1944
THULE	4.3.93	3150t	Stricken 1923, BU 1933
Oden class			
ODEN	9.3.96	3500t	Stricken 1937, BU 1943
THOR	7.3.98	3328t	Stricken 1937, BU 1942
NIORD	31.3.98	3328t	Stricken 1922, BU 1945
Dristigheten class			
DRISTIGHETEN	28.4.00	3270t	Stricken 13.6.47, BU 1961
Äran class			
ÄRAN	14.8.01	3650t	Stricken 13.6.47, sunk 1.11.68
WASA	29.5.01	3650t	Stricken 15.3.40, BU 1961
TAPPERHETEN	7.11.01	3650t	Stricken 13.6.47, BU 1952
MANLIGHETEN	1.12.03	3650t	Stricken 24.2.50, pontoon 1956
Oscar II class			
OSCAR II	6.6.05	4273t	Stricken 24.2.50, BU 1974

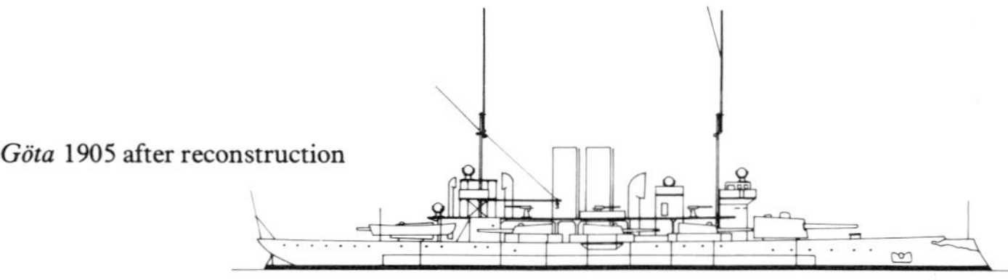
Göta 1905 after reconstruction

Svea class
The class was totally reconstructed in the first years after the turn of the century. *Göta* served from 1926 as a barrack ship for the naval air service until scrapped 1938. *Thule* became a barrack ship from 1926 and from 1928 an artillery target. *Svea* was active until 1915, was converted to a submarine depot ship 1919–1921 and served until 1940.

Oden class
All three ships underwent extensive reconstruction during 1914–18, the heavy 'military mast' and TT being removed and one broad funnel instead of two thinner. *Oden* not in active service after 1918. *Thor* from 1906 equipped as cadet ship. *Niord* from 1922 barrack ship, officially from 1926, but with her heavy guns remaining.

Dristigheten
She was a step between the *Oden* class and the *Äran* class. Rebuilt 1927–28 as aircraft depot and repair ship at Bergsund, Stockholm, with 2218t std and 2270t full load. Armament: 4–75mm AA, later also 2–40mm and 1×2 + 2×1 AA MG. After being stricken in 1947 used as an artillery target.

Äran class
Äran not in service 1933–39, then modernised, including a totally new AA armament of 4–57mm, 2–40mm guns and 2×2–8mm MG. From 1942 served as barrack ship until stricken. *Wasa* was from the beginning an unlucky ship with many small misfortunes. Not in active service after 1924. From 1939 used a dummy ship for *Drottning Victoria*. After 1945 she became a protection training ship until sold. *Tapperheten* was modernised in 1940 with AA (as *Äran*). *Manligheten* had a thorough 1940–41 modernisation, new boilers, all artillery increased range, new fire direction, totally new AA (as *Äran*) and an 'Italian' cruiser bow. Length in wl increased to 90.2m and displacement to 3685t.

Oscar II
Dimensions: 313ft 8in × 50ft 6in × 16ft 9in/18ft 3in (*95.6m × 15.4m × 5.1m/5.6m*). Armour: belt 150–125–100mm, citadel 100mm, turrets 190–130mm. ihp/speed: 9400 = 17.8kts. Armament: also 3–37mm. Complement: 326, as flagship 335. Modernised four times: 1910–11 tripod mast and rangefinder there; 1916 CT uncovered; bridge and fore mast moved astern, 2–57mm changed to 57mm AA; 1928 main mast changed; 1938–39 totally modernised: new artillery top and central instruments, all 57mm guns taken away, new AA with 4–57mm, 2–25mm and 2×2–8mm MG, all 10 boilers changed, 2 of them oil firing, all navigational equipment new. Displacement raised to 4050t and draught to 5.7m. After being stricken in 1950 served as a TS for protection service until BU.

MONITORS

Name	Launched	Disp	Fate
John Ericsson class			
JOHN ERICSSON	17.3.65	1508t	Stricken 1918. Cement barge. Extant 1984
THORDÖN	1.12.65	1502t	Stricken 1925, sold 1926
TIRFING	6.10.66	1512t	Stricken 1925, sold 1926
LOKE	4.9.69	1594t	Stricken 1908, sold
SKÖLD	11.11.68	249t	Sunk 1907
Gerda class			
GERDA	1.9.71	454t	Stricken 1922, sold 1938 to Denmark
HILDUR	14.7.71	454t	Stricken 1919, oil barge
Berserk class			
ULF	1873	454t	Stricken 1919, oil barge
BJÖRN	1874	454t	Stricken 1922
BERSERK	1874	454t	Stricken 1919, oil barge
SÖLVE	1875	451t	Stricken 1919, oil barge
FOLKE	1875	451t	Stricken 1919, heat ship for submarines, sold 1942

John Ericsson class
John Ericsson's 15in guns were a gift from the eponymous Swedish-born constructor of the USS *Monitor*, and she was built to his design. The two model Dahlgren (also a Swede in US Navy service) muzzle-loaders are now a monument at the Ericsson tomb in Filipstad (mid-west Sweden). In 1881–82 the armament was changed to 2–240mm BL guns, then changed to 2–152mm guns and 2 Nordenfelt 57mm in 1894–95. Served in the west coast squadron during 1914–18. *Thordön* and *Tirfing* had different dimensions: 223ft 1in × 45ft 3in × 11ft 10in/12ft 6in (*60.8m × 13.8m × 3.6m/3.8m*). They started with 2–267mm (10.6in) guns, changed to 240cm in 1869, after rebuilding 1902–05 replaced by 2–120mm and completed with 8 small guns, 47mm in *Thordön*, 57mm in *Tirfing*. *Loke* differed from other three. Displacement 1595t. Dimensions: 205ft 5in, 210ft × 45ft 3in/46ft, × *11ft 10in*/12ft 2in (*62.4m/64.0m × 13.8m/14.0m × 3.6m/3.7m*). Request for rebuilding refused, therefore scrapped 1908, ten years before the other three ships.

Sköld
Belong to the 'Archipelago Artillery'. Dimensions: 104ft 8in/107ft 3in × 22ft 4in/22ft 8in × 7ft 3in/7ft 11in (*31.9m/32.7m × 6.8m/6.9m × 2.2m/2.4m*). 17ihp = 3.75kts. She also had John Ericsson manual propelling machinery. Originally 1–267mm gun, changed to 1–240mm in 1870, later also 2–12mm MG. Stricken 1906, artillery target, sunk 1907 and the wreck sold.

Oden about 1918 *Author's Collection*

Gerda class
After experience with the armoured gunboat *Garmer* and the small monitors *Fenris* and *Sköld* the authorities chose a new monitor type for the outer defence of the archipelagos, bigger, better armoured and with more machinery power. *Gerda* and *Hildur* had a displacement of 454t/459t and dimensions of 106ft/130ft 3in × 22ft 4in/26ft 3in × 8ft 2in/8ft 10in *(32.3m/39.7m × 6.8m/8.0m × 2.5m/2.7m)*. Their 133ihp was to give 7.6kts but 8kts was reached, their 1–240mm (9.4in) gun was placed in a heavy armed, elliptic turret with 418mm–356mm (16½in–14in) armour. On the waterline the protection was 64mm–76mm (2½in–3in). Complement: 42. They were extensively rebuilt in 1908–10 with the 240mm gun replaced by a 120mm. A CT with 254mm armour was also added.

Berserk class
Five more small monitors were voted in 1871 and 1872. They differed only in details from the *Gerda* class, had more powerful machinery (155ihp), and therefore half a knot more speed. *Ulf* as the last of the five was really curious. She was 'the wrong way round'! Some tactician discovered that the squadron must perhaps retire – and then would not have a single gun to bear against the enemy. This last monitor was changed on the stocks at Motala Warf in Norrköping and got her heavy gun on the aft deck. As all the small monitors were nicknamed 'armoured lice' *Folke* was always called 'the wrong way louse'. All were rebuilt 1896–1909 with 1–120mm gun and 2 or 3–57mm guns.

ARMOURED CRUISER

Name	Launched	Disp (std)	Fate
FYLGIA	20.12.05	4310t	Sold 1957, BU

Fylgia, the world's smallest armoured cruiser, was intended as flagship for the scouting squadron. Most of all she was used as a cadet TS and as 'the white swan of Sweden' saw harbours the world over. Designed for 21.5kts, she reached 22.7. Totally rebuilt 1940–41. The 152mm guns had their range increased by over 30 per cent. Four boilers for oil. All small guns were replaced by AA: 4–57mm, 4–40mm, 3–25mm and 1–20mm. The side TT were taken out but two single 533mm placed on deck. She got a clipper bow and two new funnels replaced the earlier three. The very 'mixed' armament depended on her role as cadet cruiser. But after 1945 the minelayer *Älvsnabben* took over and *Fylgia* was stricken on 30 January 1953. But her four twin 152mm guns are still used as artillery in the fortifications in the north, like many other ex-naval guns, rebuilt for fortress functions.

TORPEDO CRUISERS

Name	Launched	Disp (std)	Fate
ÖRNEN	6.8.96	844t	Sunk as target 1950
CLAES HORN	9.2.98	846t	Sold for BU 1924
JACOB BAGGE	30.4.98	835t	Sold 1949, BU 1951
PSILANDER	25.11.99	814t	Sunk as target 3.8.39
CLAS UGGLA	9.12.99	800t	Sunk 30.8.17

Örnen class
The five units of the *Örnen* class in Sweden always have been called torpedo cruisers. With their 2–120mm guns they were used as flotilla or division leaders for the torpedo-boats. *Örnen* did active service in two world wars. Officially next to be stricken in 1922, she served as TS depot ship and as cadet ship until after World War Two. She was stricken in 1947 as was *Jacob Bagge*. *Claes Horn* was after four years of neutrality patrols so worn out that she was stricken in 1923. *Psilander* was stricken in 1936. *Clas Uggla* ran aground in the Gulf of Bothnia on 22 June 1917 and sank two months later.

DESTROYERS

Name	Launched	Disp (std)	Fate
MODE	22.7.02	410t	Stricken 1928, sunk as target 1936
MAGNE	21.8.05	430t	Stricken 1936, target, BU 1944

Mode
Displacement: 410t/453t, ihp/speed: 6000 = 31kts. Yard trial without armament 32.385kts at 6500ihp. Fully equipped not over 29kts. First destroyer fitted for northern weather conditions. Swedish classification 'jagare' = hunter. This Yarrow type hull not suited for Baltic short, 'stiff' waves.

Äran about 1910 *Author's Collection*

Thordön 1913 *Author's Collection*

Ulf 1914 *Author's Collection*

Magne
Displacement: 430t/460t. ihp/speed: 7200 = 30.5kts, reached 30.7kts on trials. This Thornycroft hull suitable for Baltic conditions, and therefore ensuing Swedish-built destroyers had this shape. Stricken 1936, target, sold 1943, BU.

FIRST CLASS TORPEDO-BOATS

Name	Fate
Hugin class: launched 1884, 65t deep load	
HUGIN (N:o 1)	Stricken 1923 as *Vedettbåt n:r 15*
Munin class: launched 1886–87, 67t deep load	
MUNIN (N:o 3)	Stricken 1923 as *Vedettbåt n:r 17*
FREKE (N:o 5)	Stricken 1923 as *Vedettbåt n:r 16*
GERE (N:o 7)	Stricken 1923 as *Vedettbåt n:r 18*
Gondul class: launched 1894, 69.1t	
GONDUL (N:o 9)	Stricken 1926 as *Vedettbåt n:r 21*
GUDUR (N:o 11)	Stricken 1926 as *Vedettbåt n:r 22*
Komet class: launched 1896–1904, 92t deep load	
KOMET	Stricken 1925 as *Vedettbåt n:r 20*
BLIXT	Stricken 1947 as *Vedettbåt n:r 27*
METEOR	Stricken 1947 as *Vedettbår n:r 28*
STJERNA	Stricken 1937 as *Vedettbåt n:r 29*
ORKAN	Stricken 1947 as *Vedettbåt n:r 30*

Name	Fate
BRIS	Stricken 1937 as *Vedettbåt n:r 31, sunk 1938 as target*
VIND	Stricken 1937 as *Vedettbåt n:r 32*
VIRGO	Stricken 1941 as *Vedettbåt n:r 33*
MIRA	Stricken 1943 as *Vedettbåt n:r 34*
ORION	Stricken 1947 as *Vedettbåt n:r 35*
SIRIUS	Stricken 1942 as *Vedettbåt n:r 36*
KAPELLA	Stricken 1937 as *Vedettbåt n:r 37*
Plejad class: launched 1905–1910, 106–120t deep load	
PLEJAD	Stricken 1930 as *Vedettbåt n:r 38*
CASTOR	Stricken 1940 as *Vedettbåt n:r 51*, BU 1947
POLLUX	Stricken 1940 as *Vedettbåt n:r 52*, BU 1947
ASTREA	Stricken 1947 as *Vedettbåt n:r 42*, target, sunk 1953
SPICA	Stricken 1947 as *Vedettbåt n:r 41*, BU 1951
IRIS	Stricken 1947 as *Vedettbåt n:r 49*, sold 1958
THETIS	Stricken 1947 as *Vedettbåt n:r 40*, artillery target, sunk
VEGA	Stricken 1941 as *Vedettbåt n:r 53*, BU 1948
VESTA	Stricken 1941 as *Vedettbåt n:r 54*, BU 1947
ALTAIR	Stricken 1947 as *Vedettbåt n:r 45*, BU 1951
ARGO	Stricken 1940 as *Vedettbåt n:r 46*, BU 1947
ANTARES	Stricken 1947 as *Vedettbåt n:r 43*, BU 1951
ARCTURUS	Stricken 1940 as *Vedettbåt n:r 44*, BU 1951
PERSEUS	Stricken 1947 as *Vedettbåt n:r 48*, BU 1957
POLARIS	Stricken 1947 as *Vedettbåt n:r 47*, BU 1951
REGULUS	Stricken 1944 as *Vedettbåt n:r 49*, school hulk, BU 1946
RIGEL	Stricken 1944 as *Vedettbåt n:r 50*, BU 1949

Hugin
The prototype *Hugin* was built by Thornycroft at Chiswick, rerated second class TB 1906 and patrol boat in 1915.

Munin class
Munin with her original number rerated second class TB 1906. In 1915 patrol boat number 17. *Freke* and *Gere* changed numbers in 1906 (during the Union of Sweden and Norway all Swedish torpedo-boats had odd numbers, Norwegian even) and were rerated to second class TB with number *2* and *4* respectively. Became patrol boats in 1915 with numbers given in the table.

Gondul class
After the dissolution of the Swedish-Norwegian union *Gudur* changed number to 10. Both redesignated patrol boats in 1918.

Komet class
Komet as prototype built at Schichau, Elbing with funds collected by The Women's Association for Sweden's Naval Defence. Patrol boat 1918. Remaining 11 renumbered from 1921 as patrol boats with TT removed.

Plejad class
Plejad as prototype built at Normand, Le Havre. From 1926 served as patrol boat. The 16 Swedish-built boats all became patrol boats from 1928 with the numbers given.

SECOND CLASS TORPEDO-BOATS

Name	Fate
BLINK (ex-*Rolf*) (N:o 61)	Stricken 1919 as *Vedettbåt n:r 6*, 1921, BU
BLIXT (ex-*Seid*) (N:o 63)	Stricken 1926 as *Vedettbåt n:r 7*
GALDR (N:o 65)	Stricken 1928 as *Vedettbåt n:r 8*
Narf class	
NARF (N:o 67)	Stricken 1928 as *Vedettbåt n:r 9*
NÖRVE (N:o 69)	Stricken 1928 as *Vedettbåt n:r 10*
Bygve class	
BYGVE (N:o 71)	Stricken 1923 as *Vedettbåt n:r 11*
BYLGIA (N:o 73)	Stricken 1923 as *Vedettbåt n:r 12*
Agne class	
AGNE (N:o 75)	Stricken 1923 as *Vedettbåt n:r 13*
AGDA (N:o 77)	Stricken 1923 as *Vedettbåt n:r 14*, target, sunk 1925
N:o 79 class	
N:o 79	Stricken 1926 as *Vedettbåt n:r 26*, target, sunk 1932
N:o 81	Stricken 1929 as *Vedettbåt n:r 25*, sunk
N:o 83	Stricken 1929 as *Vedettbåt n:r 24*, target, sunk
N:o 85	Stricken 1926 as *Vedettbåt n:r 23*

The inconsequent numbering as the torpedo-boats were reclassed as patrol boats (*Vedettbåtar*) has caused confusion in most reference books, even Swedish ones. This is the first work of reference with the correct numbers.

GUNBOATS

Name	Fate
Blenda class	
BLENDA	Stricken 1930, barrack ship, sold 1942
DISA	Stricken 1926 as depot ship and minelayer
Urd class	
URD	Rammed and sunk 22.8.13 in the Sound by coast defence battleship *Oden*
VERDANDE	Stricken 1928 as hospital ship, sunk 1929 as target
SKAGUL	Stricken 1928 as depot ship, sunk as target
SKULD	Stricken 1930, heating central for submarines, BU 1948
SKÄGGALD	Stricken 1922 as depot ship
ROTA	Stricken 1928 as aircraft depot ship, sunk as target
Edda class	
EDDA	Stricken 1923 as barrack ship

Blenda class
As a gunboat with 1–274mm and 1–122mm gun *Blenda* won international attention as she joined the international squadron at Constantinople in 1877. A French naval chief engineer commented: "It is without any doubt a big step forward to construct a seaworthy ship with 12kts speed and a displacement of 500 tons, that can carry one 27 and one 12cm gun". From 1887 used as 'mother ship' for torpedo-boats. Rebuilt to repair ship, 1906, rebuilt as submarine depot ship 1910–11, armed with only 2–57mm guns. World War Two blockship in Norrköping, then to South America as cargo ship – 77 years old! *Disa* got an armoured CT in 1892. Her heavy gun and carriage from Elswick were condemned and changed to 1–152mm and also 2–57mm were installed. From 1912 depot ship, from 1918 also minelayer.

Urd class
Builders: *Urd* Kockums, Malmö; *Skagul, Skäggald* and *Rota* Bergsund, Stockholm; *Skuld* and *Verdande* Karlskrona N Yd. Displacement: 533t/550t, ihp/speed 780 = 13.4kts. Armament: 1–274mm and 1–122mm gun. *Urd* rearmed 1893–94 with 1–152mm, 1–120mm and 2–57mm Nordenfelt guns. In 1908 first ship with new 75mm guns. Rammed 22 August 1913 at the isle of Ven in the Sound, sunk without loss of life, wreck salvaged by Danish Switzers, BU. *Verdande* (ex-*Verdandi*). From 1901 TS. Rebuilt 1907–09 as hospital ship. Stricken 1928 and 1929 sunk as artillery target. *Skagul* rearmed 1895–96 to same as *Urd*. Reclassified as depot ship 1923, stricken 1928 and sunk as artillery target. *Skuld* TS from 1904 and from 1907 only 1–120mm gun and 2 MG. From 1916 submarine depot ship with 4–57mm. Stricken 1930 she was used as heating ship for submarines until scrapped. *Skäggald* rearmed 1906 as *Urd*. Rebuilt as

Vedettbåt n:r 34 (ex-*Mira*) *Author's Collection*

Skäggald as a minelayer *Author's Collection*

submarine depot ship 1909–10. *Rota* got 2–57mm guns in 1896. She was disarmed in 1906 and given heavy davits to serve as a surveying vessel. In 1909–10 she was rebuilt as a radio ship. From 1918 also minelayer. Stricken 1928 and sunk as artillery target.

SMALLER PATROL BOATS

As seen under torpedo boats all were deprived of TT and reclassed as patrol boats *(Vedettbåt)*. Up to 1910 they had the letter B *(Bevakningsbåt)* before the number. Apart from the above mentioned ex-torpedo-boats there also existed 5 old spar torpedo-boats *N:o 3–7*, 27t, rebuilt 1903–05 as *B 1–5*, later *Vb 1–5*, stricken 1921–30.

MISCELLANEOUS

The wooden screw frigate *Vanadis* and the screw corvettes *Balder* and *Saga* were used as TS for cadets and ship's boys. *Balder* was stricken 1901 and *Saga* reclassed 1906 as 'canteen ship', reduced to barrack ship 1907, *Vanadis* already 1896 to barrack ship and survived as such until 1939.

Gustav V as completed

Author's Collection

MAJOR SURFACE SHIPS

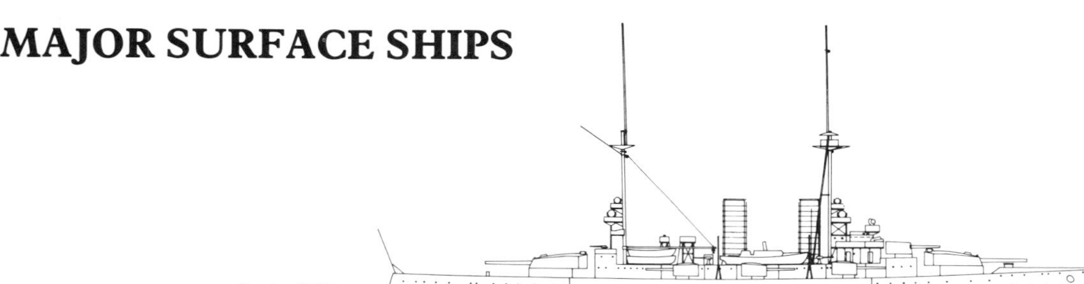

Sverige 1917

SVERIGE class *coastal battleships*

Displacement: 7125t standard; 7633t deep load (*Sverige* 6852t standard, 7516t deep load)

Dimensions: 396ft 8in wl, 399ft oa × 61ft × 20ft 4in, 22ft (*Sverige* 392ft 9in, 393ft 8in × 61ft × 20ft 8in, 21ft 4in)
120.9m, 121.6m × 18.6m × 6.2m, 6.7m (119.7m, 120.0m × 18.6m × 6.3m, 6.5m)

Machinery: 2-shaft Motala geared (*Sverige* Curtis direct coupled) turbines, 12 Yarrow boilers, 23,910shp (*Sverige* 25,400shp) = 22.5kts. Coal 340t/776t, oil 100t

Armour: Belt 200mm/150mm–60mm (7⅞in/5⅞in–2⅜in), turrets 200mm–100mm (7⅞in–3⅞in), CT 175mm/100mm–60mm (6⅞in max)

Armament: 4–283mm (11.1in)/45 M12 (2×2), 8–152mm (6in)/50 M12 (1×2, 6×1), 6–75mm/50 M 12, 2–57mm, 2 MG, 2–533mm (21in) TT (side aw)

Complement: 427 (as flagship 443)

Name	Builder	Laid down	Launched	Comp	Fate
SVERIGE	Götaverken, Göteborg	12.12	3.5.15	10.5.17	Stricken 30.1.53, BU 1958
DROTTNING VICTORIA	Götaverken, Göteborg	1915	15.9.17	1921	Stricken 1.4.57, BU 1960
GUSTAF V	Kockums, Malmö	1915	31.1.18	1.22	Stricken 1.4.57, BU 1970

From six different coastal battleship types the 1911 Parliament chose the type F to a cost of 11,636,000 SwCr and voted the first annual expenditure. The liberal government decided early in 1912 to postpone the building while waiting for a total defence analysis and decision. A nationwide campaign collected in some months more than the cost and the government was forced to accept it and begin the first ship, "the people's gift to the country", which was why the ship was named *Sverige* (= Sweden). The two other ships were voted by the 1914 parliament but material and economic difficulties meant the complete division of four battleships never became a reality.

These three ships underwent a series of rebuildings and modernisations. *Sverige* was in the middle of reconstruction when the Second World War broke out and did not re-enter service before 9 May 1940. They then all three differed very much from one another. *Drottning Victoria* and *Gustaf V* were both built as icebreakers, the first and only Swedish warships with this role, very rarely being used for civil purposes. From 1924 the three ships were successively modernised, beginning with *Sverige*. In 1924–25 she got a heavy tripod mast with a central director and a fire-control centre deep down in the forward hull. *Drottning Victoria* got the same equipment in 1926–27, her TT were also removed and there a new fire-control centre for the heavy and medium guns was installed. She also got paravanes for minesweepings. In 1927–30 *Gustaf V* got all the modernisations of the other two, but also a modern AA director: 4–75mm AA (2×2) on a stern deckhouse and a fire-control centre below. The two funnels were joined into a broad single. In 1931–33 *Sverige* was further modernised, as *Drottning Victoria*, but the stern funnel remained intact while the fore funnel was angled aft, S-shaped. In 1934–35 *Drottning Victoria* got the same AA fit and the boilers also were renewed with the six forward coal boilers replaced by two oil boilers. The coal boxes were used for better underwater protection and oil tanks. In 1936–37 *Gustaf V* was altered in the same way and her medium ammunition magazines were rebuilt for new, longer projectiles. The bow twin 150mm turret was removed and replaced by 4–40mm Bofors AA guns. In 1938–40 *Sverige* was modernised as *Gustaf V* but her twin 150mm turret was not rebuilt – instead the two middle single turrets were removed to fit the 4–40mm AA. For *Drottning Victoria* her last rebuilding was very carefully planned in shorter stages during the winters of 1940–41 and 1941–42 with the 40mm AA as *Gustaf V*. *Drottning Victoria* was also the first ship to have a Swedish-built radar on her forward gunnery director. Originally designed before 1914 large sums were needed to keep this capital ship nucleus of the Navy up to date during World War Two. Not until 12 years after were the two younger ships stricken as obsolete.

Clas Fleming in her early days
Author's Collection

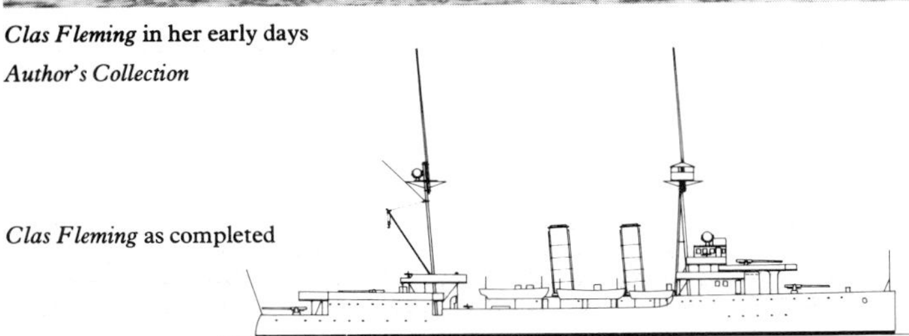

Clas Fleming as completed

CLAS FLEMING *cruiser-minelayer*

Displacement: 1550t standard; 1800t deep load
Dimensions: 263ft 4in × 34ft 1in × 14ft 1in
80.2m × 10.4m × 4.3m
Machinery: 2-shaft Parsons turbines, 8 Yarrow type boilers, 6500ihp = 20kts. Coal 265t
Armour: Deck 25mm (1in), CT 75mm (3in)
Armament: 4–120mm (4.7in)/50, 4 MG, *c*100 mines
Complement: 160

Name	Builder	Launched	Fate
CLAS FLEMING	Bergsund, Stockholm	14.12.12	Stricken 1.1.59, BU 1961

Though not of cruiser dimensions, in Sweden she was classed as minelayer cruiser (for example German minelayer cruisers were also very small 'cruisers'). Designed originally in 1908 and laid down in 1911 for the purpose of offensive minelaying operations at high speed. Between the wars she saw little active service due to difficulties with the boilers under the armoured deck. In the early 1930s Götaverken had constructed a 'warm air motor' and successfully tested it in a tug. In 1933 the yard got an order to construct heavier machinery for *Clas Fleming*. It took five years to build 'the world's first gas turbine'. In 1939–40 Götaverken totally rebuilt the 'mine cruiser'. She was lengthened 5m amidships and got diesels instead of the boilers. Also her mining capacity and speed were increased. The two thin funnels gave way to three broad ones, from stem to stern lower funnels. The middle one was a dummy, later removed. The 'gas turbines' machinery functioned well, so *Clas Fleming* survived until 1959.

Sigurd 1914 *Author's Collection*

Hugin as completed *Author's Collection*

Wale 1919

WALE *destroyer*

Displacement: 430t standard; 461t deep load
Dimensions: 215ft 8in wl, 216ft 10in oa × 20ft 8in × 5ft 11in, 9ft 2in
65.8m, 66.1m × 6.3m × 1.8m, 2.8m
Machinery: 2-shaft VTE, 4 Yarrow boilers, 7665ihp = 30kts
Armament: 2–75mm/53 M 05, 4–57mm/55 M 89B (from 1911 2–6.5mm MG M 10), 2–457mm (18in) TT (from 1916 2×2)
Complement: 54

Name	Builder	Launched	Fate
WALE	Kockums, Malmö	21.9.07	Stricken 12.10.40, sunk as target 26.9.46

The first Swedish-built destroyer laid down in 1906 and completed on 14 April 1908. She was closely modelled on the Thornycroft built *Magne*. She achieved 8971ihp and 30.7kts. Her pennant number was 3.

RAGNAR class *destroyers*

Displacement: 430t standard; 460t deep load
Dimensions: As *Wale* except 8ft 2in, 8ft 10in (*2.5m, 2.7m*) draught
Machinery: 2-shaft 4-cyl VTE, 4 Yarrow boilers, 7200ihp = 30kts
Armament: 4–75mm/50 M 05, 2–457mm (18in) TT (from 1916 2×2) (from 1911 2–6.5mm MG)
Complement: 69

Name	Builder	Launched	Fate
RAGNAR	Kockums, Malmö	30.5.08	Stricken 13.6.47, BU 1951
SIGURD	Lindholmen, Göteborg	19.9.08	Stricken 13.6.47, BU 1951
VIDAR	Kockums, Malmö	9.6.09	Stricken 13.6.47, sunk 28.8.61

First two laid down in 1907 and completed in 1909, *Vidar* laid down in 1908 and completed 1910. Carried pennant numbers 5, 6 and 4 respectively. Rearmed in 1940 with 3–75mm, 2–25mm/64 AA M 32 and 2–8mm AA MG (1×2). Pennant numbers changed to 22, 21 and 23 in autumn 1940.

HUGIN class *destroyers*

Displacement: 446t standard
Dimensions: 215ft 8in wl, 216ft 10in oa × 21ft 4in × 6ft 11in, 11ft 6in
65.8m, 66.1m × 6.5m × 2.1m, 3.5m
Machinery: 2-shaft AEG-Curtis turbines, 4 boilers, 10,330shp = 30kts
Armament: As *Ragnar* class
Complement: 72

Name	Builder	Launched	Fate
HUGIN	Götaverken, Göteborg	10.12.10	Stricken 13.6.47, BU 1949
MUNIN	Kockums, Malmö	5.12.11	Stricken 18.10.40, BU *c* 1943

First Swedish warships with turbines. *Munin* reached 33.16kts. Pennant numbers 7 and 8, 1940. *Hugin* changed to 24 (*Munin* stricken). *Hugin* rearmed in 1940 as *Ragnar* class and she was given new boilers, mine rails, depth charges.

WRANGEL class *destroyers*

Displacement: 415t standard; 498t deep load
Dimensions: 228ft 4in wl, 236ft 3in oa × 22ft 8in × 7ft 11in, 9ft 2in
69.6m, 72.0m × 6.9m × 2.4m, 2.8m
Machinery: 2-shaft de Laval turbines, 4 Yarrow boilers, 13,000shp = 34kts. Coal 105t, from 1927 only oil 105t
Armament: 4–75mm/53 M 12, 2–6.5mm MG M 14, 4–457mm (18in) TT (2×2 and 2×1)
Complement: 81

Name	Builder	Launched	Fate
WRANGEL	Lindholmen, Göteborg	25.9.17	Stricken 13.5.47, sunk as target 1960
WACHTMEISTER	Lindholmen, Göteborg	19.12.17	Stricken 13.6.47, BU 1951

Laid down in 1916 and completed 1918. Pennant numbers 9 and 10, changed in 1940 to 25 and 26. Armament changed in 1940 to 4–75mm, 1–25mm/44 AA M 32, 2–8mm AA M 36, the two single TT removed, standard displacement 498t. Two sister ships, *Ehrensköld* and *Nordenskjöld* authorised in 1914 but never built for economic reasons.

Wrangel as completed *Author's Collection*

SUBMARINES

HAJEN *submarine*

Displacement:	107t/127t, max 111t/127t
Dimensions:	65ft, 70ft 10in × 11ft 10in × 9ft 10in *19.8m, 21.6m × 3.6m × 3.0m*
Machinery:	1-shaft Avance paraffin oil motor plus 1 Luth & Rosén electric motor, 200hp/70hp = 9.5kts/7kts. Paraffin oil 2.2t
Armament:	1–457mm (18in) TT (3 torpedoes)
Complement:	11

Name	Builder	Launched	Fate
HAJEN	Stockholm N Yd	16.7.04	Stricken 1922, extant as museum boat

The naval engineer Carl Richson was sent to the USA in 1900 to learn about submarines. The 1902 parliament voted the money and Richson began construction, approved by the King on 28 November 1902. Building began with the utmost secrecy in the old 'Galley yard' inside Stockholm N Yd. The Avance motor was never fully reliable and was changed in 1916 to a 4-cyl diesel of 135hp. After *Hvalen*'s arrival in 1909 *Hajen* was classed as a second class submarine and got the number 1.

Hajen as completed *Author's Collection*

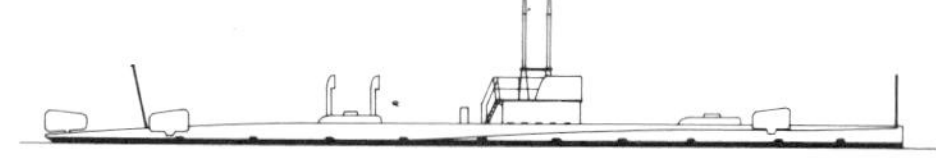

Hvalen about 1914
NB 1/750 scale

HVALEN *submarine*

Displacement:	186t/230t
Dimensions:	139ft 1in × 14ft 1in × 6ft 11in, 8ft 10in *42.4m × 4.3m × 2.1m, 2.7m*
Machinery:	1 shaft, 3 petrol motors plus 1 electric motor, 750hp/150hp = 14.8kts/6.3kts
Armament:	2–457mm (18in) TT (bow; 4 torpedoes)
Complement:	17

Name	Builder	Launched	Fate
HVALEN	Fiat-San Giorgio, La Spezia	16.2.09	Stricken 1919, sunk as target

The 1907 parliament voted a second submarine and to get new ideas from a European builder, the contract was given to the Italian yard. The boat corresponded to the Italian *Foca*. *Hvalen* received naval publicity all over the world as the crew made the voyage to Sweden without any assistance or accompanying vessel. The submarine was taken over on 9 July 1909 and on the 30th she began the 4000nm voyage to Stockholm, where further tests were made. These ended on 18 December and the submarine was accepted that day. Her wreck was sold and BU after being sunk as a target in 1924.

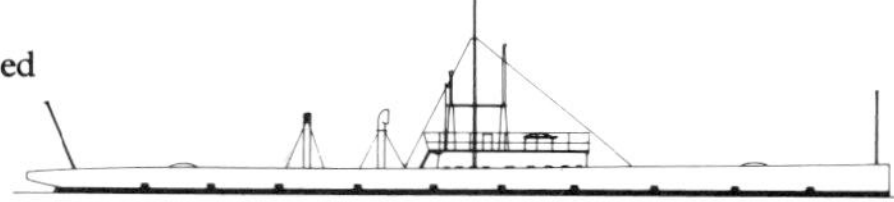

Undervattensbåten 2 as completed
NB 1/750 scale

UNDERVATTENSBÅTEN No 2 class *submarines*

Displacement:	138t/230t
Dimensions:	87ft 8in × 11ft 10in × 9ft 10in *26.8m × 3.6m × 3.0m*
Machinery:	1-shaft Polar 6cyl diesel plus 1 Luth & Rosén electric motor, 420bhp/200hp = 8.8kts/6.6kts
Armament:	1–457mm (18in) TT (bow; 3 torpedoes)
Complement:	12

Name	Builder	Launched	Fate
UNDERVATTENSBÅTEN N:o 2	Motala verkstad	25.2.09	Stricken 6.6.29
UNDERVATTENSBÅTEN N:o 3	Motala verkstad	14.4.09	Stricken 21.11.30
UNDERVATTENSBÅTEN N:o 4	Motala verkstad	16.10.09	Stricken 6.6.29

Delfinen on trials 3 October 1915 *Author's Collection*

At the same time as *Hvalen* was ordered at Fiat also three second class submarines of an improved *Hajen* type were voted, constructed by the above-mentioned Carl Richson. Like *Hajen* they were designed to operate in the archipelagos. Pennant numbers 2, 3 and 4.

SVÄRDFISKEN class *submarines*

Displacement:	252t/370t
Dimensions:	148ft, 149ft 3in × 13ft 9in *45.1m, 45.5m × 4.2m × ?*
Machinery:	2-shaft Hesselman 6cyl diesels plus 2 Luth & Rosén electric motors, 1000bhp/300hp = 14.2kts/8.5kts
Armament:	2–457mm (18in) TT (bow; 4 torpedoes), 1–37mm
Complement:	21

Name	Builder	Launched	Fate
SVÄRDFISKEN	Kockums, Malmö	30.8.14	Stricken 1936, BU 1946
TUMLAREN	Kockums, Malmö	14.10.14	Stricken 1936, BU 1946

Kockums Mekaniska Verkstad in Malmö purchased sole rights in 1910 for Sweden from Fiat-Laurenti and the next contract for first class submarines therefore went to Kockums. Since then Kockums has delivered most Swedish submarines. Later the 37mm gun was changed to a 57mm. Pennant letters S, later Sf and T, later Tu. Both served as AA batteries in Karlskrona during World War Two.

DELFINEN *submarine*

Displacement:	260t/370t
Dimensions:	139ft 5in × 14ft 1in × ? *42.5m × 4.3m × ?*
Machinery:	2-shaft Hesselman 6cyl diesels, plus 2 electric motors, 1000bhp/300hp = 13.6kts/9.4kts
Complement:	21

Name	Builder	Launched	Fate
DELFINEN	Bergsund, Stockholm	1914	Stricken 1.10.30

Delfinen had a single hull and was a development from the earlier Richson second class submarines. She had only 36t buoyancy. The hull had specially favourable underwater lines. Pennant letter D, later Df.

NORTHERN EUROPE

Gädden as completed *Author's Collection*

LAXEN class *submarines*

Displacement: 140t/170t
Dimensions: 87ft 7in, 87ft 11in × 11ft 10in × ?
26.7m, 26.8m × 3.6m × ?
Machinery: 2-shaft 6 cyl diesel plus 2 electric motors, 700bhp/200hp = 8.8kts/6.6kts
Armament: 1–457mm (18in) TT (bow)
Complement: 10

Name	Builder	Launched	Fate
LAXEN	Karlskrona N Yd	1914	Stricken 1935
GÄDDAN	Karlskrona N Yd	1915	Stricken 1931

These were second class submarines for archipelago operations, a development of the *Undervattensbåten N:o 2* class. Pennant letters L, later Lx, and G, later Gd.

ABBORREN class *submarines*

Displacement: 174t/310t
Dimensions: 101ft 8in × 11ft 10in × 10ft 2in
31.0m × 3.6m × 3.1m
Machinery: 2-shaft 6cyl diesels plus 2 electric motors, 920bhp/280hp = 9.5kts/7.4kts
Armament: 2–457mm (18in) TT (bow; 4 torpedoes)
Complement: 14

Name	Builder	Launched	Fate
ABBORREN	Karlskrona N Yd	25.5.16	Stricken 18.6.37
BRAXEN	Karlskrona N Yd	5.5.16	Stricken 18.6.37

A development of the *Laxen* class to permit 2 TT. Pennant letters A, later Ab, and B, later Br.

Hajen 1924
NB 1/750 scale

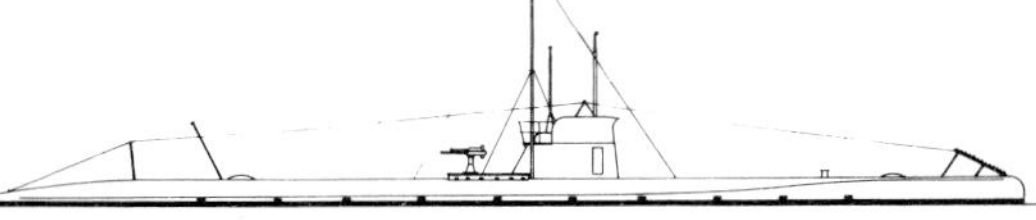

HAJEN class *submarines*

Displacement: 422t/600t
Dimensions: 177ft 2in × 17ft 1in × 11ft 6in
54.0m × 5.2m × 3.5m
Machinery: 2-shaft 6cyl diesels plus 2 electric motors, 2000bhp/700hp = 15.5kts/9kts
Armament: 4–457mm (18in) TT (bow; 8 torpedoes), 1–75mm
Complement: 30

Name	Builder	Launched	Fate
HAJEN	Kockums, Malmö	8.11.17	Stricken 19.3.43, BU 1944
SÄLEN	Kockums, Malmö	31.1.18	Stricken 24.7.42, BU 1946
VALROSSEN	Kockums, Malmö	16.4.18	Stricken 19.3.43, BU 1944

Kockums design based on German Aktien-Gesellschaft Weser drawings. Pennant letters H, later Hj, S, later Sä, and V, later Wa.

Abborren in the 1920s *Author's Collection*

Bävern as completed
NB 1/750 scale

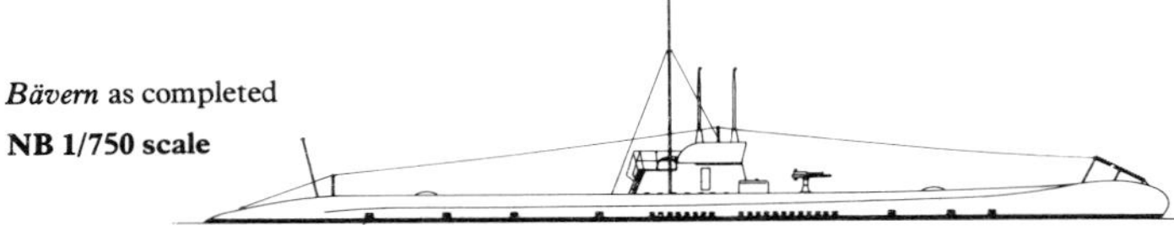

BÄVERN class *submarines*

Displacement: 472t/650t
Dimensions: 187t × 19ft
57.0m × 5.8m × ?
Machinery: 2-shaft 6cyl diesels plus 2 electric motors, 2100bhp/520hp = 15.2kts/8.2kts

Name	Builder	Launched	Fate
BÄVERN	Kockums, Malmö	5.3.21	Stricken 6.10.44, BU 1956
ILLERN	Karlskrona N Yd	30.6.21	Rammed and sunk 12.8.43, salvaged BU 1944
UTTERN	Karlskrona N Yd	25.7.21	Stricken 6.10.44, BU

Based on the Weser construction.

SMALL SURFACE WARSHIPS

VEDETTBÅTEN N:R 19 *patrol boat*

Displacement: 58t standard; 67t deep load
Dimensions: 74ft 10in × 16ft 1in × 6ft 11in
22.8m × 4.9m × 2.1m
Machinery: 1-shaft Bergsund crude oil motor, 101ihp = 10kts
Armament: 1–57mm/55 M 98B, 1–6.5mm Madsen MG
Complement: 10

Name	Builder	Launched	Fate
VEDETTBÅTEN N:R 19	Bergsund, Stockholm	1914	Stricken 1947, sold, 1983 passenger boat *Aramis*

Originally ordered as *Lysmaskinsbåt n:r 3* for the archipelago defence and served as such (searchlight vessel) with 4 60cm searchlights and no armament. Transferred to the Navy in 1917 and renamed. From 1919 tender, specially for the naval air wing.

Sveparen about 1940 *Author's Collection*

SÖKAREN class *minesweepers*

Displacement: 227t standard; 266t full load
Dimensions: 83ft 8in wl, 91ft 2in oa × 22ft 4in × 9ft 10in
25.5m, 27.8m × 6.8m × 3.0m
Machinery: 1-shaft Motala VTE, 1 Howden boiler, 465ihp = 10kts
Armament: 1–57mm/21.3 AA M16 Bofors
Complement: 17

Name	Builder	Launched	Fate
SÖKAREN	Motala Verkstad	16.8.17	Ran aground and sunk 3.10.53. Sold, salvaged, civil timber tug, extant 1983
SVEPAREN	Motala Verkstad	19.2.18	Stricken 1.1.64, sold, rebuilt as yacht, extant 1983
SPRÄNGAREN	Motala Verkstad	12.6.18	Stricken 1961, sold, harbour tug, extant 1983

These three '*vedettbåtar*' were built with the money left over from the collection for the coast defence battleship *Sverige* and used as minesweepers, tenders tugs etc. Originally pennant numbers 16, 17 and 18. Rearmed 1939–40 with 1–25mm gun and 1 MG. Pennant numbers changed to 47, 48 and 49. In the 1950s *Sveparen* and *Sprängaren* were reclassified as training vessels and renumbered 253 and 254.

Italian ORLANDO 12 ton type ('A' group, 2nd series) *motor boats*

Class:
Mtb 1 (ex-*Mas 231*), *Mtb 2* (ex-*Mas 232*)

Bought from Italy in 1920 and stricken in 1927. For use in the archipelagos. Had 1–6.5mm MG and 2–457mm (18in) TT.

COASTAL MINELAYER

Only one minelayer was built in the period 1906–22: *Ångkranpråmen n:r 9*, 1920 renamed *Minutläggaren n:r 9*, Mul 9, launched 1912, 120t, 9.1kts, stricken 1957.

Mtb I date unknown
Author's Collection

Netherlands

The Netherlands in 1906 were a nation of 5,400,000 at peace (the main domestic problem was the question of state subsidies for church schools) but menaced by German expansionism. In the Netherlands Indies the long Achin War (1873–1904), a severe drain on the colonial treasury, had ended, and administration was being centralised in Java, but the rising power of Japan was beginning to darken the future of the Dutch in the vast archipelago, much larger and more populous than the mother country and rich in sources of petroleum and other important raw materials.

At home the Army was the main defence; to prevent it being outflanked the Royal Netherlands Navy provided defended minefields and could oppose wider seaborne attacks with coast defence ships and torpedo-boats. The larger ships were, however, mainly for the East Indies, where the Navy might be required to delay the aggressor until reinforced by an ally. Five coast defence ships were constructed in the early 1900s; although in effect small, slow armoured cruisers, they had powerful main batteries and, accompanied by second-class cruisers and torpedo craft, offered a credible deterrent to the much larger armoured cruisers stationed in the area by the Great Powers.

BUILDING PLANS 1908–14

After 1905, the balance of power in the Far East altered considerably. The British battle squadron was withdrawn, and the Russian 1st Pacific Squadron no longer existed to balance the Japanese battle fleet which could be expected to operate further from home; in addition, formidable new cruisers with 12in guns were being constructed in Japan. The 1908 Dutch estimates therefore provided for a larger coast defence ship with 11in guns, the *De Zeven Provincien*, while a programme of four 7000-ton ships was put forward. In 1909, the estimates included votes for two destroyers for the East Indies and a new, larger submarine, and two *Kortenaer* class ships were to be refitted; 6 similar destroyers followed, 2 in 1910 and 4 in 1911. Also voted in 1911 were the first submarine for the East Indies and four armoured gunboats with internal-combustion motors for home waters. The planned squadron of new coast defence ships was nearly approved in 1912, when funds for the first of a class of four (7600t, 10,000ihp = 18kts, 4–11in/45, 10–4.1in, 3 TT, belt 5.9in, barbettes 9.8in, to be built in Amsterdam Dockyard) were requested. Expert opinion preferred five much stronger battleships of the Spanish *Espana* type, despite strong financial objections, so that the government proposals were rejected, the Minister of Marine resigned, and the whole question of East Indies defence was put to a Royal Commission (June 1912).

The Commission reported on 2 July 1913, and proposed building a new fleet for the Netherlands and her colonies to maintain neutrality and to defend the Indies against direct attacks. Nine battleships, each of 20,668 tons and 21 knots, should be built, five for the East Indies and four for home waters, in reserve, refitting etc. Six 36-knot torpedo cruisers (probably large destroyers) of 1200 tons, 8 destroyers of 500 tons (the existing *Fret* class would be satisfactory for the time being), 8 torpedo-boats (also present, although old); 8 large submarines and 2 large minelayers would also be required, divided between the Indies and home waters. The new fleet base on Java should be Tandjong Priok (Batavia), with three new forts. The cost of the scheme, 17 million florins annually for the next 35 years (sic), would roughly treble the usual naval budget. These recommendations caused a cabinet crisis, and, although approved by the government, which slightly enlarged the battleships specifications and invited detailed plans from leading foreign shipbuilders, no decisions to place orders or even on financing the scheme were taken before August 1914 killed it.

Between 1906 and 1914 the Dutch Navy played a typical peacetime role, with training, exercises and cruises to show the flag. During the

1912–13 Balkan Wars, the cruiser *Gelderland* was sent to Constantinople to defend Dutch interests, and the coast defence ship *Kortenaer* to Smyrna. In the Caribbean the Netherlands fell foul of the eccentric President Cipriano Castro of Venezuela, causing one 'peacetime' operation in 1908 that should be remembered. During differences that included allegations of Dutch ships carrying contraband, the coast defence ship *Jacob van Hemmskerck* and the cruisers *Gelderland* and *Friesland* blockaded Venezuelan ports, and in December the coastguard ship *23 de Mayo* was seized by *Jacob van Heemskerck*, and the *Alexis* (or *Alix*) by *Gelderland*.

NEUTRALITY 1914–18

The Dutch were able to stay out of the World War, but were the hardest hit neutral, because of their geographical position and dependence on sea trade. At the outbreak of war seaborne trade between German and non-Scandinavian countries of course ceased, but with much more German cargo suddenly arriving by the indirect route through Rotterdam and the inland waterways, the Dutch were the first to feel the weight of the British Blockade and Contraband Control. In November 1914 the North Sea was declared a war zone, in which neutral ships not following approved routes and submitting to inspection by the Royal Navy would be exposed to mines and other hazards. In December, the Dutch government agreed to make itself the sole consignee of foodstuffs, as it had already with copper and oil, with a guarantee that they would not reach the enemy. The Netherlands Overseas Trust, an association of traders, received strict guarantees from individual importers as to each consignment. The scale of the problem is shown by statistics: four times as many cotton bales entered the Netherlands in the first year of war as during the previous year, and overall imports from America in March 1915 were more than twice the March 1914 figure.

Such was the strength of the blockade, however, that by July 1915 no neutral shipping line would knowingly accept a German cargo; a recalcitrant company might be coerced by reduced coal quotas for its ships. If an importer was found to be an intermediary for the enemy, his name went on the British Black List and his next consignment went into the Prize Court. A Dutch fishing company that refused to sell its catch, intended in happier days for Germany, to the British would cease to receive its allowance of oil fuel, which had to pass the blockade. The Central Powers nevertheless received considerable support, through official fears and private greed; it was never possible to stop completely the iron ore trade from Narvik through Sweden and Rotterdam to Germany (several million tons between August 1914 and December 1915). And by March 1916 no fewer than 37,000 people had been arrested smuggling goods across the frontier.

The British for their part had the 'Beef Trip' or Dutch Convoy, losing only 6 ships out of 1031 on the 80-mile route during 1917 after their June 1916 agreement with the Dutch to take food previously sent to Germany.

On 16 July 1917 six German blockade runners from Rotterdam were pursued into Dutch waters by destroyers of the Royal Navy's Harwich Force. Two ran ashore but were destroyed by gunfire on the beach and the other four were taken. There were further interceptions.

The actual cost of the war to the Dutch was an estimated £147 million at 1920 prices for loss of trade and for maintaining a large standing army. About 230,000 tons of merchant shipping, including several large passenger liners and six out of eight ships in a neutral convoy with a German safe-conduct, fell victim to submarine warfare. The Navy, reinforced by a 1915 bill for naval (and military) extensions that provided for 2 cruisers, 4 submarines (as well as one apiece from Britain and Germany inadvertently acquired during hostilities) and 6 aircraft, was required to ensure Dutch territorial waters were not violated, sweep stray mines and otherwise enforce neutrality. British submarines on North Sea patrols frequently sighted Dutch cruisers and destroyers. In the East Indies, Allied ships and German raiders such as the *Emden* had to obey International Law when coaling and taking on provisions. November 1918 brought a return to normality, although in the peace deliberations there was the humiliation of being summoned to discuss Belgian claims for frontier adjustments, and the Allies' demands for the ex-Kaiser. Fourteen German torpedo-boats and 22 motor launches from Flanders, interned in the Netherlands during the German collapse, were handed over to Belgium in 1920.

POSTWAR PLANS

In 1920–21 a new Commission prepared recommendations for home and colonial defence in the revised circumstances created by the war and the peace treaties. The duties of the Navy were defined thus:

'In the Netherlands, barring the approaches to the river mouths while the submarines comprise the offensive elements. In the East Indies, by action at sea to impede the enemy in effecting a footing in the islands; to retard his penetration inland, if any landing is effected; to menace his transport and communication lines, and to assist in local defence. We must content ourselves with minor craft and not with capital ships or their kindred.'

The proposals for naval defence to counter threats existing in 1921 and the situations predicted for 1928 and 1934 are worth considering in detail. Fleet Establishments were proposed for 1928 (all vessels under construction on 31 December 1921, plus 12 new destroyers and 9 submarines for the East Indies, and 7 submarines for home waters) and 1934 (2 extra cruisers for the East Indies, which would then have 24 destroyers, 32 submarines and 4 minelaying submarines plus surface minelayers and auxiliaries. Forces in home waters were to total 18 coastal submarines and 1 coast defence ship. The new cruisers were to be of 5500 tons and 30 knots, with smaller and fewer guns than *Java* and *Sumatra*, but with torpedo tubes, *ie* approximating to the design of *De Ruyter* as first drafted *c*1930, and the new destroyers of 1000 tons, 30 knots, three 4.7in guns, and two twin 20.8in torpedo tubes. The main East Indies base was to be Tandjong Priok, defended by heavy guns in armoured turrets and medium calibre batteries. Soerabaja, the existing arsenal, with four floating docks, would be one secondary base, and a second was to be built in the Riouw Archipelago. Macassar (the capital and free port of the Celebes) was to be defended by medium calibre guns.

This programme was far beyond the financial resources available after a 'war to end all wars', at a time when much faith was put in disarmament and the new League of Nations. Even a reduced programme was rejected by the States-General in 1923.

BASES AND ORGANISATION

Den Helder/Willemsoord and Hellevoetsluis were the main North Sea bases, and there was a naval depot and storage yard at Amsterdam. The Navy could also use the dry docks belonging to private shipbuilders and the Rotterdam city municipality. Warship construction was almost exclusively by private companies, which obtained technical assistance from Germany for large ships, armour and heavy guns, and from Yarrow in Britain for torpedo craft. Dutch naval designers did not enjoy their deserved 1930s reputation; their coast defence ships compared badly on paper with their Scandinavian counterparts, which could sacrifice freeboard and coal capacity. Two major canals, the New Waterway between Hoek van Holland (Hook of Holland) and Rotterdam and the North Sea Canal linking Ijmuiden with Amsterdam, had considerable strategic importance, and the sea entrances were heavily fortified. Naval personnel were fairly constant at 10,000–11,000 all ranks (volunteer), and the prewar budget fluctuated between about £1,400,000 and £1,800,000 annually. The large mercantile marine (250 steamers of 330,000 tons in 1906, 500 of 560,000 tons in 1914 and 900 of 1,800,000 in 1920–21, plus 300–400 sail of *c*50,000 tons) operated out of Rotterdam, Amsterdam and Vlissingen.

The East Indies Naval Forces consisted of three separate forces:

The East Indies Squadron, of ships sent out from the Netherlands. In 1920–21, it consisted of the coast defence ship *Tromp* and eight *Fret* class destroyers.

The East Indies Marine (*Indische Militaire Marine*), of smaller ships permanently based in the East. In 1920–21, it consisted of 8 *Draak* class torpedo boats, 5 or 6 submarines, 2 gunboats, 3 minelayers and 5 survey ships, under the orders of the C-in-C, East Indies Squadron and sometimes combined with the squadron for training and exercises.

The ships of the Government Service (*gouvernementsmarine*), belonging to the East Indies Government, generally of the small patrol vessel/gunboat type for customs, police and coast guard duties, with limited military potential.

FLEET STRENGTH 1906

COAST DEFENCE SHIPS

Name	Launched	Disp	Fate
REINIER CLAESZEN	21.11.91	2440t	Stricken 1914
Evertsen class			
EVERTSEN	29.9.94	3464t	Stricken 1913
PIET HEIN	16.8.94	3464t	Discarded 1914
KORTENAER	27.10.94	3464t	Discarded 1920
Koningin Regentes class			
KONINGIN REGENTES	24.4.00	5002t	Stricken 1920
DE RUYTER	20.2.01	5002t	Stricken 1923
HERTOG HENDRIK	7.6.02	5002t	Hulk 1945
MARTEN HARPERTS-ZOON TROMP	15.6.04	5216t	Stricken 1927, BU 1932
JACOB VAN HEEMSKERCK	22.9.06	4920t	Hulk 1948

Koningin Regentes class
In 1939 *Hertog Hendrik*, renamed *Vleereede*, and *Jacob van Heemskerck*, renamed *Ijmuiden*, were brought back into service as guardships. Their 1941–45 armament as the German flak ships *Ariadne* and *Undine* was 6–4.1in, 4–40mm (*Undine* 4–37mm AA (2×2)), 16–20mm AA (4×4). The hulk of *Hertog Hendrik* was BU 1972, the hulk of *Jacob van Hemmskerck*, renamed *Neptunus*, was extant in 1983.

In addition to the above, a number of old monitors were in service in 1906; none had significant fighting value and some were practically hulks. Their names (fates) were: *Heiligerlee* (stricken 1909); *Krokodil* (BU 1906); *Bloedhond* (sold 1907); *Luipaard* (sold 1907); *Panter; Wesp* (both discarded and sold 1906); *Draak* (sold 1914); *Matador* (discarded 1908, sold 1914).

The small turret ship *Stier* was stricken in 1908 and BU in 1930.

CRUISERS

Name	Launched	Disp	Fate
SUMATRA	1890	1693t	Sold 1907
KONINGIN WILHELMINA DER NEDERLANDEN	22.10.92	4530t	Sold 1910
Holland class			
HOLLAND	4.10.96	3840t	Stricken 1920
ZEELAND	1897	3840t	Stricken 1924
FRIESLAND	1896	3840t	Stricken 1913
GELDERLAND	28.9.98	3970t	Sunk 16.7.44
NOORD BRABANT	17.1.99	3970t	Lost 17.5.40
UTRECHT	14.7.98	3970t	Stricken 1913

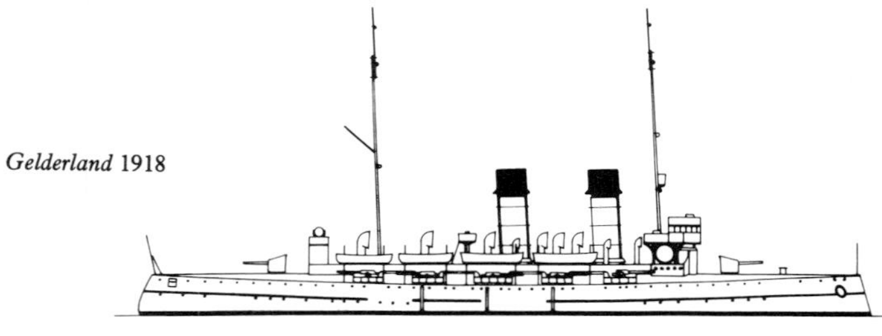
Gelderland 1918

Holland class
Gelderland, classed as non-effective in 1918, served as a gunnery TS from 1920. Her armament after 1941 as the German flak ship *Niobe* was 8–4.1in, 4–40mm AA, 16–20mm AA (4×4). She was torpedoed and bombed by 132 Russian aircraft at Kotka, Gulf of Finland. She went down in 2 hours with a 50-degree starboard list in shallow water having been hit at least nine times, but claimed 9 planes shot down. The 300 crew lost 60 dead. *Noord Brabant*, stricken in 1920, was employed on various subsidiary duties until burnt during the German invasion.

Three older ships of the unprotected cruiser type were still in existence in 1906 but without fighting value. The names (fates) were: *Adolf Hertog van Nassau* (guardship 1879, sold 1914); *Van Galen* (subsidiary service 1893, BU 1920); *Atjeh class – Koningin Emma der Nederlanden, ex-De Ruyter* (hulked 1900, captured by Germans 14 May 1940, capsized 1942, salved 1943 and scuttled).

Marten Harpertzoon Tromp 1906 — *Aldo Fraccaroli Collection*

FIRST CLASS TORPEDO-BOATS

Name/Number	Launched	Disp	Fate
Ardjoeno class			
ARDJOENO	1886	82t	Stricken 1911
BATOK	1887	84t	Discarded 1912
CYCLOOP	1887	84t	BU 1918
DEMPO	1887	82t	Stricken 1911
EMPONG	1888	85t	Discarded 1919
FOKA	1888	85t	Stricken 1913
GOENTER	7.11.88	85t	Stricken 1913
HABANG	1888	79t	Stricken 1912
IDJEN	31.7.89	90t	Stricken 1919
CERBERUS	29.8.88	82t	Stricken 1920
Lamongan class			
LAMONGAN	15.11.90	59t	BU 1911
MAKJAN	2.8.90	59t	Stricken 1919
NOBO	22.4.91	59t	Stricken 1912, BU 1918
Hydra class			
HYDRA	1900	101t	Subsid serv 1920, discarded 1927
SCYLLA	1900	101t	Discarded 1921
MINOTAURUS	3.9.02	101t	Discarded 1921
PYTHON	18.9.02	101t	Discarded 1921
SPHYNX	28.3.03	101t	Discarded 1921
Ophir class			
OPHIR, PANGRANGO, RINDJANI	1901	140t	Stricken 1919
SMEROE, TANGKA, WAJANG	1903	140t	Stricken 1919
G 1 class			
G 1, G 2	17.12.04	140t	Stricken 1919
G 3, G 4	1904	140t	Stricken 1919

SECOND CLASS TORPEDO-BOATS

Name/Number	Launched	Disp	Fate
XV	1881	30t	Stricken 1904
XVI	1881	30t	Stricken 1905
ETNA (also XXI)	1882	45t	Discarded 1912
HEKLA (also XII)	1882	45t	Stricken 1913
III (new)	25.7.91	34t	Discarded 1914
XXI (new)	25.2.90	37t	Discarded 1918
XXII (new)	29.3.90	35t	Discarded 1912
K 1 (also MICHIEL GARDEYN)	1905	47t	Stricken 1921
K 2 (also CHRISTIAAN CORNELIS)	1.9.05	47t	Lost 13.5.40
K 3 (also WILLEM WARMONT)	1905	47t	Stricken 1921

Jacob van Heemskerck 1913 — *Aldo Fraccaroli Collection*

GUNBOATS (OVER 500 TONS)

Name	Launched	Disp	Fate
Lombok class			
LOMBOK	1891	590t	Subsid serv 1910
SUMBAWA	14.11.91	590t	Subsid serv 1911
BORNEO	1892	787t	Depot ship 1916
Nias class			
NIAS	1895	812t	Subsid serv 1907
MATARAM	1896	810t	Subsid serv 1916
EDI	1897	820t	Subsid serv 1910
SERDANG	15.5.97	820t	Minelayer 1921, scuttled 6.3.42
Koetei class			
KOETEI	1898	800t	Subsid serv 1931
SIBOGA	1898	790t	Minelayer 1910, sold 1933
ASSAHAN	1900	800t	Minelayer 1917, sold 1931

Certain older gunboats of over 500t still existed in 1906 but had negligible fighting value. Their names (fates) were: *Madura* (subsidiary service 1900); *Bonaire* (depot ship 1902; sold 1923); *Bali* ex-*St Eustatius* (subsidiary service 1906); *Suriname* (stricken 1907, BU 1911); *Ceram* (subsidiary service 1907, sunk as target 1929); *Flores* (subsidiary service 1906).

Gunboats (200–500 tons)

Almost all the iron-hulled gunboats constructed in the 1870s were still in service in 1906, although many were used extensively for subsidiary duties, such as stores or accommodation hulks, as well as for surveying, minelaying, training and river patrolling. The names (fates) were as follows:

Hydra class

Hydra (stricken 1906), *Ever* (subsidiary service 1884, discarded 1926); *Das* (minelayer 1914, sold 1925); *Dog* (subsidiary service 1894, stricken 1927); *Fret* (accommodation ship 1898, deleted 1924); *Geep* (subsidiary service 1892, sold 1922); *Gier* (TS 1894, sold 1913); *Havik* (minelayer 1914, BU 1936); *Raaf* (subsidiary service 1894, sold 1936); *Brak* (hulk 1902, sold 1961); *Lynx* (renamed *Los* 1912, sold 1925); *Bever* (accommodation ship 1896, sold 1937); *Sperwer* (TS 1896, BU 1960).

The armament of the two minelayers in 1921 was 2–1pdr, 1 MG

Wodan class

Wodan (discarded 1924); *Balder* (minelayer 1910, BU by Germans); *Braga* (minesweeper 1913, gunboat then river gunboat during 1914–18, scuttled May 1940); *Freyr* (gunboat until scuttled 1940, again scuttled 1944, BU 1947–48); *Heimdall* (subsidiary service 1918); *Njord* (gunboat until stricken 1925); *Thor* (minelayer 1918, sunk 12 May 1940); *Tyr* (gunboat until taken over by Germans 1940, sold 1945); *Hefring* (TS 1907, scuttled 14 May 1940, raised, BU); *Vali* (subsidiary service 1909, BU 1940s); *Vidar* (minelayer 1915 until BU by Germans); *Bulgia* (minelayer 1925, sunk 12 May 1940, raised, BU); *Dufa* (discarded 1913); *Hadda* (minelayer 1909, scuttled 14 May 1940, BU by Germans); *Udur* (TS 1903, BU 1940s); *Ulfr* (subsidiary service 1903, sunk 12 May 1940).

The armament of the four minelayers in service in 1921 was 2–4pdr semi-auto, 2 MG in *Balder* and *Hadda*, and 2–1pdr, 2 MG in *Thor* and *Vidar*.

MAJOR SURFACE SHIPS

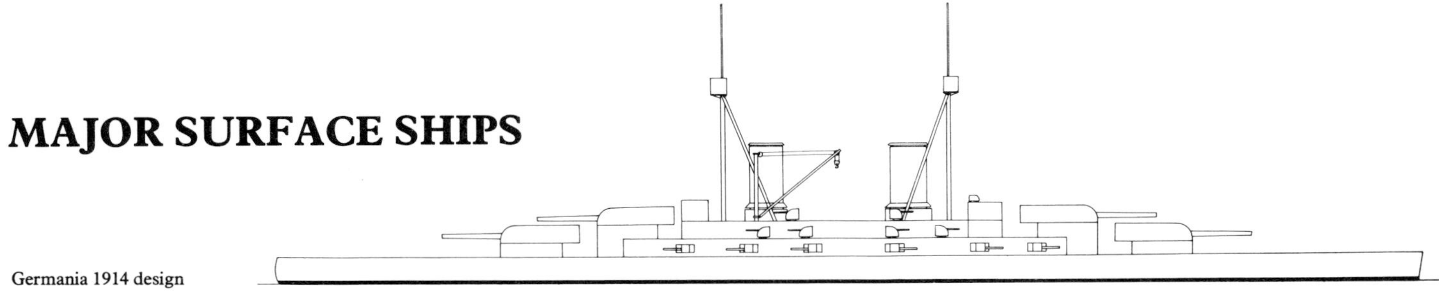

Germania 1914 design

Projected *battleships*

Displacement: 24,605t normal; 26,851t full load
Dimensions: 603ft 8in wl × 91ft 10in × 29ft 8in max
184.0m × 28.0m × 9.0m
Machinery: 3-shaft turbines, 6 double-ended boilers, 38,000shp = 22kts. Fuel 2400t max
Armour: Belt 250mm–150mm (10in–6in), bulkheads 200mm (8in), barbettes 300mm–110mm (12in–4⅓in), torpedo bulkheads 40mm (1⅝in), deck 50mm–25mm (2in–1in), CT 300mm–200mm (12in–8in)
Armament: 8–356mm (14in) (4×2), 16–150mm (5.9in), 12–75mm, 5 TT sub
Complement: –

The origins of these projected ships are described in the introduction. The Royal Commission on the defence of the East Indies (1912–13) recommended the construction of nine dreadnought battleships (20,668t, 21kts, 8–13.5in, 16–5.9in, 12–75mm guns), and the Dutch Government, after slightly enlarging the recommended proposals, invited detailed designs from Germania, Blohm & Voss and Vickers. The data for the Germania design, which seemed best to meet Dutch requirements, are listed in the table; the others were generally similar. Noteworthy features were the above-average speed and below-average belt armour, for possible gunnery duels in the generally good visibility of the Java Sea, and the strong protection against torpedoes and mines. Had the programme been approved, the first ship would have been laid down in December 1914 and completed in 1918.

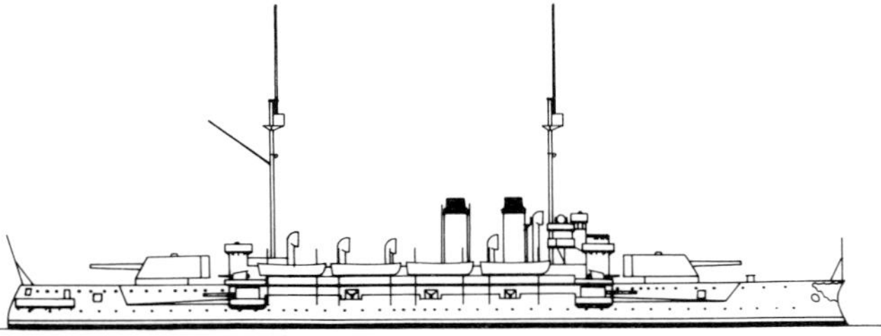

De Zeven Provincien as completed

DE ZEVEN PROVINCIEN *coast defence ship*

Displacement: 6530t normal
Dimensions: 333ft wl, 339ft 6in oa × 56ft × 20ft 3in
101.5m, 103.5m × 17.1m × 6.2m
Machinery: 2-shaft VTE, 8 Yarrow boilers, 8000ihp = 16kts. Coal 700t/1030t
Armour: Belt 150mm–100mm (5.9in–3.9in), turrets 248mm (9.8in), CT 200mm (7.9in), deck 50mm (2in)
Armament: 2–280mm (11in)/42.5, 4–150mm (5.9in)/40, 10–75mm/40, 4–37mm, 1–9pdr mortar, 2 MG
Complement: 452

Name	Builder	Laid down	Launched	Comp	Fate
DE ZEVEN PROVINCIEN	Amsterdam D Yd	7.2.08	15.3.09	6.10.10	Scuttled 2.3.42

The last Dutch coast defence ship, although improved versions were planned (see introduction). The trials performance was 8516ihp = 16.27 knots. She was sent to the East Indies in 1921, and was relieved as flagship by the new light cruiser *Java* in 1925. A serious mutiny on board (4–14 February 1933) was ended by a bomb from a Dutch seaplane that hit the forecastle, killing 23. She was laid up in July 1933 and converted to a gunnery TS in 1935–36; five boilers and the forefunnel were removed, and the

Soerabaia (ex-*De Zeven Provincien*) about 1939
Aldo Fraccaroli Collection

remaining boilers converted to burn oil fuel. The armament was also altered, and the ship re-entered service in 1937 as *Soerabaia*, with revised data: displacement 5644t standard, 7500ihp = 16kts, 1100t oil fuel, 2–11in/42.5, 2–5.9in (later removed), 2–3in, 6–40mm AA, 6–12.7mm AA, complement 447. Badly hit by Japanese aircraft at Soerabaia on 18 February 1942, and subsequently scuttled, she was raised by the Japanese and expended as a blockship, 1942–43.

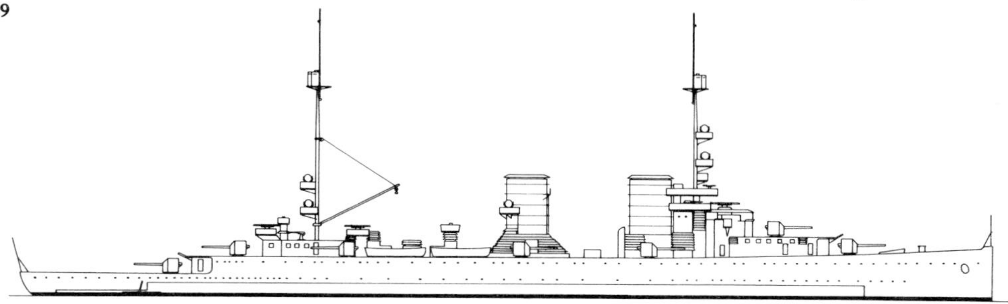

Java as completed

SUMATRA class *cruisers*

Displacement:	6670t standard; 7050t normal (*Celebes* 7205t)
Dimensions:	509ft 6in oa (*Celebes* 519ft 5in) × 52ft 6in × 18ft max *155.3m (158.3m) × 16.0m × 5.5m*
Machinery:	3-shaft Krupp-Germania turbines, 8 Schulz-Thornycroft boilers, 72,000shp = 31kts. Oil 1200t
Armour:	Belt 75mm–50mm (3in–2in), deck 50mm–37.5mm (2in–1.5in), funnel bases 50mm (2in), gunhouses 100mm (4in) (faces), CT 127mm (5in)
Armament:	10–150mm (5.9in)/50, 4–75mm/55 (13pdr) AA, 4 MG
Complement:	480

Name	Builder	Laid down	Launched	Comp	Fate
JAVA	De Schelde	31.5.16	9.8.21	1.5.25	Sunk 27.2.42
SUMATRA	Nederlandse	15.7.16	19.12.20	26.5.26	Scuttled 9.6.44
CELEBES	Fijenoord	1917	–	–	Cancelled 1919

Java and *Sumatra* were authorised on 15 July 1915 under the 1915–16 Programme to a Dutch design, but with materials, technical supervision and some skilled labour from Krupp. Much larger and better armed than contemporary British and German light cruisers, but construction was much delayed during and after World War One (they should have been ready in 1918), so that by 1925–26 they were completely outclassed by Washington Treaty designs. Two Fairey IIID seaplanes handled by small cranes mounted abeam, to port and starboard, just abaft the first funnel were added shortly after completion. During big refits in 1934–35, the mainmast was replaced by a small derrick post stepped farther forward, while a new tubular foremast, with director tower and searchlight platform, was installed. The original AA and machine guns were replaced by 6 (*Java 8*) single 40mm AA and 6–12.7mm AA. The complement was increased to 525. *Java* was torpedoed by the Japanese heavy cruiser *Nachi* in the Battle of the Java Sea, while *Sumatra*, under refit both in the Netherlands in May 1940 and at Soerabaja in December 1941, saw little operational service in World War Two; she was laid up at Portsmouth in September 1942, disarmed, and expended in the breakwater of a Mulberry harbour. *Celebes* was authorised in July 1917 and laid down under the 1917–18 Programme, but little work was done before she was cancelled. The name was revived in the 1930s for the projected light cruiser that became *De Ruyter*.

Java as completed
By courtesy of F J IJsseling

FRET class *destroyers*

Displacement:	510t normal
Dimensions:	231ft oa × 21ft 8in × 9ft 3in max *70.4m × 6.6m × 2.8m*
Machinery:	2-shaft turbines, 4 Yarrow boilers, 8500shp = 30kts. Coal 120t (+ 12.5t oil in last four)
Armament:	4–75mm/40 semi-auto, 4 MG, 2–457mm (18in) TT
Complement:	83

Name	Builder	Launched	Fate
BULHOUND	De Schelde	20.12.11	Stricken 1927
FRET	De Schelde	15.10.10	Stricken 1922
JAKHALS	De Schelde	20.1.12	Stricken 1928
WOLF	De Schelde	17.9.10	Stricken 1924
HERMELIJN	De Schelde	22.2.13	Stricken 1925
LYNX	De Schelde	24.12.12	Stricken 1928
PANTER	Fijenoord	9.9.13	Stricken 1934
VOS	Fijenoord	28.6.13	Stricken 1928

Wolf as completed
Aldo Fraccaroli Collection

The eight ships of this class were begun in 1909–12, completed in 1911–14, and sent to the East Indies in pairs, as completed. The radius of action was 2360 miles at 8.5kts and 670 miles at 20kts for the first four, and 2700 miles and 750 miles at the same speeds for the last four. Completed with short funnels, but later altered with heights reducing from the first to the fourth. *Fret* and *Lynx* were used as targets after being stricken, and were BU at Soerabaja in the 1930s. *Panter* was converted to a dispatch vessel in 1928. The torpedo tubes removed from this class were later fitted in the MTBs *TM 3–TM 21*.

DRAAK class *torpedo-boats*

Displacement:	103t
Dimensions:	130ft × 13ft 6in × 7ft 4in max *39.6m × 4.1m × 2.2m*
Machinery:	2-shaft reciprocating, 1500ihp = 24kts. Coal 21t
Armament:	2–37mm (1pdr), 2–450mm (17.7in) TT (1 bow aw, 1 deck)
Complement:	21

Class (launched, fate):
De Schelde – *Draak* (21.7.06, subsidiary service 1921, sold 1931), *Krokodil* (2.8.06, subsidiary service 1921, sold 1931), *Zeeslang* (27.4.07, subsidiary service 1921, sold 1933).

These three boats were laid down in 1905–6 and completed in 1907. They were similar to the *Hydra* class boats but with one fewer tube, and, like that class, belonged to the East Indies Marine (*Indische Militaire Marine*).

G 1 class *torpedo-boats*

Displacement:	140t
Dimensions:	152ft 6in × 15ft 4in × 8ft max *46.5m × 4.7m × 2.3m*
Machinery:	1-shaft VTE, 2-cyl boilers, 2000ihp = 25kts. Coal 40t
Armament:	2–50mm, 3–450mm (17.7in) TT (1 bow sub, 2 aw)
Complement:	25

Krokodil as completed — *Aldo Fraccaroli Collection*

G 2 as completed — *Aldo Fraccaroli Collection*

G 16 between the wars — *By courtesy of F J IJsseling*

Class (launched, fate):
Fijenoord – *G 5–G 8* (all 1906, stricken 1919), *G 9*, *G 10* (both 1908, stricken 1919), *G 11* (1908, mined 30.3.18), *G 12* (1908, stricken 1919).

For *G 1–G 4*, see the 1860–1905 volume. *G 5–G 12* were laid down 1905–8 and completed 1906–8. G = large ('*Groot*'). *G 5–G 8* had names, seldom used, as follows: *Roemer Vlacq*, *Pieter Constant*, *Jacob Cleydyck*, *Cornelis Janssen de Haan*. *G 11* was subsequently salved and broken up.

G 13 class *torpedo-boats*

Displacement:	180t
Dimensions:	162ft 5in pp × 17ft 1in × 9ft 6in max *49.5m × 5.2m × 2.9m*
Machinery:	2-shaft VTE, 2cyl boilers, 2600ihp = 25kts. Coal 44t
Armament:	2–75mm/30, 3–450mm (17.7in) TT (deck)
Complement:	27

Class (builder, fate):
De Schelde – *G 13* (18.10.13, BU 1943), *G 14* (15.11.13, BU 1919)
Fijenoord – *G 15* (3.1.14, BU 1943), *G 16* (10.3.14, BU 1945)

All four laid down 1913 and completed 1914. *G 13* and *G 15*, which escaped to England in 1940, were BU at Preston, in February 1943. *G 14* was badly damaged by a boiler explosion at Vlissingen on 11 January 1919, and was not repaired. *G 16*, scuttled at Den Helder on 14 May 1940, was salved and became the German *TFA 9*. She was retroceded in 1945 and scrapped.

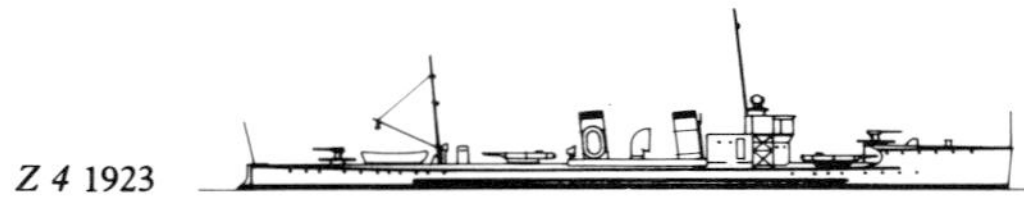
Z 4 1923

Z 1 class *torpedo-boats*

Displacement:	277t standard; 322t normal
Dimensions:	200ft 3in pp, 205ft 4in oa × 20ft 5in × 8ft 4in max *61.0m, 62.6m × 6.2m × 2.5m*
Machinery:	2-shaft AEG-Vulkan turbines, 3 water-tube boilers, 5500shp = 27kts. Coal 60t, oil 16.2t (repeats 72t coal + oil 9.4t)
Armament:	2–75mm/30, 2–12.7mm AA, 4–450mm (17.7in) TT (1×2)
Complement:	46

Class (builder, fate):
Vulkan, Stettin – *Z 1*, *Z 2* (both 26.8.14, to Germany 1914), *Z 3*, *Z 4* (both 12.12.14, to Germany 1914)
Nederlandse – *Z 1*, *Z 2* (both 1917, stricken 1933), *Z 3* (23.3.17, BU 1940–41, *Z 4* (1917, stricken 1933)

The first four boats were taken over by Germany on 10 August 1914 while still on the stocks and completed as *V 105–V 105*, with 88mm (3.5in) guns replacing the original 75mm guns. Z = very large *ie* high seas ('*Zeer groot*' or '*Zeegard*') type. Four repeat units with the same numbers and to the same plans were laid down in the Netherlands in November (*Z 1*, *Z 2*) and December (*Z 3*, *Z 4*) 1915, but owing to non-delivery of materials from Germany were not finished until December 1919-January 1921, or after *Z 5–Z 8*. *Z 1* had short funnels, a short mainmast and high foremast, *Z 4* high funnels, high mainmast and a short foremast, and *Z 2* and *Z 3* short funnels. *Z 3* was fired by her crew at Enkhuizen on 14 May 1940; the wreck was subsequently scrapped. Of the four original boats, *V 105* and *V 106*, assigned to Brazil by the 1919 Peace Treaty, were handed to Britain for breaking up; however, *V 105* went to Poland as *Mazur*, replacing *A 69*, originally meant for transfer. *V 107* was mined in the Baltic off Libau (Russian Courland) on 8 May 1915, and *V 108*, transferred to Poland by the Peace Treaty and named *Kaszub*, was lost at Danzig-Neufahrwasser on 20 July 1925 by a boiler explosion.

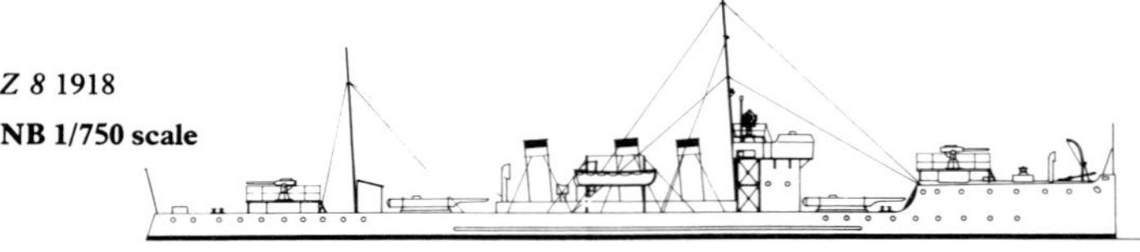
Z 8 1918
NB 1/750 scale

Z 5 class *torpedo-boats*

Displacement:	263t
Dimensions:	191ft 10in pp × 19ft 8in × 5ft 5in *58.5m × 6.0m × 1.7m*
Machinery:	2-shaft VTE, 3 cylindrical boilers, 5500ihp = 27kts. Coal 80t + oil fuel 7t
Armament:	2–75mm/30, 2–12.7mm AA, 4–450mm (17.7in) TT aw (1×2)
Complement:	46

Class (builder, fate):
De Schelde – *Z 5* (1.4.15, to Britain 2.3.42, sold 1945), *Z 6* (15.4.15, stricken 1942)

Fijenoord – *Z 7* (10.5.15, discarded 1944), *Z 8* (23.6.15, discarded 1944)

All four laid down in 1914 and completed in 1916–17. *Z 5* was converted to a patrol vessel in 1930, with one boiler and the first funnel removed, extra fuel and a lengthened forecastle; data became 3000ihp = 22kts, 100t oil, no TT, complement 34. All four reached England in May 1940 and, like the other Dutch TBs that escaped, served as tenders to RN flotillas. *Z 5* was taken over by the RN as HMS *Blade*.

SUBMARINES

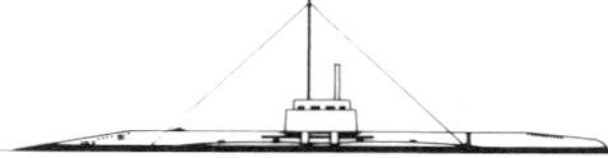

O 1 1910
NB 1/750 scale

O 1 *submarine*

Displacement: 105t/124t
Dimensions: 67ft × 16ft × 9ft 2in
20.4m × 4.9m × 2.8m
Machinery: 1-shaft petrol motor plus 1 electric motor, 160bhp + 80shp = 9kts/6kts
Armament: 1–250mm (9.8in) TT
Complement: 10

Name	Builder	Launched	Fate
O 1	De Schelde	8.7.05	Stricken 1920

The Holland-type *O 1* was laid down by De Schelde of Vlissingen in June 1904 and completed in July 1906 as *Luctor et Energo*, a private venture using plans from the US Electric Boat Co. She was purchased for the Netherlands Navy on 20 December 1906, and was known initially as *'onderzeeboot I'*. In 1914 the petrol motor was replaced by an MAN diesel motor of 200bhp.

O 2 class *submarines*

Displacement: 130t/150t
Dimensions: 102ft 1in × 10ft 2in × 9ft 6in
31.1m × 3.1m × 2.9m
Machinery: 1-shaft 2 MAN 6-cyl diesels plus 1 electric motor, 350bhp/200shp = 11kts/8.6kts. Range 500nm/10kts, 26nm/8.6kts
Armament: 2–450mm (17.7in) TT (2+2)
Complement: 10

Name	Builder	Launched	Fate
O 2	De Schelde	30.1.11	Stricken 1931
O 3	De Schelde	30.7.12	Stricken 1932
O 4	De Schelde	5.8.13	Stricken 1935
O 5	De Schelde	2.10.13	Stricken 1935

These four Hay-Whitehead type boats were based on plans from Marley F Hay and Whitehead & Co, Fiume (Rijeka). All laid down by De Schelde in 1909–12, and completed in 1911–14. They were known originally as *'onderzeeboot I–IV'*.

K 1 *submarine*

Displacement: 330t/386t
Dimensions: 159ft 5in × 15ft 5in × 10ft 2in
48.6m × 4.7m × 3.1m
Machinery: 2 shafts, 2 MAN 8cyl diesels plus 1 electric motor, 1800bhp/500shp = 16kts/8.5kts. Range 1500nm (normal), 2250nm (extreme); 30nm/8.5kts
Armament: 3–450mm (17.7in) TT (2 bow, 1 stern)
Complement: 17

Name	Builder	Launched	Fate
K I	De Schelde	20.5.13	Stricken 1928

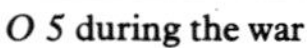

O 5 during the war — *Aldo Fraccaroli Collection*

K 1 after the war — *By courtesy of F J IJsseling*

K I, the first submarine for the East Indies, was of the Hay-Whitehead type, built in 1911–14. *K* stood for *'Koloniaal'* and with the Roman numerals, indicated service in the East Indies Marine. Home service boats were given Arabic numerals.

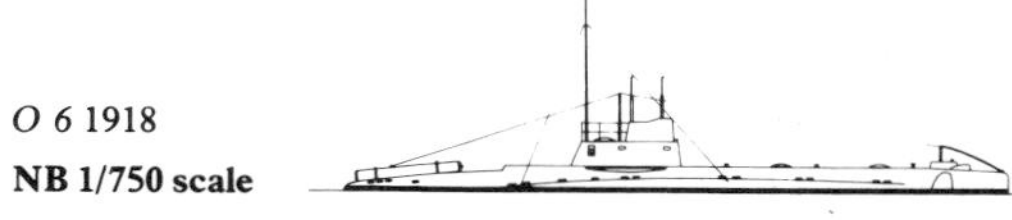

O 6 1918
NB 1/750 scale

O 6 and O 7 class *submarines*

Displacement: 189t/229t (*O 7* 176t/206t)
Dimensions: 112ft 3in pp, 117ft oa × 12ft 6in × 10ft (*O 7* 105ft pp, 112ft 4in oa × 12ft × 9ft 6in)
34.2m, 35.7 × 3.8m × 3.0m (32.0m, 34.2m × 3.7m × 2.9m)
Machinery: 1 shaft, MAN 6-cyl diesel plus 1 electric motor, 375bhp (*O 7* 350bhp)/185shp = 12kts/8.5kts. Range 750nm/10kts, 25.5nm/8.5kts
Armament: 3–450mm (17.7in) TT (2 bow, 1 stern), 1 MG
Complement: 15

Name	Builder	Launched	Fate
O 6	De Schelde	10.6.16	Stricken 1936
O 7	Fijenoord	22.7.16	Stricken 1939

O 6 and *O 7*, of the Holland and Hay-Denny types respectively, were laid down in May 1914 and completed in late 1916.

K II *submarine*

Displacement: 569t/649t
Dimensions: 177ft 2in × 16ft 9in × 12ft 6in
54.0m × 5.1m × 3.8m
Machinery: 2 shafts, 2 MAN 8-cyl diesels plus 1 electric motor, 1800bhp/500shp = 16kts/8.5kts. Range 3500nm (normal), 5500nm (extreme)/16kts; 25.5nm/8.5kts
Armament: 6–450mm (17.7in) TT, 1–75mm (13pdr) AA, 1 MG
Complement: 29

Name	Builder	Launched	Fate
K II	Fijenoord	24.2.19	Stricken 1937

K II was of the Hay-Denny type, built in 1915–22, and very similar to the later *K V–K VII*. The MAN could not complete work on the engines owing to the war, so they were finished by De Schelde. Two TT were in a training mount in the casing forward of the conning tower.

K III class *submarines*

Displacement: 574t/710t
Dimensions: 210ft × 18ft 4in × 11ft 10in
64.0m × 5.6m × 3.6m
Machinery: 2 shaft Sulzer diesels plus 1 electric motor, 1200bhp/630shp = 14.5kts/8kts. Range 3500nm/11kts
Armament: 6–450nm (17.7in) TT (2 bow, 2 deck, 2 stern), 1–75mm (13pdr) AA
Complement:

Name	Builder	Launched	Fate
K III	De Schelde	12.8.19	Stricken 1934
K IV	De Schelde	2.7.20	Stricken 1936

K III and *K IV* were of the Holland type, laid down in 1915–16 and completed in 1920–21; they were generally similar to the later *K VIII–K X*. Sulzer diesels replaced the more powerful (1800bhp) MAN diesels originally ordered but not delivered because of the war. The diving limit was 22 fathoms.

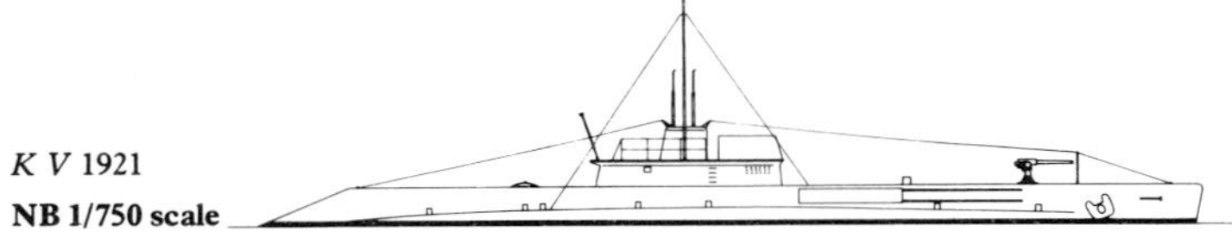

K V 1921
NB 1/750 scale

K V class *submarines*

Displacement:	560t/640t
Dimensions:	177ft pp × 16ft 9in × 12ft 6in *54.0m × 5.1m × 3.8m*
Machinery:	2-shaft Sulzer diesels plus 1 electric motor, 1200bhp/500shp = 15kts/8kts. Range 3500nm/11kts
Armament:	6–450mm (17.7in) TT (2 bow, 2 deck, 2 stern), 1–75mm (13pdr) AA, 1 MG
Complement:	31

Name	Builder	Launched	Fate
K V	Fijenoord	20.11.19	Stricken 1937
K VI	Fijenoord	23.12.20	Stricken 1937
K VII	Fijenoord	8.3.21	Sunk 18.2.42

All of the Hay-Denny type to plans from that Scottish (Dumbarton) firm, laid down in April–July 1916 and completed in 1920–22. Because of the war, the MAN declined to supply the (1800bhp) motors specified, so Sulzer diesels of less power were used. The endurance figures were as for *K II*, and they had the same trianing mount for two TT. The diving limit was 22 fathoms. *K VII* was bombed and sunk by Japanese aircraft at Soerabaja, Java.

K VIII class *submarines*

Displacement:	573t/712t
Dimensions:	210ft 4in × 18ft 4in × 11ft 10in *64.1m × 5.6m × 3.6m*
Machinery:	2-shaft MAN (*K IX, K X* Schelde-Sulzer) diesels plus 1 electric motor, 1800bhp (*K IX, K X* 1500bhp)/630shp = 15kts/8kts. Range 3500nm/11kts, 25nm/8kts
Armament:	4–450mm (17.7in) TT (2 bow, 2 stern), 1–88mm (3.5in) AA, 1–12.7mm AA
Complement:	31

Name	Builder	Launched	Fate
K VIII	De Schelde	28.3.22	Discarded 1942
K IX	De Schelde	23.12.22	Hulked 1942
K X	De Schelde	2.5.23	Scuttled 2.3.42

All of Holland type, built under the 1916 Naval Programme. They were laid down in 1917–19 and completed in 1922–23. *K VIII* and *K IX* were broken up in Australia, while *K X* was scuttled at Soerabaja (Java) after being damaged by Japanese warships.

K III as completed *Aldo Fraccaroli Collection*

K VIII as completed *By courtesy of F J IJsseling*

Ex-German UC type *submarine*

Class (original number, launched, fate):
M 1 (ex-*UC 8*, 6.7.15, stricken 1932).

This small minelaying submarine was stranded near the Frisian island of Terschelling on 6 November 1915, refloated and interned. She was acquired from Germany, and entered service in the Dutch Navy on 13 March 1917.

Ex-British 'H' class *submarine*

Class (original number, launched, fate):
O 8 (ex-*H 6*, 8.15 to Germany 1940 as *UD 1*)

This RN boat was stranded on the Dutch coast near Schiermonnikog on 18 January 1916, refloated and interned. Acquired by the Netherlands, she entered Dutch service on 7 May 1917. She was captured by the Germans at Den Helder on 10 May 1940, and was scuttled at Kiel on 3 May 1945.

SMALL SURFACE WARSHIPS

BRINIO class *armoured gunboats*

Displacement:	540t normal
Dimensions:	172ft 3in oa × 28ft × 9ft 3in max *52.5m × 8.5m × 2.8m*
Machinery:	2-shaft diesel motors (see notes), 1200bhp = 14kts. Oil fuel 34t
Armour:	Belt 55mm (2⅛in), deck 17mm (⅝in), CT 50mm (2in)
Armament:	4–105mm (4.1in)/50 semi-auto, 2–12.7mm AA
Complement:	63

Class (launched, fate):
Amsterdam DY – *Brinio* (12.8.12, sunk 14.5.40), *Friso* (29.8.12, sunk 12.5.40), *Gruno* (26.5.13, stricken 1950)

These three gunboats were built in 1911–15, and were intended to drive off destroyers in shallow and coastal waters, although too slow for this purpose. The original machinery (*Brinio* details not available, *Friso* by NV Werkspoor, *Gruno* MAN, but built by Smit, Rotterdam under licence) having given rise to various problems, all were re-engined with more powerful diesels, *Brinio* with 6-cyl 2-stroke Sulzers (1932), *Friso* with 6-cyl 4-stroke MAN motors (1928), and *Gruno* with 6-cyl 2-stroke Germania motors (1917), to give 1500bhp = 14kts. *Brinio* was disabled by German dive bombers in the Zuider Zee and scuttled by her crew. *Friso* was heavily damaged by German aircraft, also in the Zuider Zee, and sunk by gunfire from the minesweeper *Pieter Florisz*. Both were salved, in 1942 and 1943 respectively, and scrapped. *Gruno*, which escaped to England in 1940, had 2–40mm added, firing over the 4.1in guns fore and aft.

HYDRA class *minelayers*

Displacement:	593t normal
Dimensions:	163ft 1in oa × 29ft 6in × 9ft *49.7m × 9.0m × 2.75m*
Machinery:	2-shaft VTE, 2cyl Werkspoor boilers, 900ihp = 11kts. Coal 72t
Armament:	3–75mm/40 semi-auto, 2–12.7mm AA, 70 mines
Complement:	59

Class (launched, fate):
Amsterdam DY – *Hydra* (7.7.11, sunk 15.5.40), *Medusa* (23.6.11, subsidiary service 1945)

These coastal minelayers, for laying defensive fields in home waters, were built in 1910–11; both exceeded 12kts on trials. *Hydra*, sunk by collision with the torpedo-boat *Z 3* in February 1921, was salved in April 1921, repaired and re-entered service early in 1923. *Hydra* was sunk by German shore artillery; she was later raised and scrapped. *Medusa* was used as a depot ship from 1950, with armament (1953) 2–40mm AA.

Trawler type *minelayers*

Displacement:	477t (*Vulcanus* 410t)
Dimensions:	125ft × 21ft × 11ft 2in (*Vulcanus* 129ft 7in × 21ft 8in × 10ft 6in) *38.1m × 6.4m × 3.4m (39.5m × 6.6m × 3.2m)*
Machinery:	1-shaft reciprocating, 412ihp = 10.2kts (*Vulcanus* 375ihp = 10kts)
Armament:	2–37mm (1pdr), 30 mines
Complement:	34

Name (original name, where built, launched, fate):
Triton (*Onze Trawler*, N Shields, 1906, fishing service 1921), *Vulcanus* (*Azalia*, Grimsby, 1902, subsidiary service 1920).

These trawlers were taken over and converted into auxiliary minelayers in 1914 and 1916–17 respectively. *Vulcanus* was also fitted for minesweeping.

Tug type *minelayer*

Displacement: 234t
Dimensions: 102ft 9in × 13ft 5in × 7ft 9in
31.3m × 4.1m × 2.35m
Machinery: 1-shaft reciprocating, 400ihp = 10.2kts
Armament: 1–37mm (1pdr), 20 mines
Complement: 17

Class (launched, fate):
Hercules (1910, stricken 1932)

This boat was laid down as a tug for the East Indies Marine by Soerabaja DYd, but was completed as an auxiliary minelayer. She was taken over by the Dutch Navy in 1919.

VAN MEERLANT class *minelayers*

Displacement: 687t standard; 748t normal
Dimensions: 179ft 10in pp × 28ft 6in × 10ft 6in
54.8m × 8.7m × 3.2m
Machinery: 2-shaft VTE, 2 Yarrow boilers, 1000ihp = 13kts. Coal 115t
Armament: 3–75mm/40 semi-auto, 2–12.7mm AA, 60 mines
Complement: 60

Class (launched, fate):
Gusto, Schiedam – *Van Meerlant* (24.11.20, sunk 4.6.41), *Douwe Aukes* (23.2.22, depot ship 1948, sold 1962).

These larger and slightly faster versions of the *Hydra* class were built in 1919–22. *Douwe Aukes* was rearmed with 1–75mm AA, 2–2pdr AA, 2–20mm AA in 1941 as a convoy escort, while *Van Meerlant* was mined in the Thames estuary.

Tug type *minesweepers*

Displacement: 238t (*II* 205t; *III, IV* 230t)
Dimensions: 83ft 8in × 20ft 8in × 10ft 2in (*II* 97ft 5in × 20ft 6in × 9ft 6in; *III, IV* 90ft 3in × 20ft × 9ft 2in)
25.5m × 6.3m × 3.1m (29.6m × 6.25m × 2.9m; 27.5m × 6.1m × 2.8m)
Machinery: 1-shaft reciprocating, 500ihp = 10kts
Armament: 1–12.7mm AA
Complement: 16

Class (original name, builder, launched, fate):
I (*Marie I*, van der Kuyk en van Ree, Rotterdam, 20.12.16, scuttled 10.5.40, raised by Germans and German *LAZ 46*, to Dutch mercantile service 1941), *II* (*Marie II*, Koopman, Dordrecht, 12.7.18, mined 13.5.40, salved and mercantile tug), *III* (*Anna*, Schuyt, Papendrecht, 1918, scuttled as blockship 14.5.40), *IV* (*Pauline*, Schuyt, Papendrecht, 1918, scuttled 14.5.40, salved and mercantile tug).

These four tugs were taken over while building and fitted for minesweeping. They were subsequently renumbered *M 1–M 4*.

Gruno 1940 — *Aldo Fraccaroli Collection*

Vulcanus — *By courtesy of F J IJsseling*

Hydra — *By courtesy of F J IJsseling*

Van Meerlant between the wars
CPL

Portugal

Portugal, a third class power with an extensive colonial empire, entered the twentieth century troubled and divided. The Treaty of Windsor (1899), by re-establishing the ancient, Anglo-Portuguese alliance, ended the colonial disputes that had troubled Lisbon since the Congress of Berlin (1878), at one time even threatening a partition of her African territories between Britain and Germany, but the equilibrium reached by 1906 in foreign relations was not reflected at home. An unpopular government ruled by decree, and the murder in 1908 of the discredited King Carlos I was the overture to the revolution that two years later swept away the House of Braganza. The armed forces were honeycombed with socialism; effective control of many ships and regiments was in the hands of NCOs who, as Freemasons or *Carbonarias* (members of the republican secret society) or both, plotted revolution. During the three-day Lisbon revolution of October 1910 the cruisers *Dom Carlos 1, Sao Rafael* and *Adamastor* shelled royalist troops when the latter might have succeeded in overcoming republicans in the Marine barracks. The corrupt monarchy of Manuel II (who fled to Britain) was replaced by a wobbling republic proclaimed on 5 October 1910.

It was no longer necessary to sustain the naval build-up of the late 1890s, and very little new construction was undertaken in the years to 1921. The 1907–8 Naval Programme provided for 2 coast defence ships of 2500 tons (Argentine *Libertad* type); 6 5000-ton protected cruisers; 18 400-ton destroyers; and 6 320-ton submarines, but nothing was done as there was no money. Contemporary reports of more ambitious proposals, for example three dreadnoughts to be acquired immediately from Britain, recurred in the daily and technical press, but were pure pipedreams.

The Republic's naval programmes were as ambitious, and as unfulfilled, as the monarchy's. In 1912 the Minister of Marine introduced a bill for the Fleet Law of the Republic, providing for 3 21,500-ton battleships of improved *Minas Gerais* type, 3 2500-ton scout cruisers, torpedo craft and submarines, to a total of £8,800,000. Once again financial problems intervened, and in 1913 a smaller programme, of 2 cruisers (2500t, 20kts, 2–6in, 6–4in guns), 6 destroyers of 700–800 tons and 3 submarines of 300 tons were substituted. The contract for these vessels was provisionally awarded to a British consortium (John Brown, Cammell Laird, Fairfield, Palmer's and Thornycroft), with Fiat-Ansaldo associated for the submarines. Little progress was made with this plan before the outbreak of war, although the money required was voted; paper projects for the three battleships, which by 1914 had progressed through *Orion* type ships with 13.5in guns to improved *Queen Elizabeth*s, remained in the files.

In 1914 Portugal committed herself to military operations against Germany, but war was not declared formally until March 1916. An expeditionary force served on the Western Front, in the Battle of Loos, but the colonial forces could not prevent German troops marching across Mozambique. Naval operations were less important; the most notable episode being the gallant fight of the auxiliary gunboat *Augusto de Castilho*, escorting the passenger ship *Sao Miguel* from Madeira (the island's capital, Funchal, had been shelled by *U 156* at the end of 1917) to the Azores, with the much more heavily-gunned *U 139* (commanded by the top U-boat ace Arnauld de la Periere) on 14 October 1918.

In return for her contribution to the war effort, the Versailles Treaty gave Portugal ¾ per cent of the reparations to be paid by Germany, and a small piece of land in northern Mozambique, previously claimed by German East Africa. Her share of the surrendered fleets was six ex-Austrian torpedo boats, and a Turkish torpedo gunboat of the *Berk* type. The latter was not delivered, because of the Turkish revolution and the new Peace Treaty. The old interest in big ships remained. Just before the Washington Treaty the USA is said to have tried to sell Portugal the dreadnought *Utah* and five old *Connecticut* class pre-dreadnoughts, but a rational naval programme had to await the new Corporate State and the late 1920s.

The Lisbon naval base had some small slips, used to assemble and launch torpedo craft, and a small drydock; larger docks belonged to the Harbour Board. The main overseas base, at Luanda, Angola, had a small floating dock, while Lourenço Marques, Mozambique, had a similar small drydock. During 1914–18, batteries and other defences were erected at Porto Delgado, Azores, while the port was used by US transports, but the base was not developed by the Portuguese. Naval personnel figures were 890 officers and 4843 men (1921). The merchant fleet increased from 44 steamers of 29,000 tons in 1906 to 66 of 70,000 tons in 1914 and 132 of 233,000 tons in 1921; the sailing ship total stayed at 200–250 vessels of about 50,000 tons.

FLEET STRENGTH 1906

COAST DEFENCE SHIP

Name	Launched	Disp	Fate
VASCO DA GAMA	1.12.75	2982t	BU 1935

CRUISERS

Name	Launched	Disp	Fate
ADAMASTOR	12.7.96	1729t	Sold 1933
SÃO GABRIEL	7.5.98	1771t	Discarded 1924
SÃO RAFAEL	5.7.98	1771t	Wrecked 10.11
DOM CARLOS I	5.5.98	4186t	Discarded 1923
RAINHA DONA AMELIA	12.4.99	1630t	Wrecked 8.15

In 1910 *Dom Carlos I* and *Rainha Dona Amelia* were renamed *Candido Reis*, then *Almirante Reis*, and *Republica* respectively. *Almirante Reis* was dismantled for a long refit in 1918, but never re-entered service.

DESTROYER

Name	Launched	Disp	Fate
TEJO	27.10.01	522t	Discarded *c*1929

Tejo was wrecked in 1910, salved and rebuilt; she re-entered service in 1917 with White-Foster boilers and only two funnels. Revised armament data: 1–4in, 1–3in, 2–47mm, 2–14in TT

TORPEDO BOATS

Number	Launched	Disp	Fate
1 (ESPADARTE)	1881	54t	Discarded 1918
2	1886	66t	Discarded 1933
3	1886	66t	Discarded 1924
4	1886	66t	Discarded 1918

SUBMARINE

Name	Launched	Disp	Fate
PLONGEUR	1892	100t	Discarded 1910

SLOOPS

Name	Launched	Disp	Fate
RAINHA DE PORTUGAL	16.10.75	1106t	Discarded 1910
ALFONSO D'ALBUQUERQUE	9.7.84	1092t	Discarded *c*1912

GUNBOATS (OVER 200 TONS)

Name	Launched	Disp	Fate
RIO LIMA	1875	628t	Discarded 1918
SADO	1875	645t	Discarded *c*1921
BENGO	23.8.79	455t	Discarded *c*1910
MANDOVI	16.8.79	455t	Discarded *c*1910
ZAMBESE	30.9.86	631t	Hulked 1920

Name	Launched	Disp	Fate
VOUGA	5.1.82	710t	Discarded *c*1910
LIBERAL	9.8.84	549t	Lost 22.6.10
ZAIRE	9.8.84	549t	Discarded 1918
DIU	27.8.89	717t	Discarded 1918
LIMPOPO	1890	288t	Discarded *c*1943
DOM LUIZ	22.6.95	789t	Discarded 1918
PATRIA	27.6.03	626t	Discarded 1931

Liberal was wrecked at Ambriz, a fort and seaport N of Luanda, Angola. Also in service in 1906 were the 220–230t gunboats *Al Baptista de Andrade* and *Thomas Andrea*, for Mozambique and Timor, and the 375t *Chaimite*; the former were discarded *c*1910 and the latter *c*1920.

RIVER GUNBOATS

Name	Launched	Disp	Fate
Cacheu class			
CACHEU	1902	70t	Discarded 1918
FARIM	1902	70t	Discarded 1918
TETE	1903	70t	Lost 2.17
SENA	1904	70t	Discarded 1918
RIO MINHO	1904	38t	Discarded 1940s

Tete was destroyed by a boiler explosion on the Zambezi.

MAJOR SURFACE SHIPS

Douro as completed

GUADINA class *destroyers*

Displacement: 515t standard; 660t full load
Dimensions: 240ft × 23ft 6in × 7ft 8in max
73.2m × 7.2m × 2.3m
Machinery: 2-shaft Parsons turbines, 3 Yarrow boilers, 11,000shp = 27kts. Coal 146t. Range 1600nm/15kts
Armament: 1–4in (102mm/40, 2–3in, 4–18in (457mm) TT (2×2)
Complement: 80

Name	Builder	Launched	Fate
DOURO	Lisbon DYd	22.1.13	Discarded 1931
GUADIANA	Lisbon DYd	21.9.14	Discarded 1934
VOUGA	Lisbon DYd	19.4.20	Lost 1.5.31
TAMEGA	Lisbon DYd	21.10.22	Discarded *c*1945

These Yarrow-type boats were built by Yarrow and assembled in Portugal.

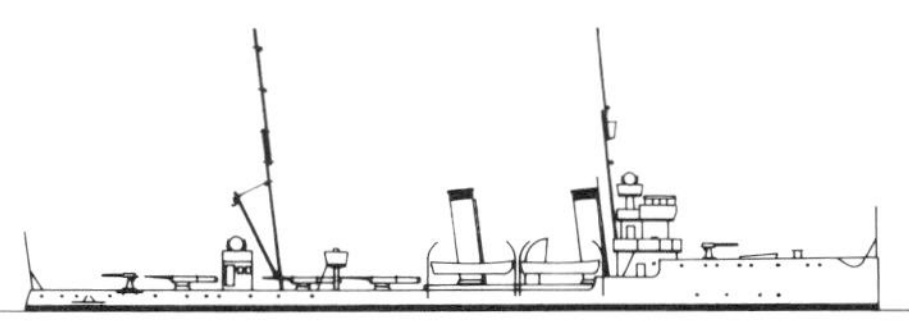

Liz 1915

LIZ *destroyer*

Displacement: 550t
Dimensions: 230ft × 22ft × 7ft
70.1m × 6.7m × 2.1m
Machinery: 2-shaft Parsons turbines, Thornycroft boilers, 8000shp = 28kts
Armament: 4–3in (76mm)/40, 3–18in (457mm) TT
Complement: 70

Name	Builder	Launched	Fate
LIZ	Ansaldo	22.12.14	To Britain 1915

This destroyer, generally of the Italian *Bersagliere* class (but with raised forecastle, enlarged bridge, only two funnels and repositioned TT) was laid down for Portugal at Genoa; however, she was purchased for the RN in May 1915 before delivery and commissioned as HMS *Arno* (June 1915). *Arno* was sunk in a collision with the destroyer HMS *Hope* off the Dardanelles on 23 March 1918.

Ex-Austro-Hungarian 82F type *torpedo-boats*

Class (former number, fate):
Zezere (ex-*85F*, wrecked 1921), *Ave* (ex-*86F*, discarded 1940), *Cavado* (ex-*88F*, wrecked 1921), *Sado* (ex-*89F*, discarded 1940), *Liz* (ex-*90F*, discarded 1934), *Mondego* (ex-*91F*, discarded 1938)

All made over to Portugal in September 1920 by the Peace Treaties for police duties only, and transferred in 1921. The proposed Portuguese armament was 1–66mm Skoda (11pdr), but all were later fitted with an additional 1–57mm Hotchkiss and 4–18in TT (2×2), and formed a training flotilla for stokers' and torpedo courses. *Zezere* and *Cavado* were wrecked near Bone (Algeria) while on the way from the Adriatic to Portugal.

SUBMARINES

PLONGEUR *submarine*

Displacement: 100t
Dimensions: 72ft 1in × 11ft 6in × ?ft
22.0m × 3.5m × ?
Machinery: 2-shafts, electric motors, ?hp = 6kts
Armament: 4 Nordenfelt TT
Complement: 6

Name	Builder	Launched	Fate
PLONGEUR	Lisbon	1892	Discarded 1910

This boat was designed by Fontes Pereiro de Mello, and was cylindrical in shape, ending forward in a cone. She dived and surfaced by use of ballast tanks and horizontal rudders; the motors were powered by accumulators.

ESPADARTE *submarine*

Displacement: 245t/300t
Dimensions: 148ft × 13ft 9in × 9ft 8in mean, 10ft max
45.1m × 4.2m × 2.9m, 3.0m
Machinery: 2-shafts, 2 Fiat-Diesel 6-cyl motors plus two electric motors, 550bhp/300shp = 13.8kts. Range 1500nm/8.5kts, 24nm/8kts, 100nm/4kts
Armament: 2–457mm (18in) TT (bow; 4 torpedoes)
Complement: 21

Name	Builder	Launched	Fate
ESPADARTE	Spezia	5.10.12	Discarded 1931

This Laurenti-Fiat type boat was built in 1910–13.

Espardarte date unknown *Aldo Fraccaroli Collection*

FOCA class *submarines*

Displacement:	260t/389t
Dimensions:	147ft 9in × 13ft 10in × 10ft 3in mean, 10ft 6in max *45.0m × 4.2m × 3.1m, 3.2m*
Machinery:	2-shafts, 2 Fiat-Diesel 6-cyl motors plus electric motors, 550bhp/400shp = 14.2/8.2kts. Range 650nm/14.2kts, 3500nm/8.5kts, 18nm/8.2kts, 100nm/4kts
Armament:	2–457mm (18in) TT (bow; 4 torpedoes)
Complement:	21

Name	Builder	Launched	Fate
FOCA	Spezia	18.4.17	Discarded 1935
GOLFINHO	Spezia	1917	Discarded 1934
HIDRA	Spezia	9.8.17	Discarded 1935

These Laurenti-Fiat type boats, generally enlarged *Espardarte*s with better endurance, were built in 1915–17. The *Foca*s were replaced in service by the *Delfin* class.

Golfinho as completed — *Aldo Fraccaroli Collection*

SMALL SURFACE WARSHIPS

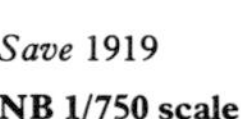

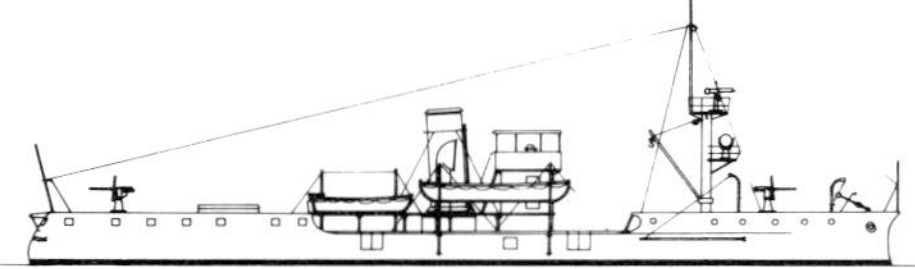

Save 1919
NB 1/750 scale

LURIO class *gunboats*

Displacement:	305t normal
Dimensions:	140ft 5in × 23ft 7in × 5ft 11in *42.8m × 7.2m × 1.8m*
Machinery:	2-shaft reciprocating, cyl boilers, 500ihp = 12.5kts. Coal 61t
Armament:	2–47mm (3pdr), 1 MG
Complement:	51

Class (builder, launched, fate):
Lurio (Lisbon DYd, 1907, discarded 1931), *Save* (Lisbon DYd, 1908, discarded 1931)

BEIRA class *gunboats*

Displacement:	397t standard; 492t full load
Dimensions:	147ft 8in × 27ft 3in × 7ft *45.0m × 8.3m × 2.1m*
Machinery:	2-shaft TE, Yarrow (*Beira*, *Ibo* cyl) boilers, 700ihp = 13kts. Coal 85t
Armament:	1–3.5in, 1–9pdr, 2–3pdr (*Ibo, Mandovi* 1–3in, 2–6pdr, 2–3pdr; *Bengo* 1–3.5in, 4–3pdr; *Quanza* 2–3in)
Complement:	67

Class (launched, fate):
Lisbon DYd – *Beira* (1910, survey ship 1936, discarded *c*1945), *Ibo* (1911, survey ship *c*1948, discarded 1953), *Mandovi* (1917, survey ship *c*1945, discarded late 1950s), *Bengo* (1917, discarded 1935), *Quanza* (1917, discarded 1935)

Beira in the late 1930s — *Aldo Fraccaroli Collection*

The armament first reported for this five ship class was only 2–47mm: data for 1921 are listed above. Armament of surviving units in 1943 was 2–3in, 2–47mm (*Mandovi* 4–47mm only). Three slightly modified ships of the *Zaire* class were launched in 1925–27.

Ex-British 'FLOWER' class *sloops*

Class (former name, fate):
Republica (ex-*Gladiolus*, discarded *c*1943), *Carvalho Araujo* (ex-*Jonquil*, survey ship 1937, discarded 1959).

These two ships were sold to Portugal in 1920.

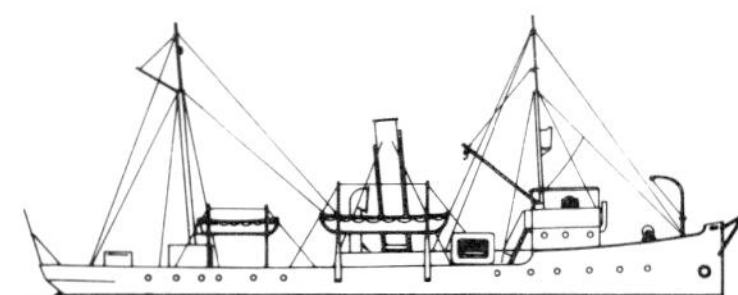

Vulcano 1919
NB 1/750 scale

VULCANO *minelayer*

Displacement:	151t
Dimensions:	110ft × 19ft 6in × 7ft 3in *33.5m × 5.9m × 2.2m*
Machinery:	2-shaft reciprocating, cyl boiler, 412ihp = 12kts
Armament:	See notes
Complement:	24

Class (launched, fate):
Thornycroft – *Vulcano* (1910, discarded late 1940s)

Exercise ship, carrying various arrangements of minelaying and torpedo-dropping gear.

Note – a small Army mining tender, known as *Mineiro*, *ie* 'mining vessel', for laying defensive minefields was built in 1892 and discarded *c*1943 (77t, 58ft 6in × 13ft 5in × 7ft, 2-shaft reciprocating, 1 cyl boiler, 150ihp = 8kts, coal 10t, complement 18).

MACAU *river gunboat*

Displacement:	133t normal
Dimensions:	119ft 8in × 19ft 9in × 2ft *36.5m × 6.0m × 0.6m*
Machinery:	2-shaft reciprocating, Yarrow boilers, 250ihp = 11.8kts
Armament:	2–57mm (6pdr), 3 MG
Complement:	24

Class (launched, fate):
Yarrow – *Macau* (1909, to Japan 1943)

This boat was seized by Japan at her name port in 1943 and renamed *Maiko* on 15.8.43. She became the Chinese *Wu Feng* in 1946.

FLEXA *river gunboat*

Displacement:	44t normal
Dimensions:	68ft 10in × 13ft 1in × 2ft 2in *21.0m × 4.0m × 0.7m*
Machinery:	1-shaft reciprocating, 45ihp = 10kts
Armament:	1–37mm (1pdr)
Complement:	7

Class (launched, fate):
Flexa (1909, discarded 1933)

This boat was also listed as *Flecha*. She was built to the order of the Colonial Department.

TETE *river gunboat*

Displacement: 100t standard
Dimensions: 76ft 8in × 20ft × 2ft 3in
23.4m × 6.1m × 0.7m
Machinery: Stern-wheel reciprocating, 1 Yarrow boiler, 70ihp = 8kts
Armament: 2–47mm, 2 MG
Complement: –

Class (launched, fate):
Yarrow – *Tete* (1918, discarded early 1970s)

This boat, built originally to the order of the Colonial Department for service on the Zambezi to replace her blown up namesake also named after the port high up the river, was re-launched at Chinde in 1920.

DILI *patrol vessel*

Displacement: 495t
Dimensions: 140ft pp × 25ft × 10ft 3in
42.7m × 7.6m × 3.1m
Machinery: 1-shaft reciprocating, 500ihp = 11kts
Armament: ?
Complement: 72

Class (builder, fate):
Dili (–, discarded 1938)

Station ship in Portuguese Timor and named after the island colony's capital.

LINCE *patrol vessel*

Displacement: 77t standard
Dimensions: 88ft 6in pp × 14ft × 6ft
27.0m × 4.3m × 1.8m
Machinery: 2-shaft semi-diesels, 300bhp = 12kts
Armament: ?
Complement: 20

Class (launched, fate):
Orlando – *Lince* (1911, discarded *c*1945)

Used in home waters for torpedo training.

CINCO DE OTOUBRO *dispatch vessel*

Displacement: 1343t
Dimensions: 226ft 10in × 28ft 11in × 14ft
69.2m × 8.8m × 4.3m
Machinery: 2-shaft reciprocating, cyl boilers, 1800ihp = 15kts
Armament: 2–47mm, 4–37mm (1921: 2–37mm)
Complement: 225

Flexa as completed *Aldo Fraccaroli Collection*

Class (launched, fate):
Ramage & Ferguson, Leith – *Cinco de Otoubro* (ex-*Amelia*, ex-*Banshee*, 1900, survey ship 1924, discarded 1937)

Former Royal Yacht, rated as 'aviso' (sloop) or dispatch vessel. Renamed after the 1910 revolution.

Ex-British *motor launches*

Class (former number, fate):
No 2 (ex-*ML 557*, discarded 1933), *No 3* (ex-*ML 574*, discarded 1933)

Purchased in 1920, and attached to Aviation Services.

In addition to the above, there was the fishery protection vessel *Carregado* (1912, 105t, 80ft pp × 18ft × ?, 1-shaft reciprocating, 300ihp = ?kts, stationed in the Algarve and deleted in 1920).

AUXILIARY WARSHIPS

Various ships were taken over from commercial owners during World War One and equipped as auxiliary warships. The most important are listed below:

The passenger ship SS *Malange* of the Empreza Nacional, Lisbon, was renamed *Pedro Nunez* and refitted as an armed merchant cruiser (1889, 3574grt, 5486t, 363ft 6in pp × 42ft × 21ft, 1-shaft reciprocating, 3600ihp = *c*16kts, armament 2–4.7in, 2–3in, 2–47mm, complement 209, stricken 1923).

The minelayer *Sado* (II) was a converted freighter (2518t, 229ft 7in × 36ft × 14ft 9in, 1-shaft reciprocating, cyl boilers, 500ihp = 11kts, 100t coal, 1 MG aft, complement 69, deleted by 1920).

The trawler *Elite* was requisitioned in 1917, renamed *Augusto de Castilho* and fitted for minesweeping (1909, Cochrane, Selby, 487grt, 1–65mm, 1–47mm); she was sunk by *U 139* on 14 October 1918 between Madeira and the Azores.

The SS *Gomez VII* was renamed *Açor* and armed as a gunboat (1874, 330t, 136ft 1in × 19ft × 9ft, 360ihp = 9kts, 1–3pdr, complement 53); she was used on fisheries and surveying duties until discarded in 1933.

Spain

The Spanish Navy in 1906 had scarcely recovered from the traumatic events of 1898. New construction had been very slow: the redesigned *Cataluña* was still not complete, while the cruiser *Reina Regente* had been seven years on the stocks. However, the long years of neglect and peculation that had sent antiquated ships and gallant men to their doom in Manila Bay and off Santiago de Cuba were almost over. In November 1907 a major programme of naval reorganisation was adopted by the Cortes, and became the Navy Law of 7 January 1908.

NAVY LAW OF 1908

The Law was in three parts. The Naval dockyards would be placed on a new and more efficient footing. The works and plant at the dockyards would be leased to private Spanish companies for the construction of large ships. Foreign technical assistance was essential; the Sociedad Española de Construccion Naval (SECN), a new company in which a British consortium of Sir W G Armstrong, Whitworth Ltd, John Brown & Co and Vickers Ltd was the managing authority holding 40 per cent of the capital and providing intially 5 per cent of the workforce), took over the dockyards at Ferrol, Cartagena, Matagorda (Cadiz), Sestao (Bilbao) and Santander, and created shipbuilding yards. The SECN also built large factories for producing heavy guns, gun-mountings and shells at Carraca (Cadiz) and Reinosa (near Santander), for which the British firms supplied materials and skilled supervision of work; armour plating was also supplied by the consortium. Further modernisation work undertaken included the building of a large graving dock at Ferrol, 573ft × 82ft × 37ft depth, with 28ft of water over the sill at low water – the harbour and basin were also dredged to this depth. New turbine shops were built at Ferrol and Cartagena. The essential infrastructure thus provided, and the Ministry and personnel also reorganised by the Law, work on the new construction programme of 3 battleships of 15,000 tons, 3 destroyers or submarines, 24 torpedo-boats and 4 gunboats could begin. Designs for the new ships were competitive and not exclusively British. For example, in considering the new battleships, it was found that the British 12in gun mountings guaranteed 2 rounds per minute, with loading at all angles of elevation and training, whereas the German equivalent could only manage one round per minute, as loading was at all angles of elevation but central training. The French Normand Company gave extensive assistance with the new torpedo-boats.

The 1907 Programme was to be ready by 1914; in 1913, with work going to plan, the government introduced a second programme, for 3 battleships of 21,000 tons to constitute a Second Squadron, 2 scout cruisers of 5000 or 6000 tons, 9 destroyers and 3 submarines. New naval bases were to be built, the most important at Port Mahon (Minorca) and Ceuta (Spanish Morocco). In 1914 a bill providing for an annual vote of £1,440,000 to pay for the new programme was introduced in the Cortes.

NEUTRALITY 1914–18

Some ships of the 1907 programme were still building at the onset of World War One; the trio of battleships proposed in 1913 were never begun. The Law of 30 July 1914 provided for one cruiser, and the Law of 17 February 1915 for 2 more cruisers, 3 destroyers, 10 submarines and 3 gunboats, but naval construction during and just after 1914–18 was very slow. The British consortium was fully occupied at home, and could not deliver materials without great delay.

Spanish neutrality was successfully maintained, although a strong section of authority, including the Conservative and Clerical factions, favoured the Central Powers. The country was able to enjoy the fruits of neutrality yet was relatively unaffected by the war, with living conditions almost normal. Allied pressure was necessary to ensure that German agencies in Spain were closely supervised, and private radio stations sending out cipher messages suppressed. German influence in the Canaries was strong, and the authorities reluctant to intern German auxiliaries that dodged in and out of the islands. Spanish control of her African coast was also weak; for nine days of August 1914 the raider *Kaiser Wilhelm der Grosse* used territorial waters at Rio de Oro as a base, where she met four colliers and supply ships. She was attacked and sunk there by HMS *Highflyer* because she refused to move out.

U-boat warfare produced many converts to the Allied cause, already supported by Republicans and some Liberals. In October 1916 Spain prevented U-boats using her waters for refuelling or revictualling. When they continued to attack Spanish fruit carriers, in contravention of guaranteed immunity, Madrid went further. After the stay of *UC 52* at Cadiz (11–27 June 1917) to repair defective engines, it was decided to intern any belligerent submarine entering Spanish territorial waters. Four U-boats, damaged in action or otherwise strained by events, were interned by November 1918: they were *UB 23* at Corunna (30 July 1917), *UC 48* at Ferrol (3 March 1918), *U 39* at Cartagena (18 May 1918) and *UC 56* at Santander (24 May 1918). To these were added *U 35* and *UC 74* at Barcelona after the armistice; all were handed over to the Allies early in 1919, except *UC 48*, scuttled by its crew on March 1919. *UB 49*, damaged in action with an armed yacht, entered Cadiz on 9 September 1917 and was interned, but the captain broke parole on 6 October and to Spanish annoyance the submarine escaped. *U 35* had landed two agents and an immediately seized consignment of anthrax germs (12 cases) off Cartagena on 14 February 1918 having collected Leutnant zur See Wilhelm Canaris (destined chief of Hitler's *Abwehr*) from his efforts to set up U-boat fuel points in October 1916. In 1918 Germany and Spain reached an agreement arising from friction over the submarine sinkings: to offset Spanish losses, German ships in Spanish ports would be made over to Spanish companies. This measure, poor recompense for the 260,000 tons of Spanish ships sunk, was not recognised by the Allies, and none of the seven ships actually transferred sailed before the end of the war. Ironically, British Naval Intelligence's Spanish section, led by Royal Marine Colonel Charles Thornton from Gibraltar, had been so active and effective that the Spanish Government requested Rear Admiral 'Blinker' Hall not to close it down.

The year after 1918 brought no domestic peace, and rising tension in Morocco, where brigand-like Riff tribal chiefs refused to submit to the Spanish Protectorate established in 1912. Attempts to force a military solution were halted temporarily by the disastrous Spanish defeat at Annual (1921). The British consortium returned to its functions, and the SECN yards were kept fully occupied completing the ships provided by the 1908, 1914 and 1915 Laws; an ambitious postwar programme of new construction, proposing 4 battlecruisers of *c*30,000 tons, 4 light cruisers of 6000 tons, 12 destroyers of 1000 tons, 25 ocean-going submarines and 30 minesweepers was so unrealistic in the new international climate that it was not presented to the Cortes. The Navy was, however, reinforced by six ex-British motor launches to patrol the North African coast.

BASES AND ORGANISATION

The principal naval bases were at Ferrol, which had the big shipyard and large fuel depots and was strongly fortified, Cartagena, with a smaller yard and a repair establishment for submarines, and Carraca (Cadiz), the base for Moroccan gunboats. They were supplemented by smaller stations at Port Mahon (Balearic Islands), Vigo, Marin and Arosa Bay. The Navy could also use private docks in the commercial ports of Barcelona, Bilbao, Santander and Gijon. The organisation of the fleet varied according to the season. In the winter of 1920–21, it fully manned Training Squadron of battleships *Alfonso XIII* and *España* and 4 destroyers.

Training Division: cruiser *Carlos V* (flagship), battleship *Pelayo* (gunnery), 1 destroyer, 5 torpedo-boats and old corvettes *Nautilus*, based at Vigo.

The cruiser *Reina Regente* detached for foreign training cruises.

For service on the African Coast, Canary and Balearic Islands, fishery protection, coast guard etc: the cruisers *Cataluña*, *P de Asturias*, *Rio de la Plata*, *Estramadura*, gunboats, 17 torpedo-boats and 4 submarines.

Naval personnel totalled about 10,000 in 1912 and 18,000, including 4200 marines, in 1921; in 1908 the naval vote was approximately £1,900,000 and in 1921 £4,750,000. The mercantile marine in 1914 consisted of 479 steamers of 420,000 tons and 80 sailing ships of 23,000 tons. These figures increased to 600 steamers of 1,000,000 tons and 230 sailing ships of 55,000 tons in 1920–21.

FLEET STRENGTH 1906

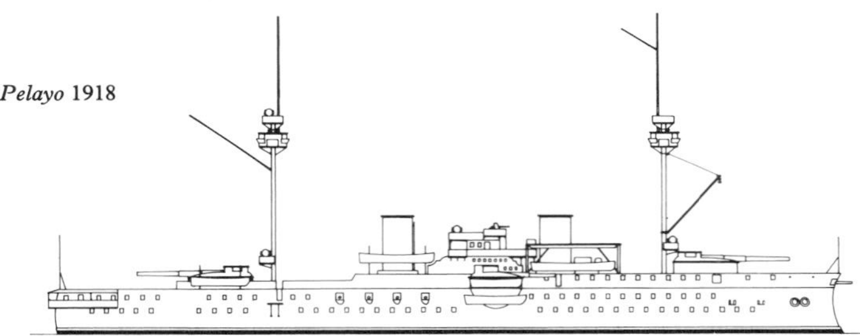

Pelayo 1918

BATTLESHIPS

Name	Launched	Disp (deep load)	Fate
PELAYO	5.2.87	9745t	BU 1925

Pelayo underwent a major refit in 1910, when the TT were removed. She was in use in 1920–21 as gunnery TS in the Training Division.

The old broadside ironclads *Numancia* and *Vitoria*, which had been rearmed with modern guns in 1897–98, were in service as TS in 1906. Neither had much fighting value except for harbour defence; *Numancia* was non-seagoing from 1909 until BU *c*1920, while *Vitoria* was non-seagoing from *c*1906 until BU *c*1910.

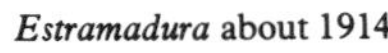

Estramadura about 1914 *Aldo Fraccaroli Collection*

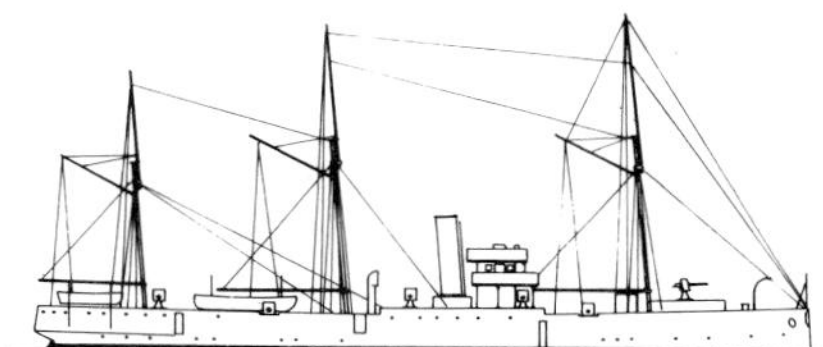

Infanta Isabel 1920

CRUISERS

Name	Launched	Disp (deep load)	Fate
Velasco class			
INFANTA ISABEL	26.6.85	1152t	Stricken 1927
ISABEL II	19.2.86	1152t	Stricken 1907
CONDE DE VENADITO	15.8.88	1152t	Stricken 1907
Alfonso XII class			
ALFONSO XII	21.9.87	3042t	Sold 1907
Reina Regente class (old)			
LEPANTO	1892	4725t	Discarded 1912
Emperador Carlos V class			
EMPERADOR CARLOS V	13.3.95	9090t	BU 1933
Cataluna class			
PRINCESA DE ASTURIAS	17.10.96	7524t	Discarded 1929
CATALUÑA	24.9.00	7524t	Discarded 1929
Plata class			
RIO DE LA PLATA	17.9.98	1875t	Discarded 1929
Estramadura class			
ESTRAMADURA	30.4.00	2030t	Discarded 1930
Reina Regente class (new)			
REINA REGENTE	20.9.06	5287t	Discarded 1926

Infanta Isabel was rebuilt in 1911; her 1921 armament was 1–66mm and 10–57mm, and complement 194, with other data unchanged.

Rio de la Plata was equipped for minelaying *c*1920.

DESTROYERS

Name	Launched	Disp (deep load)	Fate
AUDAZ	6.2.97	430t	BU 1925
OSADO	16.3.97	430t	BU 1925
PROSERPINA	25.10.97	457t	BU 1931
TERROR	28.8.96	450t	BU 1924

All four were equipped for minelaying *c*1920.

FIRST CLASS TORPEDO-BOATS

Name	Launched	Disp	Fate
ACEVEDO	1885	66t	Discarded 1910
JULIAN ORDONEZ	1885	66t	Discarded 1908
ORION	24.11.85	88t	Discarded 1908
BARCEZÓ	1886	65t	Discarded 1908
BUSTAMENTE	1887	65t	Discarded 1910
HABANA	1886	67t	Discarded 1910
AZOR	1887	100t	Discarded 1925
HALCÓN	1887	100t	Discarded 1925

Azor and *Halcón* were refitted with Yarrow water-tube boilers in 1907.

The 3 third class 'vedette' boats built by White in 1892 (60ft × 9.3ft × ?, 18.3 knots) were discarded in 1908.

SUBMARINE

Name	Launched	Disp	Fate
PERAL	8.9.88	87t	Discarded 1909

TORPEDO GUNBOATS

Name	Launched	Disp	Fate
DESTRUCTOR	29.7.86	348t	Discarded 1911
Temerario class			
TEMERARIO	1889	562t	Sold 1920
NUEVA ESPAÑA (ex-*Velox*)	1889	562t	Discarded 1916
MARQUES DE MOLINS	1891	562t	Discarded 1922
MARTIN ALONZO PINZON	1889	562t	Discarded 1914
VINCENTE YANEZ PINZON	1891	562t	Discarded 1914
Dona Maria de Molina class			
DOÑA MARIA DE MOLINA	9.10.96	830t	Discarded 1926
MARQUES DE LA VITORIA	4.2.97	830t	Discarded 1926
DON ALVARO DE BAZAN	14.9.97	830t	Discarded 1926

Temerario class
Temerario became a commercial tug in 1920. *Marques de Molins* was reboilered with one funnel *c*1918 (both this ship and *Temerario* were built with two closely spaced funnels); the armament in 1921 was 4–57mm, 3 MG.

Doña Maria de Molina class
By 1921, the three ships of this class differed completely in appearance. The class nameship retained her two closely spaced funnels, but the *Marques de la Vitoria* was reconstructed in 1917–18 with a single funnel, and the *Don Alvaro de Bazan* had two widely spaced funnels; the 1921 armaments were 8–57mm (*Don Alvaro de Bazan* 6–57mm, 2–47mm), 2 MG.

SLOOPS AND GUNBOATS

Name	Launched	Disp	Fate
GENERAL CONCHA	28.12.83	515t	Lost June 1913
Hernan Cortes class			
HERNAN CORTES	1895	295t	Discarded 1927
VASCO NUNEZ DE BALBOA	1895	295t	Discarded 1927
PONCE DE LEON	1896	250t	Discarded 1910s
MACMAHON	1887	114t	Discarded 1932

General Concha was wrecked on the Moroccan coast

RIVER GUNBOAT

Name	Launched	Disp	Fate
PERLA	1887	42t	Discarded 1925

MISCELLANEOUS
In addition to the above, the Royal Yacht *Giralda* (built Govan 1894, bought 1898) could be employed as a sloop/dispatch vessel/patrol boat in wartime (2450t, 20kts, 2–57mm); she was specially refitted for oceanographic research in 1921 and loaned to the Prince of Monaco.

Don Alvaro de Bazan about 1921
Aldo Fraccaroli Collection

MAJOR SURFACE SHIPS

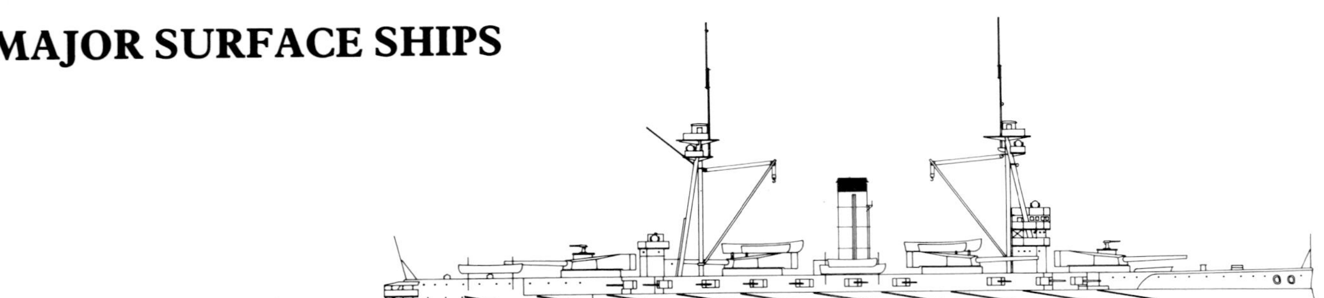

España 1914

These ships were authorised by the Navy Law of 7 January 1908 and built by the SECN syndicate; they were the smallest battleships of the dreadnought type ever constructed, the speed, protection and freeboard (about 15ft amidships) being well below average. To avoid rebuilding existing docks, they were built shorter than if a fully rational design were possible. The main belt was 6ft 7in deep (2ft above water) and extended between the end barbettes. The Bullivant net defence was fitted. For the end 12in turrets, the arcs of fire were about 270°, and for the echelon turrets 180° and 80°; the guns were 24ft 6in above water, manoeuvred by hydraulic power, with all-round loading at any elevation. The Vickers-type directors were in the lower top on each mast. *Jaime I* first went to sea in 1917, but her completion was much delayed by non-delivery of material, particularly armament, from Britain 1914–19. *España* hit an uncharted reef off Cape Tres Forcas (Morocco), near Melilla, in dense fog. *Alfonso XIII* (renamed *España* in April 1931) was laid up at Ferrol in 1934 awaiting disposal; refitted in 1936, she was sunk on a mine laid by her own (Nationalist) side off Cape Penas, near Santander. *Jaime I*, although refloated after the 1937 magazine explosion and fire, was officially discarded on 3 July 1939 as beyond economic repair.

ESPAÑA class *battleships*

Displacement: 15,452t normal; 15,700t max
Dimensions: 435ft wl, 459ft 2in oa × 78ft 9in × 25ft 6in max
132.6m, 140.0m × 24.0m × 7.8m
Machinery: 4-shaft Parsons turbines, 12 Yarrow boilers, 15,500shp = 19.5kts. Coal 900t normal, 1900t max + 20t oil. Range 5000nm/3100nm at 10kts/16.75kts
Armour: Belt 8in–4in (203mm–102mm), upper belt 6in (152mm), barbettes 10in (254mm), gunhouses 8in (203mm), deck 1.5in (38mm), CT 10in (254mm), anti-torpedo bulkheads 1.5in (38mm)
Armament: 8–12in (305mm)/50 (4×2), 20–4in (102mm)/50, 4–3pdr, 2 MG, 2 landing
Complement: 854

Name	Builder	Laid down	Launched	Comp	Fate
ESPAÑA	Ferrol DYd	6.12.09	5.2.12	23.10.13	Wrecked 26.8.23
ALFONSO XIII	Ferrol DYd	23.2.10	7.5.13	16.8.15	Mined 30.4.37
JAIME I	Ferrol DYd	5.2.12	21.9.14	20.12.21	Lost 17.6.37

Jaime I date unknown
CPL

Projected *battleships*

Displacement: *c*21,000t normal
Machinery: 4-shaft Parsons turbines *c*21kts
Armament: 8–13.5in (343mm)/45 (4×2), 20–6in (152mm)

The construction of three battleships, A (possibly to have been named *Reina Victoria Eugenia*), B and C was proposed in 1913; they were to be laid down in 1914–15 and completed in 1920. The World War caused the whole project to be abandoned; full particulars are not available, but the ships would probably have resembled contemporary British practice, with two closely-spaced funnels and superimposed turrets fore and aft.

Republica (ex-*Reina Victoria Eugenia*) about 1934
Aldo Fraccaroli Collection

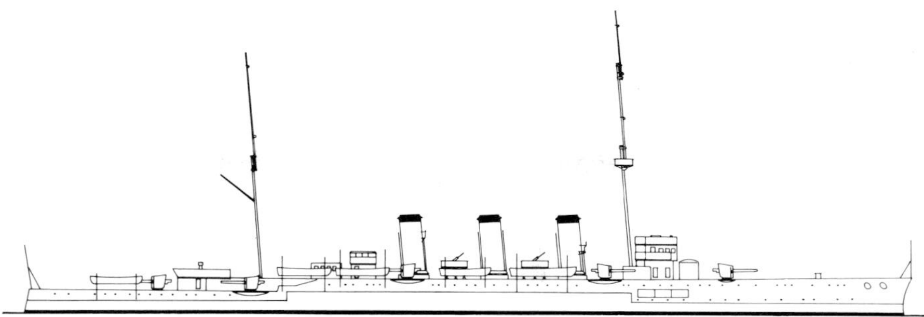

Reina Victoria Eugenia as completed

This ship was built under the Navy Law of 30 July 1914, to a design practically identical with improved *Birmingham* class British light cruisers, but with the boilers rearranged in three boiler rooms, and one less funnel. Her construction was greatly delayed by the Great War. At least one and possibly three more ships of this design were proposed, but the smaller *Mendez Nunez* type was preferred. *Reina Victoria Eugenia* was renamed *Republica* in 1931 and *Navarra* in 1936, and rebuilt 1937–38

REINA VICTORIA EUGENIA *cruiser*

Displacement: 5502t normal
Dimensions: 440ft pp, 462ft oa × 49ft 8in × 15ft 9in mean
134.1m, 140.8m × 15.1m × 4.8m
Machinery: 2-shaft Parsons turbines, 12 Yarrow boilers, 25,500shp = 25.5kts. Coal 660t
Armour: Belt 3in–1.25in (76mm–32mm), deck 3in (76mm), CT 6in (152mm)
Armament: 9–6in (152mm)/50, 4–3pdr AA, 4 MG, 1 landing, 4–21in (533mm) TT (2×2)
Complement: 404

Name	Builder	Laid down	Launched	Comp	Fate
REINA VICTORIA EUGENIA	Ferrol DYd	3.15	21.4.20	15.1.23	Stricken 1956

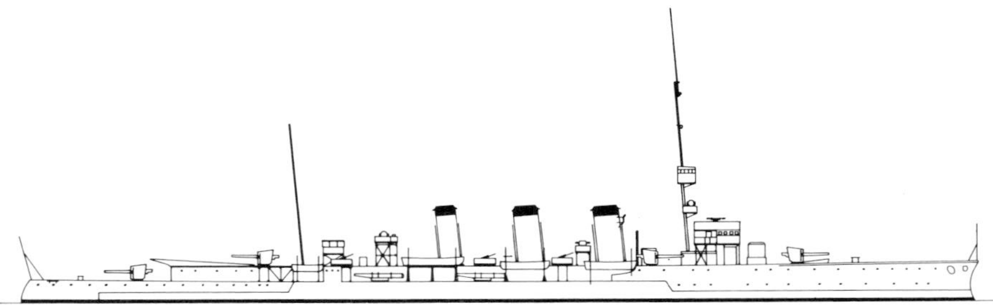

Blas de Lezo 1926

These ships were built under the Navy Law of 17 February 1915 to a design generally similar to that of the British 'C' class light cruisers. Their construction proceeded very slowly because of shortages of shipbuilding materials during and after 1914–18. Six boilers were for oil burning, six for mixed firing. Two further ships of this class, previously projected, were cancelled in 1919. *Blas de Lezo* grounded on the Centollo Reef off Cape Finisterre at speed, and although refloated, sank in deep water. *Mendez Nunez* was damaged on the same occasion. She was reconstructed as an AA cruiser in 1944–47.

MENDEZ NUNEZ class *cruisers*

Displacement: 4650t normal
Dimensions: 410ft pp, 462ft oa × 46ft × 14ft 4in mean, 15ft 6in max
125.0m, 140.8m × 14.0m × 4.4m, 4.7m
Machinery: 4-shaft Parsons geared turbines, 12 Yarrow boilers, 45,000shp = 29kts. Coal 250t normal, 787t max + 492t oil
Armour: Belt 3in–1.25in (76mm–38mm), deck 1in (25mm), CT 6in (152mm)
Armament: 6–6in (152mm)/50, 4–3pdr AA, 4 MG, 1 landing, 12–21in (533mm) TT (4×3)
Complement: 343

Name	Builder	Laid down	Launched	Comp	Fate
MENDEZ NUNEZ	Ferrol DYd	28.9.17	3.3.23	1924	Discarded 1963
BLAS DE LEZO	Ferrol DYd	9.4.17	27.7.22	3.25	Wrecked 11.7.32

Mendez Nunez about 1939

Villamil as completed — *Aldo Fraccaroli Collection*

Velasco between the wars — *CPL*

Torpedo-boats *14* and *16* — *Aldo Fraccaroli Collection*

BUSTAMANTE class *destroyers*

Displacement: 530t normal
Dimensions: 221ft 3in × 22ft × 5ft 6in
67.4m × 6.7m × 1.7m
Machinery: 3-shaft Parsons turbines, Yarrow or Normand boilers, 6250shp = 28kts. Coal 80t. Range 900nm/15kts
Armament: 5–57mm (6pdr), 4–18in (457mm) TT (2×2) (*Cardarso* 4–15in TT (2×2))
Complement: 70

Name	Builder	Launched	Fate
BUSTAMANTE	Cartagena DYd	1913	BU 1931
CARDARSO (ex-*Requesens*)	Cartagena DYd	1914	BU 1930
VILLAMIL	Cartagena DYd	5.12.13	BU 1932

This class was built under the Navy Law of 7 January 1908 by the SECN syndicate to a Vickers design. All were fitted for minelaying. Plans to sell the class to Mexico in 1924 fell through.

ALSEDO class *destroyers*

Displacement: 1145t normal; 1315t full load
Dimensions: 275ft pp, 283ft oa × 27ft × 15ft max
83.8m, 86.3m × 8.2m × 4.6m
Machinery: 2-shaft Parsons geared turbines, 4 Yarrow boilers, 33,000shp = 34kts. Oil 272t. Range 2500nm/15kts
Armament: 3–4in (102mm)/45, 2-2pdr AA, 4–21in (533mm) TT (2×2)
Complement: 70

Name	Builder	Launched	Fate
ALSEDO	Cartagena DYd	26.10.22	Stricken 1957
JUAN LAZAGA	Cartagena DYd	3.24	Stricken 1961
VELASCO	Cartagena DYd	6.23	Stricken 1957

This class was built under the Navy Law of 17 February 1915, and the first unit was laid down in 1920. The design generally resembled the British *Nimrod* class. The name of the second unit was later shortened to *Lazaga*, and the three were identified by the initial letters of their names painted on their bows. The 2pdr AA were replaced by 4–20mm AA in the 1930s, while *c*1945 2 DCT were added, and the complement increased to 86. A proposal to replace the 4in gun between the funnels with 1–3.5in (88mm) AA was not implemented. *Velasco* and auxiliaries sank the Republican submarine *B 6* off Cape Penas (near Santander) on 19 August 1936 at the start of the Civil War.

No 1 type *torpedo boats*

Displacement: 177t normal
Dimensions: 164ft × 16ft 6in × 6ft 4in max
50.0m × 5.0m × 1.9m
Machinery: 3-shaft (*Nos 8–22* 2-shaft) Parsons turbines, Normand boilers, 3750shp =26kts. Coal 33t
Armament: 3–47mm (3pdr), 3–18in (457mm) TT (1×2, 1×1)
Complement: 31

Class (launched, fate):
Cartagena DYd – *1* (1912, BU 1931), *2* (1911, discarded *c*1939), *3* (1912, wrecked 3.9.36), *4* (1912, scuttled 4.39), *5* (1912, BU 1931), *6* (1912, BU 1932), *7* (1914, BU *c*1944), *8* (1914, BU 1932), *9* (1915, discarded *c*1943), *10* (1916, BU 1932), *11* (1915, BU 1931), *12* (1915, BU 1932), *13* (1914, BU 1932), *14* (1915, discarded 1952), *15* (1916, BU 1935), *16* (1916, discarded *c*1943), *17* (1918, BU 1952), *18* (1918, discarded *c*1939), *19* (1918, discarded *c*1943), *20* (1918, scuttled 4.39), *21* (1919, scuttled 4.39), *22* (1919, scuttled 4.39)

A total of 24 boats of this Vickers-Normand type were authorised by the Navy Law of 7 January 1908, but *23* and *24* were cancelled in 1919. In later years, the number of TT installed was less than in the table, the single or even both mountings being removed, and the boats were used for minelaying. The four boats scuttled in April 1939 were raised and scrapped.

SUBMARINES

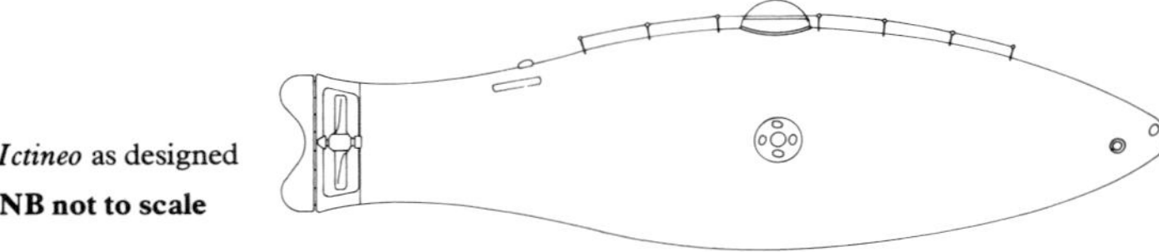

Ictineo as designed
NB not to scale

PERAL *submarine*

Displacement: 87t
Dimensions: 70ft × 8ft 6in × ?ft
21.3m × 2.6m × ?m
Machinery: 2-shaft electric motors, 60hp = 10kts
Armament: 1 TT (bow; 3 torpedoes)
Complement: 6?

Name	Builder	Launched	Fate
PERAL	Carraca, Cadiz	8.9.88	Discarded 1909

This boat was designed by Lt Isaac Peral y Caballero (1851–95), laid down on 23 October 1887 and commissioned 7 June 1890 after running trials, including a trip to Cartagena. She dived and surfaced using ballast tanks and vertical screws, below the cigar-shaped hull forward and aft. The motors were powered by accumulators, and two spare Schwartzkopf torpedoes could be carried. The dimensions are also given as *22.0m × 2.3m*. Listed in 1906, but of no fighting value.

Peral was the second Spanish submarine: the single shaft, steam-powered *Ictineo*, designed by Narciso Monturiol, was launched at Barcelona in 1859 and ran trials from September 1860 to March 1861, when extensive official tests were carried out at Alicante. A second, larger *Ictineo* was proposed in 1864–66 but never built.

Peral preserved as a monument — *Aldo Fraccaroli Collection*

Isaac Peral 1919
NB 1/750 scale

ISAAC PERAL *submarine*

Displacement: 488t/750t
Dimensions: 197ft × 19ft × 11ft
60.0m × 5.8m × 3.4m
Machinery: 2 shafts, 2 Nelseco diesels plus electric motors, 1000bhp/480shp = 15kts/10kts. Range 240nm/70nm at 4.5kts/11kts
Armament: 4–18in (457mm) TT (bow), 1–3in AA
Complement: 24

Name	Builder	Launched	Fate
ISAAC PERAL	Fore River Co	27.7.16	Hulked 1930, numbered *A 0*

This Holland type boat was built under the Navy Law of 17 February 1915 and was very similar to the US submarine *M 1*. Nelseco diesels were MAN diesels built in the USA under licence. The gun was on a disappearing mounting. Her name was transferred to submarine *O 1* in 1930.

'A' class *submarines*

Displacement: 260t/382t
Dimensions: 149ft 7in × 13ft 10in × 10ft 2in
45.6m × 4.2m × 3.1m
Machinery: 2 shafts, 2 Fiat 6-cyl diesels plus electric motors, 600bhp/450shp = 13kts/8.5kts. Range 1600nm/650nm at 8.5kts/13kts surfaced, 85nm/18nm at 4kts/8kts submerged
Armament: 2–18in (457mm) TT (bow)
Complement: 18

Name	Builder	Launched	Fate
NARCISO MONTURIOL (A 1)	Fiat San Giorgio	1917	Discarded 1930s
COSME GARCIA (A 2)	Fiat San Giorgio	1917	Discarded 1930s
A 3	Fiat San Giorgio	1917	Discarded 1930s

These Laurenti-Fiat type boats were built at Spezia in 1915–17 under the Navy Law of 17 February 1915. The maximum diving depth was about 130ft (about 40m) and there were eight watertight compartments.

'B' class *submarines*

Displacement: 491t/715t
Dimensions: 205ft pp, 210ft 4in oa × 17ft 4in × 11ft 3in
62.5m, 64.1m × 5.6m × 3.4m
Machinery: 2 shafts, 2 Nelseco 8-cyl diesels plus two electric motors, 1400bhp/850shp = 16kts/10kts. Range 8000nm/125nm at 10.5kts/4.5kts
Armament: 4–18in (457mm) TT, 1–3in
Complement: 28

Name	Builder	Launched	Fate
B 1	Cartagena DYd	2.6.21	Scuttled 4.39
B 2	Cartagena DYd	1922	BU 1948
B 3	Cartagena DYd	1922	Scuttled 4.39
B 4	Cartagena DYd	1922	Scuttled 4.39
B 5	Cartagena DYd	1923	Sunk 12.10.36
B 6	Cartagena DYd	1923	Sunk 19.9.36

These six Holland type boats, of an enlarged and improved *Isaac Peral* type, were built under the Navy Law of 15 February 1915; construction began in July 1916. They were originally to have been numbered *A 4–A 9*. The three boats scuttled at Cartagena or Pormon by the Republicans at the end of the Civil War in April 1939 were subsequently salved and scrapped; *B 2*, scuttled at the same time, was raised and used as a generator plant until scrapped. *B 5* was sunk by Nationalist aircraft off Malaga.

B 6 about 1930 — *Aldo Fraccaroli Collection*

SMALL SURFACE WARSHIPS

RECALDE class *gunboats*

Displacement: 811t normal
Dimensions: 213ft 9in × 30ft × 9ft 6in max
65.2m × 9.1m × 2.9m
Machinery: 2-shaft VTE, Yarrow boilers, 1100shp = 14kts. Coal 148t. Range 3000nm/10kts
Armament: 4–3in (14pdr), 2 MG
Complement: 126–129

Class (launched, fate):
Cartagena DYd – *Recalde* (31.12.10, discarded 1932), *Laya* (1910, sunk by Nationalist aircraft at Valencia 15.6.38), *Bonifaz* (1911, discarded 1932), *Lauria* (1912, discarded 1930s)

These four ships were built under the Navy Law of 7 January 1908.

CASTILLO class *gunboats*

Displacement: 1314t standard; 1335t normal
Dimensions: 236ft 4in pp, 251ft 4in oa × 33ft 9in × 11ft 9in
72.0m, × 76.6m × 10.3m × 3.6m
Machinery: 2-shaft VTE, 2 Yarrow boilers, 1700ihp = 15kts. Coal or oil fuel 324t. Range 6500nm/10.5kts
Armament: 4–4in (102mm), 2–47mm AA, 2 pompoms (landing)
Complement: 132 (later 220)

Class (launched, fate):
Cartagena DYd – *Antonio Canovas del Castillo* (21.1.22, stricken 1959), *José Canalejas* (1.12.22, stricken 1953), *Eduarto Dato* (July 1923, stricken 1954).

This class of three gunboats was authorised by the Navy Law of 17 February 1915, but was not ordered until January 1920 nor completed until 1923–24. The names were shortened *c*1930 by the omission of the first word. The post-Civil War armament was 4–4in (*Canalejas* 4–4.1in), 2–3in AA, 2 pompoms (landing).

Recalde date unknown — *Aldo Fraccaroli Collection*

Eduarto Data as completed — *Aldo Fraccaroli Collection*

Cosme Garcia as completed — *Aldo Fraccaroli Collection*

Cartagenera 1919
NB 1/750 scale

CARTAGENERA *river gunboat*

Displacement: 27t
Dimensions: 53ft 6in × 11ft 10in × 3ft 11in
16.3m × 3.6m × 1.2m
Machinery: 1-shaft reciprocating, 120ihp = 12kts
Armament: 1–2pdr (40mm) pompom

Class (launched, fate):
Cartagenera (1908, discarded 1925)

Ex-British *motor launches*

Class (former number, fate):
M 1 (ex-*ML 179*), *M 2* (ex-*ML 185*), *M 3* (ex-*ML 205*), *M 4* (ex-*ML 239*), *M 5* (ex-*ML 503*), *M 6* (ex-*ML 532*)

All six purchased in 1921 for use as patrol boats on the Moroccan coast. *M 3* was destroyed by fire *c*1925, and *M 2* and *M 4* deleted *c*1926; the remaining boats, apparently renumbered *H 1–H 3*, were discarded in the 1930s.

AUXILIARY WARSHIPS
There were three coastguard and fisheries vessels, *Delfin*, *Dorado* and *Gaviota* (launched 1910–11, 158t, 11kts, 1–57mm (5pdr)), and the tug *Anteo* (launched 1903, 342t, 131ft 2in × 21ft 7in × 6ft 9in, 650ihp = 11kts, 32t coal, fitted for minelaying and minesweeping, 40 mines). They were discarded in 1927, 1929, 1932 and 1932 respectively.

The proposed construction of the 15 coast guard vessels *Esmeralda*, *Intrepida*, *Pronta*, *Liebre*, *Santa Maria* (or *Santa Marta*), *Serpiente*, *Cuervo*, *San Juan*, *Cedida*, *San Matteo*, *Dolores*, *Radiante*, *Flecha*, *Garza* and *Pez*, projected in April 1917 (300t, 114ft 9in × 19ft 8in × ?ft, 2-shaft diesels, 16kts, complement 70, fitted for minelaying and sweeping in wartime), was abandoned in 1921.

Greece

The Greek Navy played a major role in the 1821–1829 War for Independence against the Ottoman Empire. From that time the Turks were the most probable enemies and relations between the two nations dominated the development of their naval forces. Greek warships were for years inferior to Turkish ones. The Greek Fleet was too small to support the Cretan Insurrection of 1866–68 so its contribution was confined to running arms and volunteers from the island of Syra in a number of fast steamers. When during the 1860s and 1870s Turkey built several ironclads and a number of smaller units Greece built only two capital ships, the *Basileus Georgios* and *Basilissa Olga*, which for 20 years were her biggest ships. At the time of the Balkan crisis of 1885, comparatively large sums were spent by Greece to increase the Navy with three coastal defence ships and a number of torpedo-boats and gunboats. The 72ft-wide, 26ft-deep, 4-mile long Corinth Canal opened in 1893. In the Thessaly war of 1897 the Fleet supported land operations with no opposition from the Turkish Fleet, which remained inactive, but forceful Great Power naval intervention stopped major hostilities in Crete until Turkey relinquished the island by 5 December 1898.

Little changed in the first years of the new century, although three new battleships were envisaged in 1905, but finally only eight destroyers were built in Britain and Germany in 1906–7. In 1907–8, the French Admiralty had worked out plans to make Greece a naval power, with French material. A suitable law was enacted in Athens to allow French officers to work in Greece, but the scheme was abandoned in the face of violent opposition from Greek naval officers. The sweeping changes in the constitution in 1910–11 allowed the Greek Government to employ foreign specialists in the public service. Thereupon, the Italian Government was asked to help in reforming the gendarmerie, the French, the Army, and the British, the Navy. Between then and 1916 there followed successively three British missions, but at the same time a British naval mission was sent to Constantinople.

GEORGIOS AVEROF BUYS A CRUISER
Growing tensions between the Balkan states caused a naval race and finally a series of wars. Shortly before the outbreak of hostilities in 1912 the Greek Fleet acquired a number of ships of various origins. Using a gift from the millionaire Georgios Averof an armoured cruiser, built as speculation by Orlando, was bought. Four former Argentine and two former German destroyers were acquired. In addition 2 submarines, 6 torpedo-boats were ordered and 9 merchantmen were converted into auxiliary cruisers. Moreover the 3 old *Hydra* class coast defence ships had been rearmed with modern guns.

THE BALKAN WARS 1912–1913
This completely renewed fleet was successfully led by Rear-Admiral Paul Kondouriotis against the Turks during the First Balkan War (from 17 October 1912 to 30 May 1913). Kondouriotis' task was to stop the Turkish Fleet issuing from the Dardanelles and to support the Army in expelling the Turks from Epirus. The latter aim was achieved by Captain Damianos' 2 torpedo-boats and 6 gunboats entering the Gulf of Arta on the night of 18–19 October 1912 past the Turkish forts of Preveza (causing the Turkish torpedo-boat *Antalia* to scuttle) which fell to land attack on 4 November. Kondouriotis sailed from Athens on 18 October with *Averof* , the 3 *Hydra* class ships, 14 destroyers, 5 modern torpedo-boats, the submarine *Delfin*, the minelayer *Ares*, a hospital ship and auxiliaries. On the 21st the Fleet put ashore 500 men to take Lemnos as the base for watching the Dardanelles. Tenedos, Thasos, Imbros, Strati and Samothrace were all occupied unopposed. In November it was the turn of Mitylene and Chios although their garrisons held out until either side of Christmas. Greek ships transported Bulgarian troops from Salonika (taken on 8 November) to Dedeagatch (Alexandroupolis) on the coast of Thrace.

On 3 December an armistice freed Turkey from fighting Bulgaria, Serbia and Montenegro and her fleet was able to concentrate in the Dardanelles. The cruiser *Medjidieh* and 4 destroyers sortied on the 14th only to be driven back under cover of the forts by 7 Greek destroyers. On the 16th the two main fleets met and bombarded each other indecisively for 40 minutes before the Turks retired. Another sortie was countered on the 22nd although the fast cruiser *Hamidieh* broke out undetected on 14 January 1913. Four Turkish armoured ships, *Medjidieh* and 13 torpedo craft came out four days later to within 12 miles of Lemnos before *Averof* began a two-hour gunnery action that sent them scurrying back.

In February 1913 the Greeks made the first use of aircraft in naval warfare when the pilot Mutusis and an observer took off in a seaplane from Mudros Bay (Lemnos). They dropped four bombs on the Turkish squadron, all missing, and spent most of the 2½ hour flight scouting the Gallipoli Peninsula. A destroyer picked them up. The war's last naval operation was the Greek capture of Samos on 14 March. The submarine *Delfin* had already carried out the first twentieth century submarine torpedo attack.

To strengthen the fleet a new battleship was ordered from Vulcan in July 1912. The British naval mission, although it played a part in sea-training and the reorganisation, was irrelevant to Greek purchasing policy. The Greek naval programme of 1911, as suggested by the British mission, included modernisation of the *Hydra* class coast defence ships and building two battleships of 12,000t plus another cruiser of the *Averof* class, but with the sign of peace in May 1913 the British mission was changed and its command was given to Rear-Admiral Sir Mark Kerr who became Chief of Staff to the Greek Navy. The Greek construction programme, as proposed by him, depended on the country's strategic options, whether trouble was envisaged from Turkey-Bulgaria, or from the Triple Alliance. That would determine the priority given to naval bases. In either case, however, dreadnoughts were vulnerable in narrow waters, especially to detection by aircraft in contact with torpedo craft. The latter needed protection from light cruiser attack and their protective forces should be sufficiently powerful to act as bait to draw the enemy dreadnoughts into the danger areas. Kerr identified a balanced Greek Fleet as 3 armoured cruisers, 3 light cruisers, 34 destroyers, 20 submarines, 2 airships, 12 seaplanes and auxiliary vessels. But Turkish attempts to buy dreadnoughts scotched Kerr's programme, even with the suggested addition of buying a dreadnought then under construction for Chile. The official Greek programme called for 2 23,000t battleships, 1 cruiser, 4 destroyers and 1 submarine. This programme was realised with few changes. A French *Provence* class dreadnought was ordered after the Italian *Sardegna* class had been considered, one cruiser was bought in America and some light forces were ordered, including two light cruisers. The approaching delivery of the Turkish dreadnought caused the purchase of two American *Mississippi* class battleships in June 1914, which put Greece ahead for a short time.

THE FIRST WORLD WAR

The situation in August 1914 rapidly meant that the new ships from Germany and especially France were unlikely to materialise so the Greek Minister of Marine asked Admiral Kerr to find out unofficially if the British Government would finance the construction of a *Valiant* type battleship, a *Southampton* type light cruiser and a repair ship by the Coventry Ordnance Works, 4 submarines and a repair ship by Vickers – all to be paid for out of interest on a loan to be raised by Greece at the end of war. The request was turned down.

Greece remained neutral at the outbreak of the First World War. She understandably declined to attack Turkey (especially Gallipoli), when Churchill prompted Admiral Kerr to make soundings in September 1914, unless Bulgaria was on her side. That kingdom had treacherously attacked her in the Second Balkan War of the previous year. But a constitutional crisis that began in March 1915 was compounded by the policies adopted by the Allies under French inspiration after their landings at Salonika in October of that year. The growing animosity in Greece and between the pro-German (Constantine I) King of Greece and the Allies culminated on 19 October 1916 with French forces seizing the Greek Fleet, putting the light flotilla under the French ensign, reducing *Lemnos*, *Kilkis* and *Averof* to skeleton crews, removing the breech blocks from their guns and landing all torpedoes and ammunition. The Greek crisis formally ended when King Constantine rejected an Allied ultimatum and then was forced to abdicate in favour of his son George II. A pro-Allied Government was formed in Salonika by the former prime minister and Cretan statesman Eleutherios Venizelos. Finally on 2 July 1917 Greece declared war against the Central Powers. The Allied Fleets had already made heavy use of Mudros Bay (Lemnos), Imbros, Suda Bay (Crete) and Corfu as bases. There were 12 associated RNAS/RAF stations.

The capitulation of Turkey moved Greece to realise her ambitions for dismembering the Ottoman Empire. On 15 May 1919 Greek forces landed at Smyrna (Izmir) and occupied the western part of the Anatolian peninsula. The Treaty of Sevres (10 August 1920) gave Greece the area around Smyrna, Thrace and islands of Tenedos and Imbros, but the final victory of the Turks in 1922 ended Greek hopes of a foothold in Asia Minor. The Greek Navy, strengthened by former Austro-Hungarian torpedo craft and a number of auxiliary cruisers, supported land operations, made patrol duties and participated in the chaotic final evacuation of the Greek army and civilians (250,000 people) in September 1922. There was no seaborne Turkish opposition as the Allies had interned the Ottoman Fleet at Ismit or Constantinople since 1918. Greek naval personnel numbered about 4000 (2-year conscripts or volunteers) throughout the period. The main arsenal was Salamis with a floating dock (3000t capacity) and the Piraeus had two private dry docks.

FLEET STRENGTH 1906

ARMOURED SHIPS

Name	Launched	Disp	Fate
Basileos Georgios class			
BASILEOS GEORGIOS	28.12.67	1774t	Stricken 1912
Basilissa Olga			
BASILISSA OLGA	26.1.69	2060t	BU 1925
Hydra class			
HYDRA	15.5.89	4885t	BU 1929
SPETSAI	26.10.89	4885t	BU 1929
PSARA	20.2.90	4885t	BU 1929

Basileos Georgios class
She was re-engined and rearmed in 1897 with 1–150mm, 9 MG, 1 TT, retaining her 2–210mm Krupp BL guns. Stricken in 1912 she was sold in 1915.

Basilissa Olga class
She was re-engined in 1897 and rebuilt as a gunnery TS. Deleted *c*1905 she was BU 1925

Hydra class
Rearmed with 5–5.9in/45 QF guns in 1908–10. *Hydra* was deleted 1919 and placed on the sale list 1921, not sold, became a gunnery TS in 1922. *Spetsai* deleted 1919 served after 1922 as a stationary TS. *Psara* deleted 1919, placed on the sale list 1921, not sold, hulk retained as boys school at Poros Island.

CRUISERS

Name	Launched	Disp	Fate
Navarchos Miaoulis class			
NAVARCHOS MIAOULIS	1879	1770t	Sold 1931
Hellas class			
HELLAS	1861	1654t	Stricken 1906

Navarchos Miaoulis class
Stricken in 1912 she was hulked as gunnery TS, then seamen's TS, and then finally sold in 1931.

Hellas class
Originally built as *Amalia* she was renamed *Hellas* in 1862, reconstructed in 1878, she served as school hulk for cadets after 1890.

GUNBOATS

Name	Launched	Disp	Fate
ACHELAOS class	1884	420t	See notes
AMBRAKIA class	1881	440t	See note
KISSA class	1884	86t	See notes
ALFA class	1880	52t	See notes
PARALOS class	1858	360t	See notes
PLIXAVRA class	1857–58	220t	See notes

Achelaos class
Formerly rebuilt in 1895–97, they were seized in December 1916 by the French and served under their flag. The class included *Achelaos* stricken 1925; *Eurotas* stricken 1925; *Pineios* lighthouse tender 1919, stricken 1930; *Alfeios* surveying vessel 1919, renamed *Naftilos* 1925, stricken 1936.

Ambrakia class
Two ships rebuilt in 1910 were *Ambrakia* discarded *c*1931 and *Aktion* deleted 1920. *Aktion* served 1917–18 under French flag.

Kissa class
The class of three ships included *Aidon*, wrecked 1924 off Aegina Island; *Kissa*, ended career as lighthouse tender *c*1937; *Kichli*, used as auxiliary to 1941, then seized by Germans, recovered intact 1944, stricken *c*1945.

Alfa class
Four gunboats, listed also as TBs due to spar torpedo carried were *Alfa* (ex-*Sfaktiria*), *Delta* (ex-*Ambrakia*) both stricken *c*1915 and placed on the sale list 1921; *Gamma* (ex-*Nafpaktia*) sunk 1918 and *Beta* (ex-*Mykali*) sold by 1912 to private owners, repurchased by Serbia, became *Serbija* (qv).

Paralos class
Two ships: *Paralos* stricken 1907 served as floating warehouse to 1913, *Salaminia* became lighthouse tender in 1907, then during 1910–20 served as ferry at Salamis, stricken 1923.

Plixavra class
The class included: *Plixavra* sold 1926; *Afroessa* stricken 1904 and served as hulk, BU 1909; *Syros* (ex-*Panopi*) stricken 1920, placed on the sale list 1921.

TORPEDO-BOATS

Name	Launched	Disp	Fate
NF 11 class	1885	85t	See notes
NF 6 class	1881	48t	See notes
NF 18	1879	31t	See notes

NF 11 class
Apart from *NF 11*, which was wrecked on 13 April 1913 near Mudros Bay (Lemnos) and *NF 12* sunk on 28 March 1900 by boiler explosion in the Salamis Channel, remaining ships, *NF 12* (ii) (ex-*NF 13* renamed 1909) and *NF 14–NF 16* were stricken 1919 and placed on the sale list in 1921.

NF 6 class
The class include *NF 6* (ex-*Samos*), *NF 7* (ex-*Chios*), *NF 8* (ex-*Mytilini*), *NF 9* (ex-*Kos*), *NF 10* (ex-*Rodos*), *NF 17* (ex-*Kypros*), all stricken *c*1910.

NF 18
She was former *Ionia* and was sold in 1913, while her sister ship *Sfinx* stricken in 1901 was used as a water barge till the 1930s.

MINELAYERS

Name	Launched	Disp	Fate
AIGIALEIA class	1881	300t	See notes
KANARIS	1878	870t	See notes

Aigialeia class
The class consisted of *Aigialeia* stricken 1933, *Monemvasia* and *Nefplita*, both stricken *c*1924.

Kanaris
Mine depot ship, till 1889 *Psara*, formerly SS *Gettysburg* (ex-*Walrus*) bought in 1880. Seized in December 1916 by the French, returned in 1918 she was placed on the sale list in 1921, sold in 1923 as a merchant ship, BU 1933 in Italy.

MAJOR SURFACE SHIPS

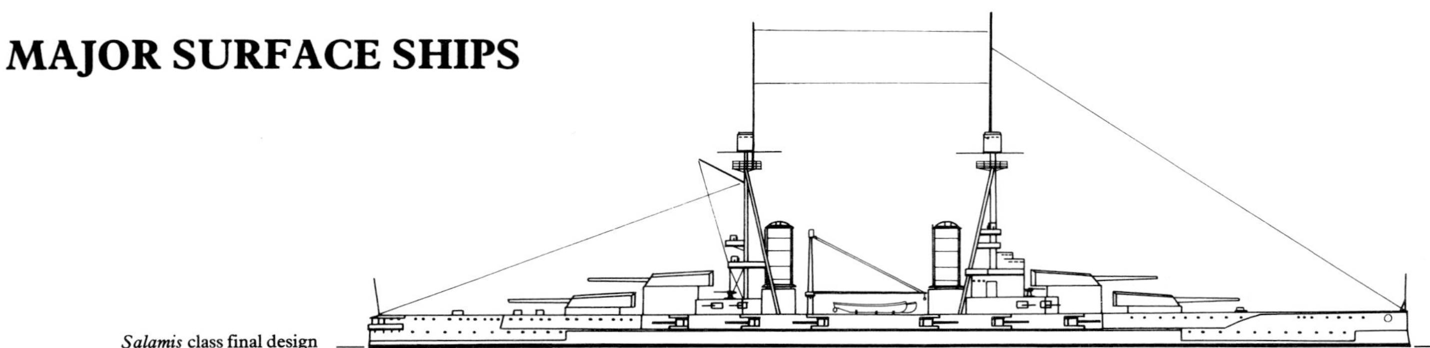
Salamis class final design

SALAMIS class *battleship*

Displacement:	19,500t
Dimensions:	569ft 11in wl × 81ft × 25ft *173.7m × 24.7m × 7.6m*
Machinery:	3-shaft AEG turbines, 18 Yarrow boilers, 40,000shp = 23kts
Armour:	Belt 250mm–100mm (9⅞in–3⅞in), deck 75mm–40mm (2⅞in–1½in), barbettes 250mm (9⅞in), turrets 250mm (9⅞in), CT 30mm (1¼in)
Armament:	8–14in (356mm)/45 (4×2), 12–6in (152mm)/50, 12–75mm QF, 5–500mm (19.7in) TT

Name	Builder	Laid down	Launched	Comp	Fate
SALAMIS	AG Vulcan, Hamburg	23.7.13	11.11.14	Unfinished	BU 1932

She was ordered in July 1912, originally designed for operations in the Aegean with the following particulars: 13,500t, 458ft (pp) × 72ft × 24ft, *139.6m × 22m × 7.4m*, 2 shaft turbines 26,000shp = 21kts, 6–14in/45 (3×2), 8–6in/50 in casemates, 8–3in, 4–37mm AA and 2–450mm (17.7in) TT and protection of belt 10in, barbettes 10in and 12in CT. Design was soon enlarged by the Greeks to 16,500t and finally on 23 December 1912 the contract was changed to a battleship of the particulars mentioned above costing £1,693,000 for delivery in March 1915. Construction work suspended on 31 December 1914. After the war the Greeks refused to accept the incomplete ship and the builders sued the Greek Government in 1923. On 23 April 1932 the arbitrators judged that the Greeks must pay a further £30,000 (apart from £450,000 paid before the war) to Vulcan while the ship remained the builders' property. She was scrapped at Bremen in 1932. Her main and secondary armaments were ordered from Bethlehem Steel (USA) and apart from two barbettes delivered without guns her 14in guns were purchased by Britain and used for *Abercrombie* class monitors.

French PROVENCE class *battleship*

A 23,500t battleship was ordered from C et A de St Nazaire – Penhoët in April 1914 and was to be similar to the French *Provence* class except an additional 12–76mm guns. Work on her began on 12 June 1914 but stopped at the beginning of August and never resumed. She was to be named *Basileus Konstantinos*. Contract dispute settled in 1925.

American MISSISSIPPI class *battleships*

Two American battleships were bought on 30 June 1914 and named *Kilkis* (ex-USS *Mississippi*) and *Limnos* (ex-USS *Idaho*). Their boilers were retubed in 1926–27. In 1932 *Kilkis* was deleted from effective list and used as gunnery TS, whilst *Limnos* was placed in inactive reserve and her armour was used in fortifications on Aegina Island. In 1940–41 *Kilkis* served as floating battery at Salamis where she was sunk on 23 April 1941 by German Ju 87 dive bombers together with her sister.

Kilkis as purchased
CPL

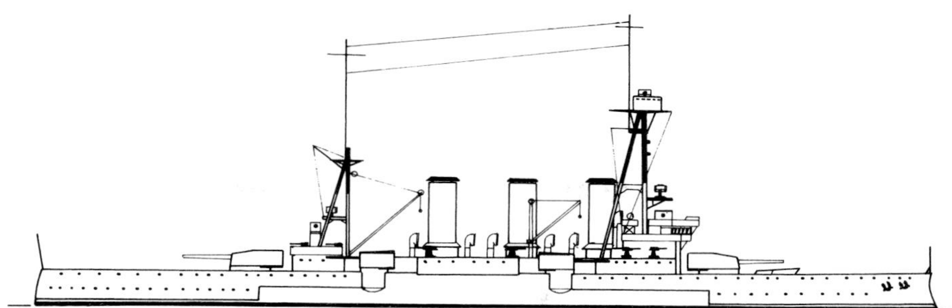

Averof in the 1930s

A near sister to the Italian *Amalfi* and *Pisa* armoured cruisers, the *Averof* was a speculation built ship, formerly known as Italian 'X' cruiser. Bought in October 1909, she was named after a Greek millionaire who left about £300,000 for increasing the Navy. Unlike her Italian sisters, which carried 10in guns, *Averof* was armed with Armstrong 9.2in guns. As the Greek flagship she played an important role in the Balkan Wars of 1912–13. During 1914–18 1–76mm AA was added. She was partially refitted at HM Dockyard, Malta in 1919, then in 1925–27 *Averof* was reboilered and refitted by Forges et Chantiers de la Méditerranée at La Seyne and rearmed with 4–9.2in, 8–7.5in, 4–3in, 2–3in AA, 4–47mm, 5–40mm AA, while TT were removed. She escaped to Alexandria by 25 April 1941 during the German invasion of Greece and did convoy duty in the Indian Ocean after that. In that time she carried apart from her main and secondary armament 8–3in, 4–3in AA, 6–37mm. In 1944–45 *Averof* served as a station ship at Piraeus. Stricken in 1946, she still exists as a memorial at Poros Island, 40 miles south of Athens.

Italian PISA type *armoured cruiser*

Displacement: 9958t normal
Dimensions: 462ft oa, 426ft pp × 69ft × 24ft 8in
140.8m, 129.8m × 21.0m × 7.5m
Machinery: 2-shaft VTE, 22 Belleville boilers, 19,000ihp = 22.5kts (designed). Coal 660/1500t. Range 7125nm/10kts
Armour: Belt 203mm–83mm (8in–3¼in), deck 50mm (2in), turrets 203mm (8in), CT 178mm (7in)
Armament: 4–9.2in (234mm)/45 (2×2), 8–7.5in (190mm)/45 (4×2), 16–76mm (3in), 2–47mm, 3–457mm (18in) TT
Complement: 670

Name	Builder	Laid down	Launched	Comp	Fate
(GEORGIOS) AVEROF	Orlando & Co, Livorno	1907	12.3.10	5.11	Stricken 1946

Averof as completed
Aldo Fraccaroli Collection

Helle before 1939

She was ordered in 1910 by the Chinese Navy, but due to the Chinese Revolution *Fei Hung* (as she was named) was offered to sale and finally bought in 1914 by Greece and renamed *Helle*. On trials she made 8640shp = 21kts. The armament was supplied by Armstrong. She served under the French flag 1916–17. In 1926–28 she was reconstructed as cruiser/minelayer by FCM, La Seyne. Her poop and rigging were removed, her engine renewed and boilers replaced by 3 Yarrow oil burners only, the superstructure was transformed by a modern style bridge, new tripod mast and new funnels. A Vicero type fire control system was installed. Her new particulars were:
Displacement: 2115t (standard)
Machinery: 7200shp = 20.5kts (in 1940 only 18kts)
Armament: 3–6in/50, 2–3in AA, 2–40mm, 2–18in TT, 110 mines

Helle was torpedoed and sunk by the Italian submarine *Delfino* while at anchor off Tinos Island before Italy invaded Greece.

Chinese CHAO HO class *cruiser*

Displacement: 2600t normal
Dimensions: 322ft oa, 320ft pp × 39ft × 14ft
98.1m, 97.5m × 11.9m × 4.3m
Machinery: 3-shaft Parsons turbines, 3 Thornycroft watertube boilers, 6000shp = 18kts (designed). Coal 400/600t and oil 100t
Armour: Deck 1in (25mm) on flat, 2in (50mm) on slopes
Armament: 2–6in (152mm)/50, 4–4in (102mm)/50, 2–3in, 6–3pdr, 2–37mm automatics, 2–18in (457mm) TT
Complement: 232

Name	Builder	Laid down	Launched	Comp	Fate
HELLE	New York SB Co	1910	4.5.12	11.13	Sunk 15.8.40

Helle about 1930
Aldo Fraccaroli Collection

KATSONIS class *cruisers*

Two 5200t cruisers were ordered in June 1914 from Cammell Laird called *Katsonis* and *Kountouriotis*. They were requisitioned and purchased on the stocks and completed as HMS *Chester* and HMS *Birkenhead* respectively. See British *Birkenhead* class for full treatment.

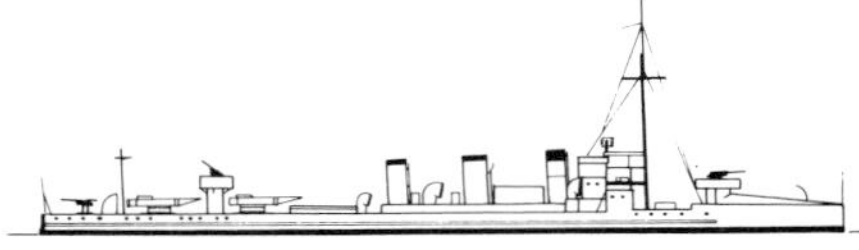
Aspis as completed

NIKI class *destroyers*

Displacement:	350t full load
Dimensions:	219ft 10in × 21ft 8in × 8ft 10in *67.0m × 6.6m × 2.7m*
Machinery:	2-shaft TE, 4 Navy type boilers, 6800ihp = 30kts (in 1940 25kts). Coal 90t
Armament:	2–12pdr (76mm or 3in), 4–6pdr (57mm), 2–18in (457mm) TT
Complement:	58

Class (launched, fate):
Niki (30.5.06, stricken 1945), *Doxa* (18.7.06, sunk 27.6.17), *Aspis* (3.4.07, stricken 1945), *Velos* (8.5.07, stricken 1926)

Four destroyers ordered from A G Vulcan of Stettin in 1905 and completed in 1906–07. In December 1916 they were seized by the French and in 1917–18 served under the *tricoleur*. *Doxa* was sunk by the German submarine *UB 47* off Sicily while in French hands. *Velos* discarded in 1926 was sold in 1931. The remaining pair was rebuilt in 1925–27 and rearmed with 2–88mm/30 and 1–40mm AA. They served in the British Mediterranean Fleet after April 1941. *Niki* was a station ship at Volos 1944–45.

Sfendoni as completed

THYELLA class *destroyers*

Displacement:	352t normal; 380t full load
Dimensions:	220ft 3in × 20ft 6in × 6ft *67.1m × 6.2m × 1.8m*
Machinery:	2-shaft VTE, 4 Yarrow water tube boilers, 6000ihp = 30kts (designed). Coal 88t
Armament:	2–76mm Hotchkiss, 2–57mm Hotchkiss, 2–18in (457mm) TT (revolving)
Complement:	70

Class (launched, fate):
Thyella (1906, sunk 21.4.41), *Nafkratousa* (1906, wrecked 3.21), *Lonchi* (1907, stricken 1926), *Sfendoni* (1907, stricken 1945)

Four funnelled destroyers, ordered from Yarrow in 1905 and completed in 1906–07. On trials they made 6263–6524ihp = 31.8kts–32.4kts. *Nafkratousa* was wrecked on Milos Island. *Lonchi* discarded in 1926 was sold 1931. They served under French flag 1917–18 after seizure in December 1916. *Thyella* and *Sfendoni* were refitted in 1926–18 and rearmed with 2–88mm/30 from the *Keravnos* class and 1–40mm, 2–18in TT. *Thyella* was sunk by German aircraft in Vouliagmeni Bay, Athens. *Sfendoni* served with the British Mediterranean Fleet 1941–45 was rearmed with 2–3in and 3–20mm, became station ship at Kalmas in 1945.

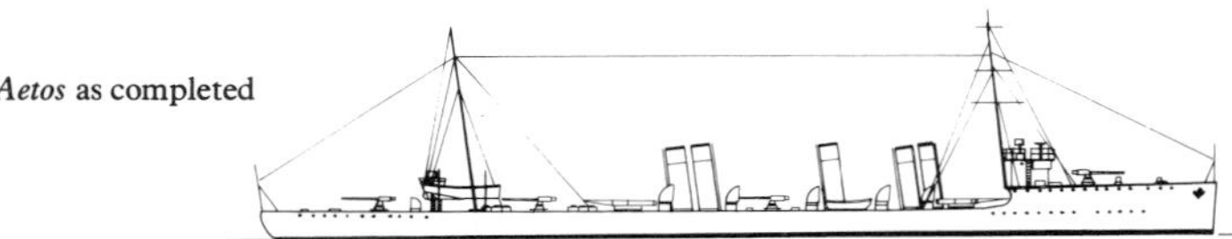
Aetos as completed

AETOS class *destroyers*

Displacement:	980t normal; 1175t full load
Dimensions:	285ft wl, 293ft oa × 27ft 8in × 8ft 6in *86.9m, 89.3m × 8.4m × 2.6m*
Machinery:	2-shaft Parsons turbines, 5 White Foster boilers, 22,000shp = 32kts (designed). Coal 230t and oil 90t
Armament:	4–4in (102mm), 4–21in (533mm) TT
Complement:	90

Class (launched, fate):
Aetos (2.11, stricken 1946), *Ierax* (3.11, stricken 1946), *Panthir* (4.11, stricken 1946), *Leon* (7.11, sunk 15.5.41)

Five funnel destroyers originally ordered from Cammell Laird in 1909 by the Argentine Navy as *San Luis*, *Santa Fe*, *Santiago* and *Tucuman* respectively. Bought in October 1912 they were seized in December 1916 by the French and served under their colours during 1917–18 except *Panthir*. The 4in guns were supplied by Bethlehem Steel Co. They were rebuilt in 1924–25 by White, Cowes, being reboilered with 4 Yarrow oil burner boilers and rearmed with 4–4in, 2–40mm AA (fitted in 1930s), 6–21in TT (2×3). *Ierax* and *Panthir* were fitted also to carry 40 mines. They received two new funnels which replaced the five old. Four single TT mounted abeam were replaced by two triple turntable TT. *Leon* was sunk by German aircraft at Suda Bay, Crete. The remaining ships served with the British Mediterranean Fleet thereafter and were rearmed by 1944 with 2–4in, 1–3in HA, 2–40mm AA, 2 MG and 3–21in TT. They became station ships in 1944–45.

Ex-German V 1 class *destroyers*

Class (former name, launched, fate):
Keravnos (ex-*V 5*, 22.5.12, stricken 1919), *Nea Genea* (ex-*V 6*, 29.2.12, stricken 1919)

Two German destroyers, built by A G Vulcan of Stettin, respectively bought in July 1912. They served in 1917–18 under the French flag. Stricken in 1919 they were placed on the sale list in 1921.

KRITI class *destroyers*

Four 1000t destroyers ordered in June 1914 from John Brown – *Kriti* and *Lesvos* and at Fairfield – *Samos* and *Chios*. Requisitioned after the outbreak of the war and purchased in August 1914 by Royal Navy being renamed *Medea*, *Medusa*, *Melpomene* and *Melampus* respectively.

Ex-Austrian HUSZÁR class *destroyer*

The former Austro-Hungarian destroyer *Ulan* was received in 1920 to replace *Doxa* (the *Niki* class ship lost in 1917) and was renamed *Smyrni*. She was sold *c*1931.

AIGLI class *torpedo-boats*

Displacement:	120t normal
Dimensions:	147ft 8in × 9ft 4in × 4ft *45.0m × 5.0m × 1.2m*
Machinery:	1-shaft VTE, 2 Navy type boilers, 2400ihp = 24kts (designed). Coal 25t
Armament:	2–6pdr, 3–457mm (18in) TT

Class:
Aigli, Alkyoni, Arethousa, Doris, Dafni, Thetis

Six torpedo boats ordered from A G Vulcan, Stettin, in 1912 and completed in 1913 with Bethlehem guns. They were: *Aigli* (scuttled 24.4.41 near Fleves Island, Saronic Gulf, after damage by German aircraft), *Alkyoni* (scuttled 23.4.41 in Vouliagmeni Bay), *Arethousa* (scuttled 24.4.41 off Varkiza), *Doris* (scuttled 23.4.41 at Porto Rafti), *Dafni* (stricken 1926, sold 1931), *Thetis* (stricken 1926, sold 1931). Seized in December 1916 at Salamis by the French Navy, they were manned under the French flag and returned in late 1918. In 1926 they were refitted with 1–37mm and 2–18in TT.

Ex-Austrian Tb 82F class *torpedo-boats*

Three torpedo boats 92F, 94F and 95F from the former Austro-Hungarian Navy were acquired in 1920 and renamed *Prousa* (scuttled 4.4.41 at Corfu after heavy damage by Italian aircraft), *Panormos* (wrecked at Aegina Island 11.3.38) and *Pergamos* (scuttled 25.4.41 at the Salamis dockyard after damage by German aircraft) respectively.

Ex-Turkish AKHISAR class *torpedo-boats*

Two Turkish torpedo-boats *Tokat* and *Antalya*, sunk at Prevesa by the Italians on 29 November 1911 were salved by Greeks in 1912, repaired, rearmed with 2–1pdr and 1 TT and enlisted as *Tatoi* and *Nikopolis* respectively. They were stricken in 1916, *Nikopolis* was placed on the sale list in 1921.

SUBMARINES

NORDENFELT I *submarine*

Displacement: 60t surfaced
Dimensions: 64ft × 9ft diameter × 11ft depth
19.5m × 2.7m × 3.4m
Machinery: 1-shaft Lamm steam locomotive compound engine, 1 cylindrical return tube marine boiler, 100ihp = 9kts/4kts
Armament: 1 Nordenfelt 25mm QF, 1–14in (356mm) TT
Complement: 3

Name	Builder	Launched	Fate
NORDENFELT I	Ekensberg	1885	BU *c*1901

The first boat (laid down in Sweden in 1882 and completed in 1885) built to a Nordenfelt and Rev George Garrett (1852–1902) design. She was bought by Greece in 1886 for £9000. Built of wrought iron frames with iron plating, she was steam powered on the surface, and steam was raised to provide latent heat for heating water stored in two 4t special tanks. She was claimed to have an endurance of 14 miles at 4 knots submerged using hot water held in tanks. The Whitehead torpedo was fired from a bow tube placed in an external casing over the bow. Never operational, she was BU *c*1901.

DELFIN class *submarines*

Displacement: 310t normal; 460t submerged
Dimensions: 164ft × 15ft 5in × 9ft
50.0m × 4.7m × 2.7m
Machinery: 2-shaft Schneider diesels plus electric motors, 720bhp/460shp = 13kts/8.5kts
Armament: 5–450mm (17.7in) TT
Complement: 24

Name	Builder	Launched	Fate
DELFIN	Schneider, Châlons	1911	Stricken 1920
XIFIAS	Schneider, Châlons	1912	Stricken 1920

These Laubeuf type submarines were ordered in 1909 and delivered in 1912. They had one internal TT in bow and four external TT, one additional torpedo was carried for the bow TT. *Delfin* was based at Tenedos island in the Balkan War from where she carried out the first modern submarine torpedo attack (unsuccessful) on 9 December 1912. Lt-Cdr Paparrigopoulos sighted the Turkish cruiser *Medjidieh* leaving the Dardanelles with 5 escorts. An hour later he fired a torpedo from 500 metres but it did not run properly and sank. Both served under the French flag 1917–18, they were discarded in 1920 and placed on the sale list in 1921.

Laubeuf type *submarines*

Two submarines, temporarily named X and PS were ordered in 1912 at France. Requisitioned in 1915 before completion they were incorporated into the French Navy as *Amazone* and *Antigone* respectively.

German U 31 *submarines*

At the beginning of July 1914 negotiations between the Greek Navy and Germaniawerft, Kiel for sale of *U 33–U 37* were far advanced, however, the outbreak of war effectively put a stop to this proposed sale.

SMALL SURFACE WARSHIPS

TENEDOS *minelayer*

Displacement: 450t
Dimensions: 142ft × 24ft × 11ft
43.3m × 7.3m × 3.4m
Machinery: 1-shaft VTE, boilers, 560ihp = 13kts. Coal 40t
Armament: 40 mines

Name	Builder	Launched	Fate
TENEDOS	Glasgow	1906	See notes

A former salvage tug with one funnel, swan bow, two masts schooner rigged. She was seized from Turkey on 14 October 1912. Also used as dispatch vessel and lighthouse tender. Seized by the French in December 1916, served under French flag 1917–18. She was sunk on 23 April 1941 by German aircraft in the Saronic Gulf, refloated by Germans and served as *UJ 2106* was sunk on 21 June 1944 by HM submarine *Unsparing* off Cape Maleos, Peloponnese.

KORGIALENIOS *minelayer*

Displacement: 380t
Dimensions: 150ft × 21ft 6in × 10ft
45.7m × 6.6m × 3.0m
Machinery: 1-shaft TE, boilers, 550ihp = 13.5kts. Coal 35t
Armament: 1–6pdr, 50 mines

Name	Builder	Launched	Fate
KORGIALENIOS	Rotterdam	1916	See notes

She was bought in 1916 with funds (£40,000) bequeathed by M Korgialenios, served also as dispatch vessel. Sunk on 23 April 1941 by German aircraft off Corfu, she was refloated by them and served as German *UJ 2110* till 25/26 October 1944, when she was scuttled at Salonika.

In 1918 four trawlers were bought from the British Navy and renamed *Y 1* to *Y 4* and served as minesweepers. They had 140t, 10kts, 1–12pdr Krupp gun. *Y 2* and *Y 4* were discarded in 1922 and the other two in 1925. Moreover two steamers requisitioned as minelayers in 1912: *Aris* (deleted 1920) and *Mykonos* (returned to owners 1913).

SMALL CRAFT
In 1920 three British Admiralty type motor launches, built 1916 of 37t, 19kts and armed with 1 MG were acquired and named *B 1* to *B 3*. They were discarded 1923–25. Moreover in 1921 a Thornycroft 45ft CMB was purchased for experiments and existed till *c*1933.

AUXILIARY CRUISERS
During the Balkan War of 1912–13 a total of 9 merchant steamers were requisitioned, armed and served as auxiliary cruisers. They were: *Sapfo, Themistoklis, Pelops, Athinai, Makedonia* (sunk 2 January 1913 by the Turkish cruiser *Hamidiye* at Syros), *Esperia, Arkadia, Mykali* and *Sfaktiria*. Moreover in 1922 the following vessels were converted to auxiliary cruisers and received letter designations: *Konstantinoupolis* (A), *Chios* (B), *Vasilissa Sofia* (G), *Aigaion* (D), *Hermis* (E), *Naxos* (Z), *Adriatikos* (H), *Aktion* (TH) and *Mykonos* (I).

Turkey

The fate of the Turkish Navy was heavily influenced by the events of 1870s. The Turkish Navy contributed in 1876 to the downfall of the Sultan Abdul Aziz, who was succeeded by Abdul Hamid II. The new Sultan lived in fear of the Navy starting a new revolution. After the Russo-Turkish War of 1877–78 half its crews were dismissed, numerous ironclads ordered from Constantinople and Britain were cancelled. Ships were left to rot in the Golden Horn and their crews became demoralised. Nevertheless, by a strange anomaly, aiming to impress his neighbours Abdul Hamid II, for whom the fleet was a scarecrow, gave an impression of reinforcing his navy by increasing its number of ships. Some attempts were made in the late 1880s, when two small cruisers were built, using engines from old discarded ships and a few torpedo-boats and auxiliary vessels were built. A pair of British-built Nordenfelt submarines delivered in 1888 never became operational. According to a contract with Germaniawerft, signed in 1886, various torpedo craft were delivered, but they were not followed by home-built ships.

In 1890 a comparatively large programme was announced. It included rebuilding a number of old ships, two new French *Hoche* class battleships, cruisers and smaller units. None of these ships were built although the frames of some cruisers were seen until after 1910. As a result only some gunboats were built for coast defence and obsolete ironclads were modernised. At the beginning of the century the cruisers *Abdul Hamid* and *Medjidieh*, some destroyers, dispatch vessels and others of less importance were built. As soon as these new ships reached Constantinople, they were condemned to a miserable inaction like their predecessors. Great Power naval intervention had ensured Crete became Greek in 1898. By 1906 naval personnel totalled 31,000 with 9000 marines; that year the Ottoman Empire possessed 100 steamers (58,000grt) and 900 sailing ships (180,000grt).

THE ITALIAN AND BALKAN WARS 1911–1913

After the revolt of the Young Turks in July 1908 naval affairs did change. The Fleet programme announced in 1908 called for 6 battleships, 12 destroyers, 12 torpedo-boats, 6 submarines and smaller craft, but these were by no means complete when the war with Italy broke out in September 1911. As a stop gap 2 small German battleships and 4 newly built destroyers were purchased, while 4 fast yachts and some new merchantmen were bought. A British Naval Mission (headed by Rear-Admirals Williams and Gamble) was sent to Turkey in 1910, but the first years of its activity were not very successful. During the two years of the Italo-Turkish War and the immediately following Balkan Wars, the Turkish Navy played a minor role. In 1911–12, after the main force of 2 battleships, 2 cruisers and 5 destroyers sailed from Beirut straight to the Dardanelles, the Turkish ships stationed at Preveza, Beirut, Izmir, Tripoli and Red Sea were virtually annihilated by the Italian Navy. The Turkish fleet was used occasionally in the Balkan Wars (October 1912–August 1913) and took some losses, but the few sorties and two actions with the Greek Fleet were indecisive. It was powerless to save Turkey's Aegean islands from Greek or Italian capture.

Two dreadnought type battleships were ordered in June 1911 from British yards. The growing tension between Greece and Turkey caused the Turks to try to acquire some foreign capital ships. Two Brazilian *Minas Gerais* class and also four French-built destroyers were mooted, but finally only *Rio de Janeiro*, building in England for Brazil, was ordered. Another dreadnought was ordered from Vickers in 1914 in reply to the Greek order for a second dreadnought. Shortly before World War One numerous other ships were ordered in Britain, France and Germany. Some attempts were made to modernise the home shipbuilding industry. In December 1913 Turkey had concluded an agreement with the British companies of Armstrong and Vickers under which the government shipyard in Smyrna (Izmir) was to be renovated and extended. These British companies were supposed to manage this newly established shipyard for 30 years, for both shipbuilding and repair purposes. The outbreak of World War One killed these plans and none of the capital ships were finally delivered to Turkey.

THE FIRST WORLD WAR

In late 1913 General Liman von Sanders' German Military Mission was sent to Turkey and from that date the Turkish Army came under German control. The seizure on 1 August of the Turkish ships, then being built in Britain was one of the events that caused Turkey to declare war against Russia, England and France. The Turkish Navy only consisted of 2 old battleships, 2 small cruisers, 9 destroyers, 3 torpedo gunboats and several torpedo-boats, gunboats and auxiliary ships, excluding obsolete ships of little fighting value. It received a considerable aid in the German battlecruiser *Goeben* and the light cruiser *Breslau*, which arrived at Constantinople on 11 August 1914. At that time Turkey was still neutral, but on 16 August the Turkish Government announced that they had bought both ships. The Ottoman Empire formally declared war on the side of the Central Powers on 1 November 1914, although her ships bombarded Sevastopol, Novorossiysk and Odessa on 29 October. The German ships retained their crews, and moreover the whole Turkish fleet was placed under Rear-Admiral Wilhelm Souchon who led it rather successfully in the Black Sea. On the Dardanelles front coastal guns, mines and U-boats were more successful than warships against the Anglo-French Fleets. During the war various military equipment, including small ships were transferred from Germany via Bulgaria to Turkey. With German aid, flotillas on Euphrates and Tigris rivers and on the Palestinian lakes were organised and operated against British forces. Late in 1918 the war was going badly for Turkey and on 31 October 1918 the Mudros Armistice came into force. On 2 November *Goeben* was formally handed over to the Turkish crew under Admiral Arir Pasha at Constantinople and she became known by her proper name of *Yavuz Sultan Selim*. After the arrival of Allied occupation forces the Turkish fleet was interned in the Gulf of Ismit on the Asiatic shore east of the capital, being manned by 6000–8000 men in 1919.

THE TREATY OF SÈVRES

The Treaty of Sèvres signed on 10 August 1920 limited Turkey to the Constantinople area and a part of the Anatolian Peninsula. Other territories were to be divided between Allies. The Army was limited to 50,000 (including 35,000 gendarmerie). Heavy conditions were also imposed on the Navy which was allowed only 7 gunboats (*Aydin Reis, Sakiz, Preveze, Hizar Reis, Kemal Reis, Isa Reis* and *Burak Reis*, heavily damaged, replaced later by *Berika I Zafer*) and 6 torpedo-boats (*Sivrihisar, Sultanhisar, Drac, Musul, Akhisar* and *Yunus*). Their armament was limited to 2–77mm guns and 2 MG for gunboats and 1–77mm for the torpedo-boats from which all torpedo armament was to be removed. After 20 years the gunboat could be replaced by 600-ton new units (the torpedo-boats by 100-ton patrol vessels). Submarines and other ships were prohibited. The rest of the fleet was to be divided between Allied powers, namely to Japan: *Turgut Reis*, to Britain: *Yavuz Sultan Selim; Hamidiye; Mecidiye; Muavenet-i-Millet; Numene; Tasoz; Basra;* and *Samsun* and to other powers: *Berk I Efsan, Pelangi Deria; Zuhaf; Peyk I Sevket* and *Nusret*.

THE NEW NAVY

During the summer of 1919 the Turkish Nationalist Movement was created in Anatolia under Mustafa Kemal (Ataturk). The treaty was rejected by the nationalists, resulting in civil war and the eventual expulsion of the Sultan Mohammed VI (he finally left on 18 November 1922 in the battleship HMS *Malaya* bound for Malta) and his foreign advisers. The Nationalist forces operated two gunboats, *Aydin Reis* and *Preveze*, which had been released in February 1919 by the Allies and sent to the Black Sea to combat smuggling. These ships were temporarily incorporated into the Red Russian Navy to avoid capture and they were used to carry arms and ammunition to Turkey purchased from Soviet Russia by the Turkish Nationalist Government. The Nationalist victory over the Greek forces caused the new Treaty of Lausanne, signed on 24 July 1923. This allowed Turkey to keep her fleet, but several years passed before enough money was available for repairing the largest ships and building new ones.

FLEET STRENGTH 1906

ARMOURED SHIPS

Name	Launched	Disp (normal)	Fate
Osmaniye class			
OSMANIEH	2.9.64	6400t	Stricken 1913, BU
MAHMUDIEH	13.12.64	6400t	Stricken 1913, BU
ORHANIEH	26.6.65	6400t	Stricken 1913, BU
ABDUL AZIZ	1.65	6400t	Stricken 1913, BU
Assari Tewfik class			
ASSARI TEWFIK	30.11.68	5600t	Wrecked 25.1.13
Assari Shevket class			
ASSARI SHEVKET	1868	2050t	Stricken 1910, BU
NIJIMI SEVKET	1868	2050t	Stricken 1929, BU
Avni Illah class			
AVNI ILLAH	21.4.69	2325t	Sunk 24.2.12
MUIN-I-ZAFFER	6.69	2330t	Stricken 1929, BU
Idjalieh class			
IDJALIEH	1870	2266t	BU *c*1922
Fethi Bulend class			
FETHI BULEND	1870	2720t	Sunk 31.10.12
MUKADDAMI KHAIR	28.10.72	2806t	Stricken 1910, BU
Messudieh class			
MESSUDIEH	28.10.74	9120t	Sunk 13.12.14
Hamidieh class			
HAMIDIEH	1.85	6700t	Stricken 1910, BU
Feth ul Islam coast defence gunboat			
FETH UL ISLAM	1864	336t	Stricken 1910, BU

Osmanieh class
The ships were laid up in 1904 waiting for rearming with 1–210mm Krupp gun

in the fore barbette and 1–150mm Krupp gun in the aft one. The 8–150mm Krupp guns were to be unchanged. The stricken ships in 1913 survived as 1914–18 hulks and were scrapped postwar.

Assari Tewfik class
She was the former Egyptian ironclad *Ibrahmieh* taken over before completion by Turkey. She was damaged in the Dardanelles action on 18 January 1913 with the Greek Fleet and a week later hit a rock off Podima, 15 miles S of Midia (Turkey in Europe) when she was supporting an unsuccessful Turkish Black Sea landing operation. She was further damaged by rough seas and Bulgarian field guns, becoming a total loss.

Assari Shevket class
Assari Shevket was originally the Egyptian *Kahira* and *Nijimi Shevket* was originally the Egyptian *Musafer*. Both taken together with *Assair Tewfik*. *Nijimi Shevket* survived 1914–18 and served as a depot ship till 1929.

Avni Illah class
During 1903–7 reconstruction they had also been fitted with 1–14in TT. They were designed by G C Mackrow. *Avni Illah* had one screw and *Muin-I-Zaffer* two to observe differences and profits of these two solutions. *Avni Illah* was sunk (probably scuttled on fire) off Beirut by the Italian armoured cruisers *Giuseppe Garibaldi* and *Varese*. *Muin-I-Zaffer* became TS in 1913 and her 4–3in QF and 8–6pdr guns were removed. In 1916–17 all her guns were landed. She survived till 1929 as a torpedo TS.

Idjalieh class
She was laid down in May 1868 and completed in January 1872. In 1900 she became a stationary TS and then as an accommodation ship during 1914–18.

Fethi Bulend class
They were designed by Reed. *Mukaddami Khair* was the first ironclad built in Turkey. Originally they had also 1–7in Armstrong MLR replaced in 1890 by 2–120mm Krupp guns. *Mukaddami Khair* was discarded in 1910, while *Fethi Bulend* was sunk as guardship at Salonika by two 14in torpedoes from the Greek torpedo-boat *NF 11*, 14 of the 148 crew died.

Messudieh class
Her particulars after reconstruction were as follows: Displacement 9200 tons normal, draught 27ft max (she was not lengthened, but received complete new stern), two sets 4-cylinder TE machinery. On trials she reached 11,135ihp = 17.5kts. Shortly before World War One her main guns were landed and replaced by wooden dummy guns. In 1914 she was moored as stationary guardship in the Dardanelles Narrows off Chanak (Canakkale), and she was torpedoed and sunk there by the British submarine *B 11*.

Hamidieh class
She was laid down at the new Imperial Arsenal Haskeni at Constantinople in December 1874 as *Nusretiye* and renamed in 1881. Originally she was to be armed with 10–260mm Krupp BLR in battery and 2–170mm Krupp BLR pieces on the upper deck. She was deleted in 1910 and scrapped.

Feth ul Islam class
Feth ul Islam was the only survivor of the class originally consisting of 5 armoured gunboats built for Danube service by FCM, La Seyne. Other ships were *Burdelen* (1864, stricken 1886), *Memduhiye* (1864, ex-*Semendria*, stricken 1900), *Iskodra* (1868, captured 6.10.77 by Russians at Nikopol, renamed by them *Sistovo*, stricken 23.11.89), *Podgoriza* (1868, captured with *Iskodra*, renamed *Nikopol*, stricken 23.11.89). Their particulars were as follows:
Displacement: 336t (normal)
Dimensions: 99ft 9in pp, 103ft oa × 32ft 2in × 5ft 3in, *30.4m pp, 31.4m oa × 9.8m × 1.6m*
Machinery: 2 sets high pressure 1 cyl 80hp/290ihp = 8kts. Coal 30t
Armour: Iron. Belt 3in, ends 2in, battery 3in, CT ⅜in
Armament: 2–4in (in 1890 rearmed with 2–7in, 2–9pdr Krupp). Iron hull central battery type gunboats, two funnels amidships, one on each side. The upper deck only .48m over water line. They were built in eight months (each).

CRUISERS

Name	Launched	Disp	Fate
Mehmet Selim class			
MEHMET SELIM	8.79	1280t	BU *c*1913
Heibetnuma class			
HEIBETNUMA	30.1.90	1958t	Stricken 1909, BU
Lutfi Humayun class			
LUTFI HUMAYUN	16.8.92	1350t	Stricken 1909, BU
Abdul Hamid class			
ABDUL HAMID	25.9.03	3830t	Stricken 1948, BU
Abdul Mecid class			
MEDJIDIEH	25.7.03	3250t	Stricken 1948, BU

Mehmet Selim class
A wooden, fully rigged frigate laid down 1875 at Ismid, completed 1880 at Constantinople. She had 450nhp and 1800ihp. In 1880 she became cadet TS and in 1907 was deleted from list, her armament was removed except TT and she became a stationary torpedo TS till 1913, when she was scrapped.

Assari Tewfik about 1910 *CPL*

Messudieh about 1910 *CPL*

Medjidieh about 1910 *CPL*

Heibetnuma class
She had 2 funnels and was a 3-masted barque-rigged corvette with ram bow. On trial she made 14.6kts. She was used as a cadet TS. In 1905 rearmed with 2–150mm, 2–120mm, 4–6pdr, 1 TT aw. Stricken in 1909 and scrapped after 1914–18.

Lufti Humayun class
She was rearmed by 1900 with 4–150mm Krupp which replaced 170mm guns. In 1903 she retained only 2–150mm and 2–120mm, 4–47mm, 1 Nordenfelt and 2 TT aw. She was stricken in 1909 and scrapped after 1914–18.

Abdul Hamid class
She was renamed *Hamidieh* as the result of the 1908 revolution. On 21 November 1912 she was torpedoed off Varna by a Bulgarian torpedo-boat, only just making Constantinople with bows awash from a 10ft starboard hole and 8 dead crew. She bombarded Odessa on 29 October 1914 in the surprise attack with *Goeben* and *Breslau*. After 1914–18 she became a cadet TS.

Abdul Mecid class
She was renamed *Medjidieh c*1903. In 1914 she received 6–47mm in place of 3pdr and 1pdr guns. She sank on 3 April 1915 on mines 15 miles off Odessa after bombarding Nikolayev (*Hamidieh* rescued her survivors), but was salvaged by the Russians in June and commissioned on 29 October as *Prut* armed with 6–130mm (5.1in), 4–75mm, 2 MG later changed to 10–130mm and 4–75mm AA. She was recaptured at Sevastopol by the Germans and returned to Turkey on 12 May 1918, returning to her original name. In 1927 she was rebuilt with Babcock and Wilcox watertube boilers and two funnels. Her armament varied from 4 to 6–130mm/56 Vickers QF and 2 to 4–76mm/50 Schneider QF, 2 MG, 2–18in TT, finally she had 4–130mm and 4–76mm.

SLOOPS AND DISPATCH VESSELS

Name	Launched	Disp	Fate
Blockade runner type			
RETIMO	1862	767bm	Stricken 1909, BU
HANIA	1863	829bm	Sold 1910
Iz-ed-din class			
IZ-ED-DIN	1864	1075t	Stricken 1926
ISMAIL	1865	1075t	Stricken 1910
TALIAH	1865	1075t	Stricken 1910
FEVAID	1865	1075t	See notes
Sureyya class			
SUREYYA	1865	624t	
Zuhaf class			
ZUHAF	31.8.94	643t	Stricken post 1918
KILID UL BAHIR	31.8.94	643t	Sunk 16.12.14

ASIA

Blockade runner type
Retimo rebuilt in 1876 and 1896 was bought by Turkey in 1869. Originally she was armed with 1–40pdr and 2–12pdr, disarmed in 1896, not serviceable *c*1905. *Hania* was probably Dudgeon built *Run Her*. She was bought 1867 and rebuilt 1894. Originally she was armed as *Retimo*. Complement 93/137. Not operational *c*1905.

Iz-ed-din class
They were officially listed as yachts. *Iz-ed-din* was built by Thames Iron Wks, *Taliah* by Samuda and *Fevaid* by Millwall. Their armament varied. They were rebuilt in 1888. *Fevaid* was scuttled at Salonika and on 8 November 1912 seized there by the Greeks, became *Fuad*, on Navy List to 1919, on sale list 1921 as hulk.

Sureyya class
She was built by Samuda Bros and engined by Penn. The paddle ship was originally served as Imperial yacht armed with 2–11pdr and 2–8pdr, later rearmed with 3–3.5in, 2–1pdr and 1 MG and served as guardship at Smyrna.

Zuhaf class
They were built by Germaniawerft at Constantinople, carried 80 tons of coal. *Kilid ul Bahir* was sunk off Beirut by the Russian cruiser *Askold*'s gunfire. *Zuhaf* was rearmed in 1914 with 4–57mm and fitted out as a minelayer.

GUNBOATS

Name	Fate	Name	Fate
Firat class: launched 1885, 197t			
FIRAT	Stricken 1913	SAT	Stricken 1910
Resaniye class: launched 1899, 120t			
RESANIYE	Scuttled 20.4.12	TIMSAH	BU 1922
Sevket Numa class: launched 1894–1908, 198t–200t			
SEVKET NUMA	Sunk 10.11.15	SAIK I SADI	Unknown
SAYD I DERYA	Scuttled 10.11	NASR I HUDA	Survived 1914–18
SEYYAR	Unknown	BERIKA I ZAFER	Stricken *c*1925
NUR UL BAHIR	Sunk 1.5.15		

Resaniye class
Resaniye was scuttled at Vathi, Samos. *Timsah* mined in 1918, remained beyond repair at Constantinople till 1922.

Sevket Numa class
Name ship sunk by HM submarine *E 11* in the Sea of Marmara. *Berika I Zafer* reportedly sunk at Smyrna by HM destroyers *Wolverine* and *Scorpion* in Britain's first action against Turkey (1 November 1914) but survived the war. *Nur ul Bahir* sunk off Merefte (Sea of Marmara) by HM submarine *E 14*.

There were also the small gunboats and dispatch vessels *Mosul* (1865, 220t), *Seyyar* (1865, 220t), *Seyr I Derya*, *Mujde Resan*, *Shahiddin* (all three 1866/68, 258t), *Sahir* (1868, 225t), *Ainaly Kavak* (1869, 195t), *Yali Kiosk* (1869, 195t), *Istankoi* (1870, 203t). All were stricken in 1906–10.

TORPEDO GUNBOATS

Name	Launched	Disp	Fate
SHANANI DERIA	16.8.92	443t	Stricken 1910
NAMET	30.1.90	900t	Stricken 1910
PELENGI DERIA	1890	900t	BU *c*1922

Pelengi Deria was rearmed in 1914 with 3–75mm and 4–47mm. She was torpedoed on 23 May 1915 by the British submarine *E 11* SW of Seraglio Point, Constantinople, but salvaged and scrapped postwar.

DESTROYERS

Name	Launched	Disp	Fate
BERK I EFSAN	1892	266t	Sold *c*1927
TAYYAR	1893	266t	Stricken 1913

TORPEDO-BOATS

Name	Launched	Disp	Fate
TIMSAH	1885	30t	Stricken 1910
SIMIR I HIDSUM	1884	14t	Stricken 1910
MECIDIYE class (6)	1885–1890	42t	Stricken 1910
MAHABET class (2)	1887	83t	Stricken 1910
GILYOM class (5)	1886	85t	Stricken 1910
NASR class (7)	1888–1892	87t	Stricken 1910
EJDER	1890	118t	Stricken 1910

Mecidiye class consisted of *Burhan ed Din*, *Tevfik*, *Mecidiye* (she was renamed

Pelengi Deria about 1910 — *CPL*

Alice Roosevelt prior to 1904), *Eser I Teraki*, *Sanaver*, *Nimet*. *Mahabet* class comprised of *Mahabet*, *Satvet*. *Gilyom* class consisted also of *Seyfi Bahri*, *Tir I Zafer*, *Vesile I Nusret* and *Saika*. *Nasr* class comprised also of *Fatik* (stricken 1911), *Nusret*, *Sahab*, *Tarik*, *Pervim* and *Seham*.

ARMED YACHTS

Name	Launched	Disp	Fate
SULTANIYE	1861	3029t	Scuttled 20.4.12
ISTANBUL	1865	909t	BU *c*1924
BEYLERBEY	1873	96t	Stricken *c*1913
SERIFIYE	5.4.93	55t	Stricken *c*1913
ERTUGRUL	1.03	900t	Stricken *c*1948
SOGÜTLÜ	25.9.03	110t	Stricken *c*1938

Sultaniye
Paddle, iron, one funnel, fore and aft rigged yacht built in Britain, used as Imperial yacht and from *c*1910 as navy transport: 2902bm tons, 364ft 7in × 40ft × 16ft (*111m × 12.2m × 4.9m*), 800nhp = 14kts, coal 300t. Armed with 2–120mm Krupp and 2 small guns. Complement 275 men. Scuttled at Smyrna as blockship against the Italians.

Istanbul
Iron, paddle, two funnels, two pole masts Imperial yacht built in 1865 by Samuda Bros as *Partev I Piyale*. Dimensions: 264ft × 28ft 10in × 10ft 6in (*75m × 8.8m × 3.2m*), 350nhp/2400ihp = 16kts. Coal 350t. Complement 137 men. In 1882 renamed *Istanbul*, 1888 rebuilt and armed with 2–120mm, 1904 rearmed with 7–47mm, then with 4–47mm, in 1911 rearmed with 2–80mm Krupp and during 1914–18 again with 2–120mm. After *c*1913 she served as stationary guardship at Constantinople.

Beylerbey
A small wooden, screw Imperial yacht, built as *Serifiye* and renamed in 1893. She measured 91ft 10in × 14ft 9in × 8ft 10in (*28m × 4.5m × 2.7m*), 35nhp = 12kts, not armed.

Serifiye
A small wooden, screw yacht, built at Constanze. She measured 95ft × 9ft 10in × 6ft 4in (*29m × 3m × 1.9m*). Listed as dispatch vessel and yacht. Her speed was 15kts.

Ertugrul
Steel Imperial yacht built by Armstrong and engined by Hawthorn-Leslie. She had a clipper bow, two funnels, one fore and one aft, and three pole masts with yards on fore one. Dimensions: 260ft × 27ft 9in × 11ft 6in (*79m × 8.4m × 3.5m*), 2 shaft VTE with cylindrical boilers 2500ihp = 21kts. Armed with 8–3pdr.

Sogütlü
Steel screw yacht for Sultan, built by Armstrong, with one funnel and two pole masts. She measured 188tm, 123ft 6in × 18ft × 5ft 9in (*37.6m × 5.5m × 1.7m*), 250ihp = 14kts.

MAJOR SURFACE SHIPS

Ex-German BRANDENBURG class *battleships*

Two old German battleships *Kurfürst Friedrich Wilhelm* and *Weissenburg*, (1891, modernised 1903–05, 9900t, 6–280mm) were bought on 12 September 1910 and named *Heireddin Barbarossa* and *Torgud Reis* respectively. *Torgud Reis* helped bombard Varna on 19 October 1912 and with her sister gave vital gunfire support to the Turkish Army holding the Chatalja lines (covering Constantinople) against the Bulgarians, especially on the Turkish left flank (Chekmeje Bay) during 17–18 November. Both ships (*Barbarossa* as flagship) fought the Greek Fleet off the Dardanelles in the indecisive actions of 16 December 1912 and 18 January 1913. Both had one barbette disabled and caught fire during the latter action. Most of the 800 Turkish shells fired on both occasions came from their 11in guns. *Torgud Reis* helped free with her propellers and then towed the grounded *Goeben* in the Dardanelles (January 1918). Their guns were partially removed during 1914–18 and used in coast defence or mounted on small vessels. *Heireddin Barbarossa* was sunk on 8 August 1915 by British submarine *E 11* off Bulair, Sea of Marmara. *Torgud Reis* became a school hulk in 1928 armed with 2–280mm and was BU 1956/57.

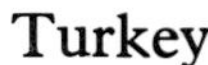

Torgud Reis as purchased *CPL*

RESADIYE class *battleships*

Displacement:	23,000t (normal); 24,700t (*Fatik*, normal)
Dimensions:	525ft pp, 559ft 6in oa × 91ft 7in × 28ft 10in (design) *160.0m, 170.5m × 27.9m × 8.8m* 565ft oa × 90ft × ? (*Fatik*) *172.2m × 27.4m × ?m*
Machinery:	4-shaft Parsons turbines, 15 Babcock & Wilcox boilers, 26,500shp = 21kts (designed), 27,500shp = 21kts (*Fatik*, designed), see *Erin* for particulars
Armament:	10–13.5in/45, 16–6in/50, 4–3in, 4–21in TT (as designed)

Name	Builder	Laid down	Launched	Fate
RESADIYE	Vickers	1.8.11	3.8.13	Confiscated 1.8.14
MAHMUD RESAD V	Armstrong	6.12.11	–	Cancelled 1912
FATIK	Vickers	11.6.14	–	Dismantled 1914

First two ships were ordered in June 1911 by the Turkish Navy. Following the outbreak of the First Balkan War Armstrong demanded better guarantees of payment and work was suspended, not being resumed afterwards. The order was cancelled, when work on Vickers ship was continued at increased pace from May 1913 onwards. *Resadiye* was requisitioned for the Royal Navy as HMS *Erin* in August 1914, when almost complete. *Fatik* was ordered from Vickers on 29 April 1914 as a response to the Greek order for a second dreadnought. She was to have been delivered by 29 April 1917 and would be slightly enlarged *Resadiye* and generally similar in respect of layout, armament and protection. She was dismantled on the slipway after the outbreak of war in August 1914. For further remarks see *Erin*.

SULTAN OSMAN I *battleship*

A 27,500t battleship laid down for Brazil as *Rio de Janeiro* on 14 September 1911 by Armstrong, bought by Turkey half finished on 9 January 1914 for £2,725,000 and construction proceeded for Turkey's account as *Sultan Osman I*. The 500-strong Turkish crew arrived on the Tyne on 27 July 1914. Handing over and start of voyage home planned for 3 August 1914 but occupied and confiscated by the Royal Navy on 2 August, then commissioned as HMS *Agincourt*.

German MOLTKE class *battlecruiser*

The German battlecruiser *Goeben* served with the Turkish Navy, under the Turkish flag as *Yavuz Sultan Selim* from 16 August 1914 with German command and crew, officially transferred to Turkish Navy on 2 November. *Yavuz Sultan Selim* made a 25-minute surprise bombardment of Sevastopol on 29 October 1914, firing 47–11in and 12in–5.9in shells – the first shots of Turkey's war with Russia. Two 12in shells from a fort holed her aft funnel killing 14 men. A 12in Russian battleship shell knocked out her 3rd port 5.9in casement and ammunition in a foggy 18 November action but *Goeben* hit the battleship *Ivstafi* four times in 19 rounds of 11in. She fired 15 more at Batumi on 10 December. She was heavily damaged on 26 December 1914 by 2 Russian mines in the Bosphorus, but was repaired. In 1915 two 150mm guns were landed and sent to the Dardanelles (she was hit by 2 12in shells in a 10 May 1915 action with the Black Sea Fleet), in 1916 the 4 aft 88mm/45 guns were replaced by 88mm AA. Again damaged on 20 January 1918 by 3 British mines and bombs, repaired. Altogether she fought 17 surface actions and 60 air raids, being hit by 6 12in shells, 5 mines and 3 bombs. Interned on 5 October 1918 at Ismit, she lay there until 1926 and became completely unserviceable. In 1927–1930 (thanks to a new 26,000t dry dock from Germany) she was rebuilt at Ismit by A C De St-Nazaire-Penhöet, receiving new particulars.

Displacement:	23,100t
Dimensions:	610ft 3in × 97ft × 27ft *186.0m × 29.6m × 8.2m*
Machinery:	new boilers, on four hour trial made 27.1kts
Armament:	(with French fire control system) 10–280mm, 10–150mm, 2–8mm, 4–88mm AA, 4 MG, 2–500mm TT
Complement:	1300

In 1936 she was renamed *Yavuz*, received a short refit in 1938 (she took the body of Kemal Ataturk from Istanbul to Ismit in November) and in 1941 received 4–88mm AA, 10–40mm AA and 4–20mm AA, increased finally to 22–40mm AA and 24–20mm AA. From 1948 stationary in Ismit, decommissioned 20 December 1950, deleted on 14 November 1954. In 1963 an offer of sale to W Germany was rejected. Sold 1971, BU June 1973–February 1976.

Armstrong type *scout cruisers*

Displacement:	3550t normal
Dimensions:	400ft pp, 423ft oa × 41ft × 13ft 6in *121.9m, 128.9m × 12.5m × 4.1m*
Machinery:	3-shaft Parsons turbines, 11 Yarrow small tube boilers, 1 cruising turbine, 24,000shp = 27kts. Coal 700t and oil 250t
Armour:	Deck 1½in, CT 6in
Armament:	2–6in (152mm)/50, 6–4in (102mm)/50, 4–3pdr, 2–3in, 2–21in (533mm) TT

Two scout cruisers ordered by the Turkish Navy from Armstrong Whitworth & Co, Newcastle-upon-Tyne in 1914, with machinery to be manufactured by Vickers. When war broke out the little work done on them ceased. They were neither named nor laid down. The 6in were to be mounted fore and aft, 4in guns and 3pdr were to be on either beam. The 3in guns, for anti-balloon and landing purposes were to be amidships on the centreline and the broadside deck TT were to train.

HAMIDIEH class *protected cruiser*

One cruiser laid down by Ansaldo, Genoa to the Elswick *Hamidieh* design and purchased by Turkey in 1910 and named *Drama*. She was seized in 1911 on ways at the outbreak of the Italo-Turkish war and became the Italian *Libia* (qv).

German MAGDEBURG class *light cruiser*

The German cruiser *Breslau* from 16 August 1914 served under the Turkish flag, with German command and crew as the Turkish *Midilli*. She served as the inseparable 'little sister' of *Goeben* alias *Yavuz Sultan Selim*. Their war had begun on 3 August 1914 with 10-minute shellings of Bône and Philippeville (Algeria) respectively, Germany's first blow at France. They both fired at the pursuing cruiser HMS *Gloucester* in the Ionian Sea on 6 August. In the Black Sea *Breslau* shelled Novorossiysk on 29 October 1914, sinking 14 steamers and firing 40 oil tanks. She sank a Russian transport and captured a steamer blockship (intended to block the port of Zonguldak) on 23 December. They sank 2 cargo steamers in April 1915 and then *Breslau*, aided by *Goeben*'s searchlights, sank 3 Russian destroyers in succession. She sank 2 more in August for heavy casualties. On 4 July 1916 the two ships shelled Tuapse and Lazarevskoye, sinking the steamer *Kniaz Obolensky*. *Breslau* took bow splinter damage from the Russian battleship *Imperatritsa Maria* on 22 July and mined the sea of Azov afterwards. In 1916 she was rearmed with 2–150mm, 10–105mm and in 1917 with 8–150mm. First mined on 18 July 1915 by a Russian mine near Kata Burnu, salvaged and repaired, again mined and sunk on 20 January 1918 by 5 British mines off Imbros. Her stern was blown off and she sank 30 minutes from the first detonation with the loss of two thirds of her 370 crew.

French DURANDAL class *destroyers*

Displacement:	284t
Dimensions:	184ft × 20ft 8in × 9ft 2in *56.0m × 5.3m × 2.8m*
Machinery:	2 shaft VTE, 2 Normand boilers, 5950ihp = 28kts. Coal 60t
Armament:	1–65mm/40, 6–47mm/40, 2–450mm (17.7in) TT
Complement:	67

Class (fate):
Yarhisar (sunk 3.12.15), *Tasoz, Samsun, Basra*

Four destroyers of the French *Durandal* class (Normand '300' tonne), ordered in 1906 and built 1907–08 by A C de la Gironde, except *Tasoz*, built by Schneider et Cie. *Yarhisar* was torpedoed by HM submarine *E 11* in the Gulf of Ismit. *Tasoz* was refitted at Constantinople in 1924 and stricken in 1948 along with her two sisters.

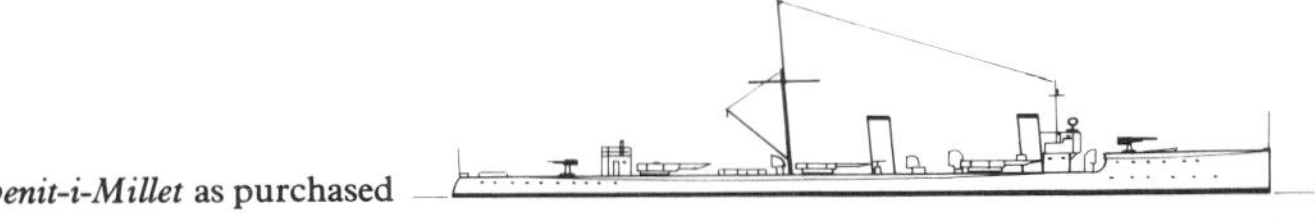

Muavenit-i-Millet as purchased

Ex-German S 165 class *destroyers*

Class (former name, launched, fate):
Muavenet-i-Millet (ex-*S 165*, 20.3,09, stricken 1924), *Jadhigar-i-Millet* (ex-*S 166*, 24.4.09, sunk 10.7.17), *Numene-i-Hamije* (ex-*S 167*, 3.7.09, stricken 1924), *Gairet-i-Watanije* (ex-*S 168*, 30.9.09, beached 28.10.16)

Former German Schichau-built destroyers bought in 1910. They made on trials 36.2kts to 34.5kts. Rearmed with 2–88mm and 2–37mm, probably never carried 3in guns. *Gairet-i-Watanije* was beached and scuttled off Varna. *Jadhigar-i-Millet* was bombed and sunk by British RNAS aircraft in the Golden Horn. Refloated in October 1917 she was scrapped. Other two ships were scrapped postwar.

Normand type *destroyers*

Displacement:	1040t
Dimensions:	287ft × 29ft 6in × 10ft 6in *87.5m × 9.0m × 3.2m*
Machinery:	2 shafts, 4 Parsons turbines, 4 Yarrow boilers, 22,000shp = 32kts. Oil 200t
Armament:	5–100mm (3.9in) Canet, 6–533mm (21in) TT
Complement:	?

Six destroyers with temporary names No 1–6 were ordered in May 1914 from A Normand, Le Havre to be laid down in July 1914. Six more were planned to be laid down in 1917. Designed in 1913 they were shortened version of *Izyaslav* class Russian destroyers, designed by the same firm. Two of the Parsons turbines were to be reversible. Construction work suspended at the beginning of the war.

Hawthorn Leslie type *destroyers*

Four 1100t destroyers were ordered in June 1914 for the Turkish Navy from the Armstrong-Vickers syndicate and subcontracted to Hawthorn Leslie. Material prepared for them was used for British *Talisman* (ex-*Napier*) class ordered in November 1914 by the RN. Two more were planned to be built in Turkey.

Italian IMPAVIDO class *destroyers*

Four 700t destroyers ordered from Orlando, shortly before the war but never begun.

Unknown Turkish *destroyers*

Six fast destroyers of unknown particulars were authorised in March 1917. They were never begun.

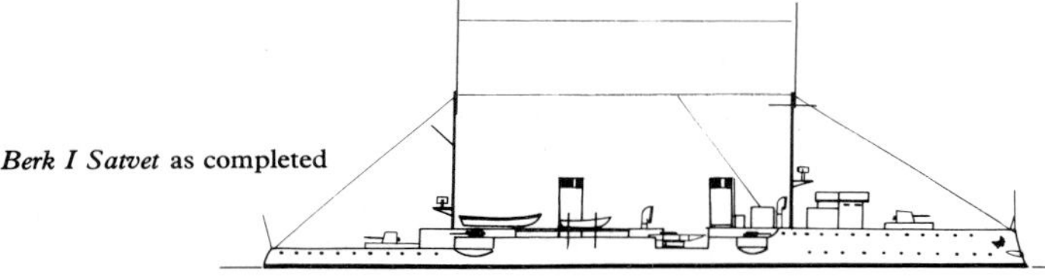

Berk I Satvet as completed

BERK I SATVET class *torpedo gunboats*

Displacement:	760t normal; 775t trial
Dimensions:	262ft 5in × 27ft 7in × 8ft 2in *80.0m × 8.4m × 2.5m*
Machinery:	2-shaft VTE, 5100ihp = 21kts. Coal 240t. Range 3240nm
Armament:	2–105mm (4.1in), 6–57mm, 2–37mm, 2 Hotchkiss QF, 3–450mm (17.7in) TT (1 bow, 2 deck)
Complement:	105

Class (launched, fate):
Berk I Satvet (12.06, stricken 1944), *Peyk I Sevket* (15.11.06, stricken 1944)

Steel hulled, torpedo gunboats with two funnels, two pole masts, one fore, one aft, ram bow and cruiser type stern. The 105mm guns were mounted forward and aft. The small guns were mounted alongside. They were ordered from Germania in 1905, laid down in 1906 and completed in 1907. *Berk I Satvet* was heavily damaged on 2 January 1915 by a Russian mine NE of the Bosphorus, but salved and repaired. *Peyk I Sevket* was torpedoed on 6 August 1915 off Silivri (Sea of Marmara), but she was beached and salved. Both ships were rebuilt in 1937–39 having been renamed *Berk* and *Peyk* respectively in 1923. Their new armament consisted of 2–88mm/45, 4–37mm/40, they were fitted to carry 25 mines, the TT were removed from *Peyk*. During refit, they received modified superstructure and raked stem. Both stricken and then hulked at Goluk Navy Yard in 1950.

ABDUL MECID class *torpedo-boats*

Displacement:	145t
Dimensions:	166ft × 18ft 7in × 4ft *50.6m × 5.7m × 1.2m*
Machinery:	2-shaft VTE, 2 locomotive type boilers, 2400ihp = 27kts. Coal 50t
Armament:	2–37mm revolver guns, 2–14in (356mm) TT
Complement:	20

Class (launched, fate):
Abdul Mecid (1901, sunk 30.9.11), *Hamidiye* (1901, stricken 1927)

Two torpedo boats built by Ansaldo, Armstrong & Co, Genoa and delivered in 1902. *Abdul Mecid* sunk by Italian destroyers *Artigliere* and *Corazziere* at Reshadiye, N of Prevaza (Ionian Sea) in the first naval action of the Turkish-Italian War. *Hamidiye* renamed *Yunus* in 1908.

AKHISAR class *torpedo-boats*

Displacement:	165t
Dimensions:	165ft 6in pp × 18ft 6.5in × 4ft 3in *50.5m × 5.7m × 1.4m*
Machinery:	2-shaft VTE, 2 locomotive type boilers, 2700ihp = 27kts (the first 2 ships and 2400ihp = 24kts (other 7 ships). Coal 60t
Armament:	2–37mm revolvers, 2–14in (356mm) TT
Complement:	20

Class (launched, fate):
Akhisar (1904, stricken 1927), *Alpagut* (1904, sunk 30.9.11), *Drac* (1906, stricken 1927), *Musul* (1906, stricken 1927), *Angora* (1906, sunk 24.2.12), *Antalya* (1906, scuttled 29.9.11), *Kütahya* (1906, sunk 13.9.16), *Tokat* (1906, beached 29.9.11), *Urfa* (1906, lost 1914–18?)

All 9 built by Ansaldo, Armstrong & Co, Genoa. They had 9 watertight compartments. The TT were mounted on deck, one forward, one aft conning tower. Each tube had stowage for one extra torpedo. The first boats ordered in 1902 and delivered in 1904 were *Akhisar* and *Alpagut*, sunk by Italian destroyers *Artigliere* and *Corazziere* at Reshadiye, N of Preveza in the first naval action of that war. Seven boats were then ordered in 1904 and delivered in January 1907. *Angora* sunk in Beirut harbour, despite hiding behind neutral shipping, by Italian cruisers *Garibaldi* and *Varese*; *Antalya* scuttled at Preveza during the Italian attack, salved 1912 by the Greeks and became *Nikopolis*; *Kütahya* sunk by Russian mine near Kara Burna; *Tokat* hit frequently by 12pdr fire from 3000 yards and driven ashore by Italian destroyers off Preveza, the first Turkish loss of the war, salved in 1912 by the Greeks, became *Tatoi*. They were enlarged Italian *Condore* class.

French 38-metre type *torpedo-boats*

Displacement:	97.5t
Dimensions:	131ft 11in oa, 124ft 8in pp × 14ft 5in × 8ft 6in *40.2m, 38.0m × 4.4m × 2.6m*
Machinery:	1-shaft TE, 2 du Temple boilers, 2200ihp = 26kts (designed). Coal 11.2t
Armament:	2–37mm revolvers, 3–450mm (18in) TT (1 bow, 2 trainable)
Complement:	20

Class (launched):
Hamidabad (1906, sunk 31.10.17), *Demirhisar* (1906, beached 17.4.15), *Sivrihisar* (1906, stricken 1928), *Sultanhisar* (1906, stricken 1928)

Four torpedo boats of the French 38-metre type, ordered in 1904. Same as the French Navy TBs *309–311* and *353–358*. Built by Ch Schneider, Creusot. *Hamidabad* sunk near Cape Igneada (Turkey in Europe) by Russian destroyers *Bystryj* and *Pyl'kij*, *Demirhisar* (beached on Chios Island to escape HM destroyers *Jed*, *Kennet* and *Wear*), salved, scrapped postwar.

Peyk I Sevket about 1910
CPL

SUBMARINES

Nordenfelt type *submarines*

Displacement: 100t surfaced; 160t submerged
Dimensions: 100ft × 12ft diameter
30.5m × 3.7m
Machinery: 1 shaft Lamm locomotive steam compound engine, 250ihp = 8kts surfaced. 1 steam tank for submerged motion giving speed 4kts to 5kts. 1 cylindrical boiler. Coal 8t
Armament: 2–14in (356mm) Whitehead torpedoes in outside bow tubes. 2 Nordenfelt 1in (25mm) MG on deck
Complement: 7

Name	Builder	Re-launched	Fate
ABDUL HAMID	Des Vignes Co, Chertsey	6.9.86	See notes
ABDUL MEDJID	Des Vignes Co, Chertsey	4.8.87	See notes

Two boats ordered 23 January 1886 (as a counter to the supposed Russian and Greek submarine threat) to the second Nordenfelt design built on the Thames and after trials were dismantled and sent in sections to Constantinople. They were improved and half as long again as the *Nordenfelt I* built for Greece. An attempt was made to improve longitudinal stability by using two downhaul screws located in sponsons on either side of the vessel. *Abdul Hamid*'s trials on surface were successful (February 1887 60nm trial run to Işmid), but the stabilising system failed during submerged tests. *Abdul Medjid* was nicknamed the 'Whale Ship'. There were not enough volunteers for their crews and both boats were laid up in the Naval Arsenal. One was reported in July 1909 as being in a shed on the Golden Horn with knee-deep grass growing round it. They were discovered by Germans in the First World War and attempts to make them operational failed.

Laubeuf type *submarines*

Two boats were ordered in April 1914 from Schneider type to be delivered by December 1915.

British E class *submarines*

Two ships ordered on 29 April 1914 by Turkey from Vickers Ltd and subcontracted by Vickers to Beardmore & Co (Dalmuir). Material was requisitioned in August 1914 and used in the British submarines *E 25* and *E 26*, ordered November 1914. They were probably ordered as Laubeuf type.

Ex-French EMERAUDE class *submarine*

The French submarine *Turquoise* stranded in the Dardanelles on 30 October 1915, was seized by the Turks and renamed *Müstecip Ombasi*. She was returned in 1918 and deleted in 1919.

SMALL SURFACE WARSHIPS

MARMARIS *gunboat*

Displacement: 422t normal; 531t full load
Dimensions: 172ft oa × 24ft 7in × 11ft 10in
52.4m × 7.5m × 3.6m
Machinery: 1-shaft VTE, 2 Scotch boilers, 950ihp = 14.8kts. Coal 75t
Armament: 4–9pdr, 2–1pdr, 1–18in (457mm) TT aw
Complement: 66

Name	Builder	Launched	Fate
MARMARIS	A C de la Loire	1903	Sunk 5.6.15

Scout type gunboat. Designed for coast guard work in the Red Sea and the Persian Gulf. She was brigantine rigged, had a sail area of 5160 sq ft. One 9pdr gun was mounted fore, one aft and two others amidships in sponsons. The TT was in the bow above the water. She was scuttled at Basra after being disabled on 2 June 1915 by the British sloop *Odin* S of Amara on the River Tigris.

YOZGAT class *gunboats*

Displacement: 185t
Dimensions: 131ft 2in × 29ft 6in × 9ft 10in
40.0m × 9.0m × 3.0m
Machinery: 1-shaft VTE, 1 boiler, ?ihp = 12kts. Coal 40t
Armament: 2–47mm

A Nordenfelt submarine as delivered *Aldo Fraccaroli Collection*

Class (fate):
Yozgat (sunk 10.12.15), *Kastamonu* (sunk 7.1.12)

Small craft built at Constantinople and launched in 1906 for customs' survey duties and the suppression of smuggling in the Red Sea. *Kastamonu* was rearmed in 1910 with 1–77mm and *Yozgat* with 1–75mm, 1–37mm and in 1914 *Yozgat* had 2–57mm and 2–47mm pieces. *Kastamonu* was sunk in the Red Sea action at Kunfuda by the Italian squadron and *Yozgat* off the Kirpen Islands by Russian destroyers.

SEDD UL BAHIR class *gunboats*

Displacement: 192t normal; 309t full load (Loire). 213t normal (Schneider)
Dimensions: 154ft 2in × 18ft 10in × 7ft 11in
47.0m × 5.7m × 2.4m
Machinery: 1-shaft VTE, 1 Scotch boiler, 480ihp = 12.4kts. Coal 44t
Armament: 3–3pdr, 2–1pdr, 1–18in (457mm) TT
Complement: 47

Class (launched, fate):
A C de la Loire, Nantes – *Sedd ul Bahir* (1907, sunk 10.11.12 by Greek TB at Aivala, N of Smyrna), *Ordu* (1907, sunk 7.1.12), *Bafra* (1907, sunk 7.1.12), *Aintab* (1907, sunk 7.1.12), *Malatya* (1907, damaged on 17.9.16 by Russian mine off Kara Burnu, stricken 1920)
Schneider et Cie – *Nevsehir* (1908, sunk 30.1.15 by Turkish mine in the Bosphorus), *Tasköprü* (1908, sunk 10.12.15 by Russian destroyers off Kirpen Is), *Gocedag* (1908, sunk 7.1.12), *Refahiye* (1908, sunk 7.1.12)

A total of 8 gunboats built for coast guard work, suppression of piracy and smuggling and settlement of various disputes along the Turkish coasts in the Red Sea and the Persian Gulf. They had two masts rigged, carrying a 2205 sq ft sail area. The 3pdrs (usually only 2 mounted), were placed one forward, one aft and the TT was a turntable mounting on the deck, forward of the superstructure. Five of them were sunk in the Red Sea action at Kunfuda, Asir, Arabia by the Italian light cruisers *Piemonte*, *Puglia* and *Liguria* plus the destroyers *Artigliere* and *Garibaldi*.

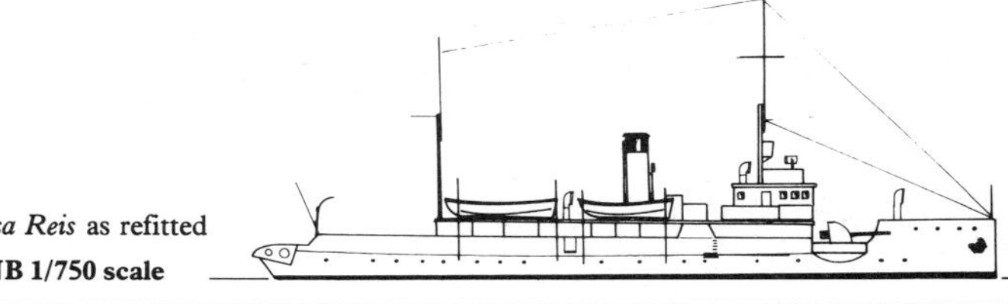

Isa Reis as refitted
NB 1/750 scale

ISA REIS class *gunboats*

Displacement: 413t
Dimensions: 154ft 3in × 25ft 9in × 4ft 3in
47.0m × 7.9m × 1.3m
Machinery: 2-shaft VTE boilers, 850ihp = 14kts
Armament: 3–75mm, 2–3pdr, 2 Hotchkiss MG

Class (launched, fate):
Isa Reis (12.11, mined 11.7.15, stricken 1953), *Hizir Reis* (2.12, mined 21.1.15, stricken 1948), *Duruk Reis* (2.12, mined 10.1.15, stricken 1948)

Three gunboats built by FCM, La Seyne for various purposes. All of them were mined in the Bosphorus, salved and repaired, *Duruk Reis* was renamed *Kemal Reis* in 1918. Two 3in guns were mounted forward on sides in sponsons and one 3in aft. They were refitted in 1923 and rated as minesweepers and temporarily served as gunnery TS (*Hizir Reis*), customs vessels (*Isa Reis* and *Duruk Reis*) and survey vessels. They were stricken after World War Two.

PREVEZE class *gunboats*

Displacement: 502t
Dimensions: 178ft 2in × 27ft 11in × 8ft
54.3m × 8.5m × 2.4m
Machinery: 2-shaft VTE, boilers, 1025ihp = 14kts
Armament: 2–100mm/50, 2–47mm, 2 MG

Class:
Preveze (1.12, TS 1915), *Aydin Reis* (6.12), *Sakiz* (2.12), *Burak Reis* (5.12, damaged 10.1.15 by mine in Bosphorus).

Four gunboats built by A C de Saint Nazaire – Penhöet. *Aydin Reis* was 'given' by the Kemal Government to Soviet Russia on 18 September 1920 and *Preveze* on 13 October to avoid capture by intervention forces. They joined the Russian Black Sea Fleet on 27 October 1920 and then returned in 1922, rearmed with two 3in guns. All ships, except *Aydin Reis*, were stricken in 1924 and she was reclassified as survey vessel and armed with 2–3in (removed 1936) and 2–57mm and reboilered with Babcock boilers. Stricken in 1948.

BEIRUT *armed yacht*

Displacement: 520t
Dimensions: 164ft × 22ft 8in × 12ft
50.0m × 6.9m × 3.7m
Machinery: 1-shaft TE, boilers, ihp = 12kts
Armament: 2–6pdr, 2–1pdr

Name	Builder	Launched	Fate
BEIRUT	Ramage & Ferguson	30.1.99	Sunk 1.11.14

A screw steel yacht bought and armed in 1910. Formerly *Lady Gipsey*. In 1913 she became a survey vessel and was sunk by British cruisers during the landing operation off Urla, W of Smyrna.

GALATA *armed yacht*

Displacement: 140t
Dimensions: 110ft 6in × 16ft 1in × 8ft
33.7m × 4.9m × 2.4m
Machinery: 1-shaft VTE, boilers, ihp = 12kts
Armament: 1–1pdr

Name	Builder	Launched	Fate
GALATA	Day, Summers & Co, Southampton	1898	Stricken 1927

A screw, steel yacht *Amalie* (ex-*Lobelia*) bought in 1910.

CIPKA *armed yacht*

Displacement: 560t (metric)
Dimensions: 189ft 6in oa, 162ft 5in pp × 22ft 10in × 12ft 5in
57.8m, 49.5m × 7.0m × 3.8m
Machinery: 1 shaft VTE, boilers, 700ihp = 15kts
Armament: 1–6pdr, 2–1pdr
Complement: 35 (Italian)

Name	Builder	Launched	Fate
CIPKA	Ramage & Ferguson, Leith	5.92	To Italy 7.1.12

A screw, steel yacht *Fauvette* bought and armed in 1910. She was damaged and seized by the Italian squadron at Kunfuda, Asir, Arabia. Renamed as *Gunfida*. She was stricken on 13 November 1924.

TARABULUS *armed yacht*

Displacement: 639t; 705t
Dimensions: 193ft 2in oa, 167ft pp × 25ft × 11ft 10in
59.0m, 50.9m × 7.7m × 3.6m
Machinery: 1-shaft VTE, boilers, 355ihp = 10.5kts
Armament: 1–6pdr, 2–1pdr
Complement: 31 (Italian)

Name	Builder	Launched	Fate
TARABULUS	Murray Bros, Dumbarton	7.87	To Italy 30.9.11

The screw steel yacht *Thetis* was bought and armed in 1910. Scuttled to avoid capture at Preveza by the Italian destroyers *Artigliere* and *Corazziere*. Refloated, repaired and commissioned into the Italian Navy as *Capitano Verri* on 19 November 1911. Stricken 19 December 1926.

INTIBAH *minelayer*

Displacement: 616grt
Dimensions: 202ft × 30ft 1in × 12ft
61.6m × 9.2m × 3.7m
Machinery: 2-shaft TE, boilers, 1670ihp = 12kts
Armament: 1–76mm, 2–57mm, 50 mines

Name	Builder	Launched	Fate
INTIBAH	R Duncan, Glasgow	1886	Stricken 1957

The salvage tug *Warren Hastings* bought in 1910 and converted to minelayer. Iron hulled with two funnels, the ship was engined by Rankin & Blackmore. In 1928 temporarily loaned to Seri Sefani Co, renamed *Uyanik* 1926, completely refitted in 1933.

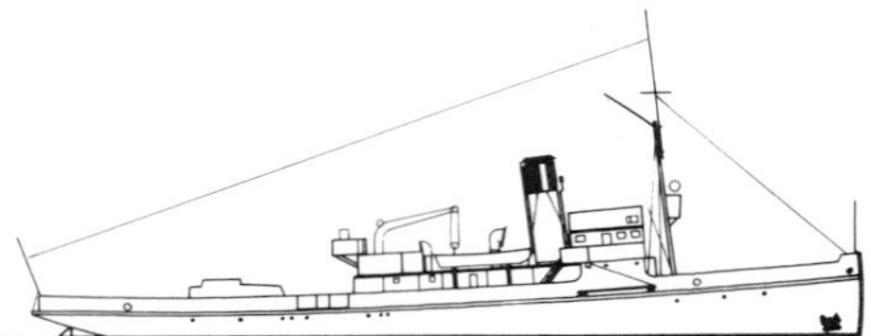

Nusret as completed
NB 1/750 scale

NUSRET *minelayer*

Displacement: 365t
Dimensions: 131ft 10in × 22ft × 8ft 2in
40.2m × 6.7m × 2.5m
Machinery: 1-shaft TE, 1 boiler, 1200ihp = 15kts
Armament: 2–47mm, 40 mines

Name	Builder	Launched	Fate
NUSRET	Germaniawerft	4.12.12	Stricken 1958

She laid the crucial parallel minefield in the Dardanelles (Arenkioi Bay) on which the British battleships *Irresistible* and *Ocean*, and the French battleship *Bouvet* were lost on 18 March 1915. In 1936–37 she was named *Yardim* and again returned to the previous name. After being stricken she was converted into the coastal motor vessel *Nushat Kaptan*.

AUXILIARY MINE WARFARE VESSELS

The following vessels served as auxiliary minelayers: *Giresun* (1877, 3056grt, mine depot ship), *Selanik* (270t, former tug served till 1928), *Gayret* (1885, 139grt), *Nilüfer* (1890, 1088grt, sunk 22.11.14), *Samsun* (1884, 275grt, sunk 14.8.15) and *Muzaffer*.

Moreover the following vessels were converted to minesweepers: *Rhone* (1895, 216grt, sunk 30.12.14), two former German coast guard vessels *Castor* (ex-*Wega*) and *Sirius* (both 1890, 52grt), four trawlers purchased in 1913–14 and also the Golden Horn ferries, of which *No 2* was sunk 27.5.15 and *No 5* was sunk 15.5.15.

Thornycroft type *motor launches*

Displacement: 12t
Dimensions: 60ft × 11ft × 2ft 6in
18.3m × 3.4m × 0.8m
Machinery: 2-shaft Thornycroft C/6 petrol motors, 140hp = 11kts (designed). Oil 740 gallons
Armament: 2–37mm

A total of 21 boats were built in 1911–12 by Thornycroft to the above particulars. All, except four boats built of steel, were built of teak. Three more boats were built of steel in 1912 of the same power and of similar general arrangement, but of shallower draught. Their dimensions were 70ft × 13ft × 1ft 10in *(21.3m × 4.0m × 0.6m)*. The boats, numbered *No 1* to *No 24*, originally designed for prevention of smuggling, and various purposes along Turkish coast were widely employed in the 1911–18 wars. One boat was lost in 1912, 5 more were lost in 1915–18 in the Bosphorus–Dardanelles area, where they were employed as minesweepers. A number served on Messopotamian rivers, where they were sunk by British forces, and one seized in 1914 became HMS *Flycatcher*. Only 5 boats survived the Great War and *Mülazim Hayati* (ex-*No 14*) served till 1948.

MOTOR GUNBOATS

Two former Russian motor gunboats *Zivoj* and *Zutkij* (built 1916 in USA, 30t, 20kts, armed with 1–47mm, 1–37mm and 2 MG) were received by the Turkish Nationalist Government from Soviet Russia in October 1921. Known as *No 1* and *No 2*, these boats were in bad condition in need of repairs and after long negotiations were sent back to Novorossiysk in December 1921.

MESOPOTAMIAN FLOTILLA

The Turkish flotilla on the Tigris and Euphrates rivers in August 1914 consisted of the gunboat *Marmaris* and several Thornycroft boats which served, till war broke out in the Persian Gulf. Later a number of river steamers were armed, of which the most significant was *Doghan* (ex-German tug *Pionier*, 130t, 12kts, 1–60mm). Beginning with 1916 a number of 50ft–54ft motor boats built by Holtzwerft, Hamburg and Kremer Sohn were delivered via Bulgaria. Moreover three sternwheel motor steamers and a number of armed lighters were built by Germans in Dsherablus. The flotilla supported land operations in Mesopotamia. In 1915 three British armed steamers and a gunboat *Firefly* were seized and incorporated into the flotilla, the latter as *Sulman Pak*. Some ships were sunk or captured by the British when they captured Baghdad in March 1917.

AUXILIARY WARSHIPS

A number of various vessels were armed during 1911–1918 wars and served as auxiliary gunboats and patrol vessels. Among them were *Sakiz* (1877, 246grt); *Moha* (tug, 600t, sunk 7.1.12); *Ferman, Mahmud Sevket Pasa* (1886, 2690grt, sunk 8.8.15, refloated and returned to mercantile service); *Djeyhun* (1890, 3510grt, sunk 7.6.15). Coast Guard Cutters *Nos 1–4*, *Iskodra* (ferry, 25t); ferries of the Bosphorus Steam Navigation Co, of which 7 were sunk or heavily damaged during 1914–18.

China

The Chinese Navy for hundreds of years consisted of a large number of junks. These ships were easily defeated by the European steamers during the Opium Wars. Steam was introduced into the Chinese Navy during the 1860s when a few steamers were built and purchased abroad. In 1868, with American and French aid, the Kiangnan and Foochow Arsenals began to build steam ships, mainly transports. During the 1880s a comparatively modern and strong fleet was built by Li Hung Chang using the Sea Defence Fund, established in 1875. Rumour has maintained that the Dowager Empress spent 21 million taels (about £3 million) allocated to the Fund on building her Summer Palace in Peking. Although the Chinese Navy was defeated by Japan in 1894–95, its sailors behaved in a manner of which any nation might have been proud. The traditions of that time were passed down. Little money was expended to the upkeep of vessels for some years and their engines and boilers were generally in poor state of repair. Lack of periodic docking left their bottoms in a very bad condition and reduced the speeds possible from deteriorating machinery.

However in 1898, four years after the Sino-Japanese War, China purchased five cruisers, their best ships for a number of years. The 1900 Boxer Rebellion and the Empire's chaotic condition meant that until 1906 only a few small ships were built for the Navy. In 1906–10 a number of gunboats and torpedo-boats were built in Japan and in Shanghai for the Northern provinces.

The Chinese Navy was organised by paired provinces grouped and placed under governor-generals. Four such pairs operated naval fleets: Kwantung and Kwangsi (Canton Fleet); Fukien and Chekiang (Foochow Fleet); Kiangsi and Anhwei (Shanghai or Nanyang = South Fleet); and Chihli – a single province (Peiyng = North Fleet). Some armed vessels were also operated by local authorities. The provincial authorities were almost independent and seldom cooperated. Such a navy lacked any unity, though nominally the whole Fleet was under the Imperial court's orders.

THE 1908–1911 PLANS

In 1908 an approximate programme of modernisation and reorganisation of the Navy was prepared. The Chinese Navy was to consist of three fleets (North, South and Central), each with 1 battleship of 14,000 tons, 1–2 first class cruisers, 4–5 second class, 5–6 third class and 6 fourth class and an uncertain number of dispatch vessels, gunboats and torpedo craft. The large ships were to be built in Japan and the smaller in China. An edict of 15 July 1909 created a naval and military advisory board to centralise administration. A Chinese naval commission was sent abroad and on its return at the end of 1910 two new programmes were announced. The first 'small' four-year programme called for 3 training cruisers of 3000 tons, 8 gunboats of 500 tons, 1 destroyer and 1 naval transport of 2000 tons at a total cost of 19.5 million taels (about £3 million). Nearly all of these ships were ordered and built. The 'large' seven-year programme called for 8 battleships of 16,000 tons, 20 cruisers, 30 destroyers and torpedo-boats as well as numerous gunboats and auxiliary ships at a total cost of 160 million taels (about £53 million) or one and a half times the Empire's estimated revenue in 1908. Two new naval bases in Nimrod Bay (on the coast of Chekiang, East China) and Nienshan (North China) were planned. Moreover coast defences, river flotillas and the training squadron were to be strengthened.

THE 1911–12 REVOLUTION

The army mutiny in Wuchang on 10 October 1911 began the Revolution that toppled the Manchu Dynasty in 1912. The boy-emperor Pu-bi abdicated and the Republic of China was proclaimed under the presidency of Marshal Yüan Shih-kai on 12 February 1912. The first warship to join the rebels was the cruiser *Hai Chou* and her commander Huang Chung Ying became the Chief of the Revolutionary Navy and then the first Marine Minister of the Republic of China. The 'large' building plan was never realised due to the shortage of money. Instead China tried to sell ships already nearing completion, but finally only one cruiser was acquired by Greece. In 1913–14 numerous ships were ordered to gratify President Yüan Shih-kai's imperial dreams but most of them never materialised due to the outbreak of the world war. China also planned to built several armoured cruisers and nearly 100 submarines, but these plans were too ambitious for the young republic. Despite these plans there had been a steady deterioration in naval discipline since 1911. The Navy ceased to exist as a national force and its different units fell under the control of various warlords. China of the late 1910s and early 1920s was a divided country and so was the Navy.

China declared war against Germany on 14 August 1917. German and Austro-Hungarian vessels were seized by the Chinese Government and some of them were incorporated into the Chinese Navy, where they served until the Sino-Japanese War of 1937–45.

SHIPBUILDING INDUSTRY

Despite 50 years of development, the shipbuilding industry in China was still in its infancy. Shortly after its establishment in 1868, the Kiangnan Arsenal at Shanghai built 5 ships for the Chinese Navy, but after 1873 the funds of the Kiangnan Construction Bureau were devoted to the use of arsenals and the manufacture of guns. Shipbuilding became so neglected that during the ensuing 30 years (1875–1904) only one ship was built. The output of the next period (1905–1911) totalled 133 vessels, including gunboats and merchantmen, of which only 18 were over 180ft in length, but more progress was made with the advent of the Republic in 1912. The Foochow Naval Dockyard built a number of warships at the outset, but appropriations for the Dockyard were greatly reduced from 1876. From 1874 to 1907 the Dockyard built 24 ships, but between 1908 and 1917 it failed to launch any. The Chinese Navy also controlled Whampoa Dock at Shanghai, engaged both for building and repairing, and Taku Dock, mostly used for docking the ships.

In 1919 China had 72 steamers of 95,560grt and sailing craft but during 1908 no fewer than 28,445 British vessels of 34,405,761 tons had entered and cleared the 40 Chinese treaty ports (including inland river ports open to foreign steamers since 1898). This was 40 per cent of her total trade, double the tonnage brought in China's own ships, more than all other foreign vessels combined and almost twice Japan's volume of trade. It was no more than typical of the period that the US Navy set up a Yangtze River patrol on 5 August 1921 'to protect US interests, lives and property . . .' On 14 August 1922 the defeated President Sun Yat Sen was rescued from Canton by a British gunboat and taken to Shanghai. On 6 December 1923 warships of all five Great Powers plus Portugal arrived at Canton to protect its foreign-administered customs house from Chinese seizure. They remained until China relented in April 1924.

FLEET STRENGTH 1906

CRUISERS AND SLOOPS

Name	Launched	Disp	Fate
Wei Yuan class			
CHAO WU	19.6.78	1209t	Stricken 1930
KANG CHI	21.7.79	1209t	Stricken 1910
Fu Po class			
FU PO	22.12.70	1258t	Stricken 1930
YUAN KAI	4.6.75	1258t	Stricken 1930
TENG YING CHOU	23.6.76	1258t	Stricken 1920
TAI AN	2.12.76	1258t	Stricken 1915
Hai Ching class			
CH'EN HANG	6.1.74	1450t	Stricken 1930
Nan T'an class			
NAN T'AN	12.12.83	2200t	Stricken 1910
NAN JUI	8.1.84	2200t	Stricken 1920
Pao Min class			
PAO MIN	1885	1477t	Stricken 1920
Kai Chi class			
KING CHING	17.1.86	2100t	Stricken 1920

Name	Launched	Disp (load)	Fate
Tung Chi class			
TUNG CHI	1895	1900t	Sunk 11.8.37
FU AN	1895	1700t	Stricken 1932
Hai Yung class			
HAI YUNG	15.9.97	2950t	Scuttled 11.8.37
HAI CHOU	11.12.97	2950t	Scuttled 11.8.37
HAI TAN	12.2.98	2950t	Scuttled 11.8.37
Hai T'ien class			
HAI CHI	24.1.98	4300t	Scuttled 11.8.37

All old sloops and cruisers built 1870–85 and *Fu An* served as transports. *King Ching* and *Tung Chi* were employed as TS. The ships that survived until the Sino-Japanese conflict were scuttled as blockships in the Yangtse 11 August 1937. *Hai Chou* having been the first ship to rebel against the Manchu in 1911.

ARMOURED GUNBOAT

Name	Launched	Disp	Fate
CHIN OU	1875	200t	Stricken *c*1914

Formerly *Tiong Sing* renamed in *c*1905, she served in the Nanyang Fleet till *c*1914.

GUNBOATS

Name	Launched	Disp	Fate
SUI CHING	1867	350t	Stricken *c*1918
AN LAN class	1868	439t	Stricken *c*1929
PENG CHAO HAI	1869	600t	Stricken *c*1913
TSE HAI	1869	730t	Stricken *c*1918
CHING YUAN class	1872	578t	Stricken *c*1918
LUNG HSIANG class	1876	320t	Stricken *c*1910
TSE TIEN	1876	420t	Stricken *c*1929
SI CHEW	1878	500t	Stricken *c*1929
HAI CHANG CHING	1880	440t	Stricken *c*1929
HAI TUNG HUG	1880	430t	Stricken *c*1918
KUANG YUAN class	1886	300t	Stricken *c*1929
KUANG WU class	1887–89	560t	Stricken *c*1929
KUANG CHIN class	1890–91	600t	Stricken *c*1929
KUANG CHING class	?1894	300t	Stricken *c*1929

A group of gunboats of various types and origins. They served mainly in provincial fleets for suppressing smuggling and piracy on inland and coastal waters. Some of the oldest ships were also used for customs duties. The *An Lan* class comprise *An Lan* (ex-*Kwang Tung*) and *Chen Tao* (ex-*Shang Tung*), both renamed after delivery. *Ching Yuan* class comprised also *Chen Hai*. *Lung Hsiang* class consisted also of *Hu Wei*. *Kuang Yuan* class comprised also *Kuang Chen, Kuang Li, Kuang Hsiang*. *Kuang Wu* class consisted also of *Kuang Chi* and *Kuang Keng*. *Kuang Chin* class consisted also of *Kuang Yü*. *Kuang Ching* class comprised also *Kuang Pi*. In addition to the above boats the provincial fleets possessed a number of small gunboats armed with light guns and a number of armed customs vessels. Moreover some armed steamers were in private hands.

TORPEDO GUNBOATS

Name	Launched	Disp	Fate
FEI YING	17.7.95	837t	Stricken 1932
KUANG TING	1891	1030t	Stricken *c*1914
CHIEN WEI	29.1.99	871t	Scuttled 11.8.37
CHIEN AN	3.3.00	871t	Scuttled 11.8.37

Fei Ying's engines were removed in 1926 and she finally was discarded in 1932. *Chien Wei* and *Chien An* were completely rebuilt in 1927–31 and renamed *Tse Chiang* and *Ta Tung* respectively. They were rearmed with 2–4.7in, 1–3in, 2–6pdr and 1–20mm AA, 6 MG.

TORPEDO-BOATS

Name	Launched	Disp	Fate
LEI LUNG class	1883	58t	Stricken 1925
LEI CHIEN class	1885–86	27t	Stricken 1925
CHANG	1895	89t	Stricken 1929
LIEH	1895	89t	Stricken 1931
SU	1895	120t	Scuttled 11.8.37
CHEN	1895	120t	Scuttled 11.8.37
CHIEN I	1902	30t	Not operational

Lei Lung and a sistership *Lei Hu* were the only survivors of the Vulcan-built class. Schichau's *Lei Chien* class comprised also *Lei Ken, Lei K'an, Lei K'un, Lei Li, Lei Sun, Lei Tui, Lei Chen* and *Lei Chung*. All the above boats belonged to the provincial Canton Fleet and at the end of their careers were employed by water police. *Su* and *Chen* were scuttled at Kiangyin in the Yangtse as blockships. *Chien I* the Foochow-built torpedo-boat was probably never operational.

MAJOR SURFACE SHIPS

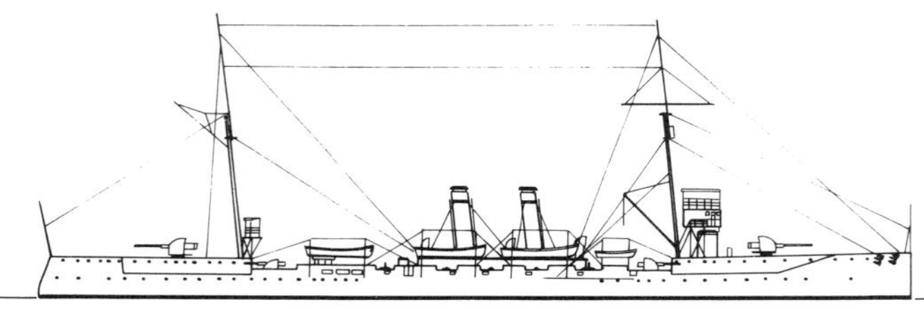

Ying Swei as completed

CHAO HO class *light cruisers*

Displacement: 2750t *(Chao Ho)*, 2500t *(Ying Swei)*, 2600t *(Fei Hung)*
Dimensions: 320ft pp (330ft pp, *Ying Swei)*, 346ft (oa) × 39ft–42ft × 13ft–14ft
97.5m (100.6m), 105.5m × 11.9m–12.8m × 4.0m–4.3m
Machinery: 3-shaft Parsons turbines, 3–6 boilers (see notes), 6000shp = 20kts (designed). Coal 550t plus oil 100t. Range 4500nm–5000nm at 10kts, *c*2900nm at 18kts
Armour: Deck 2in–¾in (51mm–19mm), CT 3in (76mm) *(Ying Swei* deck 1½in–¾in)
Armament: 2–6in (152mm)/50, 4–3in/50, 2–3in, 6–3pdr, 2–1pdr, 2–18in (457mm) aw TT
Complement: 331

Name	Builder	Laid down	Launched	Comp	Fate
CHAO HO	Armstrong-Whitworth	7.11.10	23.10.11	12.12	Sunk 28.9.37
YING SWEI	Vickers	1910	14.7.11	12.11	Sunk 25.10.37
FEI HUNG	New York SB	1910	4.5.12	11.13	To Greece 1914

A class of cruisers designed specially for training purposes. The special features of the design were the great variety in the size of the guns fitted, adoption of alternative systems of auxiliary machinery and different types of boilers on board – cylindrical and watertube as follows: *Chao Ho* 2 Yarrow watertube and 4 cylindrical; *Ying Swei* 4 White Foster watertube and 2 cylindrical; *Fei Hung* 3 Thornycroft express type. *Fei Hung* and *Chao Ho* had Armstrong guns, while *Ying Swei* carried Vickers pieces. After the Chinese Revolution of 1912 *Chao Ho* and *Fei Hung* were offered for sale, but finally only the *Fei Hung* was sold by her builders to Greece. In 1930 they received 2–2pdr AA guns. *Chao Ho* was disabled by Japanese ships at Canton and ran aground, while *Ying Swei* was sunk by Japanese aircraft in the Yangtze at Chiangyin.

CNT Monfalcone type *light cruisers*

Three small cruisers ordered in September 1913 that were to be built in 22–26 months from start of construction. Their armament was to be supplied by Skoda. All three were begun by early 1915, seized on the stocks by the Italians, recaptured intact in October 1917 by Austro-Hungarian forces, but there is no surviving evidence of Austrian intentions concerning these ships.

Displacement: 1800t (metric)
Dimensions: 350ft oa × 36ft × 13ft
109.7m × 10.9m × 4.0m
Machinery: 2-shaft AEG turbines, Yarrow boilers, 30,000shp = 32kts. Coal 150t plus oil 130t
Armour: Deck and shield protection
Armament: 10–4in, 4–1.8in (47mm), 2–18in (457mm) TT (2×3)

Name	Builder	Laid down	Launched	Comp	Fate
No 65–67	CNT, Monfalcone	1915	–	–	

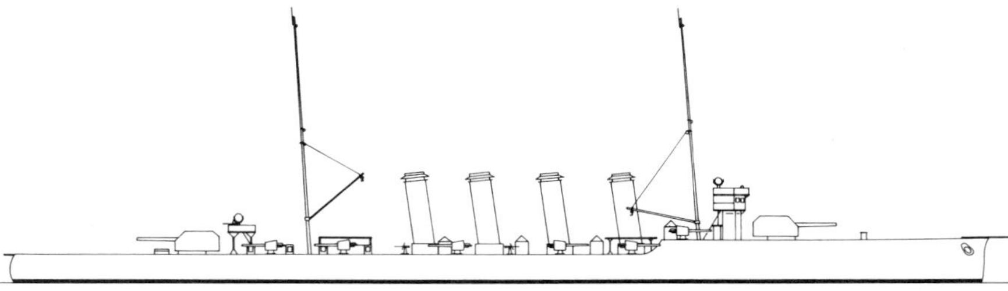

CNT Monfalcone large cruiser design

CNT Monfalcone type *large cruiser*

Displacement: 4900t normal
Dimensions: 456ft oa, 450ft wl × 48ft × 16ft
137.0m, 135.3m × 14.7m × 4.9m
Machinery: 2-shaft Parsons type turbines, 14 Yarrow watertube boilers, 37,000shp = 28kts
Armour: Belt 4in–2⅜in (102mm–60mm), deck 2½in–1in (63mm–250mm), turrets 4in (102mm), CT 4in
Armament: 4–8in (203mm)/50 (2×2), 12–4.7in (120mm)/45, 10–1.8in (47mm)/44, 4–1.5in (37mm), 8–7.9mm MG, 2–18in (457mm) TT

Name	Builder	Laid down	Launched	Comp	Fate
No 68	CNT, Monfalcone	3.15	–	–	BU *c*1919

She was ordered in November 1913 by the Chinese Navy. Construction work began on the ship at the end of 1914. Her armament and the armour were to be provided by the Skoda Works, while turbines were to come from Ganz & Danubius AG, Budapest. After the outbreak of the war work on her stopped and later Monfalcone was occupied by the Italian forces. When Monfalcone was recaptured in October 1917 the Austro-Hungarian Navy intended to complete her with modified armament (April 1918), of 8–150mm/50, 2–90mm/50 AA, 4–450mm TT (2×2). She was actually scrapped unfinished on the stocks postwar.

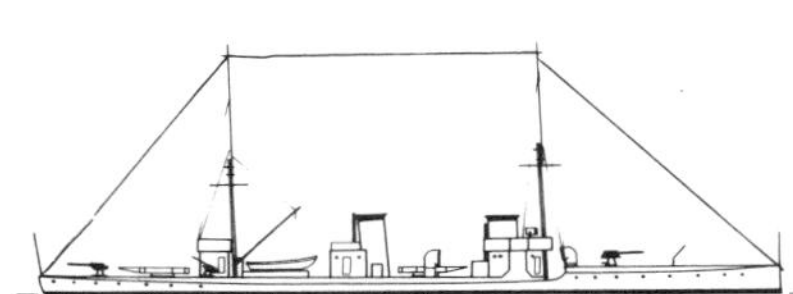

Chang Feng class

CHANG FENG class *destroyers*

Displacement: 390t
Dimensions: 198ft × 21ft 4in × 5ft 11in
60.4m × 6.5m × 1.8m
Machinery: 2-shaft VTE, 4 Schichau boilers (watertube), 6500ihp = 32kts. Coal 80t
Armament: 2–3in (12pdr), 4–3pdr (47mm), 2–18in (457mm) TT
Complement: 69

Class (launched, fate):
Chang Feng (6.11, wrecked 21.1.32), *Fu Po* (1912, sunk 27.9.37), *Fei Hung* (1912, scuttled 26.9.37)

Chang Feng was ordered from Schichau (Germany) in 1910 and the remaining two in 1911. On trials they made up to 36.8kts. In 1918 they were renamed by President Yüan Shih-Kai *Yu Chang*, *Chien Kang* and *Tung An* respectively. *Chang Feng* was wrecked at Nantung Chao, was salved and BU. *Chieng Kang* was sunk by Japanese aircraft at Chiangyin on the Yangtze, refloated by the Japanese, she was incorporated into the IJN as *Yamasemi*. *Tung An* was scuttled at Tsingtan.

LUNG TUAN class *destroyers*

A 400t destroyer, which was to be armed with 2–12pdr, 4–3pdr, 2–18in TT, was ordered in 1912 from Stabilimento Tecnico Triestino, Austria-Hungary. Launched in 1913, named *Lung Tuan*, completed and ready for delivery in 1914, she was seized by the Austrian Navy on 28 August 1914 and renamed *Warasdiner*. She was a prototype for 12 destroyers ordered in 1913 at STT to be delivered by 1916. None of them was laid down.

CHING PO class *destroyers*

A 400t destroyer, which was to be armed with 2–12pdr, 4–12pdr, 2–18in TT, was ordered in 1911 from Ansaldo, Sestri Ponente. She, named *Ching Po*, was taken over with China's agreement by the Italian Navy at the outbreak of the war with Turkey in 1911 and completed as *Ascaro*. Three more 500t, 30kt destroyers were to be built by Ansaldo in 1914, but due to World War I none was laid down.

HU PENG class *torpedo-boats*

Displacement: 96t
Dimensions: 135ft oa, 131ft 7in pp × 16ft 2.5in × 6ft 9in
41.1m, 40.1m × 4.9m × 2.1m
Machinery: 1 shaft TE, 2 Kampon type watertube boilers, 1200ihp = 23kts. Coal 28 tons
Armament: 1–2.5in, 1–6.9mm MG, 3–14in (356mm) TT (1 bow, 2 deck)
Complement: 31–32

Class (no, launched, fate):
Hu Peng (nr 7, 10.6.06, sunk 1.10.37), *Hu Ngo* (nr 8, 10.6.06, sunk 8.10.37), *Hu Chung* (nr 10, 17.11.06, sunk 3.10.37), *Hu Ying* (nr 9, 17.11.06, sunk 8.8.37)

Four steel Normand type TB were ordered from Kawasaki for the Nanyang Fleet by Vice Admiral Hu Peh. They were laid down on 25 February 1906 (the first pair) and on 11 May 1907 (the second pair) and delivered after a year. On trials they made 23.08 to 23.74kts with 1375–1484ihp. In 1922 they were rearmed with 2–2.5pdr and in 1931 with 1–3pdr and 1–1pdr and their crew increased to 41 men. They all were sunk by the Japanese aircraft on the Yangtze. *Hu Ngo* was refloated by the Japanese serving until 1940 as *Kawasemi*.

SUBMARINES

In 1915 Chinese sailors under Vice Admiral Wei Han arrived in the USA for instruction on US 'H' class submrines, but due to China's lack of money no boats were actually ordered. Finally in 1918 China tried to acquire six submarines ordered by Russia from the Electric Boat Company but no sale was made.

SMALL SURFACE WARSHIPS

CHIANG YUAN class *gunboats*

Displacement: 565t
Dimensions: 177ft 2in oa, 170ft pp × 28ft × 7ft
54.1m, 51.8m × 8.5m × 2.1m
Machinery: 2-shaft VTE, 2 watertube boilers, 950ihp = 13kts. Coal 113 tons
Armament: 1–4.7in (120mm), 1–12pdr (75mm), 4–3pdr (47mm), 4–6mm Maxim MG
Complement: 85

Class (launched, fate):
Chiang Yuan (16.11.04, stricken 1963), *Chiang Hung* (25.6.07, wrecked 8.9.31), *Chiang Li* (18.8.07, scuttled 26.9.37), *Chiang Chen* (18.9.07, sunk 20.7.38)

These 4 gunboats were ordered from Kawasaki Yd, Kobe (Japan), by the Viceroy of Kiangsu and Kiangsi, being named after rivers. *Chiang Yuan* was laid down in 1904 and delivered in 1905 and remaining ships were laid down and delivered in 1907. On trials they made 14.6kts to 15.1kts. *Chiang Yuan* survived 1937–45 on the Yangtze and was in the Chinese Communist Fleet from 1949 to 1963. *Chiang Li* was scuttled at Tsingtao. *Chiang Chen* was heavily damaged by Japanese aircraft on the Yangtze, seized by the Japanese on 15 November 1938 and salvaged.

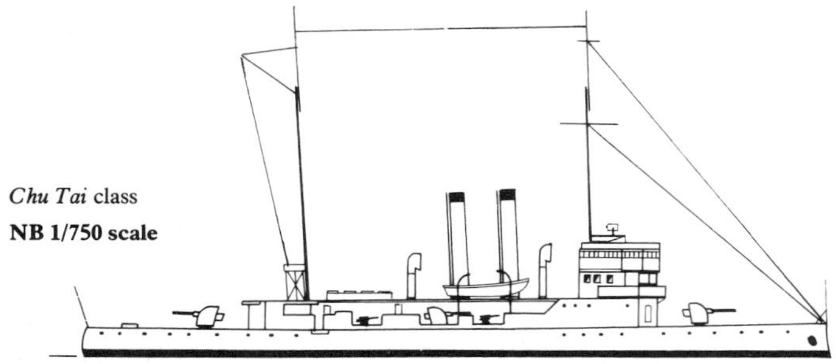

Chu Tai class
NB 1/750 scale

CHU class *gunboats*

Displacement: 752t
Dimensions: 200ft oa, 190ft pp × 29ft 6in × 8ft
61.0m, 57.9m × 9.0m × 2.4m
Machinery: 2-shaft VTE, 2 watertube boilers, 1350 = 13kts. Coal 150t
Armament: 2–4.7in (120mm), 2–12pdr (3in), 2–25mm, 2–6mm MG
Complement: 85

Class (launched, fate):
Chu Tai (25.9.06, wrecked 1.6.38), *Chu Tung* (12.6.06, discarded 1960s), *Chu Chien* (31.7.06, scuttled 11.8.37), *Chu Yu* (21.2.07, sunk 29.9.37), *Chu Yiu* (1.4.07, sunk 2.10.37), *Chu Kuan* (14.8.07, stricken 1960s)

These 6 vessels were ordered in 1904 from Kawasaki Yd, Kobe (Japan) by the Hukwang Viceroy Chang Tse tung, who appointed Lao Hueiwen to supervise construction. Laid down in 1905–1907, they were delivered in 1906–1907. On trials they made 13.9–16.3kts. *Chu Tai* beached off Nankang, Fukien was destroyed by Japanese aircraft on 19 April 1941. *Chu Chien* was scuttled in the Yangtze. *Chu Yu* was sunk off Tayu by Japanese aircraft and *Chu Yiu* on the Yangtze. The remaining 2 ships survived World War Two on the Yangtze, *Chu Tung* falling in 1949 to the Communist forces while *Chu Kuan* served till 1960s in Taiwan's Navy.

Chiang Hung as completed *Aldo Fraccaroli Collection*

KUAN CHUAN *gunboat*

Displacement: 305t
Dimensions: 119ft oa × 20ft × 7ft 7in
36.3m × 6.1m × 2.3m
Machinery: 1 shaft compound vertical, 1 cylindrical marine type boiler, 300ihp = 7.9kts. Coal 35t
Armament: 2–37mm, 1 Maxim
Complement: 26

Name	Builder	Launched	Fate
KUAN CHUAN	Kiangnan Dock	1908	Stricken 1929

AN FENG *gunboat*

Displacement: 169t
Dimensions: 122ft × 18ft 6in × 5ft 5in
37.2m × 5.6m × 1.7m
Machinery: 1 shaft engine, 1 watertube boiler, 350ihp = 12.1kts
Other particulars: not known

Name	Builder	Launched	Fate
AN FENG	Kiangnan Dock	1908	

She was built for An Hui Sheng, for provincial use.

LIEN CHING *gunboat*

Displacement: 500t
Dimensions: 175ft × 25ft × 9ft 6in
53.3m × 7.6m × 2.9m
Machinery: 2-shaft TE, cylindrical multitubular boilers, 925ihp = 13.5kts. Coal 95 tons
Armament: 4–3pdr (47mm)
Complement: 60

Name	Builder	Launched	Fate
LIEN CHING	Kiangnan Dock	1910	Sunk 26.8.37

She was a steel hulled gunboat, built by order of the Department of the Navy as a royal yacht, for Tsa Tsun. Completed in 1911, she had one funnel and two masts. In November 1930 she was renamed *Chi Jih* and used as surveying ship. Two MG were added and the crew increased to 92 men. She was sunk near Suzhou on the Yangtze by Japanese destroyers.

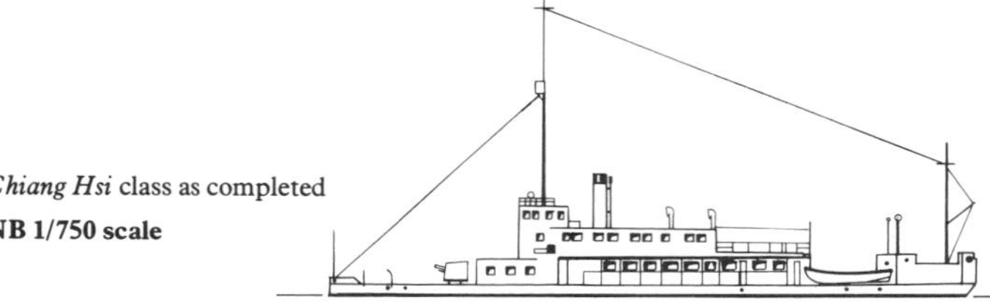

Chiang Hsi class as completed
NB 1/750 scale

CHIANG HSI class *river gunboats*

Displacement: 140t
Dimensions: 144ft × 24ft 6in × 2ft (146ft × 24ft × 2ft *Chiang Kun)*
43.9m × 7.5m × 0.6m (44.5m × 7.3m × 0.6m Chiang Kun)
Machinery: 2-shaft VTE, 2 Schultz watertube boilers, 450ihp (500ihp *Chiang Kun*) = 12kts. Coal 30t
Armament: 1–87mm howitzer, 4–8mm Maxim MG
Complement: 49

Name	Builder	Launched	Fate
CHIANG HSI	Germania	1911	Sunk 24.8.41
CHIANG KUN	Vulcan	1912	Sunk 24.8.41

Steel hulled river gunboats (named after rivers) for the Nanyang Fleet. Their design based on *Otter* class German gunboats. *Chiang Hsi* was originally laid down as *Chin Pei*. The planned 2–57mm guns were never fitted. In 1930 *Chiang Kun* was armed with 2–1pdr and *Chiang Hsin* with 1–1pdr. Both ships were sunk by Japanese aircraft at Patung, Szechuan.

Chiang Hung as completed
Aldo Fraccaroli Collection

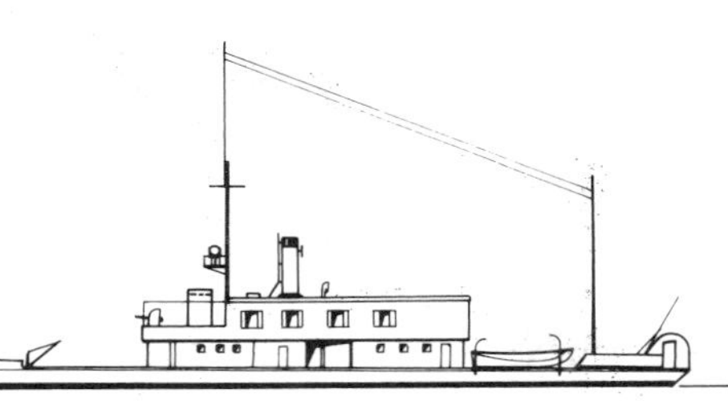

Chiang Kung as completed
NB 1/750 scale

CHIANG KUNG class *gunboats*

Displacement: 250t
Dimensions: 144ft 4in × 19ft 7in × 7ft 6in
44.0m × 6.0m × 2.3m
Machinery: VTE = 14kts
Armament: 1–3in, 1–57mm (see notes)
Complement: 62

Class (fate):
Chiang Kung (sunk 10.38), *Chiang Tai* (sunk 26.9.37), *Chiang Ku*, *Chiang Ching*

Small gunboats built at Hankow in 1908 for provincial purposes. The two last ships were probably never begun. The 57mm gun was not fitted, as 4 Maxim were mounted. By 1936 they were rearmed with 2–3in, 1–40mm AA, 1 MG. *Chiang Kun* was sunk by Japanese aircraft in the Tsuin river, near Canton and *Chiang Tai* by Japanese aircraft off the Kwantung coast.

YUNG HSIANG class *gunboats*

Displacement: 780t normal
Dimensions: 216ft oa, 205ft pp × 29ft 6in × 8ft
65.8m, 62.5m × 9.0m × 2.4m
Machinery: 2-shaft VTE, 2 watertube boilers, 1350ihp = 13kts. Coal 190t
Armament: 1–4.1in (105mm), 1–12pdr (75mm), 4–3pdr (47mm), 2–1pdr
Complement: 108

Name	Builder	Launched	Fate
YUNG HSIANG	Kawasaki, Kobe	30.3.12	Scuttled 26.9.37
YUNG FENG	Mitsubishi, Nagasaki	1912	Sunk 24.10.38

Yung Hsiang was scuttled at Tsingtao, refloated by the Japanese and returned in 1945, served as Taiwan gunboat armed with 2–3in, 8–25mm, 6 MG till *c*1959. *Yung Feng* was renamed *Chung Shan* in 1934, she was sunk off Kinkou in the Yangtze by Japanese aircraft.

WU FENG *gunboat*

Displacement: 200t
Dimensions: 124ft × 20ft × 7ft
37.8m × 6.1m × 2.1m
Machinery: 1-shaft VTE, 1 cylindrical multitubular boiler, 300ihp = 10kts. Coal 30t
Armament: 4–3pdr (47mm)
Complemen: 46

Name	Builder	Launched	Fate
WU FENG	Tsingtao	1912	Scuttled 11.8.37

She was built as the Admiralty yacht for Peiyang Fleet, but officially served as a gunboat. In 1922 she was rearmed with 2–65mm. She was scuttled at Kiangyin as a blockship.

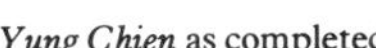

Yung Chien as completed

YUNG CHIEN class *gunboats*

Displacement: 860t
Dimensions: 215ft 6in oa, 205ft pp × 29ft 6in × 11ft 6in
65.7m, 62.5m × 9.0m × 3.5m
Machinery: 2 shaft VTE, 2 watertube boilers, 1350ihp = 13.5kts. Coal 150t
Armament: 1–4in, 1–12pdr (3in), 4–3pdr (47mm), 2–1pdr (37mm)
Complement: 105

Class (builder, launched, fate):
Yung Chien (Kiangnan Dock, 1915, sunk 25.8.37), *Yung Chi* (Kiangnan Dock, 1915, sunk 21.10.38)

A *Chiang Hsi* class gunboat on trials *Aldo Fraccaroli Collection*

Yung Chien was sunk by Japanese aircraft while lying under repair at Shanghai's Kiangnan yard and captured by the Japanese in November 1937. She was refloated, repaired and on 25 October 1938 became the Japanese depot ship *Asuka* being sunk on 7 May 1945 in the Whangpoo River by US aircraft. *Yung Chi* was sunk by Japanese aircraft near Hsin-Ti on the Yangtze and seized by the Japanese on 8 November 1938. She was salvaged, repaired and transferred on 22 May 1940 to the Nanking Government's Navy as *Hai Hsing* (armed with 1–100mm, 1–90mm, 9 small guns). Recaptured by the Chinese in mid-September 1945 and renamed *Yung Chi*, she was sunk in the Yangtze by Communist gunfire on 25 April 1949.

CHIEN CHUNG class *river gunboats*

Displacement: 90t
Dimensions: 110ft oa × 18ft 6in × 2ft
35.5m × 5.6m × 0.6m
Machinery: 2-shaft VTE, 1 watertube boiler, 450ihp = 11kts. Coal 33t
Armament: 1–3.4in (87mm) howitzer, 4–7.9mm Maxim MG
Complement: 42

Class (launched, fate):
Chien Chung (6.15), *Yung An* (1916), *Kung Chen* (1916, sunk 10.38)

River gunboats built at Yangtze Works, Hankow. They were paid off in 1931 and later probably returned to service. *Kung Chen* was sunk in Canton by Japanese aircraft.

HAI YEN *river gunboat*

Displacement: 56t
Dimensions: 65ft × 12ft × 2ft 2in
19.8m × 3.7m × 0.7m
Machinery: 2-shaft VTE, 1 return fire boiler, 60ihp = 10kts. Coal 8t
Armament: 1–37mm, 2–7.9mm Maxim, MG

Name	Builder	Launched	Fate
HAI YEN	Taku	1917	Sunk 29.7.37

River gunboat, sunk in Canton by Japanese aircraft.

HAI FU class *river gunboats*

Displacement: 166t
Dimensions: 109ft oa, 105ft pp × 17ft × 7ft 9in
33.2m, 32.0m × 5.2m × 2.4m
Machinery: 1-shaft VTE, 1 boiler, 220ihp = 10.5kts. Oil 35t
Armament: 1–37mm QF, 2 Maxims
Complement: 22

Class:
Hai Fu, *Hai Ou*

River gunboats built by Kiangnan Dock, Shanghai in 1917. In 1931 another 1–37mm was added and the crew increased to 35. Their fates are unknown.

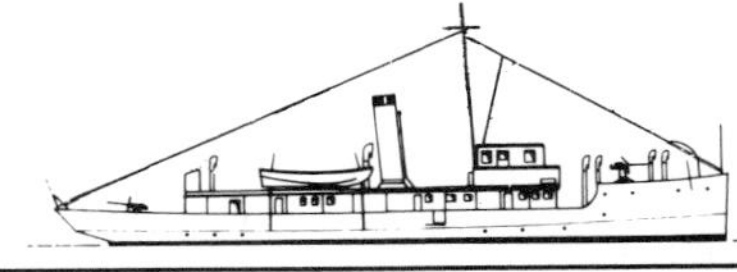

Hai Hung as completed
NB 1/750 scale

HAI HUNG class *river gunboats*

Displacement: 190t
Dimensions: 112ft × 18ft × 8ft 6in
34.1m × 5.5m × 2.6m
Machinery: 2-shaft VTE, 1 cylindrical boiler, 300ihp = 10.5kts *(Hai Ku)*, 11.0kts *(Hai Hung)*. Coal 20t
Armament: 2–37mm QF, 2–7.9mm Maxim MG
Complement: 22

Class:
Hai Hung, *Hai Ku*

River gunboats built at Foochow in 1917. Their fates are unknown though still in service in 1930.

HAI HO class *river gunboats*

Displacement: 211t
Dimensions: 106ft × 18ft × 6ft 6in
32.3m × 5.5m × 2.0m
Machinery: 1-shaft VTE, return tube boiler, 200ihp = 12kts. Coal 20t
Armament: 4–37mm, 2–7.9mm Maxim
Complement: 22

Class (builder, launched):
Hai Ho (Taku Dock, 1917), *Hai Peng* (Taku Dock, 1920)
River gunboats. Fates unknown.

EX-GERMAN RIVER GUNBOATS
Two German river gunboats *Vaterland* and *Otter* were taken on 20 March 1917 by the Chinese Navy and commissioned as *Li Chien* and *Li Sui* respectively. *Li Sui* was damaged by Soviet aircraft off Fugdin on 19 October 1929 and BU 1932. *Li Chien* was seized by the Japanese and was given to the Manchurian Flotilla being renamed *Li Sui* in 1937.

MOTOR TORPEDO BOATS
In 1921 two Italian MTBs *Mas 226* and *Mas 227* were purchased and renamed *No 1* and *No 2*. They were stricken in 1933.

Argentina

The period 1906–21 was one of financial exhaustion for the Argentine Navy. Argentina and Chile had engaged in an expensive naval arms race that had just ended with the naval limitation treaty, the Pact of May, signed in 1904. However, the Brazilian building programme of 1904 did force Argentina to respond. Brazil's acquisition of dreadnoughts alone outclassed the entire Argentine fleet. The necessity of more naval expenditure was hotly debated in Argentina. A continuing border dispute with both Brazil and Uruguay helped decide the issue in favour of buying two dreadnoughts with an option to buy a third depending upon what Brazil did. In 1907 the Argentine government adopted a naval programme to build or buy 3 armoured ships (dreadnoughts), 9 torpedo-boat destroyers, and 21 torpedo-boats at a cost of 145 million francs. In addition 45 million francs were set aside for gunboats and transports. Most of this programme was never completed due to a shortage of funds.

FIRST WORLD WAR
Argentina remained neutral during World War One. On three occasions in 1915 German merchantmen were interned for violating Argentine neutrality: *Patagonia* on 18 January; *Seydlitz* on 23 January; and *Holger* on 26 February. The Argentine Navy, like most in Latin America, was dependent upon Great Britain for its hard coal. The war interrupted this source, and the activity of the fleet was greatly reduced during the war years. During the early years U-boat activities had little effect on Argentine public opinion. Argentina had a modest merchant fleet, and it rarely ventured beyond coastal waters. But, as the shortage of merchant shipping grew world wide, Argentine ships were forced to sail into U-boat patrolled waters. In April 1917 the Argentine merchant ship *Monte Protegido* was sunk by a U-boat. Though Germany paid compensation in this case, two more Argentine merchantmen met similar fates in June and a fourth in January 1918. The effect of these sinkings was compounded by the ruthless actions (deciphered by the Royal Navy's Room 40 diplomatic section) of the German Ambassador at Buenos Aires, Count Luxburg, who telegrammed Berlin in July 1917: 'As regards Argentine steamers (*Oran* and *Guazo*) I recommend either compelling them to turn back, sinking them without leaving any traces, or letting them through [to Bordeaux]'. Eventually Argentina severed diplomatic relations after the Allies revealed this and other telegrams in the American press.

Argentine sheep, beef and mules (the latter being sold to Britain for the Indian Army in Mesopotamia) were shipped weekly from Buenos Aires. In 1916 Herr Arnold, Germany's most effective agent in Latin America, lethally infected 200 mules, destined for the SS *Phidias*, with anthrax germs concealed in sugar beet cubes. This deadly piece of germ warfare, which cost another shipment of mules, was owed to a German diplomat's French mistress carrying the ampoules aboard the Buenos Aires-bound Spanish liner *Reine Victoria Eugenia*. The Admiralty's Room 40 Intelligence Unit knew of her lethal cargo but the cruiser HMS *Newcastle* missed a planned interception due to fog. The British Minister dissolved one of the cubes in front of President Hipolito Irigoyen, but it took combined British and American espionage efforts to counter Arnold, whose methods included infecting grain with fungus and stirring up strikes.

As throughout Latin America, the First World War impacted very heavily on the Argentine Navy, thus restricting its operations and acquisitions for many years.

In 1910 Argentina had begun the construction of 12 torpedo-boat destroyers. Four were to be built by Cammell Laird of England, four by Chantiers de la Bretagne of France, and two each in the German yards of Krupp and Schichau. The ships building in Great Britain were sold to Greece in October 1912, and those building in France were taken into her own navy in August 1914. Argentina did order four more units from Germany in 1912 to replace those sold to Greece but they were never delivered.

Personnel totalled about 8500 in 1906 and rose to about 9500 in 1919 with 8000 reserves and 10,000 special reserves. Buenos Aires, the main base, had two drydocks. Puerto Belgrano received two by 1919 and Rio Santiago emerged as a new base with three docks (2 floating). The merchant marine totalled 317 steamers of 222,533grt (including sailing ships over 100 tons) in 1919.

FLEET STRENGTH 1906

BATTLESHIPS

Name	Launched	Disp	Fate
El Plata class			
EL PLATA	29.8.74	1500t	Stricken 16.11.27
LOS ANDES	29.10.75	1500t	Stricken 16.11.27
Almirante Brown class			
ALMIRANTE BROWN	6.10.80	4300t	Stricken 17.11.32
Libertad class			
INDEPENDENCIA	26.2.91	2300t	Stricken 1951
LIBERTAD (ex-*Nueve de Julio*)	11.12.90	2300t	Stricken 16.12.46

CRUISERS

Name	Launched	Disp	Fate
Patagonia class			
PATAGONIA	1885	1400t	Stricken 16.11.27
25 de Mayo class			
25 DE MAYO	5.3.90	3180t	Stricken *c* 1921
9 de Julio class			
9 DE JULIO	26.7.92	3500t	Stricken 23.10.30
Buenos Aires class			
BUENOS AIRES	10.5.95	4500t	Stricken 17.5.32
Garibaldi class			
GARIBALDI	27.5.95	6700t	Stricken 20.3.34
GENERAL BELGRANO	1896	7100t	Stricken 8.5.47
PUEYRREDON	25.7.98	6800t	Stricken 2.8.54
SAN MARTIN	25.5.96	6700t	Stricken 18.12.35

DESTROYERS

Name	Launched	Disp	Fate
Corrientes class (modified RN 'A' class)			
CORRIENTES	1896	280t	Stricken 23.10.30
ENTRE RIOS	11.7.96	280t	Stricken 23.10.30
MISIONES	1897	280t	Stricken 23.10.30

In addition to the above, the Argentine Navy in 1906 also operated the torpedo-boat *Espero* (launched 22 April 1890, 520t, stricken 28 June 1916); 6 *Bathurst* class (modified RN *TB 79* type) coastal torpedo-boats, *Bathurst, Buchardo, Jorge, King, Pinedo* and *Thorne* (launched 1890, 90t, stricken 1926–27); 2 *Comodoro Py* class (modified *Ariete* class) coastal torpedo-boats, *Comodoro Py* and *Comodoro Murature* (launched 1891, 110t, stricken 1926–27); the sea-going torpedo gunboat *Patria* (launched 1893, 1100t, stricken 1927); the coastal gunboat *Uruguay* (launched 6 March 1874, 550t, converted to a hydrographic ship in 1903, decommissioned 16 November 1927 and now preserved in Buenos Aires; and the training ship *Presidente Sarmiento* (launched 31 August 1897, 2733t, decommissioned 1961, preserved in Buenos Aires); and numerous transports.

MAJOR SURFACE SHIPS

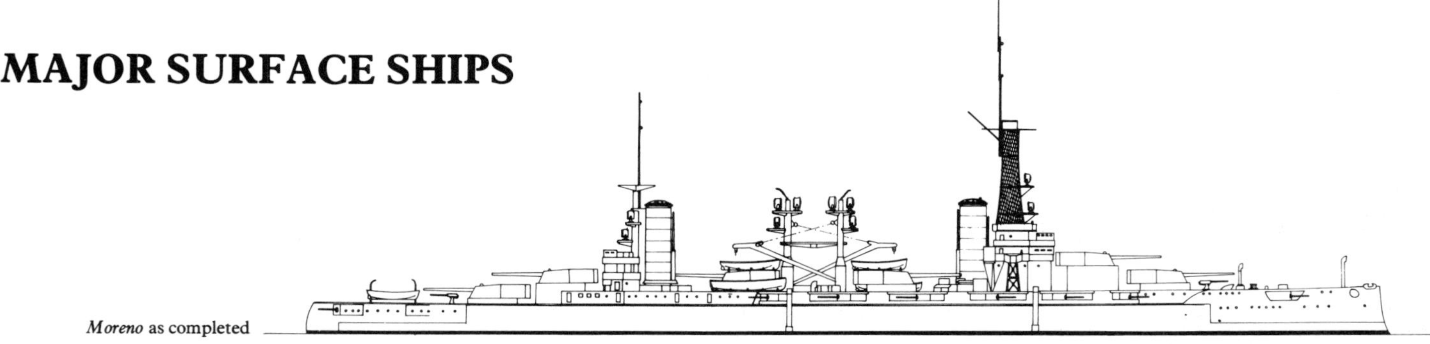

Moreno as completed

RIVADAVIA class *battleships*

Displacement: 27,940t normal; 30,600t full load

Dimensions: 594ft 9in oa, 585ft pp × 98ft 4½in × 27in 8½in normal
181.3m, 178.3m × 30.0m × 8.5m

Machinery: 3 shafts, Curtiss geared turbines, 18 Babcock and Wilcox boilers, 40,000shp = 22.5kts. Coal 4000t, oil 600t. Range 7000nm at 15kts, 11,000nm at 11kts

Armour: Belt 12in–10in (305mm–254mm), casemate 9⅓in–6⅙in (238mm–159mm), turrets 12in, CT 12in

Armament: 12–12in (305mm)/50 cal (6×2), 12–6in (152mm)/50 cal, 16–4in (102mm)/50 cal QF, 2–21in (533mm) TT

Complement: 1130 (130 officers and 1000 men)

Name	Builder	Laid down	Launched	Comp	Fate
RIVADAVIA	Fore River	25.5.10	26.8.11	12.14	Sold 8.2.56
MORENO	New York SB	9.7.10	23.9.11	3.15	Sold 8.2.56

The *Rivadavia* class was authorised in 1908 primarily as a response to the *Minas Gerais* class being constructed in Brazil. An intense internal debate took place in Argentina concerning the need to purchase two such expensive dreadnoughts, costing £2.2 million each. Argentina's recent border controversies with Brazil, Chile, and Uruguay helped win the day for those in favour.

The Argentine method for acquiring the best possible design stirred controversy among the building nations. In 1908 Rear-Admiral Onofre Betbeder set up office in London and requested all interested parties to submit plans for the construction of two dreadnoughts with the option to build a third. The guidelines were sketchy to allow the bidders to develop the best possible plans. Fifteen companies submitted plans. The Argentinians reviewed the submissions, chose the best features from each, and gave the revised guidelines to the competing firms. This process was then repeated. The competitors were in a furore and considered this as a looting of their trade secrets.

The contract was awarded to Fore River Shipbuilding Corporation of Quincy, Massachusetts, at a saving of over £224,000 per ship over the nearest competitor. European builders were shocked because the United States, which then lagged far behind Great Britain and Germany in the dreadnought race, was not considered to be a serious competitor.

The *Rivadavia* class closely paralleled American battleships in appearance and design. The machinery was placed amidships with the boilers grouped in separate rooms equally forward and abaft the engine room. This arrangement reduced trimming problems and separated machinery vitals into three separate compartments.

The 'en echelon' 12in amidships turrets could in theory fire on a 180-degree arc on the side of the ship were located and 100 degrees on the opposite side. The secondary 6in guns were mounted on the upper deck behind 6in armour. The 16 4in QF guns were for protection against torpedo attack; 8 of these guns were mounted in the between decks, 4 on the gun deck aft, and 4 on the upper deck forward. The 8 remaining guns were located on the weather deck – 6 on the superstructure deck and 2 on the upper deck aft. The 4in guns were not protected by armour. Two submerged side-loading TT were located in the torpedo room forward, firing broadside. The ships' magazines stowed 120 rounds of 12in shell per gun, 300 rounds for each 6in, 350 rounds per 4in gun, and 16 Whitehead torpedoes.

The ships were initially fitted with two 15ft Barr & Stroud rangefinders mounted in revolving armoured towers above the forward and after CT for controlling the 12in guns. Two 9ft Barr & Stroud were mounted on the platform on top of the king posts for the boat booms.

Typical of American-built dreadnoughts, protection received special attention. The main belt was 12in amidships tapering to 5in and 4in at the stem and stern respectively. The belt extended 5ft above and 6ft below the normal waterline. The turret armour was 12in on the face, 9in on the sides, 9.5in on the rear and 4in on the top. The forward and aft CT were 12 and 9in respectively. The protective deck extended the ship's length 24in above the waterline amidships, sloping down to the lower edge of the main belt armour. The protective deck varied from 20lb medium steel to 80lb of nickel steel. The inner bottom extended most of the length of the ships. An inner skin was fitted around the magazines, boilers, and machinery. This was for added protection against mines and torpedoes.

Rivadavia on trials *Aldo Fraccaroli Collection*

The electrical plant consisted of 4375kW turbogenerators located under the midship magazines forward and aft of the engine rooms. Two 75kW generators run off of diesel engines provided electricity when the boilers were cold. An 8kW Telefunken radio had an optimum range of 1500km.

The USN Board of Inspection and Survey for Ships made the following observations concerning *Rivadavia* on 21 October 1913. 'On the high speed runs the vessel made the exact contract speed, 22.5 knots; but it is believed that she can do a little better . . . She . . . handles remarkably well . . . The Board prefers our adopted centerline arrangement of turrets [*Wyoming* class]. While theoretically the *Rivadavia* has an ahead and astern fire of six guns, this is not so in reality, as it is almost certain that the blast from the waist turret guns would dish in the smokepipes and damage the uptakes . . . The Bethlehem Steel Company designed and made special [12in guns] breech-blocks, all of which were rejected, and the regular US Navy type of breech-block was finally made and installed. With comparatively minor modifications the vessel would practically meet the requirements of our own vessels.'

A third dreadnought was authorised in 1912 in response to Brazil's third dreadnought, the *Rio de Janeiro*. Since neither this ship nor the Brazilian *Riachuelo* ever materialised, Argentina's third dreadnought was never laid down. *Rivadavia* and *Moreno* were extensively modernised in the United States between 1924 and 1926. They were converted to oil-firing and received a new fire control system. They were sold for scrap on 8 February 1956.

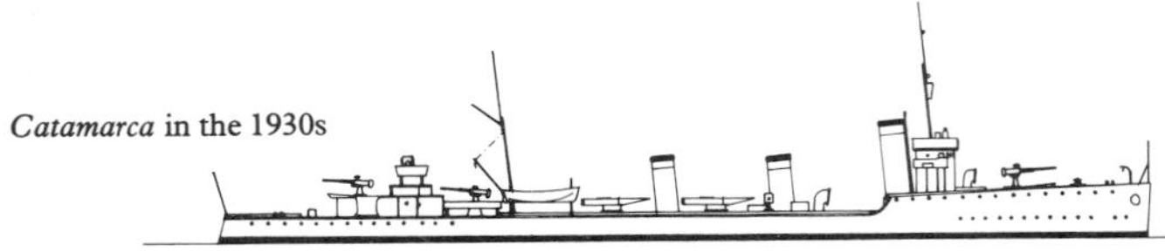
Catamarca in the 1930s

CATAMARCA class *destroyers*

Displacement: 995t normal; 1357t full load
Dimensions: 289ft 2in oa × 27ft × 17ft
88.1m × 8.2m × 5.2m
Machinery: 2-shaft Curtis AEG turbines, 2 Schulz-Thornycroft boilers, 25,765hp = 27kts. Coal 250t, oil 110t. Range 3000nm at 15kts
Armament: 4–4in (102mm)/50 cal, 4–21in (533mm) TT
Complement: 150

Name	Builder	Launched	Fate
CATAMARCA	Krupp	1911	Sold 1959
JUJUY	Krupp	4.3.12	Sold 10.1.57

The *Catamarca* class (named after Andean provinces) were two of 12 destroyers ordered by Argentina in 1910, being laid down next year and completed on 13 April and 15 April 1912 respectively. These destroyers cost £124,360 each and were numbered D1 and D2. They sailed from Germany with Argentine crews in the summer of 1912.

Jujuy (outboard) and *Cordoba* — *By courtesy of R L Scheina*

LA PLATA class *destroyers*

Displacement: 875t normal; 1368t full load
Dimensions: 295ft 4in oa × 29ft 6in × 16ft 5in max
90.0m × 9.0m × 5.0m
Machinery: 2-shaft Curtis AEG turbines, 5 Schulz-Thornycroft boilers, 28,000hp = 35kts. Coal 290t, oil 50t. Range 3000nm at 15kts
Armament: 4–4in (102mm)/50 cal, 2–37mm AA, 4–21in (533mm) TT
Complement: 150

Name	Builder	Launched	Fate
LA PLATA	Schichau, Elbing	1911	Stricken 10.1.57
CORDOBA	Schichau, Elbing	1912	Stricken 10.1.56

Two of 12 destroyers ordered from Germany by Argentina in 1910. Each ship cost £124,360. *La Plata* was completed on 30 March 1912 and *Cordoba* on 8 July 1912. Trials speeds were *Cordoba* 34.7kts and *La Plata* 36.8kts.

La Plata between the wars — *CPL*

SAN LUIS class *destroyers*

Displacement: 980t trial; 1175t full load
Dimensions: 292ft 11in oa × 27ft 7in max × 9ft 10in
89.2m × 8.4m × 3.0m
Machinery: 2-shaft Curtis turbines, 5 White Forster boilers, 20,000shp = 32kts. Coal 225t, oil 75t. Range 3000nm at 15kts
Armament: 4–4in (102mm)/50cal, 4–21in (533mm) TT
Complement: 110

Class (launched):
San Luis (2.11), *Santa Fe* (3.11), *Tucuman* (9.11), *Santiago* (4.11)

In 1910 Argentina ordered 12 torpedo-boat destroyers – four from Cammell Laird and four each from French and German yards. These English boats (laid down in 1910) had five funnels whereas the French and German ones had three. Magazine capacity was 250 rounds of 4in shell. The characteristics cited above are as designed, as was the case with the German boats actually delivered, changes in plans would probably have resulted in larger crews, increased drafts, and slower speeds. These four destroyers, named after Argentine towns, were sold to Greece in October 1921 for the First Balkan War and became *Aetos*, *Ierax*, *Leon* and *Panther*. See *Aetos* class under Greece.

MENDOZA class *destroyers*

Displacement: 940t trial; 1170t full load
Dimensions: 289ft 8in oa × 28ft 3in × 10ft 2in
88.3m × 8.6m × 3.1m
Machinery: 2-shaft Curtis turbines, 5 White Forster boilers, 19,500shp = 32kts. Coal 256t, oil 82t. Range 3000nm at 15kts
Armament: 4–4in (102mm)/50cal, 4–21in (533mm) TT
Complement: 110

Class (launched):
Mendoza (18.2.11), *Salta* (25.9.11), *San Juan* (18.2.11), *Rioja* (1911)

In 1910 the Argentine Navy initiated construction of 12 TBD, these 4 to be built in France (laid down by Ch de Bretagne, Nantes, in 1910). The French boats had three funnels. Magazine capacity was 250 rounds of 4in shell. The characteristics cited above are as designed; as was the case in the German boats actually delivered, changes in plans would probably have resulted in larger crews, increased drafts and slower speeds. These destroyers were bought by France immediately after the outbreak of World War One. They became the French *Aventurier*, *Intrepide*, *Opiniâtre*, and *Temeraire*. See *Aventurier* class under France. Four new boats were ordered from Krupp to replace them. Reportedly they were to have diesel engines. They were never delivered due to the war.

SMALL SURFACE WARSHIPS

ROSARIO class *gunboats*

Displacement:	1055t full load; 709t light
Dimensions:	250ft 6in oa × 32ft 2in × 14ft *76.4m × 9.8m × 4.3m*
Machinery:	2-shaft VTE, 2 Yarrow boilers, 1300shp = 14.5kts. Coal 160t, 1000nm radius at 8kts
Armour:	Belt amidships 4in (102mm), deck 1½in–1in (38mm–25mm), CT 3in (76mm)
Armament:	2–6in (152mm) howitzers, 6–12pdr (3in/76mm), 8 MG
Complement:	145

Name	Builder	Launched	Fate
ROSARIO	Armstrong, Tyne	27.7.08	Sold 4.12.59
PARANA	Armstrong, Tyne	28.4.08	Sold 28.8.58

These gunboats cost £81,445 each. *Parana* was laid down in 1907 and completed on 8 August 1908, *Rosario* was laid down in 1908 and completed on 7 August 1909. Argentina had numerous unresolved border disputes with Brazil and Paraguay. The ships were acquired to patrol the river waters, notably the Parana and Paraguay, bordering these nations.

Ex-German M 27 class *minesweepers*

Class (original no, fate):
M 1 (ex-*M 48*, renamed *Bathurst* 1936, stricken 16.12.46, BU 1951), *M 2* (ex-*M 51*, renamed *Fournier*, stricken 5.4.37, hulk BU 1943), *M 3* (ex-*M 52*, renamed *Jorge*, sloop *Cormoran* 26.1.40, stricken 26.8.46), *M 4* (ex-*M 53*, renamed *King*, stricken 27.7.37, torpedo TS *Teniente de la Sota* from 11.41, stricken 16.12.46, BU 1948)

These 4 German Type 1915 minesweepers were sold out commercially in 1921 and resold to Argentina around 1922. They were given names (of early naval heroes) about 1936 and later converted to oil-firing. Some carried 3–3in (76mm) guns in a patrol role.

Parana 1938 *Aldo Fraccaroli Collection*

Ex-German M 57 class *minesweepers*

Class (original no, fate):
M 5 (ex-*M 74*, renamed *Murature*, museum ship 1940), *M 6* (ex-*M 79* renamed *Pinedo*, stricken 25.7.51), *M 7* (ex-*M 80*, renamed *Py*, capsized in dock 1936, stricken 13.1.37), *M 8* (ex-*M 90*, renamed *Segui*, salvage vessel 1934, stricken 29.4.50), *M 9* (ex-*M 101*, renamed *Thorne*, stricken 16.12.66, hulk until BU in 1959), *M 10* (ex-*M 105*, state yacht *Golandrina* 1925, stricken 8.10.55)

Six German Type 1916 minesweepers acquired with the previous class, and the same remarks apply.

Brazil

Brazil entered the twentieth century with high aspirations. The country was in an era of prosperity. Brazil controlled the world's coffee and rubber markets. Gold had been discovered and offered the hope of great wealth. The political unrest that had occurred in the transition from Empire to Republic seemed to be over. True, problems lay ahead, but it seemed that many had been solved.

The Brazilian Navy launched a massive acquisition programme to create a modern fleet. Titled the Building Programme of 1904, it was refined for a few years before orders were placed for warships. The major controversy was about the size of battleship to be purchased. Those favouring the new dreadnought design ultimately won. Brazil ordered in a short period 2 dreadnoughts, 2 scout cruisers, 10 destroyers, 3 submarines, and 1 submarine tender. The ordering of two dreadnoughts, *Minas Gerais* and *Sao Paulo*, in 1906 created quite a stir in naval and diplomatic circles. This would mean that Brazil would have dreadnoughts before major powers like France and Russia. Speculations abounded that Brazil was acting in someone else's interests. This was not true. On 6 August 1910 Brazil announced the contruction of a third dreadnought, *Rio de Janeiro*. Overnight Brazil was becoming a major naval power.

This euphoria was premature. On 22 November 1910 the crew of *Minas Gerais* mutinied. This was a reflection of the nation's economic and social condition, prosperity having been shortlived. Brazil had to turn her interest inward again. At first the size of *Rio de Janeiro* was reduced and finally she was sold. The Navy began plans for a fourth dreadnought, the *Riachuelo*, but this ship never got past the planning stages.

The warships built (including Brazil's first three submarines and their purpose-built depot ship from Italy during 1914–17) as part of the Building Programme of 1904 did all commission and were the backbone of the Navy for the next 40 years.

WORLD WAR ONE

Brazil fought alongside the Allies for the last year of World War One. Her entry into the war parallelled that of the United States. Brazil had declared herself neutral in 1914. In fact, her economy, largely based on coffee, was devastated by the war. U-boats sank a number of Brazilian merchant ships. Finally on 24 October 1917 Brazil declared war on the Central Powers. A Brazilian squadron made up of the scout cruisers *Rio Grande do Sul* and *Bahia*, destroyers *Paraiba*, *Rio Grande do Norte*, *Piaui* and *Santa Catharina*, plus a few support ships was dispatched to operate off NW Africa. They spent three months on station before the war ended. The two dreadnoughts were sent to the United States to be overhauled before joining the Grand Fleet at Scapa Flow. The yard work was not completed before the war ended.

Brazil shared in the spoils at Versailles. She received two German destroyers which she promptly sold. More importantly, Brazil was awarded the 43 German merchant ships she had commandeered upon entering the war.

Between 1906 and 1919 personnel strength rose from about 8000 to 10,000. There were 19 boy sailors' schools in which 12-year-olds spent 3 years followed by 10 months special instruction and 12 years with the Fleet. Volunteers served 3–20 years. A marine corps wearing British-style white helmets and without commissioned officers existed by 1906.

FLEET STRENGTH 1906

BATTLESHIPS

Name	Launched	Disp	Fate
Brasil class			
BRASIL	1864	1518t	BU *c*1905
Lima Barros class			
LIMA BARROS	21.12.65	1330t	BU *c*1905
Riachuelo class			
RIACHUELO	7.6.83	5610t	Stricken 1910
Aquidaban class			
AQUIDABAN	17.1.85	4921t	Sunk 22.1.06
Marshal Deodoro class			
MARSHAL DEODORO	18.6.98	3162t	Sold 1924
MARSHAL FLORIANO	6.7.98	3162t	Stricken 1936

SOUTH AMERICA

Riachuelo class
Riachuelo rebuilt at La Seyne in 1893–95; she was fitted with a tower-like military mast. The additional weight caused the ship to roll and be a poor sea boat. The mast was removed in 1905.

Aquidaban class
Aquidaban rebuilt at Stettin in 1897–98; she was fitted with a tower-like military mast. The additional weight caused the ship to roll and be a poor sea boat. The mast was removed in 1905. *Aquidaban* exploded and sank at Jacarepagna, near Rio de Janeiro. Loss of life was very heavy.

Marshal Deodoro class
Deodoro and *Floriano* were extensively overhauled at Rio de Janeiro in 1912. The machinery, boilers and armament were all replaced.

CRUISERS

Name	Launched	Disp	Fate
Trajano class			
TRAJANO (ex-*Toneleiros*)	12.7.73	1414t	Stricken 11.4.06
Guanabara class			
GUANABARA	18.3.78	1914t	Stricken *c*1905
Parnaiba class			
PARNAIBA	18.3.78	472t	Stricken *c*1905
Primeiro de Marco class			
PRIMEIRO DE MARCO	7.10.81	726t	Stricken *c*1905
Almirante Tamandare class			
ALMIRANTE TAMANDARE	20.3.90	4537t	Stricken 27.12.15
Benjamin Constant class (TS)			
BENJAMIN CONSTANT	1892	2820t	Disarmed 2.3.26
Republica class			
REPUBLICA (ex-*Quinze de Novembro*, ex-*Republica*)	26.5.92	1300t	Disarmed 1920
Barrozo class			
BARROZO	25.8.96	3437t	Stricken 1931

DESTROYERS

Name	Launched	Disp	Fate
Tiradentes class			
TIRADENTES	26.5.92	795t	Stricken 5.7.25
Gustavo Sampaio class			
GUSTAVO SAMPAIO	1893	480t	Disarmed 1.5.12
Tupi class			
TUPI	1896	1190t	Stricken 27.12.15
TIMBIRA	1896	1190t	Disarmed 27.10.17
Tamoio class			
TAMOIO	1898	1080t	Stricken *c*1920

In addition to the above, the Brazilian Navy in 1906 also operated 5 Yarrow type coastal torpedo-boats, *Nos 1–5* (launched 1882, 40t–52t, discarded *c*1910); 3 *Alfa* class torpedo-boats, *Alfa, Beta, Gama* (launched 1883, 3.5t, discarded *c*1905); 3 *Araguari* class coastal torpedo-boats, *Araguari, Iguatemi, Marcilio Dias* (launched 1893, 110t, discarded *c*1910–15); 5 *Panne* class torpedo-boats, *Panne, Pedro Afonso* (ex-German *Zwei*), *Pedro Ivo* (ex-German *Eins*), *Pernambuco, Silvado* (ex-German *Drei*) (launched 1892–3, 130t, discarded 1911–15); 1 *Moxoto* class (launched 1893, 16.5t, discarded *c*1905); armed merchantmen *Andrada, Jupiter, Marte* and *Mercurio*.

MAJOR SURFACE SHIPS

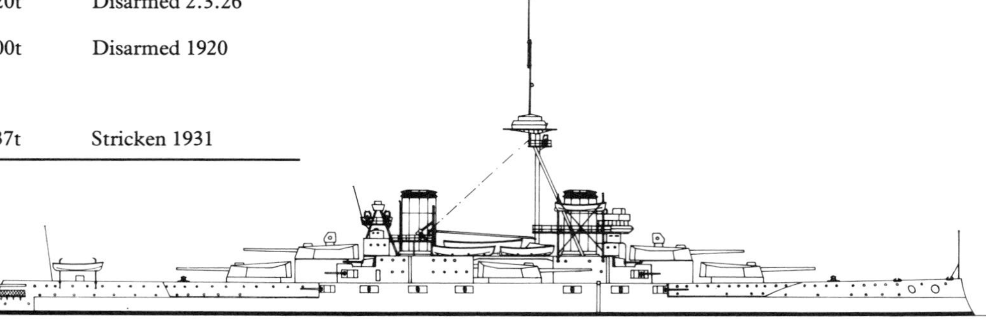
Sao Paulo 1917

MINAS GERAIS class *battleships*

Displacement: 19,281t normal; 21,200t full load
Dimensions: 543ft oa, 530ft wl, 500ft pp × 83ft × 28ft max, 25ft mean
165.5m, 161.5m, 152.4m × 25.3m × 8.5m, 7.6m
Machinery: 2-shaft Vickers VTE, 18 Babcock boilers, 23,500shp = 21kts. Coal 2350t, oil 400t. Range 10,000nm at 10kts
Armour: Krupp steel, belt 9in (229mm), belt extremities 6in–4in (152mm–102mm), casemate 9in, turrets 12in–9in (305mm–229mm), CT 12in
Armament: 12–12in (305mm)/45cal (6×2), 22–4.7in (120mm)/50cal, 8–3pdr (37mm)
Complement: 900

Name	Builder	Laid down	Launched	Comp	Fate
MINAS GERAIS	Armstrong, Elswick	17.4.07	10.9.08	6.1.10	Sold 1953
SAO PAULO	Vickers, Barrow	30.4.07	19.4.09	7.10	Sold 1951

The class was authorised in 1906 and was the heart of the 1904 Building Programme. These ships were the largest and most powerful dreadnoughts in the world when completed. Professional magazines were full of rumours that Brazil was in fact acting as an agent for one of the leading naval powers and would in fact turn the ships over to their real owner when completed. The English press speculated that Germany, Japan, or the United States were the real backers and the European press believed that England had in fact built the ships for herself. These speculations had no basis in fact.

Also, overnight expressions such as 'Pan Americanism' and 'Hemispheric Cooperation' began to appear in US naval journals. Brazil, now possessing the two most powerful warships in the world, was being courted as a potential ally. A depression in the Brazilian economy coupled with the serious 22 November 1910 mutiny aboard *Minas Gerais* (named after the inland province) halted the dreadnought programme.

On 24 October 1917 Brazil declared war on the Central Powers. It was decided to send both units to Scapa Flow to join the Grand Fleet. *Minas Gerais* and *Sao Paulo* were in poor condition and lacked modern fire control equipment. *Sao Paulo* sailed for the New York N Yd in June 1918 to correct these problems. She broke down along the way and required extensive aid from US warships. *Sao Paulo*'s overhaul outlived the war and she remained in New York for two years. *Minas Gerais* underwent a similar refit following the return of her sister.

The most unusual design feature in the class was the engines. Unlike most contemporary dreadnoughts, they were powered by reciprocating engines instead of turbines. The armour plates were Krupp cemented type. The belt was 9in thick, tapering slightly fore and aft, while the same thickness was carried to the height of the upper deck over the citadel. This afforded protection to all of the barbette machinery, the boilers, magazines, and uptakes. The deck slopes were 2¼in and the aft conning tower 9in. The armour for both ships was manufactured by W G Armstrong, Whitworth & Co.

Minas Gerais in the 1920s

CPL

On 6 August 1910 Brazil astonished the naval world by announcing that she would have a third dreadnought built, *Rio de Janeiro*, to be the largest, most powerful warship in the world. Also, there was a strong movement in Brazil, led by the Navy League, to provide for a fourth dreadnought.

Two events undid these hopes and plans. On 22 November 1910 the *Minas Gerais* mutiny undermined public support for the Navy, and the Brazilian economy suffered a severe setback. On 3 May 1911 the newly elected President Hermes Rodrigues da Fonseca, shocked leading warship constructors by implying that *Rio de Janeiro*, then in the early stages of construction, was an unmanageable white elephant. The president stated that the Navy needed sound reform and additional shore installations more than extra dreadnoughts.

RIO DE JANEIRO *battleship*

Displacement: As designed 32,000t normal
As redesigned 27,500t normal
Dimensions: 652ft oa, 631ft 6in pp × 90ft 6in × 27ft mean as redesigned
198.7m, 192.5m × 27.6m × 8.2m
Machinery: 4-shaft Parsons geared turbines, 22 Babcock boilers, 45,000shp = 22kts. Coal 3000t, oil 500t
Armament: 12–14in (356mm)/45cal (6×2), 16–6in (152mm)/50cal, 14–4in as designed
14–12in (305mm)/50 cal (7×2), 20–6in (152mm)/50cal, 12–14pdr, 3–21in (533mm) TT sub as redesigned
Complement: 1100 (as redesigned)

Name	Builder	Laid down	Launched	Comp	Fate
RIO DE JANEIRO	Elswick	14.9.11	22.1.13		Sold late 1913 while outfitting

To answer these criticisms, the builders revised *Rio de Janeiro*'s plans, reducing her tonnage and armament. This was totally inconsistent with contemporary decisions and sound judgment. Finally, in late 1913 Brazil sold the uncomplete *Rio de Janeiro* to Turkey, citing the reason as tactical incompatibility with the *Minas Gerais* class. Brazil soon reversed her decision and opened negotiations for a larger dreadnou[illegible]t, the *Riachuelo*.

In 1921 Great Britain offered to sell *Agincourt* (ex-*Sultan Osman I*, ex-*Rio de Janeiro*) to Brazil for £1 million. The proposal was seriously considered but decided against.

Riachuelo suffered the same fate as *Rio de Janeiro*. Brazil asked Armstrong (Elswick) shipyard to prepare four designs. Construction was never begun, and Brazil had not selected from the four design variations before she cancelled the project. Brazil's economy was too weak to support the construction of another dreadnought.

RIAÇHUELO class *battleship*

Displacement: 31,500t normal (design A), 32,500t normal (design B), 36,000 normal (design C and D)
Dimensions: 685ft oa × 96ft × 28ft normal – design A
208.8m × 29.3m × 8.5m
689ft oa × 96ft × 28ft 6in normal – design B
210.0m × 29.3m × 8.7m
740ft oa × 98ft × 29ft normal – design C and D
225.6m × 29.9m × 8.8m
Machinery: 4 Parsons geared turbines, Yarrow boilers, 45,000shp = 23kts (design A), 24kts (design B); no data for design C and D
Armour: Krupp steel. Belt 12in (305mm) design A, 13in (330mm) design B; turrets 12in designs A and B; coal 4000t, oil 1000t; no data for designs C and D
Armament: Design A: 12–14in (356mm)/45cal (6×2), 16–6in (152mm)/50cal, 12–3in, 4–3in AA, 4 or 6 TT sub
Design B: 10–15in (381mm)/45cal (5×2), 20–6in (152mm)/50cal, 10–3in, 4–3in AA, 6 TT sub
Design C: 10–16in (406mm)/45cal (5×2), 20–6in (152mm)/50cal, 10–3in, 4–3in AA, 6 TT sub
Design D: 12–15in (381mm)/45cal (6×2), 20–6in (152mm)/50cal, 10–3in, 4–3in AA, 6 TT sub
Complement: 1200

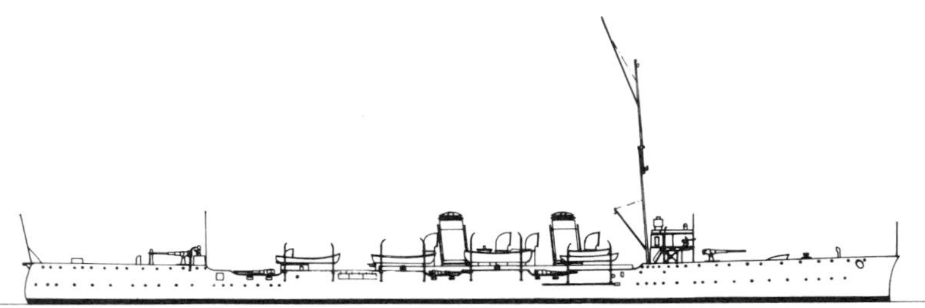

Bahia as completed

This design was based on the British scout cruiser *Adventure*. *Bahia* made 27.016kts on her trials and *Rio Grande do Sul* 27.41kts. When completed they were the world's fastest small cruisers. Both ships were part of the Brazilian squadron that operated off the NW coast of Africa during 1917–18. They were re-engined and re-boilered in 1925 and 1926. This increased their speed to 28kts. *Bahia* and *Rio Grande do Sul* saw extensive service during World War Two. On 4 July 1945 Bahia exploded and sank within three minutes while serving on US plane guard duty, midway between Brazil and Africa; 294 lives were lost.

BAHIA class *cruisers*

Displacement: 3100t normal
Dimensions: 380t pp × 39ft × 14ft 6in mean
115.8m × 11.8m × 4.4m
Machinery: 3-shaft Parsons geared turbines, Yarrow boilers, 18,000shp = 26.5kts. Coal 500t
Armour: Deck ¾in (19mm), CT 3in (76mm)
Armament: 10–4.7in (120mm), 6–3pdr (47mm), 2–18in (457mm) TT
Complement: 350

Name	Builder	Laid down	Launched	Comp	Fate
BAHIA	Armstrong, Elswick	19.8.07	20.4.09	1910	Sank 4.7.45
RIO GRANDE DO SUL	Armstrong, Elswick	30.8.07	20.1.09	1910	Stricken 1948

Bahia in the 1930s

By courtesy of R L Scheina

Mato Grosso towards the end of her career — *By courtesy of R L Scheina*

PARA class *destroyers*

Displacement: 560t normal
Dimensions: 240ft pp × 23ft 6in × 7ft 10in mean
73.2m × 7.2m × 2.4m
Machinery: 2-shaft 4cyl VTE, 2 Yarrow boilers, 8000shp = 27kts. Coal 140t. Range 3700nm at 14kts
Armament: 2–4in (102mm), 4–47mm (3pdr), 2–18in (457mm) TT aw
Complement: 130

Class (no, launched, fate):
Para (2, 14.7.08, stricken 1933), *Piaui* (3, 7.9.08, stricken 1944), *Amazonas* (1, 21.11.08, stricken 1931), *Mato Grosso* (10, 23.1.09, stricken 13.9.46), *Rio Grande do Norte* (4, 1909, stricken 1944), *Paraiba* (5, 18.5.09, stricken 1944), *Alagoas* (6, 29.7.09, disarmed 1939), *Santa Catharina* (9, 26.10.09, stricken 1944), *Parana* (8, 27.3.10, disarmed 20.10.33), *Sergipe* (7, 25.5.10, stricken 1944)

The 10-ship *Para* class, all Yarrow built, closely resembled the *River* class built for the Royal Navy. These units were built under the 1907 Naval Programme, designed to modernise the entire Brazilian Navy. All units exceeded their 27kt design speed by at least a fraction during trials. The best speed was *Parana* at 28.736kts. The ships were divided into ten watertight compartments by bulkheads from the outer bottom plating to the upper deck. The *Para* class proved to be very manoeuvrable. The diameter of the turning circle at full speed was about 375 yards and at two thirds speed about 330 yards. In the stopping and starting trials, the boats began to move astern from full speed ahead in 30 seconds from the time the signal was given. *Piaui, Rio Grande do Norte*, *Paraiba* and *Santa Catharina* served in the 1917–18 active squadron off NW Africa. Numbers were painted on the after funnel as indicated.

Ex-German V 105 class *destroyers*

Class (former name, launched, fate):
No name assigned (ex-*V 105*, ex-Dutch *Z 1*, 1914, transferred to Poland in 1919), no named assigned (ex-*V 106*, ex-Dutch *Z 2*, 1914, transferred to Great Britain in 1919)

These two destroyers were awarded to Brazil under the Versailles treaty.

GOIAS *torpedo-boat*

Displacement: 150t normal
Dimensions: 152ft pp × 15ft 3in × 4ft 4in mean
46.3m × 4.7m × 1.3m
Machinery: 3 shafts, combinations reciprocating and turbine engines, Yarrow boilers, 950shp = 26kts
Armament: 2–47mm (3pdr) QF, 2–18in (457mm) TT aw
Complement: 30

Built by Yarrow & Co, England, for £14,000 and completed on 9 October 1907. Named after a central state of Brazil. She ran a trial speed of 26.493kts; by 1919 in poor condition she was stricken on 6 May 1933.

SUBMARINES

F 1 class as completed
NB 1/750 scale

F 1 class *submarines*

Displacement: 250t/305t
Dimensions: 150ft 11in pp × 14ft 6in × 12ft 2in mean
46.0m × 4.4m × 3.7m
Machinery: 2 shafts, 2 Fiat 6cyl diesels, plus electric motors, 700bhp/500shp = 13.5kts/8kts. Range 800nm at 13.5kts, 18mi at 8kts
Armament: 2–18in (457mm) TT bow
Complement: 20

Class (launched, fate):
F 1 (11.6.13, stricken 18.11.33), *F 3* (9.11.13, stricken 18.11.33), *F 5* (1913, stricken 18.11.33)

These Laurenti-Fiat type submarines were ordered from Fiat-San Giorgio of Spezia (Italy) as part of the 1904 Building Programme. The tender *Ceara* was acquired at the same time to service the boats. The 'F' boats were the first submarines to be acquired by Brazil. In the late nineteenth century Brazil had made a part payment on the submarine *Goubet II* designed by and named for the French inventor who did much work for the Russian Imperial Navy. *Goubet II* never left France and was ultimately sold at auction. Numerous contemporary English-language naval magazines reported that Brazil had purchased the original submarine *Goubet* and five of the second generation *Coubet II* but these reports were erroneous.

SMALL SURFACE WARSHIPS

CEARA *submarine depot ship*

Displacement: 4200t normal; 6400t full load
Dimensions: 328ft 9in pp × 49ft 3in × 13ft 9in mean, 20ft max with dock flooded
100.0m × 15.0m × 4.2m, 6.1m
Machinery: 2 shafts, 2 Fiat 6cyl, 2 cycle diesels, 6400shp = 14kts. Oil 400t. Range 4000nm at 10kts
Armament: 4–4in (102mm), 4–6pdr (57mm)
Complement: *c*200

Name	Builder	Launched	Fate
CEARA	Fiat-San Giorgio, de Spezza	1915	Stricken 1926

Ceara (named after a NE province and its seaport) was specifically designed to serve as a depot ship for 6 submarines and completed on 25 April 1917. The ship had a central dock (180ft 5in × 24ft 10in – *55.0m × 7.6m)* between the double hulls able to take a submarine, making her the world's most advanced submarine depot ship. Two cranes with a 400t deadweight capacity were fitted near the stern. Depot facilities included two 150kW charging generators, 3 air compressors, refrigerating plant and workshops. She carried enough fuel to supply 6 submarines four times; pumps could empty the dock in 2 hours.

JAVARI class *river monitors*

Particulars: As British *Humber* class

Class (launched):
Javary (17.6.13), *Madeira* (30.9.13), *Solimoes* (19.8.13)

Like so much of the 1904 Building Programme, these ships, ordered from Vickers in January 1912, never made it into the Brazilian Navy. Named after Brazilian rivers, they were taken over on 3 August 1919 by the Royal Navy and served as HM ships *Mersey* (ex-*Javary*), *Severn* (ex-*Madeira*), and *Humber* (ex-*Solimoes*). However, prior to the outbreak of the war, naval periodicals were speculating that Brazil was in the market to dispose of the ships because 'of their unsuitability for river navigation'. It is more plausible that Brazil could not afford the ships as the British Admiralty paid £155,000 for each ship.

Ceara as completed — *By courtesy of R L Scheina*

PERNAMBUCO *river monitor*

Displacement:	470t
Dimensions:	146ft × 24ft × 5ft 3in *44.5m × 7.4m × 1.6m*
Machinery:	800hp = 11kts. Coal 45t
Armour:	Belt 6⅔–4in (168mm–102mm), turret 6in (152mm), deck 4in, CT 3½in (89mm)
Armament:	3–4.7in (120mm), 10 MG
Complement:	?60

Built at Rio and launched in 1910. Stricken in 1948.

ACRE class *river gunboats*

Displacement:	200t
Dimensions:	120ft × 20ft 2ft *36.6m × 6.1m × 0.6m*
Machinery:	300hp = 11kts
Armament:	1–3.4in (15pdr) howitzer, 1–6pdr, 4 Maxim MG
Complement:	30

Class (launched):
Acre (1904), *Missoes* (1904)

Yarrow-built gunboats. There were also the 33t, 90ft *Jutohy* and *Teffe* (built 1890–92, refitted 1917, 1–3pdr, 2 MG, 11kts, coal 7t).

AUXILIARY WARSHIPS

By 1919 Brazil had the 1800t auxiliary minelayer (550 mines max) *Carlos Cromez* (ex-*Itaipu*, 1892, 301ft × 39ft × 10ft, 4000hp = 16kts, coal 400t) and 2 tug minesweepers (*Jaguarayo* and *Maria do Conto*) in the Mining Flotilla. In addition there was the AMC *Belmonte* (ex-German SS *Valesia*, Rostock 1912) an interned mechantman seized in October 1917. She displaced 5227t grt, measured 364ft × 51ft, could steam 12kts at 2700hp, and was armed with 4–4.7in and 6–6pdr.

Chile

Following the conclusion of the 1902 Disarmament and Arbitration Treaty with Argentina and its 5-year term moratorium, Chile was the last of the three big South American powers to enter the dreadnought race. Not until 1911 were tenders for two dreadnoughts called, specifying English armament, thus effectively excluding American competition. An assortment of ageing 1890s-vintage Elswick cruisers, and the battleship *Capitan Prat* comprised the main fleet until this date. The major naval programme of 1910 established a well-balanced advance, with dreadnoughts, destroyer leaders and Chile's first submarines. The First World War interrupted the programme, leaving Chile less one dreadnought and 4 destroyers, but boosted with six submarines (July 1917) and 50 naval aircraft (1918) donated by the British government in compensation. In addition the costs of the dreadnought *Cochrane* converted into the aircraft carrier HMS *Eagle*, were refunded. Essentially the most anglophile of South American navies, Chile contracted a small British advisory mission in 1911, which established a Naval War College at Valparaiso. Although neutral throughout the war, Chile failed to enforce this position after German and British squadrons clashed off Coronel on 1 November 1914.

A number of factors influenced Chile's neutrality. First, Germany held substantial influence in Chile. Germans held considerable investments in Chile. Also, a large number of immigrants had come from Germany to Chile. Second, Chile, like Argentina, had a modest merchant marine (87 steamers of 89,515grt and 33 sailing ships of 26,178grt in 1919); thus U-boat activities did not substantially influence foreign policy. Throughout the war Chile did negotiate with Germany for the use of interned German merchant ships without success; 32 steamers (3 colliers did resupply von Spee's squadron) and 57 sailing vessels lay idle in Chilean ports. On 3 September 1918, as the war drew to a close, the crews of seven of these interned ships tried to sabotage their ships and partly succeeded. Two days later, Chilean troops were ordered on board to protect the ships.

Personnel during the period numbered about 7500–8000 (1000 conscripts, the rest volunteers). By 1919 a second drydock was building at Talcahuano, with two more projected for Valparaiso. At this juncture Chile had South America's largest air arm. A vice-admiral commanded the Navy.

FLEET STRENGTH 1906

BATTLESHIPS

Name	Launched	Disp	Fate
Huascar class			
HUASCAR	6.10.65	1130t	Extant 1984 as museum
Almirante Cochrane class			
ALMIRANTE COCHRANE	25.1.74	3370t	Stricken 1933
Capital Prat class			
CAPITAN PRAT	20.12.90	6901t	Stricken 1936

Huascar class
Huascar was used as a submarine depot ship by 1919.

Almirante Cochrane class
She was hulked by 1908 after becoming a gunnery and torpedo TS in 1900.

CRUISERS

Name	Launched	Disp	Fate
Presidente Errazuriz class			
PRESIDENTE ERRAZURIZ	21.6.90	2047t	Stricken 1930
Blanco Encalada class			
BLANCO ENCALADA	9.9.93	4568t	Stricken 1946
Ministro Zenteno class			
MINISTRO ZENTENO	1.2.96	3437t	Stricken 1931
Esmeralda class			
ESMERALDA	14.4.96	7000t	Stricken 1929
O'Higgins class			
O'HIGGINS	17.5.97	8500t	Stricken 1926
Chacabuco class			
CHACABUCO	4.7.98	4160t	Stricken 1952

Presidente Errazuriz class
Gunnery TS by 1919 having been refitted in 1908 with a 4–6in/45 QF and 2–4.7in/45 QF armament.

O'Higgins class
Reported to be being rebuilt as a seaplane carrier in 1919.

DESTROYERS

Name	Launched	Disp	Fate
Almirante Lynch class			
ALMIRANTE LYNCH	1890	713t	Stricken 1919
ALMIRANTE CONDELL	1890	713t	Stricken 1919
Almirante Simpson class			
ALMIRANTE SIMPSON	1896	800t	To Ecuador 1907

Name	Launched	Disp	Fate
Capitán Orella class			
CAPITAN ORELLA	1896	300t	Stricken 1924
CAPITAN MUNEZ GAMERO	1896	300t	Stricken 1924
TENIENTE SERRANO	1896	300t	Stricken 1924
GUARDIA-MARINA RIQUELME	1896	300t	Stricken 1924
Capitan Merino Jarpa class			
CAPITAN MERINO JARPA	1901	321t	Stricken 1924
CAPITAN O'BRIEN	1901	321t	Stricken 1924
Capitan Thompson Class			
CAPITAN THOMPSON	1902	480t	Stricken 1924

In addition to the above, the Chilean Navy in 1906 also operated 2 *Colocolo* class torpedo-boats (*Colocolo* and *Tucapel*, launched 1880, 5t, discarded *c*1915); 4 *Glaura* class torpedo-boats (*Glaura, Guale, Rucumilla, Tegualda*, and *Janequeo* (ii), launched 1880–81, 35t, discarded *c*1915 – the first *Janequeo* was sunk in 1880); 3 *Fresia* class torpedo-boats (*Fresia, Lauca* and *Quidora*, launched 1880–81, 25t, discarded *c*1915). Numbers 7–9 torpedo-boats (launched 1891, 110t, discarded *c*1906); 6 *Injeniero Hyatt* class torpedo-boats (*Injeniero Hyatt, Cirujano Videla, Injeniero Mutilla, Guardia-Marina Contreras, Teniente Rodríguez* and *Capitan Thompton*, launched 1896–98, 140t, by 1919 torpedo school tenders, stricken *c*1920); *General Baquedano* TS (launched 1898, 2500t, 4–4.7in, 2–12pdr, 2–6pdr, 12kts, stricken 1955); transport *Maipo* (launched 1901; 6600t, stricken 1929); transport *Rancagua* (launched 1898, 8600t, discarded 1931); transport *Angamos* (ex-*Spartan*, purchased 1891, 5975t, discarded 1928).

The gunboat *Pilcomayo* had been discarded in 1905, and the torpedo-boat *Sargonte Aldea* in 1900.

Almirante Latorre as returned to Chile
By courtesy of J M Maber

MAJOR SURFACE SHIPS

Chile ordered dreadnoughts to counter those ordered by Argentina, which of course, had been ordered to counter Brazil's acquisition. Tenders were solicited in both Europe and the United States. But as Lt Cdr R W McNeely USN, observed, 'there was being carried on in Chilean newspapers a systematic propaganda against American naval materials . . .' The Chilean Navy had strong ties with the Royal Navy, and it was not surprising when Armstrong was awarded the contract.

Almirante Latorre continued the time honoured tradition of outclassing all preceding dreadnoughts in size and power. *Almirante Latorre* was bought by the Royal Navy on 9 September 1914 and renamed HMS *Canada*. *Almirante Cochrane* was purchased and taken over by the Royal Navy in 1917, renamed *Eagle* and converted into an aircraft carrier. Following the war, *Almirante Latorre* was rebought by Chile in April 1920. Chile also negotiated for *Eagle*, but she wanted the ship converted back to a battleship. This was impractical. The Royal Navy offered, among other ships, two *I* class battlecruisers in her place. This proposal was not accepted. Ultimately, Chile settled for the one dreadnought.

ALMIRANTE LATORRE class *battleships*

Displacement: 28,000t standard; 32,300t full load
Dimensions: 661ft oa, 625ft pp × 103ft × 28ft 6in mean, 30ft max
201.5m, 190.5m × 31.4m × 8.7m, 9.1m
Complement: 1176
Other particulars: As British *Canada* class

Name	Builder	Laid down	Launched	Comp	Fate
ALMIRANTE LATORRE (ex-*Canada*, ex-*Libertad*, ex-*Valparaiso*)	Armstrong, Newcastle	27.11.11	17.11.13	30.9.15	Sold 1959
ALMIRANTE COCHRANE (ex-*Santiago*)		22.1.13			See notes

Armour protection varied considerably throughout the ship. The belt had three thicknesses – lower 10in, middle 7in, and upper 4.5in. The belt ends were 6in to 4in; this protection extended from the end of the barrel of the forward 15in gun for about 25ft and from the aft 15in gun turret for about 50ft. This left 50ft of the bow and stern unarmoured. The secondary battery was protected by 6in of armour. The turrets were 10.5in–9in thick. Deck armour was as follows: shelter decck over casemates 1in, forecastle deck over 6in battery 1in, upper deck over 6in battery 1in, main deck aft 1.5in, protective deck 1in, lower deck forward 2in and aft 4in.

When completed, the range of the 14in guns were limited only by the maximum visibility. Initially, *Almirante Latorre* carried a total of 16–6in guns. The two which had been mounted on the upper deck abeam the aft funnel had to be removed. These guns had been damaged from the muzzle blast from the 'Q' 14in turret, located just abaft the stack and removed.

Almirante Latorre was modernised during 1929–31 in Devonport D Yd. She was fitted with new Vickers-Armstrong machinery, bulges, new turbines and converted to oil fuel. The ship was fitted to carry 4300t of oil and had an endurance of 4400nm at 10kts. The main topmast was raised to 60ft and controls were fitted at the ends of the upper bridge. In September 1931, having just recently returned to Chile, *Almirante Latorre*'s crew participated in a short-lived mutiny.

ALMIRANTE LYNCH class *destroyers*

Displacement: 1430t normal; 1800t–1850t full load
Dimensions: 320ft pp × 32ft 6in × 11ft max
97.5m × 9.9m × 3.4m
Machinery: 3-shaft Parsons geared turbines, White-Forster boilers, 30,000shp = 31kts. Coal 427t, oil 80t. Range 2750nm at 15kts 15kts
Armament: 6–4in (102mm), 4 MG, 4–18in (457mm) TT
Complement: 160

Name	Builder	Launched	Fate
ALMIRANTE LYNCH	White	1912	Stricken 1945
ALMIRANTE CONDELL	White	1913	Stricken 1944

Initially, this class was composed of six ships. Only two, *Almirante Lynch* (completed 1913) and *Almirante Condell* (completed 1914), had been delivered to the Chilean Navy prior to the outbreak of the First World War. The remaining four destroyers were taken over by Great Britain. Since they were considerably altered during the war, they have been considered a separate class, the *Almirante Williams* class. *Almirante Lynch* made 31.8kts for 6 hours while on trials and *Almirante Condell* did 33.4kts for 6 hours. These ships were extremely large destroyers for their day. *Almirante Condell* forced the German light cruiser *Dresden* from Sholl Bay (Mt Lizzie, W Side of Tierra del Fuego) to Punta Arenas on 11 December 1914 after the Battle of the Falklands by reminding her of the 24-hour limit on staying in neutral waters, but the authorities at Punta Arenas did not receive the Government's orders not to let her coal there.

Almirante Williams in the 1920s

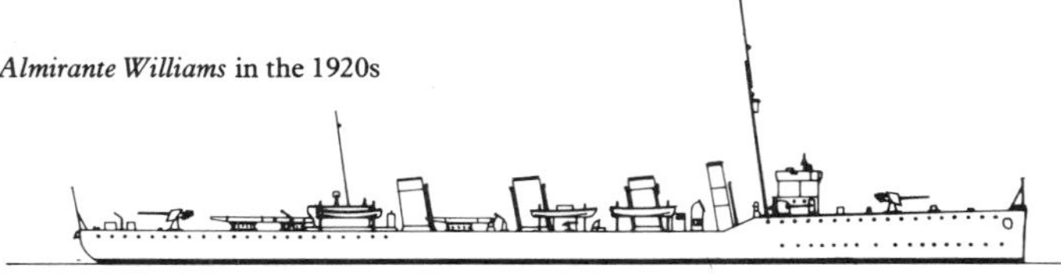

ALMIRANTE WILLIAMS class *destroyers*

Displacement: 1704t normal; 1829t full load
Dimensions: 331ft 4in pp × 32ft 6in × 11ft 7in max
101.0m × 9.9m × 3.5m
Machinery: As British *Faulknor* class
Armament: 2–4.7in (120mm)/45cal BL, 2–4in/45cal Mk VI, 2–2pdr Mk I pompoms, 4–21in (533mm) TT (2×2)
Complement: 205

Name	Builder	Launched	Fate
ALMIRANTE WILLIAMS (ex-*Botha*, ex-*Almirante William Rebolledo*)	White	2.12.14	Stricken 1933
ALMIRANTE URIBE (ex-*Broke*, ex-*Almirante Coni*)	White	25.5.14	Stricken 1933
ALMIRANTE RIVEROS (ex-*Faulknor*, ex-*Almirante Simpson*)	White	26.2.14	Stricken 1933

Initially, these ships were members of the *Almirante Lynch* class. Taken over by Great Britain with the outbreak of World War One, they were considerably altered and thus considered a class of their own. Initially they carried the same armament as the *Almirante Lynch* class; they were rearmed by the Royal Navy in 1918. One class member, *Tipperary* (ex-*Almirante Riveros*), was sunk at the Battle of Jutland. The remaining 3 ships were repurchased by Chile in April/May 1920.

SUBMARINES

'H' class as completed
NB 1/750 scale

'H' class *submarines*

Dimensions: 105ft 9in pp × 15ft 9in × 12ft 4in max
33.5m × 4.8m × 3.7m
Machinery: 2 shafts, 2 sets Nelseco diesels plus electric motors, 480bhp/640hp = 13kts/5kts. Oil 17.5t. Range 2800nm at 11kts, 30nm at 5kts.
Other particulars: As British 'H' class

Class (former name, fate):
H 1 (ex-H 13, stricken 1949), *H 2* (ex-*H 16* stricken 1945), *H 3* (ex-*H 17*, stricken 1945), *H 4* (ex-*H 18*, stricken 1945), *H 5* (ex-*H 19*, stricken 1953), *H 6* (ex-*H 20*, stricken 1953)

These were the first modern submarines acquired by Chile, although a submarine had been built during the war with Spain (1864–66). Twenty 'H' class boats had been ordered by Great Britain in 1914, when it had been hoped that these units could be purchased unarmed from the US, armed in Canada, and then brought across the Atlantic. However, the neutral US interned the boats at Boston, until she entered the war, when the boats were released. At this point, Great Britain decided to cede five boats to Chile in part payment for the Chilean warships that had been appropriated in 1914, and Chile decided to purchase a sixth boat. Formal acquisition took place on 7 July 1917. These submarines were renamed respectively *Guacolda, Tegualda, Rucumilla, Quidora, Fresia, Guale c*1936. *Rucumilla* sank in an accident on 2 June 1927. The entire crew was lost. The boat was raised and put back into service.

Almirante Lynch about 1937 — *By courtesy of R L Scheina*

Peru

The Peruvian Navy had been devastated by the War of the Pacific (1879–83). By 1906 it just began to pull itself up from the trough. The purchase of the Elswick-built *Almirante Grau* class scout cruisers gave the navy its first modern warships in decades. The most influential factor affecting the Peruvian Navy during this era was a French naval mission that started with one officer in 1908 and grew to about six. Peru bought from France two submarines, one destroyer, and almost bought a cruiser. In fact, the dispute over the purchase of this ship (see *Comandante Aguirre*, ex-*Dupuy de Lôme*) combined with the outbreak of World War One to end the mission in 1914. During the early years of the war, the cruisers *Almirante Grau* and *Coronel Bolognese* escorted merchant ships in territorial waters. One Peruvian merchantman was torpedoed during the war, the *Lorton* in February 1917. On 29 September of that year Peru placed armed guards on board eight German ships interned in Callao. On 14 June 1918 Peru broke diplomatic relations with Germany and seized the interned ships. Peru was unable to add to her fleet during the war and it remained unchanged until the arrival of the US Naval Mission in 1920. The first warships to be acquired under its influence were the 'R' class submarines in the late 1920s.

The Navy was headed by a vice-admiral in 1919 being under Colonel C A de la Fuente, Minister of War and Marine. Warships were painted brown grey. Peru's merchant marine that year numbered 12 steamers of 26,590grt and 40 sailing ships of 10,950grt.

FLEET STRENGTH 1906

CRUISER

Name	Launched	Disp	Fate
LIMA (ex-*Socrates*)	1881	1790t	Stricken 1940

The hulk of this two-funnel German (Howaldt/Kiel) built cruiser rests at Iquitos up the Amazon.

Almirante Grau between the wars *By courtesy of R L Scheina*

MONITOR

Name	Launched	Disp	Fate
ATAHUALPA (ex-*Catawba*)	13.4.64	2100t	Stricken *c*1910

MINOR WARSHIPS

Name	Launched	Disp	Fate
APURIMAC	*c*1850	1000t	Stricken *c*1915
AMERICA	1904	240t	Extant ?1984

Apurimac, a 34-gun wooden screw frigate, served as a TS from 1890. *America* was an Amazon river gunboat with 2–3pdr. She was at Iquitos and there were 1980 plans to retain her as a museum ship.

In addition to the above, the Peruvian Navy in 1906 also operated the small gunboat *Santa Rosq* (launched Glasgow 1883, 2–6in discarded *c*1920) and 6 small paddlewheel steamers.

MAJOR SURFACE SHIPS

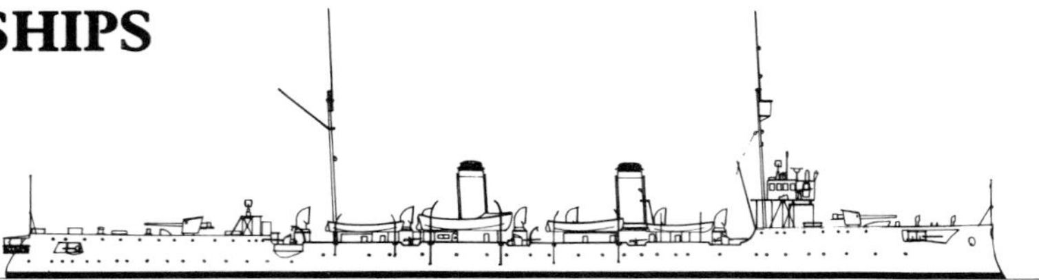

Almirante Grau as completed

Almirante Grau (named after Miguel Grau who held the Chilean Navy at bay in 1879) was fitted as a flagship and for 50 years these ships were the largest, most powerful ships in the Peruvian Navy. *Bolognesi* lacked a poop. *Grau* made 24.64kts on her trials. Between 1923 and 1925 the ships were refitted at Balboa in the Canal Zone. Their boilers were retubed and they were modified to burn oil. Both ships received Italian fire control systems. Between 1934 and 1935, they were reboilered by Yarrows. In 1936 the aft 3in guns were replaced by Japanese-made 3in AA guns.

ALMIRANTE GRAU class *scout cruisers*

Displacement: 3100t normal
Dimensions: 370ft pp, 380ft oa × 40ft 6in × 14ft 3in
112.8m, 115.8m × 12.3m × 4.3m
Machinery: 2-shaft Yarrow VTE 4cyl, 10 Yarrow boilers, 14,000hp = 24kts. Coal 500t. Range 3276nm at 10kts
Armour: Deck 1½in (38mm), gun mounts 6in(152mm), gun shields 3in (76mm), CT 3in
Armament: 2–6in (152mm)/50cal, 8–3in, 6–6pdr, 2–1pdr, 2–18in (457mm) TT sub
Complement: 320

Name	Builder	Launched	Completed	Fate
ALMIRANTE GRAU	Armstrong, Elswick	27.3.06	19.10.06	Stricken 24.12.58
CORONEL BOLOGNESI	Armstrong, Elswick	24.9.06	1.3.07	Stricken 24.12.58

ex-French DUPUY DE LÔME *armoured cruiser*

Comandante Aguirre (ex-*Dupuy de Lôme*). This 1890 armoured cruiser was to be transferred to the Peruvian Navy. However, many in Peru became critical of the wisdom of acquiring an old warship that did not influence the balance of power *vis à vis* Peru's primary rival Chile. Also a deepening financial crisis in Peru influenced the decision not to conclude the arrangement. In fact, the cruiser *Lima* had taken a Peruvian crew to France in 1912 for her before the arrangement fell through, and the ship had been photographed flying the Peruvian flag. Between 1912 and 1920 she remained in France in this state of limbo. In 1920 she was resold to a Belgian firm and used as a merchant ship named *Peruvier*.

Ferre as completed *Aldo Fraccaroli Collection*

Ex-French CHASSEUR class *destroyer*

Rodriguez (ex-*Actee*). Arrived in Peru 1914, having been detained in Brazil; name often cited as *Teniente Rodriguez*; stricken in 1939.

SUBMARINES

FERRE class *submarines*

Displacement: 300t/400t
Dimensions: ?
Machinery: 2 shafts, 2 Schneider-Carels diesels plus electric motor 13kts/8kts. Range 2000nm at 10kts
Armament: 4 TT (bow) 6 Smulders torpedoes
Complement: 21

Name	Builder	Launched	Fate
FERRE	Schneider-Creusot	1912	Stricken 1919
PALACIOS	Schneider-Creusot	1913	Stricken 1919

The acquisition of these Laubeuf type submarines was influenced by the French Naval Mission (1908–14) to Peru. They were transported to Peru in the *Kangaroo* which had been built specifically to carry submarines. Their careers were shortened due to the scarcity of batteries and spare parts. In fact, Peru had had an earlier submarine. A submarine had been built in Peru in 1879 by the inventor Federico Blume. Little is known about the craft including its dimensions. Possibly unnamed, his craft was not able to carry out any missions during the War of the Pacific (1879–83). It was destroyed to prevent it from falling into Chilean hands.

Belgium

Belgium possessed a kind of naval organisation, but she had no sea-going naval vessels. There were numerous small and fast (192t–798t net, 13kts–21kts) mercantile vessels (mostly paddlewheelers) built in 1870–1896 employed as Government packets (19 by 1900). These were the property of Belgian Government and commanded by naval officers under the Bureau of Marine. Some of them might be useful during a war on account of their high speed. There was also the 684-ton fishery protection vessel *Ville d'Anvers* built at Antwerp in 1865. There were also several river gunboats in the Congo (the gunboat *Paul Renkin* and a motor patrol boat were launched on Lake Kiru during 1914–18 and the torpedo-boat *Netta* slipped onto Lake Tanganyika in December 1915) and one on the Nile (*Vankerkhoven*).

The dire experience of 1914–18 finally led to the formation of a regular home coast defence navy; not only had Allied warships assisted the Belgian Army to keep its toehold in the country but the Germans had stationed substantial light naval forces and built lavish coastal defences in conquered Flanders. A naval commission was formed in 1919. In November that year *U 91* and *U 112* were presented to Belgium by Britain and were towed to Antwerp only to be broken up there in 1921–22, but on 19 April 1920 the 1200-ton escort sloop *Zinnia* of the British 'Flower' class was bought. She was employed on fishery protection duties. At the end of the First World War there were 14 German coastal torpedo-boats abandoned in Belgian ports: *A 14, A 12, A 4, A 5, A 8, A 9, A 11, A 16, A 20* (launched 1915, displacement 109t), and *A 30, A 40, A 42, A 43* and *A 47* (launched 1916, displacement 230t). These were put into service and renumbered respectively *A1PC—A9PC* and *A21PC—A25PC*. These boats together with sloop *Zinnia* formed the new Royal Belgian Navy and such was its strength in 1921, together with 23 ex-German motor launches *V 1—17, V 21—25*. Zeebrugge, Ostend, Bruges, Ghent and Antwerp were the available ports.

Bulgaria

Bulgaria gained her independence, together with a strip of Black Sea Coast, in 1878 as a result of the Russo-Turkish War. In 1885 the Eastern Rumelia province was incorporated, thus giving an access to the Aegean. It was only in 1896 that the first serious steps were taken to build a proper navy; until then only three steamers (*Krum, Aleksandr I* and *Simeon Veliki*) aided by the training ship *Asen* and seven other boats constituted the Bulgarian Navy on the Danube, while the Black Sea coast was defended by three small steam-driven boats. Almost all these Bulgarian ships were given by Russia.

In 1896 almost 20 per cent of military funds were to be spent on the Navy and that had to be done relying heavily on French help. In 1897 the gunboat *Nadezhda* was ordered there; the following year a French officer, Paul Pichon, became a commander in the Bulgarian Navy until 1908. A further ship built for the Black Sea by France was *Kaliakra*, an 80-ton boat; several small boats were also acquired.

In 1903 the first naval programme was prepared and it called for 12 small torpedo-boats of 15 tons, 2 of 90 tons, and 2 of 150 tons, together with training ships and some coastal equipment. The programme resulted in 6 torpedo-boats of 97t, 3 floating torpedo stations and 2–240mm and 2–100mm coastal guns with projectiles – all ordered from the Schneider Works in France. During later years the funds allocated to the Navy were spent on equipment rather than ships, though some of the latter were sometimes planned, too. Thus, in 1905 two minelayers were contemplated, while in 1910 two 470-ton destroyers, 190-ton submarines and minelayers were planned. None were built – not only because of lack of funds, but also due to the reluctance of some Bulgarians to support a navy.

In 1908 the Russians, trying to strengthen fellow Slav feelings in Bulgaria, offered to sell the Bulgarian Navy some old ships: a cruiser, two 'popovkas', gunboats, minelayers, torpedo-boats and auxiliaries. The proposition was declined on the grounds that as Bulgaria was to enjoy good relations with Russia, a large fleet was unnecessary. Russian help could always be counted on, but on the other hand the Bulgarian Navy would never be capable of opposing the Russian Black Sea Fleet. In either case the Navy was considered an unnecessary expenditure. Much more important was Russian support for Bulgaria's full independence, which was proclaimed on 5 October 1908.

THE BALKAN WARS

So little faith was placed in the Navy, that during the First Balkan War in 1912 Bulgaria did not seek any opportunity to enlarge her fleet. It was rather the shipbuilding companies which put forward proposals to the Bulgarians. For example, Yarrow and Thornycroft proposed torpedo-boats, Normand, submarines and Orlando a minelayer and other ships. Germany in the meantime proposed to sell cruisers, gunboats, torpedo-boats – all elderly having been built before 1892. All these offers were turned down.

When the Balkan War broke out in 1912, only the following warships could be mustered by the Bulgarians: the gunboat *Nadezhda*, 6 torpedo-boats, the minelayer *Kamchija* on the Black Sea and a few yachts on the Danube, adapted as warships. Five cargo ships were incorporated into the Navy. During the hostilities the Bulgarian Fleet had the duty of safeguarding the Black Sea coast and providing support for land operations. Only one skirmish was fought, when the torpedo-boat *Drski* damaged the Turkish cruiser *Hamidieh* on 21 November 1912. Other sorties by torpedo-boats brought no successes. The Second Balkan War was fought by Bulgaria on land; *Nadezhda* and six torpedo-boats were interned at Sevastopol, and naval activities were limited to minelaying. The war ended with heavy territorial losses to Bulgaria; her Aegean access was limited to a small strip of coast lacking any large harbour.

THE FIRST WORLD WAR

Two years later Bulgaria entered another war when in October 1915 she joined the Central Powers. Her most important share in the naval war was opening up the naval bases of Varna, Burgas and Euksinograd to German and Turkish ships. When in 1919 the treaty between Bulgaria and the victorious Allies was signed in Neuilly-sur-Seines the Bulgarian Navy was formally abolished and had to be converted into a police force. Moreover, she lost her access to the Aegean, as the southern part of her territory was ceded to Greece.

Bulgaria was allowed only 4 torpedo-boats (to be converted to patrol boats) and 6 patrol boats on the Danube. In 1921 the Bulgarians were able to buy 2 submarine chasers and 4 motor launches. Thus by the end of 1922 the Bulgarian Navy comprised 4 former torpedo-boats. 2 submarine chasers, 4 motor launches, 5 minesweeping and a few auxiliary boats. The Danube Flotilla comprised 2 old Russian torpedo-boats and 8 small police boats.

FLEET STRENGTH 1906

Name	Built	Disp	Fate
Gunboat			
NADEZHDA	1898	717t	Dismantled 1918

Name	Built	Disp	Fate
Torpedo-boats			
VASIL LEVSKI	1877	20t	BU 1938
HRISTO BOTEV	1877	20t	Deleted *c* 1930

Nadezhda
During the First Balkan War her guns were landed, due to her poor condition. They were later fitted again, but were landed once more in 1915. In 1918 she was sent to Sevastopol for a refit and was left there by the crew who were thus persuaded by Bolsheviks; her machinery and equipment were dismantled. Not returned by the USSR, she deteriorated and remains of her hull were reportedly still to be seen off Sevastopol in 1941.

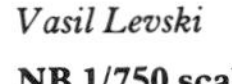

Vasil Levski
NB 1/750 scale

Botev and Levski
Former Russian small torpedo-boats *Cherepakha* and *Bychok*, respectively. Transferred from the Russian Navy in 1884, they were used as patrol boats during the Second Balkan and First World Wars. *Botev* was to be placed as a monument in Ruse in 1936, while *Levski* was shortened and rebuilt with a gasoline engine and was finally broken up in 1938.

The first Bulgarian warship, *Aleksandr I* (350t), was bought in France in 1883. Used as a royal yacht in peacetime, she had to perform the wartime roles of minelayer and transport during war. In 1913 she was scuttled off Ruse (together with some other ships), but later was raised and repaired. Deleted 1914.

Also extant in 1906 were the steamers *Simeon Veliki* (1870, 200t) and *Krum* (1859, 265t); the first was scuttled in 1913, the latter deleted in 1914. There were also 10 steam boats of 10–60t. The oil sail training ship *Asen* was deleted in 1903 and broken up in 1906.

ADDITIONS 1906–1921

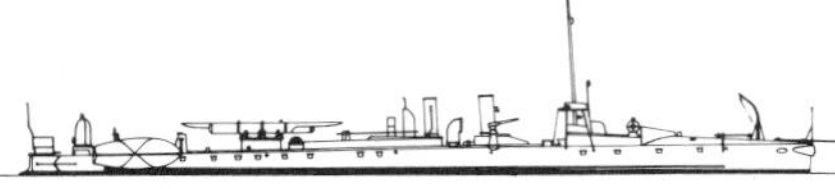
Drzki as completed
NB 1/750 scale

DRSKI class *torpedo-boats*

Displacement: 97.5t normal
Dimensions: 124ft 8in pp × 14ft 5in × 8ft 6in stern, 4ft 3in mean
38.0m × 4.4m × 2.4m, 1.3m
Machinery: 1-shaft 3cyl VTE reciprocating, 2 water-tube boilers, 1900ihp = 26kts. Coal 10.5t. Range 500nm
Armament: 2–37mm Schneider, 3–450mm (17.7in) TT (1 fixed in the bow, 1×2 deck)
Complement: 27–32

Class:
Drzki, Smeli, Hrabri, Strogi, Letjashchi, Shumni

All were built by Schneider's Châlon-sur-Saône yard. Ordered in two groups: *Drski, Smeli* and *Hrabri* were launched on 10 August 1907 and completed in January 1908. The other three were launched on 6 April 1908 and completed in August 1909. They were shipped to Bulgaria and were reassembled there. They took part in the First Balkan War, but were laid up, interned in Sevastopol, during the second. *Shumni* sank on 12 September 1916 after striking Russian mines off Varna; *Strogi* was damaged then, but repaired later. *Letjashchi* was seized by the French in October 1918 and while in their hands struck a rock off Varna and sank on 28 November 1918. The remaining four served in the early 1920s as minesweepers and later were again equipped with TT. Thoroughly modernised in 1934 they served in the Second World War as patrol boats, armed with 2–450mm TT and 2–20mm guns. In 1942 they were rearmed with the original 2–47mm guns, 2 MG and depth charge racks, in addition to TT. Reportedly, they were taken over by the Soviet Navy in 1944 and were returned when the war ended. Deleted in 1954; *Drski* has been a monument on dry land at Varna since 1955.

Ex-German *UB 1* class *submarine*

Class:
No 18

Her name is sometimes given as *Podvodnik No 18* (or *8*). Former German *UB 8* transferred to Bulgaria on 25 May 1918. Employed in defence of Varna. Surrendered to the French on 23 February 1919, towed by them to Bizerta and scrapped there from August 1921. Purchase of a second ship of this class, the *UB 7* was contemplated, but the ship was sunk before the deal could be concluded.

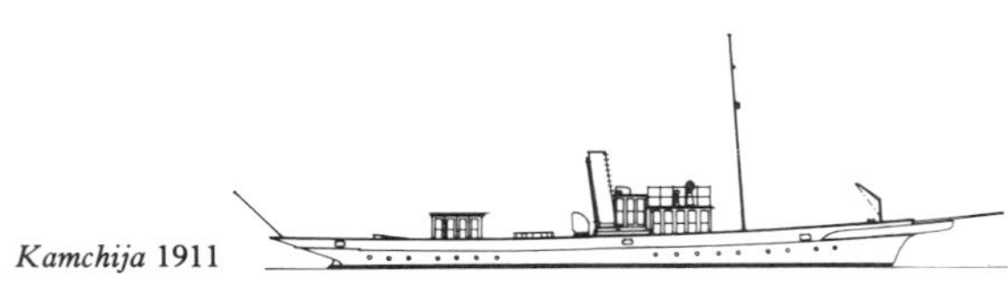
Kamchija 1911

KAMCHIJA *minelayer*

Former French steam yacht *De Romas*, bought in 1906 and renamed *Kamchija* in 1909. With a displacement of 105t and length of 118ft 9in *(36.2m)*, she was equipped with 2 boilers, one steam engine of 250hp and was capable of 11kts. In 1911 she was converted into a minelayer with a capacity of 10–12 mines. She was used as a patrol boat during the First World War. Refitted in 1924, she was employed as a survey ship; during the Second World War she was employed also on training duties, while minelaying was performed by two converted barges *Dunav* and *Svishchov*, capable of laying 50-60 mines each. After 1945 *Kamchija* was used as survey ship again, until she was deleted in 1952.

Ex-German *minesweeping boats*

In 1917 three former German minesweepers of 15t were commissioned into Bulgarian Navy as *Konduktor Dokuzanov, Kapitan-Lejtenant Minkov* and *Kapitan-Lejtenant Minor*. A year later they were augmented by three 8t boats *Nesebr, Emona* and *Kalacerka*; purchase of 18 more of this type was planned. Later the boats were renamed *Lilija, Vjara, Balik, Dobrotich* and *Momchal*. All were requisitioned by the French in 1919, but returned later and employed on minesweeping duties. Some of them took part in the Second World War (eg *Emona, Balik, Nesebr)* and were deleted only in 1955. During the Second World War they were augmented by 13 25t MChK type minesweeping boats and four 23.5t *Marica* class, all built during the Second World War.

Ex-US *submarine chasers*

In 1921 the Bulgarian Navy bought two submarine chasers of *SC* class and four 80ft motor launches. The chasers were renamed *Chernomorec* and *Belomorec*; the motor launches were renamed *Minor, Vzriv, Kapitan-lejtenant Minkov* and *Konduktor Dokuzanov*. *Dokuzanov* and *Minor* were deleted in 1934, while the remaining two were repaired and served on the Danube as patrol boats until the end of war, when they were deleted. The SC class chasers saw service in the Second World War, at first armed with 1–47mm gun and 2 MG and in 1941 rearmed with 1–37mm and 1–20mm. Both were deleted in 1952.

MISCELLANEOUS
Other Bulgarian warships in that period comprised the sail training ship *Strela* (ex-*Anemone*, bought 1906, 28t) and three floating torpedo floating batteries, or stations (built 1907 in France, 17t, armed with one 450mm (17.7in) TT).

During the 1912 Balkan War the merchant ships *Boris, Varna, Kiril, Sofija* and *Bulgaria* were temporarily commissioned in the Navy as transports. Three of them *(Varna, Bulgaria* and *Boris)* saw service again in the First World War, the latter being used as a minelayer.

Cambodia

Cambodia, which since 1863 had been a French protectorate possessed a token navy in 1906 consisting of the yacht *Lutin* (built 1874, 490t, 10kts), a former French gunboat received in 1897, 2 gunboats of 80t (8kts) armed with one small gun and 3 small steamers as well as uncertain number of armed junks. Final fates of these ships are unknown.

Colombia

Between 1906 and 1921 the economy of Colombia was very unstable. The country had lost her northern province of Panama in 1903 causing political turmoil. No new ships were added to the Fleet in this era except four 20t motor launches built by Yarrow for the Coast Guard in 1913. Only one was armed in 1919, Britain having detained the other 1pdr guns. Colombia and the USA ratified a treaty in 1921.

FLEET STRENGTH 1906

CRUISER

Name	Launched	Disp	Fate
ALMIRANTE LEZO (ex-*Cartagena*, ex-*El Bashir*)	*c*1902	1200t	Stricken *c*1925

Armed with 2–4.7in BL, 4–1pdr, 4 TT aw, 2500ihp = 18kts

RIVER GUNBOATS

Name	Launched	Disp	Fate
BOLIVAR	1870	981t	Stricken *c*1920
GENERAL PINZON (ex-*Namauna*)	1881	740t	Stricken *c*1928
Esperanza class			
ESPERANZA	1897	400t	Stricken *c*1935
GENERAL NERINO	1895	400t	Stricken *c*1935
CHERCINTO	1896	643t	Stricken *c*1935

Esperanza class
The first two were stern wheelers (built at Perth Amboy, New Jersey, USA) able to make 15kts at 430ihp. Dimensions, 140ft pp × 9ft × 3ft. They had ¼in nickel belt armour amidships and 3–1pdr guns. *Chercinto* measured 185ft pp × 31ft × 12ft with 400hp giving her *c*12kts, armament not known.

In addition to the above, the Colombian Navy in 1906 also operated the steamer *La Popa* and the transport *Cordova* (launched 1891 and stricken 1910).

Costa Rica

This Central American republic with an area of just under 20,000 square miles had a population of *c*300,000 including 7000 foreigners. Main products: coffee and bananas. Main ports Punta Arenas (Pacific) and Limon (Caribbean). The Army of 600 was supported by a 12,000 strong militia. Railway network poorly developed – only 175 miles in 1901. Governments in Costa Rica were very unstable and manipulated by the USA. The Navy consisted of one 15t Yarrow-built torpedo-launch of 1890 (stricken *c*1920) without any fighting value. There were armed border clashes with Panama in February-March 1921 but US pressure on Panama prevented war.

Cuba

Cuba won her independence from Spain in 1898 with substantial help from the United States. Cuba's internal affairs were legally intervened in eight times up to 1917 by the United States, and her international relations were dominated by the northern neighbour. The US 1st and 2nd Marine Regiments landed in September 1906 and stayed until January 1909. They came again in May–July 1912 to help put down the Negro Rebellion. Cuba began her fleet during this era with the German-built gunboat *Baire* (see 1860-1905 volume).

On 7 April 1917 Cuba declared war on Germany, one day after the United States. US Atlantic Fleet marines had been on the Sugar Intervention since February. Cuba offered to send troops to Europe, but this was discouraged by the US as not being practical. The Cuban and United States navies collaborated to patrol the islands. The Cuban Navy patrolled the more remote areas of the islands, and the US Navy concentrated in the areas primarily off Havana and Guantanamo (where a marine battalion remained until 1922). The gunboats *Baire* and *Patria* were sent to the US for overhaul and rearmament. On 21 August 1917 Cuba transferred to the US four large German steamers of 19,464grt that had been seized when Cuba had declared war. The Cuban Navy did not encounter any enemy ships during the conflict.

The island's merchant marine totalled 35 steamers of 29,286grt and 146 sailing vessels of 15,132grt in 1919. That year a government dockyard was planned for Havana Bay and was to include a 4000t floating dock. The Naval Academy at Mariel was to move to Havana.

ADDITIONS 1906–1921

CUBA *sloop*

Displacement: 2055t
Dimensions: 260ft pp × 39ft × 14ft
79.2m × 11.9m × 4.3m
Machinery: VTE, Babcock boilers, 6000shp = 18kts. Coal 250t
Armament: 2–4in (102mm), 4–6pdr (57mm), 4–3pdr (47mm), 4–1 pdr (37mm), 2 MG

Name	Builder	Launched	Fate
CUBA	Cramp, Philadelphia	10.8.11	Stricken 1971

A twin-funnel vessel very strangely classified as a light cruiser in the 1919 *Jane's*.

Cuba 1949 after reconstruction
Aldo Fraccaroli Collection

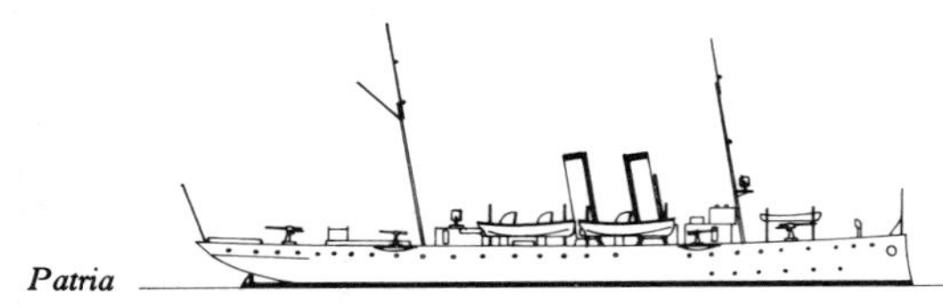
Patria

PATRIA *gunboat*

Displacement: 1100t
Dimensions: 200ft pp × 36ft × 13ft
61.0m × 11.0m × 4.0m
Machinery: = 16kts. Coal 150t
Armament: 2–6pdr (57mm), 4–3pdr (47mm), 4–1pdr (37mm)

Name	Builder	Launched	Fate
PATRIA	Cramp	10.8.11	Stricken 1955

Two-masted, twin-funnel vessel used as TS.

DIEZ DE OCTUBRE class *gunboats*

Displacement: 218t
Dimensions: 110ft × 20ft × 8ft
33.6m × 6.1m × 2.4m
Machinery: = 12kts. Coal 50t
Armament: 1–3pdr (47mm), 2–1pdr (37mm)

Class (builder, launched, fate):
Diez de Octubre (Cramp, 1911, stricken 1946), *Veinte y Cuatro de Febrero* (Cramp 1911, stricken 1946)

A pair of US-built gunboats with single funnel, two masts and a ram bow.

MISCELLANEOUS
Two 80t wooden gunboats were built at Havana in 1912: *Habana* and *Pinar del Rio*. They were 100ft × 18ft × 6ft vessels with 1–1pdr gun and capable of 12kts on 1 screw at 200ihp (coal 20t).

Four US sub-chasers *SC 274, SC 302, SC 312* and *SC 314*, were transferred in November 1918.

Armed revenue cutters totalled 13 in 1919 including 3 ex-Spanish gunboats of 1895–96 (35–45t, 1–1pdr, 10–12kts): *Cespedes, Maceo* and *Agramonte*. None mounted heavier armament than 2–6pdr.

Dominican Republic

This nation, which shares the great island of Hispaniola with Haiti, maintained a small gunboat navy during this era. In May 1916 the United States intervened in a civil war and a brigade of US Marines were stationed on the island until September 1924. There were enough skirmishes by mid-1918 to yield 53,000 firearms. The following minor warships composed the Dominican Navy during this era: *Restaurcion* (gunboat, launched 1896, 1000t, 4–4.7in, stricken *c*1916); *Independencia* (gunboat, launched 1894, 322t, 7 small guns, stricken *c*1916); *Presidente* (gunboat, rebuilt 1898, 4 small guns, stricken *c*(1916).

Ecuador

Border troubles with neighbours were somewhat relieved during this era. Peru had not recovered from the War of the Pacific (1879–83) and Colombia was suffering from economic and internal political problems. As elsewhere in Latin America, these border confrontations were caused in large measure by the fact that Spain had never defined the boundaries between her administrative areas. The French 811t 'avisos' *Papin* and *Inconstant* of 1886, bought in 1900, were stricken in *c*1915–16. The 800t Chilean torpedo gunboat *Almirante Simpson* (launched 1896) was bought in 1907 and renamed *Libertador Bolivar*. In addition the Ecuadorian Navy in 1906 also operated the old steamers *Catapari* and *Nueve de Julio* (2 guns apiece). Both were disposed of *c*1912. There was also a 300t coastguard vessel *Patria* (ex-yacht *Cavalier*) with 4 MG. Ecuador's merchant marine totalled 7 steamers (1942grt) and 4 sailing ships (1882grt) in 1919. Ecuador broke diplomatic relations with Germany during 1914–18.

Egypt

In 1906 Egypt practically had no navy. Three obsolete gunboats were the only survivors of the Khedive Ismaïl I (1863–79) purchases. With him began a period of accelerated economic development for the country which, though it led Ismail to ruin and led to the British occupation from 1882, was not without benefit to Egypt. After 1882 Egypt, although nominally under the Ottoman court, was under British control. Some coast guard vessels and yachts built in Britain and France were the only acquisitions of the 1882–1906 period. Before the Great War the Red Sea lighthouse tender *Aida (i)* was replaced by a new ship *Aida (ii)* (1911, 1428grt) built by A et Ch de la Loire, Nantes. During 14–20 October 1914 the Egyptian Government sent troops to seize 22 suspect ships in the Suez Canal and handed them over to the British Naval authorities at Alexandria. Two relatively valuable ships were added in 1920, when a sloop *Syringa* and a patrol boat *P 57*, were bought from the Royal Navy, and incorporated into the Egyptian Navy as *Sollum* and *Raquib* respectively.

FLEET STRENGTH 1906

GUNBOATS

Name	Launched	Disp	Fate
KHARTUM	1862	455t	Stricken *c*1914
DONGOLA	1863	300t	Stricken *c*1914
JEAFFERIEH	?1865	690t	Stricken *c*1914

COAST GUARD VESSELS

Name	Launched	Disp	Fate
NOOR EL BAHR	1884	450t	Sold 1928
NESIM	1885	81t	Stricken 1920
MARDA	1886	154t	Stricken *c* 1920
ZARIF	1886	144t	Stricken 1920s
SARIA	1886	71t	Stricken 1920s
ABBAS	1891	298grt	Sunk 6.11.15

Abbas was sunk by *U 35* in the Bay of Sollum.

YACHTS

Name	Launched	Disp	Fate
MAHROUSSA	1865	3417t	Extant 1984
EMIRIGHAIN	1874	11t	Stricken *c* 1920
AIDA	1882	723grt	Stricken *c* 1910
SAFA EL BAHR	1894	700t	Sold 1908
ABDUL MONAYM	1902	610t	Stricken 1930s

Mahroussa, the royal yacht built as a paddle steamer, was in 1905 transformed to a triple screw turbine-powered vessel, again refitted in 1946–47 was converted in 1951 to a school ship, later renamed *El Horria*. *Aida* served as a lighthouse tender and *Abdul Monaym* as coast guard vessel.

RIVER GUNBOATS

Name	Launched	Disp	Fate
TAMAI class	1884–85	73.5t	See notes
EL ZAFIR class	1896-97	128t	See notes
SULTAN class	1896-97	140t	See notes

Ten Nile stern wheeler (except *Sultan* class) gunboats built for the 1883–99 Sudan wars. They carried 1 gun normally a 12pdr (3in) and 2–4 Maxim MG, some had a howitzer as well. They were officered by an elite RN detachment in 1896–99. Their bombardments included Hafif (4 boats present, Dervish steamer sunk by *Tamai*, *Abu Klea* and *Metemmeh*) and Dongola in 1896; Metemmeh twice in 1897; capture of Shendy together with bombardments of Omdurman and Khartoum (9 boats present) during 1898 followed by the Fashoda incident (*El Fateh*, *Sultan*, *Nasir* and *Abu Klea* escorted Kitchener).

Tamai class consisted of *Tamai* (? lost during 1914–18 in the Red Sea), *Hafir* (ex-*Eltre*, sunk 1941), *Metemmeh* (stricken 1925), *Abu Klea* (stricken 1930s). *El Zafir* class comprised *El Zafir* (sank 28 August 1898 near Shendy in an accident, salvaged and repaired, BU 1964), *El Fateh* (BU 1953) and *El Nasir* (BU 1932). The single-screw *Sultan* class consisted of *Sheik* (disarmed 1924), *Sultan* (sold 1925) and *Melik* (converted to oil storage barge during 1939–45).

ADDITIONS 1906–1921

Ex-British ANCHUSA class *convoy sloop*

HMS *Syringa* (29.9.17, 1290t) was bought on 31 March 1920 and renamed *Sollum*. She was used for transport, lighthouse administration, inspection and other duties. *Sollum* lost when she went aground at Sidi Barrani in January 1941 while under attack by German aircraft.

Ex-British P-Boat type *patrol craft*

The British *P 57* (1917, 613t) patrol boat was sold to Egypt on 21 May 1920 and enlisted as *Raquib* in the Egyptian Navy. She was stricken in the 1930s.

Estonia

Estonia's independence was declared on 24 February 1917, but this small country still had to fight for complete liberty from her neighbours. On the following day Estonia was occupied by the Germans, who withdrew only in November 1918, leaving the country denuded of arms and open to a Soviet advance. The Soviets took Narva on 28 November 1918; they later succeeded in occupying two thirds of Estonia by January 1919. Allied assistance with arms and devastating naval gunfire support provided by Rear-Admiral Edwyn Alexander-Sinclair's British squadron (the cruisers *Cardiff*, *Caradoc*, *Calypso* and 7 destroyers) helped to counter the offensive 40 miles from Reval (Tallinn) in January, and in May 1919 the Estonian Army, aided by Finnish volunteers and Latvian regiments liberated Estonia and northern Latvia. There the Estonian Navy, created from ships left by the Russians in Reval, fought its first action in June 1919, silencing the batteries of Dunamünde, forcing its passage to the River Daugava and sweeping the bridges of Riga with gunfire.

The peace treaty between the Baltic States and Soviet Russia was signed at Tartu in February 1921. By that time Estonia possessed quite a large navy of 2 destroyers, 2 gunboats and 2 minelayers, supported by a number of auxiliaries and 3 further gunboats on Lake Peipus. All those ships, except the destroyers, were found in Estonian harbours after the withdrawal of the Russians and Germans. The destroyers were captured by a British squadron at the end of 1918 and presented to Estonia. It comes as no surprise that Estonia's Navy did not expand until the 1930s, as this small country, cut off from her former hinterland, strained hard to improve her economy. Personnel numbered 2100 in 1919 under Captain Johann Pitka. The main bases were Reval (4 floating drydocks) plus Rohukula, Pärnu, Narva and Baltic Port. The new republic's merchant marine totalled 80 steamers (30,000grt) and 177 sailing ships (20,000grt) in 1919.

Ex-Russian NOVIK class *destroyers*

Class:
Wambola (ex-*Spartak*, ex-*Kapitan I Ranga Miklucha-Maklai*), *Lennuk* (ex-*Avtroil*)

Two Russian *Novik* class destroyers were captured by a British squadron (cruisers *Caradoc*, *Calypso* destroyers *Vendetta*, *Vortigern*, *Vendetta* and *Wakeful*) under Captain Bertram Thesiger on 26–27 December 1918 off Reval in the Gulf of Finland. Both were presented to Estonia and renamed. In 1933 they were sold to Peru and again renamed *Villar* and *Guise*. *Lennuk* was armed with 5–102mm (4in), 1–40mm and 9–457mm (18in) TT and 60 mines. *Wambola* carried 4–102mm (4in), 1–40mm, 9–457mm (18in) TT and 50 mines.

Ex-Russian *gunboats*

Class:
Lembit (ex-*Bieber*, ex-*Bobr*), *Laene* (ex-*Sputnik*), *Wanemune* (ex-*Imperator*)

Three large gunboats were found in Estonian harbours during 1920–21 and were put into Estonian service. *Lembit* (875t, launched August 1907) 2–120mm (4.7in), 4–75mm, 40 mines) served between April and November 1918 as a German floating workshop; she was broken up in 1925. *Laene* (211t, 1–57mm) was taken over in August 1940 by the Soviets and put into their service as *Gangutec*; she sank on 2 December 1941. *Wanemune* (260t, 2–45mm) was later renamed *President*. She was stationed on Lake Peipus. In August 1940 put into Soviet service as *Issa* and was scuttled on 24 June 1941.

There were also four more gunboats (converted Imperial Russian passenger steamers) on Lake Peipus. Two of them were taken over by the Soviet Union in August 1940: *Ahti* (1908, 140t, 2–76mm) was renamed *Embak*; *Tartu* (108t, 2–76mm) was renamed *Narva*. Both were scuttled in September 1941.

Ex-Russian No 18 class *minelayers*

Class:
Ristna (ex-*No 18*, ex-*Apostol Piotr*), *Suurop* (ex-*No 19*, *Apostol Pavel*)

Two paddle steamers, rebuilt by the Russians as minelayers and abandoned by them in Helsinki. In 1918 they became part of the Estonian Navy. In Estonian service they carried 1–75mm and 1–40mm guns and 175 mines. Both were put into Soviet service in 1940.

Ex-Russian *minesweepers*

Class:

Kalev (ex-*M 8*), *Olev* (ex-*M 10*)

Two former Czarist minesweepers of 50t were incorporated into the Estonian Navy under the above names. In 1936 they were renamed *Vaindlo* and *Keri* respectively. Both were seized in August 1940 by the USSR and renamed *T 295* and *T 296* respectively. The latter was scuttled in August 1941, but *T 295* became *KATShch 1* in June 1941 and *KATShch 1501* in July 1941, and from 1944 was known as *VRD 84*. She was broken up in the 1950s.

MISCELLANEOUS

Three former Russian naval icebreakers were incorporated into the Estonian Navy: *Tasuja* (ex-*Gerkules*, 1912, 1100t) was taken over by the USSR in August 1940 and was sunk by German aircraft in Kronstadt on 1 December 1941. Raised in 1942 and repaired, she was broken up in 1965. *Juri Vilms* (ex-*Valdimir*, ex-*Hector*, 1902, 200t) was taken over by the USSR in August 1940 and was lost during the Second World War. *Jaan Poska* (ex-German *Reval*, ex-Russian *Sneg*, 1914, 250t) was taken over by the USSR in 1940 and renamed *Parnu*. Broken up in the mid-1950s.

Other ships in service comprised 4 tugs converted to minesweepers in 1919, 2 transports, 3 hydrographic ships and 12 tugs, tenders and frontier guard ships.

Finland

As the Bolshevik revolution in October 1917 overthrew the liberal government in Russia, Finland declared herself an independent nation from 6 December. A Finnish Communist element gave rise to a civil war that ended in May 1918. At that time there was a lot of small ex-Czarist warships in many harbours, most of them in very poor condition. The bigger ships and all vessels able to steam had run for Kronstadt and Petrograd (ex-St Petersburg). A total of 6 ex-Russian gunboats, 10 torpedo-boats, 2 240t and 16 smaller minesweepers were taken over. Of these 7 torpedo-boats were later returned to the Soviet Union. For details see the Finland section in the 1922–46 volume and the Russia section in this volume.

Haiti

Haiti had numerous squabbles with maritime nations concerning the payment of debts. A clash with the Germans in 1902–03 resulted in the sinking of the 950t gunboat *Crete a Pierot* by the later famous gunboat SMS *Panther*. Between July 1915 and 1934 Haiti was occupied by US Marines when the country's finances and government collapsed. Over 2000 were landed from the battleship *Connecticut* plus the armoured cruisers *Washington* and *Tennessee*. Apparently, the ships of the Haitian Navy were sold in 1915 and the Navy ceased to exist. Only two unarmed auxiliary schooners remained for coastguard duty. On 12 July 1918 Haiti declared war on Germany.

GUNBOATS

Name	Launched	Disp	Fate
22 DECEBRE 1804	1860	900t	Stricken *c*1912
1804	1875	600t	Stricken *c*1912
SAINT MICHAEL	1875	850t	Stricken *c*1912
DESSALINES (ex-*Ethel*)	1883	1200t	Stricken 1915
TOUSSAINT-LOUVERTURE	1886	500t	Stricken 1915
Capois La Mort class			
CAPOIS LA MORT	1893	256t	Stricken 1915
ALEXANDER PETION	1893	256t	Stricken 1915

In addition to the above, Haiti also operated a few small sail transports.

Around 1910 she bought the *Erl King* which became the 500t gunboat *La Liberte* (200ft × 26ft 4in × 14ft, *60.9m* × *8.0m* × *4.3m*, 12kts, 1in belt armour midships, 2–6pdr, 2–3pdr, 2–1pdr). She was stricken *c*1912. The old Italian protected cruiser *Umbria* (launched 1891) was bought in 1911, renamed *Ferrier* and sank because of her crew's inexperience.

Honduras

Honduras is one of the larger republics (1905 official census 500,136) in Central America with an area of 43,277 square miles. The country has two coasts – Pacific and Caribbean Sea (63 miles and 375 miles). In the early years of the twentieth century she was closely associated with and her foreign trade was mainly with the USA. US Marines landed in January 1912 to protect American property. The main port was and is Puerto Cortés on the Caribbean and smaller ones Trujillo, Omoa and Amapala on the Gulf of Fonseca (Pacific). Amapala's surrender on 11 April 1907 had virtually ended the war with Nicaragua since the cruiser USS *Chicago* gave refuge to the defeated Honduran President Manuel Borilla, landed marines and arranged terms with the victors. There was a small army of 500 soldiers which was supported in emergency by 20,000 militia. The Navy was really symbolic and consisted of one 13t steam (22ihp) launch, the *22 Februar* launched on 24 December 1897 to which was added (by 1919) the 200-ton gunboat *Tatumbla* (2 small guns, 44 crew, 12kts), and the 24–ton *Liberia* (ex-Liberian revenue cutter *Mesurado,* 85ft × 12ft × 4ft 6in, 1-Nordenfelt, 1 MG, 120hp = 12–14kts, 500gal paraffin).

Latvia

Latvian independence was proclaimed on 18 November 1918 when the Government was established, but only in December 1920 was the country freed of foreign armies. On 4 January 1919 the Soviets, who had already created the Communist government of Latvia, took Riga; they had to abandon it to the Germans in May. They in turn handed Riga to the Latvian Government in July 1919 only after negotiations by the British Lieutenant-General Sir Hubert Gough, Head of the British Military Mission to the Baltic Provinces. In October Riga was attacked by the West Russian Army (organised with German help) which was defeated with the vital help of Anglo-French naval gunfire especially the 15in guns of the monitor HMS *Erebus*. Only on 11 August 1920 was a peace treaty signed between Latvia and the USSR after an armistice on 1 February. It brought much needed peace to the one of most industrialised provinces of prewar Russia.

The course of the war prevented any warships of importance being preserved for Latvian use. What were left in harbours were at first organised into the Soviet Latvian Flotilla (see Russia) and later scuttled. Thus, apart from a few auxiliaries, the Latvian Navy comprised in 1922 only one warship, the patrol ship *Virsaitis*, salvaged in 1920. Only during the mid-1920s were funds found for expansion of the Navy. One former German minesweeper *M 68* (that sank on 29 October 1917 off Dvina outlet) was salvaged in 1920; the repairs were finished in November 1921. Served as guard/patrol ship in the Latvian Navy with armament of 2–75mm guns and 2 MG. In August 1940 taken over by USSR and renamed *T 297*. She sank on mines on 2 December 1941 and was raised after 1945 and broken up in 1960.

Two icebreakers were incorporated into the Navy in 1919: *Varonis* (ex-Russian *Passat*, 1908, 250t), taken over by the USSR in August 1940, sank in 1941, later salvaged and broken up in late 1950s; and *Lacplesis* (ex-Russian *Matros*, 1914, 253t), taken over by the USSR in August 1940, scrapped in mid 1950s.

Liberia

The steam Liberian Navy was created in the early 1890s, when the steel gunboats *Gorronommah* and *Rocktown* were built. Unfortunately both were lost by 1900. Some vain efforts were made to acquire new gunboats from France. In 1907 a new vessel was acquired for government use, when the steam launch *Cecil Powney* was seized from a private chartered company, and subsequently used to convey officials in the harbour and rivers around Monrovia. In 1906 another vessel was ordered and in 1908 delivered to Liberia; she was formerly the Rothschild yacht *Eros* (1876, 770t), which as *Lark* served in the Liberian Navy. In 1915 her crew were laid off since they could not be paid, and she was broken up over several years. In 1916 the auxiliary schooner *President Howard* (1912, 73grt) was bought from a German owner. She was sunk by *U 154* off Monrovia on 9 April 1918. A revenue cutter ordered from Blandy Brothers of Las Palmas in the Canaries was never delivered and sold to Honduras by 1919.

Mexico

As the twentieth century began, Mexico had been one of the most stable countries in Latin America. The dictator President Porfirio Díaz had been the dominant force in Mexican politics for almost forty years, and he promoted foreign investment, in part, by guaranteeing internal tranquility at any price. Díaz was overthrown on 25 May 1911 and died in Paris exile (1915). The Mexican Revolution, which began in 1910, lasted for almost a decade. This was fought almost entirely on land and none of the combatants developed much of a naval force. This contest among the Mexicans was closely watched and at times interfered with by the United States. Between April and November 1914 United States troops landed in strength at Vera Cruz and every two years or so an American warship intervened to protect national interests. In 1919 Mexico's merchant marine totalled 31 steamers of 33,975grt and 16 sailing vessels of 2630grt.

FLEET STRENGTH 1906

CRUISERS

Name	Launched	Disp	Fate
Zaragosa class			
ZARAGOSA (ex-*Porfiro Diaz*)	9.4.91	1200t	Stricken *c*1924

Zaragosa was rebuilt in 1910.

Zaragosa 1894 — *By courtesy of R L Scheina*

DESTROYERS/GUNBOATS

Name	Launched	Disp	Fate
Independencia class			
INDEPENDENCIA	1874	480t	Stricken *c*1920
LIBERTAD	1874	480t	Stricken *c*1920
Democrata class			
DEMOCRATA	1875	445t	Stricken *c*1915
MEXICO	1875	445t	Stricken *c*1915
Plan de Guadalupe class			
PLAN DE GUADALUPE (ex-*Dolphin*)	1892	824t	Stricken 1924
Tampico class			
TAMPICO	1902	980t	Sunk 16.7.14
VERA CRUZ	1902	980t	Stricken 1924

MINOR NAVIES

Name	Launched	Disp	Fate
Nicholas Bravo class			
NICHOLAS BRAVO	1903	1227t	Stricken 1945
MORALES	1903	1227t	Stricken 1924

Nicholas Bravo (named after the general who was thrice president, 1839–46) was renamed *Blanquet c*1917.

The Mexican Navy also operated a few small transports.

ADDITIONS 1906–1921

PROGRESO class *gunboat*

Displacement: 1590t
Dimensions: 230ft 2in × 34ft × 9ft 9in mean
70.1m × 10.3m × 3.0m
Machinery: 1 shaft, VTE, 1400shp = 13kts. Coal 209t
Armament: 4–6pdr (57mm)
Complement: 140

Name	Builder	Launched	Fate
PROGRESO	Odero, Sestri Ponente	1907	Stricken 1947

In February 1915 the Italian-built *Progreso* was blown up while lying off the port of Progreso in the Yucatan. Ten on board were killed. The one-funnelled, two-masted warship had been sent to the port to support the forces of General Venustiano Carranza, the then president. She was raised and returned to service.

GENERAL GUERRERO class *cruiser transport*

Displacement: 1850t
Dimensions: 245ft pp × 35ft × 17ft 6in max
74.6m × 3.2m × 5.3m
Machinery: VTE, 1500shp = 12kts
Armament: 6–4in (102mm), 2–3pdr (47mm)
Complement: 300 crew plus 550 troops

Name	Builder	Launched	Fate
GENERAL GUERRERO	Vickers, Barrow	1908	Stricken 1924

She could carry 45 horses and a few field pieces for the embarked troops. Three 4in guns were mounted on the forecastle and three on the poop deck. Name is also cited as *Vicente Guerrero*. Either way she commemorated the War of Independence guerilla leader and the third Mexican president (1829).

Morocco

The steam Moroccan Navy was founded in 1882 when Emperor El Hassan ordered a 1164-ton barquentine-rigged steamer, which received his name, from R Craggs & Sons, Middlesborough. She was armed with 1–6.6in old Krupp gun and 4 MG by the turn of the century. At that time Morocco was under Spanish influence and a Spanish crew served in that ship. The Spanish expedition of 1894 and the treaty of that year, while conceding only insiginficant frontier rectification to Spain, involved the Sultan in the payment of about £650,000 indemnity and so in 1895 a German crew replaced the Spanish one. Moreover Germany became the first deliverer of military hardware to Morocco. In 1891 an 18-ton steamer *El Tirki* and three steam launches were bought from the German owners.

In 1892 came the most modern Moroccan ship – a small cruiser *El Bashir* (1150t) was built by Orlando of Leghorn, Italy, but due to high cost she was sold in 1902 to Colombia. Moreover in 1892 the gunboat *Es Sid el Turki* (460grt) was ordered from Krupp and subcontracted by them to A G Weser of Bremen. *El Hassaneh* was sold in 1902 and *Es Sid el Turki* (2–9pdr, designed 1200ihp = 14.5kts) in 1908. In 1898 another vessel *Noor el Bahr* (672t) was ordered from F Barachini, Sampierdarena (Spain), but shortly after completion she was sold to Turkish merchant owners. In 1902 Krupp delivered two small steamers for transport and coast guard purposes. The years 1905–11 were taken up with maritime rivalry over Morocco between France and Germany, which ended with the treaty of 4 November 1911 and then, as it was ratified in 1912, the French protectorate over the empire (partitioned with Spain after a secret agreement in 1904) was established, but at that time Morocco had no navy.

Nicaragua

This Central American republic possessed 2 steamers and 18 sailing vessels (10,032grt) and enjoyed 8 presidents during this period. Her railway network stood at 147 miles in 1904 with 1200 foreigners in a 1905 population of 550,000. The regular Army stood at 4000, 40,000 on mobilisation. Between February and April 1907 Nicaragua defeated her northern neighbour Honduras, occupying the latter's capital Tegucigalpa. Nicaragua's superior seapower had already enabled her to capture Puerto Cortes and La Ceiba on the Honduran Caribbean Coast. Not surprisingly Nicaragua's present flag was adopted in 1908. On 19 May 1910 the gunboat USS *Paducah* landed her marines at Bluefields on the Atlantic coast to revive General Juan J Estrada's Catholic 'conservative' side to a civil war victory against President Jose Santo Zelaya's anti-clerical 'liberals' in Managua. (Zelaya had already fled to Mexico in 1909 aboard a Mexican gunboat). The main port was Corinto on the Pacific where Butler's US Marine battalion from Panama landed into a civil war on 14 August 1912 (it had done so in December 1909–March 1910 without going farther) to march up the 90-mile railway to Managua. Reinforced to a regiment, it opened the SE railway to Granada although the last 15 miles took 5 days. Two hilltop forts were stormed by 850 marines and sailors (with 3 field guns) in a 40-minute fight during the early hours of 4 October. By January 1913 only 100 marines remained as US Legation Guard. In 1919 Nicaragua had a 400-ton gunboat *Momotombo* (2–12pdr/3in and 1–6pdr/57mm) as well as the armed transport *Maximo Jeraz* (ex-USS *Venus*) and the *Ornotepe*.

Paraguay

Paraguay has been called the Poland of South America because she is surrounded by powerful neighbours, with whom she was frequently in conflict with during the nineteenth century. The landlocked Paraguayan Navy was almost non-existent during the 1906–1921 era. Between 1864 and 1870, Paraguay had waged the disastrous War of the Triple Alliance or Lopez War against Argentina, Brazil, and Uruguay. Reportedly four out of five Paraguayan males were killed in the conflict, and much disputed territory was lost. The nation did not recover from this war until well into the middle of the twentieth century. In 1919 the Paraguayan Navy was reported as the dispatch vessel *Triumfo* (and another), the presidential yacht *Adolfo Riqueilme*, the armed steamers *Constitucion* and *Independencia*.

Persia

The modern Persian Navy was born in 1885, when an iron 1200-ton gunboat *Persepolis* and a small river patrol vessel *Susa* , both built by A G Weser, Bremen, were erected at Mohammerah in the Tigris-Euphrates delta. *Persepolis*, delivered completed with a German crew, proved expensive to maintain and her machinery was neglected. The majority of the crew were repatriated and the ship spent most of her time at her moorings, outwardly smart but rarely serviceable. By 1906 her armament was reported as 1–4in BL, 2–30pdr BL and 2 smaller guns. She was scrapped about 1936. The Navy in 1906 also comprised a gunboat *Muzaffer* (1899, 400t) and the steam yacht *Selika* bought in 1902. *Muzaffer* served with and in the Royal Navy during 1914–18 and was reconditioned by HM Dockyard at Bombay before being returned. She was finally stricken about 1936. Some other vessels of the Persian Navy were a river customs steamer *Azerbaijan*, based at Muscat and which served during 1918–19 in the Royal Indian Marine, and an armed steamer *Perebonia*, which was taken on 18 May 1920 by the Soviets at Enzeli on the Caspian Sea but probably returned to Persia.

Poland

The Polish Navy was called into being on 28 November 1918, seventeen days after Polish independence was declared. The new Navy had two aims: the first was to support Polish claims for the Pomeranian coast; the second was to secure inland waterways in the newly emerged Polish state. A number of civilian ships were put into naval service, mainly on the Vistula river and the construction of river warships was contemplated. These plans resulted in four gunboats (called monitors in Poland) built in Danziger Werft; a further two were ordered in 1923 at Krakow. Another flotilla was hastily created in the east, preparing for war between Poland and Soviet Russia, comprising mainly ex-German motor boats.

The Polish river flotillas, created in 1919 on the Vistula and Pina rivers were at that time the only units of the Polish Navy with any military value. They proved themselves during the Polish-Soviet War of 1919–20 (the only war lost by the USSR), when they fought gallantly and victoriously against an overwhelming enemy.

On 10 February 1920 Poland took over a 42 nautical mile strip of coastline, which lacked a harbour of any importance. Gdansk (called Danzig by the Germans) became a Free Town; though nominally Poland had certain rights there, practice and law prevented its use as a naval base. Therefore the Polish Navy used the small harbours of Puck and Hel initially but already in 1922 a decision was taken to build a new harbour in the village of Gdynia.

In December 1919 only six ex-German torpedo-boats were allocated to Poland, though strong protests were issued by the Polish delegation to Versailles. The delegation demanded 2 light cruisers, 2 destroyers and a number of submarine chasers, motor boats and auxiliary ships. These claims were based on the economic potential of inland Polish industrial districts, which until 1918 had been under German and Austrian administration for more than a century: the protests were not approved.

NAVAL CLAIMS AGAINST THE USSR

Poland also claimed her share from the Russian Navy during the Polish-Soviet peace talks in Riga in 1921. At these negotiations 2

Gydnia in the late 1920s with the ex-Russian gunboats in the background
Twardowski Collection

Gangut class battleships, 10 large destroyers, 5 submarines, 10 minesweepers, 21 auxiliaries and transports, 2 uncompleted *Svetlana* class cruisers and other equipment (guns, mines, etc) were demanded. Though the claims were later reduced to 5 destroyers, 5 submarines, 5 minesweepers, 2 auxiliaries and 1 uncompleted cruiser, they were not considered and Poland received nothing to add to her fully-conceded territorial claims when the Treaty of Riga was signed on 18 March 1921.

In the meantime various ships were being bought. The first of them was a small passenger coaster, which became the first Polish warship under the name of *Pomorzanin*. She was followed by 2 gunboats purchased in Finland and 4 minesweepers bought in Denmark. There were also boats, launches and tugs, bought mainly in Gdansk and 5 river patrol boats bought in 1920 in Austria.

These ships formed the Polish Navy until 1926, when 2 destroyers and 3 submarines were ordered in France. Meanwhile, the fleet expansion programmes were drawn up. The 1920 programme called for a fantastic 2 battleships, 6 cruisers, 28 destroyers, 45 submarines, 28 minesweepers and auxiliaries. Four large and twenty small monitors had to be built on Poland's rivers together with 49 motor boats. This programme had to be completed by 1929. This date was totally unrealistic, due to Poland's economic situation, and in the same year another programme was drawn up, which called for 1 cruiser, 4 destroyers, 6 ex-German torpedo-boats, 2 submarines and some smaller ships. This programme could not be realised either, though talks were underway with the British Admiralty for transferring 1 cruiser, 4 destroyers, 2 floating workshops and some CMBs to Poland. Personnel in 1919 were reported to number 1500 officers and sailors from the former Imperial Austrian-Hungarian and Russian Navies.

Ex-German V 105 class *torpedo-boats*

Class:
Mazur (ex-*V 105*), *Kaszub* (ex-*V 108*)

Allocated to Poland on 9 December 1919 and were renamed as above. These ships arrived in Poland in September 1921 when they were disarmed. While in Polish service they received 2–47mm guns and 2 MG. During 1924 they were armed with 2–75mm, 2 MG and 2–450mm (17.7in) TT. *Kaszub* was destroyed on 20 July 1925 in dry dock at Gdansk, due to a boiler explosion.

Mazur was refitted in 1931 as a TS with 4–75mm and 2 MG. In 1935 she was rebuilt (the after funnel was struck) and her armament consisted of 3–75mm, 1–40mm AA and 2 MG. On 1 September 1939 she was sunk by German aircraft in Gdynia harbour; the first warship lost in World War Two.

Ex-German A 56 class *torpedo-boats*

Class:
Slazak (ex-*A 59*), *Krakowiak* (ex-*A 64*), *Kujawiak* (ex-*A 68*), *Goral* (ex-*A 80*)

Allocated to Poland on December 1919 and renamed. *Goral* was renamed *Podhalanin* in 1922. All arrived in Poland during September 1921 without armament and only in 1925 received 2–75mm, 2 MG and 2–450mm (17.7in) TT. All were deleted in 1936/37 and used as floating magazines, targets, etc. *Krakowiak* was scrapped before the war; the other 3 were captured by the Germans and probably broken up by them during the war.

Ex-Russian GOLUB class *gunboats*

Class:
General Haller (ex-*Turunmaa*, ex-*Vodorez*), *Komendant Pilsudski* (ex-*Karjakla*, ex-*Lun*)

Former Imperial Russian Navy gunboats purchased in 1920 when they were renamed after the founders of the Polish Legion and heroes of the Polish-Soviet War. While in Polish hands they were armed with 6–47mm and 2 MG. This was changed in 1925 to 2–75mm, 2–47mm and 2 MG. Final rearmament in 1938 became 2–75mm, 2–13.2mm, 4 MG and 30 mines. Both took part in the Second World War; *Haller* was sunk by German aircraft on 6 September 1939 in Hel harbour, while *Pilsudski* was seized by the Germans, renamed *Heisternest* (later *M 3109*) and sunk by Allied aircraft on 16 September 1944. Some sources claim them to be named *Kondor* and *Berkut* when ordered by Russia.

Ex-German FM class *minesweepers*

Class:
Czajka (ex-*Finlandia I*, ex-*FM 2*), *Jaskolka* (ex-*Finlandia II*, ex-*FM 27*), *Mewa* (ex-*Finlandia III*, ex-*FM 28*), *Rybitwa* (ex-*Finlandia IV*, ex-*FM 31*)

Four *FM* class minesweepers were bought on 24 September 1920 in Denmark. They came to Poland under provisional names and were later renamed after birds. While in Polish service each was armed with 1–47mm, 2 MG, 20 mines and 2 sets of minesweeping gear. They were deleted in 1931 and sold for civilian use, while *Mewa* was rebuilt as a survey ship and renamed *Pomorzanin* (she replaced the first ship of that name). She was sunk on 14 September 1939 in Jastarnia by German aircraft.

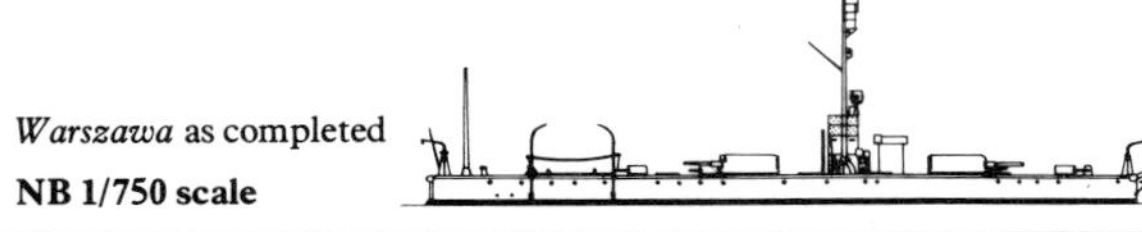
Warszawa as completed
NB 1/750 scale

WARSZAWA class *river monitors*

Displacement:	110t normal; 126.5t full load
Dimensions:	113ft 4in × 16ft 9in × 2ft 7in *34.5m × 5.1m × 0.8m*
Machinery:	3 shafts, 3 Maybach 4cyl diesels, 180hp = 10kts
Armour:	11mm (⅜in) deck
Armament:	2–105mm (4.1in), 5 MG
Complement:	34

Class (completed):
Warszawa (13.8.20), *Horodyszcze* (20.8.20), *Pinsk* (20.10.20), *Mozyrz* (10.12.20)

Ordered in January 1920 from the Danziger Werft and named after cities, these monitors served on the Vistula, and between 1925–26 on the River Pina. In June 1923 *Mozyrz* was renamed *Torun*. In the late 1920s all were rearmed with 2–75mm guns and 1–100mm (3.9in) howitzer and one MG turret was dismounted, while the remaining four were adapted for AA fire. During late 1930s all were rebuilt (*Torun* in 1936, *Warszawa* in 1938, *Pinsk* in 1938–39, *Horodyszcze* in 1939): their silhouette was lowered, draught reduced, and the 3 Maybach diesels were replaced with 2 Glennifer of 100hp each. Three 75mm guns were mounted in place of previous ones, 4 MG were installed on the CT and in its casemates. All four were scuttled on 18 September 1939 in the River Pripjat. Raised by the Soviets and repaired, they took part in 1941 campaign as *Vinnica, Smolensk, Zhitomir* and *Vitebsk*, respectively. All were blown up in 1941 to prevent their falling into German hands.

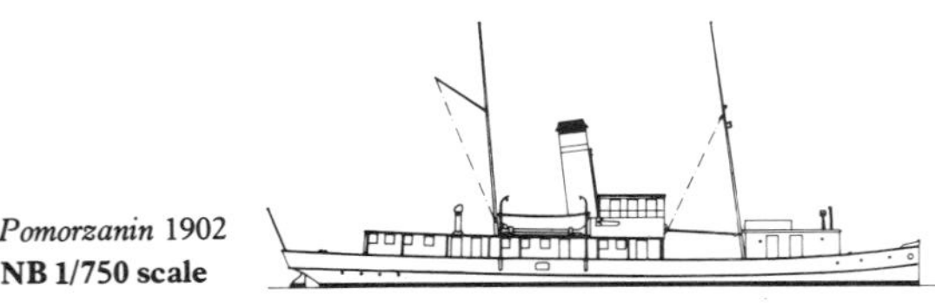
Pomorzanin 1902
NB 1/750 scale

POMORZANIN *survey ship*

Former German coastal passenger ship *Wotan* (1893, 220t, 8kts). Bought in 1920 in Gdansk, entered service on 4 May 1920 and was used for hydrographic duties until 1922, when she was sold into private hands and renamed *Kaszuba*. Returned to the Polish Navy in 1924, again as a survey ship. Finally deleted in 1931 and sold to a private owner, renamed *Pomian*. During the Second World War used by the Germans and scuttled by them in 1945 at Gdansk. Raised after the war and broken up in the early 1950s. Although she was not a fighting ship and never carried any armament (though she is sometimes credited with 2 MG), she has the distinction of being the Polish Navy's first ship.

In addition to the above units, the following ships were bought by the Navy up until 1923: tugs *Castor, Pollux, Krakus, Wanda* (120–160hp), several large steel launches and barges and the patrol boat *Mysliwy* (former British motor launch, deleted 1926).

POLISH RIVER FLOTILLAS 1918–1921

Although the Polish river flotillas comprised only civilian ships, hastily armed and seldom armoured, the military role they played justifies their inclusion here.

Vistula Flotilla

Created in late 1918 in order to secure the 630-mile Vistula, the flotilla comprised 1 armoured steamer and 5 motor boats, left by the withdrawing Germans in Warsaw. All received armament only in August 1919. By the end of 1919 the flotilla possessed 14 steamers (passenger ships and tugs, armed mainly with a few MG each) and about 20 motor boats (armed with 1–37mm or 1 MG each). When the Red Army neared Warsaw and the Vistula in August 1920, the flotilla took an active part in the nine-day decisive Battle of Warsaw. The first action was fought on 14 August; three steamers (*Moniuszko, Neptun* and *Stefan Batory*) were sunk by Soviet artillery during skirmishes on 14 and 18 August.

By mid-September 1920 the Vistula Flotilla was organised thus:

First Division: 4 monitors nearing completion in Gdansk. *Second Division:* 6 small passenger/cargo steamers of under 50t displacement, armed with 2–8 MG. *Third Division:* 5 large passenger/cargo steamers of about 120t displacement *Wawel, Stefan Batory, Sobieski, Minister* (each armed with 2–75mm or 80mm guns and 4 MG) and *Andrzej Zamojski* (armed with 2–104mm (4.1in) howitzers and 4 MG). *Fourth Division:* 16 motor boats armed with 1–2 MG. *Reserve Flotilla:* 5 steamers.

Most of the above ships were returned to their owners after the war ended. Those few that remained (some monitors, a few small steamers and motorboats) were transferred to the Pinsk Flotilla by 1926, when the Vistula Flotilla was dissolved.

Pinsk Flotilla

The Pinsk Flotilla, in the east of Poland, was created in the spring of 1919 and was made up initially of six motor boats 9–12m long, each armed with 1–37mm gun. All were rebuilt from wrecks left by the Germans. At first its main duty was as a means of transport, but on 3 July 1919 the first action was fought off Horodyszcze. Later the flotilla was supplemented by 3 small tugs and 3 motorboats, transferred from the Vistula Flotilla, while in March/April 1920 the greater part of the Soviet Pinsk Flotilla was captured by this tiny force almost intact, with army help. Of the ex-Soviet vessels 2 armoured ships were put into Polish service as *P 1* (ex-*Trachtomirov*) and *P 2* (ex-*Burzhin*) together with 6 tugs and 19 transports.

When during May 1920 Polish armies reached Kiev and the Dnieper river, the Polish Dnieper Flotilla was to be created. This attempt was prevented by a Soviet general offensive in the summer 1920. Only a few ships of the Pinsk Flotilla were evacuated, mainly by rail, while the majority had to be scuttled, as the water was very low at that time. The new Polish Pinsk Flotilla was created in February 1921 when a naval salvage team began work there. The flotilla then comprised ships salvaged or transferred from the Vistula.

Rumania

Though Rumania's independence from Turkey was gained only in 1878, she already had some degree of autonomy that allowed her to possess a small flotilla of warships stationed on the Danube to protect her interests there.

Active participation in the Russo-Turkish War in 1877–78 brought not only independence (which was finally accepted by the great powers only in 1880), but also direct access to the Black Sea via the Danube estuary and the region of Dobrudja to the south, which were incorporated into Rumania. The new Constanza Black Sea harbour was built on the Dobrudja coast and funds for warship building were provided. The ships came in two groups: the first comprised seagoing ships (the gunboat *Grivita* and a sail training vessel, *Mircea*) and several ships for the Danube (a patrol ship, *Alexandru cel Bun*, and 16 small boats of under 45t). All those ships were delivered in the early 1880s. The second instalment comprised the cruiser *Elisabeta* and 3 torpedo-boats arrived during the late 1880s and 1890s, followed by 6 large and 6 small patrol ships for Danube. Meanwhile, in 1891 the Department of the Navy was formed, speeding up both the training and expansion of the naval forces. The Navy was subsequently divided into Maritime and Riverine Divisions.

A certain improvement in the economy, small as it was (about 80 per cent of Rumanians lived off the land) enabled Rumania to start a large rearmament programme at the end of the 1890s. The naval expansion programme was drawn up in 1899 and called for 6 coastal battleships, 4 destroyers of 300t and 12 torpedo-boats of 80t; none of them were built. The Danube Division had to be strengthened by 8 river monitors (4 of which were built) and 12 river torpedo-boats (8 built). These ships came into service between 1906 and 1908, signifying both the importance of Danube security to Rumania, and Rumanian difficulties in realising planned programmes. By 1906 personnel numbered about 1500.

During the 1912 Balkan War Rumania remained strictly neutral, despite Turkish pleas for help. In return for her neutrality she received from Bulgaria the Silistria district which lengthened her coastline. This gain was thought to be too small and when in July 1913 Bulgaria challenged her late allies, thus opening the Second Balkan War, she found her northern border attacked by the Rumanian Army which occupied the territory down to Sofia. This war brought further territorial gains for Rumania and her coastline stretched down almost as far as the Bulgarian port of Varna.

By that time the original 1899 naval programme had developed into the 1912 programme, which called for 6 light cruisers of 3500t (none of which were begun), 12 large destroyers of 1500t (4 were built and requisitioned by Italy) and 1 submarine. The Danube Flotilla was supplemented by a staff vessel and two patrol boats. Other plans for naval expansion were even more unrealistic; one of them called for a battleship of 13,000t, armed with 4–305mm (12in), 4–203mm (8in) and 12–150mm (6in).

THE FIRST WORLD WAR

When the First World War broke out, the pro-French feelings (which had increased in importance in Rumania since the beginning of twentieth century) together with the Allies' promises of large territorial gains, induced the Rumania to join the Allies in 1915. The military misfortunes of Russia halted this step temporarily, but on 27 August 1916 war was declared on Austria-Hungary with catastrophic results as by December German troops entered Bucharest. The remnants of the Rumanian Army survived only as an adjunct of the Russian Front having suffered 50 per cent losses or seven times the losses of the Central Powers.

Rumania's Maritime Division was in 1916 hopelessly outdated and of little value due not only to requisitioning of ships building abroad (such as 4 modern destroyers in Italy or 2 tugs of 300ihp each, building at Budapest), but mainly because of the stress laid upon the Danube Division which was constantly improved at the cost of seagoing ships. Not surprisingly it was promptly supplemented by four modern auxiliary cruisers taken from the country's 41 steamers of 75,174grt. The Danube Division was made up of modern ships and therefore proved a valuable addition to the Russian forces in that area; it supported the southern wing of the Rumanian Army and effectively barred the Danube estuary to the Austro-Hungarian river flotilla, however it remained on the defensive. The four auxiliary cruisers of the Maritime Division participated in Russian Black Sea Fleet operations.

The Russian October Revolution of 1917 left Rumania as the only state in that area to oppose the Central Powers and the peace treaty drawn up with them, of 7 May 1918, was harsh, demanding reliquishment of the Dobrudja (conquered by Field Marshal August von Mackensen's German-Turkish-Bulgarian Army of the Danube) among other conditions. Six months later the situation changed completely when the Central Powers capitulated and during 1919–20 Rumania was able not only to regain her losses, but also to make further gains. The Dobrudja region was returned, while in the north the Rumanian coastline stretched up to the Dniester river, doubling its length when compared with the pre-war one.

Greater care had to be taken of the Maritime Division of the Navy and five French ASW gunboats were bought in 1921. They were supplemented by 2 destroyers (from 4 ordered in 1912) from Italy and by 7 large torpedo-boats allocated to Rumania in 1920 from the divided Austro-Hungarian Navy. Purchase of the coastal battleship *Gorgon* and six 'M' class destroyers from the Royal Navy was also contemplated, but nothing came of it. The Danube Division was also developed and was strengthened with 3 ex-Austrian river monitors and 7 ex-Italian ELCO submarine chasers.

FLEET STRENGTH 1906

CRUISER

Name	Built	Disp	Fate
ELISABETA	1888	1320t	BU post 1919

Disarmed in 1916 due to her age. All her 4–4.7in and 4–12pdr were mounted ashore, while *Elisabeta* became a guardship at Sulina (Black Sea central exit of the Danube). After the war she was hulked at Galatz on the Danube and later scrapped.

TORPEDO-BOATS

Name	Built	Disp	Fate
NALUCA	1888	56t	Unknown
SBORUL	1888	56t	Unknown
SMEUL	1888	56t	Sunk 16.4.17

The French-built *Naluca* class except *Smeul* were rebuilt in 1907. The 2–1pdr revolvers were replaced by 1 MG. They drew only 7ft and had 20-man crews. Coal capacity was 7t. *Smeul* sank on a mine in the Danube estuary.

GUNBOATS

Name	Built	Disp	Fate
GRIVITA	1880	110t	See notes
Oltul class			
OLTUL	1888	116t	See notes
SIRETUL	1888	116t	See notes
BISTRITA	1888	116t	See notes
Rahova class			
RAHOVA	1882	45t	See notes
SMARDAN	1882	45t	See notes
OPANEZUL	1882	45t	See notes

Grivita

Grivita was a 198½ft × 17ft × 5ft 10in (*60.5m × 5.2m × 1.8m*) gunboat built by STT, Trieste of Austria-Hungary. She mounted 2–57mm (6pdr) and 2–37mm (1pdr) guns and 2 MG; her speed was 9kts (180hp, coal 18t) and her crew 30. She was employed as a seagoing TS. Her fate is unknown.

Oltul class

Gunboats (100ft × 13ft 6in × 5ft 9in, *30.5m × 4.1m × 1.7m*) built by Thames

Iron Works and armed with 1–57mm (6pdr) and 1–37mm (1pdr) guns being crewed by 30 men; the speed was 13kts (380hp, coal 12t). All 3 were used on the Danube. Fates unknown.

Rahova class
Gunboats built by Thames Iron Works and armed with 1–37mm gun and 1 MG. Their speed was 8.5kts. Also used on the Danube, their fates are unknown.

GUARDSHIPS

Name	Built	Disp	Fate
MONTEANO	1893	95t	Unknown
OLTEANO	1893	95t	Unknown
IMEO	1893	95t	Unknown

Armed with 1–57mm and 2–37mm guns and had a speed of 13.5kts. All 3 were used on the Danube.

Other ships extant in 1906 comprised the sail training brig *Mircea* (1882, 350t) and warships stationed on Danube: the guardship *Alexandru cel Bun* (1882, 104t) and about 10 boats used for patrol or police purposes, ranging from 32t to 10t.

ADDITIONS 1906–1921

VIFOR class *destroyers*

Particulars: See Italian *Aquila* class *flotilla leaders*

Class:
Marasti (ex-*Sparviero*, ex-*Vijelie*), *Marasesti* (ex-*Nibbio*, ex-*Vartez*)

Four large destroyers of 1500t – *Vifor, Vijelie, Vartez* and *Viscul* – were ordered in 1913 from Italy under the 1912 naval programme. Their armament was to consist of 3–120mm (4.7in)/45 and 4–75mm/50 guns and 5–450mm (17.7in) TT. In May 1915 they were in various stages of completion (*Vifor* 60 per cent, *Vijelie* 50 per cent, *Vartez* 20 per cent and *Viscul* not yet begun) and were requisitioned after Italy entered the war. On 1 July 1920 two of those ships were returned to Rumania and received the names *Marasti* and *Marasesti*.

Ex-Austro-Hungarian Tb 74 T and Tb 82 F *seagoing torpedo-boats*

Class:
Viforul (ex-*Tb 74 T*), *Varteful* (ex-*Tb 75 T*), *Vijelia* (ex-*Tb 80T*), *Sborul* (ex-*Tb 81 T*), *Naluca* (ex-*Tb 82 F*), *Smeul* (ex-*Tb 93 F*), *Fulgerul* (ex-*Tb 84 F*)

Seven large Austro-Hungarian 250t torpedo-boats were allocated to Rumania in 1920. *Fulgerul* capsized and sank in the Bosphorus on 8 February 1922 while being transferred to the Black Sea.

340t type *submarines*

Particulars: See French *O'Byrne* class

Three submarines of 340t were ordered during the war in France. All were requisitioned and entered French service when completed in 1921.

Ion C Bratianu as completed *Twardowski Collection*

Ex-French FRIPONNE class *ASW gunboats*

Class:
Locotenant Lepri Remus (ex-*Chiffonne*), *Locotenant-Comandor Stihi Eugen* (ex-*Friponne*), *Capitan Dumitrescu C* (ex-*Impatiente*), *Sublocotenant Ghigulescu* (ex-*Mignonne*)

In 1920 four ASW French *Friponne* class ASW gunboats were purchased and put into service with the above names. The *Boudeuse* belonging to the similar *Ardent* class was also bought to provide spare parts for the four operational ships. *Lepri Remus* sank on 11 January 1940 in the Danube estuary. *Dumitrescu* was in very bad shape in 1944 and was broken up by the Rumanians in 1946. *Stihi Eugen* and *Ghigulescu* were taken over by the Soviet Union in August 1944 and put into service with the Soviet Black Sea Fleet as *Akhtuba* and *Angara* respectively. Both were returned on 22 September 1945 and served until the 1960s in the Rumanian Navy; *Ghigulescu* is known to serve as a survey ship with the name of *NOD 113*.

ION C BRATIANU class *river monitors*

Displacement:	680t
Dimensions:	208ft 4in × 33ft 10in × 5ft 3in *63.5m × 10.3m × 1.6m*
Machinery:	2 shafts, 2 sets of TE reciprocating engines, Yarrow boilers 1800ihp = 13kts. Coal 60t
Armour:	Sides 75mm (3in), deck 75mm (3in), turrets 75mm (3in), CT 50mm (2in)
Armament:	3–120mm (4.7in)/35, 2–120mm (4.7in)/10 howitzers, 4–47mm, 2–6.5mm MG
Complement:	110

Class:
Ion C Bratianu, Lascar Catargiu, Michail Kogalniceanu, Alexandru Lahovari

Built by STT, Trieste in 1907 (the last one in 1908) in sections, transported to Galatz and assembled there. The class was named after Rumanian prime ministers, the name ship honouring her Prime Minister and Minister of War in the period. All four took part in both World Wars; after the first they were rearmed and carried 3–120mm (4.7in), 1–76mm AA, 2–47mm guns and 2MG. *Catargiu* and *Kogalniceanu* were sunk by Soviet aircraft on 24 August 1944 in the Danube estuary. *Bratianu* and *Lahovari* were taken over by Soviet Union in August 1944 and incorporated into Soviet Danube Flotilla as *Mariupol* and *Berdjansk* respectively. Four more ships of this class were planned under the 1899 programme, but were not begun.

Ex-Austro-Hungarian *river monitors*

Class:
Ardea (ex-*Temes*), *Besarabia* (ex-*Inn*), *Bucovina* (ex-*Sava*)

Three Austro-Hungarian Danube monitors were allocated to Rumania in 1920, after being interned in Yugoslavia (see Yugoslav entry). They entered Rumanian service with the above names. All took part in the Second World War and in August 1944 fell into Soviet hands when they were into service as *Azov* (ex-*Ardeal*), *Kerch* (ex-*Besarabia*) and *Izmail* (ex-*Bucovina*).

Captain Nicolae Lascar Bogdan as completed
NB 1/750 scale

CAPITAN NICOLAE LASCAR BOGDAN class *river torpedo-boats*

Displacement:	45t normal; 51t full load
Dimensions:	98ft 5in × 13ft 1in × 2ft 7in *30.0m × 4.0m × 0.8m*
Machinery:	2 shafts, 2 sets compound engines, 550hp = 18kts. Oil 7.6t
Armour:	Bulletproof sides and deck
Armament:	1–47mm Skoda, 1–6.5mm Maxim MG, 2 spar torpedoes
Complement:	16–20

Class:
Major Ene Constantin, Capitan Nicolae Lascar Bogdan, Capitan Romano Michail, Major Giurascu Dimitrie, Major Sontu Gheorge, Major Grigore Ioan, Locotenant Calinescu Dimitrie, Capitan Valter Maracineanu

All were built by Thames Iron Works in 1906–07 and were transferred to Rumania via inland waterways. They bore numbers 1 to 8, respectively. All participated in the First World War; *Capitan Maracineanu* sank on a mine at the end of 1916. By the 1940s they were still in service, though *Capitan Bogdan, Major Ene* and *Major Grigore* were used as frontier patrol boats with their armament reduced to one MG. Apparently three of them survived the Second World War in shape good enough to be incorporated in August 1944 into the Soviet Black Sea Fleet as *SKA-754* (ex-*No 1*), *SKA-755* (ex-*No 3*) and *SKA-756* (ex-*No 4*). They were returned on 22 September 1945. When built they had torpedo dropping gear amidships apart from spar torpedoes. Four more boats were planned under the 1899 naval programme, but were never begun.

Ex-Italian ELCO 44 ton type *submarine chasers*

Class:
M 1–M 6 (ex-*MAS 268, 273, 348, 350, 373, 349, 351*)

Seven former Italian submarine chasers were bought in 1921 for service on the Danube. Renamed as above which was later changed to *VAS 1* to *VAS 7*. They were employed as patrol boats and were discarded in 1931–32.

AUXILIARY CRUISERS AND SEAPLANE CARRIERS
Four Rumanian passenger ships *Regele Carol I* (1898, 2369t gross), *Romania* (1904, 3152t gross), *Imperator Trajan* (1907, 3418t gross), *Dacia* (1907, 3418t gross) were refitted in 1916 as auxiliary cruisers and proved to be the most valuable ships of the Maritime Division of the Rumanian Navy. Their speed was 18kts and each was armed with 4–152mm (6in) and 4–76mm guns; each could take four seaplanes and all had minelaying capability. They were in service during 1916–18 and operated together with the Russian Black Sea Fleet.

San Salvador

In 1906 this Central American republic possessed the 75-ton gunboat *Cuscatlan* (built San Francisco, 1890) with 1 small QF gun and capable of 10kts. She was not extant in 1919, but the country included a naval ensign with the present flag which was readopted in 1912. San Salvador had been Honduras' most active ally in the 1907 war with Nicaragua.

Sarawak

Sarawak on the north coast of Borneo was an independent state during this period and also a British protectorate (since 1888). Her area of 48,000 square miles was populated by 600,000 including *c*100 Europeans. Armed forces included about 500 soldiers of the Dajak tribe under the command of a British officer. At the time there was still a slave trade (price US1$ for a person). Sarawak had only one railway line of 95 miles. There were no real ports but a good anchorage was located in Kidorong Bay. Foreign trade was served mainly by British and German ships. The Navy consisted of 5 old and small gunboats: *Aline* (1875, 175grt, 1 screw gun), *Lorna Doone* (1881, 118grt, screw, 2 small guns), *Aden* (1884, 300grt, paddle, 1 gun), and *Kaka* (1901, 400grt, paddle), the yacht *Zahora* (1894) and a few armed launches. All these ships were discarded by 1920. The Government owned the *Alice Lorraine* (1904, 125t) and *L'Aubaine*.

Siam

The modern Royal Siamese Navy was born in 1860, when the French mercantile steamer *Formosa* was bought and converted into a gunboat. In 1865 one steam corvette and four gunboats were ordered in France and since that time numerous ships of various origins have been incorporated. For many years the Royal Siamese Navy was commanded by a Dane, Admiral de Richelieu, until his retirement in 1903. During his command the ships of the Fleet were mostly captained by Danish and Norwegian officers, many of whom served till 1914–18. The Navy controlled three forts near the mouth of the Menan Chao Phraya river garrisoned by 2000 marine infantry. The Royal Dockyard and Arsenal at Bangkok, which began to build steam warships in the 1870s, was capable of handling ships up to 3000t and contained slipways, sheerlegs and workshops as well as a drydock (plus 2 private ones). The Fleet in 1906 had obsolete ships, mostly of merchant or yacht origins. Before the First World War it was strengthened by torpedo craft built in Japan and a small gunboat built in Britain. The armoured gunboat ordered shortly before the war was not built until 1925. The state-controlled Siam Steam Navigation Company formed *c*1910 possessed 7 vessels. Personnel totalled 5000 (compulsory service) in 1919 with 20,000 reserves. The Royal Naval Academy at I'hra Rajwangderm took 120 cadets and there were 6 provincial training establishments. Naval radio stations existed at Bangkok and Singora.

In July 1917 Siam declared war against Germany and Austria-Hungary. All enemy subjects were interned and a quantity of German shipping taken as prize. Some small German vessels were taken into the Siamese Navy as transports.

FLEET STRENGTH 1906

CRUISER AND SLOOPS

Name	Launched	Disp	Fate
MAHA CHAKRI	27.6.92	2600t	Stricken 23.6.16, BU 1917
THOON KRAMON	1866	800t	Sail TS, stricken *c*1916
SIAM MOUGKUT	1870	950t	BU *c*1912
MAKUT RAJAKUMARN	5.2.87	610t	Stricken 22.4.30

Maha Chakri was a British-built protected cruiser doubling as royal yacht. She was credited with 6 MG in 1906. *Thoon Kramon* was a wooden corvette armed with 4–4in ML and 4 smaller guns by 1906. *Siam Mougkut* was a floating battery with 8–4in 32pdr BLR. *Makut Rajakumarn* carried 3–4.7in BL, 4 MG, and 1–TT aw, designed 800hp = 14kts (*c*11kts by 1906).

TORPEDO-BOATS

Name	Launched	Disp	Fate
MORADOPH	1888	45t	Stricken *c*1908

GUNBOATS

Name	Launched	Disp	Fate
YONG YOT	1863	340t	Stricken 27.4.08
NIRBEN	1866	260t	Stricken *c*1906
HAN HAK SAKRU	1866	140t	Stricken *c*1910
MAIDA	1867	260t	Stricken *c*1910

Name	Launched	Disp	Fate
RAN RUK	1879	450t	Stricken 17.10.08
KOH SI CHANG	1890	100t	Stricken *c* 1910
UDHAI RAJAKICH	1890	134t	Stricken *c* 1910
THEVA SOORARAM	1898	115t	Stricken 1.6.19
Muratha class			
MURATHA	1898	447t	Stricken 26.12.29
BALI	1900	462t	Stricken 20.7.35
SUGRIB	1901	462t	Stricken 20.7.35

Yong Yot (10kts) carried 1–4.7in and 3 smaller guns. *Nirben* (9kts) 1–4in and 6 small guns. *Han Hak Sakru* (7kts) 1–4in and 2 small guns. *Maida* (11kts) 1–4.7in ML and 2 small guns.

DISPATCH VESSEL

Name	Launched	Disp	Fate
PRAP PORAPAK	1899	210t	Stricken 12.5.22

PADDLE YACHT

Name	Launched	Disp	Fate
CHAH KANG No 1	1875	95t	Stricken *c* 1908

ADDITIONS 1906–1921

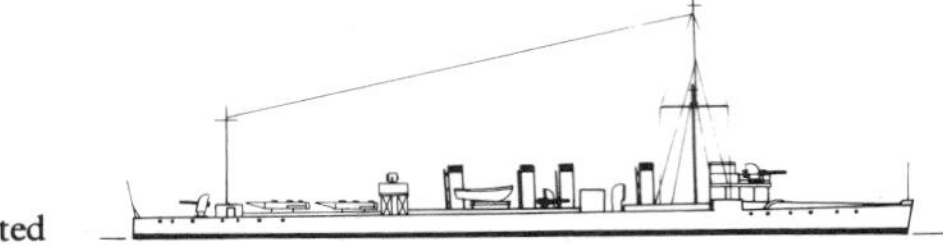
Sua Thayan Chon as completed

SUA THAYAN CHON class *destroyers*

Displacement: 375t
Dimensions: 227ft pp × 21ft 6in × 6ft
69.2m × 6.6m × 1.8m
Machinery: 2-shaft VTE, 4 Kampon type watertube boilers, 6000ihp = 29kts (designed). Oil 75t
Armament: 1–12pdr (76mm), 5–6pdr (57mm), 2 MG, 2–18in (457mm) TT
Complement: 75

Name	Builder	Launched	Fate
SUA THAYAN CHON	Kawasaki, Kobe	27.4.08	Sold 22.8.39
SUA KHAMRON SIN	Kawasaki, Kobe	5.2.12	Sold 17.1.37

They were similar to the 1903–5 Japanese *Harusame* class destroyers.

Ex-British 'R' class *destroyer*

Name	Builder	Launched	Fate
PHRA RUANG (ex-*Radiant*)	Thornycroft	7.20	Stricken 7.59

Sold on 21 June 1920.

No 1 class *torpedo-boats*

Displacement: 89t
Dimensions: 135ft oa, 131ft 7in pp × 16ft 2in × 6ft 9in
41.1, 40.1m × 4.9m × 2.1m
Machinery: 1-shaft TE, 2 Kampon type watertube boilers, 1200ihp = 23kts. Oil 19t
Armament: 1–6pdr (57mm), 1–3pdr (47mm), 2–18in (457mm) TT
Complement: 24–29

Class (launched, fate):
No 1 (9.5.08, stricken 1.4.33), *No 2* (9.5.08, stricken 17.1.37), *No 3* (14.5.08, stricken 17.1.37), *No 4* (19.4.13, stricken 19.9.37)

Steel Normand type TB built by Kawasaki, Kobe.

MAHA CHAKRI *armed yacht*

Displacement: 2500t
Dimensions: 335ft oa, 298ft wl × 40ft × 25ft depth, 18ft 6in draught
102.1m, 90m × 12.2m × 7.6m, 5.6m
Machinery: 2-shaft TE, 4 Kampon watertube boilers, 2000ihp = 14.5kts. Oil 200t. Range 2000nm
Armament: Light saluting guns only
Complement: 200

Name	Builder	Launched	Fate
MAHA CHAKRI	Kawasaki, Kobe	1918	Stricken 1952

Built with money from a voluntary public subscription, her engines and numerous fittings were taken for her from *Maha Chakri (i)* which was dismantled in Japan during 1916–1917. In 1936 she was rated as transport and depot ship for submarines and renamed *Angthong*.

SURIYA MONTHON *gunboat*

Displacement: 225t
Dimensions: 137ft oa, 130ft pp × 18ft × 6ft 8in
41.8m, 39.6m × 5.5m × 2.0m
Machinery: 2-shaft TE, 1Thornycroft boiler, 7500ihp = 14.5kts. Coal 66t
Armament: 2–6pdr (57mm)
Complement: 34

Name	Builder	Launched	Fate
SURIYA MONTHON	Thornycroft, Southampton	1907	Stricken 20.7.35

A coastguard vessel.

ARMOURED GUNBOAT

An armoured gunboat of 1070t was ordered from the British Armstrong, Whitworth Company. Her engine which was to be 850hp was subcontracted to Hawthorn Leslie. She was laid down in 1914 with yard No 872 but, at the outbreak of war, the hull was dismantled to free the slipway for British use. Reordered after the war, she was laid down again on 29 September 1924 as *Ratankosindra*.

Uruguay

Uruguay sits between two powerful neighbours. For this and other reasons she has maintained at least one warship of modest size to represent her rights. This era, like the nineteenth, was plagued with border disputes. Uruguay remained neutral during World War One. During the war three Uruguayan merchantmen were sunk by U-boats. On 24 November 1918, having broken diplomatic relations, Uruguay seized eight German steamers. In 1919 the country had a merchant fleet of 27 steamers (20,298grt) and 48 sailing ships (24,537grt). Montevideo had a 459ft × 55ft national dock for ships drawing up to 19ft. There were 3 other smaller docks.

FLEET STRENGTH 1906

GUNBOATS

Name	Launched	Disp	Fate
GENERAL SUAREZ (ex-*Tactique*)	1887*	400t	Stricken *c* 1913
MALVINAS	1885	400t	Stricken *c* 1912
GENERAL ARTIGAS	1883	270t	Stricken *c* 1913

*Date of purchase. *General Suarez* was still a harbour TS in 1919. *General*

Artigas was named after the Uruguayan liberator general who captured Montevideo in 1815. In addition to the above, the Uruguayan Navy in 1906 also operated the transport *General Flores* (260t, stricken *c*1920), named after the president murdered in 1868. There was also the old paddlewheel gunboat *Baron de Rio Branco* (ex-*Maldonado*, 300t, 12kts, 4 small QF and 2 MG) transferred for surveying to the Ministry of Interior in 1912.

Uruguay 1935 CPL

ADDITIONS 1906–1921

Ex-Italian DOGALI *protected cruiser*

Montevideo (ex-*24 de Agosto*, ex-*Dogali*) was bought in January 1908, initially named *24 de Agosto*, renamed *Montevideo* in 1910; laid up 1914 not discarded 1932.

18 DE JULIO *gunboat*

A 678t, 4-gun (85 men) and 2 MG presidential yacht. Purchased *c*1909; stricken *c*1950.

URUGUAY *gunboat*

Displacement:	1400t
Dimensions:	278ft 9in pp × 30ft 9in × 11ft 9in max *85.0m × 9.4m × 3.6m*
Machinery:	VTE, 4 Normand boilers, 5700shp = 23kts. Coal 210t, range 3000nm at 12kts
Armament:	2–4.7in (120mm), 4–12pdr (76mm), 6–1pdr, 2–18in (457mm) TT aw
Complement:	125

Built by Vulkan, Stettin and launched on 12 April 1910; fitted as a TS for midshipmen; stricken 1953.

Venezuela

During this era Venezuela had numerous disputes with major naval powers primarily over the payment of her international debt, but remained neutral in 1914–18. On 7 December 1902 the gunboat *Restaurador* was seized by the German Navy. She was returned three months later, on 24 February 1903. Only one significant warship, the 950t/1125t gunboat *Maresal Sucre* (ex-*Isla de Cuba*) was acquired during this era, being bought from the US Navy on 2 April 1912. Puerto Cabello, west of Caracas, was the main base with a 3000t capacity steel floating dock. Venezuela had a 1919 mercantile marine of 11 steamers (5298grt) and 8 sailing ships (1097grt).

FLEET STRENGTH 1906

GUNBOATS

Name	Launched	Disp	Fate
LIBERATOR	1883	832t	Stricken *c*1910
RESTAURADOR	1884	740t	Stricken 1946
BOLIVAR (ex-*Galicia*)	1891	571t	Stricken *c*1920
MIRANDA	1895	200t	Stricken 1945
JOSE FELIX RIBAS	1894	300t	Stricken *c*1930

Restaurador was renamed *General Salom c*1920. *Bolivar* was renamed *Zumbador c*1910. *Miranda* (named after the Napoleonic era Venezuelan general who devised the country's original flag in 1806), measured 135ft × 19ft × 8ft *(41.2m × 5.8m × 2.5m)*, carried 36t of coal (315hp = 12kts) for a range of 850nm at 8kts, a crew of 45 and 4–6pdr in 1918.

ADDITIONS 1906–1921

Ex-Spanish gunboat ISLA DE CUBA

In 1918 her armament was 2–4in, 2–6pdr, 6–3pdr, 2–1pdr, her range 2640nm at 10kts and crew 92 with 2000ihp machinery. Named *Maresal Sucre* after Bolivar's Venezuelan chief lieutenant and Bolivia's first, murdered president (1795–1830).

Yugoslavia

The state of Yugoslavia emerged on 1 December 1918 and was called then the Kingdom of Serbs, Croats and Slovenes. It also encompassed the Montenegro, Bosnia, Macedonia and Herzegovina regions. The frontiers were settled in 1919 and Yugoslavia took possession of 350 miles of coastline with over 600 offshore islands.

Before the First World War Serbia and Montenegro, both leading factions in the aspirations towards independence of the Southern Slavs, wanted to gain access to the sea. As a result of the Berlin Treaty of 1878 a 37 nautical mile strip of the Adriatic coastline was allocated to Montenegro, but remained subject to Austrian maritime law until 1908. Nevertheless Montenegro managed to create the beginnings of a merchant marine and the Duke's yacht *Rumija* was armed with 47mm guns. Serbia had no direct access to the sea until November 1912, when her armies arrived at Durazzo on the Adriatic coast during the Balkan War. On 17 December 1912 she was deprived of her conquest by the Great Powers conference in London.

When the Serbian armies were defeated in late 1915, they were evacuated to the island of Corfu by the end of March 1916. While stationed there the first warship (an old Greek torpedo-boat) of future Yugoslavia – *Srbija* – was bought. She served in the Salonika area up to Armistice Day.

The next step in Yugoslavia's naval development came after the fall of the Austro-Hungarian Empire, when on 31 October 1918 the National Council of Serbs, Croats and Slovenes took control of Austro-Hungarian warships. This move was quickly countered by the Italians, averse to creating another naval power in place of Austro-

Hungary. Thus the battleship *Viribus Unitis* was promptly sunk on 1 November 1918 by Italian frogmen. The rest of the former Austro-Hungarian Navy was seized by the Allies, with the Italians capturing the Pola group of warships, the French, the Cattaro, the Americans the Split and the British the Beograd group, the latter consisting of river warships.

According to the Treaty of Saint-Germaine-en-Laye the Austrian Navy was divided in September 1919 between the victorious countries. The Kingdom of Serbs, Croats and Slovenes received only 1 obsolete battleship, 12 torpedo-boats, 4 river monitors and some other ships, despite claims for 4 cruisers, 17 destroyers, 27 torpedo-boats, 20 submarines, 6 river monitors and numerous auxiliaries. Even when reduced to 2 cruisers, 6 destroyers, 30 torpedo-boats and 4 submarines, the claims were not considered and the warships allocated were taken over by Yugoslavia in the beginning of March 1921.

The next acquisitions were 6 ex-German 'M' class minesweepers, bought on 20 July 1921. With them the first stage of Yugoslavian naval development ended, though in 1922 the first Fleet expansion programme was drawn up, which proposed a fleet comprising 24 destroyers, 24 submarines and a large number of minelayers and seaplanes.

Austro-Hungarian *torpedo-boats* (F and T classes)

Class:
T 1 (ex-*76 T*), *T 2* (ex-*77 T*), *T 3* (ex-*78 T*), *T 4* (ex-*79 T*), *T 5* (ex-*87 F*), *T 6* (ex-*93 F*), *T 7* (ex-*96 F*), and *T 8* (ex-*97 F*)

The only modern seagoing warships allocated to Yugoslavia and renamed in 1920.

Ex-Austro-Hungarian KAIMAN class *torpedo-boats*

Class:
T 9 (ex-*60 T*, ex-*Schwalbe*), *T 10* (ex-*61 T* ex-*Pinguin*), *T 11* (ex-*69 T*, ex-*Polyp*), and *T 12* (ex-*54 T*, ex-*Wal*)

Acquired and renamed in 1920. Broken up in 1924, except *T 11* which was scrapped in 1926.

Ex-Austro-Hungarian *minesweepers*

Particulars: See Austro-Hungarian Schichau 78t type *torpedo-boats*

Class:
D 1 (ex-*No 21*), *D 2* (ex-*No 36*, ex-*Uhu*), *D 3* (ex-*No 38*, ex-*Kranich*) and *D 4* (ex-*No 19*, ex-*Kibitz*)

Four former torpedo boats of Austro-Hungarian Navy, converted to minesweepers between 1911 and 1917. Acquired by Yugoslavia and renamed. All except *D 2* were broken up in 1924, though deleted only in 1927. *D 2* seized by Italians in April 1941 and renamed *D 10*. In September 1943 she was taken over by the Germans and sank off Kumbor while in their hands.

Ex-German 'M' class *minesweepers*

Class:
Galeb (ex-*M 100*), *Jastreb* (ex-*M 112*), *Kobac* (ex-*M 121*), *Cavran* (ex-*M 106*, renamed *Jabud* in 1923), *Orao* (ex-*M 97*), *Sokol* (ex-*M 114*)

On 20 July 1921 6 former German minesweepers were bought as 'tugs' for 1.4 million marks each and renamed.

Ex-Austro-Hungarian *river monitors*

Class:
Morava (ex-*Körös*), *Sava* (ex-*Bodrog*), *Drava* (ex-*Enns*), *Vardar* (ex-*Bosna*)

These four river monitors were among the most valuable additions to the Yugoslav Navy. Though temporarily manned by the Yugoslavs in 1918–19, they were acquired in 1920 and renamed after the new country's major rivers.

In addition to the above four monitors, the following Austro-Hungarian river warships were interned in Yugoslavia and temporarily manned by Yugoslav crews during 1918–19: *Drina* (ex-*Temes*, later Rumanian *Ardeal*), *Soca* (ex-*Sava*, later Rumanian *Bucovina*), *Bregalnica* (ex-*Wels*, later Hungarian *Szeged*), *Neretva* (ex-*Barsch*, later Austrian *Barsch*). Other Austro-Hungarian river warships, and the majority were interned in Yugoslavia, were not renamed.

Ex-Greek *torpedo-boat*

In early 1916 a Greek ship *Paxo* (or *Paxoi*) was bought from private hands (for 50,000 drachmas or about £2000 then) for use by the Serbian Army stationed on Corfu. Renamed *Srbija* her displacement was 50t, dimensions 75ft 9in × 13ft 1in *(23.1m × 4.0m)*, speed 16kts and she carried a crew of 13 men. She was probably the Greek torpedo-boat *Beta*, sold in 1912. Armed with 2 MG, she was used at first off Corfu as a dispatch ship and transport. From May 1916 to November 1918 she served as a patrol ship in and around the Gulf of Salonika. In 1919 she arrived at Dubrovnik, becoming the first Yugoslav warship. Instead of being repaired there she was left to rust and deteriorate, finally being scrapped in 1928.

RUMIJA *yacht*

Built in 1899 by J Reid & Co, Glasgow as *Zaza* for Prince Nicholas of Montenegro (later King). With dimensions of 137ft 1in × 20ft × 11ft 6in *(41.8m × 6.1m × 3.5m)* she displaced 140t and was powered by a steam engine of 65nhp. Renamed later as *Rumija*, she was armed with two 47mm guns – the only armed ship belonging to the pre-1914 nations that were to become the future Yugoslavia. Torpedoed and sunk on 2 March 1915 by the Austrian torpedo-boat *T 57* in the Adriatic port of Antivari, Montenegro.

The Yugoslav Navy also had 6 ex-Austro-Hungarian auxiliaries allocated in 1920, with a seventh following in 1923.

Apart from combat ships and auxiliaries the Yugoslav Navy possessed the following 7 hulks (former large warships) allocated from the Austro-Hungarian Navy: *Sibenik* (ex-*Donau*, 1875, 2440t, former corvette), later renamed *Krka*, captured in 1941 by Italians, later fate unknown; *Tivat* (ex-*Kaiser Max*, 1863, 3588t, former ironclad), later renamed *Neretva*, fate after 1941 unknown; *Skradin* (ex-*Aurora*, 1874, 1340t, former corvette), BU 1927; *Zlarin* (ex-*Frundsberg*, 1873, 1355t, former corvette), later renamed *Krivosije*, BU 1935; *Prvic* (ex-*Schwarzenberg*, 1874, 3423t, former frigate), seized by the Italians in 1919 and not returned, in exchange the Yugoslavs received *Frundsberg;* ex-*Prinz Eugen* (1877, 3600t, former ironclad), seized by the Italians and not returned to Yugoslavia, nor any ship for exchange was offered; *Kumbor* (ex-*Kronprinz Erzherzog Rudolf*, 1887, 6829t, former battleship) served as staff vessel in Kotor Bay until sold for scrap in 1922.

Zanzibar

This East African sultanate became independent in 1856 but suffered a gradual diminution of her islands and mainland territories as a result of German colonial claims and the international suppression of her infamous slave trade. A disputed succession to the sultanate in August 1896 led to the celebrated 38-minute bombardments of the royal palace's gun batteries by Rear-Admiral H H Rawson's squadron of 5 ships. The most persistent resistance afloat came from the Zanzibar 7-gun single-screw warship *Glasgow* (Denny of Dumbarton, 1878, 195ft × 30ft × 80ft). She engaged Rawson's flagship, the first class protected cruiser *St George*, three times before, on fire, she struck her colours and sank. The gunboat HMS *Thrush* suffered the only British casualty, one wounded seaman (Zanzibari casualties were about 500), although hit over a hundred times, while the third class cruiser *Racoon* sank the Zanzibari launch *Chwaka*. Zanzibar was still credited with her 6 other small armed steamers (acquired 1864–85, 2 from Germany) in 1906.

Index

Note: Dates and countries given after entries are to distinguish ships of the same name; dates are for launch where known or else building dates for the class or simply an extant date. Accents are omitted for simplicity, and numbered vessels such as U-boats are not included.

A

B

C

D

E

F

G

H

I

J

K

L

M

N

O

P

W

X

Y

Z